CDP® REVIEW MANUAL

A DATA PROCESSING HANDBOOK

Fourth Edition

by

Kenniston W. Lord, Jr., CDP, CSP

VNR VAN NOSTRAND REINHOLD COMPANY
New York

Library of Congress Catalog Card Number: 85-29442
ISBN: 0-442-26052-0

Published by Van Nostrand Reinhold Company Inc.
115 Fifth Avenue
New York, New York 10003

Van Nostrand Reinhold Company Limited
Molly Millars Lane
Wokingham, Berkshire RG11 2PY, England

Van Nostrand Reinhold
480 La Trobe Street
Melbourne, Victoria 3000, Australia

Macmillan of Canada
Division of Canada Publishing Corporation
164 Commander Boulevard
Agincourt, Ontario M1S 3C7, Canada

15 14 13 12 11 10 9 8 7 6 5 4 3 2

Library of Congress Cataloging-in-Publication Data

Lord, Kenniston W.
CDP® review manual.

Includes index.
1. Electronic data processing—Handbooks, manuals, etc. 2. Electronic digital computers—Handbooks, manuals, etc. I. Title.
QA76.L577 1986 004 85-29442
ISBN 0-442-26052-0

PREFACE

And now it is time to do a fourth edition of this manual. I undertake the work with just a little anxiety, primarily because compression has set in. The first edition lasted six years; the second lasted five; the third lasted but three. And I know how much the field has changed and something of the speed at which the change is taking place. The effect seems exponential.

About the greatest change which has happened to the CDP Exam since the 1983 edition is the change of testing intervals from annually to semiannually, in the months of May and December. Also, there has been movement of the examination into overseas locations. Having asked for both to happen in 1971, I'm gratified. The Society of Certified Data Processors, the society I helped to form in 1971 and for whom I served three terms as President (1974–1976), has now become the Association of the ICCP. When you obtain the CDP, or any of the other ICCP certifications, please consider joining. Contact both ICCP and AICCP at Suite 268, 2200 E. Devon Avenue, Des Plaines, IL 60018. The telephone number is 312-299-ICCP / 312-299-4270. For an application to take the examination, contact ICCP or their testing office at P.O. Box 12383, Lexington, KY 40583. The cost for the entire examination is now $150.

Greater changes have taken place, however, in the world of certification. To begin with, the CCP (Certificate in Computer Programming) is gaining stature. Next, the Association for Systems Management (ASM) has joined ICCP and brought with it a fledgling certification program, the Certified Systems Professional (CSP). You'll note that the author has qualified for that certificate. Movement is in the works for the Office Automation Society International (OASI) to bring into place an office automation certificate. Perhaps by the time this book is to be rewritten one more time, that will be fait accompli. Look also for a college-level certification called the ACP. Increased interest is certain to be brought about by the proliferation of new directions using the microcomputer.

The years 1983 to present have been momentous for our career field. During that time, the microcomputer has taken a dominant position in our offices, our organizations, and the world of data processing. With the rapidity of a gatling gun, one reads of boon or boondoggle surrounding the microcomputer. Users who hadn't been successful to get service got micros and then demanded access to databases. Users who had invited the microcomputer into their world found that the device permeated their surroundings, becoming the indispensable office productivity tool of the decade. Typewriters gave way to electronic typewriters which gave way to the nondedicated microcomputer/word processor/database manager/spreadsheet/forecasting tool. Gradually the office is being automated, and communications leads the way. Because communications and the local area network are certain to be a part of the data processing future, discussion of those principles are included in this book. Also included are some details of some new hardware you'll be certain to encounter.

Major changes are happening under our noses. COBOL is still the standard language of the business data processing community, and FORTRAN is still the standard language of the scientific community despite the efforts of many to make it otherwise. We still have PASCAL being used (though it may be gradually giving way to Modula-2), and with the advent of the UNIX Operating System, there has been a heightened interest in C. And, of course, there is some interest in ADA—but that interest is not yet strong enough to merit inclusion in this book. But the biggest news insofar as I am concerned is the major move to *driver* software, and chief amongst the driver software has to be Lotus Symphony. We'll talk about both, for they are the harbinger of change in our field. In the last edition of this book I called this driver software "specification translators." The description remains apt, but not necessarily explanatory.

This time we'll look more closely at Theory Z and at some implementation of traditional yet new management concepts which may be changing the staid management types into managers of compression. No predominant theories have emerged in this time, but we're going to change the focus of the management chapter and the data processing management chapter to emphasize technique and other considerations.

The mathematics and statistics sections have changed little, though we've tried to find alternate ways to present some of the information—ways which will hopefully be an improvement. A slight change has been made also to the accounting principles chapter, to better convey the message. We've added to the chapter on mathematics to place a focus on the business math which the data processor encounters.

The CDP Exam is still divided into five sections, of 60 questions each. The last edition of this book was divided into eight chapters. This edition still has eight chapters, but we are changing the mix, combining chapters and adding new information in the accounting and systems sections. The rationale for this is that the analysts' responsibility is broadening as the microcomputer field is growing. One of the first ways it is broadening is in the structuring of the task, and you'll find that we've incorporated some systems structuring into this edition. Also, some additional principles and practices of project management have been incorporated into this chapter. Likewise, we are expanding the accounting chapter to include discussion about EDP auditing.

While database has traditionally been a part of the systems portion of the exam and the review manual, the micro, again, has made changes to the concepts of holding data. In addition, because the micro-to-mainframe manipulation of data promises to be a major part if the next decade of computing, communications discussion becomes part of this book in this edition.

The systems person has been undergoing a transformation, a metamorphosis, if you will, to the point that in many companies of size, the analyst has become an in-house consultant in the use of the computer in data processing and office automation. The operative phrase here is Decision Support Systems, and we'll discuss the concepts of modeling the organization.

This, then, is a reference book for the CDP Examination, yes. But it is designed to go far beyond the examination itself. I happen to think there are things involved with the field which have not yet found their way to the test. This is the approach taken in this book:

- Chapter 1. Data processing history and equipment
- Chapter 2. Computer programming and software
- Chapter 3. General management
- Chapter 4. Data processing management and project management
- Chapter 5. Accounting and EDP auditing
- Chapter 6. Mathematics and statistics
- Chapter 7. Systems analysis and design
- Chapter 8. Miscellaneous systems topics:
  Communications, Database, Decision Support Systems, and Office Automation

Like its predecessor, this edition anticipates where the field, and the examination will go. It has not been prepared simply for one to pass the present-day CDP Examination. What is here is probably more than enough to get you through the exam and any professional examination dealing with these topics in this career field.

My CDP had been acquired in 1969—just how current could I possibly be in 1985? To find out, and to see just how good a tool the manual was, I sat for the exam in May of 1985 in Portland, OR. It had been my intention to show my grade report, but alas it has disappeared. I did not get 100%. Why not? Aren't you the expert, Ken? Perhaps. There were but three questions on that test which were not specifically covered in my book, and those will be discussed in this edition. That's a 99% coverage, and I'm pretty proud of that, particularly in view of the fact that I've not seen the exam since 1969 and ICCP has steadfastly refused to review the book for coverage. Privately they'll tell me how good the book is, but nothing officially.

At the same time, I misread the questions and answers just like everybody else—or worse yet, the questions still aren't as good as they could be. There were, to my mind, too many of the "NOT" type of question, but at least the "all of the above/none of the above" questions are gone. I'll bet all my answers were defensible. Percentage-wise, however, I'm very close to where I passed in 1969. Consistent at least. Is this book a guarantee that you can pass the exam? No. But the best possible review preparation may lie between these two covers, and the book—while it's becoming more expensive—is still the best single sourcebook available. Note, however, that this book—and any class which may use it—cannot a substitute for fundamental education.

We've made some other changes in this edition, as well. Because I become a little shell-shocked when pounced upon for the very few questions where there is an answer open to disagreement (or for some reason I failed to ensure that the printed answer matched my manuscript), included in this edition are some very brief explanations as to why it is felt the answer is correct. If you disagree, you disagree.

But don't write unless you can defend your answer. It's easy to be critical. In each edition suggestions are solicited from candidates about how the book can be improved; what is received is only criticism because the book is expensive and it's not perfect. Even the young man who so roundly criticized the book in the test room prior to the exam (not knowing the author was present), when contacted, had no specific contributions to make. If the book helped you to pass, give the publisher your testimonial. If it's the worst thing you've ever seen, give us your constructive suggestions. This is a gargantuan effort. If you help us, you help the profession and the certificate.

A few political things:

- The accounting which is incorporated in this book has been drawn from or verified against standard college accounting texts. The auditing which incorporated into this book has been drawn from publications of the Institute of Internal Auditors. Authoritative references have been used.
- With each edition I catch brickbats because I haven't taken pains to identify Ms. Susan Jones as a Manager, or I haven't gone back through the manuscript to ensure that there are an equal number of women and men mentioned. Webster doesn't do you any favors, ladies, by identifying "manager" as a male noun. I've tried. Keep the "sexism" comments to yourselves, ladies, and help me to improve the book's technical content. This book is neither sexist, racist, nor anti-gay. The same could be said of the author.
- To those who are disturbed because the book goes beyond the test, ask yourself whether the book has furthered your career in other areas, as well. I know this: the same comment was included in the 1983 edition; the 1985 test was adequately covered by the materials which were added in 1983. Look upon the book as the kind of reference you can make extended use of in your career.
- To those who feel the book is too expensive and that I'm making a killing, this: this book and every other book you'll purchase today are too expensive. I teach at the college level; I'm sensitive to that. But if a topic that wasn't in the book showed up on the test, you'd not feel too happy about that. Look upon this book as an investment in your career. And if I do make a killing, which is doubtful, I'll retire and not work so hard. If you think writing such a book is easy, I encourage you to try; see the next page.

I've tried to make this the most valuable reference book to the career field possible. Included in this edition are many of the things that have been requested. There are several hundred more questions in this edition than in prior editions. And this time there is a tutorial answer to each question. These new questions, by the way, are not simply drawn from my other publication, *1001 Questions,* published by another publisher. They are entirely new and cover fully the material.

Finally, while this is the fourth edition of this publication, it is my third rewrite of the book in a ten year period. It's time for another to pick up the handle and keep the book current with the state of the art. The rights to this publication are for sale. Contact the author through the publisher. And make an offer.

KENNISTON W. LORD, JR., CDP, CSP

ACKNOWLEDGEMENTS

Ten years ago, with the encouragement of Gerry Galbo, my editor, I purchased the rights to the first edition of this book. First acknowledgement, then, must go to Gerry for his support in this and other publishing projects throughout that period.

My wife Nancy has again performed yeoman service on the manuscript of this book. Not only has she kept things flowing around me and kept me from being interrupted, she has also taken care of the production of the final manuscript. My thanks to her.

Thanks to Joan Hulse who used an IBM PC to do the initial entry and has provided indexing services of various components of my books.

Finally, my thanks to Jim Stirbis, who has taken upon himself the task of editing both the last edition and this edition. He has taken a rough manuscript, with dumb mistakes (are there any other kind?) and shaped it into the finished product you have in hand.

CONTENTS

EXAMINATION SECTION 1

1

DATA PROCESSING EQUIPMENT

COMPUTERS AND PERIPHERAL EQUIPMENT

Evolution of EDP

One cannot underestimate the importance of the history of EDP. Yes, we can live without knowing it, but some knowledge of that history may serve to explain why we are where we are and how we got here. If you think about it, everything written about the history of EDP has been about EDP hardware. The reasons for this are simple—a piece of hardware, being physically tangible, can be pinpointed in time. It is more difficult to determine the precise time of the birth of an idea or concept, much less the successful implementation of that concept. Thus, this part of the chapter will of necessity deal with the history of EDP hardware. The information contained in this book, however, will detail the history of much more than hardware.

Abacus

The abacus is the oldest known mechanical computing device. It evolved from the natural tendency of man to count in a manner similar to the digits on his hands. Numbers are stored on the abacus using the biquinary numbering system, which includes a "bottom five, 1–5" and a "top five, 1–5" approach.

Napier's Bones

Logarithms provided the next logical step in the development of a system of mathematics. Napier devised a set of sticks, or "bones," upon which logarithmic functions had been inscribed. With these devices, for the first time, large numbers could be calculated, based upon roots (bases) and powers (exponents).

Jacquard's Loom

The first "automatic program" was probably the mechanism which controlled Joseph Jacquard's loom. In 1801, Jacquard patented a device which controlled the pattern produced by a loom. Weaving directions were "programmed" by using holes in steel plates. Jacquard wove a portrait of himself using 20,000 steel "cards."

George Boole

The ability of the modern computer to "think" is based upon a book written by an Englishman, George Boole. The book described the mathematics of symbolic logic, today called Boolean Algebra. Boole's principles provided the framework around which the complex digital machines were later developed.

Charles Babbage

In 1812, Charles Babbage, with a grant from the British Government, designed and developed a device for performing simple calculations. It was called a "difference engine." It operated on the principle of constant difference to evaluate mathematical formulas.

Had metals technology been more advanced, Babbage might have realized his dream of building the "analytical engine." As it was designed, the analytical engine would store intermediate answers on cards similar to those used by Jacquard. The machine was designed to read the intermediate answers and then go on to subsequent calculations. As is frequently the case, the machine was never built. Babbage ran out of money and the British government, embroiled in war, could not be persuaded to provide additional resources. A hundred years later, the principles developed by Babbage would be embodied in electronic and electromechanical devices.

The programming language ADA, which will not be dealt with in this edition, was named for Babbage's assistant, Ada Lovelace, first known computer programmer.

Herman Hollerith

Dr. Herman Hollerith developed a method for storing and processing census data. By the time of the 1880 census, Hollerith had concluded that it would take more than 10 years to tabulate the figures, unless some more mechanized means were obtained to process census data. He expanded Jacquard's concept of storing yes/no selections and devised a coding scheme to store data. That coding scheme is today used in tabulating cards. Tabulating cards, on the other hand, aren't used very much anymore. Time marches on.

For the 1890 census, Hollerith's Tabulating Machine Company provided equipment for storing and processing census data. After several mergers and considerable growth, this company is now IBM.

James Powers

James Powers, who also worked at the Bureau of the Census, developed a line of card-tabulating equipment. His equipment was used to tabulate the census of 1910. The Powers Accounting Machine Company was later acquired by Remington Rand Corporation. We now call them UNIVAC.

Mark I

The Mark I was a large electromechanical calculator designed by Professor Howard Aiken at Harvard University. Although it was designed in 1937, it was not completed until 1944.

COLOSSUS

Americans like to be credited with the first electronic computer, the ENIAC. However, the first electronic computer might well have been a code-breaking device developed by the British Government early in the Second World War. Dubbed COLOSSUS, the device was was produced for the British Foreign Office in 1943, and successfully broke the German code generated by a highly secret device called ENIGMA.

ENIAC

Credit is customarily given to ENIAC as the first large-scale electronic computer. ENIAC (Electronic Numerical Integrator and Calculator) was built by J. Presper Eckert, Dr. John W. Mauchly, and their coworkers at the Moore School of Electrical Engineering at the University of Pennsylvania.

The ENIAC was completed in 1946 and used by the Ballistic Research Laboratories of the Army

Ordnance Corps in Aberdeen, Maryland, until 1955. Elements of ENIAC may be seen, in working order, at the Smithsonian Institute, Washington, D.C. It still works. ENIAC had less power than today's microcomputer.

General Purpose Stored Program Computers

In 1945, Dr. John von Neumann, part of the ENIAC team, wrote a report proposing for the first time a stored program computer. This resulted in the EDVAC (Electronic Discrete Variable Computer) project, started at the Moore School in 1946. Eckert would later suggest that Dr. von Neumann had represented as his own certain ideas original with Eckert and Mauchly.

Professor Maurice Wilkers spent the summer of 1946 with the Moore School computer group. A year later he began the EDSAC (Electronic Delay Storage Automatic Calculator) at Cambridge University, England. It was completed in 1949, before the EDVAC, and was the first stored program computer to operate.

Princeton

By 1946, von Neumann had moved to the Institute for Advanced Study at Princeton University and had begun the IAS computer. This computer, which had parallel binary computational capability and random access storage, was faster than the older, serial machines.

Massachusetts Institute of Technology

The Whirlwind I computer was started in 1947 at the Servomechanisms Laboratory of the Massachusetts Institute of Technology (MIT). The development of the coincident-current magnetic core memory was a significant contribution of the MIT group, headed by Dr. An Wang, who received its patent. Wang went on to build a very successful computer company with patent infringement monies from a court judgment against IBM.

Manchester University

The University of Manchester, England, is credited with the Williams Tube Memory, the first practical electrostatic storage system, in 1947. Other developments included index registers and hierarchies of memory devices.

The National Bureau of Standards

While waiting for two very large Hurricane Computers to be produced by the Raytheon Corporation, NBS started to build two interim computers, the SEAC (Standards Eastern Automatic Computer) and the SWAC (Standards Western Automatic Computer).

The SWAC had a very small electrostatic memory, but it was one of the fastest of the early computers. The SEAC was the first stored program computer to run in the United States; it was placed into operation in 1950 and used for more than ten years. It had a mercury delay line memory to which other types of memory were later added.

UNIVAC

The Eckert-Mauchly Computer Corporation, formed in 1947, contracted for delivery of a UNIVAC (UNIVersal Automatic Computer) to the Bureau of the Census for use in the 1950 census. The UNIVAC was delivered in June 1951 and was used for more than 12 years. The company became the Eckert-Mauchly Division of Remington Rand Corporation. In 1952, Remington acquired Engineering Research

Associates, developer of the ERA 1103, a large and powerful scientific computer, and some of the best early drum memories. Drum memories would be the main memory mainstay until the invention and dissemination of core memories.

International Business Machines Corporation

The road to predominance in the computer mainframe world began with the introduction of electromechanical calculation punches in the 1930s. Largely the funding source for the Mark I in 1944, IBM developed the Card Programmed Calculator (CPC) in 1948. While CPC was not a stored program computer, it did serve as a pre-electronic computing device.

Early in the Korean War, IBM announced the Defense Calculator, a large-scale scientific computer. Known as the IBM 701, it was delivered in 1953. The IBM 702 was intended for the commercial data processing field. It had 10,000 characters of electrostatic Williams Tube Memory. Announced in 1953, the first IBM 702 was delivered in 1955.

The Critical Years

In the mid-1950s, UNIVAC computers were clearly superior to those produced by IBM. IBM had announced the 705 and UNIVAC had announced the UNIVAC II. The first 705 was delivered in late 1955, less than a year after the first 702. It was 1957, however, before the first UNIVAC II was delivered.

In these two very critical years, IBM would make the philosophical, technical, and manufacturing breakthroughs necessary to forge ahead in the large-scale commercial computer field. They would later take a commanding position and would be the subject of extensive and intensive litigation relative to alleged monopolistic domination of the computer industry. By the late 1970s and into the early 1980s the focus of the industry changed from mainframes to microcomputers—personal computers, desktop computers. After more than a decade, the Justice Department abruptly dropped its suit against IBM, freeing the latter to exploit its commanding position. In relatively short order, IBM took the lion's share of the microcomputer world and delved into the business of land and satellite communications.

First Generation

The first generation of commercially produced digital computers appeared in the 1951–1960 time period. Today these machines are considered slow, with small internal memories, able to work on only one job at a time, and dependent on magnetic tape and magnetic drums for the bulk storage of data. First generation computers were characterized by the vacuum tube, with its problems of reliability, heat dissipation, power requirements, air-conditioning requirements, and extensive maintenance.

Second Generation

The second generation of computers were built between the years 1958 and 1965. With larger internal memories, faster execution times, lower maintenance requirements, cooler running, and more power, second-generation computers provided more computer power for the dollar. Mass storage devices had been adopted, but magnetic tape was still the primary medium to store data files. Data communication between computers was introduced. What we now know as multiprocessing didn't really happen in the second generation; however, enterprising software developers found ways to successfully use the newly implemented I/O overlap features.

The major component of the second-generation computer was the transistor, with its faster speed, greater reliability, etc. New concepts of architecture began to appear: channels, data communications, multiprogramming, and time-sharing became part of the data processor's lexicon.

Third Generation

The third generation of computers began to arrive in 1965. With larger internal memories, the ability to handle multiple programs, the sophisticated interrupt systems which allowed the intermingling of system services, the extensive use of data communications, and the provision of mass storage devices (notably removable disk packs, which had also begun to show up on later second generation equipment), third-generation computers were an architectural departure from their predecessors.

The third generation was characterized by microminiature integrated circuit fabrication techniques, which at once reduced the physical size of the circuits by one or two orders of magnitude, reduced maintenance experience, reduced the heat generated by the computer, and improved operating speed.

Fourth Generation and Beyond

It had been predicted that the number of years between computer generations was decreasing and that the fourth generation would appear in 1970. It never happened quite as anticipated. New mainframe computers made significant advances in what has been termed "plug compatible equipment." Fourth generation techniques have been an evolution of, not a departure from third generation concepts. Read only memories (ROM), integrated circuits (ICs), and sophisticated adaptations of solid logic technology (SLT) have provided computers which are more powerful, more capable, and less expensive. New computers of the large mainframe type will continue to appear, but less and less frequently as the world of computer hardware is taken over by the microcomputers, which may logically be labeled as the fifth generation.

The supercomputer still exists, but since the last edition of this book, the ILLIAC IV (designed by the University of Illinois, built by Burroughs, and used by NASA) has been disassembled. The CRAY I, built by Cray Research, has been placed where large number crunching has become important—history repeats itself—the Bureau of Census. The CRAY II supercomputer has come to market during this time, as well.

Minicomputers

Until 1965, the cost of computers limited their use to high-payoff applications of mathematical analysis and commercial operations such as payroll, inventory control, and general business record-keeping. Although the cost of printers, card readers, card punches, and magnetic storage devices remains high, the cost of the basic electronic components used to make computers had been significantly reduced, a process which continues to the present day. This allowed the use of small computers in monitoring and controlling production lines and laboratory processes.

The development of the minicomputer brought forth new concepts in storage technology. We began to see the first random access memory (RAM) here, used with the read only memories (ROM). The computer on a chip had yet to be invented, but the components which would ultimately make the microcomputer successful found their genesis in the efforts of Digital Equipment Corporation (DEC) and Data General (DG). There were other minicomputer manufacturers (DEC was called Snow White—and the other seven minicomputer manufacturers were called . . .). Today, DEC has a dominant position in the minicomputer world, and a large share of the mainframe market. Their microcomputers didn't fare all that well.

Minicomputers differ from large-scale mainframe computer systems only in the manner in which each is used. The same peripheral devices and programming languages are available for minicomputers as are available for large-scale computers. Several minicomputers are being teamed up to provide large-scale computing power. Because of their low cost, minicomputers are being used as dedicated processors for on-line real-time data processing applications. Other uses of minicomputers include distributed processing, data collection, and various control functions. Interestingly, the minicomputer has taken a somewhat different direction with a concept known as the "office automation." In this context, the minicomputer is being used to function as a word processor, and electronic filing and retrieval system, a terminal to send and receive electronic mail, etc. Despite the onslaught of microcomputers, the mini has held its own in an increasingly specialized market.

Microcomputers

In 1976 the Mits Corporation of Albuqueque, NM, produced a kit computer, using the new "computer on a chip" from Intel. Known as the Altair 8800, this device launched us into the era of the personal computer. A year later, Radio Shack would introduce the TRS-80 home computer, and we have subsequently seen such devices as the IMSAI, the PET, the APPLE, the NORTHSTAR, the SOL, the ATARI, the COMPAQ, the CORONA, etc. While many have come and gone, IBM continues to dominate.

Microprogrammable Computers

The microcomputer, the "computer on a chip," has appeared everywhere—with applications to automobiles, televisions, microwave ovens, video games, hand-held toys, chess challengers, etc. One of the more productive uses, however, has been in what is called the world of robotics. Used in industrial robots, machines are reducing human tedium, and, unfortunately, displacing a few people. Programmable controllers, as they are called, route manufactured products, apply processing technology (such as welds), and even make rudimentary decisions based upon what they have learned. We will see the field of AI (artificial intelligence) mushroom in the upcoming years, as these industrial robots help us to compete.

More exciting, however, are the various ways in which the microprogrammable computer has been put to use to help people, particularly in aid to the handicapped. The microprogrammable computer helps the blind to see, the incoherent to express himself, and the halt to become mobile. What then may be seen as the scourge of the working class has become a most welcomed benefactor to a whole class of people unable, without it, to function.

Solid State Memories

The computer on a chip has literally set designers of computing hardware, and to a great extent, software, free of the design limitations of previous computers. Given the basic architecture of the chip, machine structure is now implemented via microcodes, more commonly called firmware. Each machine language instruction is defined by a set of microprogram instructions which have been located in an inaccessible place (to the problem programmer) referred to as Read-Only-Memory (ROM). ROM is used for unmodifiable microcode and is customarily distributed by the manufacturers of—interestingly—both hardware and software. The Microsoft BASIC interpreter is one example of a piece of software which has been distributed in hardware (ROM) form.

The ROM has found very wide use in the so-called notebook microcomputers, such as the Radio Shack TRS-80/100, the NEC 9201, and the Epson HX-20, HX-40, and PX-8 series. In the first four, the ROM units that contain the programs are built into the device. In the last, also known as the Geneva, the ROM may be changed, allowing popular software to be entered to the computer as easily as plugging it in. To change the characteristics of the machinery, it is necessary only to alter or replace the ROM.

Closely related to ROM is RAM or Random Access Memory. This is the memory which is customarily available to operating systems and to user programs. RAM has emerged as a bulk storage memory which is similar in nature to any random access device, in that addressing schemes allow direct access through a delicately controlled system of registers.

Advances in memory technology have occurred at a very rapid pace since the advent of the computer on a chip. Manufacturers have found ways to increase the number of memory positions in the chip while reducing the size of the chip itself.

There are others. EROM, or Erasable Read-Only-Memory, is similar to ROM except that it is accessible locally under specialized controls. Once realigned, it functions just like ROM. Programmable Read-Only-Memory (PROM) functions in a manner similar to EROM, except that it may be accessed under user program control.

Bubble memories made their debut in calculators and some computer memories, and where operating temperatures will remain critical, they will be further implemented. However, applications of silicon technology continue to hold the day. Sand, which contains silicon, is plentiful and inexpensive. The cost of computing hardware is coming down as the cost of computer personnel is escalating. As with industrial robots, more and more of the work is being shifted to the machine. And, as we will see when we discuss management, the computer-knowledgeable micro-equipped user presents special challenges to DP.

Computer Components and Functions

Irrespective of the computer—be it the Apple IIc or the Cray II—all computers have some common functional components. In the early days there was a box called memory, a box called CPU, a box called ALU (arithmetic/logic unit), and several boxes called Input and Output. They were singular in purpose and easily identified. As technology advanced, new concepts were added and the packaging changed. Despite the change in packaging, some functions remain identifiable. The sections of a computer are, therefore, detailed as to function here.

Memory Section

The memory section of the computer performs several fundamental functions. Memory, of course, is an older analogy to the human brain. The types of storage have changed throughout the computer's history from electromagnets to vacuum tubes, to transistors, to core storage to solid state storage (or simply RAM), but the function has been essentially unchanged.

Memory is used to store both programs and data. The programs may be an operating system, a language compiler, or the spreadsheet calculation mechanism used to predict the budget. It may also be one or more concurrently processing application programs.

The data may be data which had been entered and is now positioned in a buffer; intermediate data, on which some calculations have been made; output data, perhaps also positioned on a buffer; communications data, coming and going through a communications device; or constant data.

The memory which is part of the installed computer is commonly called main memory. This memory is that which is customarily directly controlled by the computer's control section. In recent years, the concept of remote memories has gained acceptance. These remote memories are a function of a hierarchy of memories and a variety of control unit mechanisms. Components of main memory are memory cells (positions of memory), the memory address register, the memory work register, and the associated electronic circuits for reading, writing, restoring, checking, and clearing. Memory is divided into cells, each of which can be uniquely referenced by the computer's control circuits. Memory cells are able to store some fixed number of binary digits (bits). Occasionally, these bits are divided into specific word lengths. Fixed-word-length computers have word lengths which will range from 8 bits to 256 bits, in increments of 8.

Since the last edition of this book, the preponderance of microcomputer memory sizes have changed from 8-bit to 16-bit machines, with a minor number of 32-bit machines. Minicomputers will generally have 16- or 32-bit word lengths. Larger machines will have 32, 64, or 128 bits to the word. Word lengths of 256 bits will be found in large scientific machines.

Each memory cell is referenced or accessed according to the memory address where it is located and according to the size of the memory word register. Memory is customarily organized into fixed or variable word. Fixed-word memories are composed of standard (fixed) memory cells. Each cell is the same size and will hold a data work, number, or instruction word in the system. Use of multiple cells may be required. The design choice of the word length (size of each cell, in bits) is a compromise among conflicting factors of speed-of-access and memory cycle considerations. Variable-word memories are also composed of fixed-size memory cells. All cells are uniform, but each will hold only a single byte or character code. The assembler programmer decides in each case what constitutes the length of each word, selecting the required number of cells to make up the word. The high-level language programmer need not be concerned about this.

Computers of recent manufacture have traded heavily upon the concepts just presented. Efficiency and speed are obtained from fixed word lengths. The programmer, however, can reference parts or multiples of the word length design, as appropriate. Some refer to this organization as fixed-word, byte-oriented. These concepts change somewhat with the microcomputer, as the data and program are literally moved around within memory via a bus. The bus is an electronic vehicle upon which program and data travel, with random entrance and exit points.

The memory address register holds the absolute (often called relocated) address that is to be accessed for reading from or writing into. Information in transit to and from the memory cell is held in the memory word register (just like a bus), which must be large enough to hold the largest portion of memory which can be accessed. The memory address register must be large enough to hold the largest absolute address in the memory.

Arithmetic and Logic Section (ALU)

The arithmetic and logic section is the calculating and processing part of the computer, where the work is done. The primary function of this section is to perform the arithmetic functions of addition, subtraction, multiplication, and division. Also, it performs the functions of logic, using Boolean Algebra, wherein testing for magnitude (greater-than, less-than, equal-to, not-equal-to) is performed. In most computers, this section is also responsible for bit manipulation (tests under mask, ORs, ANDs, NORs, bit shifting, bit rotation, etc.). Positionally this may or may not be a separate section of the computer nowadays. Functionally it is unique.

All computers of recent manufacture work in some form of binary arithmetic. Designers of computing hardware, however, have promoted notational concepts of data representation for ease of handling. Thus, we talk of binary machines, decimal machines, fixed-point arithmetic, floating-point arithmetic, octal and hexadecimal notation, single- and double-precision arithmetic, subtractive adders, and complementary arithmetic.

Control Section

In a general purpose digital data processing computer, it is the function of the control section to control, direct, and time the operation of all of the other components of the computer. The control section functions as directed by the instruction set of the computer, according to the individual instructions of an internally stored program. This stored program is a unique sequence of instruction words and symbols which form the machine-language version of the algorithm or process to accomplish the task to be performed.

While there have appeared some standard source languages, or at least some which purport to be standard, there is no standard machine language among computing machines. There is a notable exception to this: the microcomputers. While there are several different microcomputer chips, they have been evolutionary in nature. The 4004 chip gave way to the 8008, to the 8080, the 8085, and the Z-80. These, in turn, gave way to 8086, 8088, 80186, 80286, etc. Other chips have been designed (6502, 1802, 68000 etc.), but the preponderance of the current crop of microcomputers have settled on the 16-bit series (8086/8088, 80186/80286—IBM or IBM compatible) or the 32-bit series (68000, used in the Apple McIntosh). This, then, means that the machine language is identical among machines.

In general, the control section includes a master clock, a program address (or control) register, an instruction word register, an operation code decoder, an instruction word modifier decoder, and an instruction word operand address field register. While the titles of these will change from manufacturer to manufacturer, conceptually they are the same. Other components may be the interrupt system, foreground and background control mechanisms, memory protect mechanisms, index registers, base registers, associative page registers, and status-word registers.

Some functions of the control section are directly attributable to the number of active addresses working within the design of the computer itself. We have seen three different types of instruction formats: one address, two address, and three address.

One-Address Format

The one-address format normally contains the address or location of one of the operands specified by the operation code. If other operands are required in the specific operation, they must have been prepositioned by earlier instructions. This concept is extensively implemented in the microcomputers.

The shifting result of registers is a prime example of this concept. The register is referenced by the instruction itself, while the modifier designates the number of bits to be shifted. Another example of the one-address instruction which does not contain an address is the instruction which contains immediate data, that is, data which is a part of the instruction itself.

Thus, a one-address system may contain instructions which hold an address (either data or instruction), a constant which may be an instruction modifier, or immediate data. One-address systems have not been used extensively since the second generation for the larger mainframe computers, but one-address instructions are still used on those systems.

Two-Address Instructions

When the instruction word format contains two address fields in addition to the operation code, there are many combinations of usage possible. The instruction may literally contain two addresses, such as MOVE from a source address to a destination address; or one or both of the addresses could be that of a fixed location, such as registers; or one address could be a memory address and the other could be a register. A single two-address instruction word format can be used to transfer the contents of one memory cell to another memory cell. Occasionally, one of the addresses is used to detail the next instruction to be accessed. This system is used for just about every type of current computer.

The two-address format comprises an operation code and two address fields. Each address field may be either a data address, an instruction address, or a constant. The constant may be either a modification of the operation code or immediate data.

Three-Address Instructions

Some of the first generation of computers and a few of the second generation used the three-address system. Under this scheme, in some instances, the operation is similar to a two-address machine, but with a significant difference. For instance, in a two-address machine, if it is desired to perform the functions of A + B = C, A would have to be added to C and then B would have to be added to C, with C retaining the result—and following two separate instructions. In the three address system, A is one address, B is the second, and C is the third, allowing the entire function to be performed in a single instruction. The number of addresses in a machine instruction is strictly in the design of the machine itself.

Variable-Length Instructions

The variable length instruction consists of an operation code and as many addresses and modifiers as necessary (to a maximum permissible size) to perform the desired operation. The length of the instruction must either be implied by the operation code or indicated by some discrete signal which is not part of the instruction.

The control section of the computer exerts control over all other sections by sending out control signals and timing pulses in a periodic fashion. The fundamental cycle of control is called the computer cycle or instruction cycle. The number of substeps in these cycles varies with each computer, but for general purposes there are four phases: fetch the instruction, get the data, perform the action, and store the results. When these phases are specified by a RAM-based program, rather than by hard-wired electronic circuits, the program is called a microprogram. Some machines allow the user to implement microprograms which specify the method of operation of special machine-language instructions that the user has defined. This is called EPROM, Erasable Programmable Read-Only Memory.

Fetch the Instruction

To fetch the instruction, the computer must determine the location of the next instruction in the internally stored program. Generally this information is contained in a register which has been designated for the purpose. This program address register (or program control register) holds this address. During fetch, the contents of this register are transferred to the memory address register; the instruction is moved from memory to the memory word register and on to the program control register, where it is decoded (interpreted) and performed. The program address register is incremented to the next sequential instruction.

Get the Data

In this phase, the operands are obtained and/or positioned. In its simplest form, the address of the operand is moved from the address field of the instruction word to the memory address register. The desired data are then moved via the memory word register to the appropriate register for action. Prior decoding of the operation code will have enabled all of these moves. In a more complex case, it may be necessary to decode several modifiers in order to determine if indexing, indirect addressing, displacement, or some combination of the three will be used and which registers and memory cells are involved in determining the operand address. For register-to-register transfers of data, a single modifier is sufficient to specify each register.

Perform the Action

This is the actual execution of the intended operation, determined by the prior decoding of the operation code. Iteration of these steps is determined either by the data or by additional information from the instruction address or modifiers.

Store the Results

By convention, some operations leave the results where they were produced. Others return the results to specified memory locations. Where the results must be moved, the store-results phase is similar to the get-data phase, except that the movement of data is reversed.

And Again . . .

The cycles continue until ordered to stop. If the control section proceeds through the steps and phases of the cycle at a predetermined rate, determined by clock pulses or some other timed arrangement, the computer is termed *synchronous.* If it proceeds to a step upon completion of the preceding step, the computer is called *asynchronous.*

Input/Output Section

The function of the input/output (I/O) section is to control the flow of information to or from the computer (and in some cases expedite the flow, alter the packaging of information, and encrypt/codify the information). The I/O section can be considered an extension of the control section. If proper distinctions are made between I/O data, I/O media, and I/O devices, the I/O function can be understood.

It is difficult to describe simply the components of the I/O section, because from one computer manufacturer to another the techniques used to implement these concepts have been really very different. The operation to be performed may be identical but the mechanisms (both hardware and software) will vary widely from computer system to computer system. In the early days card and tape input and output were most commonplace. Today it is not uncommon to find whole computer systems as I/O appendages to larger computers. Plug-to-plug peripherals have been commonplace for many years. Plug-compatible-mainframes (PCM) are more recent.

The I/O components must include timing and control circuitry; registers to hold and decode the commands to I/O drivers, controllers, and devices; and enough registers and buffer space to store and forward the data information flow both in and out. Buffer considerations to compensate for slower devices must be a part of the design of this section. Designs which place control functions away from the mainframe and into channels and control units are commonplace. Also required are registers which handle priorities, interrupts, lockout or security, buffers, device activities and status, etc.

Internal Processing

The Stored Program Concept

The concept of the internally stored program is a significant feature that contributes to the power of the modern electronic digital computer. The purpose of a program is to direct the computer to perform a sequence of steps or procedures. The steps in the sequence constitute an operation upon data which has been presented in either an extended or coded format. The internally stored program is generally called "code" and will be co-resident in memory with the data upon which it is to perform its work.

Code Structure for Data Representation

Recall that the computer stores programs and information in binary form. Binary has only two basic characters: zero and one. Thus, irrespective of the method in which data has been *noted*, it will be *encoded* in binary. Binary, being bi-stable, represents the presence or absence of a pulse, the presence or absence of a hole in a card or paper tape, or a space (gap) or recording on a tape or disk. Because binary encoding has only two characters, very few laws are required to cover the possible combinations of the characters in addition, subtraction, multiplication, and division. Ease of complementing is also a consideration.

It's important to distinguish between the *encoding* via binary and the *notation* used to present that coding. That notation may be binary, octal, hexadecimal, ASCII (American Standard Code for Information Interchange) or some other. Unless someone develops an entirely new system, all encoding will be binary. Notation, however, is how the computer will accept and present the data. Data are pieces of knowledge about a given class or subject. In and of themselves, they may be meaningless. Combined with other pieces, tabulated, calculated, summarized, and presented, they are customarily termed information. Information can be subdivided into words, which further break down into alphabetic letters, numbers, and special symbols. Those data elements which occupy a single position of memory are often defined as characters.

Normally, 26 letters, 10 digits, about 7 punctuation symbols, and some other special symbols are used. Further, modern computers will extend-or double-these by implementation of both upper-and lower-case symbols. Thus, depending upon the specific computer, from 43 to 112 individual codes will be represented. The most common character set currently being used is ASCII. ASCII is one of a class of bit groups at the seven-level. Seven-bit groups provide for 128 code groups, enough for upper- and lower-case letters and many special control symbols. ASCII has been a requirement of the U.S. Government since 1969. Even those systems which are 8-bit (or 16/32-bit) oriented will handle ASCII.

The smallest practical code was devised for the teletype by Jean Baudot. A five-level code, it is called, interestingly, the Baudot Code, and was for many years the mainstay of communications. The "IBM Extended Binary Coded Decimal Interchange Code (EBCDIC)" is an example of an eight-bit code. It permits 256 different codes.

First and second generation computers, and some later third generation computers, used six-bit codes. Groups of six bits allow 64 (26) codes, and were used for Binary Coded Decimal (BCD), XS-3 (Excess-Three), FIELDATA, Flexowriter, etc. A serious problem with these code sets is that no two are identical. More difficult yet is the fact that the collating sequences are not standard. A collating sequence is simply the order-by-numerical-weight method to determine code sequence.

The concept of a binary code is as simple as binary itself. Any binary code is just that: an arbitrary combination of symbols upon which there is an agreed-to standard interpretation. In a binary number, the binary digits have both digit and positional value.

Accessing

Fundamental to the existence of the computer is the ability of the control unit to access internally stored program instructions and data.

Direct addressing is the most straightforward method to access data or instructions. The instruction word contains the number (address or displacement modifier) that is decoded to develop the absolute and "direct" address of the location to be accessed. Thus, the concept of Random Access Memory (RAM). The only requirement of this mechanism is that the instructions must be able to contain the fully developed address.

Indirect addressing allows the computer to place not the address of a data field or instruction within the address itself, but rather the address of a memory cell which contains the address of the operand. In this manner, it is possible to cascade addresses, a concept which will be described in the data base discussions within this manual.

Base/displacement addressing requires that a relative (or relocatable) address be contained within a program and that the program or system software must load a valid beginning address into the base register. The displacement address contained in the instruction word is added to the base address in the base address register to give the absolute memory cell address. In some systems it is the programmer's responsibility to supply the displacement address relative to more than one base register. Generally, however, everything is coded relative to zero, with the system supplying the base address and resolving the relocated address.

Indexing by using a register as a displacement to modify data access is a simple scheme which adds the contents of the index register (offset) to the address contained within the instruction to produce an *effective address*. The concept is precisely the same as base/displacement addressing.

Pushdown stacks is a form of addressing which became popular with the microcomputer. Under this concept, instructions and data are handled in a last-in, first-out concept, the way dishes are stacked in a restaurant. The software language FORTH capitalizes on this stacked environment for fast, efficient manipulation of programs and data.

Beginning at the second generation of computers, it became possible to access parts of words, rather than the whole word. Partial word accessing has been available in one form or another since. Under the current implementation of the scheme, a small group of modifier bits can designate the part of a fixed word which is to be accessed.

Registers

It would be an accurate statement that nothing works within an electronic computer without the aid and assistance of a register. Registers cause, permit, control, facilitate, or track action within the computer. The register is the central point in a network of internal communications.

Register types vary, of course, from computer to computer, and their use in microcomputers varies significantly from those of their larger cousins. Registers are used in microcomputers also as a form of ''stack'' memory. There are, however, common functions of registers among various computers. These include the program address register (locates the next instruction), the program control register (decodes the present instruction), the general purpose registers (used by the arithmetic and logic section for arithmetic and logical operations), and the memory section registers which control the movement of data through buffers, among memory cells, and among the input/output units.

Data Flow

Great strides have been made in the transmission of data between parts of computers and across communication lines. Originally, data flow was transmitted serially, a bit at a time, and this method is still in use. Parallel transmission followed, as channels were pressed into service for communications not only with devices but with other communication recipients.

There have been exciting changes and developments in the process of data flow. Integrated network architectures have been interfaced with large-scale computing hardware to provide parallel digital communication at high rates of speed across conventional communication lines, through microwave communication, and using satellites.

More details about communications may be found in the new material on communications and databases, found later in this book.

Channels and Trunks

Early in the first generation of computers it became evident that it was not at all economical to drive and control I/O devices with the CPU. Things simply locked up pending satisfactory completion of input/output operations. The channel is a device which performs all of the functions of the computer with respect to the driving and controlling of I/O devices, but does so removed from the computer itself. The devices are connected to control units, which are connected to channels, which are, in turn, connected directly to the CPU—generally. As computing systems have become more powerful, the need to add yet another hardware device in this sequence has become apparent. Thus, today, mini- or microcomputers are inserted in the line for the sole purpose of handling data communication among devices or communication media. These devices will provide buffering capability, speed compensation, interrupt handling capability, remote data bases, and in some cases host independence.

A trunk is a multiple and standard connection between components of the computer system. It will have as many two-way conductors as there are bits in the computer transmission word, plus those connections necessary for control purposes.

Interrupt

The interrupt is a hardware feature that allows a computer to change from one state of control to another under an orderly scheme and upon some kind of agreed-upon external stimulus. Further, an interrupt might be a function of an internal clock.

The interrupt generally instigates selected sequence of events. A register will note the location the computer was working with at the time of the interrupt. Another register or status word may contain the location of the interrupt handler for the class of interrupt which caused the change. That interrupt handler will then assume control of the machine for the period of time necessary to dispose of the cause of the interrupt. Then the sequence of events reverses itself, finally allowing the computer to resume what it was doing at the time of the interruption.

A minimum of hardware is required: the termination of the interrupt signal, the interface with software which will manipulate the "push down stack" of memory to allow the process to be reversed later.

In smaller computers, there may be as few as one or as many as fifty more classes of interrupt. In the larger, more complex machines, the reasons for the interrupt may vary, but sixteen levels of interrupt is the usual minimum.

Memory Protection Mechanisms

In multiprogramming, time-sharing, on-line real-time systems, software supervisory modes, and in other instances, it may be desirable to allow access to memory under very controlled circumstances. This is a hardware feature which, through software control, protects large blocks of memory from accidental and unauthorized access in the normal course of business.

Counters, Accumulators, and Adders

Counters are registers or memory cells that can be incremented or decremented either automatically or by program control. When combined with initiation and testing, the registers can hold control information, such as loop control (Jump Loop, DO, DO UNTIL, DO WHILE, PERFORM, or FOR . . . NEXT) processes.

Accumulators are registers of fundamental importance, in that nearly all computers use registers to contain the elements, intermediate results, and final results of all calculations. In some instances, it is the programmer's responsibility to retrieve information from the accumulator. In yet others, the intervening software will perform those tasks.

In its simplest form the half-adder adds two binary digits and produces a one-digit sum and a one-digit carry. To add two binary digits and the carry from the preceding stage, two half-adders in cascade are required. Each will produce only a one-digit sum and a carry to the following stage.

Floating Point

Scientists use logarithms and scientific notation to represent very large and very small numbers. Similarly, computers use "floating-point" notation. In all computers that handle floating point, the number to be represented is converted to a two-part number or expression, which is called normalized form. The first part is the fractional part, called the *mantissa.* The second part is the *exponent*, which is the power to which the numbering system base is raised to make the expression equal to the original number. This scheme is called floating point because, using the exponents-times-a-fraction method to express a number, the exponent can vary and then the point can float correspondingly, without changing the value of the number. In the decimal system, the point is a decimal point; in other systems a binary point or a hexadecimal point. When the point falls just to the left of the high-order one-bit of the fraction, the expression is normalized.

When no sign position is allowed for the exponents, a value in the center of the total range of possible exponents is chosen to represent the exponent zero. All exponents are biased by the selected value. Thus, biased exponents are always positive. They are called characteristics, and are also referred to as a scale factor or scaled exponent.

As arithmetic operations are performed on floating point numbers, the points may float to the right or the left, becoming unnormalized. The computer will normalize the final result.

Microprograms

Some computers allow the user to define machine language instructions by leaving a block of operation codes undefined and providing a means for the user to define them. The user must understand the format of the computer's operation codes, set up the desired microprogram in main storage, and execute the standard instruction for loading the microprogram into the appropriate location (EROM) or RAM). The computer will then refer to the user's microprogram to determine the definition of a user-defined machine instruction. As we continue to mature, we will find more and more software systems moving into microcode—and that software which may be subject to patent or copyright being placed into microcode to preclude modification or piracy.

Other changes in this area include the ability of one computer to function as another—or in a multiprocessing mode to function as more than one computer. An example of this would be the operating system which could cause a portion of a mainframe computer to look like and function like another operating system or indeed as another entirely different computer, through simulation or other means.

Input/Output Media and Devices

Card Reader

Nothing would have made this author more glad than to be able to tell you that since the last edition of this book, the punched card has taken its place in the annals of history as a precusor to something more modern. However, about the best that can be said is that the punched card is no longer the file medium of choice and has been largely relegated to the entry of data. One of these days it will definitely become a thing of the past as bar readers, scanners, or terminal entry will become the vogue.

The punched card reader (device) is a peripheral input device whose purpose is to transfer the data from the punched card (medium) to the CPU. There are two types of punched card readers: the brush type and the photoelectric cell type. In the brush-type reader, the card is fed under reading brushes which, making electrical contact through the holes, sense the presence or absence of holes in each column of the card. The photoelectric-cell type reader operates on the same principle, except that photocells are activated by light which will pass through holes and not through an unpunched portion of the card. Card reading speeds range from about 30 to 2,000 cards per minute.

Regardless of the method of timing the movement of the card through the reader, it takes a command from the CPU to begin the movement. Basically, there is only one instruction to read a card. However, several other functions may be controlled. If a multistacker reader is used, the selection of the stacker into which the card will be put upon completion of the read cycle, the selection of the section in memory in which the card image will be stored, and tests for possible conditions of the card reader, such a read errors, hopper-out-of-cards, or stacker-full condition, will be performed.

Normally, the card goes through two different read situations to check for validity of the read operation. The holes are sensed at the first read station and a count of holes is established. Then the card passes through the second read station. If the count is the same, then the information is transferred into memory; if the count is not the same, the error signal is generated, and the card is dropped into a reject stacker. The error signal and the selection of the reject stacker are controlled by the program in the CPU. Some readers also compare what was actually read at each station. Many card punches, especially lower-speed units, are "end-feed." They operate one column at a time.

The move away from the punched card has brought with it new classes of data entry personnel and users directly involved with data entry and program operation. Also, key punch machines are fast becoming obsolete, particularly in large systems.

Card Punch

The card punch is used to punch coded holes in a punch card, as a means to prepare input to another segment of the data processing system. The information is punched in column-parallel, all columns simultaneously. Before a card can be punched, all of the information to be encoded to the card must be placed into a buffer. The on line card punch works differently from a manual card punch, which can punch only a single column at a time.

Since the whole card image is stored in the punch buffer, it is possible to punch all columns and rows at one time. It is more practical, however, to punch all columns of one row, then subsequent rows, one at a time. After the card has been punched, it then moves past a read station where the card is either checked for the proper number of punches or logically checked.

Punched cards are by and large disappearing from the modern-day data processing scene. The expanded use of on line systems and use of microcomputers and minicomputers in distributed data processing networks have made cards an impractical means to store file or intermediate data. Today, bulk storage devices are available on all computer systems of moderate size, and even smaller systems have fixed disk or diskette systems for the storage of data—as well as cassette tape. Because the punched card is on its way out, very little card punching is done nowadays. You will find cards most often used to prepare turnaround documents, such as a utility bill.

Magnetic Tape Units

Historically, magnetic tapes have been nickel-cobalt-beryllium steel and have appeared in a variety of widths, from $\frac{1}{2}$ inch to 3 inches. By far the preponderance of large system tapes today are $\frac{1}{2}$ inch, magnetic-oxide-coated mylar, $1\frac{1}{2}$ mils in thickness. The usual length of a tape is 2,400–3,600 feet. Some computers in the minicomputer and microcomputer classifications still use tape, using cassette tapes of $\frac{1}{8}$ inch or $\frac{1}{4}$ inch width. Tapes are largely used for microcomputer backup, and tape backup (often called the Bernoulli Box) to hard disk microcomputer systems is becoming quite popular.

Magnetic tape can be used both for the storage of data and programs and for the input and output of intermediate data. Any way it's used, it is considerably cheaper than available alternatives. However, speed of recording may be a determining factor when one is considering tape.

Information recording on cassette tapes via microcomputers has been largely with tones within audio frequencies, as opposed to the digital recording techniques used on the larger computers. Information is generally recorded in one of two modes—binary coded or straight binary. The two most common track sizes are seven-and nine-track, with the nine-track being the standard. Seven-track tapes accommodated several six-bit codes, e.g., Binary Coded Decimal (BCD), Excess-Three (XS-3), etc. Nine-track tape reserves eight bits for the data, and can accommodate the Extended Binary Coded Decimal Interchange Code (EBCDIC, the so-called "IBM Standard"), and the American Standard Code for Information Interchange (ASCII). Nine-track can hold an eight-bit code or two four-bit hexadecimal codes, or one eight-bit binary group plus a parity bit. It is quite common in systems which have held to six-bit codes for the nine-channel tape to carry four six-bit characters in three eight-bit frames.

Several methods of recording are used for magnetic surface media, such as drums, disks, and tape. In one method, a magnetized spot represents a one-bit, and the absence of a magnetized spot represents a zero. Several other recording methods have been used to minimize recording and sensing errors and to optimize recording and sensing efficiencies. These schemes include return-to-zero, return-to-bias, non-return-to-zero, modified non-return-to-zero, and phase modulation (often called phase encoding).

Similarities: two hubs upon which to mount the tape and a take-up reel; read- and write-heads, capstans for each, vacuum columns or other speed compensating mechanisms, motors to drive the hubs, and electronic circuitry to perform reading, recording, and sensing; controls for the operator. Differences: physical size of tape reels, tracks on the tape, methods of recording, levels of recording, arrangements of the bits, parity coding and checking, tape speed, recording density, code used, methods of error correction and end-of-tape detection.

Tape speeds were originally 50 inches per second. Today, speeds in excess of 300 inches per second are not uncommon, though 200 is more customary. Recording densities range from very low to more than 6,000 characters per inch. Common densities in use are 200; 556; 800; 1600; and more than 5000, with the 1600 density being currently predominant.

Accuracy of transmission is attained via a pair of redundancy checks. The vertical redundancy check counts the bits within the character. If the number of bits is odd, the parity bit is turned on. If the number of bits is even, the parity bit is turned off. Memory tends to be odd parity, tape tends to be even parity. Horizontal redundancy check performs the same checking, but horizontally throughout the record.

Data transfer rates will vary according to densities and tape speeds, as well as for the electronics which must control the process, check for parity, etc. Today, rates above 300,000 characters per second are common. Thirty years ago, 10,000 were common.

Data are recorded on magnetic tape in groups called *blocks*. The block is read sequentially (linearly) into some form of buffer or into main memory. The maximum length of the block is certainly constrained by the size of the available memory, but more probably by the length of the input buffer. Also, it is useful to have more that one block of memory in the computer at the same time, limiting the available space to memory divided by N blocks. A different kind of limit must be considered for the minimum size of a block, because of the constraints of tape equipment. Because the tape unit must slow down and stop and speed up and start, there are spaces between blocks, called the interblock or inter-record gap. This approximates $\frac{6}{10}$ of an inch.

Consider a density of 800 characters per inch and a record length of 80 characters. If only one record was located in the block, the data would be recorded in sets of $\frac{1}{10}$ inch separated by $\frac{6}{10}$ inch. Not very efficient. Where the records are this short, the general practice is to group several logical records into one physical record (or block). This is called, aptly, blocking. The primary consideration in establishing block size will be the CPU's timing and the I/O facilities and needs.

Diskettes

No media has more revolutionized the data input, storage, output process than has the diskette. A diskette is a platter of magnetic material enclosed within a square protective jacket with a felt inside coating. See Figure 1.1. The actual diskette itself is defined in tracks and sectors, as shown in Figure 1.2. The number of tracks and sectors will vary with the size of the diskette, whether one or two sides is to be used, and which equipment will use it. At the moment, diskettes are available in two sizes: 5.25 inch and 8 inch. The former is most used for mainframe microcode or personal computers. The latter is most used for personal computers and standalone word processing systems. Recently, a smaller, 3.5 inch diskette, encased in plastic, has become available. Designed by Sony, it is used on the Apple McIntosh and

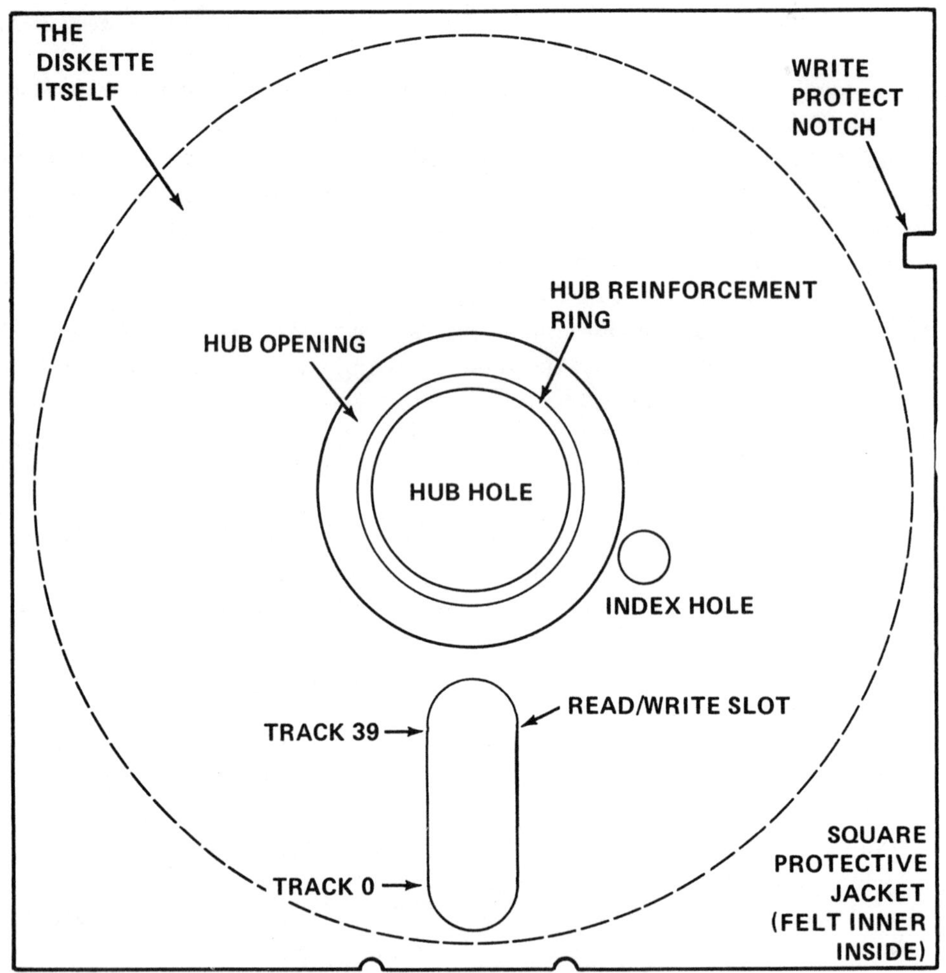

Figure 1.1. Diskette schematic.

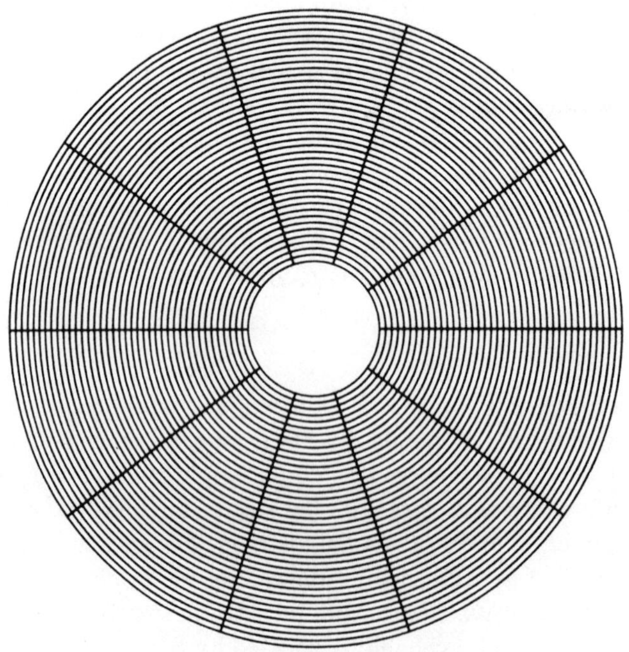

Figure 1.2. Tracks and sectors.

the Epson PX-8 Geneva, and is beginning to appear on more systems. Whereas the larger diskettes are susceptible to dirt, the smaller diskette has few environmental problems—magnetic forces affect them all, however.

Laser Disks

Among the more exciting of the peripheral devices shortly to emerge will be the laser disk. As of this writing, the laser disk has just been released. The Laser CD is, of course, one of the more recent success stories in the world of ultra-high-fidelity music. Not only have the disks gotten smaller, their capacity has grown exponentially. The same will be true of the laser disk which will be used with the computer. It will be first used with the microcomputer, and will ultimately be used to replace the mass media disk we have come to know and love.

At this point, the 3M Corporation has developed an erasable-optical disk—a 5.25 inch disk that can hold 300–500 megabytes, depending on the disk drive. This is 50–60 times the capacity of a standard hard disk. The problem, at this point, is the paucity of drives—but they're coming. Foreign manufacturers already have them on the market, and the 3.5 inch size is coming. The device is also being touted as a mass memory option, called CD-ROM.

It works this way: to write, a laser heats up a spot on the surface of the disk, which is made of either terbium iron or gadolinium cobalt. While the spot is hot, it is magnetized with an imposed field, which becomes stable once the spot has cooled. To erase, the laser heats the spot while a reverse field is on.

Reading a disk uses a phenomenon called the *Kerr effect*. When the laser light bounces off the surface of the magnetized spot, the direction of polarization is rotated. By passing the reflected light through a polarizing filter, the rotated component can be measured, and the state of the magnetization of the spot can be read. According to 3M releases, from which this information was obtained, changes in the wavelength of the light will affect the density of the disk. Early models are, however, quite slow, compared to the older diskette recording modes.

Permit us to be a bit futuristic here. When the video disk finds its use for data storage with the computer, the co-residence of voice recording (i.e., voice data) can't be far behind. Take that one step further and we can see that camera input—an "electronic microfilm," if you will, cannot be far behind. The laser disk will all but eliminate the filing cabinet. Reports, letters, articles, catalogs, books, bills, checks, memos, and almost all the other business paperwork will be storable in electronic format. Tie that concept to the newly emerged laser printer, and you can see the radical change which is descending upon us.

Direct Access I/O Terminals

The advent of the microcomputer has made a direct access input/output terminal available to anyone for very little cost, either to prepare diskette media or to communicate directly in a local area network or on line to a mainframe host. Today, whole networks have been devised to allow personal computer owners to communicate with each other, with library services, and with larger users. New types of machines and devices have become tied directly to the computer emerge daily, it seems. Included in these are, of course, the microcomputers, remote keyboards, touch-tone telephones, automatic copying equipment, facsimile equipment, word processing systems, voice response units, etc. The voice/data communication combination is just beginning to emerge as this book is written.

Paper Tape

Paper tape, like punched cards, is just one of several historic media which refuses to disappear completely. Until recent years, paper tape was used as a medium for some microcomputers, for transmission purposes, and for numerical control programs. Other recording media, such as the diskette, and other forms of control, such as the microcomputer on a chip, have obsoleted paper tape for these functions.

The function of a paper tape reader is to move a continuous piece of paper (or metal or mylar) tape past a read station, to sense the presence or absence of holes punched in multiple channels along the tape, and to convert the information thus obtained into electrical signals for further use.

Paper tape is a continuous recording medium, in contrast to cards, which are fixed in length. It is organized into channels, with 5, 6, 7, or 8 tracks. The original paper tape, used with teletype machines, was structured in a five-code configuration by Jean Baudot in 1870. Even today, it is referred to as the teletype or "Baudot Code," from which we derive the term "baud." The five channels permitted 32 combinations of holes and no holes, including six control characters, such as shift-up and shift-down, each of which can make an additional 26 combinations available.

Six-channel code is sometimes called *press code* and is used for newspaper data transmission. The 7-channel code is used almost exclusively with computers. There are several binary codes used: 6-bit plus parity; 6-bit plus control bits, etc. The 8-channel is similar to 7-channel; it has an extra channel for parity or control, as needed.

Early punched paper tape readers used metal fingers to sense the holes in the tapes. Later models use photoelectric sensing. Some low-speed devices use pinfeed sprocket wheels to move as indicated, or a takeup hopper, or a fanfolding mechanism. Speeds of current paper tape equipment vary from 1,000 to 1,800 characters per second, reader speed, and up to 300 characters per second, punch speed.

Paper tape punches punch holes in the paper tape, mylar, or metal, one frame at a time, as directed. There are two basic methods of punching; chad-producing and chadless. The chadless tape process is more of an embossing method, wherein the codes are pressed into the paper and the chad does not fall away. Chadless paper tape is all but obsolete and is not in common use. Chad-producing paper tape has the holes cut completely through the medium; the chad falls away. This is more suitable for photoelectric sensing.

Magnetic Ink Character Recognition

MICR (Magnetic Ink Character Recognition) is the process of machine-sensing of information which has been encoded on a document with magnetic ink. This process was developed through the cooperation of the banking profession and the computer manufactures. MICR is used almost exclusively in the banking industry.

The standard set of characters, font E13B, includes the ten digits, 0 through 9, and four special symbols; account, "on us," transit number, and dash. While the shapes of the characters are rather peculiar, they are easily interpreted visually. Look at a check for an example of these codes.

The ink used for these numbers has special magnetic qualities. They are printed within $\frac{1}{2}$ inch of the bottom of the document in three carefully defined and prescribed areas. In the reader, the special ink is magnetized, permitting sensing and interpretation as the document is moved past the read head. A reader will provide several output stackers to allow the documents to be physically classified after they have been read.

Optical Character Recognition

Optical character recognition (OCR) is a scheme to allow a machine to sense alphabetic characters, digits, and special symbols and translate them into some kind of binary code. OCR equipment can be standalone (producing a tape or disk which the computer can then read), or it can be on line with the computer itself. Most readers are self-contained systems consisting of a document handler, a scanning unit, stackers, a small general-purpose computer, and an output unit that make up an off line system.

In general, there are three types of document handlers: the document reader, which can handle relatively few lines of information; the journal tape reader, intended for reading paper tapes created by cash registers, accounting machines, and strip printers; and the page reader, which is designed to read printed material in normal page format. Some of the above may be combined. Also to be considered are the OCR font selection. There are, again, three general classes: optical mark sense readers, stylized font readers, and the multifont reader.

There are several types of character recognition schemes; analog waveform matching, matrix matching, stroke analysis, inbuilt curve, curve tracing, feature matching, and feature analysis.

The objective of OCR, of course, is to reduce the written document to computer-readable form as quickly as possible. Without OCR, it is doubtful that some credit card organizations could operate their business.

There are a couple of variations of the OCR concept. The first is the scanner which reads the Universal Product Code (UPC) which now has been emblazoned on just about every market product other than perishable products. Look at your favorite soup or cereal, and you will see an example of how the UPC is placed on the item—and you'll find it on your favorite magazine as well. The scanner at your local grocery store is able to determine the start of the code and the length of the code, irrespective of the direction of the product being passed over the scanner.

A second variation is the bar code reader, discussed later.

Key-Driven Devices

Walk into nearly any major fast-food chain and you will see an example of the special purpose key-driven terminal. These devices are designed to accept input from labeled keys and return information to the operator in the form of labeled lights. These terminals may be connected to a large central computer or to a dedicated minicomputer or microcomputer, or can produce a computer-readable medium, such as punched paper tape or magnetic tape.

Key-to-Tape/Disk

In systems where batch input is still the rule, large volume data input has traditionally been done via keypunch machines. Over the past several years, however, there has been a change to devices which allow the data to be entered directly to a magnetic medium (which is more easily readable).

The concept is not new. UNIVAC's first entry into the market was a device called the Unityper, back in the 1950s. The concept of the device was the ability to enter data directly to tape. But because computers were new, because there were so few UNIVAC computers in the field, because training and maintenance needs were so extensive, the concept never made it. Perhaps the first serious entry into the marketplace was made by Mohawk Data Sciences in the mid 1960s. Again, it was a key-to-tape device, and was widely used for data transmission for central batching. However, as fixed disks and especially diskettes (or floppy disks) became more widely available, the growth of the data entry device has become phenomenal.

There are basically three categories of key-to-media equipment: the standalone data recorder, with which one operator records data on one medium; the compact data inscriber, where the operator will enter information only, as in a hand-held terminal which records on cassette tape; and the key processing system, which uses a processor to control a number of key stations.

A typical standalone data recorder contains a conventional keyboard, a control panel, a small memory, and a magnetic tape or disk handler. Among the most significant advantages of key-to-medium machines over card punches are higher data entry efficiency, visual error checking, conversion cost savings, and a more plentiful supply of operators. The keypunch operator is limited by the design of the machine to approximately 16,000 keystrokes per hour, whereas a typist can make 23,000 keystrokes per hour.

Higher efficiency also results from faster error correction procedures. Also, the same data recorder is used for both data entry and verification.

In the compact data inscriber, a tape cartridge is used, as mentioned. Both of the standard cassettes and mini-cassettes are used. Data can either be transmitted to the computer via telephone lines or brought back for processing. Also, it is possible to convert these tapes to a larger media, such as floppy disk.

The key processing data preparation system is a shared-logic processor which contains features of source data automation. Typically, there is a small computer, perhaps a hard disk drive, a tape mechanism for dumping the disk to tape, and/or a floppy disk mechanism for easy portability of the data. The number of stations on line to this shared logic processor may be as few as 2 or as many as 64. Because a computer is central to the configuration, it is possible to do considerable editing as the data is captured.

Program Direction Devices

Computer manufacturers are constantly trying to find a replacement for the keyboard. Until that happens, we'll see devices that make entry easier, more convenient, and usable by untrained novices. This last goal i very, very important. Included in this category are:

The Mouse

A mouse is a small device which sits on the desk beside the computer and is moved around the desk to adjust the cursor position. The mouse is particularly useful for use as a drawing device or as a marking device. In software designed for using the mouse, the mouse is used to move either the primary cursor or a secondary cursor to the position on the screen where the desired command is displayed. The mouse does have its drawbacks—the hand must be moved from the keyboard, and the cursor is moved on the screen, and it necessary to have a clear desk surface to use it. But all in all, the mouse is here to stay.

Plotters and Digitizers

A plotter is a machine that can draw a line or symbol on paper or film—generally the former. Plotters which are pen-configured and controlled by the computer are, for all intents and purposes, automated drafting machines. The functional components of such a plotter are: storage for a sequence of directions; a carriage that can be moved under control in two coordinates; a pen or combination of pens that has, at least, up-down control and which is mounted on the carriage; a paper-holding device; and a control system for reading the directions (commands) and translating them into the proper pen movements. The more modern computers move the paper along one axis and the pen(s) along the other axis.

Plotters are available in a variety of sizes, shapes, and capabilities. They are rated as to their accuracy, precision, repetition, speed of paper movement, and the sophistication of their internal control system. Needless to say, the higher the accuracy, the higher the expense. Plotters are generally available in two distinct groups: utility plotters and precision plotters. Utility plotters are accurate to $\frac{1}{100}$ inch, while precision plotters have accuracies in the range of $\frac{1}{1000}$ to $\frac{5}{1000}$ inch. The accuracy must hold over the entire working surface, which may range from book size up to 40×60 inches.

Pen-moving plotters are either flat-bed or drum. The flat-bed type accepts any type of drawing medium that will fit on the table. This may be either utility or precision. The drum plotter drives the pen on only one axis, while the paper feed drum can also be moved in either direction on the other axis. Limitations of the drum plotter are low accuracy and the requirement for special paper.

The pen can be moved by either an analog servomotor or a digital stepping motor drive, similar to those used in a diskette (floppy disk) drive. High-accuracy plotters require a feature known as pen positioning.

Film plotters expose photographic film from a CRT image. The drawing has been done by the computer—this process exists merely to get the drawing to film, as a means to obtain duplicates. The limitations of film plotters are those caused by the CRT. In general, the resolution is one one part in 2,000; positional accuracy is roughly 1%.

The Graphics Pad

The most interesting thing to emerge in this equipment area in recent years has been the ability to take a rough drawing, lay it out on a digitizer bed (also called a graphics tablet) which forms the coordinate aces for the computer, and with a special input device, to allow the artist to trace the lines from the rough drawing. The computer then corrects all errors, presents a visual illustration of the drawing, and then allows it to be plotted directly. It would seem that these devices would have significant use in architectural activities.

Graphics pads, sometimes called graphics digitizers, are devices used to trade, write, or draw graphic images. There are several competing technologies used in graphics pads. Some require use of a special graphics pen. others use a mouse-type device. Still others are sensitive to the touch of a finger. All of these do approximately the same job. They tell the computer the position of the writing or pointing instrument on the pad. Special graphics programming uses a continuous stream of this information to build a digital image of what is being traced or drawn on the graphics pad.

The Light Pen

The term *light pen* is a misnomer. This is one of many types of devices which have been designed to communicate human directions to the face of an active CRT connected to an operating digital computer. The light pen is simply a photoelectric cell mounted in a pen-shaped holder and having an on-off switch. In practice, the operator presses the switch to identify the function to be performed with the light pen. He then touches the light pen to the portion of the tube face in which he is interested. Touching the glass tube face activates the "on" switch, and the photocell in the pen picks up light from the phosphor of the CRT. The signal from the photocell is fed back to the computer program, which can thus determine the area of the tube by checking the position of the electron stream with the time of the photocell signal. The process is applicable to computer-aided design (CAD) systems and to multiple-selection educational processes.

The Touch Screen

A recent innovation to the CRT is the touch screen. Essentially a touch screen is a misnomer. It would be more accurately described as an "interrupt the beam" system, where the screen has been filled by some form of menu from which an option may be selected. A facing is added to the screen and a photoelectric light beam is placed across the screen to a corresponding receiver at the opposite side. When the finger is extended to "touch" the screen, the light beam is interrupted, and the program interprets the selection according to the switching created by the broken beam.

Voice Commands

Speech recognition and synthesis capability has been available for several years. Speech recognition is achieved using analog-to-digital conversion. The speech recognition module samples the analog signal coming from a microphone and sends the computer a digital equivalent of the signal. By prompting the user to say each word in a preassigned command table, the computer is able to assemble a digital pattern of the user's voice saying each word. Thereafter, when the computer recognizes the digital pattern corresponding to a command, it issues that command to the application software.

Speech recognition tables occupy much space. One second of speech provides about 1,000 bytes of digital information. Although some manufacturers use linear predictive coding and other advanced techniques to lower the memory overhead, the process is still memory intensive, and limited in vocabulary. Despite this, there exist reasonably priced devices for speech recognition and for audio synthesis. The device which can recognize the speech of "just anyone" has not yet been invented. But it is possible to speak into a variety of devices and to enter the analogy of that speech to the computer. Vocabulary limitations require that only command sequences be used. There is no doubt that further advances will be made in this area before this book is revised again.

Response systems employ two different methods. In the more common method, human voice recordings are recorded on a magnetic drum or on rotating photographic film. The multiple voice tracks are accessed by one or more sensors, according to the input obtained. An example of this is in use in the Bell Telephone System. Based on the dialed input or upon input keyed by an interrupting operator, the computer will access a limited sequence of prerecorded messages. "The number you have called—5.5.5.1.2.1.2. . . . has been changed to . . . 5.5.5.2.1.2.1."

The second method is with the use of phonemes. Phonemes are synthetically produced sound, wherein words are developed within the computer in a phonetic alphabet.

Application of speech recognition and synthesis have extended even to the microcomputer, where they are being used to enhance educational programming. More exciting are applications where OCR scanners prepare auditory text for blind persons.

Voice commands may prove to be the best alternative to the mouse for directing the cursor, as it is not necessary to move your hands from the keyboard. However, if voice commands become popular, an increased noise level in the office will result, requiring redesign of the office for soundproofing. See Voice Entry, below.

Direct Eye Commands

The U.S. military already uses gun sighting devices that follow eye movements to aim weapons. This same technology may be developed as a means to move the cursor on the CRT. Computer operators using visual sighting devices would be required to wear glasses that contain intrinsic electronics. A small crosshair sight on the lens would be used to aim the cursor at the desired spot on the screen.

Bar Code Readers

Bar code readers are used in grocery markets and department stores for scanning of product numbers. The concept is precisely the same as the UPC, with but one exception. There are devices which record the scan code (from hand-held calculators to notebook computers), and the process is often combined with some keystroke entry of unit numbers.

Printed Entry Pads

Printed entry pads allow entry of text into the computer by printing the text on a piece of paper which overlays the pad. In actuality, these are graphics pad systems that include additional software for interpretation of the printed entry. These are most valuable where typing is not a common skill. Variations on these follow the pen strokes and through a series of algorithms can enter block letters from handwritten information.

Optical Digitizers

Optical digitizers are really a type of electronic camera. They convert a visual image into a digital representation which the computer can use, store, and retrieve. Charge-coupled device (CCD) technology and optically sensitive random access memory chips are changing the way electronic imaging is done. Unlike the television video tube, which required digital sampling of an analog signal, the new CCD reads the picture directly in digital encoding, with high resolution. The most significant application of this principle, at the moment, will be electronic microfilm, permitting the entry of blueprints, illustrations, document entry, handwriting recognition, and facsimile. Watch the next edition for more exciting news of this capability.

Handwritten Entry

One day you can "scribe" a report, feed it to the optical digitizing camera, and get back a typed report. Sounds like the paperless office might not happen.

Voice Entry

The time isn't too far away when you will be able to speak to the computer and get a report back. Again, voice entry is now possible, but two situations must be overcome before voice entry will be a viable technique. The first will be the laser disk, already discussed, wherein a massive vocabulary will be stored. The second will be discrimination software, and the English language is certain to give such software fits, with words like "read" and "reed," "read" and "red." And, of course, "to, too, two, and tu" are certain to provide difficulty.

Multiple Screens

There is a move toward having more than one monitor attached to the computer, particularly a microcomputer. Some of the major software applications packages support two monitors. This permits display of a secondary application without the interruption of the primary application.

Cathode Ray Tube (CRT) Terminal

The CRT terminal (often called a *video display terminal*—VDT) is a commonplace fixture in the modern office. Not only is it part of the on line computer network, but also it is a part of the data entry process and the office management or word processing process, and may even be a part of the training effort. Wherever it is employed, its main attraction is the ease of entering, visually verifying, and transmitting data to the computer and receiving data from the computer.

A typical alphanumeric CRT terminal has four major components: the cathode ray tube and its associated deflection circuitry, the memory and control logic, the keyboards and other control devices, and the interface to the computer. A filament heater heats the cathode and causes a stream of electrons to be emitted. The electrons are either accelerated toward the phosphor on the tube face or turned back by an appropriate voltage on the control grid. The number of electrons striking the phosphor determines the degree of illumination at the spot on the tube face. The focusing electrode controls the spread and ultimate convergence of the beam, the same as focusing light with a lens. The deflection of the beam to strike the desired spot on the face may be caused by an electrostatic or an electromagnetic field, or both.

Most terminals have phosphors that glow for a very short time (have short persistence). Therefore, the picture must be refreshed constantly. Three general methods of beam deflection are used to generate the picture: video, saw-tooth, and programmed scan. One of three methods is used to display the character on the screen. The monoscope and shaped beam methods have the individual character definitions built into the CRT, representing the character as a position on a plane. The more commonly used method is the dot or stroke pattern for each character stored in digital form in the control logic.

Most terminals display a cursor symbol to indicate the position of the next character to be typed. Keys are available to move the cursor symbol to indicate the position of the next character to be typed. Keys are available to move the cursor as desired. Most terminals are made to work with specific software systems which provide editing features, such as character replace, line insert, line deletion, split screen, and scrolling.

Light-Emitting Diode and Crystal Displays

Other forms of display are available and widely used. Among these are the LED (light-emitting diode) and liquid crystal displays (LCD). You know these from their more common use in digital watches. LED watches are those which have "9-bar" numbers. These displays are in used in some microcomputer equipment, but are not a predominant feature of computer equipment, essentially because they cost more than CRTs to produce, for a marginal difference in ease of use. You will see them used largely in monitoring equipment.

The crystal (LCD) displays use the same numbering configuration on a gray, metallic, background. In the smaller more portable microcomputers, the LCD display is being widely used, from the very small 5-line, 20 character display of the Epson HX-20 to the 25-line, 80 character display of the Data General DG/1.

Large Screens

Larger screen size, coupled with higher resolution has begun to happen. Full page monitors (66 lines), such as those produced by Xerox, are on the market and will become more common in word processing applications, in particular. Another stimulus to larger screens is the concept of windowing. Some monitors now have the capability to support up to four normal (80 characters by 25 lines) screens of information.

High Resolution Graphics

Screen resolution is the number of individual dots that can be displayed on a screen. Those dots are frequently called "pixels," which is short for "picture elements." However, pixel imaging is on the way out, as increased resolution and intensity controls are improved. As the electronic microfilm becomes available, users will demand photographic resolution of flesh tones every bit as much as the stark colors of a financial bar graph.

Printers

There are two classes of printers for obtaining printed output from computers: those which impact the paper and those which do not impact the paper. Impact printers fall into five basic types: drum, chain, bar, spline, and matrix. Further, impact printers may be line printers or character printers. And further still, character printers may be unidirectional or bidirectional. Non-impact printers are those which are designed to work with lasers, thermal or heat processes, electrostatics, or xerography.

Drum Printers

There are two types of drum printer in common use. The first casts the drum as a solid cylinder, with tracks corresponding to the appropriate print positions, generally 132. The cylinder rotates as a unit, and when the character which matches a corresponding print buffer moves into place, a hammer presses the paper against the printer's ribbon, against the cylinder. The second style of drum printer works similarly, with the exception that the print cylinder is really a series of print "wheels" which rotate into place in much the same manner as the tumblers of a combination lock used for bicycles.

Chain Printers

The chain printer works on the same impact principle. The only significant difference is that the type is cast as separate characters and placed onto a chain which revolves in a path that is parallel to the line being printed. The chain may have several sets of the characters fastened to it, and will continue to rotate parallel to the line until each character has been placed and hammered onto the paper. Chain printers (full line printers) can operate at speeds ranging from 300 to 2,000 lines per minute.

Bar Printer

Functionally, the bar printer works in the same manner as the chain printer. The difference is that the bar shifts and reciprocates, whereas the chain revolves. Bar printers are used on printers where high-speed printing is not required.

Matrix Printer

The matrix printer prints the character by selecting wires which protrude from a fixed matrix collar, striking the ribbon, and pushing it against the paper. Since matrix printing is generally character-oriented, the printing mechanism moves quite fast. Again, printing may be unidirectional or bidirectional, depending upon the hardware and upon the software support. Matrix printers can be used to produce printing of differing sizes and densities, generally under program control. Matrix printers are capable of draft quality, near-letter-quality (NLQ), and letter-quality (LQ), often at the pressure of a switch. Matrix printers are likewise ideal for computer-generated graphics. Figures 1.3 and 1.4 show the detail of the matrix printer.

Daisy Wheel Printers

The spline printer, or so-called daisy wheel printer, is the newest of the impact printers to appear on the scene. Using a print wheel on which characters have been placed on spokes or splines, the printer works by the rotation of the wheel above the face of the paper. The wheel is rotated until the proper character is in place and then a single character hammer pushes the spline against the ribbon and onto the paper. Spline printers are commonly found in the word processing systems. Spline printers currently work at between 30–60 characters per second, depending upon whether the printer has single-direction or bidirectional printing capability (and/or software support). A variation of this theme is the thimble printer, which rotates on its axis until the letter is positioned, and then prints by impact. Spline printers tend to be noisy.

Non-Impact Printers

Non-impact printing techniques are faster and have seen the most extensive development since the last edition of this book was written. Great strides have been made in producing xerographic and laser output from the computer. Speeds in excess of 30,000 lines per minute have become commonplace for those whose output needs have required that type of equipment. As will be detailed later, however, the amount of paper produced by organizations has gotten to the point where other techniques, such as microfilm and microfiche have had to be used.

Ink Jet Printers

Ink jet printers are new to the microcomputer printer market, but they have existed for some time in the mainframe environment. They operate by squirting ink droplets at the paper. Some of them have multiple

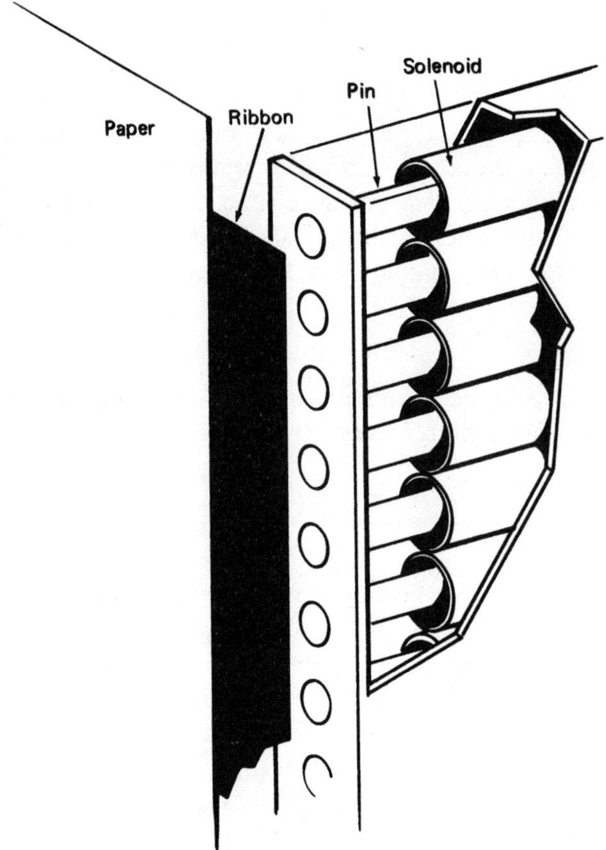

Figure 1.3. Solenoids push pins.

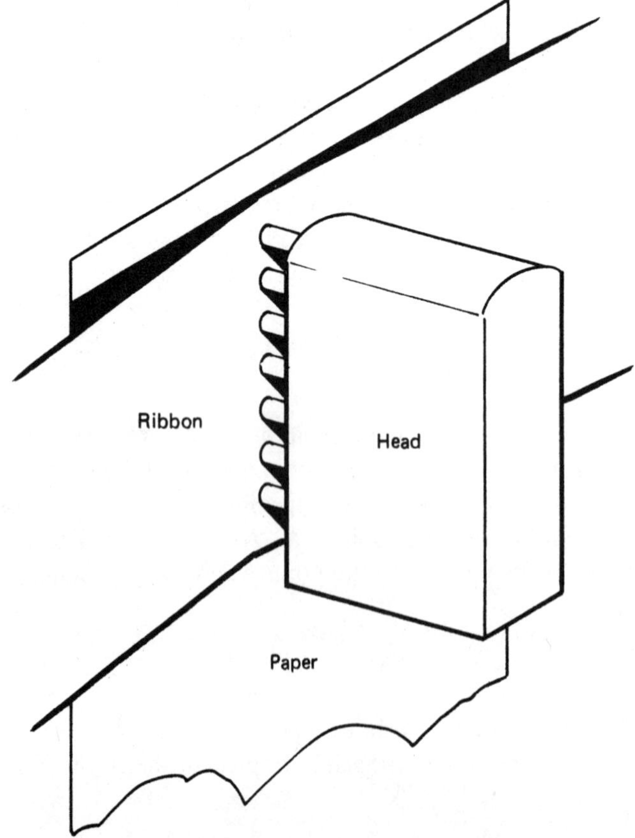

Figure 1.4. Pins push ribbon against paper.

ink nozzles allowing them to do color printing. Ink jet printers create better looking characters than most dot matrix printers, but do suffer from some ink splatter. Mixture of the ink to operate under high pressure has been difficult. The most important advantages of these printers are low cost and quiet operation.

Laser Printers

Laser printers have been around for a while in the mainframe environment, and are useful to produce both forms (completed) and reports on normal page size. They are quite expensive, but also quite capable. Somewhat less expensive are the laser printers which are becoming available for use with the microcomputer. These are modified office copiers which use the laser to produce the desired image upon the copier drum, transfer that copy to paper, clean the drum, and repeat the process. These printers are likely to become primary printers for business applications. Not only do they produce letter quality printing, they can produce typeset quality text. Add to this the local area networking (discussed in the chapter on Communications), and the ability to use this device for the entire office exists. Again, as with the laser disk, comes now the ability to print mass volumes of data. Figures 1.5a and 1.5b show, schematically, the operation of the laser printer and the Canon laser print engine, respectively.

Thermal Printers

Another type of printing based on the electrostatic copying process will put words to paper. The thermal printer creates the image on the sensitized side of the electrostatic paper—designed expressly for the thermal printer. It's a treat to take an exam on a notebook computer and print it right there on the thermal printer. It's not very fast, but it is quite effective.

Color Thermal Printers

A parallel development is taking place in photography which will affect our printing future. You'll note that the 8 mm camera is disappearing from the scene, in favor of the portable videotape camera. The

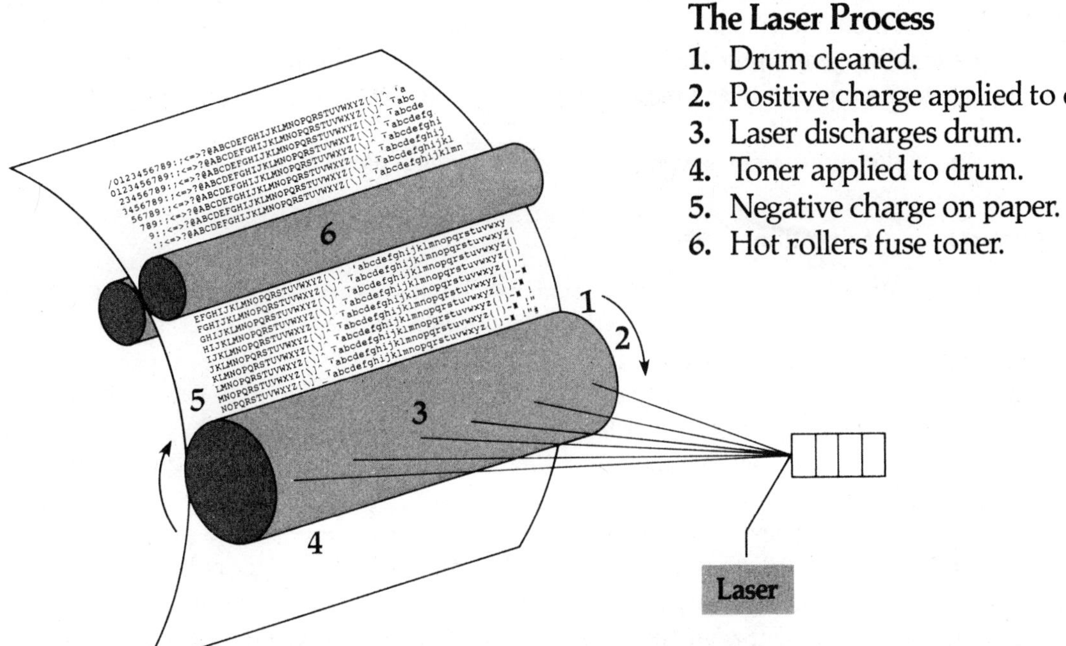

The Laser Process
1. Drum cleaned.
2. Positive charge applied to drum.
3. Laser discharges drum.
4. Toner applied to drum.
5. Negative charge on paper.
6. Hot rollers fuse toner.
1
2
3
4
5
6
Laser

Figure 1.5a. Laser printer schematic.

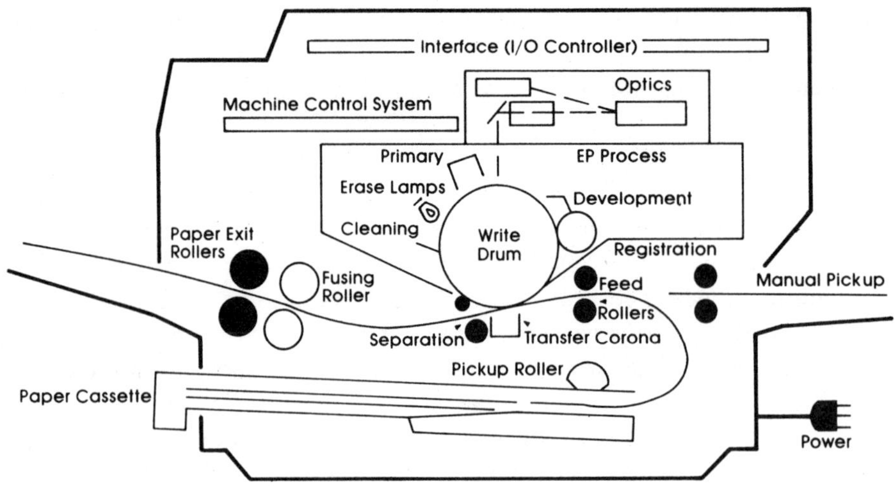

Figure 1.5b. Canon laser print engine.

next step in this process will be the creation of an electronic camera—one which doesn't use film (and all that silver). Because the picture has been taken electronically, it must be imaged electronically, and the color thermal printer will be the first effort here. This will be a specialty printer, not the normal business printer used.

Console

The console is the interface between the computer and a human operator. Early computers had large consoles which could display all information pertinent to the operation of the program. Also included were displays and switches needed by engineers to repair the computer equipment.

Some second-generation computers reduced the size of the console by preparing a test board for the engineer. Third-generation computers and beyond have built-in diagnostic capabilities which allow for the testing of the system through terminals. In fact, several computer mainframe manufactures maintain diagnostic facilities which periodically sample the computer's diagnostic history via communication media.

Today, a console looks and functions in much the same manner as a terminal.

COM (Computer Output Microfilm)

The conversion of computer output to microfilm and microfiche has speeded up the output process and reduced the bulk of paper to be stored. COM may be direct output, or there may be conversion units which will take a magnetic tape and change the medium.

Roll microfilm and microfiche are currently used because they are considerably less expensive to produce and store than paper. As the price of silver has escalated, however, microfilm has become considerably more expensive, owing to the fact that the microfilm process uses silver halide. Can you see the change that electronic microfilm will bring?

Microforms can be duplicated and mailed at a tremendous savings, an important point at a time when postage rates are also escalating. Where the COM equipment exists, however, users have to be very discriminating about the use of the equipment. It's simply too easy to commit everything to COM. The selection and use of COM equipment is an economic decision which requires the justification of every product.

COM equipment generally offers a wide selection of type fonts and graphic symbols not readily available on standard mainframe computer printers. But that may change with the use of other types of microcomputer-based printers.

It looked at first as if development of an input process from microfilm would be developed. In the short term, users simply made copies of the microfilm and then had them scanned. But the input process has not been successfully implemented, and with the advent of electronic microfilm, may never be.

Computer Characteristics

Analog and Digital

An analog computer operates on continuous variables that represent continuous data. The physical variables are represented by analogs. Your wristwatch is an analog computer, as is the speedometer of your car. They are not time or speed, respectively, they are but an analogy to time and speed.

In the analog computer, interconnected operational amplifiers perform various kinds of arithmetic operations, including summation, multiplication, integration, and differentiation. The computer has analog inputs and produces analog outputs.

Analog computers are not suitable for data processing or business applications. Their design is strictly for measurement computations. The components of an analog computer (operational amplifiers, function generators, potentiometers, etc.) are "patched" together by the user to solve the specific problem at hand. By adjusting the potentiometers, the computer is "programmed." When the computer is released to work on the problem, the signal voltage at various points then varies with the independent variable—time—in accordance with the potentiometer settings and established interconnections. The solution will be presented via a plotter, strip chart recorder, or oscilloscope. Analog computers are faster, less expensive, and easier to program than digital computers. Digital computers are applicable to a wider range of problems.

A digital computer operates upon data expressed in discrete form. Digital computers are today typified by the presence of an internally stored program. The internal mode of operation is binary and performs logic and the fundamental arithmetic operations of addition, subtraction, multiplication, and division upon discrete, discontinuous data. The digital computer has five distinct components: control, arithmetic/logic, memory, input, and output. These may be grouped in a variety of methods, but all digital computers will have these in common.

A digital computer accepts and produces one-dimensional streams of discontinuous data. It is sequentially controlled to execute one operation (or one instruction) at a time, whereas the analog computer performs its many operations simultaneously. Modern advances of multiprogramming simulate the operational functions of the analog computer in the digital computer. However, the digital computer still operates sequentially, one instruction at a time.

It is possible to combine the two. Using analog-to-digital and digital-to-analog converters, the marriage of techniques best suited for the particular task is made. Process control applications make great use of these hybrid computers.

Serial and Parallel

The terms *serial* and *parallel* are used four different ways in the discussion of computers.

Serial:

- A *serial memory* is a device in which information is read from or written into memory in a time sequence. Serial memories are no longer common.
- A *serial operation* processes instructions in a time sequence. For example, in an addition opera-

tion, the two right-hand or least significant digits are processed first, followed by the next pair to the left, etc.

- *Serial data transmission* requires that all bits or characters of a unit be transferred in a time sequence. This may require one or more clocking pulses.
- A *serial processor* with a single arithmetic unit operates upon a single stream of tasks.

Parallel:

- A *parallel memory* is a device in which data are placed, held, and taken out in such a way that each part of the data is handled simultaneously. Time is not a factor coordinated by the recipient.
- In each *parallel operation* all parts of the operand are processed simultaneously. Parallel operation is faster than serial operation.
- *Parallel data transmission* transfers all bits of the unit simultaneously. There must be as many transmission wires as there are bits in the computer word.
- A *parallel processor,* which may also be called an *array processor* or *multiprocessor,* is a computer in which many arithmetic units can be applied to a job or task simultaneously.

Process Control

Computer process control makes automatic adjustments to regulate a process. To do so, a feedback mechanism is necessary in the system. Either analog or digital signals are fed back, to be interpreted by the process control system, which will produce output direction according to the stimuli received. Some current process control applications include power transmission, continuous chemical process flow, steel-rolling, beer-brewing, bread-making, etc.

At this point in our history, the computer on a chip is finding many uses in this area. Microcomputers are gradually taking over process control operations. Just as with larger systems, the logging function is a byproduct of the operation. But it is interesting to note that as microcomputers take over, the degree of local control vs. central control will become larger.

Multiprogramming

Multiprogramming is the interleaved execution of multiple programs under concurrent operation. These multiple programs use the central processing unit (CPU) on a one-at-a-time basis.

In multiprogramming, large amounts of memory are required. Sufficient channels and devices are needed to develop the ''wait time'' available to assign to other tasks, an interrupt feature is required to allow other programs to take control of the CPU, hardware memory protection must limit access to authorized users, software is needed to control the process, and there must be a real-time clock which is used solely by the executive program for time allocation, control, and accounting purposes.

Virtual

Since the time a suitable means to multiprogram was discovered, hardware and software efforts to expand the use of the computer have been very effective. The concept appears on nearly every major computer system available in the mini- and maxi-range, and experiments are underway with the microcomputer.

Two virtual concepts are appropriate—*virtual memory* and *virtual machine* (which is, in reality, simply another way to utilize virtual memory). Virtual memory is the memory space defined by a range of addresses which are not a part of the physical addressing scheme of the computer. Simply stated, the program begins at the 1,024th megabyte of a 512K machine, of course, an impossibility. In other words, the virtual concept assumes that the storage capacity of the machine extends beyond the physical capabilities of the machine itself. To accomplish this, some extreme sophistication is necessary in the movement of relocatable modules to and from direct access storage, advance scheduling of memory space, tight allocation of cycles and communication services, and dynamic adjustment to rapidly changing variables.

In the virtual system, the management of the machine is transparent to the programmer and the programmer need only structure his applications in a manner which permits ease of module movement. Once those features have been established, the working of the virtual method becomes a function of hardware capability and system software facility.

Virtual memory gains its strength from two principal methods: dynamic memory allocation and paging.

- Dynamic memory allocation is a technique in which the location of computer programs is determined by criteria applied at the moment of need. Using primary and secondary memory, the technique assigns memory segments as they are required. Control software manages the availability of memory segments and connects the incoming module to the program in function within the computer. The control routine links internal and external modules in a chained effect, managing both the permanent and transient program modules as necessary.
- Paging is a technique wherein programs are divided into fixed-length blocks called pages. The pages can be effectively exchanged or swapped between primary and secondary memory as required. When a page is needed, its location must be immediately determined. If it is located within primary memory, it is bound (relocated, attached). If it is in secondary storage, it must be obtained from that medium. Control software generally accomplished the task of bringing the pages into the system through its look-ahead capabilities.

Under the concept of *virtual machine,* one machine can be subdivided, with each of the component subdivisions functioning, as it were, as an independent machine. The attractiveness of this method allows the mixture of operating systems within the computer itself. It also allows the tandem operation of a pair (or more) of programs within the definition given below for multiprocessing.

Microcode

Modern computers now have, either as read-only-memory (ROM) or as PROM (programmable-read-only-memory) certain system functions which used to be part of the software programming of the the control program, monitor, or operating system. However, some of this code can be tailored to the configuration on which the code is to operate. Thus, many current systems will feature the ability to load certain "hard-wired" programming from diskette (floppy disk) to the CPU. In this manner, source code modules need not be maintained, protecting the vendor's investment in that programming. More important, however, is the ease of loading and the fact that once entered, the programming is functionally a part of the control circuitry.

Multiprocessing

Perhaps 90% of the readers of this book have never seen computers operating in a configuration wherein one computer exercises control over another. The concept of appending a minicomputer or a microcomputer to a larger mainframe is not new. Every manufacturer has such a subordinate computer. Sometimes the item is a "designed-in" device, such as the one used with the Control Data Cyber-70 series. Sometimes the device is placed on a channel to function as a controller, as in the placement of a DEC11/40 into the DEC 2060. Sometimes it is a separately designed unit, such as an attached support processor, which might be a front-end communications processor (FECP).

Frequently, the multiprocessing activity is a function of two or more computers working in tandem, for example, the much-plagued computers used by the various space shuttle craft. Tandem processing, in this instance, involves each of the computers working through the same program and producing results which can be correlated to those obtained from the other system(s) with which the device has been placed in tandem.

Alternatively, the computer systems may share input/output devices and computing load. Theoretically, the same virtual scheme would work among computers. One processor is in control of the combined system, while the other processors are subordinate to it.

Communications and Data Transmissions

With this edition of the book, the subject of communications has been treated extensively. We will, however, deal with the topic generally at this point.

Changes and improvements in communications services have kept a close pace with other changes in the computer world, a fact best typified by the divestiture of AT&T services, incursion of AT&T into the computer business, and incursion of IBM into the communications business by acquisition of the Rolm Corporation and the Satellite Business Systems joint endeavor.

The introduction of data-carrying/communicating satellites has placed the movement of data on a scale of which few would have dared to dream a few short years ago. Today, discussion of the computer as a communications device abounds, and the card punch is giving way to the on-line real-time terminal aspects of information and control handling.

Collection Devices

The number and spectrum of these devices boggle the imagination. A great number of devices and device types abound in the marketplace. There are devices which collect data in its most raw state at its point of inception. Whole schools of management theory have been applied to these concepts, but most the most commonly used term is source data automation. The most apparent type of collection devices would then be of the type known as point of sale equipment.

The simplest of the data collection devices has to be the touch-telephone. Using it, data may be transferred accurately, if not very speedily. On the opposite end of the scale are the digitizers—devices which allow the operator to scan a drawing while simultaneously translating the data to digital form.

Between the two extremes are a plethora of devices—smart terminals (those which have an embedded computer), dumb terminals (which function solely as data-entry keyboards), cartridges, badge-readers, teletype paper (mylar) tape, scanning pen (OCR) readers, formatted input terminals, sensors, transponders, etc. And more are coming to light daily, as our ingenuity is applied to the movement of data. We've even come to the point where a letter generated in New York is delivered in San Francisco within minutes utilizing the fast transmission of text. As electronic mail takes its place beside electronic banking, there will be ever more varied and competitive services for us to use. Services such as MCI Mail, CompuServe E-Mail, etc., are compressing the work activities of widely scattered business interests.

Major changes have occurred with the "office of the future" (now called office automation or office information systems) concepts which are emerging. Not only word processing, but also the intercommunication capabilities of systems have placed the "power typewriter" squarely into the world of information processing. The control of sophisticated copying machines, the handling of message traffic, the entry of data directly to the computer, the production of some very sophisticated graphics, the production of computer output on the system, and the concept of electronic filing may well bring us to the state of the "paperless office." Time will tell. Before that happens, however, users will need to be convinced that the protection from loss is absolutely foolproof.

Communication Services

There are three basic types of connection of data communication equipment: simplex, half duplex, and full duplex. A simplex connection permits data transmission in a single direction only, and is commonly used only for data collection purposes. A half duplex connection permits the transmission of data in either direction, one direction at a time. A full duplex connection allows simultaneous data transmission in both directions.

Recent advances in data communications have been made at an unprecedented rate. As before, communications services utilizing direct wire (twisted pair), acoustically coupled (requiring a modem), direct-connection modem, or telephone-technology communication (requiring modems, multiplexors, node-point processors, narrow-band, voice-band, and wide-band services) remain available. You can still purchase some forms of the TELPAK services with 60–240 voice-grade circuits. You can still connect to the Direct Distance Dialing network. You can still obtain transmission services via microwave (from a variety of sources, such as Western Union or Southern Pacific Railway, among others), or infrared. You can get acoustically coupled circuits or obtain hard-wired modems from a variety of sources. You can still buy a modem-oriented telephone system from a plethora of sources. Still relatively new to the communications field is the SNA protocol. The last edition of this book stated: "System network architecture (SNA) will, no doubt, become the standard communications protocol of the future." That's probably still true, but not quite so much a given, as other protocols, such as the Micro-Network Protocol (MNP), and a variety of services, such as Ethernet (XEROX), Novel, Omninet (Corvus), and IBM's token-passing PC-Net will attest.

For the mainframe world, the SNA has emerged pretty much the victor, and seems destined to become the standard of the industry. With due consideration, it should be obvious to anyone in the field long enough to be reading this manual that there is a very large move toward IBM compatibility in plug-compatible mainframes (PCM) and peripherals, specifically those which are on-line or terminal oriented.

SNA is not new. IBM has been working on it for nearly a decade, as their own products have been developed using a variety of protocols. However, as the International Standards Organization (ISO) has been developing its seven-level network architecture model, called the open system interconnection (OSI), the similarity between OSI and SNA has become unmistakable. Thus, it can be concluded, SNA is at least a de facto standard, if nothing more. SNA (System Network Architecture) will be discussed in the final chapter, the section on communications.

For heavy data communications, the Bell System Network has changed to include an all-digital network. Using a switched digital capability (SDC) which began coast-to-coast operation in 1984. Incorporated into the system will be a digital terminal system (DTS), a wideband, two-way microwave facility. A DTS can transmit up to 1.5M bits per second in either direction. Unlike current DTS channels, the SDC will be placed in homes and offices. Features of the SDC mechanism will include analog voice communications and analog data transmission, as well as digital data transmission. In its early steps, there will be a limited number of digital intercity trunk circuits accessible to geographically dispersed users. Again, divestiture of AT&T services has this world upside down, and a plethora of products and services are emerging from all directions.

As if that were not enough, there is the CCIS network, the Bell System common channel interface signaling network, provided for packet-switching customers. Packet switching is not new, of course, but CCIS is different. Using CCIS, which is designed for heavy traffic volume, data will be intermingled with speed synthesis and recognition.

Data Terminal Equipment

In speaking of data terminal equipment (DTE), the concentration lies heavily upon that equipment which is, in some manner, interactive. Today's on-line, real-time or time-shared system uses communications to make possible access to centralized data bases with the touch of a few keys. Those keys may be in the form of words entered to a microcomputer, or they might be in the form of formatted, pre-coded keys from a cash register.

All terminal equipment products have in common a means to enter data to the system and a means for the system to acknowledge that the data have indeed been entered. The CRT display terminal has its greatest strength in its ability to display a great amount of information rapidly and in a more visual format than is possible with hard-copy devices. Alternatively, light-emitting diode (LED) or liquid crystal displays (LCD) will generally provide the same or similar data, a line at a time. Even in the so-called one-way terminals, some means exist for the system to acknowledge receipt of the input.

Direct data conversions, commonly called data acquisition systems, vary by design and function. Basically, they are input devices which may be remote from the central computing site and which accept data to be fed to the computer. Such data acceptance may be in the form of direct connection, such as telemetry or hydrothemographic data. Other input may be manually fed by cards, badges, cartridges, and the like. When a machine-sensible medium is remotely developed and introduced to the system at that location, the process is commonly called *source data automation* (SDA).

There was a time when the data collection device was a mute object to be feared and/or despised. Employees viewed with distrust the fact that the computer was keeping tabs on the time clock and on the piece part production. However, modern efforts to humanize interaction with the computer have largely alleviated the fear. People may still dislike the use of such devices (''I've been reduced to just a @#$% computer number''); however, the increasing median education and increased exposure have made the use of the computer at least tolerable for such. The greatest obstacle to be overcome recently is management's, even DP management's, fear of the microcomputer. We'll deal with that in the chapters on management.

There is no doubt that the number of data entry devices has increased, but the nature of the data entry devices has shifted to the microcomputer and a concept called *distributed data processing* (DDP). Under DDP, data are still collected at the source, but now processed remotely (at least certain edit functions) before the purified data are passed on to the central site. DDP allows local computing capability, terminal input to the host system, communications with other terminals in the network, remote job entry and output, and a host of other concepts which stretch our capabilities far beyond.

Point of sale terminals capture the data at the source—the ''point of sale''—with a view to protecting the seller from the wiles of the unscrupulous customer. Point of sale is just one element of the *point of origin* concept, which holds that information is captured as close as possible to the point where it is generated; the device should be easily operated by a person at that location. The person should be able to make the appropriate entries to the system with a minimum of supervision. For this reason, function keys which generate precoded information are customarily installed on point of origin systems.

Under office automation concepts, a word processor may well be this point of origin. Integrated systems are quite popular at this juncture: systems which provide word processing, data processing, message handling, image processing, etc. are becoming commonplace. Office automation will utilize communications extensively.

Data Communication Equipment

As currently constituted, data communications accept as input both analog and digital signals. The 3000 Hz telephone line uses an analog signal, which is translated into digital format through the use of a MODEM (MOdulate/DEModulate). Modems come in a variety of styles from a multitude of vendors. They all exist for the single purpose of converting analog to digital, and back again.

More devices are being produced which will permit parallel digital transfer of data, rather than the serial analog method. As these devices are pressed into service, more communications services, up to and including satellites, will come into being. Modems may be hard-wired to the communications circuit or they may be interfaced through other types of hardware—RS-232 communications interface, terminal control units (TCU), or front end communication processors (FECP).

In addition to the front end communication processors, there are other network elements—concentrators, multiplexors, node point processors, and the like. As the concept of distributed processing grows, these elements will become increasingly more important, particularly as the concepts of SNA and packet-switching are added. Also, as microcomputers are established in their own local area networks (LANs) and those LANs are interfaced to larger networks, we will see an exponential growth in the use of communications connected to the mainframe CPU, whether it be large, mini, or micro.

Networks exist because direct connection to the host isn't very practical. Not every terminal is busy all the time. Some terminals are at sufficient distance to make such a solution very costly. What then happens is that several terminals (with individual control units and input/output devices) are connected to the end of a single communication medium, generally a voice-grade line. Data arriving from each of the terminals are "concentrated" into packages for transmission. Each package may contain data and identification from a variety of sources. Once at the CPU, the packages are unpacked and each component is handled appropriately. Concentration is generally a one-way option, from terminal to CPU or from CPU to terminal—in essence a sophisticated half-duplex system.

In the situation where interaction is required, along with two-way communication, a multiplexor is required. The node point processor is a remotely located subhost which supports its own mini-network. It may have independent data base features and will generally request services and report out of its own network only on occasions which require it.

An example will help to clarify this. Suppose your firm is a retailing firm, with offices in the Midwest, say Chicago. Ideally, you might like to have each of your stores on line to your main office. But that isn't very practical, and the cost is prohibitive. Since the computer is used largely for credit sales, you've noted that 75% of the company's credit business is derived from credit cards issued at the store where they are used; an additional 15% of the credit business is done within a 250-mile radius of the store at which the card was issued; 8% within 600 miles; and the balance may show up anywhere in the chain, as people travel. So, if you're smart, and you are, you set up mini-networks which incorporate the stores into an ever-increasing set of concentric circles. Thus, 75% of the "hits" will be derived on the store's own computer; the next 15% will fall within one concentric circle; the next 8% within two concentric circles; and the balance will ultimately be passed along the network to the home office. The beauty of this system is that it allows local store-to-store communication for the proximate location and movement of inventory, centralized purchasing of goods and commodities available within the covered area, summarized sales statistics grouped according to node, etc. In short, much of the field processing is complete before data ever arrive at the home office.

The computer utility has becoming a reality. It has been said that individuals and organizations can now dial into more than five thousand information networks, sources, or bulletin boards. Networks exist for message-handling and bulletin-board mail transmission. Intercompany information networks exist for joint research. The idea is not new. The ARPA network, built around the now discontinued ILLIAC IV, has had that for years. But with the advent of the personal microcomputer and the use of the microcomputer in businesses of all sizes, these services will grow. Today you can get a dial-up encyclopedia in Boston, a micro-bank in Seattle, a reader's source in New Jersey, a grocery-ordering service in Nashville, and what not. It's an exciting time to be involved in this field. As soon as the various networks work out the compatible sets of protocols, access to the commercial services around the world via satellite will be well within technical possibility, if not economic advisability.

Be sure to continue reading about communications in the last chapter of the book.

Auxiliary Memory

Laser Memory

Laser memory rightfully belongs in the auxiliary memory section of this chapter, as it is built upon the newly emerging CD-ROM. CD (for "compact diskette") and ROM (or even RAM) offer three very important considerations for future use of auxiliary memory.

- The first is its gargantuan capacity. Sony's entry, for example, stores 540 megabytes, which may be translated to 270,000 double-spaced pages of text. How's that for a manuscript? Likewise, diminished size will facilitate storage. The Sony disk is 3.5″.
- The second is indestructability. Dirt, magnetic fields, temperature extremes, etc. have no effect.
- The third is software protection—early writing on the subject indicates that it is possible to prove extreme protection from software piracy.

Of course, what this really means is that whole books will be stored upon a diskette. Imagine what that will do for library storage and to those parts of the publishing industry that remain bound to paper output. Combined with graphics and logic-based, the CD-ROM will become a boon for education and simulation. Chemical reactions can be realistically simulated without danger, for example. Microsurgery can be practiced without endangering the human patient. Fire control simulators and flight simulators can be developed which waste neither ammunition nor fuel. It's an exciting time to be in this field. The CD-ROM, and the CD-RAM coming behind it, are indeed revolutionary.

The Data Base Machine

A cartoon of a few years ago showed two buildings, side by side. The smaller, by far, of the two buildings, was labeled "Computer Center." The larger was labeled "Disk Storage." Such was the popular conception of the time that data would reside on larger and more extensive disk systems. The CD-ROM may reverse the building sizes.

Magnetic drums, which were one of the older forms of mass storage, were widely used—and quickly discarded. While faster than disks, they were much more expensive and difficult to maintain—and, it was found, with sophisticated paging and spooling software systems, quick media access was no longer a necessity. In fact, the cycle has recycled itself in that disks, which were once large and not demountable, became small and were demountable, and are now small and once again not demountable—but with considerably greater capacity. There are still demountable packs, of course.

In recent years, the "data base machine" has emerged. The concept is simple, if not its execution. Machines with large-volume solid-state memories are appended to a host CPU as would be any other input/output device. The data may be on-loaded to these data base machines from tape or disk, but until dumped again, the data are available at electronic speeds. Consider, please, the impact of tying several data base machines into the new supercomputers, such as the Cray II or the Cyber 205, the latter of which has a memory of 16 trillion bytes. The concept is called *very large scale integration* (VLSI).

Thus, extraordinary impact is being made at both ends of the computing spectrum. When one considers the current size of memory chips (the Japanese have cornered the 256K market), very, very, very large scale integration isn't very far away.

Magnetic Tape

Magnetic tape has been with the computer from nearly its inception. It was also one of the first available auxiliary memory units. With certain exceptions (a now obsolete concept called Hypertape), magnetic tape is a sequential file memory medium, which means that the records must be read from tape in the same sequence in which they were written onto the tape. Some attempts have been made to obtain random access to tape-the most recent being a micro-based device called the *stringy floppy,* and a hard disk backup device which uses tape—the *Bernoulli Box.* For ease of movement, storage in secure spots, holding considerable data, and backup capabilities, tape still provides the most economical means of holding data. At today's prices, densities, and speed, it is a much less expensive storage medium than punched cards—which are, themselves, slowly becoming obsolete. Hurrah! But wait—tape itself becomes obsolete with the introduction of the CD-RAM. Amazing, isn't it?

Drums and Data Cells

A *magnetic drum memory* is a metal cylinder coated with magnetic oxide. It is rotated at a constant speed, and has one or more read/write heads positioned against the surface. Generally, the heads are fixed, while the cylinder rotates. The position of the heads defines the tracks on the magnetic surface. Some of the heads are movable, generally within a range, while other drums have permanent heads, one for each track. The location of information on drum is by address location—generally the head number and/or the track within the head's reach. Data are read from or written to the drum by sensing or changing the magnetic compositions on its surface. Not many drums are in use nowadays.

Another device available but not commonly used is the *data cell.* It consists of cartridges of magnetic cards which are rotated into place, individually wrapped around a drum, and read in much the same manner as is the drum memory. The concept has been used in NCR computers of a few years ago, IBM computers, and RCA/UNIVAC computers. They all have a single characteristic—they are slow in comparison to other forms of auxiliary storage and are fraught with mechanical problems. They have all but disappeared from the computing scene.

Disks

A magnetic disk auxiliary memory comprises one or more thin metal disks, one or more read/write heads on movable access arms, and a motor. The disks are coated on both sides with the same kind of ferrous oxide magnetic coating as found on tapes and drums. Usually multiple disks (from 5 to 25) are mounted on the same driving shaft, with sufficient separation to allow the access arm to move the heads in and out of the unit. The tracks are concentric circles, such that the arm and head must move in a path perpendicular to the axis of rotation. In the case of a multiple-surface disk pack, each of these heads combs one disk surface, producing a cylinder effect-the number of tracks which can be accessed by the heads with the arm in a specific position.

As previously stated, some disk units have demountable packs. Some are permanently mounted and cannot be removed. Capacities and transfer rates vary widely, but typical capacities range from 2 million up to 200 million characters per disk pack. Transfer rates range from 100,000 to 800,000 characters per second.

Micro-Media

The diskette (commonly called floppy disk) is a flexible mylar sheet upon which data are recorded. Diskettes come in two common sizes—"standard," which is 8 inch, "mini," which is 5.25 inch; and "micro," which is 3.5 inch. The storage capacities per surface are changing daily. The micro-sized diskette, fully encased in plastic, holds more than 300,000 characters. The diskette's internal structure returns to the older, sector-oriented form of organization, and there are two types, known as soft-sector and hard-sector diskettes. Look back at Figures 1.1 and 1.2. The latter shows the sector lines. The former shows the "index hole," often called the "pilot hole." If the diskette is soft-sectored, and many are, there is one hole punched in the mylar diskette. When that hole aligns with the pilot hole, the measurement of the sectors begins at that point. The hard-sectored diskette has a hole at every sector mark.

OTHER OFFICE EQUIPMENT

Desk Calculators

The mass production of electronic logic chips has made possible desk and hand-held calculators which are powerful, quiet, fast, and inexpensive. It is possible to obtain calculators which have extensive mathematical functions for less than $20. Further, hand-held calculators have derivatives which are used to teach mathematics (such as the Texas Instruments' Little Professor). It is even possible to obtain a small calculator which can fit inside a wallet or checkbook cover. And it's possible to obtain an entire computer (produced by Casio, Sharp, Panasonic, or Radio Shack) which will fit in your pocket or purse. The device even comes with tape drive and printer.

Desk calculators may be programmable or nonprogrammable, may have LED or crystal display, may or may not produce a paper tape, and may or may not have resident memory. Generally, the nonprogrammable type are fixed function. The programmable types may have conditional branching, access to storage registers, etc.

It wouldn't take a whole lot of imagination to introduce the notebook or "lap portable" computers here again. With advanced software, printing, and communications capabilities, these devices are very much modern office equipment.

Duplicating Devices

Duplicating refers to the process of reproducing original documents by transferring an image to a "master" and then reproducing from that master. Copying refers to reproducing an original without an intervening master. Duplication is normally used for large quantities, but as the cost of copying is lowered, the choice between duplication and copying becomes less important for moderate quantities. Convenience and response time may be more important than cost.

Because of its high quality of reproduction, the most popular type of copier is the photocopier. Photocopies generally come in two types—electrostatic and xerographic. Xerographic is generally preferred, in that the process is dry, it does not require special paper, and the quality of copy is excellent. The electrostatic process is probably more widespread, however, because it is considerably less expensive than xerography. Modern advancements to the process permit the changing of cartridges to diminish maintenance, the intermixing of color, and two-sided copying. Here, also, electronic publishing will find its way using the laser copier.

Duplication by mimeograph stencils and spirit masters has been largely replaced by the offset duplication processes. Offset duplicators use masters of paper, plastic, or metal. Paper masters may be produced by a copying process, by a photographic process, or by direct typing or computer printing. Metal masters are more difficult to produce, requiring a photographic process and chemical processing; however, they can be used for very large print runs and are the correct choice if the master is to be stored for later use.

The mimeograph duplication process generally stores ink in the center of a rotating drum. The ink is forced out through the surface of the drum, through the cut stencil, and onto the paper. The density of print can be controlled. The spirit process applies alcohol to a pigment-based image on the spirit master. The master can be produced by typing, by computer, or with heat-treatment. So long as there is some pigment backing to the spirit master, there can be printing, and the intensity of the image is controlled by adjustments to the flow of alcohol. Offset printing is somewhat more interesting. The process works upon the principle that grease and water do not mix. A master is optically "burned" and chemically etched. It is placed on a drum and ink is applied to the master, adhering to the image. The inked image is then placed on a "blanket," in reverse. The reversed-image is then re-reversed by application to paper.

Factors to be considered when selecting duplication and copying equipment are the size and shape of the original documents, the number of originals, the number of multiple copies, whether there is collating to be done (this can be done automatically by some machines), the desired quality, response time, and cost.

Filing Devices

Irrespective of how successful electronic microfilm will be, paper will be with us for a very long time. Filing cabinets vary in size, shape, ease of retrieval of documents, and amount of information readily visible. When a small amount of information must be readily available with supporting information nearby, strip files are used. The file cabinet is generally used in filing systems with moderate volumes requiring moderate file maintenance activity. Files can easily be located and updated. However, for filing systems requiring frequent file maintenance, the opening and closing activities become a burden to users. The lateral file cabinet has the advantage of allowing folders with side taps and thus allows a user to locate and remove a folder without opening the drawer.

Shelf-Filing

The open-shelf approach eliminates the drawers associated with file cabinets. Higher shelves may be used with the aid of ladders and more users have access to file sections simultaneously. Many who use open-shelving, such as insurance companies, find it absolutely necessary to use color-coding of file-holding materials.

Mobile Shelving

When infrequent access is required, mobile shelving may be used to eliminate the aisles associated with shelf filing. All shelves ride on tracks and may be positioned face-to-face without any aisle between shelves. Access is gained by creating an aisle, perhaps by selecting the desired section on a control panel. Mobile shelving makes good use of the available floor space but allows only limited simultaneous access by users and if not properly used may result in low user productivity.

Automated Files

Automated files allow the user to select the desired file; the equipment then delivers the file rather than requiring the user to locate the file. Once the file drawer or shelf is delivered, the user selects the desired folder. The entire folder must be removed to allow other users access to the automated file equipment.

Bookkeeping Machines

Bookkeeping machines have traditionally been used in ledger card posting applications such as accounts receivable and accounts payable. These applications required typewriter-type printing capabilities and simple adding machine operations. The principal advantage of the bookkeeping machine is that it performs the required ledger card operations but is not far removed from a purely manual system. The operator and the accountant can see all of the ledger card entries and can quickly correct any errors.

Advances in electronics have allowed bookkeeping machines to take on the characteristics of computers. This allows many businesses to automate additional accounting functions such as payroll, billing, and inventory control. Again, because things change, bookkeeping machines are gradually disappearing from the scene, in favor of the desktop microcomputer and computerized accounting systems which are available for reasonable prices from software vendors.

Microfile Equipment

The most common microform media are roll film, both 16 mm and 35 mm, microfiche, which are film sheets (4 inches × 6 inches), microfilm jackets that contain strips of microfilm and can be easily updated, and aperture cards, generally used for engineering drawings, which are film inserts for the standard 80-column punch cards.

There are three types of film in common use. Original documents are photographed on silver halide film, while either negative or positive duplicates are made on diazo or vesicular films.

The advantages of the various microforms include the following: space savings due to the smaller size as compared to paper documents, inexpensive duplication and distribution, physical means to keep records together and avoid accidental loss of individual records, and (in the case of computer output microfilm) very high rates of output using special fonts and graphics.

Microfilming, except for COM, is done either with rotary microfilmers designed to provide fast, continuous filming of high-volume documents, or with planetary microfilmers designed to produce high-quality film, such as that needed for engineering drawings. Film processing may be done with on-site equipment or provided by an outside service organization. High-speed, economical duplicators allow distribution to numerous users. Microfilm readers vary from small, hand-held units used by field personnel to "read" selected portions of large technical libraries up to large, computer-controlled retrieval systems. Reader-printers can provide instant copies of selected material.

When microform files must be updated, microfilm jackets are used to allow inserting recent additions and changes. Sometimes it is more economical to completely replace a microform file (copy) with an updated version than to attempt to update the file.

Some systems combine microform and digital retrieval. This provides the benefits of microfilms (photographic quality, high-density storage, ease of duplication and distribution, etc.) and the benefits of digital storage (ease of updating, sophisticated data communications, ease of computer processing, etc.) in one integrated system.

We've been using the term "electronic microfilm," so let's spend a bit of time with it. The advent of the laser/video disk will make this concept very much a reality. Electronic microfilm may one day become the primary storage and retrieval use of the business computer. Video disk will provide easy-to-use document storage and retrieval. Its massive storage capabilities and low cost make it the first viable substitute for a file cabinet. New developments in still frame digital photography will allow production of an inexpensive camera that can produce a digital image of any document for storage on an optical disk. The random access feature of the video disk will provide instant retrieval of documents using an ordinary microcomputer. You are but steps away from the removal of paper clutter from the office.

Local area networking will enhance the utility of electronic microfilm. Local area networks will allow anyone on the network to remotely access the electronic microfilm files, if authorized to do so. The network will act like a messenger, allowing you to find files anywhere in the network, irrespective of their physical location. Retrieval of the information will be relatively easy; paper reduction of the images will be fast, using laser printing devices. There will be major changes in communications speed, storage requirements, graphics imaging and presentation, and the use of color.

Forms Handling Equipment

This equipment removes carbon paper (deleaving), separates multiple copies (decollating), separates the continuous forms into individual pages or sections (bursting), slits off the pinfeed margins, slits forms which have been printed side-by-side, and imprints information such as signatures, destination address, batch numbers, etc. As COM becomes more popular for batch output and as on-line real-time systems eliminate the need for hard-copy output, the need for forms handling equipment will be reduced. And by now it should go without saying—put a laser printer and binding equipment into the process, and reports combined with text will appear in book form. We have the technology, and it's affordable.

Typewriter Data Encoders

Typewriters capable of producing human-readable characters while at the same time producing machine-readable characters are being used to generate computer input. The advantages are that the information can be visually inspected by the originator, forms can be processed annually, and optical character readers can read the forms at high rates. The development of typewriters which have quick font change capability and availability of inexpensive hand-held optical character readers make fast, accurate input systems feasible.

These are, of course, the electronic typewriters. Some of these have internal buffers. Some have display screens. Most have RS-232 serial communication capabilities. And these devices, impact devices, are selling right alongside the various implementations of the microcomputer.

Unit Record Equipment

The Card Unit Record

The 80-column card is divided into 80 vertical *columns* or card columns. The columns are numbered from 1 to 80 beginning with the left side of the card. The columns are divided into 12 punching positions called *rows*. The rows are designated from the top to the bottom of the card by 12 (referred to as the "R" punch), 11 (referred to as the "X" punch), 0, 1, 2, 3, 4, 5, 6, 7, 8, and 9. The top edge of the card is known as the 12 edge, and the bottom of the card is known as the 9 edge. Cards are fed through machines either 9 edge first or 12 edge first, and either face-up or face-down.

Each column of the card accommodates a code for either a letter or a special character. Digits are recorded by punched holes in the digit punching positions of the card from 0 to 9. The top three punching positions-12, 11, and 0-are known as the zone punching positions. Obviously, the 0 punch can be either a digit punch or a zone punch. A combination of a zone punch and a digit punch is used to represent one of the 26 letters. The 11 special characters are recorded by one, two, or three punches in a column.

The letters A to I are coded by the combination of a 12-punch and a digit punch (1 to 9). Letters J to R are coded by an 11-punch and a digit punch (1 to 9). The letters S to Z are coded by a zero punch and a digit punch (2 to 9). The above codes are standard, and the set is known as the Hollerith Code. The special character punch codes, however, vary in both number and code.

There are many uses for a convention called the control punch. Simply stated, this is a regular punch in the 80-column card that is unique and is not part of the regular data. For instance, it could be an X-punch in a particular column which would normally hold only a numeric data punch or nothing. The control punch could then be sensed and used to control some desired machine action.

Items of information are recorded on a card in groups of consecutive columns called fields. A field may consist of from 1 to 80 columns, depending upon the length of the item of information to be recorded on it. Field length is generally determined by the maximum length of information to be punched into it.

Machine Functions

As you read this section, keep your mind open to the fact that even though we're discussing punched cards, the functions are those of any recording medium. Hopefully the fifth edition of this book can chronicle the demise of unit record media and equipment.

The first function of a machine is *recording*. Regardless of the method used in capturing necessary data, the importance of recording them accurately at the time of origination cannot be overemphasized. Manual means of recording the data are usually not machine-sensible; therefore, a human transcription which may introduce errors is required.

Machine-sensible media are produced by a variety of devices as byproducts of the transaction. These machines produce punched paper tape, punched cards, edge-punched documents, MICR characters, and others, such as optical character font. Some machines can produce magnetic tape, and some produce no medium but rather send the character code directly to the computer communications buffer. These devices include bookkeeping machines, flexowriters, adding machines, cash registers, time clocks, credit card imprinters, etc.

The basic method of converting source information into machine-sensible form is through the use of card punch equipment. In this method the operator reads the source document for information and depresses keys on the keyboard of the equipment which causes coded holes to be punched into the proper vertical columns of the card.

The second function is *classifying.* The classifying function is arranging the cards in some predetermined sequence. Classifying techniques include those of sorting, selecting, sequence checking, merging, and programming. A class of specialized equipment has been developed for sorting which is, perhaps, the classification function most frequently required in punched card processing.

The process of selection may be done on either sorters or collators. Sequence checking, matching, and merging can be done on the collator machines.

Programming, in punched card processing, refers to the function by which the machine can distinguish cards from different groupings and thus provide individual group totals, as performed on the accounting machine by the wiring of external "boards."

The third function is *calculating.* Calculating is the process of performing arithmetic operations and punching the results into a card. Calculation is performed on calculators and calculating punches in punched card systems, but it is better performed by the electronic computer.

The fourth function is *report preparation.* Report preparation is performed by accounting machines which are called tabulators. The accounting machine processes data and produces printed reports through instructions which are wired into a removable control panel.

The fifth function is *summarizing.* Summarizing is the product of calculations which present new data in a more concise and presentable form.

While not a unit record concept, the sixth, and final step, will be *communication*—transmission and receipt.

Standard Card Unit Record Equipment

The *card punch* is used to punch cards and, perhaps, to print on cards. When the key is depressed, a hole or combination of holes is punched into a card. The main difference between the layout of the typewriter keyboard and that of the card punch is the close grouping of the numeric keys, which also punch letters as well as digits. The shift from letters to digits is made manually by a shift key or automatically by the program unit.

A hopper supplies blank cards to the punching mechanism. The first two cards to be punched must be fed by depressing the feed key. All other cards can be fed automatically under control of the automatic feed switch.

The punching is performed at the first of two stations along the card path. The second station is the *read station.* Cards in both stations move along in unison as the keys or the space bar are depressed. Often, some fields in a group of cards contain repetitive information. When the duplicate key is depressed, the holes in the column under the read station activate the punch station, where those holes are duplicated. After the card leaves the read station, it is fed into a stacker.

Repetitive operations can be accomplished automatically through the aid of a card punch component called the *program unit.* The program unit can control automatic skipping over columns not to be punched, automatic duplicating of repetitive information, and the shifting from numerical to alphabetic punching mode and back.

In some shops, after a batch of cards has been punched, it is verified to check the work of the card punch operator. With the source documents and the punched cards in the same sequence, the *verifier* operator duplicates the keystrokes of the card punch operator; however, no holes are punched. The card verifier's error light goes on when there is disagreement. After two more tries the top edge of the card is automatically notched above the column with the error. All cards that have no detected errors are automatically notched on the right-hand end at the 1 row.

The *interpreter* is capable of interpreting the holes found in a punched card and printing the appropriate characters. In punched card terminology, interpreting is the translation of already punched holes into printed information on the same card.

The *sorter* performs the basic functions of the numerical sorting, alphabetic sorting, and selection. Numeric sorting involves the rearrangement of cards in numeric order by sorting on a specific digit field in the cards. The selection switches must first be set for numeric sorting; then the cards must be sorted on each column of the field to be classified.

An outstanding feature of the sorter is the 13 pockets which hold the cards after they have been read. The pockets are numbered from right to left: Reject, 12, 11, 0, 1, 2, 3, 4, 5, 6, 7, 8, and 9.

Alphabetic sorting requires two sorts on each column, because a letter is recorded by two holes punched in a single column. There are two methods of sorting alphabetic data. In one method each column is sorted first on the numerical punch with the zone punch detector turned off. On the second sort of the same column, the numeric detector is turned off and the sorting is on the zone punch only.

The other method follows a different procedure. On the first sort of the column, the letters A through I are directed into pockets corresponding to the letter's digit punch; letters with 0 zone punch are directed to the 0 pocket; and letters with 11 zone punch are directed to the 11 pocket. Now, the cards in pockets 1-9 are already in sequence; they do not require a second pass. The 11 zone punch group is sorted and placed behind the first group. Next, the remaining cards are sorted and placed behind the others. Alphabetic sorting using the second method is faster, because the deck of cards to be sorted decreases progressively.

One of the principles of data processing is good source data automation. One of the principles of source data automation is to record source data only once. When information is recorded in the form of holes in a card, a punched card machine can reproduce some or all of the information in other cards. The *reproducing punch* is one of these machines.

Card punch equipment can also duplicate part or all of the information from one card into another. Duplicating reduces the work performed by the operator on each card, improves accuracy, and increases the productivity of the equipment operator.

Whereas duplicating transfers data from one card to another, which then passes the data to the third, and is performed one punch at a time, *reproducing* is performed by transferring data from one deck of cards to another, card by card. Reproducing can be the complete copying of one card into another, or only selected data may be reproduced.

Gang punching is like duplicating and also like reproducing in that data are punched from one card to another. However, gang punching is punching all or part of the data in a master card into succeeding cards. Master cards are identified by control punches, which when sensed, prevent unwanted data being punched into master cards. Most reproducers operate at speeds of 100 cards per minute.

Summary punching is the automatic conversion of data developed by one of the account machines into coded punched holes in a card.

The *collator* performs the operation of merging, sequence checking, selection, and matching. Sometimes all of these operations can be performed simultaneously. At other times it is necessary to perform each operation individually.

Two files of cards are compiled to produce a single file in the process called *merging*. Each of the two files must be in proper sequence prior to the merging operation. While it is sometimes possible to perform this operation on a sorter, merging on a *collator* normally provides a faster means of placing related sorted cards together in a single file.

The operation in which the ascending or descending sequence of cards is checked for proper sequence is called *sequence checking*. This procedure is performed on the collator by comparing each card fed into the machine with the previous card. As long as the proper sequence is maintained, the operation continues through the deck of cards.

Punched cards containing punches representing specified characteristics may be selected from decks of cards. Typical selection criteria might be as follows: cards punched with specific digits, all cards containing digits higher than a specific number, all cards containing digits lower than a specific number, cards containing digits between two specific numbers, first card of each group, last card of each group, unmatched cards, and cards out of sequence.

Matching determines if the cards in two files are exactly the same, usually as regards only specific data. Matching involves sequential checks on pairs of cards or groups of cards previously arranged in a sequence. After the check is completed, the two files of card can be stacked separately or combined.

The accounting machine performs the majority of the reporting functions required. There are several different accounting machine types, but they differ in general only in their input/output speeds and in their accumulating capacity. They perform the functions of accumulating data by addition and subtraction, comparison, selection, programming, and printing detail data and group data. If a summary punch machine is connected, the function of summary punching can also be performed. Automatic control of the accounting machine is based upon a prewired control panel (or ''boards'').

Ordinary punched card accounting machines can add and subtract, but they cannot multiply and divide. Punched card machines that can perform all four arithmetic operations are called *calculators.*

The punched card calculator, like the punched card machines, is controlled by means of a wired control panel. The function of the calculator has been taken over by the new small electronic computer, where volumes of work are involved. Calculator machines operate at rates of between 20 and 150 cards per minute.

This is no doubt the last edition which will carry information about the unit record or punched card equipment and techniques. There are people now in our field who have never seen, and probably will never see, this equipment.

QUESTIONS

It is important to note that these questions are not directly tied to any subject or concept given in the text. These have been collected with a view to providing an approach to the test and preparation.

1. The ENIAC was built by:
   A. Eckert and Mauchly
   B. Ballistic Research Laboratories
   C. IBM
   D. Univac Division, Sperry Rand

2. If you have a low relative I/O to processing time, the input/output buffers
   A. Are most efficient
   B. May be full
   C. May not be full
   D. Are least efficient

3. Which of the following communications channels has the fastest transmission rate?
   A. Telegraph grade
   B. Broadband grade

C. Voice grade
D. Subvoice grade

4. An asynchronous communications system
A. Is a low-overhead system
B. Carries data in eight-bit bytes
C. Is a high-overhead system
D. Carries only ASCII into packet switching

5. The National Bureau of Standards produced which of the following computers:
A. SEAC
B. EDSAC
C. Whirlwind I
D. Cray-II

6. Associative memory is best described by the following:
A. A technique for connecting two memory locations
B. A technique for handling fixed-memory locations
C. A technique for handling auxiliary memory
D. A technique for virtual memory and paging

7. What is the basic principle used in offset duplication?
A. Dye transfer
B. Fluid process
C. Pressure
D. Grease and water will not mix

8. The CRT refresh cycle presents the information on the screen which was formerly in the:
A. Screen buffer
B. Memory address
C. Keyboard buffer
D. Input/output buffer

9. Which computer section interprets the instruction word?
A. Control
B. Word organization
C. Memory
D. Input/output

10. Boolean algebra is commonly used
A. To manipulate digital logic gates
B. To calculate simultaneous equations
C. To handle distance/rate/time problems
D. To compensate for variations in speed

11. Direct reference, indirect reference, base/displacement, and indexing are ways to perform:
A. Computer arithmetic
B. Word organization
C. Memory accessing
D. Data transmission

12. When a check is processed through the MICR encoder, the operator's primary responsibility is to
A. Magnetize the spots
B. Add the amount and account number
C. Add the date
D. Add the check digit

13. Which of the following is NOT a function of the address field of a single-address instruction format?
    A. Location to store the result
    B. Location of the next instruction
    C. Location of one of the operands
    D. Immediate data
14. The fastest communications protocol of those listed is:
    A. Teletype
    B. Bisynchronous
    C. MNP
    D. Asynchronous
15. A general register:
    A. May be used for relocation
    B. May be used for double-precision arithmetic
    C. May be used for indexing
    D. All of the above are correct
16. An analog computer
    A. Performs hundreds of calculations per second
    B. Is slower than a digital computer
    C. Measures variable data
    D. Measures discrete data
17. Which of the following is NOT one of the general phases of the compute instruction cycle?
    A. Fetch instruction
    B. Get data
    C. Perform action
    D. Fetch next instruction
18. FDM and TDM are types of:
    A. Hardware ports
    B. Modems
    C. Multiplexors
    D. Acoustic couplers
19. When an interrupt occurs, which of the following should be stored?
    A. The contents of the critical registers
    B. The location of the interrupt
    C. The latest checkpoint
    D. Pointers to the data buffer
20. The Electronics Industry Association devised a serial communications interface known as
    A. IEEE-488
    B. SAE-40
    C. RS-232
    D. PL-296
21. What is the function of the program address register?
    A. To hold the address of the next instruction
    B. To monitor the sequence of instruction addresses
    C. To decode the address portion of the instruction work
    D. To mark the present program step in case of an interrupt
22. Parity is calculated on the basis of the number of bits in the character and the system used. That change is made in:

A. The primary parity medium
B. The single-bit memory area
C. The character movement buffer
D. The secondary storage area

23. Which of the following is found in the control section?
A. The channel command words
B. A sequence of instructions
C. Single current individual instruction
D. The next sequential instruction

24. The basis for asynchronous communications require that data be:
A. Encoded for digital transmission
B. Be clocked at each end of the transmission line
C. Be encoded and decoded by a modem at each of the line
D. Be transmitted in synchronous parallel mode

25. In any modern computer the only kind of internal arithmetic is:
A. Binary
B. Octal
C. Decimal
D. Hexadecimal

26. Which type of memory has the fastest access time?
A. Drum memory
B. Bubble memory
C. Associative memory
D. Semiconductor memory

27. The register which decodes the operation code is the:
A. Program address register
B. Memory address register
C. Data address register
D. Program control register

28. Of those listed, which medium is most commonly used on the microcomputer:
A. Cassette tape
B. Magnetic drum
C. Magnetic tape
D. Winchester disk

29. Which of the following is a seven-bit code?
A. BCD
B. FIELDATA
C. EBCDIC
D. ASCII

30. Elite, Roman, Courier, and Clarendon are each examples of a:
A. Print matrix
B. Print head
C. Character set
D. Character font

31. An acoustic coupler is an example of a:
A. Direct data device
B. Time-shared terminal

C. Modem
D. Multiplexor

32. What is the difference between multiuser and multitasking?
A. A multiuser environment is hardware based
B. Multitasking offers file- and record-level locking
C. Multiuser is sequential; multitasking is simultaneous
D. Multiuser partitions one or more processors for use by more than one person; multitasking lets a single processor keep many tasks active at the same time

33. The telecommunications standard which is finding widest acceptance in the mainframe world is:
A. DDD
B. SNA
C. SDLC
D. EFT

34. CMOS stands for:
A. Conductive Magnetic Ordered Sequences
B. Character Matrix Operating System
C. Complementary Metal Oxide Semicondictor
D. Capacitance Managed Octagonal Switches

35. When are MICR characters magnetized?
A. When additional characters are added
B. When the characters are printed
C. Just prior to being read for processing
D. When being selected

36. A communications line where data may be transmitted in both directions, one direction at a time is:
A. Simplex
B. Half duplex
C. Full duplex
D. Complex

37. A floating point expression is said to be normalized when:
A. The point is to the right of the low-order one-bit of the fraction
B. The point is to the left of the high-order one-bit of the fraction
C. The point is halfway between the high and the low one-bits
D. The point is the same number of places to the left of the high-order one-bit as the value of the characteristic

38. The laser printer used with a microcomputer is most useful for presenting:
A. Color graphics
B. Matrix continuous form output
C. Letter quality font-oriented printout
D. High-speed collating of different forms

39. Under which type of communications system will the communications monitor periodically check to determine "device ready" status?
A. Contention
B. Polling
C. Distributive
D. Demand

40. The laser disk may provide order of magnitude improvements in:
A. Storage capacity
B. Communications speed

C. Parity checking
D. Memory movement

41. Liquid crystal displays may most often be found
A. On CRT faces
B. In conjunction with LED displays
C. On digital readouts on test equipment
D. On calculators, wristwatches, and notebook computers

42. The two parts of a floating point number may be called
A. Mantissa and exponent
B. Exponent and characteristic
C. Mantissa and fraction
D. Fraction and floating point

43. The concept of electronic microfilm involves
A. The use of the diazo process and silver halide
B. The use of digitizing cameras and laser disks
C. The use of matrix and daisy wheel printers
D. The use of phonemes and photons

44. Most current operating systems provide two operating modes. In the problem mode, privileged instructions CANNOT be executed. What is the mode in which all instructions can be executed?
A. Standard processing mode
B. Supervisor mode
C. Interrupt mode
D. Problem mode

45. The cylinder concept on a direct access device is based upon the number of:
A. Tracks on the disk
B. Tracks on a cylinder
C. Multiple heads positioned at a single track
D. Disks in operation

46. Data will reside in the computer as a function of the:
A. Control section
B. Arithmetic and logic section
C. I/O section
D. Memory

47. Seek time is:
A. The time it takes to position the access arm on the correct cylinder
B. The time it takes to find the correct record in a file.
C. The time it takes to find the correct disk in operations.
D. The time it takes after the hide to find the person

48. Parity checking is also called:
A. Vertical redundancy checking
B. Horizontal redundancy checking
C. Cyclical redundancy checking
D. Memory

49. What type of storage is most volatile?
A. Card
B. RAM
C. Tape
D. Disk

50. Data are recorded on magnetic tape in groups called
A. Blocks
B. Characters
C. Bits
D. Bytes

51. The location of an indirect address is probably:
A. In a data register
B. In an address register
C. In a general register
D. In an accumulator

52. Dot and stroke generators are commonly associated with:
A. CRT systems
B. Character modes
C. Plotting systems
D. Graphic displays

53. The concept of interrupt levels include:
A. You cannot interrupt an interrupt
B. An interrupt will always branch to the next sequential instruction
C. Interrupts upon interrupts, as conditions change
D. Protection from interrupts under certain conditions

54. The maximum length of a magnetic tape block is constrained by:
A. The size of the record
B. The size of the computer word
C. The size of memory available
D. The size of the internal buffer

55. A matrix printer with graphics capability can:
A. Print in draft, NLQ, or correspondence mode
B. Print only in capitals
C. Print only in lower case
D. Print bidirectionally only

56. Drum printers function by:
A. Striking the axial row of the drum
B. Rotating the individual characters to align to the print line
C. Pushing the drum against the paper
D. Striking the reciprocal row of the drum

57. Privileged instructions may be executed only by:
A. The monitor
B. The supervisor
C. Application programs
D. Utility programs

58. Baudot or teletype code is:
A. 5-channel
B. 6-channel
C. 7-channel
D. 8-channel

59. The Daisy wheel printer functions with a:
A. Pin element
B. Bar element

C. Spray element
D. Spline element

60. Chain printers require:
A. Rotating cylinders
B. Heat-sensitive paper
C. 48-character slugs
D. Impacting hammers

61. What is the smallest unit of information that can be stored in RAM?
A. Bit
B. Byte
C. Word
D. Character

62. Analog computers operate upon:
A. Continuous variables that represent continuous data
B. Discrete data
C. Integer data
D. Communications interfaces

63. The primary advantage of ROM over RAM is that:
A. ROM is random access memory
B. ROM is nonvolatile
C. Information cannot be stored in RAM by a program
D. Information in ROM can be read without destroying it

64. The Extended Binary Coded Decimal Interchange Code will permit a maximum single character binary value of:
A. 15
B. 63
C. 127
D. 255

65. Which is NOT an advantage of a floppy disk over a cassette tape?
A. Higher data transfer rate
B. Faster access
C. Larger capacity
D. Less expensive

66. The terms *serial* and *parallel* are NOT used to describe which of the following attributes or components of the digital computer:
A. Precision
B. Memory
C. Operation upon operands
D. Transmission of data

67. Dot matrix printers
A. Produce letter-quality output
B. Are fast impact printers
C. Form letters from patterns of dots
D. Can print only a finite set of characters

68. "Scrolling" is a technique most commonly associated with:
A. CRT display devices
B. Direct access devices

C. Memory devices
D. Electronic calculators

69. Data buffering may be described as:
A. Basically, placing a storage area between the slow-acting devices and the fast-acting device
B. Necessary for time sharing and multiprogramming
C. Involved in allowing more than one input/output operation and one internal computer operation to occur simultaneously
D. All of the above

70. Read-only-memory (ROM) is used:
A. For storage of a permanent program, e.g., controller firmware, an executive routine, or special subroutines
B. To prevent store instructions which address the page from being executed
C. To provide for indirect addressing
D. As random access access memory

71. In a fixed-word length computer:
A. Each memory cell and most registers are of the same length
B. Internal transmission of data is quite inefficient
C. Data are handled serially, one bit at a time
D. Memory is sector-oriented

72. Computer performance evaluation software measures:
A. Execution efficiency
B. I/O efficiency
C. Privileged/nonprivileged instruction ratio
D. All of the above

73. In a variable-word-length computer:
A. Data are handled serially, a character at a time
B. The size of the data cell varies
C. Efficiency is higher than for fixed-word-length computers
D. The size of the register varies

74. The function of a channel is:
A. To connect I/O devices to a program
B. To connect control units to I/O devices
C. To provide broadband transmission capability
D. To connect I/O devices to the CPU

75. Which of the following is NOT required for multiprogramming?
A. Multiprocessing computer components
B. A large memory
C. More than one channel
D. Hardware interrupt

76. A terminal control unit performs which of the following services:
A. Shifting bits "end to end"
B. Polling multidrop lines
C. Assemblage of characters transmitted from a terminal
D. All of the above

77. Which type of communications connection allows simultaneous data transmission in both directions?
A. Simplex
B. Half duplex

C. Full duplex
D. Modem

78. In a one-address machine, which of the following is NOT included in the instruction itself?
A. Address of the next sequential instruction
B. Address of one of the operands
C. Immediate data
D. The target field

79. The tracks on a disk are
A. Concentric circles
B. Adjacent circles of equal diameter
C. Each associated with a specific read/write head
D. Helical or spiral, depending upon the number of disks

80. The de facto standard for BASIC was developed by:
A. ANSI
B. Microsoft
C. IBM
D. Wang

81. Some bookkeeping machines are designed to utilize information stored on the back of ledger cards in the form of:
A. Magnetic stripes
B. MICR
C. Mark sense markings
D. Small, round punched holes

82. Of the following, which type of internal storage has the fastest access time?
A. Magnetic core storage
B. Thin-film storage
C. Plated wire memory
D. Drum storage

83. In direct addressing, the address field of the instruction word contains
A. The address of a memory cell that contains the address of the data
B. The address of the memory cell that contains the data
C. Immediate data
D. The address of the next sequential instruction

84. An audio response unit:
A. Has an unlimited vocabulary
B. Functions by fitting prerecorded or synthesized word patterns together
C. Is an example of a sequential access device
D. Cannot be contacted from a terminal

85. The first, second, and third generations of computers are distinguished by:
A. Silicon technology, VLSI, chips
B. Vacuum tubes, ICs, deForest bridges
C. Transistors, Wheatstone bridges, and SLT
D. Vacuum tubes, transistors, integrated circuits

86. The microprogrammable controller is often used to:
A. Handle input data
B. Control robots
C. Print reports
D. Communication asynchronously

87. Distinguish between EROM and PROM
A. Both are erasable, and they are the same
B. Neither is erasable and must be burned in at the factory
C. Both are erasable; EROM may be reburned; PROM may be established by the user
D. Neither is erasable; neither can be reprogrammed

88. Relocation of a program involves
A. Ones-complement of the hexadecimal shift register
B. Twos-complement of the binary relocated address
C. A restructured general register complement
D. A base register and a displacement offset

89. The first and last parts of a character transmitted asynchronously will be:
A. The ASCII character beginning and ending bits
B. The start bit and the parity bit
C. The baud rate and the stop bit
D. The start bit and the stop bit

90. Indexing develops what kind of address?
A. Displacement
B. Effective
C. Relative
D. Base

91. Pushdown stacks function in a ________ manner:
A. FILO
B. LIFO
C. FIFO
D. LILO

92. The function of a front end communication processor is to:
A. Operate the network independent of the host
B. Function as a terminal control unit to another host
C. Do process monitoring on a communications network
D. Handle multiprocessing "busy" assignment

93. Memory protection is accomplished
A. As a hardware feature of the CPU
B. As a software feature of the operating system
C. As a hardware feature of the applications system
D. As a software feature of the applications program

94. Most diskettes have:
A. 25 tracks
B. 32 tracks
C. 40 tracks
D. 96 tracks

95. The Kerr effect is caused by:
A. Punching a card
B. Bouncing a laser beam on a compact disk
C. Sending a pulse train on a communications service
D. Reading a paper tape with photoelectric cells

96. The UPC is just one implementation of:
A. OCR
B. EFT

C. CPM
D. DOS

97. The Mouse is a program directing device which is used to:
A. Fill windows with color
B. Select options from a menu
C. Point the cursor
D. Provide discrete data input

98. A plotter, as implemented on the microcomputer, is an automated drafting machine which:
A. Can use only one colored pen at a time
B. Moves the pens along one axis and the paper along another
C. Moves the pens only along two axes
D. Moves the paper only along two axes

99. Voice commands for speech recognition and synthesis is achieved using:
A. Analog-to-digital conversion and storage tables
B. Digital inflection and storage tables
C. Analog deflection and storage tables
D. Controverted deflection and storage tables

100. The touch screen is a method to:
A. Isolate a portion of the screen for examination
B. Transfer commands from voice to visual execution
C. Interrupt the beam placed across the face of the screen
D. Interrupt the voltage scanned across the phosphor

ANSWER KEY

1. A	**26.** D	**51.** C	**76.** D
2. D	**27.** D	**52.** D	**77.** C
3. B	**28.** D	**53.** C	**78.** D
4. C	**29.** D	**54.** C	**79.** A
5. D	**30.** D	**55.** A	**80.** B
6. D	**31.** C	**56.** A	**81.** A
7. D	**32.** D	**57.** B	**82.** B
8. A	**33.** B	**58.** A	**83.** B
9. A	**34.** C	**59.** D	**84.** B
10. A	**35.** C	**60.** D	**85.** D
11. C	**36.** B	**61.** A	**86.** B
12. B	**37.** B	**62.** A	**87.** C
13. A	**38.** C	**63.** B	**88.** D
14. B	**39.** B	**64.** D	**89.** D
15. D	**40.** A	**65.** D	**90.** B
16. C	**41.** D	**66.** A	**91.** B
17. D	**42.** A	**67.** C	**92.** A
18. C	**43.** B	**68.** A	**93.** B
19. A	**44.** B	**69.** D	**94.** C
20. C	**45.** C	**70.** A	**95.** B
21. A	**46.** D	**71.** A	**96.** A
22. B	**47.** A	**72.** D	**97.** C
23. C	**48.** A	**73.** A	**98.** B
24. C	**49.** B	**74.** D	**99.** A
25. A	**50.** A	**75.** A	**100.** C

TUTORIAL

1. Dr. John Mauchly and J. Presper Eckert built the ENIAC in the mid-1940s while at the Moore School of the University of Pennsylvania.
2. Buffers are a speed compensating method between high memory speed and low input/output speed. If you have low relative I/O to processing time, the effectiveness of a buffer is lost.
3. The broadband grade has the fastest transmission rate because the width of the band provides the ability to transmit in parallel. Telegraph, voice, and subvoice grade channels must all be used for serial transmission.
4. An asynchronous communications system is a high-overhead system. Each character is sent separately in a "start/stop" operation, including: one start bit, seven data bits, one parity bit, and one or two stop bits.
5. The SEAC (or Standards Eastern Automatic Computer) was produced by the National Bureau of Standards, as was the SWAC (Standards Western Automatic Computer).
6. Associative memory is a paging technique for memory which is addressable by content. The locations are dynamic. The cost is the same as the cost of any large-scale memory. Its size is limited only by machine design, and it does nothing to speed up memory access time.
7. The offset duplication master is optically "burned" and chemically etched. It is placed on a drum and ink is applied to the master, adhering to the image. The inked image is then placed on a "blanket," in reverse. The reversed image is then re-reversed by application to paper.
8. Under normal circumstances, a CRT is refreshed from the screen buffer. An exception would be where the screen is memory-mapped (has its own area of main memory). The other answers have to do with display or entry methods.
9. Of the four, three (excluding B) are sections of a computer. The control section (or CPU) interprets the instruction word.
10. The language of binary math for logic manipulation was devised by George Boole. Binary is applicable to networks of switches commonly called "gates." The other answers are absurd.
11. The answer is a memory addressing technique. The addressing scheme may well be used to facilitate the others.
12. When a check is processed, the MICR encoding operator adds the amount—answer B. The account number and check digit are already a printed part of the check. The date is inconsequential.
13. In the one-address system, the target address would have to have been already stored.
14. Bisynchronous is a high-speed data communications protocol. By their very nature, teletype devices are very slow, which disqualifies answers C and D, as well.
15. While you will probably see no "all of the above" or "none of the above" questions, all of the first three answers are correct. If you can handle these concepts, you'll have the answer covered.
16. By its very nature, an analog is a continuing measurement of a changing variable. Analog computers work no faster or slower than digital computers. Analog data is changing data, not fixed data. It measures only and does no calculation in and of itself.
17. Answer D here is a duplication of Answer A, and no instruction will be fetched twice in the sequence.
18. A port is a hardware interface. A modem converts digital signals to analog signals for the telephone network. An acoustic coupler is one type of modem. A multiplexor is the means to merge several signals, even those of differing speeds, onto a wider-band communications carrier. There are two common types of multiplexor—time division (TDM), which allocates each incoming line a portion of time, and frequency division (FDM), which allocates a portion of the bandwidth.
19. Checkpoint probably will not apply; it will not apply in every case, at least. Pointers to the data buffer should be a part of the register contents. The location of the interrupt will be a part of the program address register. Therefore, save the registers.

20. The Electronics Industry Association (EIA) established the technical specification, named it as RS-232, and offered it to the International Standards Organization (ISO), which has accepted it. It is important to note that this is the *serial* and not the *parallel* connection.

21. The register is a pointer, but in this case it's the pointer to the next instruction, not the current one—besides, with high level languages, many instructions may constitute a program step.

22. The key to this answer is the phrase "single-bit memory area." With odd parity being prevalent in memory transfer operations, the flip of a bit would make the character even parity. This method would not be valid where two bits were changed.

23. The channel command words would be a part of the executable instructions of the channel control unit. Instructions are worked with one at a time, so a sequence is out of the question. The next sequential instruction may or may not be there, depending upon the nature of the current instruction. So C is the correct answer.

24. Because the question deals with asynchronous communications, answers B and D do not apply. Neither does A, as it is a serial transmission. The computer must communicate to the telecommunications carrier through a modem (MOdulate/DEModulate) device on both ends of the line.

25. Octal, decimal, and hexadecimal are merely representations of binary, the numbering system of the computer

26. Semiconductor memory has fastest access, particularly where processing functions are closely related. Drums, with either fixed or movable heads, have longer wire connections. Associative (disk page) memory is slower yet. The closest would be the bubble memory—which is slower, and not widely used.

27. The program, memory, and data address registers say where the instruction's effect will be felt. The program control register decodes the instruction's operation code.

28. Winchester disk is the correct answer. Magnetic drum has not been implemented for the microcomputer—it's not needed. Magnetic tape has been available, but is very slow and very unreliable, as it uses an audio, not a digital, recording process. This tape has been largely cassette, but recently some manufacturers have found ways to use magnetic tape for archival purposes.

29. BCD and FIELDATA are six-bit codes. EBCDIC is eight-bit. ASCII is the answer (D).

30. A font is a set of characters in a specific character style, such as OCR-B. C is close, but a font applies to a single character set.

31. The acoustic coupler is a modem into which a telephone handset may be placed.

32. Don't assume that the longest answer is, by definition, the correct answer. In this case, it is. And, if you think about it, multiuser means more than one person.

33. The systems network architecture (SNA) has become the defacto standard for at least the mainframe world. The same is not true with the microcomputer, although SNA is quite workable there. Synchronous data link control is a communications method, but IBM only—not fully accepted. The direct distance dialing (DDD) is a network of AT&T, and EFT is the electronic funds transfer system. B is the answer.

34. CMOS stands for Complementary Metal Oxide Semiconductor. This semiconductor fabrication process makes everything from memory chips and microprocessors smaller, cooler, and more efficient. You'll find CMOS chips in wristwatches and lap portable computers, like the TRS-80 Model 100.

35. So there will be no danger of loss of magnetism or interference with other magnetized fields, the special magnetic ink is magnetized as the check is entering the throat of the machine.

36. The switching necessary to provide communication on a line in both directions, but one at a time, is half-duplex. This is why, when two people are talking simultaneously on a telephone, one blocks out the other.

37. The concept of normalization is to place the value into the power. To do so, everything must be to the right of the decimal point, or the point must be to the left of the high-order one bit.

38. The laser printer may someday have color capability, but the only way to do it now is to change cartridges and then print the entire paper in another color. While the printing is still matrix, you'll never know it; but only the larger laser printers provide continuous form output. Collation of forms is possible with the laser printer, but who would want to do it?
39. Contention is a demand type of communication (A, D) which signals the host when ready. Distributive is a nonsensical answer. Polling (B) is the answer.
40. There are many improvements offered by the laser disk, the most outstanding of which is capacity.
41. Liquid crystal displays are found on calculators (which draw their power from light), wristwatches, and notebook computers. Just about all notebook computers use them because of their very low power consumption.
42. This is a definition question, to which A provides the most accurate definition.
43. Electronic microfilm will use digitizing cameras, laser disks, laser printers, etc. Diazo and silver halide are chemicals used in the COM process. Matrix and daisy wheel printers are physical printing processes. Phonemes are used for synthesized speech and photons exist in television cameras.
44. The supervisor mode permits all instructions to be executed, (B). D is nonsense. A is nonexistent. C is a suspension from execution.
45. If you were to look at a disk pack from the top, and the tracks were visible, you would realize that each track has a correspondent in the same place on every disk surface. This set of tracks is called a cylinder, and can be accessed with every available head in that position.
46. Data are stored in memory, but by the other three, and other methods.
47. The positioning of the arm is the seek time, and the time that it takes to position to the midpoint of the disk is known as the average seek time. Only afterward does the record search time begin. C and D are somewhat absurd, I think you'll agree.
48. The parity check is done as a function of the character itself, vertically. Parity is simply the addition of an odd or even bit, depending upon the scheme utilized.
49. Card, tape, and disk are semi-permanent media. RAM, on the other hand, disappears when the power is disconnected, and is therefore the most volatile. I know, some RAM will not lose its contents—look for a sustaining battery.
50. It's actually known as the *physical block.* It can also be known as the *logical block,* if more than one record is contained in the recorded space.
51. Expect to find the indirect in a general register. Data registers are few, accumulators are no longer registers, an address register isn't indirect.
52. There is some credence for A here, but the advent of graphic displays which are unique from normal CRT displays make D the best answer. B and C do not apply.
53. Interrupts have a priority; a higher priority interrupt can interrupt a lower priority interrupt. Things are placed in a pushdown stack and resolved sequentially.
54. The size of available memory is the constraint. The full memory would have to be declared a buffer in order to do so. Don't jump at "buffer." Read the question carefully.
55. The printers with graphics capability can do just about anything. The more dots, the higher the resolution. Some of the letter quality output would cause you to believe a character printer was used.
56. The drum printer must either align all cylinders (if cylinder-oriented) or rotate until the desired letter corresponds to the hammer (the axial row), at which time the hammers will hit all the appropriate letters.
57. Privileged instructions are a supervisor state activity which cannot be executed by the other three.
58. The system Baudot devised had five channels.
59. The daisy wheel printer has a spline element, wherein each character is on a "petal" offshooting from the hub. Pin is matrix, spray is ink-jet, and bar is character.

60. Chains, by definition, have no cylinders and no slugs. Neither do they require sensitized paper—simply the impacting hammers.

61. *Character* and *byte* are synonomous. A word consists of several bytes. The *bit* is the smallest unit—*bi*nary digi*t*.

62. Digital computers work on discrete and integer data. Communications interfaces do not apply to the question. The analog computer tests an analog of the data, not the data itself.

63. C is definitely not true; A is true only by splitting hairs; D is true, but not the primary advantage, which is the nonvolatility of ROM.

64. EBCDIC has 8 bits, with a range of 256 values, 0 to 255.

65. The cassette tape can be purchased for about half the cost of the diskette.

66. Be careful. It says "NOT." Serial and parallel memory were mentioned in the text. Transmission of data has been mentioned, and will be mentioned again in the communications chapter.

67. Dot matrix printers can be used for near letter quality output (NLQ). They're not very fast (but are getting faster), and even though they logically have a finite set of characters, changes in fonts and character sets extents these immeasurably. They form their letters from a matrix-arranged pattern of dots.

68. The physical screen is but a logical screen on a complete display. The process of moving to another part of the physical screen, in any direction, is called *scrolling*.

69. These are all apt descriptions, and useful to describe buffering.

70. Definition A fits the mainframe world at this time. In the microcomputer world, the ROM will contain applications software.

71. Nobody's memory is sector-oriented at this time. Fixed-word computers are very efficient. Bit-movement of data simply isn't done, with the exception of shift operations.

72. Performance measures are designed to measure anything that can be expressed as a percentage or volume measurement.

73. Variable word length computers have a lot of capabilities, but they aren't by definition faster or more efficient. While they are variable word, the word size itself is very fixed, and not necessarily at the size of the register, which itself is fixed.

74. The sole purpose of a channel is to be able to handle communications between the I/O devices and the CPU—through a controller, if necessary, but not always necessary.

75. Multiprogramming is a memory hog, channel oriented, and requires an interrupt system. Multiprocessing components (e.g., other computers) are not necessary.

76. Did it again. The TCU provides all these services.

77. Definition question. Simplex is one way only. Half duplex is two way, one at a time. C is correct. A modem may or may not be used.

78. The target field must be established first by a prior instruction.

79. The important thing here is to distinguish between a disk and a long-playing record, which has a continuous track. Because they are concentric, they cannot have equal diameter. C has a ring of truth: some disks have tracks with their own heads, but not a specific head.

80. At the moment, Microsoft has set the standard—despite the efforts of the inventors to standardize, through ANSI, a new version of BASIC called Real BASIC. Dvorak keyboards are more efficient, but QWERTY keyboards are the standard—many thousands of Microsoft-based micromputers will do the same for the Microsoft version of BASIC.

81. This question is gradually becoming obsolete. Bookkeeping machines keep the information on magnetic stripes. MICR is used for bank checks. Mark sense was used by card punches. Holes are not used.

82. Here is an example of something that is good, but is not commonly used. B is the answer. A is seldom used anymore, in favor of silicon technology. Plated wire was tried and then discarded by

UNIVAC. Drums are on the way out. Even CD-ROM would not have fit here, as the question says "internal storage."

83. Immediate data is part of the instruction. Only a branching instruction (by definition, indirect) would have the next sequential instruction. If the cell contained the address of the data, it would be an indirect reference.

84. The vocabulary is limited by storage. It is a direct access device, based on tables, and has no direct relationship to a terminal. At the moment, prerecorded word patterns are most effective, but synthesized speech is improving.

85. The only sequence which makes sense is D. First generation computers had vacuum tubes. Second generation computers utilized transistors, while the third generation was largely integrated circuits.

86. The microprogrammable controller is largely used for process control applications, such as industrial robots.

87. EROM means Erasable Read Only Memory. PROM means Programmable Read Only Memory. Both are erasable. The first must be burned at the factory; the second may be recreated by the user with special equipment.

88. Relocation requires that the first address in the new section be placed in a base register and a program located at relative displacement offset from that position.

89. Asynchronous transmission uses the start/stop bits for each character. The only other answer which makes sense is B, and that is true only part of the time (when parity checking has been specified).

90. Indexing uses a register as a displacement to develop an effective address. It does not develop any of the other types of address.

91. The pushdown stacks remove the addresses in reverse sequence to that in which entry was made—last in, first out (LIFO). LIFO is a good accounting term.

92. The front end communications processor can indeed handle the network independent of the host. More often, however, it works as the intermediary between the network and the host, providing services at the host end of the network, services which would not tie up the mainframe.

93. Memory protection is accomplished by the flagging of memory segments. This is done by the operating system at the behest of the user.

94. Most have 40 tracks, but these can be double-sided, double-density, extending the available number of usable tracks to 80 or more.

95. Named for the scientist who invented it, the Kerr effect is caused by bouncing a laser off the surface of the compact disk, passing the light through a polarizing filter, and measuring it to detect its magnetic properties.

96. The Universal Product Code (UPC) is a bar code read by a wand using the principles of optical character reading (OCR). EFT is electronic funds transfer; CPM stands for the critical path method (or, if you will, the CP/M operating system); and DOS is the disk operating system.

97. The mouse is an analog device whose purpose is to move the cursor. Once the cursor has been placed, control buttons on the mouse may be used for any of the other purposes.

98. Be careful here. B is correct for the micro at this time. C is correct for very large plotters attached to mainframe computers. A is true for some plotters, but not the very sophisticated ones. D isn't true at all, to my knowledge.

99. Voice commands are spoken to an audio (analog) circuit, converted to a digital pulse, stored in tables, and matched on future uses of the system to identify sounds.

100. The Touch Screen requires that you break the beam which crosses across the face of the screen. This is most often done with a finger, but anything which will interrupt the light will be sufficient. Depending upon what beam is broken, and the display at that beam location, the program can then function according to the external direction.

EXAMINATION SECTION 2

2

COMPUTER PROGRAMMING AND SOFTWARE

It's been almost two decades since the inception of the "computer on a chip." Intel's experiment was first with the 4004 and then the 8008, and they have gone considerably further, as discussed in Chapter 1. In that time, programming (we still don't know if it's art or science) and software have taken some awesome new directions. The driver program is upon us, and we'll never be the same.

When computers were programmed by analogs or by plugboards, the programming was the function of operations personnel. The development of stored program computers led to the birth of a new discipline—a new body of knowledge separate and distinct from anything previously experienced. Computer programming, i.e., the direction of the computer hardware by the execution of a stored program, has developed to the point where there are now self-programming computers, computers which program other computers, and a plethora of computer languages, each vying for a position of predominance.

The development of software has become a multibillion dollar business with a host of participants, ranging from cottage industries to large-scale software houses which gross millions of dollars of sales annually. Since the last edition of this book, the size of the cottage industry has diminished, and many products have left the market, simply because they could not be economically marketed and also because many in the cottage industry had not reckoned the cost of support. From our knowledge of the computer hardware and rudimentary instructions has come a large variety of prepackaged applications software, sophisticated systems operational software, and increases beyond belief in the areas of communications and user-friendly, user-directed driver software.

It is impossible in a book of this nature, and within these size constraints, to fully cover the world of programming and software. The book can cover the nature of instruction sets, collating sequences, methods and technologies for referencing memory, structure of data, commonly used programming techniques, and software systems which touch us all. When this book was last published, it was thought that language ADA would have grown to some level of prominence. It didn't. Perhaps the one language which did was the language C, and we'll talk about it briefly.

While new directions are occurring, some of the older ones refuse to die. FORTRAN, for example, continues to be a language of prime use, despite the fact that there are better scientific languages. Microsoft BASIC continues to be the de facto standard, despite the efforts of BASIC's originators to have a "standard" (non-Microsoft) BASIC, known as "Real BASIC," adopted by the American National Standards Institute. Slight changes in focus have emerged, however, and we now have Structured BASIC. And, as you might suspect, COBOL is still very much with us. We have such a huge investment in COBOL programs that we may never lose that language. In the last edition, we added discussion of PASCAL. In the years since the third edition, PASCAL has gained some popularity, and it will be further discussed here. Expect that by the time of the next edition, PASCAL may well have been replaced by Modula-2, which will not be discussed in this edition.

While still in use, discussion of ALGOL and PL/1 has been dropped. It's important to include materials here which are certain to be found on the examination. It's also important to recognize that this industry is changing—and new concepts, such as driver programs, will become part of our vocabulary.

And now we have arrived to the point where programmers and users alike are using an entirely new concept—that of driver programs, programs like Lotus 1-2-3, Lotus Symphony, Interactive Financial Planning System (IFPS), and SPSS, designed for a specific purpose—to allow the user to obtain valid output without having to resort to the use of a data processing department. It is interesting, however, to find that it is the programmers of the data processing departments who are doing the preponderance of the new and more complicated applications in these drive languages. In this chapter we will introduce you to the advanced concepts of these four packages. They may not be on the ICCP examination this year—but expect to see them soon.

THE PROGRAMMER—WHO IS S/HE?

What are the qualities of a good programmer? Ed Yourdon claims these nine are worth noting:

1. A good programmer writes good programs (or efficient programs, or well-documented programs, etc.)
2. A good programmer works well with other people.
3. A good programmer communicates well with the users of his program.
4. A good programmer takes a bath at least once a week.
5. A good programmer shows up for work on time.
6. A good programmer *never* shows up for work on time.
7. A good programmer doesn't cause trouble.
8. A good programmer works well under pressure.
9. A good programmer likes classical music.

These nine provide a good cross-section of the attributes of what we now know a programmer to be—a curious mixture of conformist/nonconformist, dullard and intellectual giant. In other words, the purveyor of what has been for some time an arcane art with glimpses of scientific approach. Yourdon observes: "Is a superprogrammer—i.e., someone who can code faster than a speeding bullet, leap over reams and reams of printout in a single bound, and generally out-program everyone else in the organization—looked upon with favor and respect by the management?" (*Techniques of Program Structure and Design,* Prentice-Hall, 1975). Has anything changed in 10 years? Well yes, and no, as we shall see.

While Yourdon's book is dated, it holds forth some excellent measurements of the value of the work of the programmer:

1. The program works and is readily observable. There is a difference between a program which works and one which works to specification. It is insufficient for the programmer to simplify work, he or she must provide the means to verify the the program is working correctly, a demarcation from just *testing* to *perpetual verification.*
2. The program should minimize testing cost. The program which is so complex that it is a monument to its author (and thereby maintainable only by its author) is an abject business failure. The time and money spent to maintain (or, more often, to recreate) the uncommented code, the use of a language other than an acceptable and transferable programming language, is better spent elsewhere. Programming which uses obtuse techniques and operating system interfaces, and indulges in self-modification and spectacular tricks, should earn the programmer a one way ticket out the front door.
3. The program should minimize maintenance costs. Larger organization have maintenance departments; smaller users aren't so blessed. Both need to confront the questions of programs that are put into execution with known bugs, programs which develop multiple versions, programs in which the rate of change exceeds the rate of progress, massive shifts of people, lack of enthusiasm for maintaining an old program, lack of understanding of another's code, and the lack of coherent documentation. Some of these issues are certainly management issues; some are certainly programmer issues; many are personal integrity issues. All are business issues.

4. Flexibility—ease of changing, expanding, or upgrading the program. The small program of today is the large program of tomorrow. Techniques for table expansion, addition of new modules, removal of obsolete routines, and changes of input or output media become a part of the professional programmer's repertoire—the kind of journeyman work not achieved by "quick and dirty" programming.
5. Minimize development costs. Getting the right program done in the appropriate amount of time is very easy—providing you have honestly estimated the work. Accidentally or purposefully misestimated work begins a series of events which can never be controlled. The programmer whose interest is in the esoteric beauty of the program and not in the time-compressed efficiency of the operational module will produce a wagon with square wheels—one which makes forward progress in spite of itself.
6. Simplicity of Design—the preparation of a program which permits the interchangeability of people and modules becomes the hallmark of a good programming practice. Avoidance of dangerous instructions (instructions which obscure the process or which change other instructions' appearance on a memory dump) must be a personal commitment to a professional practice. The easiest way to develop, test, upgrade, or change support personnel is to make the program simple and straightforward. The manager who conveys that advancement is contingent upon a programmer's ability to successfully turn over his programs to another will find that the quality of the product will increase.
7. Efficiency. A good programmer considers that operational efficiency is the best testimony to his programming skills. Unfortunately, all too often some programmers spend inordinate hours fine-tuning that last millisecond out of a program. Certainly operational efficiency is important, but so is a programmer's time and skill. It therefore behooves the programming supervisor to establish guidelines for paring the program in terms of memory usage and time. The author feels somewhat contrary in this perspective—it is no longer efficient to spend hours desk-checking a program. The first compile highlights the syntax errors and test results highlight logic errors. However, strict adherance to a "reasonable" number of test shots should be maintained. What we're saying here is that there is a breakeven point, one which is found with practice, but one which must be put into practice for the value of the economic return from both the computer and the computer programmer.

PROGRAMMING PRINCIPLES

It could be said that a program is a procedure set to code. Be it pseudocode, structured code, or source code, the computer program is the specification of a sequence of steps designed to accomplish a specific goal. These steps are those which are derived from the analysis of a problem and the step-by-step instructions for solving the problem. The ultimate form of the instructions will be that of the computer's inherent instruction set, but the steps between may be specified in a selection of cryptic, or clear procedural steps designed to cause the computer to behave in a predictable manner. A program is more aptly labeled software, the applied intelligence which causes hardware to function.

Software has traditionally been divided into two classes: that which operates the application and that which operates the hardware. The former is called application software, and the latter is called system software.

Application software (e.g., an inventory posting program) is a set of instructions designed to solve a specific problem or produce a specific output, in this case, a posted inventory. Systems software (e.g., assemblers, compilers, file management routines, database management, etc.) is generalized programming which is utilized by the application programs to perform the functions required of the data processing system. Application software may or may not be supplied by the vendor of the hardware system. System software is generally obtained from the vendor of the hardware system, although certain broad-coverage software may be obtained from a firm whose business it is to develop and market such systems software.

To this must be added a third classification of software—the driver, the intermediary in which the form of the application is specified and not the process. In that instance, the structure of the input and the structure of the output are defined and the formatting and formulating which must be done between. It then becomes the responsibility of the driver program to perform the marriage. These structures are called templates, and the templates define the input, the output, and the snapshot of gyration. The driver program, then, is a template processor, and what makes it all so beautiful is that you need only to change the template. The program itself does not need to be maintained or altered. We'll deal first with the more traditional orientation to programming.

Computer Instructions

Instruction Format

An instruction is a statement that specifies an operation and the values or locations of its operands. For programming purposes, there are three levels of instruction: machine language; the first-level symbolic, generally an assembly language of some sort; and the high-level symbolic, as exists in a problem-oriented language, such as COBOL. This section deals specifically with machine instructions, commonly referred to as *machine code.* It is machine code which most frequently appears in a memory dump.

An instruction to a computer usually consists of an operation code, operand(s), and, occasionally, modifiers. The operation code of an instruction specifies the type of operation to be executed by the computer (e.g., addition, multiplication, data transfer, etc.). In certain machines, normally known as one-address machines, and to some extent in two- and three-address machines, an operation code may be the entire instruction. An operand is that portion of the instruction upon which some action may be performed. It may be the recipient of an addend, a product, a quotient, or a transfer. It may hold an address which is an indirect reference. It may be a register name. Normally, the operand is used to represent the address of a storage location which contains the data to be processed.

The instruction format of a computer may contain one or more operands. *Single address* pertains to an instruction format containing one operand (one-address machine). *Multiple address* (two or three operands) pertains to instruction formats for two- and three-address machines. A computer which has a single address must operate directly upon the operand, frequently with data which has been set at a pre-established location. In a multiple-address instruction format, each operand generally references various locations of stored data.

Modifiers are single- or multiple-bit fields of an instruction word that can be appropriately set to change an instruction at execution time. Modifiers are customarily used for indirect addressing, indexing, as register or partial word identifiers.

In most present-day computers, the instruction length is specified by the operation code. That should not be construed as an absolute, however, in that some instructions are fixed in length, some will vary from character (byte) to several, and some may vary from instruction to instruction, within the machine's instruction set, and are denoted by the presence of a format bit within the operation code.

We've pretty much standardized upon the eight-bit "byte" for character representation. The byte system is, of course, IBM's, and other vendors have followed suit. These bytes are grouped into half, full, and double word lengths. The 8-bit character is the basis for the majority of the present day microcomputers, minicomputers, and maxicomputers. Depending upon the design of the machine itself, some machines may be seen to be 8-bit machines (byte), 16-bit machines (half-word), 32-bit machines (full word), or 64-bit machines (double word). As mentioned in the last chapter, there is a 128-bit computer on the market, which technically makes it a quadruple word machine. Couple that to the fact that chips are now being produced in 512K sizes, and you can get some estimate of the raw power at our disposal.

Instruction Execution

The execution of a computer instruction requires two separate phases. The first is the fetch phase; the second is the execution phase. In the fetch phase, an instruction is selected from main storage under control of an instruction counter (or register). The instruction counter contains an address that specifies the location of the next instruction to be fetched into the central processing unit (CPU). Once in the CPU, the operation code of the instruction is moved into an instruction register for interpretation and execution.

The operand portion of the instruction is stored in another register. Data required by the instruction are then moved to the appropriate locations. The initial location of the data may be implicit to the instruction function or may be explicitly stated in the instruction word. Before execution of the instruction, the address in the instruction counter is appropriately incremented or modified, depending upon the nature of the computer system being utilized.

This varies insignificantly with the microcomputer, in that the instruction counter is called the *program counter,* the registers have primed counterparts for reference, and the memory structure is mapped, making much of the instruction specification explicit within the read-only memory (ROM).

In the execution cycle, the instruction is performed, i.e., the operation specified by the operation code is appropriately performed. The time required for a computer to perform an operation is normally the sum of the times required to fetch the instruction, interpret the operation code, locate the needed data, execute the instruction, and store the results.

Instruction Types

Each computer is designed with a built-in set of operations it can perform. This is called the *instruction repertoire* (or *instruction set*), and it is unique for each computer manufacturer and (occasionally) model. Exceptions to this generalization are found in the microcomputer industry, where several microprocessors will be designed around a single chip, such as the Zilog Z-80 or the Intel 8088. All computers will have at least five classes of instructions: data transfer, arithmetic, decision, input/output, and special.

Data Transfer Instructions

The purpose of data transfer instructions is to move data from one storage location to another. Computers have gotten so fast now that the data can be moved from memory to register to memory much faster than data can be moved from memory location to memory location. Data transfer instructions involve loading to a register, storing from a register, moving data from one location to another, and setting up the conditions for the block movement of data.

Arithmetic Instructions

The function of a computer is, of course, to compute. A computer, in addition to its data formatting and movement capabilities, is largely a sophisticated calculation mechanism. Thus, each computer usually has several instructions for the basic mathematical operations of addition, subtraction, multiplication, and division. In addition, there will be instructions for performing the functions upon multiple words of data, for ''normalizing'' the result, for rounding the result. Beyond the more elementary of mathematical functions, instructions which perform square roots, sine, cosine, tangent, and other more sophisticated mathematical functions are available.

Instructions to add or subtract must specify the memory locations of the data to be operated upon and the location where the results are to be stored. Instructions used for multiplication must identify the locations of the multiplier, multiplicand, and the memory cell (or location) that will hold the quotient and remainder.

It's important to note that computers do not really multiply or divide. In fact, computers do not really subtract. All a computer can do is add. In order to subtract, the number to be subtracted must be complemented, added to the number from which it is to be subtracted, and then recomplemented (if negative results occur). Thus it can be seen that to multiply, a number (multiplicand) must be added to itself the number of times denoted in the multiplier, resulting in the product. Division, then, is repetitive complementary addition, with the possibility of a developed remainder (of a size smaller than the divisor).

In some instances, the execution of an arithmetic operation may result in an overflow or underflow in the register or field which holds the result. Overflow occurs when the result of an addition, subtraction, or division operation exceeds the capacity of the intended unit of storage which is designated to store the result. Underflow occurs when a machine computation yields a nonzero result that is smaller than the smallest nonzero quantity that the intended unit of storage is able to store. The existence of these conditions is usually indicated by the computer, and it is the responsibility of the programmer to detect the spill and to provide the necessary set of instructions to correct it.

Arithmetic operations may be accomplished by a fixed-point or floating-point instructions. With fixed-point instructions, the programmer must keep track of the actual decimal point locations of numerical data, since the location of the decimal point is assumed, and no actual decimal point is kept within the data words in a computer's memory. With floating-point instructions, the computer automatically keeps track of this information through either systems software or capabilities build into the computer hardware.

Scaling is the procedure for locating the decimal point in the results of an arithmetic operation accomplished with the fixed-point instructions. More specifically, it is frequently defined as a process to adjust the representation of a quantity in order to bring its range within prescribed limits.

In addition and subtraction the quantities to be added or subtracted must be aligned according to the assumed position of the decimal points before the calculation is performed. With multiplication and division the scaling problem is to locate the decimal point in the result of the executed operation.

Occasionally, the precision desired in the result of an arithmetic operation exceeds the word size of a fixed-word-length computer. In such an instance, the number of significant digits necessary to express a quantity cannot be contained in a single memory word, requiring two computer words to represent the number. This is commonly called *double-precision arithmetic.*

Decision Instructions

The ability of a computer to select a given choice from a plethora of alternatives is the result of the computer's logical ability, according to the system of mathematics devised by George Boole (see Chapter 1). The computer's decision ability involves the weighing of a single variable (is the switch set to 1?) and changing course or sequence depending upon the result. Or, it may require the weighing of two elements of data, one against the other, and proceeding on the basis of whether one is equal to, unequal to, higher than, or lower than the other. This transfer of control capability is often called *branching* or *jumping* and is accomplished on the basis of the results of decision instructions or interrupts created by the hardware. Each decision instruction tests data based on criteria. Some are designed to control hardware, while others are designed to control the sequence of program execution.

Branch, jump, or transfer operations change the contents of the instruction register, thereby changing which instruction is to be executed next, replacing the address of the current instruction. When an unconditional branch (jump, transfer) is received, transfer of control is done independently of the results of any test performed. Conditional branch (jump, transfer) causes transfer of control only if certain criteria or conditions are met when the instruction is executed. The existence of the required condition is established by the comparison or test. Testing is accomplished by the compare or logic instruction which establish the relationship between two operands.

An interrupt temporarily stops or halts a process, normally in a manner which will prevent its later resumption. Interrupts can be either hardware or software (predominantly the former), causing a transfer of control in response to a given set of conditions.

Input/Output Instructions

Data movement to and from a computer utilizes input/output operations. An output or write instruction transmit data from main memory to an output device, and an input or read instruction transmits data from an input device to main memory. Tape systems will utilize "read tape," "write tape," and "rewind" I/O instructions. Disk systems will use "seek," "search," "read disk," and "write disk," instructions. Other examples would be "print," "punch," "skip," and "space."

Special Purpose Instructions.

Editing Instructions are utilized to modify the format of data, to arrange presentation on hard copy, or to perform other functions, such as shifting, bit alteration (masking or filtering) suppression of leading zeros, addition of dollar signs, and insertion of special characters into output words (such as asterisk-fill).

Miscellaneous Instructions include those instruction of the housekeeping and control type, such as setting sense switches (or testing), setting flags (User Program Switch Indicator), set and clear word marks, no operation, halt, and test overflow indicator.

Instruction Examples

Examples of instructions from three well-known computer systems are shown in Figure 2.1.

Addressing Techniques

An address is an identification, as represented by a name, label, number, register, location in storage, or any other data source or destination. Address modification is any change or replacement operation performed on all or part of a given address.

There are five specific types of addressing schemes, with variations upon several. They are: implicit/implied, immediate, extended/absolute, direct/short, and indexed. These are shown graphically in Figure 2.2.

Implicit Addressing (or "Implied" or "Register")

Instructions which operate exclusively on registers normally use implicit addressing. An implicit instruction derives its name from the fact that it does not specifically contain the address of the operand on which it operates. Instead, its opcode specifies one or more registers.

Immediate Addressing

Immediate addressing contains a literal or constant value as part of the instruction.

Absolute Addressing

Absolute addressing usually refers to the way in which data are retrieved from or placed into memory. The address is permanently assigned by the computer designer to the storage location.

Direct Addressing (or "Short" or "Relative")

Direct addressing is customarily used for relative addressing within the confines of a specific memory page. It is frequently called *page zero* addressing.

IBM SYSTEM 4300

Instruction	Mnemonic
Add	A
Add Logical	AL
Add Packed	AP
And	N
Branch on Condition	BC
Halt and Proceed	HPR
Pack	PACK
Move Characters	MVC
Transfer Input/Output	XIO

UNIVAC SYSTEM 1108

Instruction	Mnemonic
Add to A	AA
Add to X	AX
Store to A	SA
Store Zero	SZ
Load A	LA
Multiply Integer	MI
Multiply Fractional	MF

ZILOG Z-80

Instruction	Mnemonic
Add Immediate	A,n
Cell Conditional Subroutine	CALL cc,pq
Block Compare (decrement)	CPDR
Decimal Adjust Accumulator	DAA
Enable Interrupts	EI
Jump Relative	JR
Load Indirect	LD(BC),A
Output to Port	OUT (N),A
Rotate Left Accumulator	RLA
Subtract With Borrow	SBC HL,ss

Figure 2.1

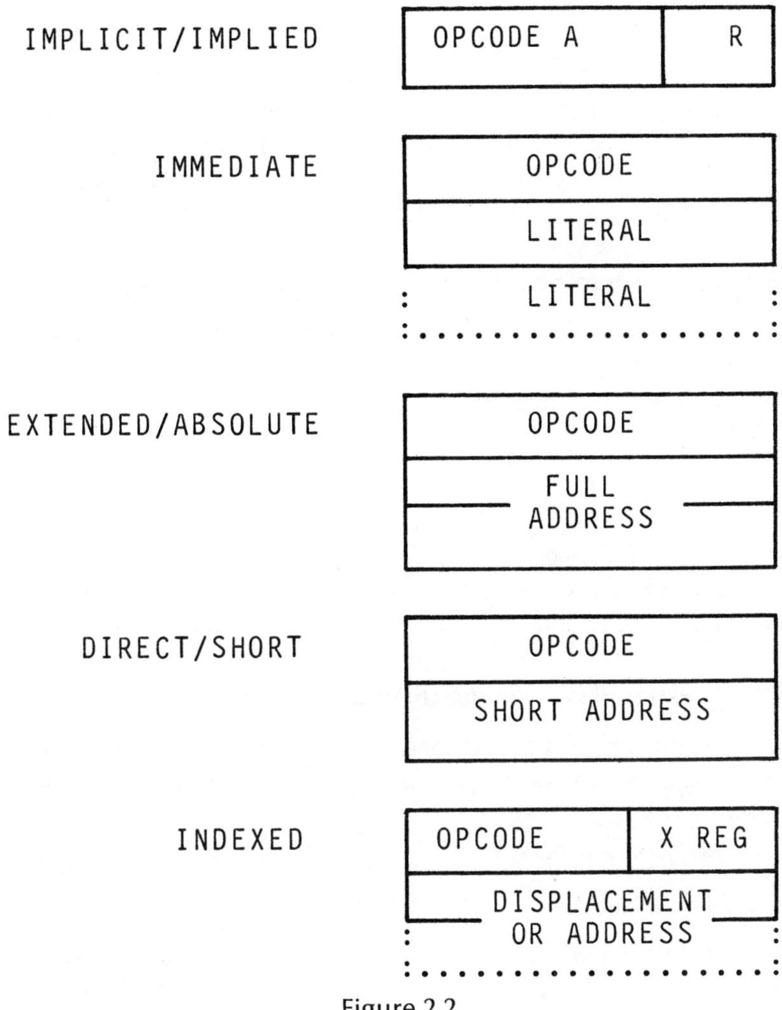

Figure 2.2

Relative Addressing

In an effort to reduce program size, relative addressing is a specification of displacement only. Relative addressing is most frequently used with direct access devices and random access memory (RAM).

Indexed Addressing

Indexed addressing is a technique used to access the elements of a table or block successively. The principle of indexed addressing is that the instruction specifies both an index register and an address. The contents of the register are added to the address to provide the final address. For instance, the following instruction:

ADD 15000(1), 15025(2).

In this example, the contents of index register (1) are combined with address (5000) to form an *effective address;* the other required effective address is obtained by combining address (15025) with the contents of index register (2). The addition operation is then performed by adding the contents of the two computed effective addresses.

Pre-Indexing and Post-Indexing

Two modes of indexing may be distinguished. Pre-indexing is the usual indexing mode in which the final address is the sum of a displacement or address and of the contents of the index register. Post-indexing treats the contents of the displacement field like the address of the actual displacement, rather than the displacement itself. In post-indexing, the final address is the sum of the contents of the index register plus the contents of the memory word designated by the displacement field.

Relocatability and Base/Displacement Addressing

Carrying the indexing concept forward, it is possible to develop a program relative to zero (or relative to page) and then relocate it according to the available space at execution time. This can be accomplished with or without the use of an index register.

Base/Displacement Addressing Without Indexing (Figure 2.3)

The value of the displacement (25) in the first operand is added to the contents of base register (3), giving the storage location of one element of data. The other element of data is obtained by adding the displacement (49) in the second operand to the contents of the specified base register (4). The contents of the computed storage locations are then added to produce the result.

Base/Displacement Addressing With Indexing (Figure 2.4)

The displacement (25) is combined with the contents of the specified index register (4) and the base register (3), giving the storage location of the pertinent data. The contents of this computed address are then added to the specified register (5).

Loops

A loop is a sequence of instructions that is executed repeatedly until a terminal condition prevails. More precisely, certain operations involve repetition of the same set of instructions, in which the last instruction triggers a repetition of the process for some predeterminded number of iterations, or until a predetermined value is reached. Figure 2.5 is a Microsoft BASIC example of a triple looping process, i.e., a loop within a loop, within a loop. It is an electronic digital clock.

This particular example is known as a nested FOR . . . NEXT loop, written in BASIC. Examine please the statements 30–50. This loop will iterate 60 times, printing the factors developed in S (seconds), M (minutes), and H (hours). In short, statements 30–50 cycle 60 times for each cycle of statements 20–60, which, in turn, cycle 60 times for each cycle of 10–70. A functional pictorial representation of this process is shown in Figure 2.6.

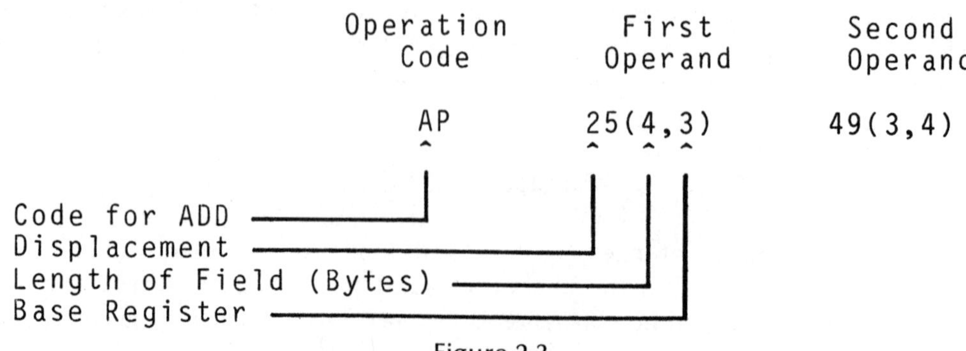

Figure 2.3

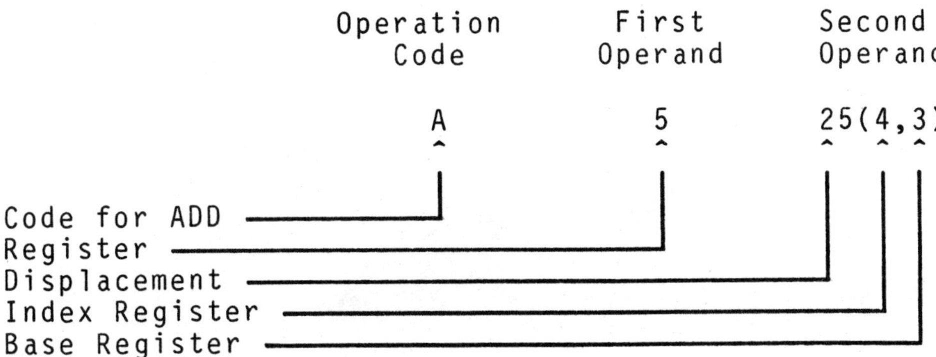

Figure 2.4

Multiply the number of iterations which are received in statements 10 through 70. You'll see that 86,400 iterations are required to go on to the instruction which follows statement 70. Without a looping feature, then, a computer program would require 86,400 instructions to process the clock through one physical day. With a looping feature, the program can be coded with only one set of instructions which control the iterations and end the operation.

The advantages of utilizing a looping technique are:

1. The coding time is considerably shorter.
2. Loops utilize less memory space that a straight-line coded program.
3. Due to the compactness of the code, loops are simpler to debug.
4. The range of a loop is adjustable with only minor modifications.
5. Time is saved throughout the entire programming effort.

A typical looping procedure consists of the four phases which follow:

1. *Initialization.* Counters, index registers, loop controls, and other pertinent control variables are set to starting values. These operations are generally executed before processing of the loop begins and are not repeated except as the loop is subordinate to another loop.
2. *Processing.* The processing step (FOR . . . NEXT in this example) is designed to perform one general case of a repetitive task. In this phase, the specified task is appropriately executed.
3. *Modification.* Addresses and data are modified for the next iteration and tests are made to determine if execution of the loop should be repeated or terminated. The modification phase consists of nothing more than a simple gauge of the addresses of instructions or contents of data fields.
4. *Control.* The control phase is ordinarily accomplished by comparing the contents of a counter or a control variable with a predetermined terminating value. If the comparison does not indicate the end of the operation (e.g., a terminating value), the total operation is repeated. At the time the terminating value is matched, the looping process is broken.

```
10 FOR H = 0 TO 24
20       FOR M = 0 TO 59
30             FOR S = 0 TO 59
40                   PRINT @150,H;":";S
50             NEXT S
60       NEXT M
70 NEXT H
```

Figure 2.5

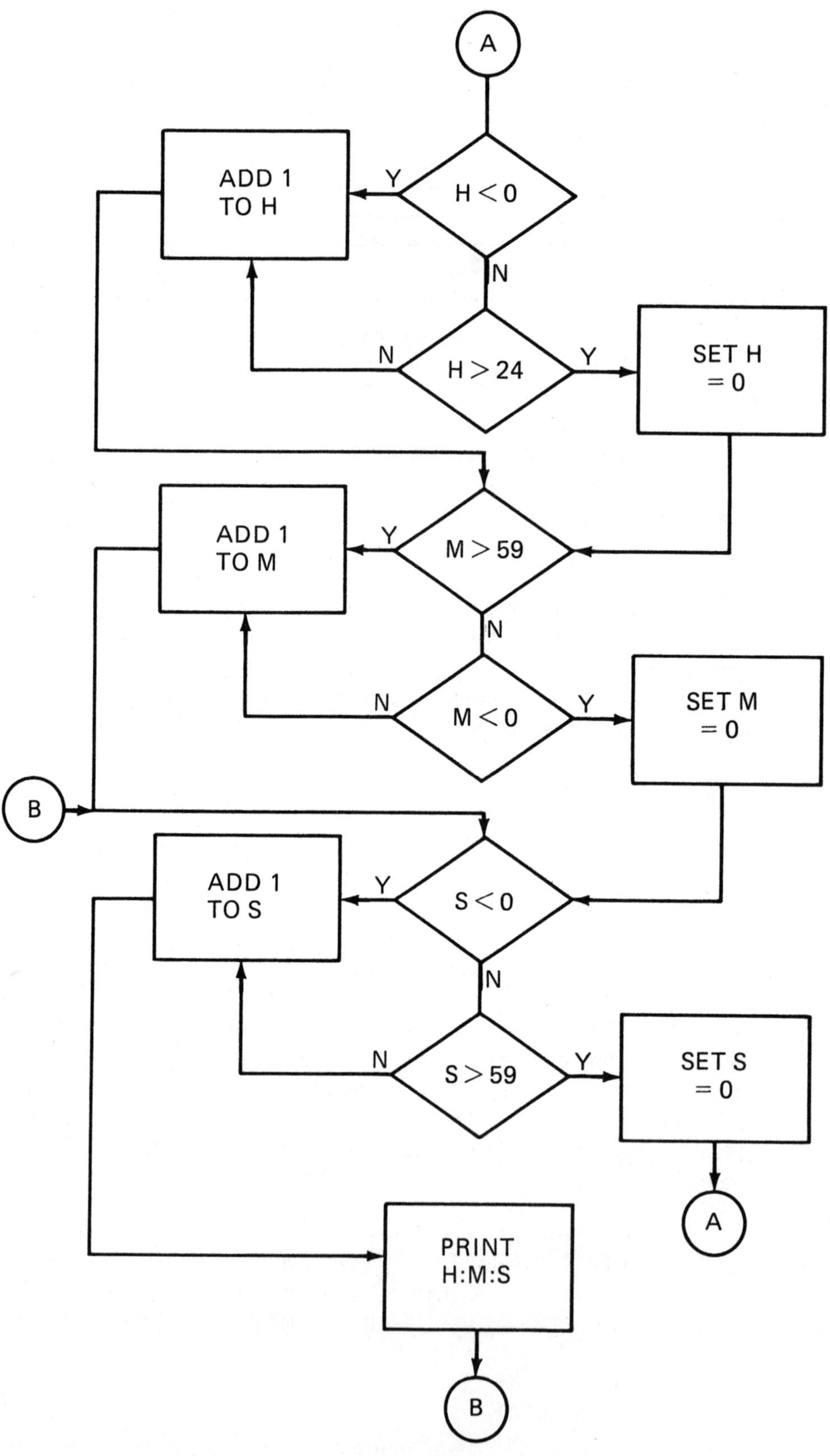
A
H < 0
Y
ADD 1
TO H
N
H > 24
N
Y
SET H
= 0
M > 59
Y
ADD 1
TO M
N
M < 0
N
Y
SET M
= 0
B
S < 0
Y
ADD 1
TO S
N
S > 59
N
Y
SET S
= 0
A
PRINT
H:M:S
B

Figure 2.6

Subroutines

A routine is an ordered set of instructions. A subroutine is a routine that may have some general or frequent use and that can be made part of another routine. Subroutines are exercised by merging with a program, calling dynamically from somewhere external to the program (for compilation or independent exercise), or by incorporation into the program as required. In general, there are two types of subroutine, the open subroutine and the closed subroutine. Beyond that are the DO . . . WHILE and PERFORM . . . UNTIL constructs which vary the theme somewhat.

An *open subroutine* is a chunk of common coding which is simply sued wherever in the program it is required, and coded separately. It may or not be identical to other uses. For instance, the BASIC routine shown in Figure 2.7.

This open subroutine is a keyboard test (in BASIC) on a microcomputer for the response to a Yes/No question. In this block of coding, if the response is a Y (for YES) then the program will proceed to statement 200. If the response is N (for NO), then the program will proceed to statement 300. Otherwise, statement 130 will repeat the process.

Many keyboard responses will be found in an interactive program. The above process is no different from a DISPLAY . . . ACCEPT sequence in COBOL. If one of the called-for responses is obtained, then the program will do something. It probably will not proceed to 200 or 300, as in this example. The coding is similar, however, and repeated use of coding similar to this will label both this and that an open subroutine.

The second type of subroutine is the *closed subroutine,* which is generalized in nature and normally has one entrance and one exit point. The BASIC coding in Figure 2.8 is similar to a paragraph which has been PERFORMed in COBOL:

This particular closed subroutine is designed simply to "freeze" the display and not proceed until the space bar has been depressed on the microcomputer. Note that it is invoked with a GOSUB (PERFORM) and then control is returned at the end of the routine by the RETURN verb. The return mechanism in COBOL would have been automatic (if a one-paragraph subroutine) or with the use of THRU where multiple paragraphs were being used. Assembly Language programmers on the IBM and IBM-compatible mainframes will recognize this as the BAL...BR subroutine process.

The DO . . . WHILE and PERFORM . . . UNTIL constructs bear mention here. The PERFORM . . . UNTIL is a single iterative exercise, comparable to a FOR . . . NEXT loop. The DO . . . WHILE depends upon the tested condition, as shown in Figure 2.9.

This BASIC routine is identical in concept to the PASCAL routine of Figure 2.10.

Subroutine Libraries

With the advent of the microcode, many things which were formerly externally placed subroutines are now intrinsic functions of the computer. However, locally produced routines which solve common computational problems, perform input/output, and provide editing and formatting operations, are frequently stored in a common file of a computer, and are generally collectively referred to as a *subroutine library.* This library is frequently linked to a language compiler and is available for inclusion in the programmer's problem program; thus, the COPY and INCLUDE functions of COBOL, the MERGE function of BASIC, the COMMON function of several other languages. Some of the subroutines are provided by the

```
100 Z$ = INKEY$
110 IF Z$ = "Y" THEN 200
120 IF Z$ = "N" THEN 300
130 GOTO 100
```

Figure 2.7

```
100 GOSUB 500
110 .....

500 Z$ = INKEY$
510 IF Z$ = " " THEN 530
530 RETURN
```

Figure 2.8

```
100 DO WHILE NOT EOF(1)
110     INPUT #1,FILE.RECORD$
120     IF LEFT$(FILE.RECORD$,1) = "Z" THEN 170
130     ____________________
140     (manipulation logic)
150     ____________________
160     PRINT FILE.RECORD$
170 WEND
180 END
```

Figure 2.9

```
PROGRAM TRACE(INPUT,OUTPUT);
VAR X,Y,Z:INTEGER;
BEGIN
     READ(X,Y,Z);
     X:=X+Y+Z;            |
     X:=X MOD Z;          |________________
     Z:=Y DIV 2;          | manipulation
     Y:=X * X+10;         | logic
     X:=(X-10) * 3;       |________________
     WRITELN(X,Y,Z);
END.
```

Figure 2.10

computer vendor. Fewer are provided by the hardware vendor nowadays than are purchased from independent software vendors.

Subroutine libraries have some inherent advantages and some functional disadvantages, as follows:

Advantages

1. A subroutine library saves memory for closed subroutines. A subroutine needs to be inserted in main memory at a single location, to be subsequently entered as needed through the use of appropriate linkage instruction (PERFORM, DO, GOSUB, CALL, BRANCH-AND-LINK).
2. It saves programming time by the elimination of redundant efforts. The same common computational problems need not be programmed by every programmer having a need for the function in his assigned programming task. Once a common task has been programmed, it is available to all programmers via the subroutine library.
3. It allows for management control of standard methods. The concept requires close management control to be operationally effective, requiring the specification of methods, techniques, and algorithms to be used.

4. It reduces training requirements. Programmers will not find it necessary to take special courses in functional areas to acquire the knowledge to program such calculations when they are encountered in the assigned programming efforts.
5. It provides a framework for structured programming. Structured programming is a process of defining a problem in terms of discrete identifiable sets of instructions, normally established as separate entities. Subroutines can be used easily with structured programming.
6. It reduces the amount of testing, because those routines have already been extensively tested. Thus, the code which has been added to the subroutine library need not be tested by the programmer.

Disadvantages

1. A subroutine library reduces flexibility. Minor modifications to subroutines for one-time programming efforts are not recommended for effective subroutine library operation. The ability of the programmers to improvise, take short cuts by minor changes to existing routines, etc., is therefore inhibited.
2. It requires maintenance, and that means people. A subroutine library is a part of systems software, and therefore requires a continuous staff effort to improve its operational effectiveness. As new techniques and approaches are developed, their use must be promoted, literature must be prepared, training classes must be held, and close supervision may be required.
3. It requires controlled distribution of user information. Each user must always have the latest information on the function, required inputs, generated output, interdependency linkages, etc., of each subroutine in the library. The absence of up-to-date information leads to costly debugging efforts and program modifications.
4. It necessitates training for proper utilization. Programmers utilizing a subroutine library must be familiar with linkages, calling sequences, and parameter-passing conventions. Some type of formal or informal training is usually necessary to learn and understand these operations.
5. It requires other software, such as linkage instructions, "get subroutine" coding, and the like for access and utilization. It may require additions to the overhead.
6. It may be demoralizing to programmer trainees. Part of the problem, from a management standpoint, with the programming effort is the fact that new people are required to do maintenance. Or, alternatively, they may be given merely pieces of the project, and never see the project work in its entirety.

Calling Sequences and Parameters

Linkage information is usually set up by the calling routine and communicated to the subroutine via a calling sequence. A calling sequence is a specified arrangement of instructions and data necessary to set up and call a given subroutine. In some instances, through the use of locations that are permanently reserved in the user's system for storage and communication of data, both the calling routine and the subroutine are aware of the locations of the data used and/or generated by the subroutine. This is referred to as implicit communication. Explicit communication occurs when either the data or their addresses are passed between the routines at the time of the linkage.

Macros

Some languages, most notably assembly languages, provide for the development of macros. A macro is an open-parameter routine into which variables may be substituted at assembly time. The subroutines may be provided with the language or they may be user-defined. The programmer uses the subroutine by specifying the appropriate symbolic and calling sequence.

For instance, the macro may look like this:

```
A &&A,CTR
A &&B,CTR
M CTR,&&C
```

The calling sequence may look like this:

```
ADD A TO B GIVING C
```

Reenterable, Serially Reusable, and Recursive

Subroutines should be reusable. That means that anything disturbed within the subroutine should be restored; a fresh copy of the subroutine should not be loaded when needed. Appropriate housekeeping procedures within the routine allow it to be made reusable. Two common types of reusable subroutines are the *reentrant* and *recursive.* A reentrant subroutine allows multiple entrances and executions before prior executions have been completed. A recursive subroutine is one that may be entered before previous executions have been completed as a result of the subroutine's having called itself. A serially reusable routine is a reentrant and recursive routine which may commence several successive iterations before the initial (and successive) iteration(s) has/have been completed. A reentrant subroutine may or may not be recursive, but a recursive subroutine must always be reentrant.

Program Checking

Years ago, a lot of desk checking was done. Programmers ''played computer'' and walked through their code, attempting to simulate the operation of the computer without the expense of the computer time. And then, with the relative cost of computing hardware falling, we came to understand that the compiler or assembler was an effective diagnostician. The tests ensured the validity (insofar as humanly possible) of the results produced and established that the program accomplished the tasks for which it was designed. It didn't meet with unqualified success. By and large, desk checking meant to determine if the keypunch operator had translated the programmer's inadequate hand-printing adequately to Hollerith Code. With the demise of the punched card and the shift to programmer terminals, desk checking is a dying artform.

Next, the era of on-line interactive compiler and translator seemed to remove any impetus for detailed checking of the program in total, due to the immediacy of the compiler's feedback. And then came structured programming, where people didn't write complete programs any more—only constructs, modules, and interfaces. While the programmer could interactively debug his or her construct, module, and interface, it was becoming painfully obvious that each did not have a clearly detailed understanding of where his piece fit into the whole—and, since programming was largely an intimate exchange between the programming person and his compiler, the concept of ego-less programming was born, and desk-checking was now no longer performed by the individual, but was rather acted out before the group and other interested parties in a melodrama called *structured walkthrough.* The concept of the structured walkthrough is the removal of the affinity of the programmer with his computer and the substitution of ''group think.'' Some will claim that with the substitution, programming became less of an intellectual activity and more one of clerical drudgery. However, with driver programs, even this may soon be an obsolete concept.

The process of detecting, locating, and removing mistakes from a program (also malfunctions from a computer) is commonly known as *debugging,* a term coined by the Mark I team, which found a crushed moth between relay contacts. Errors uncovered during the debugging process are normally syntactical errors or logical errors. Syntactical errors are errors in the structure of expressions of the programming language being used or in the rules governing the structure of the language. Logical errors are errors in the logic of the program design and result in the failure of the program to accomplish its specified function. Important point: just because a program has errors does not mean that program execution is, by definition, aborted.

Several techniques for debugging are available to a programmer during program checkout. Some examples are given next.

Structured Walkthrough and Desk Checking

As mentioned above, desk checking is a combination of manual procedures designed to locate syntactical and logical errors. The procedures usually include a review of the flowcharts, decision tables, structure charts (to be discussed), coding, etc., and if necessary, a manual stepthrough of the program. This is more frequently being done in the structured walkthrough, nowadays. In the structured walkthrough, all members of the project team participate as the programmer(s) present the structure of the developed logic to the group.

Program Listings

Program listings (often called *diagnostic data sets*) are printouts of source programs and, in the case of an assembler-level program, a listing of the related machine instructions. These printouts are available as options to the compile or assembly process. Automatic diagnostic procedures designed to uncover various syntactic errors in the user's program are also frequently contained within the assembler or compiler, and are reflected on the listing.

Console Debugging

Console debugging was—at least through the second generation of computers—a very important way to debug a difficult programming problem. And then along came multiprogramming and to debug at the console meant to tie up the entire system. That quickly discouraged console debugging. The technique is enjoying a resurgence because of the on-line aspects of program development. Likewise, for one-terminal systems, such as a small business system or a microcomputer, console debugging has again become important. The technique usually pinpoints the problem areas, through trace mechanisms, register displays, and before and after pictures of data fields. Be aware, however, that console debugging is costly in equipment time and in person time.

On-Line Debugging

It could be said that console debugging and on-line debugging are, at this stage of the computer's development, synonymous. With the increase in interpretive compilers, immediate syntactical editing is available, if not the demonstration of logical errors. Using the interpretive compiler, however, logical errors, once discovered, can be easily corrected. On-line debugging allows execution of the program without job-stream consciousness (e.g., JCL decks). The immediacy of the result would indicate that this method of debugging will be beneficial for some time to come.

Test Data

Test data are frequently employed to uncover logical errors in program design. The output of a computer run using test data can be compared to predetermined results to check the validity of a program. It would be fair to state that while test data are beneficial, the ability to generate test data (via a generator) is applicable only to batch-stream processing. On-line, interactive data, by its very nature, cannot be generated or entered to the system in quantity.

A very good test will check out every conceivable condition that could occur during actual operation of a program. Test data may include reproduced real data that the program is designed to process, hypothetical data designed to represent conditions that could be encountered in processing real data, or a combination of both.

Large, complex programs should be tested segment by segment. When all segments are working, then the complete program can be tested. Tests should be initially designed to check normal operating conditions, followed by tests of exceptions, and then tests of error conditions. Copies of the test data should be retained for future reference. Debugging aids available to a programmer may include complete or partial (snapshot) memory dumps and dynamic analysis and traces.

Memory Dumps

A dump is a process of copying all or part of the contents of memory to an external medium, specifically a line printer. It also refers to the data output from this process and the program that performs the process. The resulting display reveals the precise status of the program being executed at the time the dump was taken.

Several types of dumping procedures may be utilized by the programmer. Dumps may be made from main memory, secondary storage, disk storage, and tape, which functions as auxiliary memory. A dynamic dump is a dump of main memory performed during the execution of a program. A static dump is one which is performed at a particular point in time with respect to a machine run. A selective dump is a dump of one or more specified storage locations. A change dump is a selective dump of those storage locations whose contents have changed. A snapshot dump is a selective dump performed at varying points in the program.

Dynamic Analysis and Tracing

Dynamic analysis is the process of printing program variables and status information followed by analysis to determine whether the program has executed correctly. Several operating system/language combinations will permit the specification of external switches to internal reporting mechanisms. Also, it is not uncommon to include in the program, particularly where on-line interaction is a part of the design of the system, instructions to cause the variables to be presented on a screen.

Tracing follows the progress of the program by address, statement number, or paragraph name. Tracing routines are usually utilized during a debugging process to present status information after branch instructions, interrupts, or transfers to subroutines, although that's a function of programmer selectivity. One of the serious drawbacks to trace mechanisms in an on-line environment is the inability to direct the output of a trace to a disk or other medium. Instead, the trace data appear upon the screen which is being used for input entry and output presentation. If the screen is linear, that is, if it scrolls, there is no problem. The problem arises when a formatted screen tool is used.

Basic Programming Techniques

We begin with the more traditional techniques (which are still in use in many places) and move on to the more current structured techniques.

Specific fundamental steps are required in the development of a computer program. This development is generally called the programming process, and it usually includes the activities of problem description, problem analysis, conversion of the problem to a set of computer instructions, and testing. Interestingly, of the four elements listed above, it is problem analysis which has received the most attention in the structured process, followed by the mechanism, the program itself.

Problem Description

The problem description is a clear, accurate statement of the user's need, as interpreted by a qualified system analyst. It may include a general description of the objective, the method of solution, the design of the solution, the procedures, algorithms, and standards to be followed, and the environment in which it must all come together to perform. If the system analyst has done a proper needs analysis, the description of the problem will be specified to the program in terms from which the analysis documents may be directly produced. Be aware, however, that as users have become trained in analysis techniques, much of this problem definition will have been done at the user's location.

Problem Analysis

There is no such thing as a universal program. The driver programs we've been discussing come closer to that concept than ever before, but the problem must still be divided into small, related units which permit study, analysis, and direction. The completed study should contain an analysis of all units of a problem, define the scope of a solution, develop at least the design of the final product of these processes, determine values of pertinent parameters, develop alternatives to the primary solution, etc. While the hardware configuration is most often the one in house, specification for the acquisition of other hardware may be part of the results demanded from this process. This is especially true now that the user can obtain a desktop computing capability for $3,000 or less.

Development of Program Logic

A program's design is an outline of a solution to a problem using a computer in terms of the relationships of control, structure, and function. It requires that the problem be broken down into logical steps that can be accomplished by a specified computer; then the steps are arranged in a logical series designed to lead to the desired end result.

This frequently requires that the programmer apply pencil to paper, to chart the sequences to be followed. Several methods will be presented in this book: Decision Tables, HIPO Charts, Warnier-Orr Charts, ANSI Standard Flowcharting, and the Chapin Chart (or Nassi-Schneiderman Diagram, if you prefer). We'll also discuss pseudocode. In other words, we'll cover traditional, current, and futuristic concept of programming.

Flowcharting

Flowcharts are one method of depicting program logic-the oldest. They are used to develop and record the program logic. A flowchart is a graphic representation of operations, data flow, equipment, etc. In order for flowcharts to be universally meaningful, the American National Standards Institute (ANSI) has devised standard flowchart symbols, some of which are illustrated below:

Symbol	Name	Use
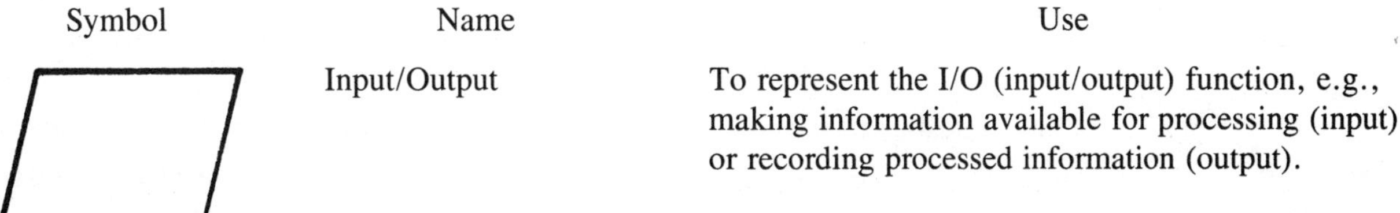	Input/Output	To represent the I/O (input/output) function, e.g., making information available for processing (input) or recording processed information (output).

Symbol	Name	Use
	Punch Card	To represent an I/O function in which the medium is punched cards, including mark sense cards, partial cards, stub cards, etc.
	Magnetic Tape	To represent an I/O function in which the medium is magnetic tape.
	Processing	To represent the processing function, e.g., the process of executing a defined operation or group of operations resulting in a change in value, form, or location of information.
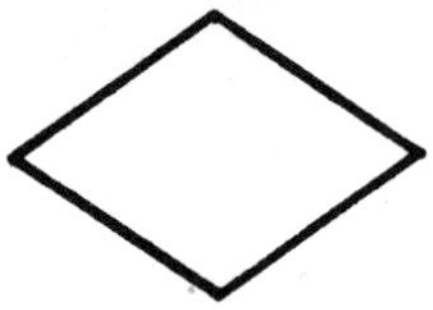	Decision	To represent a decision-type operation that determines which of a number of alternative paths is to be followed.
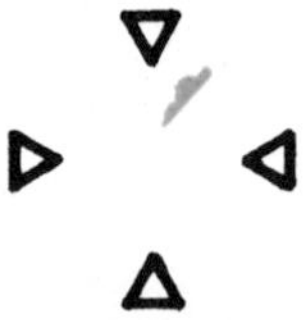	Flow Direction	To represent the flow direction, e.g., the indication of the sequence of available information and executable operations. Normal direction of flow is from left to right or top to bottom.
	Connector	To represent a connection to another part of the flowchart.
	Terminal	To represent a terminal point in a system at which information can enter or leave, e.g., start, stop, halt, delay, or interrupt.
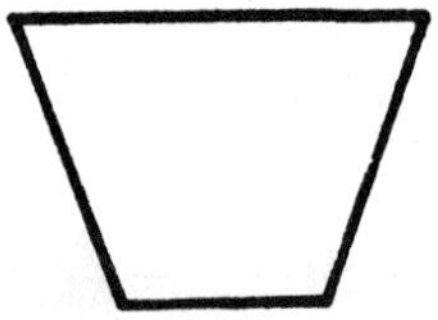	Manual Operation	To represent any off-line process geared to the speed of a human being.
	Auxiliary Operation	To represent an off-line operation performed on equipment not under direct control of the central processing unit.
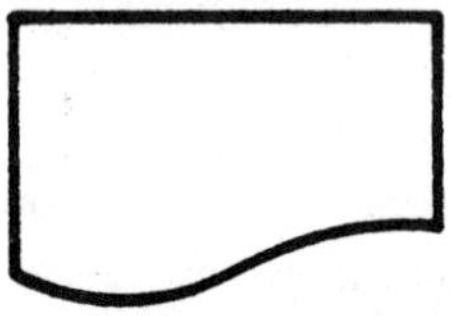	Document	To represent an I/O function in which the medium is a document primarily intended for human use.
	Communications Line	To represent an I/O function in which information is transmitted automatically from one location to another.

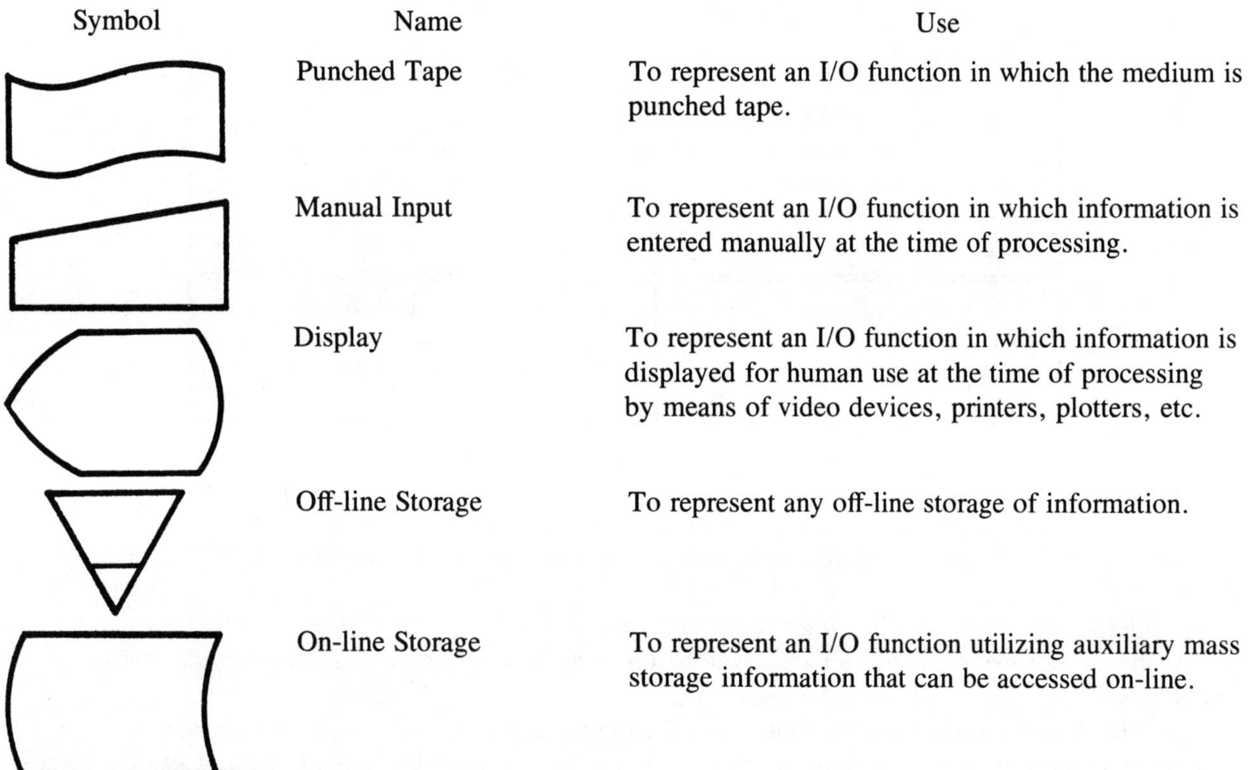

Symbol	Name	Use
	Punched Tape	To represent an I/O function in which the medium is punched tape.
	Manual Input	To represent an I/O function in which information is entered manually at the time of processing.
	Display	To represent an I/O function in which information is displayed for human use at the time of processing by means of video devices, printers, plotters, etc.
	Off-line Storage	To represent any off-line storage of information.
	On-line Storage	To represent an I/O function utilizing auxiliary mass storage information that can be accessed on-line.

Simply speaking, a flowchart can be described as a representation of the program logic steps in standard charting symbols, with each step connected to another to indicate the path through the computer solution from start to stop. Look back to the discussion of the electronic clock for an example of a program flowchart.

Decision Tables

A decision table is a tabular representation of all contingencies which are to be considered in the description of a problem, combined with actions. They are frequently used in lieu of flowcharts to represent the logical solution to a problem. There are three types of decision tables: limited-entry, extended-entry, and mixed-entry. The construct of a limited-entry decision table is shown in Figure 2.11.

TABLE HEADER OR IDENTIFICATION	RULE HEADER OR IDENTIFICATION
CONDITION STUB OR LIST	CONDITION ENTRY
ACTION STUB OR LIST	ACTION ENTRY

Figure 2.11

Department Store Purchase	1	2	3	4
Request by Brand?	YES	YES	NO	NO
Brand Available?	YES	NO		
Another Available?			YES	NO
Make Purchase	X		X	
Stop Program	X	X	X	X

Figure 2.12. X indicates action is to be executed.

Table Header or identification is the user-derived name for identifying the decision table.

Rule Header or identification is various combinations of conditions and the resulting actions to be taken.

Condition stub or *list* is a list of all conditions or alternatives.

Action stub or *list* is a list of all actions to be taken resulting from the conditions or alternatives listed.

Condition entry answers the questions contained in the condition stub.

Action entry indicates the actions resulting from the various combinations of responses to the conditions.

A completed decision table reflecting the solution to a department store purchase problem is presented in Figure 2.12. The table is read from top to bottom with one rule being analyzed at one time. If the conditions of a decision rule are met, then the indicated actions are appropriately executed.

HIPO Charts

HIPO is an acronym for *Hierarchical Input, Process' Output.* It is a system which shows the input, output, and functions of the program being charted. It draws a hierarchical structure down the page using blocks, like Figure 2.13.

Warnier-Orr Chart

Taking this structure one step further, we can produce a Warnier-Orr diagram, like Figure 2.14. This gets translated into a problem statement as shown in Figure 2.15, where (1) indicates the number of the file, (1,E) indicates that there are 1 to E employee records within the file body, and + indicates that a choice of options may be made.

Chapin Chart/Nassi-Schneiderman Diagram

Another method to describe the detailed procedural logic within a module is known as a Chapin Chart, or Nassi-Schneiderman Diagram. The process is also called a structured flowchart.

"Structured flowchart" is an appropriate term. It is similar to a conventional flowchart, in that everything "flows." Note that there are no returns–no traveling arrows from bottom to top. The three basic ideographs of the Chapin Chart correspond directly to the three basic constructs of the structured programming. In essence, the illustration is pseudocode which has been contained by diagrams. Figure 2.16 is an example of the Chapin Chart.

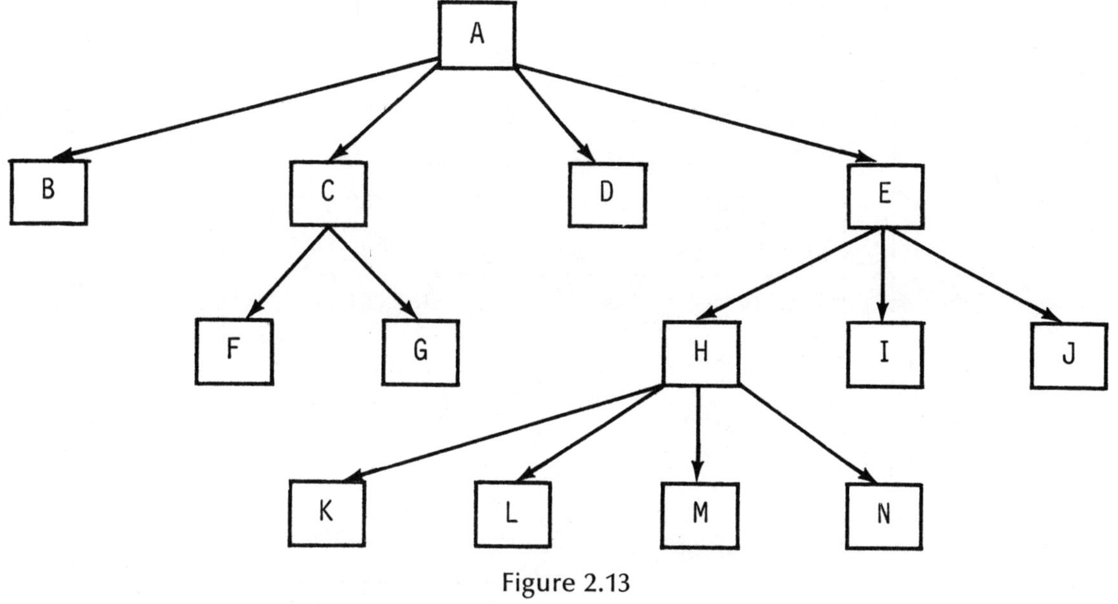

Figure 2.13

```
             ┌ B
             │        ┌ F
             │ C      │
A            │        │ G
             │ D      │              ┌ K
             │        │ H            │
             └ E      │              │ L
                      │ I            │
                      │              └ N
                      └ J
```

Figure 2.14

```
            ┌ FILE HEADER                                          ┌ STREET
            │                                   ┌ NAME             │
EMPLOYEE    │                                   │                  │ CITY
FILE        │                                   │ ADDRESS          │
(1)         │                                   │                  │ STATE
            └ FILE BODY     ┌ EMPLOYEE          │ SSN              │
                            │ RECORD            │                  └ ZIP CODE
                            └ (1,E)             │
                                                │ PAY RATE         ┌ SALARY
                                                │                  │
                                                └ EMPL TYPE        │   +
                                                                   │
                                                                   └ HOURLY
```

Figure 2.15

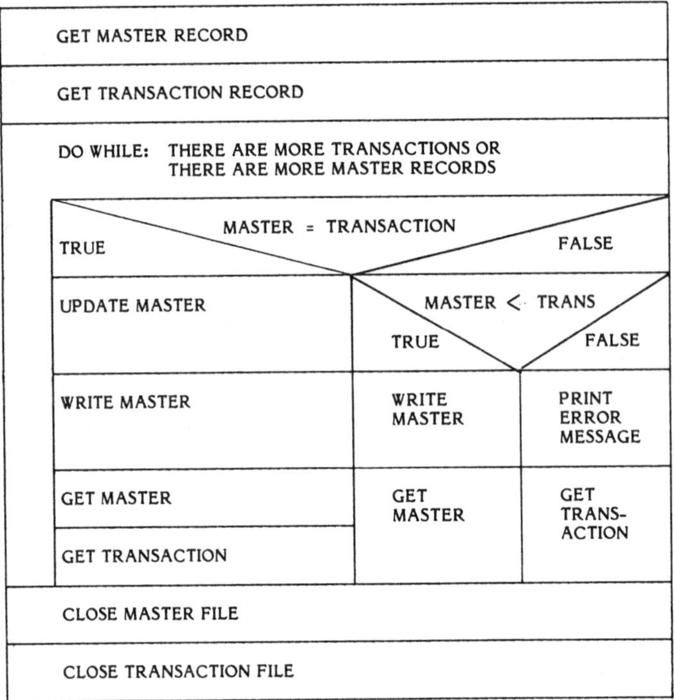

Figure 2.16. Chapin/Nassi-Schneiderman Chart

Structured English—Pseudocode

There are four basic structure types for pseudocode. They are:

- *Sequence.* The top-to-bottom steps to be followed. Requires no keywords. Sequence must be preceded by a title and terminated with the word EXIT.
- *Condition.* A choice of actions on the basis of the the condition. IF . . . THEN . . . ELSE structures, which are common.
- *Case.* A selection of options—or possible cases; mutually exclusive conditions called a case structure. IF . . . ELSEIF . . . ELSEIF . . . ELSE, used for mutually exclusive conditions. Alternately, you may use the construct SELECT . . . WHEN . . . WHEN . . . WHEN. Terminated by ENDIF and ENDSELECT.
- *Repetition.* Repeating of operations until a condition is satisfied; REPEAT . . . WHILE and REPEAT . . . UNTIL options which match the DO . . . WHILE and PERFORM . . . UNTIL options previously discussed. Also, use FOR ALL, FOR EACH, AND, OR, GT, LT, GE, and LE (Greater Than, Less Than, Greater Than or Equal, Less Than or Equal).

Figure 2.17 illustrates a structure in pseudocode, structured English which will match the program.

Decision Trees and Action Diagrams

Let's carry the structuring concepts just two steps further. Figure 2.18 is an example of the construct of a decision tree. A decision tree is simply a branching diagram which looks like a reversed double-elimination schedule. From this, we can draw the action diagram, which puts the structure right at our program (See Figure 2.19).

```
PURCHASE_ORDER

   FOR ALL receipts
       Obtain VENDOR record;
       IF VENDOR# is valid
           Set up vendor details for PURCHASE_HDR record;
           Set up order delivery address for PURCHASE_HDR record;
           Write PURCHASE_HDR record;
       ELSE
           Issue "Invalid Vendor" message;
           QUIT PURCHASE_ORDER
       ENDIF;
       FOR ALL items ordered
           Obtain INVENTORY record;
           If INVENTORY# is valid
              If quantity ordered has been received
                 Set up product details for PURCHASE_ITEM record;
                 Set up quantity ordered for PURCHASE_ITEM record;
                 Increase inventory quantity on-hand by
                     quantity received;
                 Update INVENTORY record;
                 Write PURCHASE_ITEM record;
              ENDIF;
           ELSE
              Issue "Invalid Vendor" message;
           ENDIF.
       ENDFOR
       Prepare receiving report;
       Print receiving report;
   ENDFOR;
 EXIT PURCHASE_ORDER.
```

Figure 2.17

Program Coding

After the program logic has been developed and recorded, it has to be coded in a symbolic form that can be accepted by a computer. Coding is accomplished using one of many computer programming languages. A programming language is a set of representations, conventions, and rules for the preparation of computer programs.

Programming languages are generally categorized into various levels: machine languages, assembly languages, and higher-level languages. To that, with this edition, we add the "driver language," which isn't a language in and of itself—but is, instead, a specification which interfaces with a packaged program.

A machine language is a numerical language that is used directly by the computer. An assembly or symbolic language uses mnemonic operation codes and a mixture of symbolic and absolute operand addresses. A higher-level or compiled language provides an Englishlike expression capability. The driver language is an assembly language (or a near-assembly language) which exists in operable form, but which is modified by the existence and contents of the template applied to it.

Computer programs written in either a higher-level language or an assembly language must be trans-

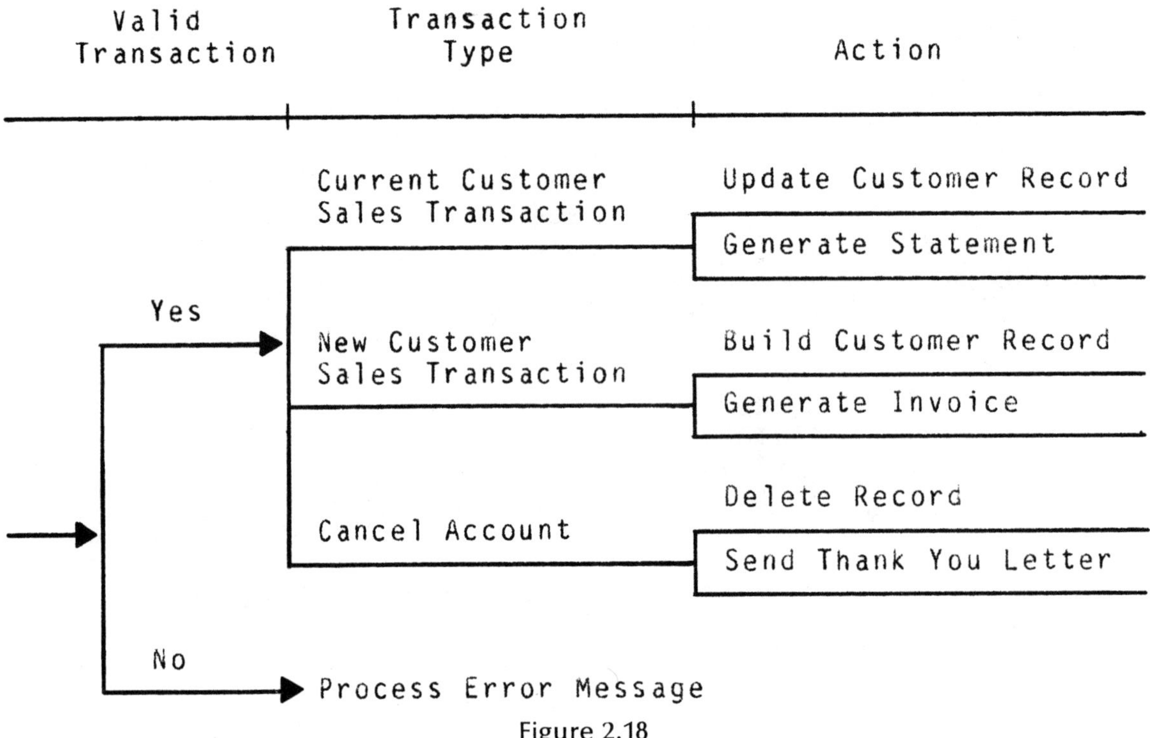

Figure 2.18

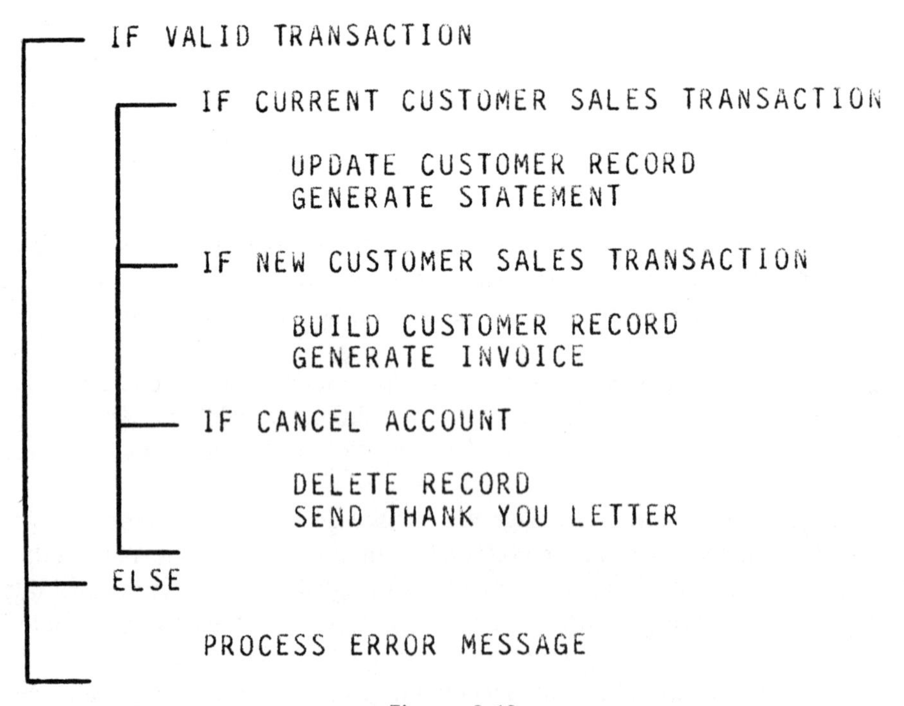

Figure 2.19

lated into machine language before they can be executed by the computer, and are known as object, load, relocatable, or executable programs. Drive modules already exist in executable form.

Program Conversions

After the encoding of the program instructions is completed, the next step of the programming process is to convert the coded instructions into machine-readable form. The instructions must be punched and entered by card, keyed and entered by tape or disk, or entered directly through interactive terminals. A program that has been coded and entered into the computer in machine-readable form is known as a *source program*.

Data Editing and Error Detection

One of the distinct advantages of on-line data entry is that sophisticated accept/reject criteria can be built into the entry package, purifying the data at its point of initial entry. In the batch system, the editing must be accomplished by modules designed for the purpose. It becomes even more exciting when one realizes that the data editing can be done at an intelligent terminal or an on-line microcomputer, permitting only "pure" data to be offered to the host mainframe.

Data editing and error detection procedures preserve the integrity of a data base by rejecting invalid or inconsistent data. Some editing procedures are designed to provide the same protection as would be the result of the effort of alert, knowledgeable employees who handle the input data. Others carry out extensive logical editing which might require many hours of searching through files if it were attempted (and it's not normally done) via a manual system.

Data editing and error detection procedures are designed to detect errors in the input data stream and during operation of the computer system itself. Some, but certainly not all, tests and edits are given next:

1. *Range check.* Data are compared with a range of predetermined values to ascertain if the values fall within the range boundaries. Values falling outside the range could indicate a potential error. In such an instance, the data might be accurate, but falling outside the prescribed range would identify it as an exception.
2. *Hash totals.* The total of employee numbers, invoice numbers, or other numbers whose total is by itself meaningless, provides the ability to check against control totals. The check verifies that all employees, invoices, etc., have been considered during the processing of the program.
3. *Record sequence check.* Although less important in an age of strictly random data, the sequence check is still valuable as a control of sequential files, irrespective of the storage medium.
4. *Record counts.* As files are passed through a program, the count of the records on those files should be maintained. As transactions are processed (specifically the add or delete transactions) the count should be incremented or decremented as appropriate and then matched against the record count of the following or output files.
5. *Relational checking.* This is the method of checking logical inconsistencies and highlighting them as exceptional conditions.
6. *Check digits.* A number's validity is proved by performing calculations upon the number and adding an extra digit to the number. That digit is developed within the calculation, and used to "decode" the number.

Edit checks exist to determine accuracy-accuracy of the program's operation and accuracy of the data that it utilizes. The checks can be intrinsic or applied via programming. An intrinsic check is performed by equipment designed for checking purposes (e.g., parity checks). A programmed check is designed by the programmer and implemented specifically as a part of the program.

Restart Points

It's unfortunate, but occasionally things don't work quite properly. And when they don't work well during long complex runs which process considerable data, it's wise to be able to establish intermediate starting points. The intermediate starting points are commonly called *checkpoints*.

Checkpoints, and their associated restart procedures, should be embedded in several places within the system for use when and if the system should fail or terminate for other than end of processing reasons, not including multiprogramming interrupts. Any termination situation should clearly demonstrate the condition which has occurred, providing information describing the status of the job and of the system itself (memory contents, registers, pointers, data under examination, etc.). The collected information can then be used for restarting the system. This collected information is, in reality, the "audit output" developed at prescribed places within the system.

Documentation

To ensure that a computer program is thoroughly understood and that it can be operated and maintained both at present and in the future, it must be documented. Documentation contains information describing a given computer program. It is also the creation, collection, organization, storage, citing, and dissemination of such documents or of the information contained within the documents.

We've come to the recognition that the programmer who programs the application may not be the best person to document it. It's fair to say that many who have the skills to make a computer "stand on its ear" have little ability to string together the words necessary to make a coherent sentence. They might spend hours shaving microseconds, but nary any extra effort to ensure that instructions are the clearest. This is a natural tendency, especially if we see documentation as a necessary evil. Managers would do well to tie financial and career incentives to the quality of documentation. More on that in the chapters on management.

Complete documentation of a computer system generally includes at least the following:

1. *Narrative explanations*—a document describing what the system process to accomplish-the objectives. These should be stated in easy-to-understand text. Assumptions should be stated, products should be identified and defined, input requirements should be identified and defined, and any rules for processing should be stated.
2. *Graphic representation* of the process. Flowcharts, Chapin Charts, HIPO charts, decision tables, structure diagrams, or any other suitable representation of the system—current in form—should be part of the package.
3. *Program listing* of the source and (if available) assembled code. Printouts of the program should be filed with the documentation each time there is a change to the program or system.
4. *Input/output formats*—forms, disk records, sizes and characteristics of data elements, linkages to data base elements, sample reports, etc., should be included.
5. *Screen formats* for on-line systems. Particularly important where the display is not linear (DISPLAY/ACCEPT) but is presented using a screen formatting tool or a macro (such as would be used in a spreadsheet).
6. Set of *test* and/or *audit data,* both actual and hypothetical, used in the testing and in the periodic auditing of the system. If your test data set has been properly constructed, the data could be used after a suitable time lapse with the same predictable results. A record of test sessions would be useful support material here.
7. *Machine-readable* and/or *hard-copies* of job stream control mechanisms which may be used. If you are using driver programs, then formula maps would be most useful.
8. *Operating instructions*—location of program(s), location of job stream control mechanisms, loca-

tion of preparation and setup procedures for use by the operations personnel, identification of input/output devices to be used, selection of communications media to be used, listing of error conditions and their responses, and key helps from user manuals which may have been developed for the system.

Estimating Run Time

It is possible to develop a system which seems to save nothing—no time, no cost, no benefit. Such a system is viewed as a waste of time for the affected users, at least. If it has been determined that an automated application is desirable, it's useful to develop some prediction as to the run time which will be consumed by the application. This run time is then added to the total running time for all applications and applied against the total real available time on the computer. For applications which will marginally exceed the available time, some assessment of the worth of all applications must be made. At some point, however, the spillover is sufficient to determine the additional computing power that is required. And let's all recognize that there are programs which *will be* written, irrespective of their economic or social worth.

The only real way to know the run time is to code, test, install, and run the application. It isn't often desirable to do so, however, and an estimate of the running time of the application may be critical to the decision about the development of the application. As a general guideline, these areas can be used to estimate run time: input/output, calculation/processing, off-line equipment functions, on-line communications response averages, and miscellaneous operations.

Given the specifications on the speed of the I/O equipment, the calculation of I/O time is relatively easy, as the size of the files and the handling characteristics are known. In many instances, I/O timing formulas are provided by the vendor.

Estimating the calculation/processing time isn't easy. The instructions can be counted according to the number of executions and multiplied by the time required for the execution of each type of instruction. Careful attention should be given in the estimating process to those instances where buffering is used and the degree to which processing or I/O overlap is used. For off-line equipment, the time expended on printing, card punching, etc., should be considered.

And now that the right way has been discussed, the simple way will be presented. Find the I/O time (for an I/O bound job), subtract 25% for buffering or input overlap, add 30% of the difference for computation, add the print time for spooled output, and add any off-line time and you have it. This formula should work:

$$\begin{aligned}\text{Run Time Estimate} &= (\text{I/O} - .25\ \text{I/O}) + .3(\text{I/O} - .25\ \text{I/O}) + \text{PT} + \text{OL}\\ &= 1.3(\text{I/O} - .25\ \text{I/O}) + \text{PT} + \text{OL}\end{aligned}$$

where: I/O = Input/Output Time
PT = Print Time
OL = Overlap

There's no authority for that estimate other than the author's personal experience.

Queue Estimating

In real-time or on-line systems, events are sometimes independent of current functions in the processing units. Consequently, queues may be developed throughout the system. The four common types of queues are as follows:

1. *Input.* New data to be processed.
2. *Channel wait.* Jobs waiting for I/O facilities or communications facilities.
3. *Current work.* Jobs being processed.
4. *Output.* Processed data to be reported.

Items are transferred to and from these queues based on considerations of timing and priority which might transcend, in a reasonably complex mix, the rather simplistic formula presented above. The calculation of time involved in the enqueuing process is an exercise in advanced statistics, and is beyond the the scope of this book. To see what is involved, it is an operations research model which includes bulk models, busy period, busy probability, delay probability, discipline, finite queue, finite source, idle period, interarrival time, multiple server, optimization model, output, preemptive, priority, self-service, service time, simulated, single-server, tandem, transient behavior, waiting line, waiting time. It's a complex topic.

Organization of Data

The mind of man seeks constantly to find ways to organize data on magnetic media in such a manner that any given item of information can be obtained in the shortest possible time, commensurate with machine capabilities, data structure considerations, and cost. Historically, there have been only two methods to store data—*sequentially* and *randomly.* Any other form of organization is but a variation of these two.

Sequential file organization is somewhat fixed in concept. The method simply requires the reading of $(N - 1)$ records prior to reading record N. The development of an information processing system around a sequential record-keeping mode assumes that there is a high probability of processing for a large number of records, where the specific sequence of access is important only in relation to the sequence of the transaction stream. Modification of a sequential file must be done in "copy mode." That is, the deletion of records from, the insertion of records to, and the modification of records within require that "before" and "after" copies of a file be taken. Further, the method requires that all data be structured relative to the method whereby the file has been given sequence. This means that similar data used under dissimilar circumstances may not be easily tied to its counterpart(s) using its organizational method.

Random file organization allows the access to the Nth record without the requirement to review $(N - 1)$ records to gain access. In theory, any record can be accessed as quickly as any other record. The most frequently used variations of random file organizations are relative access, indexed sequential access, and direct access. It is in the area of direct access where the various types of database applications have emerged. We have expanded our coverage of database to provide detailed discussion of the various types of database. See Chapter 8 for further detail.

Relative file organization allows access to the Nth record by displacement calculation from a given marking position—e.g., the 10th record from the beginning. A variation of this method is the calculation of the Mth byte of the file as determined by the product N times M.

Indexed sequential file organization combines a method of maintaining a key index with a method of maintaining a data file organized upon one or more keys. By and large, single keys are used. However, in some systems, alternate keys may be specified-and, in at least one instance, a hybridized key may be developed and used in an ISAM environment. A hybridized key is developed by bringing together non-contiguous data and using the data dynamically as a key. Some systems merely flag deletions pending reorganization of the file, at which time the flagged records merely "drop off" the file. Some vendors develop ISAM files on the basis of the record's active existence.

Direct access is the technique which allows the programmer to specify the reading/writing of data beginning at a specified physical location within the I/O device. This technique requires a programmer to calculate the physical location from the control key using an algorithm and to deal with the problem of synonyms—different control keys which transform to the same physical location.

Input/Output Considerations

Access Methods—Data Management Systems

Sequential file organization requires the programmer to accomplish the following functions correctly:

1. Read old master file records and write them to the new master only after determining that either there is no transaction activity or all appropriate transactions have been posted.
2. Adding new records, if appropriate from the new master file. Of course, this must be done without producing an out-of-service new master file and without losing any old master file records—even if the record to be added is to be the first or last record on the new master file.
3. Deleting existing records if appropriate from the old/new master file. Of course, this must be done without producing an an out-of-sequence new master file and without losing any old master file records—even if the record is the first or last record on the master file.

Some factors to be considered when evaluating the feasibility of using sequential file organization are listed below:

1. What percentage of the master file records are actually updated during an average run?
2. How many master records are added to the master file during an average run?
3. How much computer time is required to process an average run?
4. How much operator handling time is required for an average run?
5. What are the operational risks involved?

Random file organization requires the programmer to accomplish the following functions correctly:

1. Read the record to updated, update the record, and rewrite the updated record.
2. Add the record to be added.
3. Delete the record to be deleted.

In each case, if an error occurs (depending on frequency and severity), the programmer may simply issue an error message and continue processing the text transaction.

Several additional factors to be considered when evaluating the feasibility of using random file organization are:

1. On-line real-time systems will generally require instant access capability available from random file organization.
2. The cost and availability of random access storage devices and input/output units.
3. The cost of making backup files, restoring the backup files, and reupdating when the need arises.

Performance Characteristics

Sequential access organization is most appropriate when a high percentage of master file records must be accessed during a given update run and instant access inquiry capability is not required. The definition of a ''high percentage'' must be evaluated relative to the speed of the input/output devices, the blocking factors (when this is relevant), the efficiency of the operating system (or input/output control system) in dealing with data blocks, and the amount of memory devoted to input/output buffering.

Random access organization is most appropriate when a small percentage of the master file records must be accessed during an average update run. If the time (cost) required to update the data records and make the associated backup files is less than the time (cost) required to update the sequential files, then the random organization may be justified. Many applications, such as on-line real-time systems, require the use of random organization in order to meet processing speed or response time requirements.

Advanced Programming Techniques

Structured Programming

There has been a high level of acceptance and implementation of structured programming, championed by the efforts of Edward Yourdon and others, for reasons detailed earlier in this chapter. As programming technology advanced, it was found that programmers were developing systems which were inefficient, difficult to follow, difficult to modify, and nearly impossible to debug adequately . Those who studied the problem, notably Edgar Dykstra, found that a proper program was really a function of using only the control logic structures of sequence, selection, and iteration. According to the structured program experts and writers, a proper program must meet two requirements: (1) Each module must have precisely one entry point and precisely one exit point and (2) the module must be self-contained.

Sequence

The sequence logic structure implies that program statements are executed in their order of appearance. Figure 2.20 illustrates the sequence logic structure. This, of course, is no different for any program in any language, except that for the structured programming technique to work, it must be seen as a control logic structure.

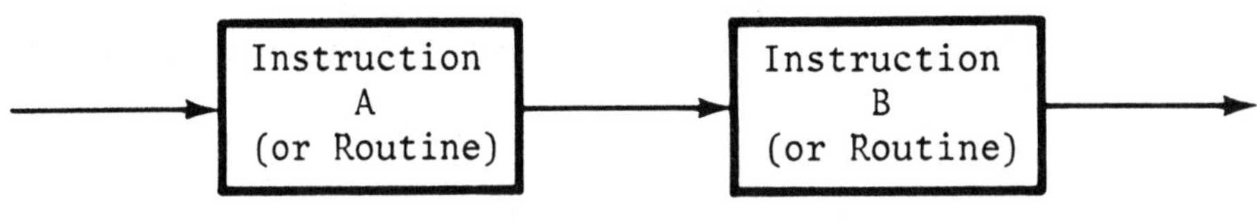

Figure 2.20

Selection

The selection logic structure is a function of a comparison action with both sides of the comparison being treated in the same statement. This is commonly called the IFTHENELSE structure. Figure 2.21 illustrates the selection logic structure:

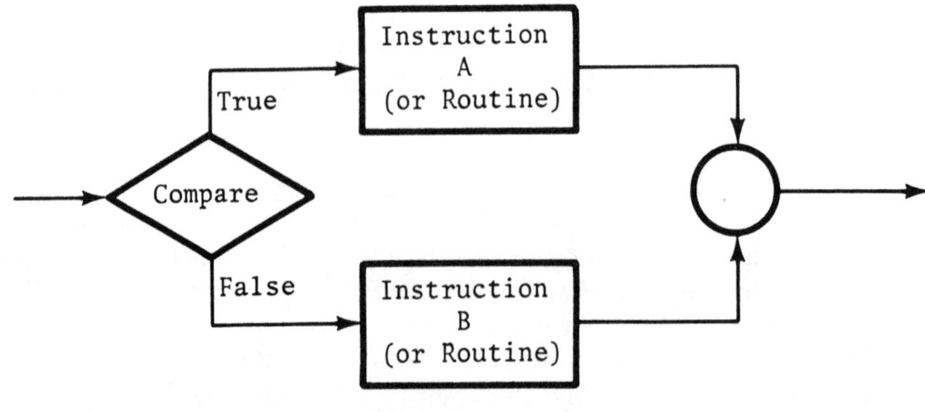

Figure 2.21

Iteration

The iteration logic structure is used for repeated execution of the program (coding structure) while a certain condition remains true. It is commonly referred to as the DOWHILE structure. Figure 2.22 illustrates the iteration logic structure.

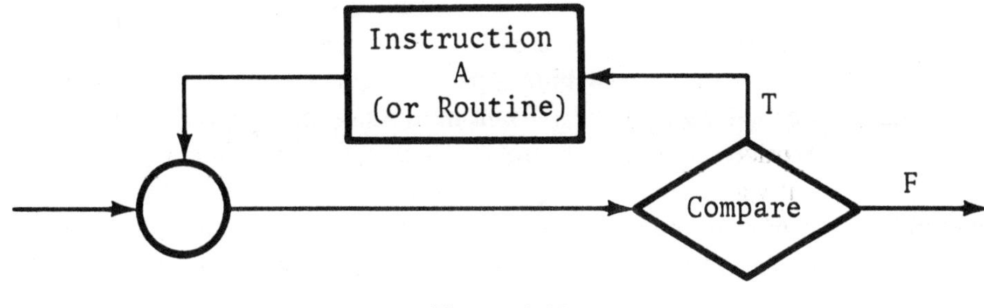

Figure 2.22

These three are the fundamental concepts of structured programming. The intent is to be able to combine them as functions within functions, such that a self-contained function could be replaced by a substituted function. Further, the method reduces the number of unconditional branches and, of course, eliminates the unconditional branches (GOTOs) which would pass program control outside the self-contained module.

The GOTO-less programming issue has sapped the strength of the structured programming movement and caused unneeded controversy, especially since the aims of structured programming are far more significant:

- Improve program reliability
- Improve program readability
- Minimize program complexity
- Simplify program maintenance
- Increase programmer productivity
- Provide a disciplined programming methodology

In one sense, the concept of structured programming centers on the presentation of the code, form, and process. Structured programming is, to be sure, a set of conventions which impose rules to follow on coding constructs, data structures, module contents, and documentation. These do discourage the use of the unconditional branch (GOTO), the use of the three constructs mentioned above, and the application of the concepts to the programming language you're using—even to BASIC.

In fact, Structured BASIC is catching on, and the WHILE NOT EOF(1) example given a short time ago is a good example. The important thing is that the clarity of thinking must be worked out in advance. We are conditioned to think about what we would do IF, and not much about what we would do IF NOT. In a true sense, sequential processing in structured programming happens only in the IF NOT (WHILE NOT) sense. Structured programming then gives us the top-down structured technique into which we can place the structured coding—the PERFORMed modules and the nested IF . . . ENDIF control constructs.

Multiprogramming

Multiprogramming is a technique for allowing a computer to execute two or more programs simultaneously by overlapping a CPU operation with the input/output operations of other programs. Multiprogramming is made possible by hardware and operating system software, which handle interrupts. When an executing program initiates an input/output operation, the operating system allows another program to execute until an interrupt is received, indicating the completion of the first program's input/output operation. If the higher priority program is an input/output-bound program, the second program will execute during computer time made available by the multiprogramming technique. When programs do not have frequent input/output operation, the execution of one program may be suspended in order to allow a second program to execute. This would happen when the first program failed to initiate an input/output operation after a previously specified length of time called a time slice.

When an application program operating within a partition (or region) manages a multiprogramming environment, the process is called *multitasking*. When more than one program is being run on a computer, a storage protection feature protects each program's memory area from alteration by another program.

Multiprogramming must be distinguished from multitasking. Multitasking is essentially a hardware concept which details the overlap of functions attributable to control units placed on channels or other forms of functional overlap, such as the time necessary to print a hard copy of a console log.

Multiprogramming should also be distinguished from *multiuser*. Multiuser operation of any computer, from mainframe to micro, involves more than one access to the specific user's own area of the computer. Multiuser operation becomes complex when more than one user wants access to the same record in the file. Thus, order entry clerks who are on-line to the computer and who each want access to the same inventory record must take their respective turns. System design schemes for handling this will include semi-batch processing, where the order clerk enters a group of sought-after items, and the computer can sort out its own contention problems.

Multiuser applications of microcomputers are making tremendous inroads into the larger mainframes. At the moment, multiuser/multiprogramming applications are done with some difficulty on the micro. One approach is the isolated/embedded micro, such as that employed by the NorthStar Dimension. In that device, several individual CPUs are imbedded in the same cabinet, and each is connected to a terminal. The hard disk file is not so isolated, however, and modifications of existing microcomputer operating systems have been made to accomodate the handling of contention problems.

For some time, the CP/M operating system (more specifically the MP/M version) has been able to handle multiple users, using specific USER areas. One such system is produced by Altos. It isn't very fast, but it does show that multiuser systems are a viable concept. (CP/M means ''Control Program for Microcomputers.'' MP/M means ''Multiprogramming for Microcomputers.'')

Meta-Programming Systems

Strange as it may seem in this day and age, there are people who continue to love to program a computer in machine language—more so now on the microcomputers. Since a computer must be busy to pay its own way, there must be ways to instruct it to do its work. They are called programming systems. Programming systems generally include assemblers, compilers, translators, interpreters, report generators, program generators, driver programs, various utility programs, etc. All have one thing in common (*meta*) and that is the structure into which a specification is placed. The purpose of programming systems is to increase the productivity of an application for operation on a computer. The programming language is a set of representations, formats, and rules used to communicate the solution of a problem to a computer for handling.

However the application is programmed, it's going to end up in the machine in machine language. Machine language is a series of numbers which are accepted by the computer and which cause the computer to behave in a predictable manner. In the machine-language instruction, a portion of the instruction is reserved for the operation code and the balance of the instruction is reserved for one or more addresses. For instance, one machine language instruction for one small UNIVAC computer is 22532. The

INSTRUCTION LOCATION	OPERATION CODE	OPERAND
500	30	000
501	04	000
502	23	435
503	33	014
504	64	502
505	76	562
506	64	307

Figure 2.23

op code (22) is for an add instruction, while 532 is the address of the data. These numbers are in hexadecimal. Continuing with this computer's repertoire, Figure 2.23 illustrates the machine code to add a list of 15 numbers which have been stored in memory.

The excessive amount of time required to write programs in machine languages, the clerical work involved in keeping track of storage positions and assignments, the difficulty of remembering all the various operation codes, etc., led to the development of symbolic languages that use mnemonic (meaningful) terms. (Mnemonic merely means "committed to memory.")

Assemblers

Assembly languages (also referred to as symbolic languages closest to machine language) utilize alphabetic, numeric, and special characters to identify and name data or instruction locations (mnemonic addresses). Mnemonic operation codes and mnemonic addresses consist of symbols chosen to assist the human memory. Examples of two prevalent assembly language systems are shown in Figure 2.24.

A symbolic language is machine dependent (with each symbolic instruction corresponding precisely to the particular machine's internal instruction set) and must be converted to machine language before it is usable on a computer. This is accomplished by a language processor known as an assembler. An assembler is a program that prepares (or assembles) a machine language program using a symbolic source language, substituting absolute operation codes and absolute or relocatable addresses for symbolic addresses. With one minor exception, one machine language instruction is produced for each and every source instruction.

The symbolic language program that must be assembled into machine language is called the *source program.* The resulting machine language is called the *object program.* The object program may exist in absolute (not to be relocatable) or in relocatable form. In the process of translating the former to the latter, the assembler performs other tasks, such as assigning memory locations to instructions and to data, checking the language source statement for syntax, etc.

There is one exception to the one-for-one concept-the macroinstruction. The *macroinstruction* (*Macro*) is a single command, placed in the source program, which may generate a set of machine language instructions. The ADD A TO B GIVING C macroinstruction, previously discussed, illustrates this.

Symbolic Input/Output

The premise of enhancements to the programmer's bag of tools is based upon making the machine do work which the machine language programmer used to have to do. One of these involves the movement

Z-80 ASSEMBLER

LABEL	OP CODE	OPERAND
	ORG	4A00H
	LD	A,31H
	LD	(3E20H),A
LOOP	JP	LOOP
	END	4A00H

IBM 4300 ASSEMBLER

LABEL	OP CODE	OPERAND
	CSECT	
	CNOP	6,8
	BALR	2,0
	USING	*,2
	LH	9,=H'14'
	L	4,=A(FIVR)
	SP	SUMPX,SUMPX
	B	BRNCT
ZENT	AP	SUMPX,0(5,4)
	AH	4,-H'5'
BRNCT	BCT	9,ZENT
	B	END

Figure 2.24

of data from memory to media and vice-versa. In addition to performing the actual input/output operation, with its attendant error and condition checking, it's necessary for the programmer to be concerned with efficient I/O—to somehow compensate for the internal speed of memory (fast) and the external speed of I/O (less than fast). This work is now accomplished by elements of the operating system.

Initially called an Input/Output Control System (IOCS), the access method is a software package invoked by the programmer using symbolic input/output coding. This symbolic input/output coding performs the movement of data to and from media and memory, the verification of accuracy, the establishment and maintenance of relative linkages, etc. Label functions, password functions, administration of schema and subschema services will be performed by the access software, and will therefore be transparent to the programmer.

Compilers

Compiler languages (also referred to as higher-level languages) are designed for the convenient expression of procedures used in the solution of a wide class of problems. Though the languages are artificial (not immediately translatable to machine language), their syntax and grammar follow rules similar to

```
PROGRAM AVE100NUMBER(INPUT,OUTPUT);
(*PROGRAM AVERAGES 100 NUMBERS*)
VAR NUMBER:ARRAY 1..100 OF REAL;
 SUM,AVERAGE:REAL;
 COUNT:INTEGER;
BEGIN
 SUM:=0.0;
 FOR COUNT:=1 TO 100 DO
      BEGIN
              READLIN(NUMBER[COUNT];
              AVERAGE:=SUM+NUMBER[COUNT]
       END
 AVERAGE:=SUM/100.0;
 WRITELN('AVERAGE=',AVERAGE);
END
```

Figure 2.25

conversational language. Further, such languages have some degree of machine independence and transportability, in that they can be developed for one machine and, given similar capabilities, can be used on another machine. As with assembly languages, programs written in higher-level languages (source programs) must be translated into machine language (object programs) before they can be executed on a computer. An example of the higher-level language PASCAL is given in Figure 2.25. The program is designed to average 100 numbers and print the result.

The program works this way. Initially SUM: =0. Then, the program enters the loop. For each time through the loop, the value of NUMBER is increased by 1, until 100 times through the loop have been accomplished. Then, the SUM is divided by 100 and the average is printed.

The program which translates a program such as that presented above is called a *compiler.* A compiler is a program which prepares a machine language program from the specifications of a higher-level language by generating one or more than one machine instruction for each symbolic instruction written.

The compilation process has several phases. First, a *parsing* function is executed. Parsing is the process of breaking down a statement grammatically in terms of its function, syntatic relations, etc. The statements of the source language are examined and analyzed; a dictionary of data descriptions is built; a coded representation of the statements is created; a copy of the source program is printed; and, if necessary, appropriate diagnostic messages issued. In the second phase, a *mapping* process is performed. The dictionary entries are examined, and the declarations are mapped into the data formats of the object computer. In the final phase, appropriate *object code* is generated to handle the expressed operations.

Some compilers have an additional phase, in which an attempt is made to *optimize* the object code generated in the final phase of the compilation process. In this phase, the object code is reviewed, superfluous code is appropriately eliminated, and an attempt to improve the efficiency of the program is made.

As with the assemblers, there is a preparation step for compilers. Unless the program is to be entered and executed under an *interpretive compiler,* the source program must be entered into a machine-readable magnetic medium; the compiler must be loaded in the same manner as would any other program (compilers are generally service programs of the installed operating system); the translation must be performed; and the output of the listing and diagnostics must be accomplished. The object module must be produced and it must be loaded and executed.

As with the assemblers, the higher-level languages may be compiled and executed immediately. The process is known as *compile and go.* If the source program is successfully translated, the object program is simply transferred, bound to its designated location in memory, and executed. Any program written in a symbolic or higher-level language must be assembled or compiled before it can be executed (even including the interpretive compilers); only machine language programs are immediately executable.

In recent years great strides have been made with *cross-compilers.* The cross-compiler runs on a large computer and prepares object modules for another, and generally smaller, computer.

Translators

Translators transform statements from one language to another without significantly changing the meaning. Assemblers and compilers are examples of basic translators, in that they generate machine language instructions from symbolic instructions and higher-level language statements. A program called a *disassembler,* which will take machine language and structure it into a form of assembly language, is also a translator. What it does is to take the contents of memory from the program's starting point and develops a pseudo-source language. Thus, it is possible to translate a COBOL source language into an ASSEMBLER source language by going through the disassembler process.

The more common function of a translator, however, is its use as a programming aid. When significant changes have been made in a version of a language, or a conversion is to be made from one language to another, a Language Conversion Program (LCP) is generally developed to assist the translation. The newly generated code isn't always wholly executable, but it is a place to start.

Interpreters

An interpreter is a computer program that translates and executes each source language statement before translating and executing the next one. With an interpreter, the source program is not assembled into an object program. Instead, results are computed immediately after an instruction has been translated. The interpretive process allows very efficient use of computer and programmer time during the programming and debugging of the application.

The interpreter, or more accurately, the interpretive compiler does not need to be a software program which is loaded from sources external to the computer. It may be a permanently resident read-only-memory (ROM) program, such as the Microsoft BASIC Interpreter, widely used in the first and second generations of microcomputers.

The principal value of the interpreter has to be its ability to test a program "so far," or to test only a selected portion of a program, particularly in an on-line mode. Using this approach, the programmer may insert instructions for the display of run-time variables, may insert stop codes from which he may continue execution, or may establish routines which will print select portions of data during the execution of the test.

Some interpretive (and interpretable) languages, such as BASIC, are also available as compilers. This allows programs which must be executed repeatedly to be compiled into the machine language only once and then executed efficiently. Other interpretive languages are those which are threaded-list oriented (such as LISP and FORTH) and those which are time-sharing in nature, such as APL. As the cost of hardware decreases, and as the cost of programmer time increases relative to the hardware, there will be further development in interpreters.

Generators

A generator is a controlling routine that performs a creative function, e.g., report generator, report program generator, and program generator.

A report generator creates reports requiring little or no calculation or complex logic. Generally, these reports are simple lists of data. With the report generator, the programmer writes specifications for the report rather than the program instructions necessary to generate the report. The specifications may include the print positions in which each data field is to be printed, control fields, totals required, etc. The specifications are subsequently converted into a set of specifications and interfaced with the report generator processor. The appropriate data are then passed through the system, and a report is produced according to the format described in the specifications. This report generator may be embodied within a language (such as the REPORT WRITER feature of COBOL) or may be a standalone package (such as ASI-ST). Further, some data base/data management systems have extraction and reporting mechanisms. One such example of this is ADR's ROSCOE.

This is also an area where much work has been done with the microcomputer. Using packages such as QUICKPRO and PERSONAL PEARL it is possible to specify the contents of an input screen and an output report and the generator will provide the code to marry the two. One of the more widely known of this kind of generator is actually a driver program—dBase II. But even dBase II has its own statement generator, AUTOCODE. And there are no doubt others. Again, the driver program is revolutionizing the programming field.

A report program generator differs from a report generator in that it does not generate a report directly, but rather generates a program which is then, in turn, used to generate the report. The report program generator language RPG is structured to provide a machine-acceptable form for describing both the data and the report, generating the coding to accept the former and produce the latter.

A program generator is a system which accepts program specifications or parameters and produces a tailor-made program as an output. One example of this is DEC's CONGEN. Another is a user-specified sort/merge routine.

Operating Systems

An operating system or monitor is software which controls the execution of computer programs and which may provide scheduling, debugging, input/output control, accounting, compilation, storage assignment, data and task management, and related services. Without an operating system, certain functions (such as multiprogramming) wouldn't be available at all, many functions (such as input/output completion testing) would have to be performed directly by the programmer, and machine time and computing power would be largely underutilized. The operating system and its guru, the systems programmer, have become a pervasive force in modern day computing. Even at the microcomputer level, a variety of Disk Operating Systems and a standard operating system (CP/M—Control Program/Microcomputer) have emerged.

Generally, an operating system consists of an executive control program and a number of processors. Each processor has a specific function that it performs upon the command of a control provided by the operator or by the user. The function of each processor can usually be considered either that of job management, data management, or task management. These terms are, of course, IBM terms, but the functions are the same, albeit under different names, for other manufacturers.

Job Management

Job Scheduling

The job scheduling mechanism must read and interpret the control statements, allocate computer time, form job queues, handle priorities, load programs, allocate memory, and respond to traps and interrupts.

Input/Output Allocation and Control

This function dynamically matches and assigns I/O channels and devices with job requirements, monitors their status, and controls their operations. Where on-line features are part of the system, communication with the terminal control unit (TCU) or front-end communication processor (FECP) will be included in these duties.

Operator Communication

This function handles all communications with the system operator and with remote "virtual" operators, as well.

Errors, Diagnostics, and Recovery Processes

These uncover errors, issue diagnostic messages, and handle system recovery procedures.

Utility and Miscellaneous Services

These handle special I/O considerations, intercommunications between terminals, sharing of data base mechanisms, and device-to-device transfers.

Data Management

File Control

This function describes a file, inputs data into the file, maintains the file, handles linkage and search mechanisms among major data base modules.

Open/Close Files

This function opens and closes files as required by a specific tasks. It provides label, password, and access protections.

I/O Supervision

This controls the movement of data between elements of memory.

Task Management

Task Supervision

This function loads the task into main memory for execution and controls the movement of tasks between primary and secondary storage.

Interrupt Handling

This handles all interrupts to the execution stream, providing services where possible, providing direction where service is not possible.

Facility and User Time Accounting

This handles accounting of user and system program execution time and of individual component use time. These statistics will then be used for direct customer charge for services.

Language Translation

This provides capabilities to assemble or compile application programs.

Operating system requirements for batch objectives differ from those for on-line environment. In the batch environment, job-to-job transition must be provided; the computing system must be applied to a computing mix which will include diverse applications and operating modes. Increased throughput and improved turnaround time; use of diagnostic aids; and increased utility to the programmer must be provided. In the on-line environment, those things must be provided plus reasonable response times; multi-user lockouts on a given record; recovery from system failures which are not necessarily easily detectable; limitations to access; and access to a wide variety of language processors, utility programs, and application programs. Except for remote job entry (RJE) systems, most on-line applications involve job stream segments, rather than the job streams themselves.

Microcomputer Operating Systems

There are essentially three specific operating systems which are utilized in the microcomputer world: CP/M, MS-DOS, and UNIX.

CP/M

CP/M, or Control Program for Microcomputers, is the oldest. First developed by Digital Research (Gary Kildall) for the Altair 8800, and then extended to a whole host of machines, it became the industry standard for 8-bit microcomputers, excepting those produced by Radio Shack and Apple, which chose to go their own way. Interestingly, both would subsequently add hardware to permit the use of the CP/M operating system, essentially because of the wealth of CP/M programs available in the marketplace. CP/M hasn't fared so well in the world of 16-bit microcomputers, losing ground to the rival MS-DOS operating system from Microsoft.

CP/M provided just about all the services of its larger relatives:

- *The monitor.* A group of programs that manages the detailed operation of the system.
- *The file commands.* Small and often-used programs which manage the file systems and I/O devices.
- *The utilities.* Programs whose function is to copy and transform files.
- *Language translators.* Programs used to convert statements in some programming language (source code) to machine language.
- *Applications.* It is said that CP/M has the largest number of available applications.

There are several versions of CP/M, but the most prevalent is the MP/M multiprogramming operating system. Both CP/M and MP/M have an 8086 version, which was a last ditch (and somewhat futile) attempt to capture the burgeoning market created by IBM and IBM-compatible products. It hasn't worked.

MS-DOS

MS-DOS, or Microsoft Disk Operating System, has usurped the position of CP/M in the support of the 16-bit market, now largely the purview of IBM and compatible products. Developed by Seattle Computing Systems and subsequently bought by Bill Gates (Microsoft), MS-DOS found its great success in its PC-DOS version, used by the IBM PC. From a structure point of view it duplicates most of the features of CP/M. Its services are conducted differently, and the language translators are separately obtained, but conceptually the two are similar in nature, and little can be done on the one that cannot be done on the other.

MS-DOS does offer one capability not found in CP/M, however. That capability is the use of subdirectories and the associated concept of pathing. It is possible under MS-DOS to create levels of subdirectory and to isolate the programs of a certain type to that subdirectory, reading other subdirectories through a series of path structures, each denoted by a backslash (\). Thus, if it is desired to reference the document KEN.DOC in the WordStar Subdirectory of the Word Processing Subdirectory, it might be coded like this:

\WP\WS\KEN.DOC

Conceptually, this pathway system works very much like Apple Computer's PRODOS. MS-DOS certainly owes its success to two things: its low price and the machines to which it is attached.

UNIX

UNIX is an operating system which predates even CP/M. This system was developed by Bell Labs for use on the Digital Equipment Corporation PDP-7, and was generally drawn from design effort on the now defunct General Electric 645 (that operating system was known as *Multics*). Because the cost of running Multics was excessive, certain functions were transferred to the DEC equipment. Later AT&T would license UNIX to other DEC users. Unlike most operating systems, which operated in the host's native language, UNIX was developed in a high-level language, for which a compiler could be written for each machine. That high-level language, initially called B, was modified extensively and rechristened C, and the name stuck. Because UNIX was written in C, it could then be transported to other machines—and, of course, today is found prevalently on the AT&T 3B series of minicomputers and the Olivetti-produced 6xxx and 7xxx series of microcomputers which carry the AT&T name. UNIX also has some lookalikes—notably XENIX, produced by you-know-who—Microsoft.

Unlike the other operating systems, UNIX has buried within it many of the features of currently available integrated software—word processing, database systems, electronic mail and networks, programming tools, graphics, and some business applications. They aren't intended to be as capable as WordStar™ (MicroPro International) or as grandiose as Symphony™ (Lotus Development Corporation), but they don't pretend to be. But UNIX is there with editors, text formatters, spellers, and syntax checkers which test sentence structure. The electronic filing capabilities of UNIX compare favorably with many of the database packages currently available. Electronic mail and networking capabilities of the system are unparalleled, but of course, that is AT&T's business.

And there are the programming languages and compilers which are a part of the system—FORTRAN, BASIC, Pascal, COBOL, RPG, SPITBOL, APL, LOGO (which we will discuss shortly), Forth, and, of course, C. That's right, an operating system which is written in C running a C compiler.

UNIX's Command Line Interpreter, called the *shell,* is the link between users and the computer and functions just like a BASIC interpretive compiler. The standard shell is called the *Bourne shell,* after its developer. There is also a *C shell,* which was developed at the University of California, Berkeley. The shell has also the power of a "pipe," a pathway feature not dissimilar to that described in MS-DOS. We'll provide an example of the C language shortly, but you'll be pleased to know there is a UNIX command called *finger.* As you might suspect, it is a "pointer" command.

The Driver Program

Well, we've been hinting at it—now is the time to explore the concept in some detail.

The spreadsheet is possibly the best example of the driver program. The spreadsheet vendor has developed a program which takes the cells of the analysis pad, size defined by use, and with the template applied by the user against those cells performs movement, transformation, and calculations, displaying the results nearly instantaneously in those very cells.

Spreadsheet Format

Figure 2.26 provides a general idea of the structure and intended contents of a spreadsheet.

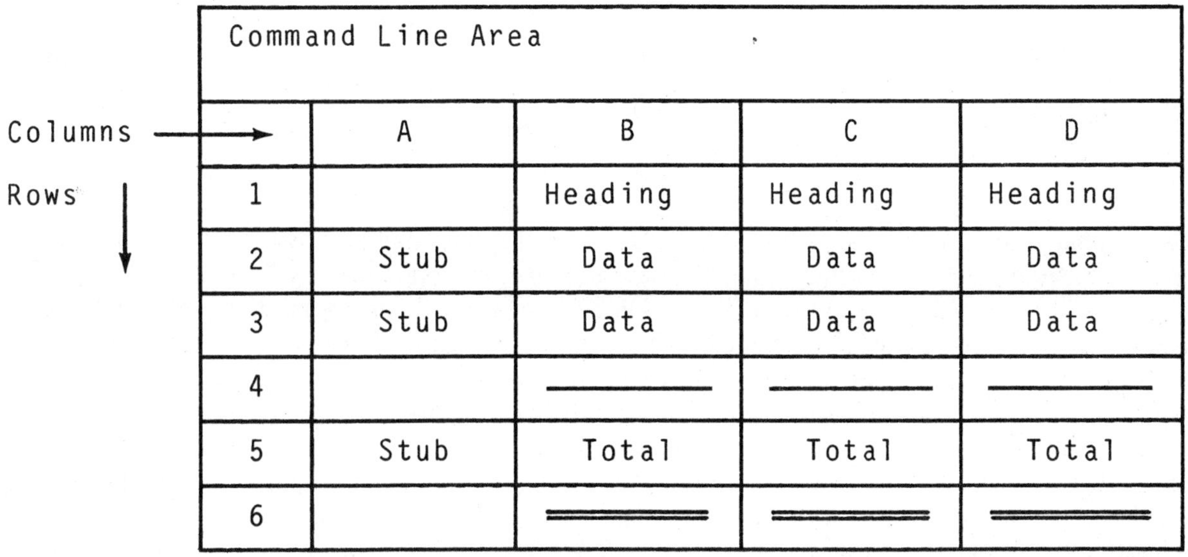

Command Line Area				
Columns →	A	B	C	D
Rows ↓ 1		Heading	Heading	Heading
2	Stub	Data	Data	Data
3	Stub	Data	Data	Data
4		————	————	————
5	Stub	Total	Total	Total
6		====	====	====

Figure 2.26

Command Structure

Most spreadsheets have a command structure located in one of two places—at the top or bottom of the screen. Several have menus from which to select. All have subselections from which to choose. Figure 2.27 is an example drawn from Lotus 1-2-3.

Movement

Most worksheet programs will provide the ability to move around within the worksheet itself. Most generally the movement attributes are a function of the package's design. In general, however, you'll find that movement among the cells is accomplished by the cursor (arrow) keys.

From that point, they may differ. But even while the mechanics of operation differ, the concept is precisely the same. The purpose of the GoTo function is to move directly to a specific line and column somewhere on the worksheet. On the surface that might not seem like much, and while you're on the same screen, it isn't. However, the screen as you see it is simply a window (the logical spreadsheet—that portion you can see) upon the entire spreadsheet (the physical spreadsheet). The logical spreadsheet is frequently called the "active area." The concept is not dissimilar to reading the newspaper through a magnifying glass.

The GoTo function is used to move you from your present location to somewhere off the logical spreadsheet to elsewhere on the physical spreadsheet, with the requested cell appearing in the "home" (upper left-hand corner of the screen) position. Should you do this a row or column at a time, the process could become very lengthy, as with the emergence of each new row or column, the spreadsheet would be repositioned, and that can become time consuming.

Another movement feature of the spreadsheet package will be the ability to move right or left, up or down, in increments of one logical screen. In Lotus, this is accomplished, generally, by the PgUp, PgDn, Ctrl, or Alt keys (of an IBM PC), either alone or in combination with the cursor keys. Yet an-

```
Worksheet  Range  Copy  Move  File  Print  Graph  Data  Quit
Global, Insert, Delete, Column-Width, Erase, Titles, Window, Status
```

Figure 2.27

other pair of movements is accomplished on computers equipped with Home and End keys. The Home key will move the cell cursor to the upper left corner of the logical spreadsheet. The End key will move the cell cursor to the lower right corner of the logical spreadsheet. Used with another key, each may move to the very beginning or the very end of the spreadsheet.

Cell Entry

Data are entered to a cell by one of four methods: keyboard entry, copy or move data from another cell, loading data from a disk file, or by communication from another option directly into the worksheet. Two sorts of data may be entered from the keyboard—alphabetic data and numeric data. A cell may be declared as alphabetic or as numeric. Generally the alphabetic is used for titles, frames, and the like. Once the type of data has been sensed, the spreadsheet will declare it as such. Some spreadsheets offer the opportunity to identify that data as left justified, right justified, or centered.

Most spreadsheets provide both copying and movement capabilities. The concept here is not complicated. In the case of the COPY, you are merely replicating a cell in another location, providing two copies of the value. In the case of the MOVE, you are removing the cell from the source location and placing it at the destination location.

Loading the spreadsheet from file is another important feature. Many of the commercially-used spreadsheets use the Data Interchange Format (DIF) for input and export of data. This format is one which was designed by the designers of VisiCalc and has found somewhat universal acceptance among other software producers not only of spreadsheets, but also of word processors and graphics programs. Naturally no spreadsheet file can be loaded which has not first been saved by either the spreadsheet or by another software package.

Figure 2.28 shows the nature of the data which is to be entered, vs. the data which is to be derived or calculated.

Formulas

The raison d'etre for the spreadsheet is the calculation process, and this calculation process is the driver program itself, modified by the contents of the template, the actual formulas. The formula methods for

Command Line Area

Columns →	A	B	C	D
Rows ↓ 1		Alphabet	Alphabet	Alphabet
2	Alphabet	Num/Ent	Num/Ent	Num/Calc
3	Alphabet	Num/Ent	Num/Ent	Num/Calc
4		————	————	————
5	Alphabet	Num/Calc	Num/Calc	Num/Calc
6		════	════	════

Figure 2.28

Command Line Area

Columns →
Rows ↓

	A	B	C	D
1				
2				(B2+B3)
3				(C2+C3)
4		————	————	————
5		@SUM(B2:B3)	@SUM(C2:C3)	@SUM(B5:C5)
6		====	====	====

Figure 2.29

all spreadsheets are algebraic, with all the rules of algebra. Requirements for the formula will be operands, operations, and results. It will be necessary to specify the spreadsheet row and column as an operand. Often, because the result will be located in the same location as one of the operands on the spreadsheet (such as if you were adding a value to an accumulator), it will be necessary that the location where the answer is to be located be specified first. Naturally all the algebraic calculation symbols may be used. Spreadsheets also includes function operation, such as @SUM, @AVG, etc., as well as the logical operators #AND#, #OR#, and #NOT#.

Figure 2.29 shows the positioning of the formulas to perform the desired calculations. Figure 2.30 shows the final step after the entries have been made and the calculations have been performed. Conceptually, any change made to the entry positions will effect a change in the calculated results.

Command Line Area

Columns →
Rows ↓

	A	B	C	D
1	Region	Product A	Product B	Combined
2	1	100	250	350
3	2	210	475	685
4		————	————	————
5	Tot Sales	310	725	1035
6		====	====	====

Figure 2.30

Formulas are the central function of the electronic spreadsheet. The whole concept of spreadsheeting is based upon the use of formulas. The formulas used are similar to the formulas you have used in algebra. Here, however, you will instead use cell locations or range names.

There are three types of information that can be entered into an electronic spreadsheet cell:

- *Numbers.* Each cell can contain one number value. The number entered into a cell will automatically be displayed using the format and width that have been preset for the spreadsheet. Either can be changed. The number must begin with a numeric character, a period ("."), a plus sign (+) a minus sign (−) or a dollar sign ($) to be recognized as a number.
- *Formulas.* Formulas consist of values and operators, and/or @functions ("at functions"). The formulas specified will have a designed maximum size and must start with a numeric character or one of these characters: double quotation mark ["], period [.], plus sign [+], minus sign [−], left parenthesis [(], commercial "at" [@], pound sign [#], or dollar sign [$]. The formula must not contain spaces except those spaces that are part of a range name. The values that can be provided to a formula are numbers, text strings in double quotation marks, cell addresses, and/or range names. Depending upon whose spreadsheet you are using, there may be a fixed set of formulas, or an extended set, including some not normally available in the algebraic system.
- *Mathematical @functions.* The mathematical @function provides an extension to the normal functions provided by algebraic equations for the purposes of accomplishing numeric functions. Although some of these functions will be used rarely, when they are needed, you need them, as they are often the only way to get the required answer. Others of these functions will become vital portions of your programming inventory of functions. Such functions as rounding, integer, and absolute will become normally used functions for business programmers. Others, such as sine, cosine, and tangent, will be the interest of the scientific people. Some (not all) of the mathematical functions of one driver program are given in the next subsection. No attempt has been made to explain the meaning of the function beyond the stated purpose of the function.

Driver Language

All well and good, you say—but this is a *driver* program, you said. Thus far you have detailed only interactive entry, despite the fact that the program did drive through the formulas. Does the spreadsheet driver have any other functions? To give you some idea of the capabilities of a top-notch spreadsheet driver program, these are the functions built into Lotus Symphony:

@ABS	Returns the absolute value of a number
@ACOS	Returns the arc cosine of a number
@ASIN	Returns the arc sine of a number
@ATAN	Returns the arc tangent of a number in radians
@ATAN2	Similar to @ATAN, with a result in the range of −pi to +pi
@AVG	Provide an average of an argument list
@CELL	Multifunction tasks, depending upon argument
@CELLPOINTER	Multifunction test at this pointer
@CHAR	Display the character associated with the number
@CHOOSE	Look up an argument based upon a numeric variable
@CLEAN	Strip control codes from strings
@CODE	Decodes the first character in the string provided to it
@COLS	Determines the number of columns used in a specific range
@COS	Returns the cosine of a number in radians

@COUNT	Used to provide a count of the number of items in the list
@DATE	Generates a date serial number
@DATEVALUE	Interprets the date string
@DAVG	Average of selected values
@DAY	Uses a whole date serial number and converts it to the day of the week
@DCOUNT	Number of selected values
@DMAX	Maximum of selected values
@DMIN	Minimum of selected values
@DSTD	Standard deviation of selected values
@DVAR	Variance of selected values
@ERR	Display the numeric value or an error
@EXP	Returns the exponential of a number
@FALSE	Returns a value of 0
@FIND	Used to find the location of any occurrence of the search string within the string
@FV	Calculates the future value of a series of interest payments (ordinary annuity)
@HLOOKUP	Determine a value from a horizontal look-up table
@HOUR	Uses the whole time number and interprets from that time number the hour of the day
@IF	Performs decision-making and redirection tasks
@ INT	Returns the integer portion of a mixed number
@ISERR	Returns ERR if a cell contains ERR
@ISNA	Restricts available numbers
@ISNUMBER	Tests cell for a number
@ISSTRING	Tests cell for a string (alphabetic)
@INDEX	Look up a value in a table
@IRR	Calculates the internal rate of return
@LEFT	Displays a leftmost subset of a strings
@LENGTH	The @LENGTH function returns the length of the target string
@LN	Returns the natural logarithm of a number
@LOG	Returns the logarithm, to the base 10, of a number
@LOWER	Converts a string into lower case
@MAX	Determines the largest value in argument list
@MOD	Returns a remainder on a divide
@MID	Extracts information from the middle of a string
@MIN	Used to determine the smallest number in an argument list
@MINUTE	Uses the whole time number and interprets from that time number the minute of the hour
@MONTH	Takes the whole date number and interprets from that the month that the date number represents
@NA	Hides some of the entered numbers
@NOW	Creates a serial number based upon the current date and time
@NPV	Calculates the net present value
@PI	Returns the value of pi
@PMT	Standard amortization formula
@PROPER	Converts a string to initial capital, balance lower case
@PV	Calculates the present value
@RAND	Returns a random number between 0 and 1
@REPEAT	Repeats a string a given number of times
@REPLACE	Replaces one string with another, at specific coordinates

@RIGHT	Displays a rightmost subset of a string
@ROUND	Rounds a number to a specified length
@ROWS	Used to tell the program the number of rows in a range
@SECOND	Takes the whole time number and interprets from that number the second represented within that number
@SIN	Returns the sine of a number
@SQRT	Produces the square root of a number
@STD	Used to determine the standard deviation in an argument list
@STRING	Converts decimal numeric to alphabetic string
@SUM	Used to provide a total of an argument list
@TAN	Returns the tangent of a number
@TIME	Generates a decimal serial number based upon time variables
@TIMEVALUE	Uses any of the current time formats to interpret the time string
@TRIM	Eliminates spaces within the string
@TRUE	Always produces a 1
@UPPER	Converts a string into entirely upper case letters
@VALUE	Converts a number from string to numeric format
@VAR	Calculates the variance in an argument list
@VLOOKUP	Finds information based upon a vertical tabling system
@YEAR	Takes the whole date number and interprets from that number the year represented within that number

That rather takes one's breath away—but it does show the range of capability available in a working piece of driver software.

Macros and Ranges

Of course it's our concept that a program, once run, is self-running. Most of the programming languages are process, not product oriented. COBOL, BASIC, Pascal—they all deal with the process. Ah, yes, but RPG, COBOL Report Writer, Personal Pearl, and Friday all deal with the product. The more sophisticated spreadsheet drive packages provide the ability to work within ranges of the spreadsheet and to develop keyboard macros which which may be used over and over. A macro is a program for automatic use of the spreadsheet. A macro will be a command, function, or formula that can either be generated by the touch of one or two keyboard keys or incorporated into macro programs. Macros are commonly used to save repetitive typing.

The range concept has to do with the spreadsheet's ability to identify subordinate portions by the assignment of names, to calculate within that specific range, and to perform a number of services upon that range along within the spreadsheet. This is frequently used where the spreadsheet is developed as an entity, but is subdivided. Figure 2.31 is an example of part of a spreadsheet which shows the logic and formulae used.

The "program" which is developed to cause the driver to drive these logic and formula statements is called a keyboard macro. Figure 2.32 is an example of a keyboard macro.

There are other driver programs—a word processor is a driver program, as is a relational database processor. In the sections on database and decision support systems, we'll talk again briefly about the spreadsheet driver and delve into other elements of the various driver systems which make up the ever widening selection of integrated software available not only on the microcomputer, but also upon the mainframe. At that time we'll also talk about the Interactive Financial Planning System and SPSS, both of which have their own programming languages.

At the same time, we should mention the growing integration of micro/mainframe applications and

```
COMPANY:      Winkin, Blinkin, and Nod, Architects
YEAR:         1985
                          YTD                                YTD
 YTD HOURS               LABOR                             SUPPLIES
=====================================================================================
 13,500.00   (C2) @IF(G7=$B$5,K7+$C$5,K7)       (C2) @IF(G7=$B$5,L7+$D$5,L7)
COST/HOUR:   (C2) +K7/$J$7                      (C2) +L7/$J$7
% OF COST:   (P2) +K7/$R$7                      (P2) +L7/$R$7

  2,420.00   (C2) @IF(G11=$B$5,K11+$C$5,K11)    (C2) @IF(G11=$B$5,L11+$D$5,L11)
COST/HOUR:   (C2) +K11/$J$11                    (C2) +L11/$J$11
% OF COST:   (P2) +K11/$R$11                    (P2) +L11/$R$11

  1,500.00   (C2) @IF(G15=$B$5,K15+$C$5,K15)    (C2) @IF(G15=$B$5,L15+$D$5,L15)
COST/HOUR:   (C2) +K15/$J$15                    (C2) +L15/$J$15
% OF COST:   (P2) +K15/$R$15                    (P2) +L15/$R$15
```

Figure 2.31

```
{calc}{home}{goto}b5~0{right}0{right}0{right}0{down}
{down}{down}{down}0{left}0{left}0{left}0{up}{up}{up}{up}
```

Figure 2.32

other drive programs which are making that transition. Expect to see two packages emerge in this area—T/Maker III (from the T/Maker Company, California) and Metafile (Sensor-based Systems, Minnesota). Both companies and their software have been around a while, have mainframe and microcomputer credentials, and extraordinary integrated software capability. Expect also that Lotus Development Corporation's Symphony will be a hot contender.

Sorting

It is frequently necessary to arrange information into some specific sequence for the extraction and reporting of information, or for matching another file in a specific sequence. Often, the time to sort a file into prescribed sequence plus the time to report from that file is less than if the reporting process alone were done on the unsequenced (or sequenced in different order) file. To sort a file requires a systematic technique for carrying out the sequencing tasks. Such techniques are widely used and have been since information has been processed in any form. However, there are different sorting methods, each with specific advantages and disadvantages.

The sorting process assumes some specific things. It assumes the existence of a collection of records called a *file,* as well as the existence of a *field* within each record (at precisely the same relative location) which may be used to order the records within the file. This is frequently called a *key* or *key field.* In some data organizations, there is a *symbolic key* which will be used to locate data. This symbolic key may be contained within a group of similar keys. It is possible, therefore, to reorganize data according to the reorganization of the keys alone, and sorting does not necessarily require the reorganization of the data itself.

The choice of sorting technique is seldom a choice made by the programmer him(her)self. Normally, a sorting technique is obtained with the hardware and its operating system, and that's the end of the question. However, for those with a choice, the techniques demonstrated here may prove useful. The technique selected is dependent upon both the hardware and software considerations of the type of data, number of records, size of available secondary or auxiliary work storages, size of primary memory, the computer instructions available, the characteristics of the input/output system, etc.

Basically, there are two types of sorting techniques: internal and external. An internal sort is a program that arranges a list of elements in main memory. An external sort is a program that arranges the records of a file by creating intermediate sequences of records in secondary stage and then reducing them to a single ordered data set. Several common internal sorting techniques are selection, exchanging, insertion, and radix. Examples of external techniques are straight merge and probability merge. These techniques are discussed below, as is the Shell-Metzner Sort.

Sorting by Selection

Sorting by selection consists of determining the record with the smallest key (lowest in the collating sequence), placing it at the beginning of the group of records to be sorted, determining the record with the next largest key, placing that record second, etc., until the entire group of records is appropriately ordered. This concept is illustrated in Figure 2.33.

The sorting procedure works as follows:

Pass 1. The lowest key (02) is placed first. The next three keys are in sequence, so they are merely copied over. The last key (19) is out of sequence, but is tagged for movement.

Pass 2. Note that between Pass 1 and Pass 2 nothing has been moved. This is because it's only the last entry which is out of sequence. Once that sequence disarrangement has been found, the penultimate record is past. The disarrangement will be corrected in Pass 3.

Pass 3. In correcting the disarrangement, the final element is placed in its correct position, but the balance is not merely punched down. An exchange has taken place which cannot be corrected until Pass 4.

Pass 4. And it is. This pass leaves the records in the proper sequence.

The sorting by selection technique is easy to understand and program, but it has certain disadvantages: considerable time is utilized in the movement of records; a large amount of primary storage is required; the use of sequential storage is impractical, since the technique basically requires immediate availability of all records; and because of sort time requirements, the technique is time-consuming when used with large files.

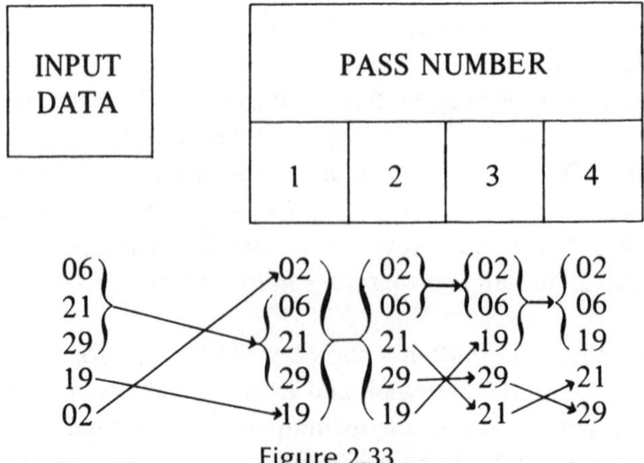

Figure 2.33

Sorting by Exchange

The exchange sort, often called a bubble sort, looks at the keys of records in pairs, successively exchanging each pair that is not in the desired sequence. The keys of the first pair are compared, exchanged if the key of the first record is greater than the key of the second record. Then, the second and third record are treated as a pair, and the same process continues. Once an exchange is made, however, there is nothing to guarantee that both elements of the exchange are in the appropriate order. For example, the fourth record may have a higher key than the fifth record and be exchanged with it. Once exchanged, however, the new fourth record may be reversed to the third record. This then, means that once the sort pass is complete, if an exchange has been made, another pass would be required. Thus, if a list of keys (records) were in completely reverse order, the "bubble" (the lowest record) would work its way up the top of the list in successive passes, one record at at time. Upon completion of the sort, one additional pass is required where no exchange is made, to ensure that the records are in the proper order, as shown in Figure 2.34.

Pass 1. The first pair (06,21) are already in sequence, and are passed forward. The same is true of the second pair (21,29). However, the third pair (29,19) are in reverse sequence, are exchanged, and 19 is passed forward. The 02,29 pair are exchanged, and passed forward.

Pass 2. Exchange occurs on the 02,19 pair. Everything else is carried forward.

Pass 3. The 02,19 pair is exchanged.

Pass 4. The 02,06 pair is exchanged.

Pass 5. This is the checking phase.

Sorting by exchange is a technique that is relatively easy to program; it requires less primary storage than sorting by selection; and the time consumed is dependent upon the original ordering and the number of records to be sorted.

Sorting by Insertion

Sorting by insertion consists of determining where each record should be inserted in a sequence of records as each record is encountered and appropriately moving all other records to make room for it, as shown in Figure 2.35.

Step 1. The first record (06) is moved into the work area.

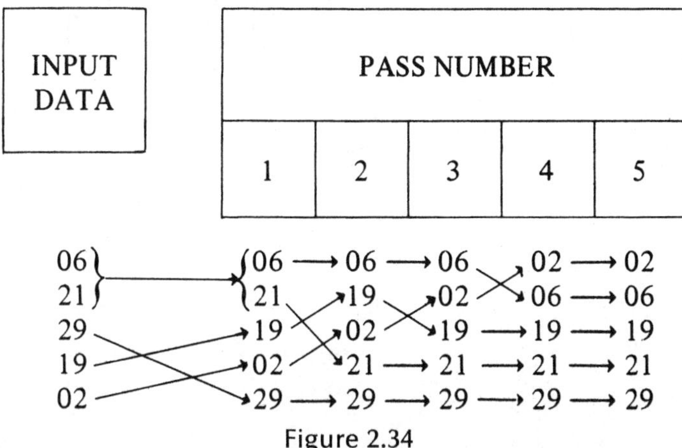

Figure 2.34

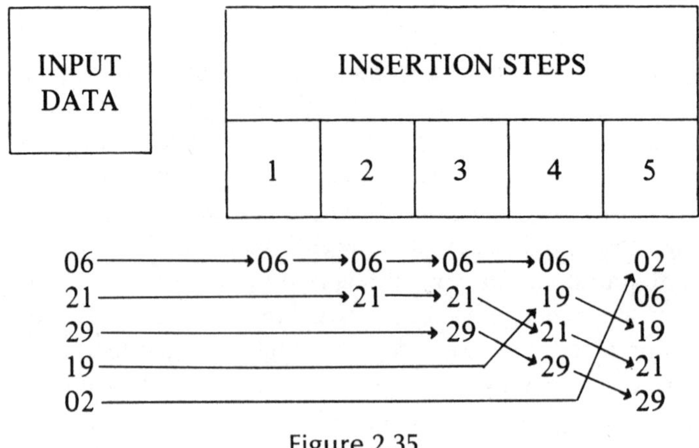

Figure 2.35

Step 2. The second record (21), being higher is transferred behind the first record.

Step 3. The same with record (29).

Step 4. Record (19) is inserted in its appropriate place, all records which follow are "pushed down."

Step 5. The same as with Step 4, but with record (02).

Sorting by insertion requires considerable search time to determine the correct location for each record that is encountered. It involves a large amount of record movement, since there are as many insertion steps required as there are records. It can be effectively utilized for sorting files with a small number of records.

Radix (Digit) Sorting

Radix or digit sorting consists of distributing all the records of a group of records among storage areas. Distribution is based on the position and value of the individual digits in the key or control field. For a decimal key, ten storage areas must be available for each pass. The first distribution (see Figure 2.36) is based on the key's unit position. Each key's unit position value is examined, and the record is placed in a correspondingly numbered storage area in appropriate sequence (e.g., zeros, ones, twos, etc.).

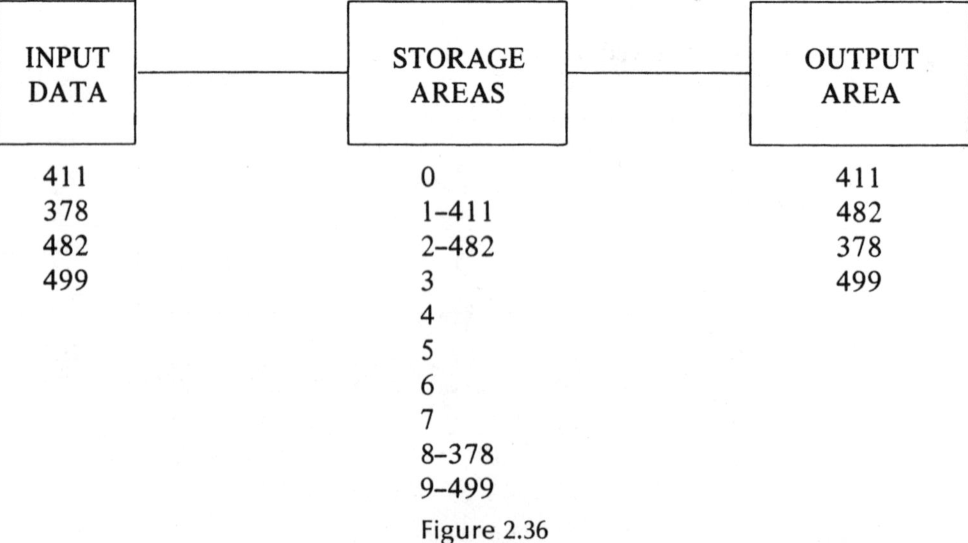

Figure 2.36

INPUT DATA	PASS NUMBER		
	1	2	3
411	411	411	278
378	482	378	411
482	378	482	482
499	499	499	499
	Sorted on Units Position	Sorted on Tens Position	Sorted on Hundreds Position

Figure 2.37

The second allocation is based on the ten positions, the third on the hundreds position, etc., until as many passes have been made as there are digits in the key. The basic principle of radix sorting is illustrated in Figure 2.37.

Radix sorting is most commonly used for sorting punched cards with punched card machines and is not recommended for use with random access storage.

Straight Merge Sorting

Straight merge sorting consists of sorting only a segment of records of a file on an individual pass, recording the results on an output device, sorting the next segment, recording the subsequent result on an alternate output device, etc., and then merging the output into larger strings. Merging is the process of combining two or more strings into one, generally in a specified sequence. The process is repeated until a single sorted string is obtained, as shown in Figure 2.38.

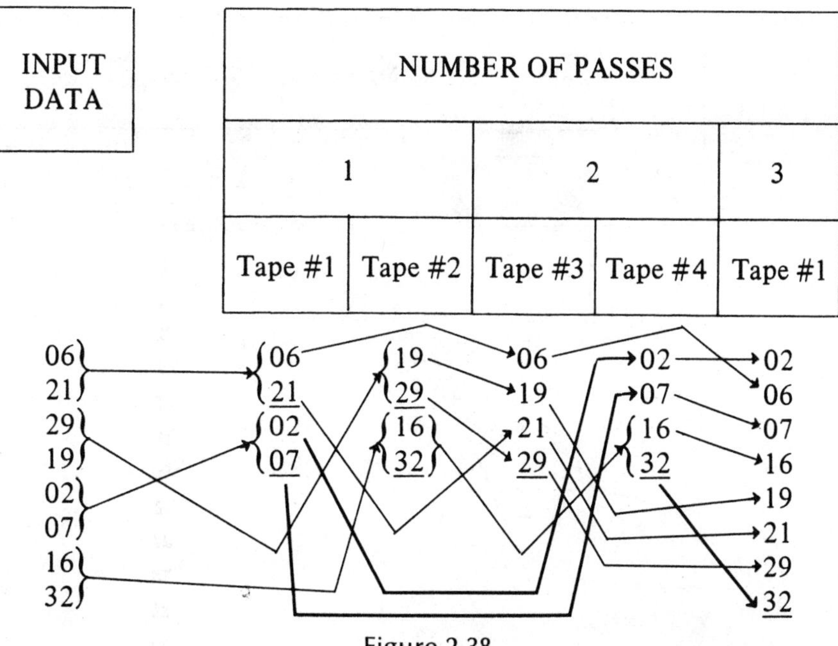

Figure 2.38

Pass 1. Pass 1 is a dispersal onto two tapes. Records 06 and 21, already in sequence, are placed on Tape #1. Records 29 and 19 are reversed and placed on Tape #2. Records 02 and 07 (in sequence within the pair) are added to the bottom of Tape #1, as are records 16 and 32 to the bottom of Tape #2.

Pass 2. This pass reads from both Tapes 1 and 2, dispersing to Tapes 3 and 4 a like amount ot data, with sequences properly merged. Record 06 moves from #1 to #3, followed by Record 19 from #2, and so on.

Pass 3. Once the strings are finally dispersed such that each tape's records are in sequence within themselves, then the entire file is written back to one tape, in this case Tape #1.

Straight merge sorting is extremely effective for sequential file systems. Key length, key range, original ordering, and record length have little effect upon its efficiency.

Probability Merge Sorting

Probability merge sorting and straight merge sorting are based upon the same concept. They differ, however, in the manner in which probability merge sorting takes advantage of the natural sequences of the data. Strings of sorted records are formed on alternate output devices, as with the straight merge sort, but so long as a record is found with a key larger than or equal to the key of the last record written, the string development continues. The procedure is illustrated in Figure 2.39.

Shell-Metzner Sort

The logic of the Shell-Metzner sort is that it divides the data into two equal parts and then begins exchanges of the first half against the second half, item for item. Where an exchange cannot be made, the top-half data item is merely carried forward, and the next top-half item is matched against the same bottom half item, and the exchange is made. The number of passes made is a function of the organization of the data at the time the sort is entered, the degree of exchange required, etc. Two examples are presented in Figure 2.40.

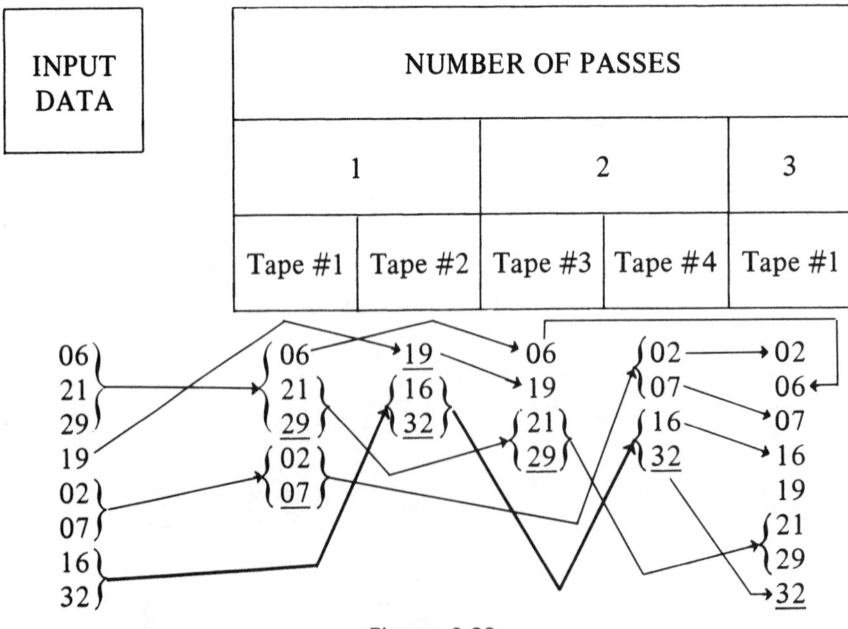

Figure 2.39

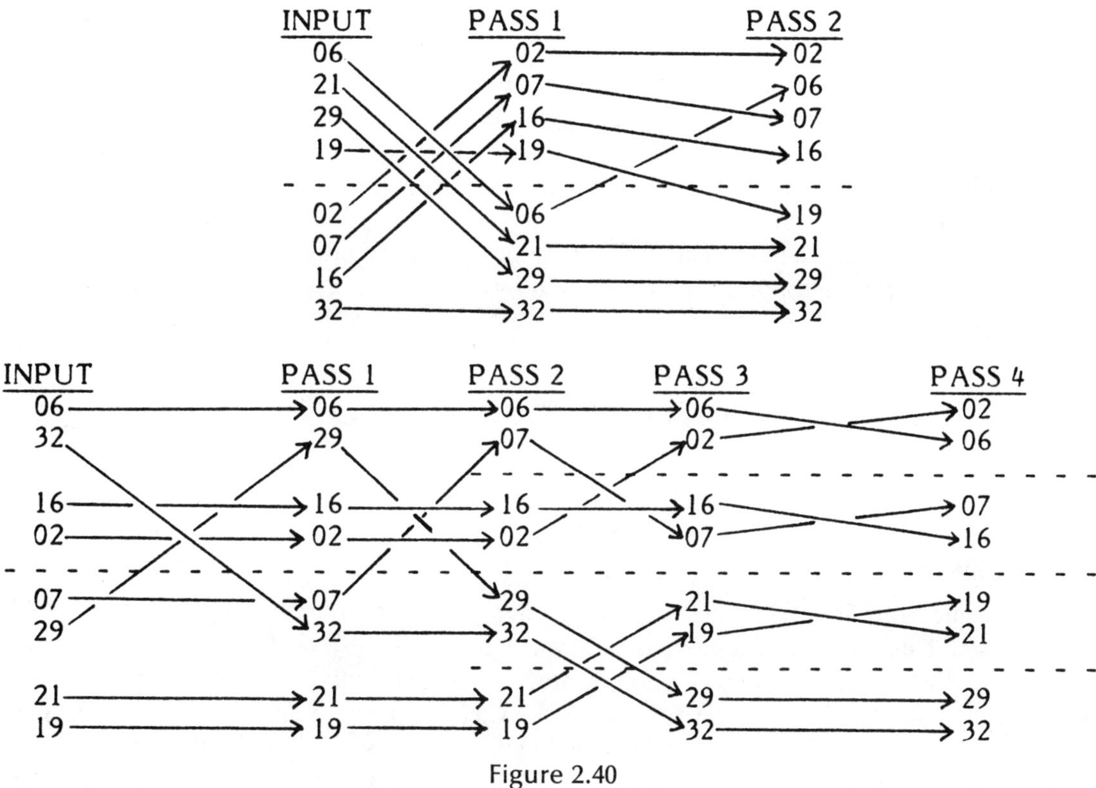

Figure 2.40

In the first illustration, the data are presented based on previous examples in the text, and two passes are required. In the second example, the input data is recorded, and the process now requires four passes. After the first pass (in this example) the system is divided into quarters, and the exchange is made between the quarters. The determinant of when to shift from semi-sections to quarter-sections is made when all top-half data are in the top half, and all bottom-half data are in the bottom half.

Tests on the Shell-Metzner Sort, done on a microcomputer, are startling. A thousand-number data set (generated randomly) took approximately 9.5 minutes to sort via the exchange method. Using the Shell-Metzner method, the same thousand numbers were sorted in approximately ten seconds.

Database Management Systems

Database management systems have been developed for applications which require separation of the logical data relationships from the physical data locations. Such an approach allows a programmer to define a logical record (called a *subschema*), a nonentity in physical form, without regard for the actual physical location of the data items. The physical location of the desired data items may be spread over several different physical storage devices. The software system gathers together, based on a previously defined logical database description or schema, the various physical records and data items necessary to provide the requested data items at run time. Infrequently used data items might be stored on relatively slow access devices, while frequently used data items will be stored on the faster devices. As mentioned in Chapter 1, there have been and there will continue to be advances in the use of computers as database machines.

The selection of a database management system is a management decision, sequence of access, ease of reporting, interface with other system components, etc. This edition adds a major section (Chapter 8) on the subject of database. See it for more detail.

Utility Programs

Utility programs are service routines that are frequently used by a programmer in the development or operation of a program. Examples are memory dump routines, print routines, card-to-tape (card-to-disk, tape-to-disk, disk-to-tape) mechanisms, sort routines, etc. Generally, utility programs fall into one of the following categories: load or restart enters the program to be executed into main memory and sets or resets pertinent registers. Housekeeping sets storage areas to predetermined values. File conversion transfers information from one medium to another. Testing aids assist the programmer in the testing of his program. Application aids are routines frequently used by the programmer in application programs, such as formatted report utilities.

PROGRAMMING LANGUAGES

General Computer Languages

Procedure Languages

There are many questions about the differences between a procedure-oriented language and a problem-oriented language. This book defines them as follows: A *procedure-oriented language* is a programming language defined for the convenient expression of procedures used in the solution of a wide class of problems. With the language, the user is able to define a set of operations to be executed in a specified sequence. A *problem-oriented language* is a programming language designed for the convenient expression of a given class of problems. Using a problem-oriented language, the user need only state the problem, not the steps of a solution.

COBOL remains the most widely used procedure-oriented language. It was developed and maintained by a committee of representatives of users, manufacturers, and universities initially called together by the Department of Defense. It has been implemented on virtually all large mainframes, most minicomputers, and several microcomputers. The original committee was called the Committee On Data Systems Languages (CODASYL), which now is part of the American National Standards Institute (ANSI). A more detailed discussion of COBOL is given later in the text.

RPG (Report Program Generator) is probably the most widely used problem-oriented language, in that RPG has been implemented as the prime language for some middle-scale computing systems. As you can tell by our prior discussion, RPG may well be losing its position to driver programming.

Interactive Languages

As time-sharing became popular back in the 1960s, it was necessary to develop special languages suited to work with time-sharing resources. Some of these are discussed here.

BASIC (Beginners All-Purpose Symbolic Instruction Code) is a language which was developed at Dartmouth College in 1965. As it was initially designed, it had about 17 commands, was simple to learn, and easy to translate. But as time went on, the BASIC language has been enhanced to the point where it is both an interactive time-sharing language and an interpretive language which has found extensive use in both minicomputers and microcomputers. BASIC simply isn't very basic anymore. BASIC has defied standardization, and because of that, some portability has been lost. The closest thing to standard has been ROM BASIC, developed by a firm called Microsoft, which has been used in several competing brands of microcomputers.

FORTRAN is a widely used interactive language in the scientific community. Generally, it has not been extensively used for business activities. QUICKTRAN, an on-line version of FORTRAN, has been with us for more than 20 years.

APL (A Programming Language), PL/1 (Programming Language / One), ALGOL (Algorithmic Language), JOVIAL (Jules' Own Version of An International Algebraic Language), C (from Bell Labs), and a host of others are also in use. Advocates of APL indicate that the language is gaining popularity. So say advocates of PASCAL, ADA, FORTH, etc. Time will tell. One thing for certain—the C language is definitely gaining ground.

Simulation Languages

SIMSCRIPT is a special purpose language developed by the Rand Corporation two decades ago for programming discrete simulation programs. SIMSCRIPT allows for the description of a system in terms of its entities, attributes, and sets. Attributes are properties associated with the entities, and sets are groups of entities. The language has been widely implemented and is operational on several computers.

GPSS (General-Purpose System Simulator) is a simulation language used for discrete models. The basic elements of GPSS models are transactions, blocks, and equipment. Transactions move from one block to another and blocks define physical processes which require equipment elements.

DYNAMO is a simulator language used for continuous, closed-loop information feedback systems. The six phases of a simulation are Input, Generation, Running, Printing, Plotting, and Rerun.

SPSS is a data analysis system designed to define, manipulate, manage, and present statistical data, with emphasis on frequency distribution and descriptive statistics, variable to variable relationships, correlation coefficients and scatterplots, multiple regression analysis, factor analysis, discriminant analysis, survival analysis, analysis of additive scales, nonparametric statistics, log-linear models, univariate and multivariate analysis of variance, and time series analysis.

Assembly Languages

There will always be an assembly language for each machine which operates on a machine language. The degree of exposure to the assembly language, however, will become limited to a select few, as the need to obtain more productivity from the system increases. As the cost of data processing personnel increases and the cost of computer hardware decreases, it becomes economically infeasible to develop and debug programs in assembly language. Even compilers are being developed in higher-level languages called systems programming languages. Some will, of course, dispute this point—but the fact is that programming positions call for a knowledge of the subject and the ability to translate that subject area into high-level code.

Graphics Languages

As we are able to develop our graphics processing capabilities, languages emerge to assist us. One of the better business graphics packages is the BPS Business Graphics package, installed on the Apple systems and on the IBM PC. Whereas a driver program, such as Lotus 1-2-3, would take spreadsheet data and present a picture, BPS Business Graphics have an entire graphics presentation language whereby entered data can be manipulated prior to presentation. Add plotters and graphics cameras, and you have some pretty potent graphics presentations.

Another graphics programming language which has found a great following is LOGO. The facility here is the turtle, and children of all ages can attest to the power and beauty of turtle graphics. As we find more useful and interesting ways to use the microcomputer, LOGO may provide a considerable facility.

List Processing Languages

List processing languages (also referred to as symbol manipulation languages) are designed to simplify the programming of applications which require storage allocation of both numeric and symbolic information. List processing is a method of processing data in the form of lists. Usually, chained lists are used so that the logical order of items can be changed without altering their physical locations. List processing languages make it possible for the user to build, copy, compare, scan, and modify lists. Four list processing languages have been around awhile. The last one, mentioned below, has been around since the advent of the minicomputer, but is finding favor with the microcomputer users.

IPL-V (Information Processing Language V) is a list processing language similar to an assembly language, designed and implemented at Carnegie Institute of Technology in 1957-1958. It's still in use there, but not widely used elsewhere.

LISP (List Processing) is a symbol manipulation and list processing language designed for use in applications requiring list processing, large amounts of recursion in operations, and symbol manipulation. Original work on the language was performed by the Artificial Intelligence Group of MIT in 1959, and its use has been general restricted to that activity. See comments on LOGO.

COMIT is a string-handling and pattern-matching language developed by MIT in 1957. It was designed to provide the professional linguist with the capability to write computer programs required in his research. It was the first language to provide for an effective technique of searching for a particular string of information and subsequently manipulating its symbols into another format.

SNOBOL is a programming language developed by Bell Telephone Laboratories in 1963 to facilitate handling strings of symbols on a computer. It's widely used in a limited segment of the scientific processing community today.

FORTH is a threaded-list system which is only today gaining any popularity among users. FORTH has five elements: dictionary, stack, interpreter, assembler, and virtual memory. It is its own operating system, and operates effectively through a series of push-down stacks (the parameter stack and the return stack). FORTH does not have a complete list of reserved words. There are about 100 standard words, but the command set is open ended, described by the programmer. FORTH is finding favor with those persons who are working on Artificial Intelligence (AI) systems, the so-called "Expert Systems."

Report Program Generator

The Report Program Generator (RPG) language was originally developed to meet the need for programs to produce reports from data files. Improvements and expansions in processing capabilities have resulted in a language which can be used to perform most data processing functions. The desired program is represented on five program coding specifications: control card and file description specifications; file extension specifications; input specifications; calculation specifications; and the output-format specifications. The RPG programming language was designed to facilitate preparation of computer programs by those individuals who wanted to concentrate more upon the problem to be treated by the computer than upon details of computer system operation or the specific procedure by which the problem was to be solved by the computer. Today, RPG is being widely used on the minicomputers and on some small mainframes. Its use on mainframes is sparse. It ias not used on microcomputers.

Inasmuch as the output of RPG programs is most frequently in the form of reports that present information concerning the status of data files, the language is called Report Program Generator. RPG can, however, be used for a variety of EDP applications that do not involve report production in the traditional sense of the term "report." Chief among these nonreport applications are those which update files stored on magnetic tape or disk or other nonpaper media.

FORTRAN

FORTRAN, of course, stands for FORmula TRANslation. The language is predominantly written for the scientific community. It is, however, taught to the majority of data processing students at one time or another. Since this text is aimed at the business data processor, FORTRAN is mentioned here solely for

```
      DIMENSION X(25),Y(25)
      DO 12I = 1,24
      IP 1 = I + 1
      DO 12J = IP 1,25
      IF (X(I) - X(J)) 12, 12, 13
13    TEMP - X(I)
      X(I) = X(J)
      X(J) = TEMP
      TEMP = Y(I)
      Y(I) = Y(J)
      Y(J) = TEMP
12    CONTINUE
```

Figure 2.41

expository reasons. The FORTRAN routine shown in Figure 2.41 is a bubble sort, similar to that discussed in the earlier section on sorting.

The IF statement compares the Ith element of the X array with the Jth element of the X array to determine sequence. Only if a "greater than" is encountered is there a switch, which involves moving the Ith element to TEMP, substituting the Jth element and placing TEMP back into the Jth element, for both array X and array Y.

C

As previously stated, the programming language C is gaining high marks for portability in the UNIX environment. Figure 2.42 is an example of C coding, an input routine.

```
/*      get an input string from a file
*/

#include "fileio.h"

fgets(line,maxline,fd)
unsigned char *line;
int maxline;
unsigned fd;
{
  int j,cc,k;
  struct bufstr *buf;

  buf=_checkfd(fd-=0x8000)      /* convert from stream to fd */
  for(j=0;j<maxline-1;){
    cc=read(fd,line+j,1);
    if(cc<1)break;
    if(line[j++]=='\n')break;
  }
  line[j]=0;
  if(j)return line; else return 0;
}
```

Figure 2.42

Pascal

The programming language Pascal was designed by Niklaus Wirth in 1968. He named it after the French mathematician Blaise Pascal (1623–1662).

Pascal was created to avoid many of the problems and pitfalls of the programming languages then in existence. Because it is a highly structured language, it lends itself well to modern programming techniques. Its simplicity and readability make it one of the best languages for tracing the concepts of programming and instilling good habits. After learning Pascal, you will find it easy to learn other languages, as the methods, techniques, and habits you learn with Pascal are applicable to other languages and to increasing your programming skill.

LOGO

LOGO was designed in Cambridge, MA in the late 1960s, as part of an experiment to test the idea that programming might be a useful educational discipline to teach children. Built upon the concepts of LISP, at first LOGO had no graphics. Later, graphics were incorporated into the language, in the form of "turtle graphics." It wasn't until this decade that computing power sufficient to perform LOGO with turtle graphics could be made available to schools at a reasonable cost.

Figure 2.43 is an example of a LOGO program:

```
TO START
HOME CS SPLITSCREEN
CURSOR 6 20 PRINT1 "X
CURSOR 20 20 PRINT1 "DISTANCE
CURSOR 6 21 PRINT 1 "Y
CURSOR 20 21 PRINT 1 "HEADING
SKETCH
END

TO SKETCH
MAKE "X XCOR
MAKE "Y YCOR
SETH 360 * (PADDLE 0 ) / 255
MAKE "D PADDLE 1
CURSOR 8 20
(PRINT1 ROUND :X "'    ' )
CURSOR 29 20
(PRINT1 ROUND :D "'    ' )
CURSOR 8 21
(PRINT1 ROUND HEADING "'    ' )
CURSOR 29 21
(PRINT1 ROUND HEADING "'    ' )
PC 6
FD :D
PU SETXY :X :Y PD
FD :D
PU SETXY :X :Y PD
IF PADDLEBUTTON 0 THEN PC 1 FD :D
SKETCH
END
```

Figure 2.43

Specialty Languages

Did you ever think you's encounter a computer command named SKUNK? If you're not a programmer for an IBM machine, have you encountered the Job Control Language (JCL)? Now's the time.

Dossier

Dossier is a scanner language for National Computer Systems' Optical Mark Reader. In simple terms, it's a test scoring machine, generally used as a source data conversion mechanism.

Figure 2.44 is a very brief Dossier program. The program is incomplete, and not very germane to most. It's presented simply as an example. You will probably not see it on the ICCP examinations.

```
        DOSSIER       BD,BEGIN,RECB,RECE,NAME
BEGIN   POCKET,S      A
        SKUNK,U       2,2,1,14,1,I,START
START   LIMIT         47,62
        BIAS          2
        NUMERIC,V     10,10,33,7,1,1,SPCDE
        ALPHA,V       27,14,13,20,1,1,NAME
        RESPONSE      1,=M,9,40,0,0
        ITEM,V        7,3,15,54,0,1,HS
        ARRAY,V       3,60,2,45,3,-1,1
        EDIT,V        14,NAME,ED.1
        FLAG,R        N,NAME
        EVALUATE,T    INVCT
```

Figure 2.44

Job Control Language

There is probably no IBM programmer, from the early S/360 up to the 8000 series, who hasn't cussed the Job Control Language (JCL). With the expansion of the plug compatible mainframes (PCM), the number of organizations using IBM-like equipment (Magnuson, Amdahl, NCS, Omega, and others) has grown. With a legal decision or two that these items may be offered with standard IBM software, suddenly the JCL is applicable to far more than just IBM-only programmers.

The standard text for JCL approaches two inches in thickness, so no attempt will be made here to include very much. The purpose of the JCL, of course, is to communicate with the operating system, to tailor the executive to meet the requirements of the job being processed, to initiate and control the processing of the job.

Figure 2.45 is an example of a two-step job procedure called CARDS.

```
//CARDS    PROC
//STEPA    EXEC    PGM=FIGURE
//DDA1     DD      DSNAME=NUMBERS,DISP=OLD
//DDA2     DD      DSNAME=PROCESS,DISP=(,PASS),
//                 UNIT=3350,SPACE=(TRK,(1,1,1))
//STEPB    EXEC    PGM=RESULT
//DDB1     DD      DSNAME=VSC,DISP=OLD
//DDB2     DD      DSNAME=*.STEPA.DDA2,
//                 DISP=(OLD,KEEP)
//DDB3     DD      SYSOUT=C
//         PEND
```

Figure 2.45

COBOL

During May 1959, a meeting of representatives from users in private industry, government installations, computer manufacturers, and other interested groups was called by the Department of Defense to consider the development of a common language of business electronic data processing applications. The group unanimously agreed that such a language was desirable and feasible.

Appropriate committees were formed to undertake the development project. By the end of 1959, the first version of the COBOL Language (COBOL-60) was prepared and distributed. By 1960, it was implemented on the UNIVAC-II and RCA 501 computers. COBOL-61 extended COBOL-60 with minor changes. COBOL-63 made major changes to COBOL-61, with the addition of such facilities as the Report Writer and a SORT verb. Arithmetic operation was improved. COBOL-65 extended the language, adding table handling facilities, and I/O capabilities for mass storage equipment. COBOL-65 would become the base standard for COBOL as approved by the American National Standards Institute (ANSI).

For nearly nine years, COBOL remained relatively static, though the CODASYL/ANSI committee continued work on the language. In the 1974 version, ten modules were defined: Nucleus, Table Handling, Sequential I/O, Indexed I/O, Sort/Merge, Segmentation, Report Writer, Telecommunications, Library, and Cluster-Program Communication.

A move was made to make radical changes to the language, in 1980–1981, and was defeated, primarily because the proposed changes were not upwardly compatible with COBOL-74. Work continues in ANSI to upgrade and update the capabilities of the language while protecting the very large user investment. The Defense Department, on the other hand, tried to introduce and standardize the programming language ADA. It hasn't happened yet.

COBOL Program Divisions

Using COBOL-74 as a basis of discussion, we find that COBOL consists still of four divisions: *identification, environment, data,* and *procedure.* Each division contains specification information and must be incorporated into the source program in the sequenced listed.

The *identification division* provides a standard method to identify the source program. It generally contains the name of the program, the identity of the programmer, the date the program was coded and compiled, the purpose of the program, and any other identifying information.

The *environment division* contains information about the type of computer to be utilized for both compiling and running the program (they need not be the same—but good luck if you try crossing vendors). It includes also the memory size, the type of input/output equipment, and the number of media stations to be included in the program. Specification of symbolic keys is made here for indexed files.

The *data division* describes the data files, records, and schema/subschema to be utilized, as well as other data to be processed or created during execution of the object program.

The *procedure division* contains the steps the user expects the computer to perform. The steps are expressed in terms of meaningful words, statements, sentences, paragraphs, and sections.

Character Set

The COBOL character set consists of 51 characters. These include the 26 uppercase letters, 10 digits, the hyphen (-), and 14 special characters (+ * = $ / , . ; ( ) " < > blank), which are generally used for punctuation, editing, arithmetic functions, etc.

Names

Names or words in COBOL are composed of a combination of not more than 30 characters chosen from the letters, digits, and hyphen. Names may not begin or end with a hyphen and are ended by a space, by a period, by a right parenthesis, or by a comma and a space.

- A *data name* is a user-created word containing at least one alphabetic character. It is used to name a data item in the program.
- A *procedure name* is used to name a paragraph or section of purposes of referencing a specific procedure or set of procedures. A procedure name consisting of all numbers is allowed.
- A *condition name* is assigned to a specific value or range of values that a data name may assume.
- A *literal* is a data item which has a value identical to the characters of which the item is composed. The value remains constant during program execution.
- A *figurative constant* is a value that has been assigned a fixed data name (e.g., ZERO represents the value of 0).
- A *reserved name* is a word of the COBOL language that should never be used by a programmer except when they are designated for use by a specific COBOL format.

Verbs

The steps that the user desires the computer to perform in the solution of a particular problem are contained in the procedure division. The steps are expressed in sentence forms which are constructed according to specific formats and utilize various COBOL verbs. The verbs denote a specific action to be taken, such as ADD, PERFORM, and STOP. Figure 2.46 is a list of typical COBOL verbs.

Expressions

Arithmetic statements in COBOL may be expressed with symbols (called arithmetic operators), data names, numeric literals, or a mixture of symbols and words. Arithmetic operators used in forming expressions are given in Figure 2.47 together with their functions.

The COBOL compiler evaluates arithmetic expressions left to right in the following sequence: exponentiation; multiplication and division; addition and subtraction. Parentheses specify the order of computation, beginning with the innermost set and proceeding to the outermost set.

Figure 2.48 shows two different ways to write the same arithmetic expression.

Conditional expressions in COBOL allow the user to perform tests to determine where the program should go or what it should do, depending upon the result of the condition tested. A number of relational operators are provided in COBOL to allow the user to perform the tests by combining operators with data names, literations, etc., to create conditional expressions. Examples of the relational operators are: GREATER; EQUAL TO; and LESS. An example of a simple conditional statement is given in Figure 2.49.

```
ADD         COPY        GENERATE    PERFORM
ALTER       DISPLAY     GO TO       READ
CALL        DIVIDE      HOLD        SEEK
CANCEL      ENTER       MOVE        SORT
CLOSE       EXAMINE     MULTIPLY    USE
COMPUTE     EXIT        OPEN        WRITE
```

Figure 2.46

OPERATOR	FUNCTION
+	Add
-	Subtract
*	Multiply
/	Divide
**	Exponentiation

Figure 2.47

```
ADD  A,B GIVING C
COMPUTE C = A + B
```

Figure 2.48

```
IF SALES IS GREATER THAN 600 GO TO START-1
```

Figure 2.49

Simple conditional expressions can be combined with the logical operators to form compound conditions (the logical operators are AND, OR, and NOT). IF SALES IS GREATER THAN 600 AND CUSTOMERS NOT GREATER THAN 50 GO TO START-1 is an example of such expression.

Statements.

Imperative statements in COBOL begin with an imperative COBOL verb and specify an unconditional action to be taken. For example, MOVE SUM TO TOTAL.

A compiler-directing statement causes the COBOL compiler to take a specific action during the compilation process (e.g., STOP).

Structured COBOL Sample

Figure 2.50 is an extraction from an inventory transaction processing routine, written in structured COBOL. This extraction is the mainline processing routine.

COBOL Structured Programming Conventions

Recall that the three constructs are sequence, iteration, and selection. The iteration structure can also be referred to as the DO-WHILE, DO-UNTIL, or PERFORM-UNTIL structure. The selection structure can be referred to as the IF-THEN-ELSE structure. In COBOL, any nonconditional, nonbranching statement is a sequence structure. Similarly, a succession of two or more of these statements is also a sequence structure. Thus, a series of MOVE statements is a sequence structure; a series of arithmetic statements *without* ON SIZE ERROR options is a sequence structure.

The elements of COBOL Structured programming include:

- The sequence of coded modules
- Vertical formatting of the source listing
- Meaningful Data Division names

```
000-EDIT-INVENTORY-TRANS.
    OPEN INPUT  PARTNUMS
                INVTRANS
         OUTPUT ITRANLST.
    MOVE CURRENT-DATE TO HDG1-DATE
                         TOT1-DATE.
    PERFORM 100-LOAD-PART-NUMBER-TABLE
         VARYING PN-TABLE-INDEX FROM 1 BY 1
         UNTIL PART-NUMBER-EOF.
    PERFORM 200-EDIT-INVENTORY-TRAN
         UNTIL TRAN-EOF.
    PERFORM 300-PRINT-TOTAL-PAGE.
    CLOSE PARTNUMS
          INVTRANS
          ITRANLST.
    STOP RUN.
```

Figure 2.50

- Appropriate indentation to show structure of data items
- Grouping data items according to type and use
- Condition names which increase the clarity of the program
- Sequencing of Data Division items to effect ease of location
- A single (and only one) STOP RUN statement
- Section names should not be used, if possible
- Indentation of procedural statements to effect understanding
- Use, where possible, of compound conditions if the problem statement calls for them
- Use of the case structure wherever possible
- Use of the internal sort feature
- Use of declaratives

BASIC

BASIC has developed into a significant language for business use. It has been installed on virtually every microcomputer, and retrofitted into many mainframe and minicomputers. Some of the implementations of BASIC vary. For example, the Basic-4 minicomputer specifies a channel for PRINT instructions, and whether or not the output goes to a screen (terminal) or to the paper printer, the channel specification makes the difference. This problem is solved in Microsoft BASIC with the PRINT and LPRINT instructions. The former can be changed dynamically; the latter cannot, so the defacto standard isn't necessarily the most flexible.

However, implementations of the microcomputer BASIC vary, even though they are similar in nature. CP/M systems, for example, use MBASIC, otherwise known as BASIC-80. MS-DOS systems use BASIC, BASICA, and GWBASIC. The first is a ROM BASIC. The second adds graphic capabilities. And the third—"Gee-Whiz BASIC"—simultaneously pats its head and rubs its tummy.

There is still no "national standard" for BASIC, though BASIC developers Kemeny and Kurtz have attempted to get their Standard BASIC (Real BASIC) accepted at ANSI. There is, however, a move to Structured BASIC, using many of the same concepts of Structured COBOL, just discussed. While there is no standard BASIC, the more or less standard implementation of Microsoft BASIC may prove to be the de facto standard.

```
100 REM ****************************
110 REM * THE ARRAY MUST BE LOADED *
120 REM * FROM DISK OR KEYBOARD TO *
130 REM * PREPARE FOR THIS ROUTINE *
140 REM ****************************
150 M = LAST
160 M = INT(M/2)
170 IF M = 0 THEN 430
180 J = 1
190 K = LAST - M
200 I = J
210 L = I + M
220 IF A$(I) < = A$(L) THEN 360
230 PRINT
240 PRINT I,L,M,K
250 REM ****************************
260 REM * T$ IS A TEMPORARY HOLD   *
270 REM * AREA.  OTHER VARIABLES   *
280 REM * ARE EXPLAINED IN TEXT.   *
290 REM ****************************
300 T$ = A$(I)
310 A$(I) = A$(L)
320 A$(L) = T$
330 I = I - M
340 IF I < 1 THEN 360
350 GOTO 210
360 J = J + 1
370 IF J > K THEN 160
380 GOTO 200
390 REM ****************************
400 REM * THE ARRAY IS NOW SORTED  *
410 REM * AND IS READY TO BE USED. *
420 REM ****************************
430 REM INSTRUCTIONS BEGIN HERE
```

Figure 2.51

Sample BASIC Program

To serve as a basis of discussion of the BASIC system, Figure 2.51 is a BASIC program which will perform a Shell-Metzner sort.

Sequence Number

Every BASIC statement is sequence-number controlled, generally in increments of ten, although other options are available. The sequence number is strictly numeric. Instructions may be entered randomly and will appear in the proper location. Renumbering software is available should more than 10 instructions be inserted between instructions. On some systems there is an AUTO command to the keyboard editor. This AUTO command will allow you to specify a beginning number and the amount of the increment. On others, it is a function of a control key. On still others, it must be entered manually.

As previously mentioned, the majority of the microcomputers use and interpretive compiler, one which compiles the source code immediately before the code is executed. Thus, the program is retained in source format. The source statement sequence numbers, then, are key to the BASIC program, since they are the labels (tags) of the instruction and the object of a sequence control instruction and of a variety of other functions, including the equivalent of the COBOL PERFORM (GOSUB), the COBOL GO TO . . . DEPENDING ON (ON *n* GOTO . . .), the FORTRAN DO instruction (FOR), and the PL/1 NEXT instruction, etc.

The LET Instruction

The majority of the non-input/output functions of a BASIC program can be obtained with a form of the LET instruction. The LET performs the data transfer, initializes counters, and performs arithmetic. For instance:

LET N = A is a data transfer instruction;

LET N = 1 is a counter initialization;

LET N = N + 1 is an arithmetic expression (increments the counter).

Two variations of LET are important. First, LET is a default instruction. Therefore, N = N + 1 is a legitimate instruction. Also, there are no spacing requirements, as in COBOL: N=N+1 works just as well.

Data Classification

BASIC compilers deal with both numeric and alphabetic information. There are several methods to identify numeric data, while the use of the dollar sign ($) seems to be the standard way to identify alphabetic data, more commonly the string data. The types are shown in Figure 2.52.

Length Characteristics

Length is a function of data representation. In most BASIC compilers, numeric data are stored binarily, and the number of characters (bytes, words, or cells) is a function of the size required to express the number binarily, up to the maximum allowed by the design of the computer. Alphabetic characters take the single storage unit (byte, word, or cell) for representation. Length becomes a problem only when transfer from one mode to another is attempted. For instance A = A$ is a type mismatch, and is therefore invalid. If this transfer is necessary, the accepted statement would be A = VAL(A$).

Variable Type	Declaration Character	Examples
Integer (whole number)	%	A%,B9%
Single Precision (6 significant digits)	!	A!,BB!,Z5!
Double Precision (16 significant digits)	#	A#,ZZ#
Double Precision with scientific notation	D	"A#=1.234D+12"
String (up to 255 characters)	$	A$,GT$,H1$
Array (3 dimensional string)	A$(X,Y,Z)	
Array (2 dimensional single precision)	A!(I,J)	or A(I,J)
Array (1 dimensional double precision)	G#(I)	

Figure 2.52

```
IF INT(N/2) = N/2 THEN 20
```

Figure 2.53

Comparison Operations

Comparison operations in BASIC do not differ significantly from COBOL in that they are IF. . .THEN relationships. IF N = 5 THEN 50 is a valid instruction. In this case a counter is tested for a value (5) and when it is found, a branch to statement 50 is effected.

The expression may be a more complex one, as in Figure 2.53. This is a means to determine if the number is a whole number (no remainder). INT means INTeger. Seen another way, this statement could determine if the number is odd or even.

Data Size Definition

In addition to the definition of class (alphabetic or numeric) and length characteristics mentioned, larger units of data or memory can be reserved by means of a CLEAR statement or DIMENSION statement. The former opens up string space. The latter defines an allocation of memory. Thus DIM A(5,5) would produce a two-dimensional 5 × 5 allocation of memory. Some compilers are limited to two-dimensional arrays. The majority allow three dimensions and allow the DIMENSION statement to dimension several arrays. For example, Figure 2.54 would be legal.

```
DIMENSION A$(5,5,5), B(5,5), C(5)
```

Figure 2.54

The dimensioned area of memory may be used linearly, as with a buffer operation, or accessed by any number of subscripting or matrix operations. Using a triple dimension statement as shown in Figure 2.55 would allow the operation MAT A = B + C to add the corresponding positions of matrices B and C and place the sums in the corresponding positions of A, sort a superpowerful LET. Similar operations can be performed with input/output and other arithmetic operations.

```
DIMENSION A(5,5), B(5,5), C(5,5)
```

Figure 2.55

Input/Output Operations

Methods of allocating input/output devices in BASIC vary from manufacturer to manufacturer and even from compiler to compiler. In some, they are a function of a SELECT statement which will identify a device assignment and perhaps even identify the size of the buffer, e.g., SELECT PRINT 215(132) from the BASIC Four Computer. In others, the designation may be the channel to which the device is assigned: e.g., PRINT (7) from the WANG 2200. In yet others, the device has a fixed channel. PRINT in Microsoft BASIC targets the object to the video screen, while LPRINT will target it to a line printer. The same is true for other devices. On some machines, simple reassignment of the channel will target the output to another device, such as a diskette.

Since the majority of small business systems now have some form of visual display (CRT), some input/output operations default to the keyboard associated with that CRT (input) and the CRT itself (output). Thus, the INPUT or INKEY$ statements would expect a response by the keyboard operator upon the keyboard. The input statements, however, also function as an output operation, pending receipt of the input, as shown in Figure 2.56.

```
INPUT "ENTER PRINCIPAL"' P
```

Figure 2.56

This INPUT statement would display the message "ENTER PRINCIPAL" on the CRT and the operation would stop pending the entry of a number which is then stored in the numeric variable P.

For one-character responses, the INKEY$ function is used. When using the INPUT statement, the appropriate entry must be made, followed by the use of a carriage return or ENTER key. The INKEY$ function bypasses the ENTER key, but allows only a single character response.

```
100   PRINT "DO YOU WISH TO RUN THE PROGRAM AGAIN (Y/N)?"
110   Z$ = INKEY$
120   IF Z$ = "Y" THEN 10:  REM 10 IS BEGINNING OF PROGRAM
130   IF Z$ = "N" THEN 1000:  REM 1000 IS END OF PROGRAM
140   GOTO 110
```

Figure 2.57

In Figure 2.57 a Yes/No question has been posed. A "Y" response provides a definite direction, as does a "N" response. If neither is pressed on the keyboard, if something else has been pressed, or if nothing is pressed, the program will function in a 110–120–130–140–110 loop.

Iteration

The BASIC equivalent of the COBOL PERFORM . . . VARYING is the FOR . . . NEXT loop. Under the system, the FOR establishes the range of the loop, while the NEXT causes the reiteration. The coding which comprises the routine is inserted between. Further, FOR . . . NEXT loops can be nested. The best example of this is the electronic clock BASIC program contained earlier in this chapter.

Keywords, Compiler Functions, and Operator Controls

Words such as INPUT, INKEY$, PRINT, FOR, NEXT, etc. are BASIC keywords. On some systems, it is possible to enter the keywords as a function of entering a single key. On all systems, the keywords can be spelled out, of course. But the entry of what is called a token does shorten the programming effort. Single entry keywords are available for most small business systems either as a form of hardware design (such as the WANG 2200) or a function of keyboard interception (such as the Z-80).

Documentation is a function of the compiler, by inclusion of a remarks statement (REM). Generally, these are notes about the program's function and do occupy space in memory. Occasionally, restrictive memory considerations require the removal of REMarks statements and the compaction of spaces. Utilities exist for this function.

Other compiler functions include STOP statements and CONTinue commands. These vary among systems. Other statements permit halting and stepping of the program, but these, too, are not available on all systems. Trace routines (TRON and TROFF) assist the programmer by displaying the statement number on the screen. There is now no means to direct the trace to the printer or to a data file.

Operator controls are also available for the mechanical operation, interaction with system software for program storage, reallocation of devices, calling of modules, etc.

Sequence Control

Like any other language, BASIC has an unconditional branch. It is the GOTO. Thus, GOTO 250 will cause sequence to proceed to statement 250.

BASIC also has the equivalent to the COBOL GO TO . . . DEPENDING ON . . . It is known as the ON . . . GOTO . . . . The two routines of Figure 2.58 are equivalent:

```
Routine #1   IF A = 1 THEN 400
             IF A = 2 THEN 500
             IF A = 3 THEN 600
             IF A = 4 THEN 700

Routine #2   ON A GOTO 400, 500, 600, 700
```

Figure 2.58

Conversions and Notation

All BASIC compilers have data conversion and/or separation capabilities. Binary can be converted to decimal and vice-versa; string variables which contain numbers can be converted to numeric variables, and vice-versa. Signs can be added, deleted, changed. Intrinsic functions of SINE, COSINE, TANGENT, SQUARE ROOT, RaNDom numbers, etc., are included, as are INTeger statements, exponentiation, absolute value, separation of mantissa and exponents (E-Notation), etc.

Subroutines

BASIC has the ability to execute routines, as do other languages. Its function is similar to the PERFORM in COBOL and the BAL/br combination in IBM Assembler. In BASIC, it takes the form GOSUB and RETURN. Figure 2.59 would be a valid linkage. Of course, all the usual conventions of not leaving control of the subroutine via GOTO statements and the possibility of alternate returns apply.

Other Console Capabilities

One of the nice things about BASIC is that a statement is replaced simply by repeating the appropriate statement number. Since the compiler is interpretive in nature, the statement is simply replaced. It may be replaced in the same memory allocation as the former statement (assuming equal or smaller length), or it may receive a new memory allocation, which requires appropriate linkage in RAM.

EDITing of statements is done from the console. By and large there are edit functions to do searching, replacing position to specific characters, move to the end of the line, change from and to, etc.

BASIC Summary

We're beginning to see some reference to BASIC, as I predicted in the last edition. This is not surprising in view of the proliferation of BASIC-based systems since the last edition was published.

It has not been the intention here to teach BASIC, but rather to demonstrate the capabilities and form of the language. BASIC compilers differ among manufacturers, but there is a possibility that with the proliferation of microcomputer BASIC a standard may be in the offing.

```
10 GOSUB 1000      1000 LET...
20 LET...          1010 INPUT...
                   2000 RETURN
```

Figure 2.59

QUESTIONS

Note: there is no guarantee that every question presented here has been covered in the text.

1. Three classes of software are:
   A. Application, system, and functional
   B. Application, driver, and system
   C. System, compiler, and language
   D. System, translator, and utility
2. A subscript is defined
   A. When the descriptor is valid under execution
   B. Only if the specification is valid
   C. Under execution, whereas indices are not
   D. After the horizontal redundancy check has been defined
3. A closed subroutine may be defined as:
   A. A self-contained section to which the mainline routine refers
   B. A routine located within the mainline routine
   C. A routine for input and output only
   D. A routine for controlling calculations only
4. A file consists of 2,500 records. It takes 500 milliseconds to effect the input and the output on this file when updating *for each record,* plus between 100 and 200 millisecond per record to perform the updating, and 100 milliseconds to print a proof copy of the record. Assuming normal I/O binding, what would be the processing time for this file?
   A. 2,500 milliseconds
   B. 500 minutes
   C. 3 minutes
   D. (100 − 200 * 2,500)
5. You have decided to create a subroutine library. The reason you are doing this will most probably be:
   A. Programmers are not creative enough to write the necessary routines
   B. Management has mandated that all coding shall be structured
   C. It compresses the programming time for commonly used functions
   D. Macros will shorten the compile time for the program
6. The process of creating a file of records which has a defined interdependency of one record onto another by means of chains and pointers produces what kind of database?
   A. Random
   B. Indexed sequential
   C. Relative
   D. Relational
7. What are the two major phases of an instruction execution cycle?
   A. Fetch and store
   B. Fetch and mix data
   C. Fetch and execution
   D. Fetch and rotate
8. When using a reusable subroutine, the policy on modification of that subroutine should be:
   A. It is not necessary to restore variable values
   B. The subroutine should be restored by the housekeeping routines
   C. Reusable subroutines should not be modified
   D. Restore the initial values at the end of the routine

9. Which of the following programming techniques would be most appropriate in trying to match a sequential transaction record with a sequential master record?
   A. Indexing
   B. Looping
   C. Immediate addressing
   D. Formatting

10. Is is possible to transform data to program through a compiler?
   A. Data cannot become program
   B. A machine-code program can be reduced to source code
   C. Data are never a part of the program itself
   D. Data are never transient

11. An open subroutine may be described as:
   A. A subroutine inserted in the mainline routine and without any need of a return
   B. A self-contained routine referred to the mainline routine
   C. A complete program
   D. A routine for input and output only

12. The only valid reason for modifying an instruction is:
   A. To assist in the debugging
   B. To minimize execution
   C. To complicate the subroutines
   D. Tɔ diminish the memory occupied by the program.

13. An indirect address is:
   A. The number that specifies the difference between the absolute address and the base address
   B. The resulting information of an address modification process
   C. An address that specifies a storage location that contains either a direct address of another indirect address
   D. The address stored only in ROM

14. In a COBOL DO-WHILE structure, the initialization is established by:
   A. Routines at the beginning of the loop
   B. Incorporating those routines into the loop
   C. Placing those routines outside of the loop
   D. The DO-WHILE structure itself

15. When programming a CALL statement in COBOL:
   A. All coding is the responsibility of the programmer
   B. All parameter passing is controlled by the called routine
   C. All parameter passing may be done through WORKING STORAGE, the FILE SECTION, the COMMUNICATIONS SECTION, or the LINKAGE SECTION
   D. No parameters may be passed

16. A program should be tested in this manner:
   A. From its inception, because of the risk of error
   B. By the user only, as s/he is certain to know of any errors.
   C. Hardly ever, because modern high-level languages are error-free.
   D. By the programmer to check for technical errors; by the analyst to check for design errors, and by the user to check for subject errors.

17. When writing in assembler language which permits the use of a mantissa, the language is most probably one which:
   A. Has been implemented in a business-oriented language
   B. Has been implemented on a floating-point environment

C. Has been implemented on a machine with E-notation
D. Has been implemented on a bit-discriminating minicomputer

18. Evaluate—programming should be done in pseudocode because:
A. Pseudocode can be processed by a translator
B. Pseudocode defines the intellectual processes
C. Pseudocode is more efficient that machine code
D. Pseudocode may be written in any language

19. A loop is a:
A. Special addressing technique
B. Basic computer instruction
C. Sequence of instructions executed a predetermined number of times
D. Special purpose index register

20. Program module tests should be conducted:
A. On contrived data
B. On live files
C. On prior-used files
D. On representative samples of contrived and live data

21. Magnetic drums are often used for auxiliary storage. Which of the following would NOT be true?
A. Paging techniques may be used
B. Fast transfer rates are required
C. Cost per character of storage is very low
D. Virtual memory concepts may not be utilized

22. The purpose of a checkpoint is:
A. To magnetize demand deposit agreements
B. To transmit asynchronous data
C. To provide a restart point
D. To verify the balances in a system

23. Given the following COBOL record description, what is the size of the record?

```
01    INVENTORY-RECORD.
      02    NAME                PIC IS X(30).
      02    CLASSIFICATION.
            03 CODE-A           PIC IS 9(2) COMP-1.
            03 CODE-B           PIC IS 9(2) COMP-1.
            03 CODE-C           PIC IS 9(2) COMP-1.
            03 FILLER           PIC IS XXX.
      02    TYPE-CODE REDEFINES CLASSIFICATION.
            03 CODE-D           PIC IS 9(2) COMP-3.
            03 CODE-E           PIC IS 9(2) COMP-3.
            03 CODE-F           PIC IS 9(2) COMP-3.
      02    BIN-LOCATION        PIC IS X(8).
```

A. 36 bytes
B. 40 bytes
C. 44 bytes
D. 62 bytes

24. In a database involving the inverted structure, it is necessary to do which of the following in order to use it?
A. Read the file sequentially

B. Build a ring structure
C. Create a sequence of unsorted keys
D. Reorganize the file into every desirable sequence

25. The product of the process whereby a symbolic program is translated is called a(n):
A. Object program
B. Source program
C. Relocatable module
D. Reiterative module

26. Which of the following occurs during a restart?
A. The program returns to the last checkpoint
B. All files are returned to their origins
C. The contents of main storage are ''frozen''
D. Terminals on the line are notified that restart is in progress

27. The calling sequence in any programming language refers to the sequence of events necessary to:
A. Tailor the called module
B. Build a parameter execution
C. Invoke a utility program
D. Modify the calling module

28. In communications-based system, the programmer must concern himself with which of the following:
A. The polling scheme on a multi-drop line
B. The shift from baud to bit
C. Programming the multiplexor
D. The transaction handling mechanisms

29. When a move instruction has been executed,
A. The source and the target fields are different
B. The source and the target fields are identical
C. The source field is blank and the target field is not
D. The source field is not blank, but the target field is

30. In a two-address system, it is necessary to:
A. Store the length in a third address
B. Perform the translation of the operation code
C. Identify source and target address in the same format
D. Ensure that the data at the source address is smaller than the size of the target field.

31. In a 64K RAM memory, the number of bytes available is:
A. 65,535
B. 64,000
C. 6,400
D. 2 Kilos

32. The two major parts of a decision table (to the left of the vertical double lines are the:
A. Condition stub and identification rules
B. Condition stub and action stub
C. Table identification and action stub
D. Indirect table specification

33. A bubble sort is:
A. The same as a key field sort
B. Faster than a partition sort

C. An algorithm for sorting elements of a file
D. An algorithm particularly useful in sorting large files

34. Which of the following is not important when estimating program run times?
A. Size and organization of file and the programming language used
B. The number of closed subroutines included
C. The size of the object module
D. The number of registers used

35. To calculate parity, you:
A. Add the number of bits—the 0s and the 1s—in a 7-bit ASCII character as decimal numbers
B. Add the value of the 7-bit ASCII character as binary numbers
C. Add the number of bits in a 7-bit ASCII character and square the sum
D. Don't—parity doesn't apply to ASCII characters

36. With all sorting methods there is one specification that will influence the sorting speed. It is:
A. The number of tape units
B. Characteristics of the sort key
C. Internal speed of the computer
D. Speed of the disk units

37. Spooling permits you to:
A. Dump a screen display to disk
B. Print a file while working on another
C. Apply recursive techniques to the modem
D. Integrate a database program

38. Higher-level language programs are translated to machine language by a(n):
A. Interpreter
B. Simulator
C. Assembler
D. Compiler

39. A serial port is to a parallel port as
A. 1 byte is to 1 bit
B. 1 parity bit is to 1 stop bit
C. 8 bits are to 1 byte
D. 1 bit is to 1 byte.

40. The rationale behind a data extractor is:
A. Standardization, but permitting no modification
B. Standardization with variable parameter input
C. Processing of nonstandard labels
D. Operating systems lack capability

41. What are ASCII and EBCDIC?
A. Chip manufacturers
B. Signals that means "ready to send" and "ready to receive"
C. Code systems that represent data characters
D. Pulse trains

42. In programming CRT applications, the programmer must concern himself with:
A. The light intensity of the tube
B. The color scheme used on the tube
C. Control of the cursor
D. Parameterization of input data

43. Which term DOESN'T belong in this list?
A. GET
B. PUT
C. SUM
D. DIM

44. A checkpoint is utilized in:
A. Run time estimating
B. Queue timing estimates
C. Restarting a program
D. Loop controls

45. A cross-assembler is:
A. A utility that notes where variables are used throughout a program.
B. A program that runs on one processor and generates machine language code for another
C. A program that links modules of assembly language code and generate appropriate microprocessor-specific subroutines.
D. A utility that translates assembly language programs into BASIC.

46. Blocking does NOT:
A. Increase the efficiency of I/O operations
B. Increase the efficiency of storage medium utilization
C. Reduce the amount of main memory required
D. Reduce the number of IRGs required

47. What's the difference between nested and recursive subroutines?
A. Nested subroutines are static; recursive subroutines are altered by others
B. Nested means one within another; recursive subroutines call themselves
C. Nested subroutines are restricted to FOR loops
D. Nested subroutines are illegal in BASIC

48. Truncation errors are usually caused by:
A. Failures in circuit-checking routines
B. Failure to execute wrap-around-carry instructions
C. Using only the least significant digits
D. Incorrectly sized target fields in move instructions

49. An asynchronous computer will execute instructions:
A. At fixed time intervals
B. Whenever the channels are in device-ready status
C. One after another, not at fixed intervals
D. By changing to synchronous mode

50. The two types of auxiliary memory devices are:
A. Sequential access and direct access
B. Sequential access and serial access
C. Main memory and direct access
D. ROM and RAM

51. An open subroutine
A. Is a subprogram completely outside the problem program
B. Is a recursive subroutine within the mainline
C. Is reentrant and requires housekeeping routines
D. Is placed in the main line wherever required

52. Which of the following would be most successful in detecting errors resulting from transposition
A. An inventory code system which incorporates a check digit

B. A disk library system which uses removable external labels and standard internal labels
C. A tape library system which uses volume serial number for identification, storage, retrieval, and release activities
D. A tape library system which shows a high number of errors of omission

53. A closed subroutine
A. Is in the problem program once and branched to whenever necessary
B. Is a recursive subroutine within the mainline
C. Is reentrant and never requires housekeeping routines.
D. Is placed in the mainline whenever necessary

54. The unique portion of data record is known as the:
A. Label field
B. Key field
C. Reference field
D. Constant field

55. A recursive subroutine basically uses which data structure?
A. Chained data method
B. Stacking method
C. Queuing method
D. Sequential processing

56. The translator of an assembly language program is called a(n):
A. Assembler
B. Compiler
C. Generator
D. Translator

57. If Matrix R is the size of U * V, Matrix S is the size of V * W, and Matrix T is the size of W * Y, multiplying Matrix R by Matrix S will yield a Matrix Z whose size will be:
A. V + W
B. U + V + W
C. U * W
D. V * W

58. Which of the following is not an advantage of using COBOL condition names?
A. The meanings of the different values of a condition variable can be established independently of the procedure division
B. The amount of coding in the procedure division is reduced
C. The relational operators can be eliminated from the procedure division
D. The PERFORM structure can be simplified

59. Increasing the data recording capacity of a magnetic tape can be accomplished by:
A. Shortening the interrecord gaps
B. Using thinner and wider tape
C. Using higher density per square inch
D. Using bondage tape

60. A routine which is reenterable and serially reusable would be used:
A. When memory is limited and the subprogram is needed by several different tasks
B. When fast turnaround is required and housekeeping can be ignored
C. In a standalone dump program
D. When the target computer is not the same as the source computer

61. A magnetic tape is to be written with 3/4'' interrecord gaps and logical records of 100 characters at a recording density of 1600 bpi. What is the blocking factor which will produce a 50% utilization of a 2,400 foot tape?

A. 12
B. 10
C. 24
D. 16

62. The definition of a programming problem in a structured manner would use:

A. A GOTO structure
B. A Nassi-Schneiderman chart
C. A block diagram
D. A bubble chart

63. An increased blocking factor will NOT:

A. increase I/O wait time
B. increase the number of interrecord gaps
C. increase the amount of required storage
D. increase the CPU processing time.

64. A dynamic dump would not display the contents of:

A. The relevant instruction
B. Data fields being referenced
C. General registers
D. Data files

65. In COBOL, which statement will define a numeric value of 298?

A. 77 FIELD-NAME VALUE 298 PIC ZZZ.
B. 77 FIELD-NAME VALUE 298 PIC 999.
C. 88 FIELD-NAME VALUE 298 PIC 999.
D. 77 FIELD-NAME VALUE 999 PIC 298.

66. Privileged instructions:

A. Are executed by the supervisor program
B. Are reserved for I/O operations
C. Can, in some cases, be executed by a problem program
D. Cannot, under any circumstances, be instigated by the problem program

67. Which of the following is a string variable?

A. ANSWER%
B. ANSWER#
C. ANSWER$
D. ANSWER!

68. A computer program that translates and executes each source language statement before translating and executing the next one is called a(n):

A. Simulator
B. Translator
C. Interpreter
D. Generator

69. Given:

```
01   MY-TABLE.
     03   X      OCCURS 6 TIMES.
          05     Y PIC X(6)   OCCURS 5 TIMES.
```

In order to find the third Y element in the fourth X element, you would code:

A. Y(3,4)
B. X(4,3)
C. X(3,4)
D. Y(4,3)

70. Virtual memory would NOT be stored on:
   A. Drums
   B. Core planes
   C. Magnetic strip memory
   D. Disk

71. An end-of-reel condition will be sensed by:
   A. An end-of-file mark
   B. A crimp in the tape
   C. A tape mark
   D. A reflective spot

72. A routine which is reenterable and serially reusable should:
   A. Be reused only if the housekeeping subroutines are executed prior to reuse
   B. Be known as a recursive subroutine
   C. Be known as an open subroutine
   D. Permit no modification of the routine

73. Indirect addressing implies:
   A. The address part of the instruction contains the address of the sending field.
   B. The address part of an instruction contains the base and displacement of the target field.
   C. The address part of the instruction contains the address of an operand.
   D. The address part of the instruction contains the absolute location of the operand.

74. The PL/1 language could easily replace
   A. FORTRAN, COBOL, and ALGOL
   B. APL, SIMSCRIPT, and JOVIAL
   C. IPL-V, LISP, and COMIT
   D. FORTH, C, and APT

75. What is the purpose of condition codes?
   A. To determine the nature of the immediately preceding logical operation
   B. To test the status of the input/output operation
   C. To shape the contents of the data file according to predetermined conditions
   D. To branch to a specific location unconditionally.

76. The generalized computer audit packages used by accountants and auditors to test the contents of transaction or master files are:
   A. Severely limited in capability
   B. Used by trained people with limited EDP knowledge
   C. Subroutines for other report preparation and filing updates
   D. Incapable of handling other than sequential tape and disk files

77. A program that is I/O bound is said to be:
   A. Processing large amounts of scientific data
   B. Waiting for the channel
   C. Processing small amounts of business data
   D. Anticipating the channel command

78. In a virtual storage system:
   A. Pages are fixed in length and are a design feature of the hardware
   B. Pages are variable in length and are a design feature of the hardware
   C. Page sizes are dynamically allocated according to program size
   D. Page sizes are fixed according to the physical size of a disk track

79. A disassembler is used to:
   A. Troubleshoot the hardware
   B. Interactively run the source code

C. Translate from machine code to assembler
D. Take the system apart for maintenance

80. A basic tenet of structured programming is:
A. No program module can exceed 500 statements
B. Moves, transforms, and executes are eliminated
C. The GO TO is eliminated whenever possible
D. All programming must follow a well-defined flow or HIPO chart

81. Which of the following is a simulation model processor?
A. ALGOL
B. Pascal
C. LISP
D. GPSS

82. BASIC, QUICKTRAN, and APL are examples of:
A. List processing languages
B. Interpretive languages
C. Business application languages
D. Compiler languages

83. A printer with both lower and upper case is:
A. Faster than a printer with an upper-case only
B. The same speed as a printer with an upper-case only
C. Slower than a printer with upper-case only
D. Used for script only

84. In a direct access file organized relatively:
A. The physical and logical positions are identical
B. The physical and logical positions are dissimilar
C. The system creates pseudonyms
D. The system creates extents

85. Page fault can be described as:
A. The page requested is not in real storage at the time.
B. The page requested is not in virtual storage at the time.
C. The page requested is not in storage anywhere.
D. The error-detect mechanism has detected paging hardware errors.

86. In a Report Generator (RPG) program:
A. All formats must be 96 characters
B. All calculations must be binary
C. All format statements must indicate position
D. All input/output is the responsibility of the programmer

87. A binary value of zero can be represented in one's complement form by:
A. 011111111 and 00000000
B. 111111111 and 11111110
C. 000000000 and 11111111
D. 100000000 and 00000001

88. In the Report Writer feature of ANSI COBOL:
A. A sort may be invoked
B. The DATA DIVISION must be defined first
C. Data conversion may be done
D. Reports may be generated in multiples

89. The INVALID KEY clause in COBOL can be coded in a(n):
- A. OPEN
- B. CLOSE
- C. FILE DESCRIPTION
- D. READ

90. In an indexed sequential file structure:
- A. All records must be written with keys
- B. If no key is assigned, the software will assume the first five positions to be the key
- C. All indicies must appear on direct access
- D. Keys may or may not be included in the record

91. Object code would be input to the:
- A. Compiler
- B. Linkage editor
- C. Relocable module
- D. Load module

92. In a ring-structured database:
- A. The presence or absence of data can be determined with a bit mask
- B. The data will always be present on a single cylinder
- C. The data will always be separated volume-for-volume
- D. The data chain cannot be followed

93. If you multiply a single precision number by a double precision number, the answer will be a:
- A. Single precision number
- B. Double precision number
- C. Triple precision number
- D. The precision cannot be determined

94. The purpose of a Warner-Orr Diagram is to:
- A. Logically grouping of functions
- B. Identify the unincluded module
- C. Determine the logical precedence sideways
- D. Determine the logical groupings of data groups

95. Two record keys hash to the same disk address. Usually one would use which procedure in this case?
- A. Use an absolute address for the second record
- B. Sort the two records
- C. Reindex with a new key
- D. Use a chained data structure

96. Given the following PL/1 statement, which answer best describes its function?

```
ABC:PROC (A, S, D, F)
```

- A. It is used to define a procedure called ABC which needs four parameters A, S, D, and F
- B. It is used to define a procedure called ABC with alias names of A, or S, or D, or F
- C. It will cause the value "ABC" to be stored in locations called A, and S, and D, and F, respectively
- D. It is syntactically incorrect and will not function for any purpose

97. Overflow occurs when:
- A. Target fields are too small for the sending field
- B. The operands are too large for the instruction used

C. Bits are shifted out the right side of a register
D. The jump register fails to connect with the target

98. Given the following BASIC routine, what will be the value of the variables J and X at the end of the routine?

```
10   FOR I = 1 TO 9
20       LET J = I * I
30       LET X = SQR(I)
40       PRINT I,J,X
50   NEXT I
60   END
```

A. J will equal 1, X will equal 9
B. J will equal 3, X will equal 81
C. J will equal 9, X will equal 1
D. J will equal 81, X will equal 3

99. When using an N-dimensional table, you need to specify how many selection arguments?

A. N * N
B. N–1
C. N + 1
D. N

100. Given the following FORTRAN statement, which value will be computed first?

A = (((B+C-D*E/F)(6.*X**2.))**3.)**4

A. B + A
B. E/F
C. X**2
D. D*E

ANSWER KEY

1. B	**26.** A	**51.** D	**76.** B
2. C	**27.** A	**52.** A	**77.** B
3. A	**28.** D	**53.** A	**78.** A
4. C	**29.** B	**54.** B	**79.** C
5. C	**30.** D	**55.** B	**80.** C
6. D	**31.** A	**56.** A	**81.** D
7. C	**32.** B	**57.** C	**82.** B
8. C	**33.** C	**58.** D	**83.** C
9. B	**34.** A	**59.** C	**84.** A
10. A.	**35.** A	**60.** A	**85.** A
11. A	**36.** B	**61.** A	**86.** C
12. D	**37.** B	**62.** B	**87.** C
13. C	**38.** D	**63.** D	**88.** D
14. D	**39.** D	**64.** D	**89.** C
15. C	**40.** B	**65.** B	**90.** D
16. D	**41.** C	**66.** A	**91.** B
17. B	**42.** C	**67.** C	**92.** A
18. B	**43.** C	**68.** C	**93.** A
19. C	**44.** C	**69.** B	**94.** C
20. D	**45.** B	**70.** C	**95.** D
21. C	**46.** C	**71.** D	**96.** A
22. C	**47.** B	**72.** A	**97.** A
23. C	**48.** D	**73.** C	**98.** B
24. C	**49.** C	**74.** A	**99.** D
25. A	**50.** A	**75.** A	**100.** D

TUTORIAL

1. Application software solves user problems, driver software is a class of software against which a template is placed, and system software includes operating systems and utilities. Of course, both the first and second can be construed to be the same—the text makes a point to discern between the two.
2. A and B are not relevant to the question. D applies in the case of I/O errors. Subscripts are defined under execution. Indexes are defined under compilation. IF statements with indexes run faster.
3. The key to this question is the word ''closed.'' A closed subroutine has a single entrance and a single exit. The routine is placed outside the mainline and referred to as required.
4. The definition of ''normal I/O binding'' is ''buffer to process overlap.'' Thus, the computation time and print time are free. Total lapsed time is then 2,500 * 500 = 1,250,000 milliseconds, or nearly 3 minutes.
5. The rationale for preparing a subroutine library is to have the ability to write and debug the routine and then use it as required.
6. Be careful. This one has four very close answers. A does not apply. Of those listed, only relational has the dependency needed, else they would not be ''relational.''
7. We could be faulted for not including an interpretation step here. In any event, the instruction must be fetched and then executed. The other options don't make a lot of sense.
8. To use a piece of code again, don't change it. D has a ring of truth, though the restoration of initial values should be the first thing done, not the last. A does not apply. B is possible, but not necessary, given C.
9. Looping is the correct answer. Both files—the transaction file and the master file, are in ascending sequential order. Once a transaction sequence number has been located, the master file must be read in a loop until a match has been found.
10. This is a tricky one. Data never becomes a program through compilation, except that the source program is technically ''data'' to the compiler program. D is not correct. Neither is C, for nearly the same reasons., The process in B is called ''disassembly.'' A is correct—BUT—not to the assembly language programmer who is capable to enter machine-language code through BASIC DATA statements. There's always an exception.
11. An ''open'' subroutine is a duplicated amount of coding which is included where it is needed. For relatively short programs, an open subroutine is acceptable. For a very long program, where this routine would have to be duplicated several times, it would be terribly inefficient.
12. An instruction is modified to keep the number of instructions low, taking fewer bytes (perhaps), but not necessarily reducing either the execution time or the debugging effort. D is the correct answer. It can most effectively be done where instruction parts can be addressed, as in assembly language.
13. Indirect address is the description of an address that is stored in a common place. The address at this common place can be changed at will. Thus, when an indirect address is referenced, it is referenced at the common address. An indirect address is not easily debugged.
14. To say ''at the beginning of iteration'' is a nonsequitur, as the iteration is established by the DO-WHILE structure and does so at the beginning of the loop. It is not the programmer's responsibility to establish and utilize the routines.
15. Calling of a subroutine requires that common information be established and passed to the called routine. In COBOL, the sections referenced in C are required. In FORTRAN and some other languages, a COMMON area is used.
16. D is the sensible answer. The emotional answer would be A. The political answer would be B. C is an absurd answer.
17. The whole point of a floating-point environment is the ability to handle scientific notation, with or without E-notation. A business-oriented language may or may not utilize floating-point hardware. I wonder what a bit-discriminating minicomputer is.

18. Pseudocode is an English narrative which cannot be processed by a translation program. Some feel this is a more effective way to specify the logic of a program. It cannot be used to operate the computer and whether it can be written in French or German—Pascal or Forth, that answer is immaterial.

19. The basic concept of a loop involves the steps of initialize, increment, test. In some cases the testing is done outside the loop (PERFORM VARYING). In other cases, the testing is done inside the loop (X=X+1:IF X=50 THEN. . .). In the structured environment the testing is a function of a condition [DO WHILE FILE NOT EOF(1)].

20. The first test should be on a representative sample of live and contrived test data. Live file tests are never a valid shakedown, either in full or in sample, essentially because these files have already been edited. Short test files for early tests will minimize wasted time.

21. In those places where drum is still being used—and there are few of those—it is being used for virtual systems, where paging to and from the drum is relatively fast, but the cost per character is very high. Drum is faster than disk, but a lot more expensive. For that reason, drum is disappearing from the field in most instances.

22. A checkpoint is a picture of memory, transactions, and files taken at a specific interval. Its purpose is to establish a recent restarting point.

23. Name = 30; classification = 6 (under both definitions); quantity = 8; 30 + 6 + 8 = 44.

24. The concept of the inverted structure is that the data on the original file are either copied and extracted according to the required data. When this selection has been done, the new key will be in the new file in the sequence of the key from the source file. To use this system, the new file must be sorted on the new key.

25. A symbolic program *is* a source program (B). C and D both start as a symbolic program. The product of assembly (or compilation, or translation) of a source program is an object program. A is the answer.

26. The answer D might be correct, but if there are no terminals, it is not. A restart needs to pick up where it left off. Main storage is anything but frozen, as this restart is not necessarily done immediately after the system has died. The last checkpoint is where the process starts.

27. The term "calling sequence" responds to the sequence of events necessary to tailor the "*called*" module by passing data from the "*calling*" module. Establishment of parameters to be passed is done here, though they are not "executed." C does not apply.

28. The polling scheme is a function of the communication driver software. The shift from baud to bit is really an impractical process, and meaningless. Programming the multiplexor will be a network activity not related to the programmer. No, the programmer is presented a transaction and has only the responsibility to handle that transaction.

29. The concept is called "nondestructive copy." A "move" is actually a "copy" from source to destination. In no computer are A, C, or D correct.

30. A two address system doesn't need a third address. Translation of the operation code is done by the operating system and involves no activity on the part of the programmer. The source and target address do not have to be in the same format. The only requirement is that the data target be large enough to accept the data source, else there will be a shortening of the data at the target location.

31. Multiply 64 times the value of K (1,024) and the answer is 65,535.

32. Decision tables have four main components: Condition Stub and Action Stub (to the left of the vertical double lines, and separated by the horizontal double lines) and Condition Entry and Action Entry (to the right of the vertical double lines and separated by the horizontal double lines).

33. A bubble sort is a common algorithm used to sequence files that consist of relatively few elements. It relies on a series of comparisons and swaps in which the successive elements of lower value rise like bubbles to the top.

34. Of the choices given, the size and organization of the file and programming language used is most accurate. A sequential file will have different timing characteristics than will a random file, a database structure, etc. If the language involves statement by statement interpretation, then it is certain to operate more slowly than one which exists is a compiled object module.

35. Take the count—if it is even, then a bit will be added, as a computer's internal memory is odd parity. If it is already odd, no parity bit is set.

36. Of course, nothing was said in the question about tape. Certainly internal speed will affect the process somewhat, but in this day and age, that is marginal. The speed of the disk units would have little to do with access. But the size and characteristics of the sort key—particularly if there happened to be a split or consolidated key—would make a tremendous difference.

37. The acronym SPOOL means "simultaneous peripheral output on line." No other explanation should be necessary.

38. The concept of a compiler is a many-for-one transformation of a high-level language to an assembly language. Assembler is one-for-one. Simulator and interpreter are different concepts.

39. Serial ports transmit data 1 bit at a time; parallel ports transmit data 1 byte at a time.

40. The data extractor is a utility which allows you to specify a varying parameter list—conceptually, it is not too different from the driver program described in the text. It very much permits modification, may handle any kind of label it needs to happen. D is irrelevant, and not true.

41. EBCDIC is an 8-bit code used primarily on IBM equipment. ASCII is a 7-bit code used on just about everything else. Both are character representations.

42. I'm not sure how parameterization of input data applies to the question. The color scheme used on the tube may be a determination set for color systems for background and foreground color contrast. Light intensity is controlled by the operator. The program must know where the cursor is at all times. Fortunately, there are instructions which assist this.

43. A, B, and D are BASIC verbs. C would be a spreadsheet command.

44. Remember the phrase "Checkpoint/Restart." Checkpoints are taken as a means of recovery at a known position, rather than having to completely redo processing.

45. The cross-assembler produces code on one processor for another—a technique used for distributing standard programs to a distributed processing activity.

46. If anything, blocking INCREASES the amount of storage required to hold the physical record.

47. Nested subroutines are very legal in BASIC and are not restricted to FOR loops. They should not be altered; neither should recursive subroutines, which can call themselves.

48. If your target is smaller than your source, truncation will be the result. More often that not, that truncation is an error, though you could certainly anticipate the truncation. What's a "wrap-around-carry" instruction?

49. Asynchronous anything means one following one, or one after the other. The same will be true of communications, when we study them.

50. Auxiliary memory generally means disk and tape. Tape is sequential access only; disk can be either. Auxiliary media are always external.

51. The open subroutine is simply repeated instructions, placed wherever required.

52. There is a world of difference in the methods to catalog media and the method to isolate internal error. Use a check digit.

53. The closed subroutine is written once and used as necessary.

54. There are two parts of a record: the fixed part, or key field; and all the other stuff. That key field is unique to the record.

55. Recursive subroutines use a stacking system similar to that which is used by FORTH and by microcomputers. The idea is to be able to work your way back from the lowest point in the subroutine.

56. Too easy. An assembler assembles assembly language; a compiler compiles a high-level language; a generate generates a program; and a translator simply redefines.

57. The size of matrix T is irrelevant to the problem. V is common to both matrices R and S, it need not be counted. The ultimate size will be the size of the other two variables.

58. The condition names radically cut the variable testing time during processing in a COBOL program. That variable can be established in the data division, reducing the amount of coding in and eliminating the relational operators from the procedure division. It really does nothing for the PERFORM structure.

59. The interrecord gap is fixed by the design of the tape transport. Thinner and wider tape would not fit the read/write heads. Increasing the bits-per-inch (bpi) should do.

60. The concept of a routine that is reenterable and serially reusable is its ability to make the maximum use of memory.

61. You can make this one too complicated. At 50% utilization, you must have as much space recorded with records as you have not recorded with interrecord gaps. The sum of the interrecord gaps is 1.5 inches. At 1600 bps, 1200 bits can be recorded in 1.5 inches. Since the records are 100 characters (bits, linearly), the blocking factor will be 12.

62. A Nassi-Schneiderman (or Chapin) Chart was discussed in the text, as a means to identify the processing structure of a structured program. Recall that HIPO charts and Warnier-Orr charts assisted here, as well.

63. Increasing the blocking factor decreases the number of interrecord gaps, increases the wait time on the I/O channel, and increases the size of the storage for buffer and work area. However, CPU processing time will not be changed, because the number of logical records has not changed.

64. Dynamic means ''right now.'' It would include contents of memory only—the instruction, the registers, the data fields (which are in buffers and main memory). It would not show you the contents of the data files.

65. Statement A has an incorrect case. You cannot assign a value to an 88 statement. Statement D is syntactically incorrect. B is the answer.

66. The operating system has a whole classification of privileged instructions which are useful for (but not reserved for) I/O operations. These are not initiated by the problem program in any manner.

67. A string variable is denoted by the dollar sign ($). Answer D is syntactically incorrect, while B and A are single- and double-precision specification, respectively.

68. This might best be described as an interpretive compiler. This is the way a BASIC program is run (other than that which has been compiled by the BASIC compiler), one instruction at a time.

69. The key to remember is that we're looking at the X dimension of the array—the 4th X, to be precise. Then, we're looking at the third Y item in the X dimension.

70. Magnetic strip memory was a main memory technique used by the National Cash Register Company. It's not used in modern computers. Core planes are disappearing, as well, not because they were not practical, but because of solid logic technology (SLT), otherwise known as the chip.

71. When you're running out of tape—about 14 feet from the end (close to the hub) the manufacturer has placed a reflective spot—an aluminum sticker which will be sensed by the tape unit—and that condition can be tested.

72. A serially reusable subroutine must be reset—and resetting is a housekeeping feature which must be accomplished outside the routine itself.

73. The operand is at the indirect location. The instruction contains a reference to the indirect location as a means to acquire the contents (operand) at that indirect location.

74. I'm going to leave this question in, despite the fact that PL/1 has never lived up to its promise. It's intended to be a scientific language which should have, by now, replaced FORTRAN, COBOL, and ALGOL. ALGOL is still around on a few machines, but FORTRAN and COBOL are still very much with us. It wouldn't surprise me to see PL/1 remain only in the IBM environment, but be replaced by Pascal, C, or even ADA.

75. When a logical test is made, the condition codes are set to indicate the outcome of that test. One may then branch to a specific location on the basis of the setting of the condition code.

76. Part of the difficulty in the audit situation—especially the in-house audit situation—is that there is little understanding of the computing process. That is, of course, changing, and we've taken steps in this issue to assist that process by expanding the Accounting chapter to include some auditing subject.

77. Though it seems like an impossibility in this day and age, a business program with a high I/O to compute ratio and low priority could very well be waiting for the channel.

78. Pages have a defined length. That defined length does not necessarily have to be completely full, but it cannot be overrun. That defined length makes it far easier to work with from the system programmer's point of view.

79. A disassembler has nothing to do with the maintenance of the hardware. Source code cannot be interactively run, except for those for whom interactive processors have been developed. No, a disassembler takes the machine code and develops a workable assembler statement from it.

80. It was the GO TO which created all the fuss, though, as the chapter states, there is much more to the concept of structured program. It does attempt to diminish the excessive use of the unconditional branching instructions and what the programmers have come to call "spaghetti code."

81. GPSS, the general purpose systems simulator is our answer. The rest are programming languages.

82. Academic answer based on the text—interpretive languages. The use of those languages is, of course, up to the user, but they are generally not compiled.

83. I know—C can't be the correct answer—what about. . .? With the exception of the matrix printers, one of two reasons lengthens out the time for both upper- and lower-case printers: the single lower-case character set, against a large number of upper-case character sets; and the amount of time necessary to shift, if required.

84. The concept of a relative file is that there is a contiguous—or at least near-contiguous block of records. If the number of breaks in the file sequence is small, then the wasted space on the file will be more than compensated for the fact that an index structure will not have to be chased to find the record. The record's key then becomes its location on the file, even if that key has something other than the number "1" as a beginning.

85. All page selection from the program is done in real storage. It is the responsibility of the operating system to see that the page has been obtained from virtual storage and placed in real storage, where it may be used.

86. The whole concept behind RPG is that you will provide positional specifications. I/O has specifications; calculations can be done in any mode, with the number of characters contained on the computer on which the RPG has been implemented.

87. The one's complement of a binary number merely replaces 1s with 0s and vice-versa.

88. COBOL permits you to sort, but outside the report writer. B is a false statement. C can be done in other parts of the procedure division. But, once ready, the report writer can generate as many reports as are wished.

89. INVALID KEY has meaning only when the program attempts to READ a record and cannot locate its key.

90. A key is not absolutely necessary for an ISAM structure—though they are most often used. It is possible to separate the key from the record.

91. This may seem to be an IBM only question—but other computers have the Linkage Editor, which is the correct answer. A compiler does the conversion. A relocatable module is the output of the Linkage Editor. And a load module is the executable code placed on a media or handler.

92. Here we've tossed you a curve. There was absolutely nothing in this chapter about database. We will discuss the subject fully in Chapter 8. A is the answer. Data can be arranged across any number of cylinders and volumes, and would require a chain to follow the ring.

93. The product will be expressed in the lowest precision of the factors used in the multiplication.

94. The Warnier-Orr Diagram presents the problem structure in a precedence diagram, written left to right. This precedence diagram breaks out the vertical structures on the basis of their rank in the horizontal flow.

95. D is the best answer of the available choices, but not the only answer. The file management system will often provide pseudonyms or alternate storage areas and chain linkages.

96. This is an informational question only, assuming you might run into such a statement. It's doubtful that you'll see a PL/1 program on the test. Expect some COBOL, or BASIC, or ultimately some of the others we've discussed.

97. Of the choices offered, the diminished size of the target field will cause an overflow. So will a developed total which is too large for the accumulator.

98. You'll have to map out this process to see these. The first half of the routine squares the number. The second half finds the square root. J is the square root of the square root in this instance.

99. In most cases, you would need only the number of arguments for which you have array (table) elements. Exceptions to this would be when you are using a sentinel at the end of the array or using a zero-position of the array as storage.

100. These are the precedence rules—the multiplication is cleared first, then the division, then the addition, subtraction, and exponentiation. The process always begins on the inside of the parentheses.

EXAMINATION SECTION 3

3
GENERAL MANAGEMENT

A former pastor, speaking on the subject of management to the convention of his fellowship, defined management in these fifteen tasks:

- To decide what has to be done.
- To tell somebody to do it.
- To listen to reasons why it should not be done, why it should be done by somebody else, or why it should be done a different way.
- To follow up to see if it has been done.
- To discover that it has not been done.
- To inquire why it has not been done.
- To listen to excuses from the person who should have done it.
- To follow up to see that it has been done, only to discover that it has been done incorrectly.
- To point out how it should have been done.
- To conclude that as long as it has been done, it might as well be left where it is.
- To wonder if it is all right to get rid of a person who cannot do a thing correctly.
- To reflect that he probably has a wife and large family and certainly any successor would probably be just as bad and perhaps even worse.
- To consider how much simpler and better it would have been done if you'd done it yourself in the first place.
- To reflect sadly that one could have done it right in twenty minutes, and now one must spend two days to find out why it has taken three weeks for somebody else to do it wrong.
- To resolve that the next time you (will/will not) do it yourself.

Whether or not you agree with these points, one fact is abundantly clear—management is the art/science of getting things done *through people.* It is a science in that there are formulas to be used, reliance on the disciplines of economics, mathematics, statistics, psychology, sociology, and anthropology, in addition to the traditional techniques of business and public administration. It is an art, because so much of it hinges on the successful use of human relations techniques.

Were it imperative to provide a definition, the definition of management would most certainly have to be *the process through which goals are defined, achieved, and measured by a structured, cooperative group.* That definition covers the majority of what we know about *traditional* management, and that definition will hold through the bulk of this chapter—until we get to Theory Z, which shows that management is indeed an art form.

What, Then, Is Management?

This chapter can have absolutely no meaning if we cannot agree that management exists for the accomplishment of goals through the skillful employment of the people resource. To this end, then, there are innumerable tasks, including *planning* (determining what to do), *organizing* (arranging the resources and means to accomplish the plan), *leading* (directing or influencing) the available resources toward the accomplishment of the goal, and *control* (comparing all that effort to the plan). These are the four classical functions of management. Would you be surprised if you found out there were more? Some would include "making do" on this list.

And Who Are The Managers?

Who are the managers? Where they are located in the organization? How do they achieve their positions? What do they do once they are managers?

Here is a general definition: A manager is anyone, at any level, who directs the efforts of others toward accomplishing goals. The definition is important, because the term *manager* is not always a classification of rank. You may well direct others without a reporting relationship. Neither is it a classification of gender. In this day and age, *manager* is NOT a male noun, even though Webster defines it as such (see the introduction to this book). There, does that make everybody happy?

Managers, then, are people assigned to and functioning at various levels of responsibility. At the lower levels of the organization, the managers are called *supervisors.* Supervisors are responsible for daily operations, for the direct interaction amongst the workforce. They are responsible *to* the middle level of formal management (department heads/division directors). These *middle management* personnel are, in turn, responsible for the coordination of programs and activities. Theirs is a twofold responsibility. they are responsible upward for the accomplishment of organizational goals and objectives, and responsible downward as representatives of top-level management.

Top-level management (Chief Executive Officer, Executive Director, President, Vice President) is responsible for overall direction of the organization, responsible to stockholders or to the public, and responsible for establishing measurable and achievable objectives which will guarantee the perpetuation of the enterprise.

What Does a Manager Do?

At whatever level, the manager is tasked to make decisions and to develop his team. It is his or her responsibility to do the data gathering, risk assessment, decision-making—even under uncertainty—necessary to accomplish the goals and objectives. If the manager does this, then his or her position is secure. If not, others are willing to try to manage.

Within the classical management functions, the manager is responsible for a variety of items, as described next.

Planning

The manager must assist in setting objectives and in establishing specific achievable steps to accomplish those objectives. He or she must evaluate the goals selected and the techniques felt necessary to achieve them.

Organizing

The manager must obtain and handle the human and physical resources which may be obtained. To do so requires some knowledge of organizational structures and styles, the corresponding people structures and styles, and how they mesh.

Leading

This is often called influencing or directing. The manager's responsibility is to cause things to happen, not simply to react to stimuli. The manager must create and maintain communication and keep people moving toward goals within the organizational climate.

Controlling

The manager is responsible for the establishment of controls, for measurement systems and performance appraisals. Here the mixture of emphasis lies between the dynamic redirection of resources and the fine tuning of the organization.

Managerial Skills

Not just anybody can be a manager, and organizations which promote employees into management without proper preparation do both the employees and the organization a disservice. Some of the skills a manager must have are described next.

Technical Skill

Technical people without managerial training are upwardly mobile to technical managerial positions within a very narrow spectrum. Their downward communication deals with technical subjects. Their interaction is generally with technical peers. And their upward communication is generally end-line, owing to the fact that their management may not understand, may not know what they do not know and understand, and may not be motivated to assist in the process.

Organizational managerial positions require other skills. For example, they require a knowledge of the organization at large, an interdisciplinary orientation, and a different feel for the interaction of people. It is a different level of team play, and the quicker an individual who desires upward mobility learns that, the more quickly the personal ambitions are likely to be realized.

Communication Skill

As one moves up on the organizational ladder, the requirements for communications skills change—radically. At the shop level, presentations are oral and informal. Nobody cares that the supervisor isn't a good orator; the audience is former peers.

When it is necessary to communicate horizontally and upward, however, the rules change. Now formal oral and written communications skills are required, and the technical student who hasn't taken time to learn his communication lessons properly will be at a serious disadvantage. When one analyzes the statement of the business school graduate who "took just enough to get a job and 'nuthin' else," one who knows quickly comes to the realization that he or she has just established the upward limit of mobility.

Human Skill

If it is true that management is the process of getting work done through people, then people-handling skills are of paramount importance. A knowledge of people's needs and motivations now becomes the leverage for achieving the entire range of ambitions, from lofty goals to achievable quotas. People are complex, and unfortunately there are no moulds into which people can be neatly formed. There are indicators of commonality, however, and the manager's knowledge and implementation of motivators will play a crucial part to his or her success.

Management, then, is the art of gaining and using cooperation. Leadership does not always mean "up front." Management of people occurs successfully through the manager's insights and what one does with them.

Analytical Skill

As precise as this field claims to be, some of its most successful practitioners could survive in it only through inordinate common sense, consistently logical approaches to problem resolution, knowledge of the available scientific techniques, and an intuitive sixth sense.

Decision-Making Skill.

I have often felt that except for very narrow circumstances (like handling dynamite) there is always room to make an error. I would much prefer to work for a manager who was willing to make a decision (which could be wrong) than for a manager who would make no decision whatsoever, and who preferred to study everything to death. The good manager develops a skill for assessing risk at each managerial function, for applying scientific tests of analysis, and making that decision which, given all logical tests, appears to be a ''good'' decision. The ineffective manager may have a safer position, but—as Dr. Lawrence Peter states—will rise to the level of his incompetence.

Conceptual Skills

In this world there are the dreamers and the doers. The best manager can find some mix of both. One of the difficulties inherent in advancing technical people into management is that they are so hung up on the trees that they fail to (or perhaps simply cannot) see the forest. A worthy manager, then, must be one of the ''big picture'' people, a visionary, a creative solution-maker, and an image-shaper, every bit as much as the person who is the field general.

THE MANAGERIAL CONTINUUM

Were we to examine management history, we would find that management as we know it in the latter part of the 20th Century dates back about 7,000 years to the Sumerians, where it is known that records were kept. A thousand years later, the Egyptians were building pyramids. Two thousand years after that, written documents appeared in Egypt. Less than 2,000 years before the birth of Christ, Babylon's Hammurabi was defining laws, authorities, and responsibilities. A couple of hundred years after that, organizational structure was centralized in Egyptian society. The modern-day concepts of organizational theory, decentralization, and management by exception appeared during the exodus of the Hebrews from Egypt. Exodus Chapter 23, verses 25 and 26 state:

> And Moses chose able men out of all Israel and made them heads over the people, rulers of thousands, rulers of hundreds, rulers of fifties, and rulers of tens, and they judged the people at all seasons: the hard cases they brought unto Moses, but every small matter they judged themselves.

As history continued up to the birth of Christ, managerial advances can be documented in Babylon, China, and Greece, with such diverse contributions as the classical functions of management (to plan, organize, lead, and control), for management standards, development and use of work measurement tools, production controls, quality controls, scientific measurements, and the like.

The money aspect of management was developed in the years from 1300 to 1500. Double-entry bookkeeping, for instance, was developed in Italy in 1340, the procedures of which were documented in 1494. Cost accounting came along later in Spain, to be followed shortly by inventory and work-in-process accounting. In 1436 in Venice, Italy, an organization called the Arsenal of Venice is known to have incorporated cost accounting; checks and balance for control; numbering of inventoried parts; interchangeability of parts; use of the assembly line technique; use of personnel management; standardization of parts; inventory control; and cost control.

The 1500s found calls for specialization (Sir Thomas More) and the concepts of Niccolo Machiavelli, who felt that management must rely upon mass consent, the acceptance theory of authority-that authority flows from the bottom up and not from the top down. He felt that the organization required cohesiveness and that there were two kinds of leaders—the appointed and the anointed.

The Industrial Revolution

Modern management techniques began to emerge in the late 18th and early 19th Centuries. Prior to 1700 most manufacturing utilized limited capital and uneducated workers on a small scale. The emerging technical developments of this period, however, provided a new opportunity for the application of some of the newer managerial skills. Though the advances were small, they served as the foundation of greater strides in the 1800s.

Production moved through three specific stages in this period. First was the *cottage industry* (*domestic system*), wherein an entrepreneur produced his goods at home, ventured into the marketplace to sell them, and returned home to produce more goods. While it kept Dad at home, there was no incentive to grow, no ability to extend an individual's managerial skill, and no demands beyond the survival of the family unit. The second method (the *putting-out system*) found agents or middlemen contracting for and purchasing the entire output of a family, combining that with similarly contracted goods, and moving those goods to market. Since more time could be spent in the production of goods, both the producers and the middlemen made out well. But, there were problems—more goods could be made than raw materials obtained. Growth, then, had a damper which could only be overcome by what has become known as the *factory system.*

The attraction of capital to the centralized location required massive changes in perspective. Thomas Watts, an accounting teacher, took the concept of the Arsenal of Venice and applied it to the factory system as early as 1716. Adam Smith's concept of the division of labor and performance accountability appeared in his book *Wealth of Nations* (short title) in 1793. To Smith is also attributed the concept of depreciation. Sir James Steuart preceded by a hundred years Frederick Taylor's equal division of work concepts. Richard Arkwright (c. 1750) identified the four factors of production: men, money, materials, and machines, and applied them to the newly emerging cotton industry in England.

Production planning had its genesis in Great Britain at the Soho Engineering Foundry of Matthew Boulton, James Watt, and Sons. Formed to manufacture Watt's steam engines, they instituted practices of market research and forecasting, planning of site location, machine layout and work-flow studies, established production standards, standardized components, cost control applications, cost accounting, employee training, work study and incentives, and an employee welfare program. Many of these techniques predate Taylor. Experimenting with piece rates, Soho's managers measured and standardized each operation, predating Babbage, Taylor, and Gilbreth. Soho, in fact, may have been the first recorded Theory Y company (to be discussed later) in that the employee's physical well-being was more carefully considered than in any other contemporary industry. Special entertainment was provided, overtime pay was given, the work environment was improved, houses were built for workers, an insurance society was provided, bonuses and Christmas presents were provided for employees and their families, and fair wage adjustment were made. Clearly, Soho was ahead of its time.

The industrial revolution was capital intensive and dehumanizing to people, a practice which would continue in some form into this century, as readers of Sinclair Lewis' *The Jungle* can attest. However, there was at least one place where the individual's worth was predominant. New Lanark, Scotland, had a factory built to test the theories of Robert Owen. Owen was the man who showed England that industrialism need not be built on cheap and brutally abused labor. Workers were provided homes and services, rewards on the job, and schooling for young laborers on the job. The factory showed a consistent profit, allowing Owen to develop his theories of management as a profession. Under his direction, houses and streets were built, the minimum working age for children was raised, working hours were decreased, meal facilities were provided, schooling was introduced, and evening recreation centers were opened to meet the problems of leisure. Robert Owen has been identified as the father of modern personnel management.

Eli Whitney is generally credited with the concept of interchangeable parts in the production process. Though some will claim he did not originate the concept and that it predated him substantially, he certainly capitalized on it. He is credited with efforts at quality control and with the recognition of span-of-control problems.

Early Management Writers

The 1800s produced a plethora of literature on the subject of management. Economists conceived and wrote about management concepts, the functions of management, and the applications of management theory. It's at this point that the qualities of a manager were defined. Adam Smith had said a manager should have order, economy, and attention. To that were added foresight, calculation, perseverance, constancy of purpose, discretion, and decision of character (Samuel Newman). James Mill added fidelity and zeal.

We normally think of motion and time study as an innovation of the Taylor–Gilbreth era. However, time and motion study is clearly indicated in the writings of James Mill. Mill is also credited with the inception of a capital control system.

Carl von Clausewitz was a Prussian general who wrote on war and the management of large armies at war. He felt that business was a form of human competition which greatly resembled war. Clausewitz's greatest contribution was the contention that managers must accept uncertainty and meet the uncertainty with thorough analysis and alternative planning.

Human factors engineering was detailed in the writings of Charles Dupin, a 19th century French engineer. Today those human factors engineering practices are called *ergonomics,* and we will discuss the concept of ergonomics in the systems chapter.

Charles Babbage, a name well known in computing circles, was also known for his management writings. His contribution was to lay down the concepts for the initiation and development of the scientific approach to the study of management. He was predominantly concerned not with the production of machines, but with their use and the organization of humans in relation to them. Babbage recommended that data be gathered and used as the basis for management decision. It also appears that he was well into time and motion studies, as his writings detail the methods to be followed to time operations with a stopwatch, thereby detailing the procedures of what would become known, in this century, as an efficiency expert. Babbage detailed eleven proposals for management:

1. Analyze manufacturing processes and cost.
2. Use time study techniques.
3. Use printed standard forms for investigation.
4. Use the comparative method method of studying business practices.
5. Study the effects of various tints of paper and colors of ink to determine which is least fatiguing to the eye.
6. Determine how best to frame questions.
7. Determine demand from statistics based on income.
8. Centralize the production processes for economy.
9. Inaugurate research and development.
10. Study factory location relative to the proximity of raw materials.
11. Use a beneficial suggestion system.

Babbage, though not given the credit for the actual work, was definitely the harbinger of the new scientific management concepts which were to follow. And, as can be seen, he had some concerns for ergonomics, as well.

Prelude to Scientific Management

The scene now shifts to America, where we, though we started late, had now climbed on the bandwagon of the Industrial Revolution. The introduction, in 1862, of the limited liability joint stock company formed the basis for employment of capital funds provided from outside the organization. Bankers such as Jay Gould, J. Pierpont Morgan, and Cornelius Vanderbilt invested heavily in the building of stock companies, including a newly emerging and dramatic enterprise, the railroads. Henry Poor, editor of the American Railroad Journal, established basic managerial principles for the railroads: organization, communication, and information. Daniel McCallum of the Erie Railroad implemented Poor's recommendations with job descriptions, system, common sense, reports, and control. Individuals were made both responsible and accountable for successes and failures. McCallum is credited with early use of the organizational chart.

The quest for new knowledge in the management of enlarging enterprises resulted in a call for paper by the American Society for Mechanical Engineers, what we now call ASME. They published the papers, which dealt with wages, wage systems, labor efficiency, incentives, etc. It is said that the contribution of Henry Towne, "The Engineer as an Economist," may well have been the inspiration of Frederick Taylor's work on scientific management. Simultaneously, Henry Metcalfe, an Army captain, assumed command of an arsenal, and developed a method of system and control, utilizing information cycles and flows. His theories, published in 1885, were acknowledged by Taylor and the American Management Association as contributory to the advancement of managerial practice.

It has been said that Andrew Carnegie developed the incentive system in the U.S. Perhaps not. In 1891 Frederick Halsel's paper for ASME developed the concept of a "premium plan" for demonstrable time savings. Utilizing the most recent productive output as a base, premiums were paid as soon as additional production was realized, with one-third of the improvement going directly to the worker.

Scientific Management

Finally, Frederick W. Taylor, known as the "Father of Scientific Management." Taylor was an engineer who worked for steel firms in Pennsylvania. At Midvale Steel (1878), he recognized that there was no clear concept of worker-management responsibility, no effective work standards, no incentives, decisions were based on rule of thumb, no work flow studies were being done, workers were misassigned, etc. Responsible for production processes including tools, speeds, metals, and the like, Taylor invented methods for cutting steel which revolutionized the process. He wrote, however, on the subject of management as it was applied in the shop environment. Having heard Towne's paper at ASME, Taylor began work on his own theories, presenting two papers to ASME. The last, "Shop Management," contained the germ of the scientific approach:

- The objective of good management is to pay high wages and have low unit production costs.
- Apply scientific methods of research to formulate principles and standard processes which would allow for control of the manufacturing operations.
- Employees must be scientifically placed on jobs where materials and working conditions are scientifically selected so that standards can be met.
- Employees should be scientifically and precisely trained to improve their skills in so performing a job that the standard output could be met.

- An air of close and friendly cooperation should be cultivated between management and workers to make possible the application of the other principles.

These ideas Taylor developed into five specific principles of management:

- Research
- Standards
- Planning
- Control
- Cooperation

to which Taylor added these scientific steps:

- Define the problem
- Gather data
- Analyze the data
- Develop alternatives
- Select the best alternative

and these human steps:

- Improved work methods (motion study)
- Work/rest alternates (fatigue and rest study)
- Output standards (time/unit study)
- Payment by output unit (incentive)

Taylor's ideas received world-wide publicity during the Interstate Commerce Commission's hearings on railroad efficiency (the Eastern Rate Case, 1911), when Harrington Emerson, an early advocate of efficiency engineering, testified that the application of scientific management principles would save the railroads one million dollars per day. While Taylor has been criticized for stressing the ''impersonality of measurement'' and resolving the individual/organizational conflict in favor of the organization, the improvements in factory management resulting from his techniques cannot be denied.

Around Taylor there gathered a group of management thinkers who became known as the Taylor Society. The Taylor Society enunciated thirteen aims of scientific management:

1. To gauge industrial tendencies and the market in order thereby to regularize operations in a manner which will conserve the investment, sustain the enterprise as an employing agency, and assure continuous operation and employment
2. To assure the employee not only continuous operating and employment by correct gauging of the market, but also to assure by planned and balanced operations a continuous earning opportunity while on the payroll
3. To earn through waste-saving management and processing techniques, a larger income from a given expenditure of human and material energies, which shall be shared through increased wages and profits by workers and management
4. To make possible a higher standard of living as a result of increased income to workers
5. To assure a happier home and social life to workers through removal, by increase of income, of many of the disagreeable and worrying factors in the total situation
6. To assure healthful as well as individually and socially agreeable conditions of work

7. To assure the highest opportunity for individual capacity through scientific methods of work analysis and of selection, training, assignment, transfer, and promotion of workers
8. To assure by training and instructional foremanship the opportunity for workers to develop new and higher capacities, and eligibility of promotion to higher positions
9. To develop self-confidence and self-respect among workers through opportunity afforded for understanding of one's own work specifically, and of plans and methods of work generally
10. To develop self-expression and self-realization among workers through the stimulative influence of an atmosphere of research and valuation, through understanding of plans and methods, and through the freedom of horizontal as well as vertical contacts afforded by functional organization
11. To build character through the proper conduct of work
12. To promote justice through the elimination of discriminations in wage rates and elsewhere
13. To eliminate factors of the environment which are irritating and the causes of frictions, and to promote common understandings, tolerances and the spirit of team work

The above 13 points are quoted from *Scientific Management in American Industry,* edited by H.S. Person (New York: Harper & Bros., 1929).

The concepts of scientific management would be further enhanced during the early part of the century by such people as Frank and Lillian Gilbreth and by Henry L. Gantt, and of Henri Fayol, in whose work there are some elements of scientific management, some elements of the humanist school of management, and also some elements of what we now know as the process approach. Suffice it to say that these individuals were contemporaries of Taylor and used his work as the launching platform for their own perspectives.

Frank Gilbreth, for instance, is commonly known as a time and motion study person, and indeed his work as a bricklayer gave rise to his concerns about wasted motions. But the interest of his wife Lillian would lead them to the mingling of management science and management psychology. Using motion picture film, and using subjects with lights attached to their arms, the Gilbreths developed motion pictures known as *cyclegraphs.* Timing of film was difficult in those days, so Gilbreth introduced a device of his invention called a *chronocyclegraph.* With this device, they could determine acceleration, deceleration, and direction of movement, the now famous *therbligs* (''Gilbreth'' spelled backwards with the *th* transposed). Their interests went beyond motions, however, into the workplace. Training, work methods, environments, tools, healthy worker psychology outline the contributions of the Gilbreths. More than this, however, they taught managers to question feasibility and applicability.

Gantt also was a contemporary of Taylor, and in fact had participated in the Midvale Steel experiments. We know of Gantt's major contribution today in the so-called Gantt chart, a device used by management to compare actual to planned performance. But Gantt had other, more humanistic interests relative to management, including the task-and-bonus plan for paying workers wherein the base rate was guaranteed and the excess production was the basis for the bonus. He held forth for training of workers and for in-house training programs to build skills, form better work habits, cut loss time, and increase reliability. Finally, Gantt held that organizations exist more for service than for profits. In short, Gantt's major contribution to management thought had to be industrial responsibility.

The Process Approach

A separate and distinct management philosophy, whose advocates are frequently referred to as the *Management Process School,* evolved during the same period. The first was an American by the name of Harrington Emerson, to whom we can give credit for efficiency engineering. Emerson developed twelve principles of efficiency, the first five of which deal with interpersonal relations between employer and employee; the remaining seven of which deal with management systems methodology:

1. Clearly defined ideal—know what you are attempting to accomplish. Eliminate vagueness, uncertainty, and aimlessness.
2. Common sense—strive for knowledge and seek advice from every quarter.
3. Competent counsel—seek advice from competent individuals.
4. Discipline—adhere to rules.
5. Fair deal—justice and fairness.
6. Reliable, immediate, adequate, and permanent records upon which to base decisions.
7. Dispatch—scientific planning of each function relative to the whole.
8. Standards and schedules—task methods and timing.
9. Standardized conditions—unity of method.
10. Standardized operations—unity of method.
11. Documentation of standard operating procedures.
12. Reward for efficiency.

During the same period, a little-known Frenchman postulated an executive's view of management. It was not until after the Second World War, however, that Henri Fayol's concepts gained credence, essentially because the Americans brought their management system to war with them. Fayol's perspectives are quite applicable today. He said:

- The question of centralization or decentralization is simply a matter of proportion—finding the optimum degree for the particular firm.
- Each employee intentionally or unintentionally puts something of himself into his work. He does not operate merely as a cog in a machine.
- There is a scalar chain—the chain of supervisors ranging from the top to the bottom ranks.
- For order to prevail, there must be an appointed place for every employee and he should be in his appointed place.
- Dividing enemy forces is clever, but dividing one's own team is a grave error.

These concepts formed the basis for Fayol's theories. Though they differed in approach, Taylor and Fayol were working on the same problem—Taylor from the shop up, Fayol from the top down. Fayol observed that management was an activity common to all humans, requiring some degree of planning, organizing, commanding, coordinating, and controlling. Since management applied to all, Fayol felt that it should be taught.

He had some other ideas about top down management: Centralization or decentralization was the responsibility of management's decision about products, processes, or markets. Management should identify the employee's intentions about work, and establish a scalar chain of supervision to accomodate that. Emphasis should be placed upon punctuality and position, team building, technical advancement (production, manufacture, adaptation), involvement of the employee in commercial activities (buy, sell, exchange). The organization had the responsibility to provide financial resources (search for and optimum use of), security (property and people), accounting for resources and responsibilities thereof (stocktaking, balance sheets), and managerial functions (planning, organizing, commanding, coordinating, controlling).

His theory of management, then, included two models:

Industrial Model

1. Technical (production, manufacture, adaptation)
2. Commercial (buying, selling, exchange)
3. Financial (search for and optimum use of capital)

4. Security (protection of property and persons)
5. Accounting (stocktaking, balance sheets, costs, statistics)
6. Managerial (planning, organizing, commanding, coordinating, controlling)

Managerial Model

1. Planning—examining the future and drawing up a plan of action
2. Organizing—developing the dual structure of human and material resources. The manager has these duties to perform:
   a. Ensure that the plan is judiciously prepared and strictly implemented.
   b. See that the human and material organization is consistent with the objectives, resources, and requirements of the organization (firm, agency).
   c. Establish a single, competent, energetic building authority.
   d. Harmonize activities and coordinate efforts.
   e. Formulate clear, distinct, precise decisions.
   f. Arrange for efficient selection of personnel.
   g. Define duties clearly.
   h. Encourage initiative and responsibility.
   i. Compensate fairly and suitably for work performed.
   j. Establish sanctions against faults and errors.
   k. Maintain discipline.
   l. Subordinate individual interest to the interest of the group.
   m. Develop unity of command.
   n. Supervise both material and human order.
   o. Control everything.
   p. Resist regulatory excesses, red tape, and controls.
3. Commanding—maintaining activity among the personnel of the organization. The manager should:
   a. Have a thorough knowledge of his personnel.
   b. Eliminate incompetent personnel.
   c. Have a thorough knowledge of agreements which bind the organization and its employees.
   d. Set a good example for employees.
   e. Conduct periodic audits of the organization.
   f. Convene subordinates on a regular basis.
4. Coordinating—binding together, unifying, and harmonizing all activity and effort
5. Controlling—determining that everything has been accomplished in conformity with the established plan and command

Fayol's management theory, in summary, states that management, as a discipline, falls squarely upon these 14 points.

1. *Division of work.* Specialization belongs to the natural order.
2. *Authority and responsibility.* Responsibility is a corollary of authority.
3. *Discipline.* Discipline is what leaders make it.
4. *Unity of command.* Employees cannot bear dual command.
5. *Unity of direction.* One head and one plan for a group of activities having the same objectives.
6. *Subordination of individual interest to the general interest.*
7. *Remuneration.* This should be fair, rewarding of effort, and reasonable.

8. *Centralization.* Centralization belongs to the natural order.
9. *Scalar chain.* This is the line of authority.
10. *Order.* There is a place for everyone and everyone is in his place.
11. *Equity.* This results from a combination of kindness and justice.
12. *Stability of tenure of personnel.* Prosperous firms are stable.
13. *Initiative.* This is a great source of strength for business.
14. *Esprit de corps.* Unity is strength.

Because the publication of Fayol's work was delayed by World War I, during which Europeans had an opportunity to observe Taylor's theories at work in the U.S. military forces, Fayol's work would pass a second war until the value of his concepts would be recognized. His contribution and the fact that he demonstrated that management was an acquired art, has caused this period to be dubbed "the age of classical management doctrine."

However, the amount of space spent here on Fayol should provide some indication of how important his work was.

The Human Behaviorists

The 1930s witnessed a dramatic shift from the task orientation of the scientific management practitioners. A new group, the neoclassicists, turned the thrust of management thought to a microanalysis of feelings and attitude of people within the organization, to a new concern for human relations. The roots of this new Human Relations School could be traced as far back as the Philadelphia Textile Plant experiments of Elton Mayo in 1923, the tenets of Oliver Sheldon, and the writings of Mary Parker Follett on group cooperation, coordination, and conflict resolution. Through Follett's eyes, power, leadership, and authority became dynamic concepts—not heavy tools which only burdened managers. Sheldon held that management has a social responsibility to the community and to the employees. Further, it is said that Sheldon contributed a managerial philosophy which moved management from the materialistic toward the conceptual.

The real inspiration for this new movement, however, was the Hawthorne experiments of Elton Mayo and associates, conducted at Western Electric's Hawthorne Works in Chicago in 1927. Because of a Rockefeller Foundation study of attitudes and reactions of groups under varying conditions and a study of the effects of illumination upon output which found that groups' productive outputs varied, but not in the manner anticipated, Mayo, a Harvard professor, began the Hawthorne study under controlled circumstances.

In the experiment, the conditions of work of a six-woman team were changed one at a time to determine effects on production. Some of the changes were rest periods of differing length and number, shorter work days or week, soup or coffee at the morning coffee breaks, etc. With each change, the effect was consistent: output increased, and the people felt less fatigued. Mayo's conclusion, then, was that logical factors were far less important than emotional factors influencing employee behavior, with those most powerful being those which emanated from the worker's participation in social groups. Thus, it was further concluded, if the needs of the workers are met, the needs of the organization will be met also. Others have felt that this set of concepts brought forth extraordinary manipulation. It is known that during this period there was an unprecedented rise in trade unionism. Others, notably Abraham Maslow, Douglas McGregor, and Rensis Likert, would have more to say on the subject of human interaction.

The Hawthorne experiments irrevocably altered the concept of man as an interchangeable part operating in an exclusively physical setting. As a result of Mayo's work, the industrial woods abound today with behavioral scientists, personnel counselors, industrial chaplains, sensitivity trainers, group dynamicists, sociogram analysts, nondirective interviewers, role-playing instructors, critical incident teachers, and industrial psychologists—each trying to satisfy management's demand for the creation of a work situation conducive to maximum long-run productivity.

The Social System School

A broader sociological approach was later taken by a group called the *Social System School.* The father of the concept was Chester Barnard, president of the Jersey Bell Telephone Company when he wrote his expository *The Functions of the Executive* (1938). Barnard's theory of cooperation and organization was a system of consciously coordinated activities or forces of two or more persons, in which the executive is the most strategic factor. He held that the individual should be induced to cooperate and that employees would perform work if (1) they understood what work was to be done, (2) believed it to be consistent with the purposes of the organization, (3) believed it to be compatible with their own personal interests, and (4) were able to comply with the request. To Mayo's work, Barnard introduced social concepts into the analysis of managerial functions and processes.

Lyndall Urwick made no innovative contribution to management thinking. He did, however, consolidate the works of Fayol, Taylor, Follett, and others into a comparative analysis, *The Elements of Administration,* published in 1943. His work crystalized the similar concepts that had been independently developed, thereby giving them more credence and serving to mold them into a system of managerial thought.

The Quantitative School

Beginning in 1941 with the introduction of linear programming, the application of quantifiable models to management has become the fastest-growing managerial phenomenon. The following list of quantitative techniques includes the work not only of recent people but also of others, dating back, whose ideas applied to the quantitative school of management:

Decision theory, including organization theory, learning theory, cybernetics, and suboptimization. These techniques are applied to a determination of the objectives of the firm, an assessment of group conflicts and interactions, job performance estimates, and organizational analysis.

Experimental design. Experimental design techniques are basic to the construction of any predictive model.

Game theory. This is applied to timing and pricing in a competitive market and to military strategy.

Information theory. This is applied to data processing systems design, organization analysis, advertising effectiveness in market research.

Inventory control, including economic lot size and inventory control.

Linear programming. This is used in the assignment of equipment and personnel, scheduling, input/output analysis, transportation routine, product mix, and allocation processes.

Probability theory. Probability theory enters almost all areas of application.

Queuing theory. This applies to inventory control, traffic control, telephone trunk systems, scheduling of computer systems, etc.

Replacement theory. This governs the replacement of equipment which has been taken from service through failure and deterioration.

Sampling theory. This is applicable to quality control, simplified accounting and auditing, consumer surveys, product preference research.

Simulation theory, including Monte Carlo methods. These techniques are used in system reliability evaluation, profit planning, logistic-system studies, inventory control, and manpower requirements.

Statistical decision theory. This is applicable to circuit design, legal inference.

The Systems School

We are still heavily into the quantitative school of management. But for the last quarter century, the Systems School of Management has been heard from. Under the concepts of this school, the business is a system and must be managed as a system. This system has resources which are its inputs. Those inputs are materials, physical capital and human capital. The system also has outputs which are produced and offered to those who reside outside the system. Those outputs are, naturally, the products and/or services offered by the organization. These, plus the managerial workforce and the standards by which the organization is managed, form the internal environment of the organization.

The external environment of the business includes the public, the stockholders, government, competitors, unions, the labor force, suppliers, and customers. Each applies a pressure upon the "system," which responds to stimulus—primarily external environment to internal environment.

It's important to recognize why a systems school may be necessary. Under the concepts of this school, goals become the raison d'etre of management and values have been assigned to a somewhat lower plane. We're into technology now, and middle management, at least, has felt that technology for its own sake might be a worthwhile goal. Not necessarily. But at the same time, there have changes in the structure of work, the psychosocial interactions of organizations' relationships with employees and those outside the organization, and in the managerial practices employed. Student uprisings of the 1960s had a profound effect on the way business is conducted. Social responsibilities of corporations were brought under the microscope, and under intense inspection were found wanting. Government-mandated hiring programs brought managers and employees together under duress, be it sexual, racial, gender, or classification. Extreme competition and labor and market practices claimed to be unfair opened up pressures to defeat trade unionism's desire to maintain control. The highest incidence of white-collar crime in history has shown that many who commit these crimes don't necessarily do it for the money—they do it for the thrill or the challenge.

A quarter century of postwar affluence produced a cadre of workers to whom money and security were not predominant. It brought about at least one generation classified as the "me" generation, permeated by selfish interests and interested in exploiting organizations and corporations for personal gain. The population dropped, the work force dropped, the prices rose to extreme heights, and the country resorted to undocumented aliens as a means to compete, to protective tariffs as a means of exclusion, and to any means possible to compensate for the fact that productivity was dropping at an alarming rate and that foreign imports were simply of a higher quality and durability.

The invention and production of productivity tools has failed to regain much of the ground lost to others. The computer, for all its power, did not return the steel mills, the agricultural losses, the wood products business. And we who are teaching management in schools of higher learning are subtly discouraged from impressing upon our students that returning to the Puritan work ethic may well be the only salvation.

Wait a minute, Ken. You're suggesting that the business system approach may not be what it's cracked up to be. Right. There is a preponderance of evidence which strongly indicates that "modern" is not by definition "best." The systems approach to management—expecting employees and processes to function as a well-oiled machine—may just not be working to our advantage.

The Situational Approach

The same concept which gave us "if it feels good, do it," has now begun to suggest that the manager need not be concerned with absolutes, that he must adapt to meet the particular circumstances and constraints that a firm may encounter. This should not be construed to mean flexibility—but it should be taken to indicate that the cadre of management emerging from the graduate schools in the last quarter century is taking us to where we've never been—to an operation with few, if any, rules. Except their own. And you can see the result.

Under the situational management concept, the external environment may change rapidly. The objectives have changed, however, in that striving to earn only enough profit to survive has become more acceptable than striving for a specific profit objective, supposedly in favor of more social concerns. Objectives have been decentralized, which isn't all bad, but because the external environment may change significantly, contingency becomes the watchword.

High-tech firms have found that technology imposes a strain on the management of an organization. Being the basis of the "state of the art," technology can be a blessing, a bane, or a boondoggle. It leaves people behind, creates stress and anxiety, and in the final result produces marginal, if any, improvement. The situational management style, being bent upon reacting to external change, introduces technology brusquely, throwing fear and trembling into the workforce—and, for all intents and purposes, ensuring that the workforce is a younger, more adaptable workforce. Nobody questions the need to adapt to changing stimuli. The question which may become the undoing of this management style is whether the people of the firm *need* to undergo the horror of unprepared change for the sake of situational management's concept of an ephemeral market.

Under the situational school, the argument over centralization and decentralization rages once again, because it's the top-level management strata who may make the most decisions, imposing an unreasonable will upon the subordinates. This situation is only exacerbated by distance, compression of communications, and the need for instantaneous decision. Productivity may well vary inversely to applied managerial pressure.

Situational management says "Hire good people and let them do their thing." Will it work? Can it work? Some think it can, and in a highly motivated, technologically oriented startup company, it probably will. In the older industries, where performance and loyalty still count, chances are it will not. Since high-tech is not in a majority position in our country, situational managers may well have difficulty coping with work force that holds more traditional values.

Management in the situational school falls into one of two categories—*autocratic* and *participative.* The only rules the autocrat recognizes are his rules, and aberration from his rules are grounds for dismissal. The participative manager recognizes that in concert there is strength; so participation becomes the basis for management. If productivity is the result, so much the better.

It is this author's profound impression that this concept of management won't last very long. Or could you tell that?

Don't conclude that the author feels the systems school of management concept is all bad. As management has evolved through these various schools of thought, it has enlarged its historical focus on the administrative process to encompass first psychology and sociology and then mathematics and economics. In the Systems School of management, the organization is viewed as a complex of internal subsystems interacting within a dynamic (and sometimes decentralized) environment. Kast and Rosenzweig, for example, have proposed a structure of five organizational subsystems: (1) goals and values; (2) technology; (3) structure; (4) psychosocial; and (5) managerial.

The Empirical School

One additional school of management thought is the Empirical School. Best typified by Ernest Dale of the Wharton School of Finance and Commerce at the University of Pennsylvania, this group looks at management as the study of experience. Rather than preparing a list of universally applicable principles, the successes and mistakes of a manager are evaluated in terms f specific situations. This group places a strong emphasis on the analysis of case studies as the primary teaching vehicle.

Conclusion

While the distinctions between some of the schools of management thought have become blurred, some of the questions remain. Is management an art or a science? Are management's decisions a result of intuition and experience or a result of mathematical modeling? What happens when the intuition proves to be the better choice? Is directive power "power over" or "power with?" To all this, the author adds a definition not seen in any of the works discussed: A manager is one who is responsible for more work than he can physically perform himself. If this is true, then the manager's ability to get work done through people becomes tremendously important.

THE ENVIRONMENTS IN WHICH AN ORGANIZATION MUST FUNCTION

An organization cannot—must not—function in a vacuum, else it ceases to be a social entity. No, the organization is best by both an external and internal environment which conditions the means whereby they conduct business.

The *external environment* consists of government, competitors, the labor force, unions, stockholders, suppliers, customers, and the public. The *internal environment* consists of the business system—resources (inputs), processing, outputs, management, standards—and situational requirements. Let's take them in that sequence.

External Environment

The Governmental Environment

All organizations are subject to Federal, State, and local statutes. To all levels of government they pay taxes, if they are for-profit organizations. If they are not, they certainly file reports with government.

There are, however, many government and labor relations laws for which they have responsibility. On the local scene, these will include distribution and movement laws and local zoning laws. More are enacted at the federal level. These include the following:

Sherman Anti-Trust Act of 1890. Prohibits monopolies and contracts or combinations in restraint of trade.

Pure Food and Drug Act of 1906. Prohibits the manufacture, sale, or transport of adulterated or improperly labeled food or drugs in interstate commerce.

Clayton Act of 1914. Supplements the Sherman Act by prohibiting certain actions which would substantially lessen competition or create a monopoly in any line of commerce.

Federal Trade Commission Act of 1914. Prohibits unfair methods of competition in commerce and sets up the Federal Trade Commission (FTC).

Wagner Act—National Labor Relations Act of 1935. Determines the responsibilities of business and labor in the field of collective bargaining and labor relations; recognizes the right of workers to organize, elect representatives, and bargain collectively.

Robinson Patman Act of 1935. Defines price discrimination as unlawful.

Wheeler–Lea Amendment of 1938 to Federal Trade Commission Act. Broadens FTC jurisdiction to include unfair or deceptive practices and those that injure the public.

Fair Labor Standards Act of 1938. Treats wages, hours, and working conditions for individuals engaged in interstate or foreign commerce; sets minimum wage and time-and-one-half for more than 40 hours per week.

Taft–Hartley Act—Labor Management Relations Act of 1947. Modifies the responsibilities of business and labor in collective bargaining; bans featherbedding, the closed shop, and other restrictive practices.

Anti-Merger Act of 1950. Broadens the Clayton Act to prevent intercorporate acquisitions which would have a substantially adverse effect on competition.

Landrum–Griffin Act of 1959. Safeguards the rights of union members against unions.

Federal Civil Rights Act of 1964. Prohibits discrimination on the basis of race, color, religion, sex, or national origin.

Environmental Protection Act of 1970. Expands the role of the Federal Government in the regulation of activities contributing to environmental pollution.

Occupational Safety and Health Act (OSHA). Establishes rules of safety for the workplace and the watchdog agency to oversee enforcement.

Fair Credit Act of 1973. Places the responsibility upon the seller to disclose, in terms understandable to the purchaser, the credit terms of any purchase or contact. Also permits the borrower to have access to his credit files and to request that changes or modifications be made to those files.

Privacy Act of 1975. Requires the registration of computer-based information systems (within the Federal Government) and makes available publicly held information about private individuals.

Small Business Computer Security and Education Act of 1984. Establishes a computer security and education advisory council consisting of ten members to advise the Small Business Administration (SBA) on the nature and scope of computer crimes committed against small business concerns; the effectiveness of Federal and State law in deterring computer-related criminal activity or prosecuting computer-related crimes; the effectiveness of computer technology and management techniques available to small businesses for increasing their computer security; the development of information and guidelines to be made available to the Administrator (SBA) to assist small business concerns in evaluating the security of computer systems; and other such appropriate functions of the small business computer security and education program.

These examples of the many Federal acts which affect the internal and external activities of business highlight the need for a legal representative on every management staff to interpret the legality of all that the business does or does not do.

The Competitor Environment

The organization faces both product and people competition. Product competition pits price against features, and sadly, quality foreign product against what seems to be inferior domestic product. There is people competition, as well. The labor pool in this country is diminishing. Competitors have a part in the market penetration and absorption for similar products. As many microcomputer manufacturers have discovered, the ability to produce is not ability to market.

The Labor Force Environment

Growth in the labor force is slowing. The median age of workers is increasing, and the mixture of that work force is changing. At the same time, the level of employment is increasing; in other words, those of our citizens who are employed want better jobs, leaving the menial jobs unattended.

There is a larger percentage of women in the work force. Increased levels of education have made it possible for everybody so motivated to achieve a higher standard of living. Manufacturing is stable or on a decline, as this country moves to a service economy and service-oriented businesses are increasing. As Victor Kiam (President of Remington Razor) says, ''We may all one day sell insurance to each other.''

Agriculture is declining, as misguided capital investment and often unscrupulous banking executives have encouraged capital expansion in the wake of a diminished price market created by the overproduction—while part of the world starves.

The Union Environment

The Union Environment is changing. The concept of a trade union was that labor needed a third party to unify member's interests. Shifts in the economy and shifts of manufacturing jobs overseas has raised the question as to whether a union is still a viable need. Over the years, as they have gained concessions, the union has changed from a horizontally opposed force to the point where it is not so anymore. While trying desperately to maintain its strength, management is fast gaining the upper hand by shutting down nonprofitable facilities, consolidating marginal facilities, and downsizing wage and benefit packages in the bargaining process.

The Stockholder Environment

The separation of ownership from management has been instrumental in the growth of professional management. In the United States, fragmentation of ownership allows thousands of people to own shares in our corporations, allowing them to share in the profits (if any) and in the determination of direction of the business. Represented by a Board of Directors, the stockholder, unless he has a large block of shares, has little voice. Management is answerable to the Board of Directors. Historically, the responsibility of the Board has been profits and premiums on stockholders' holdings, for the stockholders have had at least a monetary interest in the firm and have been sensitive to unexplained changes (losses).

In recent years, however, opinions of the stockholders have been solicited, causing the stockholder to take a larger interest in the firm's operation. This has often come about because the stockholder has often sought control or participation. Because of this, firms have taken an interest in certain social issues which may or may not have been legislated—environment, minority rights, women's movement, etc. Some of these have been addressed as a function of social responsibility; some as a function of internal and external pressures. Through this, we have seen the rise of public-interest stockholders.

The Social Environment

The public environment has drawn its share of concern. People have come to feel that a firm has a social responsibility to explain its purpose. Incidents of this include nuclear plants and disposal of hazardous materials. There has also been a heightened concern for ethics—contemporary standards or principles of conduct. Some of this represents a swing in the pendulum.

In his book *The Protestant Ethic and The Spirit of Capitalism,* Max Weber interpreted the Protestant ethic as the driving force behind capitalism. This ethic stemmed from the Calvinistic interpretation of earthly success as the mark of salvation. Idleness was viewed as sinful, while industry and thrift were accepted religious duties. Thus, amassing of capital and generation of profit became morally desirable.

In the mid-1950s, William Whyte identified a major shift in the ethical outlook from the individual to a more societal orientation. In *The Organization Man,* Whyte portrayed the individual who had become a cog in the wheel of the business enterprise, wherein the social pressures dictated right versus wrong, becoming the fountain of all knowledge and the source of all creativity. Whyte's social ethic required man to subordinate his goals to the objectives of the organization.

Today, society and business are swinging back toward center. According to Amitai Etzioni in *Modern Organizations,* the following is occurring:

1. Society becomes its own bureaucracy.
2. Science and technology have accelerated.
3. There has been an increase in mobility and decline of family.
4. Educational standards have risen.
5. Political consciousness has spread.
6. There is affluence for the majority.
7. There has been a liberation of the limits of socially acceptable conduct.

But the student of society would indicate that these very things are the harbingers of decay in our modern society. The decline of family alone has given rise to a welfare-oriented cadre of nonworkers who have become convinced that work is not necessary, and with good reason—it isn't. Educational standards may be rising, but educational practice has not followed suit. Scores are the worst they have been in history, unruly pupils make education unmanageable, and the rise of the private secular and religious educational facilities would indicate that there are more who would ascribe to the Protestant ethic than to other forms of societal description. They contend that the reason for all this decay is the seventh point of Etzioni's list, above. Enough said.

The Supplier Environment

We've learned a lot about cooperation in this country. We've learned that no auto parts means no cars, no coal means no electricity, and no gas and oil can mean no commerce. Again, as concerns for "me" have mounted, then perceived leverage and contentious labor strikes have created a force upon the organization that isn't conducive to growth. The pendulum has swung to the extreme, and is swinging back.

The Customer Environment

The customer is the ultimate judge. If the customer purchases the product, the organization profits and grows through its three stages of development: survival, profit, and growth. If it does not—the answer should be obvious. But customers may also be interested in peripheral issues: boycotts or minority hiring, etc. As product quality lapses have opened the door to foreign competition, customers have indicated that they've had enough and have evidenced a concern for both quality and quantity.

The Business System

Irrespective of the type of work you're in, that work is part of a business system. I constantly encounter the student who is so wrapped up in technology that he can't seem to see how that technology fits into the world of enterprise and that he could possibly one day be in a directing position within it.

The business system begins with inputs—the resources of people, materiel, capital, and financial. Traditionally, we have called these the factors of production—the 4Ms: Men (sorry, ladies), Money, Machines, and Materials. The second element of the business system, processing, is conversion and movement oriented, and does not include the managerial staff. Outputs are the organization's reason for being, and must conform to organization's goals and objectives.

To make this happen, management must create standards, performance guidelines which provide constant feedback and measurement. A business system is dynamic—it must have the ability to change. If it cannot change, it may not die, but it could be something less than successful. History is full of those organizations whose success was lower, but lived: Sears vs. Montgomery Ward; KMart vs. Woolco. There are those whose success was great, but who failed nonetheless: e.g., W. T. Grant and Robert Hall.

A business system must be dynamic, recognizing that any of these environments are subject to change: the external environment, the objectives of the firm, the state of the art of the technology, the structure of the organization, the personnel employed by the organization, and the managerial approaches which must be taken to correspond to these changes.

THE FUNCTIONS OF MANAGEMENT

Since the inception of Scientific Management, *planning* has been recognized as the fundamental and primary task of management and the foundation upon which all other management activities must be based. It is the process of preparing a set of decisions for future action directed at achieving goals in the best manner predictable. The key concepts of planning are that (1) it is oriented toward the future; (2) objectives must be preselected, and (3) rational and efficient strategies must be defined.

Planning need not be perceived from this viewpoint, however. Peter Drucker points out that planning is not forecasting but rather is needed because forecasts are inaccurate; planning does not deal with future decisions but rather with the future actions and consequences associated with present decisions; and planning is not the elimination of risk but rather the recognition of the costs associated with future uncertainty.

Objectives may be overlooked in the press of day-to-day operations. Planning forces management to consider all actions, both short-range and long-range, in terms of the organization's ultimate objectives. Planning also provides a basis for other functions of the manager. *Organizing* requires an understanding of objectives, processes, and resources in order to assemble a coherent structure. *Directing* requires a plan to establish the normal or desired manner of performance for efficient use of resources. *Controlling* depends upon the plan to define benchmarks, milestones, or standards so that actual versus forecasted environmental conditions can be evaluated.

Figure 3.1 shows graphically the functions of management.

The final element, *staffing* is perhaps the most important from the perspective that if there are insufficient or inadequate manpower resources, the best planning, organizing, directing, and controlling in the world will avail nothing. It's about this last element, staffing, that we know the least.

Figure 3.2 shows business as a flow process.

PLAN

The Planning Process

It has been said that if you fail to plan, you plan to fail. There are many ways to visualize the planning process. Figure 3.3 indicates the relationship of the planning factors encountered in planning. To some extent, there are a series of constraints which successively refine the courses of action available to move the enterprise toward its predetermined objectives. Perhaps the most important part of the illustration is the budget. The budget is the screen through which all the resources will pass. It is the primary control tool of any organization. The initial planning parameters are set by estimates or forecasts of external environmental conditions and anticipated resources. These parameters can be modified to some extent, as would be the case in a technological environment. Modification in that arena would come as a result of research and development.

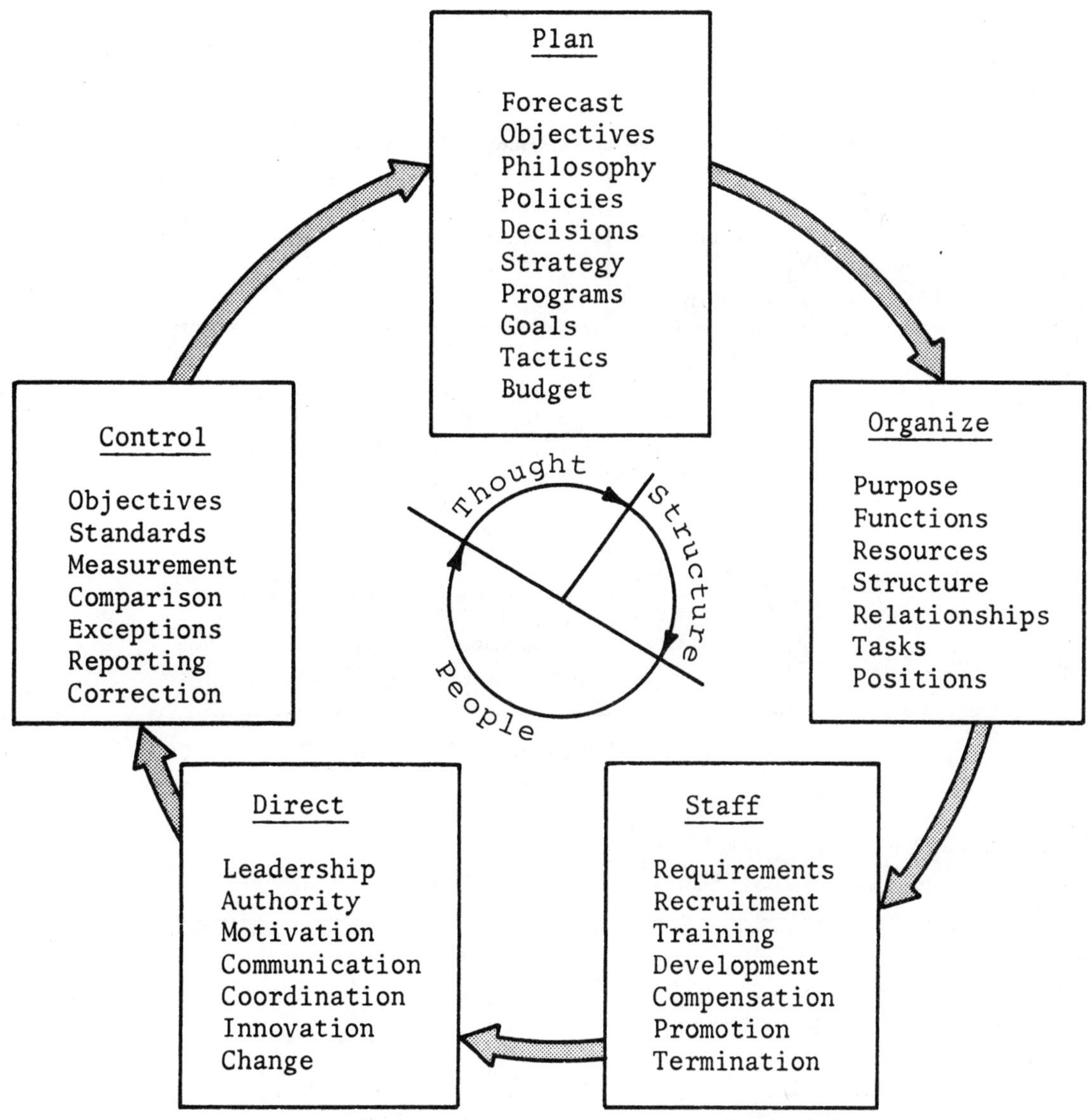

Figure 3.1. The functions of management

Most gratifying to the author in Figure 3.1 is the presence of creed, which we'll discuss presently. The creed here, however, is the organizational creed—the statement of the enterprise for publication to the world. Inherent in the organizational creed will be some formal statement of purpose and the method in which business will be conducted. Some will label it as a statement about nothing. But many will view the creed as an effort on the part of top management to define the organizational outlook. The most important part of the planning process is the mission—the goal set by the Board of Directors or other oversight board. These are the expected key results.

Policies are written statements or general understandings which guide the decision makers of the organization. Most policies are unwritten, for both good and bad reasons. 'We will never knowingly be undersold,'' says Ralph Williams (used car dealer immortalized on *The Tonight Show*). Whether he lives up to it, however, is another question. The statement is one of policy. Policies are forms of future plans, wherein the methods to achieve those plans are defined in a general sense. To some extent, they act as constraints upon the documented future plans of the organization. And, believe it or not, policies fre-

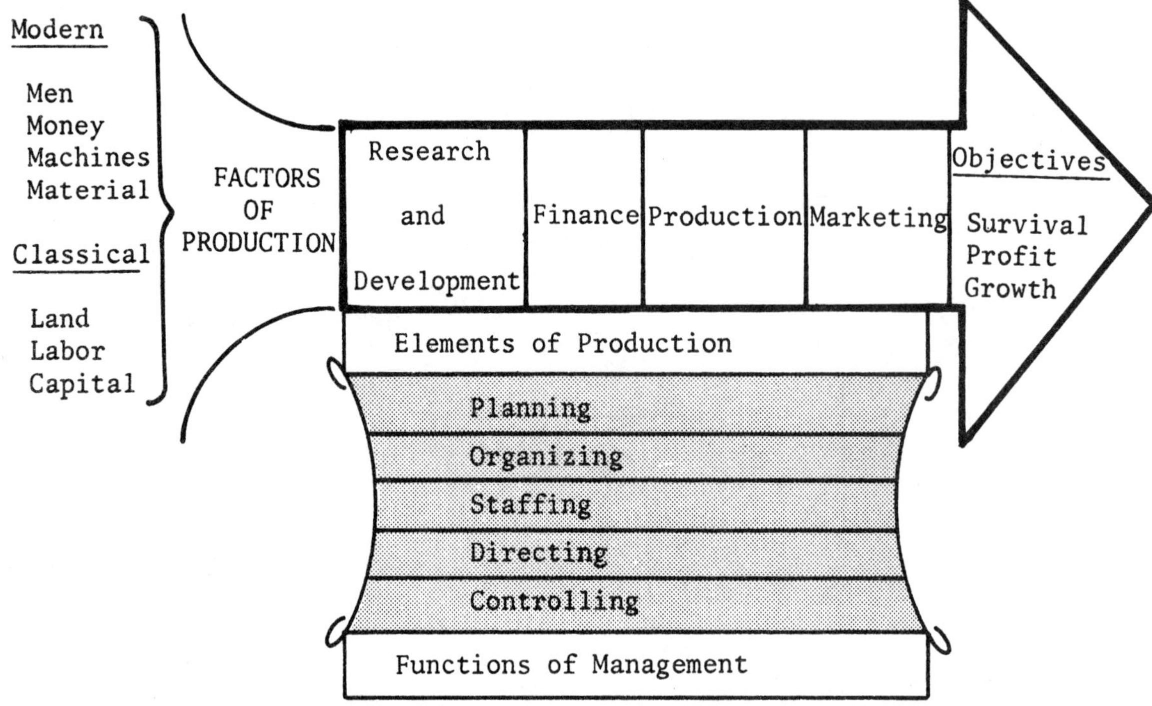

Figure 3.2. Business as a flow process.

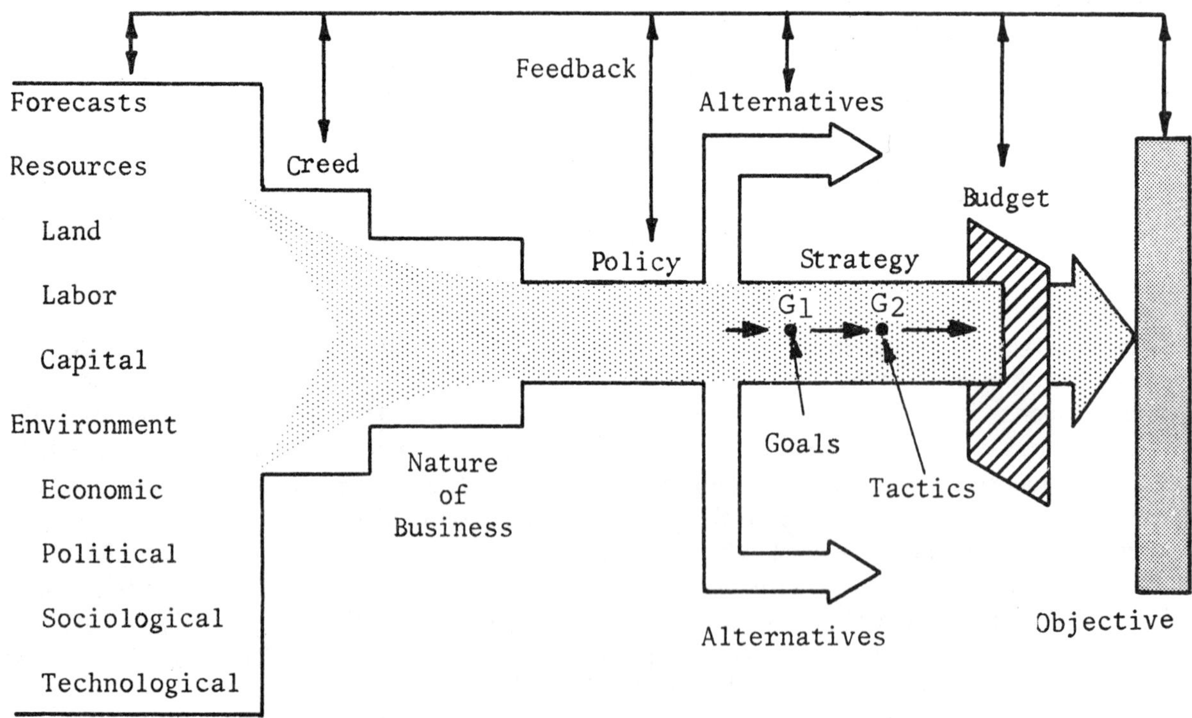

Figure 3.3. The relationship of planning factors.

quently get changed. They have to. 'We'll make the best buggy whips in the world'' no longer computes.

Procedures are detailed methods to handle future and present business in a more-or-less standardized manner. Generally, they are documented in some form of procedural manual or are stated in the forms of managerial philosophies and creeds.

Developing Strategies

Within the constraints of the creed, nature of the business, policies and procedures, the planner can now develop strategies or courses of action designed to reach objectives. To do so, he must define three things: (1) the specific goal to be achieved; (2) the specific method whereby the goal is to be achieved; (3) and the measuring technique whereby it can be determined that indeed the goal has been met.

Once the strategy has been selected intermediate goals and objectives are set. These are called *milestones* (though some would prefer to call them millstones). The plan is then translated into numerical terms, which now become the basis for a budget, which will be both a planning device and a control device. At each stage (the accomplishment of each milestone) there must be a feedback process for monitoring progress and adhering to budgetary constraints. The process of planning is therefore a continuous one, which must be constantly adjusted and redirected—not merely followed blindly.

In *The Effective Executive,* Peter Drucker lists six steps in the planning process:

1. Establish objectives.
2. List planning assumptions.
3. Determine alternative courses of action.
4. Evaluate alternative courses of action.
5. Select best course of action.
6. Formulate derivative plans.

Objectives

Objectives are the starting point. An organization's performance must be stated, against which all else will be measured. The planning function is meaningless unless objectives are clearly defined, realistically attainable, and accepted as valid by top management. Multiple objectives are normally established. The goal, having been established at the highest level, now needs the addition of methods and measurements, action words and target dates, set at every managerial level. These must be upwardly consistent with the established goals.

Peter Drucker suggested in *The Practice of Management* that, as a minimum, performance objectives are required in one of eight areas: (1) market standing; (2) innovation; (3) productivity; (4) physical and financial resources; (5) profitability; (6) manager performance and development; (7) worker performance and attitude; and (8) public responsibility.

One obvious problem is the selection of conflicting objectives. The objective of increased profit and the objective of increased market penetration may be mutually exclusive. Obviously a performance objective implies measurement, which implies, at the corporate level at least, some generally stated objectives.

There are several types of objectives. They might be economic, service, or personal. *Economic objectives* include survival—at or near breakeven; profit—economic incentives; and growth—long term survival. *Service objectives* include consumer orientation, product support, and product reliability. And the *personal objectives* which exist must match organizational interests. The specifics will vary with the internal vs. external forces upon the organization.

The process of setting objectives is not easy. There may be misstated or unstated goals, a practice which is common in highly political organizations. It is easy to set impossible-to-achieve goals or mutually exclusive goals, though they might all be very worthwhile. Shifting emphasis (situational management) makes measurements difficult to define in other than absolute terms.

Planning Considerations

A plan is as a plan does. A rigidly executed plan will probably fail, particularly if the enterprise is tied in any manner to the economy. The greater the uncertainty of the future, the longer alternatives must be kept available. The plans are the task lists for accomplishment of objectives, the specific achievement steps which are both people and task specific. *Strategic planning* identifies methods and alternatives—over a long-term plan. To do so, there must be a long-range mission statement, an analysis of the organization, a forecasting of the potential situation, organizational goals, operational objectives, and operational plans and programs.

There are short-range plans, intermediate-range plans, and long-range plans. Those plans which deal with the investment of capital into productive equipment with a useful life of 20 years will, no doubt, be considered long-range, and must be kept as flexible as possible in the face of future uncertainty. Short-range plans will be from a month to a small number of years. These plans can be discarded if proved to be infeasible. Intermediate-range plans may involve support for the long-range plans, such as a building program to enhance future production.

One factor is absolutely certain—all persons affected by the plan must have a hand in its development—for the secret ingredient in any planning situation is commitment.

Planning alone is not enough. Planning must be done against standards—the measurements of the objectives and of the plans—and policies, which are the organizational decision-making guidance documents. These can be established at any organizational level, and must be upward consistent. They include the procedures and rules—the "how to" methods, addressed to specific tasks and containing the embodiment of experience. And what makes it possible is the reactive planning—the feedback and modification cycle.

This makes the development of performance standards extremely important. These standards must contain statements of quantity, quality, time, and cost. And it requires that the process be supported by functions and Standard Operating Procedures (SOPs), rules of conduct and both exclusionary and inclusionary rules.

Planning Techniques

One of the best planning techniques is also embodied in the planning process. This is the process known as *Management By Objectives*—or MBO.

MBO holds that it isn't enough to set them—you must operate by them. It further holds that MBO is a participative establishment (all affected must be involved); is goal, not activity, directed; and forces forecasting and planning.

This century's Mr. Management, Peter Drucker, in *The Practice of Management,* states that a participative approach to management gets everybody involved in establishing goals, methods, and measurements for the following areas: market standing, innovation, productivity, worker performance and attitude, physical and financial resources, profitability, managerial performance and development, and public responsibility.

The MBO Process

MBO requires that long-range goals and strategies be set and that they be worked into specific organizational objectives. Next, the organization must establish individual performance objectives and standards, in the form of action plans tailored specifically to the individual. After some period of time, the results must be appraised, corrective action (if required) must be taken, and reward (if merited) or reprocessing need to occur.

Objective types selected should include those that are routine (recurring activities), problem-solving (the fundamental management task), innovative (forward progress objectives) and personal (growth and development). Individual objectives should be those which cause the person to stretch a step beyond yet be realistic and attainable, specific, measurable, and timed. Organizational objectives should define the principal thrust of the organization, the conditions and premises under which the organization must operate to achieve the objectives, identify individual contribution to the unit's direction, and the major results—the milestones to be achieved. Further, goals—significant end-targets—must be set, joint accountability—the who must be identified, and the range of progress behaviors must be established. And then, assessment weights must be assigned to specific achievement.

MBO Benefits and Problems

It is said that MBO has some very specific benefits:

- Builds tighter management; higher achievement
- Provides a planning system
- Forces priorities and measurable accomplishments
- Clarifies the roles, authorities, and responsibilities of people
- Obtains participative involvement
- Provides the primary control structure
- Provides career development opportunities

It also has some problems:

- It must be supported from the top level down to be effective
- Objectives are tough to write—it is hard to be specific
- It must be tightly monitored
- The short range is planned; the long range is avoided
- It takes large amounts of time

Graphic Techniques

Planning techniques and systems vary in complexity from the simple Gantt Planning Chart (discussed in Chapter 4), which shows task sequence against time, to the more systematic concepts, such as the Program Evaluation and Review Technique (PERT), a time-event network planning and analysis tool, also discussed in Chapter 4.

Simulation of business conditions by computer provides rapid analysis of multiple courses of action. Other quantitative decision-making techniques, such as breakeven analysis, linear programming, and game theory have also been applied to the planning processing. In general, any technique which provides more accurate forecasting data, a systematic consideration of alternatives, or a quantitative basis for decision-making could be categorized as a legitimate planning technique. Look for more discussion of these concepts in the section of the last chapter, where Decision Support Systems are discussed.

ORGANIZE

Organization

"Today we sit with our feet on the desk—tomorrow we've got to get organized." The quote implies "order." Order implies structure. Structure is largely a question of leadership. Organization implies formal and informal organizational entities, comprised of people, functioning as a unit which is group and goal-oriented, existing as a structure which defines and limits the behavior of individuals. It is hierarchical in nature, involves the movement of authority, and the movement of responsibility. And it has an information network, both formal and informal.

Organizing—like planning—is associated with an orderly process of getting things accomplished. The process of organization can be people-oriented or task-oriented. A synthesis of available definitions of organization includes the concept of a structural grouping, a defined relationship by individuals and subgroups of the structure, and a purposeful pattern of conduct, directed toward the goals/objectives defined as a part of the planning process.

Max Weber, in *The Theory of Social and Economic Organization,* indicated that the administrative bureaucracy is a particularly efficient form of organization, in which labor is clearly divided, a hierarchical authority structure exists, there are formal rules and regulations, impersonal management orientation, and a tendency toward career employment. It could be said that this is a Theory X orientation. The Management Process School stated that organization was a function of the tools used by the manager in the process of increasing complexity and organizational growth. Mutual benefit associations, service organizations, most commonwealth or governmental organizations are organizationally structured along the lines of services provided and tend to be more along the lines of Theory Y, as are some service industries, e.g., insurance, banking. Business activities may adopt a Theory X, Y, or Z posture relative to the product line or service, but the Theory Z will be implemented into organizations which have found participative cooperation to be desirable. We'll talk about Theories X, Y, and Z later.

Organizational Theories

Just as changes in areas of management focus can be historically traced through the various management schools, so too can similar changes in emphasis be seen in the field of organizational theory. Taylor and Fayol were interested primarily in the structural patterns of the task relationships within the organization. The most important organizational principle to this group was the division of labor, or specialization.

Taylor carried this concept to the extreme by proposing a single, repetitive task as the optimum for each worker—making the individual a machine. In practice, the concepts of specialization/division of labor dominated the managerial scene for many years. The classical principle of unity of command, wherein each worker had a single boss, emphasized the reliance on a structural pattern. Numerical limitations of numbers to be supervised (span of control) would be a critical determinant to the structure of the organization.

With the Hawthorne experiments, emphasis shifted from the formal structure of the informal patterns of human interrelationships and organization. If people, as parts of the organization, were different, so, too, were the tasks different, and certainly the results would be different.

The mixture of the classical theory with the behavioral school is not easy to define. Modern writers find that:

1. The individual is an organizational component.
2. Both structural (scalar, vertical) and functional (horizontal) relationships must exist.
3. The informal organization is real and productive.
4. The role and status system operates, but is not always productive.
5. The environment (both physical and emotional) is becoming more important to the practical operation of the organization.

These parts are linked together by communications, by the decision process, and by the limits (policy) within which the organization functions.

Departmentalization and Support Activities

Because of span-of-control considerations, an organization can only grow—and then can grow indefinitely—along the lines of functionalization, fractionalization, or departmentalization. Functionalization implies, of course, that the organization is divided along the lines of product, clientele, or other natural division. An example of functionalization would be the Caterpillar Tractor Company, whose several plants produce unique (albeit interrelated) equipment. Fractionalization is more evident in organizations whose divisions compete for either the same market or significant overlaps of the same market. One example of fractionalization would have to be IBM. Finally, departmentalization is evident in nearly every organization with a variety of business functions to be performed—the accounting department, the shipping department, the purchasing department, and the like.

There are many different criteria which can be used as the basis for departmentalization. A few follow:

1. *Numbers.* An organization can be divided simply by numbers—so many people involves a specific organization. The Army has nine men to a squad, three squads to a platoon, three platoons to a company, and so on.
2. *Time.* The shift foreman, responsible for an eight-hour slice of continuous operation, is an example of time departmentalization.
3. *Location.* The division of a company into geographic units is another method of organization along the lines of materials sources, transportation access, repair facilities, or consolidated warehousing.
4. *Clientele.* Here the company is structured to support specific markets or places of doing business. Again, IBM, with its General Division and its World Trade Division exemplifies this.
5. *Function* or *process.* Grouping in terms of product similarity. This has the advantages of maximum specialization, direct representation, and good communications, but lacks organizational unity.
6. *Product.* Departmentalization by product may group disparate functions together to contribute to the singular end product.

Each method of departmentalization has distinct advantages and problems. In some instances, one division doesn't want to know about another division. Communications may suffer where organizational entities are remotely located from one another. Competition for resources is keen where similar products are produced or similar customers are served. It must be noted that departmentalization is not an either/or proposition. Depending upon the size of the organization, departmentalization may be absolutely necessary. Larger organizations cannot operate without divisions. Smaller organizations probably can't function very effectively with them.

Allied to the question of basic departmentalization is the assignment of service activities. Those organizational elements not directly concerned with the major function of the organization but which cut across organizational lines are included here. Production, finance, research, customer service, marketing, personnel, data processing, etc., might be classified as support activities. The location of these activities is generally dictated by the needs of the organization. In the computer area, centralized expensive hardware has been the only possible way to obtain computing power. The advent of the microcomputer and distributed data processing concepts has changed on that. The larger organization might have the personnel and finance functions, but smaller groups at remotely located sites might perform certain of the otherwise centralized functions. Some functions, such as public relations and legal services exist at the staff level alone.

Structure and Purpose

There is a clear relationship between the purpose of an organization and its structure. This occurs because the purpose is to perform certain tasks for which a unique structure is evolved. Structure is most often the result of dictum. But if Ouchi is to be believed (we will discuss his Theory Z later), the following procedure will produce a workable structure:

1. Determine the nature or purpose of the unit.
2. Establish collective objectives.
3. Select a course of action and establish policies and plans to achieve objectives.
4. Establish subgoals which are achievable by one or more members of the group.
5. List the specific activities and functions required to meet the goals established by the group.
6. Categorize activities and functions into related groups.
7. Determine the resources required and balance against the resources available for each function or activity.
8. Establish a systematic pattern of related groups of activities, considering group and individual limitations.
9. Link the pattern of groups into a structure with lines of control and areas of responsibility. This can be either a formal or an informal structure.
10. Provide for horizontal and vertical communication systems and information flow.

Evaluating the structure is somewhat more difficult, and requires one of the following approaches:

1. *Problem approach.* Define existing problems through analysis of performance, interviews, or observation; analyze each problem for causal factors and interrelationships; take corrective measures to solve specific problems.
2. *Functional analysis.* Evaluate the specific functions of each activity or subsystem and list the contributions of these functions to the accomplishment of overall objectives; consider regrouping of functions in terms of contribution.
3. *Interaction analysis.* Evaluate the extent to which each subactivity supports, is dependent on, or interacts with other subactivities; regroup subactivities so that maximum interaction occurs within rather than between organizational subunits.
4. *Work-load analysis.* Evaluate the organizational resources used by each subactivity for attainment of specific outputs; reallocate total organizational resources so that each subactivity has the same proportion of organizational resources per unit of output.

Regardless of the specific approach taken, the organization must be considered as an interrelated whole, rather than a summation of discrete parts. However, each part must be examined in terms of its contribution to the ultimate objectives of the organization.

Centralization and Decentralization

Just as a discussion of line and staff (see below) revolves around authority rather than function, the terms *centralization* and *decentralization* also hinge on authority relationships. The two apply to decision-making, not to geography or function. Distinguish, please, among *decentralization* (decision-making authority is pushed downward), *departmentalization* (group activities on the basis of characteristic), and *delegation* (entrusting work to others by assigning tasks, granting authority, and exacting responsibility). Consider Table 3.1.

FACTOR	FAVORING DECENTRALIZATION	FAVORING CENTRALIZATION
Cost of decision	Low cost	High cost
Policy	Uniform	Broad, vague
Economic	Large	Small
History of expansion	External acquisition	Internal growth
Local environment	Dynamic	Stable
Output	Objective standards	Difficult to measure
Subordinate	Well trained	Inexperienced

Table 3.1

Each situation must be examined individually. As organizations become larger and more complex, the trend in the production and marketing functions is toward decentralization. However, external pressures has driven business to increased centralization of common functions.

Line and Staff

It has become common to classify some organizational activities as line activities and other as staff activities. It is the nature of the authority relationship, however, rather than the category of activity which differentiates the two. In the line organization, there is an uninterrupted chain of authority from top to bottom. The staff elements are advisory or support.

Much of the line/staff confusion stems from a failure to recognize different kinds of staffs:

1. *Advisory staff.* Provides technical or specialized advice and counsel to superiors; advises, recommends, but does not decide.
2. *Service staff.* Advises superior in technical area of expertise; provides selected services to operating managers. The chief of the service staff exercises line authority over own work force and has strong influence over line managers in service area.
3. *Control staff.* Advises superior in own technical area and monitors line activities within designated area of responsibility. Policies and procedures are developed and monitored continuously by the control staff, prescribing definite limits to the authority of the manager.
4. *Functional staff.* Functions as a line manager within designated area of responsibility; functional authority cuts across normal command lines for specific activities.

The potential for line/staff conflict is high, since the line manager normally bears ultimate responsibility for operating functions. The kind of staff authority, the duties of the individuals, and the ultimate responsibilities must be clearly defined and understood by all parties.

In general, Line = Manager. Line personnel are directly involved in the product. They are a critical part of the scalar chain and derive authority from the scalar chain. Staff, on the other hand, are people of a specialized component. They are an expansion of executive activities, filled by the rotation of individuals among staff positions. The staff person advises, guides, counsels, and serves line personnel. His or her authority is derived by extension of executive authority, via the policy route. That authority is functional authority, permitting the exercise of authority over individuals outside the scalar chain. There are definite delegations of functional line authority and functional staff authority.

There are specific types of functional staff who provide service, advice, control, initiation, and innovation within a specialized function, e.g:

- Maintenance—service
- Market research—advice
- Quality Control—control
- Production control and scheduling—initiation
- Research and development—innovation
- Personnel—functions
- Accounting—functions

The levels of staff participation will vary. There may be companywide services (e.g. personnel), services with a function (e.g. accounting), multi-divisional administration (e.g., labor contract). Because of the growth of technology-based staff positions, staff growth has been faster (or earlier) than line. The same is true with any startup organization.

Teamwork is not easily achieved between line and staff personnel. Line complaints include the statement that staff wants to usurp line authority; is academic, theoretical, unrealistic; proposes untested, untried ideas; is too technical; thinks in a vacuum; is not enterprise-oriented; takes credit for successes, blames line for failures. Staff complaints include that line managers resist new ideas; are unwilling to accept progress; do not use resources wisely; do not ask for sound advice for fear they will look bad or defeated; distrust staff advisor because of the Mt. Olympus Syndrome. Staff further complains that it does not have enough authority—must trade on line's willingness to implement; that its authority is based on position rather than on expertise.

Coordination

It takes the skills of many to get a modern technologically based task completed. Coordination, then, is brought on by division of labor (specialization). Division of labor is, by definition, decentralization. It is necessary to production processes and it is necessary to management.

Coordination is not cooperation. Cooperation is the assistance of function, the attitude of a group of people, the passing of information; it is beyond desire and willingness.

Let us then give coordination this definition: Coordination is the conscious process of assembling and synchronizing differentiated activities so that they function harmoniously in the attainment of organizational objectives.

There are several methods of coordination. There is self-coordination—crossing a functional line at the lowest possible level. Often people maintain the coordination of linkages among tasks. There is the coordination by standardization (programmed decisions)—the project plan, coordination by plan—the project group; and coordination by mutual adjustment.

Coordination requires notices of deviation from plan, stabilization of varying conditions. It also requires vertical movement (among levels): first, by delegated authority and next, by demonstrated performance. Finally, it requires horizontal movement at the same organizational level, and amongst other departments. Coordination works best where there are good personal relationships, good communication, and the wisdom to institute such early in the process.

Coordination plays a critical part in the functions of management: in planning, as planning affects all; in organizing, to achieve workable structures; in staffing, to find the necessary skills to fill positions; in leading, to achieve harmonious and reciprocal performance, and in control, for the evaluation of operations; and one more—in liaison, where coordinators must operate without authority to commit.

Committees

Committees are a way of life in just about any organization. But a committee evokes reactions:

> A camel is a horse designed by a committee.

A group of the unfit, assigned by the unwilling to perform the unnecessary.

For God so loved the world that he *didn't* send a committee.

Committees have a variety of functions and levels. They are classified according to the level to which they are attached. There are policy, executive, finance, audit, bonus and salary, product, and nominating committees. The are high-level committees which investigate, debate, discuss, and recommend; and there are low-level procedural committees. There are staff committees which provide guidance, counsel, and advice; and line committees where the plural executive provides decisions. There are temporary or standing committees—classified by longevity. A temporary committee is one formed for a project or issue. A standing committee has a permanent place in the organization and deals with recurring problems.

There are, of course, advantages to the committee structure. These include combined opinion, coordination and cooperation, the development of executives, and representation of interest groups. There are also liabilities: the high cost—particularly time and meeting costs; limited effectiveness, as committees often solve problems which are not creative in nature; divided responsibility; the possibility of weak compromising decisions and of a mindset of "go along to get along."

There is one major disadvantage of committees: *groupthink.* Groupthink creates the illusion of invulnerability, super optimism which ignores danger signals. There is the danger of rationalizing, of assuming the committee has been constituted for some high moral purpose. And the major disadvantage of that is that the "good guys" need not live with conclusions. Such committee composition tends to stereotype adversaries, apply pressure to deviants, and apply pressure to themselves to agree in public. The illusion of unanimity foregoes critical thinking, creates mindguarding (don't confuse me with facts), and places a strain on interpersonal relations.

Despite this, committees must exist, so it is imperative to determine effective means to operate the committee. These are some of the things which can be done:

- Clearly define function, scope, and degree of authority.
- Select appropriate members
- Select a reasonable size (number of members)
- Thorough preparation for meetings
- Establish procedures for minutes, etc.
- Select an astute chairperson—with leadership ability
- Foster group interaction
- Follow up the committee action for results
- Evaluate committee work

Organizational Structure

Organization relates to planning. It is followed by functionalization—what work is to be accomplished? Of course, functionalization has dangers—the dangers of too many functions and the dangers of too few. Knowledge of what to do is required for wise allocation of resources, human and physical. The division of function and departmentalization has several criteria for distribution, several strengths and weaknesses. The opportunity to establish an organization requires the assignment of responsibility, authority, and accountability. Accountability must be verified and the interfaces—the information network must be established.

Functionalization is made more interesting by the dissimilarity of tasks and functions, the requirements for both horizontal integration and vertical integration. There is a specialization, a division of labor, and work simplification pressures.

There are advantages:

- Output is increased by repetitive tasking, common in production shops and piecework shops where the utilization of people and quality increases are important.
- Uniformity allows increases in the span of control. The platoon sergeant can march 10 or 100; the traffic cop reaches beyond his sight. Narrow focus eases training and assignment. Time compression is available. Specialized skills and complex projects don't qualify.

There are also disadvantages:

- Fatigue and boredom are mind dulling to those involved in repetitive tasks. This affects absenteeism and disrupts quota systems. It affects turnover, where flexibility exists.
- It adds levels to the hierarchy, creating downward differentiation, requiring management personnel to fill many hats in a tri-level activity—management, supervision, and operations. Naturally, this will create span of control concerns.

Unlimited control is impossible. One cannot thoroughly supervise a hundred people; one is better able to supervise only two or slightly more. The manager must also manage interfaces, calculated by the formula $n(n - 1)$. If he or she supervises two: $2(1) = 2$ interfaces; if supervises three: $3(2) = 6$; if supervises four: $4(3) = 12$.

When divisions are added to the organization there is outward differentiation. New specializations, new business ventures, and divisions of complexity create a revision of the original functionalization. Areas of functional similarity become targets for consolidation unless they are geographically diverse. Combinations of similar businesses are done on the basis of similarity of work, skills, and functions. Exceptions include the purposeful duplication or separation of control, audit, and challenge activities.

Management as a Human-to-Human Activity

If the manager's task is to be effective leader charged with the responsibility to see work accomplished through people, then the structure of the organization matters not. In the transition from the perspectives of the manager to the perspectives of the managed, it is necessary to discuss the concepts of authority versus responsibility and responsibility versus accountability.

There are four predominant theories of the authority-responsibility combination:

1. The *acceptance theory* of authority means that those who are to be managed accept the fact that Manager X has been placed in charge and is being held responsible for the productive output of that unit. This is the concept of consent of the governed.
2. The *institutional theory* holds that power is bestowed by position. The manager, therefore, has those authorities and responsibilities as defined by fiat—nothing more and nothing less. The managed persons therefore look upon the manager as one for whom the minimum acceptable work will be performed.
3. The *competence theory* holds that the individual with the technical expertise or who knows the answers must, by definition be the manager. It assumes that people will follow. A television commercial recently demonstrated this admirably: "When E. F. Hutton speaks, people listen." This was before E. F. Hutton was convicted of account kiting.
4. The *charismatic theory* holds that the individual who by force of personality is placed in a management position will be able to provide the necessary leadership to manage well. This works well for a time, but charisma is a shell; subordinates learn of the shell game very quickly.

5. One variation of the charismatic theory is the *quota theory.* This theory holds that leadership can be effectively provided if a suitable number of women, ethnic minorities, or other disadvantaged individuals are placed in a position of leadership. Women, ethnic minorities, and others have been effective leaders in their own right because of those characteristics exhibited by themselves. But employees, aware of the quota management, accommodate the system at best, eventually moving away from the situation.

It has said that authority can be delegated, but responsibility cannot. Responsibility is inherent in the individual himself and must be accepted to be successful. Accountability is responsibility viewed from the perspective of the board of directors. Responsibility is accountability viewed from the perspective of the individual. In short, the manager must have a personal management credo to be successful. One such credo is presented next:

If I created it and it is good, you owe your thanks. I will convey your thanks to my people, as they created it, and not I. If I created it and it is not good, express your concern, but withhold your anger. It is a problem and I shall, with the help of my people, attempt to correct it expeditiously. It is I—and not my people—who am responsible.

If you need a job done and it is within our capabilities, we will attempt to accommodate your wishes. Be prepared, however, to recognize that work requires the resources of people and time—your people and time as well as mine. Your work will be entered to the plan and prioritized among the needs of others. You will be told the truth, insofar as truth can be determined, as to what can and what cannot be done and when it can be done. If it cannot be done, you will know it, and we will seek other alternatives.

My people, like your people, work within a discipline. They are no more or less qualified than your people in their respective fields. They cannot work miracles. They are subject to the same human errors. They react well to praise and rail against criticism, just as any human being will. I am their buffer. I will define their work, seek their understanding and commitment, and measure their performance. You will measure mine. People seek to do a good job and to take pride in their work. We can both enhance the accomplishment of our specific objectives if we but remember that all work is accomplished through people.

Be prepared always to hear the truth, despite the fact that it may not coincide with your wishes. I do not tell people what they wish to hear for the sake of pacification, nor promise to do what cannot reasonably be done. In the final analysis, the accomplishment of work within my area is my responsibility and mine alone. My people's successes are my successes. Their failures are my failures. There will be no finger-pointing, blame allocation, or individual derision. We succeed or fail as a unit. If that is not acceptable, then another, more malleable person should be sought to replace me. Flexibility will always be offered, but will be tempered with restraint, as realistic expectations are achievable.

I am a person who is responsible for more work than I can physically perform myself. For that reason, I do not know, and do not wish to know, all the details of every task for which I am responsible. The work in this unit will be performed by people whose skills match the tasks to be done. If those skills cannot be matched to the tasks, then the people will be developed to the point where a match can be made. Success is always the result of the product of people whose needs are met, working within a framework of reasonable allocation of resources, and progressing toward a goal worthy of accomplishment. If I can elicit such, we can be successful, and your needs will be met. If I cannot, it is your right to replace me. I'll take the resources afforded me, plan their use as thoroughly as possible, use them as efficiently as possible, and obtain the results which are possible. Expect me to resist the impossible.

Authority must equal responsibility. Authority without responsibility will lead to power for the sake of power. A management credo is a healthy effort to establish yourself as a manager who can accept responsibility, demands commensurate authority, and willingly places upon his or her own shoulders the mantle of accountability. If you are a manager and do not have such a credo, try mine.

Organizational Climate, Change, and Development

Organizations must change. Management must create the psychological environment of the firm, composed of friendliness, supportiveness, risk-taking, etc. There are factors which will affect how this is done.

Organizational characteristics—the size, complexity, formalization, and autonomy given to the group.

Administrative processes—including the reward system, communications system, conflict/cooperation mechanisms, and the tolerance of risk.

Manager and supervisor aloofness or involvement—what is the emphasis on output? Is there an atmosphere of consideration and trust?

The work group—what is the commitment to it, hindrances to it, morale, and friendliness?

There are some definite types of organizational climates: they may be participative or they may be closed and threatening. In the participative climate, subordinates are trusted, communication is open, leadership is considerate and supportive, there is group problem solving, there is worker autonomy, there is information sharing, and high output goals. In a closed and threatening environment, there are high output goals, but they are declared and imposed goals. Leaders are autocratic and threatening and have a high degree of rigidity. There is strict adherence to rules and structures, and emphasis on the individual, rather than groups. People move as if they were simply going through the motions.

In the participative climate, where there is psychological involvement, there is an increased acceptability of management's ideas, an increased cooperation with members of management and staff, reduced turnover, reduced absenteeism, reduced complains and grievances, greater acceptance of changes, improved attitudes toward the job and the organization. There is a positive relationship between employee participation and issues of morale, turnover, and absenteeism. It doesn't come free, however. It requires more time, is dependent upon the ability of the participants, is subject to the restrictions of the structure and system (if any), requires self-government, and requires an inquisitive mind. It's not palatable to all involved, and imposes workload and time restrictions.

Organizational development begins with the acceptance of the need to make changes. First, the organization must recognize the need for change:

We've ALWAYS done it this way.

That won't work HERE.

He's a newcomer. What can HE know?

If it works, don't fix it.

There has to be a curiosity and discontent—a rallying for change; finding out what in the system doesn't work or doesn't work well; seeking new activities and keeping an open mind.

The process of change means leaving the status-quo, overcoming or diminishing resistance to change, recognizing that ineffectiveness is undesirable. It means moving to a new level, initiating the change (by order, recommendation, or self-starting). That is, of course, workable only if person feels a need to change. It may even require a catalyst. Finally, it means acquiring a new status quo, the adoption of permanent change.

People resist change—perhaps because of insecurity. A change of environment brings uncertainty. It is highly charged emotionally, for there is a change of mode. We get comfortable in our organizational cocoons. Change may means social loss, economic losses, or inconvenience.

So if you must make changes, make only necessary changes. Justify the change and make no change for the sake of change, else there will be an imbalance. Keep as much the same as possible, don't violate the group norms, and quickly align to the organizational culture. Work on trust; justify the change and involve subordinates in the planning. Make no surprises, encourage participation, guarantee against loss wherever possible, and *COMMUNICATE.*

Developing the Organization (OD)

Organizational development is a planned and calculated attempt to change the organization to a more behavioral environment. It begins with a survey of attitudes and treatment with respect. Next, teams and work groups are built. Where necessary, sensitivity training will provide increased openness, greater concern for others' needs, increased tolerance, reduced prejudice, an awareness of group processes, enhanced listening skills, training in the management approach. MBO becomes a very good plan for organizational development, and the introduction of a change agent, an outside catalyst, is often very positive.

STAFF

The Management of the Human Resource

Staffing involves three activities—personnel planning, recruiting, and selection. Personnel planning is the anticipation of future skill needs for growth and turnover. Recruiting is the location of and inviting of people with the skills to apply for employment. And selection matches the availability of skills to the needs of the organization.

Another part of the staffing activity involves training and (organizational) development. There is general training—indoctrination; there is technical training—job related training; and there is development—shaping for the future.

Staffing activities also include goal-oriented performance appraisal—a two-part appraisal of both employee and employer. On the heels of that comes compensation—the handling of pay, benefits, and nonmonetary rewards.

Likewise, there are the health and safety concerns—freedom from illness, freedom from danger; employee relations; and personal research—with an aim toward improvement.

Personnel and the Law

There are a few laws which govern how staffing is done:

Equal Pay Act (1963/1972). Prohibits wage discrimination on the basis of sex. Set up the Equal Employment Opportunity Commission (EEOC).

Civil Rights Act of (1964/1972). Prohibits discrimination on the basis of race, color, religion, sex, or national origin. It is enforced by the EEOC, and assures affirmative action via quota systems. Expect this law to be changed to remove quotas.

Age Discrimination Act of (1967/1978). Prohibits discrimination of people in the age bracket of 40–70. Controls the selection, retention, promotion, and compensation of that age group. It, too, is enforced by the EEOC.

Occupational Safety and Health Act of 1970. Assures healthy working conditions; enforced by the Occupational Safety and Health Administration.

Privacy Act of 1974. Restricts access to files containing personnel information.

Employee Retirement Income Security Act of 1974 (ERISA). Protects the interests of employees in benefit plans; establishes standards and fiduciary obligations.

Pregnancy Discrimination Act of 1978. An amendment to the Civil Rights Act; affords medical consideration for maternity.

EEOC Guidelines—Sexual Harassment. The employer is responsible.

The Staffing Process

The staffing process begins with *human resources planning.* It's tied to the work plan and anticipates shortages. It permits forecasts of recruitment needs.

The next step is *job analysis.* Job analysis begins with a job description which outlines the duties to be performed, the supervision given and received, the relationships of this job to other jobs, equipment and materials needed to do the job, and the physical working conditions. This is then used to produce a *job specification,* wherein the requirements of the job, the educational qualifications, the experiential qualifications, the personality and the desired physical abilities of the candidate should be.

The job analysis involves a *workload analysis,* which estimates the work to be done (type and quantity), performs time and motion studies, extrapolates work statistics, and matches these factors to a table of organization. The *workforce analysis* includes skills inventories, the history and experience of employees, their skills and qualifications, and any other related information.

An opening exists. A personnel requisition is created. Recruitment begins. Shall we promote from within or seek an outside source? There are advantages to promoting from within—is increased morale, evaluations of these people are already available, and the people are encouraged to be prepared. There are also some disadvantages—it promotes inbreeding, and often there are too few people available from whom to select.

Next comes *selection* from the available candidates. There is a resume or application, perhaps some test scores (typing, aptitude, or psychological tests), interviews (screening, patterned, or stress), and then reference checks. In this last area, there is often some difficulty. The Privacy Act has removed most of what you can find out. That information is usually limited to verification of employment, and generally must be permitted by the candidate.

Next comes the *approval*—the final decision is departmental, often through channels. An offer letter is sent to the candidate by the Personnel Department. If the candidate accepts, then the process continues.

A *physical examination* might be a requirement of the insurance carrier which carries major health and accident benefits for the organization. It might be occasioned by the physical demands of the job (e.g., fireman, longshoreman). It is also designed to preclude any claims arising from prior situations. Sometimes it is waived (EEO).

And finally, there is *orientation*—indoctrinating the candidate in the ways your organization performs its business.

Selecting managerial personnel is a bit more crucial. Managers should be selected for abilities in planning, communication, decision-making skills, organizing ability, motivation and leadership skills, conceptual skills, adaptability to change, and personal qualities.

DIRECT

Directing involves the total manner in which a manager influences the actions of his subordinates. Since the word carries a Theory X connotation, some people prefer the term *actuating*. The whole idea is to persuade the individual to work toward the accomplishment of specific goals through his own volition. Only when that cannot be successfully accomplished does the Theory X connotation of direction come into focus. Recall, however, that Chester Barnard indicated that authority was also a function of the consensus of the group. Thus the acceptance theory of authority. Barnard felt that the individual will not accept a communication (order) unless he understands the communication, believes it is consistent with the purpose of the organization, perceives that it is compatible with his personal interests, and is physically and mentally able to comply.

This concept is difficult to accept because of the power of the manager to promote, denote, discharge, establish pay, assign work, transfer, and control benefits. Thus the question is whether the worker accepts the manager's recommendation or whether he, in fact, recognizes the rewards and sanctions in the hands of the manager.

Any discussion of authority inevitably raises the question of responsibility. Recall that this chapter contains the author's perspective that the manager is responsible for more work than he can physically perform himself. Responsibility is the obligation one owes to his superiors. It is synonymous with accountability for entrusted duties. It is not authority. Authority can be delegated. Responsibility cannot. While the subordinate may be accountable (responsible) to his superior, the superior continues to be absolutely responsible (accountable) for the actions of his subordinate. Ideally, authority must equal responsibility. A manager cannot be responsible for the results of responsibility without adequate authority. Conversely, authority without responsibility may lead to the indiscriminate application of power.

Unity of command applies to authority, as well. Within a given functional area, the line of authority, delegation of duties, and scope of responsibilities should be clearly defined.

Leadership

Leadership is the process of influencing others to work together willingly in a common effort to achieve a goal, whether or not that goal coincides with the individual's goals. It has been observed that managers should be leaders but leaders need not be managers. Or, in other words, a good manager is a successful leader—but a successful leader could be an ineffectual manager who, though capable of leading might lead in an incorrect direction. Such can have the title, but not the ability. Others can have the ability, but not the title.

There are, it is said, two kinds of leaders—the appointed leader and the annointed leader. The appointed leader is, of course, that individual who has been placed into the position of leadership. The annointed leader is the natural leader, the one individual whom each member of the group will follow. Occasionally, upper-level management will appoint the natural leader. When that happens, that group makes considerable progress. When the natural leadership and the positional appointment do not reside in the same individual, there is always a contest, the group makes marginal forward progress (if any), and there will be a higher than anticipated turnover. Were upper-level management to recognize that, changes in the leadership positions could more easily be made by allowing the natural leader to emerge. Thus, Theory Z, which will be discussed later.

Leadership can be dictatorial; it can function through fear. It can be autocratic, where conformance is rewarded. It can be laissez faire, where any direction, within reason, will be tolerated as long as the impression of general progress is maintained. A leader has several bases of power. It may be formal, based on legitimate authority. It may offer reward, through the ability to administer and control perquisites. It may be coercive, carrying the ability to administer and control punishment. It may be expert, based on special knowledge or skill. Or it may be referent, based on personal characteristics.

Or, leadership can be democratic, where the management will consult with the group—where the group participates but does not vote. This, essentially, is consensus leadership. The so-called Z-groups will require consensus for decisions, but unanimity of direction.

There are two specific leadership roles by which a manager is considered to lead—task and emotive. In the *task role,* objectives are imposed—from above, from the side. The leader accepts the objectives and moves the task along. The *emotive role* handles the individual's needs, provides social and psychological supports. The issue is solely task performance.

Leadership Theories

Of course, there are several theories of leadership, just as there are several theories of management.

The *genetic theory* of leadership holds that the individual is a "born leader." This leader's leadership traits are inherited and class barriers preclude building education and skills This theory has been pretty much discredited.

The *trait theory,* according to Edwin Ghiselli, holds that one demonstrates supervisory ability by performing the functions of management. This individual has a need for occupational achievement, has intelligence—creative and verbal ability, judgment, reasoning, and thinking capacity; decisiveness—capability and competence; self-assurance—the individual's view of himself or herself; initiative—independent action, self-starting. He also holds that there are certain leadership traits—the leader is somewhat taller, is outgoing, is self-confident, and has higher intelligence—all traits which are not limited to leaders.

The *follower theory* of leadership indicates that leadership is a function of group dynamics. People follow a person for fulfillment of their needs. Leadership happens when the leader emerges, not when he's appointed.

Behaviorial Theories of Management

Let's now begin to examine some theories of managerial behavior, beginning with Rensis Likert's Universal Theory of Management.

Rensis Likert, in *New Patterns of Management,* held that management would fall into one of four categories: (1) exploitive authoritative; (2) benevolent authoritative; (3) consultative; and (4) group participative. Likert believed that in the short run peak performance would come from the exploitative authoritative style (commonly called Theory X or Grid 9,1). He preferred the group participative form of leadership, with the leader/manager as a linking pin between the organization at large and the group being managed. Figure 3.4 demonstrates this concept.

There are other approaches, of course. Mary Parker Follette held that here is such a thing as situational leadership. This concept has been expanded by Paul Hersey and Kenneth Blanchard in the model shown in Figure 3.5.

Note from the illustration that there are two axes: task behavior (directive behavior), whose range is low to high, and relationship behavior (supportive behavior) whose range is also low to high. The matrix is divided into four quadrants (situations), each with specific levels of action and maturity. Quadrant 1

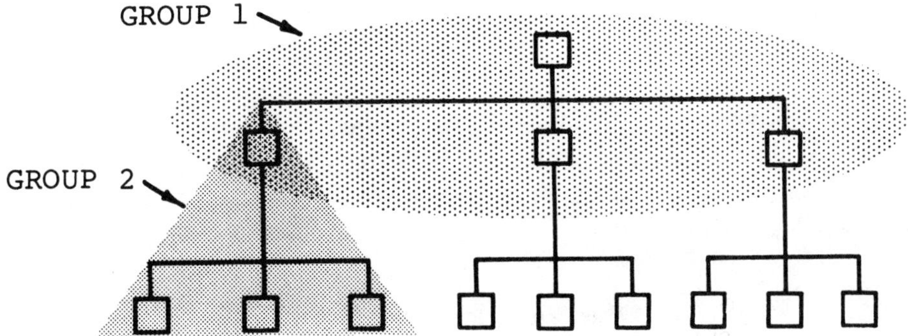

Figure 3.4. The manager as a linking pin (Likert).

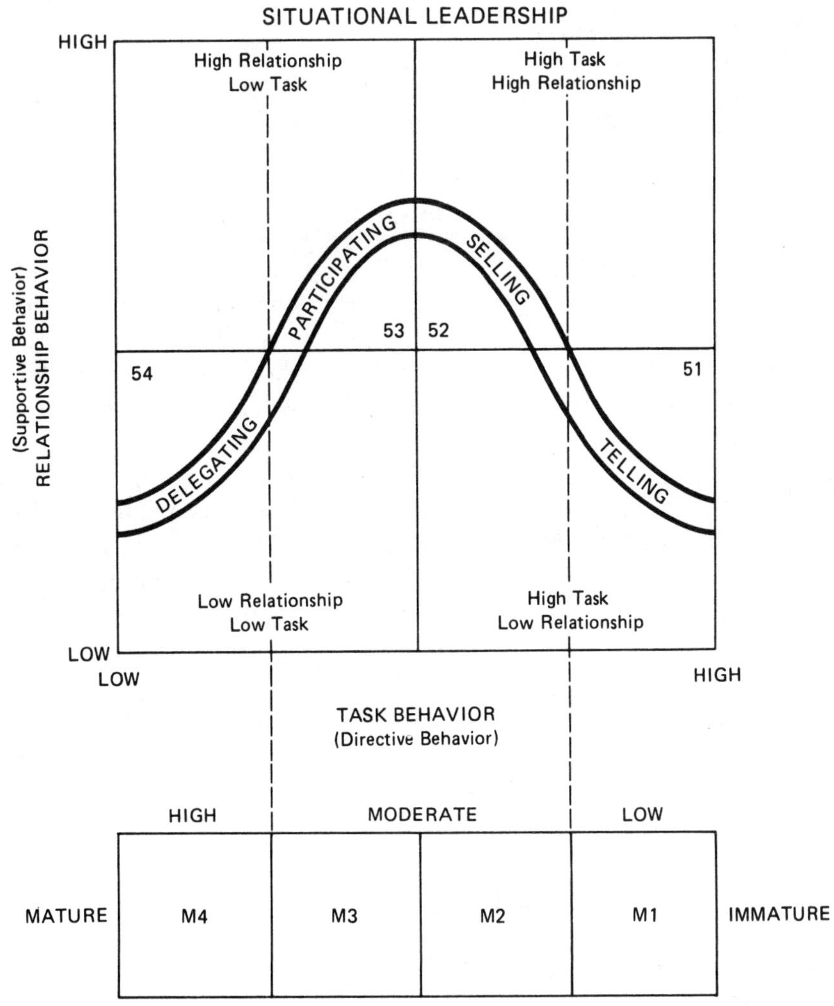

Figure 3.5. The model of Paul Hersey and Kenneth H. Blanchard.

(high task, low relationship) involves telling, or, if you will, commanding. This is consistent with the full Theory X and Grid 9,1, to be discussed. The second quadrant has a high task, high relationship dictum, wherein the selling concept of leadership is apparent. It corresponds to the Grid 9,9. The third quadrant has high relationship, low task, wherein all individuals participate in the decision. This is full Theory Y and Grid 1,9. Finally, the fourth quadrant is the low relationship, low task delegation activity, Grid 1,1. Note at the bottom of the illustration that there are four levels of maturity involved. Thus, leadership is as leadership does.

The Principles of Leadership

The principles of leadership include at least these steps:

1. Take responsibility for your actions regardless of their outcome.
2. Set the example.
3. Know yourself and seek improvement.
4. Seek responsibility for yourself and develop a sense of responsibility among your subordinates.
5. Be certain the task is understood, supervised, and accomplished.
6. Know your staff and be concerned for their welfare.
7. Keep your staff informed.
8. Employ subordinates according to their capabilities.
9. Train your staff as a team.
10. Know your job.

Span of Control

It has been said that there is a practical limit to the number a supervisor can manage effectively. The simplistic formula for the number of interrelationships is $n(n - 1)$. Thus, with five subordinates, the number of relationships are $5(4) = 20$. The addition of a sixth subordinate $[6(5) = 30]$ increases the number of relationships by 10. There are, of course, theories which state that something more is required, and there are sophisticated formulas which state that optimum number of subordinates is three to six, while twelve to twenty may be permissible. That concept would probably be rejected by the Lance Corporal with a 81-man company. Thus, it can be said that appropriate span of control is a function of the organization type. The Theory X organization, where structure is paramount, will require more levels and shorter spans than the Theory Y organization, which has fewer levels and wider spans.

Historically, the addition of levels to an organizational structure, in addition to increasing the number of interrelationships, also increases costs, problems of communication, structure, coordination, and control. Managers have found that the wider the possible span of control (efficiently and effectively used), the more economical the organization will be, diminishing the need for additional organizational levels, paper reports, meetings, etc. However, every individual in a particular level of management has some upper limit on the number of subordinates he can effectively manage. The Lance Corporal has certain dictatorial powers of control over his subordinates. Most managers have only the permission of the managed.

Prelude to Management Styles

But there are several other types of managers, and before we begin to look at the various management styles, we should explore them.

The Exploitative Autocrat

The manager makes all decisions, no matter how petty. He or she will decide who will do what, and when. Failure to complete work results in threats or punishments. Do you wonder that there is a low level of trust and confidence in this individual?

The Benevolent Autocrat

This manager makes all decisions, as well, but employees have some degree of freedom in performance within procedures. The manager may have paternalistic attitudes. There is still a low level of trust, but this individual is treated with caution.

The Consultative Manager

This manager consults and then make decisions. Employees have the freedom to make many of their own decisions. There is a free and open climate for discussion, and a high level of trust.

The Participative Team

This is the currently recommended system of management. Purportedly, it gets full involvement of employees in goals and decisions. Refer back to the figure on the Likert Linking Pin to see the link between employees and other units higher in organization.

Management Theories

Theory X, Theory Y

So far in this discussion, concentration has been strictly upon the organization as it views, and works with, the workers--and that perspective will be maintained until all of the managerial concepts have been discussed. However, from this point the reader should be aware that individuals take on the same posture concepts as organizations. Those attributes exhibited by the man or woman called "manager" are also exhibited by the organization at large and to some extent by the subordinates who are managed. Concepts of reality leadership, job enrichment, individual needs, imply a certain understanding or empathy on the part of the superior to the work situation imposed upon the subordinate. Douglas McGregor, in *The Human Side of Enterprise,* develops two distinct sets of assumptions, which have become known as Theory X and Theory Y, and will be termed "pure" or "absolute" Theory X and Theory Y.

Theories X and Y may be pictured strictly as the positive sections of two axes, X and Y. McGregor held that the assumptions of the individuals being managed would cause managers to react in kind (and usually opposite), and normally at the extreme. Bear in mind, please, that the introduction of an individual named manager indicates a separation of ownership on the part of the organization from the one or more individuals who maintain predominant interest in the organization. Theory X assumptions hold that:

1. Work is inherently distasteful, and people will rebel against distasteful work.
2. People have no desire for responsibility and prefer to be directed. This direction might just as easily take on the form of written instructions.
3. People have little capacity for creativity. Creativity is only in the preview of authority, which should be credited with all such evidences of creativity.
4. Most people must be closely controlled or coerced to achieve organizational objectives.

Theory Y assumptions hold that:

1. Work is as natural as play, if conditions are favorable.
2. The worker is motivated by satisfaction of ego and social needs as well as bread and butter needs.
3. The capacity for creativity is widely distributed and underutilized in organizations.
4. Self-control on the part of all workers is essential in achieving organizational goals.

Scientific Management, of course, is Theory X, and remains today well entrenched in the military services. Theory Y reflects the inputs of social psychologists and others, and of the progress made in the business world itself. Because a manager deals with immediate subordinates, and therefore has little concept of the surrounding organizational world, it is often quite possible that the subunit's strategy is not reflected by the organization at large.

The Managerial Grid

Management, according to Robert Blake and Jane Mouton, is really a combination of Theories X and Y, mixed into the reaction of the manager to an externally applied stimulus. Blake and Mouton took the Theories X and Y, called the X axis Concern for Production and the Y axis Concern for People, and stated that each manager has one predominant managerial style coupled with one lesser managerial style to which he will revert when the stronger one fails. While there are many points within the grid, five uniquely identifiable points can be labeled, as shown in Figure 3.6.

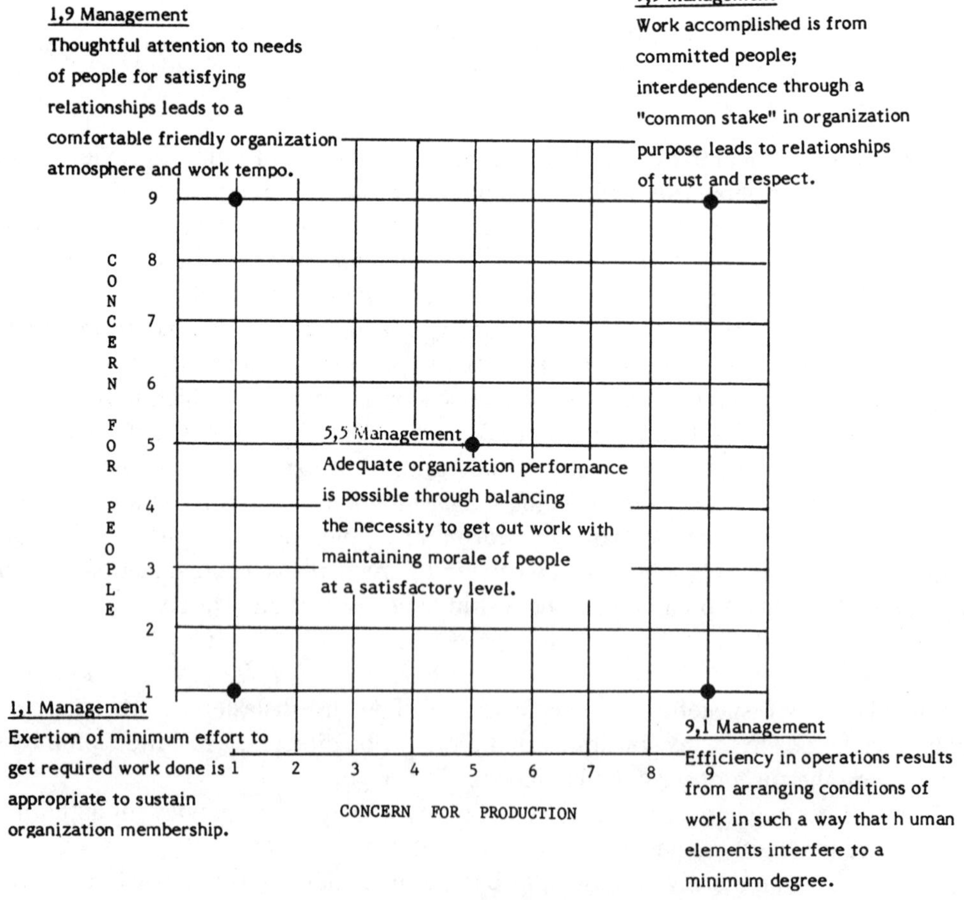

Figure 3.6. The managerial grid (Blake and Mouton).

Let's change the orientation just a bit:

1,1 is *impoverished management*—there is little concern for either people or production.
9,1 is *authority-obedience management*—the manager controls—human elements cannot interfere.
1,9 is *country club management*—the manager has maximum concern for people, little concern for production.
5,5 is *organization man management*—the manager seeks balance, is a fence rider, compromiser; often without deciding.
9,9 is *team management*—there is a commitment to people, mutual trust, respect, interdependence.

Motivation

Management as externally applied persuasion relies heavily upon factors which influence the workers and upon factors which may be known only to the individual himself. It has been well established that workers' highest priorities do not include remuneration. A worker would often rather have his manager show an interest in an ill spouse than give a raise in salary. Money may be important, but is not the total motivation.

Motivation is the process of influencing or stimulating a person to take action by creating a work environment whereby the goals of the organization and the needs of the people are satisfied. The evidence of motivation is that people perform their jobs efficiently and effectively.

Motives explain why people behave and are the drives and impulses that cause behavior. It is a complex process and creating motives is equally complex. Motivation is enhanced by increased pay, job security, working conditions, punishments, dismissal actions, and the withholding of rewards. Successful management's awareness of human needs, planning for and satisfying them, creates a climate where motivation can happen.

Of course, both the Blake and Mouton grid and Douglas McGregor's Theory X and Theory Y have a motivation component. But we should examine a couple more.

Chris Argyris' Maturity Theory

This theory holds that the difference between mature personality and demands of the organization for the basis of organizational maturity.

If the organization is fully prescribed in plans, policies, and methods/procedures, the person will need to be passive and has minimal control over the job. He will be expected to be passive, dependent, subordinate. It's an extremely short time perspective, avoid sharpening what are considered to be shallow abilities, and performs in anticipation of failure. There are three possible reactions: escape, fight, or adapt.

Abraham Maslow's Hierarchy of Needs

Abraham Maslow, in *Motivation and Personality,* indicated seven basic factors of human behavior, as shown in Figure 3.7. The concept is that when the lower number has been satisfied, the higher number can be approached.

1. *Physiological.* These are the survival needs–air, water, food, clothing, shelter and sex, pay, benefits, and working conditions.
2. *Safety.* These needs include protection against danger, freedom from fear, benefit programs, job security, safe and healthy working conditions and consistent and fair leadership.
3. *Social.* These include love, belonging, affiliation, acceptance, friends, organized activities, and social events.

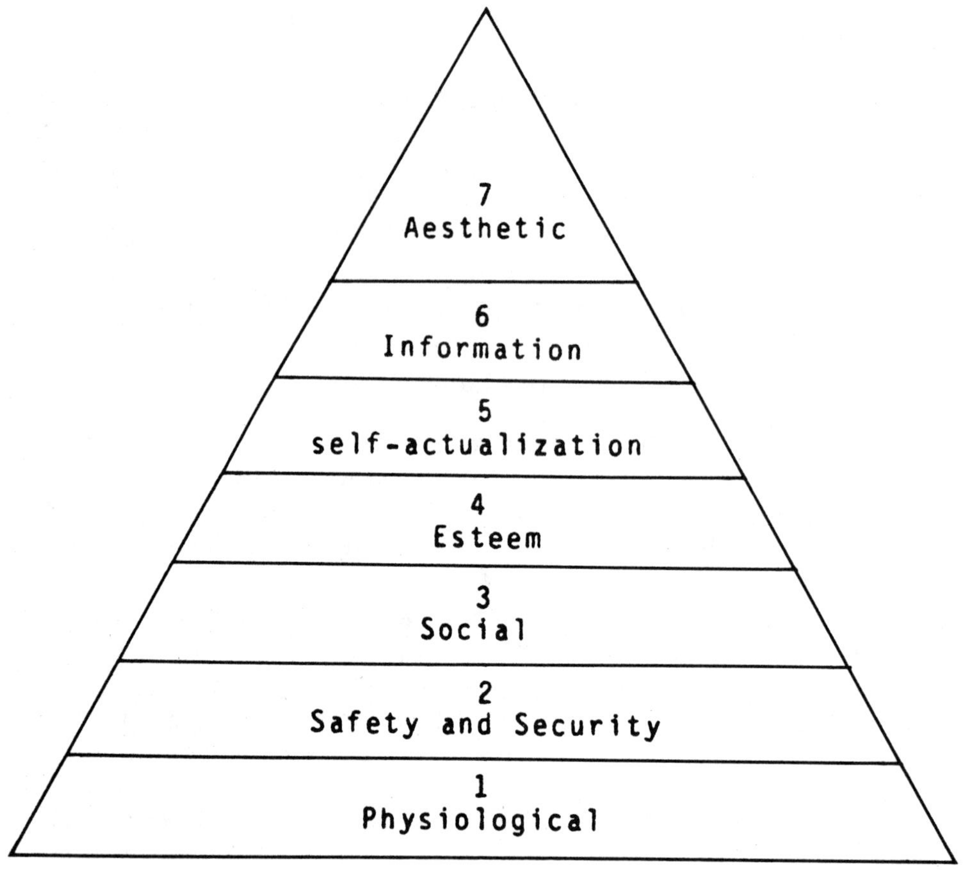

Figure 3.7

4. *Esteem.* Among these needs are achievement, recognition and status, title and responsibility, recognition for work done, promotions, status, prestige.
5. *Self-actualization.* These needs include realization of potential, challenging work, creativity, personal growth and advancement.
6. *Information.* This is the need to be aware of one's environment and the impact of changes upon one's circumstances.
7. *Aesthetic.* These needs encompass the arts, music, levels of aspiration, and higher intellect.

The first five are part of Maslow's original hierarchy. The remaining two were added in his later years.

Thus, an individual's existence is a constant struggle to satisfy needs; behavior is the reaction of the individual to achieve a reduction of need pressures, directed toward some desired goal. It's the task of management to capture and employ the satisfaction of those needs in the satisfaction of organizational objectives. According to Maslow, a person can have a percentage of each. A need that has been relatively well satisfied ceases to motivate.

Clayton Alderfer's ERG Theory

People have existence needs (the physical or material needs), relatedness needs (relationships with other people), growth needs (creative efforts to gain recognition to satisfy esteem), and fulfillment needs. These are taken in series—and if the individual is unsuccessful, then he will fall back to the next lower level.

Herzberg's Motivation-Hygiene Theory

There are two classes of factors—hygiene and motivation. Hygiene factors do not make one healthy, but do maintain health. Included are pay, status, security, working conditions, fringe benefits, policies and administrative practices and interpersonal relations. Motivation includes meaningful and challenging work, recognition for accomplishment, feeling of achievement, increased responsibility, opportunities for growth and advancement and the job itself.

David McClelland's Manifest Needs Theory

According to McClelland, the individual has a need for achievement, a need for power, and a need for affiliation. The need for achievement includes the desire to take responsibility, the individual is goal oriented and seeks a challenge and sets goals of moderate but achievable risk. The individual desires feedback, has high energy and is not afraid of work.

The individual with a need for power wants power or influence over others. He likes to compete in "sure-win" competitions, enjoys confrontation, has a need for affiliation, friendships, and close emotional relationships, and wants to be liked. This individual may be a socialite, and seeks a sense of belonging.

Under this concept, the behavior is dependent upon the strength of the motive, the probability of success, and the drive produced by the incentive or reward.

Reinforcement Theory of B. F. Skinner

Skinner, the father of programmed instruction, holds that behavior is learned, and therefore modifiable. According to him, punishment to be avoided. According to him, people act in personally rewarding ways, and because of this people's behavior can be shaped with the use of positive reinforcers. Punishment is rejected as a reinforcer. When undesired behavior is not rewarded, it disappears.

Theory Z

In 1981, William Ouchi, a Japanese-American UCLA professor, placed his name into the continuum of management thought when he published his thesis of management, Theory Z, in the book, *Theory Z—How American Business Can Meet the Japanese Challenge.* In the process he crystallized much of the thinking of the advocates of participative management throughout the years. Summed into a phrase (his phrase), Theory Z is "Management By Walking Around." In the world of automobiles and in some cases electronics, the Japanese were outstripping U.S. production so substantially that American manufacturers and unions sought, and received, import quotas and higher than necessary protective tariffs. And yet, despite it all, Japanese production remained high, due not to low wage scales in Japan (which have climbed as high as our own) nor to increases in quality (which have exceeded our own), but to a life-long philosophy of the Japanese people which fosters a loyalty between the company and the employee, in both directions, and between employees, also in both directions. Reading of the book is highly recommended; it is available from Addison Wesley. Following are the thirteen steps to the Theory Z philosophy:

1. Type Z organizations are those in which individuals have a part in the decision-making process. The participating group shares in both the decisions and the results of those decisions.
2. Theory Z is a philosophy as much as it is a managerial style. An organizational philosophy provides a guidance for behavior of the employees of the organization.
3. Define the desired management philosophy and involve the company leader. The Z form of organization requires that the people participate in the direction of the organization.

4. Implement the philosophy by creating both structures and incentives. Reserve the structure to be imposed upon the problem when there are lapses of team cooperation.
5. Develop interpersonal skills. The Z organization succeeds by modifying its form as it needs change. An active training program is required. Incentives, many of which are not monetary, promote inter-organization cooperation.
6. The cooperative Z style requires independent audit. The success of the system rests in the amount of questioning subordinates do of supervisors, supervisors do of managers, managers do of directors, etc.
7. Involve the union. Z involves substantive change in working conditions. An increase in the trust of the employee by the organization and the trust of the organization by the individual, negates the need for the union.
8. Stabilize employment. Where Z has been applied, it has worked because employment has been stabilized. Organizations can overcome employees' voluntary termination by changes in work environment, challenge, and participation in decisions which affect them.
9. Decide on a system for slow evaluation and promotion. In an atmosphere of stable employment, there will be less turnover and therefore fewer open positions to which an employee can be promoted.
10. Broaden career path development. This means training. But it also means that the individual must become involved in systematic programs of training which are extra-organizational. Career paths must be broadened as a function of the interest the individual shows in himself.
11. Theory Z changes must be made at the top. The reason is key: a low-level individual can not participate unless the next higher level allows it. Change from the bottom of the organization is revolution. Change from the top of the organization is evolution.
12. Seek out areas to implement participation. Those areas where the practice should be begun are those areas which have experienced the use of suggestion mechanisms. From that point, the concept spreads as a function of the workers themselves.
13. Permit the development of holistic relationships. The holistic organization gets that way because of the co-participation (as temporary equals) of individuals who come from varietal levels of the organizational structure. It can't be delegated by upper management—but it can be killed. Once begun, it should be encouraged to grow. Once killed, it might never again bud.

Self-Perception

The perception of himself by the individual is a large determinant in the ability of the individual to be managed. As with every interpersonal relationship, the self-image will act as a screen to provide different signals which beat against the received signal. One of the better examples of this to emerge in recent years is the Johari Window, as shown in Figure 3.8.

Arena. There is free and open exchange of ideas. Behavior is public. The arena area increases trust and increased information.

Blind Spot. This is nonverbal behavior. It indicates insensitivity, contains faults and hidden attributes of the individual. However, it can contain good characteristics of which we are totally unaware.

Facade. The real feelings are suppressed (big boys don't cry). This area contains the deep, dark secrets. These are the areas where we feel we could not obtain support or where we might be judged by peers and superiors. It requires that we constantly resist assumptions, exposing part of ourselves (moving into the arena). And it involves the constant seeking of approval.

Unknown. These are the things which are available only through digging; those things which are dis-

	THINGS I KNOW	THINGS I DON'T KNOW
THINGS OTHERS KNOW	ARENA (PUBLIC AREA)	BLIND SPOT
THINGS OTHERS DON'T KNOW	FACADE (HIDDEN AREA)	UNKNOWN TO SELF AND OTHERS (SUB-CONSCIOUS)
		UNCONSCIOUS

Figure 3.8

covered by accident—or those things which may never be discovered. It also includes those things which are denied, rejected, and will remain unknown.

When the arena widens into the blind spot—then the introspective process has begun and the individual begins to see himself and his peers in a light of confidence. However, the blind spot can widen into the arena area by constant attack and withdrawal, to the point where the individual, withdrawn and "right" in the face of reality, will "drop out" of interpersonal relationships and become a loner.

When the arena widens into the facade, then the individual begins to evaluate himself in terms of reality, measuring his performance in relation to his peers and in relation to goals he will set for himself, either formally or informally.

Motivation Enhancements

There are several ways to ensure that motivation is kept at its peak. Job fulfillment, job enrichment, and nonfinancial rewards head the list of most surveys. People often feel that money is a prime motivator—it is, certainly, but not necessarily *the* prime motivator. With it you can attract and retain qualified personnel and provide some motivation to higher levels of performance. But it's not necessarily desired, as you can recall from Maslow. It can produce peace, but not growth.

A more certain motivator has been found to be equity—ownership, yes, but even-handed treatment. The degree of perceived equity is the amount of fair treatment the employee gets. As a comparison to compensation, people want compensation relative to their personal effort, education, training, etc., even before any concern for other people. How do you deal with the person who has pushed herself through college, making substantial sacrifices, when she becomes aware that a man, doing the same job, gets paid more? Or either of the college-educated people when faced with a janitor earning more than they can in a "profession." You must then appeal to their future and their professionalism.

But there is one other that works for everybody—the self-fulfilling prophecy. Expectations beget performance; if performance is expected, it will be received. If you can get your subordinates to do what they believe they are expected to do, even though they may not wish to, you have it.

Job Design, Job Enrichment, and Job Enlargement—building the motivational climate

There is a basic dichotomy in this discussion. The organization doesn't exist to pamper its people—but it does need people to fill the organization's basic needs, while at the same time, it must provide satisfaction and fulfillment for those people—particularly in a tight recruiting situation. There are constraints on this process: the influence of technology, the influence of economics, government requirements and regulations, and management and union philosophies all play a part in what can be done and what actually is done.

The purpose of job design, then, is to find a fit between the individual and the work. Rather than taking the individual and stuffing that individual into a mold, modern firms find more satisfaction on both sides of the equation if the person can be helped to fit the job and the job can be tailored to fit the person.

Job enrichment is a slightly different concept. Here, the idea is to increase the demands of the job, to increase the worker's accountability for that job, and in turn to provide work scheduling freedom, within limits, feedback via reports; and new learning experiences.

Job enlargement is the horizontal expansion of duties tied to increased freedom to do the job.

In recent years we have seen the increase in a concept called *quality circles,* where these concept have been successfully put to work. 'At Ford, quality is Job 1,'' says the commercial. Under the concept, people work in teams, establish their own quotas, establish their own problem solving mechanisms, provide and obtain feedback on the performance needed, and derive satisfactions from the whole piece of work.

Conclusion

So, the factors which affect performance are the skills and abilities of personnel, their levels of education and training, existing technology and the availability of tools to do the job. Motivation is not a task that the manager does—it's the creation of a climate which has a recognition of human behavior and needs, and deals with them. The result: an increase in utilization and a decrease in management.

Communications

Communication ties together the individuals and the departments of the organization into a purposeful structure seeking common objectives. It is more than the transfer of information; it is the transfer of meaning between individuals by written, oral, or symbolic means. Claude Shannon pointed out three levels in the communication process:

1. The accurate transmission of symbols of communication (the domain of information theory).
2. The determination of how precisely the transmitted symbols convey the desired meaning.
3. The effectiveness of the received meaning in influencing conduct in the desired fashion.

Management is primarily interested in those aspects of the communication process which have an impact on the functioning of the enterprise. Those aspects may be divided into person-to-person and organizational communication.

Factors which affect transmission person-to-person are listed next:

1. *Appearance.* If person A is a large, overpowering individual, person B may feel threatened. The fear, rather than the transmitted words, could become the dominant theme of the interaction, and the intent of the message could be lost. Conversely, a pleasant smile or well groomed appearance may have a positive effect.
2. *Attitude.* If person A has had a bad day, or if dislikes person B, his attitude will be communicated by this tone of voice, gestures, or the phrasing of the message. The attitude, rather than the message, gets transmitted.
3. *Clarity.* Person A's idea must be encoded into words which will convey it clearly. Generalizations, poor logic, high abstraction, or poor word selection can detract from the idea.

4. *Consistency of words and action.* If person A communicates an idea which is contrary to his observed action, his credibility and sincerety will be open to question.
5. *Noise.* Interference, office noise, misuse of language, and externally applied stimuli will become a filtering barrier through which communication will be extremely difficult.
6. *Semantics.* The meaning of a word to person A may be different from that intended by person B, based on differences in background. The frequently used term "cost savings" provides such confusion.
7. *Evaluation.* We tend to evaluate messages on the basis of our evaluation of people—or, more often, on the basis of our biases. This, then, becomes a screen through which few ideas can pass.
8. *Expectations.* We hear what we want to hear and tune out what we don't wish to hear. That, in effect, means that we hear what we expect to hear.
9. *Faulty listening habits.* We can talk faster than we can listen. The ability of the speaker to pace his presentation to the ability of his audience to absorb the thoughts promotes communication.

In much the same manner, person-to-person communication is affected by certain factors:

1. *Status.* Person A is president of the firm. Person B delivers the mail. A message from person A to person B carries some urgency, irrespective of the content of the message.
2. *Perspection.* Person A, president, carries a different orientation than person B. Because of this, there is a term-confusion. What term Z means to person A may be entirely different to person B. The term "system" fits this situation.
3. *Intermediate interpretation.* A message passed from the president, through the division director, to the manager may change content, urgency, or other attribute during transmission.
4. *Overload.* A single message cannot be treated in isolation. It is only one of many messages, written and oral. Staff and line channels can carry only so many messages before interference sets in.
5. *Informal channels.* The grapevine operates more effectively than any formal manner of communication. The wise manager utilizes it, not maliciously, but effectively.

There are steps which can be taken to increase communication. The problem or idea should be clarified. The participation of others should be used to expand the idea or develop a solution. The decision or idea must then be transmitted. Within context, the receiver of the message should be motivated to action. Finally, communication is only improved on the basis of measurement—the feedback loop. Most managers will spend up to 75% of their time in communication, of which at least half involves listening. A listening course is a wise investment of time and funds.

The Communications Process

The source (sender)—has the idea and attempts the transmission. The message becomes encoded into symbols the sender feels the receiver(s) will understand.

LUCAT BENE DEREDEGO
AHONNIT BUSIS INERO
ONOMO DEMIS TRUX
SUMMIT CAUSIN SUMMIT DUX

That should be perfectly clear to anyone from New Jersey. The rest of you will have to write for translation. We communicate by speaking, writing, acting, and drawing.

The target (receiver) must decode the message, converting the symbols into meaning. The effect of the communication is evidenced by feedback and/or action/compliance.

There are filters and barriers to this process. If you happen not to speak New Jersey, you've encountered one of them. Technical filters, such as those affect us greatly. Timing is another—there is a need for immediacy. Sometimes, our communications become overloaded. There are cultural differences among us. American are preoccupied with time. Orientals are preoccupied with space. Language presents filters. Our vocabulary is a large one, and society places the responsibility upon the better educated to speak in terms the less well educated can understand. Sometimes the message received is not the message sent, despite the universality of the word—e.g., FISH—the eater, the catcher, and the tropical lover.

Jargon presents problems and words which have mixed meaning. For example, we use the word ''input'' as a verb. Webster calls it a noun. Think about those mixed or misused words—less/fewer, podium/lectern—verbal/oral.

Psychological communications present us with problems also. We mix business and interpersonal relationships to our communications detriment. We give forth mixed messages—do what I mean, not what I say. There are any number of filters. Among these are the personal—physical attributes; the cultural—taboos; the ethnic—unique attributes; the emotional—not always related; censorship (reshaping the message); trust (the dissimilar line), the short-circuited feedback; and jealousy.

Others may not wish success for you. Your competency may be viewed as a threat. Your personality, position, or social associates may be desired. And we all suffer from preoccupation—the mind is a million miles away.

And there are perception sets.

''He never has anything valuable to contribute anyway.''
''The Moral Majority is neither.''
''Chairman, salesman'' vs ''chairperson, salesperson.''
Changes in the language—''Miss, Mrs., Ms.''
What you think it is, makes it what it will be.
Preferences and convictions.
Predictable reactions.

Making Communication Work

Communication is learned. Information about empathy, improvement in reading skills, observation, choice of words and tact, kinesics (body language), and Transactional Analysis (TA) are beneficial for this activity.

Empathy may be a primary skill to achieve: ''Walk a mile in my shoes,'' says the song. Empathy is an appreciation of the forces upon the correspondent.

I grieved because I had no shoes
Until I met a man who had no feet.

Listening is an acquired skill which is not possible to do when one is talking. It is affected by speed of delivery and your own preoccupations. It is too often evaluative and argumentative. It's easy to become projective, to become a part of the process.

Management of Conflict

Conflict is not all bad. It begets competition. Its absence begs mediocrity and apathy. There are a number of reactions in this thing called interpersonal conflict management. Here's a list:

- Force—the boss is still the boss

- Withdrawal—drive it inside (personal)
- Smoothing—drive it under the surface (organizational.)
- Compromise—most typical
- Mediation and arbitration—used in Management/Union relations
- Superordinate goals—bury the differences; do what is needed.
- Problem solving—conflict can be healthy.

Some of the ways to handle structural conflict management include changes in procedure, changes in personnel or functions, changes in space or layout, and the acquisition of resources.

Delegation—Granting the Right or Power to Perform

Since it is true that the manager cannot do all the work, then delegation becomes the way to assign responsibility, authority, and opportunity. If nothing else, delegation follows the scalar chain—flow of organizational structure. There is a unity of command. The subordinate is accountable to the superior from whom the authority is obtained. Divided accountability is seldom successful: ''No man can serve two masters.'' Of course, there is a relationship of coordination to the unity of command.

The process of delegation begins by assignment of duties by the manager to his immediate subordinates. This assignment grants permission (authority) to make commitments, use resources, take all actions necessary to perform the duties. It is the creation of a subordinate obligation (responsibility) to the delegating executive to perform the duties satisfactorily.

The assignment of duties calls for a balance of work among subordinates and a balance between span of control and managerial levels. There are the routine duties which must be accomplished, as well as the assignment of specialized duties, with some reservation of certain tasks to the managerial level.

Granting authority is not an easy task, especially when you are ultimately responsible. There are the contingency considerations, real and imagined. This is generally solved by granting authority to the position, not to the person. Granting of anything requires a clarity of understanding, a complete definition that is clear to both subordinate and superior, and to others involved. We tend to solve this by using charts, manuals, and job descriptions. The grant must be germane to duties, related to the assigned responsibilities, related to the expected results, and provide responsibility commensurate with authority.

There's much more to it than this—types of delegation; division of authorities and responsibilities, centralization vs. decentralization, etc. That's all the space we have for it here.

Performance Appraisal

Performance appraisal is a formal evaluation of an employee's job-related activities, conducted by a superior, covering a specified period of time, and a source of information about training and development needs. The appraisal system include several purposes:

- Administrative—salary increases, promotions and transfers, terminations, and development potential
- Informative—to supply data on strengths and weaknesses, often done in the ''not for salary'' review
- Motivational—the learning experience which permits performance self-adjustment
- Work analysis—the job to be done
- Formal appraisal process—skill and motivation applied to the job

There are many uses of an appraisal system, including the planning of executive requirements, transfer and promotion (or termination), merit salary rating, executive development, feedback, reinforcement (the top 10%), performance correction (the bottom 5%), and to formulate a development plan to overcome problems.

Who should appraise? The immediate supervisor—one-on-one; the group at the supervisor level—to enforce objectivity, and the immediate supervisor and his superior. There should be some regularity of appraisal—routinely one each year, six months in new and responsible positions. It should be done at all levels of the organization. Review of the appraisal should be done by a higher executive. This keeps both the superior and the subordinate informed, and whatever level.

Specific appraisal methods will be largely a matter of organizational policy.

Compensation and Reward

Compensation depends upon economic health of the stock market, the economy and the organization. Compensation practices include salary, bonuses, pensions, stock options, and perquisites. Factors which will be salary determinants will be organizational size, the type of industry, and the amount of managerial responsibility.

In any compensation scheme, there is internal consistency and external competitiveness. The manager should reward jobs according to their importance to the organization. At the same time, there is reality. The organization must meet the executive compensation of other firms. The alignment to external compensation systems must ensure equitable alignment to other firms and significant supplementary benefits, where appropriate. Compensation adjustment happens because there is an internal evaluation of management positions. Is the job worth the salary? Climbers make their own jobs. Direct financial compensation methods include these:

- Incentive compensation—given for dollar profit improvement, increased return on investment, and improved individual performance on the part of the individual being evaluated. Bonus amounts will vary, but are a substantial portion of executive income. There is no standard scale, and these monies are generally paid for something extraordinary. There are also cash or deferred payment plans, stock options, and profit sharing and pension plans.
- Stock options—used to create a proprietary attitude towards costs and profits; creates a dollar profit improvement.
- Stock plans—used to attract executives. It is most often used in research and development firms. Stock plans are generally given in the form of options. The value of the stock plan is dependent, however, on the condition of the market. And, of course, the Internal Revenue Service is the ever-present deterrent.
- Profit sharing plans—used to increase individual attention to company profits. Distribution of the profits is based on organizational performance. Often, the distribution is a stock, not a cash distribution, and that stock is accumulated. The investment is toward the future appreciation of the stock. Profit sharing plans are often mixed with retirement plans.
- Qualified retirement pension plan—used to promote greater loyalty to the company and to lessen employee turnover. It may appear in the form of deferred compensation, which will diminish the tax bite. It assures income for the individual after retirement from the organization.

There are also several forms of indirect financial compensation, commonly called perquisites. Included in this could be tuition for the employee's children, employee membership in clubs, hospitalization plans, dental benefits, discounts on company products, or use of company facilities. This form of reward is not performance related.

The Influencing Process

And now we come down to it. All the above ways haven't worked, and the job still needs doing. There's got to be another way. It's called "influencing." Influencing is the process by which people are induced to act in ways they otherwise might not. The basis of influence is some sort of power or authority.

There are several bases of authority, according to Max Weber. There is the *traditional*—rooted in tradition or custom; the *legal/rational*—rooted in the official and rationally enacted rules of the organization; the *charismatic*—personal devotion of the follower. There are several types of authority, according to Robert Peabody. There is the *positional*—acceptance of the position that a manager holds; the *functional*—based on expertise; and the *personal*—based on personal magnetism.

People will comply with legitimate authority. People comply where leader's goals are consistent with theirs. That compliance may be dependent upon employee's acceptance of the scalar chain, or upon lateral relations with technical experts. The interdependence of functions fosters compliance, cooperation, and coordination.

Compliance often comes as a result of creative problem solving—brainstorming sessions. It might also come as a function of bargaining and negotiation—exchange of resources to improve performance of departments. Or, it can come as the function of a win–lose conflict, in which one wins and one loses.

Power is, hopefully, the last resort. It is a form of domination and leverage to cause people to do things and things to happen. It requires control of resources: money, opportunity for advancement, security, and satisfying work assignments. It produces action when authority fails, when employees will not accept authority, when employee needs do not correspond to organizational needs, or when there is an incongruence between personal and organizational goals.

Power is derived from incentive and sanction systems. It is institutional and impersonal and appears when legitimate authority is not perceived by subordinates. The successful application of power depends on leadership ability. It's a matter of personal administrative skill to know when authority has failed and power must be used.

But power is not a one-way street, according to Herbert Simon. It may be wielded by an individual, but employees may retaliate by absenteeism, waste, minimum compliance, slowdown, or malicious obedience—following the letter of the order in opposition to common sense (only following orders). Even the control of positive motivators—e.g., control of financial rewards—may backfire. You may well find that using power is more expensive than compliance through attendance.

The mixture of authority, power, and influence exists in any concrete administration situation. It is desirable that authority be accepted. Otherwise, there is an influence gap—there is a point where authority fails, and power takes over. Both authority and power are present to some extent in any organizational situation: authority and power are a continuum, where at any given time the mixture is different. That mixture will be toward power where there is not professional respect and toward authority where the respect exists.

Today's manager must submerge power beneath the surface of superior-subordinate relations. He or she must assess what is required by the situation and the variables confronted by the manager. Part of the art of management requires selecting the mode of influence that will lead to accomplishment of the objectives and still provide satisfaction to the employee.

CONTROL

Controlling, from the perspective of management, is the process which evaluates organizational performance relative to predetermined goals. Efficiency is evaluated in the sense that optimum output for a given input is traceable. Effectiveness is evaluated in the sense that the specific performance contributes to achievement of organizational goals in the desired manner. Critical to the control process is the timely action to modify operations to coincide with predetermined standards. The control system must contain a logical description of goals, objectives, or standards in quantitative and qualitative terms; a means to measure current operations in terms of the same units of measure used to establish the goals; an adequate information system to transmit operational performance data to the decision-maker for comparison; and an action system to adjust the operation to conform to the standards.

Each of these elements is essential. The best possible system of on-line sampling and analysis is of little value if the manager is unable to influence the process in a timely manner. The control process may be treated as a series of distinct steps:

1. Establish standards.
2. Define performance criteria or limits of acceptable deviation.
3. Measure actual performance.
4. Compare actual versus standard performance.
5. Take corrective action and reevaluate standards if required.
6. Initiate preventive actions for similar future deviations if required.

The control process overlaps the planning function. The setting of standards is accomplished in the planning process, most frequently in the budget, where general objectives or programs are translated into specific measurable units such as cost, revenue, time, or items. Quantitative standards may be set by evaluation of historical data, by forecasting or planning, or by design. An obvious problem is that many objectives, such as those dealing with executive development, commitment to social responsibilities, or improvement of morale, are not clearly quantifiable. It is extremely difficult to set standards which actually measure progress toward desired objectives in these areas, but if no standards are set, management cannot control the activity.

A system which controls all factors within tight limits is prohibitive in cost and function. Some long-range objectives may require no defined control limits but only a simple comparison of planned and actual performance on an annual or semiannual basis. Other objectives, such as those in quality control, may require constant monitoring and close control limits. However, the preciseness of these limits should give consideration to tolerance of the operating equipment, tolerance of the measuring process, and the cost of making adjustments.

The measurement of performance is the easiest task of the entire control process, in that the units of measure were established when the standard was set and only a physical count of the units, labor hours, or other measurement is required. Special measurement problems, if any, are technical rather than managerial in nature.

In order to control the process, it becomes necessary to measure, to compare against standard, and to correct. This involves both an open loop and a closed loop. The closed loop is an automatic control, such as self-adjusting brakes. An open loop is where a human is placed into the loop, samples the data, compares it to predetermined standards, and reports variations to a higher level, orally or perhaps in report form. Decisions are then made at the higher level, direction flows back down the scalar chain, and the worker implements the directive, as filtered through the several levels. If timing is no problem, this is adequate.

Caution must be exercised when taking corrective action, since an improper standard rather than a process deficiency may be at fault. Standards developed in the planning process are frequently based on forecasts which may no longer be realistic.

The final step in the control process is the preventive action. This is basically a planning task which requires careful analysis of the actual rather than the apparent causes of the deviation, consideration of future courses of action which will adhere more closely to the standards, and a decision as to any changes required in goals, processes, sensors, or standards. This preventive action may require major changes and call for a repetition of the entire planning process.

Although control has been discussed in terms of a single system, there are really many control systems: finance, procurement, manufacturing, quality control, program management, etc. These control systems can be categorized as decision systems or technical systems. While the fully integrated control system cannot be achieved, a most effective common denominator is dollars—cost, profit, expenditures. For this reason, the integrated budget is a universal control device.

Some general considerations for control systems follow:

1. Control systems must generate returns in excess of cost. The cost of a control should resemble the cost of loss without the control.
2. Control systems must consider behavioral impact and provide lattitude for personal initiative. Control must not mean only restriction.
3. Controls must focus on the critical factor, that element essential to the performance of the organization.
4. Control systems must be flexible. In dynamic change, response to external change is a must.
5. Controls must provide for a timely response—from sensing to correction the process must allow change in time to affect processes and output.
6. Control systems must be future-oriented. Control and planning go hand-in-hand.
7. Control systems are unique. External control systems (even successful ones) cannot be adapted without change.

Control Techniques

1. *Management by exception.* MBE is a principle of control to be used to free management from involvement in total detail.
2. *Management by objectives.* MBO involves establishing performance objectives for the individual, group, department, division, etc. particularly important in a decentralized atmosphere. It is a control tool for performance only and will supplement other systems.
3. *The management audit.* A checklist inspection to analyze organizational operations. On a periodic basis, inspection by a higher authority hones skills and conformance to policies, plans, and procedures.
4. *Network analysis.* Time/cost event network analyses (PERT, CPM) are most powerful tools for planning and control. Each element of the program has its milestones against which performance can be measured.
5. *Budgets.* The budget is a plan of operations expressed in numeric terms. It is also a statement of standards to be met, and a control device.

The introduction of the computer has added a new dimension to the control process, presenting greater opportunities for closed-loop control systems, providing the means for more timely corrective action and, unfortunately, providing the capability for undue proliferation of internal controls.

Regardless of the control techniques and automated capabilities, the best possible means of control is, and has always been, the selection of high-quality subordinate managers. If an organization is a framework to provide a good person a place to work, then perhaps the best form of control is to provide a good subordinate with the resources needed to achieve his specific objectives.

GENERAL MANAGEMENT ACTIVITIES

The functions and principles of management are applicable to a wide range of managerial activities. Within each area of management, however, there are subtle differences in the application of principles

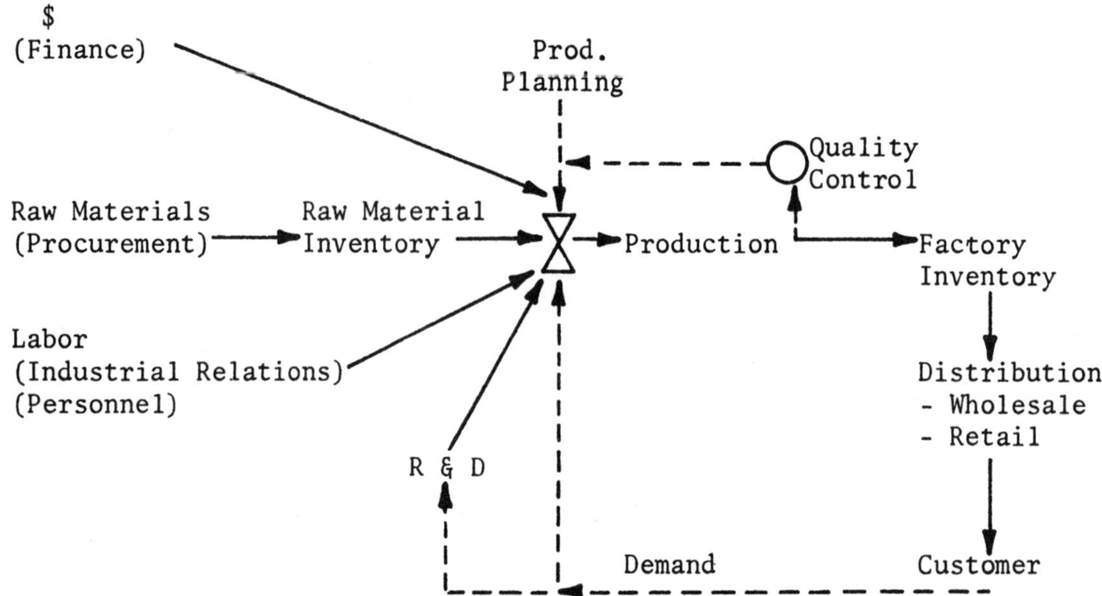

Figure 3.9. The total production system.

because of differences in the nature of the activity. To understand the nature of many business functions, it is essential that the business be visualized as a total system so the relationship of subactivities will be apparent. Figure 3.9 shows an example of the total production system.

The ratios of the actual output to the input and the actual production output to the theoretically possible capacity of the system are measures of the relative efficiency with which the capital expenditure for planned facilities and equipment, the rate of input of raw material and utilization with inventory and demand requirements, allocation of resources to production vs. marketing vs. research/development, and balance of quality control vs. customer utility. To assist in making these decisions, information flows to the manager from numerous sources of planning and control data.

In the production system, there may be a number of different flows, each presenting unique management problems. An intermittent flow would refer to a job shop or batch process. The job shop is best represented by the machine tool industry, where work in the shop consists of a number of similar products which have different specifications. A number of identical jobs might call for batch techniques where either end items or components could be made in economically efficient lots with limited applications of assembly line techniques.

In a continuous flow process, classical assembly-line techniques would apply, with careful management attention given to balancing the equipment capacity, labor force, and materials input. Many consumer products are manufactured in a continuous flow process. In this process, close attention is given to aggregate unit cost figures. For a given investment in capital equipment, as shown in Figure 3.10, the more units produced, the lower the average unit fixed cost associated with each item. However, the variable costs will decrease initially as the equipment is used to capacity; then costs will increase as overtime labor and excessive maintenance costs build up on overutilized equipment. This is referred to as the *law of diminishing returns.*

This means that the business, to obtain higher capacity with no loss in efficiency, must increase investment in capital equipment, as shown in Figure 3.11. With each incremental increase in plant investment (point A to point B) more efficiency and lower unit costs could be expected when producing at optimum capacity.

As the facility becomes larger and larger, however, management becomes more and more complex

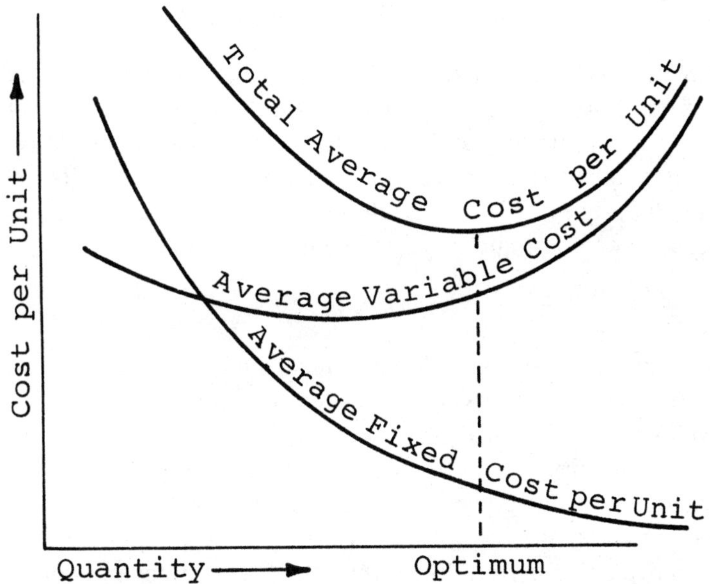

Figure 3.10. Unit costs for a fixed plant capacity (a short-run concept).

(point C) and unit costs at full production capacity will increase. This means that even though increasing returns to scale is often mentioned in any operation a point may be reached at which increased sale or size will result in decreased returns. A solution is to divide the business into relatively autonomous sub-units, which can each operate near optimum production levels.

A final type of flow process is the unique product flow, as in ship building or construction of a dam. The production of a one-of-a-kind product which represents a major portion of the activity of a single business presents management problems far different from those of the assembly line.

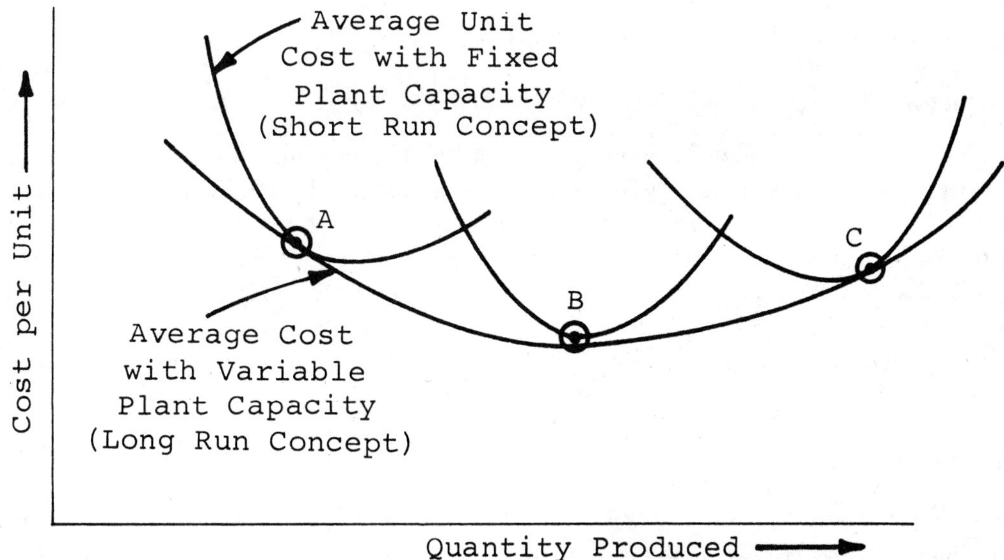

Figure 3.11. Increasing and decreasing returns to scale (a long-run concept).

Manufacturing Management

Manufacturing management (production management) focuses primarily on the technical aspects of the industrial process but, of necessity, also includes consideration of the man/machine interface within the plant. The general management principles and concepts discussed earlier are fully applicable. These functions have been highly automated using materials requirement planning (MRP), master scheduling, forecasting, computer-aided design (CAD), computer-aided manufacturing (CAM), bills of material (BOM), and other techniques which simulate the manufacturing process.

Plant Location

Selection of the optimum plant site is at best a compromise among proximity of input resources, markets, labor supply, and special considerations. No one site will possess all factors desired. Initial planning must therefore develop a list of critical factors and will provide some subjective weight to each. Raw materials and market proximity should be measured not in terms of distance but in terms of transportation cost. Input resources such as power or cooling water; regional legislation on taxes, workmen's compensation, and pollution; general labor availability; future competition for labor or materials; average land and utility costs; and even climate will affect the selection of a general community location. The long-term profitability of the plant will be governed more by these regional conditions than by the costs of developing a local site. Local development costs such as land purchase, construction, utilities hookup, and aesthetic treatment must, of course, also be considered. Also to be considered are the regulations of the Environmental Protection Agency (EPA) and the Occupational Safety and Health Act (OSHA).

Process Analysis

When a product has been accepted as a marketable commodity, the development of the lowest-cost production process becomes one of the major factors in the success or failure of the product. After fundamental decisions such as degree of quality and rate of production are made, a cost analysis will assist in the evaluation of general purpose versus special purpose equipment, hand operation versus sophisticated automated equipment, manufacture versus buy decisions, and comparison of specific processes to be used. If all factors are considered, the decision is essentially reduced to a cost comparison. The manager's task is to closely monitor the assumptions and forecasts used in setting the framework for the quantitative analysis and to ensure that no pertinent considerations are omitted.

Human Engineering/Working Conditions

Human engineering refers to the effective integration of the man/machine effort and considers the physical demands of a particular machine or work function. Working conditions refer to the physical and psychological conditions encountered by the worker in his day-to-day job activities. Essentially, this is the product of the Hawthorne experiments. Analysis of the task may lead to the conclusion that while physically compatible, a man should not be subjected to the task for psychological reasons. Hence, despite higher initial cost, automation would be desirable. The relationship between man and system is of continuing concern to the manager, the organization, and OSHA. Look for further information on the subject under the heading of Ergonomics in the Systems chapter.

Layout and Design

Layout and design refer to the translation of diagrammatic flow processes into an efficient physical flow of work and materials throughout the plant. The layout must consider the work process itself, the relationship between various activities, the space required for each activity, specialized requirements such as storage areas, utility connections, isolation of hazardous activities, and centralization of common service activities. Ideally, a detailed scale drawing of the proposed layout should be prepared and the physical path of each important process or function examined.

Material Handling

The handling of material increases the cost of the end product but makes no contributions to product utility, since it is primarily intended to facilitate other processes. The obvious management problem is to minimize the handling of material by reducing distance, volume, and power consumption whenever possible. In the classic case of a plant processing bulk raw materials into an end product, material should flow from machine to machine (process to process) with gravity providing the power for movement and with no intermediate storage points. Although this seldom happens, material flow can be closely integrated with plant layout to minimize movement distances, rehandling, and buffering stockpiles and to use the lowest cost form of transport.

Inventory Control

Inventory represents material retained in nonproductive status because of, or in anticipation of some economic gain (or delay of economic loss). Inventory may be raw material, component/subassembly, work-in-process, or finished goods. Finished goods may be held at the factory, in distribution warehouses, at wholesalers or retailers, or even in transit. Large amounts of capital are tied up in this inventory throughout the entire production and distribution system. Some of the major costs associated with retention of this inventory are (1) the cost of obsolescence and deterioration; (2) cost of taxes and insurance on inventory as an asset; (3) warehouse handling and storage costs; and (4) cost of capital invested in inventory.

Despite these costs, business retains some kind of inventory to ensure that the product is available when the customer wants to buy it. Since demand fluctuates, the retention of safety levels throughout the marketing structure is desirable. In addition to the varying customer demand, the business may build up inventory in anticipation of sales campaigns. Inventory may be built to smooth the production process, to diminish the crisis purchase of raw materials at increased cost, and to reduce lost sales due to the lack of finished good. Economic purchase quantities and the opportunity to avail the firm of the lower prices of other suppliers may affect the investment in inventory, and therefore in the control of inventory.

Maintenance Programs

Until the device breaks down, maintenance is frequently overlooked as unnecessary. Good maintenance programs require careful planning, direction, and control. The heart of the program is preventive maintenance, avoiding the cost of the crisis long before the crisis will occur.

Work Measurement

Work measurement is most frequently associated with the setting of standards for purposes of control or incentive compensation. This management tool is equally important for work planning and work improvement. A proper work measurement program will provide a basis for production scheduling, training, cost control, and pricing policy, in addition to performance evaluation and comparative analysis. Focusing on a step-by-step methodological approach to each job can lead to an improved way to perform each task. Work measurement techniques include:

1. *Time study.* A stopwatch is used to measure the way a job is normally performed by a proficient worker. This becomes a de facto standard, but is not necessarily the most efficient means to do the task.

2. *Methods time measurement (MTM).* The task is analyzed and subdivided into the basic motions required. Emphasis is on the proper method to perform each task. Predetermined standard times are assigned to each motion. The sum of motion times plus a prescribed overhead allowance sets the job standard.
3. *Work sampling.* Worker tasks are statistically sampled to determine the percentage of time devoted to each subtask. Time standards are then established on a proportionate basis, giving some consideration to operator performance and methods.

Work Improvement Programs

Work measurement, particularly by the methods time measurement technique, and human factors engineering are forms of work improvement. Work improvement programs include any organized management effort to improve the effectiveness of its workers. The term *methods improvement* normally applies specifically to a scientific and systematic analysis of work methods in the search for improved procedures.

Work improvement also includes such programs as suggestion awards, zero defects, and value engineering. These programs are distinct from routine management functions in that they are separately identified programs which depend heavily on creativity or innovation for effectiveness. Once initiated, these programs will face into ineffectiveness without continuing management emphasis. Behavioral modifications generated by employee participation in these programs may be of more significance than the changes in work methods.

Marketing Management

Historically, marketing was concerned primarily with distribution. Today the term brings to mind advertising and selling. Both definitions are too narrow. A more accurate definition is provided by Philip Kotler in *Marketing Management: Analysis, Planning, and Control*: ''Consumer behavior cannot be accurately predicted. The marketing situation faces a tremendous number of variables and complex interrelationships. Factors in the marketplace change so dynamically that, as data are being collected, the situation changes.'' Thus, the marketing mix, while difficult to define, can be divided into five areas: product, price, promotion, place, and research.

Market Research

Market research is aimed at defining the customers' needs and indicating how the firm can best satisfy those needs. The marketplace is an aggregation of individuals; statistical analysis of data is important. Observations of customer behavior, interviews, research surveys, and other data-gathering methods are used extensively to collect a sample of consumer behavior as a means to predict the aggregate reaction to the marketplace. These data, then, becomes the basis for policy decisions.

Product

Every product has a unique life cycle. Upon introduction, sales volume increases relative to the advertising and expanse of knowledge. As people become fully aware of the item, volume levels off and declines as demand becomes replacement demand. As competing packages are introduced, demand drops sharply. The decision to drop a product is made through a marginal analysis (contribution to offset fixed costs and provide profits). Marginal profit decisions are tricky, and firms will often discontinue unprofitable lines as an entree to more profitable lines or as an adjunct to cash flow considerations. Product decisions also involve packaging. Packaging is the major product identifier, part of a promotion plan, and a competitive tool. Advertising on TV, brand name associations, loyalty to producer, etc., may be sufficient to ensure product success.

Price

Pricing policies have an obvious and immediate impact on consumer demand and company revenue. Prices are a tool of competitive strategy and a prime target of consumer concern. Prices are subject to regulation by laws governing price discrimination. Prices can be set on the basis of cost (cost plus a fixed percentage), demand (what the traffic will bear), and competition (generally slightly less expensive than the industry leader's umbrella). From a practical point of view the firm is inhibited from changing prices too frequently or drastically, with the exception of known trends of supply and demand or world markets, since both will generate adverse customer reaction. Early consideration or pricing may lead to redesign of the product to conform to desired profit margins.

Promotion

Marketing activities, other than pricing, designed to persuade the buyer to purchase the product, are described as promotion. Promotion includes personal selling (salesman to customer), sales promotion (displays, trading stamps, or other giveaways), advertising (nonpersonal presentation on a paid media), or publicity (dissemination of information at no charge).

The most widely discussed form of promotion is advertising. Advertising serves the consumer by informing him of the nature and availability of products. The actual advantage to the seller is difficult to determine, though some sales impact is obvious. If the message is spread to enough people, even a small percentage is a large dollar value.

Place

The final element of the marketing mix is the place of selling, which includes location and physical channels of distribution. Two aspects are important: the physical distribution of the product through the transportation system and its distribution through "middle men." A company may set up its own distribution system by direct ownership or franchises, exclusive dealerships, or full distribution. Each of these options, and others, will vary the degree of control the company exercises over the system, the degree of risk, financing requirements, and warehousing needed.

Depending on the distribution channel established, a *push* or *pull strategy* may be arranged. The pull strategy is designed to influence the customer, through promotion, to ask for and create demand for the product at the retail level, pulling the product through the system. Push strategy depends on influencing the wholesaler and retailers to stock the product, through contractual arrangements, price concessions, availability, etc.

R&D Management

The organization exists in the midst of technology. And technology changes—rapidly. The source of new products within an industry must come from research and development (R&D). *Basic research* is directed toward the expansion of the frontiers of scientific knowledge. *Applied research* seeks scientific knowledge with direct application to a commercial objective. *Development* deals with the conversion of basic and applied research to specific products of processes with marketable utility. It has been well established that one idea in 67 makes its way into the marketplace.

The key to management of R&D is *planning*. Ideas just do not happen. Research is future-oriented and must be related to forecasts of future technology. Research objectives must be based on the future needs of the company environment in which it will operate and of the future position in the marketplace. Because of the length of time from idea to market, objectives must be under continuous scrutiny and modification. Figure 3.12 shows the process from idea to market.

As illustrated, there are many decision points. These decisions are important, since each added step necessitates the investment of an added amount of capital which becomes increasingly tied to the success

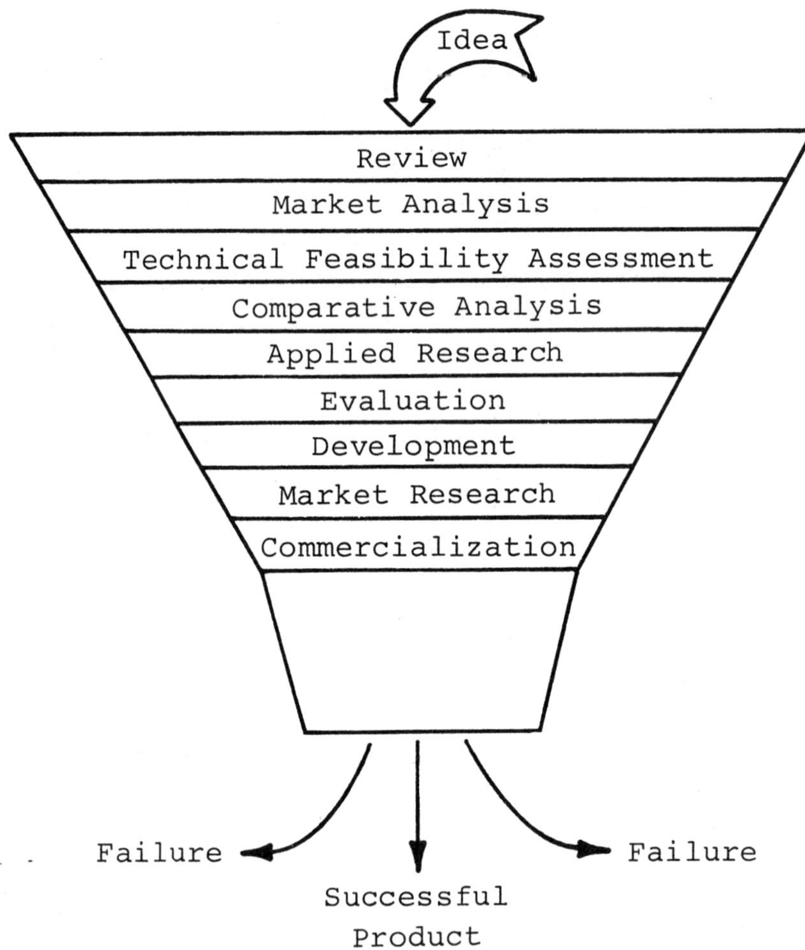

Figure 3.12. The product cycle, idea to realization.

or failure of a single product. Basic research may uncover ideas which lead to several products. Applied research will deal with several ideas on their way to market. But development deals with the individual product. It must go through the objective process from "can it be made" to "will it sell?"

Industrial Relations Activities

The most valuable asset of any organization is its people. The basic responsibility for the effective integration of people in the pursuit of organizational objectives rests with the line manager. However, comprehensive guidelines may be needed to provide for uniform policy application in sensitive areas, and some personnel-related activities may be centralized for control or efficiency. In many organizations these activities have been grouped within the staff service activity of Industrial Relations, sometimes called Personnel Relations or Personnel Administration. In others, these functions may be delegated to the line manager.

Staffing

Two diverse standards apply: one for the hourly worker entering the organization's workforce at an apprentice or low-skill level and the other for salaried/managerial personnel entering the organization at a relatively senior position. Because of the potential impact on the company of errors in judgment, far more stringent, centralized, and personalized procedures are required for this latter category.

In the critical recruitment and selection phase, employee tests are used extensively with mixed results. At the low entry levels where mechanical skills or mental ability are the primary criteria for success, results have been good. Tests for specific interest areas have been effective in limited situations. Personality tests which attempt to measure social development, persistence, stress reaction, or character have been very questionable. In fact, more and more certain minorities have been successful in getting legal support to force organizations to discontinue testing as discriminatory. If the tests are recognized as tools and have been evaluated for reliability and validity, they can be a powerful aid to the personnel staff.

A key staffing policy is that the criteria for promotions and transfers should be known, understood, and applied in an equitable fashion.

Compensation

Compensation can take many forms: wages and salaries, bonuses, incentive payments, profit-sharing, perquisites, and stock options. While not so evident, contributory retirement plans, paid vacations, education plans, and recreation facilities are also forms of compensation. All of these benefits provide prompt and immediate satisfaction to the worker when increased, but are quickly accepted as entitlement, reducing long-range benefit.

Wage and salary administration is touchy—and has a high potential for destroying morale unless equitably administered. Job descriptions and wage/salary ratings must be keyed to the manager of supervision, and amount of responsibility as well as to an objective or accepted manner of performance evaluation.

Executive compensation is a separate field, tied to tax considerations, legal restrictions, and the extent to which the executive is to be bound to the organization.

Incentive systems are common, but have drawbacks, among which may be a reduction in quality (favoring volume), generation of friction, increase of clerical costs (to keep the record), difficulty of setting rates (because of the star performer), disregard for safety, and higher than normal earnings. On the opposite side of the same issue, however, are the benefits; greater output, lower costs, higher earnings, stimulated creativity, reduction of lost time, and reduction of supervision.

Labor Relations

The term *labor relations* refers to the interaction of management with labor on matters covered by collective bargaining procedures such as wages, hours, and conditions of employment. These procedures are established by the National Labor Relations Board, which also regulates the bargaining process, determines the bargaining unit, and rules on unfair labor practices. See the previously listed relevant acts of Congress.

Labor law is complex and professional legal staffs are maintained by larger organizations to cope with this complexity. The complexity also dictates that labor relations policy and bargaining be centralized.

Three terms are important in labor relations:

1. A *grievance procedure* is a formal procedure for dealing with employee problems arising from administration of the collective bargaining agreement. In this procedure, the union steward is interposed between the worker and the foreman.
2. If a mediation service is called into the dispute, the first action taken by that mediation service is the *fact finding*. The mediators will take statements of both labor and management and document them, using them in three-way negotiations.
3. Upon failure of the mediation service, and depending upon whether included in the contract, an arbiter may be appointed and the *arbitration* begins. When the arbiter has made a decision it is incumbent upon both parties to accept the decision; this process is called *binding arbitration.*

Training

There are several kinds of training. The first is training for the newly hired employee, covering organization policy, working conditions, safety rules, and what is expected. From this point on, training for a suitable skill required will be performed. Formal classroom instruction, programmed learning courses, apprenticeship programs, or informal on-the-job training are all possible options. Each method provides advantages depending on skill level, equipment required, availability of instructors, and numbers of new employees acquired at a time.

A second category of training is required to introduce the existing work force to new equipment and techniques, or to improve skills to meet quality or time requirements. Here, because of the numbers involved, some form of centralized instruction is required, to allow instruction and follow-up performance. It can be demonstrated that as workers are trained, the cost to produce widgets declines in proportion to the amount of training received until the cost levels.

A third category of training is managerial development, which might involve several levels of individuals, from the project manager, shop foreman, or supervisor complete to the top of the organization. There are several peculiar principles of training which apply solely to this level.

A fourth category of training might be classed as educational incentives, such as providing opportunities for off-duty classes at company expense. Direct benefits of the organization may be marginal for any one course, long-run payoff in job satisfaction and long-term growth make such programs worthwhile.

Services

The Industrial Relations staff function often includes a number of miscellaneous service activities; these may include medical, accident/safety, recreation, company publications, security, and community affairs. Each must be managed and each must contribute to the objectives of the organization in terms of productivity, improved morale, or satisfaction of social responsibilities.

Financial Management

Financial management deals with the planning, directing, and controlling of the company's monetary operations. The financial manager is concerned with forecasting the need for funds, acquiring funds at minimum cost, evaluating alternative uses of funds, ensuring that available funds are used to provide maximum returns, maintaining the company's financial position and reputation, minimizing risk, taking full advantage of tax legislation, and measuring results of company operations in financial terms.

Financial Flow

There is a continual flow of funds through an enterprise. If cash, the most liquid or convertible form of funds, is viewed as a central reservoir, the reservoir level will continuously fluctuate under the dynamic conditions of day-to-day operations. Figure 3.13 illustrates some of the inputs and outputs which affect this reservoir. The financial manager is faced with the task of retaining sufficient liquidity to satisfy current requirements and minimizing the quantity of funds which are not working or earning some return. The maintenance of this dynamic balance is a primary task of the financial manager.

Ratio Analysis

An important tool available to the financial manager in analyzing the present and projected position of the organization is ratio analysis, a comparative analysis of figures on current or projected (pro forma) income statements or balance sheets. There are hundreds of ratios which may be established, but some

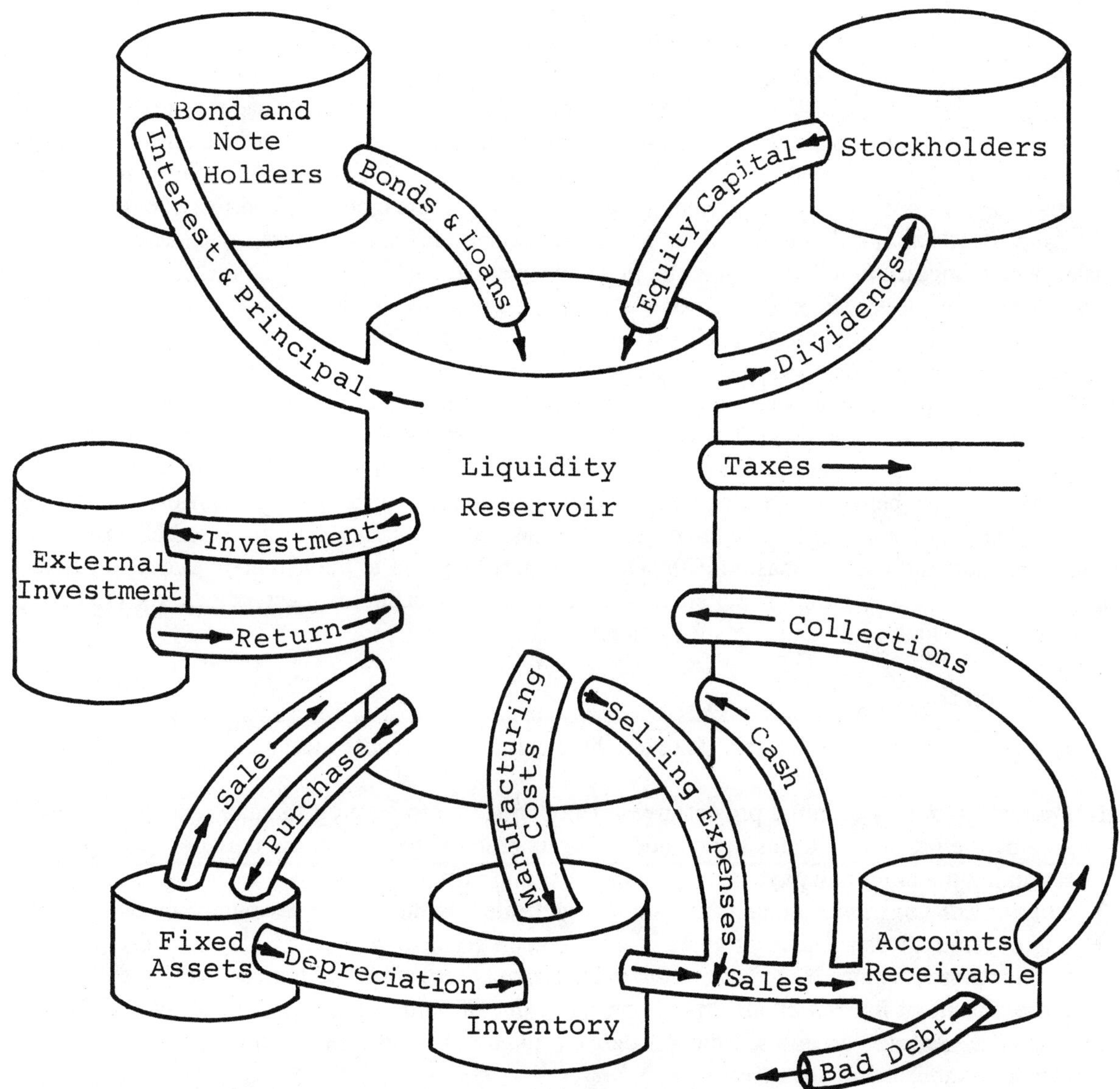

Figure 3.13. Corporate financial flow.

are more meaningful than others to an individual organization. A ratio taken alone is virtually meaningless. When compared with organizational ratios from past years or with industry experience of organizations of similar size in similar businesses, however, meaningful comparisons can be made. See the chapter on accounting for examples of these ratios.

Sources of Capital

The financial manager has several alternative sources of capital available to support the operations and growth of the organization. These sources must be analyzed in terms of cost for use of the capital, the degree to which the interests of current stockholders are diluted, the risk involved in meeting fixed interest payments, and flexibility in case of future changes in capital structure.

Capital can be obtained internally and externally. Internally, funds are generated by cash available from operations or by the sale of fixed assets, which is the more common. Cash from operations comes from profits not paid out as dividends and from depreciation expense realized but not disbursed. While low-risk sources of cash, these do not normally provide sufficient funds for expansion programs.

Funds may be obtained from several external sources. Short-term and long-term notes from banks are common, particularly where collateral is secure or reputation would lead the financier to feel safe in extending the consideration. Bonds, generally a long-term device, are used to finance expansion. Mortgage bonds (secured by specific assets) or debenture bonds (secured by credit position of the organization or of the owners) may be used. Bonds have fixed and tax deductible interest charges and must be repaid at a specific time. Bonds do not dilute the ownership structure, and may carry features, such as convertibility to stocks, which appear attractive to investors in an adverse market.

The issuance of capital stock which provides for payment of dividends at a fixed rate is another means to attract capital. Common (for full partnership) stocks add funds, but dilute partnership; the dilution occurring both in voting rights and in distribution of earnings.

Each form of capital has an associated cost. The cost of debt, capital, notes and bonds, is a function of the financial position of the organization and the market conditions at the time of debt issuance. In simple terms, it is the fixed interest payment divided by the net amount received. Net amount is used, since a bank note may be discounted, and a bond may be sold below or above par. However, since interest is tax deductible, the actual cost to the organization should be computed after taxes. The cost of equity capital is more difficult to measure. Consideration must be given to the net amount received from the stock issue, anticipated earnings per share after the additional capital is received, and the effect of earnings per share dilution on existing stockholders.

Investment Opportunities

In evaluating investment opportunities, there are three commonly accepted techniques:

1. *Payback period.* The initial project investment divided by the average annual cash inflow generated by the product indicates the number of years required to recover the initial project cost. Determining the minimum payback period is a function of policy.
2. *Present value method.* The annual cash flow generated by the project discounted by the desired rate of return gives the present value of the income stream. Investment outlays are also discounted to their present value. If the net present value exceeds zero, then the project is acceptable. The present value of inflows divided by the present value of outflows is called the *profitability index* (PI). The project is accepted if the PI is greater than 1. This method requires that the rate of return be established in advance.
3. *Internal rate of return.* This is a trial and error approach requiring the use of discount tables. The rate of return which will discount future dollar return from the project so as to equal the present value of the project cost is found. This internal percentage rate of return may then be compared with the cost of capital available to determine if the project should be approved.

Of the three methods, only the last—the internal rate of return—provides a means to evaluate project return versus future cost of capital, providing a sound basis for decision-making.

Working Capital

To the accountant, working capital equals current assets less current liabilities. To the financial manager, however, working capital equals current assets. Hence the management of working capital refers to the management of the organization's liquid assets: cash, accounts receivable, and inventory. The firm needs cash for current transactions, as a reserve to meet unexpected contingencies, and for speculation.

From a purely financial point of view, inventory levels should be as low as possible to minimize investment carrying costs. Overall policy must balance many other factors. Tight credit will result in a fewer funds tied up in outstanding credit. A liberal credit policy will encourage sales, but will also increase the risk of bad debts.

Office Management

The same rules that apply to the production line apply to the office. Before setting up a new production process, a careful flow analysis is developed to minimize rehandling of material and to group related activities together. The office is no different. Before investment is made in the office—for copy machines to computers—cash flow and investment analyses must be made.

Discussion of office management demonstrates a cross between people management, through tool management, into results management. The management of the office involves the office system, which is generally undergoing an overhaul at this time. The change to the office system is being dubbed *office automation.* Office automation brings together the concepts of decision support systems, the basic elements of secretarial science, and some very new and sophisticated hardware systems. As you look at office automation, be aware of the concept of integration—the integration of word processing, electronic filing, graphics and other document production activities, and communications. Also be aware of heightened security concerns, increased pressures for productivity, and entirely new training requirements.

See the chapter on systems for more detail on the office automation opportunity.

QUESTIONS

1. Modern management concepts such as decentralization and spanof control can be traced historically to:
   A. Taylor's Scientific Management
   B. Ancient civilizations of Egypt
   C. The Industrial Revolution
   D. The Bible
2. Coordination involves the integration of which of the following functions *except:*
   A. Planning and controlling
   B. Organizing and planning
   C. Controlling and influencing
   D. Assignment and responsibility
3. The people communications process may be enhanced if:
   A. All directives are written
   B. There is immediate feedback
   C. It is standardized
   D. Directives follow the formal organizational structure
4. Which of the following is *not* a proper aspect of the management function of directing?
   A. Giving orders
   B. Offering instructions
   C. Appraising employees
   D. Establishing rules and regulations
5. Frederick Taylor's Scientific Management did not include:
   A. Use of scientific standards
   B. Cooperation of labor and management
   C. Importance of the informal organization
   D. Use of functional authority

6. Which statement may *not* be said about delegating?
   A. Delegate enough authority to get the job done
   B. Delegating lets others cover the details
   C. The best way to get the job done is to do it yourself
   D. It assigns the responsibility for the task
7. Decentralization refers to:
   A. Moving staffs to the user's site
   B. Integrating company functional areas
   C. Subdividing management decision-making authority
   D. Developing duplicate facilities
8. The management function of selecting the future courses of action for the organization—its goals, policies, and strategies—is called:
   A. Planning
   B. Organizing
   C. Staffing
   D. Directing
9. As contrasted with Frederick Taylor, Fayol looked at management from the viewpoint of:
   A. An efficiency expert
   B. A chief executive
   C. The shop foreman
   D. Academic theory
10. The first step in the process of *control* is to:
    A. Hire only people who can do the work
    B. Measure employee performance
    C. Compare performance against personnel standards
    D. Set standards against which to measure
11. Objectives require identification of:
    A. Goals, methods, and measurements
    B. Profit maximization points
    C. Cost minimization points
    D. Break even points
12. Which of the following is customarily given staff authority?
    A. Production Manager
    B. Sales Manager
    C. Inventory Manager
    D. Personnel Manager
13. The most recent identifiable approach to management thought is the:
    A. Decision Theory School
    B. Human Relations School
    C. Mathematical School
    D. Systems School
14. Employees of a firm whose function is to advise those in the direct chain of command have:
    A. Chain authority
    B. Line authority
    C. Staff authority
    D. Functional authority
15. An organization which is divided into departments is generally termed a:
    A. Line organization

B. Staff organization
C. Decentralized organization
D. Compartmentalized organization

16. When the manager defines the jobs to be done, she is performing what function of management?
A. Planning and Controlling
B. Organizing and Staffing
C. Directing and Controlling
D. Controlling and Staffing

17. The factors of production, in the classical sense, do *not* include:
A. Land
B. Labor
C. Inventory
D. Capital

18. Organization charts best portray:
A. The structure of power
B. The status definition
C. The authority structure
D. The salary schedule

19. Disciplining a subordinate's work would be most closely associated with which principle of management?
A. Delegation of authority
B. Unity of command
C. Management by exception
D. Division of work

20. The first step in organization should be:
A. The division of work
B. Set up the coordination methods
C. Define the objectives
D. Determine the financial status

21. The National Labor Relations Board was established by the:
A. Robinson–Patman Act (1936)
B. Wagner Act (1935)
C. Taft–Hartley Act (1947)
D. Federal Civil Rights Act (1964)

22. The management function of supervising and coordinating the activities of subordinates is called:
A. Planning
B. Organizing
C. Directing
D. Controlling

23. As contrasted with Frederick Taylor, Blake and Mouton looked at management from the viewpoint of:
A. Production vs. people
B. The line organization
C. The staff organization
D. Interpersonal motivation

24. The management function of measuring and correcting the actions of subordinates to ensure that plans for the business are fulfilled is called:
A. Planning

B. Organizing
C. Directing
D. Controlling

25. A firm obtains maximum profit by:
A. Selling as many units as possible
B. Setting marginal revenue equal to marginal costs
C. Setting prices as high as possible
D. Producing to full capacity

26. Control is:
A. Making sure people obey orders
B. Keeping books and issuing financial statements
C. Determining the degree of fulfillment of objectives
D. Establishing an informal communications network

27. When it is necessary to relocate a department, the manager should concern himself most with:
A. Adaptation to new surroundings
B. Complaints caused by the change
C. Returning to pre-move efficiency
D. Justifying the move to the staff

28. The "closed shop" was outlawed by the:
A. Fair Labor Standards Act
B. Wagner Act
C. Anti-Closed Shop Act
D. Taft–Hartley Act

29. Planning as a process requires:
A. Consideration of alternative strategies
B. Establishment of objectives
C. Continuous reevaluation
D. All of the above

30. Price discrimination is regulated by the:
A. Price Discrimination Act
B. Lanham Act
C. Wheeler–Lea Act
D. Robinson–Patman Act

31. The method whereby a corporation model is built is called:
A. Simulation
B. PERT
C. Linear Programming
D. Operations Research

32. The rights of self-organization and collective bargaining are guaranteed by the:
A. Fair Labor Standards Act
B. Wagner Act
C. Robinson–Patman Act
D. Taft–Hartley Act

33. A program is best defined as a:
A. One-time plan aimed at a single objective
B. Statement of a plan in financial terms
C. Determination of the scope of the firm's economic activity
D. Short-run operational plan

34. The first federal antitrust legislation was the:
   A. Clayton Act
   B. Sherman Act
   C. Robinson–Patman Act
   D. Miller–Tydings Act

35. The common stock in the ABC Widget Company has just risen from $20 to $25 per share.
   A. The stockholder's return has been diminished
   B. The stockholder's return has been increased
   C. The stockholder's return remains level
   D. The stockholder's return is nonexistent

36. A manager's main role in communicating:
   A. Is getting others to do what she wants them to do
   B. Requires that the receiver not be permitted to respond
   C. Is ensuring that she is understood
   D. Is ensuring that the receiver will comply

37. Objectives are:
   A. The starting point for all planning activity
   B. The same at every level of the business
   C. Always compatible with other objectives of the firm
   D. The results of the business plan

38. The staffing function of management falls primarily to:
   A. The Purchasing Department
   B. The Personnel Department
   C. The Payroll Department
   D. The Painting Department

39. According to Peter Drucker, the job of a manager consists of:
   A. Forecasting, budgeting, and controlling
   B. Managing a business, workers, and work
   C. Planning, organizing, activating, and controlling
   D. Supervision

40. Objectives should be stated
   A. In a general and unstructured manner to fit people's needs
   B. In unattainable terms, to ''stretch'' the people
   C. In a quantifiable manner, to permit measurement
   D. In a logically related manner

41. Operations research:
   A. Is synonymous with quantitative decision methods
   B. Starts with a clear statement of the problem by the manager
   C. Applies the scientific method to the definition and solution of problems
   D. Is able to portray complete business situations realistically

42. The manager's decision-making process
   A. Requires making decisions under probabilistic conditions
   B. Requires responsibility for decision-making
   C. Requires a limiting factor
   D. Requires a full understanding of the causes and effects of the decision stimulus

43. Abraham Maslow's hierarchy of need includes:
   A. Safety, social, and monetary
   B. Social, monetary, and self-esteem

C. Safety, monetary, social, and self-esteem
D. Self-esteem, safety, and social

44. A manager's decision must *never* be made under:
A. Duress or crisis
B. Intuition and insight
C. A paucity of available facts
D. A plethora of available facts

45. The Hawthorne experiments:
A. Discovered that individual output was governed by the norms of the informal group
B. Developed a method of task analysis which led to improved work planning
C. Confirmed the importance of incentive payments as a motivating force
D. Applied quantitative techniques to management problems

46. Planning is best done when it is done
A. By top level officials
B. By line subordinates
C. By an official planning group
D. By the manager responsible for the plan

47. The prime function of a manager is:
A. Managing his or her staff
B. Planning the project
C. Accomplishing work through people
D. Progress reporting

48. The organization's business plan should go through what steps?
A. Growth, Survival, Profit, Organization
B. Organization, Profit, Growth, Survival
C. Organization, Survival, Profit, Growth
D. Organization, Growth, Profit, Survival

49. The most commonly used control technique is the
A. PERT network
B. Budget
C. Internal management audit
D. Cybernetic approach

50. The business environment in which local zoning action is likely to fall is known as the:
A. Internal, Governmental
B. Internal, Social
C. External, Governmental
D. External, Social

51. You are called upon to take part in an adversary interview, and have been given the direct adversary role. You must
A. Adopt a benefactor position
B. Adopt a neutral position
C. Adopt an antagonistic position
D. Adopt no position—there is no adversary interview

52. A prosperous firm:
A. Enjoys stable employment
B. Experiences a high turnover
C. Cannot attract qualified talent
D. Cannot retain qualified talent

53. Ouchi's Theory Z holds that the:
A. Manager has the sole responsibility for all decisions
B. Manager must take a straw poll to determine direction
C. Workers must have a democratic part of all decisions
D. Workers must be allowed participation in the direction of the group

54. Eli Whitney is credited with the use:
A. Of the cotton gin
B. Of interchangeable parts
C. Of the assembly line
D. Of the quality circle

55. A company's acid ratio is 1.5:1. The company is:
A. Insolvent
B. Insolvent, but early recovery is possible
C. Solvent, but just barely
D. Solvent, and in good financial condition

56. Robert Owen showed
A. That the predominant feature of the industrial revolution was cheap labor
B. That industrialism need not be built on cheap labor
C. That machinery, not people, were required to industrialize
D. That people, not machinery, would be required to industrialize

57. In Likert's linking pin concept:
A. The manager links subordinates into a cohesive group
B. The manager displays a consultative form of leadership
C. The manager is a member of two distinct groups of individuals
D. The worker functions effectively as an element of the man/machine interface

58. In addition to early computer concepts, Charles Babbage is credited with these contributions to management theory:
A. Data gathering as a basis of decision
B. Data processing as a basis of decision
C. Data declination as a basis of decision
D. Data inference as a basis of decision

59. The Human Relations School of Management began with:
A. The Hawthorne experiments
B. The National Labor Relations Board
C. The Taft-Hartley Act
D. The Uniform Commercial Code

60. The payback period of an investment is:
A. The investment divided by the return on investment
B. The investment divided by the payoff period
C. The investment divided by the cost of money
D. The investment divided by the average annual cash inflow

61. The informal communication channel or grapevine in the organization should be:
A. Used to transmit a large percentage of nondirective type messages
B. Manipulated to transmit information favorable to the company image
C. Recognized and considered in communication programs
D. Never used because it could be dangerous

62. The issuance of capital stock with fixed dividends
A. Is not possible

B. Is not advisable
C. Attracts capital
D. Attracts expenditure

63. The planning process requires a manager to:
A. Make decisions under uncertainty, use probability theory, and consider job characteristics
B. Know all facets of the performance of a project
C. Give precise schedules and estimates
D. Gather sufficient staff to complete the project in the shortest possible time

64. Management must have a concept of ratio analysis because ratios are required for:
A. Planning purposes
B. Organizing purposes
C. Directing purposes
D. Controlling purposes

65. The Theory X manager assumes that:
A. People must be closely controlled
B. The worker is motivated by social as well as monetary needs
C. There is a basic conflict between man and organization
D. The worker is a self-starter

66. Organizational Development is a concept which
A. Concerns itself strictly with management training
B. Concerns itself with the total organization
C. Concerns itself with clerical workers
D. Concerns itself with line workers

67. Which of the following is the most important consideration when preparing reports upon which management will make decisions?
A. Format
B. Brevity
C. Detail
D. Timeliness

68. A grievance procedure is that which
A. Interposes the union steward between the worker and the foreman
B. Avoid the effects of labor law
C. Resolves on the job difficulties
D. Selects the adjudication of the difficulty

69. The first step in developing a new organization would be to:
A. Categorize functions into related groups
B. Define authority relationships and position descriptions
C. Determine the purpose of the organization
D. Compute the personnel and equipment resources required

70. The industrial relations activity has *no* responsibility for:
A. On the job performance
B. Staffing
C. Compensation
D. Labor relations

71. Max Weber is best known for his:
A. Concept of social Darwinism
B. Universal principles of management
C. Theory of bureaucracy
D. Analysis of microeconomic theory

72. The product cycle begins with an idea and ends with:
A. Research and development
B. Commercialization

C. Applied research
D. Comparative analysis

73. Division of labor is *not:*
A. Another name for specialization
B. Related to the individual as departmentalization is related to the organization
C. A classic principle of organization
D. The means to parcel out work to be done

74. Suggestion awards are customarily a feature of:
A. A needs analysis
B. A work improvement program
C. A performance evaluation
D. A work sampling program

75. The term *oligopoly* refers to a marketplace in which there:
A. Are a few buyers, all of whom are dominant
B. Is a single seller in a controlled industry
C. Are a few sellers, each of whom is semidominant
D. Is a single buyer who can utilize a firm's total capacity

76. As the average fixed cost per unit drops
A. The total average variable cost will also drop
B. The total average variable cost will rise and then fall
C. The total average cost per unit will fall and then rise
D. The total average cost per unit will rise and then fall

77. A decrease in production output as the proportions of labor and material are increased for given size plant is referred to as:
A. The law of diminishing returns
B. A decreasing return to scale
C. A long-run concept
D. Negative work improvement

78. In the production system, the factory inventory
A. Includes all raw materials
B. Includes accumulated cost to that point
C. Includes sales and distribution costs
D. Includes research and development costs only

79. A bureaucratic organizational structure is characterized by
A. Excessive procedures, forms, and policies
B. A "chain of command" hierarchical structure
C. Duplicated and inefficient administration
D. Its inability to expand and/or contract

80. Control Systems must
A. Structure the nature of the acquired data
B. Generate returns in excess of cost
C. Align themselves to objective plans
D. Be used only by accountants

81. The work measurement method which provides for best focus on the proper method of performing each task is:
A. Methods time measurement
B. Work sampling
C. Time study
D. Scientific management

82. Power is *derived* from:
A. Incentive and sanction systems
B. Assumption of absolute control
C. Bestowal from above
D. Assignment as a job function

83. The equation of authority commensurate with responsibility at a given organization level will mean that:
A. Both must be delegated equally
B. Both are necessary to the degree of the tasks to be performed
C. Both should be clearly and separately defined for each position
D. Responsibility will be derived from the conferred authority

84. Incentive compensation should be given for
A. The suggestion program
B. Increased return on investment
C. Greater communications
D. Greater homogeneity

85. An agreement between the union and management to call a third party to assist in seeking an acceptable solution to negotiation problems is termed:
A. Arbitration
B. A grievance procedure
C. An unfair labor practice
D. Fact finding

86. In an administrative performance appraisal the manager should:
A. Promote without advancing pay
B. Transfer for cause
C. Assign salary increases
D. Avoid terminations

87. In the following list, which is the direct responsibility of management?
A. Allocation of computer time to "bread and butter" functions
B. Maintain state payroll tax reports
C. Maintain bills of material and time cards
D. Allocation of work in process to various departments

88. Delegation grants the
A. Ability to do the job without the responsibility
B. Right or power to perform the job
C. Decision to divide the work amongst employees
D. Responsibility to do the job if the ability is present

89. The management function which is concerned with stimulating members of the organization to take action consistent with the plan is:
A. Controlling
B. Influencing
C. Organizing
D. Planning

90. Communication is first facilitated by
A. The symbols used to communicate
B. Knowledge that the receiver is hearing
C. An appreciation of forces upon the correspondent
D. Listening before speaking

91. This school of management thought has often been referred to as the "organization theory" approach.
A. Group behavior approach

B. Decision theory approach
C. Social system approach
D. Systems approach

92. When the manager is faced with managing conflict
A. Any reaction is acceptable
B. No reaction is acceptable
C. Avoidance begs apathy
D. Existence begets competition

93. The issue of additional common stock by a firm may result in:
A. Reducing the preferred stock dividend
B. Increasing the fixed interest payments due each year
C. Increasing the stockholder's financial leverage
D. Diluting the voting rights of current shareholders

94. A perception set is a statement of
A. The filters through which a manager sees things
B. Practices employed in worker supervision
C. Person preference of the top managers
D. Pitfalls to avoid for proper management

95. The basic difference between Theory X and Theory Y concepts of management is:
A. Theory Y advocates an authoritative management–employee relationship while Theory X advocates a participative management–employee relationship
B. Theory X advocates an authoritative management–employee relationship while Theory Y advocates a participative management–employee relationship
C. The letters used to identify them
D. There is no valid answer here

96. Job enrichment is designed to:
A. Find more work for the employee
B. Horizontally expand the empoyee's responsibility
C. Find the fit of employee to job
D. Increase the demands and rewards of the job

97. In the large corporation, management's responsibility to the stockholder:
A. Focuses exclusively on profits
B. Gives major consideration to such ethical issues as environmental pollution and minority employment
C. Is defined only in terms of end results
D. Is defined primarily in economic terms

98. In the Arena area of the Johari Window exist:
A. Things both I and the public know
B. Things the public knows, but I do not
C. Things neither the public nor I know
D. Things which cannot be known

99. The Fair Credit Reporting Act guarantees that:
A. Information will be used as the citizen intends it to be used
B. Any organization offering credit services must make interest charges known
C. All citizens have a right to correct data themselves
D. Information kept by the government is freely accessible

100. In the Blake and Mouton Managerial Grid, Impoverished Management is:
A. 9,1 B. 1,9 C. 1,1 D. 5,5

ANSWERS

1. D	26. C	51. C	76. C
2. D	27. C	52. A	77. A
3. B	28. D	53. C	78. B
4. C	29. D	54. B	79. B
5. C	30. D	55. D	80. B
6. C	31. D	56. B	81. A
7. C	32. B	57. C	82. A
8. A	33. A	58. A	83. B.
9. B	34. B	59. A	84. B
10. D	35. B	60. D	85. D
11. A	36. C	61. C	86. C
12. D	37. A	62. C	87. B
13. D	38. B	63. A	88. B
14. C	39. B	64. D	89. B
15. A	40. C	65. A	90. C
16. B	41. C	66. B	91. C
17. C	42. A	67. D	92. D
18. C	43. D	68. A	93. D
19. A	44. C	69. C	94. A
20. C	45. A	70. A	95. D
21. B	46. D	71. C	96. D
22. C	47. C	72. B	97. D
23. A	48. C	73. D	98. A
24. D	49. B	74. B	99. B
25. B	50. C	75. C	100. C

TUTORIAL

1. Refer to the text, where the Bible reference is given.
2. Assignment and responsibility do not relate to coordination. Coordination is the combination of all the other functions amongst the various organizational units.
3. Communications is a human activity. Immediate feedback can resolve tremendous problems.
4. Directing involves guiding the employee toward the accomplishment of the task. Appraisal is a management function, but not of directing.
5. Even Taylor acknowledged the existence of the informal organization, but it was not part of his proposal.
6. Recall that our premise is that a manager is a person who is responsible for more work than he can perform himself. This means that he or she simply cannot do it alone.
7. Decentralization requires that some of the decision-making capability be placed at the decentralized location. Duplication occurs, but is not a necessity of the decentralized structure.
8. They're all management functions—but *planning* is the best answer here.
9. Refer to the chapter for the writings of Fayol—who looked at the organization from the top down, from the perspective of the chief executive.
10. As has been stated, one does not control without a standard; setting the standard must then be the first step, else you'll never know how successful you have been.
11. An objective has three parts—goals (where am I going?), methods (how will I get there?), and measurements (how will I know I have arrived?).

12. The Personnel Manager is the only person in the list who is not in the line organization—the only person for whom the mandate is service, not product.
13. Again, refer to the text—the Systems School is the most recent approach to management thought.
14. Chain authority, if anything, would be line authority. Functional authority generally is applied to a specific project. Advisory capacity is a staff, not line function.
15. The definition of line and staff should be obtained here. Staff is an assisting capacity. Line is the direct operating entities of the organization. Departmentalization is the distribution of those operating entities.
16. The manager is organizing the work and arranging the people to do it. She is definitely performing B.
17. The classical factors are land, labor, and capital. See the figure in the chapter which compares the traditional to modern factors of production.
18. When an organization develops a chart which maps the organizational functions and the people assigned to them, they are mapping the authority structure, C. Whether it is the definition of power and status is another question. It certainly should not be the salary schedule.
19. Since authority has been delegated, there is a responsibility commensurate with that authority, and it is that to which the discipline is applied. Division of work is an assignment function; management by exception is a premise of operation, and unity of command is a structure.
20. If I hit it hard enough, will you remember that nothing should ever happen in an organization without first setting the objectives?
21. The Wagner Act is also known as the National Labor Relations Act of 1935.
22. Supervising denotes the ongoing activities of overseeing the activities of subordinates.
23. In the Blake and Mouton Grid, the X axis is the concern for production and the Y axis is the concern for people.
24. The key here is *measuring*. The answer is *controlling*.
25. The point where marginal revenue equals marginal costs is otherwise known as the upper break-even point—where the revenue has begun its decline (according to the law of diminishing returns) and the cost has exceeded its ascent.
26. A may be absolute control; B and D are not applicable. C, fulfillment of objectives, is the purpose of control.
27. The idea is to get things working again. Adaptation will be a function of the capabilities of the people involved. Justification should be done early, so that it will not occupy an inordinate amount of time. Until things are working, complaints of crisis should be handled immediately; complaints of inconvenience should be deferred.
28. The Taft–Hartley Act outlawed the closed shop (where a union is not permitted) and allowed for an 80-day cooling off period in the event of major labor strikes.
29. You won't see a question like this on the test. These are all valid answers.
30. Knowledge question only—the Robinson–Patman Act.
31. Model building is a function of operations research.
32. Knowledge question only—Wagner Act.
33. A program has a single objective and is structured toward that objective. It need not be a financial or economic plan. It is most certainly not an operational plan.
34. It's also known as the Sherman Anti-Trust Act.
35. Since stockholders are paid dividends on the basis of the value of the common stock, an increase in the value of the common stock is an increase in return to the stockholders.
36. Of course, the manager wants others to do what she wants them to do, but all communications are not directive. It's far better to ensure that she is understood.
37. It has been said that if you don't know where you're going, you're certain to arrive. Objectives

must be specified before you can have any chance to achieve them. They vary at the business level, should be compatible—but sometimes are not—with other objectives. They are the beginning, not the results, of the business plan.

38. Under normal circumstances, the manager's department will apprise the Personnel Department of staffing needs. The Personnel Department will then take the steps necessary to obtain qualified candidates.

39. Answers A and D are tasks, of course. Answer C is more the traditional function. Drucker, according to his writing, ascribes to C.

40. Objectives should be set in a quantifiable manner, as a prelude to measurement (*control*).

41. Operations Research is a mathematically-based modeling system, utilizing the scientific method.

42. A manager does not have the luxury of always having all the facts available when a decision must be made. Limiting factors, if any, are the degrees of risk through which the decision must be made.

43. Please review the illustration of Maslow's hierarchy in this chapter. Monetary does not lie within the hierarchy.

44. Vocabulary time. Plethora means an overabundance. Paucity means highly lacking. Since in both cases the facts are "available," C is the answer. A manager should not make decisions on a few facts, if many facts are available.

45. The Hawthorne experiments were conducted with people assigned to an informal control group. No task analysis was made, nor were there any incentive payments. The quantitative school happened later.

46. If top level officials do the planning, nobody will be able to live with the plan. They should set goals and objectives. Line subordinates have little understanding of the big picture, and should not do the planning. An official planning group is hardly in touch with each element of the organization. The manager who will be responsible for the plan should do the planning—with input from all.

47. A manager cannot physically do all work herself; therefore the work must be done by others. Project planning and reporting are tasks, and staff management must be done, but are not the *prime* function.

48. An organization, once organized, must aim first for survival; then profit; then growth.

49. Budget is the filter through which all organizational activities must pass. See the figure in the chapter.

50. Since it's outside the organization, it's external; since it's regulatory, it's governmental.

51. C is the best answer—and is a judgment call brought about by experience. It may not be wise, but despite this, the adversary interview remains.

52. A prosperous firm is generally a well managed firm, and enjoys a most stable employment, attracting the best of talent.

53. "Manage by walking around" involves management by participation of the workers in decisions.

54. While he invented the cotton gin (and didn't drink it), Whitney is best known for the interchangeable parts he used in the manufacture of weapons. He didn't invent the assembly line, but interchangeable parts had a profound effect on Henry Ford's (who did) automobiles.

55. There are 1.5 times as many current assets as their are current liabilities.

56. Robert Owen held that cheap and abused labor need not be the grease in the wheel of industrialism.

57. The manager is in the middle ground—a part of the staff and a part of the line, simultaneously. The manager is a direct participant, not a consultant.

58. Babbage held that to make decisions, the manager must gather data and determine its relationship to the decision situation.

59. It was not until the experiments of Elton Mayo that the early concepts of the Human Relations School of Management began. The NLRB, Taft-Hartley, and UCC are all law-related.

60. The payback period is the period when the investment is repaid. This means that the proceeds must be divided into the investment.

61. It is a wise manager who can use the grapevine effectively. It should never be a vehicle for official messages, and would appear manipulated if stuffed with nonsense.

62. The issuance of capital stock with a fixed dividend will attract capital looking for a safe investment. Rates tend to be somewhat lower in this instance.

63. If you know of a manager who knows all the problems and all the answers to those problems, become his agent. No, the process of management is one of making decisions under uncertainty, without complete information.

64. A ratio is a "how am I doing" measurement, most useful in the controlling process.

65. Theory X is directive (Grid 9,1) and must control everything. D is Theory Y, as is B. C does not apply.

66. The Organization Development concept involves the organization as a whole, seeking to improve communications, relationships, knowledge, and results.

67. There will be every opportunity to alter format, detail, and conciseness after the fact. Decision support means *now,* and timeliness (and the currency of the data) is the answer.

68. The grievance procedure is the first step in a labor unrest situation. It immediately interposes the union steward between the worker (labor) and the foreman (management). From that point, the fact finding process begins.

69. If you wish to avoid the "why are we here" questions, you'd better determine the purpose of the organization—be it a social organization or a business organization. Nature abhors a vacuum. People avoid directionless activities.

70. The industrial relations activity handles the staffing, compensation, and labor relations (usually bargaining) activities of the organization. It has only after-the-fact involvement with performance reviews.

71. Weber wrote about organizations and how they encumbered themselves. He wasn't an economist, it is not known what he felt about evolution—and are there any universal principles of management, except the businessman's Latin: I came, I saw, I concurred.

72. When the product steps are done (review, market analysis, technical feasibility assessment, comparative analysis, applied research, evaluation, development, and market research), the final step is the commercialization of the product.

73. Division of labor is not an assignment schedule—it is a responsibility schedule which defends departmentalization.

74. The suggestion awards should result in work improvement.

75. There are but a few players in the oligopoly game, most of whom are holding all the cards, as many now-defunct microcomputer manufacturers have found out.

76. There will be an optimum point, to which the total average cost per unit will fall, after which it will rise. The change is a function of a rising average variable cost, at the point where capacity is nearly full.

77. When the curve hits the apex on the Y axis and starts to move again toward the X axis, you have found the law of diminishing returns. It may be a long-run concept, but not necessarily. I don't know what a decreasing return to scale is, and negative work improvement is a contradiction.

78. The factory inventory will include all costs up to that point, from raw material through work in process. Some costs, such as research and development costs, will be factored into this figure.

79. There has never been a bureaucratic organization in history that didn't have a scalar structure. It isn't necessarily inefficient, but it usually is. It expands more than it should, and contracts only when it seems out of control. Such tend to have excessive procedures, forms, and policies—but only where there is no strong dictatorial leadership. A is certainly a close answer under normal circumstances.

80. Any control system's cost must resemble cost of loss due to the lack of the control. Since it is desired to spend less than that, it must generate returns in excess of cost.

81. Work sampling and time study are part of the MTM system. Scientific management may use MTM, but A, methods time measurement (MTM) is the answer.

82. The key word is *derived*—some power is bestowed by authority, to be sure, but derived from a system of rewards and punishments.

83. The annals of managerial history are strewn with the failures of those who are given responsibility without authority. They must be given to the same individual, and blessed by the hierarchy.

84. Incentive compensation should be given for profit improvement, increased ROI, and increased performance.

85. The process *starts* as fact finding. If the dispute cannot then be settled, arbitration will result.

86. The administrative performance appraisal is used to handle organizational issues. Promotions, terminations, and transfers are all handled here, but not under the circumstances indicated. Salary increases are the answer.

87. There is some management in any of these. But one one which is management's alone is the report to the external legal authority. A nonmanagement person may prepare the report, but it is management's responsibility.

88. Delegation assigns the right or power to do the job—the authority and the responsibility.

89. B, influencing is the best answer here. The book presents influencing as a subtopic to directing and discusses the fact that in the final analysis when action has not been induced, it may be influenced.

90. Empathy is an appreciation of forces upon the correspondent, and becomes the initial point of communication.

91. The social system school devised the organization theory. The other three do not apply.

92. Conflict begets competition. Its absence begs mediocrity. Reactions include force, withdrawal, smoothing, compromise, mediation, superordinate goals, and problem solving.

93. Preferred stock dividends are paid to preferred stockholders, not to common stock holders. Neither has a fixed interest payment, or any change in leverage. The amount of ownership has been diminished, however.

94. We all have perception sets—they are the eyes through which we see, and evaluate things. Objectivity is required to deal with them.

95. Theory X is indeed authoritarian, but Theory Y is not necessarily participative. It is more socially oriented, laissez faire.

96. A and B fall in a category known as *job enlargement.* C is *job design. Job enrichment* presents new challenges and provides the rewards for those challenges, D.

97. Management has a responsibility to maintain the value of the stockholder's shares, and to cause them to grow, where possible. That does not mean profits (though they help); it could mean cutting losses.

98. The Arena area of the Johari Window includes things known to both the public and me.

99. C and D apply to the Freedom of Information Act. A is not always possible. B is the answer.

100. I like to call the 1,1 manager a person who has retired on the job. The authors, however, prefer to identify him as impoverished, as he cares for nobody but himself—not much for either the job or the people.

4

DATA PROCESSING MANAGEMENT with Project Management

Modern data processing requires the technical skills of many highly qualified personnel. The individual who must manage data processing must possess exceptional technical knowledge or be able to draw persons with the appropriate knowledge to his assistance to guide the operation and all his personnel in this complex environment. He ought to be skilled in the art (though there are scientific elements, management is still an art) of managing—of getting work done through people.

It would be nice to know with certainty that we have learned, through much trial, that the management of data processing is not a task for the uninitiated. There is strong evidence, however, that top level management continues to assume that because an individual is a superb computer technician, he or she is endowed with the skills necessary to run the operation. And, worse, there's strong evidence that few individuals who are faced with installation as top computer executive (TCE) ever get the necessary training. That's certain to create openings for aspiring technicians, but not much stability. And now, with the widespread use of computing capabilities within user departments via microcomputers, the TCE is faced with managing—or at least getting a handle upon—computer resources over which he or she has absolutely no control.

The impact of data processing on the organization's business has become total. The operation of the entire organization now functionally rests in the hands of the TCE. It didn't start that way, of course. It was to have been a support tool. But the computer is all-pervasive, and there is no stopping it now, as it has become the means to reduce labor costs, to increase productivity, and to find new ways to compete. Organizations cannot now back away, even if they wished to do so.

The timely and accurate handling of business records and the presentation of "management information" as the basis for valid decisions have become vital to all organizational departments, so vital that they have acquired not just one or two, but hundreds (in larger organizations) of microcomputers, and are knocking on the doors of traditional DP organizations looking for help. Therefore, the need for fully qualified management in the data processing entity becomes extremely important.

GENERAL DP MANAGEMENT CONCEPTS

Background of the DP Organization

Although computing history was extensively covered in Chapter 1, it is helpful to examine that history from the perspective of the data processing function as it exists within the average organization. Unless the firm's primary business is the *business* of data processing, the DP function is generally a support function for the organization as an entity. Since the organization is not organized to be in the computer business, it no doubt has a greater interest in the manufacture, sale, and distribution of widgets. Because data processing was introduced to the organization as a means to keep records, it was natural to relegate it to some organizational function whose business it was to keep records. And because punched card equipment (in those days) was more amenable to numbers, that equipment was used initially in accounting applications.

Because accounting applications were the purview of the controller (used interchangeably with comptroller), data processing (nee punched card accounting) reported to the controller. There has been a shift away from that form of organization because DP came to serve other than financial users and the investment in computing resources required the centralization of equipment. As if history were repeating itself, the move to distributed data processing may remove the centralizing impetus. Most certainly the existence of an inexpensive microcomputer has already had a discernible impact upon the management of data processing activities.

The assignment of the punched card accounting equipment to the controller was a natural assumption, because it had to be put somewhere, and the majority of the applications would be financial, it was thought. So, accounting and payroll applications formed the backbone of data processing activities.

An interesting paradox confronted the organization during the 1960s and 1970s. While the cost of computing was dropping rapidly in terms of capability and power, i.e., the cost per computer operation, the total cost was escalating rapidly, because the machines were at the same time expanding in sophistication. Thus, the controller was faced with a very basic economic question: could he afford to devote the larger expense solely to the functions he controlled, especially when the unit cost of the work being performed now approached pre-automation levels.

So, new applications had to be found. And those applications had to come from other departments. The controller reluctantly began to give up some control in exchange for cost-sharing of the equipment. As more applications were found adaptable to electronic data processing (EDP), other sections of the organization sought not only to use the controller's equipment, but also the authorization to acquire equipment and establish their own data processing units. With his applicable ''experience,'' the controller was the key figure in discussions about equipment utilization and acquisition. And, so long as he controlled the budget, all of DP was in his empire. However, critics often noted that financial systems activities always seemed to be complete, while other applications either were not complete or were not attempted.

Many questions which then arose are still unresolved. Should management authorize separate functional data processing units? Ten years ago the answer would have been negative. Today, because of the cost of microcomputers and distributed data processing, it is becoming progressively positive. The information revolution is a revolution out of control, seeking its own head, its own direction, its own speed. Happily, it is largely a beneficial situation. However, then it was necessary to discourage duplication of equipment and proliferation of systems, because costs which were once in the range of $500 to $1,000 were now approaching $10,000 (per month). The move to centralization was made necessary by the need to gain the most work from the device.

The centralization of the hardware brought the decentralization of the staffs. Large companies began to move the staffs back out to the users' areas, keeping the hardware centralized, as it was discovered that an identification with a user and the knowledge of his business was imperative. Today, the shift is to put some of the hardware back out into the user's area, and where that has not been done voluntarily, the user has accomplished it for himself by acquiring a microcomputer. Further, distributed processing now means that some of these users are doing their own computing. We were not the speediest in recognizing that the microcomputer would be in the user area and that we would have to live with it. This has been accelerated by the fact that the schools at all levels have been teaching computing. The field is no longer a mystery.

Installed and considered only an exceptionally fast and sophisticated tabulator, the transfer of applications from the punched card accounting equipment to the computer often occurred with little change in procedure; sometimes the punched card continued to be the sole source of input to the system and punched card protocol dictated the file construction and report development. Only after the computer was perceived to be a mind-extender and not an accounting-only tool was any significant headway made.

Some firms found it convenient to adopt other DP organizational structures. When workload volumes became large and highly specialized, it was found that individual functional data processing units were practical, true for that period of EDP history.

Organizational Factors

There is no standard pattern for the positioning of the data processing function within an organization. There are several approaches which are common.

The Sole-Custody Approach

Under this approach, the largest single user has custody of EDP equipment and provides DP support to the other departments of the firm. Historically, this has been the controller. Under this scheme, then, DP has reported to the controller. Simultaneously, it has been necessary for the DP unit to be given a measure of autonomy to ensure fair and equitable service to other departments. Under the scheme, the use of equipment and personnel has been good, but priority has been given to the controller.

This is the major drawback of the single-user approach, and has been a source of conflict. The small or marginal user lacks access to the system and the necessary systems and programming services, and must fight for them, often going to outside services. In recent months, however, he has simply found a way to purchase a microcomputer and has done the application himself. Therefore, under today's environment, the approach is questionable.

The Totally Decentralized Approach

Under this approach, each major functional activity has its own computer and EDP operation. This concept assigns a computer and related EDP resources to each functional activity having an adequate work load. What constitutes an adequate workload is debatable. Generally EDP capabilities are acquired after frequent frustration over the inability to obtain service through a centralized facility.

Using this approach, there may be three, four, or more data processing units within the firm. Each unit tends to be highly specialized, with insufficient flexibility to handle significant workloads from outside its own sphere of influence. Although the computer may be operative for a large part of each workday, the actual processing time of the central processing unit may be quite small, and much of the available computer resources may be idle or wasted. The approach provides fast response and excellent service to the host department, but equipment and personnel costs are higher than necessary. Administrative procedures, including economic leverage for negotiations with vendors of equipment and supplies, are less efficient than in a centralized EDP organization.

While it would be a fair assessment to say that organizational management has brought this situation upon itself, the addition of remote job entry devices to central-site hosts, with the devices located away from the central site, has provided the best of both the decentralized and centralized procurement, control, and data movement while providing considerable capability in a decentralized manner.

The Service-Center Approach

A separate and independently organized DP service center may be established under a high-level neutral official (normally a VP for Information Services) to provide services for all company activities. This approach has been favored and is the best organizational approach for larger systems users. It is generally a highly efficient approach in the use of personnel and equipment. It serves users equitably and recognizes that EDP pervades the policy decisions of the organization at all levels. With all aspects of the organization depending upon data processing, there are really very few other realistic approaches. Figure 4.1 depicts the service-center approach:

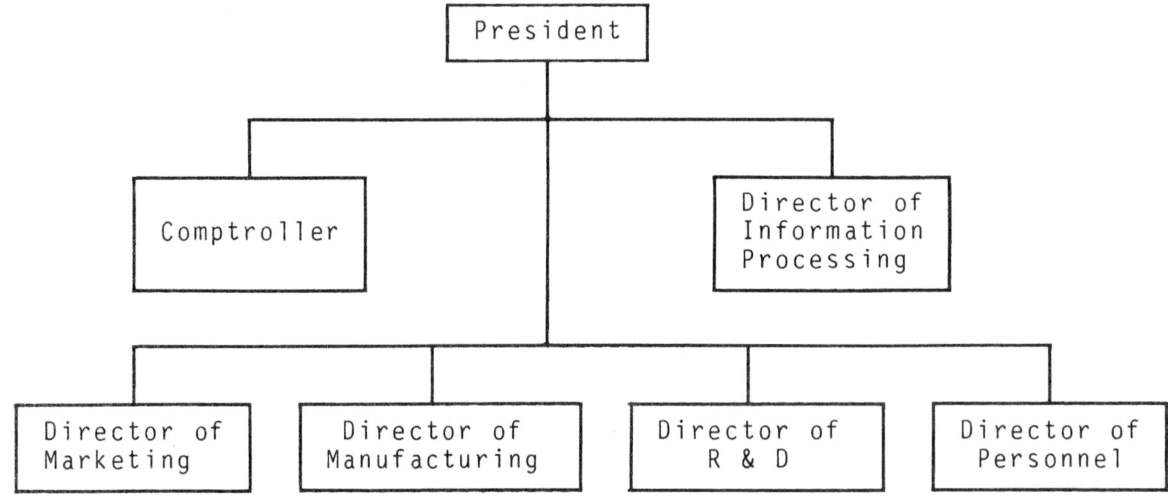

Figure 4.1. Service-Center Organization.

Using this approach, the systems analysis and programming functions are centrally grouped, specialized, and responsive to all requirements of the organization. Since the manager is at a management level equal to the heads of the departments served, he must establish priorities in the interest of the organization as a whole. Experience, however, has been a better teacher, since it has often been discovered that fairness and impartiality do not exist. To overcome this, some organizations have established steering and priority-screening committees. Either way, the organizations have found success in establishing long-range plans for their DP activities and in developing or making progress toward a management information system designed to support the organization's objectives. Lower cost per computation can be achieved and users who are on-line feel that they have exclusive use of the machine.

There are disadvantages. The larger users may complain about not getting all the service that they expected. Computer downtime, programming, or software problems may cause all computer products to become delinquent in a single stroke. Management of so complex a facility is a difficult and demanding task; professional management and top-quality technicians are essential for execution of the rigid schedule required by the service-center approach.

The Distributive Approach

The distributive (processing) approach to computing is a combination of each of the above-listed methods. This facility has been made possible through the advent of mini- and microcomputers. Organizational functions may now have available both local computing capability and the ability to communicate with and utilize the central service-center computing facility. This has required some decentralization of computing people or some training of users. Before this book will again have been published, many sophisticated users, using preprogrammed packages, will be doing much computing on their own. The expansion of BASIC-operating microcomputers and the number of people able to program them will hold some surprises for EDP managers throughout the next decade.

The User's Access

In actuality, the surprises have already begun. Initially, the user acquired a microcomputer and used it for isolated tasks, but somebody had the bright idea that there was no need to wait for data processing to do the job that needed doing—just download the database and let the user do his thing. But data processing wouldn't stand still for that. After all, the database was theirs. The user could go bark up a pipe. Here was the user and he was getting the job done with *VisiCalc, Lotus 1-2-3,* and a large variety of word processors and database packages. So the contest has come down to ownership. The DP people say that the user shouldn't have access to the data, that they have no controls over the modification of the data, that there would be no audit trails. And, if there are any programs to be done, it should be the DP people who should do them.

Acquisition of uniform systems has also become an issue. Unfortunately, there has been little standardization among the various microcomputers—which has meant that it is IBM and compatible systems that have been selected. That, of course, doesn't bother IBM at all, and IBM has gone to great lengths to find ways to transmit data to and from the micro, to use the micro as an intelligent terminal, etc.

It is no part of the purpose of this book or this author to adjudicate this dispute, but you as a potential DP manager should know that the issue exists, that a meeting of the minds must be achieved with users, and the necessary cooperation must found. I will tell the user that he has a right to the data, but a responsibility to ensure that the data are audited and protected, and that changes are coordinated. The issue for you is not the availability of data, but the protection of the data when the user has it, the restrictions upon updates and changes, particularly where there are legal-based systems involved, and the normal concerns of security and safety for the data. More is to be learned and experienced in these circumstances—and you may be an active participant in the fray.

Organizational Levels of EDP

One of the functions of management is to organize or divide the work of the group into logical parts which may be efficiently managed as subunits. The division of work normally follows natural patterns. For instance, individual units may be readily identified by their different purposes, processes used, personnel skills, or location. This division of work or specialization of labor allows these groups to become extremely skilled and the organization to become more efficient as a unit, with emphasis on applications-oriented specialization.

Data processing is a distinct process which calls for separately managed units. Within data processing there are several different operations and specializations. The management and administration of the activities keep the entire process working as efficiently as possible. Systems analysts investigate users' DP needs and organize them into system outputs, inputs, and processes. Programmers reduce the design to program logic charts and code computer instructions. Machine operators load the computer system and monitor the operation to ensure that the desired output is obtained. Database analysts perform appraisals upon the file structures, and the database administrator keeps the file structures honed. Systems programmers keep the operating system and utility programs functioning. Data control personnel will verify the accuracy of the output before delivering the product to the user. This assumes, of course, that these services are not being performed by the user himself at the end of a communications line.

The DP organizational structure forms a pyramid with operators and data controllers at the base, followed by programmers, systems analysts, and managers. The director of DP is at the top, although he may be in the middle management level of the overall organization. A separately situated DP organization will have a head which is at or above the organizational levels the DP shop will serve.

Centralized vs Decentralized Structure

When centralized, management and staff are concentrated at a single location to obtain the benefits of greater specialization and facility of coordination, communication, and top-level decision-making. Generally, if management is centralized, information processing is also centralized so it can support the staff. In a fully centralized computer operation, all data to be processed are fed into the centrally located computer—through on-line applications, through remote job entry devices, and through the more traditional means of card or key data entry. Because of the centralization, communications costs tend to be high. If the central location is in a place where high costs of labor prevail, then the organization will be faced with higher than average costs of programming and systems services, if not for every task in the department.

In a decentralized operation, the authority for action and responsibility for results will settle to the level where efficient management will permit it. Decentralization may imply that there are problems of turnaround, problems of volume, and problems of transmission. Or it may mean that the process has simply become too unwieldy. Or it may mean that under centralization one or more users have had difficulty in obtaining service and have sought ways around the logjam.

There is a definite swing back toward decentralization with microcomputers and with distributed data processing, smart terminals, and remote job entry devices. There may still be large mainframes, but users will obtain computing power—with or without the cooperation of EDP.

Open Shop vs. Closed Shop

Sadly, the day of the open shop concept in the large computing center is gone. Some would still prefer it. But it is disappearing for a very good reason—abuse. Violations of security, violations of program integrity, evasion of controls, and a plethora of anti-computer sentiments have abounded. The investment of many millions of dollars has required the computing center to shut its doors to all but those individuals with the highest authorization. Unfortunately, we're learning that these authorized individuals may also include the janitor, in uniform, without challenge. In earlier days—and, realistically, in some smaller shops today—the open shop was a reality. In the open shop concept, the computer is centralized but the DP/user staffs are decentralized and have constant access to the computer facility. In the closed-shop environment, all systems and programming people are under a centralized control and only those individuals who can pass a rigidly controlled access mechanism are given access. Scheduling is quite sophisticated, and discrete accounting of machine utilization has a high priority. The challenge for DP security specialists today is the control of access to the system from remote locations where security and personnel scrutiny are not so acute. One of the largest problems in this area will certainly be the microcomputer sitting right out in the open in the users' offices.

Selecting a Direction

The DP resource is so valuable that its use must be carefully planned, its alternatives prudently explored, and its functions carefully controlled. One mechanism to effect this, and one which is mandatory in organizations of substantial size, is the EDP Steering Committee. It would be nice if systems could be developed without problems and implemented smoothly. Realistically, however, they are not. The resource is, by definition, among the largest capital and expense items on the financial statements—a nightmare to control. It is not uncommon for the EDP resource to consume a high proportionate share of the before-tax profit on goods sold or services rendered. Yet, because it remains a novel enterprise within the confines of the actual organizational enterprise, and because its function and operation remain mystical to the greatest part of the management team, the course of least resistance has often been to allow the EDP function to float.

The reasons for having an EDP Steering Committee is the determination of priorities among users with differing needs, and whose pressure bases may be significantly different. Equally important is the resolution of political, policy, and operational conflicts relative to those EDP systems which cross functional boundaries. Since an EDP system, by definition, imposes change, the EDP Steering Committee becomes the functional harbinger of organized, planned, and delivered change.

Some organizations have found it beneficial to establish a Permanent Steering Committee (PSC) which will function as supervision for one or more Project Level Steering Committees (PLSC). The following functions and authorities should be included:

1. Dollar approval levels
2. Staffing approval levels
3. Conflict resolution procedures
4. Political issue resolution procedures
5. Organizational issue resolution procedures
6. Methods to dovetail plans to the organization's goals and objectives
7. Referral and resource procedures
8. Resource allocation and reallocation authorities
9. Administrative and reporting procedures
10. Project-level communication procedures

The Role and Responsibility of Top Management

Top organizational management has become acutely aware that its direct involvement in the data processing activity is mandated by the manner in which the computer has permeated the organization. It simply doesn't pay not to know what's going on in DP. There is considerable evidence, also, that the organization whose DP director reports directly to the top is more likely to be successful.

The computer and information processing have a considerable effect on the profitability of the organization. The value of the information on inventory levels, sales analysis, and other key information, when processed in a proper and timely manner, may make the difference between significant profits and losses. There are few, if any, "computer errors." The fault can nearly always be traced to poor planning, inadequate systems design, lack of controls, and related factors for which management must shoulder responsibility.

With the organization's EDP capability suddenly removed, for whatever reason, the organization would cease to exist. Top management knows that. They know it, but they don't want to hear it.

Data and Information

Data processing is functionally only the execution of a systematic sequence of operations performed upon data. A broader term may be data automation, which implies other activities—the collection, storage, and processing of data automatically. Generally, the term *data* is used to denote numbers, letters, or symbols of the facts, figures, conditions, or factors which are basic elements used to communicate information. Organizations cannot function solely upon data or even upon the processing of data. The result of that processing, however, is information, and information is the interpreted presentation of data in a form which supports intelligent decisions. Thus, the EDP activity may more aptly be described as information processing.

The processing of data will nearly always include the classification, recording, communicating, sorting, calculating, summarizing, and presentation of raw data. Master data are contained in master files and are the basic material for processing. They are relatively static; used frequently, changed infrequently. Transaction data are the record of the occurrence of a new event pertaining to an individual record in the master file (also referred to as detail data). Occurrences are random and unpredictable. Test data are specifically developed to test computer runs or programs. They are often actual data from prior runs with additional artificially created data added to test the program's handling. Control data are coded entries to identify a record for subsequent processing.

The Economics of Data

Computers are not inexpensive. That may be the understatement of the book. Because they are not inexpensive, the proportional share of the cost shouldered by an element of data becomes expensive—but, note this: only if that data element is processed. Raw data residing unprocessed may or may not have a cost. Data which do not have a cost are data which have not been collected. Once collected, the processing has begun and the cost is allocated. It therefore behooves organizational management to make some assessment of the worth of data once processed. The precise cost and ultimate value of information to an organization may be difficult to obtain on a specific item basis—but must be collected in aggregate. The value of the information must exceed the cost of getting it, and the return on investment (ROI) must meet the organization's investment criteria. If it cannot, use of the computer for that application must be examined. If legal regulations require it, DP management must find a way to absorb the cost, irrespective of payback.

There are many alternatives available which can result in reduced costs. Normally, these are trade-offs between the use of people and the use of machines. Translating both into dollars, the selection of equipment often prevails. People with pencils may be able to do all calculations, with the assistance of some tools, but a computer can do them faster. This does not mean a direct trade-off. People are still needed, but in a race, the computer is certain to outperform.

Error control and accuracy are a different matter, however. Humans make mistakes when they handle numbers, transposing a pair of adjacent numbers, calculating incorrectly, etc. Computers can be expected to run error free for days, performing billions of operations without error. Timing of the data, checks and controls of systems, and reliability of the equipment can produce nearly infallible information so long as the power remains connected.

It is rather difficult to comment upon the state of the computing in business when one has an insight into what it is becoming and what it will be before this book is published in its next edition. That EDP has pervaded everybody's life, there is no question. In the most minute of ways, the computer has taken over some of the more mundane operations of our lives. Management of EDP has a responsibility to improve the quality of corporate life with the effective and efficient use of EDP resources. But the user has a responsibility to learn what the system can do, study what must be specified for a successful installation, and to take a strong hand in the installation of the system. No longer is it sufficient to blame the computer for people failures.

The Data Processing Department Organization

The DP Manager's Profile

You're faced with writing the job description for a data processing manager. What skills should he have? To what degree? Should they be technical skills or managerial skills? Should the individual be a professional manager? Should he have "come through the ranks?" Would it be best to have an introvert or an extrovert? How do you measure a candidate's ability to handle people? These and many other questions are pertinent to the selection of a DP manager.

In the last chapter, you were presented with a management credo—the author's. You may not ascribe to it, but it goes far in defining the kind of leader who should occupy the DP manager's position. A DP manager must have high skills both in managerial areas and in computer areas. The technician who has advanced through the ranks most probably hasn't received the determination of aptitude and the prerequisite training to assume the position. Thus it has been; thus, it seems, it will ever be. It may be a moot point—by the turn of the century the face of computing will have changed so that the central-site computer operation simply may not exist. So long as we have to have these people, however, both skills are desirable—but, if both are not available, then the preferred choice is that individual whose skills of planning, organizing, leading, and controlling have been honed. Competent technical support can be obtained, and while it is desirable in a DP manager, the other skill is more important.

There are several important traits normally found in a good leader: superior intelligence, confidence, and recognized technical ability. The technical competence criterion is not that the individual must be the best analyst, programmer, operator, or other position. Often one of these is appointed manager simply because of demonstrated technical skills—and then goes on to fail miserably—even occasionally getting fired. Dr. Peter knew of what he was talking when he stated, "an individual rises to his level of competence."

Any manager must know how to motivate his people. The manager of DP is no different. He must be responsible for more work than he can physically perform himself, requiring him to be able to get work accomplished through people. It is not the intention here to duplicate the last chapter, but to isolate those things which are applicable solely to DP managers.

The director of data processing supports and services other functional agencies across the spectrum of company activities. He must have a broad understanding of company operations. He needs to communicate in the language of business with all departments. Thus, he best performs his duties with the dual knowledge of DP and organizational operations.

Job Descriptions and Specialization

Ten years ago the position of database analyst was not common. That position, and several others have been newly added to the spectrum of DP positions. The U.S. Department of Labor has classified 15 distinct positions in EDP. AFIPS talks in terms of 25. It really doesn't make much difference how many positions there are. As the technology changes, skill classifications are added or deleted. Today, persons with microcomputer knowledge are in demand. Conversely, there is little demand for a person capable of working with a UNIVAC I.

DP jobs require special talents and attributes. Aptitudes are difficult to predict with total accuracy; those mechanisms which exist to test aptitude and suitability should be used—but not as the sole criterion for acceptance. Aptitude tests should be balanced with other positive indicators of knowledge, education, experience, skill, and motivation.

It should be noted that every adult who can wade through a programmed instruction course on BASIC will not, by definition, make a good data processor. The DP specialist must read and follow complex and exacting instructions. Those whose love is for the machine to the exclusion of those who must use the machine will quickly become bored with the less esoteric applications. Data processing requires a considerable amount of self-motivation, maturity, perception, and understanding. The role of the DP manager is to provide the intellectual challenge which will exploit those attributes.

There can be only one manager of a unit. He reports to the functional chief of the organization, depending upon the nature of the organization. He has the responsibility to provide systems analysis and design services, maintenance services, programming, machine operations, and input/output control services. He may supervise three to five subordinate branch or division chiefs (each with a staff) if assigned to a large organization—or he may supervise one programmer and one operator in a small shop. Whether these skills are spread around or concentrated upon a handful of people is strictly a function of organizational size.

Here are some typical job descriptions for the principal employees in a DP department of substantial size:

> The *Manager of Data Processing* reports to the VP for Administration. He supervises the Chief of Systems Analysis, the Chief of Programming, the Chief of Machine Operations, the Chief of Production Control, and the Chief of Plans and Standards. (If that seems like too many chiefs, substitute "supervisors.") The narrative elaborates on his duties as the administrative and technical head of all the data processing activities of the organization. Responsibility includes management specifics of planning, organizing, leading, and controlling. Technical duties include the review and evaluation of computer systems, requests for additional services, new equipment or vendors' proposals, equipment and personnel utilization, education, and training. Administrative duties include budgeting, personnel

recruitment, evaluation, policy matters, and departmental coordination and planning. Desirable qualifications should include a business-oriented degree, specialized training in the currently installed hardware system, if possible, and five to ten years of directly related experience.

The *Chief of Systems Analysis* reports to the Manager of DP. He supervises two or more senior systems analysts. His responsibilities include providing technical and analytical assistance in the identification and solution of data systems problems; defining information requirements and prescribing procedures; organizing studies on systems matters, including resource costs of time, personnel, and money; and evaluating the advantages of and alternative efforts to management. Desirable qualifications should include a business-oriented degree, specialized training in systems and pertinent hardware capabilities, and four to seven years of direct experience.

The *Chief of Programming* reports to the Manager of DP. He supervises two or more senior programing supervisors. His responsibilities include providing technical and administrative assistance in the development of new programs and the maintenance of operational programs. He also schedules revisions to operational programs. The candidate for this position must be knowledgeable in the details of the data bases, programs, and products of all systems. Qualifications may specify a business degree as desirable, but not mandatory, specialized training in appropriate hardware systems and programming languages, and four to six years direct programming experiences.

The *Chief of Machine Operations* reports to the Manager of DP. He supervises shift leaders, tape librarians, data entry and support equipment supervisors, software support activities (in some instances), data base administration (in some instances), computer performance monitors, and distribution personnel. His responsibilities include supervision of the I/O control function; ensuring effective utilization of EDP equipment and personnel in accordance with schedules, operation run books, standards manuals, and equipment operation manuals; he maintains logs of operation, equipment utilization, down-time and maintenance, tape library controls, and input/output. The candidate must be acquainted with file structures, procedures, and products of major applications systems. Qualifications should include some college courses, as desirable, and specialized training in the current hardware system, as well as four to seven years of directly related experience.

I'm not exactly certain what the title should be at this juncture, but until one emerges from common use, let's call the next one the *Chief of Internal Consulting.* There have been major changes in the field of systems analysis—changes which have been reflected in this revision of the book. With the new departures in the field of office automation and with the proliferation of microcomputers throughout the entire organization, many data processing activities have decided that if they can't beat the user, they'll join (help) them. This assistance has taken the form of in-house assistance, and such groups as the Bank of America have created a cadre of in-house consultants who can assist users with the applications that are to be done within the users' areas.

These qualifications are but one person's perspective. The principal functions are common to most organizations. Some items, such as planning, standards, production control, development control, management science, operations research, etc., are the purview of large, well funded organizations. Smaller organizations frequently cannot afford the luxury of such diversification and may place multiple duty requirements upon a limited number of people. The functions, however, remain the same.

The DP Organization

There is no one ideal organization for data processing. The simplest consists of the manager, who reports to a functional activity chief, and two subunits. One subunit operates the computer equipment. The other

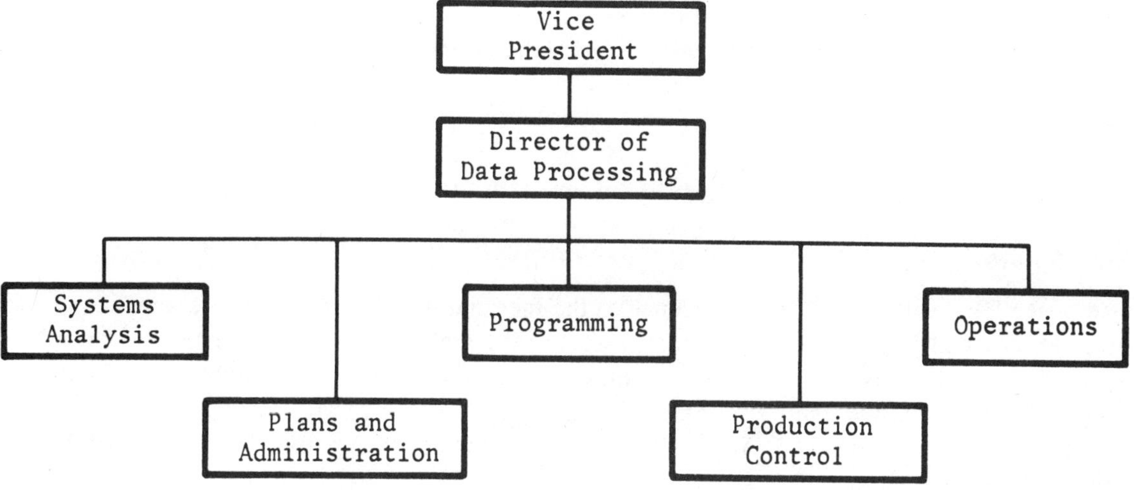

Figure 4.2

performs the clerical input/output control and operates a limited number of data entry mechanisms. Programming and systems analysis work is either done under the open-shop concept or by a centralized design and programming center serving the entire organization.

If the installation is one of several similar facilities belonging to the same organization and performing similar support at a number of decentralized locations, there may be centralized groups to do the systems analysis and programming. The systems and programming functions may then be merged into one unit at the decentralized locations. This unit would be responsible for program and system maintenance and for the preparation of programs for inquiries or one-time reports.

It is becoming increasingly popular to organize data processing as a separate, high-level department. This organizational concept lends itself to a larger-scale facilities in organizations which use data processing extensively. The organizational structure may appear as in Figure 4.2. Alternatively, it may appear as in Figure 4.3. No claim is made that either of these structures is the one best form of organiza-

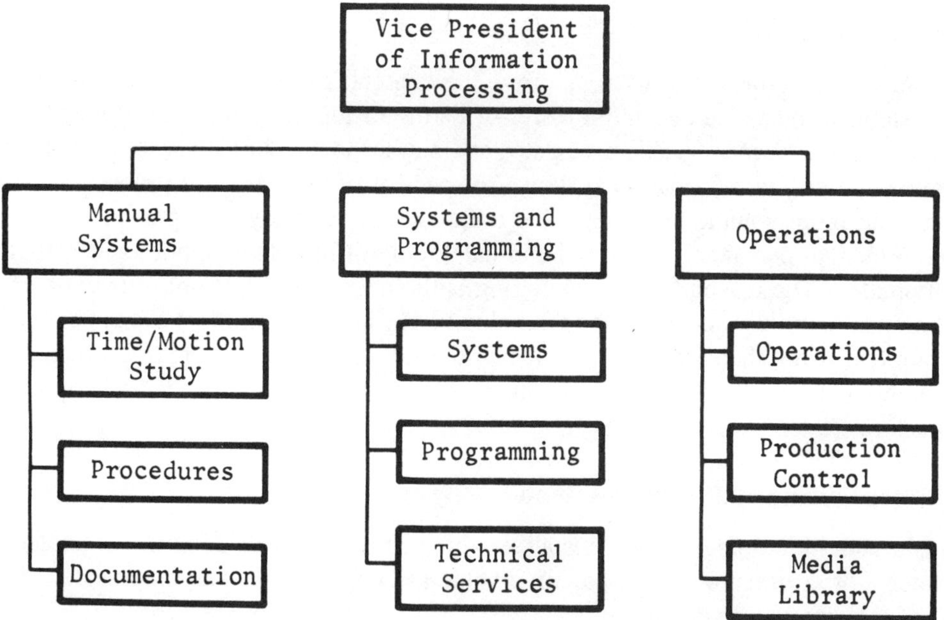

Figure 4.3. Alternate DP Department Organization.

tion. However, each does segment similar duties and responsibilities, permitting work specialization, and identifies separate and manageable units with clearly defined lines of authority and good spans of control. These principles are essential in a well organized unit.

Establishing Control and Monitor Procedures

The EDP Auditor

The rise of the EDP auditor has given credence to the fact that the information processing activity and the information which it processes are, in fact, assets of the highest value. The perspective of information as an asset is relatively new, but a few notorious computer frauds have brought us to a point of sensitivity. We're also at the point where there is emerging a cadre of EDP auditors and a professional-level examination (contact the EDP Auditor's Foundation, Steamboat Springs, IL). The EDP Auditor performs the following tasks:

1. Application systems control review
2. Data integrity review
3. System development life cycle (SDLC) review
4. Application development review
5. General operational procedures controls review
6. Security review
7. Systems software review
8. Maintenance review
9. Acquisition review
10. DP resource management review
11. Information system audit management

These are the general headings. The subheadings provide the meat of the EDP auditor's function. Please refer to the chapter on accounting for more on the subject of auditing.

Reports Approval and Catalog

Management must reserve the authority to approve the content, form, and frequency of the output of the information system. It must also demand a roster or listing of reports and products with such pertinent information as the title, frequency, effective date, and similar identifying or descriptive characteristics.

The organization has an information system, irrespective of how data are processed. Computers permit faster retrieval, more voluminous or detailed data, greater accuracy, and generally lower cost through the reduction of clerical personnel. Approval and cataloging of reports is important whether the system is manual or automated. The reason for the cataloging is the desire to keep from reinventing the wheel. It is important to monitor report production, for the value of the information must always exceed the cost to obtain it. When that is not the case—or the value of the information has decreased—then that report should be discontinued. To continue to spend the money to gather that data, massage it, summarize and report it is wasteful.

Reporting Frequency and Submission Methods

Information is a bona-fide organizational resource which should be considered as valuable as labor or material. The cost of information and its relative value are important factors to consider in the overall management of information processing.

Like any economic resource, processed information has both marginal cost and marginal utility. Marginal cost is the additional cost of producing one more unit; marginal utility is the additional usefulness of having that additional unit. Having already invested in computer equipment and the staffs necessary to use it, the cost to produce an additional report may be small. This is an example of marginal cost. The concept of marginal utility is similar. For example, monthly reports of inventory are useful management reports, but the value of that information is not necessarily increased by producing the report weekly.

The method of presenting data is a deciding factor on the utility of the report. It would not be useful to obtain an inventory list (of say 100,000 items) daily to determine balance on hand. But some means of extracting the data, perhaps an inquiry capability, may be extremely useful. Such a facility allows for the production of voluminous reports on a longer lapsed-time basis.

One of the advantages of EDP is its responsiveness; data can be made available at frequent intervals in current and useful form. The optimum frequency depends on the user's preferences and habits, the sensitivity of the operation to change, and on the rate at which changes take place. Delay (or lag) is the time between the end of a cycle or reporting period and the moment when the data become available to the user in some presentable format. Conversely, several weeks may elapse between the end of the year and the preparation of annual financial report prepared for stockholders.

Frequency and delay time are important considerations in the systems analysis and reports approval processes. They affect data scheduling—priority problems are increased. Immediate response or minimal delay times may be achieved by on-line real-time systems wherein the user interacts directly with the computer through some communications facility. His data are updated as events occur and he can access information rapidly enough to influence decisions and the conduct of the business operation.

Report submission timing is critical if electronic means to display, remote I/O devices, or electrical transmissions are to be used. The format of a submitted report is important is output is printed. Reports may be presented in a prescribed format on paper (hard copy) or may be presented on the face of a CRT or microcomputer screen. A selection of very fine tools is available for use on the microcomputer. A recent integrated software package is called *Symphony,* from Lotus Development Corporation. The package incorporates a word processor, a spreadsheet, a database, a graphics processor, and a communications package.

The wise organization standardizes its report formats. The cost of changing presentation methods might never be recouped.

Periodic Reports Surveys

Reports are security blankets. Users may never use the report, but are loth to discontinue its production. A periodic survey is a wise move—and that survey will highlight some cooperation to remove duplicate or unused reports. Perhaps you should perform that survey annually. However, on a controlled basis, some DP managers have learned that reports not distributed and not missed are frequently not used. They periodically disrupt the distribution of reports long enough to determine if they are missed. If they are not missed, then there is an investigation into the value and the cost of producing the report.

Key to this survey is the knowledge of what data appear on what report, and who gets what. Users feel that an unused report, in hand, is better than no report, if perchance they might need the data. As EDP moves closer to a totally on-line environment or through distributed processing or microcomputer capabilities, the need for the hard-copy security blankets should diminish. See Chapter 8 for suggestions for determining data distribution among reports.

Log and Control of Reports

The production of reports is controlled. Distribution of the reports should also be controlled. Any batch input should be logged and the distribution of the reports should also be logged, to prevent any question surrounding the responsiveness of the DP unit. Since reports are the basis of decision and since a late report can affect the validity of such a decision, it behooves the EDP manager to keep a strict record of the movement of data. It may not change a thing—but it will highlight any bottlenecks for resolution.

There is a critical perspective here. The owner of the data is the user department. The user should provide updating data. The processor of the data is the EDP department. Its sole responsibility is to accept the data as it has been updated by the user and to process it expeditiously. Incorrect data will result in incorrect reports. You may continue to run such reports, but the user should bear the cost.

Data Processing Departmental Administration

Budgets and Control

Budgets are those resources provided to support the department's responsibilities for achievement of its portion of the organizational objectives. They are plans while they are being created and controls while they are being used.

Because the EDP resource is expensive and pervasive, the estimated future budget data requires extensive planning. If a significant overrun occurs, it is prima facie evidence of the manager's inability to plan—assuming no extraordinary contingencies.

To budget for the EDP activity, the manager must have a detailed knowledge of current costs. Historical records will provide guidance for the budgeting activity. He must know the equipment rental costs, extra-use charges, consumables and miscellaneous supplies, salaries, conversion costs, and a host of other such related variables. Often, at least in larger organizations, a good cost analyst can provide much of this data.

Further, some organizations have budget specialists who provide detailed instructions for the preparation and submission of budgets and who will assist the budget preparation process. The actual planning must be done by the EDP department itself, since budget specialists cannot be expected to know about report size, frequency, preparation steps, processing, etc.

The budget is the most common control technique—followed closely by the installed accounting system. In all business activities, the common denominator is money. The budget/accounting systems allow management to plan what should take place, note what did actually occur, determine the differences, and direct correcting action to the appropriate places. The log of input and output is a control mechanism to ensure that work is accomplished according to plan. Time and attendance reports for employees and project-accomplishment reports are necessary controls to ensure that employees respond properly.

Records Management

The data processing center has management custody of many files in some form of media; these files require accurate logging, controlling, inventory accountability, and ultimately, disposition.

In addition, systems and programming units require long-term maintenance of paper records, custody of documents or papers pertaining to feasibility studies, applications studies, systems analysis, documentation, programming documentation, source listings, object listings, test results, and other reference materials. This documentation is needed to trace the development of each program or job processed. These are records, and as such require management. Records management within the DP center is synonymous with maintaining good documentation, a vital part of the function. Recovery and backup procedures are the responsibility of the DP manager. He must ensure the safety of an adequate number of up-to-date copies of files and data.

Personnel Administration

Many key functions pertaining to department personnel are handled by DP management itself. Detailed position descriptions for each job must be written, and experience has indicated that the personnel department has been less than successful in developing them. Some form of personnel record must be maintained by each supervisor for each subordinate.

Periodically, each supervisor is required to report on the effectiveness of each of his subordinates. The accumulation of information in a local personnel record provides the documentation to thoroughly and fairly evaluate the subordinate. In view of laws, regulations, union policies, and other restraints, it is wise to maintain a close liaison with the personnel department when doing this.

Personnel Training

Because the individuals in the DP department are customarily hired based upon specific educational criteria, it is often felt that training is not necessary. True, with the prerequisite backgrounds persons often have the broad training necessary to fit. But—their education has just prepared them to accept additional training.

Training, as differentiated from education, is more procedure-oriented than problem-oriented. It is short-range instruction in the precise steps necessary to perform a specific task. It includes instruction in the operational methods necessary to use the computing system installed. Training enables the employee to perform a specific job in the organization in accordance with applicable procedures. While there is some transferability among jobs, it should be remembered that another job requires additional training.

Four specific types of training are available: formal classroom training, on-the-job training, self-based individual study, and external training. To be effective, one department member, whose assigned task is training, should make each element a part of a tailored training plan for the individual.

Classroom training is generally oriented to the use of the equipment or the use of a software package, and is frequently conducted away from the facility. There is a school of thought that says that vendors are best used for training relative to their product. On-the-job training should be formalized, controlled, and dovetailed with other forms of training. OJT is customarily a tutorial relationship between supervisor and subordinate. Records should be prepared and posted, and at periodic intervals the employee should demonstrate proficiency. Finally, external training (such as a course in management) may be obtained from a local academic institution. This training should be integrated with other forms of training, and, if possible, should be underwritten by the organization.

Coordination

The DP department provides a multitude of services to all the organizational entities. To do so effectively, there must be good coordination; that coordination must stretch across organizational lines to reach mutual agreement and understanding with other groups. Procedures to ensure coordination must be established and may well require a binding agreement between departments. This is especially important where significant costs could be engendered by nearly duplicate efforts.

Coordination must take place in the project level steering committees, by any committees, in fact, and in any forum where communication and agreement are essential. Where such coordination is achieved, efficiency is improved, morale is enhanced, and intragroup conflicts are removed. It need not be a formal activity, but general guidelines can increase the efficiency of coordination.

Special Project Administration

Work is accomplished in work centers where individuals with certain skills apply those skills toward the completion of the assigned task. Often, these tasks are sufficiently isolated from the day-to-day tasks as to require drawing together individuals with skills required for a special activity. This is customarily called a project, and the project is generally convened for the purpose of investigating a need, designing a solution, and implementing a system. Because the project is customarily focused, its separate nature requires organization and control. It is, after all, but a microcosm of the entire organization. It is unique, of vital importance, and must have measurable objectives. It is clearly a one-time effort, should have economic, legal, or political justification, requires a plan of action and dedicated effort.

Many jobs could qualify as separate projects in the implementing of an information processing system. Chronologically, they are: preliminary or feasibility study; application study; equipment proposal; equipment selection; installation, of the equipment; design of the software; development of the software; testing, implementation, and follow-up—and the continued operation of the project's results. Those are but parts of what is called the systems life cycle.

The Feasibility Study

From the perspective of the DP manager, the feasibility study is the means to determine if an application is needed, if it can be done, what are its likely characteristics and costs, will it accomplish the objective, and what commitment of resources will be required to function according to the proposed plan.

The test of feasibility should not be political alone. It should not be legal alone. We know that both these aspects will exist. But the true test of feasibility should be economic. The feasibility study, by investigating costs and benefits, enables management to chose intelligently among competing alternatives.

The study will define the risks of moving forward. Management, including DP management, must determine if the risk of the move warrants making the move. To do otherwise is fine if the organization is in a good cash flow position. Generally, major system movements are a function of management-sanctioned projects. Occasionally it may be apparent to the DP manager or to his staff that certain major changes need to be made. Sanction is still required—for the approach must be sold. The key to success of such is this: if the project requires little additional resource and can be installed with a minimum of ripple, go ahead. If not, the approval process, though lengthy, will be more effective.

Character of the Project

Composition of the study team varies. Members of the feasibility study team should provide a good cross section of talent and experience. Available skills should be used, and often one alternative will be to use solely those skills. The addition of external persons with requisite skills is a wise means to advance the project. The product of this study group will develop the overall picture, itemizing current costs, estimating proposed costs, and contrasting the two. Alternatives will be presented, advantages and disadvantages will be noted, costs and benefits will be detailed. When the facts and figures of the months of study are consolidated and presented, management is served best with an estimate of advisability. This is especially important, as many changes are not advisable, even though they may very well be feasible.

Justification for Resources

The feasibility study is perceived to be the basis for EDP justification—that computers are justified through the study. Actually, it should also be the basis for not procuring EDP equipment or systems where warranted. No matter what the change is, however, there are changes to be made—and because of changes, there will be costs to the organization. These costs will be reflected in training, programming, disruption of the status quo. Further, it's a learning curve, where the data obtained are compared to historical costs.

The justification of any change competes with other needs of the organization. The study must show how a great contribution to profit or net benefit can be derived by the method under study than can be demonstrated by another project which would use similar resources.

Application Study

Extending the feasibility study, the application or system study deals with the systems or problems to which the computer will be applied. Approval to proceed into this effort must come as a result of the feasibility study. The systems designer will first consider the need for output. He will then work backwards to the means to obtain the necessary input. This phase, often called the detailed analysis, will achieve the collection and cross-matching of the available data and an estimate of the desired characteristics. The difference becomes the statement of design intention. More detail on these phases will be found in the systems chapter.

The manager's perspective on these activities must be oriented toward accomplishment of specific goals and project milestones. He must insist that the project planning is accomplished and that project progress adheres to the schedule.

Vendor Relations

Whether in the acquisition of hardware or the acquisition of expendable supplies, the DP manager must deal with a multitude of vendors—some of whom are qualified, some of whom are not.

For most items for which there is likely to be either a high price tag or an ongoing use, there should be a bid competition. Theoretically, such a bid competition is the means to obtain the best value, and it is frequently required by law.

Qualified vendors are frequently notified of an upcoming bid by a request for quotation (RFQ)—sometimes called a request for price quotation (RPQ). They are then invited to bid. Those vendors who express an interest are then given specifications of the bid request. "Qualified" means simply that—not necessarily your usual vendor; not the one with the nearest branch office; not the one with the most aggressive salespeople; or not the one with the political pull. It is simply the vendor who can provide a performance-to-cost ratio of +1 or greater.

A special project team or committee may be assigned to review proposals and make recommendations on the selection. The actual selection process rests with the upper echelon of management, which tends to follow recommendations, but which may apply different weights to some selection criteria.

In the case of equipment, where performance is an important criterion, the vendor(s) may be asked to perform certain simulations (such as SCERT) to determine the best mix of products to achieve the appropriate answer to the bid request. Further, benchmarking may be required to provide the actual numerical basis for comparison.

Relations with the Development Team

When the project doesn't come in on time or within approved budgets, somebody must answer. That somebody is the DP manager. He, in turn, will look to the project manager or leader for answers. If the project group has done its job correctly, the reasons for slippage (or acceleration) will be clearly understood.

Post-Project Audit and Review

There is little agreement on the matter of review and evaluation of a project or system after it has been installed and in operation. Six months to a year seems like a likely time. If a review is conducted much before one year, it may not allow the DP manager time to accumulate his experience, evaluate it, and take corrective action. Too long an interval extends costly errors unnecessarily.

Unfortunately, this review is frequently not done, seemingly for two specific reasons: (1) A poor job of setting objectives was done, so there is little conception of what should be measured, and (2) departments and managers fear that the answer to the question may be negative, so the question is never asked. Normally, these reasons are explained away with the statement "Not enough time; too many other projects to do." It seems inconceivable that the organization which spends thousands of dollars to install hardware, software, and application systems is unwilling to monitor the investment.

The addition of a cadre of DP auditors is beginning to get a handle upon those activities which are required. Top management should issue a formal letter announcing the review and giving its purpose, scope, starting dates, team members, and the requirement for an evaluation report. The team should be instructed to check on actual system operation versus that which had been planned and to compare actual costs to the costs which had previously been projected. Also, it should be instructed to compare anticipated benefits to actual benefits derived. Prepared checklists can be used to record the status of the operation. Only from such a study will a specific, economically based, determination about continuing the system be made.

Long-Range Planning

If it is true that the DP activity is support for all the organizational entities, then it logically follows that long-range planning is essential for DP. The concepts of planning described in Chapter 3 apply here. Time and change are implied in planning. Business and society are dynamic, in a constant state of change. The so-called information revolution has changed the way we think and act about everything. The addition of personal computers has changed the way we will think tomorrow. So far as the organization is concerned, if it fails to plan, it then plans to fail.

The world of EDP requires long-range planning if for no other reason than the lead times necessary to install equipment, prepare sites, train users, develop software, etc. Without the long-range planning, the programmed decision-making process will not work. Planning allows certain decisions to be made in advance. Planning exists in one of two forms—standing plans and single-use plans.

Standing plans provide uniformity of operation throughout the organization. Similar situations can be handled in a similar manner, and decisions can be expedited by referring to the manual. This type of plan is programmed decision-making, an efficient way to handle routine and repetitive matters that fall within normal expectations. It avoids the need to go through complex research each time a common situation arises. A standing plan or policy manual provides those guidelines, but certain of those plans or policies become part of the prescribed decision-making process installed in an automated system.

Single-use plans are not programmed. In fact, the criteria for the plans may not even be known at the time standing plans are developed. More often, it is possible to establish a plan which is sufficient for the time—on the basis of a model, an input, an on-the-spot set of criteria. These things fall outside the customary plan and require managerial judgment at the point of their occurrence. Emergency plans fall into both categories. Some items are permanent, can be documented, and can be trained. Some, however, are functional, and while the functional alternatives can be defined, the on-the-spot judgment may be essential.

Establishing the Planning Team

In large organizations, the planning function may be organized and staffed by specialists. These planners establish policies, broad guidelines, and goals. They coordinate with lower levels on detailed plans and may integrate a number of departmental plans into a master plan.

Detailed planning must be done where the work is done, in the department or functional location. Long-range planning can be done at a staff level. Staff planning has weaknesses if used for short-range planning, as it is difficult to separate the "planning for" from the "doing" of the job being planned. The person doing the work is most qualified to estimate and do the planning, including the preparation of any documentation. His estimates may be colored by his experience, but that experience is still the best judge.

Staff planning must concentrate upon objectives, standing plans, and plans which are designed for single use only.

Steps to Effective Planning

There are seven distinct steps to effective planning: (1) define the problem; (2) gather facts; (3) determine the organization's role; (4) select alternatives; (5) evaluate alternatives; (6) detail the selected course of action; and (7) document and communicate the plan.

A clear statement of the situation will distinguish between the problem to be solved and the symptoms of the problem which instigated the planning. Future technological, economic, competitive environments, and reasonable forecasts must be appraised. Care must be exercised when trading the history of economic data, as patterns may emerge, move, or trend. Economic models should provide best-case/worst-case parameters for contingencies.

The role of the organization will detail the needs of the customers, stockholders, and employees and must be examined as alternatives are developed. Those alternatives which are possible or nearly so must be considered. When possible, the alternatives should be weighted as a means to select the best. When the alternative has been selected, it must be developed, documented, and communicated.

Plans are equated to future dollar costs by each department; individual plans are then combined into a financial plan or budget for the entire organization. Future costs are categorized and coded by the controller and the budget specialists, with adjustments made as necessary for the good of the entire organization.

Written Plans

There are essentially two future-oriented plans for any organization: the business plan and the emergency plan. Both deal with operation of the organization under uncertainty. Formats of these plans are at the discretion of the user, but organizations have found it beneficial to detail these plans in a standard format.

The contents of the business plan should be: (1) introduction and purpose; (2) authority; (3) scope and applicability; (4) concepts, terms, and definitions; (5) goals, assumptions, limitations, and objectives; (6) forecasts; (7) alternatives and analysis; (8) course of action and sequence of events; (9) Gantt, PERT, or other project management documentation, checkpoints, and milestones; and (10) implementation and reporting procedures.

Emergency planning is of such critical importance that you should obtain expert guidance from some of the available texts on the subject. Management is dependent upon that computer. Should a disaster or disruptive emergency damage or destroy the DP operations facility, the continued operation of the organization is paramount. Planning must take prevention, recovery, remote operation, and other means of protection into account. Fireproof buildings, fire alarms and protective devices, media vaults, fireproof file cabinets, restricted personnel access, and similar means and methods are usually taken to protect the facility and records. Planning should detail the copying, movement, protection, and recovery procedures, including alternate site considerations.

Project Management Charting

Long-range planning for EDP invariably uses flow diagrams to illustrate the sequences and timing of events and activities. These take the form of Gantt planning charts, milestone tables, or PERT charts. Gantt charts represents jobs with horizontal bars, the length of which is proportional to time, calendar or time-lapse. When this type of scheduling is used, it shows job overlap and project duration in relative form. Milestones are used in conjunction with the Gantt chart, are indicated on the chart and are separately documented. Figure 4.4 is a Gantt planning chart with milestones.

The best way to show duration of jobs and their relationships to each other in intricate, detailed, and complex plans is by using the Program Evaluation and Review Technique (PERT) Chart. Figure 4.5 is a PERT network chart.

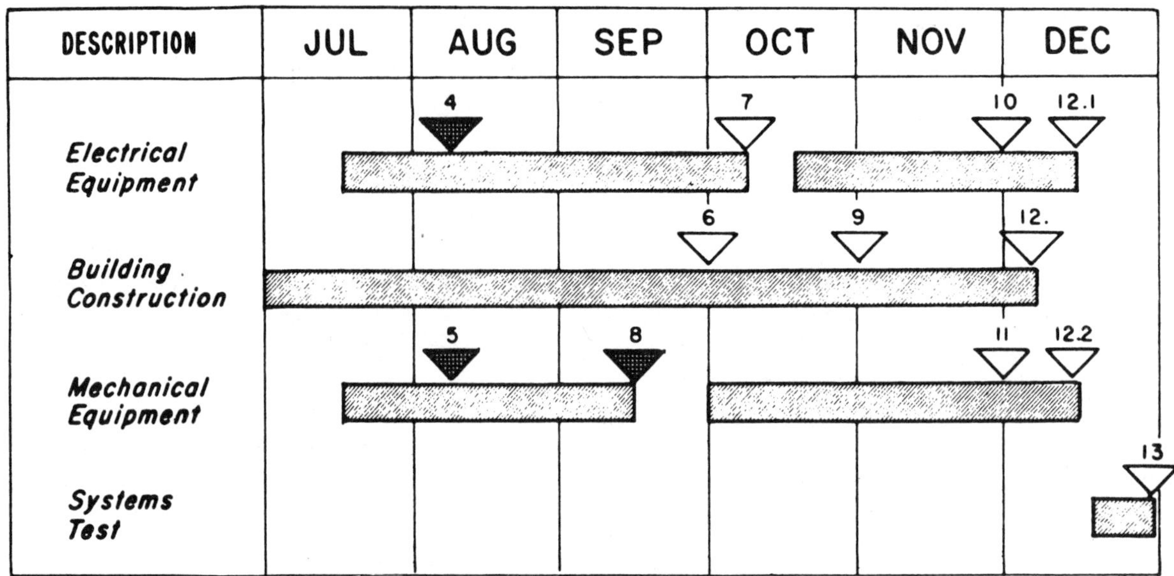

Figure 4.4. Gantt planning chart.

The PERT method of planning has found considerable use in EDP planning, largely because of its use in R&D projects, which are similar to EDP plans. Here, in a few short sentences, are the fundamentals of PERT:

1. The circles (A-G) are called *events.* An event is the completion of all work which precedes it.
2. The lines (e.g., AB) are called *activities.* The length of the line is relative and is not an accurate measure of time, as would be the Gantt line/scale.
3. Three times are assigned (AB is 1-3-5). The first is the optimistic time, what it would take if everything went right. The third time is the pessimistic time, what it would take if everything went wrong. The second time is most likely time, or the intuitive estimate.
4. A line which consumes no time is known as a *dummy* and is generally broken.
5. The longest route through the network is called the *critical path,* and is that route along which the project is shortened (accelerated) or lengthened (delayed). It is not good to have more than one critical path.

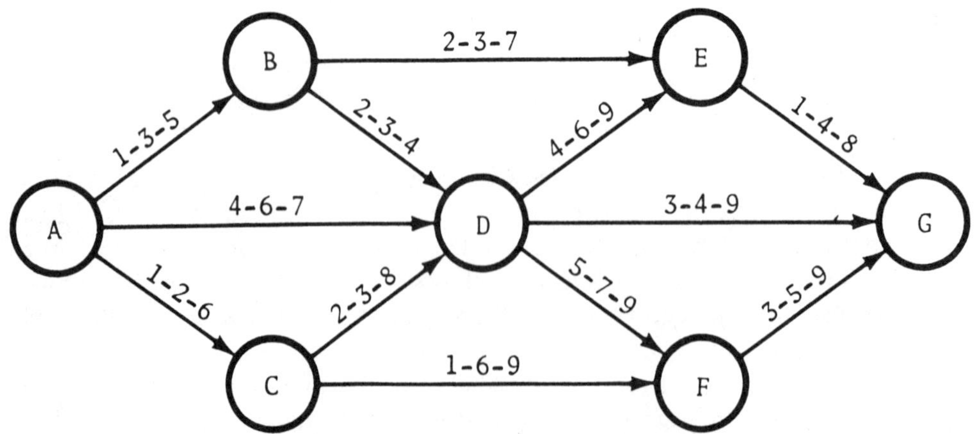

Figure 4.5. PERT network chart.

6. Using PERT's time estimates, it is possible to derive a PERT time estimate with a 50/50 probability. It is:

$$\frac{\text{Optimistic} + \text{Pessimistic} + 4(\text{Most Likely})}{6}$$

Data Processing Standards

Requirements and Scope

Standardization is the process of establishing a recognizable, measurable, acceptable, and useful degree of uniformity. By achieving this uniformity, efficiency is normally enhanced. Prescribed weights and measures, time zones, dictionaries, and glossaries bring common understanding and uniformity to people's relationships. Accounting could not function without standard procedures of generally accepted practice. Mass production would not be possible without standardization.

Standards must be developed, formulated, and accepted. They are not automatic—but they can be de facto. The DP industry has witnessed several forms of nonstandard and incompatible equipment elements, as each vendor sought to force customers to stay with the sole supplier. The move has been to standardization, however, with the efforts of the American National Standards Institute. Unfortunately, no standard is binding and most standards have been derived after some considerable time and difficulty. An example of this is the 128-bit American Standard Code for Information Interchange (ASCII), which was several years in derivation.

Standards are a must within the DP organization. Without them, special equipment is required, conversion programs must be written, additional training is required. The scope of the problem cuts across the entire industry, involving manufacturers, users, and general interest groups. Fortunately, the problem is recognized and resolution is in everybody's interest in the long term. At the same time, the effort has been concentrated upon technical standards. Thus it has been; thus will it ever be.

Some things become standards by default. Microsoft BASIC has become the standard BASIC language—something the ANSI was never able to do.

Standards within the DP Organization

Though some will feel that standards are restrictive, the worth of an organization's DP standardization program will be in reduced project/program development time, reduced bugging efforts, and increased facility. Standard methods will establish uniform techniques, design, size, or other criteria to aid in the performance of and planning for the organization. Method standards prescribe how, what, where, and when of the job is to be done in what has been determined to be the best and most effective manner. For the DPer, this may means structure charts, decision tables, flowcharts, coding aids, invoked COBOL paragraphs—whatever it takes to accomplish a uniform method of operation. This is not to state that a uniform method is necessarily the best method. It does state, however, that the investment in people and machinery is so significant, that there must be some facility for interchangeability of either.

There is a danger that standards are developed for the sheer exercise of someone's power. To avoid that, upper-echelon management should monitor the development of standards. However, standards, once established, should be universally applied and should be withdrawn once it has been demonstrated that the standard is no longer useful.

Establishing the Standards Program

To be successful, the support and endorsement of top management must be obtained at the start. The DP manager appoints the nucleus of a team composed of the most knowledgeable people to develop the program. Group meetings are conducted to announce the program, discuss its purpose and value, solicit suggestions, participation, and cooperation.

Some people will feel that such standards stifle initiative—but the key for the DP manager is productivity. It simply is a fact that persons who use a standardized approach surpass the production of people with no such discipline. Standards provide uniform and dependable performance and the basis for precise communications relative to the job.

To Be Included

Standards developed for DP should include those things which are necessary to make uniform certain activities, to provide policy and practice guidance for other activities, and to provide the basis for preplanned action.

Included in the standards manual which must be developed are such things as programming and documentation standards, records retention and backup standards, and security standards. They should encompass standard coding for program inclusion, standard packaging for program and system documentation, detailed procedures for copying, transporting, storing, and rotating magnetic media. They should also include those items which would allow the organization to become operational again in the event of a contingency. Security considerations, such as passwords, physical access, off-site backup media and operational facilities, storage of emergency stores of supplies, and consideration of personnel all become part of the standards.

Records Retention and Backup

Included in the job specification manual or the job run procedure should be a statement regarding the retention of master files, print tapes, and hardcopy reports for each product obtained. Retention dates should be coordinated by the database administrator with the using agency.

The destruction of a master file or a data base backup may cost considerably more than the cost to copy the media—occasionally, through carelessness, single copies only are kept. Recapturing the data should that single copy be purposely or inadvertently destroyed might cost tens of thousands of dollars. If cyclical copies of master data and transactions from that point to date are kept, then restructure of current master data can be accomplished. Storage of backup data should be in two places—on site for the most recent backup; off site for the previous backup and all intervening transactions.

Security Standards

The classification of data, either in government or industrial circles, requires extra precautions in the handling, processing, movement, and backup. Included in this category might be those items dealing with national security or dealing with the executive payroll. Either way, careful selection of personnel is paramount. Specific access is required and should be monitored by another having similar access, with logging of the access by both being reviewed by yet another. Any media, programs, reports, or other evidence of the processing should be carefully guarded.

The concern for security covers not only data, programs, movement, etc., but also physical access to the facility. A comprehensive security program is mandatory, involving concerns for physical and logical access, fire detection and suppression, power and air-conditioning supply, and a whole host of other concerns which cannot be detailed here. A text on data center security is highly recommended.

Programming and Documentation Standards

The whole purpose of program standards is ease of maintenance. The whole purpose of documentation standards is ease of maintenance. We have erred greatly when we have avoided either, and yet historically this is an area of DP practice which has suffered great neglect.

Some will say that standard programming methods are demeaning and negate creativity. Management should respond with a perspective which includes DP people as part of the production process of the organization—which no doubt has standardized methods in use in other departments. Documentation is seen as a nuisance, as it inhibits the same creative people from getting on to the next project. That is truly only where the DP manager insists (or allows) the project be completed without concurrent documentation activities. This means that under the pressure to complete the task, documentation is left undone; a certain means to guarantee that it will never be done. A well worn maxim is "No time to do it right; always time to do it over." We may never learn this lesson.

A standards program should be comprehensive, thoroughly trained, and enforced. That takes time, staff, and money. But it pays extensive dividends. In some instances, standards become the training tools for novices. In others, standards are guidelines for the preparation of predictable and familiar products. Contents should be all-inclusive in file documentation; pointed and pertinent in run documentation; comprehensive in audit documentation; and brief in the executive handling of exceptions and user documents.

Hardware Evaluation

The selection of equipment is, and should be, the result of a very careful needs analysis, conducted in conjunction with a very detailed cost analysis. The function is so important that large organizations detail specific staffs to select from among the myriad of devices to meet the future needs of the organization. Hardware evaluation is also an emotional issue which needs to be defused. This is particularly true where a single vendor has a long history of service to the organization and a close competitor trims the price substantially while offering compatibility, performance improvements, and service which is equal to or better than the single vendor.

Equipment acquisition is a project like any other project. There must be a feasibility study, the gathering of data (prices, benchmark results, experiences of other customers), evaluation of alternatives, and recommendation to top-echelon management. In the situation where there is presently no computing hardware, the need for computing hardware can no doubt be amply demonstrated by examination of the so-called "bread and butter" applications. Where hardware currently exists and the study is for the upgrading and/or replacement of installed hardware, the selection criteria must be more precise.

In recent years the development of a plug-compatible market (compatible to IBM-series equipment) has made available a wide variety of equipment which either exceeded the original vendor's capabilities or was substantially lower in price—or both. The plug-compatible mainframe market alone has produced equipment of superior quality and price/performance characteristics. And in the instance where the equipment has been compatible, the software has also been compatible, a factor enforced by recent court decisions.

Where major vendor changes have been contemplated, consideration becomes open to a host of other concerns. Software portability is probably the most important consideration, and has been ever since the decision was made to standardize COBOL. While there has never been a pure COBOL standard compiler (each vendor has its own enhancements), where programs have been developed in ANSI-standard COBOL (alone), the portability has been present. Training is a huge consideration when changing vendors, except for those organizations which are of sufficient size to allow a variety of in-house and vendor courses to be taught on site.

The process should begin with a request for proposal (RFP), wherein a variety of vendors are asked to bid. Those bids should contain actual configurations proposed, specific costs, delivery information, benchmark or performance data, and other locations where the equipment is installed. Availability of software should be detailed, as should be service considerations. System software is a major consideration of any such bid, and the portability of applications programming to the system software of the proposed equipment system should be treated, including any necessary conversions. It is not unusual for the purchaser to provide a benchmark application to each proposing vendor, which will then make its results known, providing a basis for equipment timing and cost comparison.

The selection of equipment is not a price or vendor issue alone. Growth in file and transaction volume should dictate selection, as well as price/performance data. Generally the organization will detail mandatory features (which are used as an across-the-board comparator) and some desirable features which will enhance the vendor's proposal. It is known that the cost per calculation will decrease, but it should be noted that that is the cost per available calculation—not the cost per performed calculation. If the new machine, for 20% more cost, can do the entire workload in 60% of the time, the cost per calculation decreases, but you must still pay the cost of the increased capability. For example, if a CPU which costs $100,000 performs the workload in 100% of the available time is replaced by a CPU which for $120,000 can perform the workload in 60% of the available time, the calculation cost would be $72,000 while the actual cost would be $50,000 more. Thus there would have to be an immediate increase of nearly 70% of the workload to justify the additional expenditure—a nearly impossible feat. While the workload is building across a gradual curve toward that cost-effective factor, the cost per calculation has not decreased 40%. It has, in fact, increased 20% on its face, and 60% on its available range (cost less 40% plus 60% equas original cost plus 20%). In short, like the farmer who resisted the new-fangled gadgets which cost lots of money, we need to farm as efficiently as we know how before the new tractor is purchased.

No equipment should be purchased on the basis of performance alone, or even upon cost. But all equipment acquisition should be done on the basis of sound financial analysis. Should the equipment be purchased outright or leased? What sort of financing must be obtained before the equipment may be purchased? Are there alternatives? If the equipment is to be leased, are there provisos for costs relative to operation time, including extra-shift charges? Is the depreciation sufficient to justify expenditure of available cash? Will the discounted cash flow provide survival funds if equipment funds are expended? Is the return on investment or internal rate of return sufficient to make the equipment attractive compared to other investment alternatives? Is the flexibility of a lease necessary to allow the organization to upgrade as equipment models change? Will the purchase leave the organization with a white elephant which the organization cannot sell when the device is no longer necessary? These and other questions are a prerequisite part for the equipment selection process.

SYSTEMS AND PROGRAMMING MANAGEMENT

Shifts In The Programming Discipline

Now we're going to take a bit of departure and introduce a new way of doing things. Of the information presented in the next few pages, most of it is new in concept, and deals with the concept of the driver program, presented in a prior chapter. We'll deal with the driver as an integrated package.

Part of this discussion rightfully belongs in the programming chapter. Some of it belongs here in DP management. Some of it belongs in the systems design chapter. But it's futuristic, and though it may not apply to the discipline as we know it today, it will emerge before this book is again revised. And because of that, it will be a responsibility of the DP manager to deal with it.

Symbiotic Parallel Programming

Driver programs don't contain a new type of programming language. They *are* a new type of programming language. The driver (and that's the way we'll refer to it from here on) exemplifies a type of programming totally dissimilar to anything in current use and a mode of programing that will expressly dominate future software development efforts.

Prior to the advent of the microcomputer, programmers talked about programming standards that would allow the development of "canned" programming that could be marketed widely. Although some canned software was developed, most of the mainframe software was developed by the particular company that was using the computer. In other words, most software was developed "in house."

The reasons for the limited availability of canned software were largely economic. Prior to 1976, the entire history of computers had produced fewer than 250,000 computers. This panoply of computing machinery included many brands and many models of computers. Although each computer was more expensive than today's microcomputer, the total number of each type of computer was relatively small, even the number of computers placed in the field by IBM. The production of canned software was therefore limited. The producers had a small market within which to sell their product. Each software package therefore had to carry a large price tag in order to cover the costs of development and to allow for a profit.

To further complicate matters, the programmers of that era had a natural prejudice against canned software. Each programmer felt that he could probably produce a better program than the developer of the software. Additionally, the canned programs were considered harder to modify to the particular requirements of the company than start from scratch programs. Considered, nothing—they were. The software was seldom totally general purpose and the vicissitudes of a package designed for purpose A were really not compatible with purpose B.

As a consequence of the small market, high price tag, and programmer resentment to canned software, the number of preprogrammed applications was relatively small. Each brand and model of computer had only a limited number of prior-developed packages available. When the microcomputer came along, much of the audience was the consumer who had had virtually no exposure to the mainframe world and its vagaries. The audience was larger, and though the number of computers and models was equally large, gradually those which did not conform to a standard protocol (generally IBM or Apple) didn't survive. And this audience wasn't hung up on the "not invented here" syndrome—they didn't have the skills or patience to work out such applications—and many of them had the kind of money necessary to allow software vendors to suitably distribute the development costs. Some of us paid too much for software, but we helped to reduce the price to some others.

In the days of million dollar computers it was economically affordable to develop software from scratch. The customers looked at the million dollar price tag for a computer and it did not seem impractical to hire a few $25,000 (a year) programmers to provide the programming to make the million dollar computer functional. However, in the days of a computer which can be purchased for less than $5,000, few users are going to be willing to spend that kind of money for programming. At least not if there is an acceptable alternative. Those who are willing to spend that much are demanding greater output from the programmers than previously.

Additionally, the users, as a group, are becoming sophisticated. They are demanding levels of quality for in-house-developed software that match the quality standards inherent to packaged software. The users will no longer stand for cryptic programming, which performs inconsistently, or crashes the computer regularly. And they are showing their displeasure with obtuse, technically written documentation suitable for other programmers.

Custom software has a hard time competing with canned software with regard to quality levels. The canned software developers can spend large amounts of time perfecting their software. Because the software will be sold to many users, the canned software producers spend the time to develop software which is nearly impossible to "crash." An enormous amount of time is devoted to debugging the canned software and making it user friendly. Thousands of buyers provide feedback to the software producers telling the producer of weaknesses, errors, or logical design flaws.

Custom software, by contrast, requires fast development and powerful results. To achieve this increased programmer efficiency, new programming techniques have had to be developed. The first of these techniques was the spreadsheet program.

The new generation of programming is specifically tailored to achieve major programming output in a limited amount of time, with a radically reduced number of programming bugs. Functionally, the application looks like it had been accomplished by a "quick and dirty" method. Operationally, because of "software engines" such as the driver, canned software efficiency and sophistication has become available through custom-developed programming. To achieve the end result of powerful programming, programming that is easy to use, has limited debugging, and is quick to write, the programmers have been forced into taking the building block approach to programming. These programmers must now place more and more reliance upon the manufacturers of software to provide the building blocks that can be assembled quickly into custom programming.

To illustrate this concept, an analogy would be appropriate. Consider frontier housing construction. The frontiersman built his own house from scratch. He chopped down the trees, split the logs, designed the house, built the house, and in some cases, even made the nails used in construction. This totally independent construction gave the frontier builder a lot of freedom. Depending upon the amount of time, effort, and skill used in the assembly of the house, the results could vary from a masterpiece to a shanty. Often, because of constraints in time or skill, the roofs leaked, the floors were mud, and there was no heating.

The traditional type of programming is similar to the frontier style of housing construction. Starting with a computer language (the equivalent of the frontiersman's set of tools), you did everything. If you wanted to process text within the application, you built your own rudimentary editor. If you wanted to create a report, you either created the report directly and laboriously, or you created your own rudimentary report generator. If you wanted to sort information, you built you own sorting program. The list goes on infinitely.

The new type of programming is much like contemporary modular house construction. To achieve the house that fits your needs, contractors use preconstructed components to create. Although there is reduced freedom, you can accomplish more in a short period of time, the results are typically more professional, and the required skill level is typically reduced. We've come a long way since the Aladdin precut home in 1944. We've come a long way since high quality, low cost software became widely available.

The driver program is a warehouse full of preassembled programming components waiting to be assembled. Using your skills, you can quickly assemble a veritable programming masterpiece. If you want to manipulate text, you use the word processor as a building block. If you want to manipulate numbers, you use the spreadsheet, etc. The pieces are simply added as you need tools to complete the job.

Parallel Programming

But the driver is more than just a warehouse of programming components. It is also a new type of programming. This new type of programming includes a departure from the traditional technique of programming in a linear fashion. It involves the concept of concurrent processes that act independently of each other but can also work together as a whole.

Imagine for a moment, that you are going to be the general contractor who oversees a group of skilled workers who are building a house. The way a house is normally built, many workers might be working independently in order to finish the house. They are all working toward the common goal of the completion of the house, but many different tasks are being accomplished concurrently. One group of workers might be working on installing the roof of the house, while simultaneously other workers could be refinishing the basement.

In traditional programming, activities oc̹cur singularly, one after the other. That would be like having the same group of workers, but allowing only one worker at a time to work on the house. Traditional programming uses the step-by-step approach. Applied to the house, the first worker would dig a foundation hole. Next another worker would develop the forms for pouring concrete into the shape of a foundation. Next, another worker would come in and install the plumbing in the correct location. Following that, another worker would pour the cement. And so on.

The driver uses the team approach to programming. While the foundation is being dug, walls are being assembled. While the plumbing is going on, work on the electrical system is well underway. How can this be, if computers can do only singular tasks, one at a time? Although in actuality, only one task at a time is being performed, it will sometimes seem as though many things are happening independently. For instance, your macro program might change the contents of a cell. That cell might have been referenced as an important ingredient to a spreadsheet. The spreadsheet will take off (self-recalculate) without instructions from your macro program and adjust itself to reflect the new data. A graphics partition might likewise adjust a graph to reflect the new information.

Macro programming is impacted by programming done in the various driver environments. All of your programming must be trained to work together. Like building a house with a crew of workers, you might give one set of instructions to one worker and another set of instructions to another worker. Some of the activities must be performed in sequence (e.g., the roof of the house cannot be constructed before the frame and the walls). Other activities can function in parallel (e.g., the bathrooms can be installed while the walls are being painted).

If you're the general manager who has a crew of workers, you know that it is possible to have more than one worker of a particular skill working on different tasks. For instance, when building a house, one carpenter might lay the house's flooring while another might be working on installing kitchen cabinets. Likewise with the driver, one spreadsheet partition might be working on payroll while another spreadsheet partition might be working on calculating corporate profits.

Macro programming is similar in concept to a foreman who directs a crew of workers. The macro program directs the driver crew in the performance of preassigned duties. Some of the duties will be performed under the direct supervision of the macro program, other duties will be performed independently as a result of the instructions given by the architectural drawing, done by workers who are reading the blueprint.

The driver program is the precursor to concurrent programming. As operating systems develop, the microcomputer will be performing multiple tasks concurrently. The computer's memory will be divided into sections that act like independent computers. In each of the partitions, a separate program could be operating in total independence of the other programs. All of the programs would share common resources (i.e., the same disk drives, monitor, keyboard, etc.), but operate quite independently.

As concurrent programming evolves, the programmer or operator will begin to use one of the programming segments to supervise other partitions of the computer. For instance, you might provide a program that tells the database in one partition to sort one group of records while telling the database in another partition to sort yet another group of records. When both of the partitions are done with their functions, you might tell a report generator in yet another partition to marry the data which was sorted by the two database partitions, into a single report.

The problem that concurrent programming will have, however, is that prepackaged applications which will work in that environment will be scarce. The developers of prepackaged software would like to use the best word processor to process text in one partition, while in another partition send other text files to a remote location via the telephone. The problem is that the developers cannot be certain what word processor the system user will have. Nor will they know which communications package is being used, which graphics program, etc. Because of this, additional systems integration will be required to utilize nearly any such package. Because such integration is not now widely available, super-sophisticated packages, such as Lotus *Symphony,* more than fill the requirements.

The driver program provides a solution to the problem of using the building block approach to programming. It provides enough common tools that the programmer can know, in advance, what the user has. Consequently, the advanced programmer can provide the instructions to each of the programming environments and know that the user will have precisely that environment.

Although custom programming that uses concurrency to achieve building block programming will gradually evolve, the evolution of canned building block software will be restricted to packages like the integrated driver programs now emerging.

In the meantime, the driver will provide the tools necessary to learn concurrent parallel programming. It provides a restricted environment within which to program, but it provides the essential facilities for learning the technique. Eventually, you may want to broaden your horizons and provide supervisory (building block) programming that includes other programs. When that occurs, the driver program will become just one building block in your inventory, albeit one of the most powerful.

A Methodology for Professional Programming

As the driver provides an environment to support professional programming, the programmers using the driver should adhere to some of the evolving standards of professional programming. The advent of the driver forecasts some changes in programming techniques and as such alters the long established time frames for programming, as well as the funding that is typically associated with long software development projects. In short, the driver program is but the harbinger of difficulty between the long-entrenched data processing departments that take too long and charge too much to produce a substandard product and the user who now has his own, very sophisticated, data processing facility. And here is the key . . . over which he has total control. Will the driver program do away with the programmer as we know him? No, but it will drastically change the way he programs, the quality of the product, the cost of the programs produced, and the timeliness of solutions applied to the problems. And, as you can now tell, managing that person or that team will be quite a challenge.

If a programmer is expected to accomplish a major programming effort within a week's time, there is a definite restriction in the amount of time that can be allocated to systems design, as well as to systems documentation. At the same time, users are becoming more demanding in their expectations from the programming being done. Why? Because they have seen what can be done. The developed program not only has to be "bug free," it also has to look and act professionally. Help screens are a requirement and the programs have to be runnable by a novice user with very little training. Advanced users will expect to be able to "stumble bum" their way through the program without reading any documentation. Like it or not, that is the situation.

This speed of development provides major challenges to the professional programmer. Although the development time is substantially reduced for the advanced driver programmer, the other time normally spent in developing an application package (program plus documentation and systems work) is still there. These elements of the applications development must experience comparable time reductions while concurrently providing the levels of service typically associated with the development of professional programming. The programs must adhere to an overall systems design. The programs must be fully documented on both the systems level (programming) and on the user level (operating instructions and file documentation). The programs must be fully debugged. The users must be properly consulted and the concepts of the integrated programming conveyed simply and easily.

This seemingly impossible task is indeed possible. That's comforting, isn't it? The tools provided by the microcomputer age may be able to accelerate the development of documentation, systems design, and debugging, but they are most certainly not a substitute for them. Happily, they do provide relatively easy ways to obtain the elements. The overall system can be illustrated quickly and easily. The appropriate help screens can be easily integrated into the system, and the entry operator can be protected against obviously inappropriate entries.

The View is Traditional

Any systems project must begin with a systems design. The fact that it is to be done on the microcomputer doesn't change that one iota. To accelerate the program development cycle, exact programming specifications are required. Those specifications must result in a program that fully complies with the contracting user's demands. The contracting user must know exactly what the capabilities of the ultimate software product will be, as well as understand the exact nature of the software. The traditional end of program development alteration period must be stopped. The microcomputer and most driver software are most capable, but not a substitute for realistic thinking. During the alteration period the user typically tells the programmer all of the things that the program still fails to accomplish and all of the things that it must still do before payment can be received. The microcomputer and the driver program provides the tools to allow the user to sign-off on a finished system before the first line of code is created.

Although this may seem like an impossible task to accomplish, the solution is surprisingly simple. The labor saving device that is an essential ingredient to the achievement of this goal is nothing other than the common, ordinary word processor.

Once Upon A Time . . .

The new programming technique that allows a contracting user to sign-off on a systems design is called *storyboarding*. Storyboarding is an adaptation of a cartooning and advertising procedure. Before selling an animated cartoon to a movie producer, the cartoon manufacturer creates a series of simple drawings which convey the ideas to be illustrated in the full length cartoon. Unlike the eventual cartoon, these pictures are ''still'' frames. They do not move and are not fully functional representations of the eventual cartoon. Advertising agencies use the same procedure to illustrate their ideas for television commercials. They create four or five still pictures that are used to represent the scenes that will eventually be filmed in the final commercial. These scenes illustrate the final product and allow the contracting advertiser to interact with the creators of the commercial. The contracting advertiser can thus have a complete and comprehensive understanding of the eventual commercial before the first scene is actually filmed.

The pioneers of storyboarding in the computer field were the games software manufacturers. These games manufacturers got into the practice of building models of all of the screens to be used in the game before the first line of code was entered. Although screen layout sheets have been available for years in the business programming arena, they have never been considered a part of the systems design function. Instead, the system design has typically started with the flow chart of the system. The programmers typically had freedom to design the screens to their own specifications, then alter the screens later to the exact requirements of the user.

But the Process is Changing. . .

In today's programming environment, the programmer doesn't have to be concerned with the intricacies of programming logic. In fact, it is only the interfaces which are of concern. The driver program then becomes a program generators. Instead, the screens to be used and the reports to be generated by the program have become the primary elements of the programming. The screens represent the user interface to the program. The reports represent the eventual results of the programmed function. The word processor is the ideal tool for creation of illustrative models of both elements of the programming.

In this environment, the professional programmer must start the system development process by working with the contracting user, or his representative, to create a precise model of the ultimate product. This is done by following this procedure:

- User consultation on systems design and function
- User consultation as to screen layout for the entire system
- User consultation as to report requirements
- User consultation as to system restrictions
- User participation as to precise layout of screens reports, and data files
- Contracting user sign-off as to total system specifications
- Systems design using word processor or free form graphics software
- Programming and concurrent voice documentation (dictation to a tape recorder) of programming (systems level documentation)
- Debugging and testing
- User review of compliance with system design
- Help screen integration
- Print screen illustration with dictated documentation
- User training, sign-off, and payment

In short, the Micro System Development Life Cycle (MSDLC) represents a complete change from the way we've done things. And a completely different way of doing things. We should look at the MSDLC.

MSDLC Phase I—System Definition

The process starts by sitting down with the contracting user and defining orally the function to be programmed. If at all possible, this phase should be tape recorded and transcribed by the contracting user's secretary.

Throughout this modern process for software development, as many tasks as possible should be removed from the programmer's responsibility and assigned to less expensive personnel. In traditional programming this phase would be an extended process resulting in several renditions of a flow chart. Using the streamlined method, the secretary transcribes all elements of the conversation. Although wasteful in words, both the contracting user and the programmer are able to visually review the elements of the original conversation. If the programmer has doubts about elements of the desired function of the product, they will become apparent when the draft of the conversation has been transcribed. Questions can be asked, and the resulting modifications to the original conversation can be incorporated into the original transcription as appendices.

MSDLC Phase II—Model Building

Depending upon the skill of the programmer and the complexity of the task, the second stage of the process can often be incorporated into the first phase of the process. If the function and the requirements of the system are readily apparent to the programmer, he or she can move directly into the storyboarding segment of the task within the structure of the original task definition consultation.

During this phase of the development, the programmer and user sit down together at a computer and construct mock-ups of the entry screens and the reports. The contracting user directly participates in this process. The user must sit with the programmer and orally approve the precise structure of the screens and the reports. The constraints of each of the input fields, the data lookup expectations, and the file structures should also be brought up at this session. By the completion of this session, the user should be fully aware of the appearance and functionality of the final product. The programmer must take a cautious approach during this session to ensure that all elements of the system are completely specified. Of particular importance is the precise definition of the functions of the final program. Which are optional, which are possible, which are certain? Precision and agreement are the keys to successful specification during this session or a subsequent session. The second session may be necessary when the contracting user is unsure of his final needs or is indecisive. In those instances, the system should be defined to the limits of the user's capabilities during the first session, and then completed during a second session when the contracting user is able to answer the questions identified during the first session. Together the user and the programmer are building a model of the proposed system's likely characteristics.

The reason that the systems design portion of the system development process can be compressed to such a degree is that by taking this approach, the output first, followed by the input which is used to obtain the output, the user is able to communicate with the programmer in a manner and form that is both exact and understandable. Unlike the traditional method of flow charting and systems design, the new system involves use of simulated output and simulated entry screens. The user is not required to visualize a nebulous entity, but instead sees a representative model that uses a familiar structure. The user is used to seeing an entry screen. Because the word-processing-produced rendition of the entry screen has exactly the same appearance as the final entry screen, the user is able to understand the final form of the program. He can then determine the exact nature of entry by the operator, the supporting information that must come from existing databases, restrictions upon operator entry, and entry field sizes.

The entry screen storyboarding supplemented by voice documentation of the restrictions and requirements provides a framework for the data acquisition phase of most programs.

MSDLC Phase III—Storyboarding

Once the entry screens have been defined and specified, the second phase of the storyboarding effort begins. The user is required to participate in the creation of a word processing based mock-up of the eventual reports that are to be produced by the program. These reports should include both screen-oriented and printout-oriented versions.

Because the reports represent exact models of the eventual output from the program, the user is again able to participate in the design phase of the project more fully than in the past. The user will be able to identify the elements of the reporting system that are necessary but unachievable using the prescribed entry mechanism. The entry screens can then be quickly modified to incorporate the additional data requirements identified during the report definition process. As part of the report definition process, each element of the report must be fully specified by the user as to how results would be obtained in a manual process. These specifications are again recorded and incorporated into the systems design transcription.

Thus, at the completion of one, two, or at most three sessions, the programmer is able to work from a comprehensive set of specifications at a level of detail not dissimilar to those prepared by an architect for a house.

MSDLC Phase IV—Pseudocoding

Next, it is necessary to pseudocode the application. Pseudocode merely means writing out the steps in a narrative form, to ensure complete handing of the process. During this phase of the project, the programmer should lay out a highly generalized but complete rendition of the code to be completed. This code can be completed with pencil and paper or on a word processor. The purpose of this code is not to identify the precise programming to be done, but instead to discover and document all of the subroutines necessary for the completion of the program and the function of each subroutine.

The use of pseudocode accomplishes a great deal in accelerating the development of any function. It illustrates the flow of the programming to be accomplished. It identifies the separate tasks to be performed by the different driver environments. And it provides the method for subdivision of the tasks for concurrent development of segments of the program by multiple programmers should the project experience a time crunch. Finally, the pseudocode provides another layer of documentation that will be useful to any future programmer (or yourself) who may have to maintain the program some months or years in the future.

Surprisingly, the previous steps can be accomplished simply and quickly. They are natural steps and provide the equivalent to a blueprint for programming.

MDSLC Phase V—Programming

Now comes the point when the application must be programmed. One of the big differences between the programming techniques prescribed here and the traditional programming techniques is the use of voice documentation. Because of the memory and location-dependent nature of driver programming, the programming style does not lend itself to integrated programming and documentation. The documentation has to be separate anyway. There is not room for remarks, for example, unless you are willing to devote unused cells in the spreadsheet (for example) to contain that documentation. This breakdown of the traditional remark-oriented programming style provides a reason to change to a less labor-intensive documentation method: the use of dictated documentation. Although the procedure is different in that the programmer talks about the program while constructing it, it is still similar to the remark method of programming. The programmer is required to talk about the programming at the completion of each line of code or programming session. The process of voiced program documentation can be greatly facilitated by the use of pedal-activated or voice-actuated dictation machines.

Dictation also gives the programmer a sense of awareness of the intricacies of the program. By talking about each section and line of code generated, the programmer is often able to recognize programming errors as they are entered. This aspect of the voice documentation again compresses the debugging and program alteration cycle.

Although more text is generated using this method, the text transcribed by lower paid personnel and the documentation function is thus abbreviated. The transcribed version can then be edited and shaped to a suitable output document. In the event that several programmers have participated in the programming effort, the project leader may then integrate the modules created by the group effort and document the integration effort in the same manner.

MSDLC Phase VI—Debugging

Once the programming has been completed, the program must be completely debugged. All elements of the program must be thoroughly tested to ensure that the system functions as expected. If one of the user's operators is capable of quickly learning the system in the absence of complete user documentation, the user's personnel time should be employed in the debugging effort when possible. Again as many tasks as possible should be off loaded from the programming personnel. Users can do a better job of discovering the problems with the system than can programmers in most instances. The program should be relatively bug free at this stage, because each module should have been tested upon its completion. The major bugs that will surface will be those involving integration and compatibility.

Be sure that during the debugging stage the use of entry restrictions is maximized, and entry editing procedures and other operator features and conveniences are maximized. Attempt to follow standard protocols for assignment of options and conveniences to function keys and other user implemented macros.

MSDLC Phase VII—Documentation

Once the program has been completed, the user documentation phase can be initiated. In some instances, the user can get a running jump on the documentation by creating documentation independent of the programmer based upon the screen design and the report design. However, in most instances, the user will require the programming personnel to construct the user documentation.

A new technique for user documentation creation involves a lot more paper but results in easy and quick-to-construct documentation. This technique is called ''print screen documentation.'' Again, the programmer uses a dictation device. By acting as the user of the program, he should start the program and comment about it as it is used. Each time the screens change even minutely, the programmer should use the computer's ''print screen function'' to create an illustration of the screen modifications that result from the actions he or she has taken. The same techniques should be used to illustrate the use of on-screen reporting. The resulting documentation will be thorough and complete. The users should have very little problem in following the flow of procedures throughout the program.

The primary drawback to this technique is that it results in large amounts of documentation. The programmer's time is optimized, but the resulting manual will be hard to reproduce because of the size. Each illustration typically takes a page of the text. The text between illustrations may only be one sentence. And the text might again be illustrated by another screen print. However, unless you have considerable resources necessary to reduce pictures and typeset documentation, this is by far a step ahead of most available documentation.

Once the dictated text of the documentation has been transcribed by a secretary into word processor text, the text can also be subdivided for help screens. Refer to the chapter on advanced word processing for assistance on the development of help screens and the word processing search functions used for selection of the proper help section. Your macro programming should then be modified to incorporate the help functions.

MSDLC Phase VIII—Turnover and Training

A final test and debugging of the system should result in a program that is ready for delivery. It is now necessary to train those individuals who will use the program on a regular basis how to do so. Each individuals should be given a copy of the documentation at the earliest possible time, with a view towards studying what is there. For the most part, each user will be familiar with the data; it will be only the form of the data entered and reported that will be different.

Naturally the individuals who do this work are doing other work, as well. Timing for the training is important, as are the attitudes of those persons to be trained. While volumes have been written on how to teach and how to prepare the materials for teaching, that will not be duplicated here. Two elements of the teaching process will be covered, however. First, start small. Trace each feature of the most minute entry process all the way through to its logical conclusion. Gradually increase the complexity of the process, but each time, follow it through to its ultimate conclusion. Second, be lavish with praise and understanding. Many of these people will be new to the microcomputer as well as the application system you have just installed. Go slow and be encouraging.

MSDLC Phase IX—Follow-up

Because the contracting user has fully defined the system, the problems with delivery of the system should be minimal. Any enhancements to the programming that are specified at the time of delivery should be easily converted into supplemental contracts, because all the original specifications have been met. The resulting program should be easily maintained, because all elements of the creation process are documented from system design to user activities.

Each modification to the original program should be treated as a separate programming effort. Each modification should incorporate all of the elements of the original program procedure. The modifications should be entered as appendices to the original documentation files both on the system programming files and the user documentation files.

MSDLC Phase X—Review

The final phase is a simple one. Study the process just completed. Identify the mistakes and learn from them. Find out what worked and resolve to capitalize upon them.

Back to today—there's a lot to be learned from what has been stated, and you will see it come to pass.

Systems Maintenance

Perhaps the most difficult function for the DP manager to manage is the function of maintenance. The function of maintenance is actually several maintenance functions—from systems software, through operations, to applications software. This selection concentrates on software maintenance. It is assumed that hardware maintenance will be relegated to the vendor or to an organization whose function is to provide such service. Some computing activities hire their own maintenance personnel, however.

Maintenance of systems software is generally pretty straightforward. Vendors provide updates and systems software people install them. They troubleshoot problems with the vendor software and with in-house standardized software and publish usage documentation. Since systems software is generally highly modularized, systems software maintenance is an attractive career. The position may also be responsible for hardware performance analysis and improvement.

The maintenance of poorly documented applications systems, however, is another matter. This is one of the most difficult, unrewarding, boring, and discouraging of activities within the DP department. Yet it is the one place where the most learning is accomplished. This makes it a profitable place to position trainees—so long as time is not of the essence. It's a curious paradox that at a point where operation of the DP facility reaches crisis proportions, the least experienced person is assigned to trouble-shoot and correct the deficiency. In the author's experience, persons assigned to maintenance responsibility should possess skills necessary to correct the deficiencies in direct proportion to the worth of the system. The novice might well maintain common reporting programs, but cash flow and investment monitoring systems should demand a high level of skill in maintenance—and should compensate the position-holder accordingly. One thing is for certain—application system maintenance is willingly done by people who know one specific fact: the precise day they'll be assigned to something else.

Programming Management

Software

The term *software* means programs, attributes of the computer necessary to make it operate, exclusive of the hardware. Systems software does not normally include those programs whose purpose is to solve or manipulate a business problem, but only those programs which facilitate use of the computer and the application programs. Systems software has usually been developed by the equipment manufacturer, or by a software vendor. We've learned that predeveloped programming is as important as the hardware itself.

Large installations often require specialized systems software. Usually this software is programmed and maintained in house. Specialized software companies have found a market because they frequently produce systems software that is more efficient, has special disadvantages, or more readily available when needed.

Most installations have some systems software in the computer at all times. Operating systems, executive software, and other features of systems software keep the computer humming, managing the communications network, scheduling the input/output devices, producing monitor output. Simply stated, systems software is a necessary feature of large-scale hardware.

Management of systems software personnel has, in recent years, been the responsibility of the Operations Manager, as the function has been moved. There are still organizational systems software groups, however. Systems software support attracts a unique type of programmer. Blessed with a penchant for detail, an introverted nature, an understanding of the bizarre, and an ability to deal with logical complexity, the systems programmer may well be the odd person out and be regarded as such. These people will be highly productive and creative and should be managed in terms of products derived, not processes followed.

Applications software personnel should be those who are more communicative and business-knowledgeable. Their management is a function of assigned projects and contributory products, for which they are held responsible and accountable. They should be managed on results of their contributions and not on the results of the product of the combination of contributions. They should, however, be encouraged to observe the entire project in operation, as a morale booster. Very large companies with very large applications which have been around for a decade or more may find some difficulty trying to motivate the programmer whose only tangible product is a calculation module. That's somewhat like an auto worker who makes only fenders and never sees a completed automobile.

Vendor Support

The vendor is called upon to perform a variety of services. Competition between hardware vendors and between software vendors has opened fringe services such a consulting, usage classes, and the like.

Vendor support can be vital, irrespective of whether it is priced with the hardware/software or priced separately. The years of vendor experience, and, in many cases, the focus of that experience make the availability of vendor talent an invaluable asset. Training manuals, brochures, technical publications, and consulting advice will be excellent. Acquired and proven software packages will be tested and reliable—or will be maintained. Vendors will participate with users' groups to enhance the comparative value of their product while providing support to customers.

Contract Programming

Despite the growth in the number of people who are DP-trained, there is evidence that the field is being de-emphasized in college-level academic programs while there is a proliferation of computer systems. This means a shortfall of people, which often means that people can not be hired directly—and consulting people may simply be too expensive. Contract programming is an occasional necessary evil. That individual at the consulting company may simply have the experience needed for this one application and will not be needed beyond the development of that project. Or, programmer X does a little moonlighting, for a reasonable fee, in the development of inventory control systems. Because he has Y years of inventory control experience, the use of programmer X may be a wise investment.

The assigned programmer talent may be devoted to maintenance, with but marginal expansion into new development —and new people are not available or are not available for an affordable price. The contract programmer brings with him or her applicable knowledge with low overhead. Often, these programmers can obtain access to your system through on-line services. You may provide the terminal. Or, as in the case of the microcomputer, the contract programmer may have a copy of your system.

Programmer Training

Training is a continuous occupation. On-the-job training by a qualified senior-level programmer, supplemented by vendor or contracted classroom instruction, is undoubtedly best. Some skills, once learned, stay with us indefinitely; other skills, if taught but not used, are lost rapidly. Programming and a foreign language are comparable in that, if they are taught in a classroom and unused, retention time is short. The process of training is an employee benefit and should be administered as part of a total program of employee education.

Audits and Controls

Internal control is the plan, procedure, and alerting mechanism that safeguards assets, checks on accuracy, and ensures adherence to policies and standards within an organization. EDP can aid in internal control if the proper steps are taken. We don't worry about the accuracy of the equipment anymore—one error in a hundred million calculations is high. Instead, the emphasis must be placed on the control of the application systems. This has given rise to the position of the EDP auditor.

The auditors monitor the integrity of the computer facility, systems design, programming steps, and output reports. They continue to check with the source of data for use of proper procedures and to institute controls as necessary. By sampling, they may trace an individual entry into the computer file and note its effect on totals or balances. They are concerned with security, backup, file retention, accuracy, safeguards, procedures, and those elements which pose a threat to the assets of the organization.

Documentation

Too much cannot be stated about the importance of documentation to the EDP department. It should not be a make-work project or one which is sandwiched between projects as time is available. It should be an assigned task which is given the same importance as the development of applications program code.

Documentation may become the historical record of the project, the basis upon which management decisions have been made, the procedures by which the system will be operated, the training plan for teaching the users, etc. An organized documentation plan is required and an active records management activity should encompass all aspects of the DP function. Documentation is the "wayback machine" should there ever be a question as to how, where, when, and why.

Testing

Before a program is made operational, it must be verified. Does that program in fact do what it should? The programmer who wrote it, the systems analyst who designed it, the auditor who specified the controls, and the user who must live with it should be a part of the testing process.

The structured programming move brought to us a new consciousness about program error-checking. No longer did we simply desk check. Our approach had to become "ego-less," while others examined our code. Structured walkthroughs became the method whereby mass input to the testing process was derived. See Chapter 2 for more detail.

So long as there is the possibility of an error, it could be said that the program is being tested. But once sample data has been passed through the system, once users have reviewed and approved reports, once every known possible combination has been checked, there comes a point where the bridges to the older method are burned and a commitment to make the new approach work is made. There will continue to be errors—oversights, erroneous specifications, changes in legal constraints, etc., but these will have to be resolved while the system is in operation.

INSTALLATION AND OPERATIONS MANAGEMENT

Processing the Data

Business data processing is normally performed under the closed-shop concept. The machine room operation is run on a production basis where programs and data files are processed by schedule. Programmers and operators report to separate heads and their functions remain distinct and separate. The systems and programming unit, in liaison with user activities, establishes due dates and frequencies of reports. Following the priorities and guidance provided by the systems analyst, the operations unit builds a daily schedule.

All production runs are scheduled and, if appropriate, placed under the control of the operating system. The normal daytime work shift is usually designated as the prime shift. The procedures under the operating system usually specify that program malfunctions, improper data, or transaction error will cause the system to flush the job stream in progress and continue to the next job stream. Problems will be resolved by systems and programming units and the aborted job is rescheduled for the next processing cycle.

To allow for flexibility, a machine burden should not be 100%. The time which is not scheduled may then be used for testing or for compensation for problems previously encountered. In PERT parlance, the operations manager should adopt the pessimistic outlook on scheduling and make plans accordingly.

A designated period each day should be reserved for compilation, assembly test, or other program development work if the shop operates strictly in the batch mode. In an on-line, real-time effort this may not be necessary, as development and testing may be run concurrently. However, even in that environment, it is the responsibility of the operations manager to monitor machine usage and demand and to inhibit those applications which may consume resources needed for critical applications.

Regularly scheduled preventive maintenance work must be worked into the schedule—often as a part of the requirements of a formal lease or maintenance agreement. Emergency maintenance or off-prime-shift maintenance may engender higher costs. During that time, normal usage of the computer is curtailed—hopefully with sufficient advance knowledge to the users of the system.

Job Accounting

The cost of data processing is the price paid for data acquisition, equipment, processing, people, and a host of other considerations which are too numerous to detail here. Since cost accounting is a financial and managerial measurement and control, accurate cost accounting for the use of the EDP resource is a must. Unfortunately, too many organizations merely lump the EDP activity into an overhead account and distribute the cost across the entire organization. In addition to the obvious drawbacks to such a system, there is no consciousness on anybody's part of the cost using the resource. Therefore, the resource is used most unwisely very often.

Costs are classified into categories for management and economic analysis. Fixed costs are generally static, changing slightly or not at all in the volume of activity. Variable costs change with any change in system usage. An example of the former is the cost of the building; of the latter is the cost for preparing reports.

Costs can be direct or indirect. Direct costs can be specifically traced and charged. Manpower applied directly to operation of the computer is a direct cost. Indirect costs cannot be easily identified with a specific job, but must be arbitrarily apportioned. Cost of the floor space consumed by the hallways falls within this category.

Cost accounting must be done on a job basis—with larger systems, the job accounting software is fairly accurate and can be used to determine accurately the usage of resources such as time and data passed. Formulas applied to that output are customarily a function of local design, but the charge for the service must include the direct costs which can be identified plus the indirect costs which are to be distributed. After all, EDP is an expensive resource, the value of which can only be determined by accurate accounting. To provide uncharged-for services will allow the user to request anything at any time, irrespective of its cost effectiveness. Charges must then be levied formally (funds transfer) or informally (funny money) against the user.

Hardware Costs

The cost of hardware is not difficult to determine. Equipment rental is prescribed by contract with rates for prime and extra shifts. Some machines are equipped with meters that record time used. Those without meters rely on the installation to log and report time used. Some contracts allow unlimited use; the vendor bills the installation for equipment rental monthly.

Purchased equipment can be equated to equivalent rental by the following ratio: purchase price, less salvage value, divided by projected life. In this instance, depreciation allowances will amortize costs.

Communications costs for on-line systems are increasing in proportion to other costs. These costs should be chargeable as a direct cost to those jobs and systems involved. Time-shared computer systems presents a formidable problem in the breakdown of shared costs. Fortunately, accounting software has made this easier.

Supplies

Supplies are a larger part of costs than many organizations care to admit. The volume of paper or microfile consumed can be a major expense. Although consumption of paper may be a controllable cost, it must be considered with other cost factors. If extended amounts of set-up time are required to change paper with each run, it may be less costly to use standard paper and save the computer and operator time.

On-line reports may be charged as a function of computer time—but large-volume hard-copy reports must be charged to include the cost of the paper. The allocation of paper costs to indirect costs may be a solution.

Equipment Maintenance

Since the last issue of this book, maintenance costs have nearly doubled. It is not uncommon to find costs of $65 to $100 per hour. Skilled repairmen are a scarce resource. The minimum amount of maintenance may be specified by contract.

Maintenance services will be outlined in the hardware contract. Between 5 and 10 percent of the available prime shift time may be reserved for preventive maintenance. Equipment maintenance costs are an indirect cost which must be distributed—perhaps as an add-on to the hourly machine rate.

Performance Measurement

Much effort has been expanded in recent years to get a handle upon, monitor, and improve the performance of the computing resource. Monitor software has been installed which will develop usage histograms. Using these histograms the systems software people can trim the systems software overhead. Programming personnel can restructure the program to make more efficient usage of resources. It would be a fair statement to say that most of the improvement will be derived in I/O channel usage. Statistics on performance will become the basis for expanding the equipment inventory, so utilization statistics will be useful both for program improvement and for run scheduling.

Controls

Operations management must install and enforce controls over those activities likely to cause trouble if unobserved or unchecked. Logging of media, movement of transactions, quality control procedures, transaction and file balancing procedures, and product utility will be among the concerns. Strict control of media library and backup facilities become the responsibility of the operations manager. Fireproof safes, records rotation programs, and inventory and control of the media become part of that responsibility.

Site Preparation

Physical Configuration

Computers occupy space and that space is unique. When constructing a data center, the key has to be lead time. The steps necessary to prepare the facility should be part of the planning which has been done. DP management is certainly involved in the specifications for construction, equipment location, movement of people and supplies, etc. Working with construction people and engineers of many descriptions, the DP manager will represent management's interests.

Size, weight, power requirements, and other pertinent data about the equipment to be installed is, of course, available from the hardware vendor. Also, the requirements of OSHA (see Chapter 3) must be taken into consideration. This will generally require a paper mock-up, drawn to scale, with movable pieces which will allow the planner to try the configuration in a variety of arrangements.

Engineering considerations become an important part of the process. Cable length, flow of air, air conditioning, flow of water, power transmission, etc., must all be considered. Raised flooring, fire detection and suppression equipment, access control, etc., will also be required. Alternate sources of power should be evaluated. Again, it would be wise to review documentation of such considerations should you be faced with the task.

Environmental Considerations

EDP equipment produces heat. Each item of equipment has a BTU rating. Excess heat must be removed, as it could damage equipment. In recent years, organizations have found ways to capture this heat and to distribute it through the building, thereby reducing the cost of heating fuel.

Air movement must be free. Normally distributed underfloor, air conditioning must be filtered and circulated through floor vents and returns. Humidity control using hydrothermographic equipment may be necessary. High humidity warps cards. Low humidity generates static electricity, causing shocks, electrical malfunctions, paper jams, and tape errors.

Acoustical treatment is desirable to reduce or absorb machine noise. Cleaning is a must—both above and beneath the raised floor. Dust is the enemy of computer media.

Vendors of large-scale equipment recommend acceptable temperature and humidity ranges—generally 72 plus or minus 5 degrees F and an ideal humidity of 50 plus or minus 10%.

Entry, Exit, and Access

Security is, of course, a concern for any data center. In the early days, data centers were located in showplaces, where much traffic moved, and where the computer could be seen. Not so today.

Removal of the DP site from the mainstream of organizational activity has become a must, like it or not. There have simply been too many incidents of interdiction. The center should be designed so that it can be made secure, access doorways should be wide enough to accommodate the largest items of equipment, ramps to the raised floor should be provided at every door, which should function automatically. Some loading ramp access to the exterior of the building is desirable.

Supply Storage

Consumable supplies and media should be stored in the same environment as the data center for at least 24 hours prior to use. This does not mean that they should be part of the facility—merely that the environments should be the same. These items need time to acclimate to temperature and humidity before use. There should be remote storage (for fire protection), and the vendor should be asked to keep some minimum shelf stock.

Office Space

Office space for the computer operations center is the scarcest resource available. The computer center is seldom large enough, the office space seems always to be inadequate, and certain items of equipment or supplies always seems to encroach upon the available space. Space enough for people to work comfortably, for users to spend time with appropriate people, and for ease of movement is necessary.

On-Line Real-Time Computer Systems

Hardware Checkout

With the increase in on-line systems and distributed data processing, the use of terminal and communications-oriented equipment abounds. Developers of such systems will admit that such systems seldom seem to work initially. The same equipment which functions perfectly in the computer room becomes quite uncooperative when positioned in a remote office. Between the two are several interfacing equipment items and communications services, all of which must be fine-tuned to work. Again, standardization is the issue. As more and more systems utilize the RS-232 connection, communications capabilities will become more easily installed. However, at the same time, new communications facilities are becoming available, with new problems. See the treatment of communications facilities in Chapter 1 for further insight.

Vendor assistance may be required during the checkout—but selected portions of the system will be instituted, tried, checked, tried again, and again, until there is confidence that the hardware will perform as expected.

Recovery

A certain amount of redundancy is required with every communications-based system. Depending upon the critical nature of the application, some systems may be installed in tandem—two or more computers which are used are used to load share, work in parallel, or to function in lieu of the other should the need arise. The duplexing of hardware is expensive, but necessary in some instances. Where equipment is not duplexed, hardware networks are frequently operated under controlled conditions on time schedules which will permit monitoring of the system.

Network Communications

As indicated in Chapter 1, great things are happening to digital communications networks, and the application of those networks to the transmission of data. As the communications-based system expands, a person should be devoted to monitoring the network, working out greater efficiencies in communications packaging, monitoring the functioning of the equipment, etc.

Communications costs are a sizable portion of the modern data processing installation. A commitment to install on-line and/or real-time systems should not be made lightly.

Conversion

Conversion to a new computer system has begun when someone has accepted the feasibility study and the project is underway. But conversion is its own project. Not only must the new applications be tested under operation, but also the older systems must continue to operate—to keep the organization afloat. Thus, computer time must be found for both operations, until sufficient confidence is experienced to allow the older system to be discontinued.

In the meantime, data needs to be reformatted, controls need to be applied, bridges must be built between the two systems, some one-time programs will have to be run, the benchmark will have to be established, and the phase-in of applications begun. Concurrent with this effort will be user training, phase-out of the older system, and adaptation of media to the new mode of operation.

Personnel involved in the machine conversion should be briefed—especially where two systems must operate in the same space—as to what the responsibilities will be. A key supervisor should be designated as the conversion team head so that the many activities underway have a common center of authority. If possible, that person should be part of the planning-for-conversion activity. Status briefings will handle problems and advise upper-echelon management of progress.

Other Management Concerns

The Project

The project team approach to building large EDP systems is, to be certain, not new. But it is different, because we're learning to convene skills instead of availabilities. A project task force is a blend of individuals who have an intense involvement in the operation of the organization coupled to an intense involvement in EDP activities. The Project Manager may or may not be a middle-level manager, but will be required to function in much the same manner. His or her technical skills must be superior, but the necessary attributes of people-managers are required as well.

It is not the purpose of this book to detail what a systems analyst should do, what a programmer should accomplish, and how—or if—the functions should be blended. In some organizations, analysts analyze and don't program. They concentrate upon the business aspects of the problem, and are best suited for their knowledge of the system as applied to their knowledge of the business. Programmers reduce specifications to machine code, testing, installing, and generally handholding. In some larger organizations, program coders are used. Frequently the two functions of systems analyst and programmer are mixed. There is widespread speculation as to the viability of that approach.

Other project team members may be: auditors, who will detail the necessary controls; user representatives for those users who will be affected; clerical support services; and graphic arts support for presentations.

Communications will be a critical part of the project team's duties. Interteam communications will tend to be informal and will concentrate on the understanding and modifications of specifications and the tasks which are to be accomplished. Intrateam communications will tend to be more formal and will concentrate on time, cost, and problem considerations. To the user, the team will communicate about objectives accomplished, cost and time expended, progress encountered, anticipated slippages, and problems envisioned. To the organizational management, communication will be in terms of milestones, budget allocations, and factors which require their assistance. And to others, communications will be restricted to schedules, projected impacts, and resource planning.

Time-Sharing Services

The expansion of business languages into time-sharing services has made possible the take-home terminal, off-hour development, work-at-home programming, and other services which would not be available in the office batch environment. While some amount of intellectual diversion should be allowed, it should be remembered that telecommunications costs are high. Monitoring of line usage, CPU usage, and resource usage is encouraged.

Telecommunications Services

The long-distance transmission of data—or the across-town transmission of programs—become a concern for the management of telecommunications. This differs from time-sharing services in that point-to-point communications are involved and the value added of the host computer is nonexistent. This will probably be more applicable to larger, rather than smaller, installations.

Distributed Processing

Management of distributed processing is management of a variety of functioning micro- or minicomputers co-located across a communications network. This may be the remote job entry (RJE) devices, functioning systems which will communicate with a host computer, or tandem systems which pass and receive data. Pure distributed processing will pass both program and data to the remote location—or, alternatively, will used packaged and standard software. There will be administrative message traffic, word processing, data processing, electronic mail, etc. It will be around the distributed processing concept that the office of the future will develop.

Centralized/Decentralized Activities

The centralization versus decentralization question has confronted us for years. Decentralization is often a function of placing the service at the location of the user's service. In earlier days, this was one way to determine actual costs. Today, under distributed processing, it is the way to achieve a greater utilization of computing power. But the staffs functioning at the remote location must function in much the same manner as at the central location. Only the distance across the reporting line changes.

Audit and Control Services

Management of the audit and control function is an obligation of the EDP manager. This does not necessarily mean that the function is assigned to that position. But, the EDP manager must establish policy, devise standards, and set practice—and make it stick. Theoretically, such clout should be the function of an internal or external auditor who has a pipeline to the top echelon of the organization. In reality, the EDP manager must manage the function. Historically, while there has been concern for security and safeguards, incidents of computer-related fraud and misuse have brought this vulnerability to the foreground.

Motivating and Managing Computer Personnel

Computer personnel are very much like non-computer personnel in many of the traditional ways. But they're also very different in many ways, and this section will concentrate upon the differences. In-depth research in this area may be obtained from the book *Motivating and Managing Computer Personnel,* J. Daniel Couger & Robert A. Zawacki, John Wiley & Sons, Inc., 1980, which served as my research for this section. Information in this section has been obtained from that volume; in some cases, by direct quotation.

The Expanding Backlog of Work

According to Couger and Zawacki, backlog is a serious problem, caused by five major factors:

1. The increasing complexity of systems. New techniques have not increased productivity. The DP budget is rising significantly and personnel costs are rising within that budget (30%–50%) between 1970 and 1980. The increasing percentages are attributable to reasons identified in other parts of this book. Today DP applications are far more complex ('lifestream''—life and growth) and more effort is required. Labor costs are affected by inflation.
2. Increasing quantity of systems. Knowledgeable users have multiplied their requests for service. And, as has been stated before, have turned to the microcomputer. In short, DP personnel have done a pretty good job of acquainting user departments with what is possible—and have awakened a sleeping giant.
3. Turnover. The book quotes *Datamation* surveys which show that turnover lies between 28 and 34 percent. This means a new employee learning curve—it also means that a large number of people simply aren't very happy. Later in the book is this statement: ''Companies that concentrate solely on financial inducements will be disappointed with the results. The job itself is the major motivator. . . .''
4. Increasing maintenance cost—more than 50% of department budgets are spent on keeping applications afloat—and this ranges to 75% in some places.

5. Shortage of qualified personnel—states that universities and colleges are not producing enough people and those people don't have enough training, and this situation is a drain on time and budget resources.

Loyalty to the Profession

The situation seems to be that many personnel in the DP career field do not feel it necessary to follow a company's objectives and career paths. Rather, these persons select another in the profession against which to prepare a model. This is spurred by a shortage which allows positions and other rewards to be escalated by changing organizations.

Key Factors

Couger and Zawacki used a measurement instrument as they gathered data for their book. It is the Job Diagnostic Survey (JDS), developed by J. Hackman (University of Ilinois) and Greg Oldham (Yale). They felt that the JDS, while not aimed at data processing people exclusively, would be the best basis for their survey, and they expanded it to include data processing personnel.

There were five characteristics of the job (called core job dimensions) which were gathered to study: *skill variety, task identity, task significance, autonomy,* and *feedback.* They found that systems analysts and programmer/analysts rated very high on the scales, compared to other professionals. These were explained by three psychological states: *experienced meaningfulness, experienced responsibility,* and *knowledge of results.* These three bear definition:

Experienced meaningfulness—individuals must perceive their work as worthwhile or important by some system of values they accept.

Experienced responsibility—they must believe that they personally are accountable for the outcomes of their efforts.

Knowledge of results—they must be able to determine, on some regular basis, whether the outcome of their work is satisfactory.

The outcomes of the JDS model compute a single summary index of the "motivating potential" of a job. The index is called the motivating potential score (MPS), and the formula for that is shown in Figure 4.6.

I'll not present any of their mathematical findings from the perspective of this formula, because you are encouraged to obtain the book. It is quite eye-opening.

Growth Need Strength

One of the things tested by the survey was the strength of the indicator of growth need amongst data processing professionals. In this area they could determine if a person who had a high growth need

$$\left[\frac{\text{skill variety} + \text{task identity} + \text{task significance}}{3}\right] * \left[\text{autonomy}\right] * \left[\text{feedback from the job}\right]$$

Figure 4.6. MPS Formula.

strength (GNS) absolutely required a position with the potential to satisfy that need. A person with a high GNS could not perform well in a job which didn't require it. When compared to the MPS, there was a direct correspondence. The highest GNS corresponded to the highest MPS. Revealing.

Social Need Strength

The question has often arisen as to whether or not a DP professional is a "loner" because he or she was a DP professional, or whether in fact loners are drawn to the field. Couger and Zawacki answer this by saying that they were very surprised that DP professionals were consistently and substantially lower than all other professionals in the need to interact with people. Programmers, it would seem, got along well with other programmers (so long as it wasn't overdone), but with few others. A major cause for this is that the job itself was a key indicator of performance—the programmer knew just how well he or she was doing on the basis of interaction with the computer. Systems people, on the other hand, are doing interpersonal relations as a part of their jobs—and yet their SNS was equally low—until it is realized that in both colleges and businesses the supply of people to the systems ranks comes largely from the programmer ranks.

Recognizing that people with inclinations to music have always fared well in this career, some parallels may be drawn. The cello player (for one) is instantly aware of his or her position in the orchestra—yet the cello player is playing only to the cello player. The instrument (computer) is in direct communication with the player (programmer), and there is instant feedback. The only significant difference seems to be that the music director is instantly aware of an audible boner—but the head cello player may not be. In short, according to Couger and Zawacki, DP people are critical of and unsatisfied by their supervision—and the reason may be that of the three types who make up the bulk of the department (programmer, systems, and operations), only the programmer has the immediate feedback.

The authors state: ". . .a low social need may indicate the need for additional training on supervisory techniques and joint goal-setting processes when DP professionals are promoted to management positions." I hear an echo. They go on to state that we have put an enormous amount of effort into improving techniques and a very little into improving the motivation for using the techniques. They cite the fact that what is happening to the DP professional world right now is what was happening to the automobile production world 40 years ago—that we have specialized the DP field so much that we should perhaps instead go heavily into job enlargement.

Motivating People in Computer Operations

According to Couger and Zawacki, the motivation situation is most acute in computer operations, where employees may be only two-thirds as motivated as other DP professionals. According to the authors, the MPS of these jobs is lower than any of the other 500 jobs in the Hackman/Oldham data base—the computer operator is the least motivated of all employees anywhere. Frightening, isn't it? Operators, in this sense, include data entry, data control, and computer operators. According to the authors, in four of the five categories mentioned earlier in this section, operations personnel rated lower than the norm. In the fifth, task significance, they are similar to the other groups. The people feel their job is just as important, but feel that the organization does not agree, and gives more support to the programming and systems people.

Summary of Findings

1. While their general satisfaction is higher than that of other professionals, DP professionals are less satisfied with supervision.
2. Growth need strength is high for DP professionals compared to other professionals and other job categories.

3. Social need strength is substantially lower for DP professionals compared to other professionals in other fields.
4. DP job specialization could be improved by reversing the trend toward specialization and concentrating as much upon the fulfillment of the employee as upon the techniques he or she is called upon to employ.

Growth and Social Need Strengths of Operations Personnel

The authors state that there is a very high GNS for operations personnel, essentially because they do not feel challenged by the work they must do. It is much closer to those of programmers and analysts than to other employees, but only about two-thirds of those in the systems department.

SNS for this group is, interestingly, much higher than that of programmers and analysts. They interact with more people. And there is generally a high feeling of satisfaction (except for pay) among these people, for growth is available in DP operations, in general growth of the department, and there is enough pay satisfaction (it may not be high enough to suit, but is substantially higher than other persons in the organization) to offset lack of challenge. Despite this, there was evidence that these people recognized that the future would be bright in the DP career field and were willing to pay their dues. Of concern to me is that it could appear that for those whose path included DP operations, something changes in these people who move from a high to a low SNS status. Obviously, management of these people is different, and—they found, this portion of the DP career field lacks the key factors for motivation.

Feedback

Throughout the book, the authors emphasize the need—and yes, the desire—for human feedback. Because a programming manager is frequently an ex-programmer, the SNS doesn't measurably increase simply because the individual's position has escalated and the need for an increased SNS is evident. They do, however, offer these suggestions:

1. Persons who do not inherently possess communications skills can acquire them. Formal training in both behavioral concepts and communications techniques can aid in offsetting the negative effects of low social need.
2. Departments where feedback is not produced naturally—because of low SNS of personnel—need more formalized feedback procedures. Training in effective feedback approaches can improve application of the procedure.
3. Persons with high growth need must be provided substantive training programs and challenging jobs.

The balance of the book explores various motivation and management theories and practices. Having set a norm for data processing personnel across the country, managers are encouraged to evaluation their own operations in the light of what they learn. Buy the book—and read it.

OFFICE AUTOMATION

We should not complete this chapter without some mention of the nature of a parallel activity of the DP management variety which is just now beginning to blossom. Office automation, once thought to be the wave of both the near and distant future for large organizations, is well on the way to becoming solidly entrenched in the daily activities of business at every level, in organizations large and small. The reason for this is that more and more businesses are discovering word processing—but word processing is just the beginning.

Once there is a word processing system, it is only logical and sensible to proceed from there to obtain the highest possible productivity by combining already-available equipment, software, and personnel. Office automation does not fall far behind. In reality, the DP manager has a large role to play in the evaluation, installation, and operation of the office automation scenario.

If you were to survey the available literature which combines information about office automation and management of the OA function, you would find little difference in that section from standard management practice tomes. Managing an OA facility is little different, then, from managing any facility. However, what is different is the fact that the OA facility is an integration of disciplines, each which must be handled, and some of which will be different from those traditionally used. In other words, while the theory may be the same, the practice may be very different—an office manager managing an in-department DP facility—a DP manager managing a major part of an office function.

It's important to realize that OA is not just data processing in the office. The applications run in the office address managerial, secretarial, and clerical functions formerly handled manually or by simple electromechanical devices. The term *office* is becoming archaic, and it no longer fits the standard description of a room in which the business of an office takes place. The current definition of an office must describe wherever business information is created, stored, replicated, and distributed. In other words, office may be taking over DP—not the other way around.

The computer-based word processor was—and is—far more than just a faster typewriter. It was the first integrator of office functions, opening the door to the electronic office by enabling the communication of two devices with each other. Soon computers were working with word processors and phototypesetters. Software-based systems then became prevalent, enabling word processors to perform computing functions and computers to type. By the late 1970s, other breakthroughs inundated the office: communications, personal computers, shared resource systems, OCR, intelligent printing, local area networks, and intelligent typewriters.

These will continue to be important, and there are certain to be more technological strides. But the challenge will be for those who work in the information processing environment to analyze office tasks, applications and procedures, and then find ways to raise the performance level and lower the cost. That is the role of the information manager today (as distinguished from the term "DP manager"). The DP manager who is wise will try less to control the function and more to understand and assist it, for if Couger and Zawacki are correct, and there continues to be a gigantic shortage of personnel, somebody will have to administer the office systems function, as well.

Some of the information for this section has been drawn from the book *Office Automation: A Management Approach,* by Kathleen P. Wagoner, PhD and Mary M. Ruprecht, CMC, and published by John Wiley & Sons, 1984. If you are faced with participating in the development of office automation systems, it would be a very good book to read.

A Revolution Within a Revolution

The more I study the phenomenon, the more I'm convinced that we are facing a revolution (office automation) within the information revolution of which we are already a part. Because of this, the DP manager has a hot potato on his hands, and the more quickly he or she face up to it, the more successful will be both.

Figure 4.7 appears on the brochure for some of the James Martin Seminars. It should give you some idea of the dimension of the management opportunities in the latter half of the 1980s and beyond.

The data processing manager is on the side of a boiling kettle with regards to office automation. On the one hand, "Who are they to obtain computing power?" is a very logical question. "Why can you not provide support?" is a logical retort. The fact is that they do have it, can well justify it, and now need to be led about how best to use it. You, as DP manager, have the responsibility to take leadership without taking control—to protect the information asset without preventing its use. The computer is not just a passing fancy—it is about as passing as Direct Distance Dialing—and you know, we've done a

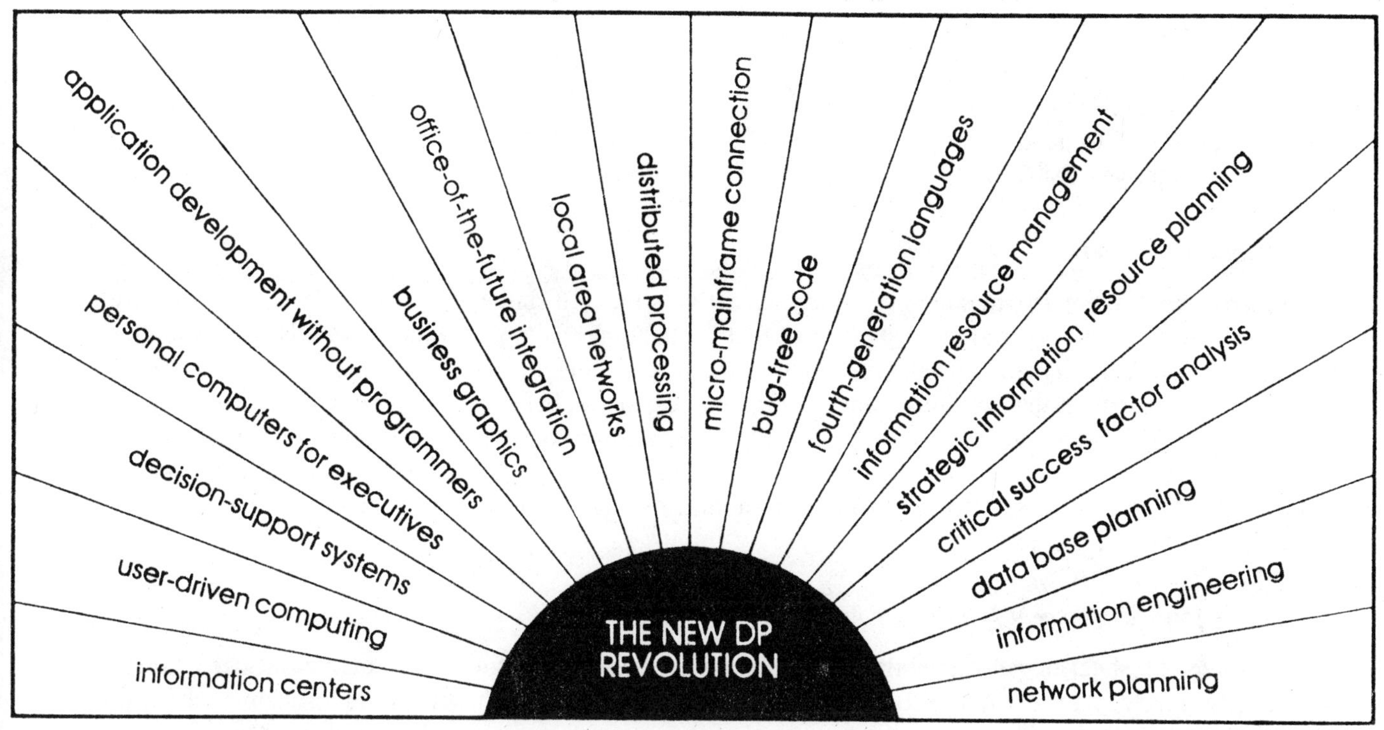

Figure 4.7. The new DP revolution.

pretty good job of training telephone operators. But the nature of the composition is changing. It's as germane to ask where all the programmers will be in the year 2000 as it was to ask where all the blacksmiths were in 1940. There are still some, to be sure, but they are not the prevailing force they once were. Benjamin Franklin once said that those who don't learn from history tend to repeat it. That could very well be true here in the world of data processing. My own observations on the basis of this conference is that there is a crying need for OA analysts now. The field seems to be populated by two types—the data processing analyst who hasn't quite yet acknowledged that OA is people and not computers, and the former WP supervisor who is but casually into the computer technology which is necessary.

Let's take the major headings from the illustration above.

Information Centers

While data processing managers are fighting over control of computers in other departments and who has access to the organizational database, new DP centers are springing up around the nation. The information center is becoming another information processing center, and the organization chart is expanding to accomodate it. New functions are being consolidated under the title of Chief Information Officer, which is finding that it must report to the vice presidential or assistant director level. Don't fight it—help it. Recognize that proper control of operational functions leads to the integrity you seek to keep.

User-Driven Computing

The distributed data processing concept was to place computing power out in the field. So it didn't happen quite the way you would like it to—so what? If the user's need can be satisfied, if your control needs can be satisfied, and if the auditor's accuracy need can be satisfied, user-driven computing may well be the way to clear the outstanding backload. The issues here are accuracy, integrity, standardization, and a valid information policy.

Decision-Support Systems

We have devoted a section of this book to this topic, so little will be said about it here other than the fact that the computer now sits in the manager's office as a means for that manager to tap the pulse of the organization and to make decisions on the basis of the most current, most accurate information available. Isn't that what you really want?

Personal Computers for Executives

In many cases, the personal computer in the executive's office is gathering dust, as he or she deals with the lack of typing or other clerical skills. But that is changing, as those skills are acquired, or as other means which don't demand those skills, such as the use of icons, are developed. Get used to it. There will be more. Just let that executive find the first successful application, and there will be more, working from no automation whatsoever, through to fully-integrated multifunction, multiuser, and multimedia systems. As the sophistication of the user increases, the complexity of the applications and the integration will likewise increase. You can fruitlessly fight it or you can help it. We'll talk more about this in the last chapter of the book.

Application Development Without Programmers

The topic is a shocker, isn't it? Have we, the avant guarde of the information revolution, been caught in the very trap we have eschewed for others? Are we, the change merchants, afraid of change ourselves? The truth is apparent. The programmer, as we knew him, in the numbers that we knew her, will gradually disappear from the scene, in favor of the knowledge worker. This knowledge worker, using driver programs and fourth-generation languages, will obviate the need for the large numbers of highly qualified automated procedure writers—and let's face it, that's what a programmer is. The DP manager who cannot accomodate the computing resource to the information center and its knowledge workers may have a very difficult adjustment period. Will programmers to away entirely? No, of course not, and there will be analysts and operators, and tape librarians, and the lot. But things are changing. The sooner that is recognized, the sooner we can respond to the users' real needs.

Business Graphics

No space will be devoted in this book to business graphics. Not that it isn't important—it is. The CDP test hasn't much about the subject at this point. But let's recognize that graphics is much more than cartoons and cute charts. Graphics becomes the information reduction and analysis mechanism which makes much sense in a decision support environment, so you will find some information there.

Office-of-the-Future Integration

Key to this subject is the single word *integration.* We've gone a long way to produce standalone systems of enormous capability and have found that these do not talk to each other. Look for more information about this in the final chapter of the book.

Local Area Networks

Communications is the grease which will make the information processing activities work. No matter if we call them DP Operations or Information Centers, the distribution of information into the office continues to be a prime goal of the data processing manager. But while he was planning to use the Beehive Terminal online to the DEC/VAX host, something changed—that something was the microcomputer and with it the local area network which functions independently of the host. In fact, DP managers have been shocked to discover that the host computer—that giant machine in the data processing center—has just become a peripheral of the microcomputer, by way of the local area network. More on that in the chapter on communications.

Distributed Processing

The microcomputer may have obviated the need for DDP (Distributed Data Processing), and it may not. Many of the minicomputer manufacturers, such as Datapoint, are hoping not. They may have faith in Allah, as Mohammed said, but they've tied their camel to the tree nonetheless. The movement into the user site of large scale distributed data processing capability continues, and provides many of the same control and use issues to the DP manager that the OA functions will offer.

Micro-Mainframe Connection

The crux of the matter. Users now have computing power and want the database. DP managers are willing to provide information, but the user's area isn't so secure, isn't so tightly controlled, and isn't so complete as the carefully worked out procedures for the protection of data and processes as is the DP. There's a tug-of-war, no doubt, and there will continue to be until these issues are resolved. But they will be resolved. Control of changes to the data and their subsequent return to the mainframe must be resolved. Dumping information for general use without modification is not very different from preparing reports, so that will happen, with some sharpening of control activities. There may be a larger issue here, as well—since the user will now find the computing resource to be so valuable and powerful, the temptation will be strong to store in the micro and then on the mainframe information which was deemed not to have been put on the mainframe in the first place. And there is a very large constraint looming on the horizon—legal-based personal accountability for information.

Bug-Free Code

Is it possible? It most certainly is. Debug the driver program and then program only the parameters. This will make a significant change in the cost of maintenance services. And it's about to become a very important issue for DP managers.

Fourth Generation Languages

What's a "fourth generation language" and why didn't you put it back in the software chapter, Ken? The fourth generation language isn't software—it's English-like specification of the extraction and criteria inherent in today's supersophisticated software. There are some examples in the last chapter of the book.

Information Resource Management

Somewhere in the fray we decided that the DP manager was really a resource manager and that resources extended to microfilm and to manual records. All over the country, as the change is being made to the Chief Information Officer concept, the information—in any form—is being consolidated. Change, or it will change for you.

Strategic Information Resource Planning

We've done a lot to try to find information to support organizational objectives. But we haven't done a whole lot to plan the information resource itself into anything other than next year's plans. There will become an increased emphasis on long-term planning for the new DP manager. Time to get some management training?

Critical Success Factor Analysis

The DP manager has never been called upon to account for the success experienced from the information provided. It's happening. You may be next.

Database Planning

Until now, we've been very concerned with the aggregation and access to consolidate information. Be prepared to be forced into the planning mold here, also, as the tradeoff of storage capacities (cheaper) against data gathering strategies (very expensive) is being evaluated by those who control the purse strings.

Information Engineering

It's a bit too soon to start chasing this concept, but information handling as an engineering discipline is right around the corner. Expect that it will be communications-based.

Network Planning

And it is fitting that the network be listed last, as the means to tie it all together. More on networks in the chapter on communications.

When one recognizes that the current microcomputer laser printer can produce in one week enough information to require more than 600 people to read in 8 hours, the scope of where we are going becomes evident. We haven't reduced paper at all. We've merely redirected it. And with its redirection, major changes are occurring everywhere within the DP spectrum. And created new challenges for DP management.

QUESTIONS

1. The environment control system for the data processing facility:
   A. Maintains a hydrothermograph to warm the air and increase humidity
   B. Is designed to maintain approximately 68–76 degrees Farenheit
   C. Determines the influence that various levels of society have on the quality and quantity of work performed
   D. Has a feedback system to increase processing when conditions are ideal
2. The demand and wait time for terminals is best estimated by:
   A. PERT analysis
   B. Monte Carlo analysis
   C. Queueing Theory
   D. Simplex Method
3. In the traditional data processing organization, the manager usually reported to the comptroller. This has fallen out of favor because:
   A. Financial systems were the only ones being developed
   B. Centralized systems crossed functional lines
   C. Comptrollers don't understand data processing
   D. Companies want data processing to be cost effective
4. The critical path lies
   A. Where the difference between the earliest date and the latest date shows a slack of zero
   B. Where there is slack on the critical path
   C. Where activity slack is zero
   D. Where PERT's expected time is divided by 6

5. In the early development of data processing organizations, the chief or manager usually reported directly to the:
   A. President
   B. Vice-president
   C. Senior systems analyst
   D. Controller (comptroller)

6. The difference between physical and logical access to the computer system is:
   A. Physical access lets you into the room; logical access lets you into the software system
   B. Physical passwords allow access to the entire system
   C. Logical passwords are built into the system
   D. Passwords are not currently necessary

7. When developing and evaluating a computer benchmark problem, which of the following criteria is *least* important:
   A. Benchmark hardware configuration and a representative program selection
   B. Representative program selection
   C. Instruction mix used in benchmark and hardware configuration
   D. Representative program selection and hardware configuration

8. A good turnaround time policy is necessary because:
   A. Programmers can only work on one application at a time
   B. Operations needs to clear out the application log
   C. Supervising programmers can only be done by the number of test shots taken
   D. Programmer time is a valuable asset and compilers reduce the amount of desk checking required

9. When all data to be processed are transmitted or submitted to one location and data processing is concentrated rather than dispersed, the organization is usually referred to as:
   A. Centralized
   B. Intra-dependent
   C. Saturated
   D. Input/output bound

10. A PERT event is:
   A. The beginning of an activity
   B. The completion of all incoming activities
   C. The completion of an individual task
   D. The point where you should introduce a Gantt chart

11. What is the minimum amount of records that should be kept by the computer operations manager?
   A. Programming documentation, computer maintenance log, and output log
   B. Programming documentation, computer schedule, and output log
   C. Input/output computer schedule, and computer maintenance log
   D. Computer schedule, computer maintenance log, and programming documentation

12. Programmers operating in a multiprogramming are able to:
   A. Code multiprograms simultaneously
   B. Do nothing different than normally
   C. Execute parallel modules concurrently
   D. Debug on-line modules and batch modules in concert

13. Surveys have indicated that not all data processing applications are completely successful and that a number do not contribute to the company objectives as well as they should. Reasons for this lack of success are most often attributed to the degree of:
   A. Equipment of technological inadequacies
   B. Source data creation

C. Top management support
D. Lack of programmer motivation

14. The organization has a critical on-line system up and working. It should:
A. Backup the on-line system with a duplicate on-line system.
B. Backup the on-line system with a parallel batch system.
C. Backup the on-line system with a copy at another organization only
D. Backup the on-line system and keep a copy on premises only

15. The basis for liquidating data processing installation expenses is usually:
A. Machine time used
B. Operator time required
C. Materials and supplies used
D. A rate that includes all of the above

16. An auditor is assisting with setting up a financial data processing application. He should:
A. Program an audit routine into the system
B. Specify the audits and controls necessary
C. Program a routine to check after-the-fact totals
D. Do nothing; an auditor's input is not required

17. The manager of data processing has the chiefs of his divisions or branches under his supervision. They are:
A. Line, staff, and administration
B. Systems analysis, programming, and operations
C. Personnel, logistics, and financial
D. Production and marketing

18. You are arranging a backup agreement with a firm across the city. You should agree to:
A. Ensure that the parallel equipment remains almost compatible
B. Provide prime shift test time to the other party
C. Provide operations management to the other party
D. Make no changes without coordination between you and the other party

19. Which of the following is not normally a direct responsibility of the data processing operations manager?
A. Computer scheduling
B. Planning computer applications
C. Maintaining a tape library
D. Supervising unit record operations

20. The data processing organizations is most participatory in company directions when it reports to:
A. The comptroller
B. The vice-presidential level
C. The finance and accounting manager
D. The presidential level

21. The time between the end of a reporting cycle and the availability of the output report is referred to as:
A. Setup time
B. Lag time
C. Output bound
D. Real time

22. A major advantage of a Gantt chart is the:
A. Scheduling of critical activities
B. Ability to make accurate estimates

C. Presentation of relative time projections
D. Ability to accomplish all milestones within projected time frames

23. Direct costs involved with producing a computer report include:
A. Forms, documentation, and computer maintenance
B. Computer, forms, and computer maintenance
C. Computer, operator, and forms
D. Forms, operator, and documentation

24. The effectiveness of an objective is determinable only by its
A. Preparation
B. Verification
C. Measurement
D. Review

25. Standards need to be formulated, developed, and accepted. They do not automatically exist in data processing. The principal organization concerned with establishing the voluntary acceptance of standards is:
A. USSA
B. NASA
C. NBS
D. ANSI

26. When an auditor has reviewed a system, he or she will issue:
A. An opinion
B. Review notes
C. Revised programming
D. Recapitulated documentation

27. An advantage of corporate data processing standards is that they:
A. Eliminate ''prima donna'' programmers
B. Increase maintainability
C. Allow software sections to be callable
D. Justify the selection of COBOL

28. When an employee is bonded, his or her management is testing his or her
A. Veracity and mendacity
B. Fiduciary responsibility
C. Financial position
D. Honesty and openness

29. Identifying the prescribing job functions and responsibilities is a function of data processing management best identified as part of:
A. Controlling
B. Directing
C. Organizing
D. Motivating

30. An application project has the following steps:
a. Examine the information
b. Pick the team
c. Obtain design approval
d. Prepare the design

The sequence in which the project should proceed from this list is:
A. a, b, c, d
B. b, a, c, d

C. b, a, d, c
D. d, c, b, a

31. During the planning phase of a project, the Project Manager is primarily responsible for:
A. Reprogramming to meet last-minute specification changes
B. Providing operational cost estimates
C. Training clerical personnel to operate the system
D. Using an estimating algorithm based on his work records

32. During the implementation phase of a project, the Project Manager is primarily responsible for:
A. Reprogramming to meet last-minute specification changes
B. Overseeing the details of training and experience
C. Training clerical personnel to operate the system
D. Estimating the installation time based on the lapsed time schedule

33. The data processing activity prepares a number of reports from a database. Another report from this same data base is being considered. When assessing this job and its costs, it is most likely to prove economically feasible when considered under the concept of:
A. Variable utility
B. Marginal utility
C. Marginal cost
D. Variable cost

34. Office Automation concepts should be of interest to DP management because:
A. DP must control personal computers
B. Office automation is information systems
C. Office automation cannot use computers
D. Office automation hasn't yet happened

35. Which of the following would probably *not* be a valid comment resulting from an internal control review of data processing?
A. Test data are not used to validate all new programs or major program modifications
B. Specific applications have not been run on off-site equipment using off-site files for input
C. A media librarian is not employed to control file movement
D. Personnel reassignment is not permitted among projects

36. Persons assigned to data processing operations
A. Have a high growth need strength and a high social need strength
B. Have a high growth need strength and a low social need strength
C. Have a low growth need strength and a high social need strength
D. Have a low growth need strength and a low social need strength.

37. Output products may become useless or of little value with the passage of time. In order to maintain reports that are useful it is advisable to:
A. Conduct a periodic reports survey
B. Discontinue all reports over one year old
C. Change the frequency of reports
D. Insert errors and see if they are caught

38. Persons assigned to programming sections
A. Have a high growth need strength and a high social need strength
B. Have a high growth need strength and a low social need strength
C. Have a low growth need strength and a high social need strength
D. Have a low growth need strength and a low social need strength

39. Two common approaches to scheduling a system design are the PERT and Gantt charts. The major advantage to PERT over Gantt is the:
A. Time-estimating algorithm

B. Task-dependency relationships
C. Ability to identify critical tasks
D. Location of slack time

40. Persons assigned to systems analysis activities often:
A. Have a high growth need strength and a high social need strength
B. Have a high growth need strength and a low social need strength
C. Have a low growth need strength and a high social need strength
D. Have a low growth need strength and a low social need strength

41. Procedures are established to assign job numbers for program identification to data processing applications. These numbers or identifications are used principally to:
A. File documentation
B. Log machine utilization
C. Arrange job sequence
D. Record card consumption

42. The motivation of data processing personnel
A. Is not possible, as this field defies motivation
B. Is not necessary, because they can motivate themselves
C. Is absolutely necessary, as they have none
D. Is not different from motivating any employee

43. The best way to provide a project progress report is:
A. Percentage completion based on the task list
B. Percentage completion based on a task difficulty index
C. Tasks completed
D. Dollars expended

44. Among the more important tasks when managing computer personnel is:
A. Task identity and significance
B. Autonomy
C. Feedback
D. Skills variety

45. The background information leading to the decision to acquire or convert to a new computer system is usually referred to as the:
A. Feasibility study
B. Computer selection process
C. Background investigation
D. Conversion

46. One of the most important management problems faced by a DP manager is:
A. A programmer's loyalty to the organization
B. A programmer's loyalty to the profession
C. An operator's loyalty to the organization
D. An operator's loyalty to the profession

47. When preparing resource schedules for the system design phase, the Project Manager would most likely assign resources based upon:
A. Guidelines developed in the preliminary study phase
B. Program specifications and file conversion methods developed by the system design team
C. Milestones and critical paths
D. Hardware delivery dates promised by vendors

48. Backlog is cited as a serious problem for five reasons: increasing complexity of systems, increasing quantity of systems, increasing maintenance cost, turnover, and
A. Low productivity

B. Shortage of qualified personnel
C. Low social need
D. High growth need

49. After the feasibility study has been put together, the next step is to:
A. Buy equipment
B. Obtain formal approval of the recommended decision from top management
C. Begin programming of applications
D. Design the most important data system

50. Management of the audit and control function is an obligation of the:
A. DP manager
B. EDP auditor
C. Control section
D. Testing analyst

51. The audit of computer operations would normally include:
A. Organization of the EDP department
B. Methods and procedures standards
C. Security
D. Forms suppliers

52. Distributed processing is a way to place:
A. Control upon user operations
B. Processing power in user operations
C. Programmers in user departments
D. Remote job entry sites wherever needed

53. PERT is concerned with variables in the job of completing a project. The one variable that is of the most concern to plan and schedule is:
A. Money
B. Time
C. Material
D. Machine utilization

54. The one thing a distributed processing situation absolutely cannot do without is a:
A. Communications network
B. Host computer
C. Remote job entry device
D. Co-located computer operator

55. One of the best approaches to the prevention of fraud in the data processing organization is:
A. The separation of duties among systems, programming, and operations
B. The consolidation of systems, programming and operations duties
C. The use of packaged software
D. The installation of an on-line real-time computer system

56. When managing a time-sharing service, the DP manager should monitor resource, CPU, and __________ usage.
A. I/O device
B. line
C. FECP (TCU)
D. NASDAC

57. Advantages gained are numerous; they include consistency of training, reduction in the adverse effects of personnel turnover, and less dependence on one individual. This technique or practice is the use of:
A. Standard operating procedures

B. Programming routines
C. Top management support
D. Centralization of authority

58. The project manager must have all the attributes of:
A. The programmers on the team
B. The analysts on the team
C. The top computer executive
D. Any middle-level manager

59. A feasibility study has been performed. It tells us of the advisability of developing a system, but need not include:
A. Costs and benefits
B. Detailed design plans
C. Problems of conversion and testing
D. Which data to use

60. Management, according to the text, is the art of:
A. Getting the job done
B. Appearing to have everything run smoothly
C. Getting work done through people
D. Running a system without the user's help

61. A sole source vendor has been preselected for EDP hardware. This was necessary because:
A. The vendor had the reputation for good equipment
B. The cost appeared less for this vendor
C. One vendor had exclusive capability for a vital process
D. It costs too much to put out numerous bid requests

62. The building of bridges between two systems most often happens when:
A. Two systems are running together
B. Two systems are running in parallel
C. A backup batch system is being built
D. An on-line system is being built

63. A project control system requires all *but* which of the following:
A. Objectives to be defined
B. Milestones to be established
C. A project reporting structure
D. A skills inventory

64. A communications-based system must have considerable:
A. Facility for transactions
B. Recovery capability
C. Tenacity of purpose
D. Capability of updates

65. A EDP systems proposal selection must rank criteria in some priority. Of first importance, the proposed system must:
A. Come within prescribed cost limitations
B. Be capable of doing the job
C. Be compatible to current systems
D. Meet the wishes of the employees

66. Systems which have an RS-232 connection are generally systems which have:
A. Parallel printing capability
B. Serial printing capability

C. Analog communications capability
D. Digital communications capability

67. Motivation of data processing personnel by management can best be achieved by:
A. Higher pay and benefits
B. Meeting security needs
C. Recognition and pride
D. Increased technical education

68. Ergonomics is the study of:
A. A unit of resistance measurement
B. The relationship of programs to systems
C. The relationship of people to machines
D. The physical positioning of equipment

69. A computer system has been selected, and the rental contract calls for extra shift charges. It is also possible to buy the equipment. Management is considering the lease/buy decision. The first consideration among those itemized is:
A. Multiple shift usage
B. Technical obsolescence
C. Residual value
D. Tax considerations

70. Environmental control is very important because:
A. Personal computers must have tight temperature control
B. High humidity causes static electricity
C. Low humidity causes static electricity
D. Mainframe computers require no temperature control

71. Which of the following is the least important consideration in the purchase of software?
A. The out-of-pocket cost of the software package
B. The operator's ability to run the package
C. The vendor's licensing rights to resell the package
D. The support which is available after purchase of the package

72. Hardware performance measurement is frequently done using
A. Poisson distributions
B. Markov chains
C. Histograms
D. Pie charts

73. Software systems designed to organize and control the application programs and use of the peripheral equipment are usually referred to as the:
A. Application system
B. Coordinating system
C. Operating system
D. Operations research

74. The cost of paper used for a large hard-copy report should be:
A. Absorbed by the DP Department
B. Conveyed to the user department
C. Conveyed with the charges for the report
D. Charged to operations

75. An audit of data processing operations should begin by reviewing:
A. Program run manuals
B. Program block diagrams, HIPO charts, and decision tables

C. Tape library and disaster procedures
D. Systems documentation

76. An example of a direct cost attributable to data processing operations would be:
A. Cost of ribbons
B. Cost of cleaning people
C. Cost of management
D. Cost of computer multiprogramming

77. Internal control concepts applied to the data processing environment include keeping:
A. Programmers from engaging in ''moonlighting'' jobs
B. Programmers and operators independent of each other
C. Operators from examining work records
D. Cash accounts in the machine room

78. The machine burden for a computer should be:
A. At least 100%
B. Less than 50%
C. Less than 100%
D. Less than 10%

79. The ''Pilot Installation'' is one form of conversion. It is most appropriate where:
A. The system is very complex or geographically dispersed
B. The system is simple and requires little or no conversion
C. The system involves only scientific programs
D. The system involves only business programs

80. The testing team should include:
A. Programmer, auditor, operator, and user
B. Programmer, analyst, auditor, and user
C. User, programmer, auditor, and operator
D. Operator, programmer, user, and auditor

81. Auditors should concern themselves with EDP systems:
A. From systems analysis aspects only
B. When called upon to do so
C. When errors or shortages occur
D. From systems design through implementation and operation

82. Programmer training is:
A. Not necessary once BASIC is learned
B. A never ending ongoing process
C. Necessary only when computer languages are changed
D. Necessary only when computer hardware is being changed

83. One item of concern for the data processing manager is fire protection. Which of the following statements is not true?
A. Fireproof vaults designed for documents are not adequate for magnetic media
B. Ionization can be activated by sources other than fire
C. Sprinkler systems are not suitable for data centers
D. H_2SO_4 will extinguish a fire more quickly than CO_2

84. The outstanding value of contract programming to an organization is that:
A. It is not necessary to hire full-time expertise in a narrow area
B. Contract programming is less expensive than in-house programming
C. In-house programming isn't as professionally done as contract programming
D. Contract programmers can't hold full time programming employment

85. Costs that clearly belong to a particular job and that also increase in proportion to the size or volume of the job can be said to be both:
A. Direct and variable
B. Indirect and invariable
C. Fixed and variable
D. Controllable and tangible

86. Vendor support bring with it a variety of services, including:
A. Operations personnel
B. Programmers
C. Training and manuals
D. Substitute management

87. The data control function should maintain a current log of activities. That log should be used for:
A. Receipt of data transactions from user departments
B. Routing of program decks or files to computer operators
C. Balancing columnar totals on output reports
D. Transmitting completed work back to the user

88. Management of systems software (operating systems and such) is frequently assigned to the:
A. DP manager only
B. Operations management
C. Database analyst
D. Key entry operations

89. Data processing management should participate in the planning prior to the renovation or construction of the facility except for:
A. Temperature and relative humidity specifications
B. Lengths of cable connecting DP components
C. Selection of the contractor to perform the job
D. Location of the master electrical switch

90. Successful management of the program maintenance activity can be accomplished by:
A. Increased salary
B. Extra compensatory time
C. A defined tour of duty
D. Permanent assignment

91. Which of the following is not a factor in the cost considerations of software?
A. Lease versus buy
B. Guarantee, warranty, or maintenance agreements
C. The confidential nature or integrity of the software programs
D. Current systems compatibility

92. The book introduces a Micro Systems Development Life Cycle which has a pseudocode phase. The purpose of the pseudocode phase is:
A. To detail logic in a native tongue
B. To provide input code to a pseudocode translator
C. To detail the logic in a narrative form
D. To dictate programs to tape recorders

93. The objective of duplication of data files for backup is to see that:
A. All data are being duplicated
B. Oldest files are kept off-site
C. Data are being duplicated accurately
D. Quick recovery is possible

94. The book introduces the concept of storyboarding. Storyboarding is:
  A. A new concept of pseudocoding
  B. A means of preparing a report mock-up
  C. A picture, in cartoon form, of the program
  D. A substitute for Nassi–Schneiderman charts

95. Evaluating the costs of lease versus purchase of equipment would be least concerned with:
  A. Tax considerations
  B. Maintenance
  C. Depreciation
  D. Costs of parallel or conversion runs

96. The model building aspect of the Microcomputer Systems Development Life Cycle prepares:
  A. The appearance of the final product
  B. The structure of the logic
  C. The sequence of the reports to be produced
  D. The output of sort processes

97. When changing computers, you should *not*:
  A. Run in emulation as long as practicable
  B. Convert all files possible on old computers
  C. Remove the older computers immediately so that all work can be processed on the new systems
  D. Start new applications in the native language of the new machine

98. And advantage of the driver program is:
  A. The confusion of traditional systems
  B. The open-ended design of the driver
  C. The shortened development time
  D. The machine efficiency of the driver

99. Which of the following is not an acceptable procedure for library standards?
  A. Requiring signatures to sign out tapes and disks
  B. Assigning one person to be responsible for the library
  C. Leaving tape files at the computer room and returning them to the library at the end of the shift
  D. Having supervisory personnel check periodically for conformance

100. Macro programming is a feature of the driver program which:
  A. Permits the specification of a report format
  B. Permits the specification of a free-standing process
  C. Permits the specification of input processes
  D. Permits the specification of documentation

ANSWERS

1. B	**11.** C	**21.** B	**31.** D
2. C	**12.** B	**22.** C	**32.** B
3. B	**13.** C	**23.** C	**33.** C
4. A	**14.** B	**24.** C	**34.** B
5. D	**15.** D	**25.** D	**35.** D
6. A	**16.** B	**26.** A	**36.** A
7. C	**17.** B	**27.** B	**37.** A
8. D	**18.** D	**28.** B	**38.** B
9. A	**19.** B	**29.** C	**39.** D
10. B	**20.** D	**30.** C	**40.** B

41. B	**56.** B	**71.** C	**86.** C
42. D	**57.** A	**72.** C	**87.** C
43. B	**58.** D	**73.** C	**88.** B
44. C	**59.** D	**74.** C	**89.** C
45. A	**60.** A	**75.** A	**90.** C
46. B	**61.** C	**76.** A	**91.** C
47. C	**62.** B	**77.** B	**92.** C
48. B	**63.** D	**78.** C	**93.** D
49. B	**64.** B	**79.** A	**94.** B
50. A	**65.** B	**80.** B	**95.** D
51. C	**66.** C	**81.** D	**96.** A
52. B	**67.** C	**82.** B	**97.** C
53. B	**68.** D	**83.** D	**98.** C
54. A	**69.** A	**84.** A	**99.** C
55. A	**70.** C	**85.** A	**100.** B

TUTORIAL

1. Experts agree that it is necessary to maintain the facility at approximately 68–76 degrees.
2. PERT is a project planning tool. Monte Carlo is a technique for risk-taking under uncertainty. Simplex is a method of linear programming. Queueing theory, on the other hand, will identify the demand and wait time for terminals. The answer is C.
3. Because the systems which were being developed served more than one user, the comptroller was no longer the predominant user.
4. Slack is the difference between the earliest possible date and the latest possible date an event may occur. If those dates are the same, slack is zero, and the event is said to fall on the critical path. A is correct.
5. For more information of this question, look at the explanation for Question 3.
6. The key is "logical access." The password allows controlled access to the entire system, assuming that it is handled correctly. The answer is A.
7. A benchmark application should have the same high-level language, which has been compiled into the machine's native language. The mix will be different anyway, and cannot be controlled.
8. Turnaround time is critical to the effective use of programmer time. D is the best answer. Honestly, however, it does promote carelessness.
9. Hopefully, this is a self-explanatory answer.
10. An event is the completion of all activities which immediately precede it, a point in time. The answer is B.
11. There will always be other concerns, of course, but certainly the schedule and a maintenance log should be required. The programming documentation doesn't belong there anyway. Output logs would be somewhat redundant—and would be a byproduct of the console log anyway.
12. The multiprogramming environment is a hardware operations environment—not a people environment. The answer is B.
13. It often happens that applications are constructed simply because there is top management leverage. Top management should be measured on their use of the computing resource every bit as much as they are measured on their use of other organizational resources.
14. The organization with no batch backup to an on-line system invites difficulty. The answer is B.
15. You will need to know all of these costs for a complete liquidation.
16. The auditor is not a programmer. He should specify auditing (security and control) functions and activities, practices and software. B is the answer.

17. These questions are just too easy. The minimal functions of at least a middle-sized installations would be systems analysis, programming, and operations.
18. One of the major requirements of any backup facility agreement is the agreement not to make significant changes in hardware or software without coordination. ''Almost compatible'' could very well mean ''not compatible.'' The answer is D. In addition, among the more successful of these agreements is the proviso that the opposite operations team train on and operate the computer operations for the other's applications. It works.
19. The planning of applications should fall to top management or to systems management—but the operations manager should have the responsibility to plan for the application's fit within the resources of time and cost—and to petition for additional resource, if necessary.
20. Hopefully it stands to reason that if you report to the top, you have a broader participation in company directions.
21. The effective date of the report could be the first of the month. The production date might be the fifth of the month. There is a lag time of five days to get this report.
22. The Gantt chart shows a task line across a time line. It may or may not have milestones. It leaves something to be desired for estimating. Critical activities are better plotted on a PERT chart, though they can be placed on the Gantt chart.
23. Direct costs mean those directly attributable to the running of the application itself.
24. The key is ''measurement,'' and you'll never know how effective your objectives are until they are measured.
25. The American National Standards Institute (ANSI) is the answer. The National Bureau of Standards (NBS) does get involved in some standards, but not DP. The USSA (United States Standards Association) doesn't exist. And NASA is that organization which never seems to get a launch off on time.
26. The key is ''opinion,'' or, if you will, the auditor's ''best professional judgment.''
27. The key to any such improvement is maintainability. Standardization begets maintainability. The other answers are absurd.
28. The answer is B. Bonding is a fiduciary insurance—not a test of honesty. All the other choices are extra-employee.
29. DP or any management, this is an organizing function.
30. Pick the team, examine the information, prepare the design, obtain design approval. To do it in another sequence might result in commitments you cannot keep.
31. The key to successful estimations are records kept of the prior projects of the estimator. Recognize that if such records are not kept, the estimate is no better than the roll of the dice.
32. When the system is about to be implemented, there is little of more importance than making sure that users know how to use the system. That is training and experience.
33. Marginal cost is the assessment of ''one more.'' In this case, the ''one more'' has to do with the accommodation of the next application without the acquisition of additional hardware.
34. Office automation is an extension of the information processing capabilities of the organization. They may not come under the direct control of the DP manager, but they are certainly under the logical support of the entire data processing activity.
35. There is no valid reason to have the program and system documentation available to operators. Everything else listed could fall within the responsibilty of operations personnel.
36. According to Couger and Zawacki, operations personnel have both a high GNS and SNS, as opposed to programming personnel who have a high GNS and a low SNS. Note, from the text, that there is some unhappiness in the operations ranks, however.
37. It would be nice to skip report distribution and see if the reports are missed, but you would be making a decision based on incomplete information. You do need to create an instrument which really defends the useful report.

38. According to Couger and Zawacki, programming personnel have a high GNS and and low SNS, as opposed to operations personnel who have a high GNS and a high SNS. The reason for this may be that the programmer obtains feedback from the program being developed.

39. If it is true that the critical path (which has no slack time) is the line along which tight management must be placed, then the slack time on parallel paths is the flexibility to place into that management activity.

40. According to Couger and Zawacki, systems personnel have a high GNS and and low SNS, as opposed to operations personnel who have a high GNS and a high SNS. The reason for this may be that the systems person is drawn from the ranks of programmers.

41. At first blush, it would seem to be useful to use this method to budget by functional area. However, the actual charge must be made on the basis of machine utilization.

42. There is no evidence to suggest that DP personnel need motivation any less than any other employee or that the needs and techniques are any different simply because of the nature of the work in which they are involved.

43. When done by a percentage basis, the figure could be meaningless, if the work were disproportionately distributed. Variations in task difficulty cause variations in the time used.

44. The common thread through any management situation is feedback as to the kind of job which is being done. Computer people need such feedback, particularly those in the systems and operations ranks.

45. Feasibility (advisability) study should have been the answer here, as it should be the initial investigation when a major change, such as acquiring a new computer, is undertaken.

46. An operator has far less flexibility than a programmer, and the programmer's loyalty to the profession rather than to the organization has been cited as a very important problem for DP manager.

47. A resource schedule is a plan for expenditure of the resource according to the project plan—milestones and critical paths.

48. There is a high turnover, and a very important shortage of qualified personnel from which to choose—exacerbating the turnover problem.

49. A finding is not the same as an approved plan. Gather your facts and get top management support and approval.

50. In the organizations large enough to have an audit and control function, responsibility of that activity falls to the DP manager. The EDP auditor needs to be aloof from the day-to-day operations.

51. There are many things to look for in a computer operations audit, but of those on the list, security is the best answer.

52. The basic idea of distributed processing is to place the computing power out in the user operations area. Sometimes there are programmers there and those programmers may use the remote job entry facilities inherent in the distributed processing system.

53. Time is the dimension best utilized by PERT. Other resources may affect time, and thereby affect PERT indirectly.

54. The distributed machine may be set up to work without an operator; it can operate without a host computer or RJE device. But it cannot function without a communications network.

55. One of the best ways of preventing fraud anywhere is the separation and isolation of duties. It's inflexible, but necessary.

56. Line usage is a very expensive commodity, and deserves extreme attention. I/O devices don't really need monitoring in this case. The FECP (TCU) could be clocked, but generally isn't for the same reason of the I/O device. NASDAC will monitor the usage of racing vehicles.

57. The use of standards has many, many benefits—use them and you'll certainly have top management support.

58. While it is useful for the project manager to have enough of a technical background to have an understanding of the project, it is also true that he or she needs of the traditional knowledge and skill of any middle-level manager in order to get the job done.

59. It's a bit premature to determine what data to use—which is somewhat analogous to selecting your brand of gasoline before purchasing your automobile. First things first.

60. The premise here is that a manager is a person who is responsible for more work than he or she can physically do—requiring that the work must be done through people. It's not a DP management-only concept—but is very applicable.

61. The answer is certainly a valid answer. Let's also be realistic enough to recognize that it happens for a number of reasons, not the least of which is that the equipment maintenance personnel are good.

62. One of the most important reasons for building bridges is to allow the user to be able to duplicate the results of the old system with the output of the new system, when the outputs are not precisely the same. This is normally done during the times of parallel processing.

63. A skills inventory is generally a personnel system, not a project control system.

64. An on-line, communications-based system must have an inordinate amount of backup and recovery capability—including portions of the system which are duplicated in batch mode—should it happen to fail irrecoverably.

65. The best, most economical, compatible, and desirable of systems is worthless if it is incapable of doing the work.

66. Analog communications are a function of the RS-232 and a modem, and that was the best answer. In some cases, a serial printer can be made to operate on the RS-232.

67. It works for non-data processing people; if fact, it works for anyone.

68. Somebody is certain to claim that ergonomics is the relationship of people to machines—it is, except that we're talking is a physical sense.

69. There are many things to be considered, including the financial questions like the cost of money. Technical obsolescence doesn't enter this question—neither do the accounting things—but costs of multiple shift usage become a very critical part of the operational planning for the devices.

70. Personal or mainframe, static electricity is the enemy of computers and data (and stings for the people, as well), and is often caused by low humidity in the air.

71. It is very difficult to go out of the DP business (with a specific vendor, for example) without losing your shirt. Even with a personal computer, the licensing agreements preclude you from selling software.

72. Any hardware performance software will prepare histograms of usage. A and B are statistical techniques. D is a presentation technique.

73. It's an operating system—and in addition to your own operating system, you were advised that you would quite possibly encounter MS-DOS, CP/M, and UNIX.

74. We don't know from the question for whom the report has been prepared. The charge, then, should accompany the report.

75. Auditors frequently wish to know how something is supposed to operate and to use that as a basis for comparison against how it actually operates. There is good reason to keep documentation up to date.

76. A ribbon is a better example of a direct cost than the others. D has a ring of truth, except we're talking about other programs. Management could be either direct or indirect, depending upon how applied. Even as a direct cost, it would be difficult to apportion economically. What generally happens is that costs of ribbons, and other supplies as well, are factored into the direct cost.

77. Just as it is that the bookkeeper is not the same person as the one who handles the cash register, the programmers and operators must be kept independent of the other—else strange things can happen to accounts and records, to say nothing of special priorities given to nonorganizational work.

78. You'll have to find the best mix of applications which provide the best burden percentage for your own organization—but 85% seems a reasonable figure.

79. The pilot is generally a new application and not a copy of a system which had a prior existence. It is generally wise to debug it at one location rather than 50.

80. The programmer who wrote the program, the systems analyst who designed the system, the auditor who specified the controls, and the user who must operate the system should all be part of the testing team.

81. An auditor should have specified the controls, and should verify the veracity of those controls, all the way from the time the system is designed through—and possibly after—the installation and operation of the system.

82. There's always something new—this field is hardly static. Training is a never ending, ongoing process, and if the organization isn't doing it, a measure of the professionalism of the programmer is whether he is doing it for himself.

83. H_2SO_4 is sulfuric acid—it doesn't extinguish fire.

84. If I need a program on linear programming expressions and I need only one program, rather than hire to meet that need, I should obtain the services of a contract programmer. The cost will be slightly higher, but it will not be an ongoing process.

85. Those costs which vary with the process are direct.

86. Vendor services include training and manuals—experience, specialized software, etc.

87. One of the purposes of the data control function is to prove output from the computer to any manual records or totals which may exist.

88. More frequently we are finding that the software types are being assigned to the operations activity.

89. The responsibility of the DP manager ends with the preparation of the specifications. Selection of the vendor belongs to another department.

90. Increased money would certainly be an incentive, and is often overlooked as a means to balance a boring work assignment. Permanent assignment would take a special sort of person to accept. Compensatory time probably isn't enough of a motivator. But . . . tell that person the precise day the maintenance assignment is over, and the assignment will be accepted willingly.

91. Confidentiality is not a cost consideration—memory protection might be.

92. Pseudocode permits you to detail the logic in narrative form—hopefully in a native language.

93. Grandfather-father-son rotation and duplication are for recovery from archives. There is no other valid purpose.

94. Not only mock-ups of reports, but also screens and file layouts.

95. The first three answers are accounting considerations. The last is an operational cost, and not of consideration when evaluating lease/purchase options.

96. The analyst and user sit down and prepare a model which is the appearance of the final product.

97. Hang onto the old computers until you're sure the new ones work. You need that safety decision—but limit its time so it doesn't become a crutch.

98. Drivers may seem to be open ended, but are not. But they do save a considerable amount of development time.

99. When the tape is finished, get it back into the vault, and away from the proximate cause of any incindiary activity.

100. The idea of the macro programming is to automate the driver program to work with another integrated program.

EXAMINATION SECTION 4

5
QUANTITATIVE METHODS
Accounting

For the many of you who have worked through the hours of business courses in search of the knowledge of the way business operates, this treatise on accounting will seem woefully inadequate. For those who have not had that exposure, this section will be simple enough to stand you in good stead for the examination. The knowledge you will really need lies somewhere between.

If you're old enough to have a specific reason to read this chapter, you are somehow involved in the practice of business, be it corporate, partnership, sole proprietorship, or wage earner. To that extent, then, you are a business person by avocation, if not by vocation. This chapter concentrates on the business practices of corporations, partnerships, and sole proprietorships. By and large the majority of us are wage earners and must deal with corporations. The other two, however, are a part of our personal lives. Each of us is a business entity.

How so? If you are married, then you are a partner in a co-partnership. You find this out for certain every April 15th. If you are single, then you are a sole proprietorship. To the extent that you are a co-partner or a sole proprietor, then you are in a business for yourself.

Every business, be it personal or corporate, exists for a specific purpose. It develops, produces, sells, provides, or otherwise transmits something. To the extent that it obtains sufficient income to exceed its expenditures, then that business is said to be solvent. Despite the fact that there always seems to be so much of the month left at the end of the money, it's a plain fact that a corporate or personal business cannot survive for long by spending more than it takes in. In other words, by not making a profit (savings) or at least breaking even, the business entity is in jeopardy.

Let's examine this personal business in which you are involved. You have *assets*:

1. One of those assets is a commodity known as *cash.* Cash can exist as two specific types, cash-in-hand and cash-in-bank.
   a. Where you have cash-in-hand, it most probably is contained in your wallet, purse, or in the cookie jar. It is said to be the most *liquid,* in that if you were to gather it all up venture out, you would be able to exchange (purchase) for some item or commodity.
   b. You have cash-in-bank (excluding safe deposit boxes, which is considered to be cash-in-hand) when the ownership of your cash remains with you, but the utility of your cash has been exchanged for some specific reason or service. This may be of one or two types:
      (1) Your checking account, commonly called a *demand deposit,* wherein you exchange the liquidity of your funds for the security of the bank's transmittal mechanisms. In this instance, your cash-in-bank is liquid only to the extent that the payee of your check is willing to accept your draft in lieu of legal tender. The bank, in this instance, makes money on your money, meeting only what is required as a reserve requirement against the demand deposit.
      (2) Interest-bearing accounts, such as savings, escrow, or Christmas Club accounts. For the ability to use your money, the bank pays you a dividend known as *interest,* say at 6%, while they turn around and lend it out at 14%, making money for the bank on what is

known as the *spread.* The interest-bearing accounts are also demandable, with accrued interest, upon withdrawal. They are only slightly less liquid than pure cash, and may be treated as cash. Certificates of deposit, all-savers certificates, individual retirement accounts (IRAs) and other accounts with time constraints differ from this definition only slightly in that the demandability is restricted until the account is due, with penalties incurred upon early withdrawal.

2. Another of your assets is known as *plant and equipment.* Plant and equipment assets (often called *fixed assets*) are depreciable; that is, their values are reduced through use or over time.
   a. If you own an automobile, it is a depreciable asset. Generally, it is depreciated about a third when you drive it out of the showroom (it's then a "used" car) and continues to depreciate, as miles are accumulated or years pass. (Automobiles are depreciable for tax purposes only if they are used for business purposes).
   b. If you own a house, it is a depreciable asset in that its utility is consumed. Many homes have *appreciated* in recent years, but the appreciation is a function of the value of the land more than the value of the building. Market forces—supply and demand—control the market price, along with inflation, the cost of selling, etc. If you own a home in which you live, it cannot be depreciated for tax purposes. If you own rental property, however, you can depreciate the property for tax purposes irrespective of what happens to the value of the property itself.
   c. Equipment—your furniture, etc.—are also depreciating devices.
   d. Any of these items depreciate in value, but not necessarily for tax purposes, unless that asset also is a part of an operating business.
3. You have other assets as well. Included in these may be bonds, insurance, inventory, and specialized tools.
4. Inventory, you say? Yes, inventory. Assuming that you are a person who eats, then you consume goods which you have purchased and stored, perhaps in the cupboard, pantry, freezer, or refrigerator.
5. But what do you sell? What is your product? What is your source of revenue? Simply stated, service—labor, be it physical or intellectual. If you work for a wage, then you are selling your services.

FINANCIAL STATEMENTS

The Balance Sheet

The "asset side of the ledger" is also called the asset element of a Balance Sheet, one of the principal financial documents of a corporation. Consider Figure 5.1.

Note the format of the balance sheet. Note the positioning of the dollar signs, always at the head of any given column. Note the intermediate totals where they are appropriate. And note that the final total is double-ruled, a standard accounting practice.

The $1.00 figure for Goodwill is not reflective of its worth, just recognition of its existence. In this case, Ken's Goodwill is worth just as much as that accounted for by the country's largest company—General Motors.

Now let's look at the other side of the Balance Sheet. Two categories of items are contained therein, known as *liabilities* and *ownership* (sometimes referred to as "proprietorship"). If you have ever had to pay a bill for your rent, telephone, utilities, or charge accounts, you're aware that generally those bills are payable "on demand." Using the carrot and stick approach, those to whom you owe money will provide an incentive if you pay early (discounts, perhaps) or get downright nasty if you fail to pay or are not very prompt in payment (penalties, service charges). Some of these *payables* are due in a specific

Ken's Personal Business
Balance Sheet
as of December 31, 19xx

Assets		
Current Assets		
Cash	$xx,xxx.xx	
Cash in checking	xx,xxx.xx	
Cash in savings	xx,xxx.xx	
Prepaid insurance	xxx.xx	
Wages receivable	x,xxx.xx	
Inventory	xxx.xx	
Total current assets		$xxx,xxx.xx
Fixed Assets		
Land	$xx,xxx.xx	
Plant and Equipment	xx,xxx.xx	
Total fixed assets		xxx,xxx.xx
Intangible Assets		
Goodwill		1.00
Total Assets		$xxx,xxx.xx

Figure 5.1. Balance Sheet, left side of equation.

time frame, and if that time frame is within one year, they are said to be a *current payable,* or more specifically, a *current liability.*

Sometimes it's necessary to make a purchase "on time" (such as an automobile) or to otherwise obtain the use of someone else's money, generally paying extra for the privilege. Thus, you have a *note payable,* or long-term debt. (With a note payable, there will always be a part of it due within one year, which is technically a current liability.)

Together, short-term and long-term indebtedness make up the liability element of the Balance Sheet, but you'll recall that there is another element—ownership. We all think that we "own" our own homes or automobiles. In fact, we share ownership of those items with a bank or some other financial institution (unless the asset is free of encumbrances). Over time, our specific ownership increases proportionately as we make payments, until the title to the asset passes into our control. We gain increasing ownership in an asset which is decreasing in value. At any point, however, we have a commodity known as *net worth,* that is, if we subtract what we owe from what we have, what we have left over is our ownership in our personal business. Hopefully, we owe less than the worth of our assets, so our ownership is a positive absolute number. Where we owe more than we have, however, it may well be a negative absolute number. We would then be what is termed "in debt" or technically insolvent. In any event, if we combine

```
                 Ken's Personal Business
                      Balance Sheet
                 as of December 31, 19xx

Liabilities

Current Liabilities

    Charge Accounts                     $xxx.xx
    Utilities                             xx.xx
                                        -------
        Total Current Liabilities                     $xxx.xx

Long-Term Debt
    Home Loan                        $xx,xxx.xx
    Auto Loan                          x,xxx.xx
                                     ----------
        Total Long-Term Debt                         xx,xxx.xx

Ownership                                           xxx,xxx.xx
Total Liabilities and Ownership                    $xxx,xxx.xx
                                                   ===========
```

Figure 5.2. Balance Sheet, right side of equation.

ownership and liabilities, the two categories should be equal to our assets. So,

$$\text{Assets} = \text{Liabilities} + \text{Ownership}$$

This is known as the *accounting formula.* Consider Figure 5.2.

And, of course, this final figure should be equal to the total struck at the end of the Asset side of the Balance Sheet. The same rules of format apply here as well.

Before progressing, let's review the salient points of a Balance Sheet, using Figures 5.3 and 5.4. The "as of" date will be the closing date of the period covered in the report.

Notes to Figures 5.3 and 5.4:

(1) These are assets which are either cash or convertible to cash within one year.
(2) These are the more permanent tangible assets which could be converted to cash, but would probably take more than one year.
(3) These are the capitalized assets which have resale value but no physical quality.
(4) These are the items on which payment is due within one year.
(5) These are the items on which payment will exceed one year.
(6) These are the entries which represent the interest in the business by the owners of the corporation.

Note that this statement didn't differ significantly from that of a personal business.

Of course, the Balance Sheet exists in aggregate; that is, it is a collection of accounts. Accounts Receivable, for instance, is a collection of all accounts receivable which are receivable by the corporation. Thus, if the corporation were to accumulate a pile of invoices (an invoice is what your company has billed to its customer), the aggregate total of that pile of invoices would be equal to the total reflected on

Gizmo Corporation
Balance Sheet
as of December 31, 19xx

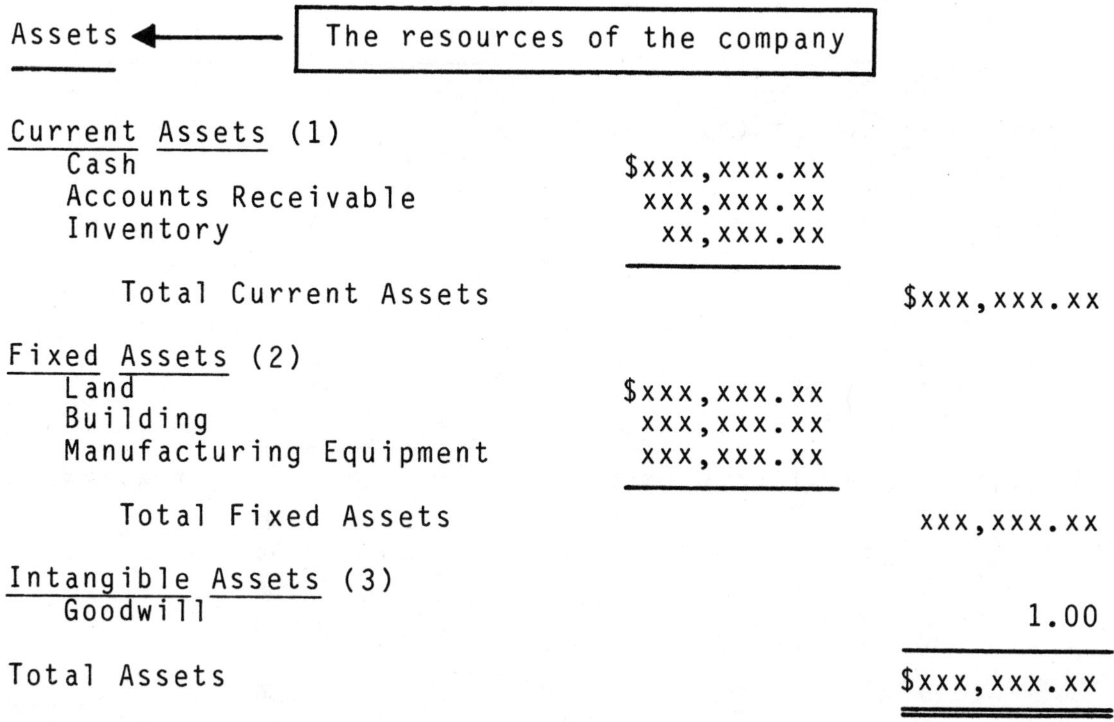

Assets ← The resources of the company		
Current Assets (1)		
Cash	$xxx,xxx.xx	
Accounts Receivable	xxx,xxx.xx	
Inventory	xx,xxx.xx	
Total Current Assets		$xxx,xxx.xx
Fixed Assets (2)		
Land	$xxx,xxx.xx	
Building	xxx,xxx.xx	
Manufacturing Equipment	xxx,xxx.xx	
Total Fixed Assets		xxx,xxx.xx
Intangible Assets (3)		
Goodwill		1.00
Total Assets		$xxx,xxx.xx

Figure 5.3

the Balance Sheet. Thus an entry on the Balance Sheet may be either a single account (e.g., Goodwill), or a collection of accounts (e.g., Accounts Payable). *Current Liabilities,* by the way, are frequently referred to as *Accounts Payable.*

In our personal business, we generally deal with a form of account known as single-entry bookkeeping. Generally there is a set of singular chronicles which permit us to keep track of what transpires. On the asset side, we keep checkbooks, passbooks, or bond and stock certificates. On the liability side, we keep payment books with tearable coupons, or simply a collection of or list of payments we must make. At any time, we can sort out asset accounts and liability accounts into separate piles on the dining room table, and go from there. The checkbook is the tying document. It *does not* tell us what we have due or what is owed, but those data are easily listed, assuming the bills have been received (or whose value is known) and the receivables are also known. We don't generally worry about ownership until we wish to sell some asset or must detail our net worth in order to get a loan.

T-Accounts

The checkbook is the tie between accounts receivable and accounts payable, but generally after the fact, when the accounts are received and when the accounts are paid. In other words, the checkbook functions as a *journal* of transactions, and the account always exists *in net.*

Suppose that you had sufficient sources of income that required you to list them in order to keep track. Say, for instance, you owned rental property, and you kept a mini-ledger on each of your tenants. You would then keep track of what is due, in installments, over the period of a year, against the value of

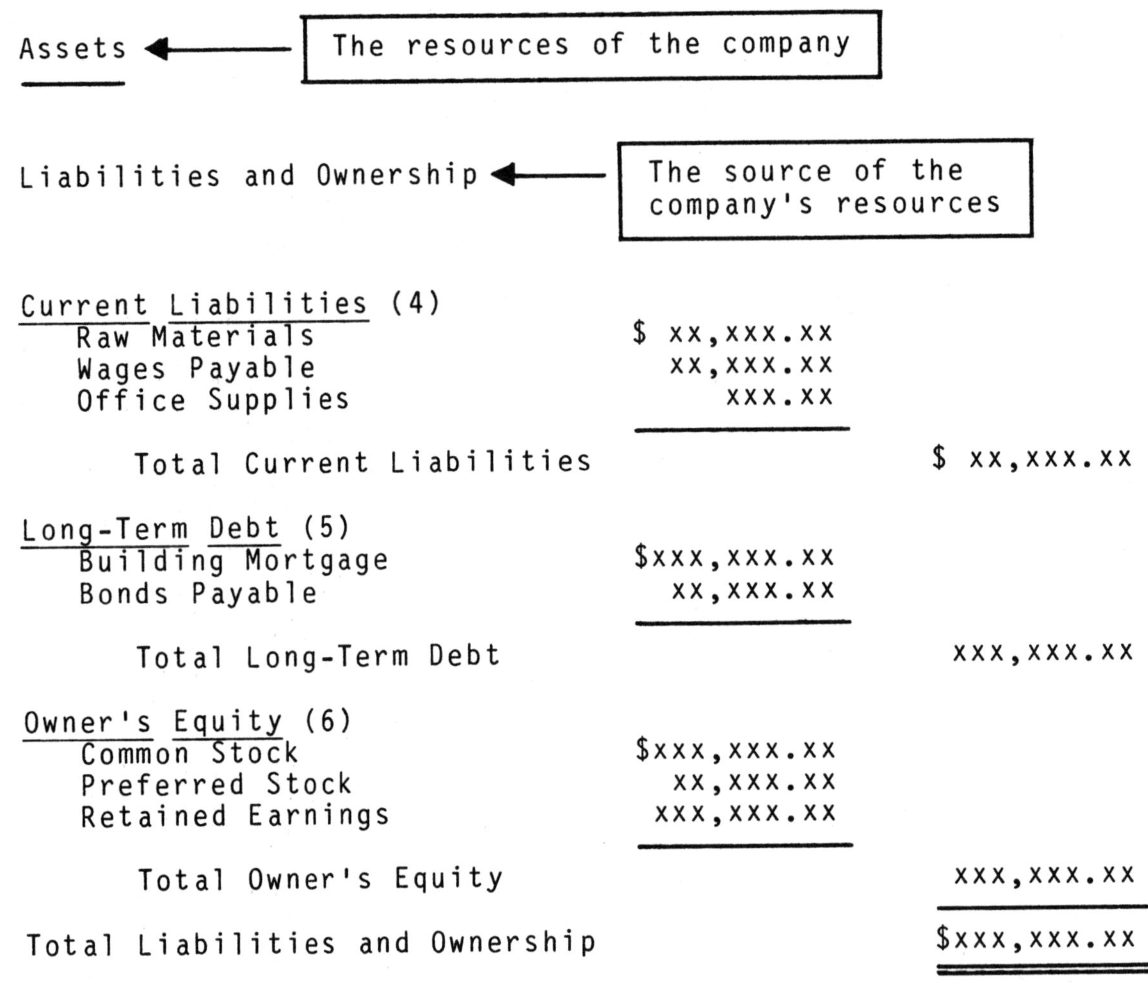

Current Liabilities (4)		
Raw Materials	$ xx,xxx.xx	
Wages Payable	xx,xxx.xx	
Office Supplies	xxx.xx	
Total Current Liabilities		$ xx,xxx.xx
Long-Term Debt (5)		
Building Mortgage	$xxx,xxx.xx	
Bonds Payable	xx,xxx.xx	
Total Long-Term Debt		xxx,xxx.xx
Owner's Equity (6)		
Common Stock	$xxx,xxx.xx	
Preferred Stock	xx,xxx.xx	
Retained Earnings	xxx,xxx.xx	
Total Owner's Equity		xxx,xxx.xx
Total Liabilities and Ownership		$xxx,xxx.xx

Figure 5.4

a lease. Suppose that the value of the lease is $1,200, obtainable in $100 increments each month. Thus, you might record in an account the $1,200 like this:

Rent Receivable		Cash	
Dr	Cr	Dr	Cr
1200			

"Dr" is the abbreviation for *Debit.* It is the column used when adding to an asset account. "Cr" is the abbreviation for *Credit.* It is used when subtracting from an asset account. A full explanation of debits and credits will follow. Thus, the payment of one month's rent would cause your accounts to change like this:

Rent Receivable		Cash	
Dr	Cr	Dr	Cr
1200	100	100	

Note that the Rent Receivable account exists with a balance due of $1,000 in net. Not until it is necessary to transfer the figures to another format or at the end of a time period are the elements totalled, and the net carried forward. This is called the *T-account.* Its function is basic to accounting.

The Income Statement

Back to our personal business. Each April 15th, each of us must make a report to the Government detailing what we have earned, what we may deduct (such as interest, contributions, and medical expense), what our exemptions are, and then compute a tax according to a table system, on the net. In essence, we have prepared what the accountant calls an *Income Statement.* The Income Statement is also one of a corporation's prime financial documents, and is also known by the title *Profit and Loss Statement* (*P&L*). An income statement for a personal business would look like Figure 5.5.

Note that the sources of income are shown first on the statement, followed by deductions, or exemptions, from that income, giving net income. This, then, produced a *net revenue* figure, which was taxable. From that figure a tax was determined and subtracted, leaving a post-tax income. Hopefully, this number was positive, in which case it was a *profit.* Had it been negative, we would have experienced a *loss.* Negative or loss figures are customarily shown in parentheses, e.g., (loss).

The question arises as to where the figure derived will show up on the financial statements. To begin with, the term *profit* is not to be confused with the term *cash.* It is very possible to have made a profit and not have that specific amount available as cash.

Things *increased* in a year's operations must also be shown on the Balance Sheet. On the asset side of the ledger, those profits could show up as cash, investments, fixed assets, or even some form of intangible assets. If you happen to have produced a loss, then the loss would be reflected as a decrease in one of those assets, owing to the type of liquidity represented in the Income Statement. If, for instance, you had obtained some item of equipment for which you would pay over time (long-term debt), only that portion which represented a *current liability* could be charged off to the expense of doing business. But the item had been purchased. It has to be reflected somewhere. Thus, part of that profit has been plowed

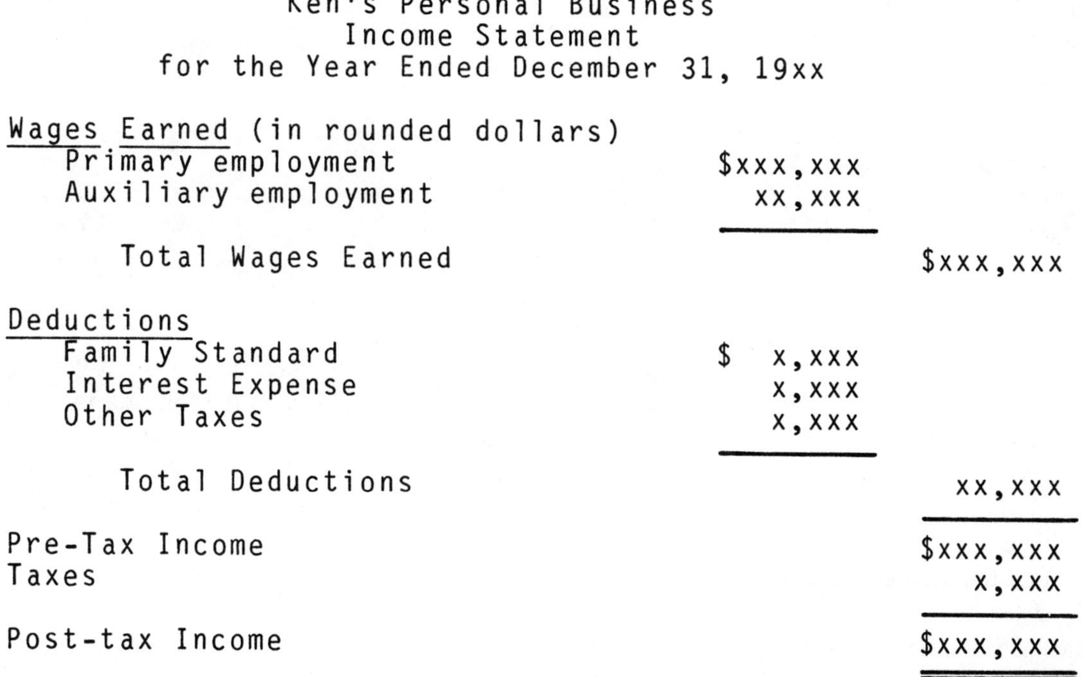

Ken's Personal Business
Income Statement
for the Year Ended December 31, 19xx

Wages Earned (in rounded dollars)		
Primary employment	$xxx,xxx	
Auxiliary employment	xx,xxx	
Total Wages Earned		$xxx,xxx
Deductions		
Family Standard	$ x,xxx	
Interest Expense	x,xxx	
Other Taxes	x,xxx	
Total Deductions		xx,xxx
Pre-Tax Income		$xxx,xxx
Taxes		x,xxx
Post-tax Income		$xxx,xxx

Figure 5.5. Income Statement.

Gizmo Corporation
Income Statement
for the year ended December 31, 19xx (1)

Sales (2)			
Gross Sales	$xxx,xxx		
Less Returns	xx,xxx		
Net Sales			$xxx,xxx
Cost of Goods Sold (3)			
Raw Materials	$xxx,xxx		
Direct Labor	xx,xxx		
Indirect Labor	x,xxx		
Total Cost of Goods Sold		$xxx,xxx	
Operating Expenses (4)			
Fixed costs	$ xx,xxx		
Administrative	xx,xxx		
Sales	xx,xxx		
Inventory shrinkage	xx,xxx		
Total Operating Expenses		xxx,xxx	
Total Costs			xxx,xxx
Pre-Tax Income (5)			$xxx,xxx
Taxes(6)			
Federal	$ xx,xxx		
State	xx,xxx		
Local property	xx,xxx		
Total Taxes			xxx,xxx
Post-Tax Income (7)			$xxx,xxx

Figure 5.6. Income Statement.

into permanent assets. For those assets, you might have a long term liability, or perhaps if you had paid for the asset outright, you might distribute it on the asset side of the ledger in the form of a write-off known as *Depreciation.* Depreciation is a *contra-asset.* It reduces the value of the asset.

The other option is to plow the profit (loss) into some form of ownership. Specifically it would fit into a category called *Retained Earnings*; depreciation methods and retained earnings will be discussed later in this chapter.

Consider the Income Statement of Figure 5.6.

Notes to Figure 5.6:

(1) Note that a specific time frame is covered in this report.

(2) Gross Sales will include all items which are revenue- producing for the firm.

(3) Cost of Goods Sold will normally be distributed among major items, grouped among minor items; it generally includes the variable costs attributable to the product.
(4) Operating expenses will also be distributed among major categories, with minor categories being grouped. The group distributions of both kinds of costs are generally for the purpose of cost control.
(5) What the government will expect to receive its taxes upon.
(6) What the government, at all applicable levels, will receive.
(7) What you will have left over to add to your business for the following year.

Conceptually, a corporate income statement isn't terribly different in format and contents from an income statement for personal business. And if you look at it closely, you'll find that it's not terribly different in content from the income tax form you file every year. Again, the Income Statement, or Profit and Loss Statement, is a critical statement of experience on the part of the corporation.

Statement of Retained Earnings

Retained earnings is a form of corporate ownership. Corporate ownership can be in one of three forms—stock, bonds, and self-ownership. Yes, a corporation can own itself. From the Retained Earnings account, a corporation can pay dividends on stock, premiums on bonds, or simply carry self-ownership from year to year.

The Retained Earnings Statement (Figure 5.7) is one form of *Capital Statements.* Other forms of capital statement would include stocks and bonds. More about capital statements follows.

Notes to Figure 5.7:
(1) The statement is for a specific time period—the same as the income statement.
(2) A beginning balance, the same as the final balance from the report of a year before or from the Balance Sheet.
(3) This is the figure added as a result of the Income Statement—the post-tax figure.
(4) See the explanation below.
(5) This represents the amount of reinvestment in the business as of the close of the reporting period.

Note on declared dividends: Perhaps it seems that the existence of a Dividends Declared category as a separate category on the statement conflicts with what was said previously. Dividends are not necessarily distributed with the close of the financial year. They may be distributed at any time during the year. But the retained earnings account is the pool from which dividends are drawn, and from which potential dividends may be drawn in the succeeding period.

```
                 Gizmo Corporation
          Statement of Retained Earnings
     for the year Ended December 31, 19xx(1)

Retained Earnings (2), January 1, 19xx            $xxx,xxx
    Add: Net Income (3) for the year 19xx          xxx,xxx
    Less: Dividends Declared (4) during 19xx       xxx,xxx
                                                  --------
Retained Earnings (5), December 31, 19xx          $xxx,xxx
                                                  ========
```

Figure 5.7. Retained Earnings statement.

Statements Summary

These are the prime statements of financial position of a corporation. The Retained Earnings statement, while it has no easy counterpart in a personal business, is nonetheless valuable in determining the investment potential of the firm. To whom do these statements have value?

1. They have great value to owners and shareholders in determining how their investments have been managed by corporate management.
2. Creditors and suppliers will wish to have access to these documents if they are in a position which requires the extension of credit. By law, these statements must be recorded with the State and as such are public documents.
3. Management will wish to have these to use as a progress bellwether, and to provide the basis for future planning.
4. Government, for obvious reasons.

The Same with Substance

Now that we've taken a cursory look at the Balance Sheet, Income Statement, and Retained Earnings Statement, let's go back and add substance to the skeleton. The entire Balance Sheet for the Gizmo Corporation for the year 19xx is given in Figure 5.8. Included are some categories of asset and liability which have not been previously described. On this balance sheet are a few new categories, such as uncollectable accounts, marketable securities, stocks, bonds, etc. For any total which appears on the balance sheet, there would probably be another statement detailing how the total was derived. Retained earnings is one example, but a statement of inventory could also exist to back up the inventory amount presented on the balance sheet. The same is true for any total.

This is a Balance Sheet in its entirety. Note that the ownership category has been changed to *Net Worth.* Many accounts carry multiple names and to some degree these names can be used interchangeably, depending upon the grouping beneath the title. Another name for ownership is Capital. There are differences which determine why a specific title is chosen, dependent upon the accountant's interpretation.

Debits and Credits

On the Balance Sheet, the assets are reflective of data coded on the debit (Dr) side of the T-account. The liabilities, on the other hand, as well as the other elements of the bottom (or right) side of the balance sheet, are reflective of data which resides on the credit (Cr) side of the T-account.

Recall from the rent illustration that the Rent Receivable decreased by $100 and the Cash increased by the same amount. This entire transaction was done on one side of the balance sheet (let's think of assets as ''left'' and liabilities and ownership as ''right'' from here on). The accounting formula (Assets = Liabilities plus Ownership) has not been disturbed; it is still in balance. Because funds were ''transferred'' between accounts, it was necessary to credit (take away) one account in order to debit (add to) the other. But there was an original entry made, which could have also placed the $1,200 on the ownership side of the equation. The original entry had to look like Figure 5.9.

Based on this, it can be seen that the *increment* of an account is a debit on the asset side of the ledger, while it is a credit on the liability and ownership side of the ledger. A *decrement* is a credit on the asset side of a debit on the liability side. To summarize:

A *debit* signifies:
An increase in asset accounts

Gizmo Corporation
Balance Sheet
as of December 31, 19xx

Current Assets			
Cash		$ 22,360	
Marketable Securities		34,050	
Accounts Receivable	$215,420		
Allowance for uncollectable accounts	(11,065)		
Net Accounts Receivable		204,355	
Inventory		114,400	
Prepaid Expenses		13,265	
Total Current Assets			$388,430
Fixed Assets			
Land		30,500	
Plant and Equipment	$542,680		
Accumulated Depreciation	(181,810)		
Net Fixed Assets		360,870	
Total Fixed Assets			$391,370
Intangibles			
Goodwill			3,000
Total Assets			$782,800
Current Liabilities			
Bank Loans	$ 30,000		
Accounts Payable	58,215		
Accrued Expenses and Taxes	35,435		
Total Current Liabilities		$126,650	
Long-Term Liabilities			
Debenture Bonds		150,000	
Total Liabilities			$273,650
Net Worth			
Preferred Stock $100 par 7% cumulative, non-callable	$ 75,000		
Common Stock no par $1 stated value, authorized 150,000 shares, issued and outstanding 75,000 shares	75,000		
Capital in excess of stated value	375,169		
Treasury Stock -- at cost	(75,169)		
Retained Earnings	59,150		
Total Net Worth		$509,150	
Total Liabilities and Net Worth			$782,800

Figure 5.8

```
Rent Receivable                    Ownership
_______________________            _______________________
Dr          | Cr                   Dr          | Cr
$1,200      |                                  | $1,200
```

Figure 5.9

A decrease in liability accounts
A decrease in capital accounts

A *credit* signifies:
A decrease in asset accounts
An increase in liability accounts
An increase in capital accounts

Two terms which have been used are *accounts* and *ledger.* In simple terms, the latter contains the former. Depending on the use, one ledger may contain several accounts, but there will be at least one account for every ledger. A ledger is a book of original entry.

An exception to this is one ledger called the *general ledger,* or sometimes the *general journal,* or just *journal.* The general ledger is a book of account which details the transactions which affect all other ledgers and accounts. Entries which modify all other ledgers or accounts are serialized in the sequence of their receipt. Thus, the general journal entry which documented the payment of $100 on the rent receivable would have looked like Figure 5.10.

Here are recorded two journal entries. The first dealt with the *original* entry which established the receivable. The second detailed the first *transaction* against the account, which transferred one month's rent into the cash column. Observe the following about these entries:

1. They are *dated.* The journal is a book of *original entry,* and as such will be of great interest to any auditor.
2. They identify which accounts are affected, *detailing the debit account first,* and then detailing the credit account. The dollar signs have been included here but would not be required on ledger paper.
3. There is a complete explanation of the transaction, written concisely, but fully applicable.

```
                  Gizmo Corporation
                   General Journal

1/1/xx   Rent Receivable              $1200
           Ownership                              $1200

         Establishing the receivable for Ken's rent


1/1/xx   Cash                         $ 100
           Rent Receivable                        $ 100

         Recording the payment of rent by Ken
         for the month of January, 19xx
```

Figure 5.10

```
1/1/xx  Rent Receivable                 $1200
        Cash                              100
             Rent Receivable                          $ 100
             Ownership                                 1200

        This journal entry establishes the receivable
        for one year's rent for Ken and for the payment
        of rent for January, 19xx.
```

Figure 5.11

```
2/1/xx  Cash                          $10
        Accounts Receivable (Ken)      90
           Inventory                          $100

        Purchase on time of one gizmo by Ken;
        deposit of $10 made; balance in nine
        equal payments of $10 each.
```

Figure 5.12

Each of the three accounts—Cash, Ownership, and Rent Receivable—in its own ledger, would have similar entries to explain the transaction. When there are *multiple* asset accounts to be changed, or multiple liability accounts to be changed, the entries can be journalized in a single motion, as shown in Figure 5.11.

The net result would have been the same, but something would have been lost in the process. In addition to journalizing the transactions, the general journal also functions as a type of control mechanism. So, in this case, the combination would not have been wise. In the following example, however, it would have been different.

In the former example, there might well have been two transactions—one when the lease was signed, and the other when the first payment was actually made. But in the latter, the entire transaction is consummated at a single time. Two assets accounts (cash and accounts receivable) have been debited and one asset account has been credited (inventory). Thus it can be seen that T-account transactions can happen on either side of the ledger by itself or on both sides of the ledger simultaneously.

Definitions

It would be impossible in this chapter to list each and every kind of asset, liability, or ownership and classify it. But a general set of definitions will be useful.

Assets

An asset is any specific thing (tangible) or right (intangible) owned that has a monetary value. It generally appears in two categories—current assets and fixed (plant) assets.

Current assets are those that may be converted into cash, or sold, or consumed within one year or less. Types of current assets include:

1. *Cash* (in-hand or in-bank) that a bank will accept at face value. Types of cash include bank deposits, currency, checks, bank drafts, and money orders.
2. *Notes Receivable.* These are claims against debtors evidenced by some binding document.

3. *Accounts Receivable.* These are claims against debtors arising from sales of services or merchandise on account.
4. *Prepaid Expenses.* These include supplies not yet consumed, advance payments on items such as insurance or taxes.

Fixed assets (sometimes called *plant assets*) are types of assets which, with the exception of land, wear out and are subject to depreciation, using one of the depreciation schemes detailed later in the chapter. Land is a plant asset which does not depreciate. Typical account titles are: Equipment, Buildings, and Land. There might be a further breakdown, such as Delivery Equipment, Store Equipment, or Office Equipment. Since there are no standards for naming accounts (while there are some common titles), the accountant must use account titles which are descriptive.

Accounts Receivable might well be broken into separate accounts for each receivable. As depreciation is a contra-asset, however, so, too, there is a contra-asset which applies to Accounts Receivable. That contra-asset is the *Allowance for Bad Debts.* Bad debts are real, and the process of accounting must be a snapshot of reality. If a company has enough data to make a projection of this contra-asset, that figure will be used. Where it does not have that experience, the figure will generally be determined as a percentage of either sales or accounts receivable.

Another asset for which you will have to account is *inventory.* Inventory is a tangible asset which is held for sale in the course of business, work-in-process (partially completed inventory), or raw materials inventory. There are many ways to account for inventory, discussed later in the chapter.

Depreciation methods for fixed assets will also be covered in greater detail later. Some general facts are useful here. The reason for depreciation is to permit a firm to spread the cost of a productive device over the period of its useful life. Thus, the cost of the device can be spent in association with the period of production which may justify its existence. That's not the same as withholding payment until that period, but rather the distribution of its costs. The depreciation scheme selected has major impacts on taxes and cash flow.

One asset which does not depreciate is land. While it does not depreciate, certain land is recognizably used for wasting purposes, such as that from which mineral resources are extracted. In such a case it is possible to charge against that land a contra-asset known as *depletion.* Conceptually, the two, depreciation and depletion, are the same thing.

One intangible asset—goodwill—has been mentioned. Other intangible assets (trademarks, tradenames, patents, research and development, and others) need accounting as well.

Liabilities

A liability is an amount owed to others (creditors); liabilities are customarily listed under account titles which contain the word *payable.* They are of two classes—current and long-term.

Current liabilities are those which will fall due within a year or less and which are to be paid out of current assets. You will generally find two prime accounts here—*Accounts Payable* and *Notes Payable.* Other common titles include "Wages Payable," "Interest Payable," and "Taxes Payable."

Notes Payable is also a term for a long-term payable involving a security. Long-term liabilities also include such things as bonds, secured notes, etc.

Ownership

Ownership (capital, equity, proprietorship) is a residual claim against the assets of the business once the total liabilities are deducted. It is also called "net worth" as described before. Included in its equity section, therefore, will be those stocks, bonds, and other devices which represent ownership, either by outsiders in the company or the company in itself.

Costs vs. Expenses

An important fact to understand is that costs are another way to describe "expired expenses." Thus, the corporation can have an "expense" for which it has yet to pay any cash. Recall that long-term debit has a portion which is current. The rationale for this method of consideration is known as *accrual.* In other words, we would wish to charge only to a current year the receivables and expenses derivable for that year, for the purpose of our operations statement, the Income Statement (P&L). Thus, if there is a note receivable, and it is destined to be paid back over the period of four years, only one of those years is considered to be "current" for the purposes of the balance sheet and income statement, while the other portion of the receivable remains to be entered on the books at its appointed time.

Account Balances

Earlier it was mentioned that a balance is struck on each account at the end of the closing period. It is useful, therefore, to know what kind of balance to expect from each account. Figure 5.13 illustrates the mechanics and normal balances.

Three new terms have been added here—Drawing, Revenue, and Expense. The Drawing Account is normally used for sole proprietorships. Revenue and Expense are self-explanatory.

An Example

Journal Entries

To assist you to see how the picture all fits together, let's walk through a month's activity for the Gizmo Corporation, detailing the journal entries first, showing the T-accounts next, and then coming up with a Trial Balance which will then be useful in preparing the statements. This is the first month of business for the Gizmo Corporation.

A. The Gizmo Corporation opens its business, investing $4,000 in cash (money from the principals), office equipment costing $500, and a library costing $800:

Cash	$4,000	
Office Equipment	500	
Library	800	
Capital		$5,300

B. Office Rent paid for the month, $200:

Rent Expense	$200	
Cash		$200

Account Type	Increase	Decrease	Normal Balance
Asset	Debit	Credit	Debit
Liability	Credit	Debit	Credit
Capital			
Capital	Credit	Debit	Credit
Drawing	Debit	Credit	Debit
Revenue	Credit	Debit	Credit
Expense	Debit	Credit	Debit

Figure 5.13

C. Purchase of additional office equipment, in the amount of $600:

Office Equipment	$600	
Accounts Payable		$600

D. Purchased an automobile for the sum of $2,800, paying $1,000 down and agreeing to pay the remainder in twelve monthly installments of $150 each:

Automobile	$2,800	
Cash		$1,000
Accounts Payable		$1,800

E. Purchased office supplies for cash, $100:

Office Supplies	$100	
Cash		$100

F. Paid for office equipment on account, $300:

Accounts Payable	$300	
Cash		$300

G. Received $225 in payment of fees for services:

Cash	$225	
Service Fees		$225

H. Paid for the premium for a three-year insurance policy on the equipment and the library, $75:

Prepaid Insurance	$75	
Cash		$75

I. Paid bi-weekly salaries, $600:

Salary Expense	$600	
Cash		$600

J. Received $400 for service fees:

Cash	$400	
Service Fees		$400

K. Paid a one-year insurance premium on the automobile:

Prepaid Insurance	$90	
Cash		$90

L. Received a $150 fee for service:

Cash	$150	
Service Fees		$150

M. Paid telephone and other miscellaneous expense bills, $290:

Miscellaneous Expense	$290	
Cash		$290

N. Paid bi-weekly salaries, $600:

Salary Expense	$600	
Cash		$600

O. Received $300 fee for services:

Cash	$300	
Service Fees		$300

P. Paid automobiles expenses, $80:

Automobile Expense	$80	
Cash		$80

Q. Principal withdraws $450 for personal use:

Capital	$450	
Cash		$450

R. Sent invoices to clients for services rendered during the month, $1,400:

Accounts Receivable	$1,400	
Service Fees		$1,400

These transactions are summarized in Figure 5.14.

Trial Balance

Since debits and credits are being applied equally, according to the accounting formula, the sum of the debits should equal the sum of the credits at any given time. To determine this, a trial balance should be struck. Figure 5.15 is a trial balance for the Gizmo Corporation.

If they balance, then you can be reasonably sure that the figures are accurate. Be careful, however, as the correct final totals do not always denote correct account totals. If they do not balance, then there is possibly some error, such as missing transactions, erroneous recording of transactions, duplicate transactions, or the misrecording of account information. A good shortcut used by the accountant is to either divide or multiply (or both) the differing number (the amount of the difference) by two, which will give some indication of double recording. For instance, if liabilities differ from assets by $100, then there is either a $50 or a $200 error somewhere in the transaction reporting.

Mention is made again of accrual accounting. Say, for instance, that we will be paid $1,200 for rent ($100 monthly) but will be paid in quarterly installments, beginning with an advance payment. Though we have money in hand on January 1 for January through March, we only "earn" it on a month-by-month basis. On February 1, we have "earned" January's rent. On March 1, we have "earned" both January's and February's rent. And so forth. More discussion on accruals will be contained in the text.

From the trial balance, the items necessary to make up an Income Statement (Figure 5.16), Capital Statement (Figure 5.17), and Balance Sheet (Figure 5.18) are obtained.

Closing Entries

When the end of a period has been reached, it is necessary to have *adjusting* and *closing* entries.

Consider the "office supplies" account for Gizmo Corporation. It would be foolhardy to make an accounting entry every time a box of paperclips is used. But at the end of a cycle, the figure must be balanced and then adjusted to reflect the actual inventory. To do this a credit entry to office supplies would be balanced by a debit entry to office supplies expense.

While expenses might be carried from month to month during the year, and in aggregate when the year is completed, the *expense accounts* must be started over again; thus, they must be closed. Likewise, a temporary capital account, expense, and revenue summary, is created, to which all revenue and expense accounts are transferred. The balance on the Expense and Revenue Summary is the Net Income, which is then transferred to the Capital Account. Likewise any drawing account is transferred to capital, in the name of the principal.

PRE-STATEMENT ACCOUNTING

In the previous section, we demonstrated journal entries which, if done by hand, would have been done on two-column accounting paper. We have avoided illustrating by means of actual accounting forms, because this is an overview of accounting, not a course in bookkeeping.

But it should be mentioned at this point that accounting supplies can be from two columns to n columns, which can be used to indicate either any number of pairs of debits and credits or specific ledgers which make up any given account. Thus we could make the basic journal entries and distribute the supporting accounts on a single line of the paper. Consider the following:

Assets

Cash

(A)	4,000	(B)	200
(G)	225	(D)	1,000
(J)	400	(E)	100
(L)	150	(F)	300
(O)	300	(H)	75
		(I)	600
	5,075	(K)	90
		(M)	290
		(N)	600
		(P)	80
		(Q)	450
			3,785

Account Balance
Debit $1,290

Accounts Receivable

(R)	1,400		

Office Supplies

(E)	100		

Prepaid Insurance

(H)	75		
(K)	90		

Debit Balance of $165

Automobile

(D	2,800		

Office Equipment

(A)	500		
(C)	600		

Debit Balance of $1,100

Library

(A)	800		

Figure 5.14. T-accounts.

Liabilities

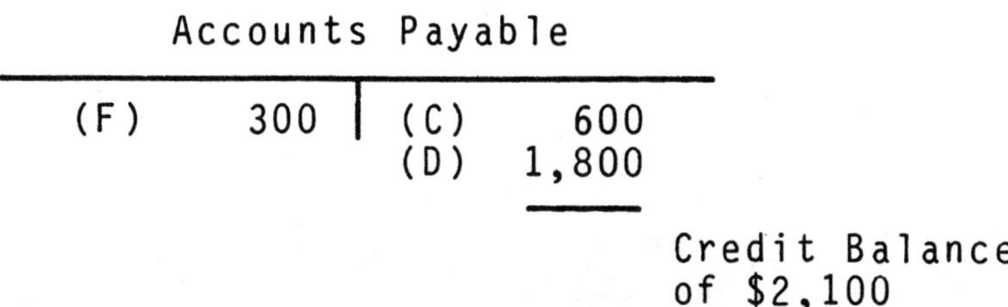

Accounts Payable

(F)	300	(C)	600
		(D)	1,800

Credit Balance of $2,100

Capital

Gizmo Corporation -- Capital

(Q)	450	(A)	5,300

Credit Balance of $4,850

Revenues

Revenues from Service Fees

		(G)	225
		(J)	500
		(L)	150
		(O)	300
		(R)	1,400

Credit Balance of $2,475

Expenses

Salary Expense

(I)	600		
(N)	600		

Debit Balance of $1,200

Rent Expense

(B)	200		

Automobile Expense

(P)	80		

Miscellaneous Expense

(M)	290		

Figure 5.14. *(Continued)*

Gizmo Corporation
Trial Balance
January 31, 19xx

Cash	$1,290	
Accounts Receivable	1,400	
Office Supplies	100	
Prepaid Insurance	165	
Automobile	2,800	
Office Equipment	1,100	
Library	800	
Accounts Payable		$2,100
Capital		4,850
Service Fees		2,475
Salary Expense	1,200	
Rent Expense	200	
Automobile Expense	80	
Miscellaneous	290	
	$9,425	$9,425

Figure 5.15

Gizmo Corporation
Income Statement
for month ended January 31, 19xx

Sales (Fees)		$2,475
Operating Expenses		
Salaries	$1,200	
Rent	200	
Automobile	80	
Miscellaneous	290	
		1,770
Net Income from Operations		$ 705

Figure 5.16

Gizmo Corporation
Capital Statement
for month ended January 31, 19xx

Capital, January 1, 19xx		$5,300
Net Income for the Month	$705	
Less: Withdrawals	(450)	
Increase in Capital		255
Capital, January 31, 19xx		$5,555

Figure 5.17

Gizmo Corporation
Balance Sheet
January 31, 19xx

Assets		
Current Assets		
Cash	$1,290	
Accounts Receivable	1,400	
Office Supplies	100	
Prepaid Insurance	165	
Total Current Assets		$2,955
Fixed Assets		
Automobile	$2,800	
Office Equipment	1,100	
Library	800	
Total Fixed Assets		4,700
Total Assets		$7,655
Liabilities		
Current Liabilities		
Accounts Payable		$2,100
Capital		
Capital, Gizmo Corporation		$5,555
Total Liabilities and Capital		$7,655

Figure 5.18

Accounts Receivable	$1000	
Sales		$1000

To record the sales of merchandise to A. Alison ($400), B. Bernstein ($300), C. Carpenter ($200), and D. Dodge ($100).

While the above entry is functionally correct, it lacks in technique and would become a nightmare to make heads or tails out of for an audit, a summary of accounts, or even bookkeeping ease. If done this way:

A/R, A. Alison	$400	
A/R, B. Bernstein	300	
A/R, C. Carpenter	200	
A/R, D. Dodge	100	
Sales		$1000

it would be functionally correct, but nowhere would the *total* Accounts Receivable figure be available,

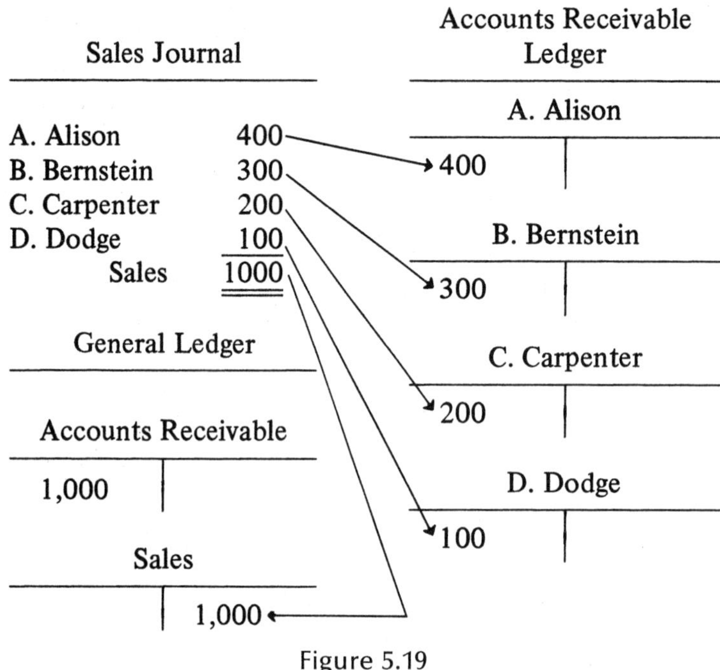

Figure 5.19

which would make for a considerable amount of work in determining financial position or making it out a statement. On top of that, if several purchases were made at divergent times, the accounting by customer would be difficult.

Now, consider Figure 5.19.

It's important to note that the books of original entry, accounts receivable and sales journals, contain the total amount of the transaction, and that the accounts receivable ledgers for the individual people contain merely a *breakdown* of the accounts by person.

In actual practice, it's entirely possible that there is a separate ledger for each of the customers (only four are shown here, and perhaps we could add a few more to a larger ledger sheet), but if on the other hand we were to have four thousand accounts, then it would tend to be somewhat cumbersome. So, there may very well be an Accounts Receivable Control Ledger, which, in turn, would have customer accounts in support. Thus, we have established a hierarchy of documents, each with a specific purpose.

In the preceding illustration, we mentioned a new type of journal—the *sales journal.* It is a special type of journal used to record the sales of merchandise on account. The emphasized words make an important point. A sale for cash would have been a deduction from inventory and an increment to cash, both elements on the balance sheet. In the instance, as illustrated, the balance sheet accounts were derived from the total of the sales journal, while the individual customer ledger accounts were derived from the transactions recorded in the sales journal.

Since special journals are supporting documentation for balance sheet accounts, there may be as many as necessary to support those accounts, and will be used depending on the complexity of the system. But there are at least four primary special journals. They are shown in the following table:

Journal	On which is recorded
Sales	Sale of merchandise on account
Cash Receipts	Receipts of cash from varying sources
Purchases	Purchases of merchandise and other items on account
Cash Payments	Payments of cash for varying purposes

For the majority of businesses, this selection of special journals is sufficient. But where the entries exceed these categories, a *general journal* may be used. Do not confuse this with the *general ledger* mentioned earlier.

The Sales Journal

Now, sales is what really begins the accounting cycle—it is the "trigger" transaction. When a sale is made (with or without a trade discount), the sale is entered in a sales journal, in a form somewhat like Figure 5.20.

As the accountant works with his several ledgers and journals, some tie to bind them all together must be determined. In this case the tie *back* to this journal would be the page number. The tie *forward* would be two account notations indicated in parenthesis at the bottom of the total. They are, respectively, the Accounts Receivable debit and the Sales credit. Note the incremental number between the date and the names. This is an *invoice number* for the sale. Note that the account is totalled at the end of the period. The total figure would then be added to the balance, either debit or credit, of the respective accounts, and a new balance struck.

For every item sold, there is a possibility that it will be returned, due to defects or other reasons. If the item is returned, then naturally the customer does not expect to pay for it, so some form of deduction from the customer's account must be made. It would be easy enough just to deduct that amount from the Sales account, except the year-end balance would indicate net sales, not gross sales, and the returns would go uncontrolled. If the return is made, then most probably the seller will issue a credit memorandum, the result of which will provide two services—it becomes a legal advice to the customer of the cancellation of the obligation, and it becomes the basis for modifying the corporation's books. To do this, an account known as Sales Returns and Allowances is established, which is an asset account and which is, until it is closed, debited. Thus, if the sale has been made for cash, and the cash were returned, the entry would look like this:

	Debit	Credit
Sales Returns and Allowances	100	
Cash		100

```
                  Gizmo Corporation
                    Sales Journal

198x                                        Page 10
Jan        1  200  A.Alden              $ 350.00
           2  201  B.Baker                210.57
           3  202  C.Collins               45.22
           3  203  D.Denver                87.64
          14  204  C.Collins              671.44
          15  205  E.Epstein                1.35
          16  206  F.Fernandel            111.88
          26  207  C.Collins               21.88
          26  208  G.Gundy                893.00
          27  209  H.Hunt                 411.40
          27  210  I.Irwin                 55.74
          --                            ________
          31                            $2860.12
                                        ========
                                      (118) (247)
```

Figure 5.20

Similarly, if the sale had been made on account, the entry would be made like this:

Sales Returns and Allowances	100	
Accounts Receivable		100

Since Sales is a capital account which has a credit balance, the effect is to decrease the Sales account while keeping it separate from the return for control purposes. The account will be closed at an ending period. The method of doing that will be discussed later.

The preceding entries assume that at some time the transaction was made *on account* and even the cash transaction was done via a delayed cash transfer. Had the cash been transferred at the time of the sale, this would not have been the case. Even though the sale had been made on account the return could have been made in cash. By and large, however, a corporation would handle its sales on account, and thus the illustration. A caution here: the accounting for the return will be slightly different if the item is returned to inventory. In that case, there would have to be a debit to Merchandise Inventory and a credit to Capital.

The Accounts Receivable ledger would then be posed along the following lines:

Widget Company
1234 Any Street
Anywhere, Idaho

Date	Ref	Dr	Cr	Bal
10/19	S35	100		100

Of course, when the payment is made, the credit will be applied to the Account Receivable and the debit to Cash. If, however, it is returned, the debit will be made to Sales Returns and Allowances and the credit to Accounts Receivable, against the ledger of the particular company.

As with any other journal, columns can be added to help explain any transaction. One such column which could be added to the sales journal would be the transportation provisions. FOB is the term in common use, meaning ''Free on Board,'' or technically the point of delivery where the buyer assumes the transportation costs. In many cases, FOB is the point of manufacture, but the seller will ''advance'' the buyer the transportation costs, billing, or invoicing the buyer for those costs as a separate category. In all cases where a discount offer has been made, the discount applies to the merchandise and not to the total figure, which includes the transportation costs.

Occasionally an accounting shop will ''shortcut'' the sales journal by using a duplicate invoice as a sales journal, dividing the invoices into a group sort, perhaps alphabetically. Of course, the EDP system performs essentially this same task.

The Cash Receipts Journal

The treatment of cash also requires a cash journal (exclusive of the EDP system). There are some basic differences, however, for the firm which offers some kind of discount scheme, such as ''2/10 n/30.'' That is said: ''Two ten, net thirty,'' and simply means that if the invoice is paid within 10 days a 2% discount will be provided, while payment is due in 30 days. Thus enter the terms ''cash'' and ''net cash.'' Where cash is not paid or discount terms provided, some type of credit terms are required, for example, a down payment with monthly payments over some stated period.

Occasionally the firm will offer discount terms but the customer will not avail himself of the terms, becoming liable for the full amount. But the corporation cannot wait until the customer has made up his mind whether to avail himself of the discount; therefore the receivable will be taken in the full amount.

Gizmo Corporation
Cash Receipts Journal

Date		Account Credited	Misc. Accts. Cr	Sales Cr	A/R Cr	Sales Disc. Dr	Cash Dr
198x							
Jan	2	Notes Receivable	150.00				150.00
	4	A.Alden			350.00	20.00	330.00
	5	B.Baker			210.57	10.00	200.57
	8	Sales		827.00			827.00
	10	C.Collins			45.22	.50	44.72
	15	Sales		200.00			200.00
	25	E.Epstein			100.00		100.00
	27	J.Jackson			50.00		50.00
	29	Purchases Return	10.00				10.00
	31		160.00	1027.00	755.79	30.50	1912.29

Figure 5.21

If the discount is taken, then the accountant must treat the discount as a special category, not merely ignore it or discount it under the table, or off the ledger, as it were.

Figure 5.12 is an example of cash receipts journal. Note that in every case the specific account to receive a debit or credit is identified, and the figures will balance. All credits, minus the sales discount, will equal the cash. There is one item missing from the illustration which would have to be added in use: that is the posting reference with each account, specifically tying this journal to the sales of discount journals. At the end of the month the columns are ruled and balanced according to the accounting formula.

There are three distinct types of columns in the cash receipts journal.

1. Individual entries to general ledger accounts, column total not posted:
   Sundry (misc.) Accounts Credit
2. Individual entries not posted, column total posted to a general ledger account:
   Sales Credit
   Sales Discount Debit
   Cash Debit
3. Individual entries posted to subordinate ledger accounts, column total posted to the corresponding general ledger controlling account:
   Accounts Receivable Credit

These categories are illustrated in Figure 5.22.

The Purchases Journal

Purchases and cash payments, like sales and cash receipts, should be journalized for control purposes. As with the receipts, the recording of payments is a sequential process, as well. An order is placed, perhaps by means of some specified form, such as a *purchase order*. This in turn will result in the receipt of an invoice from the vendor, which may precede, accompany, or follow the ordered merchandise. If yours is a sufficiently large company, a step may be inserted here, generally in the form of a *receiving report*, which notes the anticipation and receipt of the ordered product. In any event, the invoice re-

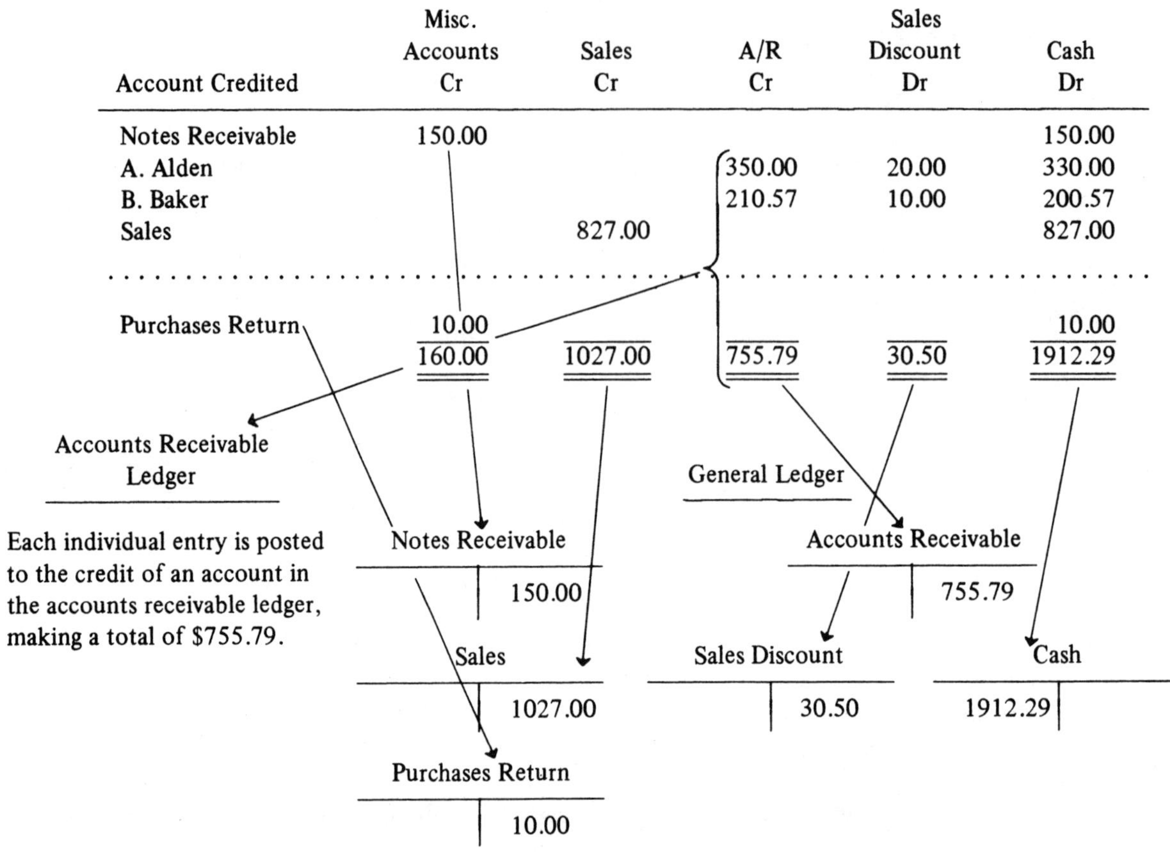

Account Credited
Misc. Accounts Cr
Sales Cr
A/R Cr
Sales Discount Dr
Cash Dr
Notes Receivable 150.00 150.00
A. Alden 350.00 20.00 330.00
B. Baker 210.57 10.00 200.57
Sales 827.00 827.00
Purchases Return 10.00 10.00
160.00 1027.00 755.79 30.50 1912.29
Accounts Receivable Ledger
Each individual entry is posted to the credit of an account in the accounts receivable ledger, making a total of $755.79.
General Ledger
Notes Receivable 150.00
Accounts Receivable 755.79
Sales 1027.00
Sales Discount 30.50
Cash 1912.29
Purchases Return 10.00

Figure 5.22

ceived from the vendor will outline costs, discounts, if any, and terms for payment. A purchases journal, like the one in Figure 5.23, is then generated:

The dollar column of the purchases journal is the Accounts Payable credit. That total will be entered into the accounts payable liability section of the Balance Sheet. In the same manner as sales are summarized for entry to the general ledger, so, too, are purchases. The purchases journal is the controlling journal for subordinate accounts. If your firm buys from a select set of suppliers, then it most probably will have a separate payables ledger for each vendor. Those vendors which fall outside the normal contents of

Gizmo Corporation
Purchases Journal

198x			
Jan	2	Consolidated Wholesalers	500.00
	2	Widget Manufacturing	225.00
	8	Framistan Suppliers	27.27
	11	Incandescent Light Bulb Co.	123.45
	29	UWAYUM Scale Corporation	88.56
	--		
	31		964.28
			(113)

Figure 5.23

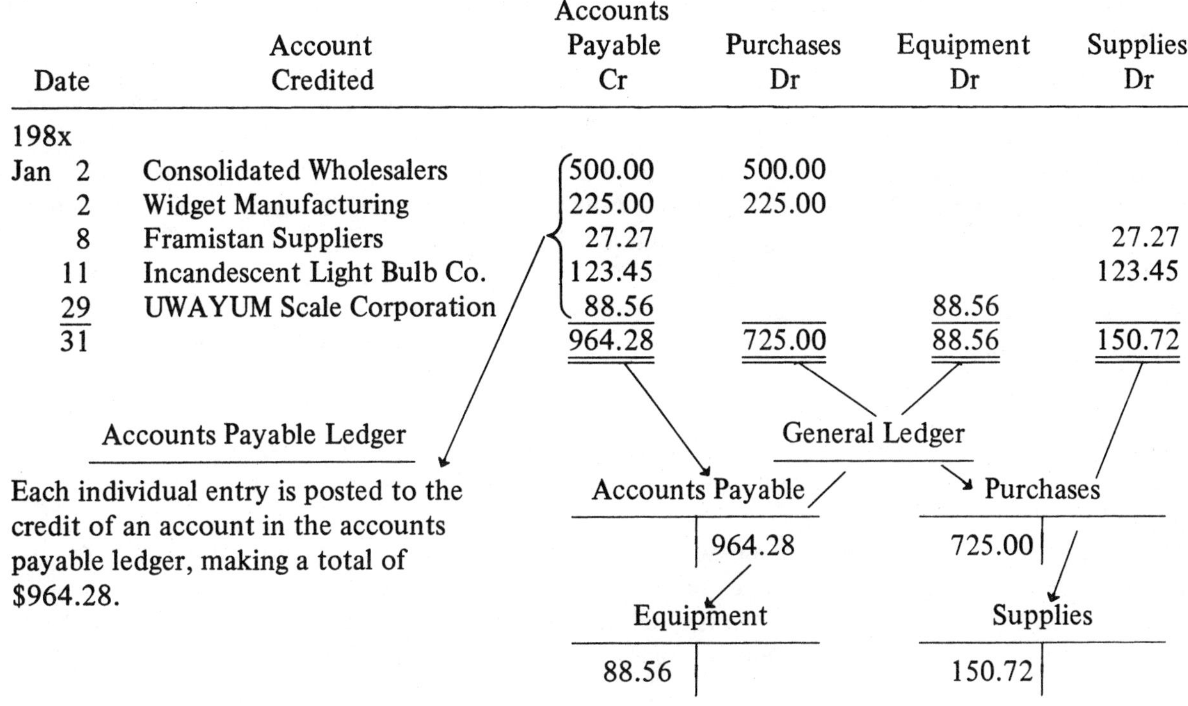

Gizmo Corporation
Purchases Journal

Date	Account Credited	Accounts Payable Cr	Purchases Dr	Equipment Dr	Supplies Dr
198x					
Jan 2	Consolidated Wholesalers	500.00	500.00		
2	Widget Manufacturing	225.00	225.00		
8	Framistan Suppliers	27.27			27.27
11	Incandescent Light Bulb Co.	123.45			123.45
29	UWAYUM Scale Corporation	88.56		88.56	
31		964.28	725.00	88.56	150.72

Figure 5.24

the purchases journal can be journalized in the general journal. Like the sales journal, the purchases journal can have columns which identify specific accounts to be treated. Consider Figure 5.24.

As can be seen, the debits equal the credits, so the Accounting Formula is inviolate. Again, as with the previous journal, the purchases journal is for items which are purchases on account. Cash transactions are not recorded here.

The purchase debit is made for items customarily bought for resale. They may be for direct resale (direct cost of goods sold on Income Statement) or they may be used in manufacturing or combining process.

The purchases journal is the source of postings to both the accounts payable ledger and the general ledger, and the sum of the individual postings to the creditors' accounts in the subordinate ledgers is equal to the column total posted to the Accounts Payable account in the general ledger.

In EDP systems, a purchase is not normally kept in the strictest sense of the word. Transaction codes will indicate which accounts will be debited or credited and a general journal run can be used to obtain a list of specific purchases from a supplier. These systems must also tie together any receiving reports and outstanding purchase orders. Also, lists of outstanding purchase orders, and unsupported receipts must be used for decision-making.

In the same manner as we had sales returns and allowances, we may have purchase returns and allowances when we (the corporation) decide to return some item which we have purchased to the vendor. In this case, the entry would take the form:

Accounts Payable—Vendor	$100	
Purchases Returns and Allowances		$100

The entry would be backed up by a debit memo, prepared either by your firm, or in confirmation by the vendor of the return receipt. The entries above are from the controlling accounts. But the specific nature of the return must be noted. If the item returned had been a piece of office equipment, purchased for use, then naturally, it would have to be deducted from the equipment asset on the balance sheet. If the returned items had been stock purchased for resale, then it would have to be deducted from Purchases. The point is that each return must be examined and specifically classified, bearing in mind that the accounting formula must always be in balance.

In the same manner as sales invoices can be used as a journal, so too may purchases invoices, group sorting as indicated before. With the EDP system, the need for a separate purchases invoice file is minimized, due to the tracking of purchases at the transaction level.

As your corporation would offer terms and discounts to its clients or customers, so too do your vendors occasionally offer them to you. In recent years this has become the basis for "sales," wherein a discount is passed on to the consumer, either in outright deduction from the selling price or from a coupon-type system. In constructing the payables system, it is important to tightly control the discount amounts and timing. The impact, for instance, of not taking a 2/10 n/30 is 36% a year in lost net profit. In a manual system, the invoice is generally filed by its discount date. In an automated system, the transaction must be dated as to its discount period. The corporation which is firmly on top of its payables will reap considerable benefit.

There is nothing special about a purchases returns and allowances journal—no cross-posting of any great difficulty or anything special about its preparation, so it will not be illustrated here. We'll just mention that the debit will be to Accounts Payable and the credit will be to Purchases Returns and Allowances. Whether or not you establish a journal for this category will depend on what the incidence of occurrence will be.

The Cash Payments Journal

A cash payments journal is an absolute necessity. It's the first place an auditor will look, as it records the cash flow of the enterprise, the cash outflow. In combination with the Cash Receipts Journal, described before, an auditor can get a pretty complete picture of the business. See Figure 5.25.

Since Cash is an asset account with a debit balance, all cash payments will be a credit to Cash and a debit to some other account. It may be an asset account, such as inventory or prepaid insurance, or it may be a liability account, such as purchases. The specific columns established to work with the cash payment journal will depend on the nature of the cash transactions and their frequency of occurrence. Thus, we would set up debit accounts for payment to a vendor with whom we frequently do business, but would most probably not establish a category for the annual fire insurance premium.

The cash receipts journal is the detail subordinate support for a single entry under Cash debit; so too the cash payments journal is the detail subordinate support for a single entry under Cash credit. These single entries are customarily made at the end of some specific account period, such as a month.

When you get to the point where the account is completed for the accounting period, the sum of the balances in the creditors' ledgers must balance with the Accounts Payable. If it does not, you must locate the discrepancy and correct it.

As in the sales your corporation makes, the point of transportation is important to your purchases as well. The same set of rules apply, relative to the FOB point. While you cannot take a discount on the total amount, the cost of transportation is a part of the total cost of the purchase. If shipping is included in the invoice, it is part of the accounts payable. If your corporation pays for the transportation on receipt, it would receive a separate entry in the books.

Gizmo Corporation
Cash Payments Journal

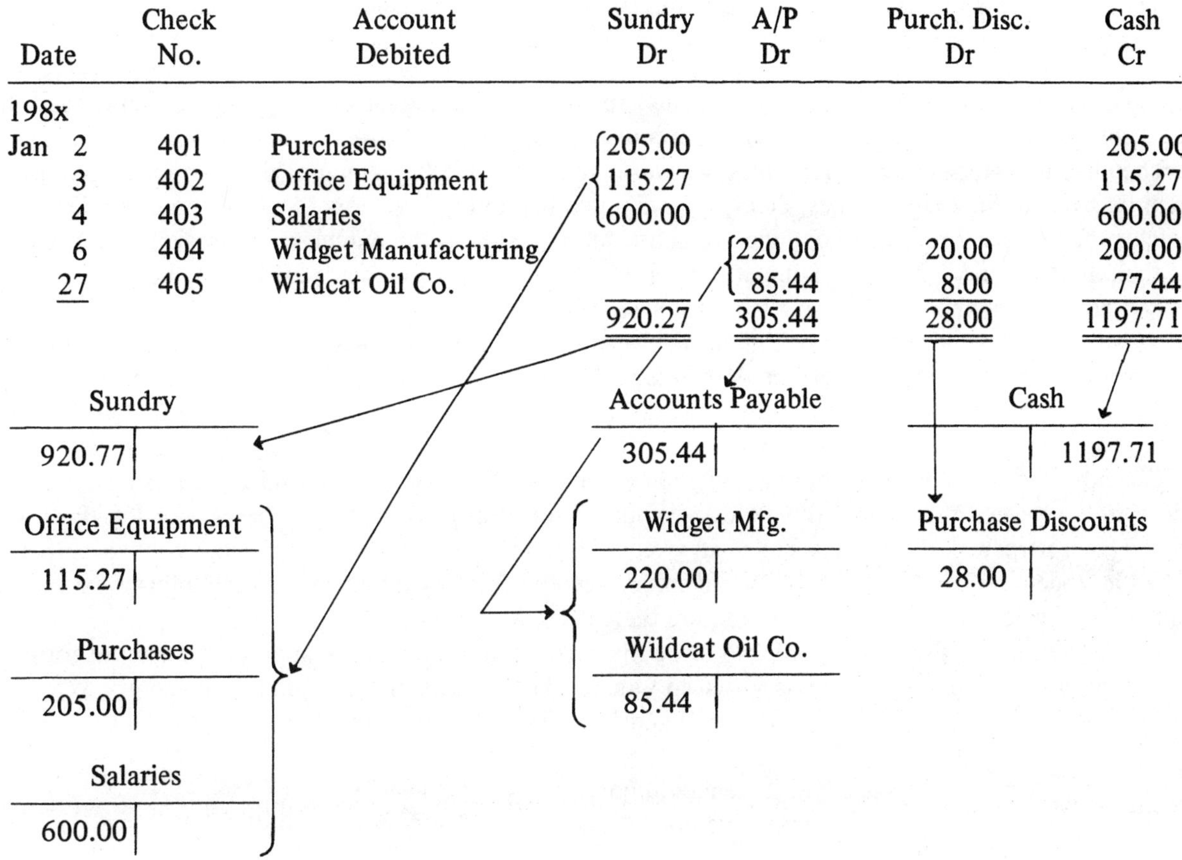

Date	Check No.	Account Debited	Sundry Dr	A/P Dr	Purch. Disc. Dr	Cash Cr
198x						
Jan 2	401	Purchases	205.00			205.00
3	402	Office Equipment	115.27			115.27
4	403	Salaries	600.00			600.00
6	404	Widget Manufacturing		220.00	20.00	200.00
27	405	Wildcat Oil Co.		85.44	8.00	77.44
			920.27	305.44	28.00	1197.71

Figure 5.25

Preparing the Statements

Everything leads to one specific point—the summarization of accounts and the preparation of the reports outlined earlier. Even though we must make interim reports monthly or quarterly, the government requires an annual accounting of position for tax and other purposes. To accomplish this, a corporation must perform the following accounting tasks:

1. Prepare a trial balance of the general ledger.
2. Determine that each subsidiary ledger is in agreement with the related controlling accounts in the general ledger.
3. Review the accounts to determine which ones should be adjusted, and compile the data necessary for making the adjustments.
4. Prepare a worksheet from the trial balance and the data for the adjustments.
5. Prepare the financial statements from data in the worksheets.
6. Record the adjusting entries in the general journal.
7. Record the closing entries in the general journal.
8. Post the adjusting and closing entries.
9. Prepare a post-closing trial balance of the general ledger.

10. Record the reversing entries necessary to prepare the books for the following accounting period.
11. Post the reversing entries.
12. File the completed nonrelevant journals, ledgers, and statements with the financial records of the year.

Let's first concentrate on inventory accounts, specifically merchandise inventory. You will recall that purchases, purchase returns, and purchases discounts all applied to the merchandise inventory account. Merchandise inventory assumes that there was an inventory at the beginning of the accounting period (it might be zero, in the case of a new enterprise). To that beginning inventory is added the purchases of inventory for resale. From that combined total are subtracted both the purchases returns and allowances and the purchases discount (to obtain net purchases). Net purchases is then added to the beginning inventory, to produce the merchandise available for sale. When the final inventory is deducted, the cost of merchandise for the entire year is available, for Income Statement purposes. Of course, the inventory carryover to the following year will be the value and count of the physical inventory taken at year's end.

Methods for valuing inventory will be discussed later in the chapter. There are several methods, and the method selected must be consistent from year to year, or the tax collection people will object.

Consider Figure 5.26. The entire acquisition of inventory and the returns and discounts against that inventory have been, throughout the period, accounted for in or against the purchases account. This will differ from a perpetual inventory accounting system which is prevalent in EDP usage. Where a perpetual system has been used, the balance of the inventory account (plus or minus the closing adjustments against the physical inventory) will not require the entries which will follow.

Under the manual method, in order to close the account and transfer the appropriate amount forward to the next year's books, it is necessary first to transfer the contents of the beginning inventory to a temporary closing account known as the Expense and Revenue Summary, like this:

Expense and Revenue Summary	17,460	
Merchandise Inventory		17,460

Since merchandise inventory is an asset (debit) account, it must be credited.

There is a second entry required, one that will establish the carryover balance of the inventory account for the following year. It looks like this:

Merchandise Inventory	20,836	
Expense and Revenue Summary		20,836

Merchandise Inventory, January 1, 198x			$17,460
Purchases		$100,450	
Less: Purchases Returns & Allowances	$2,711		
Purchases Discounts	1,234		
	3,945		
Net Purchases			96,505
Merchandise available for sale			113,965
Less: Merchandise Inventory, December 31, 198x			20,836
Cost of Merchandise Sold			$93,129

Figure 5.26

Cash	Accounts Receivable
Merchandise Inventory	Store Supplies
Office Supplies	Prepaid Insurance
Store Equipment	Accumulated Depreciation (Store Equipment)
Office Equipment	Accumulated Depreciation (Office Equipment)
Building	Accumulated Depreciation (Building)
Land	Accounts Payable
Commissions Payable	Mortgage Payable
Principal, Capital	Principal, Drawing
Expense and Revenue Summary	Sales
Sales Returns and Allowances	Sales Discounts
Purchases	Purchases Returns and Allowances
Purchases Discounts	Sales Salaries
Sales Commissions	Advertising Expense
Depreciation Expense	Delivery Expense
Store Supplies Expense	Taxes Expense
Depreciation Expense (Office Equipment)	Insurance Expense
Depreciation Expense (Building)	Interest Income
Rental Income	

Figure 5.27

The figure in inventory now represents the accurate carryover balance. The balance of the Expense and Revenue Summary, however, is a credit of $3,376, representing the *net incremental costs* of merchandise sold.

When the recording and posting of the year's transactions has been completed, a trial balance is prepared on a worksheet. To construct the worksheet, the following are required:

1. The account title
2. A column for the trial balance, including debits and credits
3. A column for adjustments, including debits and credits
4. A column for the Income Statement, including debits and credits
5. A column for the Balance Sheet, including debits and credits

Once the figures are transferred from the account ledgers to the worksheet, a trial balance must be taken, and it must balance; otherwise, the procedure cannot continue.

In preparing the worksheet, it is wise to prepare the account titles in the same manner as the statements which will be drawn from them. Figure 5.27 is a list of suggested titles for the worksheet. These account titles are not the only titles available, but are representative.

Figure 5.28 is a very abbreviated illustration of a complete worksheet. You should be able to see that using this method it is possible to gather the data necessary to prepare the corporation's financial statements.

On the surface the worksheet may be somewhat difficult to follow, but you can see that *each pair* of debits and credits must balance. An out-of-balance condition will require the accountant to verify all accounts to track down the discrepancy. The following is a general explanation of what happened with the adjustments:

- Merchandise Inventory was computed and newly forwarded inventory was placed on the books.
- The depreciation accounts accumulated the expired cost of the asset (as expense).

Gizmo Corporation
Worksheet
For Year Ended December 31, 198x

Account Title	Trial Balance Dr	Trial Balance Cr	Adjustments Dr	Adjustments Cr	Inc. Statement Dr	Inc. Statement Cr	Balance Sheet Dr	Balance Sheet Cr
Cash	10463						10463	
Accounts Receivable	8122						8122	
Merchandise Inventory	4756		6327	4756			6327	
Store Supplies	1234			834			400	
Store Equipment	12100						12100	
Accum. Depr. (St. Eq.)		8000		1000				9000
Exp. & Rev. Summary			4756	6327	4756	6327		
Sales		20498				20498		
Sales Rtns. & Allow.	3884				3884			
Sales Discounts	559				559			
Purchases	36234				36234			
Depr. Exp. (Off Eq)			251		251			
Depr. Exp. (Bldg)			7000		7000			
Rental Income		1000				1000		
Interest Expense	576				576			
	89742	89742	34420	34420	75441	144128	65496	40763
Net Income					68687			24733
					144128	144128	65496	65496

Figure 5.28

- The prepaid items' adjustment is similar to the entry for supplies consumed. You are recording the amount consumed.
- Commissions and salaries payable, but not yet paid, are treated as an expense of the year, but an outstanding payable for the following year.

Since we have already discussed the Income Statement, Capital Statement, and Balance Sheet, that information will not be repeated here, except to point out that you may wish to prepare formal schedules of accounts receivable and payable from the subordinate ledgers, in preparation for some form of annual report.

As stated before, the Expense and Revenue Summary and the various Expense Accounts are *tempo-*

rary accounts used for closing the books at the end of an accounting period. On the worksheet there was a column for adjustments. Those adjustments must be supported by general journal entries. Some examples of those adjusting entries would look like this:

Adjusting Entries

Expense and Revenue Summary	15,750	
Merchandise Inventory		15,750
Merchandise Inventory	12,456	
Expense and Revenue Summary		12,456
Store Supplies Expense	873	
Store Supplies		873
Depreciation Expense—Equipment	1,778	
Accumulated Depr.—Equipment		1,778

And so forth. Since this is an overview, no attempt has been made to do a complete company accounts, nor has there been any specific attempt to ensure consistency of numbers. Also, at this period, it will be necessary to make some closing entries. The effect of the closing entries is to reduce the balances of all temporary capital accounts to zero and to show in the capital account the present capital attributable to ownership. An example follows.

Sales	45236	
Purchases Returns	4598	
Purchases Discounts	863	
Rental Income	1000	
Expense and Revenue Summary		51697

The procedure for making the closing entries is this:

1. Close all income statement accounts with *credit* balances by transferring the total to the credit side of the Expense and Revenue Summary.
2. Close all income statement accounts with *debit* balances by transferring the total to the debit side of the Expense and Revenue Summary.
3. Close Expense and Revenue Summary by transferring the balance to a Capital (Ownership) account.
4. If there is a drawing account, also close it to the Capital account.

Once this has been completed, only the accounts for assets, contra-assets, liabilities, and owners' capital will remain open.

After all accounts have been closed, prepare a *post-closing* trial balance. This will tell you if you have made the adjustments and closing entries correctly. If you had done a pre-closing trial balance, then errors in the post-closing trial balance should be relatively simple to spot.

Some adjusting entries recorded at this point will affect the accounting period which follow. An example of this will be the Commissions Accrued account. Remember, it was said that even though the commissions had not been paid in that period, they are still an expense of the period. The payable still exists and will be paid in the following accounting period. In order to get the books in order, then, we need a *reversing entry* in the amount of the payable. An example of this reversing entry is:

Commissions Expense	1000	
Commissions Payable		1000

Where this gets a little sticky is on such an account as Salaries Payable, when the end of the accounting period falls mid-term in the pay cycle. Thus, the accountant might have to reverse only a partial pay cycle.

Occasionally—just occasionally—an accountant makes an error. If this error occurs within the accounting period, it is merely corrected by a line-out and correction, or at least the proper adjusting entries. But if the error was made in one accounting period but not discovered until the next accounting period, it will be necessary to attach the Capital Account to which the Expense had been originally closed. Thus:

To correct error in adjusting entry:

Auto Insurance Expense	350	
Prepaid Insurance		350
Capital (Ownership)	250	
Prepaid Insurance		250

It is common practice to present all corrected errors on the Capital Statement in order to show the effect on previously reported net income.

SPECIAL CONSIDERATIONS

To this point we have concentrated on the bookkeeping aspects of accounting. We have talked of ledger, journals, entries, trial balances, statement preparation, adjusting, closing—in essence, the *mechanics* of accounting. But it must be remembered that accounting is a method of financial monitoring wherein business decisions may be made. In the balance of the chapter we will deal with those decision-based subjects, including inventory valuation, depreciation methods, and financial analyses.

Methods of Valuing Inventory

In preparing any of the pertinent reports of the corporation, it is necessary to establish a standard method of accounting for the inventory purchased for resale or manufactured for sale. If we could depend upon our gizmos to always cost the same, year in and year out, there would be no problem. But unfortunately, that's not the way things are. Costs get inflated and increase, be they costs of manufacture or transportation, or whatever. Study the statement in Figure 5.29.

We know we began the year with 3 of Model 401. During the year, we acquired 11 more of them, giving us a total of 14. At the end of the year we had 4 left. But which 4 were they? We had sold 10 of them, but which 10? We had the option to sell 10 factorial (10!) ways, so which is the cost of goods sold and which is the cost which we will transfer to next year's books? In essence, what is the *flow of costs* throughout the year in regard to Model 401?

In what follows, we will deal with the commonly used methods of inventory valuation. Some will be more prevalent than others, but all are valid. There are reasons for using (and even for changing) a specific method. We'll concentrate upon the following methods:

- First-in, first-out method (FIFO)
- Last-in, first-out method (LIFO)

Gizmo Corporation
Inventory Valuation

Model	Beginning Inventory 1/1	Purchases in Chronological Order 1	2	3	Ending* Inventory 12/31	Number of Items** Sold during 198x
401	3 @ $110	5 @ $115	4 @ $113	2 @ $111	4	10
402	5 @ 280	5 @ 270	3 @ 265	4 @ 250	3	14
403	2 @ 62	4 @ 70	6 @ 75	5 @ 79	7	10
404	3 @ 344	2 @ 360	5 @ 375	6 @ 387	4	12

*These items will be shown on the balance sheet as ending inventory.
**These items will be shown on the income statement as cost of goods sold.

Figure 5.29

- Weighted average method
- Valuation at cost or market
- Retail method
- Cross profit method

First-In, First-Out Method (FIFO)

The concept of FIFO is that the inventory activity will deduct from inventory first the things it receives first. The simplest analogy is that the inventory is perishable, and it must be deducted from inventory before it spoils. But the same may not be true of gizmos. One gizmo is just like another gizmo, and we may not wish to concern ourselves with the age of the gizmos. For small items, this approach might be practical. But if our gizmo were a piece of heavy equipment, we might not wish to move it around just to get the very first one we had received out of inventory. So we're concerned with accounting for the gizmos *as if we were moving the items in their order of production or receipt.*

There are some special advantages of the FIFO system. To begin with, the book costs have a sliding envelope. We can "check off" the early items and add the latest ones to the list. In its execution, the FIFO method is the simplest to use. It is also useful as a means to track specific costs. Therefore, it is always the latest items which will remain in stock and will carry over to the following year, at a reasonably current cost.

A firm will generally wish to use the FIFO system in good times, when its costs of goods sold can be relatively low in relation to its net profit. Other methods exist for similar reasons. But be aware that a corporation will generally pick one mode of inventory valuation for tax purposes and will not alter it to suit other purposes at any given time. Alteration of inventory valuation methods is permitted under tax laws, but if the method is altered frequently, tax officials will question the changes.

The following is a depiction of the carry-forward inventory, valued under the FIFO method. Remember that with FIFO, the carry-forward cost represents the latest (and frequently more expensive) costs. The quantities on hand will be shown on the balance sheet as ending inventory.

Last-In, First-Out Method (LIFO)

The concept of LIFO is that the inventory activity will deduct from inventory first the things it receives last. The simplest analogy is that the inventory is permanent, and it is from newly acquired stock. Again, this does not mean that the very last item put on the shelf is the first one taken off, although the analogy of a grocery shelf is difficult to ignore. It merely means that the accounting of inventory is treated as if the last item produced was the first one taken out of stock.

Gizmo Corporation
Inventory Valuation
(As shown on Balance Sheet)

Model	Quantity On Hand 12/31	FIFO	
401	4	2 @	$111
		2 @	113
			$448
402	3	3 @	$250
			$750
403	7	5 @	$79
		2 @	75
			$545
404	4	4 @	$387
			$1,548

Figure 5.30

There is but one very special advantage to the LIFO method of accounting for inventory. It permits a higher cost of goods sold to be entered to the books. This is particularly good for a corporation which wishes to keep its taxes down or may wish to take a loss in any given corporate year. Again, a firm cannot just arbitrarily modify its inventory valuation methods from year to year to suit the income statement.

While there is that one special advantage, there is another advantage, as well. A firm involved in producing for inventory very often does not own its inventory. Generally, for purposes of cash flow, that firm will discount the merchandise to a bank or other institution in exchange for ready cash. Thus, the bank takes title to the goods, although they remain at the corporation's inventory location. It is not uncommon for a financial institution to charge as high as 20 or 25% for this service. So, a firm, in order to maintain working capital, will be willing to take 80 cents on the dollar in exchange for the ability to have that 80 cents as working capital. When the item is sold, the "loan" is paid off. The inventory valuation in Figure 5.31 shows LIFO. The quantity on hand will be shown on the balance sheet as ending inventory.

Now, compare the two methods, FIFO and LIFO, to the values stored on the Inventory Valuation, presented previously. Note that the two units of Model 401 listed under FIFO would appear in the third period of "Purchases Made In Chronological Order." The three units of LIFO show as the beginning inventory.

Impact on the Income Statement

In the same manner as the inventory valuation method affects the balance sheet, so too does it affect the income statement. See Figure 5.32.

When compared (FIFO vs. LIFO) as shown above, you can see the differences the figures make insofar as the balance sheet and income statement. A close comparison of the two will follow shortly.

In the case of Model 401, the range of purchase price was from $110 to $115, or an average of $112.50, and a variance of 5. As you can see under FIFO, we end up with an inventory valuation of $1,131 for 10 units, or $113.10 average per unit. Under LIFO, the average would be $113.40, certainly a negligible difference. So the method of inventory valuation would be insignificant for Model 401.

Gizmo Corporation
Inventory Valuation
(As Shown on Balance Sheet)

Model	Quantity On Hand 12/31	LIFO
401	4	3 @ $ 110
		1 @ 115
		$ 445
402	3	3 @ $ 280
		$ 840
403	7	2 @ $ 62
		4 @ 70
		1 @ 75
		$ 479
404	4	3 @ $ 344
		1 @ 360
		$1,392

Figure 5.31

Gizmo Corporation
Inventory Valuation
(As Shown on Income Statement)

Model	Quantity Sold 12/31*	FIFO	Total Beginning Inventory Plus Total Purchases**	LIFO
401	10	3 @ $ 110		2 @ $ 111
		5 @ 115		4 @ 113
		2 @ 113		4 @ $ 115
		$1,131	$1579	$1,134
402	14	5 @ $ 280		4 @ $ 250
		5 @ 270		3 @ 265
		3 @ 265		5 @ 270
		1 @ 250		2 @ 280
		$3,795	$4545	$3,705
403	10	2 @ $ 62		5 @ 79
		4 @ 74		
		$ 704	$1249	$ 770
404	12	3 @ $ 344		6 @ $ 387
		2 @ 360		5 @ 375
		5 @ 375		1 @ 360
		2 @ 387		
		$4,401	$5949	$4,557

* These items will be shown on the income statement as cost of goods sold.

** This total of beginning inventory and purchases is the same for both methods. Either method allocates this to either ending inventory (balance sheet) or cost of goods sold (income statement).

Figure 5.32

Balance Sheet as of 12/31		
	FIFO	LIFO
Cash	$ 1,000	$ 1,000
Accounts Receivable	3,000	3,000
Inventory	1,548	1,392
	$ 5,548	$ 5,392

Income Statement for the Year Ended 12/31		
	FIFO	LIFO
Sales	$10,000	$10,000
Cost of Goods Sold	4,401	4,557
Gross Profit	$ 5,599	$ 5,443

Difference	Balance Sheet	Income Statement
FIFO/LIFO	+$156	-$156

Figure 5.33

Model 404, on the other hand, has quite a difference, with a range of $43 in the purchase cost. Under FIFO, with 12 units, we have an average cost of $366.75. For 12 units this may be no big deal, but for 12,000 units, or 12,000,000 units, this might well be significant. Again, inventory methods just cannot be changed to suit a firm's fancy.

Now let's take a look at Figure 5.33, which shows the effect of FIFO and LIFO on the Balance Sheet and the Income Statement, concentrating on Model 404. Look back to the inventory balances for comparisons.

Other Methods

FIFO and LIFO are not the only methods to value inventory, albeit they are the most prevalent.

Another alternative is the *weighted average method.* This method is based on the assumption that all costs can be charged on an average basis. If you are in a business where various purchases of identical units of a commodity are mingled, this method smooths the physical flow of inventory accounting. Using the same data on the Model 401, we see that we began with 3 units, acquired 11 more, sold 10 of those 14, and had a carry-forward balance of 4. The total cost of the inventory of Model 401 was $1,579, which, when divided by 14, gives a weighted average of $112.78 each. A very interesting point is that this weighted average is mid range between the arithmetic average under the FIFO method ($112.50) and the arithmetic average under the LIFO method ($113.40). The precise midpoint between the two averages would be $112.95.

Look again a Model 404. We began with 3 units, acquired 13 units, sold 12 of those 16, and had a carry-forward balance of 4. The total cost of the inventory of Model 404 was $5,949, which, when divided by 16 gives a weighted average of $371.81 each. It, too, fits mid-range between the FIFO ($366.75) and LIFO ($379.75) arithmetic averages. The precise midpoint would be $373.25. The question arises: why not just take the average of the FIFO and LIFO arithmetic means? Remember, this is called a *weighted average.* Its function is to value inventory with due consideration given to the entire purchasing history of the inventory. Since inventory is essentially revolving, the weighted average system provides a smoother control on changes in inventory valuation than do either FIFO or LIFO. And, of course, it is not nearly so extreme as either of the methods. In a manual system, FIFO or LIFO is simpler.

In comparing the results obtained from the comparison, you should remember that both the amount reported as net income and the amount reported as inventory are affected. Again, as stated, when you have the lowest cost of merchandise sold, you also have the highest figure for gross profit and net income. The taxes will be proportionately higher, as well.

In all cases, since it represents a compromise between FIFO and LIFO, it would be better to value inventory via the weighted average technique. To figure it manually, however, is tedious. It's a candidate for EDP.

Another method to value inventory is to take the valuation at *cost* or *market, whichever is lower.* "Market" means "replacement cost." While the method is acceptable to IRS, it is not in common use nor recommended due to the data which must be collected to make it work. It's best used for an inventory system with few items.

Yet another method is the *retail inventory method,* wherein the inventory is valued on its retail price by figuring the ratio of cost to the retail price. In this method, the net merchandise inventory must be multiplied by this ratio to determine the cost price estimate.

And finally, the *gross profit method* is available, wherein the gross profit ratio is multiplied against the net sales to produce the inventory value. Again, there is a high bookkeeping cost, and the method is not recommended.

Depreciation

To get an *ap*preciation of *de*preciation, look at the Cash Flow Statement shown in Figure 5.34. This statement is based on the benefit of a system we anticipate installing. Note that the depreciation has reduced the before-tax income and thus the taxes on that income. Had we not deducted the depreciation the taxes (based on the corporate rate of 50%) would have been $50,000 rather than the $30,000 depicted.

Thus there is a very specific reason for treating depreciation from a financial (accounting) perspective. But it is valuable from another point of view—replacement. All fixed or plant assets, except land, lose their usefulness with the passage of time or productive output. The varying degrees of use, the varying degrees of wear, or simply the passage of time will all tend to take away the useful value of the physical asset. And sometimes, even though the physical use has been slight, the date of the asset will determine its value.

That 1954 automobile out in the garage may have only 25,000 miles on it, but it is still a 1954

Gizmo Corporatiov
Cash Flow Statement

Benefits derived from system	$100,000
Less: Depreciation	40,000
Taxable Income	$ 60,000
Income Taxes	30,000
Net Benefit After Taxes	$ 30,000
Plus: Depreciation	40,000
Cash Flow	$ 70,000

Figure 5.34

model. Distinguish carefully between *book value* and *market value,* however. The 1954 automobile will decline in book and market values until it reaches the point where technically the scrap metal is worth more. But if it happens to be in mint condition and just happens to be a Packard its value will be something more than scrap metal.

To gain a perspective on what to depreciate, we must first know what the acquisition costs are. The initial costs of a fixed asset include all expenditures necessary to get the asset into place and get it ready for productive use. Thus, the costs of a lathe—installed—including the purchase price of the lathe, any taxes attributable to the sale, the transportation, the installment, and the initial testing, are all part of the cost of this depreciable asset. The costs of a system, including its design, programming, testing, installation, etc.—its development costs—are all depreciable.

Depreciation is a means to expire costs over a period of time, or more specifically to match the cost against the productive or useful life of the asset. If a corporation were to merely purchase an item and then treat it as a current expense (write it off in one year), then net profit would take a dip in that year, while it would soar disproportionately in later years in relation to that asset. So while we may *pay* for the asset in a single year or on a two- or three-year contract, the cost of that asset may well have been written over a period of as long as ten years.

Thus, we concern ourselves with the *expired costs* when we talk about accumulated depreciation. Do not confuse *accumulated* depreciation with the annual depreciation rate which can be written off in any single year. Again, do not confuse depreciation with market value.

It is a common misconception that depreciation provides the means to provide a cash fund for the replacement of the asset which is being depreciated. Expired portions of the cost of the assets are transferred to the Expense and Revenue Summary. The cash account is not touched by any of that accounting. As we have seen, however, the depreciation is a direct offset to taxable income. If a corporation were to set aside the taxes not spent by virtue of the depreciation, then the 50% (or whatever corporate rate is used) of the depreciable portion of the asset could be established as a cash fund for its replacement.

In any method of depreciation used, the accounting for the asset will provide for the decrease toward a relatively negligible book value. Book value may be thought of as the wholesale value should you dispose of the asset. Book value must not be confused with salvage value, which is the value, in simple terms, which could be derived at minimum sale or if scrapped.

Three things must be considered when computing the periodic depreciation of the asset:

1. Its initial cost, including all contributing factors
2. Its estimated residual value
3. The period (or productive output) over which the asset will be spread.

Straight-Line Method

Perhaps the most common form of depreciation, and certainly the simplest, is the *straight-line method.* This method provides for equal periodic charges to expense over the estimated life of the asset.

To execute the straight line method, one must first determine or estimate the useful life of the asset. To do that, one must know something about the quality of the asset. The estimated useful life cannot be assigned arbitrarily. The rationale for that is this: If the useful life were to be set at ten years and the asset's useful life were only five years, then the per-year distribution of the depreciation would be half of what it should be, resulting in distribution of costs beyond the productive life of the asset. Of course, five years' depreciation could be written off when the asset expired, but it would seriously depress the net profit for that year.

Next, a salvage (or residual) value must be determined. This is the projected wholesale price, the benefit to be derived by resale, or the input of funds if the asset were to be sold for scrap. Using the following formula, the percentage of annual depreciation is determined: (Cost − Salvage Value)/Esti-

Year	Cost	Rate*	Depreciation Expense	Accumulated Depreciation	Book Value
1	$10,000	20%	$2,000	$ 2,000	$8,000
2	10,000	20%	2,000	4,000	6,000
3	10,000	20%	2,000	6,000	4,000
4	10,000	20%	2,000	8,000	2,000
5	10,000	20%	2,000	10,000	0

* Applied to original cost: depreciation expense - rate x original cost.

Figure 5.35

mated Life. Assume you have an asset worth $10,000 which has no salvage value, and you have determined that you will depreciate it across an estimated life of five years. The formula would look like this: ($10,000 − 0)/5 = 20%($2,000). Thus, 20% *of the original value* will be written off each year, incrementing the accumulated depreciation and decrementing the book value by $2,000 each year, as shown in Figure 5.35.

Production Units Basis

The *production units* basis for depreciation, sometimes referred to as the units-of-production method, is commonly used in machine-oriented applications, such as printing presses or punchpresses. To use the method, the productive output of the machine must be determined. This may be done in terms of number of operations, hours, or distance (if the asset happens to be a vehicle).

To demonstrate, assume an asset which cost $42,000 with a residual value of $2,000, which is expected to have a useful life of 20,000 hours: ($42,000 − $2,000)/20,000 = $2 per hour. Thus, for each hour of use, $2 will be charged for depreciation. An accountant is not about to make a $2 entry every hour of a $16 entry every day, so what is customarily done is to attached a lapsed-time meter, and periodically the meter reading is recorded.

Using the same criteria, let's assume that the device is good for a million units of output: ($42,000 − $2,000)/1,000,000 = $.04 per unit. As you can see, this is also an efficient means to determine the machine cost on a cost of production exercise. This accounting is done using an automatically incremented counter.

Assuming that the unit was run 40 hours a week for 50 weeks (effectively a year), then we would record a year's depreciation as (100 × 40 x 50 x $.04) = $8,000. The 100 factor is the assumption that the machine produces 100 gizmos every hour.

As can be seen, at that rate the entire asset would be written off over a five year period. What's the point? Why not use the straight-line method in the first place? The rationale is this: the estimate has been made based on a standard work-week for a standard work-year. Suppose, instead, that it was being worked for two shifts, or possibly even three. For illustration, let's assume that it is used 20 hours a day for 250 days to the year. Again, making the assumption that it can produce 100 gizmos for each hour it is working: (100 x 20 x 250 x $.04) = a $20,000 depreciation write-off. And, of course, this is making the assumption that it will be used for those hours, no more and no less. This will permit the device to be depreciated as its productive capacity has been consumed.

The rationale for using the production units basis for depreciation is to charge the greatest amount of depreciation at the earliest possible time, while the cost of running the machine is relatively low. Later in its useful life it will be subject to breakdown, will require greater maintenance, and will therefore lose in overall efficiency.

Declining-Balance Method

There is another method to accomplish the same goal. Known as the declining-balance method, or occasionally referred to as the double-declining-balance method, it allows accelerated depreciation. Recall that under the straight-line method there was fixed an annual depreciation percentage to be written off against the cost of the asset. The declining-balance method uses a similar rationale, except for the fact that an accelerated percentage is applied against the book value of the asset. The reason it is frequently referred to as the double-declining-balance method is that a percentage twice that of the straight-line method is commonly used. Since the straight-line depreciation was 20% in our previous illustration, the percentage will now be doubled to 40%. Review Figure 5.36.

Note that the 40% is assigned against the full cost in the first year, accumulating a depreciation of $4,000 and leaving a book value of $6,000. For year 2, the 40% is taken of $6,000, giving a depreciation of $2,400, incrementing the accumulated depreciation to $6,400 and decrementing the book value to $3,600. In like manner, the remainder of the years, until the remaining book value is written off in the final year. Again, the rationale is to use the method to write off the cost of the asset in its early years, when its productivity is at its highest.

In the example, there is an implicit assumption that the first use of the asset coincided with the beginning of the accounting period. Of course, it really doesn't happen that way. If the asset has been placed in service after the beginning of the fiscal year, a pro-rated depreciation must be taken. If, for example, it has been put into service during the fourth month, only 8 months would be eligible to receive a depreciation entry. In that case the depreciation would be rated at 75% of that 40% of the cost of the asset. The final depreciation rate for the first year would be 30%. In the following year the 40% figure would return, except for the fact that the book value would be $7,000 instead of the $6,000 shown in the illustration.

An interesting sidelight of the accelerated depreciation methods listed is that they may be done on a *mixed asset* basis; that is, the process does not have to be uniform across all the assets, but consistent as to the one considered.

Sum of the Years' Digits Method

Another commonly used method to depreciate a fixed asset is called the *sum of the years' digits method.* This is also a method to write the greater portion of the depreciation off over the early years of the asset. What it does is to write off a successively smaller fraction of the cost (less the residual value).

In using this method, the total of the digits must be added up. Look at Figure 5.37. Note that there are five years. Thus, the sum of the years' digits is 15(1 + 2 + 3 + 4 + 5). If the number of years is great, use the formula: $S = N(N + 1)/2$. Thus, if the asset were a 99 year asset, the sum of the years' digits would be 99(50) = 4950, which is considerably easier than 1 + 2 + 3 + . . . + 97 + 98 + 99.

Year	Cost	Rate*	Depreciation Expense	Accumulated Depreciation	Book Value
1	$10,000	40%	$4,000	$4,000	$6,000
2	10,000	40%	2,400	6,400	3,600
3	10,000	40%	1,440	7,840	2,160
4	10,000	40%	864	8,704	1,296
5	10,000	40%	518	9,222	778**

*Applied to book value: depreciation expense= rate x book value.
**Charged off in full in 5th year.

Figure 5.36

Year	Cost	Rate*	Depreciation Expense	Accumulated Depreciation	Book Value
1	$10,000	5/15	$3,335	$3,335	$6,665
2	10,000	4/15	2,668	6,003	3,997
3	10,000	3/15	2,001	8,004	1,996
4	10,000	2/15	1,334	9,338	662
5	10,000	1/15	662	10,000	0

* Applied to original cost; depreciation = expense-rate x original cost.

Figure 5.37

In determining the rate, the denominator, then, will be the sum of the years' digits. The numerator will then be the total of the remaining years of useful life. Thus, in the following table, one third (5/15) of the asset is written off in the first year, 27% in the second year, 20% in the third, 13% in the fourth, and 7% in the fifth and final year.

Again, the only difference in calculation would be for a period which does not coincide with the accounting period. In that case, the pro-rated method would apply. But there is a fundamental difference, in that the total cycle is carried into a split year. That is, the rate will run for a complete year, even though that complete year is split among more than one financial or fiscal year.

Depreciation Based on Averages

Up to this point we have discussed methods to depreciate which apply to a *specific* asset at a specific rate. It is possible to determine depreciation for entire groups of assets using a single rate. The basis for grouping may be similarity in useful life estimates, or other common characteristics, or a group may include all assets within a functional class, such as office equipment.

When depreciation is computed for a group of assets, it is necessary to develop an average rate. This is generally done by computing the annual depreciation for each item and dividing the total depreciation for the group by the total cost of the assets. It is a functional manner to perform depreciation, as new assets enter the mix as older ones are retired, so the total value of the asset group remains relatively unchanged.

Recording Depreciation

Handling depreciation on the books has already been discussed. However, there are some additional entries to the *Capital Expenditures* and to the *Revenue Expenditure.*

From time to time during the useful or service life of the asset, additional expenses are incurred. Perhaps the item breaks down and requires maintenance or repair. So far as normal maintenance is concerned, this would be a revenue expenditure, in that the asset is returned to its functioning state. If, on the other hand, the asset is completely overhauled such that the useful life is extended, it may mean that some of the accumulated depreciation may have to be removed from the books and restored from the Depreciation Expense account. And, of course, if the asset is in any manner enhanced, this will augment the capital value of the asset, increase the asset cost, and extend the depreciation.

Occasionally it becomes necessary to dispose of a fixed asset, either by write-off (hopefully at the completion of its useful life) or by outright sale. This must be done by a debit to the accumulated depreciation account and crediting the asset account for the cost of the asset.

Let's assume first that the asset has been fully depreciated:

To write off discarded asset

Accumulated Depreciation—Asset	$5,000	
Asset		$5,000

If the asset has been fully depreciated, it will be necessary to record a loss when it has been disposed. That would require this series of entries:

To bring depreciation account current to closeout

Depreciation Expense—Asset	$100	
Accumulated Depreciation—Asset		$100

To write off the asset

Accumulated Depreciation—Asset	$4,100	
Loss on Disposal of Asset	900	
Asset		$5,000

If the asset has been fully depreciated, but still has utility, it should not be removed from the books. To do so would remove the asset from the books with no indication of its remaining profitability.

When selling an asset, the accountant must first bring its depreciation account up to date, in the same manner as demonstrated above. From that point on, however, the sale must present the asset in terms of its revenue:

1. Equal to book value
2. Less than book value—a loss
3. Greater than book value—a gain

To record sale for book, the following entry should be used:

Cash	$100	
Accumulated Depreciation—Asset	4,900	
Asset		$5,000

To record sale for less than book, the following entry should be used:

Cash	$50	
Accumulated Depreciation—Asset	4,900	
Asset		$5,000

To record sale for more than book, the following entry should be used:

Cash	$500	
Accumulated Depreciation—Asset	4,900	
Asset		$5,000
Gain on Disposal of Fixed Asset		400

Occasionally, the asset is traded in or exchanged. This frequently involves a trade-in allowance for the formerly owned asset. Technically, the book on the first asset becomes the trade-in on the new asset, and if it is done evenly, the accounting is simple. It's where the gain or loss is recognized (or not recognized, as the case may be) that the actual accounting may be done. The gain and loss are recorded in the same manner as above, but the handling of the gain or loss is different. Where the gain or loss is recognized, it is separately expensed, with the reservation that the U.S. Internal Revenue Code does not permit the gain or loss for tax purposes. Where it goes unrecognized, however, the cost is added to or deducted from the price of the newly acquired asset.

As with assets and liabilities in general, the accountant may wish to establish several subordinated ledgers to permit him to track the accumulation of depreciation on the several unique assets while the depreciation is occurring. This will assist in financial decision making, especially in relation to functional groups of assets, such as office equipment.

There is one final topic to discuss—the appearance of the fixed assets on the financial statements—specifically the balance sheet. Where the number of fixed assets is small, it may be advisable to list the three categories (cost, accumulated depreciation, and book value) separately on the balance sheet. The fixed asset account, as reported on the balance sheet, should indicate the total of the book values of the separate assets.

Accounting for Notes, Interest, Expenses, Taxes: Deferrals and Accruals

Credit Instruments

Earlier in the chapter, the mechanism was illustrated whereby you may wish to obtain an IOU from a person to whom you wish to lend money. The IOU is merely one example of a *promissory note,* which is merely one form of credit instrument.

This promissory note, more frequently called simply a *note,* is a safer instrument for a creditor than is an account receivable. Since the note requires a signature, it provides legal documentation of a claim against the debtor. More specifically, the note is a highly liquid asset which has negotiable qualities on the open market, should the creditor, in an effort to favor his cash position, wish to discount it.

To get the terminology straight, the person who obtains the cash or other benefit in exchange for the instrument is known as the *maker.* The person who accepts the note is known as the *payee.* To the former, there is a *note payable.* To the latter, there is a *note receivable.*

Notes can be available as *interest-bearing* or *non-interest-bearing.* If a note is non-interest-bearing, then the sum returned is known as the *principal,* and is simply a bookkeeping entry. On an interest-bearing note, however, the maker is responsible to pay both the principal and the interest. For the maker, the interest would be treated as *interest expense* and is a revenue statement entry. For the payee, the interest would be known as interest income, and is also a revenue statement entry. Interest, by the way, is determined either by some legal authority (in the case of a ''small loan'') or by market forces and the fluctuation of the prime rate, that rate given by large commercial banks to its best customers.

Interest is generally stated in terms of a period of a year. Thus, the *simple interest* (no compounding) on $1,000 at 12% for one year would be $120. If the note happened to be for six months, the interest would be $60. Notes which extend beyond a year generally provide for interest to be paid annually, semiannually, or at some other interval. In commercial credit transactions, however, the term is generally less than a year. The common practice is to treat the year as a 360 day year, for division-by-day purposes.

The basic formula for computing interest is:

$$\text{Principal} \times \text{Rate} \times \text{Time} = \text{Interest}$$

To illustrate, suppose you borrowed $1,000 at 12% for 20 days. The formula would look like this:

$$\$1{,}000 \times \frac{12}{100} \times \frac{20}{360} = \$6.66 \text{ interest}$$

Of course, this illustration has been expressed in days. If the note were taken on a monthly basis, each month is considered to be $\frac{1}{12}$ of a year, or $\frac{30}{360}$.

In general practice, the time between the issuance of the note and its maturity date is expressed in months or days. Where it has been expressed in months, the calculation of due date is a simple matter. Where it has been expressed in days, the procedure is to determine the due date by the elapsed days on the calendar. There are a couple of ways to do this, but the problem is a simple one. Caution, however: a 90-day note taken out on the 5th of January is not necessarily due on the 4th of April. Recall the months with 28, 29, 30, and 31 days.

Since the notes payable of any firm are generally few, it is doubtful that a system of subordinate ledgers will be required. Duplicates of the note should provide sufficient documentation for a single account in the general ledger.

In addition to being a credit instrument for borrowing money, the note payable may also be a credit instrument for an extension to an account payable. This credit extension will require a note, and, of course, may be either interest-bearing or non-interest bearing. The entry to create the note for the extension looks like this:

Accounts Payable—Company	$100	
Notes Payable		$100
Issued a 30 day, non-interest-bearing note.		

When the note is paid, it will be a debit to notes payable and a credit to cash. In the cash payments journal, the debit will be journalized under some sundry account, unless such payables are common enough to have a special column. Expenses incurred for the money borrowed on the extension is a debit to interest expense and is recorded at the time the payment is made, either when the debt is settled or in incremental payments across time.

Up to this point we've talked about notes which secure receivables. Look now at the company which simply borrows money as you and I would borrow money. Suppose, for instance, we had borrowed $2,000 at 12% for a year. At the time we signed the note, the books would look like this:

Cash	$2,000	
Notes Payable		$2,000

When we go to pay the note, we must pay an additional $240 interest, making the total payment $2240. The entries would look like this:

Notes Payable	$2,000	
Interest Expense	240	
Cash		$2,240

Conceptually a Mortgage Payable works precisely the same way, but the difference is that a mortgage or even a long-term note will always have one part of it which must be represented on the books as being current (within one year).

Occasionally, a sales-oriented enterprise will have an account go delinquent. Normally, it treats its receipts as Accounts Receivable, and where the item may be returned to inventory at or near its sale value (such as a used car), then the delinquency can be recouped. But it often happens that the inventory activity cannot replace the item to its inventory, or for one reason or another wishes the customer to retain the item. The enterprise may then require the purchaser to sign a note (which is then negotiable) for the asset Accounts Receivable is decreased (credited). Again, this may be interest-bearing or non-interest-bearing depending upon the value of the item, the term of the extension, or the seller's wishes, and/or legalities.

If there is an interest-bearing note which is subsequently paid by the customer, then it is necessary for the firm to record the *Interest Income.* In this event, notes receivable and interest income would each be credited, while cash would be debited, like this:

Cash	$1,100	
Notes Receivable		$1,000
Interest Income		100

In this example, the interest has been added to the principal of the note. It is possible to extend a note in the manner of *discounting.* Many small finance companies work on this principle. In the instance of discounting, the interest is deducted from the face of the note. For example, if the note were for $1,000 and the interest were $100, then the borrower would receive $900 in cash and then would have to pay the full face value of the note, or $1,000. The only real difference between the terms *interest* and *discount* is the time period in which they are paid. The interest is paid in addition to the principal, and is generally paid at the end of the note, whereas the discount is taken "up front." In reality, they are both interest. *Caution:* Several financial firms have sliding interest scales, such as would be found on home mortgages, where the larger amount is taken first.

The entry to support a discounted note payable would look like this:

Cash	$900	
Interest Expense	100	
Notes Payable		$1,000

Another word of caution: Occasionally, a firm will use a preprinted form for several journals, such as the cash receipts journal. Since the cash receipts journal is an asset ledger, it records cash as a debit and the balancing accounts as a credit. But, as you can see above, Interest Expense is as a debit in a column marked to be a credit entry. The common practice in this instance, and in any similar instance, is to record the debit in the credit column and then to circle the entry, which indicates that it is a debit. This will hold true only for forms which have no corresponding debit space under the account you must debit.

As stated before, one of the reasons for getting a note receivable is that it is highly liquid and may be converted to cash, generally by discounting it to some financial institution. Consider, for instance, you had loaned $1000, on-interestbearing. The initial entry would look like this:

Notes Receivable	$1,000	
Accounts Receivable—Customer		$1,000
To record a 90 day non-interest-bearing note.		

You had decided to give the customer a break and grant him an extension of his time. But a month after you had been so kind, you suddenly developed an urgent need for cash. What to do? Well, you take the note down to the local bank and discount that note to the bank, promising to pay the full amount in exchange for the principal minus the discount. And you hope you can recoup the discount from the customer.

The situation changes somewhat when the note is interest-bearing. In that instance, the firm records the face value of the note plus the interest, minus the discount on the note, to determine the proceeds. For instance, suppose your firm had issued a note for $2000 at 12% for 90 days. This would give a face value plus interest of:

$$\$2{,}000 \times .12 \frac{90}{360} = \$60 \text{ interest}$$

$$\$2{,}000 \text{ (principal)} + \$60 \text{ (interest)} = \$2{,}060$$

Now, a month later, with 60 days still remaining on the note, you find it necessary to discount the note to a bank, and you are required to discount it at 15%. The discount you would pay would be:

$$\$2060 \times .15 \times \frac{60}{360} = \$51.50 \text{ discount}$$

$$\$2060 \text{ (principal)} - \$50 \text{ (discount)} = \$2008.50 \text{ (proceeds)}$$

The whole series of transactions looks like Figure 5.37a. The note that you have recorded on your books is $2,000. The proceeds of the note are $2,008.50. The difference, $8.50, is recorded as interest income. Had the proceeds been smaller than the original note, the difference would have been recorded as interest expense.

Two other facts bear on these examples. When the note is received and then discounted, the person or firm which discounts is then charged with the responsibility to pay the note. Thus, his ability to satisfy the note is contingent upon his receipt of the note made to him. This is known as a *contingent liability.*

The other fact, and the final comment on notes in this section, has to do with a dishonored note, one that is not settled. When that happens, the note is no longer a negotiable instrument and the account must be transferred back to Accounts Receivable, from which collection attempts will be made, and if unsuccessful, from which the account may be written off as a bad debt. In the case of a contingent liability, this dishonored note does not release the discounter from settling the debt with the financial institution.

Deferrals and Accruals

To this point, we have treated the firm's business essentially as a cash-oriented business. Yes, there were receivables and there were payables which extended beyond a year, but we made reference to the fact that even those had some portion with some elements of currency. Now is the time to talk about deferrals

Face Value of Note	$2,000.00
Interest on Note (90 days @ 12%)	60.00
Maturity Value of Note	$2,060.00
Discount on Maturity Value (60 days @ 15%)	51.50
Proceeds of Note	$2,008.50

Figure 5.37a

and accruals. Deferrals and accruals are important to determine precise costs allocations vis-a-vis the time period in which they are expended. Later, when cost accounting is discussed, you will see the value of this approach. For the time being, however, we're concerned about allocation of the revenues and expenses of a business to the appropriate elements of time, despite the specific time the receivable is received or the expense is paid

Definitions: A *deferral* is a postponement of the recognition of a revenue or of an expense *already paid.* An *accrual* is a gradual accumulation of a revenue or expense *not yet recorded.* Recall that which becomes the substance of the adjusting entry.

In making these adjusting entries, bear in mind that each adjustment affects one or more balance sheet accounts and one or more income statement accounts.

There are two types of deferral:

1. *Prepaid Expense* (frequently called a Prepayment or Deferred Charge). This is a liability.
2. Unearned Revenue (frequently called income received in advance or deferred credit). This is a liability.

There are two types of accrual:

1. *Accrued Liability* (frequently called an accrued payable). This is an asset.
2. *Accrued Asset* (frequently called an accrued receivable). This is an asset.

A *prepaid expense* is some commodity or service which has been purchased for consumption but which has not been consumed by the end of the accounting period. The portion of the asset which has been consumed is an expense of the period, but the remainder is a projected expense. Typical prepaid expenses are insurance, prepaid rent, prepaid interest, and office supplies.

Prepaid expenses are customarily recorded as assets initially. In the case of insurance, a fixed time schedule can be determined, but in the case of a commodity such as office supplies, their precise time of consumption cannot be accurately predicted, although it is known that some portion of those supplies will be consumed during that time period. Once it is determined how much of those supplies have been consumed, then the consumed portion is adjusted into an expense account.

It is possible to record the prepaid expense as an expense directly upon its initial entry, and thereby to decrease the bookkeeping required. Generally this is done when it is known that the prepaid expense will have been consumed within the accounting period anyway. In the same manner as the consumed portion may be adjusted from the asset account, the unconsumed portion may be adjusted from the expense account at the period end.

When the prepaid expense is initially recorded as an asset:

1. The adjusting entry is performed by transferring the amount consumed to the appropriate expense account.
2. The closing entry is performed by transferring the balance of the expense account to the expense and revenue summary account.
3. There is no reversing entry.
4. The balance of the prepaid expense is transferred to the asset account at the beginning of the new period.

When the prepaid expense is initially recorded as an expense:

1. The adjusting entry is performed by transferring the amount not consumed to the appropriate asset account.
2. The closing entry is performed by transferring the balance of the expense account to the expense and revenue summary account.
3. The reversing entry is performed by transferring the amount not consumed back to the expense account.
4. The balance of the prepaid expense is transferred to the expense account at the beginning of the new period.

In the same manner as the firm may have prepaid expenses, or money it has spent but not consumed, it may have received money it has not yet earned. This is called unearned revenue. Because it is unearned, it must be carried forward to future periods when its earning may be accomplished. More specifically, the earned portion must be separated from the unearned portion for accounting purposes.

An example of unearned revenue would be rent which has been received in advance, but for which the time corresponding has not passed. Subscriptions to magazines also fall in this category. When a firm accepts payment in advance for a commodity or service, it then makes itself liable to provide that commodity or perform that service. At the end of the period, the firm is entitled to claim as earned that which has been transferred or performed.

As prepaid expenses had two means of accountability, so too does unearned revenue—it may be recorded initially as a liability or as revenue. When unearned income is recorded as a liability, the amount of earned income is transferred to an income account as it is earned, or at some specific interval, such as a month. At the end of the period, that which has been transferred to the income (revenue) account may be treated in the income statement. The balance will be carried forward to the next period.

Unearned revenue may also be recorded initially as revenue as it is received. This is customarily done when it is a known fact that the revenue will be earned entirely within the accounting period, although the unearned revenue can be transferred out at the end of the period. Whenever a revenue account requires adjustment at the end of the period, the adjusting entry should be reversed after the books have been closed.

When the unearned revenue has been recorded initially as a liability:

1. The adjusting entry is performed by transferring the amount earned to the appropriate revenue account.
2. The closing entry is performed by transferring the balance of the revenue account to the expense and revenue summary account.
3. This is no reversing entry.
4. The balance of the unearned revenue is transferred to the liability account at the beginning of the new period.

When the unearned revenue is recorded initially as revenue:

1. The adjusting entry is performed by transferring the amount unearned to the appropriate liability account.
2. The closing entry is performed by transferring the balance of the revenue account to the expense and revenue summary account.
3. The reversing entry is performed by transferring the amount unearned back to the revenue account.
4. The balance of the unearned revenue is transferred to the revenue account at the beginning of the new period.

Some expenses are accrued over time but only paid at periodic intervals, such as salaries. In such an instance, we have an accrued liability (also known as an accrued payable or an accrued expense) which must be carried forward to the next accounting period. It is imperative to account for this accrual, as the expense of the salary must be recorded within the reporting period. An entry such as the following will be necessary:

Salary Expense	$300	
Salaries Payable		$300

When the salary has been paid, the $300 liability listed above will be discharged. To avoid the process of determining which portion was attributable to which period, a reversing entry is made as follows:

Salaries Payable	$300	
Salary Expense		$300

Now the salary payment can be made in its entirety, as follows, with the expense account being properly treated, and without undue account analysis:

Salaries Payable	$450	
Cash		$450

In the same manner as we can accrue a liability, so, too, may we accrue an asset. This is generally done when the revenue has been earned, but not received, such as during the middle of a contract, when the contract price or fee will be settled upon completion of the work. This is called by various terms, including *accrued assets, accrued receivables,* or *accrued revenues.* Such an accrued asset might be interest receivable, where the amount has been earned, but not yet paid. Its entries look nearly identical to those outlined above.

There is one other accrual/deferral which should be considered before the subject is closed—*taxes.* If you own a home, you're aware that that home is taxable property, just as some other forms of personal property. Such taxable property, known as *real property* (essentially lands and building and anything attached to that land) is commonly set on a tax base, locally determined, and is then multiplied by some tax rate. Taxes accrue, generally over the period of a year, and may be prepaid or paid on demand.

Since taxes are an expense of the business, they must be established as a payable, as an expense account, or as a prepaid account. In the situation where the taxes are held in escrow, the books may treat them as prepaid taxes, although the financial institution may not transfer them right away to the municipality. In fact, under current law in several states, taxes held in escrow may also draw interest, thus deriving interest income. Accounting for the prepaid, accrued, carryover, and payment of taxes has no special entries in the books, and are treated just like the other accounts with similar titles.

Two other kinds of tax bear examination: payroll taxes and sales taxes. Every employer who hires people is required by law to deduct certain taxes from the earnings of the employee. These may be state taxes, federal taxes, or other legally designated taxes (some cities have taxes as well). In addition, it is generally part of the payroll process to deduct certain other sums which are then accumulated for some specific reason. An example of this may be union dues. In the majority of cases, these items are deducted from the gross pay of the individual and are known literally as *deductions.*

The Federal Insurance Contributions Act (FICA) requires that a certain portion of a person's wages be deducted from his pay as a contribution to the funding of the Social Security Administration. From year to year, either the percentage of contribution or the gross on which it is deducted is changed (generally increased) by law. These taxes are customarily withdrawn from the employee's pay, are matched by the employer, and then must be deposited in an national bank, from which the Internal Revenue Service, at the same time the withholding funds are withdrawn, draws the FICA funds. This is customarily done quarterly, but can be done on other periods, depending on the size of the business.

Federal Income Tax is withdrawn in precisely the same manner as FICA, with the exception that the percentage withdrawn is dependent on the number of exemptions claimed by the employee, plus whatever other withholding he desires. The design of this method is to withdraw from the employee, over time, a figure relatively close to that which would correspond to the employee's gross tax on income. It, too, must be deposited in a national bank, but is not matched by contributions from the employer.

State and local taxes function in the same manner. In addition, other deductions, such as savings bonds, stock purchase options, contributions to charity, repayment of credit union loans, attachments to wages, premiums on insurance, deductions for health insurance, contributions to unemployment funds, union dues, contributions to special funds, company product accounts, etc., can all be deducted from the employee's gross pay. The formula for payroll deduction is simple: Gross Pay minus Deductions equals Net Pay. Of course, accounting for all these deductions is not so easy as merely stating the deductions. Since each is a separate account, they must be separately accounted for and then must be transferred at the appropriate time.

One of the documents used for this purpose is known as a *payroll register.* A payroll register contains column for each of the categories, including regular earnings, overtime earnings, total earning, taxable earnings, FICA tax, Federal Income tax, State Income tax, local income tax, and other deductions. The form used will correspond to the needs of the firm. In addition, columns are usually contained to show the amount paid, the check number, and an indication of the accounts to be debited, such as sales salary expense, office salary expense, labor expense, etc. With an automated system, all these figures would show up on a distribution report.

Of course, the individual's transaction base has been demonstrated, but the total individual transactions would, in sum make up the total payroll, plus all the deductions. The recording of the payroll in the books is transferred from the payroll register, in total, to the general journal in the following manner:

Sales Salary Expense
Office Salary Expense
Direct Labor Expense
Indirect Labor Expense
    FICA tax payable
    Withholding tax payable
    Bond deductions payable
    United Fund Contribution payable
    Accounts Receivable—J. Smith
    Salaries Payable
        Payroll for the week of __________

The debits and credits must balance. When the items marked "payable" are paid, the appropriate payable will be debited and cash (or cash in bank) will be credited. Each could be recorded individually, but that detail is available from the payroll register and general journal entries for each individual are not absolutely necessary. The method of payments could be either by check or cash, although the former is the most common method in use today. An alternative to that method may be found in direct bank transfers, where an employee's check may be deposited to the individual's checking account, requiring the firm merely to draw a single check payable to a specific bank in the amount of the total deposit, and then provide supporting documentation to permit the bank to properly credit the employee's account. Whatever the method selected, there will be a debit to the appropriate salary expense and a credit to cash. Where currency is used, it is advisable to support the transaction with a properly signed voucher system.

In a manual records system, occasionally the accounting (or payroll) department will keep a running record on the employee's earnings, showing the same kinds of information as in contained on the payroll register, except as applies to the individual only. In an automated system, year-to-date figures are customarily included.

To this point, the payroll and tax accounting has been discussed from the point of view of the specific employee. Firms, however, are liable for specific taxes (equal contribution to FICA), unemployment compensation taxes, etc. It is important to note that the total, whether it is deducted from the employee, contributed by the employer, or both, constitutes payroll expense. It is possible to record the taxes as a combination under Payroll Tax Expense, it is possible to debit each tax to a separate appropriately identified tax expense account, or it is possible to debit it to the respective wage or salary accounts to which they are related.

Payroll taxes are the type which require accrual, as outlined earlier. Taxes are a liability when the wages or salaries are *paid.* In fact, the IRS becomes very unhappy and assigns a penalty if they are not reported in the period of payment and an appropriate deposit is not made in a national bank. When the payroll falls within the accounting period, there is no problem. But when the payroll period crosses an accounting period, the expense must be divided according to the calendar, and the appropriate expense recorded despite the fact that the salary or wage is to be paid on some future calendar date. This problem is eliminated, or at least simplified, by a firm's decision to coincide the payroll period with the tax reporting period, or at least the final deducting cycle. This is why so many firms pay monthly or semimonthly.

In addition to deducting payroll taxes, the firm is often required to obtain, account for, and transmit *sales taxes* to the state and sometimes to the municipality. Sales tax percentages are generally fixed by law, and are required to be added to the amount of the sale. These are kept in aggregate and transmitted periodically to the taxing agency.

Sales taxes can be imposed on either the purchaser or the seller. When they are imposed upon the purchaser, the entry looks like this:

Accounts Receivable	$206	
Sales		$200
Sales Tax Payable		6

Receipt of the cash (payment by the customer) will look like this:

Cash	$206	
Accounts Receivable		$206

And when the tax is paid, the entry looks like this:

Tax Expense (Sales)	$6	
Cash		$6

Of course, the tax paid would be the total tax collected, not just the amount attributable to one sale, but the principle is the same.

When sales taxes are charged to the seller without any expectation to pass the tax separately along the the consumer, they are termed gross receipts taxes, and are a debit to the tax expense account and a credit to the payables account. Like other taxes, they are an accruable account, with the appropriate adjusting entries necessary.

One additional thought about taxes: the taxing agencies generally require a strict accounting by period, such as quarterly, and the funds must be transferred to the appropriate bank within the confines of the taxable period.

Up to this point, we have dealt with the various ways entries are made under different categories. Prior to beginning a new topic, we should discuss accounting from the perspective of a system of controls. Each area has been presented as an isolated topic, but it should be known that every account, journal, ledger, etc., actually forms a system wherein the firm can account for its revenues within the base of time, its cost within the base of expenditure, and the transaction mechanism between them.

Accounting has many functions. It provides information to the government, to stockholders, to creditors, etc. But more importantly, it provides control information to corporate management in relative proximity to that which requires control.

For purposes of the system, all transactions are recorded in terms of money—real (in hand), receivable (expected), or transient (flow). It is required to measure its revenue, allocate its costs, provide consistency over time, and to provide adequate disclosure to persons interested from the point of legality. The responsibility of the firm is to provide its information as accurately and conservatively as possible, basing judgment on the basis of materiality, not speculation.

A business is considered to be physically an ongoing entity, and must function as a legal person—that is, a corporation, and not the people who work for it, is treated like a single individual. Because it was not found on the 1985 exam, the discussion of partnership accounting has been dropped in favor of discussion about auditing, which was covered on the exam.

One final comment on consistency. A firm is expected to provide the accounting for its actions with a degree of consistency, so the stockholders and governmental agencies can depend on the truthfulness of financial statements. In some cases, this consistency is dictated by regulation, such as tax rates and inventory valuation methods, as well as depreciation schedules.

Accounting For Corporations

Incorporation

The corporation is a legal entity with all the characteristics of an individual. That concept was established more than a century and a half ago in the Supreme Court. Corporations exist to fulfill a charter. In the fulfillment of this charter, they may be *publicly held corporations* or *privately held corporations*, organized for profit or not for profit. *Open corporation* and *closed* or *closely held corporation* may be also used to denote public and private, respectively.

The rationale for a corporation is simple. Groups of people with pooled resources can accomplish goals more easily than can single individuals. Since much of industry is capital-intensive, huge sums of money must be attracted to allow the investment in such equipment, buildings, etc. These sums are available only from such a pooling type of activity. In addition, those who would invest in such an enterprise might not be able, available, or suitable to see the enterprise succeed by employment therein. So the corporation is formed, with a variety of objectives, which will include the production of a product or service, the employment of the principals of the firm and their employees, the acquisition of a profit form which the investors may reap a return for their investment, and a least one additional feature—perpetuity.

Since the corporation is a legal entity, is has some uniquely identifiable elements, among which are: a specific and separate legal existence; multiple and transferrable units of ownership of a variety of types; limited liability; perpetuity, or continuity of existence, where the stockholders, employees, principals change and the corporation goes on forever; and fees, taxes, and other forms of governmental regulation, subject to municipalities, states, and federal governments.

When a firm incorporates, it does so by the filing of a charter or articles of incorporation and the presentation of a tentative organization, including the sale of stock, if that is to be done. This is customarily done with the assistance of an attorney and with the payment of certain fees for incorporation to the state in which the organization is to be incorporated. The charter generally contains the basic rules governing the corporation. There are other rules of the corporation, known as bylaws, which may be effected by the corporation, including information about voting rules, location and time of stockholder meetings, issuance of capital stock, committees, titles, qualifications, etc.

This is the standard hierarchy of a corporation:

1. Stockholders
2. Board of directors
3. Executive committee
4. President
5. Vice president(s)
6. Junior executives
7. Administrative assistants
8. Other employees

Of course, this hierarchy changes from one corporation to another, as the needs of the organization exist, but categories 1–4 are relatively standard. In every corporation there are stockholders. The only question is whether or not they are *public stockholders*, or *stockholders at large.* It should be noted that categories 1 and 8 may represent many thousands of people, while categories 2–7 may represent relatively few people.

Stock

The owner's equity in a corporation is generally known as the *Stockholder's* (or *Shareholder*) *Equity, Capital, or Net Worth,* terms which appeared on the statements at the top of the chapter.

When we were discussing the sole proprietorship (you), recall that it was stated there would be a single category on the balance sheet for your worth. This means that you received that net worth and were under no obligation to distribute that net worth to any other person or to retain it for the business for any future date or occurrence. Under the corporation concept, there are two principal sources of capital—investment by the owners and the net income which is retained for the business (and not distributed), sometimes referred to as *retained earnings.* The net income would go into the Retained Earnings account of a corporation, from which the board, if it so chooses, may declare a dividend on earnings. Thus, net increases or gains are credited to the retained earnings account, and net losses are debited to the same account. Therefore, if the retained earnings has a debit balance, the account is in deficit.

In a corporation, the ownership is divided in shares, known as *Capital Stock.* Stock may be known as *Common Stock, Preferred Stock,* participating or non-participating, cumulative, or non-cumulative. They differ in the rights of the stocks as regards voting, sharing of earnings, maintenance of fractional percentage, and sharing of the assets under liquidation. Because of the limited liability afforded to the stockholders, the claims against the business are not claims against the personal holdings of the stockholders. If a corporation has only one class of stock, it is known as Common Stock. Under common stock, each share has equal rights and the rights are attributed to the share of stock rather than to the holder of that share of stock—a miniscule point, but very important in stock transfer situations.

If a corporation were to wish to appear to a broader investment potential, it is possible for that corporation to issue one or more higher classes of stock, known as *Preferred Stock.* The preference usually deals with the right to share in the earnings. The types of stock, the rights that attributed to those types of stock, and the voting limitations of each are found in either the charter or bylaws of the corporation.

The authority to distribute earnings rests with the Board of Directors. Since no corporation can guarantee with any certainty that it will operate at a profit, it cannot guarantee any distribution to its stockholders. The declaration of dividends, then, must require that adequate retained earnings exist to permit the distribution, and the board retains the ultimate decision as to just how much of the retained earnings will be distributed, retaining enough to cover potential future disaster situations or other contingencies. Dividends may be declared on common stock only after requirements for dividends have been made for higher classes of Preferred Stock.

Preferred stock may be participating or non-participating, which merely means that they may or may not participate in the distribution of the dividends. This does not mean that the non-participating members do not receive dividends, but rather that their dividends are stipulated to a specific return. Participating stockholders receive dividends which exceed the stipulated amount. It is safe to say that most preferred stock is nonparticipating, and if a corporation has stock available to the public, it will probably exist in just the two classes, Common and Preferred, non-participating.

One feature of the preferred stock over the common stock, however, is its guarantee of dividend. Lest that sound like a contradiction to a previous statement, let's establish that the preferred stockholder has a *right* to the stipulated dividend, *whether or not that dividend has been distributed.* Thus, dividends due to the holder of preferred stock are said to be *cumulative,* and despite the fact that dividends are not distributed, the dividend is nevertheless due to the stockholder at the time the dividends are paid. Preferred stock which does not have this right is said to be noncumulative.

Preferred stock may also be given preference over common stock in the claim to the assets upon the liquidation of the corporation. When and if a corporation goes defunct, the claims of the creditors are first satisfied, and then the remaining assets are distributed first to the holders of the preferred stock, and then if any remain, then they are paid to the holders of the common stock. Of course, this takes into account any unpaid, but cumulative, dividends.

One other difference between preferred and common is that the preferred has no voting rights, whereas the common does have those voting rights. This is a general statement, and not true in every instance, as a corporation may have several classes of preferred stock, and some of those classes of preferred stock may have stipulated voting rights.

It is not uncommon for a corporation to establish a price for each class of its stock, known as *par.* Par is a reasoned arbitrary figure, and may bear little, if any, resemblance to either the *book value* or *market value* of the stock. Occasionally, a corporation will issue preferred stock subject to its convertability to common stock. This is then "callable preferred stock," and when it is called, it is generally called for some amount in excess of par, which is known as the *redemption price.* The redemption price on callable preferred stock is stipulated when the stock is issued, and thus is an inviting guarantee to the investor. This redemption value may be either in return, dividends, or subsequent issues of common.

The book value of the stock is that value at which the stock had been issued plus the gains minus the losses. In other words, accumulations of gains and losses become part of capital. When there is just one class of stock, common, then the *book value per share* is obtainable merely by dividing the total capital by the number of shares outstanding. Thus, if a corporation had a common stock account of $200,000, there had been a retained earnings account of $100,000, and there were 3,000 shares of stock, the book value per share would be computed like this:

Common Stock	$200,000
Retained Earnings (CR)	100,000
Total Capital	$300,000

$300,000 divided by 3,000 shares = $100 book value

If the corporation had both preferred and common classes of stock, then the capital must be first allocated to the preferred stock, and then the difference divided amongst the common stock.

Consider the following illustration: The Gizmo Corporation has outstanding 3,000 shares of $100 par, 8% cumulative, non-participating preferred, and 100,000 shares of $10 par common. No dividends are in arrears. The balances are as follows:

Capital	
Preferred 8% stock, cumulative (3,000 shares outstanding)	$ 300,000
Common Stock, $10 par (100,000 shares outstanding)	1,000,000
Retained Earnings	200,000
Total Capital	$1,500,000

Allocation of Total Capital to Preferred and Common Stock	
Total Capital	$1,500,000
Allocated to Preferred Stock: Par	300,000
Allocated to Common Stock	$1,200,000

Book Value per Share

Preferred Stock: $300,000 divided by 3,000 shares = $100 per share
Common Stock: $1,200,000 divided by 100,000 shares = $12 per share

Thus it can be seen that the par value is of use in determining the payoff on the preferred stock (assuming the agreement is made at par), and that the remaining capital is attributable at par value plus $2 and assigned to common stock.

Now let's suppose for the sake of argument that the preferred stock had dividends in arrears for two years totalling $10. The retained earnings of $30,000 (3,000 x $10) would be reserved for the payment of dividends to the preferred stockholders as demonstrated here:

Total Capital		$1,500,000
Allocated to Preferred Stock:		
Par	$300,000	
Dividends in arrears	30,000	330,000
Allocated to Common Stock		$1,170,000

which would make the book value breakdown look like this:

Book Value per Share

Preferred Stock: $330,000 divided by 3,000 shares = $110 per share
Common Stock: $1,170,000 divided by 100,000 shares = $11.70 per share

Of course, in any system of allocation, the various rights of each class of stock must be known, and it can be seen that the book value is invaluable in determining the market price of the share. The book value, the history of earnings, the dividend rates, etc., are all valuable items of information when investors put their monies into the stock market.

Among the things a corporation's charter includes in the authority to issue a certain number of shares of stock. Since the precise capital needs of a firm at the outset are generally unknown, the charter will customarily set out sufficient provision for capital stock to permit the board at various times in its tenure to issue the stock it deems necessary. Thus, we have the *shares authorized,* the *shares issued,* and, of course, the difference is the *shares outstanding.*

Stockholder's Equity

Paid-in Capital:	
Preferred 8% stock, cumulative, $100 par (5,000 shares authorized, 3,000 shares issued)	$ 300,000
Common, $10 par (200,000 shares authorized, 100,000 shares issued)	1,000,000
Total Paid-in Capital	$1,300,000
Retained Earnings	200,000
Total Stockholder's Equity	$1,500,000

Figure 5.38

When we discussed the balance sheet of an individual, we simply expressed ownership in the terms of net worth. Since you were the sole proprietor in that example, you were then technically the only stockholder. Under the corporate situation, however, the owner's equity is divided among all the owners, and therefore is a summation of the stockholder's equity and retained earnings of the corporation at the time that the statement was prepared, figured at par value. Market value is not a good indicator, as the market may fluctuate radically between reporting periods. Book value is not a good balance sheet indicator, as the book value fluctuates with each earning cycle, and is only relevant during distribution activities anyway.

An example of a Stockholders' Equity section of a balance sheet is shown in Figure 5.38.

Of course, that illustration demonstrates a surplus in the retained earnings account. Had there been a deficit, and the retained earnings been a negative amount, the deficit would have lowered the total capital figure. As can be seen by the illustration, if the retained earnings figure of $200,000 were absent, the common stock would have been worth par, or $10. If, on the other hand, the retained earnings had been minus $100,000, then the worth of the common stock would have been $9.

So much for how the stock exists; how then do we do the business of transacting the stock? Well, it's not radically different from that which we've covered so far. Consider:

Cash	$1,300,000	
Preferred Stock		$ 300,000
Common Stock		1,000,000

In this example, the stock was transferred to the owner at par, and cash was received for the transaction. But cash is not always the source of asset input to the transaction. For instance, in a merger, where the assets from one firm are absorbed by another, the transaction might look like this:

Buildings	$520,000	
Land	80,000	
Preferred Stock		$100,000
Common Stock		500,000

Any business, be it sole proprietorship or partnership (excluding certain professions) may choose to incorporate, to obtain legal or financial benefits attributable through incorporation. In order to do so, however, it is necessary to make a thorough evaluation of the pre-incorporation firm, to ensure that assets, capital, liabilities, etc., are stated accurately at the time of incorporation. The general mechanism for the change follows. Those costs attributable to the incorporation, such as legal fees, permits, and taxes are all to be accounted for as an intangible asset known as *organization costs.* This cost may also be distributed across a period of years, in a method not too dissimilar to writing off a fixed asset.

The basic accounting procedures to incorporate a business are:

On the books of the partnership or sole-proprietorship:

1. Adjust and close the revenue and expense accounts.
2. Adjust the various asset accounts to the current fair market prices.
3. Record the transfer of the assets and liabilities to the corporation.
4. Record the receipt of stock from the corporation.
5. Distribute the stock, and also cash or other assets not incidental to the transfer to the sole owner or partners.

On the books of the corporation:

1. Record the assets and the liabilities acquired from the sole proprietorship or partnership.
2. Record the issuance of capital stock in payment for the net assets.

If arrangements have been made in the buyout of the sole proprietorship or partnership to pay the owners of the former organization a sum of monies over a period of time, the corporation may establish accounts payable to settle those debts of the corporation.

All depreciable assets are entered to the corporation books at their net value (their already depreciated value). In the case of receivables, however, both the total of the receivables and the allowance for doubtful accounts should be entered, as those who may default on receivables are not known at the time of the incorporation.

Up to now we have been talking about stock issued at par. Of course, par is an arbitrary but reasonable number which is given as the value of the stock for accounting purposes. As stated, stock can be issued above or below par. Insofar as the books are concerned, not only must the price of the stock sold be accounted for, but the divergence above or below par, as well. If the stock is sold above par, it is said to be sold at a *premium.* If it is sold below par, it is said to be sold at a *discount.*

Theoretically, a new firm should issue stock only at par, and would probably do so. But as the years wear on, it may be necessary to obtain large amounts of additional capital. At that time, the financial condition of the corporation can draw the capital needed at par, above par, or below par. If the company is stable and profitable, then it will behoove investors to pay a premium to get the stock. If, on the other hand, the company is in desperate straits to get the capital, then it will be more than willing to discount the stock. The sale of stock at a discount has other legal ramifications, and is not permissible everywhere. Local law should be consulted before using this procedure.

The entries for premium and discounted stock look like this:

Cash	$208,000	
Preferred Stock		$200,000
Premium on Preferred Stock		8,000

In this illustration, 1,000 shares of $200 par preferred stock have been sold for $208.

Cash	$570,000	
Discount on Common Stock	30,000	
Common Stock		$600,000

Paid-in Capital:		
Preferred 8% Stock, cumulative, $200 par (1,000 shares authorized and issued)	$200,000	
Premium on Preferred Stock	8,000	$ 208,000
Common Stock, $20 par (50,000 Shares authorized, 30,000 shares issued)	$600,000	
Less: Discount on Common Stock	30,000	570,000
Total Paid-in Capital		$ 778,000
Retained Earnings		$ 232,000
Total Stockholders' Equity		$1,010,000

Figure 5.39

In this illustration, 30,000 shares of $20 par common stock have been sold for $19.

The Discount is a contra-paid-in capital account and an offset against common stock.

Figure 5.39 is an illustration of how the Stockholders' Equity would be presented on the Balance Sheet.

As illustrated before, it is possible to gain assets in exchange for stock, but some care must be used in accounting for it. For instance, suppose that Land and Building had been accepted for 10,000 shares of $20 par stock. It would logically follow, then, that the value of the land and building would be set at $200,000. But suppose that the land and building had a fair market price of only $150,000. The accounting would have to be handled like this:

Land and Building	$150,000	
Discount on Common Stock	50,000	
Common Stock (10,000 Shares, $20 par)		$200,000

And if the fair market price had been $250,000:

Land and Building	$250,000	
Common Stock		$200,000
Premium on Common Stock		50,000

It is possible to issue stock at no-par, and that applies to both common and preferred, although the preferred is most often assigned a par value. In the instance where it issues no-par, the corporation must record the value of the stock at the value of the sale. Thus, if on one day it sells stock for $100 a share and then on the next day for $10 a share, then the recording of the transfer must be a debit to cash and a credit to common stock in the amount received. Rules for the sale of no-par stock are done on a state-by-state basis.

We have all heard of people who "play the stock market." These people, we think, buy and sell stock, and certainly some do. Others, however, subscribe to shares at a specific price. The stock certificate and the transaction are consumated, however, upon complete payment. On a corporation's books, the sale of the stock on subscription must be shown, but cannot be shown as an exchange for an asset, namely cash. It can become a receivable, however, under the title Stock Subscriptions Receivable. The person who subscribes becomes a stockholder as soon as the subscription is complete, but he does not acquire the rights of a stock until the full price is paid. Rights have a specific meaning all their own, and can themselves be bought and sold. The entry to sell a subscribed stock with a receivable is shown below:

Common Stock Subscriptions Receivable	$180,000	
Common Stock Subscribed		$150,000
Premium on Common Stock		30,000

And upon completion of the transfer, a simple entry like this is used:

Cash	$180,000	
Common Stock Subscription Receivable		$180,000

The receivable accounts for stock would become balance sheet accounts, as well.

It is possible for a company to deal in shares of its own stock. The process is called dealing in treasury stock. (Under uncontrolled circumstances, this can cause erratic market force). Thus, a firm may reacquire some of its outstanding stock, collect a payment in shares, or accept donations of its own shares. Treasury stock is not an asset of the corporation. It has no rights, participation, or control.

There are essentially four types of treasury stock:

1. That which is held and unissued by the corporation
2. That which has been issued as fully paid
3. That which has been reacquired by the corporation
4. And that which has not been cancelled or reissued

Since treasury stock can be sold, the account to be credited is Paid-in Capital from Sale of Treasury Stock. The debit is, of course to cash. Observe:

Treasury Stock	$50,000	
Cash		$50,000
Purchased 800 shares @ $62.50		
Cash	$20,000	
Treasury Stock		$18,750
Paid-in Capital from Sale of Treasury Stock		1,250
Sold 300 shares @ $66.67		
Cash	$18,000	
Paid-in Capital from Sale of Treasury Stock		$18,750

In the last two illustrations, the stock was accounted for at the purchase price. The gain or loss was reported as a credit or debit to the Paid-in Capital account. This, then, implies some sort of "inventory" system for the Treasury Stock, requiring that the stock be accounted for in purchased terms.

In the instance, rare though it may be, that you must account for donated treasury stock, it is generally accepted without a book entry. A memo is made in the ledger as to the par value, the number of shares received, and the donor. Not until that donated stock is sold will there be actual dollar figures entered on the books, and than in accordance with standard procedures.

A firm may issue preferred stock merely as an inducement to the investor. This stock may have a timed or callable redemption feature, allowing the firm to reclaim it at a price or in exchange for common stock. Sometimes these provisions will allow the stockholder the option as to when the conversion will be done. The following examples will demonstrate how this may be handled:

Cash	$115,000	
Preferred Stock		$100,000
Premium on Preferred Stock		15,000
Preferred Stock	$100,000	
Premium on Preferred Stock	10,000	
Retained Earnings	5,000	
Cash		$115,000
Preferred Stock	$100,000	
Premium on Preferred Stock	15,000	
Paid-in Capital from Preferred Stock Redemption		$ 2,000
Cash		113,000

Where the preferred stock does not have any provision for redemption, the corporation may purchase it on the open market, and then retire it from use. Retired stock may not generally be reissued.

As with all other books we have discussed, there are subordinate books and ledgers required to support the stockholders' ownership. The following is a listing of each with a brief description of their contents. It is important to remember that each of those discussed could just as easily be maintained on an EDP system as in any manual records:

1. *Minute Book.* Contains the proceedings of the board of Directors, containing stock authorizations, etc. This will generally be a manual record.
2. *Subscription Book.* A recording of the class and number of shares, the price, and the means whereby the payment will be made. This may be maintained on an EDP system.
3. *Subscriber's Ledger.* One such account is opened for each stockholder of record. This ledger is a subordinate ledger to the subscription book and is a controlling account which must balance the cash or other debit accounts. This would be well suited for an EDP system.
4. *Stock Certificate Book.* This may be a copy of or a stub of the Stock Certificate, and is treated just like a checkbook. With some care, this can also be an EDP system.
5. *Stockholders' Ledger.* In this ledger, the entries are made in terms of numbers of shares of stock versus dollar figures.

These, then, are the supporting documents to a system of stock accountability. Like any accounting system, only those which are absolutely necessary to support the remaining more general journals and ledgers will be required. In a small firm, it would not be necessary to go to the level of detail, as the majority of the detail can be contained in a higher-level ledger or journal. It should be remembered, however, that the lowest-level books are those which are key to any audit procedure, and, as such, must be in sufficient detail to allow the auditor to trace the transaction completely through from beginning to end.

The primary credits to the Paid-in Capital Account come from the issuance or sale of stock. In this regard, there must also be a premium or discount account to record the deviation from par value. While this is true for par stock, it may also be true for the no-par stock, with the difference between the *stated value* and the actual price obtained being recorded there. And, of course, there might well be accounts for the Treasury Stock and for Donated Capital. The problem here is the variation of terms you will find. Some may call the section of the Balance Sheet *Capital.* Others may call it *Shareholders' Equity,* or even *Stockholders' Investment.* They are all the same thing. Likewise, the terms retirement and redemption are used interchangeably.

When capital is acquired by virtue of a gift, such as a gift of land (or donated by the firm itself), the entries will vary slightly. On receipt, it is entered on the books at the fair market price. On a gift, however, the options are open—actual cost, depreciable cost, fair market value. The important thing to remember is that all values and differences must be fully accounted for and disclosed to the stockholders.

It is possible to increase or decrease the value of an asset and its corresponding capital. Consider, for example, the situation wherein you own a fixed asset, say a punch press. This press may have been determined to have a useful life of 10 years at the time of purchase, but at 7 years it is broken down to the point that it needs repair and is no longer of value to the corporation. In essence, it has arrived at its salvage value thirty percent sooner. If the corporation now goes ahead and repairs it, the cost of the capital investment is increased and the life of the asset may be prolonged. Conversely, suppose your corporation owned land that had been consistently appreciating. Now there is a flood which depresses the entire area. The asset value can be *written-down* to become more realistic. In general, we've been talking about the revaluation of corporate assets, and while land is always a "touchy" item to write up or down, it is nonetheless an asset which can either appreciate or depreciate based on market value.

It is hoped that the corporation has earnings. It is possible for a person to be both a stockholder of or an employee of the same corporation. His salary, then. represents an expense to the corporation, not a withdrawal of capital, as would be the case in a sole proprietorship. As such, the individual will pay taxes on earned income drawn in the form of salary, whereas the corporation will pay taxes as the legal entity it is. The rules under which a corporation must pay taxes are changeable from year to year, it seems, but in any event the corporation must file an estimate of its tax and make a payment quarterly in the U.S. This, then, necessitates these entries:

Income Tax	$10,000	
Income Tax Payable		$10,000
Income Tax Payable	$30,000	
Cash		$30,000

The assumption is that the tax is stable at $10,000 a month, for illustration; and that this is a quarterly payment. At the close of the accounting (or fiscal) period on which taxes are to be paid, the Expense and Revenue Summary account is closed to Retained Earnings. Of course, Net income increases the balance of the account. Net Loss and distributions of earnings to the stockholders will decrease the account. Increases and decreases in capital resulting from the sale, above or below par, of stock are not closed to the retained earnings account. They remain in the Paid-in Capital accounts.

From the Retained Earnings account other actions may be taken, in the forms of *reserves* or *appropriations* for specific incidents. These reserves remain as a part of Retained Earnings, however, for tax purposes. Although Retained Earnings may be appropriated for many reasons, we'll demonstrate just one series of entries, those required to account for the appropriation of the sale of treasury stock:

Retained Earnings	$100,000	
Retained Earnings Appropriated for Treasury Stock		$100,000

When the treasury stock has been sold, the appropriation is no longer needed, and it must then be returned to the Retained Earnings account, in a manner which just reverses the entries. Of course, if only part of the treasury stock is sold, the remaining portion of the appropriation may stay in effect, so only the net must be returned to the account. To the casual onlooker, this series of entries may look like "busy work," entries that are not necessary. Its prime purpose, however, is to prevent the distribution of the retained earnings earmarked for some special purpose. Retained earnings can be allocated to many uses—for capital expansion, for contingencies (like a law suit) or for other purposes.

Another area of concern when we discuss stock is the matter of dividends. Dividends may be declared by the board of directors in the form of either stock dividends or cash dividends. The stock dividends may take the form of splits, percentages, or outright grants. Cash dividends are self-explanatory. It should be stated that dividends must be supported; that is, there must be retained earnings sufficient to pay the dividend in whatever form it takes. It must be a pro-rata distribution for all shares of a given class. And if the dividend is to be a cash dividend, there must be sufficient cash to support the dividend. Three dates are important in the distribution of dividends:

1. The date of the declaration of the dividend by the board.
2. The date of record, or the "as of" date for the distribution.
3. The date of payment.

Generally, the board will declare the payable as of a given date, with payment to be made on some future date. For instance, a meeting January 5 could establish the date of record as of January 31, and be payable on February 15th. Dividends in arrears on preferred stock must be settled before new dividends for that class or for a lower class may be declared.

When it is determined that there should be a cash dividend, the entry is just like any other payable:

Retained Earnings	$20,000	
Cash Dividends Payable		$20,000

And, of course, the payment:

Cash Dividends Payable	$20,000	
Cash		$20,000

The payment is distributed pro-rata across the shares, not just to the stockholders. A subordinate ledger of some sort, or an EDP system file, would be required to record just which stockholders got which dividends. The dividends can paid in stock, and may be determined on a percentage or in an outright split. The important thing to remember about stock dividends is that they do not require distribution of the assets to the specific stockholders in the same manner as does a cash dividend. The effect of this action is to transfer funds from Retained Earnings to Paid-in Capital.

For the purpose of illustration, let's make the following assumptions:

Common Stock, $5 par, 10,000 shares issued	$ 50,000
Premium on Common Stock	5,000
Retained Earnings	75,000
	$130,000

Now, let's assume that the board has decided to declare a 10% stock dividend. For illustration, we'll keep to figures above, but the stock dividend would depend very heavily on the market price of the stock on the date of recording.

There are 10,000 shares of common stock (see above) with a value of $5.50 per share. Now with a 10% stock dividend, the distribution would look like this:

Common Stock, $5 par, 11,000 shares issued	$ 55,000
Premium on Common Stock	5,000
Retained Earnings	70,000
	$130,000

The total has remained the same, but the distribution has changed. This now drops the value to $5.45 per share, but has increased the voting distribution by 10%. If the fair market price had been $6, then the premium accounts and the Retained Earnings account would have had to be adjusted accordingly, like this:

Common stock, $5 par, 11,000 shares issued	$ 55,000
Premium on Common Stock	5,500
Retained Earnings	69,500
	$130,000

This places the per share value at $6.00. A higher market price on the date of record would increase the value of the premium and thus the value per share. The entry necessary to distribute the additional 10% of the stock would look like this:

Stock Dividend Distributable	$5,000	
Common Stock		$5,000

And of course the necessary entries to the premium account. When the stock is actually distributed, the entry would look like this:

Paid-in Capital	$5,000	
Stock Dividend Distributable		$5,000

Stock splits are a means to reduce the par value of the shares outstanding. Thus, if there were 10,000 shares of common at a par of $10 and there was a 2 : 1 (two for one) split, there would not be 20,000 shares at a par of $5. *The total amount of capital has not been increased.* The capital in this illustration would remain at $100,000, but the votes have doubled. The prime reason a firm would wish to do this would be to reduce the selling price of the stock, thus making it more attractive to the potential investor. The illustration has been a 2 : 1 split. A 3 : 1 split would reduce the value by two-thirds, etc.

Dividends are computed on the outstanding shares only. They are not paid on Treasury Stock. It would make no sense for a corporation to pay itself a dividend, as they have the capability, if they so desire, to transfer the funds from Retained Earnings to Paid-in Capital. In practice this is not done, as it inflates the capital position of the corporation without inflating the asset position.

As a final discussion of stock considerations, *quasi-reorganization* should be mentioned; this is also known as Title 10 bankruptcy. It has been determined that the firm is in rough shape financially. It cannot sell stocks or bonds and the capitalization has gotten out of proportion to the actual ''real'' capitalization at market prices. Thus, with the permission of the government, a firm may reorganize, eliminating the retained earnings deficit, adjusting the par value of the shares, taking extraordinary credits and debits to bring the accounts into line with reality, and beginning business again fresh, much as if the firm had been liquidated. Of course, the accounts payable must remain as they were, unless the firm is *actually* liquidated, but the asset accounts, depreciation accounts, capital accounts, and earnings accounts may be adjusted.

The entries for these actions will not be demonstrated here, primarily because the incidence of such reorganization is rare, and because the rules for the reorganization are constantly changing. Those needing further information should consult the Securities and Exchange Commission.

Bonds

One more area requires attention before the discussion of corporate accounting is closed—bonds, or specifically the *long-term obligations and investments of the corporation.*

Stocks are the means for a corporation to borrow against the potential of the corporation. There is no fixed return guaranteed. The buyer of stock takes risks in his investment based on the performance of the corporation, the distribution decisions of the board, and forces of the market, etc. Thus, an investor can go broke, make a killing, or fall somewhere in between. The rate of potential loss or gain may be stable or it may be extreme, in either direction. In the same manner as an investor may invest in a corporation, that corporation may, in turn, invest in another corporation. Thus, much of the assets of an insurance company, for instance, may be invested in the stocks and bonds of other corporations.

Corporations may invest in or sell bonds, or long-term investments or obligations. The selling of bonds means the long-term borrowing by the corporation, where a guaranteed return is realized by the investor (bondholder). In addition, certain bonds enjoy special tax privileges, such as municipal bonds, the return on which is, in some instances, tax free, and is thus a good tax shelter for the investor.

When bonds are sold by a corporation, there is a definite commitment on the part of that corporation to pay interest and repay the principal at some specific future date. In the liquidation hierarchy, bonds take precedence even over the class of preferred stock. A very interesting point is that bonds may be traded in the same manner as stocks, with the provision that they are traded interest inclusive.

A few definitions are necessary for the discussion of bonds:

1. The *face value* of the bond is the term used to denote the principal.
2. The contract between the corporation and the bondholder is known as the *bond indenture.*
3. *Interest* on bonds is called just that, and is payable on some calendar basis.
4. *Registered bonds* are those which may be transferred from one owner to another, with endorsement, and the corporation must maintain a record of ownership.
5. *Bearer bonds,* also known as *coupon bonds,* are transferred by delivery. Ownership is by possession. This requires that the interest payments be in the form of coupons attached to the bond, covering the entire term of the bond. When the bond is transferred, the purchaser pays the seller the amount of the outstanding interest, in addition to the agreed price for the principal.
6. *Term bonds* are those bonds which will *mature* (become payable) at the same time. If the maturity dates are spread over some calendar period, they are called *serial bonds.* Series E Savings Bonds are serial bonds.
7. Bonds that may be exchanged for other forms of securities are called *convertible bonds.* Convertible bonds in a form which can be converted to common stock are frequently available, and would be generally exercised where the price of the stock is increasing or the earnings and dividends records are outstanding.
8. If the corporation has a right, under the bond indenture, to redeem the bonds at an early date, they are called *callable bonds.*
9. *Secured bonds* are those to which some form of security has been attached, such as the pledge of certain assets.
10. Bonds issued on the credit of the corporation are called *debenture bonds.*

It can be seen that these bond classifications are not exercised uniquely. They may exist in any number of combinations, such as a callable, convertible, serial debenture.

Since the bond is a liability, it must be a payable account. The account title is *Bonds Payable.* The Bonds Payable account shows on the Balance Sheet as a long-term liability. Again, as in any long-term liability, some portion of it is current, and should, over time, be transferred to the current liability category.

Upon receipt of the bond money, or the sale of the bond, the following entry is used:

Cash	$10,000	
Bonds Payable		$10,000

Of course, this assumes that the bonds are issued at face value (they need not be so issued) and carry no interest accrual. It also assumes that the respective debits and credits were made upon the issuance of the bonds. Had they been sold including interest. The general practice for this is:

Cash	$10,500	
Bonds Payable		$10,000
Interest Expense		500

The interest expense does not represent an expense yet to the corporation, but is put in the expense account as a matter of practice, so that when the Interest Payable is made, the interest expense account carries the net amount of the interest expense. Remember, the interest expense in the preceding illustration represents interest which is paid in advance by the bond purchaser, for which he will receive reimbursement of maturity or sale of the bonds.

Bonds may be sold at discount. There is a mechanism for that, and it is the percentage system. A bond quoted at 100 is quoted to mean 100% of face value. A bond quoted at 90 would incur a 10% discount from the face value. Let's concentrate on accounting for the deviations of premium and discount sales of bonds. Bonds sold at a discount are generally sold that way by virtue of the rate of interest. The final payoff for the bonds would thus be higher than if transferred for a lesser rate but a higher face value. The entry to record the sale of bonds at premium would look like this:

Cash	$212,000	
Bonds Payable		$200,000
Premium on Bonds Payable		12,000

It's important to note that the premium on those bonds is not income to the corporation. It is, instead, and advance on interest which will be paid to the bondholders over the life of the bonds. Assume, for illustration, that on the bonds just discussed there is a ten-year life and that the bonds have an interest rate of 10%. See Figure 5.40.

The entry to record the interest payment will look like this:

Interest Expense	$10,000	
Cash		$10,000

The amortization of the premium will be:

Premium on Bonds Payable	$1,200	
Interest Expense		$1,200

The debit of $10,000 to the expense account above is partially offset by the $1,200 credit to the ex-

Cash to be paid:		
Face of the bonds	$200,000	
Interest -- 10 payments of $10,000 (5%)	100,000	$300,000
Cash received:		
Face of the bonds	$200,000	
Premium on the bonds	12,000	212,000
Total interest expense for 10 years		$ 88,000
Interest expense per year		$ 8,800

Figure 5.40

pense account in the second entry, leaving a net interest expense of $8,800 for the year. When the bonds have matured, the premium account will have been completely amortized.

A similar, but reverse, situation occurs when the bonds are sold at a discount. Taking the same $200,000 bonds, assume that they are sold at 90, or at a 10% discount. The entry to support the transactions would look like this:

Cash	$180,000	
Discount on Bonds Payable	20,000	
Bonds Payable		$200,000

In a similar manner as the premium is amortized, so too is the discount. It remains an expense, but functioning in the amortization manner, it becomes a deferred expense. Consider Figure 5.41.

The entries necessary to support the payment of annual interest and amortize the discounts are shown below:

Interest Expense	$10,000	
Cash		$10,000
Interest Expense	$ 2,000	
Discount on Bonds Payable		$ 2,000

It is also possible to amortize bond premium and discount via a compound interest method, which produces a uniform periodic rate of interest on the carrying value of the bonds, rather than a uniform

Cash to be paid:		
Face of the bonds	$200,000	
Interest (same as before)	100,000	$300,000
Cash received:		
Face of the bonds	$200,000	
Less discount on the bonds	20,000	180,000
Total interest expense for 10 years		$120,000
Interest expense per year		$ 12,000

Figure 5.41

periodic rate spread over time. The carrying value is the face value of the bonds plus unamortized premium or discount.

In the preceding illustrations, some elementary assumptions were made:

1. That the bonds were sold on the issuance date
2. That the interest was payable annually
3. That the interest payment date coincided with the last day of the fiscal year

Unfortunately, things don't generally cooperate quite that way. The sale of the bond may be later than the issuance date, requiring the accrual of and accounting for interest. The interest may be payable in other calendar periods, requiring accrual and accounting for specific interest payments. The payment may take place at any of those calendar periods, before, after, or in anticipation of those periods. The simple rule of thumb is that every item in bond accounting is time dependent, and each of those time units must be accounted for. More complex bond accounting exists.

For purposes of the Balance Sheet, discount on the bonds is seen as an advance on interest to be returned to the bondholders. Thus, it is treated as Deferred Expense. Bond premium is a deferred credit.

Sinking Funds

The contract for the bonds, or indenture, may require the firm to "lay away" the funds pending reclamation of the bonds at maturity. The firm, under such an agreement, will place, in even amounts over time, an amount sufficient to redeem the bond plus the accumulated interest, if that interest has not been paid. Such a fund is commonly called a Bond Sinking Fund. In actuality, the fund may take the form of a trust, and the cash deposited in the fund can be deposited in income-producing securities. When that is done, the fund should be placed in the hands of a trustee, such as a bank, investment firm, or trust company. The entry to support such action looks like this:

Sinking Fund Cash	$1,000	
Cash		$1,000

If the fund is used to purchase investments, the accounting would look like this:

Sinking Fund Investments	$10,000	
Sinking Fund Cash		$10,000

As interest or dividends on the investments are received, the entry looks like this:

Sinking Fund Cash	$500	
Sinking Fund Income		$500

We have dealt with the bonds and sinking funds in a straightforward manner, not concentrating on the restriction of dividends, the redemption procedures, the investment of the sinking funds, or the sale of investments which support the sinking funds. We'll look at them now. It may be necessary, in the agreement for the bond, to appropriate retained earnings each year to ensure that the bond will be retired at the appropriate time. That entry looks like this:

Retained Earnings	$10,000	
Retained Earnings Appropriated for bonded indebtedness		$10,000

The figure isn't important so long as it is an equal division of the face plus interest amount pro-rated over the term of the bond. The action bears no direct relationship to the sinking funds. It is merely the appropriation. Where the sinking fund as well as the appropriation, the appropriation is said to be funded.

Bond Retirement

When a corporation retires its bonds, it may do it by several methods. If the bonds are callable, then they probably are callable at the call value of the bond, which is generally greater than the face value of the bond. The firm may wish to redeem its bonds to prevent future interest expense.

The firm may experience either a gain or a loss on the redemption of the bonds. The following entries illustrate first a gain and then a loss:

Bonds Payable	$200,000	
Premium on Bonds Payable	8,000	
Gain on redemption of bonds		$ 4,000
Cash		204,000

Bonds Payable	$200,000	
Premium on Bonds Payable	4,000	
Loss on Redemption of Bonds	4,000	
Cash		$208,000

If the bonds are not callable, the firm may wish to purchase them on the open market and retire them. This would be especially true if the market value is a depressed value in relation to the face value. Assuming the corporation did buy $50,000 of its bonds at 95, the entry would look like this:

Bonds Payable	$50,000	
Premium on Bonds Payable	2,000	
Cash		$48,000
Gain on Retirement of Bonds		4,000

Only the premium relating to the bonds retired is written off. The excess of the carrying value of the liability, $52,000, over the cash paid, $48,000, is recognized as a gain.

Corporate Investments

In the same manner as the corporation issues bonds, and as support for the sinking funds, the corporation may invest in the bonds and common stocks of other firms. Again, that's the subject for another treatise. You should know, however, that it is the general practice for a firm with excess cash to make short-term or temporary investments. Because cash may be needed for the operation of the business in the near term, these investments are generally in a very secure investment, such as certificates of deposit or low-yield government securities, which are short term in nature. Investments are not required in the near term may be used for long-range investments and to the degree that they are not required for business operation, the investing company may be somewhat speculative.

Income from these investments is generally accounted for strictly upon receipt or sale. In other words, so far as the securities go, the firm will operate on a cash basis, adjusting the gain and loss accounts when the transaction has been totally finalized.

The corporate balance sheet will be drawn to reflect the actual investment and the potential return at the time of the investment or sale.

ANALYSIS OF FINANCIAL STATEMENTS

Perspective

The purpose of financial analysis is to diagnose the current and past financial condition of a firm and to give some clues about its future condition. At this point, some general observations about financial analysis are appropriate.

It has been said that if one does not know where he is going, any road will take him there. This saying is relevant because one must decide the objectives of a test, or what is to be measured, before deciding which diagnostic tools should be used. For example, a bank credit analyst, a security analyst, and the financial manager of a firm each have different objectives in mind when they examine a firm's financial condition, as follows:

- The bank credit analyst is concerned to know whether a debtor can make loan payments in a timely and suitable manner. He'd be concerned about the company's solvency, liquidity, and ability to meet current obligations.
- The security analyst is concerned about the future earnings and dividends of a company. He'd be concerned about those items which would have a major impact upon stock prices which represent the wealth of the shareholder.
- The financial manager is concerned about the financial well-being of his company, as well as its future. On his shoulders lay the concerns of both the bank credit analyst and the security analyst.

Because of their parochial interests, it is possible for all three individuals, operating from precisely the same data, to have three entirely distinct opinions about the financial condition of a firm. For example, the Trelawny Auto Parts Stores (TAPS), a chain of outlets in 10 states, produced reports which didn't exactly make the financial people happy:

- A credit analyst with the Bank of the Upper Glouster Leverage Exchange (BUGLE) reported to the credit supervisor that TAPS would not have sufficient earnings six months from now to repay its loan with the bank.
- The security analyst who worked for the stock brokerage firm of Fox, Leonard, Anderson, and George (FLAG) gave his entire attention to the grave situation and advised the brokerage firm's customers to continue to "hold" the stock (not to purchase or sell it), because the work stoppages that had depressed earnings would cease in the upcoming week.
- And the financial manager of TAPS, Tom B. Stone, was optimistic about the future because the company planned to sell some of its outlets to another firm, providing sufficient cash to pay the loan and eliminate some of the less profitable outlets from the chain. The result would be that TAPS' dependence upon borrowed funds would be reduced and its profitability increased.

Inflation

Inflation distorts some data and often leads to misinterpretation of information. In its most recent annual report, TAPS boasted that sales revenues increased 10 percent in each of the last four years. Management considered 10 percent to be good, until it was pointed out that inflation increased 12 percent per year. When the sales revenues were deflated (divided by an inflation index), TAPS experienced "nega-

Year	1	2	3	4
Sales (Millions):	$100	$110	$121	$123
Inflation Index:	100	112	125	140
Adjusted Sales:	$100	$ 98	$ 97	$ 88

Figure 5.42

Year	1	2	3	4
Number of Outlets:	10	11	12	13
Adjusted Sales per outlet (Millions):	$10.0	$8.9	$8.1	$6.8

Figure 5.43

tive sales growth,'' otherwise known as advancing to the rear. After dividing the sales (in millions of dollars) by the inflation index (calculated from a base year, incremented by 12%), TAPS found that its adjusted sales really weren't worth tooting about (see Figure 5.42), which goes to show that the most beautiful melody could easily consist of sour notes, and what looks like it's going up could just as easily be coming down. Wait . . . there's more.

During the same period, the number of TAPS' outlets increased from 10 to 13. The annual report stated that because the number of outlets had increased, that was a sign of positive growth, a flowering of future potential. However, even the most casual observer could see that if one divided the number of outlets into the adjusted sales for each year, those adjusted sales declined from $10 million to $7.3 million per outlet as shown in Figure 5.43.

Preaching the good news wasn't sufficient. The increased dollar volume and the increase in number of outlets had suggested that TAPS was growing, until the inflation was taken into account and the principals awakened. Then it was revealed that, on the average, sales expressed in constant dollars declined (or were lowered) by 27 percent per outlet. Inflation had distorted management's perception of reality, and they really were not ready for the undertaking. But who is?

Ratio Analysis

Let's turn our attention now to the statements of the Oregon Potato Equipment Corporation (OPEC). Its merger with the Oregon Onion Organization (O-O-O) has given it substantial assets and operations.

The O-O-O, better known as O^3 or Ozone, bolstered OPEC's financial position. The balance sheet and income statement for two years' operation are shown in Figures 5.44 and 5.45. Data from these statements will be used to calculate the financial ratios which follow in this missive. Know the limitations of these figures. Some of the ratios look for data from three or more years (five is common) as a basis for analysis. Where that is required, the data will be provided, but will not be shown in these statements.

The Balance Sheet represents a partial consolidation. It does not reflect the activities of the organization's two subsidiaries, The SPUD and EYE Potato Chip Corporation, and The Fried Onion Gallery (FOG), a ring-organized fast-food chain.

Oregon Potato Equipment Corporation
Income Statement
For years Ended December 31, year indicated

	December 31	
	1983	1984
	(in $000s)	
Revenue		
Net Sales (all for credit)	$57,546	$76,900
Rentals	7,870	4,173
Other	112	258
	65,028	81,331
Costs and Expenses		
Cost of goods sold (75% credit)	$47,057	$57,634
Selling, Gen'l & Admin Expenses	14,970	16,229

Figure 5.44

Measures of Financial Health

As the financial analyst looks at a firm, he is interested to determine certain critical relationships, among which are:

1. Measurements of financial position—liquidity:
   a. Current ratio
   b. Acid-test ratio
2. Measurements of financial activity:
   a. Inventory turnover ratios
      (1) Inventory holding period
      (2) Merchandise inventory
      (3) Raw materials inventory
      (4) Finished goods inventory
   b. Average collection period
   c. Accounts Payable turnover
   d. Fixed assets turnover
   e. Total assets turnover
3. Measurements of long-run liquidity:
   a. Creditors' equity ratio
   b. Stockholders' equity ratio
   c. Plant and equipment to long-term liability ratio
   d. Plant and equipment to stockholders' equity
4. Measurements of leverage:
   a. Debt to equity ratio
   b. Debt to total assets ratio
   c. Fixed charge coverage ratio

Oregon Potato Equipment Corporation
Consolidated Balance Sheet
As of December 31, year indicated

	December 31	
	1983	1984
	(in $000s)	
Assets		
Current Assets		
Cash	$ 578	$ 1,947
Marketable Securities	1,000	1,000
Accounts Receivable	7,082	6,960
Inventories	34,542	38,925
Prepaid Expenses	158	114
Total Current Assets	$43,360	$48,946
Investments and Other Assets		
Long term portion of installment contracts receivable	$ 1,097	$ 304
Investments in unconsolidated subsidiaries	312	751
Other	705	668
Total Investments & Other Assets	2,114	1,723
Property Plant and Equipment, at cost	8,513	7,627
Total Assets	$53,987	$58,296
Liabilities and Shareholder's Equity		
Current Liabilities		
Accounts Payable	$ 4,526	$ 4,562
Current Maturities of Long-Term Debt	1,004	1,007
Customer Deposits	454	230
Accrued Income Tax	1,484	1,935
Total Current Liabilities	$ 7,468	$ 7,734
Long-term Liabilities		
Notes Payable	9,747	13,051
Long-term debt, less current maturities	4,784	7,232
Other non-current liabilities	558	519
Total Long-term Liabilities	$15,089	$20,802
Total Liabilities	$22,557	$28,536
Shareholder's Equity (6,000,000 shares)	31,430	29,760
Total Liabilities and Shareholder's Equity	$53,987	$58,296

Figure 5.45

  d. Times interest earned ratio
  e. Times preferred dividend earned ratio
  f. Times bond interest earned ratio
5. Measurements of profitability and long-term growth potential:
  a. Profit margin on sales ratio
  b. Return on total assets ratio
  c. Return on net worth ratio
  d. Net income to stockholders' equity ratio
  e. Operating ratio
  f. Sales to plant and equipment (plant turnover) ratio
6. Measurements of the market:
  a. Earnings per share of common stock ratio
  b. Price/earnings ratio
  c. Return on total investment and leverage ratio

The purpose of performing such analyses is to determine the profitability versus the liquidity of the firm and the return versus risk experienced by the firm. It is an art, rather than a science, despite the firmness of the figures produced, primarily because there is little in the way of standards for comparison.

There are 29 unique ratios listed above, but they are not all the ratios which can be extracted from the financial statements of the corporation. They are the most commonly used ratios, however.

Measurements of Financial Position

The Current Ratio

$$\frac{\text{Current Assets}}{\text{Current Liabilities}} = \frac{\$388{,}430}{\$123{,}650} = 3.14$$

This is the most commonly used ratio. It is supposed to measure the degree of safety or margin in the current assets relative to the current liabilities. In this instance, the numerator (assets) must be larger than the denominator (liabilities) for the company to be "technically" solvent. This, of course, includes all long-term assets and liabilities, so the specific liquidity of the firm is better where the quotient exceeds 1, and better yet by the degree to which is exceeds 1.

Acid or Quick Ratio

$$\frac{\text{Cash 7 Securities Receivables}}{\text{Current Liabilities}} = \frac{\$260{,}765}{\$123{,}650} = 2.11$$

This is much more conservative than the current ratio. It eliminates inventory because there may be difficulty and delay converting inventory to cash. The acid ratio reduces the variables in determining the liquidity of the firm. By taking only the current factors, one can determine the quick value of the firm—the worth of the firm if it were dissolved today.

Measurements of Financial Activity

Inventory Holding Period (Inventory Turnover)

This ratio is calculated in terms of days. It is also known as Sales in Inventory.

$$\frac{\text{Inventory}}{\text{Daily Cost of Goods Sold}} = \frac{\$114{,}440}{\$667{,}940/365} = 62.5 \text{ days}$$

This ratio measures the velocity with which inventory items move through the business. A longer period may indicate an accumulation of unsalable or slow moving goods. Ideally, the denominator should be daily cost of goods sold. Sometimes the ratio is computed using sales (generally the cost of goods sold data would be unavailable). This creates a problem because sales are at retail and inventory is at cost.

Merchandise Inventory Turnover Ratio

$$\frac{\text{Cost of Goods Sold}}{\text{Average Inventory}} = \frac{\$800{,}000}{\$250{,}000} = 3.2 \text{ times}$$

This ratio records the number of times the inventory (merchandise) was replenished during the period, or the number of dollars in the terms of goods sold for each dollar of inventory. This is the inventory turnover factor which must be considered if inventory is financed and there is a carrying cost. When the quotient is a number, the number itself is the number of turns in a year. The firm would do well to find a means to increase the value of the quotient (specifically by decreasing the average inventory) while providing the sales activity with a comparable amount of sales—the same or higher level of service. If the ratio is less than 1, then the amount of inventory is absolutely too high, which may, in turn, point to overproduction for the period. For a given period producing for inventory may be acceptable, but this is not true over the long run.

Raw Materials Inventory Ratio

$$\frac{\text{Raw Materials Used}}{\text{Average Raw Materials Inventory}} = \frac{\$600{,}000}{\$125{,}000} = 4.8$$

This ratio relates the number of times the raw materials inventory was replaced during the period, or the number of dollars of raw materials used in manufacturing for each dollar of inventory on hand. This measure is useful, when tied to work-in-process and finished goods in inventory figures. If this ratio is less than 1, then at some point in time the production facility will be waiting for raw materials to use in the production process. Conversely, if the figure is relatively high, then the firm will be stocking too much raw materials. There are mitigating circumstances. Was the raw materials inventory obtained at a large discount? Was the raw materials inventory made up of rare and difficult-to-obtain materials? Was the raw materials inventory purchased as a hedge against the ability to obtain it or against the possibility of an anticipated price rise? In weighing this factor to determine just how much raw materials inventory is sufficient, you must consider such factors as the capital tied up in the raw materials inventory, the carrying cost, if any, of the materials, the critical nature of the raw material in terms of production, and the available space and cost of that space for raw material production.

Finished Goods Inventory Ratio

$$\frac{\text{Cost of Goods Sold}}{\text{Average Finished Goods Inventory}} = \frac{\$500{,}000}{\$450{,}000} = 1.11$$

This ratio depicts the number of times the finished goods inventory was sold and replaced during the period, or the number of dollars of cost of finished goods sold for each dollar of finished goods on hand. This is similar to, but should not be confused with merchandise inventory, which may be recorded in some instances at the sales price, rather than in the cost of goods sold.

If the finished goods inventory ratio produces a factor less than 1, then it is entirely possible that the firm is not producing up to its demand. A factor greater than 1 is healthy, and the closer to 1 the factor is, the more healthy the situation is, at least in relation to the demand for the firm's product.

Average Collection Period Ratio—Receivables Turnover in Terms of Days

$$\frac{\text{Accounts Receivable}}{\text{Daily Sales}} = \frac{\$204{,}355}{\$969{,}065/365} = 77.0 \text{ days}$$

This ratio should be compared to the credit terms. If the credit terms provide for net payment in 30 days, it may be reasonable to expect 45 days sales in receivables, and anything in excess of that should be questioned. This ratio should be used in conjunction with an aging of the accounts.

Payment Period Ratio or Accounts Payable Turnover in Terms of Days

$$\frac{\text{Accounts Payable}}{\text{Daily Purchases}} = \frac{\$58{,}215}{\$678{,}130/365} = 31.3 \text{ days}$$

This ratio measures how rapidly the company is paying its trade suppliers. It can be compared against the terms of credit the suppliers are offering the company. When information about purchases is unavailable, the denominator may be daily cost of goods sold. This alteration is adequate if the company is a retailer or a wholesaler, in which case purchases are reasonably similar to cost of goods sold. Many creditors like this ratio because it is very sensitive ratio. Firms getting into financial difficulties frequently begin to indicate this by going slow on their accounts payable.

Fixed Assets Turnover Ratio

This ratio indicates the number of times the assets are used in producing a product.

$$\frac{\text{Sales}}{\text{Daily Purchases}} = \frac{\$3{,}000{,}000}{\$1{,}300{,}000} = 2.3 \text{ times}$$

This ratio, when high, indicates the "density of use" of the fixed assets. If it is low, then the firm may be overstocked with capital or plant assets.

Total Assets Turnover

This ratio measures the turnover of all the firm's assets.

$$\frac{\text{Sales}}{\text{Total Assets}} = \frac{\$3,000,000}{\$2,000,000} = 1.5 \text{ times}$$

This is similar to the fixed assets turnover in that it measures the use of assets in the production process. Here, again, the higher the number, the more valuable the measure is, as a higher number indicates a greater productive output. In the illustration above, the firm is simply not generating a sufficient volume of business for the size of the assets involved. In this instance, look at the Cash account. You may find that there are more than substantial amounts of cash lying around.

Measurements of Long-Run Liquidity

Creditors' Equity Ratio

$$\frac{\text{Total Liabilities}}{\text{Total Assets}} = \frac{\$500,000}{\$750,000} = .67 \text{ times}$$

This ratio measures the amount of the creditor sources of the total assets. As can be seen from the illustration, two thirds of the assets are dependent upon the liabilities. There are similarities, it can be seen, to the Current Ratio, except for the fact that this is a long-run measurement. The smaller the number, the more liquid the corporation is. It is important, however, not to confuse a higher number with a lack of liquidity. The liability may well be salaries payable, for which there is work-in-process inventory to represent the assets. These assets, then, are accounted for at cost of production, not sales which, when accomplished, will raise the asset accounts by the amount of the profit margin.

Stockholders' Equity Ratio

This ratio will show the amount of owner sources of the assets.

$$\frac{\text{Stockholders' Equity}}{\text{Total Assets}} = \frac{\$1,000,000}{\$2,500,000} = .4$$

Here is an instance where the quotient hopefully is relatively small, as the higher the number, the more the stockholders' claims on the assets would be in case of dissolution.

Plant and Equipment to Long-Term Liabilities Ratio

$$\frac{\text{Plant and Equipment (net)}}{\text{Long-Term Debt}} = \frac{\$5,000,000}{\$1,750,000} = 2.9$$

This ratio tests the adequacy of protection to long-term creditors. The larger the number, the more secure against adverse possession the firm will be. The firm should be concerned when the number approaches or drops below 1.

Plant and Equipment to Stockholders' Equity Ratio

$$\frac{\text{Plant and Equipment (net)}}{\text{Stockholders' Equity}} = \frac{\$5,000,000}{\$2,456,000} = 2.1$$

This ratio tells the extent to which owner sources are being used to finance plant and equipment acquisitions. Again, the number should be as high as possible, and the firm should be cautious as the number approaches or drops below 1.

In addition to the ratios developed in this section, that portion of long-term debt represented by bonds (versus notes payable), when added to the Stockholders' Equity, can also provide a useful measure of long-term liquidity, as in the following:

$$\frac{\text{Plant and Equipment (net)}}{\text{Bond Indenture and Stockholders' Equity}}$$

Here, naturally, the margin would be somewhat more narrow and it would seem that ratios whose range begins at .75 would be adequate. Again, any number above 1 is a sign of a financially healthy firm.

Measurements of Leverage

Debt/Equity

$$\frac{\text{Total Debt}}{\text{Tangible Net Worth}} = \frac{\$273,650}{\$506,150} = .54$$

This ratio indicates the source of the assets between creditors and owners. That is, for every dollar of equity the owners have invested in the firm, the creditors have put in 54 cents. The better the quality of a firm's assets and earnings, the higher ratios are permissible.

Debt to Total Assets Ratio

$$\frac{\text{Total Debt}}{\text{Tangible Total Assets}} = \frac{\$273,650}{\$779,800} = .35$$

This is virtually the same ratio as the debt/equity ratio. It shows the percentage of the total assets financed by debt.

Fixed Charge Coverage Ratio

$$\frac{\text{Income Available for Meeting Fixed Charges}}{\text{Fixed Charges}}$$

Fixed charges are what are called by the name "fixed cost" by the economist. It is that group of charges you must pay to remain in business, such as rent, tax sinking funds, key salaries, etc. Stated differently, the ratio might look like this:

$$\frac{\text{Gross Income} + \text{Other Income}}{\text{Interest} + \text{Tax Sinking Fund} + \text{Key Salaries} + \text{etc.}}$$

Simply interpreted, it means do you have enough income to cover those things which will keep you in business. In the numerator are all the sources of income, while in the denominator are all those charges which are fixed (not tied to production) in nature. Don not confuse this factor with ''breakeven analysis. Only in rare instances will they be the same.

Times Interest Earned Ratio

This ratio measures the extent to which earnings can decline without resultant financial difficulty to the firm because of its inability to meet annual interest costs. If a firm did not meet its interest payments, the creditors could bring an action against the firm, possibly resulting in the dissolution of the firm.

$$\frac{\text{Profit Before Taxes} + \text{Interest Charges}}{\text{Interest Charges}} = \frac{\$200{,}000 + 45{,}000}{\$45{,}000} = 5.4 \text{ times}$$

Times Preferred Dividend Earned Ratio

This ratio is the primary measure of the safety of an individual's investment in preferred stock—the ability of a firm to meet its preferred dividend requirement.

$$\frac{\text{Net Income}}{\text{Annual Preferred Dividend}} = \frac{\$200{,}000}{\$\ 75{,}000} = 2.67$$

Since preferred dividends are paid from the Net Income (Retained Earnings), this measure will give evidence of coverage, which is done before any dividends are distributed to any other classes of stock.

Times Bond Interest Earned Ratio

This is the primary measure of the safety of an individual's investment in bonds—the ability of a firm to meet its bond interest requirements.

$$\frac{\text{Net Income} + \text{Income Taxes} + \text{Annual Bond Interest Expense}}{\text{Annual Bond Interest}}$$

$$= \frac{\$2000{,}000 + \$100{,}000 + \$50{,}000}{\$50{,}000} = 7$$

Measurements of Profitability and Long-Term Growth Potential

Profit Margin on Sales Ratio

$$\frac{\text{Net Profit}}{\text{Sales}} = \frac{\$36{,}790}{\$969{,}065} = .038$$

This ratio is an important measure of the ability to convert sales into the ultimate objective, profits. This illustrates how the revenue dollar is spent and how percentage return on sales is earned.

Return on Total Assets Ratio

This ratio measures the return on the total investment in the firm.

$$\frac{\text{Net Profit after Taxes}}{\text{Total Assets}} = \frac{\$120{,}000}{\$2{,}000{,}000} = .06$$

Obviously, the higher the percentage, the better, but the figure should certainly be above the prime rate, and somewhat approximate the rate of return on investment.

Return on Net Worth Ratio

$$\frac{\text{Net Profit}}{\text{Net Worth}} = \frac{\$36{,}790}{\$506{,}150} = .073$$

This ratio indicates the income generated relative to the owner's investment. This is a very important ratio to the owner because he may well sacrifice return to sales (for instance by adding more debt and interest costs) if he can increase his rate of return on his investment.

Net Income to Stockholders' Equity Ratio

This ratio demonstrates the profitability of the business expressed as a rate of return on the stockholders' equity.

$$\frac{\text{Net Income}}{\text{Average Stockholders' Equity}} = \frac{\$100{,}000}{\$2{,}565{,}000} = .04$$

Again, the higher the percentage, the better, but a low percentage is not an indication of disaster, as it will relate to the specific time that the measurement has been taken.

Operating Ratio

This ratio will identify the number of cents in cost needed to generate one dollar of sales.

$$\frac{\text{Cost of Goods Sold + Operating Expenses}}{\text{Net Sales Revenue}} = \frac{\$150{,}000 + \$25{,}000}{\$250{,}000} = .70$$

In this instance, we've determined that it takes 70 cents to generate a dollar of sales. There is no way to indicate what is a "good" measure, as it will depend upon the industry.

Sales to Plant and Equipment (Plant Turnover) Ratio

This ratio identifies the dollar amount of sales per dollar amount of investment in plant and equipment assets.

$$\frac{\text{Net Sales}}{\text{Average Plant and Equipment Assets (Net)}} = \frac{\$80{,}000}{\$2{,}350{,}000} = .034$$

In this illustration, we see that nearly 3.5 cents in plant and equipment must be invested to produce a dollar's worth of sales. Again, there is no "right" figure to come up with, because it depends on the industry of use. The illustration depicts a relatively low capital cost per sales (and net sales at that) dollar.

Measurements of the Market

Earnings Per Share of Common Stock Ratio

$$\frac{\text{Net Profit} - \text{Preferred Dividend}}{\text{Number of Common Shares}} = \frac{\$36{,}796 - \$8{,}400}{\$75{,}000} = \$.38$$

Earnings per share, however, can be an extremely difficult ratio to compute. The accounting profession requires the computation be made as though all convertibles, warrants, and options were exercised. The owner is interested in determining how much earnings there were to his portion of the business.

Price/Earnings Ratio

$$\frac{\text{Market Price of Common Stock}}{\text{Earnings Per Share}} = \frac{1.75}{.38} = 4.61$$

From the standpoint of the stock market, this is a critical ratio. It is an indication of the value that the "market" places on the potential of the future earnings for a given company.

Return on Total Investment and Leverage Ratio

This ratio identifies the return on prior obligations (bonds) compared to the return on the stockholders' equity. There are two methods to obtain this:

$$\frac{\text{Net Income} + \text{Bond Interest}}{\text{Average Total Assets}} = \text{Percent Earned on Total Investment}$$

$$\frac{\text{Net Income}}{\text{Average Stockholders' Equity}} = \text{Percent Earned on Stockholders' Equity}$$

These are the prime financial ratios for use in evaluating a firm's success. They are, by no means, the total number of ratios and factors which must be considered in running a firm. To that extent, other types of factors should be considered.

Economic Measurements

Rate of Return on Investment

In a discussion of return on investment, or ROI, you will find as many ratios as there are firms, and it would be impossible to present even a small section in sufficient extent to demonstrate the point. We we'll pick one and work it through.

Consider:

$$\text{ROI} = \frac{B - \frac{D}{P}}{D}$$

where: B = annual benefit from the action
D = development cost to obtain the result from the action
P = period over which the development cost is to be amortized

Let's give them some values:

$$B = \$100{,}000$$
$$D = \$120{,}000$$
$$P = 3$$

$$\frac{\$100{,}000 - \frac{\$120{,}000}{3}}{\$120{,}000} = 50\%$$

It is not unusual for a firm to establish a minimum acceptable rate of return on investment, say 15%, and, as can be seen above, this particular investment produced a 50% return.

The $100,000 benefit figure can be estimated by those familiar with the project. The cost (D) can also be measured that way. But the period must be determined. What, then, should be the proper means to determine the write-off period? The method selected must provide the best financial decision consistent with the company's minimum acceptable rate of return on investment. Let's substitute the values varying variable P from 1 to 10.

1. −16.7%	6. +66.6%
2. +33.3%	7. +69.0%
3. +50.0%	8. +70.8%
4. +58.3%	9. +72.2%
5. +63.3%	10. +73.3%

As can be seen, if the investment is treated as a current expense (written off in one year), there is incurred a loss of 16.7%, but the loss is actually greater than that, because if the company has a minimum 15% ROI, the combined loss is 31.7%.

Which period to pick? Look at the spread between years 1 and 2. It is 50 points. The spread between years 3 and 4 is 8.3 points. That's far enough. The spread's proper term is the value added. When the value added drops below the minimum acceptable rate of return on investment, that's where the write-off period should be. In this instance, it would fall between 3 and 4 years.

Margin of Safety

The discussion of breakeven is useful to determine the point where the firm must produce revenue to ensure covering its costs. That, however, is not the final consideration. In order to ensure that they receive the largest possible volume of sales above the breakeven point, other steps should be taken. The difference between breakeven and what the firm wishes the current sales revenue to be is called the margin of safety. If the volume of sales is $250,000 and the breakeven point is $200,000, the margin of safety (MS) is $50,000, or 20%, computed this way:

$$MS = \frac{\text{Sales} - \text{Sales at Breakeven Point}}{\text{Sales}}$$

$$= \frac{\$250{,}000 - \$200{,}000}{\$250{,}000} = 20\%$$

Profit to Volume Ratio

Another meaningful relationship is the profit to volume ratio, also called the marginal income ratio. This ratio (PV) indicates the percentage of each sales dollar available to cover the fixed expenses and to provide a given profit. For example, if the volume of sales is $250,000 and the variable costs are $150,000, the PV ratio is 40%, computed this way:

$$PV = \frac{\text{Sales} - \text{Variable Cost}}{\text{Sales}}$$

$$= \frac{\$250{,}000 - \$150{,}000}{\$250{,}000} = 40\%$$

The PV will permit the quick determination of the effect on profit of an increase or decrease in sales volume.

Rate of Return on Assets

The rate of return on assets is a useful measure. It is similar in nature to the Return on Total Assets Ratio discussed previously, except that the numerator is the Net Income of the firm:

$$\frac{\text{Net Income}}{\text{Assets}} = \frac{\$1{,}000{,}000}{\$100{,}000} = 10\%$$

This rate is an indicator of the relative efficiency of individual assets, permitting judgment as to the efficiency of the business. If used at the departmental level, it will provide the relative operating performance of the respective department.

Other Measures

The average rate of return is a measure of the anticipated profitability of an investment in plant assets:

$$\frac{\text{Average Net Income}}{\text{Average Investment}} = \frac{\$50{,}000}{\$20{,}000} = 2.5 \text{ times}$$

The cash payback period is similar in nature to the cash flow statement provided in the early part of the chapter. It measures the time necessary to cover the investment, like this:

$$\frac{\text{Expenditure for Plant Asset}}{\text{Annual Net Cash Flow}} = \frac{\$200{,}000}{\$40{,}000} = 5 \text{ years}$$

Year	Pres. Value of $1 @ 10%	Net Cash Flow	Present Value of Net Cash Flow
1	.909	$ 70,000	$ 63,630
2	.826	60,000	49,560
3	.751	50,000	37,550
4	.683	40,000	27,320
5	.621	40,000	24,840
Total		$260,000	$202,900
Amount to be invested			200,000
Excess present value			$ 2,900

Figure 5.46

Discounted cash flow is a method to determine the expected future net cash flows stemming from present or proposed capital expenditures. Such a method means the computation of present value, or the value of a dollar at compound interest discounted. Consider the following table, computed at 10%:

Years	Factor at 10%
1	.909
2	.826
3	.751
4	.683
5	.621

Thus, if we were to invest $200,000 for a period of five years at 10% discounted compounded, the cash flow would be as shown in Figure 5.46. This illustration assumes that we know the net cash flow for the future years. It was not the intention to instruct on the nuance of present value in this book—in fact, to use any of what has been herein presented, there is much more digging to do.

Thus ends Accounting 101.

AUDITING

While it is recognized that we cannot do justice to the subject of auditing in these few pages, some auditing questions have begun to show up on the CDP Examination, so some treatment of the subject is required. It has been placed behind the accounting section, rather than in the systems section for a couple of reasons: first it will probably be a person with accounting credentials (and hopefully system credentials) who will do the auditing. And secondly, we're expanding the systems section substantially in this edition of the book.

The rationale for an EDP auditing function is presented very often in the public newspaper—fraud, waste, outright theft, and lack of protection are the publicized causes. The explosive growth of EDP systems in and out of government and industry has been nothing short of phenomenal. Changes in DP technology have occurred concurrently with the expansion of information needs of management. Whether the need spurred the growth or the growth fostered the need is of little consequence when one recognizes that the plethora of terminals and personal computers, coupled with communications have made EDP systems vulnerable on a scale not heretofore experienced. As a result of the introduction and use of this and other new technology and new computer-based design concepts, traditional control techniques and procedures are becoming obsolete. New audit and control techniques are needed to meet the changing requirements and to ensure the integrity of information processing activities and systems.

The changes in systems have caused understandable changes in the traditional role of the auditor. These changes are being brought about by increasing automation and new data processing technology. In addition, audit and control must be treated as a single concern because they have become interrelated. Internal controls in the DP environment govern the processing of transactions, the keeping of records, reporting methods, and environmental security. Internal auditing relates to the evaluation and verification of these controls and the results of the information processing done not only in the DP activity, but also in the ever-burgeoning automated office.

Man vs. the Computer

There's no doubt there is a contest. The computer has no desire to commit fraud; that's in man's nature—a small number of people, of course, but enough that application and verification of controls has become imperative. Man is inherently inaccurate and slow. The computer, on the other hand, can perform its tasks at high speed, and accurately, once correctly programmed. These are the obvious things. But man is brilliant and can adjust to changing conditions. The computer, on the other hand, is stupid and has no discretion of right or wrong. The key fact which emerges is that the computer, which is basically a dumb animal that does only what it is told by man, will perform with invariable consistency as long as it is programmed to do so.

Traditionally, the auditor did his auditing by feel. If it felt right, it probably was right. The primary objective was to secure as much evidence as possible to substantiate the balances which appeared on certain key reports. Whether the system which processed the information which appeared in those reports was good or bad made no difference. If enough evidence was available, an auditor could render an opinion. But a few well-publicized computer-related frauds have raised consciousness about what we don't know about computer systems.

It wasn't that auditors didn't know how to get at the data—with some DP knowledge, they could do so. But auditing the EDP system is not cheap, and questions have been raised about the cost versus the benefits of auditing everything. The auditor's requirements, then, have been to reduce the cost of the audit while simultaneously improving the quality of the audit, handling the backlog and volume, and improving the timeliness of the audit. A tall order, especially for auditors with little or no EDP knowledge or experience. Now that we have audits who know more about EDP, we've come to learn that it is possible to audit through the system, rather than simply around it.

Back in the mid 1970s, the Institute of Internal Auditors (IIA), under contract to Stanford Research Institute (SRI) evaluated the state of EDP auditing practices. Their findings were published in 1977 in a book entitled *Systems Auditability & Control* (SAC). The conclusions from that study are as quoted:

1. The primary responsibility for overall internal control resides with top management, while the operational responsibility for the accuracy and completeness of computer-based information systems should reside with users.
2. There is a need for improved controls because inadequate attention has been given to the importance of internal controls in the data processing environment.
3. Internal auditors must participate in the system development process to ensure that appropriate audit and control features are designed into new computer-based information systems.
4. Verification of controls must occur both before and after installation of computer-based information systems.

5. As a result of the growth in complexity and use of computer-based information systems, needs exist for greater internal involvement relative to auditing in the data processing environment.
6. An important need exists for EDP audit staff development because few internal audit staffs have enough data processing knowledge and experience to audit effectively in the data processing environment.
7. Few current EDP audit tools and techniques are adequate to the needs of the EDP auditors as they approach the task of verifying the accuracy and completeness of data processing activities and results. New tools and techniques are needed.
8. Many organizations are not adequately evaluating their audit and control functions in the data processing environment. Top management should initiate a period assessment of its audit and control programs.

The above conclusions indicate needs for the attention of top management and needs for investments of money, staff, and management time to ensure the adequacy of the audit and control functions for each data processing system. Unquote. The real question is whether or not things have changed significantly. They have changed, of course, but the amount of change is still in question.

An Approach to Auditing

The EDP audit has many tools at its disposal—not the least being the programs which are used to test the systems and the data produced. But there is no tool more valuable than common sense—and its allies. Essentially, the EDP audit will be conducted in four areas: inquiry, observation, testing, and evaluation.

Inquiry. The auditor must be concerned about representations as to housekeeping controls and the functioning of different systems. Yes, the auditor really does need to know how the operations personnel dispose of trash and handle cleanliness. The loss of data and systems to fire and carelessness is highly documented. But the representations as to the functioning of the specific systems are far more important—and if the auditor has been involved in the systems development activities, he or she have some solid idea of the type of controls which have been designed into the system, for the predominant responsibility of the auditor is the safeguarding and protection of organizational assets.

Observation. Much of what the auditor finds is obtainable from a visual survey. Reviewing of the system documentation and the surrounding procedures provide a comparison against the inquiry process. The existence of standards needs to be the first observation—even the standards provided by one of the auditor's groups, The Institute of Internal Auditors (249 Maitland Avenue, Altamonte Springs, FL 32701).

Testing. The issue here is to determine if the system is used as the system is represented. This is done by discrete tests, the monitoring of system operation; simulation of system functions; testing of transactions; evaluation of external evidence to support the conclusions, and comparisons of inquiries and observations to the tests.

Evaluation. Of course the traditional methods of analyzing accounts hold here. Take a transaction and the account balances and follow them through. But, as we shall see, there has been great movement toward evaluation programs, pseudo systems, controlled interdiction, and the like.

Elements of Computer-Oriented Internal Control

Before the computer, internal controls were rooted mainly in the numbers of people and separation of their functions so that one person would check another. But with the computer, that is different. In the presence of the computer, we can no longer rely on the classic concept of separate people doing separate duties to achieve adequate internal control. What is needed now is *functional separation* of system elements. These functions are the authorization function, the recordkeeping function, and the custodial function.

Authorization

This traces the permissions to process data, the requirements to assure accuracy, and the procedures to follow if something changes abruptly. The permissions to process data encompass the function of the assurance of validity in the source documents which enter the system. To this extent, the systems person and the internal auditor must not accept on its face the fact that a document which is entered into the EDP system is accurate. The auditability of the EDP system precedes the system itself.

This authorization must assure prompt and accurate processing of valid source documents, which requires the establishment of standards, measurement against standards, and the maintenance of controls over the input, processing, and output of the data contained upon or triggered by those source documents. And it must also include the procedures to follow and assurances of accuracy of the data when the process has been interrupted, modified, or changed. Note well that the absence of standards against which to measure is the beginning of the uncontrolled system, from an auditor's viewpoint.
Questions which apply to authorization include:

1. What are these controls—specifically?
2. Are these controls thoroughly and adequately documented, using charts, descriptions, etc., to permit a review of adequacy?
3. Is the documentation periodically and promptly updated? There isn't a lot to compare against if the system has been changed and the documentation has not.
4. Whose responsibility is it to define operational controls? Are those who rely on the data a part of the definition responsibility? If the system is a credit system, for example, has the system design involved the credit people.
5. Whose responsibility is it to monitor such controls? Who must, for example, match the totals on the reports to the totals expected by the user department? Are these persons responsible to the computer department or independent of it?
6. Are all changes in processing methods supported by written authorization? Is there an authorization audit trail?
7. Are all program and processing changes reviewed for conformity with authorized changes? Who makes the review? Is that person independent of the computer department?
8. Are controls (log books, etc.) provided to record operator intervention? Whose responsibility is it to review such intervention? Is s/he a part of the computer department?
9. Are controls established over computer usage? Are users charged according to use with a representative scale of costs?
10. Are there adequate routines for retention and rotation of records?
11. Whose responsibility is it to review exception reports prepared by the computer department? Does someone follow the exceptions for resolution?
12. How are changes in the system authorized and how are those changes verified when completed?

Recordkeeping

The recordkeeping is a process of the computer itself, these days. In this phase of the activities, the auditor must concern himself that processing is done in conformity to the authorized specifications. Again, the authorized specifications are something more than just the documentation of the system, though the currency of that documentation is inherent in the auditability of the system. No, it must also include system specifications, test results, acceptances from the user, etc. It stands to reason that if nothing has changed, a repeat of an exhaustive test cycle will assure the continued accuracy of the system process.

Included in these functions will be the survey of media libraries, program libraries (physical and logical), and contingency plans. The auditor should be very interested in the procedures which have been developed to safeguard these records—and to test those procedures as a part of the audit.

Questions which apply to recordkeeping include:

1. Are computer operating personnel (e.g., console operators) independent of systems and programming personnel? If the programmer is also the operator, the climate for embezzlement is warmer.
2. Are there adequate controls over maintenance for maximum accuracy and reliability and minimum downtime?
3. Are operating logs kept to register work into and out of the computer department? Is all computer time accounted for? Are halts during operations printed out and later reviewed for conformity with programmed halts? The potential embezzler must have access to the computer.
4. Are data control amounts originated within the computer department? If data controls are established outside the computer department, does the computer department have knowledge of such controls? Can differences between processing results and controls be accounted for? Who accounts for these?
5. Are debugging routines adequate for proper program functioning? Do programmers and system department personnel initial all work done? Who reviews these tests for conformity with specifications of the authorizing function?
6. What assurances are there that processing controls and audit trails, as authorized, are included in programs? Whose responsibility is it to review compliance? How is it tested?
7. Are programs so documented as to facilitate reconstruction? Are diagramming requirements adequate for complete programming and system documentation?
8. Are program libraries maintained? Is issuance of programs for processing adequately safeguarded to assure consistency of processing and to prevent the wrong person from having the program? Are programs safeguarded against loss or destruction?
9. Are all changes to or destruction of programs authorized in writing? If not, how is consistency of processing assured?
10. Are media libraries of permanent data maintained? Are all tapes and disks externally labeled and indexed? Are tapes and disks internally identified? Whose responsibility is it to assure adequate maintenance, safeguarding, and retention of magnetic files, and to prevent the wrong person from having data files? Is essential information maintained on duplicate files kept separate from the computer area, to allow for reconstruction?
11. Is there adequate insurance protection against embezzlement and against destruction of files?
12. Do the procedures which exist permit a consist flow of data to the auditing function without first passing through a computer department control function?

Custody Over Assets

The responsibility and accountability for the physical possession of assets is a concern of the auditor. The physical movement of data and programs; the procedures for release of such assets; the intended use vs. the stated use—these are all concerns of the auditor.

Questions which apply to custody include:

1. Is the computer department authorized to issue disbursements? Is there provision for control of such disbursements, or for later review, by persons independent of the computer department?

2. Are bank reconciliations prepared by the computer department? Does some independent person review such reconciliations? What does that person look for?
3. Does the computer department authorize purchases or shipments of merchandise, manufacturing schedules, write-offs of accounts receivable, etc.? What controls over these activities are established outside of the computer department?
4. What are the overall strengths and weaknesses of the control group reviewing the computer department's authorization of release of corporate assets or of addition to corporate liabilities?
5. How is the allocation of costs for valid purposes being verified against organizational accounting records? Is it possible to spend "funny money" and have something slip by unnoticed?
6. How are costs for communications allocated and verified to be valid and appropriate communications expenditures?

If the authorization, recordkeeping, and custodial functions are being performed properly, the computer will consistently generate reliable data. To the extent that any one of these functions fails, computer output may be unreliable. To the extent that the functional separation is lacking, the danger of embezzlement or misuse of data increases.

On-Line Functional Merge

In the modern day of communications and on-line operating functions, the separation of even these functions, while not totally impossible, is nonetheless difficult. Among these difficulties are:

1. The disappearance of hardcopy output and the resulting loss of the paper audit trail, because of the time necessary to print.
2. Greater reliance on supervisory programs, job streams, etc., with the result that adequacy of the initial design of the system including the built-in safeguards, is critically important. Transactions are entered as fast as the fingers can fly in quantities which range from text message lengths to one-button functions or one-point icons. It then becomes the responsibility of the system designer to find ways to record these functions at the host computer. And it is the responsibility of the EDP auditor to ensure that such functions are isolated within the system—and verified so frequently as to preclude their change.
3. Disappearance of source documents as direct input of data—the truth is that there may not be source documentation for many forms of on-line activity. It now becomes the responsibility of the system designer to construct an archival document and for the auditor to apply traditional controls to that archival document in such a time frame as to ensure that the data provided at the point of origination has not changed.
4. The very thing that makes this generation of computer systems so powerful—integration—makes it doubly difficult to audit. Integration and the MIS concept mean that the transaction triggers a chain of events which may shake out in one or in all departments of the organization and with organizations outside your own.

The result—like it or not—must be more delegation of authority to the computer people. All too often, in the haste to get the system going, the first thing abandoned is control, especially is the small to medium size installations. Because of the already large investment in the installation, many managements are reluctant to add cost by insisting on disciplined data and documentation. In many instances, the programmer is also an operator, and the operator has access to programs rather than run books. This is a bad situation, as this person can do pretty much what s/he pleases. Naturally this is a concern for locally developed BASIC programs on the microcomputer which sits, out in the open, in the user departments.

Should you feel that this is not a concern, consider that:

- Many middle and upper management people fear the computer and lack confidence in it. Interesting that that situation didn't happen this year—it's been true from the beginning.
- Management generally has not recognized the need for an independent control group—an executive in charge of information. Perhaps with the CIO concept, previously discussed, this will change. In the case of smaller installations, it may well be the chief financial officer (CFO) who assumes the control functions. In any case, that function should be isolated from the people who control, program, and operate the computer—of any size.
- Management generally has not recognized the desirability of having a control-oriented review of the initial design and periodic follow-up to assure continuous compliance, once the system has gone into operation.

Auditing Considerations

The ability to audit "through" the computer has become a requirement. The purpose of the audit function hasn't changed, but the rules have. The auditor must know, evaluate, and test a DP system to be satisfied that the figures fairly present the financial position and results of operations of the organization.

The approach to the audit includes the obtaining of representations as to what the system is purported to be doing and the examination of the related system of internal control. Those inquiries about the computer system should be tested in actual fact, and the auditor must select specific programs for review, working in rotation until all programs have been tested. Where adequate systems and programming documentation exist, the auditor's job is easier. Where it does not exist, more effort must be expended on the actual programs themselves to ascertain that the procedures contained therein are in conformity to management's representations, and, if they are not, the extent by which they differ must be determined.

An understanding of the system is essential if the auditor is to rely on the figures it generates. There is no easy path to this understanding—it requires work and a combined team effort between computer specialists and auditors. The more complex the system or the weaker the internal control, the greater the effort required to determine that the system is working properly or the extent of the system's weaknesses.

The advantage of the computer, of course, is in its ability to process consistently once it has been programmed to do so. The system review done by the auditor should include tests of this consistency. This can be done in a number of ways:

1. Comparison of periodic memory dumps taken by the auditing team to the object code of the programs previously reviewed.
2. Mechanically compare the program libraries used by the program to those previously used at the last audit.
3. Reprocess data through an auditor-controlled program, comparing the results to the normal output results.
4. Use controlled input data in environments with good internal control.
5. Check batch controls and selected transactions for testing against known results.
6. Take snapshots of files and compare against modified files, looking for explanations of change.

Creating Functional Audits in the EDP Department

Figure 5.47 represents a suggested way to delineate the functional responsibilities of the administration, systems and programming, control and operations sections of a classically-organized Data Processing Department. The addition of an information center to serve office automation needs would be extended to the right, if the DP manager—or CIO—has that function under his or her control. If that function is not under the control of the CIO, the at the very least the communication between the information processing groups needs to be audited.

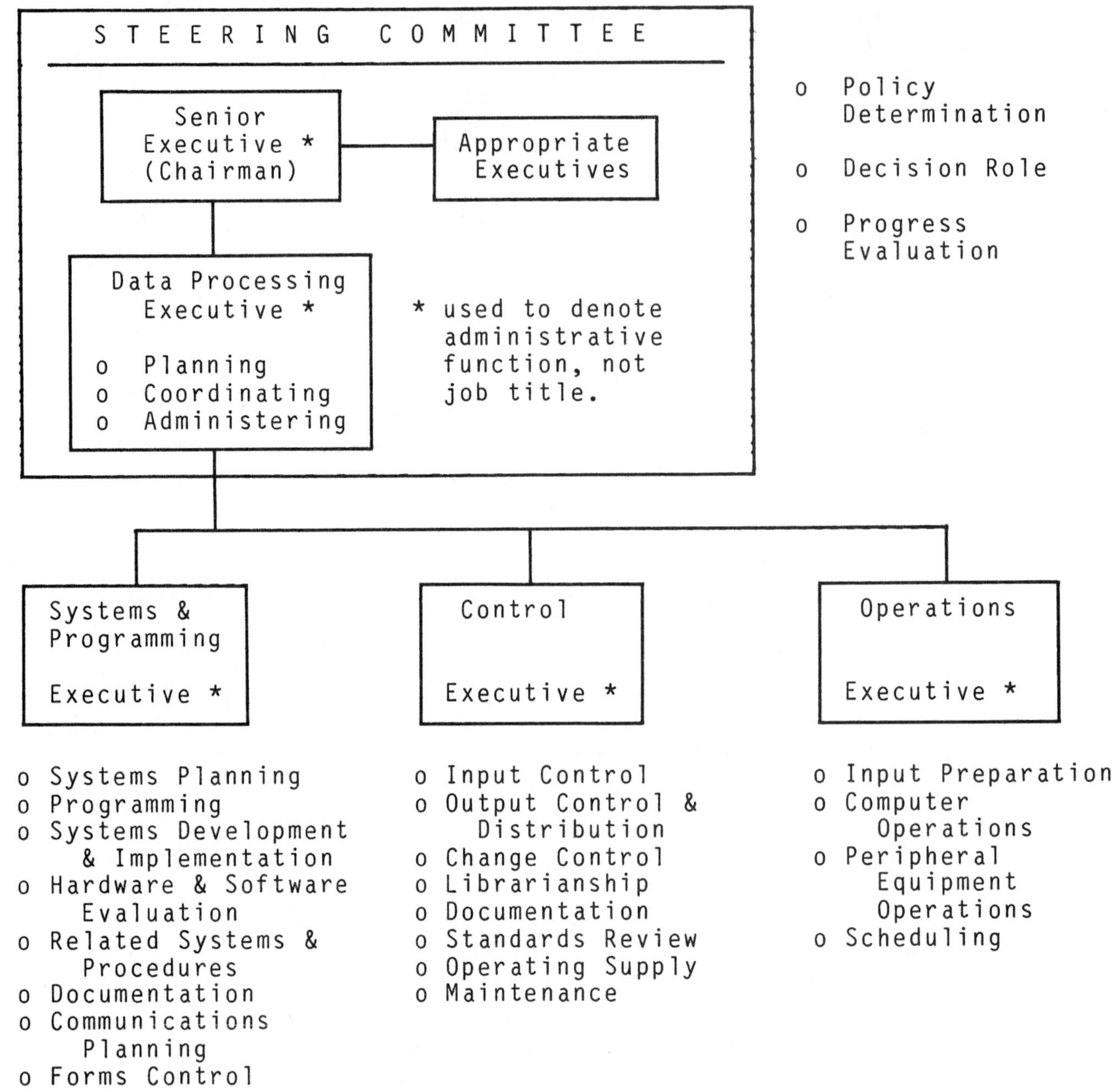

Figure 5.47

Auditor Concerns and Requirements

The need to audit systems is not new. We've been sensitive to it for about a decade. In the *Journal of Accountancy,* March 1974, Mr. E. B. Levine of IBM indicated the existence of certain auditor concerns and requirements which bear repeating here.

The Concerns

1. There is no solution to the difficulty of staying current with the developments in EDP technology. Even EDP people have the problem.

2. The documentation in support of application programs and systems is often insufficient. The auditor is forced to create documentation before proceeding.
3. User personnel and auditors do not understand DP procedures—in particular how to reconstruct transactions once they have entered the system. The reason given for this was that users and auditors have not been involved in developing the system.
4. Too much responsibility and control have been vested in EDP. The problem which arises is the lack of separation of duties, as discussed before. This forces the auditor to review the system and not the documents.
5. In advanced systems, the audit trail may be maintained within the computer and so become invisible to the auditor. The changing, reformatting, summarizing, and modification of input data makes it difficult to maintain integrity of the data and to isolate individual data items.
6. In some systems, source documents may not exist. Modifications and revisions of transactions may not be supported by documents. Loss of documentation is loss of audit trail in some instances.
7. As computer applications become more sophisticated, the interactions between systems become more complex. Time cycles for transaction processing are compressed. Errors in more sophisticated systems are themselves more sophisticated. Errors proliferate as transactions are processed through other systems, creating a snowball effect throughout the system.
8. Manual applications controls are relaxed when the application is placed on a computer, on the assumption that the machine controls are sufficient.
9. There must be adequate control over data that is rejected and/or corrected by the computer system. Many systems have no control over rejected data.
10. Program changes must be subjected to positive control and there is a tendency to store too much information, simply because it is available.

The Requirements

Having expressed their concerns, these were the requirements offered:

1. Systems should provide auditors with the capability to monitor and capture selected data as it flows through the system. The selection criteria should be flexible and easily changed. The processing should take place in such a manner that the EDP personnel would not be aware of what is being selected and would not be able to tamper with the process in any way.
2. Auditors should have the facility to retrieve data from any EDP file. ideally, this retrieval should be capable of being performed on a remote basis and should be secure against any modification by EDP personnel.
3. To provide control over software, auditors should be able to monitor and control program changes. It should be possible to compare a production program that is being executed to an audit control copy of the same program. This comparison should be protected against any intervention by EDP personnel. Further, the system should accept program changes only under certain specific conditions and should provide an effective audit trail that can be used to verify all such changes.
4. Systems should include a tagging facility that would allow an auditor to trace a transaction through a computer system. This tag would be applied to transactions selected by the auditor. From that point on, all processing that uses or affects that transaction, until it is deleted from the system, will be reported to the auditors. This capability should be secure from any modifications by EDP personnel.
5. Vendor-supplied programming should contain standard software controls. For example, verifica-

tion of standard file labels should be a mandatory part of input/output operations and there should be no provision to override or bypass this processing.

6. There should be a clear-cut way for auditors to evaluate the reliability of a system and then be able to assure themselves as to the integrity of the system during subsequent periods.
7. In order to facilitate the review of programs, there should be a system facility that could be used to completely and quickly analyze control logic. This system would highlight all decision points in a program and describe the process that would take place as a result of each alternative. It would be a useful tool for the comparison of programs to their original specifications. Taken to its logical extreme, the system would be capable of analyzing a program and determining where things could go wrong, frequency of error, significant errors, and probability of error occurrence.
8. To provide quality control over EDP operations, the system should collect operational data in a machine-readable form and have the capability to produce reports that can be used for further analysis.
9. In advanced systems, there should be a provision for control tools that will facilitate the work of the database administrator. This should provide complete control over access to the database and the functions that can be performed by each user.
10. Overall, EDP, as a profession, should try to express itself in more nontechnical language. There is too much use of acronyms that are often meaningless. Basically, EDP literature should become more user-oriented.

That was 10 years ago. Not much has changed. The concerns and the recommendations remain largely as they were formulated. There has been movement in the development of audit programs, however, and today there are programs which will track an interloper on an on-line system and analyze accounts to determine if they qualify for installment treatment under IRS regulations. These audit software packages include simplicity, immediate reaction, multiple function capability, automatic job control, self-documentation, and error detection. They can also handle multiple files, report writers, test modes, operation instructions, and security. This software can be used by auditors without EDP support, are generally available for most mainframes, can get any of the available files, and can print reports of the findings.

There are a number of audit software functions. These include footings, summarization, mathematical calculations, comparison of data fields and data files, sampling and selection of records, statistical analysis, sorting, and printing of reports and confirmations. With the software, the auditor can determine mathematical accuracy, can select the details for the audit, can reprocess the user's files, reviewing for specific attributes.

Figure 5.48 details the audit data (outcome), the audit function, and the audit language specifications necessary to extract the data with audit software. Though some things haven't changed, we have come a long way. But there is still a long way to go. The audit scope will need to be ever-widening, particularly since we now have thousands of microcomputers in the user departments. The risk of loss is increasing, but the cost of auditing is decreasing. It still has a ways to go.

Computer Audit Tests

The following are a few of the suggested tests to apply to an EDP system.

Cash and Accounts Receivable

- Assistance in bank reconciliations including cut-off
- Footing of cash books

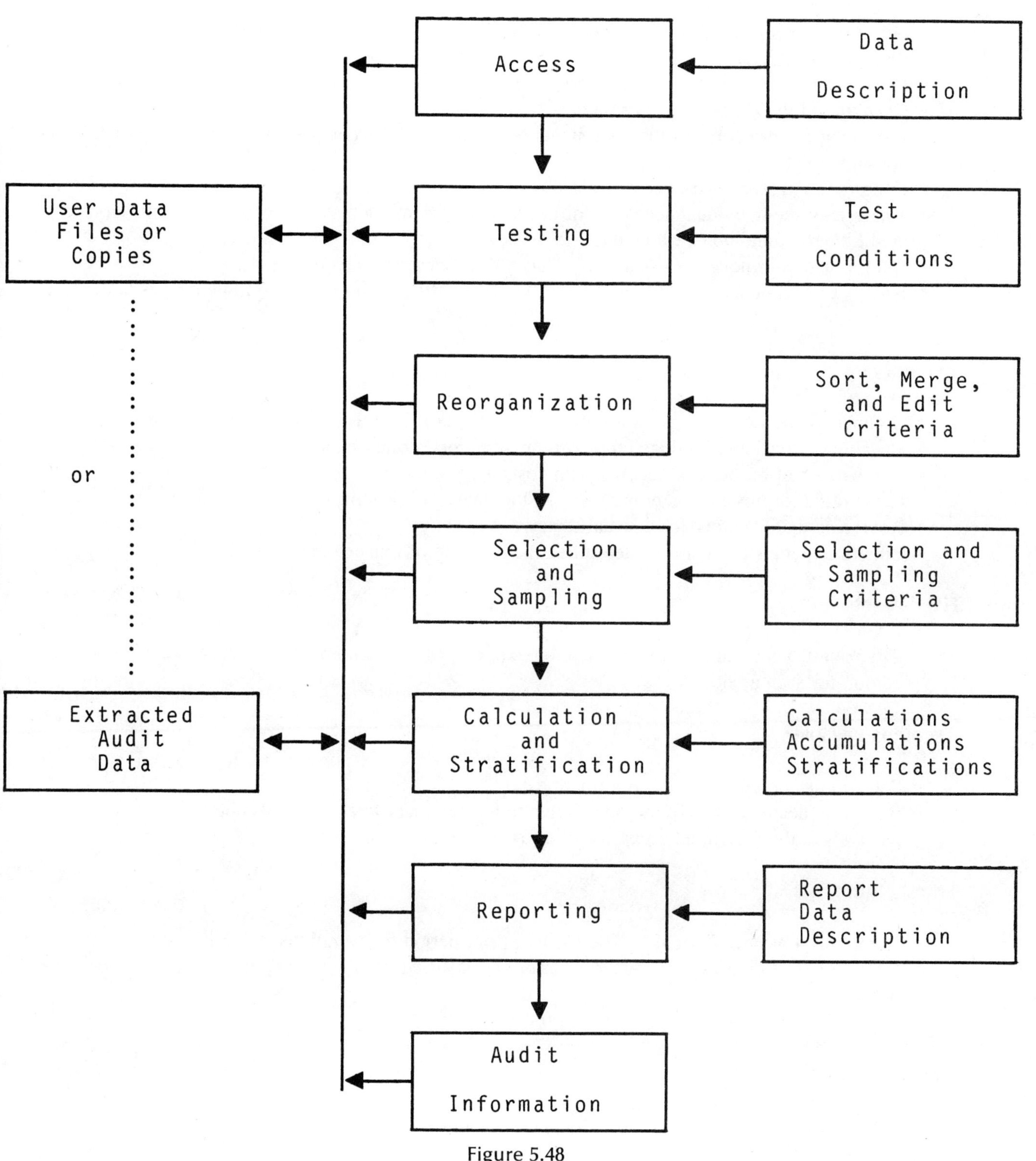
Access
Data
Description
User Data
Files or
Copies
Testing
Test
Conditions
Reorganization
Sort, Merge,
and Edit
Criteria
or
Selection
and
Sampling
Selection and
Sampling
Criteria
Extracted
Audit
Data
Calculation
and
Stratification
Calculations
Accumulations
Stratifications
Reporting
Report
Data
Description
Audit
Information

Figure 5.48

- Selection of items to be confirmed by such parameters as over x dollars, every nth, accounts over x dollars past-due, etc.
- Preparation of positive, negative, and special format confirmations including confirmation statistics
- Checking of the aging of the accounts
- Balancing detail records of the open items pertaining to the account with the summary total for the account
- Footing the trial balance
- Analysis of the individual accounts for unusual conditions such as over the credit limit, large credit balance, and non-cash credits
- Determination of noncurrent portions of installment accounts receivable
- Analysis of accounts to determine if they qualify for treatment on the installment basis under IRS regulations

Inventory

- Comparison of auditor's inventory abstracts of physical inventory with the user's costed inventory
- Checking extensions, footings, and accumulating total dollar value
- Comparison of master cost records with costs used in the inventories
- Accounting for missing ticket numbers on the physical inventory
- Analyzing the inventory for unusual items
- Bills of materials explosion to determine the build-up of finished goods costs

Fixed Assets

- Checking the computation of depreciation expense, investment credit, and the accumulated depreciation for each asset.

Accounts Payable

- Selection and preparation of confirmations
- Balancing detail records of the open items to the summary total of the account
- Analysis of the individual accounts for unusual items

Transaction Costs

- Comparison of payroll from one period to a prior period for variations
- Comparison of expense accounts with prior periods, budgeted amounts, etc., for unusual deviations
- Test of transactions updating work-in-process file

Statistical Sampling

- Selection of random numbers from a table of random numbers

Other

- Preparation of consolidated financial statements
- Preparation of tax return data
- Checking calculations of earned/unearned income on long-term leases

Of course, this is not a complete list—just a few pages to give you some idea of what the EDP auditor is all about and to prepare you for some questions about him on the CDP Exam. But note a valuable point made in this section—auditing is done against a standard, and the standard contains controls. You'll find a larger discussion of control mechanisms in the systems chapter.

QUESTIONS

1. Percentage depletion rates may be used for:
   A. Equipment
   B. Minerals
   C. Bonds
   D. Goodwill
2. Costs which are associated with a finished goods inventory do not include:
   A. Costs attributable to lost sales due to out-of-stock conditions
   B. Costs attributable to sunk or research and development
   C. Costs attributable to key salaries
   D. Costs attributable to utilities, insurance, or rent
3. Present value is the means of determining:
   A. The compound value of an annuity
   B. The compound interest to be derived from an investment
   C. The value of a discount
   D. Annual payment for accumulation of a future sum
4. A firm's ability to meet current obligations is shown by the:
   A. Accounts receivable turnover
   B. Quick ratio
   C. Debt to equity ratio
   D. Price earnings ratio
5. The best internal control to ensure the correct input tape is used for processing would be a(n):
   A. Housekeeping check
   B. Trailer label check
   C. File protection ring
   D. External tape label
6. When determining the contribution of a given product of profitability, the manager should observe:
   A. The relationship of variable costs to fixed costs
   B. The contribution of sales to profit
   C. The contribution of net revenue to profit
   D. The contribution of depreciation to cash flow
7. A company is considering introducing a new product. The marketing people have made the assumption that there is a 50/50 chance that the product will bring in $100,000 in revenues. However, there is a $\frac{1}{5}$ chance that the product will fail and they will lose a $20,000 investment. If you were the management of the company and computed the mathematical expectation of the product, what would it be?
   A. $40,000
   B. $46,000
   C. $50,000
   D. $58,000
8. Of the following statements, which is false?
   A. Accounting is based on theories and assumptions.
   B. Accounting is an information processing system.

C. Accounting provides information for reporting, planning, and controlling.
D. Accounting can be classified as an exact science.

9. In breakeven analysis:
A. Variable revenues = variable costs + fixed costs
B. Total costs = total revenues
C. Fixed costs = total costs at zero production
D. Variable revenues − total costs = profit (loss)

10. The entity assumption holds that an organization must be viewed as a unit that is:
A. An extension of its owners
B. Separate and apart from its owners
C. Controlled exclusively by owners
D. Controlled by agents of the owners

11. The current ratio is the ratio of:
A. Current assets to current liabilities
B. Current assets to gross sales
C. Net profit to taxable income
D. Quick assets to current liabilities

12. The three basic forms of business organizations are:
A. Corporations, banks, and mutual companies
B. Manufacturing, wholesaling, and retailing
C. Corporations, partnerships, and sole proprietorships
D. Public companies, private companies, and institutions

13. Allowance for depreciation would be considered a(n):
A. Liability
B. Offset liability
C. Asset
D. Contra-asset

14. The expression "For the Month Ended January 31, 198x" would be the proper dating on the heading of a corporation's:
A. Balance sheet
B. Statement of sources and applications of funds
C. Statement of retained earnings
D. Capital statement

15. Which of the following is *not* included in a P&L statement?
A. Sources and amounts of income from each
B. Types of expenses and amounts of each
C. Net profit or net loss
D. Plant assets

16. The financial statement which portrays a company at a point in time is the:
A. Income Statement
B. Balance Sheet
C. Statement of Retained Earnings
D. Sources and Applications of Capital

17. The primary financial statements consist of:
A. The Income Statement and the Balance Sheet
B. The Income Statement and the Cash Flow Statement
C. The Balance Sheet and the Funds Flow Statement
D. The Balance Sheet and the Statement of Retained Earnings

18. Of the following items, which would be found on *both* an income statement and a statement of retained earnings?
A. Net Income
B. Dividends
C. Capital Stock
D. Cash

19. A summary of information recorded in the books of original entry is known as a(an):
A. Ledger
B. Journal
C. Trial balance
D. Account analysis

20. A liability will be created and recorded for
A. Sales on account
B. Purchases on account
C. Purchases for cash
D. Sales for cash

21. Salaries payable would be classified as a(an):
A. Accrued income
B. Accrued expense
C. Deferred income
D. Deferred expense

22. Stockholder's equity will be decreased by
A. Purchasing land for cash
B. Purchasing office supplies on account
C. Borrowing cash
D. Payment of declared dividends

23. Given: fixed cost = \$5,000; variable cost = \$3.50 per unit; and revenues of \$6.00 per unit. The breakeven point would be:
A. 6,000 units
B. 4,000 units
C. 2,000 units
D. 1,000 units

24. Of the following items, which would *not* appear on the income statement?
A. Dividends Paid
B. Capital Stock
C. Dividends Payable
D. Prepaid Expenses

25. Premium on bonds may be amortized through an adjustment to:
A. Contributions in excess of par value
B. Reserve for sinking fund
C. Bonds payable
D. Interest expense

26. Ryan Corporation began operations on January 2, 198x by issuing capital stock for \$5,000 cash. During 198x, Ryan had sales of \$10,000. Ryan incurred \$6,000 of operating expenses during 198x; of this amount, \$2,500 was unpaid at year-end. Ryan Corporation declared and paid \$500 in dividends during 198x. The only other transaction was the purchase of \$3,500 of equipment for cash near the end of the year. How much was Ryan Corporation's net income for the year?
A. \$0

B. $500
C. $4,000
D. $6,500

27. Choose the correct statement regarding the various cost accounting systems:
A. A large variety of products encourages a job order cost system.
B. The process cost system captures the cost of each order.
C. Standard costs cannot be used to determine process efficiencies.
D. Job order costs are accumulated by departments of processes.

28. Rolf Corporation began operations on January 2, 198x by issuing capital stock for $5,000 cash. During 198x, Rolf had sales of $10,000. Rolf incurred $6,000 of operating expenses during 198x; of this amount, $2,500 was unpaid at year-end. Rolf Corporation declared and paid $500 in dividends during 198x. The only other transaction was the purchase of $3,500 of equipment for cash near the end of the year. How much were Rolf Corporation's total assets at year end?
A. 8,500
B. 9,000
C. 9,500
D. 11,000

29. In inventory pricing, market means:
A. Selling price
B. Current replacement cost
C. Cost adjusted for the consumer price index
D. Net realizable value

30. The balance of each account of a company may be determined by reference to the:
A. General Journal
B. General Ledger
C. Balance Sheet
D. Statement of Retained Earnings

31. The market value of a common stock can be determined from the information shown in the:
A. Par value statement
B. Newspaper
C. Amex Index
D. Dow Jones average

32. Which of the following normally has a credit balance?
A. Expense
B. Asset
C. Liability
D. Cash

33. The costing technique employed by a commercial data processing service bureau would probably be:
A. Process costing
B. Job costing
C. Standard costing
D. Direct costing

34. A common misconception about debits and credits is
A. Revenue accounts are always increased by credits
B. Asset accounts are always decreased by credits
C. Credits always increase account balances
D. Liability accounts are always increased by credits

35. Price/quantity determinations are made by finding:
A. The intersection of supply and demand curves
B. The intersection of revenue and cost curves
C. Where the highest profit margin is found
D. Where fixed cost and revenue lines cross

36. The Accounts Receivable account is a(n):
A. Asset account which is decreased by a credit
B. Asset account which is increased by a credit
C. Revenue account which is decreased by a debit
D. Revenue account which is increased by a debit

37. The best control procedure to ensure the accuracy of the inventory master file would be:
A. A periodic test against physical count
B. Control figures
C. A parity check
D. Limit tests

38. Which of the following statements is true?
A. Credits never increase stockholder's equity.
B. Assets should equal liabilities and owners' equity.
C. Debits normally indicate an unfavorable event or transaction.
D. Total debits equal total assets.

39. Bond premiums are amortized by adjusting:
A. Interest Expense
B. Reserve for Depreciation
C. Bonds Payable
D. Adjustments to Preferred Stock

40. Which of the following is sometimes referred to as the ''book of original entry?''
A. Journal
B. General Ledger
C. Chart of Accounts
D. Source Documents

41. The prime rate is the:
A. Cost of capital from the Federal Reserve
B. Cost of capital from a commercial bank
C. Cost of capital from a savings and loan association
D. Cost of capital from a savings bank

42. The chart of accounts is a detailed listing of a company's accounts
A. Along with their associated account reference number
B. Along with the rules indicating when they are to be debited and credited
C. And is prescribed by the accounting profession
D. And must contain every possible account name

43. A credit entry is required to increase a(an):
A. Asset account
B. Prepaid insurance
C. Current liability account
D. Receivables account

44. The process of posting to the general ledger:
A. Is not necessary if a journal is used
B. Precedes preparation of a trial balance

C. Is always performed simultaneously with recording transactions in the journal
D. Is performed only for revenue and expense accounts.

45. If total assets are $80,000. Current liabilities are $40,000, total liabilities are $200,000 and there are no fixed assets, the current ratio is:
A. 0.1 to 1
B. 1.5 to 1
C. 2.0 to 1
D. 2.5 to 1

46. Which of the following is *not* true about the trial balance?
A. It is used to check the equality of debits and credits
B. It provides a listing of the ending balance in each ledger account.
C. It is not a formal financial statement.
D. It should be printed in the annual report.

47. In addition to first in-first out (FIFO) and last in-first out (LIFO), inventory value may be arrived at through the use of:
A. Inventory averaging
B. Original cost plus markup
C. Original cost less reserve for bad debts
D. Selling price less overhead costs

48. Jefferson Corporation failed to record the purchase of supplies on account. The error will likely be discovered when
A. It might never be discovered
B. A trial balance is prepared
C. An income statement is prepared
D. The cash on hand is counted

49. Most inventory systems that are computerized employ the
A. Perpetual basis
B. Periodic basis
C. Physical basis
D. Average basis

50. A transposition error
A. Is also known as a slide
B. Is easily detected by reviewing the ending balance of each account included in the trial balance
C. Is to be suspected when one-half of the amount of the error is equal to the balance of an account in the trial balance
D. Is to be suspected when the amount of the error is evenly divisible by nine

51. Of the terms listed below, which describes the largest number of producers in an industry?
A. Duopoly
B. Monopoly
C. Oligopoly
D. Polyglot

52. Erroneously debiting an asset account when an expense account should be debited will result in:
A. An understatement of total assets
B. An overstatement of total debits in the trial balance
C. An understatement of total revenues
D. A trial balance that still balances

53. The best way to keep track of sensitive documents is to use:
A. Security clearances

B. An audit trail
C. Transmittal control
D. Documentation

54. Felix Corporation purchased goods on account for $4,750, paid $5,400 on accounts payable, and had an ending accounts payable balance of $7,650. How much was beginning accounts payable?
A. $7,000
B. $8,300
C. $8,975
D. $9,200

55. "Present value" means:
A. The market value of assets
B. The value of a future annutiy
C. The value of a future payment of payments
D. The value in a regional market area

56. For purposes of reporting the results of operations, the life of a business is
A. Considered to be one continuous reporting period
B. Divided into discrete accounting periods
C. Divided into one-year time intervals
D. Divided into specific points in time

57. The matching concept means:
A. Costs should be carried forward if there are no revenues to match them with
B. All revenues should be matched with all costs
C. Expenses should be allocated on the basis of net income
D. Costs which can be associated with specific revenues should be properly matched in the same accounting period

58. Which of the following would require an adjusting journal entry at the end of an accounting period?
A. Multiperiod costs that must be split among two or more accounting periods
B. Expenses to be incurred in a future accounting period and not as yet paid
C. Payments received in the current accounting period for revenues earned and recorded in prior accounting periods
D. Receipts anticipated against costs expended, before the payment has been paid for those costs

59. "Consolidated Statements" are:
A. Condensed versions of regular statements
B. The results of adding up all the statements for divisions of a company
C. A representation of all the assets and liabilities of a corporate entity
D. A method of showing all corporate financial statements on one sheet

60. The unearned revenue account could best be described as
A. A liability
B. Revenues earned by not yet collected
C. A contra asset
D. An accrual

61. If the current ratio is 1.5 to 1, then the acid test ratio would be:
A. More than 1.5 to 1
B. Less than 1.5 to 1
C. More than or equal to 1.5 to 1
D. Less than or equal to 1.5 to 1

62. At the end of the current accounting period, Malone Corporation failed to record the expiration of a prepaid expense. As a result, current period assets, liabilities, stockholders' equity, and income, respectively, are

A. Overstated, correct, overstated, correct
B. Overstated, correct, overstated, overstated
C. Overstated, correct, overstated, understated
D. Overstated, correct, understated, understated

63. In using the sum of the years' digits method of calculating the annual provision for depreciation, the rate for the last year of an asset with an estimated useful life of five years is:

A. $\frac{1}{20}$
B. $\frac{1}{15}$
C. $\frac{1}{10}$
D. $\frac{1}{5}$

64. At the end of the current accounting period, Dull Corporation failed to record utilities consumed during the period. They will be billed for the utilities during the next accounting period. As a result, current period assets, liabilities, stockholders' equity, and income, respectively, are

A. Overstated, overstated, correct, correct
B. Correct, understated, overstated, overstated
C. Overstated, understated, overstated, overstated
D. Overstated, understated, correct, correct

65. Scientifically calculated estimates are used to determine:

A. Imputed costs
B. Original costs
C. Standard costs
D. Differential costs

66. The Income Summary account

A. Will always have a credit balance
B. Will appear on a corporation's balance sheet
C. Will receive entries only during the closing process
D. Will be adjusted for the accruals experienced

67. When doing a breakeven analysis:

A. Total revenues − total costs = profit (loss)
B. Total costs = marginal revenue
C. Fixed costs = total costs
D. Revenues = total costs

68. Reversing entries are used

A. To correct a mistake
B. To post an adjusted account
C. To obtain a statistical sampling
D. To revise the figures

69. Incremental costs concepts mean that:

A. Marginal costs cannot be allowed
B. Additional personnel should not be employed
C. An additional job is not economical if the marginal utility (revenue) is less than the marginal costs
D. Incremental costs are equal to variable overhead

70. In a merchandising operation, the Sales account should include:

A. Only credit sales of merchandise
B. Only cash sales of merchandise

C. Both cash and credit sales of merchandise
D. All merchandise sales and sales of any other assets

71. Statement of sources and application of funds would be derived from a(an):
A. Statement of retained earnings
B. Cash flow statement
C. Income statement
D. Balance sheet

72. If a seller of merchandise accepts merchandise returned by a credit customer, the seller will typically issue
A. A credit memorandum
B. A debit memorandum
C. An invoice
D. A purchase order

73. The best control procedure to keep a source document from being coded with an invalid customer account number would be:
A. Document transmittal slips
B. Keypunch verification
C. A hash total check
D. A check digit

74. Which of the following statements is *false*?
A. Cash discounts are a convenient means of reducing list prices to invoice prices.
B. Cash discounts are used to encourage customers to make prompt payments.
C. From the seller's perspective, the terms cash discount and sales discount are synonomous.
D. Cash discounts may be offered in conjunction with trade discounts.

75. If marginal revenue minus marginal costs is:
A. Zero, the firm is at breakeven
B. Greater than zero, the firm is profitable
C. Less than zero, the firm is not profitable
D. Unequal to zero, the firm is too profitable

76. The audit trail provides a means to
A. Trace and access the details that underlie summarized information
B. Insure the reliability of accounting data
C. Distribute incopatible functions among different employees
D. Provide steady work for the auditing staff

77. An example of a fixed asset would be:
A. Finished goods inventory
B. Administrative supplies
C. Accounts receivable
D. Plant and equipment

78. A typical internal accounting control feature would be
A. Production quality control
B. Employee training programs
C. Prenumbered checks
D. Control diagrams

79. A certain business ratio is known as a "leverage" ratio. Which of the following is the "leverage" ratio?
A. Fixed charge coverage ratio
B. Current ratio

C. Total asset turnover ratio
D. Return on net worth ratio

80. A typical internal administrative control feature would be
A. Production quality controls.
B. Prenumbered documents
C. Requiring two signatures on checks
D. A report from an external auditor

81. Posting is accomplished by making entries in the:
A. Journal
B. Ledger
C. Trial balance
D. Adjustment

82. Which of the following would constitute an internal control weakness?
A. Limited access to assets
B. Centralization of incompatible duties
C. Verification of company records with assets on hand
D. Use of prenumbered documents

83. Proper segregation of functional responsibilities calls for separation of the
A. Authorization, execution, and approval functions
B. Authorization, execution, and payment functions
C. Receiving, shipping, and custodial functions
D. Authorization, recording, and custodial functions

84. A system is known to produce 58.3% ROI as determined by the following formula:

$$\text{ROI} = \frac{B - \dfrac{D}{P}}{D}$$

where B = benefits, D = development costs, P = write-off period. If the development cost is $120,000 and the benefit is $100,000, what write-off period has been assumed?
A. 3 years
B. 4 years
C. 5 years
D. 6 years

85. Current assets are those that:
A. Can be used to pay current liabilities
B. Will probably be converted into cash with the business' normal operating cycle
C. Will be liquidated within the business' normal operating cycle
D. Comprise the quick assets

86. The sales journal would typically include:
A. All sales
B. Only sales on account
C. The balance due from each customer
D. Sales for cash

87. When assets = net worth:
A. There are many accounts receivable
B. There are no accounts receivable
C. There are many liabilities
D. There are no liabilities

88. The purchases journal would typically include
A. All merchandise purchases
B. All purchases
C. Only merchandise purchases on account
D. All purchase on account

89. An invoice marked 2/10, n30, which is paid within the discount period will save interest at an annual rate of:
A. 12 percent
B. 24 percent
C. 36 percent
D. 48 percent

90. The cash receipts journal would typically include all but:
A. Cash sales
B. Customer payments on account
C. Sale of old equipment for cash
D. Purchases on account

91. Given a list price of $2,500, a purchase price of $2,000, and a salvage value of $200 after a 10-year depreciation, what is the book value after one year?
A. $2,300
B. $1,800
C. $1,820
D. $2,280

92. The cash payments journal will typically include
A. Virtually all cash payments
B. Only payments of accounts payable
C. Only cash payments which frequently recur
D. All cash payments except payments of accounts payable

93. If the net sales is $100,000, beginning inventory is $10,000, ending inventory is $30,000, and the gross profit percentage is 40 percent, then turnover is:
A. 2 times
B. 3 times
C. 4 times
D. 5 times

94. Which of the following terms best relates to natural resources?
A. Depreciation
B. Depletion
C. Amortization
D. Mortification

95. Which of the following accounts normally carry debit balances?
A. Assets and liabilities
B. Liabilities and income
C. Assets and expenses
D. Expenses and income

96. If a city assesses a property owner for sidewalks and curbs which benefit the property owner, how should the property owner account for the assessment costs?
A. As an expense
B. As an intangible asset
C. As an addition to a land account
D. As an addition to a property improvement account

97. Marketable bonds being used temporarily as an investment by a firm would be classified as a:
A. Current asset
B. Deferred income
C. Long-term liability
D. Stockholders' equity

98. Which of the following is not a feature of the corporate form of organization?
A. Limited liability
B. Perpetual existence
C. Separate legal entity
D. Mutual agency

99. In a company where many departments are using the services of the data processing department, the most equitable way to distribute the cost of the department is to:
A. Charge all costs to overhead accounts and distribute them equally to all departments
B. Charge all costs according to the benefit received by the department from the work performed
C. Charge all costs on a time and materials basis, with a flat hourly overhead rate added
D. Charge each department according to its resource usage

100. According to the text, the predominant concern of the EDP auditor is:
A. Complicated errors
B. Lack of competent documentation
C. High programmer turnover
D. Loss of internal control

ANSWERS

1. B	**26.** C	**51.** C	**76.** A
2. A	**27.** B	**52.** D	**77.** D
3. C	**28.** D	**53.** C	**78.** C
4. B	**29.** B	**54.** B	**79.** A
5. A	**30.** B	**55.** C	**80.** A
6. C	**31.** B	**56.** B	**81.** B
7. B	**32.** C	**57.** D	**82.** B
8. D	**33.** B	**58.** A	**83.** B
9. D	**34.** C	**59.** D	**84.** D
10. B	**35.** A	**60.** A	**85.** B
11. A	**36.** A	**61.** D	**86.** B
12. C	**37.** A	**62.** B	**87.** D
13. D	**38.** B	**63.** B	**88.** C
14. A	**39.** A	**64.** B	**89.** C
15. D	**40.** A	**65.** C	**90.** D
16. B	**41.** B	**66.** C	**91.** D
17. A	**42.** A	**67.** A	**92.** A
18. A	**43.** C	**68.** A	**93.** B
19. B	**44.** B	**69.** C	**94.** B
20. B	**45.** C	**70.** C	**95.** C
21. B	**46.** D	**71.** C	**96.** D
22. D	**47.** B	**72.** A	**97.** A
23. C	**48.** A	**73.** C	**98.** D
24. C	**49.** A	**74.** A	**99.** D
25. D	**50.** D	**75.** A	**100.** B

TUTORIAL

1. Minerals are estimated and then depleted, along the lines of depreciation. Often this depletion is taken in the form of an allowance.
2. Because lost sales means the product could not be sold because it did not exist, one can hardly charge the cost to work in process.
3. Think of it as the present value of a sum which has a given future value.
4. The quick—or acid test—ratio is the best measure of the ability to meet current obligations—everything that can be liquified goes into the value of quick assets.
5. Be careful not to jump to the labels here—though a header label would be the best alternative—the checking of which is often done in the housekeeping routines at the beginning of the program.
6. The net revenue is the actual contribution to the organization. The others may produce worthwhile measurements of something—but not product contribution.
7. The 50/50 expectation of $100,000 produces an estimate of $50,000. The $\frac{1}{5}$ expectation of a loss of $20,000 produces a −$4,000. The net is $46,000.
8. Assumptions, opinions, and other imprecise measurements render accounting as a very inexact science.
9. Breakeven is that point where costs and revenues are identical. Anything above that point has a disparity between variable revenues (hopefully higher) and total costs (hopefully lower), producing profit.
10. Because the corporation is a legal person, it, and only it, is responsible in legal actions. It is an entity, separate and apart from its owners (stockholders).
11. Divide the current assets by the current liabilities and the answer will tell you how well the current assets will cover the current liabilities. It's known as the current ratio.
12. Those given in the answer are the three types of business organization. There are others—public and private, but they are generally not business organizations.
13. Allowance for depreciation is a diminishment of the value of the asset—and is carried against (contra) the value of the asset on the asset side of the ledger.
14. This is also used on the income statement. The other statements given are snapshot pictures, not pictures of the lapse of time.
15. Plant assets (or fixed assets) is a balance sheet account.
16. You can't hide much from a balance sheet. It shows where you are on a specific date.
17. These are the predominant financial statements, and the ones which the auditor will wish to view first.
18. Net income is the product of the income statement. Net income on the statement of retained earnings depicts the movement of income during the current period.
19. The key word here is "summary." The books of original entry have the detail. The summary is consolidated into a journal. If you answered A, don't be alarmed, for the journal can be called a ledger. The reason is isn't the best answer, is that a ledger is often used only for the books of original entry. The concept is the same.
20. Liability means what the organization owes someone else. If the purchase was made for cash, there is no liability.
21. An expense is reportable as of the period, whether or not the money was disbursed. If it is owed and has not been disbursed, it is an expense, accrued until the closing period.
22. A dividend declared is a dividend payable. When paid, the cash account is reduced, and so is the ownership of the stockholders. The stockholder still gets the money, but it is separated from the books of the corporation.
23. Revenues at 2,000 units is $12,000. Fixed cost is $5,000. The $7,000 difference is 2,000 units @ $3.50.

24. Of the list, only dividends payable would not appear. The dividends paid would appear, as would the other items.

25. The premium on the bonds is an expense which is reimbursed to someone else. When the bonds are purchased, the price paid for the premium is an instant expense of the organization.

26. Calculated at sales ($10,000) − operating expenses ($6,000). The influx of cash from sale of stock does not affect net income; neither does the dividend paid. They both do affect cash, however.

27. Process cost systems must be able to capture the cost of each order, provided the accounting is done correctly. Be careful, this is a mislead to make you think about job order costing. Process cost is generally for a repetitive process.

28. Investment ($5,000) + Net Profit ($4,000) + Unpaid Expenses ($2,500) − Dividends Paid ($500). The $3,500 of equipment will not change the amount of assets, as it was exchanged for cash.

29. Irrespective of what I paid for it, if I must acquire it today, it must be at the market price.

30. The general ledger is where the summary of details on one account are located. The journal has the details. The other two are reports drawn at period end.

31. Of course, you can tie directly into the Dow Jones News Service with your personal computer, but most people simply find the information from the newspaper.

32. Since liabilities are on the right side of the accounting equation, it will customarily have a credit balance. Expenses, which are also on the liability side, will have a debit balance because they are an offset against an ownership account which does have the credit balance.

33. This is an example of a job costing technique—the process is not so repetitive that a process cost can be assigned to it.

34. Be careful of the wording of the questions. ''Misconception'' means something that is thought to be true, but is not. A, B, and D are all true. C sounds true, but is not.

35. The intersection of the supply and demand curves is the breakeven point, and there are two of them: a lower, initial breakeven, and an upper point where the maximum profit is made. So the price/quantity determinations are made between them.

36. Accounts Receivable are assets. When they are converted into cash (debit) they are decreased (credit).

37. Physical inventories are used to periodically balance the books, whether or not they are on the computer.

38. This is the accounting equation. Stockholder's equity is increased as a credit. Debits on the asset side are a very favorable event, but total debits never necessarily equal total assets.

39. Recall from a previous question that premiums paid on bonds are treated as immediate expenses. Continuing that process, the remaining premiums paid are treated as expenses.

40. The journal entry is the first place where information from the source documents gets entered into the accounting system. Totals from that are then transferred to the General Ledger.

41. Actually, it is the cost of capital from a commercial bank in rates which are most favorable to its largest customers.

42. Don't define any more accounts than you need. There are a few standard names, but no standard chart. The rules are accounting rules, and are not stored with the chart. The associated reference number is kept, however, in a manual accounting system.

43. According to the accounting formula, increases on the right side of the formula occur on the credit side.

44. The posting can be done at any time, of course, but it must be done before preparing a trial balance.

45. Divide the assets by the liabilities (current ratio) and you'll discover that there are twice as many assets.

46. The trial balance is a working balance of the general ledger. The general ledger contains both the accounts which must appear on the balance sheet and on the income statement. These accounts would not appear in the same report in the annual report.

47. Inventory averaging is a valuation method, true, but is subject to change with every transaction. C and D are not germane, but B is a valid way to value inventory—commonly called valued at sales.

48. A purchase on account would have been an increase in the office equipment asset balanced by the liability. It might be discovered upon receipt of a duplicate invoice or next month's statement, but it might never be discovered if all you have to go on is your own bookkeeping system.

49. Perpetual means constantly updated. Semi-annual physical inventories are required to balance perpetual systems.

50. It's called the "test of nines," and you can prove it to yourself if you change the number 1234 to 1324. Subtract the former from the latter and you'll see a difference of 90—evenly divisible by 9.

51. It's an economics term—but even though they may seem to hold a monopoly position (as did AT&T before divestiture), they may only be one of a few large producers—an oligopoly.

52. The trial balance simply checks the balancing of debits and credits. Errors will still balance.

53. Transmittal control is generally done via a ticket or fanfold, attached to the document.

54. Figure it this way. Start with the ending balance (CR $7,650), add the new purchase (CR $4,750), subtract the payment (DR $5,400), to get to $8,300.

55. The value *now* of a payment *then* is known as present value.

56. The accounting period is key to reporting the results of operations—generally monthly.

57. In order to get a valid picture of any single reporting period, those costs which can be allocated to revenues within the same period must be so allocated.

58. The adjusting entries are used when you cross a period boundary and the costs have not been fully amortized.

59. That's almost too easy. Consolidated statements bring together the subsidiaries with the controlling organization on one set of financial statements.

60. Unearned revenue is money received but not yet earned, like the advance on this book. As such, until receipts reach the value of the advance, it is my liability to the publisher.

61. This test will remove all noncash assets from the current ratio. It can never be any more; it will no doubt be less. It would be equal only if the assets calculated in the current ratio are cash.

62. Because the recording was not made, current period assets are overstated; liabilities have not changed, and are correct; stockholders' equity and income are both overstated.

63. Consider the numbers: 1, 2, 3, 4, 5. Their sum is 15. In the last year there is one year of useful life to be depreciated. The answer, therefore, would be $\frac{1}{15}$.

64. Current period assets are correct, as they are not affected. Liabilities are understated because they do not reflect the liability. Stockholders' equity will be overstated because the expense has not been recognized. And income, being unchanged, is correct.

65. In a standard costing system, it is necessary to calculate, with as much precision as possible, the cost of each operation.

66. Income is summarized in the closing process. It will have a debit balance and will show on the income statement, not the balance sheet. No adjustment will be made for accruals.

67. There is another breakeven question in this test. It details the breakeven point. However, at any time, total revenues less total cost will equal profit or loss.

68. A reversing entry is most commonly used to correct a mistake. It simply returns the state before the entry is made.

69. Don't assume that the longest answer is always the correct answer. If the next job cannot return its incremental cost, the incremental revenue is insufficient to justify taking it. You may not realize all your profit, but you should realize at least your costs.

70. When considering merchandise sales, you must consider all sales—cash and credit. The only difference is when the money is collected.
71. The statement of sources and applications of funds is just another name for the income statement.
72. The credit customer is an account receivable in our system. That account receivable is a debit entry. The reversing entry must then be a credit entry, and thus the credit memorandum.
73. A hash total is a total on a meaningless field, where a transposition error is not effective.
74. A list price and an invoice price may be the same. The reduction of a list price to an invoice price may be the function of bargaining, but seldom of a cash discount.
75. This is the upper breakeven point on the cost and revenue curve.
76. The audit trail provides the means to check changes in files which make changes in summaries.
77. Fixed assets are not consumed and change only by depreciable value.
78. Prenumbered *anything* will increase accounting control. These numbers will appear not only on checks, but invoices, statements, purchase orders, etc.
79. This is a leverage ratio because it measures how well financed by debt the organization is.
80. Production quality controls fall within the administrative control category.
81. Posting is done to the general ledger from the journals.
82. Auditors like to separate functions. Grouping dissimilar functions may sound like it's worthwhile, but it will confuse and lead to errors.
83. It calculates at 4 years.
84. As presented in the text, under the EDP system complete segregation of functions is not possible. Thus, the best thing to do is to separate the functions of authorization, recording, and custody of the data.
85. To this can be added "within one year." Currency in accounting means essentially a year's business cycle.
86. This journal is defense for the Accounts Receivable account, relative to merchandise sales.
87. According to the accounting formula, assets equal liabilities plus owners' equity. *Net worth* is another name for owner's equity, that is, the difference between assets and liabilities. If there is no difference between assets and net worth, there are no liabilities, and it equals the assets.
88. This is defense for the Accounts Payable account relative to merchandise purchases.
89. In order to arrive at this figure you must consider the impact of not taking the discount on an ongoing purchase.
90. The idea of the cash receipts journal is to account for cash. Purchases on account do not involve cash.
91. The list price is of no consequence. The depreciable price of the item is $1,800, or $180 per year. $2,000 − $180 = $1,820.
92. Let's be more precise—all cash payments. The exception will be the detail of petty cash purchases.
93. We started with $10,000 and ended with $30,000 for a net increase of $20,000. Then we sold $100,000, giving us $120,000. $120,000 divided by the $40,000 is 3.
94. Depletion, not depreciation, applies to natural resources. Amortization is the payoff on a mortgage, and mortified is what you should be if you didn't get the answer to this question.
95. Assets (on the left side of the equation) and expenses (on the right side of the equation) normally have debit balances.
96. This is a property improvement (as is a house), and is generally kept separate from the land itself.
97. The key is "temporary." If they were simply held, they would be classified as a long term asset.
98. The mutual agency does not qualify as a corporation. Answers A, B, and C all describe corporations.
99. One of the difficulties of costing a DP operation is the so-called "overhead" allocation. Charge according to usage.
100. The predominant concern from this list is brought about by the need to create documentation where none exists.

6

MATHEMATICS AND STATISTICS

MATHEMATICS

Modern mathematics is a precise logical representation of certain operations with numerical qualities. The ability to use mathematics to solve complex scientific problems notwithstanding, the need to understand numbers, numbering systems, and the application of mathematics to operations research is great; therefore, some understanding of numbers is required.

MATHEMATICAL NOTATION

Numbers

The numbers used in mathematics are analogous to a solar system. In the center are the *whole numbers* (0, 1, 2, 3, . . .). Note that this collection of numbers has a first number (zero) on the left, but is unbounded on the right. We can also observe that this list is *closed* under addition and multiplication. When we add or multiply any two numbers from the list, we produce another number on the list. Whole numbers, however, are not closed under subtraction; there is no whole number, say X, such that $X + 2 = 3$. To find a list which is closed under subtraction, we must move out in our solar system to the *integers* (. . ., −3, −3, −1, 0, 1, 2, 3, . . .). This list is similar to the whole numbers, but is closed under addition, subtraction, and multiplication.

To represent concepts such as half of an apple, we need *rational numbers*. Rational numbers are numbers of the form p/q where p and q are integers. Quantities such as $\frac{1}{4}$, $\frac{1}{2}$, $\frac{3}{4}$, and $-\frac{327}{52}$ are rational numbers. Rational numbers are closed under addition, subtraction, multiplication, and division (except divide by zero, which is undefined). When we speak of $3\frac{1}{2}$, we really mean the rational number $\frac{7}{2}$.

Unfortunately, not all numeric quantities can be expressed by the simple ratio of integers available in rational numbers. For example, there are no numbers p and q such that p/q is the square root of two. Proof of this fact may be found in mathematical texts. Numbers such as $\sqrt{2}$ are called *irrational numbers*. Together, the rational numbers and irrational numbers make up what are called *real numbers*.

Even this large group of numbers is not sufficient to represent all mathematical quantities. For example, what number is the square root of −1? Certainly not 1, since $1 \times 1 = 1$, and not −1, since -1×-1 is 1. Further, any number larger than 1, taken times itself, will be larger than 1. No real number can be found, so a collection of imaginary numbers is required. In this particular case, we need i, a number with the property of the square root of −1. Together, the real numbers and the imaginary numbers form the *complex numbers*.

We started with whole numbers. If you "add" the negative numbers, you get integers. If you "add" (ratios (e.g., $\frac{1}{2}$), you get rational numbers. If you "add" irrational numbers, you get real numbers. Finally, if you "add" imaginary numbers, you get complex numbers. These formulas may be helpful:

Whole Numbers + Negative Numbers = Integers

Integers + Ratios = Rational Numbers

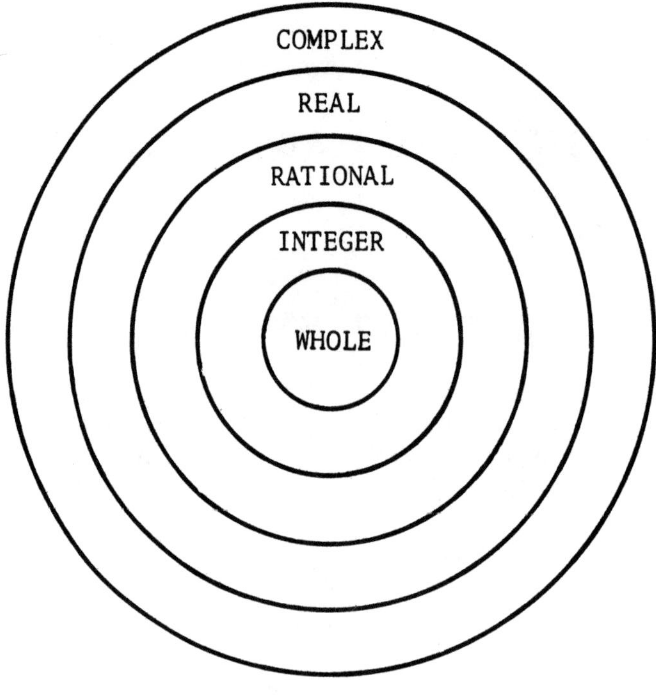

Figure 6.1

Rational Numbers + Irrational Numbers = Real Numbers

Real Numbers + Imaginary Numbers = Complex Numbers

Since every whole number is also an integer, and every integer is also a rational number, etc., we can think of each of these categories as being larger than and inclusive of the lower category.

Exponents

One of the most misunderstood terms in mathematical notation is the exponent. Given 10^2, we say that 10 is the base and that 2 is the exponent. By this notation we mean $1 \times 10 \times 10$. In fact, any number to the 0 power (a "power" is the factor by which a number is multiplied by itself) is 1 except for 0^0, which remains undefined. By a negative exponent, such as in 10^{-2}, we mean $\frac{1}{10}{}^2$. Further, by 10 to the $\frac{1}{2}$ power we mean the square root of 10; thus 10 to the $\frac{1}{3}$ power would be the cube root of 10, etc. In fact, for x and y real numbers and a and b positive, we have the following six laws of exponents:

1. $a^x \cdot a^y = a^{x+y}$
2. $(a^x)^y = a^{(x \cdot y)}$
3. $(a \cdot b)^x = a^x \cdot b^x$
4. $a^{-x} = 1/a^x$
5. $a^{(1/x)} = \sqrt[x]{a}$
6. $a^x/a^y = a^{x-y}$

Subscripts

While the superscript (exponent) denotes a mathematical operation, the subscript is only a notational convenience. By a sequence of numbers we mean an ordered collection of numerical values, not by mathematical value, but by the relative position within the list. For example, 5, 3, 7, −7, 4, 8, 2, . . . is a sequence. We can use subscripts to denote an element in this sequence so long as we decide whether the beginning 5 is the zeroth or the first element. Suppose we start at zero. Then by A_0 we denote 5; by A_1 we denote 3; A_2 is 7, etc. If we start at 1, however, than A_1 is 5, A_2 is 3, A_3 is 7, etc. If we wrote A_i and i had a value of 5 (starting at 1), then we are referring to $A_5 = 4$; $A_i + 2$ would be 2. Any operation may be performed in a subscript, but it is simply evaluated and then used to select an element from the sequence. In general, sequences start with 1, but care must be taken.

Here is that sequence pictorially:

5	3	7	-7	4	8	2
A_1	A_2	A_3	A_4	A_5	A_6	A_7

If $i = 5$, then $A_i = 4$ and $A_i + 2 = 2$.

Suppose we had a two-dimensional table X:

		COLUMN			
		1	2	3	4
ROW	1	8	4	9	-3
	2	3	5	2	-1
	3	-4	3	5	8

Then, $X_{2,3} = 2$. This is often written as ${}_2X_3$ and is called double subscripting.

Functions

A formal definition of function will be discussed with sets later in this chapter. In the meantime, a function is a box, like this:

$$\boxed{x}$$

Into the box we have placed a number, x; the function does something to x and out comes another number which is called *the value of the function at x.* To illustrate, let f be a function which adds the value 1 to the input value, which is also called the argument of the function:

$$f\,\boxed{x} = x + 1$$

If x is the input number, then the value of f at x is $x + 1$. To indicate this relationship between f, its argument, and its value, the function is written $f(x) = x + 1$. Having defined f, when we write $f(6)$ we really mean 7, since the value of f at 6 is 7. Often the function is written in the form $y = f(x)$; that means that y is to have the same value as the function f with x as input. The collection of values which x may assume is called the domain of f. For any x in the domain of f, there may be one and only one y such that $y = f(x)$. For every possible input value to the box, there is only one possible output. It cannot be the case that $f(5) = 3$ and also $f(5) = 8$.

It is possible to have a function which has two input values (and produces one output, as always). For example, the sum operation is a function. We could write $f(x, y) = x + y$. Our special rule in this case is that for every pair x and y in the domain of f, there may be one and only one z such that $z = f(x, y)$. Functions can have any name. It is just as proper to call the sum function g; then $g(x, y) = x + y$.

The operation of taking a number to a power—exponentiation—can be represented by a function. Define $h(x, y)$ to be x^y. Then we have $h(10, 2) = 100$ and $h(100, 0) = 1$; $h(0, 0)$ is undefined, since we have said that 0^0 is undefined. Thus the pair 0, 0 is not in the domain of the function h.

To evaluate a function we take each argument value and, using the definition of the function, calculate the function value. One function may be an argument to another. For example, suppose we define $f(x) = x + 1$ and $g(x) = 2x$. Then $f(g(5))$ is $f(10)$, since $g(5)$ is 10. Hence $f(g(5)) = f(10) = 11$. Note, however, that $g(f(5))$ is $g(6)$, since $f(5) = 6$. Hence, $g(f(5)) = g(6) = 12$. Thus, the order in which we evaluate the function is quite important. The rule is to work from the inside to the outside. Note also the new function, say $h(x) = f(g(x)) = f(2x) = 2x + 1$. The process of putting one function inside another is called composition of functions. We write $h = fg$ to represent this.

Calculation versus Table Look-Up

In general, the values of a function, say $f(x)$, may be found in two ways: calculation by iteration or formula evaluation—or, given x, by looking up the value of $f(x)$ in a table. The functions can be calculated by computer, and the feasibility of this will depend upon time and available memory. Tables can be used, but are only useful where the values of x are few. The amount of time and space used will depend upon the complexity of f. If the value of $f(x)$ is very difficult to calculate, and the domain of f is small, then it will be faster to use the table.

Summations and Products

It is often convenient to have a notation to indicate the sum of a group of numbers or the product of certain numbers. The Greek letter Σ (sigma) is used to indicate the sum. Let $a_1 + a_2 + a_3 + \ldots$ be a sequence. This is often written as (a_i). Then $\Sigma_{i=1}^{5} a_i$ means $a_1 + a_2 + a_3 + a_4 + a_5$; $\Sigma_{i=3}^{7} a_i$ would be $a_3 + a_4 + a_5 + a_6 + a$; $i = x$ indicates that summation is to begin at x; the summation ends at whatever value is found over the sigma.

The Greek letter Π (pi) is used to indicate the production of terms:

$$\prod_{i=3}^{6} \text{ is } a_3 \cdot a_4 \cdot a_5 \cdot a_6.$$

The selection of i is arbitrary and the expression could be indexed using any variable.

To sum double-subscripted variables, the double sum can be used:

$$\sum_{i=1}^{2} \sum_{j=1}^{3} a_{ij},$$

where $a_{11} = 2$, $a_{12} = -1$, $a_{13} = 4$, $a_{21} = 5$, $a_{22} = 0$, and $a_{23} = -4$, would be $a_{11} + a_{12} + a_{13} + a_{21} + a_{22} + a_{23} = 6$. Note that the rightmost subscript is varied first and then the left.

In the following walk-through, the comma is used for convenience and is not part of the expression:

$$a_{1,1} = 2$$
$$a_{1,2} = -1$$
$$a_{1,3} = 4$$

$$a_{2,1} = 5$$
$$a_{2,2} = 0$$
$$a_{2,3} = -4$$

Therefore:

	$j = 1$	$j = 2$	$j = 3$	
$i = 1$	2	-1	4	= 6
$i = 2$	5	0	-4	

Double products work the same way.

Functions can be used either as limit values with sigma or pi, or they may be found over the variable to be summed. Assume (a_{ij}) as above and let $f(x) = x + 2$. Then

$$\sum_{i=1}^{2} \sum_{j=2}^{2} f(a_{ij}) = f(a_{11}) + f(a_{12}) + f(a_{21}) + f(a_{22})$$
$$= f(2) + f(-1) + f(5) + f(0) = 4 + 1 + 7 + 2 = 14.$$

Factorials

A special type of function is the *factorial* function. Written $n!$ and read "n factorial," it is the production of all integers 1 through n. Thus $5! = 1 \times 2 \times 3 \times 4 \times 5 = 120$. Another possible definition is:

$$n! = \prod_{i=1}^{n} i. \qquad \text{Therefore} \qquad 3! = \prod_{i=1}^{3} i = 1 \times 2 \times 3.$$

Neither of these definitions is quite complete, since they do not work for $n = 0$; $0!$ is 1 by definition.

The first few factorials are given by the following table:

n	$n!$
0	1
1	1
2	2
3	6
4	24
5	120
6	720
7	5,040
8	40,320
9	362,880

As you can see, the value of $n!$ becomes very large as n becomes large.

Inequalities

There are certain symbols used to indicate relations such as = (equal), < (less than), > (greater than), $\leqslant$ (less than or equal to), $\geqslant$ (greater than or equal to), and < > (not equal to). An *inequality* is an expression followed by a relation and then another expression. For example, consider $x < 10$: "x less than 10." Associated with an inequality is something called the *solution* set. This is the collection of all values that cause the inequality to be true. The solution set for $x < 10$ is the collection of all real numbers that are less than 10.

More than one variable may be used in the inequality. The solution set for $x + y < 2$ is the collection of all x's and y's such that their sum is less than or equal to 2. Two inequalities are said to be *equivalent* if they have the same solution sets. We add or subtract any expression or number on both sides of an inequality and obtain an equivalent inequality. We can also multiply both sides by any positive number. Note that multiplication by 0 or a negative number may not produce equivalence. For example, $x + 1 \geqslant 1$ is equivalent to $x \geqslant 0$, but $x < 5$ is not equivalent to $-x < -5$.

COMPUTATION TOPICS

Number Representation

In any modern number system digits have two kinds of value: *absolute* value and *positional* value. Absolute value is simply the value of the digit itself. Positional value, on the other hand, is a *power of the base* of the system in question, and is expressed as follows: _ _ _ _ . The example power given has four positions. Consider the decimal number 4096; "6" has an absolute value of 6 and a positional value of 10^0 or 1; "9" has an absolute value of 9 and a positional value of 10^1, or 10. The position value of "0" is 10^2, and the position value of "4" is 10^3. We see that positional value is an *ascending power* of the base, reading right to left. The value of a numeric quantity is the sum of the absolute value of each digit times the positional value of each digit. The value of 4,096 is therefore as follows (in decimal):

$$
\begin{aligned}
6 \times 10^0 &= 6 \times 1 &= 6 \\
+9 \times 10^1 &= 9 \times 10 &= 90 \\
+0 \times 10^2 &= 0 \times 100 &= 0 \\
+4 \times 10^3 &= 4 \times 1{,}000 &= \underline{4{,}000} \\
& \text{which gives:} & 4{,}096
\end{aligned}
$$

All of the calculations and representations done so far have used the *decimal* system which has a *base* of 10.

Binary

There are as many types of digit in a numbering system as the size of the base. Because a computer is a *bi*-stable device, it uses a numbering system which has a base of 2—the *binary system*—which has only two types of digit, 0 and 1. Numbers are evaluated in the same fashion as in the decimal; each digit has absolute and positional values; the positional values are ascending powers of the base; and the value of a number is the sum of each digit times its positional value. The value of a binary 11010 is therefore:

$$\begin{aligned} 0 \times 2^0 &= 0 \times 1 = 0 \\ +1 \times 2^1 &= 1 \times 2 = 2 \\ +0 \times 2^2 &= 0 \times 4 = 0 \\ +1 \times 2^3 &= 1 \times 8 = 8 \\ +1 \times 2^4 &= 1 \times 16 = \underline{16} \\ &\text{which gives: } 26 \end{aligned}$$

We now develop a technique to convert a binary number to a decimal number. To convert a decimal number to binary, use successive divisions by 2, save the remainders, and write the remainder developed to the right (it will only be a one or a zero). To illustrate, convert decimal 13 to binary:

2 | 13	
2 | 6	remainder of 1 (first)
2 | 3	remainder of 0 (second)
2 | 1	remainder of 1 (third)
0	remainder of 1 (fourth)

Writing the first remainder on the right, we have binary 1101 (remember, *right* to *left*).

One disadvantage of the binary system is that large decimal numbers become very large in binary. The decimal number 5522109 becomes 10101000100001010111101. Such a number is difficult to read and remember, and troublesome to do the division required to convert.

Octal and Hexadecimal

To overcome these problems, a couple of numbering systems which group the binary into other bases have been developed. They are *octal* and *hexadecimal*. In simple terms, octal is represented in eight numbers, 0–7, each of which can be represented in three bits (000–111). Hexadecimal is represented in 16 numbers, 0–F, each of which can be represented in four bits (0000–1111).

Conversion of the octal number 746 is shown below:

$$\begin{aligned} 6 \times 8^0 &= 6 \times 1 = 6 \\ +4 \times 8^1 &= 4 \times 8 = 32 \\ +7 \times 8^2 &= 7 \times 64 = \underline{448} \\ &\text{which gives: } 486 \end{aligned}$$

Conversion from decimal to octal is done by successive divisions by 8, keeping the remainder in the same manner. The choice of octal permits easy conversion. Take any octal number and convert each number *individually* to bits (0–7). Going the other way, take any binary number, divide it by groups of three, beginning at the right, and convert it to a decimal-looking (actually octal) number, as follows:

Binary	Octal
000	0
001	1
010	2
011	3
100	4
101	5
110	6
111	7

Hexadecimal is a base-16 number system used for the same reasons as octal. Conversion to and from decimal is done in the same fashion, except that the base is 16, with the set of 0, 1, 2, 3, 4, 5, 6, 7, 8, 9, A, B, C, D, E, and F. The "A" has an absolute value of 10, "B" is 11, . . . , and "F" is 15. Conversion from binary to hexadecimal is done by grouping the binary digits into sets of four bits and replacing them according to the following table:

Binary	Hexadecimal
0000	0
0001	1
0010	2
0011	3
0100	4
0101	5
0110	6
0111	7
1000	8
1001	9
1010	A
1011	B
1100	C
1101	D
1110	E
1111	F

The same binary number used before becomes 5442BD.

Note that digits to the right of a decimal point (binary point, octal point, etc.) hold positional values which are negative powers of the base. Thus a base 4 number 2.123 would equal:

$$
\begin{aligned}
2 \times 2^0 &= 2 \times 1 = 2 \\
+1 \times 4^{-1} &= 1 \times \tfrac{1}{4} = \tfrac{1}{4} \\
+2 \times 4^{-2} &= 2 \times \tfrac{1}{16} = \tfrac{2}{16} \\
+3 \times 4^{-3} &= 3 \times \tfrac{1}{64} = \tfrac{3}{64} \\
\text{which gives: } & 2\tfrac{27}{64}
\end{aligned}
$$

Scientific Notation

Scientific notation is used to represent numbers which may be very large or very small in size. For example:

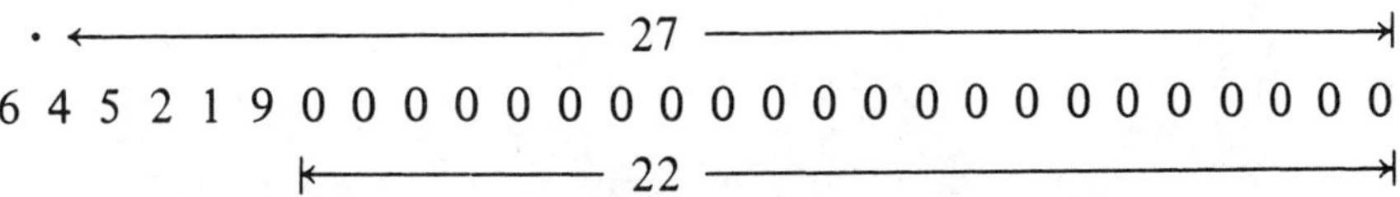

This number could be written two ways:

$$6.45219 \times 1027$$

$$.645219 \times 1028$$

The number has two parts—the *mantissa* and the *exponent*. In the preceding example, the mantissa was 645219 and the exponent is 28.

Moving the decimal point to the left *increases* the exponent by 1 for each position of movement. When the number is written in scientific notation such that the decimal point is at the extreme left with a nonzero digit immediately to the right, that number is said to be *normalized*. Thus:

6.45219×10^{27}	is *not* normalized
$.645219 \times 10^{28}$	is normalized

Floating point notation of the normalized expression is 645219 28. When using a microcomputer, you'll see 645219E + 28.

Approximate Notation

Digit Significance

Some numbers do not have exact decimal equivalents. For example, $\frac{2}{3}$ is .66666666.... Since the number of digits must be limited, the number is approximated. Further, when storing decimal numbers in binary floating-point notation on a computer, it is also possible to lose portions of numbers, and therefore accuracy. The largest number which can be stored in 23 bits is 223 = 8,388,607. If it were desired to store 8,338.609 in binary floating-point with a mantissa, the binary number would be 100000000000-000000000001. With normalization, the number would become 1.00000000000000000000001 × 224 and the mantissa would be 24 bits long. To store the number, the rightmost 1 must be discarded, reducing the number to 8,338,608. Therefore, numbers can only be stored to six decimal digits of accuracy, or six *significant digits*.

Rounding and Truncation

It is often convenient to discard excess digits. Such a procedure is called *rounding*. We might choose to round by dropping fractions, sometimes called *truncation*. Generally, a number is rounded *up* by adding 5 to the digit in the rounding position and then extracting the number *minus the position to which the 5 was added*. Consider:

	Number	Rounded	Truncated
	3.8	4	3
	7.2	7	7
	9.6	10	9
	2.5	3	2
	7.5	8	7
	6.8	7	6
Sums:	37.4	39	34

The value of either method depends on the reason for doing it and the number of numbers to be considered. As can be seen, rounding upwards may add to the sum, while truncation will usually decrease it. There is another approach—that of *balanced rounding*. The rule is to round the last significant digit to the nearest integer. If the rounding digit is a five, then round the preceding digit to the nearest even integer. Using this approach, 3.8 becomes 4.0, 7.2 becomes 7.0, 9.6 becomes 10.0, 2.5 becomes 2.0, 7.5 becomes 8.0, and 6.8 becomes 7.0. They will sum to 38.

Iteration

The act of using a process repeatedly to find the solution to a problem is called *iteration*. As an example of such a procedure, consider the following method of calculating the square root of a number greater than or equal to 1 (say x).

1. Let $P_1 = 0$
2. Let $P_2 = x$.
3. Let $Q = (P_1 + P_2)/2$ (the average).
4. If Q^2 is "close enough" to x, then stop: $Q = \sqrt{x}$
5. If $Q^2 > x$, then let $P_2 = Q$ and go back to step 3.
6. If $Q^2 < x$, then let $P_1 = Q$ and go back to step 3.

We now illustrate this procedure by taking the square root of 2. The following table gives the results:

P_1	P_2	Q	Q^2
0	2	1	1
1	2	1.5	2.25
1	1.5	1.25	1.5625
1.25	1.5	1.375	1.89062
1.375	1.5	1.4375	2.06641
1.375	1.4375	1.40625	1.97754
1.40625	1.4375	1.42187	2.02173
1.40625	1.42187	1.41406	1.99957
1.41406	1.42187	1.41797	2.01064
1.41406	1.41797	1.41602	2.00510
1.41406	1.41602	1.41504	2.00234
1.41406	1.41504	1.41455	2.00095
1.41406	1.41455	1.41431	2.00026
1.41406	1.41431	1.41418	1.99992
1.41418	1.41431	1.41425	2.00009
1.41418	1.41425	1.41422	2.00000

Actually, the square root of 2 to seven significant digits is 1.414214. The preceding table was generated by a computer program, which illustrates some of the inaccuracies brought about by loss of significant digits, rounding, and errors in floating-point notation. By and large, square roots can now be obtained through intrinsic functions in a computer, but some problems are best solved through iteration.

STATEMENTS AND SET THEORY

Statements (Atomic and Compound)

A *statement* is composed of atoms connected by logical operators to form *compound statements*. Atomic statements containing logical operators are the basis of *propositional calculus*. By an *atom* or an *atomic statement*, we mean a simple declarative statement such as "President Kennedy was a male" or $7 < 10$. There are several things to note about atoms. First, several declarative sentences may express the same atom. "John loves Marsha" is the same as "Marsha is loved by John." Of course, "John loves Mary" is an entirely different atom. Further, "$6 > 8$" is the same as "$8 < 6$" (and happens to be false). Each atom is either true (T) or false (F), and that can be determined. Finally, each atom may be assigned a name; so if "*A*: Porky is a pig" then the atom has name *A* and value *T* or *F*.

Logical operations connect atomic statements. A statement containing at least one atom and at least one logical operation is called a *compound statement*. The three primitive operations are *negation* ("not," denoted by $\sim$), *disjunction* ("or," denoted by $\vee$), and *conjunction* ("and," denoted by $\wedge$). Other symbols are sometimes used to represent these operations (particularly as they are used on a computer). Negations can be represented by $\neg$, $-$, $\overline{}$, and $'$. Hence, the negation of *A*, which is read "not *A*," could be written as $\sim A$, $\neg A$, $-A$, $\bar{A}$, or A'. Symbols used to represent disjunction include $|$ and $+$. Symbols used to represent conjunction include & and $\cdot$.

While negation operates only upon one atom, disjunction and conjunction operate upon two. Thus, we have $A \vee B$ (read "*A* or *B*,") and $X \wedge Y$ (read "*X* and *Y*"). These may be combined to give any number. The compound "*A* or not *B* and *C* or *D*" could be written as $A \vee \sim B \wedge C \vee D$. In arithmetic, we perform the operations of multiplication and division before addition and subtraction. Similarly, in propositional calculus, the order of operation is first negation, then conjunction, and finally disjunction. By $\sim A \wedge B$ we mean $(\sim A) \wedge B$ rather than $\sim (A \wedge B)$. In this manner we avoid ambiguities.

Just as each atom has a value, *T* or *F*, so also does each compound. Thus, $\sim A$ *is* whenever *A* is *F*, and *F* whenever *A* is *T*. Further, the compound $A \wedge B$ is *T* only when *A* is *T* and *B* is *T*, and is *F* whenever either *A* is *F* or *B* is *F* or both. Finally, the compound $A \vee B$ is *T* whenever *A* is *T* or *B* is *T* or both, and is *F* when both *A* and *B* are *F*. These relationships can be shown by the following three tables:

A	$\sim A$
F	T
T	F

A	B	$A \wedge B$
F	F	F
F	T	F
T	F	F
T	T	T

A	B	$A \vee B$
F	F	F
F	T	T
T	F	T
T	T	T

Truth Tables

Truth tables are used for evaluating propositional formulas. On the left, each possible value for the atomic statement is listed. For simplicity, each combination (row) is numbered:

	A	B	C
1.	F	F	F
2.	F	F	T
3.	F	T	F
4.	F	T	T
5.	T	F	F
6.	T	F	T
7.	T	T	F
8.	T	T	T

This is the stub to the table. Now, let's move gradually toward building a truth table which satisfies the expression $(A \wedge B) \vee (\sim A \wedge C)$. To do so, we must construct entries to the table for $\sim A$, for $(A \wedge B)$, for $(\sim A \wedge C)$.

Let's first look at $\sim A$. For A to be not true, then A must be false. Look at row 1 of the stub. Note that A, B, and C are all false. We said that for "not A" to be true, then A had to be false, and it is. Similarly, the same holds for rows 5–8 and does not hold for rows 1–4, like this:

	A	B	C	$\sim A$
1.	F	F	F	T
2.	F	F	T	T
3.	F	T	F	T
4.	F	T	T	T
5.	T	F	F	F
6.	T	F	T	F
7.	T	T	F	F
8.	T	T	T	F

Next, let's examine $(A \wedge B)$. For this expression to be true, both A and B must be true. If both are not true, then the resulting expression must be false. Let's build on what we have:

	A	B	C	$\sim A$	$(A \wedge B)$
1.	F	F	F	T	F
2.	F	F	T	T	F
3.	F	T	F	T	F
4.	F	T	T	T	F
5.	T	F	F	F	F
6.	T	F	T	F	F
7.	T	T	F	F	T
8.	T	T	T	F	T

Next comes $(\sim A \wedge C)$. Now, for "not A" and C to be present, we must look at the "not A" column, which was the first column developed after the presentation of the stub. For this expression to be true, there must be a T under "not A" and a T under C in the stub. Building:

	A	B	C	$\sim A$	$(A \wedge B)$	$(\sim A \wedge C)$
1.	F	F	F	T	F	F
2.	F	F	T	T	F	T
3.	F	T	F	T	F	F
4.	F	T	T	T	F	T
5.	T	F	F	F	F	F
6.	T	F	T	F	F	F
7.	T	T	F	F	T	F
8.	T	T	T	F	T	F

And finally, the target expression, $(A \wedge B) \vee (\sim A \wedge C)$: Now we have an A and B column developed and we have a "not A and C" column. For us to develop a T under this last expression, the results of each component by *itself* must be opposite to the other component, with the exception that you'll note that under no circumstances are they ever both true. They are occasionally both false, which produces a F in this last expression:

	A	B	C	$\sim A$	$(A \wedge B)$	$(\sim A \wedge C)$	$(A \wedge B) \vee (\sim A \wedge C)$
1.	F	F	F	T	F	F	F
2.	F	F	T	T	F	T	T
3.	F	T	F	T	F	F	F
4.	F	T	T	T	F	T	T
5.	T	F	F	F	F	F	F
6.	T	F	T	F	F	F	F
7.	T	T	F	F	T	F	T
8.	T	T	T	F	T	F	T

Tree Diagrams

A tree diagram is an alternative way to write an expression. The "main" operator, i.e., the innermost operator, is written at the top of the tree. From each operator are one or two branches leading to an atom (if terminal) or to another operator. This form is the "top down" form of the tree. Trees may be constructed "bottom-up." The tree diagram for the above formula is shown below:

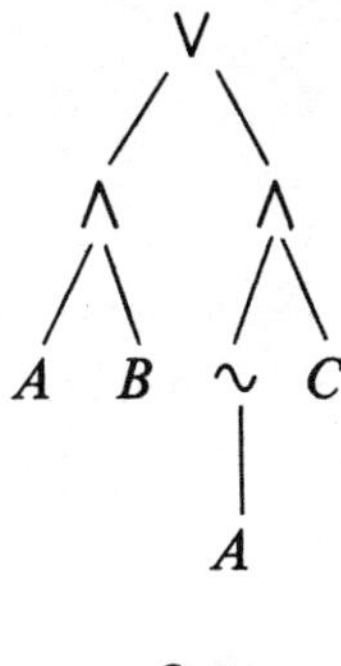

Sets

Set Operations

A *set* is a collection of numbers or things. The concept of a set is important, however, because the term "set" is used to denote more than just a collection. We think of the set as a thing in and of itself.

Closely associated with the concept of a set is the operation $\in$, read "is an element of," which operates with two arguments. Suppose A is the collection (set) of even integers. Then by $2 \in A$ ("2 is an element of A" or "two is an element of the set of even integers") we have an atomic statement which in this case happens to be true. Thus, $x \in A$ is T if and only if x is an even integer. Most mathematical concepts can be defined and studied as sets. For example, here is the precise definition of a function:

> Let D (the domain) and R (the range) be sets. A function f is the set F of ordered pairs of the form (a, b), where $a \in D$ and $b \in R$ such that if $(a, b_1) \in F$ and $(a, b_2) \in F$, then $b_1 = b_2$.

In other words, D is a collection of pairs of numbers where the first is the argument (independent variable value), and the second is the value of f at that point. The last requirement simply ensures that f has only one dependent variable value for each possible value of independent variables. If f is the function $f(x) = x + 1$, and the domain of f is the integers, then by our definition D is the set (0, 1), (1, 2), (2, 3), . . . , which is, of course, infinite in size. There is, in general, no limit to the number of elements in a set. Domain and range have no limit in size.

There are certain fundamental operations that are used with sets. IF A is a set, by A' we mean the collection of all x such that $x \in A$ is false, i.e., all x which are not in A. This is called the complement of A. If A and B are sets, by the union of A and B (written $A \cup B$), we mean all x such that $x \in A$ or $x \in B$, or both. By the intersection of A and B (written $A \cap B$), we mean all x such that $x \in A$ and $x \in B$.

The following laws hold: ϕ is the *empty* (*null*) set which contains nothing, U, on the other hand, is the *universal set* which contains everything. For any sets, A, B, and C:

1. $A \cap A' = \phi$ (the collection of elements which are in A and are not in A' is empty).
2. $A \cup A' = U$ (everything is either in A or is not in A).
3. $(A \cap B)' = (A' \cup B')$.
4. $(A \cup B)' = (A' \cap B')$.
5. $A \cup (B \cup C) = (A \cup B)' \cup C$.
6. $A \cap (B \cap C) = (A \cap B) \cap C$.
7. $A \cup (B \cap C) = (A \cup \mathrm{B}) \cap (A \cup C)$.
8. $A \cap (B \cup C) = (A \cap B) \cup (A \cap C)$.
9. $A \cup B = B \cup A$.
10. $A \cap B = B \cap A$.

It is also of passing interest to note that complementation and negation, union and disjunction, and intersection and conjunction are very similar pairs. In fact, if A, B, and C are atoms, the preceding formulae hold for propositional calculus when ϕ is replaced by F, U is replaced by T, and the operations are replaced by their paired terms.

A useful tool for visualizing the meaning of set theoretic formulas is the *Venn Diagram*. It is composed of a rectangle into which are inserted overlapping circles, one for each set under consideration. If A is a set, then A' is the area not in A. For A and B sets, $A \cap B$ is the area in both A and B. Finally, $A \cup B$ is the area in either A or B or both. The general practice is to shade the area which corresponds to a formula. The Venn Diagram for $A \cap B'$ is shown below:

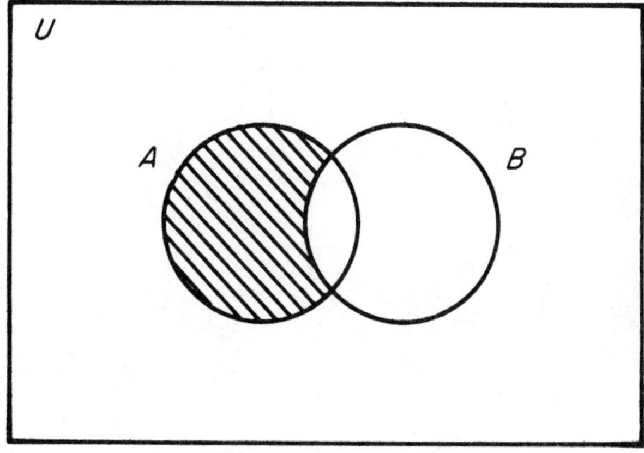

Venn Diagram

Partitions

Given a set, we may desire a break the set into partitions which group elements of the set by some property. This group is done so that each element of the set is in one and only one group. The complete definition is: A *partition* π of a set S is any collection of subsets of $S(A, B, C, \ldots)$, such that each element of S belongs to one and only one of the subjects. For example, let S be the positive integers. We may divide S into partitions by choosing subsets A and B, where A is the set of even integers and B is the set of odd integers. Note that every element of S is either even or odd and cannot be both. Each set has the same remainder when each element of S is either even or odd and cannot be both. Each set has the same remainder when each element within the set is divided by two. This will pretty much show what is meant:

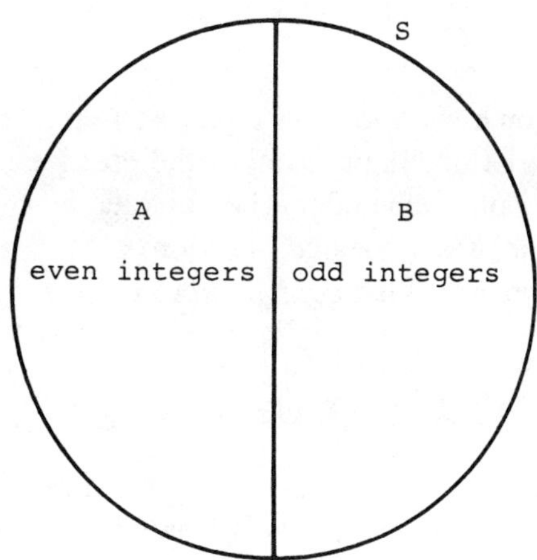

A more general case would be a partition into perhaps ten subsets:

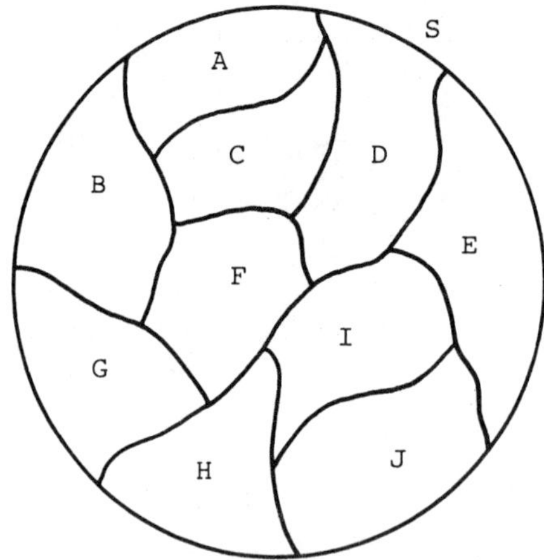

Two numbers may be related in certain ways. For example, $a = b$, $a < b$, etc. The symbol R is used to denote any relation. One then writes aRb if a stands in relation R to b. The preceding division of the positive integers into even and odd integers is an example of a type of relation called an *equivalence relation*. An equivalence relation has three properties:

1. *Reflexive:* aRa for all $a \in S$. In other words, any a will be equivalent to itself. For example, $a = a$. In contrast, it is not true that $a > a$. Hence = is reflexive but > is not.
2. *Symmetric:* if aRb then bRa for all $a \in S$ and $b \in S$. For example, if $a = b$ then $b = a$, so = is symmetric. However, if $a > b$, then $b < a$, so < is not symmetric.
3. *Transitive*: if aRb and bRc, the aRc for all $a, b, c \in S$.
   For example,

$$\text{if } a = b \text{ and } b = c \text{ then } a = c$$
$$\text{if } a > b \text{ and } b > c \text{ then } a > c$$
$$\text{if } a < b \text{ and } b < c \text{ then } a < c$$

so =, <, and > are all transitive.

For every equivalence relation on a set S there is a partition on S. Further, for every partition on S there is an associated equivalence relation. In partition of the positive integers into even and odd integers, let R be the relation "has the same remainder when divided by two." You can check that R is an equivalence relation, and that R generates the stated partition.

Finally, the subsets of a partition are called *equivalence classes*.

SEQUENCES

A *sequence* $x_1, x_2, x_3, \ldots, x_n$, sometimes written (x_i), is a list of numbers with the property that it is possible to write out the terms, in order, for as far as is desired. If the number of terms in the sequence is unlimited, then we have an *infinite sequence* otherwise, it is a finite sequence. The sequence 1, 3, 5, 7, 9, 11, . . . , $2n - 1$, . . . is an infinite sequence such that the value of the nth term is $2n - 1$ (the odd positive integers). The general term is an expression which gives the value of the nth term for any n. In our example this is $2n - 1$.

Progressions

Arithmetic Progressions

A sequence such as 2, 5, 8, 11, 14, ..., $3n - 1$, ... is a special case of sequence called an *arithmetic progression*. The general form of this sequence is a, $a + d$, $a + 2d$, $a + 3d$, ..., $a + (n - 1)d$, ..., where a is the first term and d is called the *common difference*. Assume the following notation: L is the last term, n is the number of terms (finite case), and S_n is the sum of the first n terms. Then, the following formulae hold:

$$L = a + (n - 1)d$$

$$S_n = (n/2)(a + L) = (n/2)(2a = (n - 1)d)$$

In the above example, $a = 2$ and $d = 3$.

Geometric Progressions

A sequence such as 2, 6, 18, 54, ... $2 \times 3^{n-1}$, ... is a special case of sequence called a *geometric progression*. The general form of this sequence is a, ar, ar^2, ar^3, ..., $ar^{(n-1)}$, ... where a is the first term and r is the common ratio. Again, assume the following notation: L is the last term, n is the number of terms, and S_n is the sum of the first n terms. Then the following formulas hold:

$$L = ar^{(n-1)}$$

$$S_n = a(1 - r^n)/(1 - r) = (Lr - a)/(r - 1)$$

In the example above, $a = 2$ and $r = 3$.

Sequences of Data

Weighted Moving Averages

We may relax our definition of a sequence to include any list of points or numbers. If the sequence is experimental in nature, i.e., values are affected by chance, then we may wish to use some technique for smoothing out the values in order to understand the basic movement of the points. Many techniques are available for this type of activity, including *polynomial smoothing*, *exponential smoothing*, etc., but the simplest and most straightforward method is *weighted moving averages*.

Even in this method there is a great deal of variability in technique, but the general principles are the same. Let (x_i) be a sequence. We wish to generate another sequence (y_i) which represents the values of (x_i) adjusted to follow a smooth pattern. One technique is to take $y_1 = x_1$, $y_n = x_n$, and $y_i = (x_{i-1} + 2x_i + x_{i+1})/4$ for $1 < n$. In this fashion each y_i is the average of the three points around x_i (x_{i-1}, x_i itself, and x_{i+1}) with twice as much weight given to the central point x_i. As an example of this technique in practice, consider the following closing stock quotations from AT&T (x_i); applying weighted moving averages, as given, produces the smoothed points (y_i):

x_i	y_i	x_i	y_i
53.5	53.5	52.375	52.0312
53.125	53.0625	51.25	51.4062
52.5	52.5937	50.75	50.875
52.25	52.4062	50.75	50.8125
52.625	52.5	51.	50.7812
52.5	52.5937	50.375	50.5
52.75	52.5	50.25	50.4062
52.	52.1562	50.75	50.5
51.875	51.75	50.25	50.5
52.25	51.6562	50.75	50.5625
52.25	51.9687	50.5	50.5937
52.125	52.1562	50.625	50.625
52.125	52.1875		

Of course, more or less weight could be given to the central point, or more than three points could be used. The chart below contains the points before and after smoothing:

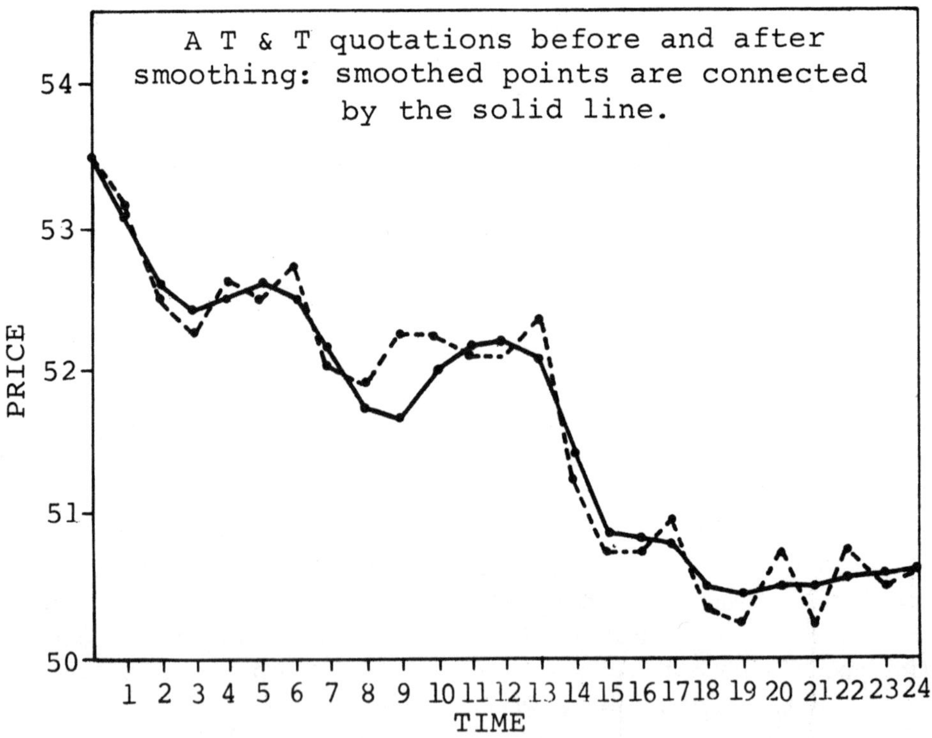

Exponential Smoothing

When moving averages are used for forecasting, the historical data must be stored and properly used in calculations. *Exponential smoothing* is a form of weighted moving average which requires only a previously calculated average, the actual results experienced for the period, and a smoothing constant which is called *alpha* (α). The mathematical calculation is as follows:

New average = (PCA + (SC = AR)),

where PCA = Previously Calculated Average,
SC = the Smoothing Constant, and
AR = the Actual Results (previously calculated average)

Example: Suppose you had experienced an actual result of 100 (PCA) and the smoothing constant is .10, the new average will be 110. If nothing were to change in the second period, the new average would be 111.1.

The smoothing constant determines the influence of the most recent actual results on the new average. If the smoothing constant is set high, the recent actual results will affect the new average more than if it is set low. Correspondingly, when the smoothing constant is set high, influence of older data is quickly lost, whereas when the smoothing constant is set low, the influence of older data remains for a longer period of time.

There is a relationship of smoothing constants to the equivalent weighted moving average, as follows:

(α) SMOOTHING CONSTANT	NUMBER OF PERIODS REQUIRED FOR EQUIVALENT WEIGHTED MOVING AVERAGE
.5	3
.4	4
.33	5
.2	9
.1	19
.05	39
.01	199

The following example shows a three-period moving average and exponential smoothing:

ACTUAL RESULTS	THREE-PERIOD MOVING AVERAGE	THREE-PERIOD WEIGHTED MOVING AVERAGE	EXPONENTIAL SMOOTHING CALCULATION	NEW AVERAGE (USING α = .5)
50.25				
50.75	50.42	50.5		50.25
50.25	50.58	50.5	50.25 + .5(50.75 - 50.25)	50.5
50.75	50.5	50.5625	50.50 + .5(50.25 - 50.50)	50.375
50.5	50.625	50.59375	50.375 + .5(50.75 - 50.375)	50.56
50.625			50.56 + .5(50.5 - 50.56)	50.53

COUNTING OR ENUMERATION

The concepts of counting or enumeration are fundamental to many branches of mathematics, but perhaps they are most important in the study of probability and statistics. In general, it is a problem of counting how many ways something can be done—drawing cards, rolling dice, arranging objects, selecting configurations, etc.

Permutations

The first class of problems include arrangements. For example, how many ways can six objects be placed onto a shelf? Any of the objects can be placed in the first position; then any of the remaining five can be placed in the second, leaving four for the third, three for the fourth, two for the fifth, and only one for the last object. Therefore, there are $6 \times 5 \times 4 \times 3 \times 2 \times 1 = 720 = 6!$ ways to arrange the objects. By definition, a *permutation* of *n* objects is an arrangement of these objects into a particular order. To ask "how many ways objects can be arranged" is to ask how many permutations of six objects exist. Permutations of *n* objects taken all at one time is written $P_{n,n} = n!$ It may be the case that we do not wish to arrange all the objects; for example, there may be six items only two of which will be placed on the shelf. Then we have the permutation of *n* objects taken *r* at a time, written $P_{n,r}$. $P_{n,r} = \text{n}!/(\text{n} - \text{r})!$, so we want $\text{P}_{6,2} = 6!/(6 - 2)! = 6!/4! = 6 \times 5 = 30$.

Combinations

We may not care about the order in which the objects are arranged, but rather just which items are selected. For example, ignoring the order of presentation of the shelf, how many combinations of two objects may be selected from the six available? The following combinations are possible: (1, 2), (1, 3), (1, 4), (1, 5), (1, 6), (2, 3), (2, 4), (2, 5), (2, 6), (3, 4), (3, 5), (3, 6), (4, 5), (4, 6), and (5, 6), giving 15 combinations in all. The duplications—for example, (1, 2) and (2, 1)—were listed only once. Order does not matter with combinations (it did with permutations). The number of combinations of *n* objects taken 4 at a time, written $C_{n,r}$ or more often $\binom{n}{r}$, is equal to $n!/r!(n - r)!$ Note that $\binom{6}{2} = 6!/2!(6 - 2)! = 6!/2!4! = 720/2 \times 24 = 720/48 = 15$.

Compositions

Recall from the section on mathematical notation the discussion of the composition of functions. We apply one function, and then another. Note that our formulas for permutations and combinations are really functions—functions with two input values. Consider this problem. How many committees of five can be selected from a group of eight people? Order does not matter, so permutations are not necessary. Combinations, on the other hand, will tell us—$C_{8,5}$, or $\binom{8}{5}$. Note, however, that for each combination there are 5! permutations which can be generated within the committee. The total number of permutations of eight things taken five at a time is therefore $\text{C}_{8,5} \times 5!$; but this is also $P_{8,5}$. It is, in fact, the case that $\text{C}_{n,r} \times \text{r}! = P_{n,r}$. Other problems may be solved in a similar manner using compositions of permutations and combinations.

RELATIONS, FUNCTIONS, AND GRAPHS

Linear Functions

Of all functions of one variable, there are certain functions which, when plotted on a graph, appear as straight lines. These are the *linear functions* and have equations of the form $y = f(x) = \text{ax} + \text{b}$, where *a* and b are real numbers. The *slope* of any equation at a given point is the ratio of the change in the value of the function (the change in y) to the change in the independent variable (x). Thus, at x_1, we have the slope $m = (y_2 - y_1)/(x_2 - x_1)$. For linear functions, the slope is independent of the choice of x_1 and x_2 and may be any two points in the domain of linear function f with $y = f(x) = ax + b$. Then $y_1 = ax_1 + b$ and $y_2 = ax_2 + b$, so $y_2 - y_1 = (ax_2 + b) - (ax_1 + b) = (ax_2 - ax_1) = a(x_2 - x_1)$. Hence, $(y_2 - y_1)/(x_2 - x_1) = a$. The slope of a linear equation is always, therefore, the constant a. If $x = 0$, note that $y = b$. To plot a linear equation, we have a point at $(0, a)$, i.e., 0 on the x axis and a on the y axis, and another at $(1, a + b)$; drawing an extended line through them gives the graph of the linear functions. The graph of the equation $f(x) = 2x + 1$ is shown in this fashion below:

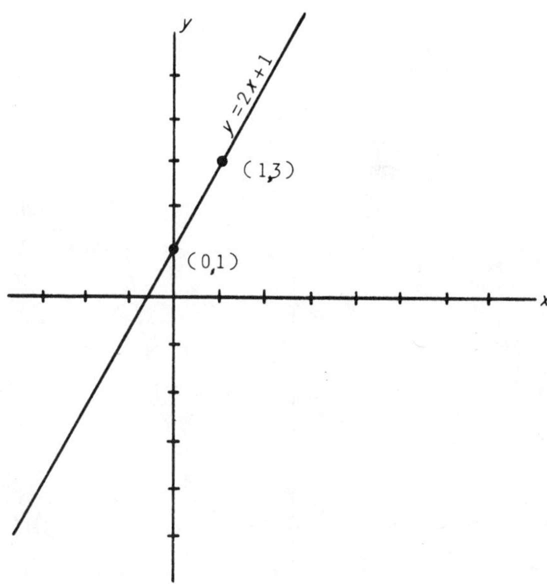

Explained another way, slope is the change in y divided by the change in x.

$$\text{Slope} = \frac{\Delta y \text{ (dependent variable)}}{\Delta x \text{ (independent variable)}}$$

$$\Delta y = y_2 - y_1$$

$$y_1 = (ax_1 + b)$$

$$y_2 = (ax_2 + b)$$

$$y_2 - y_1 = (ax_2 + b) - (ax_1 + b)$$

$$= (ax_2 - ax_1) = a(x_2 - x_1)$$

Therefore:

$$\frac{\Delta y}{\Delta x} = \frac{(y_2 - y_1)}{(x_2 - x_1)} = \frac{a(x_2 - x_1)}{(x_2 - x_1)} = a\text{(Slope)}$$

Throughout the study of equations we may be interested in the root(s) of an equation or function. By definition, the solution to an equation is a *root* of the equation; x is a root of the function f if $f(x) = 0$.

For linear equations, we want all x such that $ax + b = 0$. Work out the algebra and you find that this equation has one root: $x = -b/a$.

Quadratic Equations

A linear equation has the form $f(x) = ax + b$. We can add a term and consider equations of the form $x^2 + bx + c$. These are called quadratic equations. The general shape of such an equation when placed on a graph is the *parabola*. If $a > 0$, then the parabola will open toward the top of the graph; otherwise, it will open toward the bottom. The bottom (or top, accordingly) of the parabola will be found at $-b/2a$, and the figure will cross the y axis at c once and only once. The graph of $y = x^2 - 2x - 1$ is shown below:

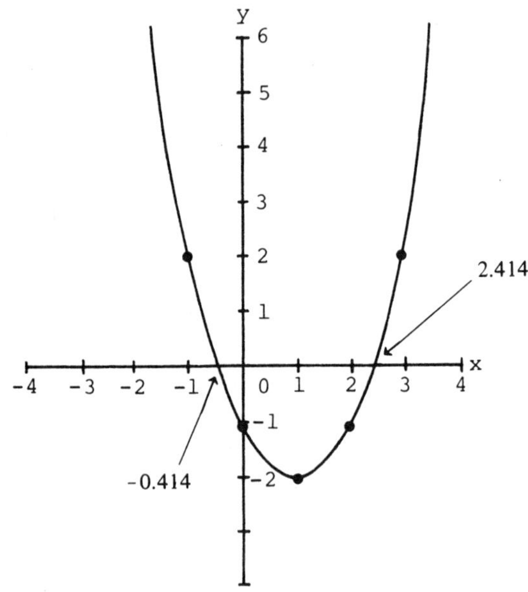

The roots of a quadratic equation are given by the quadratic formula:

$$\frac{-b \pm \sqrt{b^2 - 4ac}}{2a}$$

The $\pm$ is important, as the roots are developed using each sign individually. Note that it is possible for a quadratic equation to have 0, 1, or 2 roots. If the *discriminant* (the expression $b^2 - 4ac$) is less than zero, then there are no real roots. (Taking the square root of a negative number yields an imaginary number). If the discriminant is exactly zero, then there is one root: $-b/2a$. This corresponds to the point of the parabola resting on the x axis. If the discriminant is positive, then there are two roots. In the example $y^2 - 2x - a$, $a = 1$, $b = -2$, $c = -1$ and fit into the formula in the following manner:

$$-b + \sqrt{b^2 - 4ac} = \frac{-(-2) + \sqrt{(-2)^2 - 4(1)(-1)}}{2}$$

$$= \frac{2 + \sqrt{4 + 4}}{2} = \frac{2 + \sqrt{4 \cdot 2}}{2} = \frac{2 + 2\sqrt{2}}{2} \quad \text{(Root 1)}$$

$$\frac{-b-\sqrt{b^2-4ac}}{2a}=\frac{-(-2)-\sqrt{(-2)^2-4(1)(-1)}}{2}$$

$$=\frac{2-\sqrt{4+4}}{2}=\frac{2-\sqrt{4\cdot 2}}{2}=\frac{2-2\sqrt{2}}{2} \quad \text{(Root 2)}$$

And if you follow the roots through (the square root of 2 is roughly 1.414), you will find that the first root is 2.414 and the second root is −0.414.

Transcendental Functions

Exponential Functions

Recall the expression of the exponentiation operation as a function $f(x, y) = x^y$. A related single-variable function is found by taking a constant to a real power: $f(x) = ax$ for $a > 0$ and x a real number. We have already discussed some of the properties of the exponential operation. Given that a is a constant, we have several other properties. Let x and y be real numbers such that $x < y$. Then:

1. $a^x < a^y$ for $a > 1$
2. $a^x = a^y$ for $a = 1$
3. $a^x > a^y$ for $a < 1$ (and $a > 0$)

The graph of a^x is highly dependent upon a:

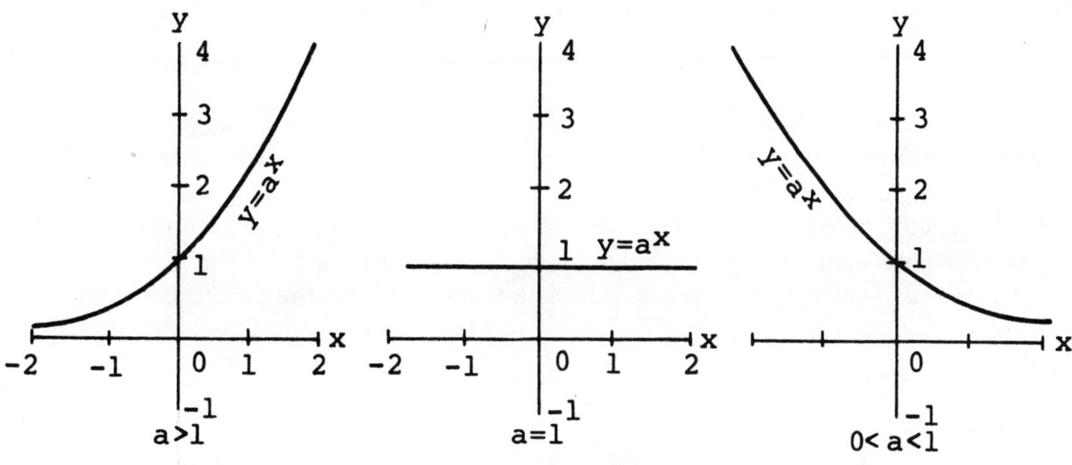

For $a > 1$, a^x is *monotone increasing*, i.e., as x gets larger, a^x gets larger; for $a < 1$, a^x is *monotone decreasing*; a^x is never negative.

Logarithmic Functions

The *logarithm* of x to the base a, written $y = log_a$, is the inverse function of the exponential. That is, $y = log_a x$ if $a^y = x$. The logarithm of x to the base a is that number y such that x is a to the yth power. Note that $a > 0$ and $a = 1$. The following laws hold for logarithms:

1. $\log_a xy = \log_a x + \log_a y$
2. $\log_a (1/x) = -\log_a x$
3. $\log_a (y/x) = \log_a y - \log_a x$
4. $\log_a (x^y) = y \log_a x$
5. $\log_a a = 1$

We can use properties 1–4 for computations. Logarithms to the base 10 or base e are normally found in tables. For example: calculate $2^{1.5}$. Let $y = 2^{1.5}$. Taking logs to the base 10 of both sides of the equation, we have $\log_{10}y = \log_{10}2^{1.5} = 1.5 \log_{10}2$. Using a table, such as the one found in *Standard Mathematical Tables* (Chemical Rubber Publishing Company), we find that $\log_{10}2 = .3010$. Thus $\log_{10}y = 1.5 \times .3010 = .4515$. Working back in the table we have $\log_{10}2.282 = .4515$, so $2.828 = 2^{1.5}$. The graphs of the logarithms look like the graphs of the exponentials turned sideways:

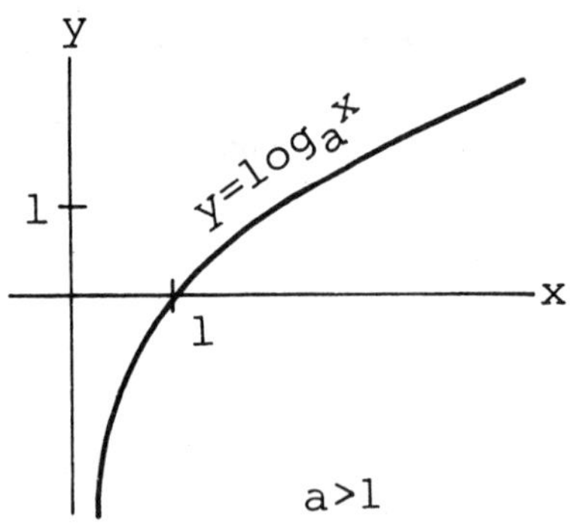

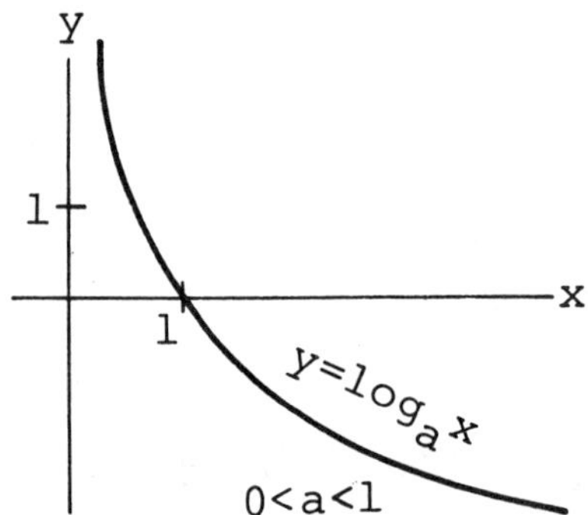

Line of Regression

We may have points of data which, when placed on a graph, seem to form a straight line. There may be, however, certain deviations because of random factors or errors in measurement. The problem is to fit a linear equation to the points so as to get the "best fit." Many tests or criteria are available, but one of the most common is to choose a *line of regression* so that the sum of the squares of the (vertical) distances between the points and the line is the minimum. This statistical problem has been studied in many aspects. The constants a and b in the equation for the line $ax + b$ can be related to the values of the points. Let pairs (x_i, y_i) be given. Assume there are n points. Then the constants for the line of regression are given as follows:

$$b = n \frac{\sum_{i=1}^{n} x_i y_i - \sum_{i=1}^{n} x_i \sum_{i=1}^{n} y_i}{n \sum_{i=1}^{n} x_i^2 - \left[\sum_{i=1}^{n} x_i\right]^2}$$

$$a = \left[\sum_{i=1}^{n} y_i - b \sum_{i=1}^{n}\right] x_i \quad n$$

These are calculations which had best be left to computers!

MATHEMATICS OF FINANCE AND ACCOUNTING

Compound Interest

In problems involving compound interest, simple interest is calculated over the principal during some interval and is then added to the principal before the next calculation is made. If P is the principal, i is the interest rate (as a decimal), and n the number of years involved, then the basic formula for the amount after n years is $A = P(1 + i)^n$. Since the interest the first year is Pi, the amount after one year is $P + Pi = P(1 + i)$. The interest the second year is $P(1 + i)i = Pi + Pi^2$. Continue on with that calculation process and you can see how the formula is derived. If the principal is compounded q times annually, the $A = p(1 + i/q)^{nq}$.

What all that means in English is this: If you have \$1,000 (P) to be invested for 10% (i) for 5 years (n), the calculations work out like this:

$$A = P(1+i)^n$$
$$A = 1000(1+.1)^5$$
$$A = 1000(1.1)^5$$

1.1	(1)
X 1.1	(2)
1.21	
X 1.1	(3)
1.331	
X 1.1	(4)
1.4641	
X 1.1	(5)
1.61051	

Therefore, A = 1,000 (1.61051) = \$1,610.51.

Depreciation Calculations

An extensive treatment of depreciation formulas is given in Chapter 5, so the space will not be devoted here to that subject. So that you might have a concept of the mathematical representation of several methods, the following formulas are presented:

Straight Line Depreciation

$$D_n = (I - F)/L$$

where I is the initial value, F is the final value, and L is the life of the asset.

Sum of the Years' Digits

$$\frac{D}{F^n} = \frac{(L - n + 1)}{\sum_{i=1}^{L} i} \times (I - F)$$

Double Declining Balance

$$r = 1 - \sqrt[L]{F/I}$$

where r is the constant percentage rate of depreciation.

Breakeven Analysis

Given a plant, factory, or industrial organization producing some product, we wish to determine the number of objects that must be produced and sold in order to break even (meet all costs). There are certain costs, such as depreciation on the building, which do not vary with changes in the productive capacity of the organization. It does not matter whether we make and sell 50 units or 50,000—depreciation remains the same. These are called *fixed costs*. Other costs vary with the productive level—more labor is needed, more raw materials, etc.—and these are called *variable costs*. A breakeven chart graphically represents the relationship of costs and sales. Along the x axis is represented production level. Along the y axis are dollars. The following lines are plotted on the graph.

1. *Fixed costs:* a straight line parallel to the x axis and intersecting the y axis at the level of fixed costs.
2. *Variable costs:* a straight line through the origin (0, 0) with the slope equal to the rate of variable cost per item produced.
3. *Total costs:* a straight line meeting fixed costs at the y axis with slope equal to variable cost per item produced.
4. *Sales:* a stright line (or curved line) showing sales as a function of the production level.

The intersection of the sales line and the total cost line is the *breakeven* point. Between these lines and to the left is the loss area. Between them and to the right is the profit area. A sample breakeven chart is shown below:

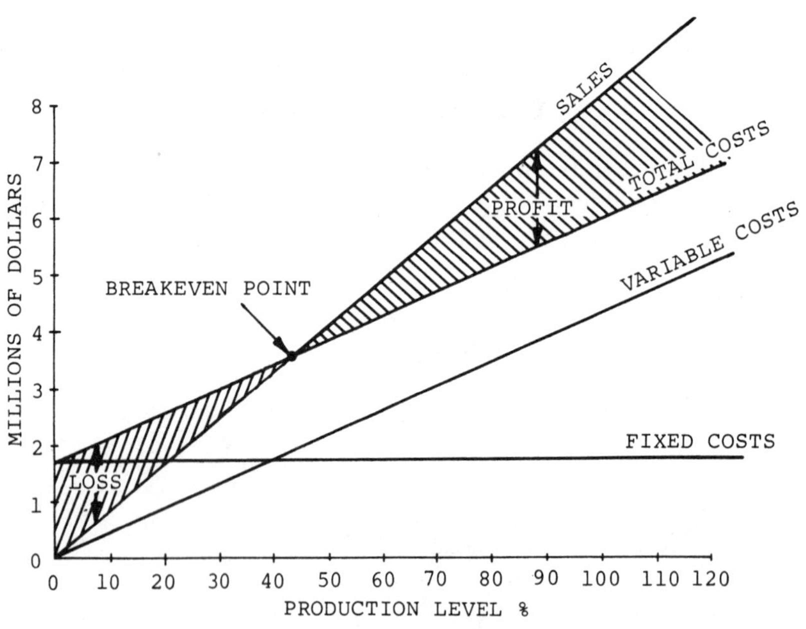

MATRICES

Theory

A *matrix* is often a convenient way to represent a set of numbers related in some fashion. In general, a matrix is a rectangular collection of numbers, called *elements*. The symobl a_{ij} can be used to represent the matrix with elements $a_{11}, a_{12}, \ldots, a_{21}, a_{22}, \ldots,$ where the first subscript indicates the row of the element and the second indicates the column. The dimensions of a matrix are used to indicate the number of rows and columns of the array of numbers. Thus, if A is a matrix with 3 rows and 4 columns, A is said to have dimensions of 3 by 4, sometimes written 3×4. A sample 4 by 3 matrix with integer elements is shown below:

$$\underbrace{\begin{bmatrix} 8 & 9 & -3 \\ 2 & 0 & 5 \\ 4 & -1 & 1 \\ 2 & 4 & 7 \end{bmatrix}}_{\text{3 columns } (j)} \left.\vphantom{\begin{bmatrix} 8 \\ 2 \\ 4 \\ 2 \end{bmatrix}}\right\} \text{4 rows } (i)$$

If the number of rows equals the number of columns, then we say that we have a *square matrix*. Two matrices, A and B, are said to be equal matrices if their elements are equal, i.e., $a_{11} = b_{11}$, $a_{12} = B_{12}$, etc. If the matrix is square, then several other definitions apply. Let the dimension be n. Then the principal diagonal is the diagonal formed by the elements $a_{11}, a_{22}, a_{33}, \ldots, a_{nn}$. The secondary diagonals are the diagonals adjacent and parallel to the principal diagonal. A 3 by 3 example is given

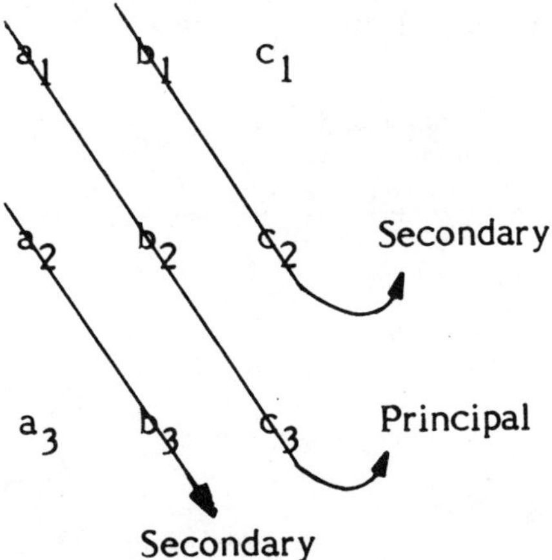

The determinant of the matrix is a number which can be calculated from the entries of the matrix. For a 2 by 2 matrix A, the determinant is:

$$a_{11}a_{22} - a_{12}a_{21}$$

For a 3 by 3 matrix A, the determinant is:

$$a_{11}a_{22}a_{33} + a_{12}a_{23}a_{31} + a_{31}a_{21}a_{32} - a_{11}a_{23}a_{32} - a_{12}a_{21}a_{33} - a_{13}a_{22}a_{31}.$$

If a_{ij} is an element in a matrix, call M_{ij} the *minor* of a_{ij}; M_{ij} is the matrix remaining when the ith row and jth column are removed from A. If $\det(A)$ is the determinant of A, then:

$$\det(A) = \sum_{i=1}^{n} (a_{ij} \cdot \det(M_{i1}))$$

Thus, we take the sum of each element in the first column times the determinant of the element's minor. This gives a method of calculating the determinant of the element's minor, which gives a method of calculating the determinant of a larger matrix.

Column Vectors

Rows and columns of matrices are also called *vectors*. Thus, the elements 8, 9, and −3 for a *row vector* in our example and 8, 2, 4, and 2 form a *column vector:*

$$\begin{bmatrix} 8 & 9 & -3 \\ 2 & 4 & 1 \\ 4 & 6 & 2 \\ 2 & 1 & 4 \end{bmatrix}$$

Column Vector ⟶ (first column: 8, 2, 4, 2)

⟵ Row Vector (first row: 8, 9, −3)

Application

Now let's see how this information would be applied. Suppose we had a pair of simultaneous equations:

$$a_1x + b_1y = c_1 \qquad (1)$$

$$a_2x + b_2y = c_2 \qquad (2)$$

Multiply equation (1) by b_2 and equation (2) by b_1, giving:

$$a_1b_2x + b_1b_2y = b_2c_1 \qquad (1')$$

$$a_2b_1x + b_1b_2y = b_1c_2 \qquad (2')$$

Now subtract (1′) from (2′) and you have:

$$(a_1b_2 - a_2b_1)x = b_2c_1 - b_1c_2$$

Solving for x:

$$x = \frac{b_2c_1 - b_1c_2}{a_1b_2 - a_2b_1}$$

Using the same procedure for y, we get:

$$y = \frac{a_1c_2 - a_2c_1}{a_1b_2 - a_2b_1}$$

Note that both denominators are the same. In matrix representation, the denominators are formed in the following manner:

$$\begin{bmatrix} a_1 & b_1 \\ a_2 & b_2 \end{bmatrix}$$

The a's and b's are now elements of a matrix is of order two, and the arrows show how the determinant is constructed:

$$\det \begin{bmatrix} a_1 & b_1 \\ a_2 & b_2 \end{bmatrix} = a_1 b_2 - a_2 b_1 .$$

The numerators may be formed by determinants as well (in this case, two different determinants. This procedure is a version of *Cramer's Rule*, which is given a simpler expression in the subsequent section on Simultaneous Linear Equations.

Operations on Matrices

If A and B are two matrices with the same dimensions, for example, n and m, then they may be added together element by element. If $C = A + B$ then $c_{ij} = a_{ij} + b_{ij}$ for each c_{ij} in C. Subtraction is performed similarly. It is not possible to add or subtract matrices having different dimensions.

Here is a fairly lengthy matrix multiplication. If you follow it, however, you should fully understand matrix addition. These are the matrices:

a	j				b	j			
i	1	2	3		i	4	5	6	
	4	5	6	X		7	8	9	$= c$
	7	8	9			1	2	3	

Factors	$1 \cdot 4 + 2 \cdot 7 + 3 \cdot 1$		**1**	**2**	**3**	**4**	5	6
Row/Col. Vectors	$a_{11} \cdot b_{11} + a_{12} \cdot b_{21} + a_{13} \cdot b_{31}$	= 21	4	5	6	**7**	8	9
Value	$4 + 14 + 3$		7	8	9	**1**	2	3

Factors	$1 \cdot 5 + 2 \cdot 8 + 3 \cdot 2$		**1**	**2**	**3**	4	**5**	6
Row/Col. Vectors	$a_{11} \cdot b_{12} + a_{12} \cdot b_{22} + a_{13} \cdot b_{32}$	= 27	4	5	6	7	**8**	9
Value	$5 + 16 + 6$		7	8	9	1	**2**	3

Factors	$1 \cdot 6 + 2 \cdot 9 + 3 \cdot 3$		**1**	**2**	**3**	4	5	**6**
Row/Col. Vectors	$a_{11} \cdot b_{13} + a_{12} \cdot b_{23} + a_{13} \cdot b_{33}$	= 33	4	5	6	7	8	**9**
Value	$6 + 18 + 9$		7	8	9	1	2	**3**

Factors	$4 \cdot 4 + 5 \cdot 7 + 6 \cdot 1$		1	2	3	**4**	5	6
Row/Col. Vectors	$a_{21} \cdot b_{11} + a_{22} \cdot b_{21} + a_{23} \cdot b_{31}$	= 57	**4**	**5**	**6**	**7**	8	9
Value	$16 + 35 + 6$		7	8	9	**1**	2	3

Factors	$4 \cdot 5 + 5 \cdot 8 + 6 \cdot 2$		1 2 3	4 **5** 6
Row/Col. Vectors	$a_{21} \cdot b_{12} + a_{22} \cdot b_{22} + a_{23} \cdot b_{32}$	= 72	**4 5 6**	7 **8** 9
Value	$20 + 40 + 12$		7 8 9	1 **2** 3

Factors	$4 \cdot 6 + 5 \cdot 9 + 6 \cdot 3$		1 2 3	4 5 **6**
Row/Col. Vectors	$a_{21} \cdot b_{13} + a_{22} \cdot b_{23} + a_{23} \cdot b_{33}$	= 87	**4 5 6**	7 8 **9**
Value	$24 + 45 + 18$		7 8 9	1 2 **3**

Factors	$7 \cdot 4 + 8 \cdot 7 + 9 \cdot 1$		1 2 3	**4** 5 6
Row/Col. Vectors	$a_{31} \cdot b_{11} + a_{32} \cdot b_{21} + a_{33} \cdot b_{31}$	= 93	4 5 6	**7** 8 9
Value	$28 + 56 + 9$		**7 8 9**	**1** 2 3

Factors	$7 \cdot 5 + 8 \cdot 8 + 9 \cdot 2$		1 2 3	4 **5** 6
Row/Col. Vectors	$a_{31} \cdot b_{12} + a_{32} \cdot b_{22} + a_{33} \cdot b_{32}$	= 117	4 5 6	7 **8** 9
Value	$35 + 64 + 18$		**7 8 9**	1 **2** 3

Factors	$7 \cdot 6 + 8 \cdot 9 + 9 \cdot 3$		1 2 3	4 5 **6**
Row/Col. Vectors	$a_{31} \cdot b_{13} + a_{32} \cdot b_{23} + a_{33} \cdot b_{33}$	= 141	4 5 6	7 8 **9**
Value	$42 + 72 + 27$		**7 8 9**	1 2 **3**

$$= \begin{bmatrix} 21 & 27 & 33 \\ 57 & 72 & 87 \\ 93 & 117 & 141 \end{bmatrix}$$

Identity or Unit Matrix

An identity matrix or unit matrix is a square matrix with 1s on the principal diagonal and 0s everywhere else; the zero matrix is a square matrix with 0s everywhere:

3 by 3 Unit Matrix

$$\begin{bmatrix} 1 & 0 & 0 \\ 0 & 1 & 0 \\ 0 & 0 & 1 \end{bmatrix}$$

3 by 3 Zero Matrix

$$\begin{bmatrix} 0 & 0 & 0 \\ 0 & 0 & 0 \\ 0 & 0 & 0 \end{bmatrix}$$

Matrix Transpose

A matrix has a *transpose*. To find the transpose, you turn the matrix on its side in a particular way. If A^t is the transpose of A, then, when $B = A^t$, we have $b_{ij} = a_{ji}$. In fact, if A has dimensions n by m, the A^t will have dimensions m by n:

$$\begin{bmatrix} 8 & 9 & -3 \\ 2 & 0 & 5 \\ 4 & -1 & 1 \\ 2 & 4 & 7 \end{bmatrix}^t = \begin{bmatrix} 8 & 2 & 4 & 2 \\ 9 & 0 & -1 & 4 \\ -3 & 5 & 1 & 7 \end{bmatrix}$$

Matrix Inverse

The *inverse* A^{-1} of a square matrix A such that the matrix product of A and its inverse equals the identity matrix. Not every square matrix has an inverse. There is a theorem which says that A has an inverse if and only if $\det(A)$ is not equal to zero. If $\det(A) = 0$, then A is said to be *singular;* otherwise, it is *nonsingular*. The process of finding the inverse of a matrix can be quite difficult. However, there are several general methods by which the inverse may be computed. One of these methods is described here.

Write the matrix along with the unit matrix having the same dimensions. Given the operations of (1) multiplying any row or column by a constant and (2) adding any row or column to any other row or column, perform the same operations on both the original matrix and the unit matrix until the original has been converted to a unit matrix. When this is done, what was originally the unit matrix has been converted to the inverse. The following is a demonstration of the inversion of the matrix:

$$\begin{bmatrix} 2 & 1 \\ -4 & 3 \end{bmatrix}$$

1. Write the matrix and the 2 by 2 unit matrix:

$$\begin{bmatrix} 2 & 1 \\ -4 & 3 \end{bmatrix} \begin{bmatrix} 1 & 0 \\ 0 & 1 \end{bmatrix}$$

2. Divide the first row of each by 2:

$$\begin{bmatrix} 1 & \frac{1}{2} \\ -4 & 3 \end{bmatrix} \begin{bmatrix} \frac{1}{2} & 0 \\ 0 & 1 \end{bmatrix}$$

3. Add four times the first row to the second row:

$$\begin{bmatrix} 1 & \frac{1}{2} \\ 0 & 5 \end{bmatrix} \begin{bmatrix} \frac{1}{2} & 0 \\ 2 & 1 \end{bmatrix}$$

4. Divide the second row by 5:

$$\begin{bmatrix} 1 & \frac{1}{2} \\ 0 & 1 \end{bmatrix} \begin{bmatrix} \frac{1}{2} & 0 \\ \frac{2}{5} & \frac{1}{5} \end{bmatrix}$$

5. Add $-\frac{1}{2}$ times the second row to the first row:

$$\begin{bmatrix} 1 & 0 \\ 0 & 1 \end{bmatrix} \begin{bmatrix} \frac{3}{10} & -\frac{1}{10} \\ \frac{4}{10} & -\frac{2}{10} \end{bmatrix}$$

Fortunately, computer algorithms are available to compute the determinant and inverses of matrices with very large dimensions.

Simultaneous Linear Equations

Matrices can be used in the solution of simultaneous linear equations. The general formula is this:

$$\sum_{j=1}^{n} a_{ij}x_j = b_i.$$

Consider these two equations:

$$\begin{aligned} 4x_1 + 2x_2 &= 60 \\ 2x_1 + 4x_2 &= 48 \end{aligned} \qquad A = \begin{bmatrix} 4 & 2 \\ 2 & 4 \end{bmatrix}$$

Representing the coefficients in a matrix A, the variables in a column vector X, and the two constants in a column vector B, we could write this as $ax = b$. The problem is to find values of x_1 *and* x_2 such that both equations are exactly satisfied. The solution is obtained by Cramer's Rule: $X = A^{-1}B$. Hence we calculate the inverse of A and multiply it by B; the result will be a column vector whose values correspond to the desired solution. In our case:

$$A^{-1} = \begin{bmatrix} \frac{1}{3} & -\frac{1}{6} \\ -\frac{1}{6} & \frac{1}{3} \end{bmatrix}, \qquad B = \begin{bmatrix} 60 \\ 48 \end{bmatrix}, \qquad X = \begin{bmatrix} x_1 \\ x_2 \end{bmatrix}$$

Multiplying A^{-1} by B we have

$$\begin{bmatrix} \frac{1}{3} & -\frac{1}{6} \\ -\frac{1}{6} & \frac{1}{3} \end{bmatrix} \begin{bmatrix} 60 \\ 48 \end{bmatrix} = \begin{bmatrix} 20 - 8 \\ -10 + 16 \end{bmatrix} = \begin{bmatrix} 12 \\ 6 \end{bmatrix} = \begin{bmatrix} x_1 \\ x_2 \end{bmatrix}$$

Hence the solution is $x_1 = 12$ and $x_2 = 6$.

Parts Requirements Listing Problem

A matrix can also be a convenient method to express relationships among several things. For example, suppose we have a plant where four different products are made from five different parts. A matrix could be used to represent the number of parts required in producing a product. Here we have a_{ij} = the number of parts i required for product j. Such a representation might be written:

	Prod. 1	Prod. 2	Prod. 3	Prod. 4
Part 1	2	4	1	7
Part 2	0	2	0	3
Part 3	1	1	9	1
Part 4	0	2	0	0
Part 5	1	1	1	1

If we have orders for three Product 1s, two Product 2s, three Product 3s, and two Product 4s, we can write this total order as a column vector:

$$\begin{bmatrix} 3 \\ 2 \\ 4 \\ 2 \end{bmatrix}$$

To find out how many of each part are needed to fill the orders represented by the column vector, we need only compute the product:

$$\overset{\textit{PARTS}}{\begin{bmatrix} 2 & 4 & 1 & 7 \\ 0 & 2 & 0 & 3 \\ 1 & 1 & 9 & 1 \\ 0 & 2 & 0 & 0 \\ 1 & 1 & 1 & 1 \end{bmatrix}} \times \overset{\textit{ORDERS}}{\begin{bmatrix} 3 \\ 2 \\ 4 \\ 2 \end{bmatrix}} =$$

$$\begin{bmatrix} 3 \cdot 2 + 2 \cdot 4 + 4 \cdot 1 + 2 \cdot 7 \\ 3 \cdot 0 + 2 \cdot 2 + 4 \cdot 0 + 2 \cdot 3 \\ 3 \cdot 1 + 2 \cdot 1 + 4 \cdot 9 + 2 \cdot 1 \\ 3 \cdot 0 + 2 \cdot 2 + 4 \cdot 0 + 2 \cdot 0 \\ 3 \cdot 1 + 2 \cdot 1 + 4 \cdot 1 + 2 \cdot 1 \end{bmatrix} = \begin{bmatrix} 6 + 8 + 4 + 14 \\ 0 + 4 + 0 + 6 \\ 3 + 2 + 36 + 2 \\ 0 + 4 + 4 + 2 \\ 3 + 2 + 4 + 2 \end{bmatrix} = \begin{bmatrix} 32 \\ 10 \\ 43 \\ 10 \\ 11 \end{bmatrix}$$

The result of the multiplication is a column vector with five components, each of which represents the total number of parts of the type corresponding to the original row labels. In other words, we need 32 Part 1s, 10 Part 2s, 43 Part 4s, and 11 Part 5s. The requirement for 32 Part 1s can be broken down into the 6 required for Product 1, 8 required for Product 2, 4 required for Product 3, and 14 required for Product 4.

Markov Chains

When the outcome of an event is dependent on the outcome of previous events, the process is called a *Markov chain* or *Markov process*. A Markov chain contains several stages, each with several possible outcomes; there are only two possible ultimate outcomes from the process.

In a production process, a product may go through several states before passing a final inspection and being placed in the finished goods inventory. The product may fail quality control testing and be scrapped during the production process or at the final testing point. A product nearing the completion of the production process has a higher probability of ultimately being placed in the finished goods inventory than a product just starting the production process.

The production process may be very complicated, but there are only two ways for a product to leave the process: It is either placed in the finished goods inventory or it is scrapped. The manager of the production process might be interested in the answers to the following questions:

1. What percentage of the products starting the production process end up in the finished inventory and what percentage end up scrapped?

2. How would the percentages change if the production process were changed in such a manner so as to change the probabilities of passing/failing a particular quality control test?
3. What is the average time a product remains in the process before either being scrapped or placed in the finished goods inventory?

The production process may be described using a matrix to represent the probabilities of a product progressing to each step. Matrix operations may then be used to answer these questions.

DIFFERENTIAL CALCULUS

Rate of Change: Basic Ideas

Recall that the slope of a line is the ratio of the change in the value of the function to the change in the independent variable, i.e., the rate of change of the line. Now extend that concept to the instantaneous rate of a function at a point, selected arbitrarily. The slope of a straight line is always constant and is independent of the points chosen to measure the slope. In general, this is not true for all functions.

Consider the slope $m = (y_2 - y_1)/(x_2 - x_1)$ and function $y = f(x)$. Calculate the slope at point x_0. Let (x_i) be a sequence which approaches x_0. As i becomes larger, $(x_i - x_0)$—the distance between the points—becomes very small. Then the points (x_i, y_i) and (x_0, y_0) for each i yield lines with slopes $m_i = (y_i - y_0)/(x_i - x_0)$. We can also write $m_i = (f(x_i) - fx_0))/(x_i - x_0)$. Further, if we let h_i be the distance between x_i and x_0 $(x_i - x_0)$, then $m_i = (f(x + h_i) - f(x_0))/h_i$.

The sequence thus developed (m_i) might approach some value m as a limit. If so, then m would be the slope of an infinitely short line, i.e., a point at x; this is what is meant by the instantaneous rate of change or the rate of change of a function at a point. This limit may or may not exist, depending on various properties of the particular function in question. The limit

$$\lim_{h \to 0} \frac{f(x_0 + h) - f(x_0)}{h}$$

if it exists, will be called the derivative of the function f with respect to x at the point x_0. Write $f'(x)$ for the function whose value at x is "the derivation of the function f with respect to x at the point x." Thus, we have built a new function, the derivative of f (written f'), which is related to the original function f by the fact that the value of f' at x is the instantaneous rate of change of the derivative. There is other notation for indicating f': $D_x f$ or $D_x f(x)$; $df(x)/ds$ or df/ds. Note also that the word derivative is used in two ways:

1. The value of the instantaneous rate of change of a function $f(x)$ at some particular point.
2. The function f' whose value at some particular point is the value defined in number 1.

The Derivative

Let's investigate some of the properties of this derivative. Let $f(x) = ax + b$, a linear equation. Then:

$$f'(x) = \lim_{h \to 0} \frac{f(x+h) - f(x)}{h} = \frac{(a(x+h) + b) - (ax + b)}{h} = \frac{ax + ah + b - ah - b}{h} = \frac{ah}{h} = a$$

Thus, f' for a linear equation is just a constant a, which is the slope. This verifies the fact that the slope of a line is a constant and is independent of the value of x chosen.

Geometrically, for any function which has a derivative, the derivative at a given point is the slope of a tangent line drawn at that point. For a linear equation, this is the line itself. This implies that if the derivative is positive, then the function is increasing at this point, since the tangent line has positive slope. Conversely a negative derivative implies a decreasing function. A zero derivative will correspond to a tangent line with zero slope, hence, parallel to the X axis. The following figure may be helpful:

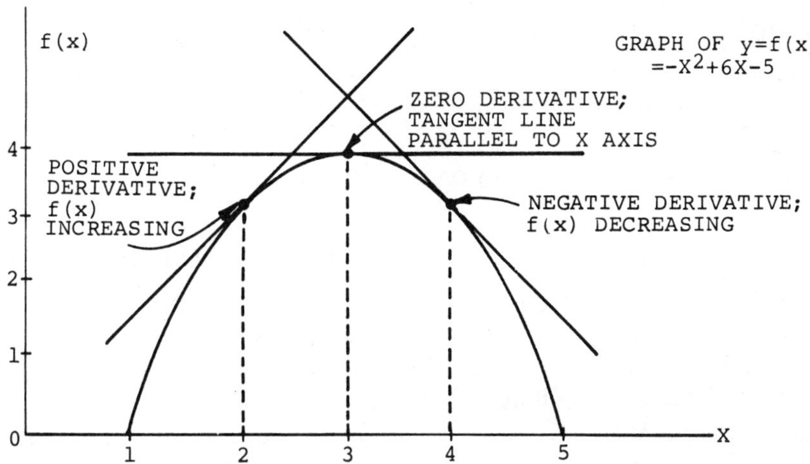

Some facts about derivative follow.

1. The derivative of the sum is the sum of the derivatives.
2. The derivative of the product is "the first times the derivative of the second, plus the second times the derivative of the first."
3. The derivative of the quotient is "the bottom times the derivative of the top, minus the top times the derivative of the bottom, all divided by the bottom squared."
4. The derivative of a constant is always zero.

Minima and Maxima

Since the derivative geometrically represents the slope of the tangent line at the point in question, we can use the derivative to determine the point(s) at which a function attains a relative minimum or maximum value. Geometrical analysis shows that the derivative will always be zero at the maximum or minimum point of a function. Using the parabola $f(x) = -x^2 + 6x - 5$ shown in the figure just given, the following can be used to find the maximum. First, calculate the derivative of the polynomial using the rules: $f'(x) = -1 \cdot 2x^1 + 6 = -2x + 6$. If the derivative is zero at the maximum, then we must find x such that $f'(x) = -2x + 6 = 0$. Thus, we have:

$$-2x + 6 = 0$$

$$-2x = -6$$

$$x = \frac{-6}{-2} = 3$$

The question as to whether this is a maximum or minimum does not arise in this case, since we can see the graph, but the following rules hold:

1. Find the derivative and set it equal to zero.
2. Find the second derivative (the derivative of the derivative), denoted $f''(x)$.
3. Evaluate the second derivative at the point designed as the maximum/minimum:
   a. If $f''(x)$ is positive, then the point is a minimum.
   b. If $f''(x)$ is negative, then the point is a maximum.

In our example, $f''(x) = -2$ for all x; hence, the point $x = 3$ is a maximum. This property of a derivative can be very useful.

OPERATIONS RESEARCH

Operations research (OR) is the application of scientific methodology to decision-making problems. We'll be talking more about decision support systems in the last chapter of this book. A decision occurs when there are two or more alternative courses of action, each one leading to a different and often unknown result. The operations researcher purports to help the decision maker seek alternatives, analyze possible outcomes, and make a rational choice.

OR can trace its roots back into studies from World War I, but had its formal beginning in World War II (Blackett's Circus), at a point in time that the quantitative method of management was receiving its genesis. Operations Research has applied quantitative techniques to decision-making. Following a scientific method, the problem is defined, assumptions are made, and then a model is constructed. A solution technique is selected, and the problem is solved. Variables are manipulated until the ''optimal solution'' is determined. Controls are applied, and the solution is implemented.

There are several techniques (theories/models):

1. *Inventory theory*, which deals with idle resources, including both physical objects and abstract resources, such as time. Costs are minimized; profits are maximized.
2. *Allocation theory*, which asks how to best allocate scarce resources to competing objectives where there are alternative strategies.
3. *Queuing theory*, involved with anything which has a waiting line. This involves simulation, and uses a computer very extensively.
4. *Replacement theory*, which deals with items of decreasing efficiency.
5. *Game theory,* which deals with conflicting interest problems.

LINEAR PROGRAMMING

Linear programming is probably the best known and most often mentioned technique of operations research. Although some elements of this method had been used for many years, it was 1947 before George B. Dantzig of the Rand Corporation presented it as a unified technique. Linear programming, then, is an optimizing technique which allocates scarce resources among competing activities while maximizing profits or, alternatively, minimizing costs. The relationships between the scarce resources and the competing activities are described in mathematical terms and the process maximizes the objective function. Alternatively, the objective function might be stated in terms of marginal costs associated with each activity and the process minimizes the objective function. All equations must be linear, i.e., their exponents cannot be greater than 1.

An Example of Linear Programming Techniques

The Processing Problem

The Handy Dandy Nut and Bolt Company manufactures two products. (You guessed!) Several machines are required to produce nuts and bolts, but we'll look at just two. Each machine can produce either product.

First Machine

Available work period:	60 seconds
To produce a nut:	4 seconds
To produce a bolt:	2 seconds

Second Machine

Available work period:	48 seconds
To produce a nut:	2 seconds
To produce a bolt:	4 seconds

Profit

On nuts:	6 cents
On bolts:	10 cents

The problem: How many nuts and bolts should be produced per work period in order to make the maximum profit (each nut or bolt must pass through both machines)?

The first machine introduces a restriction on the number of nuts and bolts that may be produced because of the limit on the number of seconds available and the fact that each part requires a fixed increment of time. Thus, letting N be the number of nuts and B the number of bolts, $4N + 2B \leqslant 60$. Likewise, for the second machine, $2N + 4B \leqslant 48$. Finally $6N + 10B$ is the total profit, which we wish to maximize. The restrictions are linear inequalities and the profit is the objective function.

The Graphical Method

We may plot the problem on a graph. Consider the first restriction. If no nuts were produced, we would have no more than 30 bolts. This gives a point (0, 30), where nuts are plotted on the horizontal axis and bolts on the vertical axis. Also, no bolts gives at most 15 nuts, or the point (15, 0). A line drawn between these points precisely consumes all 60 seconds. All other points in the triangle formed by this line and the two axes are also possible solutions to the first restrictive inequality. A similar line, from (0, 12) to (24, 0) can be drawn for the second inequality, with another triangle of possible solutions. We have the graph shown on page 456.

If a combination of nuts and bolts is actually to be produced, then this combination must satisfy both restrictions, and thus, the point on the graph must be inside both triangles. It must, therefore, be inside the figure denoted by the points (0, 0), (0, 12), (12, 6), determined by reading the coordinates of the intersection, and (15, 0). This is the region of *feasible solutions* to the problem. It remains only to examine the points inside this figure to find the one which give's the maximum objective function. The object is to find a profit line, i.e., $P = 6N + 10B$, which does not violate any restrictions and which is greater than any other profit line. One of linear programming's theorems tells us that the maximum-profit line will pass through one of the points of intersection of the constraint lines, i.e., one of the four mentioned

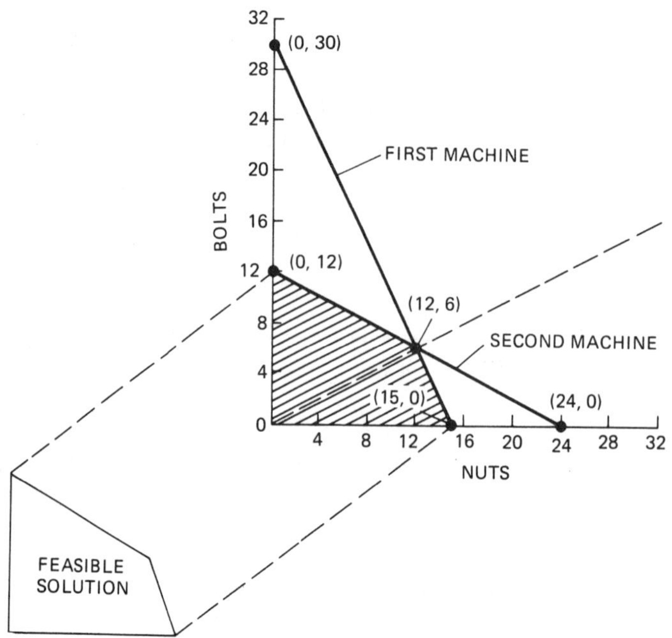

points. Evaluating $6N + 10B$ at these points shows that the maximum is at (12, 6): 12 nuts and 6 bolts. The following evaluations of the profit function should give you a feeling for the result:

Profit	Nuts	Bolts
0	0	0
24	4	2.4
48	8	4.8
90	15	0
120	0	12
132	12	6

If the slope of the profit line were different (i.e., if the relative profitability of the two products were different), then a different solution might be the maximum profit solution.

The point (2, 6) could be determined graphically, by reading the intersection of lines. The above technique is therefore limited by the following:

1. Accuracy in reading the graph.
2. Problems with large numbers of points when large numbers of equations (restrictions) are involved.
3. No more than two dimensions and, hence, only two variables may reasonably be represented.

In general, a linear programming problem may have many restrictions on several variables, where here we had two restrictions on two variables. With more equations, we have more lines. Further, with more variables, our graph becomes many-dimensional.

Simplex Method

The *simplex method* is an algebraic procedure for solving linear programming problems; it eliminates some of the confusion by the additional of *slack variables* $y_1, y_2, \ldots, y_m$ in order to transform the restrictions into *linear equalities* rather than *linear inequalities*. Start with a basic *feasible solution*. Using the nuts and bolts, we have:

$$y_1 + 4x_1 + 2x_2 = 60$$

$$y_2 + 2x_1 + 4x_2 = 48$$

The basic feasible solution here is $x_1 = x_2 = 0$, $y_1 = 60$, and $y_2 = 48$, where $y_1 = 60 - 4x_1 - 2x_2$ and $y_2 = 48 - 2x_2 - 4x_2$. In some problems the basic feasible solution may not be easily found, generally because of negative constants. In this case, *artificial variables* may be added to produce a basic feasible solution. The simplex method proceeds by testing to see if the solution is optimal. If not, the solution is changed by algebraic manipulations of the equations, and another solution is produced. This is then tested, etc. The mechanics of the procedure are best left to computers.

The Dual Linear Problem

In certain problems, we may wish to minimize the objective function, such as in cases when cost is to be reduced. The *principle of duality* says that the maximum of a given system is the same as the minimum of its dual, just as maximizing your profits is related to minimizing your costs in accounting. The dual system of equations is related to but not the same as the original system. A system of equations (restrictions) may be transformed into its dual in order to minimize its objective functions.

Transportation Problems

The *transportation problem* is a special case of linear programming. Here we have *n* factories producing goods which must be transported to *m* warehouses. The total production is equal to the total demand, but plant capacities, warehouse requirements, and costs of transporting a truck, for example, from the *i*th plant to the *j*th warehouse vary. What is the most economical method of transporting the goods? This is a linear programming problem with $n + m$ restrictions and nm variables. The size of the problem can become unmanageable by the simplex method when *n* and *m* are large, but the problem has a built-in special form which makes it solvable by a variety of techniques. Simplex would not be used. Game theory might.

STATISTICS

General Considerations

History

Until the 20th century, the use of statistics was devoted mostly to the collection of data which were then in turn presented in graphic or tabular form to show historic figures of population, income, expenditures, etc. The organization of the data and the clarity of presentation were of utmost importance. Since the function of statistics in its early years was to describe events, it was called *descriptive statistics*.

After World War I and up through World War II the nature of statistics took a different turn. To be sure, data were still collected, organized, and presented in graphic or tabular form—but the shift was to use that data as the basis for forecasting. Based upon collected information, judgment and decisions were being made for the future. Rigorous mathematical techniques were applied in the analysis of past data to determine probable outcomes of future events. Postulating a hypothesis from collected data or making decisions concerning future outcomes is generally known as *reasoning* or *inference*. This process was held to be valid by Sir Francis Bacon and later well grounded by Russell and Whitehead in their *Princi-*

pia Mathematica. Hence, the study of statistics moved from the static and descriptive to the dynamic and inferential. Modern statistics, then, is both descriptive and inferential.

Definition

One may state the definition of statistics as "a scientific methodology for the collection, organization, presentation, and analysis of numerical data for purposes of decision making under risk." The term *under risk* is included in the definition, since it certainly makes obvious the need for statistical analysis. Secondly, the inductive process is, by nature, less than total in its perspective and must therefore contain some element of uncertainty.

Inferential Statistics

Inferential statistics is of utmost importance to managers in all types of organizations, since the future of goals and objectives ultimately involves the proper utilization of limited resources. The modern world demands that managerial decisions be made rapidly and quite often in the face of risk and uncertainty. Today's managers need analytical tools to arrive at quality decisions in a complex world, and statistics can be an important aid in this effort. Decisions concerning the probability of success in a particular market or the chances of survival with a given military mix are examples of decisions that require rigorous analytical thought. Modern statistical techniques provide managers with some of the quantitative methods to arrive at sound conclusions.

Current Emphasis

In consideration of descriptive and inferential statistics, well over 90% of the techniques presented will be of the inferential variety. This is not meant to imply, however, that descriptive statistics lack importance. On the contrary, demographic data, census information, labor statistics, and publications such as the *Statistical Abstract of the United States* are replete with highly valuable historical information.

Terminology

The world *statistic* carries a very special meaning in respect to the scientific methodology of statistics. To the layman, a statistic is any numerical data, usually concerning some quantity or measurement. To the statistician, however, a statistic is any numerical data derived from a sample. For example, suppose one were to determine the average weight of male students in a given high school. From 1,000 male students, if one took a sample of 200 and averaged their heights, the average height would then be called a statistic. On the other hand, if one were to measure the heights of all 1,000 male students, the average height would then be called a *parameter*, since it was derived from the entire population (or universe) of male students in that high school.

Therefore, a *statistic* is a figure derived from a sample, and a *parameter* is derived from a population. A *census* is also synonymous with the terms *population* and *universe*. A population does not have to be large (numerically) to qualify as a population, nor does it have to concern itself with people. If the subject area under investigation is, for example, the number of statistics books in the Library of Congress, then the population is the total number of statistics books (from which the sample will have been taken).

Misuse of Statistics

As with virtually every discipline in today's world, statistics is subject to misuse and abuse. Disproportionate graphs or charts can confuse or mislead. Aslo, percentages may be misleading unless the numerator and denominator of the percentage derivation are clearly identified. "The economic growth of Tasmania is 500% greater than that of the United States'' has no meaning unless one knows the base of the percentage figures. If one samples from a select area of the population, a strong bias enters into the results and leads to erroneous conclusions. As simple a procedure as taking one's sample from a telephone book may easily exclude the indigent aged and result in some bias. Taking too few samples can also lead to false reports. There are, however, well developed sampling techniques which provide for the determination of sufficient quantity in sampling. These are mathematical techniques whch reveal the proper number of elements in the population to sample so as to eliminate a numerical bias.

Organizing and Representing Data

Frequency Distribution

Once data have been collected, they must be organized and portrayed to the user in some readable, meaningful, format. Often, the volume of data is so large that a summarizing format is required. One of the most convenient and acceptable ways to represent descriptive data is in tabular form, wherein the large masses of data are divided into classes or categories.

A *frequency distribution* groups data toagether within given classes and is determined or derived by the array (sequential arrangement) of data. For example, consider the following array of weights of 50 students in a particular class:

Student Weight in Pounds

100	112	123	130	140
102	112	124	131	141
102	112	125	132	141
104	115	125	134	143
105	116	125	135	145
106	119	127	136	146
108	120	128	137	146
110	121	128	138	148
111	121	129	138	149
112	121	130	138	149

Tables

An array of significant quantity easily becomes very difficult to read; hence, some summary method to present the data is devised. The student height may be arranged in a summary frequency distribution in the following manner:

Student Weight in Pounds

Weight	*Number of Students*
100–109	7
110–119	9
120–129	13
130–139	11
140–149	10
TOTAL	50

Note the meaning of the following italicized expressions: The *interval* of the first class shown would be stated as 100 to 110. Since there are 10 pounds within each class, the class *width* is 10. Because the intervals are measured to the nearest pound, the class interval 110–120, for example, includes all measurements from 109.5 to 120.5, and these are called the *class boundaries* or the *true class limits*. Also note that the *lower class limit* in this frequency distribution is 100 and the *upper class limit* is 150. The class mark is the midpoint of any class; therefore, (110 + 120)/2 = 115.0 is the class mark of the second class.

In addition to a tabular frequency distribution, the data may be charted using bar graphs. Bar graphs are arranged according to a particular frequency distribution are called *histograms*. The rules for forming a histogram are:

1. Rectangles are used to represent the frequency distribution.
2. The area within each rectangle must be proportional to the class frequency.
3. The width of the rectangle must be equal to the class interval.

Using the data of the student weights, one may build this histogram:

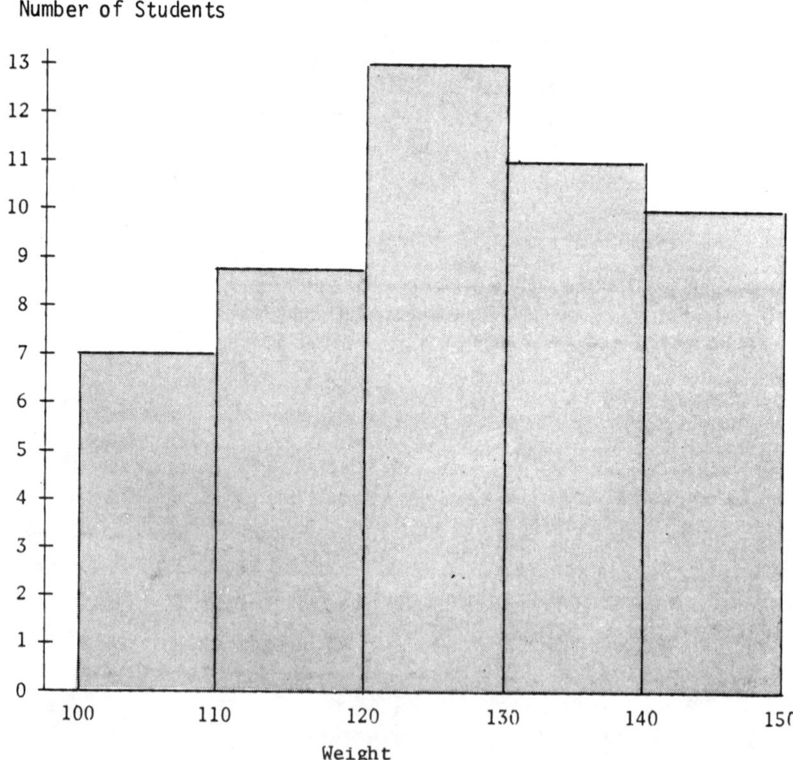

Frequency Polygon

If one connected a line to each of the classmarks of the histogram, a frequency polygon would then be produced as shown in the following histogram.

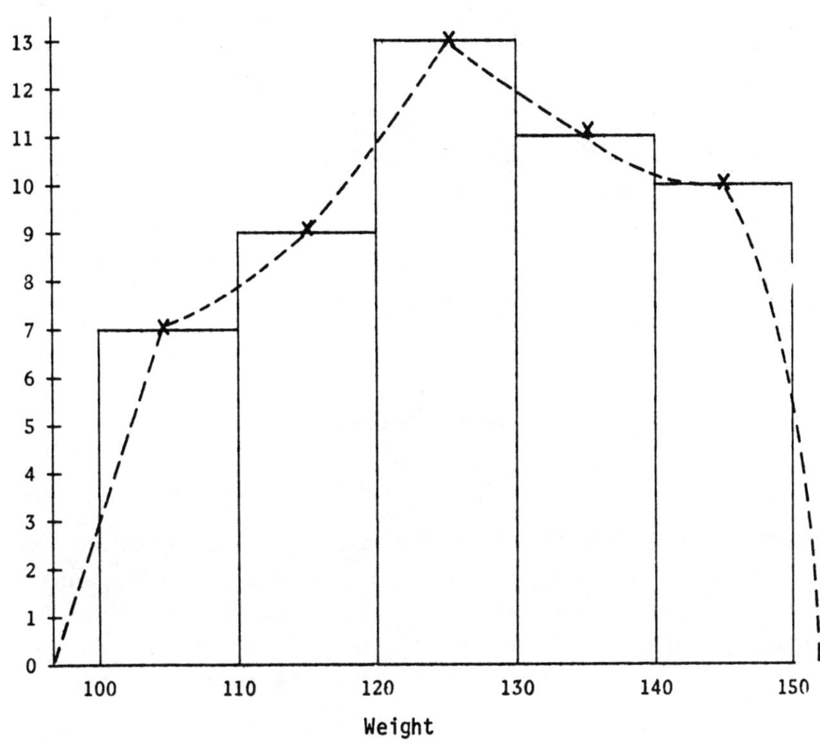

Ogive

Any frequency distribution presented in a cumulative manner is called an ogive. Ogives are of two types: "less than" or "more than." Consider the following "less than" cumulative frequency distribution.

Weight	*Number of Students*
less than 99.5	0
less than 109.5	7
less than 119.5	16
less than 129.5	29
less than 139.5	40
less than 149.5	50

The frequency polygon for the above "less than" ogive would look like this:

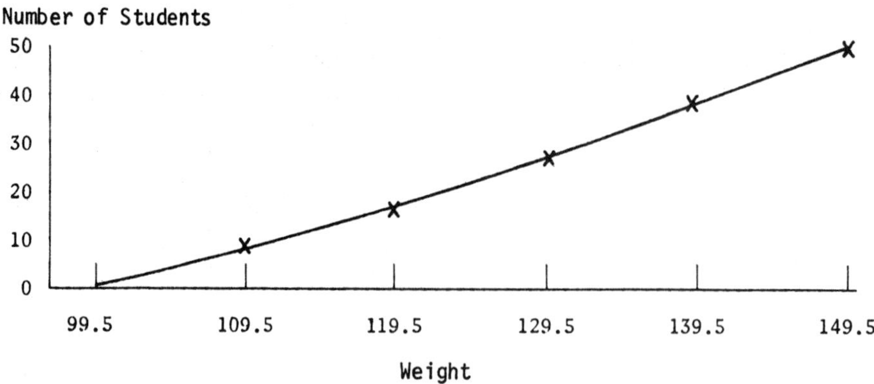

Statistical Measures

Averages

There is no one measure in statistics that has been more used and misused that the average. The average (specifically, the mean or arithmetic average) is the cornerstone of all subsequent analytical and inferential statistics. The average is primarily advantageous because it can summarize the central tendency of data. That is, data and groups of data often tend to lean toward or center around a particular value. This value or number is called the average. Three averages will be discussed: the mean, the median, and the mode.

Mean

The mean or arithmetic average is derived simply by summing the value of all the elements in an array and dividing this sum by the total number of elements in the array. If one is taking the average of sample data, the mean is designated by $\overline{X}$. This mean of population data is given by the Greek letter μ (mu).

Hence, the formulas for the arithmetic mean are as follows (where Σ (sigma) means "the sum of, "$\overline{X}$ denotes the value of each element, and n is the total number of elements in the array):

Sample Mean	*Population Mean*
$\overline{X} = \dfrac{\Sigma X}{n}$	$\mu = \dfrac{\Sigma X}{n}$

Thus, $\overline{X}$ is a statistic, whereas μ is a parameter.

The deviations about the mean have two important properties:

1. The sum of the deviations about the mean will always be equal to zero.
2. The sum of the squared deviations about the mean is a minimum (variance).

The first property can be shown this way:

$$\begin{aligned}\sum d &= \sum(\overline{X} - \overline{X}) \\ &= \sum X - n\overline{X} \\ &= \sum X - \sum X \\ &= 0\end{aligned}$$

Median

Often, the arithmetic mean may be misleading, as in the case of the statistician with his feet in the oven and his head in the refrigerator, who stated that "on the average," the temperature was just fine!!!

The median is simply that value which appears in the centermost position of an array of values. This is illustrated in the following array:

2
3
4—4 is the centermost value and is therefore the median average
7
10

(The mean of this array is 5.2). Where the number of values in an array is not odd, the one must take the middle two values and derive their arithmetic mean to find the median. For example:

2
3
3 } middle two values (4 + 3)/2 = 3.5 = median average
4 }
7
9

Mode

The following example illustrates the use of a modal average in preference to the mean average. A millionaire living on the block may considerably bias mean average income figures for that particular area of the city. Hence, a modal average, or the mode, may be used to give a more representative picture 0 income.

The mode is simply that value which appears most often in an array. For example:
Individual Incomes in Southwest Section of Plainville, USA

Individual Incomes in Southwest Section of Plainville, USA

\$2,500	
\$5,000	Mean = \$27,000 (approximately)
\$7,500	
\$7,500	Median = \$7,500
\$9,000	
\$150,000	Mode = \$7,500

In this instance, the median and the mode are far better representative averages than the mean.

Measures of Variation

Averages do not explain or show the variation in the array of data. Since the arithmetic mean is used most frequently as an average, it is often accompanied in the statistical studies by certain measures of variance within the data.

Variance

Using data from a population, one may compute the variance of that data. The variance will be denoted by the Greek letter σ as follows (where the population mean $\mu = 5$):

Array	$X - \mu$	$(X - \mu)^2$
1	-4	16
3	-2	4
5	0	0
5	0	0
7	+2	4
9	+4	16
30	0	40

The formula for the variance of population is $\sigma^2 = (\Sigma(X - \mu)^2/n$. In our example, $\Sigma(X - \mu)^2 = 40$ and $n = 6$. Thus, $\sigma^2 = \frac{40}{6}$ or 6.66.

Standard Deviation

The disadvantage of the variance, however, is that it is not represented in the same units of data from which it was derived. Therefore, to obtain a more meaningful measure of variation, one may compute the standard deviation as the square root of the variance:

$$\text{Variance} = \sigma^2$$

$$\text{Standard Deviation} = \sigma$$

The formula thus becomes $\sigma = \sqrt{(\Sigma(X - \mu)^2/n} =$ *standard deviation*. In the previous example, $\sigma^2 = 6.66$; therefore $\sigma = \sqrt{6.66} = 2.58$.

One may now say that the mean (μ) of the distribution is 5 with a standard deviation (σ) of 2.58. Notice the quality of this statement when comparing only two means:

1	5
3	5
5	5
5	5
7	5
9	5
$\mu = 5$	$\mu = 5$
$\sigma = 2.58$	$\sigma = 0$

The distribution of the first example has a σ of 2.58, which, compared to the μ of 5, reflects the relatively smooth spread of the data over the population. In the second example, there is no flexibility, as indicated by the σ of 0.

Other Statistical Measures

Skewness and Kurtosis

Not all data, certainly, follow a frequency distribution of perfect bell-shaped curves. Some curves are peaked at the top (*leptokurtic*), and some are rather flattened at the top (*platykurtic*). Other frequency polygons may be either skewed to the right (*positive skewness*) or skewed to the left (*negative skewness*). Examples and illustrations of kurtosis and skewness are shown below. Platykurtic curves have a broader central portion and lower tails than the normal (*mesokurtic*) curve. Leptokurtic curves have narrower central portions and higher tails than the normal curve.

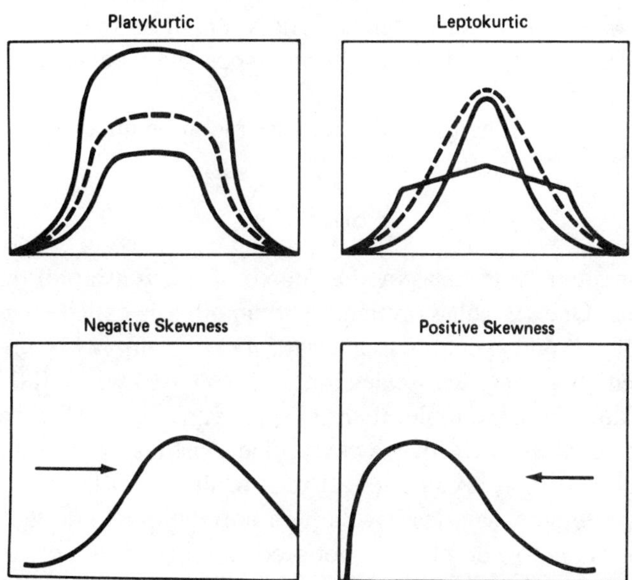

Quartiles

It is often convenient to discuss data in terms of the percentiles into which they fall. If the data are divided into ten equal parts, one would have the decile range for all the data. Perhaps the most common arrangement is made by dividing the data into four equal parts—quartiles.

Recalling the data for student weight given earlier in this section, one may wish to find the first quartile for student weight:

Student Weight in Pounds

Weight	*Number of Students*
100–109	7
110–119	9
120–129	13
130–139	11
140–149	10
TOTAL	50

The first quartile (25%) of the student weight falls were $n/4 = \frac{50}{4} = 12.5$ students. Since the first class only contains 7 students, one must take 5.5 of the 9 students who fall into the second class. The formula for finding the quartile is $Q_1 = L + (j \cdot c)/f$, where Q_1 = first quartile; L = lower class limit, f = frequency; j = number needed from next class; and c = class interval.
Hence,

$$Q_1 = 110 + (5.5 \cdot 10)/9$$
$$Q_1 = 110 + 6 \text{ (rounded)}$$
$$Q_1 = 116$$

Thus far, the discussion has been about presentation and analysis of one variable, in this case student weights. Often, however, one may wish to examine one or more variables. For example, a farmer may wish to know which fertilizer has the greatest crop yield potential or an economist may wish to determine which monetary policy has the greatest impact on disposable income: certain taxes, interest rates, credit options, investments, etc.

In order to consider and analyze the effect of one variable upon another, several statistical methodologies may be employed.

Correlation

In correlation analysis, one attempts to measure the degree of relationship of one or more variables to one or more other variables. One variable correlated with another is called *simple correlation.* When two or more variables are involved, one is dealing with *multiple correlation.*

Correlation is measured on a numerical scale from 0.0 to ±1.0, where 0.0 is no longer correlation and ±1.0 is perfect correlation. For example, there is approximately a .85 correlation between personal income and spending, as might be expected. However, one must take care to note that a high degree of correlation does not necessarily imply a cause–effect relationship. It is known, for example, that liquor consumption and college professors' salaries have a high correlation; so do the heights of ladies' hemlines and stock market trends; and so do chewing tobacco sales and automobile sales. Hence (except for obvious examples such as these) there is the danger of imputing a casual relationship between variables. In some cases, however, enough information is known to arrange a cause/effect assumption—cigarette smoking and cancer, liquor and DWI arrests, etc.

Simple Correlation

Two examples of simple correlation are illustrated in the following figure:

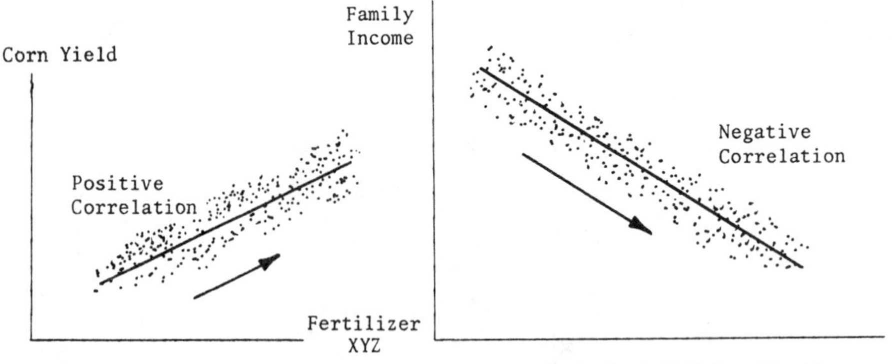

In the examples, there seems to be direct correlation between fertilizer XYZ and corn yield. When the correlation line slopes upward and to the right, it is an indication of direct or positive correlation. There is also a correlation between family income and the number of children per family. However, the line slopes downward and to the right, indicating a negative or inverse correlation. Hence, there are differences in correlation with respect to the direction of the relationship.

Coefficient of Correlation

The *coefficient of correlation* is a value which expresses not only the degree of relationship between or among variables, but also the direction or slope of the correlation line. As in the corn yield example, the coefficient of correlation may be +.75, whereas in the family income example, the coefficient may be on the opposite side at −.75: the same degree of correlation, yet in different directions.

Multiple and Curvilinear Correlation

Multiple correlation has already been discussed as being an extended case of simple correlation. Graphical representation of three variables leads to three-dimensional graphs which are awkward to read, and four variables defy pictorial representation.

Curvilinear or nonlinear correlation concerns parabolic or various other functions which are simply more general cases of correlation.

Partial Correlation

In multiple correlation, one may wish to hold other variables constant while changing only one dependent and one independent variable. This procedure within multiple correlation is called partial correlation.

Regression

Regression analysis is very closely related to correlation. The formulas used in both types of analysis are quite similar. In correlation, one seeks to determine the degree of relationship between variables; regression is a method used to project the behavior of one variable by using another variable.

Regression analysis is used mostly in efforts related to prediction and forecasting. A trend line is projected, and the regression formula is used to estimate the position of a certain variable in respect to time or some other independent variable.

For example, one may predict the future Gross National Product (GNP) of our economy by regressing past GNPs to the projected time (in years) as follows:

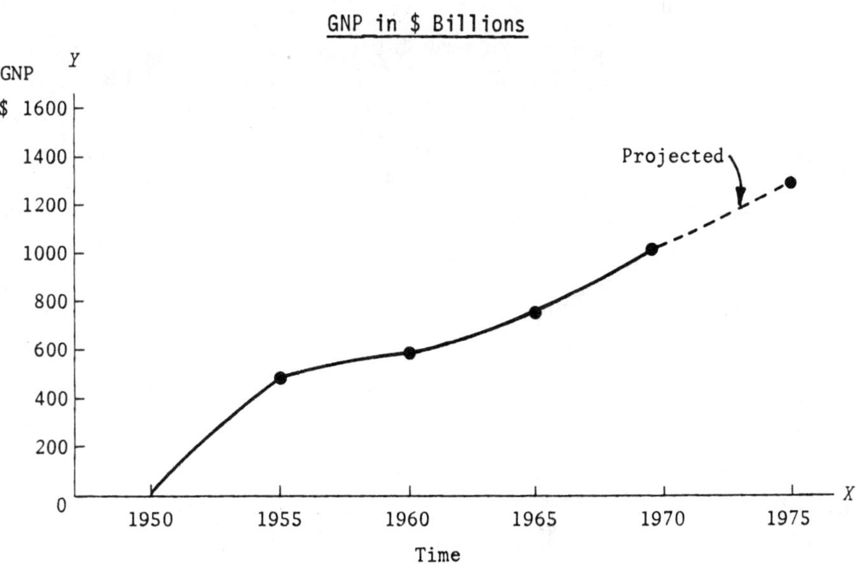

A formula for the slope of the line is derived, and future *Y* variables (dependent) are forecast by regressing *Y* on *X* (independent variable). Of course, one must reasonably assume that the same underlying casual conditions that existed in the past will continue in the future time frame of the forecast.

Least Squares

There are several techniques for determining the regression line. One may simply "hand-fit" a curve through the plotted points. Or, one can develop a line whose position is at the least square position from the plotted points. It is physically impossible to pass a straight line through random points. It is possible to find a line having a property that the sum of the squares of the deviations from the line is at a minimum. The least squares technique is demonstrated in the following diagram:

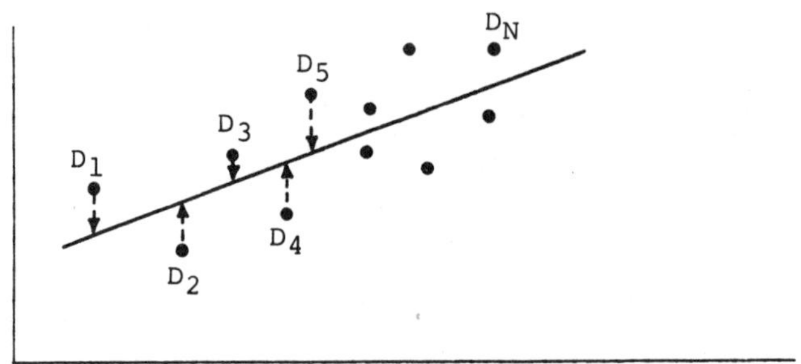

Elementary Probability Theory for Finite Sample Spaces

Statistical analysis looks to the future. Since most future events involve a considerable degree of risk and uncertainty, one must, therefore, be satisfied with trying to ascertain which events will most likely occur. Business decisions are typical of inferences which must be made in the face of uncertainty. Of one cannot materially affect the courses of activities of customers, at least knowing how they might act is the next best possible tool for managers and decision-makers. One may not be able to change the rain into sunshine, but being reasonably confident of its probabilistic occurrence may significantly influence your decisions to walk/drive, carry your umbrella, etc.

Probability

A convenient way to think about the concept of probability is to consider it as "relative frequency in the long run." On this foundation is built the structure of *classical statistics*, which is discussed under Theory of Sampling later in this chapter. The difficulty with that definition, however, is that the long run may not exist. For example, the businessman may be faced with a different or novel situation in which there is no long-run historical or empirical data upon which to rest a probability function. Much of the probability theory is concerned with *assumed* distributions, and thus lends itself to the application of what is termed *subjective probability.* In subjective probability, the decision-maker imputes a probability function or value (from 0.0 to 1.0) on a certain event; as new information comes in, this probability is revised. Ask anyone who plays the horses. The whole process of revising subjective probabilities is a part of what we know as *Bayesian inference.* The techniques of Bayesian inference will not be discussed here. This section on probability theory, however, will give some of the favor of these methods.

Experiments

In statistics, an experiment simply means "to make an observation." Noting the number of defective parts in an assembly line or data entry errors may be considered experiments.

Sample Space

The total of all possible outcomes in an experiment is called the *sample space*. *Possibilities space*, *universal set*, and *universe of discourse* are other terms which have the same meaning as sample space. All 36 possible combinations of a roll of two dice make up a sample space.

Events and Sets

One speaks of a sample space as the set of all possible outcomes. One outcome of all those possible is known as an event. Hence, an event is a subset of the total sample space:

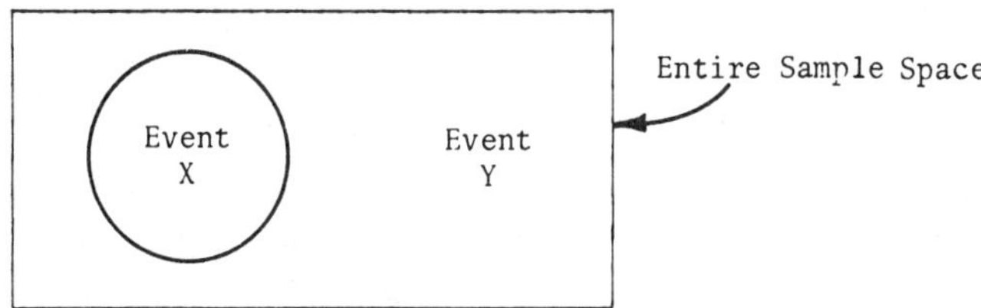

Probability Range

All probability values lie in a range between +0.0 to +1.0. There are no negative probabilities. The value 0.0 means that there is no (zero) chance of an event occurring. Although philosophically bothersome, a pragmatist would assign a 1.0 probability to the event of sunrise tomorrow and a 0.0 probability that no New Yorker will spend his winter in Florida this year. The probability of getting a head on one toss of a ''fair'' coin is .5, and the probability of a man living to be 150 years old is .00000000001, unless, of course, he is from Soviet Georgia, or is as old as Methuselah (969 years). Hence, probabilistic values range from 0 to 1.

Types of Events

Certain events depend upon others for their probability. For example, the chances of taking your umbrella to work may be a function of the weather report, cloudy skies, and time of the year. Many events, on the other hand, are quite independent, such as the outcome of a coin toss or the roll of dice. In all cases, one must consider probability functions in terms of the nature of the event or events within the sample space.

When dealing with probabilities and events, it is simpler and more efficient to use symbolic notation. In most cases, the expression *probability of an event* is stated as $P(E)$. When talking about the probability of one event or the other occurring, the $P(E_1) + P(E_2)$. The probability of one event and the other event occurring is given as $P(E_1E_2)$. Lastly, the probability of one event occurring given that the other event has occurred is noted as $P(E_1|E_2)$.

The probability of any event occurring is given as $P(E) = n/N$, where $P(E)$ is the probability of an event, n is the number of ways in which E can happen; and N is the total possible occurrences in the sample. Thus, the probability of drawing any ace from a deck of cards is $P(E) = \frac{4}{52} = \frac{1}{13}$.

Independent Events

Events are said to be independent if their probabilities are not affected by either the occurrence or nonoccurrence of other events. Tossing a coin, rolling dice, and roulette are typical examples of independent events. Contrary to popular opinion, dice have no memory. For example, the probability of rolling a seven is $\frac{1}{6}$. Simply because seven has not come up for quite a while does not mean that it is *due* to occur. Each roll of the dice must be thought of as the very first roll, since these are independent events. If the probability of tossing a tail on a coin is $P(E_1)$ and the probability of tossing a head (on the next try) is $P(E_2)$, then, since these are independent events, the probability may be expressed as $P(E_2|E_1) = P(E_2)$. This formula says that the probability of tossing a head, given that a tail was previously thrown, is still the probability of tossing a head, or .5.

The compound occurrences of the independent events is derived as the product of their respective probabilities. If one were to ask, "What is the probability of rolling two 7s in a row?", the answer given by the product of their probabilities: $P(E_1E_2) = (\frac{1}{6})\,(\frac{1}{6}) = \frac{1}{36}$. To use another example, suppose an urn contains four white marbles and two black marbles. What is the probability of drawing the two black marbles in two attempts? Notationally, the problem is stated as: $(E_1E_2) = P(E_1) \cdot P(E_2|E_1) = \frac{2}{6} \cdot \frac{1}{5} = \frac{2}{30}$ or $\frac{1}{15}$. This illustration does not assume replacement.

Mutually Exclusive Events

If two or more events cannot occur at the same time, they are said to be mutually exclusive. The probability notation is simply $P(E_1E_2) = 0$. Thus, tossing a head excludes the outcome of tails, drawing an ace excluded the drawing a king, etc. The probability of occurrence of mutually exclusive events is given as the sum of their respective probabilities within the sample space. Therefore, the probability of tossing a head or a tail is $P(E_1) + P(E_2) = .5 + .5 = 1.0$. Also, the probability of drawing an ace or a king from a deck of cards is $P(E_1) + P(E_2) = \frac{1}{13} + \frac{1}{13} = \frac{2}{13}$.

Conditional Probability

Where resources are involved in business decisions, managers often would like to estimate the probability of a certain outcome (sales volume, profit, production, etc.), given a certain mix of resource expenditure. We have already seen something analogous to this type of problem in the example above concerning marbles in an urn. Consider the following information concerning hypothetical CDP applicants:

	Male	*Female*	*Total*
College Degree	45	30	75
No College Degree	20	15	35
TOTAL	65	45	110

The probability of having a college degree is $\frac{75}{110} = .68$. The probability of having no college degree is $\frac{35}{110} = .32$. The probability of being a male is $\frac{65}{110} = .59$. The probability of being a female is $\frac{45}{110} = .41$. One may now use these marginal probabilities to determine various joint and conditional probabilities:

	Male	*Female*	*Total*
College Degree	.41	.27	.68
No College Degree	.18	.14	.32
	.59	.41	1.00

The probability that a person selected will be a female holding a college degree is $\frac{30}{110} = .27$. Looking at a subset of the entire population, one may derive the conditional probability of selecting a person with a college degree given that the person is female as $P(A|B) = \frac{30}{45} = .67$.

Random Variables, Distributions, and Distribution Properties

Many terms and expressions in our language have very special meanings when applied to a technical area. For example, in mathematics a constant is a numerical value that never changes in a given formula. In computer programming, however, a constant may be numeric or alphanumeric, and it may change. Another such special term is the word *random.* To the layman, random is taken as haphazard and accidental. In statistics, however, the term *random event* means that such an event has the same chance of occurring as any other event. When applied to sampling techniques, *random sampling* means that each element in the sample space has an equal chance of being included in the sample. This does not mean, of course, that all the probabilities must be equal, just as there is not a priority bias in the sampling procedure which would preclude one element from being selected. A *random variable* has yet another meaning, as will be explained shortly.

Random Sample with Replacement

Probability functions will change depending upon whether one samples with or without replacing the item sampled. Suppose there's a box with six tape rings in it, two of which are black and four of which are white. What is the probability of selecting two black rings in succession if the selected rings are put back into the box?

Answer: $P(E_1E_2) = (\frac{2}{6})\,(\frac{2}{6}) = \frac{4}{36} = .1111$

Random Sample without Replacement

Using the rings again, what is the probability of selecting two black rings in succession assuming that the first black ring is *not* put back into the box?

Answer: $P(E_1E_2) = (\frac{2}{6})\,(\frac{1}{5}) = \frac{2}{30} = .0666$

Random Variables and Their Probability Functions

A random variable is an entity that has been assigned a value corresponding to every possible event in the sample space. Test scores may define a random variable: If one assigns "3" for excellent, "2" for good, "1" for fair, and "0" for poor, then the random variable "test score" is specified. Recall the histogram example of students' weights presented earlier; the weights defined a grouped random variable. A variable characteristic, or observation may take any one of a specified set of values. Each value will then have an associated frequency or probability. A simple probability distribution for the random variable "test score" is presented below:

Test score	*Probability*
3	.10
2	.60
1	.25
0	.05
	1.00

Mathematical Expectation of a Random Variable

Mathematical expectation (probabilistic return) is simply the sum of the product of each value of the random variable with its respective frequency (probability). What, then, is a "fair" price to pay to enter a game in which one can win \$25 with a $P(.2)$ and \$10 with a $P(.4)$?

$$
\begin{aligned}
\$25(.2) &= \$5.00 \\
\$10(.4) &= \underline{\$4.00} \\
& \$9.00
\end{aligned}
$$

See the systems materials for an expansion of the use of this concept in selecting design alternatives.

Mean, Average, and Variance of the Distribution of a Random Variable

An arithmetic mean and variance may be calculated for the distribution function of a given random variable. The arithmetic mean is also called the expected value or mathematical expectation of the function. Using the \$9.00 example as above, variance will be calculated this way:

$$
\begin{aligned}
\$25 - \$9 = (\$16)^2 \cdot (.2) &= \$51.20 \\
\$10 - \$9 = (\$\ 1)^2 \cdot (.4) &= .40 \\
\$\ 0 - \$9 = (\$-9)^2 \cdot (.4) &= \underline{32.40} \\
\text{Variance} = \sigma^2 &= 84.00 \\
\text{Standard Deviation} = \sigma &= \$\ 9.17
\end{aligned}
$$

Probability Distribution

The following chart illustrates all the discrete combinations of throwing dice and their associated probabilities (where X is the random variable and $P(X)$ is the respective probability function):

X	$P(X)$
2	1/36
3	2/36
4	3/36
5	4/36
6	5/36
7	6/36
8	5/36
9	4/36
10	3/36
11	2/36
12	1/36

A continuous random variable could assume a theoretically infinite number of values, e.g., the diameter of blots coming off an assembly line. A continuous distribution is one in which the number of values is infinite and the values are not distinct.

Frequency Distribution

Often, a frequency distribution will be constructed while developing a probability function. If an experiment were conducted using dice and recording each combination which occurred during 36,000 tosses, the following table might summarize the results:

X	*Frequency*
2	1,000
3	2,000
4	3,000
5	4,000
6	5,000
7	6,000
8	5,000
9	4,000
10	3,000
11	2,000
12	1,000
	36,000

Joint Probability Function of Two Random Variables

The joint probability of two independent events is calculated by multiplying the individual probabilities. A pair of dice is being tossed and we wish to calculate the probabilities. A pair of dice is being tossed and we wish to calculate the probability of obtaining a "1" on both dice (snake eyes):

E_1	$P(E_1)$	E_2	$P(E_2)$
1	1/6	1	1/6
2	1/6	2	1/6
3	1/6	3	1/6
4	1/6	4	1/6
5	1/6	5	1/6
6	1/6	6	1/6

$$P(E_1E_2) = 1/6 \cdot 1/6 = 1/36 \text{ for all values of } E_1 \text{ and } E_2.$$

Now, if we wish to calculate the probability of obtaining a "4" on one die and a "3" on the other die, regardless of order, we must consider all the different ways to obtain the desired result and then add the probabilities:

$$P(E_1E_2) = \tfrac{1}{6} \cdot \tfrac{1}{6} = \tfrac{1}{36}$$

$$P(E_3E_4) = \tfrac{1}{6} \cdot \tfrac{1}{6} = \tfrac{1}{36}$$

The probability of obtaining a "3" and a "4" $= \frac{1}{18}$.

Probability Graphs for Continuous Random Variables

A variable is continuous if it can assume all values on a continuous scale. Size, height, weight, time, temperature, etc., are measured on continuous scales and their observations are referred to as continuous.

A continuous random variable has a probability that is assumes a value in any interval equal to the corresponding area under a distribution curve, as follows:

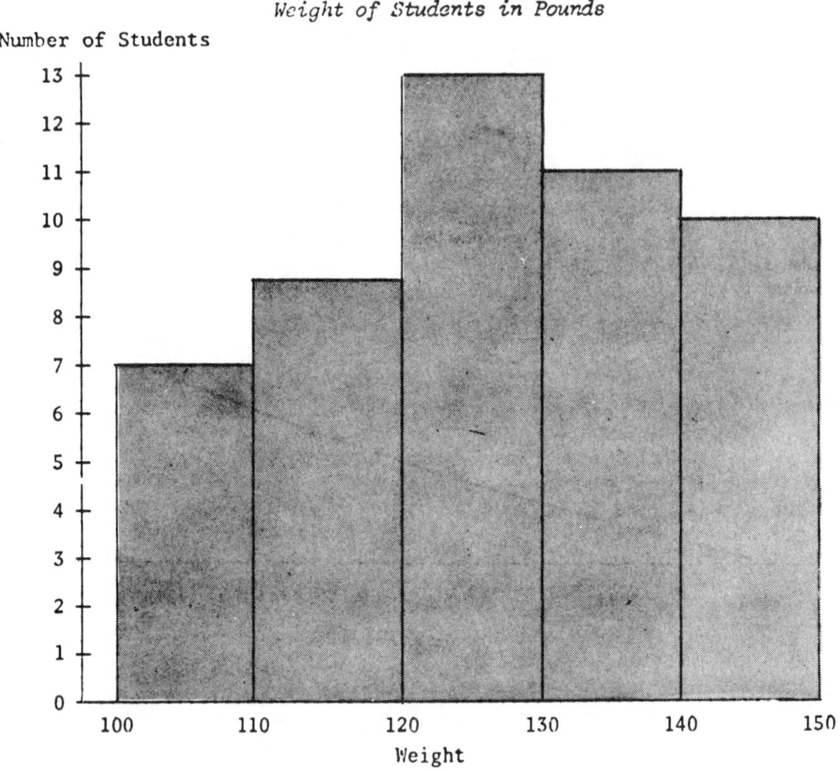

Probability Represented by Areas

By comparing the shaded area in the rectangle representing 100 to 110 pounds to the total shaded area in the above histogram (representing 100% of the sample), we can calculate that 14% of the students weighed 110 pounds or less. When a histogram is approximated by a smooth curve, the proportion of a given group is represented by the corresponding area under the curve.

Cumulative Probability Graphs

Using the student weight data from the earlier example, a cumulative probability graph may be constructed:

Weight	*Number of Students*	*Cumulative Probability*
less than 99.5	0	0
less than 109.5	7	.14
less than 119.5	16	.32
less than 129.5	29	.58
less than 139.5	40	.80
less than 149.5	50	1.00

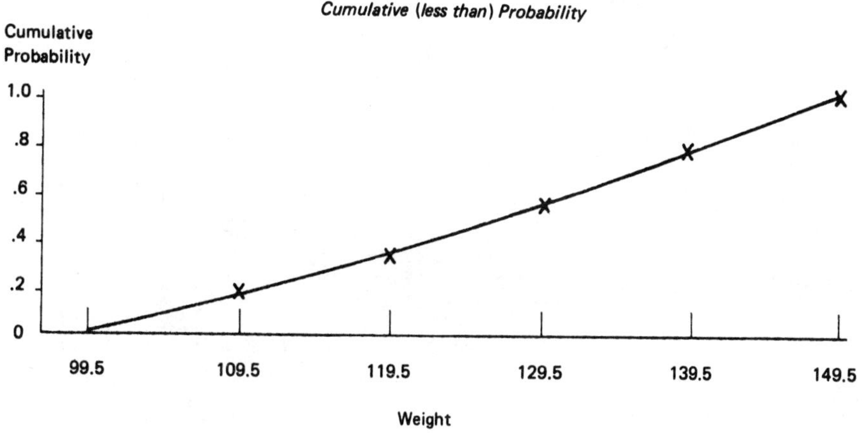

The Normal Curve and the Normal Probability Distribution

The normal curve is perfectly symmetrical distribution completely determined by the mean and standard deviation. One can determine the area under any part of the curve knowing these factors. The shape of the curve (distribution) is the familiar bell curve.

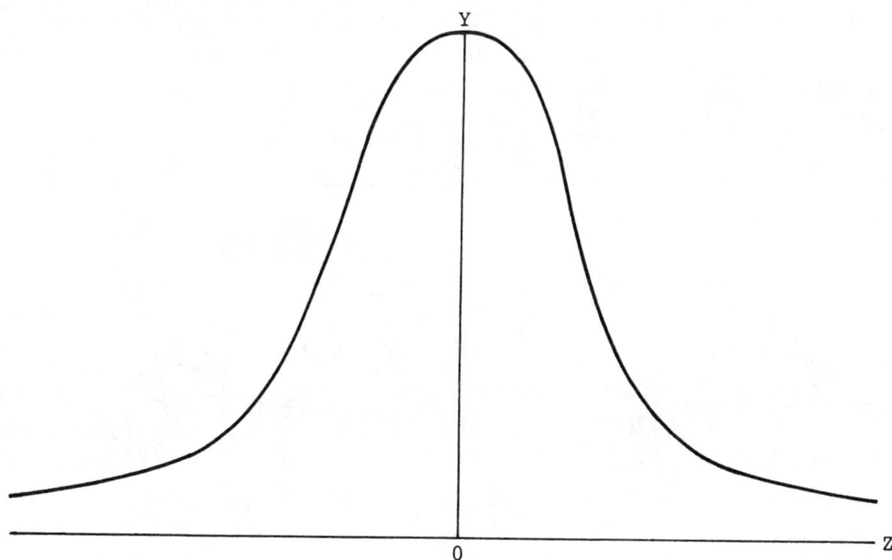

Since we are dealing with a continuous distribution, the tails'' of the curve never touch or reach the z axis, and the lines are then said to be *asymptotic* to the z axis.

In the figure presented below, the mean of the distribution is indicated by the 0 (zero) in the center of the curve on the z axis. The standard deviations are shown to the left and right of the mean. The percentage figures indicate the percentage of the area under the whole curve that falls or lies between the respective standard deviation lines, i.e., the probability that the random variable will take a value between the lines:

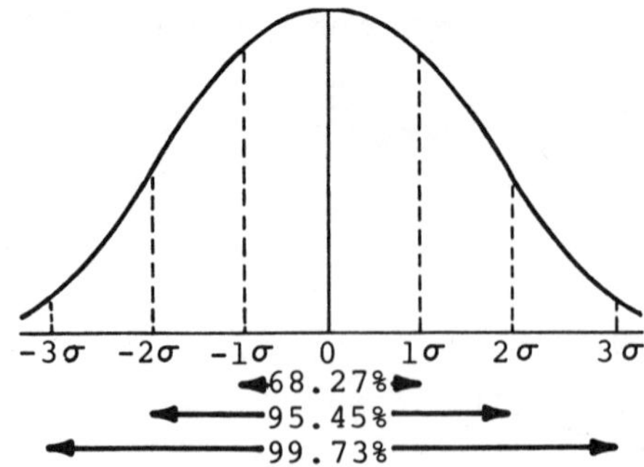

For practical purposes, anything beyond three standard deviations is not usually considered.

Table of z

The so-called table of *z*, where the unit of z is one standard deviation (+ = above the mean, − = below the mean), is necessary for calculations involving the normal distribution, since the table gives the values (from .0000 to .4999) of areas under the curve. What the table does is to match values of *z* (left column plus top row of the table) with values of P(z), the probability that *z* falls between zero and the given value. Negative values of *z* are not needed, since the symmetry of the curve provides the same results, negative or positive. A small portion of the entire table of *z* is presented here:

z	.00	.01	.02	.03	.04	.05
0.0						
0.1	.3643	.3665	.3686	.3708	.3729	.3749
1.2	.3849	.3869	.3888	.3967	.3925	.3944
1.3	.4032	.4049	.4066	.4082	.4099	.4115
1.4	.4192	.4207	.4222	.4236	.4251	.4265
1.5	.4332	.4345	.4357	.4370	.4382	.4394
1.6	.4452	.4463	.4474	.4484	.4495	.4505
1.7	.4554	.4564	.4573	.4582	.4591	.4599
1.8	.4644	.4649	.4656	.4664	.4671	.4677
1.9	.4713	.4719	.4726	.4732	.4738	.4744
2.0	.4772	.4778	.4783	.4788	.4793	.4798
3.0						

Using the table, one can easily ascertain that the probability of getting a *z* less than 1.52 (right side of mean) would be 0.5000 (left side) + 0.4357 (right side) = .9357:

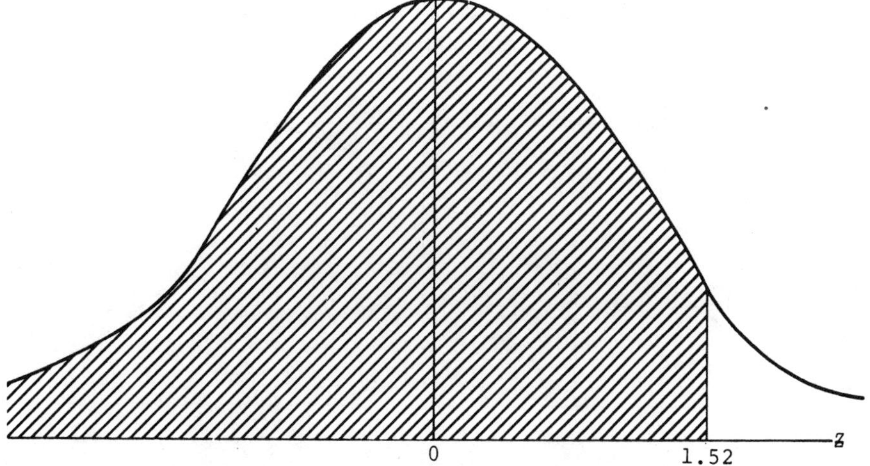

More common problems involving the normal curve are illustrated below:

1. If the mean average weight of a student population is 150 pounds with a standard deviation of 15 pounds, what percent of the students weigh less than 170 pounds? Using the z table:

   $\bar{X} = 170$

   $\mu = 150$

   $\sigma = 15 \qquad z = \dfrac{\bar{X} - \mu}{\sigma} \qquad \text{then} \quad z = \dfrac{170 - 150}{12} = 1.33$

   From the table, the percentage for $z = 1.33$ is .4082, which indicates the percentage above the mean and below 170 pounds. The percentage below the mean is by definition .5000. Hence the answer is 0.5000 (left side) + 0.4082 (right side) = 0.9082 or 90.82%
2. Of 1,000 students whose average weight is 150 pounds with a standard deviation of 15 pounds, how many students weigh between 130 pounds and 171 pounds?

   $\bar{X}_1 = 130$
   $\mu = 150$
   $\sigma = 15 \qquad z = \dfrac{\bar{X}_1 - \mu}{\sigma} = \dfrac{130 - 150}{15} = 1.33$

   $P(z = 1.33) = .4082$

   also:

   $\bar{X}_2 = 171$
   $\mu = 150$
   $\sigma = 15 \qquad z = \dfrac{X_2 - \mu}{\sigma} = \dfrac{171 - 150}{15} = 1.40$

   $P(z = 1.40) = .4192$

The 0.4082 = 0.4192 = 8274 (total area under consideration) and (.8274) (1000) = 827.4, or 827 students. The following diagram demonstrates these calculations:

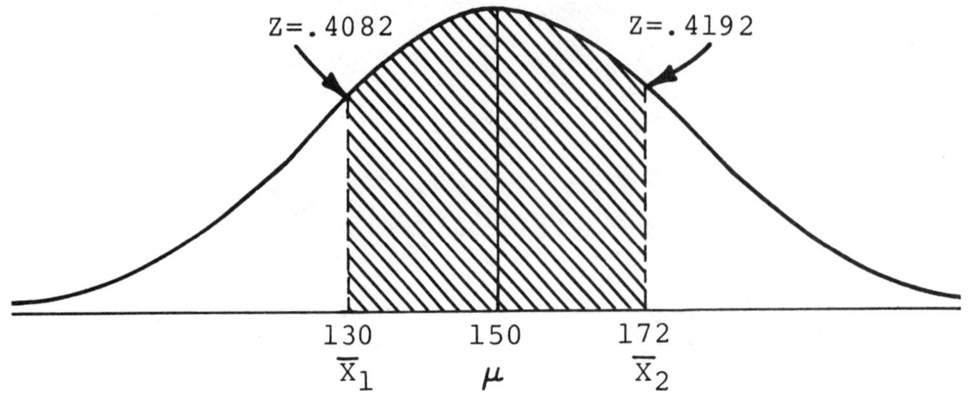

THEORY OF SAMPLING

Statistical Inference

There are many advantages to sampling as opposed to taking a census of the entire population. First, because it is timely and less cumbersome than census taking, sampling is often more accurate in its revelation of the population distribution. Second, businessmen need information upon which to base decisions, and often these decisions cannot wait until all the facts are known. Finally, some testing or quality control procedures demand sampling, since to sample everything would result in its destruction. Using the concepts already discussed concerning the mean and standard deviation, much can be learned about the population by examining the sample distributions derived from the population.

Sample Designs

A sample design is a determination—a plan—of the way in which the sample is to be conducted. There are many ways to conduct an unbiased sample; the ones presented below are the most common. The most common, simple random sample, has already been discussed—each event has an equal probability of occurrence.

Systematic Sampling

A systematic sample is one in which a very practical method of selection, say every 10th element, is devised. The starting point is usually given by selecting a number from a table of random numbers. Although not perfectly random, this method is close enough to warrant its usage.

Stratified Sampling

Where the cost of sampling is directly proportional to the number of samples taken, a method of stratifying the population into subpopulations is divised. For example, with respect to height and weight, men and women differ from each other considerably. Rather than sample from a population of their collective heights and weights, one might stratify the samples into male and female, thus getting a truer picture of the population.

Quota Sampling

This type of sample design is usually specified for personal interviews where a cross section of opinion from various ethnic, religious, or political groups is desired. Hence the interviewer may be told to question 6 Caucasians, 2 Blacks, 1 Hispanic, and 1 Oriental, with the selection of specific individuals to be at the discretion of the interviewer.

Cluster Sampling

This design is used to save time and money where the sample involves a widespread area. For example, New York City would be a natural place to use this sampling technique. The city would be divided into several block groupings and then specific block groupings are selected on a random basis. The technique is also known as area sampling.

Central Limit Theorem

The central limit theorem states, if effect, that where the sample is large, we are in effect working with a normal distribution. There are many disadvantages to using the normal curve and normal distribution. Formally stated, the central limit theorem says:

> If n (sample) size is large (greater than 30), the theoretical sampling distribution of x can be approximated closely with a normal curve having mean μ and the standard deviation $\sigma/\sqrt{n}$ where μ (mu) and σ are the mean and standard deviation of the infinite population from which the sample is obtained.

The theorem implies that irrespective of the actual or real distribution of the population, the sample means taken from it will tend to follow the normal curve pattern. This has been proved mathematically. It is useful because in statistics we are usually trying to find the mean rather than the distribution.

Standard Error of the Mean

The following formula shows that where the sample size n becomes larger, the standard deviation (standard error) of the sample means becomes smaller in inverse ratio to the square root of the sample size:

$$\sigma\overline{X} = \frac{\sigma}{\sqrt{n}}$$

The above formula is the symbolic representation of the central limit theorem.

Example of the Central Limit Theorem

Take the case where $\sigma = 4$; then $\sigma\overline{X} = 4/\sqrt{4} = 4/2 = 2$. In order to reduce $\sigma\overline{X}$ by $\frac{1}{2}$ it would require a fourfold increase in n. For $\sigma\overline{X}$ to equal 1 when $\sigma = 4$, n must equal 16; therefore, $\sigma\overline{X} = 4/\sqrt{16} = 1$. Hence, it takes a proportionately greater sample size to reduce the standard deviation.

Combinations of Two Independent Random Variables

Mean of the Sum

The sums of separate sampling distributions may be comveniently combined by straight addition if the events are independent. The mean of the sum is just the sum of the means

$$\mu D_1 + \mu D_2 + \ldots + \mu D_n.$$

For example, the mean diameters of two types of ball bearings are .10 inches and .50 inches respectively. The mean of the distribution of their sums is simply .10 + .50 = .60.

Variance of the Sum

Calculations of the variances are done in a similar manner to the mean of the sum above. The formula involves the square root of the sums of the variances, however:

$$\sigma(D_1 + D_2) = \sqrt{\sigma^2 D_1 + \sigma^2 D_2}\ \mu$$

For example $\sigma D_1 = .16$ and $\sigma D_2 = .08$; then $\sqrt{(.16)^2 + (.08)^2} = .18$.

Application

Several variables' means and variances may be combined to yield certain required information. Consider the following example:

> Brand *X* automobile tires are reported to last, on the average, 60,000 miles with a standard deviation of 3,000 miles. Brand *Y* tires advertise an average life span of 55,000 miles with standard deviation of 2,000 miles. Both brands of tires are sampled randomly with 500 tires in each sample. What is the probability that brand *X* tires will run 5,400 miles average more than brand *Y* tires?
>
> Solution:

$$\mu(\bar{X} - \bar{Y}) = \mu\bar{X} - \mu\bar{Y} = 60{,}000 - 55{,}000 = 5{,}000$$

$$\sigma(\bar{X} - \bar{Y}) = \sqrt{\frac{\sigma^2 \bar{X}}{N_x} + \frac{\sigma^2 \bar{Y}}{N_y}}$$

$$= \sqrt{\frac{(3{,}000)^2}{500} + \frac{(2{,}000)^2}{500}}$$

$$= 161$$

$$z = \frac{(\bar{X} - \bar{Y}) - \mu(\bar{X} - \bar{Y})}{\sigma(\bar{X} - \bar{Y})} = \frac{5{,}400 - 5{,}000}{161} = 2.5$$

$$P(z) = .4798 \text{ (from } z \text{ table)}$$

Answer: Probability = .5000 − .4798 = .0202

Pascal developed several ways of treating certain probabilistic functions. They were primarily concerned with the outcome of various games of chance, and so the words *success* and *failure* are carryovers from that period of probability history. Although many events in a sample space of games were possible to a gambler, all that mattered was winning or losing.

In management, the quality controllers are interested in such things as defective or nondefective; market analysts would like to know if one is a user or nonuser. This line of reasoning closely parallels the bistable device principle upon which computers are built. Also, note the analogy to the binary numbering system.

The prefix *bi* in the term binomial distribution indicates a two-condition probability distribution whose curve will represent the proportion to which these conditions fall.

Binomial Experiments

For purposes of subsequent discussion, the following notation will be used.:

$P(\text{Success}) = p$
$P(\text{Failure}) = q$ (which is always $1 - p$)
Sample size $= n$
Number of successes $= r$

When a coin is flipped three times, what is the probability of getting two heads and one tail (two successes and one failure)? One way to answer this would be to list all the possible combinations of events that could occur in this sample space:

HHH	TTH
HHT	THT
HTH	HTT
THH	TTT

We note that there are eight possible combinations and, of these, three meet the criteria of the problem (HHT, HTH, and THH). The answer is $P(2 \text{ heads and } 1 \text{ tail}) = \frac{3}{8}$. As the problem becomes larger, e.g., ten tosses, a rote enumeration of the possibilities would be a time-wasting task. A much simpler and more rigorous methods is provided in the binomial distribution.

Binomial Random Variables

The following formula gains much of its power through the use of combinatorial analysis. In the previous example, the problem was to find the probability of two successes out of three trials (or flips). Therefore, the product of this combination and the probability of a given success and failure should yield the desired probability. The formula is formally stated as

$$P(E) = {}_nC_r \cdot p^r \cdot q^{n-r},$$

which states that the probability distribution of the binomialis equal to the combination of n events taken r at a time, multiplied by the probability of success raised to the rth power, multiplied by the probability of failure raised to the $(n - r)$th power.

Using the example of tossing a coin three times, we then may say that:

$n = 3$ tosses
$r = 2$ successes
$p = .5$ and $q = (1 - p) = .5$

Then using the combinatorial formula ${}_nc_r = n!/(r!(n - r)!)$ we get $P(E) = (3!)/(2!(3 - 2)!) = \frac{3}{8}$.

$$P(E) = \frac{3!}{2!(3-2)!}\left(\frac{1}{2}\right)^2\left(\frac{1}{2}\right)^1 = \frac{3}{8}$$

This is the probability that the random variable "number of successes in 3 tosses" will take the value 2.

Although the binomial distribution formula is much easier to apply that the straight forward enumeration method, it can nonetheless become unwieldy. For example, consider the following problem:

> In a large metropolitan area, it is known that 80% of the families who belong to a certain low-level income bracket own a color television set. If 14 families are selected at random from a stratified sample, what is the probability that 11 of these families will own color television sets?

Using the binomial distribution formula, where $n = 14$, $r = 11$, $p = .8$, and $q = 2$, we have ${}_{14}C_{11}$ $(.8)^{11} \cdot (.2)^{14\text{-}11}$. Certainly, raising .8 to the 11th power would be too taxing and time-wasting for most. Therefore, a table of cumulative binomial distributions has been developed. It specifies for a given n, a given p, and a given r, precisely what the probability is. These tables typically go as high as $n = 100$, $p = .50$, and $r = 69$. For n's greater than 100, the normal distribution "takes over" as it were, and binomial approximations are no longer necessary.

Binomial Distribution Properties

Unlike the normal distribution, the binomial distribution is characterized by discrete properties. Let's reexamine the original problem of tossing a coin three times with a view toward determinating all the possible probabilities of getting heads. We know at the outset that we could get three heads, two heads, one head, or no heads. Therefore:

$$\begin{aligned}
\text{3 heads} &= 3^c3 \cdot (1/2)^3(1/2)^0 = (1)(1/8)(1) = 1/8 \\
\text{2 heads} &= 3^c2 \cdot (1/2)^2(1/2)^1 = (3)(1/4)(1/2) = 3/8 \\
\text{1 head} &= 3^c1 \cdot (1/2)^1(1/2)^2 = (3)(1/2)(1/4) = 3/8 \\
\text{0 heads} &= 3^c0 \cdot (1/2)^0(1/2)^3 = (1)(1)(1/8) = 1/8
\end{aligned}$$

A graph of this discrete binomial distribution would appear like this:

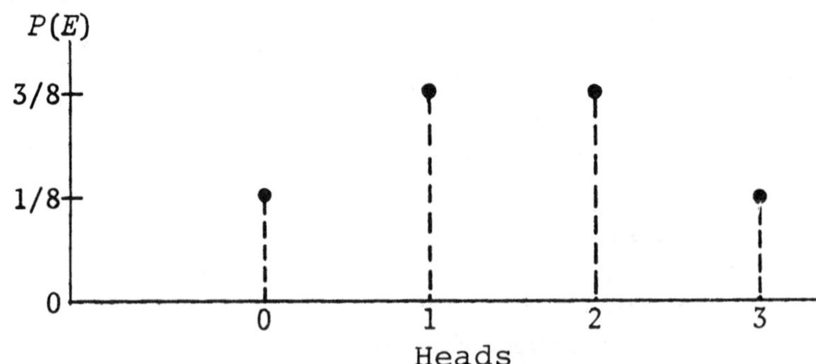

Note the symmetry of the binomial distribution, as well as its discrete quality.

The Central Limit Theorem for the Binomial

In relating the binomial to the normal distribution via the central limit theorem, it is useful to know the following properties of the binomial:

$$\begin{aligned}
\text{Mean} \quad & \mu = np \\
\text{Variance} \quad & \sigma^2 = npq \\
\text{Standard Deviation} \quad & \sigma = \sqrt{npq}
\end{aligned}$$

The normal approximation to the binomial where n is large may be used by employing the following formula:

$$z = \frac{r - np}{\sqrt{npq}}$$

The binomial distribution is used mostly to analyze qualitative factors such as defects or no defects, user and nonuser, male and female, and others. Remember that the binomial always concerns itself with a bi-stable condition.

TIME SERIES ANALYSIS

Planning is one of the most important primary functions of management. An integral component of the planning activity is the ability to predict or forecast future trends and events. In forecasting, the emphasis lies in determining the value of certain variables in the future based upon the value of those same variables in the past.

An initial step in this process is the collection of relevant past data which have become recorded at various time intervals. The data and their associated time intervals are known as time series. The statistical techniques involved in forecasting with time series is called time series analysis.

Components of a Time Series

Determination of Trends

On a graph pertaining to various fluctuations in, say, the business marketplace, it is difficult to discern a particular pattern (at least in the short run). Most activities which occur over time, however, fall into one or more of several standard trends.

A secular or long-term trend in a time series is one in which there is a general, smooth, and regular movement of the series over a long period of time. A secular trend line is usually determined by the least squares method. An illustration shows that. This chart was one which was published several years ago. It is assumed that the development of the microcomputer might have bent the line to something more pronounced after 1977:

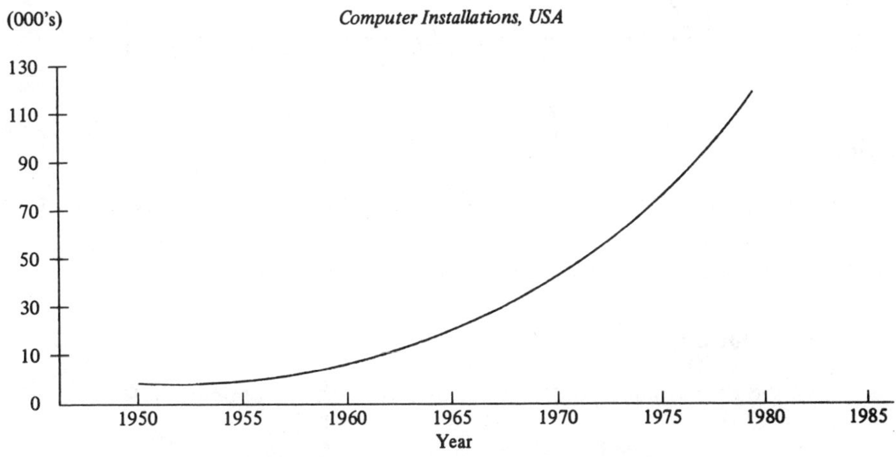

Periodic Variation

Any kind of variation which is periodic and has repeating cycles which have a duration of less than one year is called a seasonal variation. Seasonal variations are easy to understand. These variations usually occur from year to year and, as the name implies, the variation is a function of holidays, time, weather, and the like. For example:

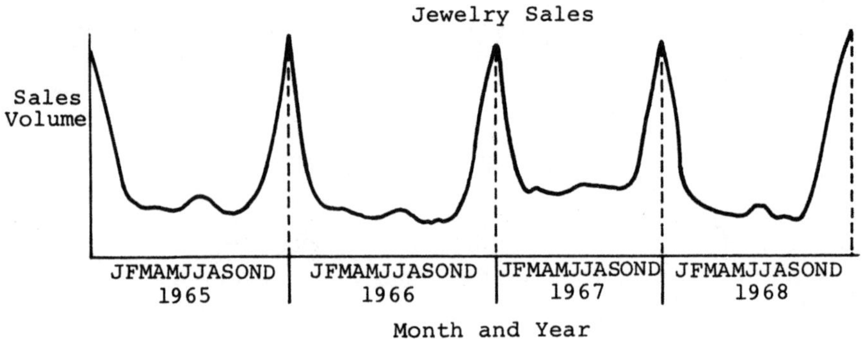

Cyclical Variation

Perhaps the most complex and important variation in time series is that of the cyclical component. Typical of these are the long-term ups and downs of the business cycle which characterize periods of prosperity, recession, depression, and then recovery. The underlying causes of many cyclical variations are as yet unknown. Theories which attempt to explain or predict business cycle variations abound, but the complexities of the nation's political and socioeconomic structure defy complete analysis. An illustration of a time series strongly influenced by cyclical variation appears below:

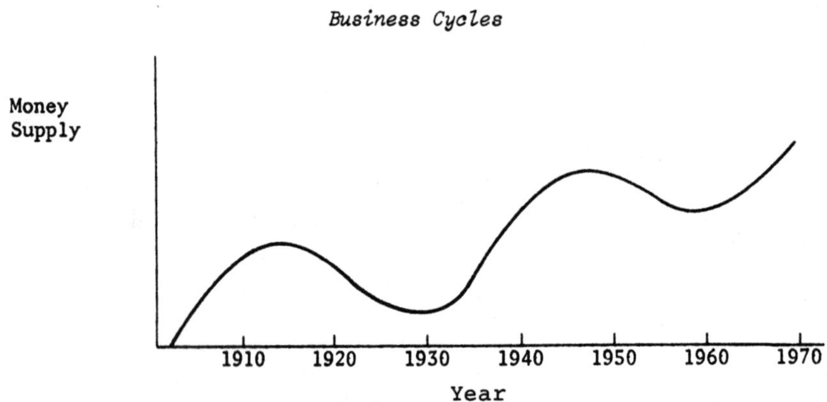

Irregular Variation

Irregular or random variations are those (usually) short-term fluctuations caused by earthquake, floods, strikes, wars, elections, and so forth. Unless they are very severe, they will usually be smoothed out by the long-term trends—the seasonal variation and the cyclical variation.

Graphic Summary of Variation

A chart which displays the three major components of a time series appears below:

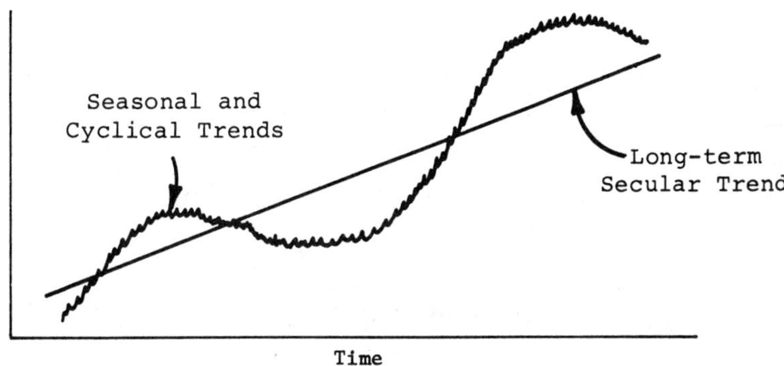

A general axiom or rule of thumb in statistics is that the predictive power of the forecasting technique is in inverse ratio to the amount of variation in the statistic. Therefore, to gain better forecasts from trend lines, variations in the trend are smoothed out for statistical purposes. The following is a brief outline, with examples, of some of the more widespread smoothing techniques. See also the treatment of these techniques in the previous chapter.

Moving Averages

A moving average for the data is taken by overlapping the separate X variables to be averaged according to some predetermined order of magnitude. This method is known as a moving average of order N. For example, consider the following list of numbers: 4, 8, 3, 7, 5, 9, 4. Given these numbers, one might calculate moving totals to the order 3:

$$\frac{4+8+3}{3}, \frac{8+3+7}{3}, \frac{3+7+5}{3}, \frac{7+5+9}{3}, \frac{5+9+4}{3}, = 5, 6, 5, 7, 6$$

Weighted Moving Average

Rather than a straight forward moving average technique, certain weights may be assigned to different variables in the data. To use the previous example, suppose the weights 2, 8, 2 are assigned to each of the 3 ordered variables in the moving average:

$$\frac{2(4)+8(8)+2(3)}{2+8+2}, \frac{2(8)+8(3)+2(7)}{2+8+2}, \frac{2(3)+8(7)+2(5)}{2+8+2},$$
$$\frac{2(7)+8(5)+2(9)}{2+8+2}, \frac{2(5)+8(9)+2(4)}{2+8+2} = 6.5, 4.5, 6.0, 6.0, 7.5$$

SAMPLING FOR QUALITY CONTROL

Control Charts

Industrial quality control typically involves the examination and testing of intermediate and end products to assure proper standards. Since discounts are available for substandard materials or these might be ruinous to regular processing, incoming materials to shop are also often scrutinized for quality. A favored method used in quality control is that of the control chart, since one does not need to know statistics or advances mathematics to use it.

Chance versus Caused Effects

Just as important as knowing whether a process is out of control is knowing whether it went out of control because of some steady causal condition or whether it happened by chance. Decisions to shut down or continue a process may hinge on the decision rule used.

Decision rules in statistics are designed to minimize the possibility of making errors. A hypothesis concerning a particular process is made, and tests are made against that hypothesis.

Type I and Type II Errors

There are two types of errors that may be made in hypothesis testing: Type I (alpha) or type II (beta) errors. A Type I error is to accept the truth of the hypothesis when, in fact, it is false. A Type II error is to reject the hypothesis when, in fact, it is true. Either of these errors are subject to analysis, or both may be analyzed at the same time.

Let us see graphically what is meant by Type I and Type II errors. The concept will be illustrated by using shaded and nonshaded portions of a normal distribution curve:

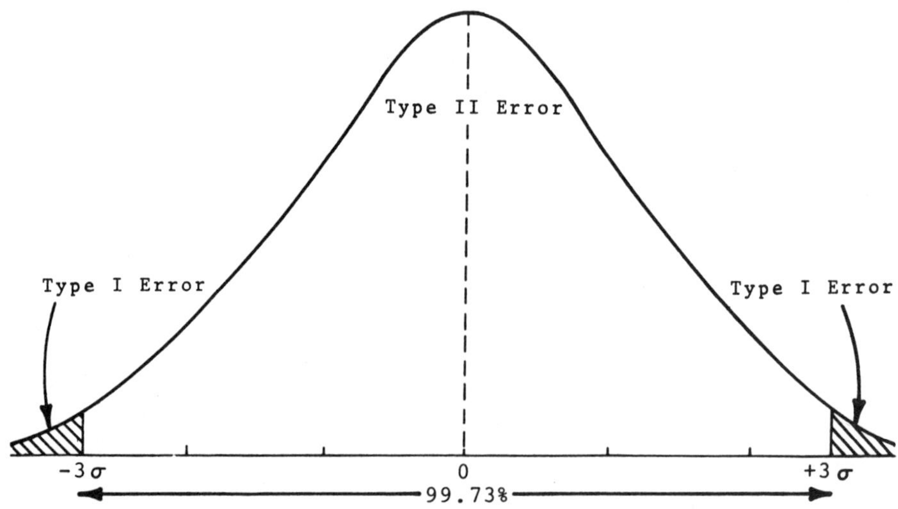

One may say that the process is in control if the mean of the sampling distribution falls within the area of 3 standard deviations from the mean. Hence, a Type I error would be to draw a sample mean from the shaded area (either side) and conclude that it fell within 3 standard deviations. The probability of this occurring is .0027 (1.00 − .9973).

A Type II error would be to draw a sample mean from the unshaded area and conclude that it fell outside the 3 (lower-case sigma) range. The probability of a type II error, in this case, is the same as that of the type I, .0027

Constructing a Decision Rule

The following example is designed to illustrate the use of control charts and decision rules:

A certain drug firm produces aspirin tablets with a machine process. The machine process is expected to produce tablets which have a mean thickness of .2310 inch and a standard deviation of .002 inch. A sample of 12 tablets is taken from the process every 4 hours to determine whether the process is in control, or working properly. The line manager for quality control wished to be more than 99% certain that the thickness of the tablets was not out of control, based upon the samples.

At the 99% confidence range, one is dealing with a 3 σ range. Therefore, we wish to know what the upper limit of our sample $(+3\sigma)$ and the lower limit $\sigma(-3\sigma)$ can be. This is given by the following formulas:

$\mu + 3\sigma/\sqrt{N}$	.2327 inch	upper control limit
μ	.2310 inch	central line
$\mu - 3\sigma/\sqrt{N}$	.2293 inch	lower control limit

Any observations which fall between the upper and lower control limits indicate a process which is in control. A sample mean falling outside of either control limit would warrant investigation.

Acceptance Sampling

Acceptance sampling uses the same procedures as those for control chart decision rules. The problems associated with acceptance sampling are usually resolved by managerial policy rather than statistical technique. For example, there are drugs whose effects may be fatal if compounded incorrectly. Hence, the emphasis in this case would by on the Type I error (accepting the hypothesis as true when it is false). It may cost the company some money in wasted product to make a Type II error, but this is negligible in the face of lives lost land potential litigation over a Type I error. Therefore, the degree of confidence for a Type I error may conceivably extend beyond the 3 limit.

INDEX NUMBERS

General Considerations

The index number is used to demonstrate, in a comparative way, the change of a certain variable over time. Index numbers are widely used. In many cases, the problems and considerations in the development of index numbers are nonmathematical in nature. Judgment may enter into the derivation of an index number. The following are some of the major considerations.

Comparability of Data

Nothing is so astounding as the growth of personal computing. The home computer, like many other electronic devices, didn't exist 10 years ago. For things that didn't exist, there is no basis of comparison. But what about changes in refrigerators during that time? Or automobiles? Often there is simply too much qualitative change to allow a valid and objective comparison.

Selection of Items

For specific areas, there is no question about the selection of the items which will be the basis of comparison. In such areas as general purpose indices, however, there is some difficulty. What items are included in the Consumer Price Index? What about the Dow Jones stock indices?

Base Year and Given Year

Any comparison involves two or more elements. Index numbers, as mentioned, usually compare changes over time. The period against which one is making the comparison is called the base year. The year or period which is being compared is called the given year. In most cases, the base year should not be in the too distant past, since economic and technological changes occur so rapidly. Also, the base year should be representative of a period of stability. One of the most common periods for a base year is 1957–1959. In comparative analysis, the base year is almost always set equal to 100: 1957–1959 = 100.

Application of Weights

Where several items are included in the composition of an index number, it is often the case that these items have varying relative significance. For example, in the Consumer Price Index, fuel oil has a greater importance to the family than theater tickets. Consequently, a subjective weighting system would be applied.

Appropriate Formula

Index numbers may be calculated according to a great variety of methods. Choosing the appropriate formula is just as important in this case as the choice among the mean, median, and mode for averages. The following sections give an overview as well as some examples of the more widely used methods in calculating index numbers. The following notation shall apply in all cases: I = number; p_0 = base year prices; p_n = given year prices; q_0 = quantities; q_n = given year quantities; v_0 = base year value; and v_n = given value.

Types of Index Number

Price Relatives

A simple price relative is the ration of a single commodity price in a given year to the price of the same commodity in a base year. This ratio may be expressed as a percentage by multiplying the quotient by 100. The percent sign is usually dropped since it is universally understood.

If the price of bacon was 60 cents per pound in 1958 (base year) and \$1.20 in a given year, the price relative is given as:

$$I = \frac{p_n}{p_0} = \frac{120}{60} = 2.0 \times 100 = 200$$

One may interpret this as follows: The given price of bacon is 200% of its 1958 price; or, the price of bacon has risen 100 percentage points over the period. Note that I for the base year is always equal to 100.

Quantity Relatives

In some cases, one is interested in the quantity (volume) increase or decrease of a certain commodity over the years. For example, what has been the relative change in the number of bushels of wheat that the United States exports from 1957 to a given year (1957 = 100)? Then:

$$I = \frac{q_0}{q_n} = \frac{50 \text{ (million)}}{30 \text{ (million)}} = 1.67 \times 100 = 167.$$

Volume exports of wheat to other countries have increased by 167% between 1957 and the given year.

Value Relatives

In economics and business, the value of any product is determined by the mathematical product of its price and quantity (pq). One may then compare values of certain products over time.

For example, in 1957, a color television cost $500 and 4 million were sold in that year. In a given year, the same TV set cost $200 and 8 million were sold. What has been the change in value of the same type of set over the period between 1957 and the given year?

$$I = \frac{p_n q_n}{p_0 q_0} = \frac{(200)(8)}{(500)(4)} = .8 \times 100 = 80$$

One may conclude this that the value of a certain TV set in a given year has dropped by 20 percent over the same set in 1957.

Link Relatives

One may link successive tears together to form a sort of moving index number. For example, if the quantities of certain commodity over a period of 5 years have been 10, 15, 25, and 50, respectively, then the link relative index numbers are as follows:

$$\frac{15}{10} = 150; \quad \frac{25}{15} = 167; \quad \frac{40}{25} = 160; \quad \text{and} \quad \frac{50}{40} = 125$$

Simple Aggregate

Using a price relative as an example, the simple aggregate index number is calculated by taking the sum of all the product prices under consideration for the given year and dividing by a similarly derived sum for the prices in the base year:

$$I = \frac{p_n}{p_0}$$

Fisher's Ideal Index

To account for the relative importance of various items and their respective units of issue, e.g., gallon, pounds, etc., the Fisher Ideal Index may be used. The formula for this index is:

$$I = \sqrt{\left(\frac{\sum p_n q_0}{\sum p_0 q_0}\right)\left(\frac{\sum p_n q_n}{\sum p_0 q_n}\right)}$$

Marshall-Edgeworth Index

This index uses a weighted aggregate method. The weights are computed as the mean of the base and given year quantities. If

$$I = \frac{\sum p_n q_t}{\sum p_0 q_t}$$

and

$$q_t = \frac{q_0 + q_n}{2},$$

then

$$I = \frac{\sum p_n(q_0 + q_n)}{\sum p_0(q_0 + q_n)}.$$

QUESTIONS

1. A total of 35 individuals failed an examination. If 14% failed, how many individuals took the exam?
   A. 590
   B. 250
   C. 49
   D. 490
2. All of the following are essential parts of a linear programming problem except one. Which one?
   A. The objective function or optimization criterion
   B. The iterative technique required to find the solution
   C. The linear restraints imposed upon the variables
   D. The matrix of correlation coefficients of all pairs of variables
3. A company *experiences* sales of \$3M, \$5M, \$9M, \$6M, \$8M, \$10M, and \$12M in consecutive years. Using the moving average technique, in three-year cycles, it could anticipate sales of the next year of:
   A. \$8M
   B. \$10M
   C. \$12M
   D. \$13M
4. ''Random'' and ''cluster'' sampling techniques are well known. A third sampling technique would be:
   A. Universal clustering
   B. Cluster averaging
   C. Logical
   D. Stratified
5. Which of the following is the binary representation of hexadecimal 4A?
   A. 01010111
   B. 01001010
   C. 10110100
   D. 00101010
6. The queuing theory may be used to determine which of the following?
   A. The Monte Carlo technique
   B. The time required for systems design
   C. The size of computer file records
   D. What delays may be expected with data collection equipment
7. In the equation $A = P(1 + i)^n$, A may be described as:
   A. An exponential function of n
   B. A quadratic function of n

C. A linear function of n
D. A logarithmic function of n

8. The probability of an event which is certain to occur is:
A. Infinite
B. 0
C. +1
D. −1

9. If A is the amount of money to be paid after n periods of time, and i is the current interest rate used in present value calculations, which of the following formulae would be used to determine the present value (P) of the debt?
A. $P = A(1 + i)^n$
B. $P = A(1 + i)^n$
C. $P = A/(1 + i)^n$
D. $P = A(1 - i^n)$

10. A bin contains 100 tape rings—60 yellow, 30 green, and 10 black. What is the probability of obtaining a black ring within the first four tries, assuming that an incorrect color is returned to the bin?
A. .6248
B. .5011
C. .4000
D. .3439

11. $500 is placed at 8% interest compounded semiannually for five years. What will the approximate final amount be?
A. $540
B. $680
C. $684
D. $740

12. What percentage of a normal distribution is included between two standard deviations above and below the mean?
A. 50%
B. 68%
C. 90%
D. 95%

13. Given:

$$A = \begin{bmatrix} 6 & 2 \\ 2 & 5 \end{bmatrix}; \quad B = \begin{bmatrix} -5 & -1 \\ 6 & -7 \end{bmatrix}$$

Add $A + B$:

(a) $\begin{bmatrix} 11 & 3 \\ 4 & 2 \end{bmatrix}$ (b) $\begin{bmatrix} -11 & -2 \\ 12 & -12 \end{bmatrix}$

(c) $\begin{bmatrix} -5 & 3 \\ 8 & 12 \end{bmatrix}$ (d) $\begin{bmatrix} 1 & 1 \\ 8 & -2 \end{bmatrix}$

14. To obtain what is known as a frequency polygon, or "curve," it will first be necessary to:
A. Define the class points of a histogram.
B. Draw a bell-shaped curve.

C. Construct a beta curve.
D. Start from a straight line.

15. Slope of the linear equation $y = 8x + 6$ is:
A. y
B. 8
C. x
D. 6

16. A "less than" ogive would:
A. Slope upward
B. Slope downward
C. Remain level
D. Not be possible to construct

17. Reduce the following to simplest form:

$$\sqrt[3]{54p^3q^5}$$

(a) $18p\sqrt[3]{3pq^5}$
(b) $27\sqrt[3]{2p^3q^5}$
(c) $6p\sqrt[3]{9q^5}$
(d) $3pq^2\sqrt[3]{18pq}$
(e) $3pq\sqrt[3]{2q^2}$

18. The central limit theorem states that:
A. The mean of a group of numbers must equal the arithmetic average
B. A converging series must approach an asymptotic limit
C. The expected value of a random variable is the arithmetic mean
D. The sampling distribution of random sample means is normally distributed.

19. Solve the following for x:

$$3x - 4 > \frac{7x}{2} + 2$$

A. $-x > 12$
B. $x < -12$
C. Either A or B
D. Neither A nor B

20. A statistical device for measuring relative changes in several variables over time is called:
A. Average
B. Stratified sample
C. Index number
D. Median

21. Using exponential smoothing, if the effect of a term is 10% in its first period (alpha is 0.10), what is its effect in the third period?
A. 12.1%
B. 10.1%
C. 9.0%
D. 8.1%

22. If two coins are tossed, what is the probability of getting a head and then a tail?
A. $\frac{1}{4}$
B. $\frac{1}{3}$

C. $\frac{1}{2}$
D. $\frac{2}{3}$

23. The Pythagorean Theorem is useful in obtaining:
A. The length of the hypotenuse of a right triangle
B. The sum of the angles of a right triangle
C. The sum of two sides of an equilateral triangle
D. The sum of the three sides of any triangle

24. Monte Carlo analysis is a simulation technique for problems having:
A. A stochastic basis
B. A probabilistic basis
C. A residual basis
D. Empirical basis

25. An integer p is a prime number if it is neither 0 nor $+1$ and if its only divisor(s) is (are):
A. $+1$
B. -1
C. ± 1
D. $\pm p, \pm 1$

26. What is the difference between a combination and a permutation?
A. Arrangement matter in combinations
B. The number of permutations may never exceed the number of combinations
C. Combinations are unique groupings without regard to arrangements
D. Combinations are factorial arrangements with no esoteric limits

27. If $y = a^x$, then $x =$:

(a) $\log_2 \left(\frac{y}{a}\right)$ (b) $\frac{\log y}{x}$

(c) $\frac{y}{a}$ (d) $\frac{\log y}{\log a}$

28. When numbers or values are arranged according to size, the value of the middle term is called the:
A. Arithmetic average
B. Mode
C. Median
D. Average

29. If $n = 8$, then n is:
A. Undetermined
B. Irrational
C. Negative
D. An integer

30. If a constant of two is added to each series of numbers, what is the effect on the mean?
A. Mean will double
B. Mean will increase by two
C. No effect
D. Depends on the number of terms

31. A statute mile is 5,280 feet and a meter is 39.37 inches. A map shows the Matterhorn as 4.50 kilometers high. Rounding where necessary, we conclude that the height *in feet* is:
A. 14,764
B. 10,560
C. 15,324
D. 14,271

32. If demand is elastic:
A. A decline of price will result in a decline in total revenue.
B. A decline in price will result in an increase in total revenue.
C. An increase in price will result in an increase in total revenue.
D. An increase in price will have no effect on total revenue.

33. Assume the dollar is traded at 2.37 Deutschemarks (DM). In the Frankfurt railroad station, a man spends 3.50 DM for a light lunch, pays 1.50 DM for a copy of *Der Speigel*, and returns $11.50 that he borrowed in New York to a friend. His total dollar expenditure is about:
A. $13.50
B. $15.20
C. $13.60
D. $16.50

34. A widget manufacturer is constantly evaluating the acceptability of its widgets in the marketplace. A means to evaluate that data is:
A. A statistical comparison of market share
B. The quality control within the firm
C. Any change in the number of styles of widgets on the market
D. a 10% sampling on the production line

35. The sum $(\frac{3}{4} + \frac{2}{3} + \frac{5}{6})$ is approximately:
A. 2.520
B. 2.250
C. 2.501
D. 1.752

36. If five men are chosen at random from a normal population whose height ranges from 48 to 84 inches, the probability that their mean height is 80 inches is best described as:
A. Impossible
B. Highly improbable
C. About a 50/50 chance
D. Highly probable

37. In the right triangle having side a opposite angle A, side b opposite angle B, and side c opposite angle C, with C being a right angle:
A. $C < B$
B. $c^2 = a^2 + b^2$
C. $a/c = \tan C$
D. $1/\sin A = \cos B$

38. The average of many samples tends to be ______ regardless of the nature of the distribution from which the samples came.
A. Discrete
B. Geometrical
C. Normally distributed
D. Truncated

39. If $A = (a_{ij})$, the multiplication of matrix A by a scalar produces a new matrix B:
A. B is the inverse of A
B. B is related to A
C. It is an impossible matrix operation
D. B is the cofactor of A

40. Which of the following is not a measure of central tendency?
A. Arithmetic mean
B. Median

C. Standard deviation
D. Mode

41. The average of the first six terms of the progression 1,000, 100, 10, . . . , etc., *to five significant digits* is:
A. 185.185
B. 18.519
C. 222.222
D. 185.19

42. Which of the following is not a measure of dispersion?
A. Standard deviation
B. Range
C. Variance
D. Mean

43. Select the *seventh* term of the series 1, 2, 4, 7, 11, . . . :
A. 16
B. 18
C. 21
D. 22

44. If individuals are arranged according to height, and the largest group having the same height consists of six people, and there is only one such group of six, their height is called the:
A. Average
B. Median
C. Mode
D. Mean

45. A farmer has a rectangular collection area of 1,000 square feet, one side of which is 20 feet. The other side is:
A. 500 feet
B. 10 feet
C. 100 feet
D. 50 feet

46. If two variables are so related that the first is determined when the second is given:
A. The first is a parameter
B. The second is a dependent variable
C. The second is a function of the first
D. The first is a function of the second

47. A measured value of 22.2 is to be multiplied by Π (3.1416). The *least* value which can be entered for Π without disturbing the accuracy of the result is:
A. 3.14
B. $\frac{33}{7}$
C. 3.1
D. 3.142

48. The derivation of a function is the:
A. Limit of the ratio of the increment of the independent variable to the increment of the function, as the latter approaches zero
B. Limit of the ratio of the increment of the function to the increment of the independent variable, as the latter approaches zero
C. Limit of the ratio of the increment of the independent variable to the increment of the function, as the latter approaches infinity
D. Limit of the ratio of the increment of the function to the increment of the independent variable, as the latter approaches infinity

49. The sum of an even number of many odd numbers is:
A. Always odd
B. Sometimes even
C. Always even
D. Either odd or even

50. If V is the variance and σ is the standard deviation, then:
A. $\sigma = 2V$
B. $\sigma^2 = V$
C. $\sigma = V^2$
D. $\sigma = 2V^2$

51. Given $m = pn^2$; if $m = 1$ and $p = 2$, then n is:
A. An irrational number
B. $\frac{1}{4}$
C. $\frac{1}{2}$
D. $\frac{\sqrt{2}}{1}$

52. The average deviation of individual values around the mean is:
A. Greater than the standard deviation
B. Less than the standard deviation
C. Zero
D. Half the range

53. Pick the set below whose elements are all prime numbers:
A. 1, 13, 12
B. 11, 3, 5
C. 7, 9, 17
D. 3, 5, 15

54. Given the array 1, 3, 5, 6, 6, 6, 7, 7, 9, 11
A. Mean = median
B. Mode = mean
C. Median = mode
D. All of the above

55. The equation $y = a + bx$ can be rewritten:
A. $x = \dfrac{y + a}{b}$
B. $x = \dfrac{y - b}{z}$
C. $x = \dfrac{y}{b} - \dfrac{a}{b}$
D. $bx = y + a$

56. Given the data 33.5, 37.5, 31.5, 34.5, 35.5, the arithmetic mean (average) of the data is:
A. 34.3
B. 34.5
C. 35.5
D. 34.4

57. There is a fallacy—find the error:

$a = b$	Let $b = a + b$
$ab = a^2$	but $a = b$
$ab - b^2 = a^2 - b^2$	so $b = 2b$
$b(a - b) = (a + b)(a - b)$	and $1 = 2$

A. $a^2 - b^2$ does not exist
B. ab can't equal a^2
C. Division by $(a - b)$ is illegal
D. $ab - b^2$ can't be factored

58. Stratified random sampling tends to:
A. Increase sample size because there are several population groups
B. Decrease sample size because special attention is given only to the significant groups
C. Provide a lower sampling error with the same sample size as compared with unrestricted
D. Increase the standard deviation of the populations

59. Given: $p = m - nq$, where m and n are positive constants. Which of the following is correct?
A. As q increases, p increases
B. As q increases, p increases
C. As p decreases, q decreases
D. As p decreases, m increases

60. A properly selected statistical sample of a large population will always:
A. Reduce the amount of effort required to ascertain characteristics of the population
B. Provide a mathematical estimate of the accuracy of the calculated population characteristics
C. Be an unbiased random sample of the entire population
D. Be of adequate size to satisfy confidence criteria if a presample was used to determine the required sample size

61. Three people in a group can have three two-person conversations. If a fourth person enters the group, the number of two-person conversations increases by:
A. 1
B. 2
C. 3
D. 4

62. In the following Venn Diagram the unshaded area represents the area defined by

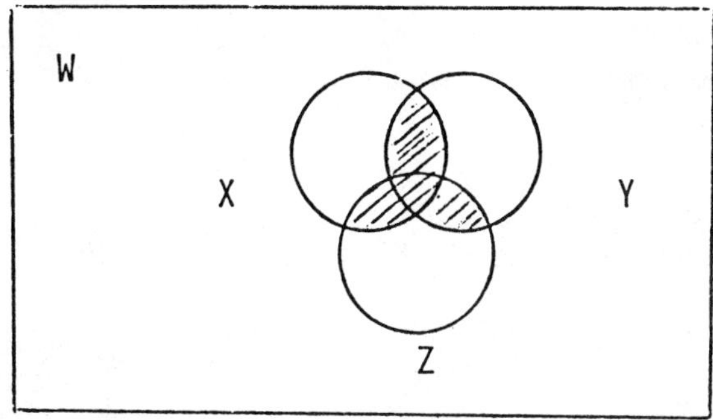

A. W − (X + Y + Z)
B. W − (XY + XZ + YZ − 2XYZ)
C. W + (X − Y − Z)
D. W + (X − Y − Z + XY + XZ + YZ)

63. How to weigh a Christmas turkey on a 16-ounce postal scale. A yardstick rests on a chair back C and the scale S, and the turkey hangs at T:

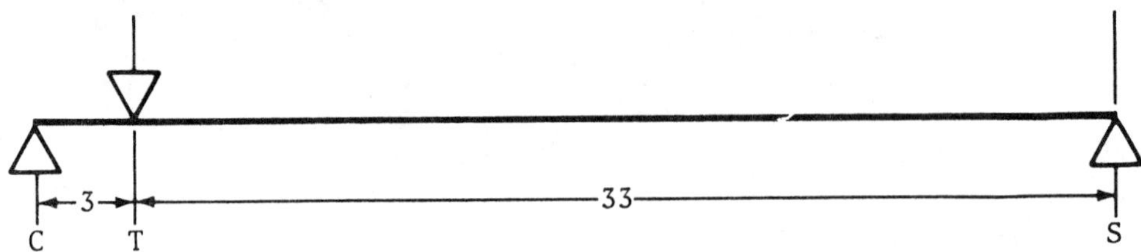

The distances CT and TS are 3 and 33 inches, respectively, and the scale registers 15 ounces. The turkey weight is:
A. 9.5 pounds
B. 17.2 pounds
C. 11.25 pounds
D. 12.4 pounds

64. The probability of getting a total of either two or three on a single throw of two dice is:
A. $\frac{1}{36}$
B. $\frac{1}{18}$
C. $\frac{1}{12}$
D. $\frac{1}{9}$

65. Multiply $(a + b)(a - b)$. The answer is:
A. $a^2 - 2ab - b^2$
B. $a^2 - 2ab + b^2$
C. $a^2 - b^2$
D. $a^2 + 2ab + b^2$

66. A program may process two types of transactions. The time consumed by a type B transaction is twice that for type A. The probabilities of occurrence are .7 for type A the .3 for type B. If 60 minutes of computer time were scheduled when all transactions were type A, how much time should be scheduled for an equal number of transactions of the potential mix?
A. 60 minutes
B. 72 minutes
C. 84 minutes
D. 90 minutes

67. The sine, cosine, and tangent are:
A. The inverse of cosecant, secant, and cotangent
B. The reciprocal of a positive number series
C. The function of an acute angle
D. The function of an obtuse angle

68. What is the number of permutations of 10 objects taken 6 at a time?
A. 10!/4!
B. 151,200
C. Both A and B
D. Neither A nor B

69. Given the sequence 2, 4, 5, 10, 11, . . . , what will the next sequential number be?
A. 22
B. 16
C. 20
D. 24

70. A scatter diagram is a useful visual aid in:
A. Regression and correlation analysis
B. Solving a polynomial equation
C. Constructing a bar graph
D. Solving a linear programming problem

71. A root of the equation $2x^2 - 4x + 2 = 0$ is:
A. 1
B. 2
C. 3
D. 4

72. To construct a frequency polygon, it is first necessary to:
A. Define the class mid-points of the frequency distribution
B. Draw a normal curve with the same mean and standard deviation
C. Form the cumulative frequency distribution
D. Compute the mean, median, and mode

73. A logarithm is:
A. The same as the cube root
B. The same as the sine of an angle
C. The exponent to which the base is raised
D. The measure of correlation between the base and the exponent

74. What is the number of combinations of 5 objects taken 2 at a time?
A. 5
B. 10
C. 15
D. 20

75. The set of *integers* between 20 and 21 is:
A. Null
B. {0}
C. 2
D. Infinite

76. If the occurrence of event A prevents the occurrence of event B and the occurrence of event B prevents the occurrence of A, what is the probability that A or B will occur?
A. The product of the probabilities
B. The sum of the probabilities
C. The difference between the probabilities
D. The quotient of the probabilities

77. In finding an answer to a numerical problem, the result cannot be more accurate than the *least* accurate number. Under those constraints, what is the sum of the following list

234.7
1.258
3.0
4.56

A. 243
B. 244
C. 242.5
D. 243.52

78. The statistical expression $B = \Sigma_{i=1}^{k} a_1 x_1$ is the same as $B = AX$, where A and X are:
A. Vectors
B. Scalars
C. Velocities
D. Radicals

79. If $f(x) = x^2 + 5$, what is $f(5)$?
A. 25
B. 5
C. 30
D. 10

80. If the probability of success is $P(s)$ and the probability of failure is $P(f)$, for an event's occurrence, which of the following is true?
A. $P(s) = 1 + P(f)$
B. $P(s) = 1 - P(f)$
C. $P(s) = 1/P(f)$
D. $P(s) = 1(P(f))$

81. What is the *maximum* number of codes that can be generated if the code consists of two letters or digits follows by three digits, *excluding* the letters 0 and 1 to preclude their confusion with 0 and 1:
A. 1,156,000
B. 576,000
C. 1,208,000
D. 90,000

82. If A and B have a correlation coefficient of 0.95, this means:
A. A and B vary similarly
B. A and B vary inversely
C. B caused A to vary in a particular way
D. A caused B to vary in a particular way

83. The following table represents what type of function?

A	B	R
1	1	0
1	0	1
0	1	1
0	0	0

A. And
B. Or
C. Not
D. Exclusive Or

84. The reason for choosing a random sample form a large set of data is:
A. To be sure to include at least 25% of the large set
B. To give greater weight to higher valued items
C. To approximate the characteristics of the large set with less expenditure of time and cost
D. To be sure that it follows the normal curve

85. Log_3 81 equals:
A. 3
B. 9
C. 4
D. 8

86. How many groups of four people can be constructed from eight people if each group must have either Mr. Smith or Mr. Jones, but not both of them (there is only one of each)?
A. 40
B. 60
C. 168
D. 210

87. The area under a curve may be found by:
A. Integration
B. Differentiation
C. Least squares
D. Regression analysis

88. If A and B are mutually exclusive events, $P(A) = .3$, and $P(B) = .5$, what is the $P(A \cup B)$?
A. .2
B. .8
C. .65
D. .5

89. The transportation problem is a special case of:
A. Zero-sum programming
B. Nonlinear programming
C. Linear programming
D. Dynamic programming

90. What is the range of the following sample?

Value	Occurrences
20	1
40	3
55	4
106	6
280	3
300	2

A. 5
B. 20
C. 280
D. 300

91. Given $A \neq B > C$; A is:
A. Less than C
B. Greater than C
C. Never equal to C
D. Cannot be determined from the problem

92. Which of the following go together in a set definition?
A. Range, median, and variance

B. Range, variance, and deviation
C. Median, variance, and deviation
D. Range, median, and deviation

93. Under Pascal's Law, what number will complete the pyramid?

1
1 1
1 2 1
1 3 3 1
1 4 ? 4 1

A. 3
B. 4
C. 5
D. 6

94. A chi-square test results in:
A. A low value for insignificant data
B. A negative value for an invalid set of data
C. A high value for results different from the expected
D. A value of 1.0 for a perfect normal distribution

95. Which of the following is not included in the Boolean Laws?
A. Distributive
B. Commutative
C. Associative
D. Conjunctive

96. Which of the following is used as a measure of the variations of a set of numbers about their mean?
A. Median
B. Range
C. Standard deviation
D. Mode

97. The residue (remainder) of 26 modulo 8 is:
A. $\frac{1}{4}$
B. 3
C. 2
D. 6

98. Exponential smoothing is best described by which of the following terms?
A. Derivative average
B. Moving average
C. Weighted moving average
D. Simple average

99. Another form of $\frac{X^2 + Y^8}{X^6} - \frac{Y^2}{X^3}$ is:

(a) $\frac{X^2 + XY^8 - X^2Y^2}{X^2}$

(b) $\frac{X^2 + Y^8 - Y^4}{X^6}$

(c) $\dfrac{X^6 + X^3Y^8 - Y^2}{X^9}$

(d) $\dfrac{X^2 + Y^8 - X^3Y^2}{X^6}$

100. Which of the following sets of data completely specifies a normal curve?
A. Mean, median, mode
B. Mean, standard deviation
C. Range, average deviation
D. Mean, correlation coefficient

ANSWERS

1. B	**26.** C	**51.** A	**76.** B
2. D	**27.** D	**52.** C	**77.** B
3. B	**28.** C	**53.** B	**78.** A
4. D	**29.** D	**54.** D	**79.** C
5. D	**30.** B	**55.** C	**80.** B
6. D	**31.** A	**56.** B	**81.** A
7. A	**32.** D	**57.** C	**82.** A
8. C	**33.** C	**58.** C	**83.** D
9. C	**34.** A	**59.** A	**84.** C
10. D	**35.** B	**60.** B	**85.** C
11. D	**36.** B	**61.** C	**86.** A
12. D	**37.** B	**62.** B	**87.** A
13. D	**38.** C	**63.** C	**88.** B
14. A	**39.** B	**64.** C	**89.** C
15. B	**40.** C	**65.** C	**90.** C
16. A	**41.** D	**66.** C	**91.** D
17. E	**42.** D	**67.** A	**92.** B
18. D	**43.** D	**68.** C	**93.** D
19. C	**44.** C	**69.** A	**94.** C
20. C	**45.** D	**70.** A	**95.** D
21. D	**46.** D	**71.** A	**96.** C
22. A	**47.** A	**72.** A	**97.** C
23. A	**48.** B	**73.** C	**98.** C
24. B	**49.** C	**74.** B	**99.** D
25. D	**50.** B	**75.** A	**100.** B

TUTORIAL

1. $.14X = 35$; $X = 250$
2. The first three are parts of the linear programming problem. The answer doesn't make a whole lot of sense.
3. ($8M + $10M + $12M)/3 = $10M
4. An example of stratified sampling would be "all male," "ages by decade," etc.
5. 0010 = 4; 1010 = A

6. The Monte Carlo method is to make decisions under uncertainty. B and C don't make sense. Queuing is analogous to "getting in line," which would make D a suitable answer.
7. *A* is, of course, the annuity. *n* is the time period. The key is the word "function."
8. The probability range is 0 to +1.
9. The explanation is that the annuity is divided by the principal plus interest for the period.
10. There are two schools of thought on this question. One holds that C (.40) is the correct answer. Here's why: Since there are 10 rings of that color in the bin, and since the incorrect one is returned each time, the probability of getting one of that color is thus $\frac{10}{100}$ (or $\frac{1}{10}$) *each* time. The probability of *not* getting a black ring is $\frac{90}{100}$ or .9. Therefore in four trials the probability of *not* getting a black ring is $.9^4 = .6561$. Since +1 is the universe, subtracting the probability of *not* getting a black ring (.6561) will leave a probability of getting one as .3439.
11. The formula is $P = 500(1 + .04)$
12. Knowledge question—look it up in a statistics book in the section dealing with degrees of freedom.
13. The process of parallel addition merely adds the algebraic sum to its correspondent. Thus, +6 and −5 become 1; +2 and +6 become +8, etc.
14. The class points of a histogram are the averages of each class. Thus, if you have a histogram of the number of people in an age class, let's say classified into decades, the class point would be the midpoint (or 5) in each class.
15. In a linear equation, the slope (*a*) is equal to the change rise divided by the change in run. In this case, the value of *a* is 8.
16. An ogive is a frequency distribution used to depict *cumulative* frequency. The ordinate at each point is the cumulative frequency. The cumulation can be either increasing or decreasing. Thus, a "less than" ogive would slope upward as additives combine to the cumulation.
17. In finding cube root, it's necessary to separate under the radical (as factors) those things which are natural cubes. 54 is not a natural cube, but the factors 2(27) will produce a natural cube ($27 = 3 \times 3 \times 3$), so the cube root (3) is extracted. The factor p^3 has a natural cube root (p). The factor q^5 can also be expressed as q^3q^2, allowing q to be extracted as the cube root.
18. The central limit theorem states, in general that if a population has a finite variance of σ^2 and a mean of μ then the distribution of sample means from samples of N independent observations approaches a normal distribution with a variance of σ^2/N and mean μ as sample N increases. When N is very large, the sampling distribution of N is approximately normal.
19. Don't be concerned about the presence of the inequality symbol. For computational purposes, you can treat it just like an equal sign. Beginning with formula, and clearing the denominator, we get $(6x - 8) > (7x + 4)$. Combining terms, we get $-x > 12$. Now, make x positive, reversing the carat, making $x < -12$.
20. Sampling technique is a statistical *method*, not a device. An index number is the method whereby *groups of data* can be determined to have changed. There are many methods whereby an index number can be determined, and the method is not critical, *provided that it is consistently used.* Let's suppose, for instance, you have a histographic distribution with class intervals of 10, such as people's ages, and you are building the histogram to depict the number of people who fit into each class. Each class has a mid-point, or it may appear as a fixed deviation from the mid-point. Let's say, for instance, that you are taking the arithmetic mean of each age with the *mode* of the age class, that is, say 60% of the ages are 2% (within the 21–30 age class). Now the key is to *measure the changes*. If this survey happened to be on the ages of a given locale, people tend to move away from or into the locale. Thus, the arithmetic mean within each class will shift. The deviation from the index number, therefore, is useful in measuring changes in the groups of data.
21. When an exponent is "smoothed," it is diminished by the value of its "alpha," in this case .10. Now, the base of the first period was 10%; for the second period, the exponent would be

"smoothed" by alpha (10%), moving from 10 to 9; at the end of the second period, 9 is the new base. 10% "smoothing" from that base would produce 8.1% for the third period. You can see that it would never reach zero, but would approach it at a diminishing rate and would never go negative.

22. The question asks about the possibility of getting a head and a tail on the toss of two coins. Note that it very careful does say a head and *then* a tail. This, therefore, implies that both coins have not been tossed simultaneously. Let's first establish that the maximum probability of a sample universe is 1.0. Therefore, all incidents or experiments will add up to 1.0. Now, let's examine the way you'd toss them (and, of course, the statistician assumes the coin is "balanced"). Now, when I flip a "balanced" coin, a 50/50 chance of getting *either* a head or a tail is possible (technically, I have a 100% chance of getting either a tail or a head, but you know what I mean—they have an equal opportunity to appear). Thus, the probability of getting a head is .5, as is the probability of getting a tail. The same holds true for the second coin. Now, when both coins are tossed, the probability is the *product* of the two because the events are independent. Thus, (.5 × .5) or .25, or $\frac{1}{4}$.
The possible combinations are:

Coin 1, head; Coin 2, head
Coin 1, head; Coin 2, tail
Coin 2, tail; Coin 2, head
Coin 2, tail; Coin 2, tail

If the problem were to ask for them in any sequence, then the probability would be .5, as opposites appear in either of two combinations.

23. Pythagoras' Theorem states: The square of the hypotenuse is equal to the sum of the squares of the other two sides. It takes the form:

$$C^2 \text{ (hypotenuse)} = A^2 + B^2 \text{ (sides)}$$

24. A and B are nearly synonymous in referring to the results of a chance experiment. Stochastic means "having to do with variables." Empirical means "observable"—the real items which can be simulated, as opposed to simulating unknowns. Monte Carlo is a probabilistic method.

25. A prime number (p) is not divisible by any integer larger than 1 and its own absolute value. Its only divisors then are ± 1 and $\pm p$.

26. The difference is that permutations are the number of unique groupings *with* regard to arrangements.

27. $y = a^x$
$y = x \log a$ and $x = \log y / \log a$

28. The key to this is the phrase "middle term," or median, not middle value. If our sequence of numbers were 1, 3, 5, 7, 9, the median is 5, which also happens to be the mean. If the sequence of numbers were 1, 3, 4, 7, 9, the median would be 4, while the arithmetic mean would be 4.8.

29. It is set equal to an integer; therefore it *is* an integer.

30. You'll have to write down a set of numbers to prove this one, but it *is* true that the mean will increase by two if a constant of two is added to every term. Consider:

$$1 + 3 + 5 + 7 + 9 = 25 \text{ (mean 5)}$$
$$3 + 5 + 7 + 9 + 11 = 35 \text{ (mean 7)}$$

31. As it works out, there is no precisely correct answer given to this (so we have rounded it off to the nearest whole number). One of the answers is very close, however. Here is how it *should* work: The product of 4.50, 1,000 and 39.37 produces the height of the mountain in inches. Divide this by 12 to produce feet.

32. The principle of elasticity of demand is a discussion of what will happen to revenue if changes in pricing structure are made. It will vary with the product and with the desire or demand for the product, as well as with the closely substitutable products which are available. If a widget goes up in price and a competing widget does not go up, then you most probably would purchase the competing widget, unless you had a preference for the original. Enough would have a preference for the original so that a stable revenue picture might be maintained, despite the fact that the units sold might decrease.

33. Here's how it's computed:

$$\begin{array}{lll} \text{Lunch} & = & 3.50 \text{ DM} \\ \text{Magazine} & = & \underline{1.50 \text{ DM}} \\ & & 5.00 \text{ DM} \\ 5.00/2.37 & = & \$2.11 + 11.50 = \$13.61 \end{array}$$

34. The simplest means is to determine the movement of market share from month to month. If it climbs, this is evidence of acceptability of product.

35. This is solved by converting to a common denominator and then adding:

$$\frac{3}{4} = \frac{9}{12}$$

$$\frac{2}{3} = \frac{8}{12}$$

$$\frac{5}{6} = \frac{10}{12}$$

$$\frac{27}{12} = \frac{9}{4} = 2\frac{1}{4} = 2.250$$

36. "Normal," means an even distribution. To achieve an arithmetic mean of 80 inches (6 feet, 8 inches), what would have to be the range, given a low point of 5 feet, for example. To find a person of this height in a normal distribution would be highly improbable.

37. This is the Pythagorean Theorem again.

38. The rule is simple—many samples produce a normal distribution.

39. If A is $\begin{vmatrix} a & b \\ c & d \end{vmatrix}$ and the scalar is 2 multiplying the matrix by two produces:

$$\begin{vmatrix} a & b \\ c & d \end{vmatrix} + \begin{vmatrix} a & b \\ c & d \end{vmatrix} = \begin{vmatrix} 2a & 2b \\ 2c & 2d \end{vmatrix} = 2\begin{vmatrix} a & b \\ c & d \end{vmatrix}$$

40. Standard deviation is a measure of tendency away (dispersion) from the center.

41. The total would be 1111.11 (for the first six terms). Divided by 6, this comes out to 185.185, or 185.19.

42. The mean is a measurement of central tendency.

43. The series begins with 1 and adds the arithmetic series 1, 2, 3, etc., i.e.,

Series	1		2		4		7		11		(16)		(22)	
		1		2		3		4		5		6		7
Term #	1		2		3		4		5		6		7	

44. Definition question—the mode has more of any one value than any other grouping.
45. A = W * L and 1,000 = 20L. L is therefore 1,000/20 = 50.
46. The second cannot be found unless the first is initially found, and the value would vary depending upon the first.
47. The *best* for a product, use as many significant digits as shown in the *least* accurate of the factors.
48. B is the correct definition. It's the limit as the increment approaches zero.
49. An even number is equally divisible by 2; an odd number leaves a remainder of 1. Look at the last digits and write 1 for odd and 2 for even, for example:

ODD number of odd numbers	1 + 1 + 1	= 3 ODD
ODD number of odd numbers	1 + 1 + 1 + 1 + 1	= 5 ODD
EVEN number of odd numbers	1 + 1	= 2 EVEN
EVEN number of odd numbers	1 + 1 + 1 + 1	= 4 EVEN

50. The variance is the square of the standard deviation.
51. In the formula, you will see that n works out to be 1 divided by the square root of 2, which is not $\frac{1}{2}$ or $\frac{1}{4}$, and is an irrational number.
52. The average deviation can be depicted in this manner: First, calculate the deviation from the mean. Next, sum all the deviations. Subtract the sum of the means from the sum of the deviations. Recall that the sum of the deviations divided by the number will be the mean. Subtract the one from the other, and the answer is zero.
53. A prime number is divisible only by itself and 1, e.g., 1, 2, 3, 5, 7, 11, 13, 17 ... Sets A, C, and D do not qualify because 12, 9, and 15 do not qualify as primes.
54. I don't generally like ''all of the above'' answers, but this question services to reinforce the meanings of the words mean, mode, and median.
55. $y = a + bx$; $y - a = bx$, meaning $x = (y - a)/b$ or $(y/b) - (a/b)$.
56. Add them up and divide by 4.
57. When division by $(a - b)$ occurs at step 4, we're dividing by zero. $a^2 - b^2$ can exist, brought about by the subtraction of identical factors on both sides of the equation. ab can equal a^2 as both sides of the equation were multiplied by a. $ab - b^2$ could be factored to $b(a - b)$. Dividing by zero is probably not actually illegal, but we would not put such a law beyond certain legislatures. Mathematically speaking, it is an ''undefined operation'' that has no meaning, in spite of the common belief that dividing by zero yields ''infinity.''
58. This method of sampling decreases the standard deviations of each population as compared to the total population, whereas the others are less precise, involving improved standard deviations and other factors of judgment.
59. Let's put it in simple terms. Suppose $p = 8$, $m = 11$, $nq = 3$. Now raise q (of the nq) by -1 to 2, and we have a value of 6 to balance against 8. In statistical terms, the derivative of $m - nq = -n$, which means a decreasing function.
60. C is incorrect because the sampling need not necessarily be unbiased. A and D are useless buzzwords.
61. When we have three people, the conversation goes 1–2, 1–3, 2–3. When the fourth person enters,

the following combinations exist: 1–2, 1–3, 1–4, 2–3, 2–4, 3–4. Any cribbage player can tell you that!

Statistically, that looks like this:

$$\frac{4!}{2!\,2!} = \frac{(3 \times 3)\,(2 \times 1)}{(2 \times 1)\,(2 \times 1)} = \frac{4 \times 3}{2 \times 1} = \frac{12}{2} = 6$$

The general case is:

$$c = \frac{n!}{(n - r)!\,r!}$$

Where n = number of things
r = how many at a time
c = number of combinations

62. W is the universe, or technically 100% (1). From W is subtracted the areas of circles X, Y, and Z, except:

a. There is a joint area XY.
b. There is a joint area XZ.
c. There is a joint area YZ.
d. These joint areas must be subtracted from the *total* area represented by $X + Y + Z$.

63. $T * 3'' = 15 \text{ oz} * 36''$
$T = 15 \text{ oz} * 12$
$T = 180 \text{ oz}$
$T = 11.25 \text{ lb}$

64. The probability of getting a two is $\frac{1}{6}$. The probability of getting a three is also $\frac{1}{6}$. There are, therefore, 12 potential faces to get the one you're looking for.

65. The first element of each factor produces the product a^2. The last element of each factor produces the product b^2. The alternate elements product $+2ab$ and $-2ab$, which cancel.

66. We know that if we were guaranteed all type-one transactions (probability of 1) that one hour (60 minutes) would be scheduled for the run. With a probability of .8, it is therefore calculable that $.8 \times 60$ minutes, or 48 minutes would be consumed by type-one transactions.

We know that the timing for transaction type-two is twice the time consumed for transaction type-one, but there is only a .3 probability that transaction type-two will occur. Since the timing is twice, then the same number of transactions will have been processed in 120 minutes. Calculating $.3 \times 120$ minutes, we have 35 minutes. Adding the two (36 minutes plus 48 minutes) gives a total of 84 minutes.

67. Knowledge question only—it's beyond this book to provide that proof.

68. A and B are both correct. Here's why: whenever you see a number with ! after it, the ! means *factorial* that each number in sequence up to the value of the number is a product. 4! would be $4 \times 3 \times 2 \times 1$. Therefore, 10! would be $10 \times 9 \times 8 \times 7 \times 6 \times 5 \times 4 \times 3 \times 2 \times 1$. $\frac{10!}{4!}$ would therefore be: 3,628,800/24 = 151,200. Now, as to why this solution is correct for the problem. Permutation merely means what are the *unique* number of ways the objects can be arranged (not combined) if we have 10 items and we arrange them six at a time. Thus, there are always four items not used. Now, we divide the number of combinations possible from all 10 items (10) by the number of combinations not used (4), therefore leaving the required 6 items.

69. This is a fairly simple numeric progression. Here's how it works: $(((((N \times 2) + 1) \times 2) + 1)$, etc.

70. A scatter diagram is used to determine regression and correlation against a trend line.

71. In order to work a root problem, it is imperative that the function of the number be set to zero (thus $b^2 - 4ac$ would also have to equal zero). In this case, it does, like this:

$$\begin{aligned} b^2 &= (4x)^2 = 16 \\ 4ac &= 4(2x^2) = 16 \end{aligned}$$

In each of the answers that which equals zero must fit the root. The only answer which satisfies that is A. In each of the other options, there would be a positive number. Just substitute the number for x and see which comes back to zero (via $b^2 - 4ac$), and you'll see it.

72. A frequency polygon is a curve drawn on points which are the mid-points of the frequency distribution.

73. This is a definition question only.

74. Let's say that we have five objects, and number them accordingly, and then pair them. They would pair as follows: (1–2), (1–2), (1–4), (1–5), (2–1) already exists in (1–2), (2–3), (2–4), (2–5), (3–1) already exists, as does (3–2), (3–4), (3–5), (4–1, 4–2, and 4–3 already exist), (4–5). So we're left with: (1–2), (1–3), (1–4), (1–5), (2–3), (2–4), (2–5), (3–4), (3–5), and (4–5).

$$\text{General case: } c = \frac{n!}{(n-p)!(p)!} = \frac{5!}{(5-2)!(2)!} = \frac{5 \times 4 \times 3 \times 2}{3 \times 2 \times 2} = 10$$

75. There is no integer between the integers 20 and 21.

76. Because the one prevents the other, the tests are independent. Being sequential, they should be added.

77. Add the list and round it to the integer.

78. A and X are vectors. B is a number (a scalar). A is a row vector of k elements a, $a(1 \times k)$ vector, and X is a $(k \times 1)$ vector. That form of multiplication of vectors is known as a "dot product" and yields a scalar.

79. We recognize that *something* squared is added to +5 to determine the answer. Since that something +5 equals 30, it's then possible to subtract that 5, giving 25, and the square root of 25 is, of course, 5. This approach is erroneous, of course, in that we started at the answer and worked backwards. The general case is to substitute $f(n)$ for $f(x)$. In this case $f(5)$ substitutes for $f(x)$, giving the formula:

$$f(5) = 5^2 + 5 = 30$$

80. The universe of any probability is 1.0. Therefore $1.0 - P(f)$ would have to equal Ps.

81. Here's how it's calculated: first, there are five positions, so the general form is the product of the values of each of the positions. Thus, the answer would be: $A \times B \times C \times D \times E$. We know the positions C, D, and E are digits (or numeric), each with a range of 10 (0–9). Thus, the multiplier for those three is 10^3. Positions A and B each have 36 values (26 alphabetic plus 10 numeric). However, we are excluding the characters (O) and (I). Thus each position is valued at 34, and positions A and B are valued at 34. We now have $34^2 10^3$ (the same as $34 \times 34 \times 10 \times 10 \times 10$), and if you do the math, you'll find that the answer comes out 1,156,000—which is quite a few license plates.

82. With a correlation of 0.95, *A* and *B* vary similarly. That high a position of correlation means that *A* increases as *B* increases, or an *inverse* relationship. Answers C and D would make a statistician ill. Statistics say something about relationships; *nothing* about the *causes* of relationships.

83. Under the general rule for Exclusive Or, $1 + 1 = 0$ (with no carry), $1 + 0 = 1$, and $0 + 0 = 0$.

84. It is a fact, you will recall that the sample drawn from a normal population will also be normal.

85. That's $3 \times 3 \times 3 \times 3$.

86. Take the general form: $c = \dfrac{n!}{(n - r)!r!}$

It is known that there are 8 people, including Mr. Smith and Mr. Jones, to be made into various teams of which one of them is to be a member. $n!$, therefore, is 6! $r!$ is 3! Therefore,

$$c = \frac{n!}{(n - r)!r!} = \frac{6 \times 5 \times 4 \times 3 \times 2 \times 1}{3 \times 2 \times 1 \times 3 \times 2 \times 1} = 20$$

87. This is a knowledge question—definition, only.

88. The conjunction is the sum of the probabilities.

89. The "transportation problem" is a classic linear programming problem, solved by the simplex technique.

90. The range is the distance between the lowest value (20) to the highest value (300).

91. We know that B is greater than C, but all we know is that A is unequal to B, and that is not, by definition, also greater than C.

92. Range defines the set's extremes. Variance defines the differences among the set's parts. Deviation is a measure of dispersion.

93. We're dealing with a binomial expansion here. The numbers in the pyramid are the coefficients of the expanded binomial, as follows:

$$\begin{array}{ll} (x + y)^0 = & 1 \\ (x + y)^1 = x + y & 1\ 1 \\ (x + y)^2 = x^2 + 2xy + y^2 & 1\ 2\ 1 \\ (x + y)^3 = x^3 + 3x^2 + 3xy^2 + y^3 & 1\ 3\ 3\ 1 \\ (x + y)^4 = x^4 + 4x^3y + 6x^2y^2 + 4xy^3 + y^4 & 1\ 4\ 6\ 4\ 1 \end{array}$$

94. Chi-square is calculated as $(f - f_o)/f$, where f is the theoretical frequency at a point in the distribution, and f_o is the observed frequency. A large value of chi-square, then, means that the observed distribution is probably not of the distribution expected. A low chi-square means the differences between the distributions are not significant. It can never be negative.

95. Conjunctive statements are part of set theory.

96. The standard deviation, by definition, is a deviation from the mean, a measure of the variations of the numbers.

97. Divide 26 by 8 and you'll see that the remainder is 2.

98. Exponential smoothing is a means of tightening the estimate. It is a form of weighted moving average, but the value diminishes.

99. It is necessary to raise the second term such that the denominator is x^6. This involves multiplying both the numerator and the denominator by x^3.

100. Complete specification may be misleading, but if the mean and the standard deviation are known, the other factors of the distribution may be calculated.

EXAMINATION SECTION 5

7

SYSTEMS ANALYSIS AND DESIGN

THE SYSTEMS TASK

This chapter and the next are the presentation of the concerns of the systems analyst, as I predict they are and will be. The systems tasks was once very simple—it was a methods and procedures position grown up to the computer age. But the computer age has gone far beyond the task as it was originally envisioned in the CDP Examination. Therefore, we're going to present the systems task in two chapters—this chapter, which deals with the updated systems task; and the last chapter which will deal with the almost unrelated subjects of communications, databases, decision support systems, and office automation. The problem is, of course, that they are very much related. They are presented in this size and in this manner as a recognition that questions about all sections are beginning to show up in the CDP Examination, and, in fact, were represented on the 1985 exam.

THE SYSTEMS PERSON

The systems analyst is the industrial engineer of the business methods world. His beginnings were of the need to squeeze the most from high-capital EDP equipment at a time when the per-unit cost of handling a transaction was approaching preautomation levels, and management was questioning the move to automation. Systems did not exist as a career from the inception of EDP. Systems work was done, of course, but more or less informally. The combination of clerical tasks, required by automation, brought with it the need to examine the way things were done, how the processes interfaced, and to explore ways to eliminate duplication and institute compression.

The definition of system was initially one of application: one application equalled one system. Soon, we found that the system was, in fact, the entire interwoven network of machines, documents, rubber stamps, mail, filing, and. . . people. We very quickly learned that rather than the automation being a part of another system, the other system was in fact becoming a part of the automated process. In that day, the electromechanical equipment gave compression. Soon there was more information than available compression. Automated equipment would solve the problem! But how to most effectively use that equipment? And what about the manual aspects of the work?

Enter the systems and procedures people (S&P). Since our perspectives at that time involved the movement or adaptation of manual systems to automating equipment, early concentration on systems improvement was concerned solely with the automation of then existing manual functions. These people designed forms to capture data for the automated system. They designed filing systems in which the products of automation and other manual reports were filed. They did some time and motion studies (recall that Gilbreth's work was recent—see Chapter 3). They wrote the procedures and sometimes the policies which surrounded the manual methods of doing business and which interfaced with the available automation equipment. Along came EDP and the S&P people had no experience with it. That didn't stop them. The first "computer systems analyst" came, naturally, with the first computers, although they did not appear concurrently. It was first thought that those to program the computers would also develop the systems design. To state that "it was fist thought" is really giving credit where credit is not due, however, since organizations sadly realized that a systems person was required only after finding that programming personnel were developing fast and efficient computer applications which bore little resemblance to the expected products and which, curiously, failed to interface with users. Many organizations haven't learned that lesson yet. Having struck out, someone suggested that the systems and procedures people could be the analysts. That, also, was a dismal failure—and we haven't learned that lesson yet either. The field is changing at this point, also, with the addition to the field of the Office Automation Analyst (OAA).

During this time, major advances were being made in computing hardware. New hardware was considerably more capable and correspondingly expensive. Equipment vendors of this era ensured sales by underbidding the cost of their own currently installed hardware. Thus, businesses were forced to update, despite the fact that in-place systems were working well. While less than successful, the S&P analyst did bring an organizational knowledge to the problem. But the pressure to find ways to use the very expensive EDP hardware quickly consumed all their time; new personnel could not be trained fast enough to have a significant impact on the process.

Having struck out with both S&P people and programmers, business then created the systems analyst and drew not only those people into the function, but also the college-educated business majors. The problem still did not go away, since two of these three kinds of people really did not understand the organization's business. As time dragged on, the number of S&P people diminished. Today, very few organizations have people devoted solely to manual systems. Programmers remained; the hardware remained; organizations muddled, convinced that the programmer could do the work. They couldn't—and they cannot—by and large, do that work successfully.

In the late 1960s, the post-World War II baby boom people were leaving graduate school with MBA certificate in hand. They were hired as systems analysts. Their understanding of classical business was dismal. At this point, business felt it would be more successful if these graduates were trained in EDP than to train programmers to know the business. The introduction of the microcomputer to user areas poses yet another dimension to the situation.

For years, EDP people have depended upon the mystique of the computer to impress users. The microcomputer has given the user a more valid perspective—not that programming is necessarily easy, but rather that it's not an arcane art. Simultaneously, there is trend to move EDP from the bowels of the organization to a position which recognizes the contribution of the selection and the vulnerability of the organization without it. If EDP people are immature in their approach to management, that responsibility rests with the entire management of the organization. Manufacturing companies apply their best management to planning capital expenditures for equipment, product effectiveness, and site selection. Financial organizations direct extensive resources to the analysis and selection of financial investment opportunities. Yet the same companies have virtually abdicated management responsibility in the acquisition of EDP machinery and in planning how that machinery can be used to maximize its contribution to the profit or well-being of the organization.

If it is true that data processing history can be neatly defined into phases, the information revolution may well be in its maturation era, as of this writing. At the moment, we have hardware which runs the gamut from the $400 desktop microcomputer to the $100,000 minicomputer, the $1M midicomputer, and the $10M maxicomputer, each with its own features and each with its own capabilities. But from the analysts' perspectives, this maturation period includes concerns for productivity, user-involvement, usability of systems, makers of decisions, the information organization as an information service (corporate resource) to the rest of the organization, communications, and the adaptation of the system life-cycle to the changing needs of the organization, not just the changing needs of the information revolution itself. Those who have been around a while can recount the massive programming changes which had to be made with each new generation of hardware. That is no longer necessary. Above that, we have gone from incompatibility to compatibility to transportability. And those changes have affected every aspect of the information system.

The systems analyst of today must reckon with information as an organizational resource. The importance of managing information systems steps has been magnified by the ever-increasing capability of technology. Today, the systems person must be capable to spreak about information technology which includes not only data, but also text, voice/communications, and image/graphics. Three important features which illustrate the complexity of the future systems task are distributed data processing (DDP), the automated office, and decision support systems. From the systems point of view, the movement to DDP represents a change in where the processing is done, not the type of processing which is to be done. Distribution of computing cycles and software programs is a combination of technological change and organizational policy. The programs will look the same, with the exception of the communications activities, and communications are covered in this section. And, as we have said, there is treatment in this section, in other chapters, of the other function.

DEFINING THE SYSTEMS RESPONSIBILITY

A system is an assembly of procedures, processes, methods, routines, or techniques united by some form of regulated interaction to form an organized whole, in support of the organization's objectives. Key to this definition is the term 'regulated.'' For anything to be ''systematic'' there must be some orderly method whereby it is to be conducted and some form of control which regulates the process against a previously established standard. Thus it follows that systems need not necessarily be computer-based, although basing a system upon a computer will tend to provide the regulation necessary for the process to be called ''systematic.'' There is a danger in this form of explanation in that the ''computer-based system'' may be incorrectly equated to a system of any generic description. Even if the computer is not used as the tool for providing the control, a system that executes business processes with the same degree of regulation can be constructed, less, of course, the computer's time compression.

Computer-based systems are not accidental. They come into being after much planning, expenditure of resources, and effort on the part of all levels of management. Top management usually delegates the responsibility for developing computer-based systems to a computer-oriented systems team. Where they have not done so, few systems have been installed.

Systems Functions

There are no standards for systems analysis and development. There is not even common a common agreement as to what the phases of systems development will be called. The closest agreement comes with the Systems Development Life Cycle, the elements of which are:

1. Systems analysis
2. Systems design
3. Equipment selection and acquisition
4. Programming
5. Testing and conversion
6. Installation
7. Operation
8. Maintenance
9. Follow-up evaluation

Because there are no standard phases and titles, this chapter concentrates upon the functions which must be considered in the development of an information processing system, despite what people choose to call them. Figure 7.1 is an 80-element PERT chart which describes the basic elements to the development of a system.

Whenever an information system is constructed, it is generally a replacement for an existing manual (or even automated) system. Few, if any, totally new processes are attempted.

System Analysis

Frequently, this part of the life cycle is divided first into a preliminary study of the existing process, and then into a detailed analysis of the findings. The preliminary study is often called the "feasibiliy study" as its responsibility is to evaluate a proposed system's likely characteristics and costs. In this activity, the objectives for the solution will be established after the determination has been made that there is, indeed, a problem to be solved. The scope of the study is defined, as a means to contain an expensive, rambling process. Early on, the initial effort is an assessment of the situation and a view to answer questions, among which are whether the problem can be cost-effectively solved using automated information-handling equipment. The early part represents a minor percentage of the total effort, but is uniquely responsible for the success of the systems project. The preliminary study report, or feasibility study, will recommend a direction to management. If that recommendation is to continue, then management must authorize the resources to perform the actual analysis.

The purpose of the detailed analysis is to learn enough about the existing system to permit the design of a better one; one which has a broader scope that the system it replaces, or one which will function in a more economical or faster manner than the current method. Improvements in speed and accuracy, while desirable, should be considered second to the utility of the data presented by the improvement in terms of the decisions which must be made by the people to whom the information will be presented.

To analyze an existing system, data must be collected, organized, evaluated relationally, and placed into a format from which a conclusion can logically be drawn as to the wisdom of progressing further. Some estimate of required resources and available benefits has been previously taken. It now is incumbent upon the analyst to prove the validity or invalidity of those estimates and to include that information in the presentation to management. Also included will be an assessment of the environment in which the present system operates and the potential change in that environment which would be experienced as a result of the proposed change.

During the phase, the systems team will prepare cost studies for the existing system, will make a projection of the costs for the systems improvement, and will supply a comparative analysis of the two, which will then serve as the basis for management's decision to continue or abandon the project.

Systems Design

The purpose of this phase is to design a system superior to the existing one. It is primarily a synthesis function. Thus, for example, the systems team prepares formats of the inputs, outputs, and data files; develops processing algorithms; and determines design alternatives. The wise system team ensures that objectives are clearly stated and understood, that reports provide information which supports decisions made relative to those objectives, and that inputs are available or can be obtained to allow the production of the reports or enquiry modules which will provide that information. In addition, a report must be prepared for management which will be used as the measurement document for subsequent phases of the project.

Equipment Selection and Acquisition

On the assumption that hardware will be obtained to support the proposed system, and such an assumption is not always certain, management's interest is to acquire the computer which will do the job most

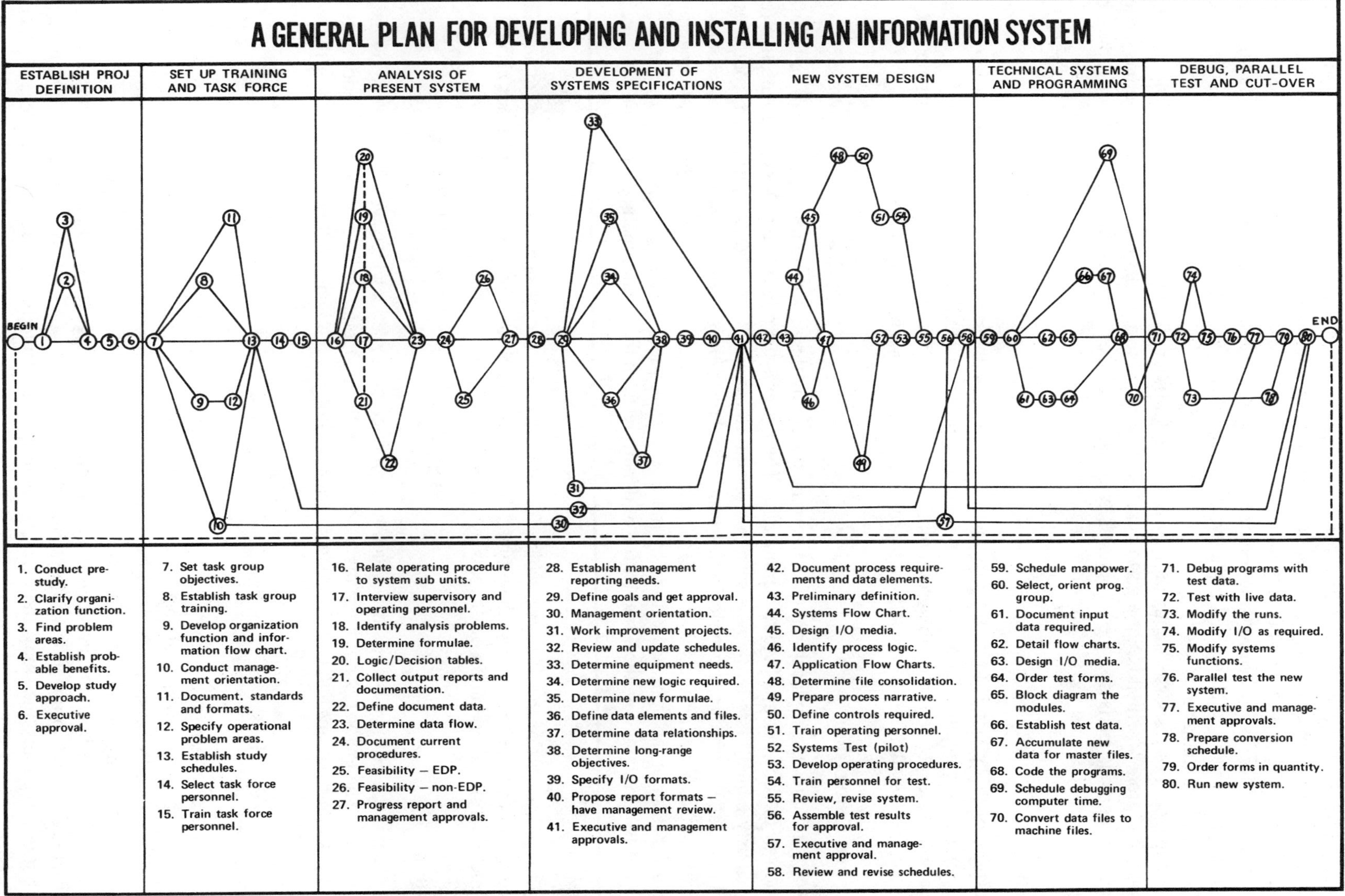
A GENERAL PLAN FOR DEVELOPING AND INSTALLING AN INFORMATION SYSTEM
ESTABLISH PROJ DEFINITION
SET UP TRAINING AND TASK FORCE
ANALYSIS OF PRESENT SYSTEM
DEVELOPMENT OF SYSTEMS SPECIFICATIONS
NEW SYSTEM DESIGN
TECHNICAL SYSTEMS AND PROGRAMMING
DEBUG, PARALLEL TEST AND CUT-OVER
BEGIN
END
1. Conduct pre-study.
2. Clarify organization function.
3. Find problem areas.
4. Establish probable benefits.
5. Develop study approach.
6. Executive approval.
7. Set task group objectives.
8. Establish task group training.
9. Develop organization function and information flow chart.
10. Conduct management orientation.
11. Document. standards and formats.
12. Specify operational problem areas.
13. Establish study schedules.
14. Select task force personnel.
15. Train task force personnel.
16. Relate operating procedure to system sub units.
17. Interview supervisory and operating personnel.
18. Identify analysis problems.
19. Determine formulae.
20. Logic/Decision tables.
21. Collect output reports and documentation.
22. Define document data.
23. Determine data flow.
24. Document current procedures.
25. Feasibility – EDP.
26. Feasibility – non-EDP.
27. Progress report and management approvals.
28. Establish management reporting needs.
29. Define goals and get approval.
30. Management orientation.
31. Work improvement projects.
32. Review and update schedules.
33. Determine equipment needs.
34. Determine new logic required.
35. Determine new formulae.
36. Define data elements and files.
37. Determine data relationships.
38. Determine long-range objectives.
39. Specify I/O formats.
40. Propose report formats – have management review.
41. Executive and management approvals.
42. Document process requirements and data elements.
43. Preliminary definition.
44. Systems Flow Chart.
45. Design I/O media.
46. Identify process logic.
47. Application Flow Charts.
48. Determine file consolidation.
49. Prepare process narrative.
50. Define controls required.
51. Train operating personnel.
52. Systems Test (pilot)
53. Develop operating procedures.
54. Train personnel for test.
55. Review, revise system.
56. Assemble test results for approval.
57. Executive and management approval.
58. Review and revise schedules.
59. Schedule manpower.
60. Select, orient prog. group.
61. Document input data required.
62. Detail flow charts.
63. Design I/O media.
64. Order test forms.
65. Block diagram the modules.
66. Establish test data.
67. Accumulate new data for master files.
68. Code the programs.
69. Schedule debugging computer time.
70. Convert data files to machine files.
71. Debug programs with test data.
72. Test with live data.
73. Modify the runs.
74. Modify I/O as required.
75. Modify systems functions.
76. Parallel test the new system.
77. Executive and management approvals.
78. Prepare conversion schedule.
79. Order forms in quantity.
80. Run new system.

Figure 7.1

effectively at the lowest possible cost, assuring compatibility exists or can be obtained with other hardware used. The systems team prepares a set of computer specifications, which are then placed out for proposal (RFP). The system team is responsible to review the vendor bids, select the vendor who most closely meets the RFP specifications, and make that recommendation to management. Where current equipment has available the required capacity, the design team will be responsible to design the system to use the available hardware.

The expansion of resource, acquisition of resource, or other changes of hardware configuration may be an ongoing process which is not a part of the life of any project at all. If an organization has designated certain persons as having the responsibility of computer performance measurement, then the loading statistics may become the basis for making the change.

Programming

The purpose of this phase is to write, test, and debug the computer programs for the new system. The installation of the computer involves the total physical plan and facilities of the organization. The manpower resources expended to do the programming in this phase are the most used for any single task in the development cycle. This may be thought of as the actual construction process.

Testing and Conversion

This phase includes the replacement of the current system by the new system in such a manner that the disruption of the operation is held to a minimum. The systems team tests the new system with live (but not previously edited) data in the new system's operating environment. The current system continues to operate in parallel with the new system until management is satisfied with the new system's operation and performance. Whether the system will function for any length of time in a parallel-mode operation will be a function of the upheaval caused by the new system (e.g., personnel displacement), the available time to run two systems together, the degree of departure from the former method of operation, etc.

Installation

Installation is the part of the life cycle which follows the user's acceptance of the new system and the replaced system ceases to exist. At this point, all user personnel must have been trained and become fully functional in the operation of the new system.

Operation

This is the portion of the system's life which will produce the benefits which were anticipated by the earlier phases. The analyst is not normally associated with the operation phase except to smooth out the rough edges and make the minor adjustments which permit smooth and unfettered operation of the system.

Maintenance

Maintenance is a programming function, but there are times when the minor adjustments to the system, particularly to the noncomputer elements of the system, become necessary. It is important to note that only adjustments to the system which support the original specifications are maintenance. Adjustments to the system whose purpose to change functions or enhance output are not maintenance and should be treated as such. It has been this acceptance of anything under the general heading of maintenance that has caused users to be so unhappy with systems efforts in recent years. Major changes are not maintenance, but deserve the same study and care that went into the building of the system in the first place.

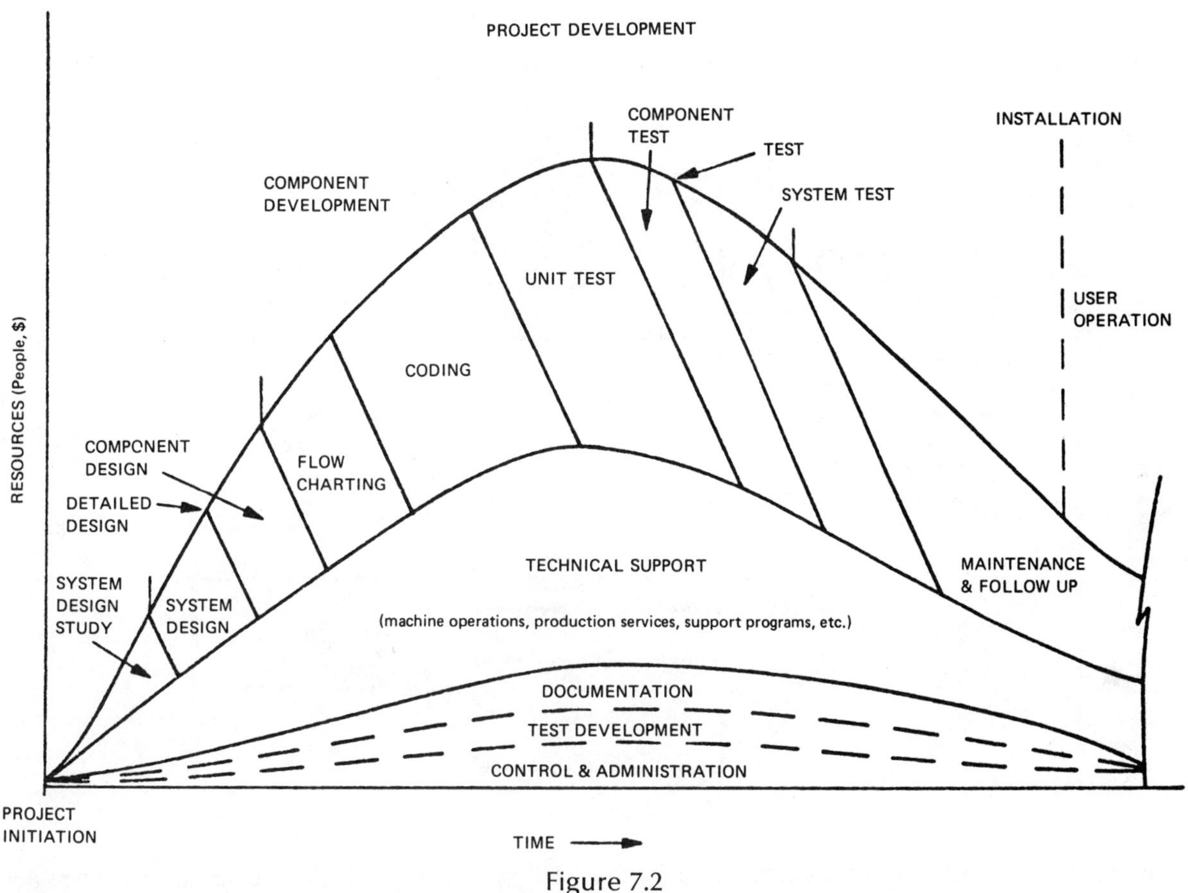

Figure 7.2

Follow-Up Evaluation

The analyst may participate in this activity, but the function rightfully belongs to the EDP auditor. The criteria for this investigation should be the objectives which were the basis for the system in the first place. These are absolutes: either the system met the objectives or it did not. In some instances, when the objectives are not met, the system should be abandoned. In the majority of cases, a mid-course correction can be made after a brief study of the reasons why the system fails to perform as anticipated.

The nine unique phases of systems development have been presented here. What matters, as stated before, is not the number of phases which are performed, but the functions outlined within the phases. A large and highly staffed organization may well divide these functions into fully manageable work projects, each building upon the work of the preceeding activity. On the other end of the scale, the entire process may be the function of one, or at least a very few, individual(s). It's useful to see what others experience. Figure 7.2 is a depiction of one software developer's experience in systems development. On the *Y* axis, resources are plotted, and on the *X* axis time is shown. Note where the apex of the project falls. Note also that the functions overlap substantially and that the resource requirements have never quite return to zero.

Systems Concepts

As was mentioned earlier, the need for systems people was not immediately apparent to management. If, they reasoned, the machine accountants had done an adequate job of converting manual systems to auto-

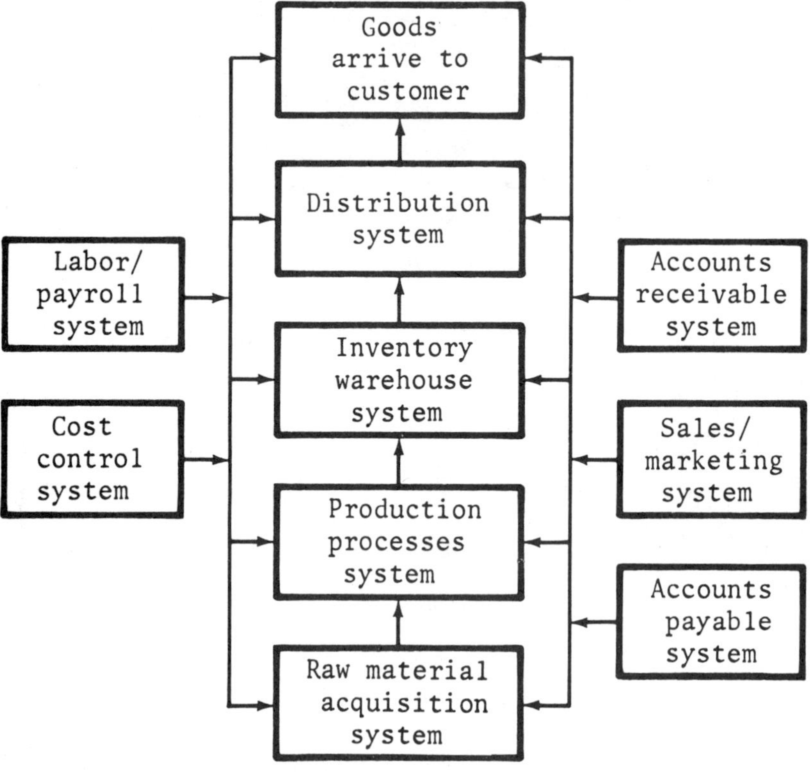

Figure 7.3

mated punch card hardware, they could do so for the EDP system as well. Time elapsed, hardware became more capable, sophisticated, and expensive, and it became obvious to management that the tasks done for one department were similar, if not identical, to tasks done for another department. It quickly became apparent that data which applied to one area also applied to one or more other areas. This, in turn, led to the concept of the "integrated system," and that, in turn, led us to the database. Figure 7.3 is a mainstreaming chart which shows the interrelationship of systems and data throughout the organization.

Communications interfaces affect the conceptual approach to systems design, and will increasingly do so as we seek to install more on-line and distributed processing systems. The need for communications is born of the need for accurate and timely information. Only an on-line access can produce timely data. Only a real-time or near-real-time environment can develop that data. As the noncomputer aspects of systems continue to find their way onto some form of computing hardware, the communications interfaces will undergo development, growth, and extensive use.

Systems Planning

Systems development requires careful planning, thorough analysis, and constant supervision to amass, coordinate, and cause to function many dissimilar elements. It's not uncommon to underestimate the cost, time, staffing, and a host of other items for this development. It's not that we have become imprecise in our estimates surrounding such efforts. It's simply that we do not wish to admit that the real cost is—until afterwards. There are three factors which are responsible for these underestimates: we fail to be honest because we want the project; the mandated target is impossible, but we want the project; we think we're better that we really are. If the project has been well defined, some of this can be accommodated, for the control points will keep the project from going substantially out of hand.

Systems planning highlights tasks that require immediate attention, even though they will not be completed until later in the cycle. Site planning, budgeting, and implementation schedules are such items. The lead time for resources and material is made and integral part of the planning. The interdependency of tasks which comprise the project is also a necessary aspect of the plan, since acceleration and slippage can be measured only if a plan which incorporates the potential alternatives has been established. If the objectives have been well defined to the systems team, the systems plan becomes a plan of action for the different segments of the development life cycle, phased for control. Regular formal reports to management will highlight delays and problems for replanning and accelerations which may provide the resources.

The Systems Team

Initially, management must question whether to venture into the entire systems development life cycle. Some view the phases of systems analysis and design as the processes of examining the way things are done with a view to having them done more efficiently. Too often, the availability of new equipment or new methods permits management to rationalize that there are no weaknesses in a specific area. Therefore, they conclude, systems analysis and design need not be done. They would begin the systems development cycle by selecting the equipment. History has recorded the impact of their mistakes.

Where the full development cycle is used, it is viewed as a means to improve the value of systems at the lowest possible cost. The cycle forces the organization to focus attention on the information flow and not on the capital asset. Top management must insist on a thorough, competent, and detailed information systems analysis and design prior to issuing any equipment specifications for computers, if computers are to be acquired. The savings to be realized will then become evident.

Despite much evidence to the contrary, people still fear for their employment because of the fear that they will be replaced by a machine. It happens, of course, but historically, the change has been one of facility and orientation. It becomes the systems team's responsibility to overcome these fears and to tap the vital knowledge held by the people who will be using the system. Top management must set the theme by making clear that they need and want effective results land that displacement will be held to a minimum. The authority of the systems team must be outlined to those conducting the study and those who are to be studied. The latter group can be expected to cooperate more fully if they understand the reason for the study, the potential outcome of the study, and the authorities and responsibilities of the systems team..

The decision as to the composition of the systems team is vital and, accordingly, requires the attention of top management. There are several alternatives available and they have been used with varying degrees of success. The discussion of committees, project teams, external consultants, etc., found in Chapters 3 and 4, are equally applicable here.

One of the most important considerations is the selection of a leader. The leader will need to be well informed on the functions and processes of the entire operation and able to plan or carry out major projects. It is advisable to select a leader from the functioning hierarchy and that there be a minimum number of levels between him and top management. It need not be the ranking member of the project team, however—and organizations should have learned that rank does not necessarily equate to leadership ability.

Systems organizations will often limit the size of the systems team to six or eight members. This does not mean that there will never be more than these people working on the study—but rather puts the team in the position of the executive who calls upon resources as they are required. The systems team itself contains only the core members who will work on the project throughout the entire development cycle.

System Study Plan

Systems teams have used a variety of techniques to plan and control the development effort. The PERT and Gantt systems described in Chapter 4 provide the best possible tools for this purpose. PERT provides a look-ahead facility not provided by Gantt. Gantt provides something very important—management understands it.

PERT represents a significant step toward an integrated management system encompassing the variables of time, resources, and technical performance. The planning and control produced by PERT offer a sound basis for scheduling as a means by which status may be measured and current and potential problems detected in time to allow corrective action. A PERT chart, carefully laid out as a Gantt Chart, becomes a very successful indicator of necessary resources, particularly when the extremes of earliest times and latest times are plotted. Part of the reason that project managers experience difficulty is that they have felt that all activities of a project should begin simultaneously.

Management is interested not only in meeting scheduled, but also in cost control and in time/cost trade-offs. A number of models which permit the inclusion of cost information in the data base and which also permit the necessary computations, projections, and analysis have been developed, such as PERT-time and PERT-cost. Because PERT is a network planning device, the predominant function is time scheduling. Cost is, of course, a function of time, but only to the extent that the resource costs are known. It therefore follows that if a network can be constructed to perform the project in the least time, it can therefore be constructed to perform it at the least cost. On what the economist calls the ''production possibilities curve,'' the *Y* axis is dollars and the *X* axis is time. The curve presents the planner with the opportunity to evaluate trade-offs available with the intermixture of time and cost. For instance, if a program module can be done in one week by a senior programmer for $1,000 (salary and overhead) but can be done in three weeks by a trainee for $1,200, there might be a valid argument for putting the trainee onto the task, even at the expense of the additional time and money. The time is, of course, longer, but may be more easily scheduled, permitting the senior person to concentrate on those tasks which require compression. The same logic prevails when evaluating outside services. Can time be purchased for money?

PERT, then, employs (1) a product-oriented work breakdown structure, beginning with objectives subdivided into successively smaller end items; (2) a network consisting of all activities and events that must be accomplished to reach the objectives, housing planned sequences, interdependencies, and interrelationships; (3) activity time estimates with identification of critical paths in the networks; (4) a schedule which attempts to balance the objectives, network flow plan, and resources availability; and (5) analysis of the interrelated networks, critical tasks, status, forecast of overruns, and the identification of problem areas.

Finally, since the budget is the prime management control tool, the progress against the budget becomes a working subset. Weekly progress reports become the sole means to measure progress and resource consumation. While management would like truthful reports, they seldom get them—for the truth is often punishing.

SYSTEMS ANALYSIS

The need for and use of computers in business has far outstripped the ability of the schools to turn out qualified computer systems analysts. Generally, these people know the computer extensively, business generally, and the specific applications not at all. Therefore, to be successful, the analyst must learn the way the activity currently operates. Further, the request for automation carries the plea, really, that the familiar remain undisturbed. While that certainly isn't technically possible, functionally the analyst must ''blend into the woodwork,'' learn what can be learned, and apply that learning to the design of a system which will overcome weaknesses, enhance capabilities, and accomplish objectives.

By the time the project has progressed to the point where the team has it, the decision to do it has been cast in bronze. The effort at this stage must either substantiate the initial estimates of time, cost, and benefit, or categorically deny them, with justification. As this phase begins, the decision has been made to at least pay for the analysis. On the basis of this analysis, a go/no go decision should be made.

The Feasibility Study

The feasibility study is a management study which concludes whether or not the use of EDP equipment appears feasible enough at this time to warrant continuation of the life cycle. It will bear the analysts' recommendations for further action. The systems people must conduct this phase in only such depth that it becomes apparent whether the present system can be salvaged and modified or whether a new system is needed.

An important input is the cost of the present system. The analysts will have sufficient data to develop cost information about a future system with some degree of accuracy. With the understanding that projections of future cost may be inaccurate, there is the facility to make cost comparisons. More meaningful and accurate comparisons can be—indeed, must be—made at other points in the life cycle.

Study Scope

Part of the reason systems teams have had such a rough time is that they have literally bitten off more than they can chew. Figure 7.4 shows the major building blocks of a manufacturing company's integrated information needs. When scoping the study, it becomes necessary to determine what elements will, of necessity, become involved in a study whose objectives include a revamping of the information systems, determining where interfaces between them exist, and determining the requirements for information to be passed between them.

Study Objectives

Systems studies are not casually undertaken. The symptom of a problem continues to rear its head, and everybody knows some improvement is required. But how much? What is a realistic change? How will that be defined? How will it be measured? Trying to build a system without an objective is an impossible and never-ending task. Even the development of the objectives is tough, and is resisted by everybody. We simply must ask uncomfortable questions for which we don't really desire answers.

A typical management directive is automation of order entry. If the system team does that, it may well find after spending the time and money that the error problem inherent in the older system not only exists under EDP but has become exaggerated. The analyst needs to be skeptical; he or she knows that if the error rate doesn't drop, the system change will not be viewed as being successful. Therefore, if reduction in error rate is the real desired change, then measurement of what the error rate is would seem to be important. If the error rate is 20%, what is a realistic improvement? 15%? 10%? Can the error rate be dropped to zero? Perhaps, but what are the time and cost constraints? Can a 75% reduction (from 20% to 5%) be acceptable? Once that has been established, the analyst has a specific, well-defined, attainable, and measurable goal—but not an objective yet. The objective happens when a decision is made as to the method to achieve the goal.

Thus, the first step in a feasibility study is to determine the study objectives. It will be necessary to modify them as the project progresses. A formal set of objectives forces management to give thought to the total environment. As objectives are defined, the problems involved in attaining them become more visible. Additionally, a framework of operation is evolved within which the systems team can work. Those objectives need to be documented and agreed-to by all. Typical objectives for new projects are:

1. Relieve management of routine decision-making

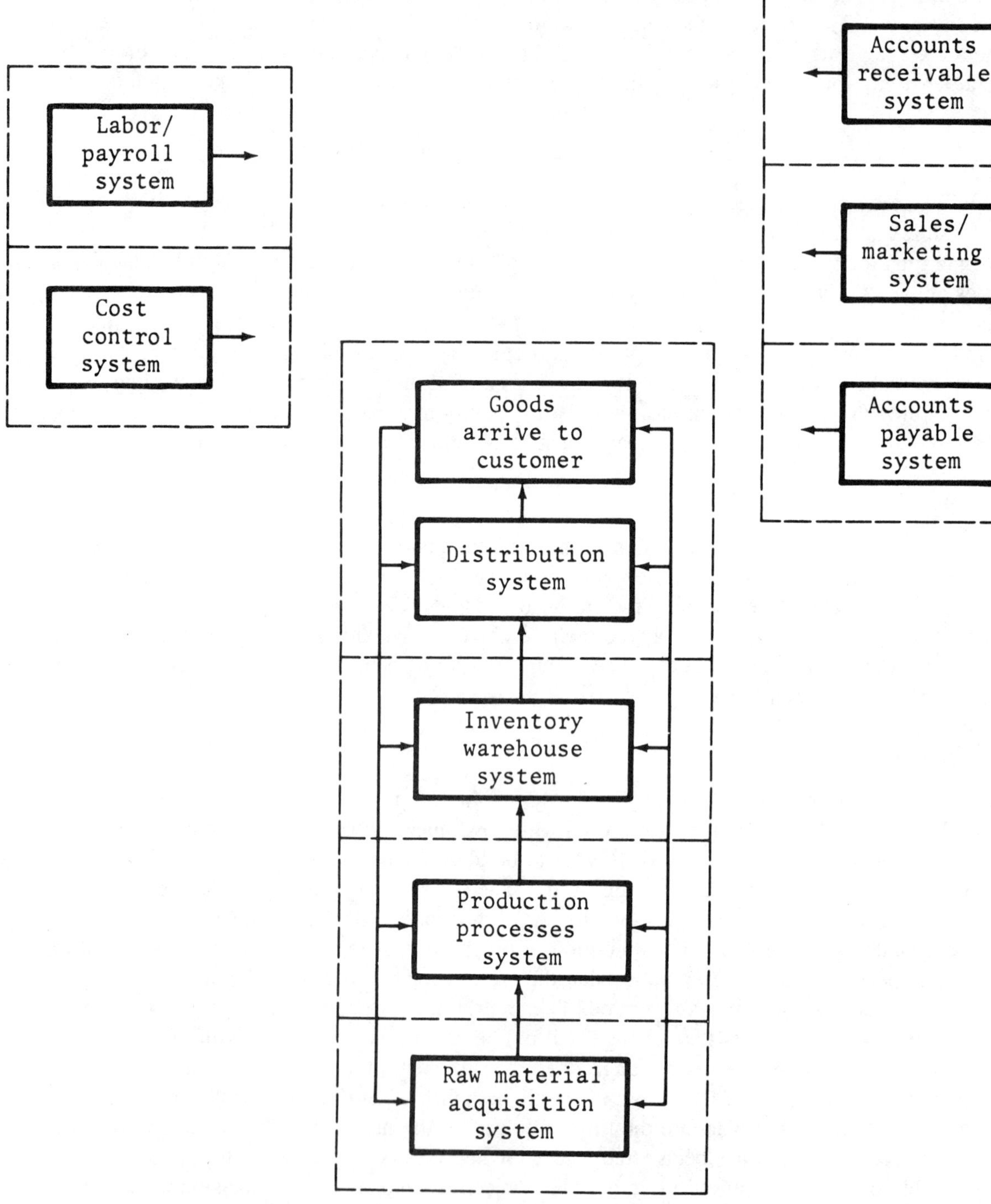

Figure 7.4

2. Increase productivity of available work forces
3. Reduce errors by reducing human involvement
4. Increase value of information
5. Reduce per-unit processing costs
6. Reduce physical storage requirements

7. Make more effective use of human resources by replacing detailed tasks with review functions
8. Permit the use of specific scientific techniques

However, to be effective, the degree of desired improvement becomes a critical part of the objectives which are set. Figure 7.5 shows how this can be accomplished. From the illustration, we can see that:

At (A) A Board of Directors has made some determination of the changes it would like to see in the organization. In a commercial organization, this change would be expressed in terms of benefits desired for dollars expended. This group will not be concerned with the method employed to derive the change desired.

At (B) A desired change is apportioned to the departments to achieve, either in the form of potential savings or increased opportunities. To illustrate, assume that the EDP department is held responsible for 5% of the change (by virtue of its interrelationship with other departments). This process is called the budget process and is the prime management tool. It is at this point when the system team(s) become(s) part of the process, since the project(s) (C) become(s) the method of accomplishing the apportioned part of the organization's objectives.

At (C) The individual projects are determined. The percentages shown are the contributions to the illustrated 5%. Such changes, however, are the contributions to that percentage made by other percentage changes at the applications level. For instance, it may take a savings of 25% in inventory carrying costs to contribute 1% of the mandated improvement in net profit.

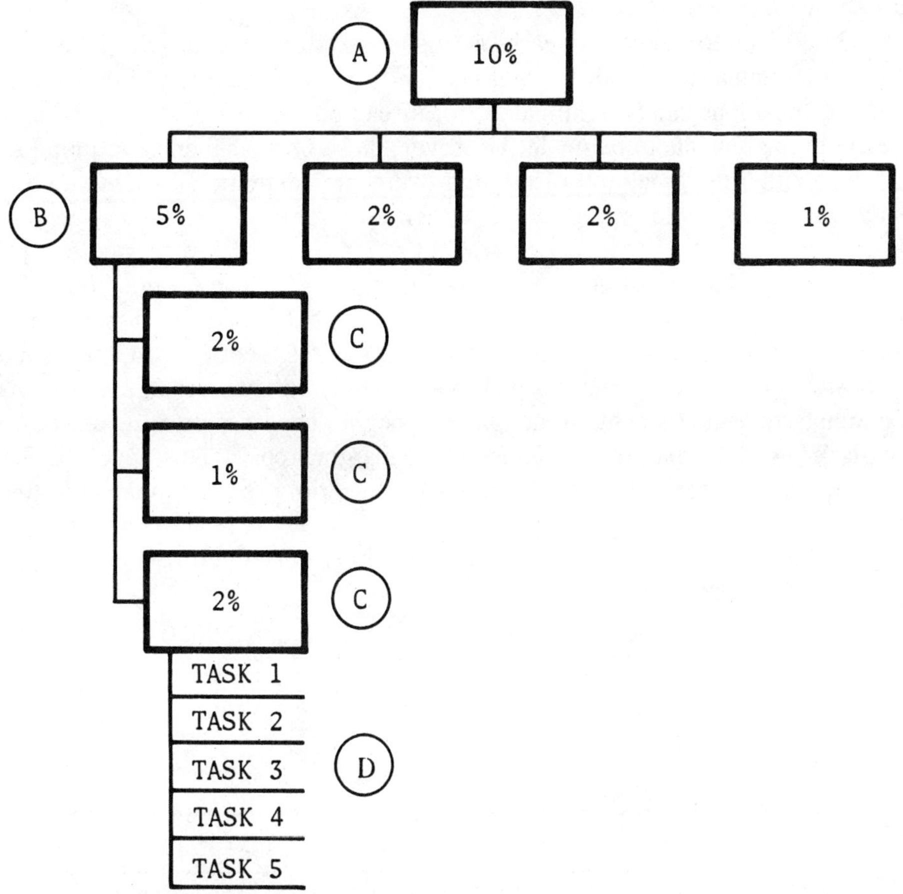

Figure 7.5

At (D) The tasks necessary to make the changes sought at C are outlined. Cursory inspection of the tasks will show that these tasks (plus their subtask breakdowns) comprise the major elements of the proposed system.

The basic objectives of most feasibility studies center on cost-effectiveness. The systems team must set its goals with cost-effectiveness at the basic objective from which all others flow. The cost savings accrue through savings in personnel and machines, while the effectiveness increases through earlier reports, improved relations with customers, and greater efficiency in the processing of data. This should not, however, minimize in any manner the potential of obtaining *X* benefits for *Y* costs, assuming the slopes of the lines are not parallel!

Tests of Feasibility

Cost has been the only aspect of feasibility which has drawn our attention so far, but costs isn't the only consideration. There are three: economic, technical, and operational.

Economic feasibility seems to be very straightforward. The system either pays for itself or it does not. Right? Not quite. While any new system should be developed to recoup the expenditures made to obtain it, we must also recognize that "breakeven" or "profit" from a systems venture is not always mandatory, obtainable, or desirable. Cost reduction exists in but a very narrow spectrum of our improvement opportunities. In a simple economic model (see Figure 7.6), savings is available only in the variable cost (*VC*) portion of the spectrum over time (*T*) or quantity (*Q*). It's doubtful that any systems improvement can improve fixed costs (*FC*).

Variable costs (*VC*) tend to increase linearly until some point where capacity is reached, at which time they then increase dramatically and the total cost (*TC*) curve bends sharply upward. So long as processes can be refined, positions can be eliminated, forms can be simplified, or volume/cost ratios can be improved, there are improvements to be made. However, those improvements are finite: there is simply a point beyond which either marginal unit of the improvement is extremely expensive on a per-unit basis or where it is physically impossible to improve it further. At this point, the process becomes more expensive.

Let's add a dimension to the illustration, as shown in figure 7.7. The benefit from a systems improvement may be difficult to measure, may appear intangible, but is present, nonetheless—even if it's only cost avoidance. The benefit curve (revenue curve—*R*) crosses the total cost (*TC*) curve in two places. The leftmost position is the true breakeven point, where systems development costs are recouped and where the marginal revenue (benefits to be derived) begin. The lines cross again, at the point which the economist calls $MR = MC$ (marginal revenue equals marginal cost). This upper breakeven is at the point of maximum efficiency, beyond which the efficiency deteriorates in proportion of the extent of the diminished returns.

Consider Figure 7.8. The systems improvement must either raise the revenue (benefit) curve or lower

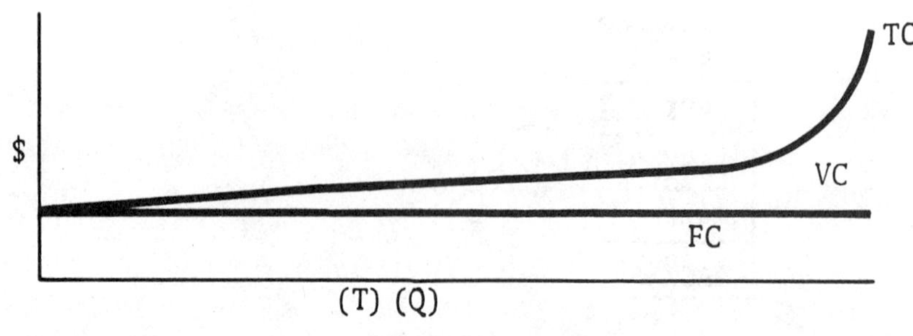

Figure 7.6

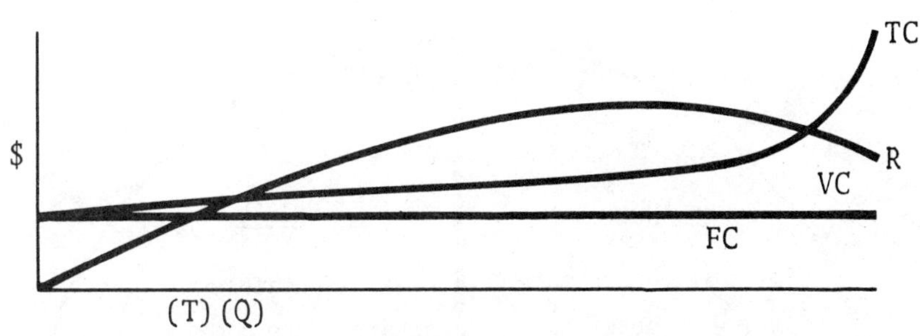

Figure 7.7

the total cost curve, or both. In the former, the system is used to exploit opportunity. In the latter, the reduction of incremental costs is required. When both can be done, the net profit figure increases and the organization grows. Here then is the rub. The analyst can quantify lost heads, discontinued forms, and simplified processes. But the benefit derivable from a new sales forecasting system is only estimable. However, merely because it eludes precise measurement, it still exists.

Insofar as computer technology is concerned, little is impossible. What is technically practical, on the other hand is another question. It is generally wisest to make important improvements in small and measured steps. Any size hardware is available, as has amply been demonstrated in this book, and the selection of hardware is important. However, having hardware without people qualified to work with it is foolish. So it's technically possible, but the people resources may be the deciding factor.

Likewise, one cannot expect people or processes to independently make difficult changes. The transformation will not be instantaneous, as methods which have been used since before people can recall them are fimrly entrenched. The best system, unused, is as beneficial as no system.

A summary of the three types of feasibility test is presented in Figure 7.9.

Format of the Feasibility Study Report

These are the minimum elements of the feasibility study report; the format will be a function of local specifications:

1. Objectives—a statement of what the systems improvement should be, in measurable terms.
2. Weakness of the present system—a description of the areas where the investigative effort should be placed and where the benefits will be found.
3. Features of the proposed solution—a description of the major building blocks of the proposed solution.
4. Benefits to be derived from the system—technical, operational, and economic.
5. Cost—a realistic assessment of all costs, including time and equipment.
6. Alternatives—other possible ways, if any, to accomplish the objectives.
7. Schedule—when it will happen; when it could happen; when the resources will be available.

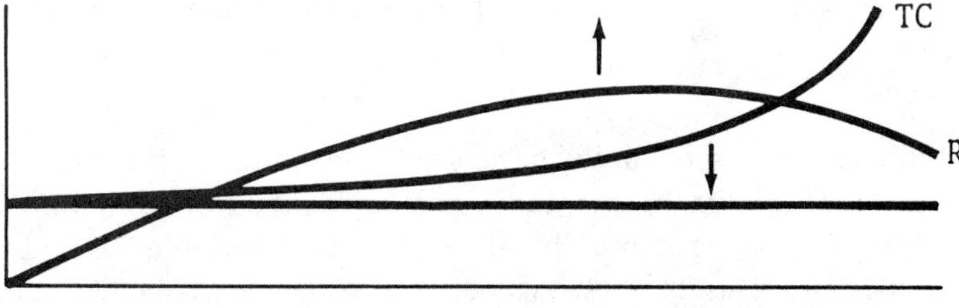

Figure 7.8

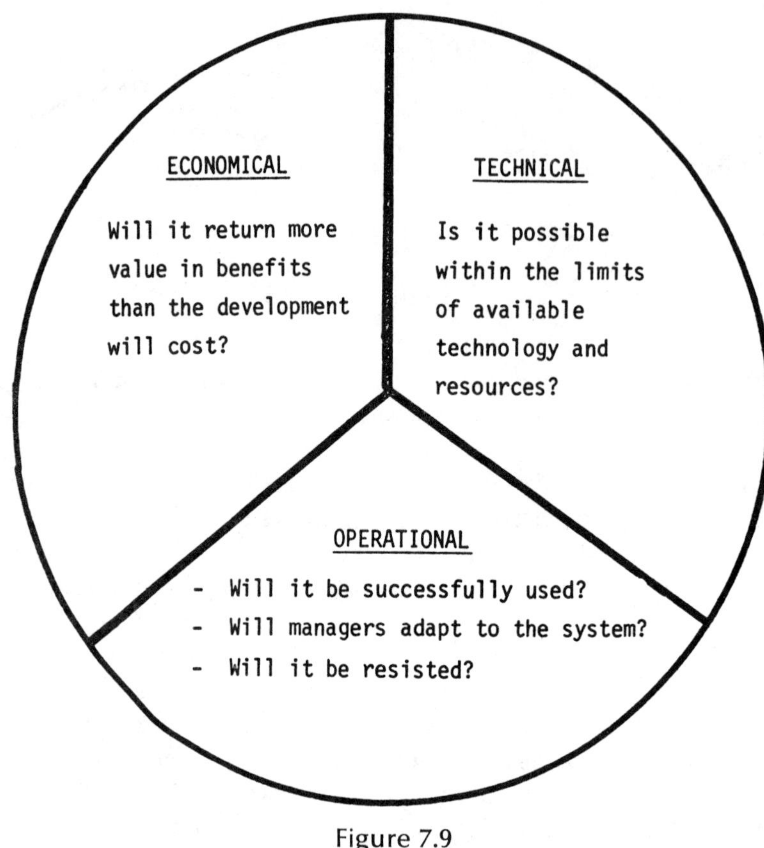

Figure 7.9

With these requirements firmly established, the next step will be the mechanics of gathering the data in search of the measureable benefits. The important thing to remember is to be measureable.

Applications Research and Problem Definition

For most analysts, systems work means not only studying the present system and designing a new one; it also may mean acquiring some general knowledge of the applications involved. This may include crash courses in finance, accounting, marketing, distribution, production, and the like.

It is most beneficial here to impart the concept of woodwork. The successful analyst must be so familiar with the process he must analyze that, if necessary, he could operate. To overcome "Mount Olympus" (superlative knowledge) syndrome, he must become part of the "woodwork" of what he is to analyze. In this manner, he can observe the operation first hand in its natural environment; he can observe the operation from inside it, where potential artificiality disappears. He can become familiar with the problems from having experienced them; he will be accepted as a bonafide member of the user's team, rather than being perceived as an outsider intent upon causing upheaval and frustration.

Systems Study Resources

Systems work is a functional area responsibility. The system team during this phase must contain several functional (user) specialists. These are the people who can guide the team to a knowledge of the area. The number of computer specialists needed at this time is small, functioning as technical consultants. They ensure that data collected are useful in subsequent phases of the systems development cycle. The functional specialists gather data while the computer specialists may or may not be the analyst.

Size of the systems team during this phase is dependent upon the environment, objectives and scope of the study. Generally, the team is the smallest it will be during the project. The members at this time are full-time employees who should remain with the project team until completion of the project. Studies have found that 30% of the firms using computers never do this phase; and there seems to be a correlation between success and a formal systems development approach. Interesting.

Consultants

Consultants make good hatchet men—they can do what must be done without fear of recrimination. Either for that purpose or to augment meager people resources, you should consider the use of consultants. Generally, the consultant has been this way before—and knows what questions to ask. Specialized experience, objectivity, and impunity are three attributes which may be found in a consultant.

Presenting the Results

The presentation of results of the study should be short and to the point. It should contain (1) the cost differential summary, (2) a major resource summary, (3) an additional benefits summary, and (4) the major recommendations. It may contain a detailed statement of recommendations, conclusions, and supporting facts, with a breakdown of cost, and explanation of extra benefits, and the detailed reasoning for the recommendations. The supporting material of the study, the objectives, all preliminary and interim reports, and outline of how the study was conducted, and a copy of the overall report findings may be included.

Some presentations will have to be made in person. The above format is sufficient, dressed in suitable presentation technique. Your audience is not concerned with the minutiae. You should be careful to avoid finger-pointing, as the prime user (who no doubt built the present system) may be in your audience. Present your conclusions in building-block form. Be prepared to give detail if asked, but present highlights. Don't expect the proposal to sell itself.

The Systems Analyst—A Change Merchant

One of the most difficult parts of the career of systems analyst is the recognition, by the analyst, that he or she is in the business of change. Figure 7.10 shows graphically the nature of change and degree of support for the change over time. There are eight distinct stages of change commitment, defined in three phases.

- *Stage 1—Contact:* At this phase, the analyst deals with the unawareness of the user. It is in the preparation phase of the project, and there is no commitment to the project at this point.
- *Stage 2—Awareness of Change.* The user now knows that something is happening, but there is confusion—What will be done? Who will do it? When will it be done? Still, there is no commitment, but we're getting closer.
- *Stage 3—Understand the Change.* At this point, something must be done, and we cross the disposition threshold, which separates the preparation phase from the acceptance phase. Unfortunately, it's at this point where all the negative perceptions are exhibited.
- *Stage 4—Positive Perception.* A little education has now occurred, and there is a go/no go decision here. The decision, if short-circuited here, will be not to attempt or support the installation of the change.
- *Stage 5—Installation.* We're now at the commitment threshold, and are entering the commitment phase. This is also a go/no go position, and if the decision is to abort, the change is also aborted.
- *Stage 6—Adoption.* The money is spent, and a decision made to abort the change here will reflect negatively upon the project team and the organization.

Stages of Change Commitment

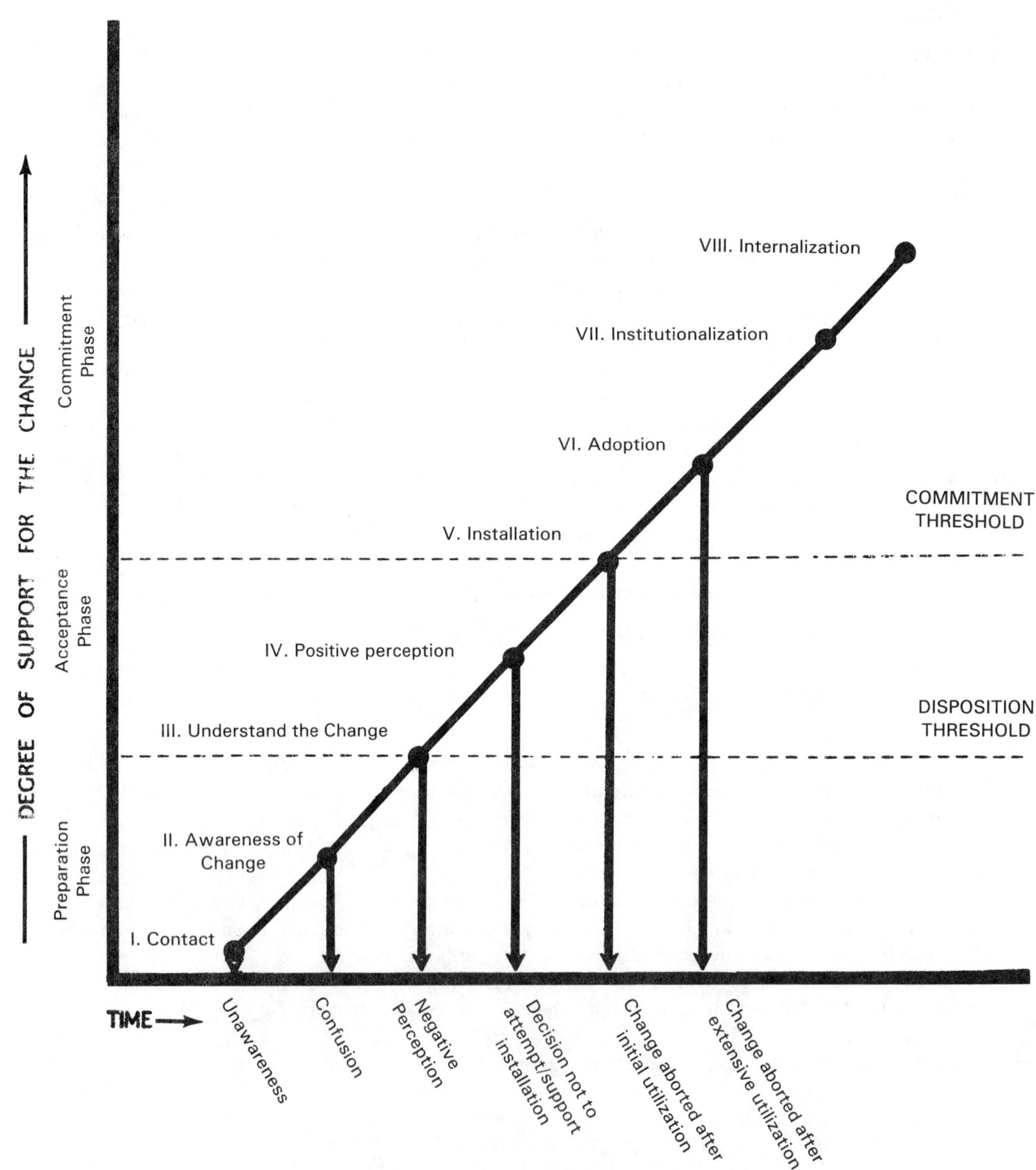

Figure 7.10

- *Stage 7—Institutionalization.* It becomes part of the ''way things are done around here,'' a part of the policy and procedures manual.
- *Stage 8—Internalization.* The change is accepted as valid, workable, and realistic. It's the way things are done because that's the way we want it done.

The Mechanics of Analysis

Systems Investigation

System and *organization* are interchangeable terms. Since most organizations now consist of appendages to one or more computers, the systems installed, in whatever form of installation, are a model of the organization the are designed to serve. This, of course, does not make the computer a master—it is still the servant—but it does mean that using a computer places a strange, new, and different protocol upon us. The analyst who studies this organization would be advised to be well prepared for certain user reactions:

Cooperative. This is the user who sees the value of an automated system and can effectively use the product in the management of his function. Be careful with the overly cooperative user who would be manipulative.

Solicitous. This is the user who will accept computerization as a means to a different end—personal desires, enhanced prestige, or authority.

Recalcitrant. This is the user who is convinced that the organization, and therefore any system, could not possibly operate without him. This individual leaves his phone number when he goes on vacation.

Resistant. This is the user who is being forced to computerize and will see the effort as a contest where winning is paramount. He will give the impression of being cooperative while withholding information.

Surreptitious. This individual will find subtle ways to scuttle the activity and is not above purposeful and conscious sabotage.

Threatened. This individual has spent many years to achieve his position and salary, and will not eagerly accept being moved by a person half his age. He will go out of his way to prove that the change in impractical.

The motivations of the user during any systems investigation effort will be largely undefinable, even to the user himself. There are a few perspectives to remember. First, when a user makes a request, be assured that it has everything to do with something which must be reported upward. He is not about to air his own dirty linen and to proclaim that he is incapable of managing—but something is not right, and somebody above him knows about it. Secondly, the user is most often reacting to the symptom of a problem, not to the problem itself. If he knew what the problem was, he would correct it. Thus, since it is the symptom that is producing the pressure, removal of the symptom convinces the user that the problem is resolved, while it may not be. If the analyst patches only the symptom and not the problem, the same or another symptom will show and the analyst will be blamed for not correcting the problem.

These are not new perspectives and have been well documented. Analysts still fall into the trap, however, whether for lack of knowledge, lack of understanding, timidity, susceptibility to pressure, or for other more subtle reasons. On the other side the user is aware of enough horror stories of poor analysis to be justified wary.

Begin with the Organization Chart

Computer or not, an organization is people, and people generate communications—on both the vertical and horizontal planes. Business operates on human communications and interaction. Thus, the present difficulties are to a great extent related to communication. In a manual system it is the communication which process the data.

The form of an organization reflects its functions. One technique of systems analysis centers on organizational data. The organization chart indicates the individual jobs within a department and the lines of authority and responsibility between them. It, along with accompanying functional statements, shows where data processing is performed. Upon reviewing the charts, a manager may decide to alter the scope of the systems study.

As the organization aspects of the present system are being considered, so too should the flow of information be charted. Specifically, the analyst should be concerned with what information flows vertically, who initiates the information flow, who receives it, when and by whom the information is interpreted, and when and by whom action is taken based on that information. Likewise, the horizontal information flow should be charted and documented, since lateral information flow will be the crux of the information processing activities. Simply stated, decision data flow along the vertical axis, while operational and functional data flows along the horizontal axis. The charting of this information should include not merely that information which resides upon or is communicated by paper, but through other communications media as well—telephone, electronic mail, telecommunications, etc.

The cost of collecting and filing documents is extremely important. If encoding is done, if there is equipment involved, if paper moves, it has a cost and time factor, and it should be included. Staffing data is also important. Staffing data tells who is doing the processing and is the basis for computing personnel costs. Capture the authorized staffing and the assigned staffing.

No Computer Demanded

Use of the computer should not be a foregone conclusion, even though you may be a computer analyst. The mission is to determine work—flow difficulties and how to overcome them—not to buy a computer and to find how to pay for it. If your determinations justify machinery, OK. More often than not, however, there are improvements which can be made which do not demand the computer.

Work Simplification

Some systems analysis techniques have existed since Taylor instituted scientific management. Work simplification consists of normal day-to-day improvements initiated by managers or employees; it is a common-sense means to eliminate waste of material, equipment, time, energy, and space in performance of work. Improvement possibilities are limited only by the ability, imagination, and aggressiveness of the analyst. The technique is not limited to systems work, but can be applied to procedures, forms, arrangements, and layouts. These are the steps:

1. Promote participation by all. A strong belief that it can be done will assist its doing. Suggestion systems work well here.
2. Justify each activity for its essentiality and eliminate all unnecessary activities. Devise simple goals which can be supported by simple processes.
3. Combine work activities wherever possible to avoid duplication.
4. Reduce travel distances to the shortest feasible distance. Move paper and not people.

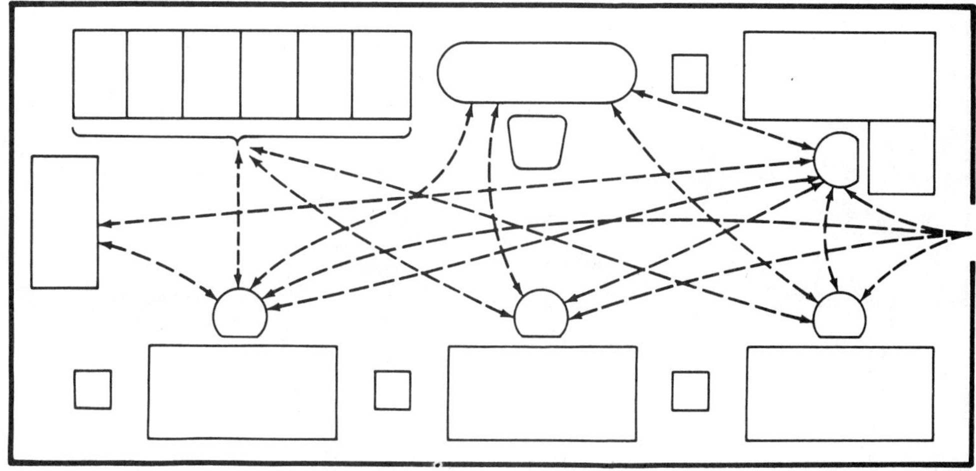

Figure 7.11

5. Arrange activities, people, furniture, and equipment to allow a smooth flow from one clerical step to another in a rhythmic pattern for an efficient workplace.

Methods and Procedures Charting

One type of chart is a movement chart, a diagram showing motion through space. A scaled layout of an office floor plan, such as shown in Figure 7.11, serves as the background so that movement can be measured and viewed in proper relationship to the physical factors. Such a chart highlights backtracking, congestion, and bottlenecks. It should be noted that this is merely an office layout chart on which the traffic pattern can be superimposed. This superimposition can be done by making several copies of the plan and then on each individual plan charting the flow of people, documents, data, or other pertinent information. Using this technique, organizations have reduced movement and other flow bottlenecks, saving thousands of dollars.

Second is the process chart. The process chart gives a detailed description of the successive steps in a process, indicated by statements and symbols arranged vertically in chronological order, arranged to give a clear picture of the office procedure. Any reasonable set of symbols may be used, such as those shown in Figure 7.12.

On the process chart, it is customary to include times required, distance covered, and a summary of activities. The steps are detailed on a form like the one shown in Figure 7.13.

There are several other types of charts which can be used. Figure 7.14 gives a little detail for the work flow, multi-column process, single-column process, forms distribution, flow diagram, and operation charts.

The Work of Analysis

The above dealt with ways to commit facts to paper, and more of that is to come. But to commit facts to paper, they must first be obtained. There are essentially four ways for the analyst to gain data: interviews, questionnaires, observation, and research. All have advantages and disadvantages.

The interview is informal and loosely structured. It permit sensitivity and observations of kinesics. It capitalizes on nonverbal communications and includes immediate feedback. It allows the analyst to be an investigative reporter in the place where the work is done. But—it's time consuming, may be impractical due to distance, requires strict control, and is highly dependent upon human relations ability. It is also highly dependent upon the interviewing skills of the analyst and upon his ability to handle risk and confrontation.

OPERATION	○	Some physical operation in the process
TRANSPORTATION	⇨	The object is moved from one location to another
INSPECTION	□	This will include reviews for accuracy
DELAY	D	For some reason, the process is interrupted.
STORAGE	▽	Most generally thought of as "filing," either permanent or temporary

Figure 7.12

FLOW PROCESS CHART

SUMMARY			
ACTIONS	PRESENT METHOD	PROPOSED METHOD	DIFFERENCE
○ OPERATIONS			
⇨ TRANSPORTATIONS			
□ INSPECTIONS			
D DELAYS			
▽ STORAGES			
TOTAL DISTANCE (FEET)			

ORGANIZATIONAL UNIT	
PROCESS	
CHART BEGINS	
CHART ENDS	
CHARTED BY	DATE

STEP NO.	DETAILS OF METHOD □ PRESENT □ PROPOSED	OPERATION / TRANSPORTATION / INSPECTION / DELAY / STORAGE	DISTANCE (in feet)	WHAT? WHERE? WHEN? WHO? HOW? } WHY? ANALYSIS { ELIMINATE SIMPLIFY COMBINE CHANGE SEQUENCE NOTES
		○ ⇨ □ D ▽		
		○ ⇨ □ D ▽		
		○ ⇨ □ D ▽		
		○ ⇨ □ D ▽		

Figure 7.13

OBJECTIVE	CHART TO USE	ILLUSTRATION OF CHART
To study the sequence of major operating steps in an activity and the organization units performing them.	WORK FLOW CHARTS give a general description of the steps in one column; other columns represent organization units. The connecting lines show the flow of work.	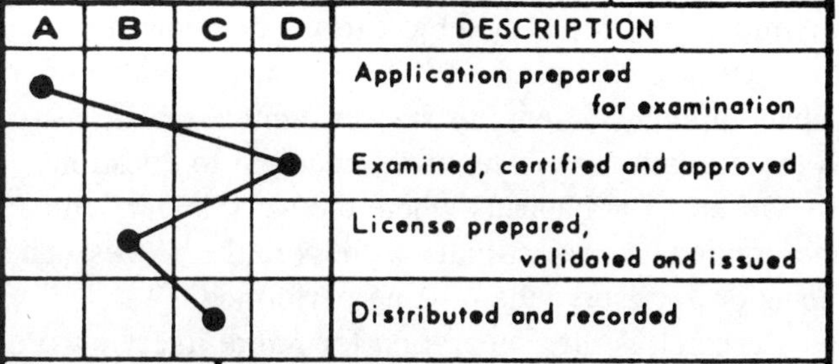 A, B, C, D, DESCRIPTION: Application prepared for examination; Examined, certified and approved; License prepared, validated and issued; Distributed and recorded
To analyze the detailed steps in a flow of work that is quite complex or involves several organization units.	MULTI-COLUMN PROCESS CHARTS show steps in greater detail than on a work flow chart -- symbols are used to describe steps.	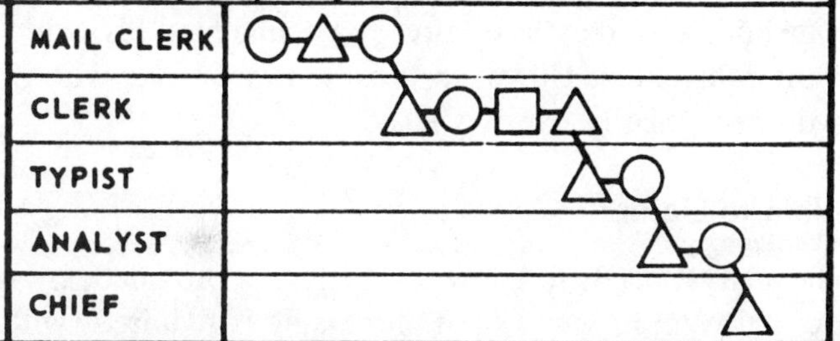 MAIL CLERK; CLERK; TYPIST; ANALYST; CHIEF
To study the detailed steps in a relatively simple procedure such as one within a single organization unit.	SINGLE-COLUMN PROCESS CHARTS are often drawn on printed forms; work flow is shown by connecting the appropriate symbols.	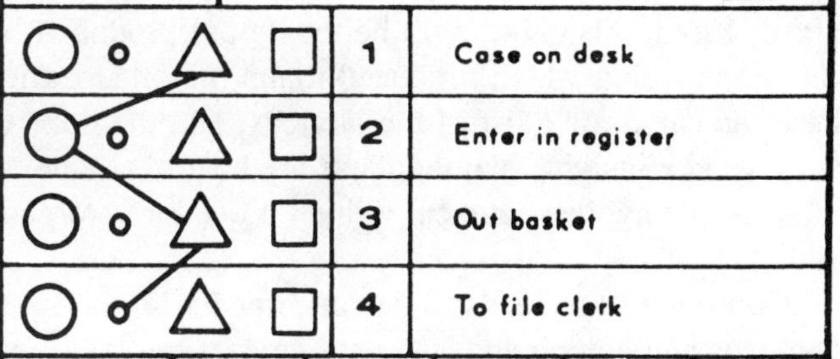 1 Case on desk; 2 Enter in register; 3 Out basket; 4 To file clerk
To study the flow of copies of a multi-copy form.	FORM DISTRIBUTION CHARTS show the number of copies in the first column. The flow of each copy of the form is traced from unit to unit.	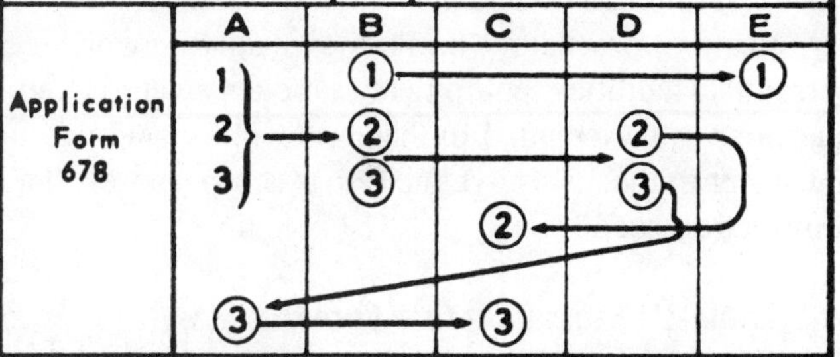 Application Form 678: 1, 2, 3; A, B, C, D, E
To improve the layout of the office so that unnecessary steps can be avoided.	FLOW DIAGRAM CHARTS involve a diagram of the office made to scale -- the flow from desk to desk is shown by arrows.	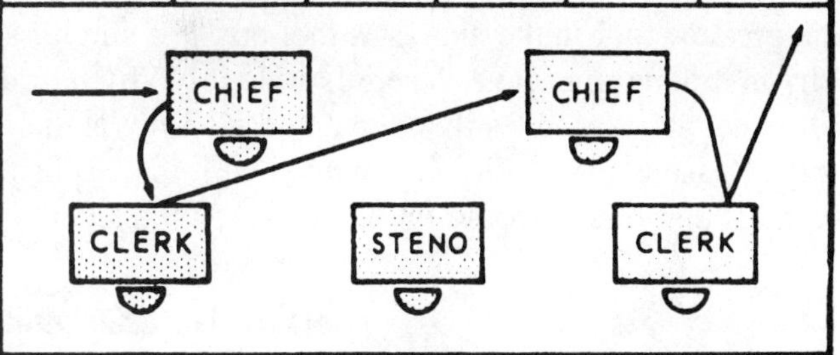 CHIEF; CHIEF; CLERK; STENO; CLERK
To simplify the steps in an operation performed by one employee.	OPERATION CHARTS are of several types; the one shown in the next column is commonly used to study the motions of each hand.	LEFT HAND: 1. Move to drawer; 2. Pick up clip; 3. Move clip to paper; 4. Attach clip to paper — RIGHT HAND: 1. Move to paper; 2. Pick up paper; 3. Idle; 4. Idle

Figure 7.14

Questionnaires are concise, easily tabulated, inexpensive, structured, time-sensitive, and provide anonymity. They are also subject to imprecision of the language and the overstructure of possible responses because they are inflexible. There is no guarantee of return or of validity. There is no opportunity to expand upon questions, to answer omitted questions, or to volunteer information. There is no incentive to respond and no means to test reaction to questions.

Observation happens where the work is performed, allowing the analyst to distinguish between fact and opinion. As a first-hand witness to the process, the analyst has an opportunity to perform measurements or to observe them being performed.

Research is the preparation for future interviews, observations, and questionnaires. Recognizing that somebody else may have already documented his work on the same problem, it prevents the wheel from being reinvented. However, situations are never wholly similar and the view, taken alone, could be dated and unnecessarily narrow.

What to Gather

The analyst needs to know what input is provided, by whom, when, what volumes, and characteristics. He will want to know what processing is required, with the method and intermediate results to be obtained. Key to his efforts will be the output produced, its format, content, decision made, and timing. The organization which produced it and the organization which received it are both important. From these, he can draw a list of the obvious, and the not-so-obvious problems. Certain types of information can give key insight. Among these are historical data, job descriptions, volume statistics, copies of reports/forms/invoices, current written procedures, organization charts, policies, and any past reviews or studies.

Continuing, he needs to be concerned with the review of current systems: the purpose of operations, machines and equipment, and data processing. Also included is an internal review, which looks at the organization, procedures and policy manuals, work measurement and production, schedules backlog, personnel, facilities, equipment, supplies, records and files, budget and cost. There are many, many questions to be included in these categories, and this book does not permit inclusion of them—but there are systems checklists available for such purposes. The purpose here is simply to highlight the areas of information need.

The Analyst's Most Effective Tool

The greatest tool in the analyst's tool box is a single, simple question: ''WHY?'' What is being done? Why is it done this way? Where is it done? Why is it done there? When is it done? Why is it done then? Who does it? Why does this person do it? How is the task done? Why is it done that way? Facts tell the story. Reasons explain it. The analyst with the inquisitive mind generally gets the facts—sometimes even the facts that others would prefer remained hidden.

Tools for Data Organization and Analysis

If the purpose is to ultimately produce structured programming, then it would be worthwhile to review the concepts of structured analysis (now) and design (later in the chapter). There are many tools for data gathering and analysis, and we'll present a few of them. But first, let's explore the current thinking on the structure of the analysis of data.

Once the data is gathered, culled, and sifted, the ultimate product will be a specification from which the structured programming should progress. These generally take the form of (1) a data flow diagram, shown in Figure 7.14, (2) a data dictionary, (3) a process specification written in pseudocode, and (4) a set of structured specification steps.

Data Flow Diagram

Let's look first at the data flow diagram. Figure 7.15 shows a portion of a diagram which is designed to handle two transactions dealing with customer activity. Those transactions are an order or a payment. The first thing we see is that it looks somewhat like a document flowchart. Not quite. Note that the files are not shown in file symbols and the processing blocks are simply rounded rectangles. The structure comes in from the numbering of the blocks, shown as 1.0, 1.1, 1.2, etc. This particular chart is at a high level. Lower level charts would take the step further—1.0.1, etc. Next, note that the chart is annotated. The words which follow the lines indicate the intermediate products. The words which lie inside the rounded rectangles identify the process or outgoing product. The files are simply flags to the processing block. Not very complicated, of course, but effective.

The Data Dictionary

Data flows are somewhat incomplete, and provide a very general description of the system. It's important to identify the data used in the system, and there are several charts on the pages following which will assist you to do that task. To identify the data, it's first important to identify the features, which include:

AND	Connected data items which will be used together
OR	A choice of options where at least one connected data item must be present
OPTIONAL	A data item may or may not be present
ITERATIONS	Zero, one, or more connected data items must be present

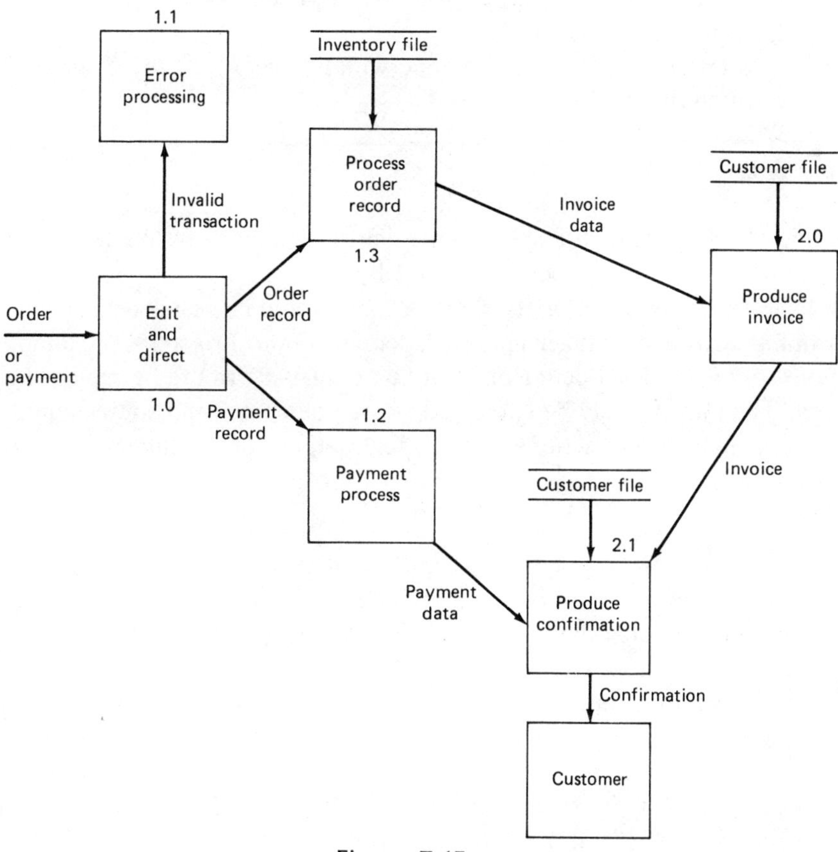

Figure 7.15

The definition starts at the top and works its way down to the level where it can be subdivided no further. Figure 7.16 shows a data dictionary.

The next step is to translate this into pseudocode—structured English, if you will. Figure 7.16a is the pseudocode for activity 1.0 of the Data Flow Diagram.

There are several ways to go from here. One is known as the De Marco Seven Steps of Structured Analysis:

Step 1: Build a current physical model.
Step 2: Build a current logical model from the physical model.
Step 3: Build a logical model of the new system to be built.
Step 4. Create a family of new physical models.
Step 5. Produce cost and schedule estimates for each model.
Step 6. Select one model.
Step 7. Package the specification into subsystems.

A model is a picture of the system as it exists. It can be flowcharted, developed in matrices, or structured as shown in the Data Flow Diagram. Looking at the current model is very important, as it becomes the basis for the new model in Step 3. At this point, some initial thinking can go into new designs—the new physical models. The balance of the steps (5 to 7), are the same no matter whose method is used.

The Decision Matrix

Perhaps no tool of analysis has been so grossly slighted as the decision matrix (table). Figure 7.17 shows a good example of a simplified decision matrix.

The decision matrix specifies what must be done without specifying the method. It's perhaps the oldest and most reliable structuring tool.

The Input/Output and Documents Matrix

This matrix classifies documents with respect to the nature of their flow, the location of the flow, and the type of action to be taken upon them. See Figure 7.18.

The function, sub-function, and activity shown at left would correspond to specific organizational units. This is the gross action to be taken, not the specific action. It is also an example for text purposes. Yours will be more complete. The document identification (A–E) would be replaced by specific document identification. The matrix could be expanded to include names and sources of data elements, distribution of files and documents, transactions which affect outputs and documents, transaction timing, and the interval and delay of the output.

The Data Elements Matrix

This matrix is a refinement of the input/output and documents matrix. In this matrix (See Figure 7.19), the data elements are uniquely classified, and then the specifications to be accomplished upon the data are posted. the matrix you develop will be more complete than this text example:.

Again, the function, subfunction, and activity shown at left would correspond to specific organizational units. The documents (X_1–X_8) would be replaced by the specific data element name. This data element structuring is extremely important in structuring the hierarchy of data for the data base. You can add size, class, transactions (which produce or modify, editing requirements, control requirements, access authority, and security considerations to this matrix.

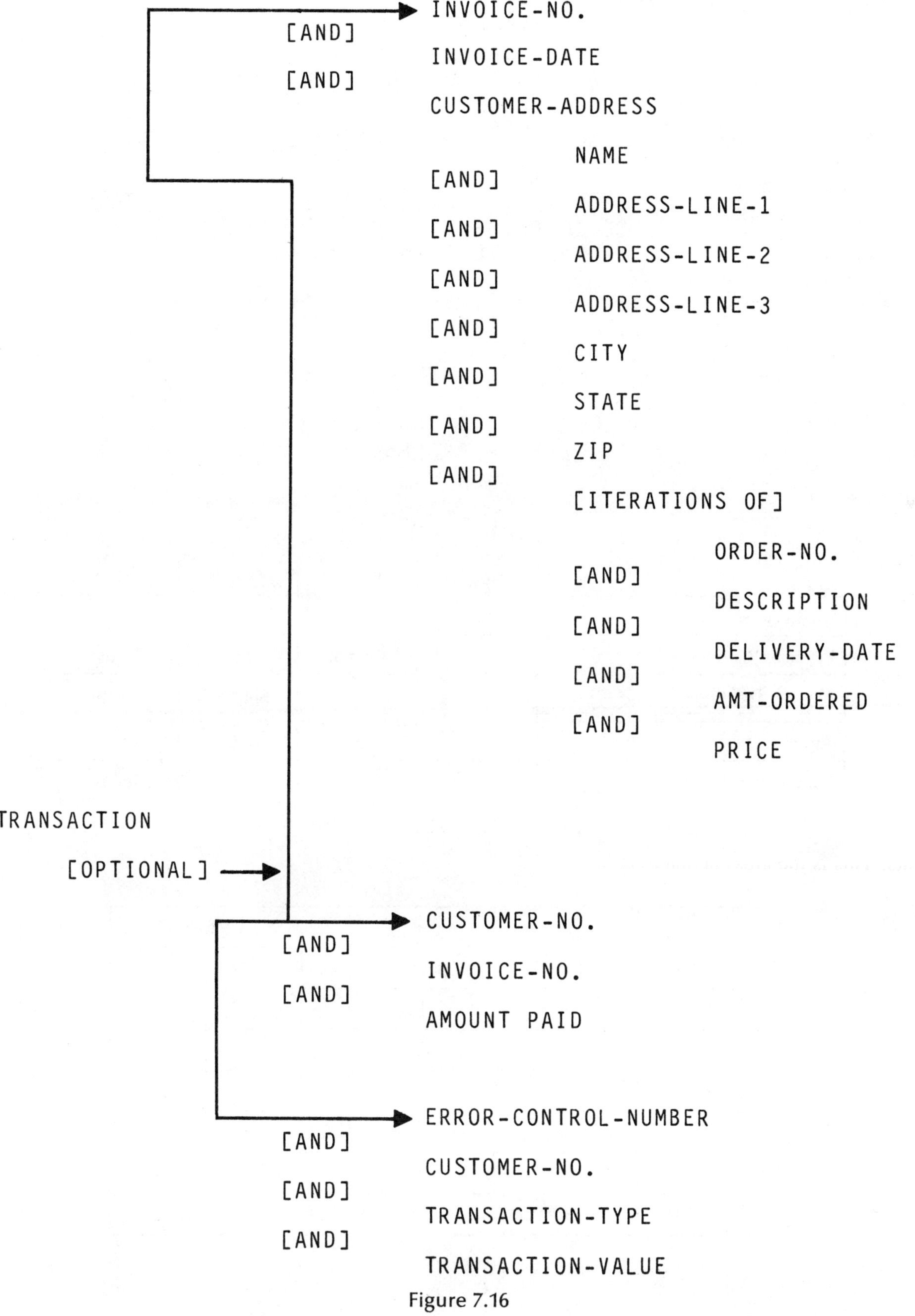
INVOICE-NO.
[AND]
INVOICE-DATE
[AND]
CUSTOMER-ADDRESS
NAME
[AND]
ADDRESS-LINE-1
[AND]
ADDRESS-LINE-2
[AND]
ADDRESS-LINE-3
[AND]
CITY
[AND]
STATE
[AND]
ZIP
[AND]
[ITERATIONS OF]
ORDER-NO.
[AND]
DESCRIPTION
[AND]
DELIVERY-DATE
[AND]
AMT-ORDERED
[AND]
PRICE
TRANSACTION
[OPTIONAL]
CUSTOMER-NO.
[AND]
INVOICE-NO.
[AND]
AMOUNT PAID
ERROR-CONTROL-NUMBER
[AND]
CUSTOMER-NO.
[AND]
TRANSACTION-TYPE
[AND]
TRANSACTION-VALUE

Figure 7.16

```
EDIT AND DIRECT.
     GET A TRANSACTION;
     IF ORDER TRANSACTION TYPE
          VALIDATE ORDER FIELDS;
          IF ERROR
               SET ERROR INDICATOR;
               PERFORM ERROR PROCESSOR
          ENDIF;
          PERFORM ORDER PROCESS
     ELSE IF PAYMENT TYPE
          VALIDATE PAYMENT FIELDS
          IF ERROR
               SET ERROR INDICATOR;
               PERFORM PROCESS ERROR
          ENDIF;
          PERFORM PAYMENT PROCESS
     ELSE
          SET ERROR INDICATOR;
          PERFORM PROCESS ERROR
```

Figure 7.16a

	Rule 1	Rule 2	Rule 3	Rule 4
Credit Acceptable	Y	N	N	N
Payment History		Prompt	Tardy	Tardy
Manager Decisions			Approve	Disappr.
Approve Order	X	X	X	
Take Action To:				Refuse

Figure 7.17

Function	Sub-function	Activity	DOCUMENT A	B	C	D	E
1	1	1		I	P	O	
1	1	2	F				O
1	1	3		P			
2	1	1	I		I	I	
2	1	2	P	I	O	F	
I = INPUT	P = POST	O = OUTPUT	F = FILE				

Figure 7.18

Function	Sub-function	Activity	Document #1				Document #2			
			X_1	X_2	X_3	X_4	X_5	X_6	X_7	X_8
1	1	1	I		I		O		P	
1	1	2		O		P		I		
1	2	1					I			
2	1	1	O		P		O	I		O
I = INPUT				O = OUT			P = POST			

Figure 7.19

The Data/File Matrix

This matrix changes the approach somewhat, placing the data element identification to the left, and the files or reports across the top. The matrix identifies the use, within files and reports, of the data elements. See Figure 7.20.

The data/file matrix can be expanded to included sources of data, distribution of reports, controls, edits, timing information, and security.

The Data Use Matrix

Figure 7.21 is a further refinement of the data/file matrix, indicating the uses of the data, the actions to be taken upon the data, and the location of the actions.

The Information Flow Matrix

Figure 7.22 is an example of how the total information flow can be placed into matrix form. Departing from the usual two-dimensional matrix, this chart is triangular in form, indicating all the sources, destinations, actions, files, data elements, and their respective relationships. This matrix is a little more difficult to construct than the others, but permits one to look at the total picture of the information system.

DATA ELEMENT	FILES/REPORTS										
	F_0	F_1	F_2	F_3	F_4	F_5	R_1	R_2	R_3	R_4	R_5
EMPL. NUMBER	R	E A	P N	O D	R	T U	S	E	R		
EMPL. NAME	C E	O N	D T	E E	S R	E	A D	R	E		
EMPL. ADDRESS	H	E	R	E							
EMPL. SSN											
ETC.											

Figure 7.20

DATA ELEMENT	USER CODES						ENTRY TYPE	
	A	B	C	D	E	F	DATA USE CODES	
EMPL. NBR.			3a				1 2 3	ORIGINATOR MAINTENANCE INQUIRY
EMPL. NAME		1b						
EMPL. ADDR.	2c						a b c	IMMEDIATE 24 HOURS OVERNIGHT

Figure 7.21

Let's trace a transaction through the matrix:

1. Left side, rightmost X, a customer inquiry.
2. Triggers one output, a manual expediting request. No files affected.
3. Used by production control, right side.
4. Left side again, customer line, leftmost X.
5. Two files are affected—the open order and customer master files.
6. Input is a regular order/approved quotation.
7. Three outputs—order register, make-order request, and short-order request.
8. Three separate distributions—internal control, production control, and the customer; the files are updated.

The transaction is complete.

The Transaction Matrix

Figure 7.22a is an example of a transaction matrix. The matrix should be flexible to permit inclusion of fields relevant to the data being evaluated.

The Payoff Matrix

The payoff matrix (Figure 7.23) is used in the determination of selective strategies and their corresponding returns, since actions taken by management may depend heavily upon the information presented.

Probabilities are assigned to each of the conditions and returns for each of the coordinates are estimated, as shown in Figure 7.24.

Possible Action #3 is the most profitable strategy:

$$\begin{aligned}\text{Possible Action \#3} &= P(3, 1) + P(3, 2) + P(3, 3) + P(3, 4)\\ &= .10(\$9{,}000) + .30(\$10{,}000) + .40(\$5{,}000) + .20(\$8{,}000)\\ &= \$9{,}000 + \$3{,}000 + \$2{,}000 + \$1{,}600 = \$7{,}500\end{aligned}$$

This is the best option (#1 = \$5,500; #2 = \$5,000; #4 = \$6,400). This is the method to use when outcome is uncertain; it is particularly useful for marketing activities.

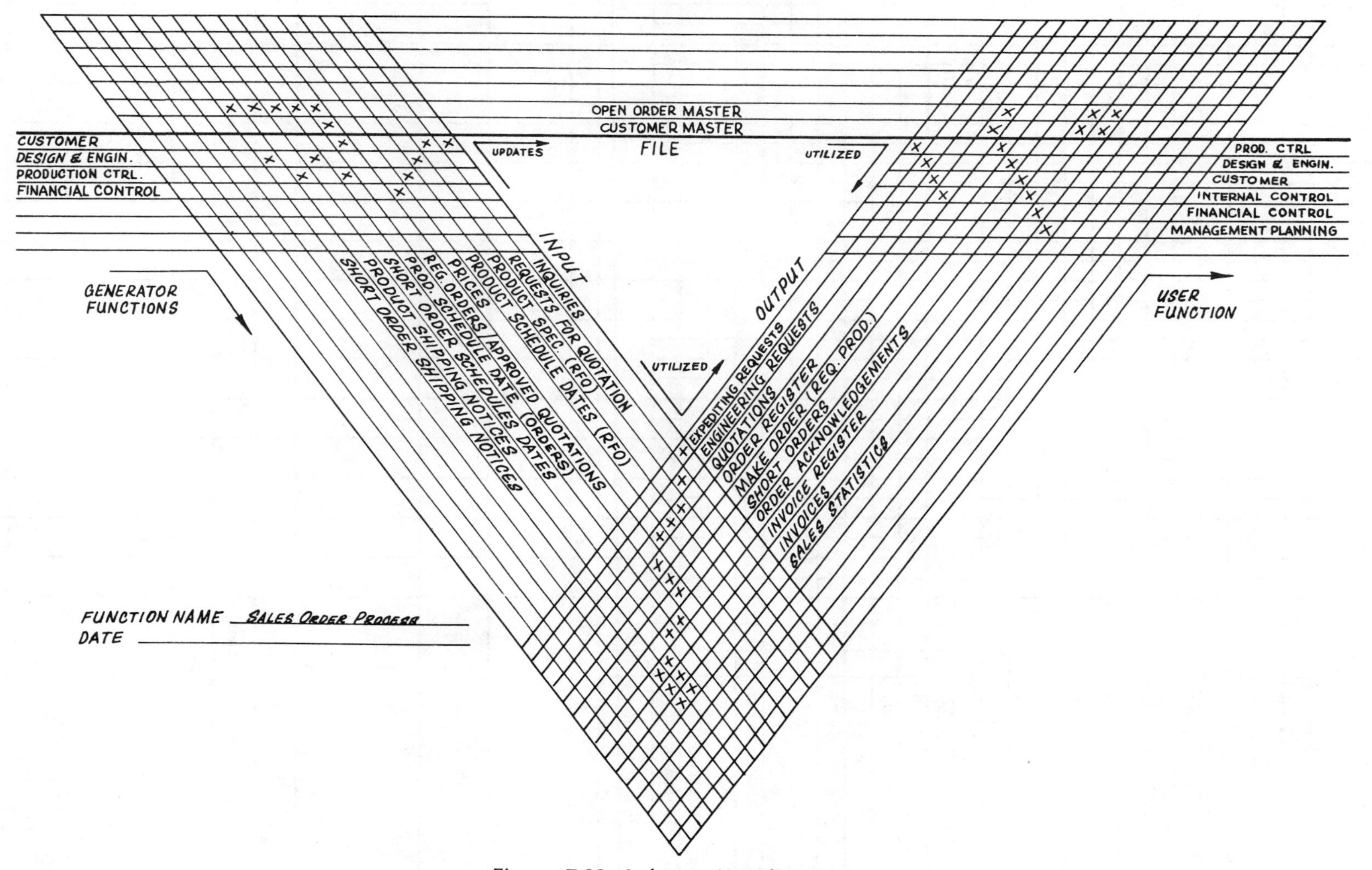

Figure 7.22. Information Flow Matrix

TRANSACTION MATRIX

Trans. No.	Transaction	Volume	Frequency	Detail/Summary	Received From:	Sent To:	Form Title	Field Size on File	Description Number	Data Element 1	Data Element 2	Data Element 3	Data Element 4	Data Element 5	Edit 1	Edit 2	Edit 3	Edit 4	Edit 5	Report 1	Report 2	Report 3	Report 4	Report 5	File 1	File 2	File 3	File 4	File 5	Security Code	Control 1	Control 2	Control 3	Total (Major)	Total (Intermediate)	Total (Minor)

Figure 7.22a. Transaction Matrix

	Cond 1	Cond 2	Cond 3	Cond 4
Possible Action #1	(1, 1)	(1, 2)	(1, 3)	(1, 4)
Possible Action #2	(2, 1)	(2, 2)	(2, 3)	(2, 4)
Possible Action #3	(3, 1)	(3, 2)	(3, 3)	(3, 4)
Possible Action #4	(4, 1)	(4, 2)	(4, 3)	(4, 4)

Figure 7.23

	P = 10%	P = 30%	P = 40%	P = 20%
Possible Action #1	$8,000	$11,000	$3,000	$ 1,000
Possible Action #2	$1,000	$ 7,000	$6,000	$ 2,000
Possible Action #3	$9,000	$10,000	$5,000	$ 8,000
Possible Action #4	$2,000	$12,000	$4,000	$10,000

Figure 7.24

Analysis Completion

The systems investigation is now complete, and the following questions should be answered before proceeding:

1. Is the existing system now fully documented?
2. Have all items on the systems documentation checklist been prepared?
3. Has user management seen and agreed to the documentation?
4. Were workers consulted during the study? Are their comments and suggestions included?
5. Did the study team review the use of all reports and files in the present system?
6. Does the user have additional exceptions not included in the documentation?
7. How much time did the user spend in reviewing the documentation?
8. What additional problems, files, and exceptions were discovered during the study phase? How will this change projected estimates?
9. Have the functional requirements of the new system been stated in detail?
10. Who in the user group has reviewed the requirements statement?
11. What design alternatives are under consideration? What factors will influence the final selection? What trade-offs are possible?
12. How was the scope of the project changed since the preliminary project statement?
13. What additional exceptions and control problems are foreseen now?

Hardware Evaluation for Systems Design

The design of many data processing systems is non-hardware-oriented. This means that the system must be designed in such a manner that many manufacturer's equipment could possibly be used. Thus, systems design generally precedes the selection of equipment. Consequently, some aspects of systems design will be discussed here to establish a foundation for a discussion of equipment selection.

The Application Study

If the system team has recommended continuing the work and management has agreed, the systems design is conducted. The application study is the documentation of the systems design. Some view the application study as an expanded feasibility study, and perhaps it is—except for the fact that the application study deals exclusively with the proposed system.

The content of the application study is varied. Perhaps most important is the systems requirement, which contains all the information needs of the organization. The system team has devoted much time to determining what information is needed; in essence, what the system's output will be. From this information, the inputs needed can be determined. Thus, the earliest design documentation will be a rough-out of products of the system—reports, file formats, input forms, etc. The essential structuring of the system flow, using a technique such as HIPO, will be done; the database structure (see the next chapter) can be determined at this time also. The record content is identified and all files to be used are segregated. Sequences are determined; storage requirements are identified. Response times are isolated and some screen design will be done. If hardware is to be obtained, the initial specifications, in terms of capability, will be written.

The anticipated systems benefits and latest cost figures are also included in the application study. The benefits are more specific and may be more factual than the general benefit statements in the feasibility study. The cost data associated with the benefits must also be more specific than previously stated. By now there has emerged a general picture of the proposed system, and costs can be reestimated with a high degree of accuracy. Three costs are important: the cost of systems development (before the money is spent); the cost of conversion from the current system to the new one; and the actual cost of operation of the new system.

The analyst must have a firm, detailed, and non-hardware-oriented systems design before any accurate cost estimate for the system can be made. The design must be flexible, but a baseline system (often called the freeze-point system) must be established. All documentation, processing methodology, and algorithms must have been set at this time.

These are the main items of the applications study. The supporting data for these items make up a rather voluminous appendix to the study, but this package becomes the documentation of the systems design. It is the sum total of tasks that the new computer must perform. The data are too detailed, however, to be used by a vendor for proposing a hardware system. But it's from this package that the hardware systems specification is developed.

Systems Specification

The systems specification is the document that the vendor uses to become familiar with the application. If the proposed system is small, the specification is basically the application study. For most systems designs, however, the application study contains much more information than is required. The cost differential, for instance, is not of interest to the vendor.

Request for Proposal

It is difficult to separate the functions of the systems team from the functions of EDP management relative to RFPs. Whether or not the systems team solicits the proposals, they should certainly review them.

The RFP is the vehicle to communicate systems development information. It is the identical specification against which all responding vendors will be benchmarked, and is the most fair method to compare differing equipment. The RFP will vary directly as the magnitude of the proposed system. It may contain the entire specification or simply an abstract.

Edward O. Joslin, in *Computer Selection,* identifies twelve elements of the RFP:

1. Systems requirements
2. Vendor support
3. Technical questionnaire
4. Benchmark data
5. Bidder's conference data
6. Check-in dates
7. Vendor questions
8. Proposal due date
9. Vendor presentations
10. Contract conditions
11. Award and debriefing dates
12. General comments

The system requirements element is the abstract of the systems specifications. Any limiting conditions must be included here. Mandatory conditions are those items essential to the organization's needs. Desirable conditions are at the vendor's option. The vendor must meet the mandatory conditions for his proposal to receive consideration. He may be comparatively penalized by not meeting the desired conditions, but is still considered.

Vendor support is necessary to fulfill the objectives; it should include training, programming, maintenance, and other kinds of technical support. The team needs information from the vendors to allow evaluation of the proposal. The technical questionnaires and systems timing tables seek to obtain information about hardware, software, vendor support, equipment cost, system timing, etc.

A *benchmark* is a routine (or group of routines) to be run on several different configurations to allow comparative analysis through performance statistics. The benchmark selected must be applied to all vendors, else there is no basis for comparison.

The RFP has all the limitations of any written document; thus, it is necessary to provide the vendor with sufficient time to analyze the RFP and to ask for clarification of items it contains. The user should include the data for the bidder's conference and a general explanation of the purpose.

The check-in dates are deadlines for the vendor to express interest in the proposal.

Many vendors will have questions about the RFP. The systems team established policy as to how questions will be handled and when answers are to be interchanged among vendors.

The proposal due date specifies the penalties that a vendor will incur if the due date is not met.

The user describes his requirements for the system to the vendor and then using demonstrations and presentations, the vendor must describe the proposal to the user. He not only describes his solution, but also demonstrates any benchmarks requested in the RFP. The conference is usually held subsequent to the submission of the bid.

The last three elements in the RFP are the contract conditions, the award and debriefing dates, and general comments. The contract conditions request that any promise made relative to the bid be put into a formal contract. The other elements are self-explanatory.

Determining the Equipment Configuration

Having completed latitude within the limitations of the RFP, the vendor can propose any configuration which will fulfill the systems requirement. Vendors can and have proposed equipment within a configuration manufactured by another vendor, but don't plan on it. It is the systems requirements which largely determine the equipment configuration to be bid. The ability to perform necessary functions determines the time needed to handle various tasks. Differences will arise among proposed systems because of differences in machine operations, handling of data, etc. The vendor must determine the most cost-effective configuration which responds to the organization's mandatory needs.

Source Data Automation

In the day and age of the microcomputer, source data automation in the traditional sense is passe. Source data automation means simply capturing the data in a form which is machine-readable at the earliest possible time. This can be done by pencil, with optical character readers, with scanning devices, acoustically, or one of several ways. However, source data automation with the microcomputer simply cannot be done less expensively. As the world of distributed data processing and on-line systems grows, the need for hand-encoding to magnetic media will diminish.

Evaluating Responses to the RFP

When you get all the answers to the questions you've raised, in the form of proposals, of course, now comes the time to figure out which is best. There are four techniques:

1. The sole source. The vendor has always been our vendor. No need for a systems study.
2. Overall impression. One proposal feels better than the others. This is the way our favorite vendor is picked from among the several to whom you went as a matter of form.
3. Cost only. The vendor with the least expensive proposal gets the business.
4. Weighted scoring. Points are preassigned to categories within the RFP. Weights are established, the vendors are measured against the weights, and the highest point-getter gets the nod.

SCERT

Computers are often used to evaluate proposed configurations. One example is the simulation package from COMRESS, Inc., called SCERT (there is also a microcomputer version). SCERT is a system of programs designed to simulate a proposed system. The are five primary functional components:

1. The introduction of processing requirements. The input is formatted to represent the workloads of the system and the computer processing requirements, and the SCERT module builds a mathematical model of the system based on this input.
2. The introduction of hardware and software to be simulated. Like the first components, this accepts input that describes the hardware configuration and the software packages associated with the hardware. The SCERT module builds a mathematical model which simulates the hardware and software configurations.
3. The presimulation algorithms. In this module, the module from component 1 is processed against the model from component 2. A series of calculations which structure and limit the non-hardware-oriented models to the particular performance abilities of the hardware are performed. In this module, SCERT assigns files to devices, structures files to operate on those devices, and computes times for various operations.
4. Simulation. The module identifies each program and performs the maximum throughput iterations for the run. Other phases of this module are used only if random processing or multiprogramming is possible or necessary.
5. The production of output reports. SCERT processes a complete series of standard output reports. In addition, exception reports or as-required reports are possible. The standard reports furnish estimates of running times, cost data, detailed analysis, and other data necessary to evaluate a vendor's configuration.

SCERT, like any simulation, has advantages and disadvantages. The advantages include:

1. The evaluation is based on the actual system.
2. The entire application is simulated.
3. Both hardware and software are evaluated.
4. Major variables including timing, cost, memory requirements, and software analysis.
5. The time to complete validation is minimized.
6. Simulation and computer shopping can be done concurrently.

And the disadvantages:

1. The results of the simulation depend on factors and algorithms which are difficult to obtain.
2. The user data must be formatted to the SCERT inputs.
3. Simulation can be very expensive and time-consuming.

Benchmarks

A benchmark is simply a problem used to evaluate the performance of several vendors' computers. Generally, the problem is a set of steps; they might even be actual applications which have been developed for the purpose of the benchmark. Benchmarks have many advantages in the selection process. They are run on the actual configuration and can be observed. They test the features of the actual hardware and software. There are disadvantages, however. Adequate benchmarks are difficult to design and prepare. They must be written in a standard language (generally COBOL) which will allow universal comparison.

Benchmarks, poorly prepared, can be more harmful than no benchmark at all. They can give misleading or inaccurate results which result in the selection of a less effective system. On the other hand, they can furnish the user with objective data relative to the performance of a vendor's system.

SYSTEMS AND PROCEDURES

To most, systems and procedures is a term applied to office management or to manual systems. They are the interfaces to the automated system, considering the space, process, papers, cost, quality, use of time, organization, and people. They are the common ingredients affecting most office work. While it is more glamorous to think about the nuances of automated systems design, the manual system is often the Achilles' heel for the organization. One simply cannot dismiss this aspect of systems. There is more than sufficient history of organizations which have paid dearly for inexpensive oversights.

Naturally, there is a massive movement to the automated office system. We're going to devote a portion of a later chapter to the subject, so we'll not delve into detail here. Known commonly as the ''paperless office'' and the ''office without walls,'' the application of the microcomputer to the office-related tasks has brought about yet another major part of the so-called information revolution.

The Role of Systems, Programming, and Operations

The objectives of manual systems are different, but many of the activities are similar. The differences between systems and procedures and systems development are rapidly disappearing. One need only compare the steps to see the similarities. Both require the establishment of objectives, the gathering of data, the analysis of that data, the development of a solution, land the installation of the improvement. The addition of programming talent and operational talent on the automated system is merely a recognition that some people processes are routine and repetitive and certain operational aspects centralized.

Tools For Systems and Procedures

The tools for manual systems are not unlike the tools for automated systems, but there are a few things which must be examined:

1. Forms. Many office problems are the result of bad forms design. The recording, communication, transferring, and operation upon data generally takes place using forms. The construction of the form, its control, the eye of movement across the form, the color, the amount of open space, and even the recording method can have much to do with the success of the system.
2. Records management. Paperwork has been strangling organizations for years. It's easily generated and nobody wants to throw it away. A new form (uncontrolled) is as close as the nearest copying machine. There is a life cycle for a record. Sometimes it's controlled by legal restrictions; often it's controlled by the activity of an account; frequently its's controlled by the inactivity and promise of an account; generally it's retained for some ''safe'' period, but then it must be destroyed or otherwise disposed of. In simple terms, obsolete records are too costly to store. The advent of microfilm has diminished the problem somewhat, but even the microfilm must be disposed of at some point.
3. Office manuals, manual of policies, manuals of procedures, SOPs, rules and regulations, and other books of organization guidance will be available and key to the successful improvement of any manual (as well as automated) system.
4. Standards. Manual systems require interfaces as well as automated systems—where this is necessary, standards must be established. If the standards system is working well, the manual system is no doubt working well also. If you must refer to an old budget code to find a new budget code to find a general ledger code to find a vendor number, then you can probably be certain there is work to be done.

DESIGNING THE EDP SYSTEM

Systems design is not systems analysis—it is the synthesis of those facts, objectives, requirements, timings, functions, etc., which have passed before. From this point, the analyst puts on his design hat and starts to put pieces of the puzzle back together in a new form—this time designed to meet the newly imposed need.

General Consideration

Begin at the End

It is true that the system exists to support the decision process of the user, then the place to begin is to find out what those decisions are, what kind of information is required to support those decisions, and how to get that information. One of the greatest failings of the designer has been ''this is the information we have available. Now what of *that* would you like to have?'' Likewise, a critical mistake is made by any analyst who willingly accepts a request to ''Give me a report that looks like this,'' even if initially prototyped on a microcomputer. When that is done, be certain that you will be given the opportunity to do it again. At this point, despite the fact that you'd like to be able to do everything for everybody whenever the need arises, a freeze of the systems concerns must be made, and the designer must now begin to look at the output. Consider the Universal Flowchart shown in Figure 7.25.

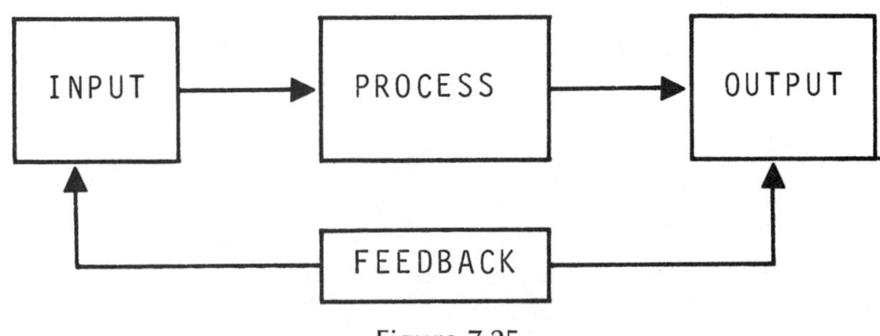

Figure 7.25

That's all there is involved for the system—and we begin by designing the third block, OUTPUT. These are the questions which should be asked:

1. What media will be used for output?
2. How much of the output content will be summarized? detailed? listed by exception?
3. What are the general requirements for format, readability, number of copies, etc?
4. What reports must be generated on schedule? on demand? on exception?
5. Are standard forms required or may non-standard forms be used?
6. Will output data be reused?
7. Will output go to another activity?
8. How many variants will there be and when will they occur?

Structured Design

The Structuring Concept

The structuring concept has been extended to the design tasks, as well; it provides a step-by-step design procedure for building the system design through the detailed design.

Structured design systematizes the design process. Design strategies like transform analysis and transaction analysis provide the means to sequence the design consideration. The product of structured design is a structure chart showing the program procedural components, their hierarchical arrangement, and the data connecting them (shown later, in Figure 7.27).

Designing programs and systems is a decision making process—and the decisions are largely technical. Structured design provides a procedure to assist designs to make those decisions. Figure 7.26 identifies the four basic steps in the structured design process:

Step 1: Draw the data flow diagram, which shows the flow of data through the sequence of steps.
Step 2: Draw the structure chart—show the functions or procedural components necessary to build the system.
Step 3: Evaluate the design of the system.
Step 4: Prepare the logical and physical program design of the system.

The first step is to show the design problem as the flow of the data through a system. This is similar in concept to flowing the documents of a manual system. The system is a combination of processes which change, or transform, the data, and become the basis for defining program components. The data flow diagram, shown in Figure 7.26, depicts the structured design process. Each circle represents a process. These four steps are the four steps of structured design.

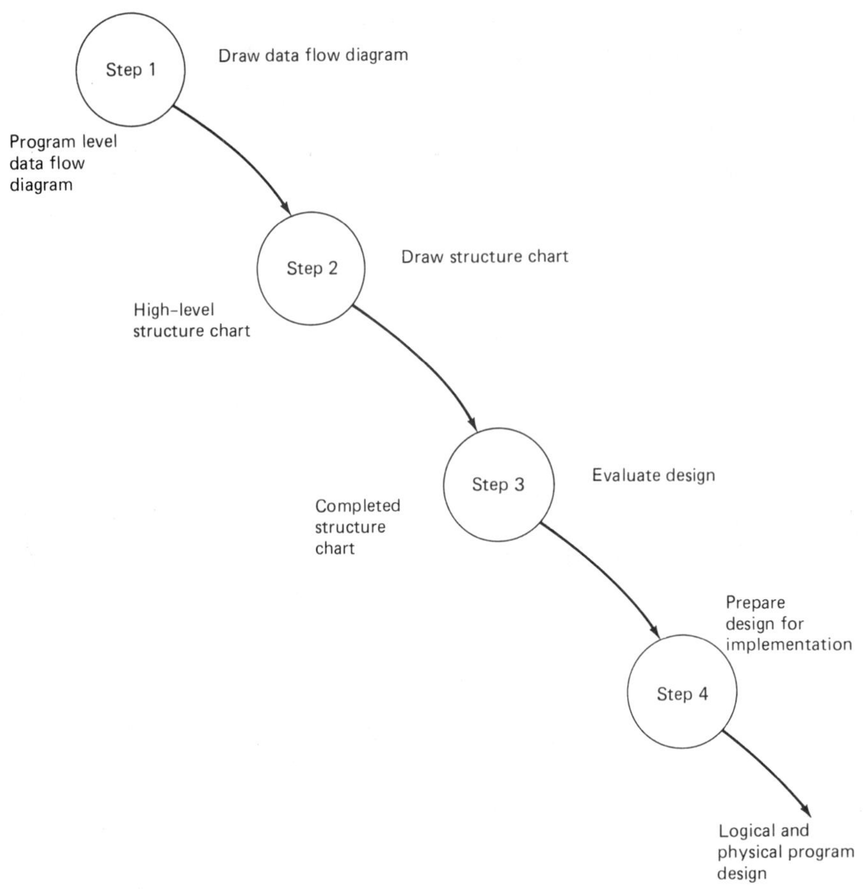

Figure 7.26

Next, it is necessary to represent the program design as a hierarchy of routines. A structure chart, shown in Figure 7.27, is used to show this view of the design. This particular structure chart matches the receipt system, previously discussed. It is derived from the data flow diagram produced in the first step. There are two strategies to follow when making a transformation of a data flow diagram into a structure chart: transform analysis and transaction analysis. These strategies, together, form a hierarchical design. The top four blocks of Figure 7.26, by the way, constitute what is known as the *High-Level Structure.*

Figure 7.28 is an example of a data flow diagram for the customer file, previously discussed.

Transform Analysis

Transform analysis is used to identify the predominant functional parts and the high-level inputs and outputs which correspond to those inputs. As you might suspect, the information is drawn from the data flow diagram. At this point, the data flow diagram is divided into those components from the universal flow chart—the inputs, processes, and outputs. The input portion of the data flow diagram details the change from the physical form in which it is received to the logical form in which it will be processed. It is called the *afferent branch.* There may be more than one afferent branches.

The output portion of the data flow diagram details the change of output data from logical form to the physical form which is a recognizable type of output. It is called the *efferent branch.* There may be more than one efferent branches.

The processing logic contains the essential logical processing (the computer program) and is furthest

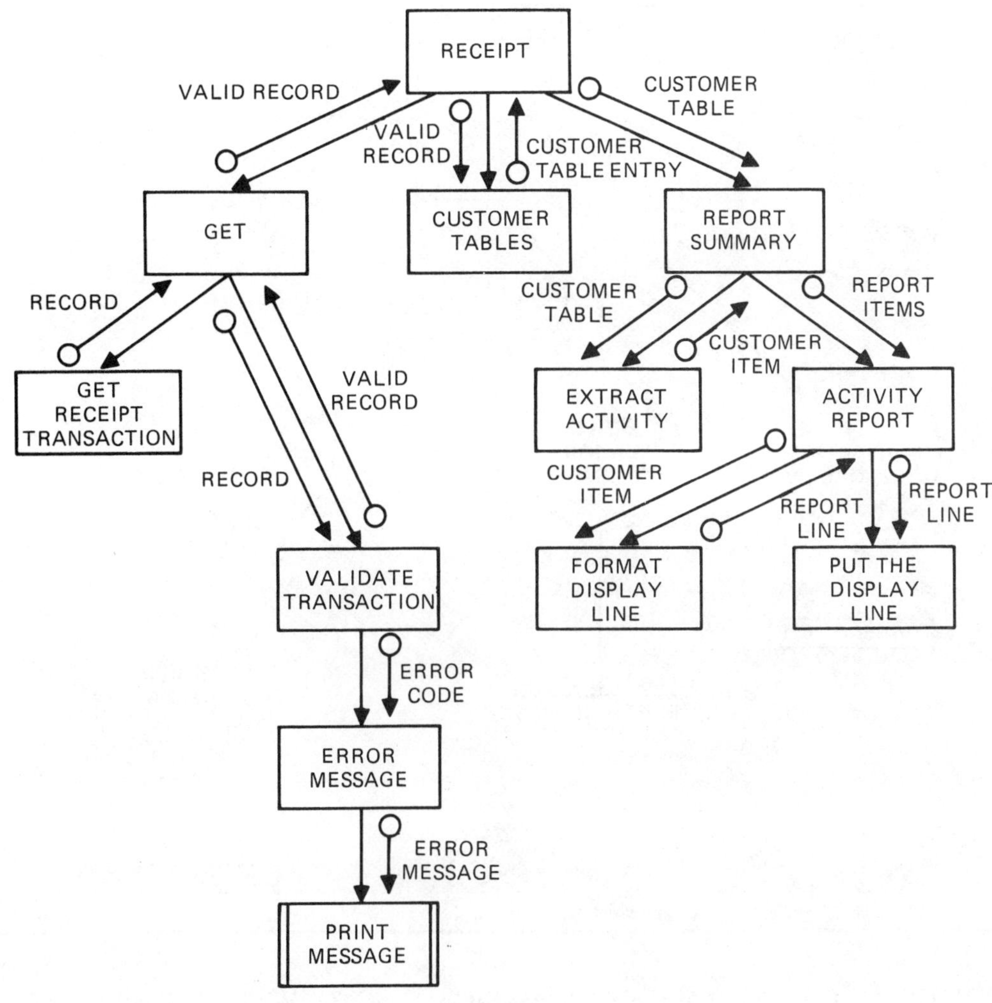

Figure 7.27

removed from either the input or output transformations. It is known as the Central Transform. There may be more than one central transforms.

Figure 7.29 shows the data flow diagram from Figure 7.28, in which the afferent branch, the efferent branch, and the central transform have been identified. The central transform will be located between the two.

In the next step, the second step of transform analysis, the structure chart is produced when you draw one functional component for each central transform, for each—the afferent branch, the efferent branch, and the central transform.

The third step is refined by the addition of subfunctions required by each of the higher-level components. This is a *factoring* of the structure chart, and may be taken to any necessary level. Factoring will require the addition of standardized input/output modules, opening and closing processing, common modules, etc. Figure 7.27 shows the fully factored structure chart.

Transaction Analysis

Transaction analysis is the second strategy. In general, it is a refinement of the high-level chart, taken to the level necessary to fully define the structure. In general, the transaction analysis structure is analogous

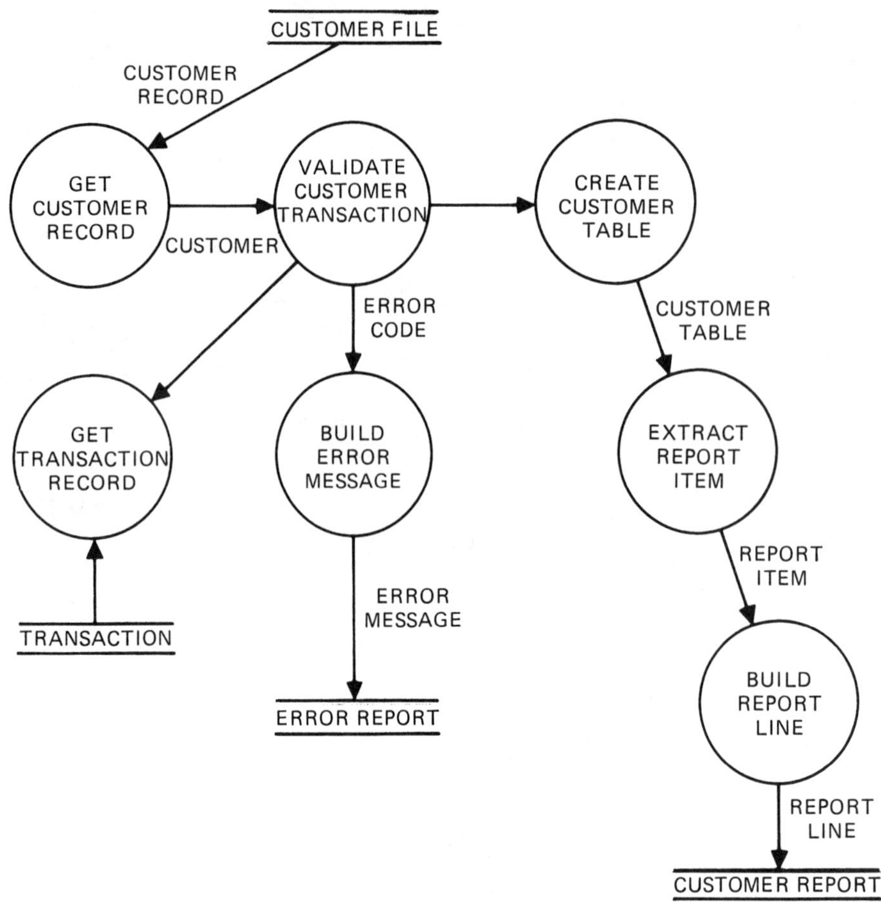

Figure 7.28

to the COBOL GO TO DEPENDING ON or the BASIC ON GOTO. We'll not detail that further here. The final structure will actually combine the transaction construct with the transform construct to form the actual hierarchical chart. Figure 7.30 details the basis steps in the transaction analysis.

Evaluate the Design

At the point where the data flow diagram identifies the processing itself, it is important to evaluate how the pieces fit together, and that is done by *coupling* and *cohesion.* Coupling is the independence between the modules. When there is little interaction, the modules are said to be *loosely coupled.* When there is much interaction, they are described to be *tightly coupled.* The most effective design is one where there is loose coupling.

Coupling

There are five types of coupling possible between two modules: data, stamp, control, common, and content. The following list is in sequence from loosest coupling to tightest coupling.

Data Coupling. Two modules of data are coupled when the data is passed through an array which is passed as a parameter between the modules. A CALL USING would fit this description.

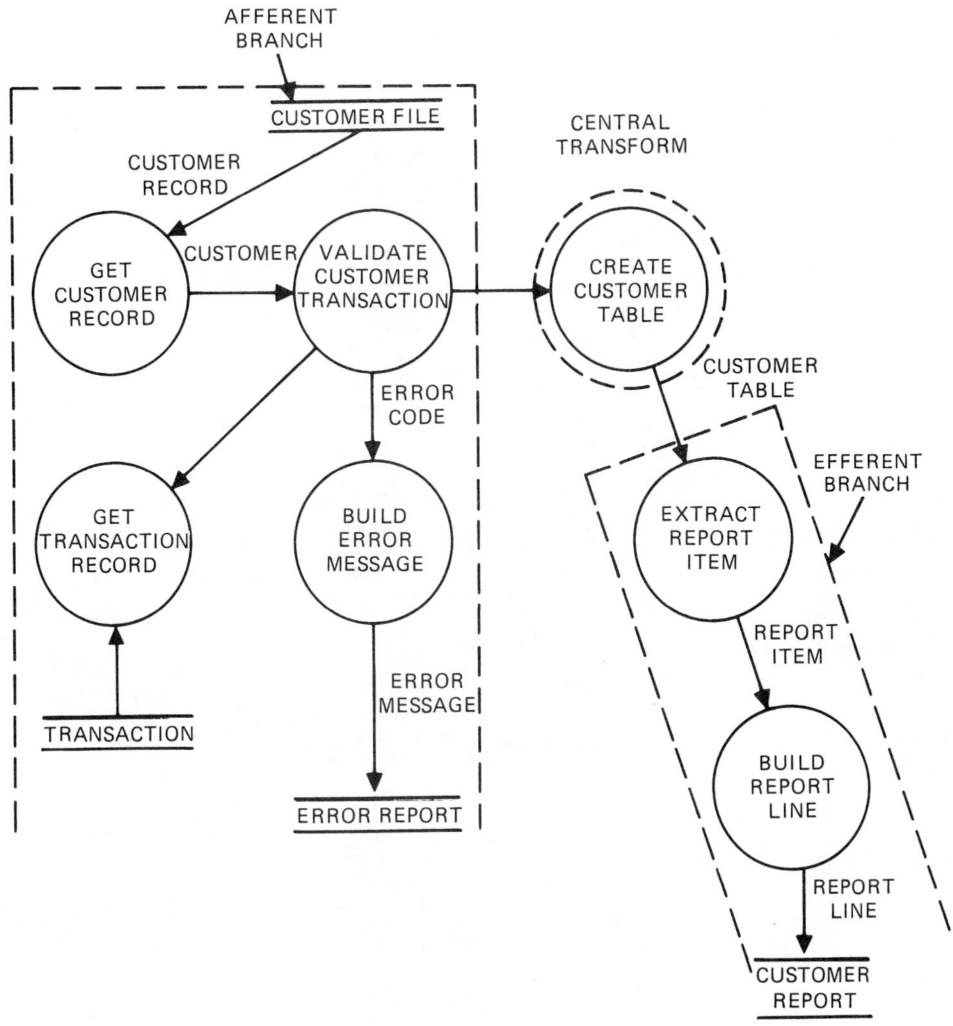

Figure 7.29

Stamp Coupling. These communicate using composite data, such as a record which consists of unrelated data. In this case, not all the data is used by the receiving module.

Control Coupling. Data from one module is used in the other to direct the sequence of instruction execution.

Common Coupling. A global area is shared, such as an EXTERNAL or COMMON definition.

Content Coupling. One module refers to the other.

Cohesion

Cohesion measures how strongly the elements within the module are related. There are seven levels of cohesion:

Coincidental Cohesion. The elements of a module are unrelated. There are no common functions, procedures, or data.

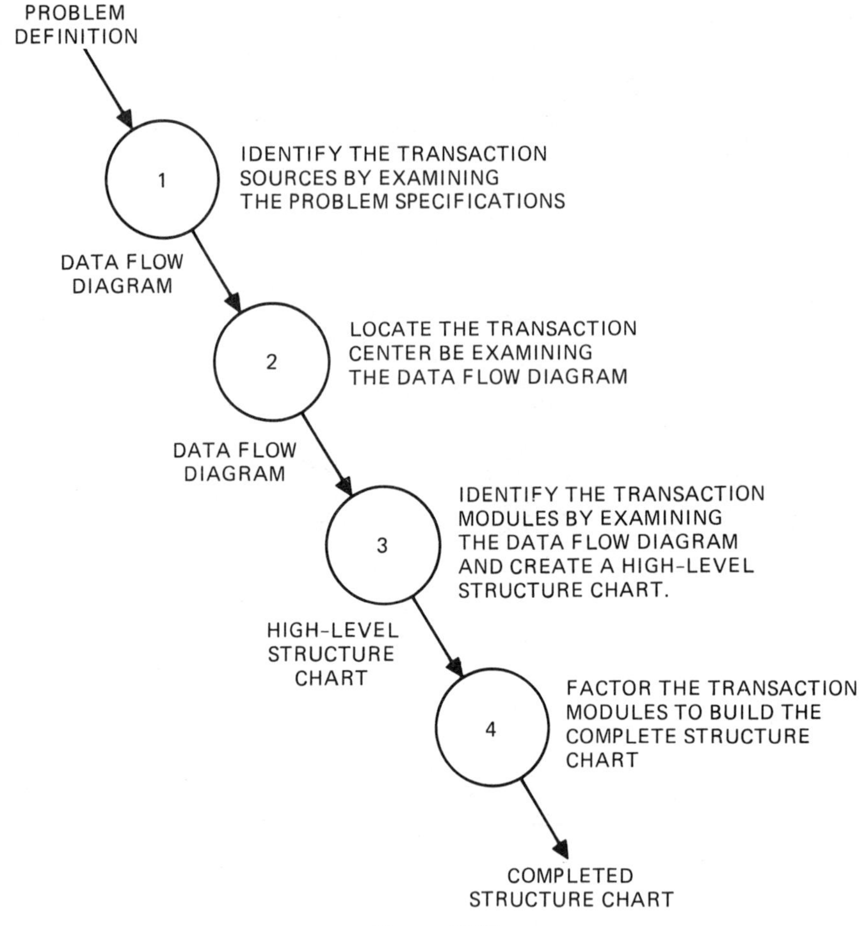
PROBLEM
DEFINITION
1
IDENTIFY THE TRANSACTION
SOURCES BY EXAMINING
THE PROBLEM SPECIFICATIONS
DATA FLOW
DIAGRAM
2
LOCATE THE TRANSACTION
CENTER BE EXAMINING
THE DATA FLOW DIAGRAM
DATA FLOW
DIAGRAM
3
IDENTIFY THE TRANSACTION
MODULES BY EXAMINING
THE DATA FLOW DIAGRAM
AND CREATE A HIGH-LEVEL
STRUCTURE CHART.
HIGH-LEVEL
STRUCTURE
CHART
4
FACTOR THE TRANSACTION
MODULES TO BUILD THE
COMPLETE STRUCTURE
CHART
COMPLETED
STRUCTURE CHART

Figure 7.30

Logical Cohesion. The elements of a module are committed to the process of a certain class of transactions.

Temporal Cohesion. The elements of a module are related by time, but need not occur in a predetermined sequence.

Procedural Cohesion. The elements of a module are all a part of the unity—the process must be followed in sequence.

Communicational Cohesion. The modules all work on the same data.

Sequential Cohesion. The elements of the module are a part of a larger sequence, where the output of one operation is the input to the next.

Functional Cohesion. Each element of a module fits in one and only function.

Packaging

The last step of the structured design process is the preparation of the design for implementation. The packaging of the design divides the logical program design into physically implementable units, called

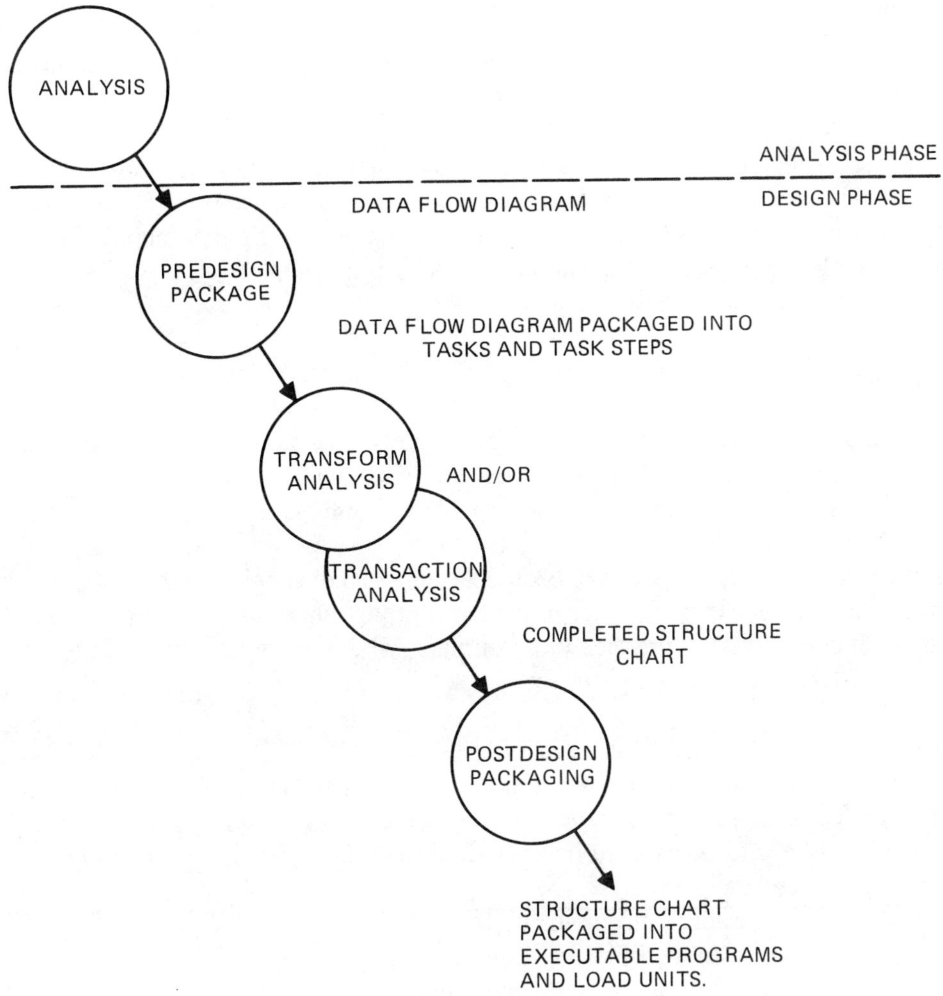

Figure 7.31

load units. Each load unit is brought into memory and executed as one program unit. It is a physical design concept and defines the system components which are executable in the programming environment. This is one of the advantages of the C programming language. There are two packaging steps—the predesign and postdesign packaging.

The system is subdivided from the data flow diagram into tasks and task steps—or, if you will jobs and job steps (for you JCL fans). The determination of the packaging limits will depend upon the available hardware boundaries, the batch/on-line or on-line/real-time boundaries. This is the predesign packaging. Once the process is complete, the postdesign packaging comes into play. These are the executable load modules, which may be combined to form load units. The rule to follow is to group into one load unit all the modules executed in sequence. Figure 7.31 shows where the packaging fits into the structured scheme.

The Remaining Elements

Structured design is a reasonable approach, but does not take into account all the business elements and ancillary items required to produce a new system.

Report Development

Space does not permit an exhaustive treatment of report design, but here are a few thoughts on the subject:

1. No user will ever receive a printer spacing chart as output. Don't show him one. All his reports will come from the computer on printed stock tab or in some other form. Show it to him that way now, if you can. If you can't produce some salient output, jury-rig that output. Emphasize to the user that a sample report does not mean that the system is complete.
2. No user will ever receive a report like this:

   $$$,$$.00   ZZZ,ZZ.00   XX/XX/XX $0.00

3. Give the user sufficient detail on a sample report—the sequence, placement of control breaks, totals, messages, etc.—just enough to show how the report will be used. Show empathy for how the report will be used—eye flow, total positioning, filing numbers, sequence presentation, etc.

Once the format utility of the output have been determined and samples have been presented to and approved by those who will use them (the actual people, not just management), then it is time to determine what inputs will be required to produce those outputs, where the inputs are, can they be economically extracted, etc. These questions are pertinent:

1. Are those data crucial to important decisions?
2. How valid would the decision be if those data were not available?
3. Can the data, or some part of it, be obtained as a byproduct of some other operation?
4. Does each input have to be handled on an as-received basis?
5. Can inputs be processed in batches?
6. How should nonprocessable form inputs be converted or handled?
7. Are inputs to be processed on a first-in, first-out basis?
8. Can the inputs be processed in a predefined sequence?
9. What is the significance of the variations of input volume on system performance criteria?
10. Will interruption be allowed? How will that affect reliability?
11. How many interruptions will there be, and when?
12. How much of this process is communications-based?

And then some questions about the processing characteristics:

1. Random or sequential processing (batch or on-line)?
2. Frequency of operations?
3. What is the predominant characteristic in the operation?
4. How complex is the logic; is it mainline or subroutine-oriented?
5. Will the processing include exceptions?
6. What are the human/machine considerations?
7. Audit trails and redundancy?
8. Frequency of referral to the files?
9. Changes or updates to the files?
10. Are referral, change, and update methods consistent?
11. What sorting is required; function of the data base management system?
12. What is the growth rate?

Once there are at least general answers to these questions, the design process can begin. What ever else the system is to be, it must be *DYNAMIC*.

New System's Objectives

As many times as this topic has been referenced, one might conclude that it's important. The objective has three parts:

1. *The Goal*—what is to be accomplished. This must be set by management in terms which can denote specific achievement. This system may accomplish the entire goal or merely a part of it. The specific set of accomplishments will allow complete project management and concise, accurate, and timely reporting.
2. *The Method*—how is it to be accomplished. Whatever type of system is developed, there are some things which rightfully belong here—like the intermediate payoffs, visibility of system products, collection of allied and alternate goals, wisdom in determining what can be used and when it can be used for maximum benefit. Cost control features will be of interest to management.
3. *The Measurement*—how it can be said to be successful. One doesn't awaken to determine that success has been achieved. Success must be planned. It is the accomplishment of the goal within time or financial constraints, productivity constraints, influx of benefits, degrees of acceptance, and the learning curve. What can be done better the next time.

System Boundaries

The identification of boundaries make the design a manageable process. Intrasystem boundaries are the more complex and are difficult to set, as the change to the standard way of doing business brings with it a certain amount of upheaval. Intrasystem boundaries define the limits of the system within the organization. The systems process would never move along if the team tried to do everything for everybody. Thus walls must be erected, interfaces designed where necessary, but the team must concentrate on the problem(s) which caused the focus initially.

Subsystems evolve from intrasystem boundaries. Certain functional areas require special treatment (and where several functional areas comingle the data, as well), and the subsystem allows unique or complex functions to be performed.

Intrasystem boundaries are less complex and often overlooked. A system, even an integrated system, cannot stand alone. It is the subsystem of some larger system, or of the organization itself. In the design process, the analyst must identify those total systems which will form an interface with the system to be designed. He determines the method of interfacing and closely cooperates with other designers over which he has no control. This is the most difficult task in determining intersystem boundaries: how to influence the design of another system so that the two can communicate. The the need for standards.

Searching for Design Alternatives

If any single area has been the system designer's downfall, it has been the failure to design alternatives. For this reason, organizations are totally vulnerable to the failure of the EDP system. Most of the reason for this is that the people who are designing the system are data processors, not business people. Their perspectives are to put together computer systems only.

An alternative is often a choice between a computer and a manual system. It is the first such system, this is a difficult choice. With or without a computer, management wants the organization to be protected, and it behooves the system designer to develop a manual counterpart to the system which can be operated (and therefore keep the organization operation) in the event of the computer's failure for an extended period.

Alternative designs depend upon the approach. First, there's the simplification, a limited approach with minor changes. Reverting to the older method would not be difficult. Next, there's the mechanization of the current system without change. All inputs and outputs remain the same; the process is merely speeded. This uses the technology without upsetting the procedure. It may use it poorly, but going back is not difficult. Third, there is the complete system redesign. It is the opposite of mechanization. The inputs and outputs may be changed to reflect the current state of the business and the same backups which were necessary before remain necessary now. And then, there is the system designed for management, in which not only the inputs, outputs, processes, concepts, and file management concerns are examined and changed, but also the people interaction with the system. Each approach has advantages and disadvantages; what may serve one user will not work for another. The key is to have another way to get the work done. The unforeseen has a way of happening.

Quantifiables During System Design

It is possible to learn many facts about system performance before its design is complete. Generally, that is accomplished with a system model for use with SCERT (previously discussed) or another model-handling program, such as IBM's General Purpose Systems Simulator (GPSS). Some applications, when written, can be put through performance monitoring software, such as Boole & Babbage's SMS-370. While these have been IBM-oriented terms, similar software is available through other vendors.

More important than simulation, however, is the recognition that close monitoring is required to ensure that management is getting what it thinks it's getting throughout this process. Frequent design reviews, document design walkthroughs, HIPO design walkthroughs, report simulations, etc., are required to ensure that the design team is moving in the anticipated, if not the right, direction.

Not Invented Here

The availability of purchasable software has made some critical decisions easy. The years and years of reinventing the wheel have extracted their toll, and we are finally awakening to the fact that some things we simply cannot—or ought not to—develop. Financial packages, such as those put out by the MSI of Atlanta, are changing the way we think about generalized systems. Simply put, there are a million copies out there of essentially the same payroll program. Data base software, such as that produced by Cullinane of Boston has been revolutionizing the way we perceive the structure of data and systems development. This is not to slight the many purveyors of fine financial or data base software, but to draw your attention to the fact that a high price tag for a proven product may be a wise investment. As soon as we learn that even though those packages are purchased, there is still much to do, then the intransigence of the user and the inflexibility of the EDP systems designers can be overcome. A change in management thinking has been required—the concept that if it wasn't invented here, it's somehow not applicable, has been largely overcome.

At the same time, vendors of software have developed extensive and useful products. Products such as those produced by ADR of New Jersey have found great acceptance. And the DATAPRO and Auerbach reader services will tell us what is available and good.

Output Products

Output from a DP system can only be intermediate or final. An intermediate output is one which is produced internally by a portion of the system as input to one or more successive portions of the machine system. It is not produced in any manner distributable to the users. Final outputs are either hard copy or some medium which is reportable by communications or can be obtained in hardcopy format with little difficulty.

Reports and Documents

It is through the reports and documents that most systems function. The systems team will design the reports to conform to the user's decision or manipulation needs, arranged in a manner which will be most useful. Human factors will play a very large role in the design of these reports.

Identification of document outputs must be accompanied by a method to control those documents. A control system must be devised to ensure that any outputs that may result in future inputs will be monitored; that no rejected transactions will be reintroduced to the system; that no accountable document becomes lost, obscuring the audit trail; and that the utility of the information is balanced with the cost of producing the information.

Graphic Hard Copy

A picture is worth (at least) *N* words. Users, accustomed to voluminous reports, may react well to summary data presented in graphic form. The graphics capabilities of an on-line system, of a microcomputer, or other terminal device may more than justify the cost. Further, distributing reports which are graphic or hard copy may be one way to ensure that the system is well used. There will still be the need for volume data, for summary data, and for transaction data. Graphic hard copy might well sell the system.

Outputs Which Function as Inputs

Wherever it is possible to close the feedback loop automatically, the systems designer should do so. If a system can produce its own inputs as outputs from a previous cycle, the number of errors will be diminished. Among the auto-encoder groups are OCR (Optical Character Recognition), MICR (Magnetic Ink Character Recognition), UPC (Universal Product Code), pre-punched cards, pre-skunked scanning documents, and microfilm.

Optical Character Recognition (OCR)

OCR is a powerful method to gain input from a source document. There are OCR fonts for output printers and the equipment can be programmed to recognize handwritten characters which conform to certain standards. The OCR systems have found wide use in invoicing and receivables applications and in certain testing applications, where pre-skunked (see Chapter 2) forms may be used. OCR systems reduce the time required for data transcription and control information is essentially unaltered by the human to whom they are addressed.

Magnetic Ink Character Recognition (MICR)

MICR is similar to OCR in that data are entered by sensing of a character. It is used largely for banking applications. More detail on MICR may be obtained from Chapter 1.

Universal Product Code (UPC)

UPC is a relatively new form of input code which may be generated by the system. It, like MICR, is generally printed and is used as a highly efficient input device. Designed for the grocery industry in an attempt to reduce inventory and price processing, it has met with stiff resistance by consumers.

Scanning Documents

The use of bar-coded scanning documents is burgeoning. The concept is not dissimilar to other scanned codes. Figure 7.32 is an example of a scanning document used by one of the major package distribution services.

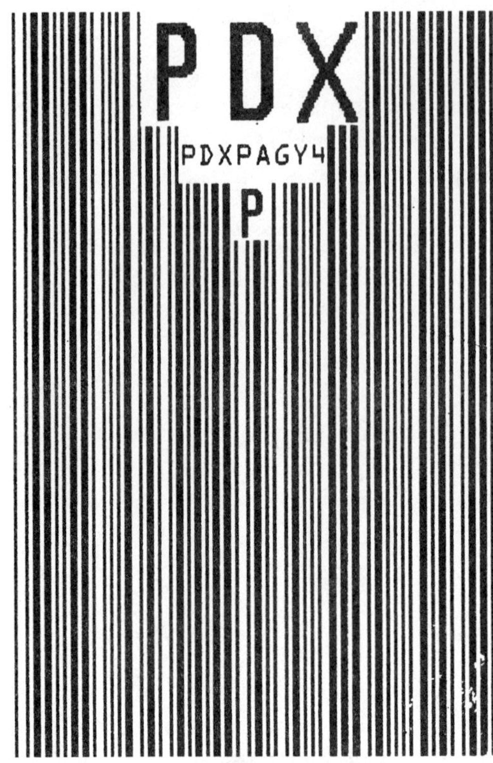

Figure 7.32

The Prepunched Card

The old standby, the punched card, is still useful for input. Fully prepunched, it is a complete record. Prepunched with a tear strip, it is frequently used for utility bills. Partially prepunched with mark sensing, it is used for meter readings. There are some porta-punch systems still in use, notably in voting systems.

Microfilm

As a means to reduce the cost of paper, microfilm outputs have been developed. For the purpose, for mail-transmission, and for storage space costs, microfilm has been a good solution, even considering its requirement of high-capital equipment. Use of CIM (computer input microfilm) has yet to get to the point of wide use, largely because there are less expensive alternatives. It's less expensive to produce COM, print it, and scan it, than to use CIM.

Other Outputs

Great strides have also occurred in printing. When last this book was written, matrix printing was relatively new; daisy-wheel printing was brand new; laser printing was available, but only for those who had the money; thermal printing was available, through little used; and xerographic printing was in the design stage. The advent of the microcomputer brought forth the need for inexpensive printers; the industry responded with a flood of matrix printers. Strip printers became available, some using sensitized paper. Laser and xerographic printers have become the hallmark for high-volume applications in large organizations. Character printers which use rotating axial print wheels are disappearing. ''Bouncing ball'' printers have seen an upswing. The newest advance, as of this writing, is the ink spray printer, widely used in office systems of a certain vendor.

The advance of the "office of the future" concept will make great changes in the way we look at outputs. Some outputs will be communicated electronically. Some will continue to be on paper. Some will be strictly a function of a CRT, LED, the ELD (electro-luminescent display), or plasma screen. But some will also be diskettes, telecopied documents, and xerographic printing. We've only scratched the surface. Find a wider discussion of these topics in the next chapter.

Output in Control Systems

There are outputs which can either be intermediate or final or both in control systems. One of these outputs in the feedback mechanism. Feedback is information generated within a system and used to modify the operation of the system. A typical control system has many feedback loops. The presence of interactive displays, the unpredictability of human operators, and the uncertainty of the system environment prevent perfect planning of system performance. Therefore, the presence of absence of feedback, the lag involved, or the manner in which the information is presented are all important and can have a profound effect on system performance. The basic idea of feedback is that performance is monitored and compared to what is expected or desired.

File Design and Organization

The next step in the systems design phase is the design and organization of the data. There are four steps:

1. Determine the file requirements. The system requirements and output requirements previously developed are the basic sources of this information.
2. Determine the data organization and media upon which the data will reside. If the process is sequential, will tape storage be sufficient? If the system is on-line, how much direct access will be required? Will this direct access have to be disk, diskette, or RAM?
3. Format the files; structure the database. The designer develops file structures and schema to fit the handling of data within the system. Those files which are high activity will be organized in a manner which best suits the reference needs.
4. Devise the data collection system. How will the data be entered? Will it be on forms and encoded or scanned? Will it be through data collection terminals? Will it be on-line data collection? What conversions must be done?

There is a danger that the present-day facilities of database environments are interpreted to mean that much data may be gathered and maintained. Certainly, for a price. For the purpose of the application, however, sufficient data to satisfy the reporting needs of the system would seem to be sufficient. The cost of retrieving and processing data is high relative to the cost of obtaining and storing data, so the current thinking goes, and therefore all available information will be stored. On the other side, it could be argued that excessive data begets excessive reporting—and the processing and media costs will exceed any reasonable expectation.

Selection of Storage Medium

No question—it's going on disk isn't it? Perhaps. Probably it ought not. However, disk storage media is becoming less expensive per byte of storage. If there is a choice between disk and tape, the question is simple—if the processing sequence is sequential and the file activity is high, then tape must be used. It's inexpensive and highly portable. If the file activity ratio (records used divided by records scanned) is low, then disk, as a standard medium, should be used. In a database environment, there is no question.

It will be disk—at least until you have a database machine installed. The inclusion of extensive RAM in hardware will ultimately make excessive disk unnecessary.

Will the file be linearly expandable? If many new accounts are anticipated, then file expansion is a predominant consideration. Addition of new data for current files will probably be minimal. The need to interrogate the file, to draw reports from it, to prove its currency may well dictate the form and media used for the file.

Timing is another important consideration. The number of disk seeks, the time required to string together the schema and the required subschemae will determined how the data is allocated in the data base environment. Chaining, data file overflow, reorganization needs, utilization experience, and the ability to remove the media will also influence these decisions. Must the data be sorted? Is the reference structure efficient? More information about database is now contained in the next chapter.

Finally, what can the organization afford? Is the equipment already installed and the data handling equipment already purchased? Is the only cost the cost of new media? What are the comparative costs of tape versus disk for storage capacities?

Unit Record Files

The days of using punched cards as files are long gone. occasionally they are used as repositories, but even that application is by the board. The use of unit record files today is largely limited to the generation of turnaround documents. Some keypunching occurs, and some transactions are generated on cards. Large users will maintain a small card-reading mechanism to allow themselves the facility, but it would be safe to say that in the majority of sizable installations, the use of the unit record has gone the way of the buggy whip.

Those organizations who have not relinquished them, however, should be concerned about their security, environmental (heat/humidity) control, movement, and storage.

Magnetic Tape Files

Tape has been around the computer from the beginning, and it's as useful today as it was then. It's flexible, inexpensive, highly portable, and has considerable capacity. The advent of word processing systems has brought use of the magnetic tape cassette, used for data collection, program storage, and even some files. It's not the most efficient—tape never is—but it's inexpensive and useful.

Disk, Diskette, Drum, Magnetic Cards

Drum and magnetic cards are disappearing from the scene, but like any feature, they'll be a while going. Magnetic cards (introduced by NCR with its CRAM and IBM and its Data Cell) never proved to be as efficient as initially thought. Magnetic cards are used with word processing machinery, but that's about all. Drum provides very fast access and massive storage—but the speed of access is seldom required (except for virtual storage) and disk has been found to be as effective.

Until the disk appeared, not much had been done to file structures other than sequential files. Disk brought random, indexed sequential, sequential, sectored, treed, chained, and a host of other organizations, each of which had some improvement to offer. Disks have gotten larger and more capable of storing data—and they've gotten smaller and more portable. And today, the diskette (in $5\frac{1}{4}$ and 8 inch sizes) can store 80,000 to 300,000 characters of information. They are in use on many minicomputers and microcomputers—and some of the larger mainframe systems, where they are generally used for microcode.

Processing

In simple terms, processing will be either batch or on-line. Batch of course, has been with us for awhile. On-line, distributed processing, and other communications-based services are changing the way we process data. There was a time when all transactions had to be processed to provide to management the reports as of the time of the processing, which would follow the latest transaction by some lag period. Today, it's possible to maintain data in a manner that the data is processed on a transaction-oriented basis, and reports are developed and maintained effective as of the latest transaction, which may have only been a few seconds ago.

Batch Processing

Batch processing was the only processing method before hardware and software developments made it possible to process transactions as they occurred. The concept of batching—accumulating transactions which require the same data processing steps—became an inherent characteristic of mechanization. The development of electromechanical data processing which used the punched card followed by the same batching principles used on an assembly line. In the tradition of mass production technology, single-purpose machines were built to perform a series of simple, repetitive operations as batches of cards were passed through each of them in succession. The batch processing techniques did not change much with the advent of the computer, with the exception that one machine replaced several. The repetitive operations were consolidated, but still existed. The processing mechanism was the only change.

There are many factors to consider in the batch processing environment. First, the scheduling of the processing run must coincide with the accumulation of the optimum amount of data. Data which are actually important to an organization may be awaiting processing, but will not be processed because the volume is insufficient. Any delay in submission might result in the rejection of future input. In the majority of cases, batch processing is independent of transaction activity; the batch can be processed whether there are four transactions or four thousand. Up to a point, the processing time is a function of file size and not of input volume, assuming sequential files.

If input volume becomes very large, it does not affect the processing time. This make it possible to schedule batch runs at specific times. Batch processing does allow for certain data to be out-of-date before processing—but the nature of the report could be that it doesn't matter. When it does matter, an on-line alternative should be selected.

On-line and Real-Time Processing

The on-line environment allows for the data files to be modified on the basis of each independent transaction as near as possible to the time of its occurrence. Editing which is done in this environment must be done as a function of the acceptance process. Sequence is inconsequential and reporting may remain in a batch mode or may be set up to provide on-line and timely reports. The growth of inexpensive terminal hardware, microcomputers, and other on-line apparatus has made on-line activities much more cost-effective. On-line applications consume much memory, however, require sophisticated handlers, and require completely different orientation to application programs. So there is a price to be paid. One often overlooked problem is this: with an on-line system you often know a piece of information much earlier than you really want to know or are prepared to deal with it.

There are several reasons why on-line processing is becoming popular. First, the computer can refer directly to all the necessary data for processing a transaction, and data can be efficiently processed in any sequence. Second, disk storage units offer flexibility in processing. Third, from a behavioral viewpoint, many jobs become more satisfying, allowing users to deal with transactions as they occur with the immediacy of editing response. No longer is it necessary to wait two days to discover that an error means you must wait two days more.

On-line and real-time are terms which are commonly used interchangeably. In the context of this discussion, the difference is inconsequential. Real-time refers to the ability of the system to respond and modify its environment in time to make appreciable difference in the outcome. For an accounting system, real-time might well be a week. For a petrochemical plant, real-time might well be fractions of seconds.

Data in the System

Reference data are often present in master files. They are reported initially and generally remain unchanged for extended periods. In a personnel file, for example, an individual's name, date of birth, or social security number rarely change. Reference data normally need not be reported after the initial submission. They are retained for use by the individual programs. Some are identifying data, such as record identification codes, while other data are quantitative constants for use in calculations; e.g., unit price. Many systems have files which contain only reference data which are called only when needed. Constant data in mathematical programs are numeric values and variables which change only as a function of program modification.

Transaction, Transient, or Variable Data

Master files contain other data which are called by various names. Since they result from transaction input, they are most often referred to as transaction data. These changes frequently and require much reporting. They are transient in nature and are actually or potentially active. It is the transaction data which reflect the detail of the processing and to which the major sections of the program apply.

There are two types of transaction data: data which are reported in the input to reflect changes in the environment, and data which are generated. These result from calculations involving either wholly reported transaction data or a combination of reported and reference data.

Engineering and scientific applications often have input variable data files that are observational or experimental in nature. Many scientific and statistical problems have intermediate files of variable data that are calculated as functions of input variables, parameters, and constants. Similarly, output variable data files are often generated in mathematical and statistical programs. In many scientific applications, generated variable data files are calculated as functions of mathematical equations, constant data, and parameter data.

Parameter Data

Many scientific applications are parameter data, numerical values that are specified by the user for each execution or run of a program. Parameters normally remain fixed during the program execution, but if the user desires many runs of a program with regular changes in the parameters, this may be accomplished by self-modification (by the program) of the parameter data. This is the way, for example, that a forecasting or simulation application works.

In the business environment, most data is generated when changes occur. Transactions which reflect those changes may be generated by the following:

1. *Purchasing* involves the procurement of the merchandise, materials, equipment, supplies, and services necessary for equipping, maintaining, and operating a business.
2. *Receiving* consists of receiving, unloading, and unpacking materials. Included in this action is the quality control function with its attendant processes.
3. *Stock-keeping* is potentially the largest data-originating function. It is the department responsible for storage and protection of all materials and support received by or made by a company that are not required for immediate use. Important responsibilities of the stockroom include the maintenance of stock records, inventory control, and replenishment of supplies which have reached the reorder point.

4. *Production* includes designing and developing products, providing facilities to manufacture the products, planning, scheduling, and routing the work, and ensuring quality control. These tasks necessitate various detailed methods so that management can exercise close control.
5. *Sales* involving both cash and credit each generate source data. Sales transactions in wholesale and manufacturing firms involve communicating with other operations to a larger degree than in retail firms, but the data needs are similar.
6. *Delivery* encompasses the packing, labeling, and transportation of goods to a customer. Data reported result from previous actions and are of a record-keeping nature.
7. *Billing* is a basic function to any business. It provides the accounting department with a record of charges to be made to a customer's account.
8. *Collection* includes the maintenance of accounts receivable, the sending of statements or collection notices, and the receipt of payment for goods sold or services rendered.
9. *Disbursing* is the final business activity which forms a source of data. Payment of payroll or invoices generates data. Payroll has been the most computerized application ever.

Systems Input

The use of design tools, particularly the data analysis sheet, makes the determination of the data requirements for inputs a relatively easy task. The formatting of the input follows from the data requirements and becomes a minor issue. Major considerations center around the processing methodology.

Editing and Input Control

Editing of input is a basic requirement of all DP systems. Input editing is done during the initial stages of data handling, shaping the transaction data to the format, standards, accuracy, and quality of data already located in the file. This portion of the system isolates exceptional data, some of which may be erroneous.

Input editing deals primarily with the transaction that causes changes in files. If good control and adequate edits are maintained over all inputs, then the files are certain to be satisfactory. Files should be passed through any editing routine which has been altered. Editing should include at least the following tests:

1. Field content. Input editing determines whether alphabetic and numeric characters are where they are suppose to be.
2. Accuracy of numeric data per se. Check digits, check sums, and hash totals are tested against previously calculated figures.
3. Data completeness. Editing can determine the presence of all data elements in each transaction record and of all records required for the particular type of transaction. This is done by examining each record, counting records, and testing for gaps in sequence.
4. Code compatibility. Editing determines whether the input data code differs from the processor code.
5. Rearrangement of data elements. Data elements in an input record are put into suitable sequence for efficient file processing, if a batch environment is used.
6. Expand or compress data. Characters are introduced or deleted to make data element and record lengths of input data correspond to lengths in files for efficient processing.
7. Remove extraneous nonnumeric data. Dollar symbols, decimal points, commas, etc., are removed from input data that will be used in arithmetic operations.
8. Examine internal consistency. Several data elements within one record, or a data element within the record and an external constant, are examined for the existence of a specified relationship.

9. Verify that the input data correspond with data already contained in the files. Proper names, descriptors, and numeric amounts are compared to see whether they agree with file content.
10. Ensure that all logical land completeness requirements are met, particularly in an on-line environment, where transactions can trigger other processing, such as shipments, payments, file modifications, etc.

The methods of performing the edits change as system capability increases. This is particularly true in the on-line inquiry based system. A special consideration in that environment lies also in the permissions to access files, to report from them, and most importantly, to change them. Because many have access, priority schemes must be established and mechanisms established for other users to be notified, and, if necessary, to approve such transactions.

There are other special input controls necessary for on-line and real-time systems. Most important, the ability to reconstruct in the event of a system failure must be retained. All input transactions are written on a processing history (log) file along with the image of the records before and after modification. Second is the concern for erroneous data arriving real-time. In such a situation, timing may be critical, and it may be more important to shut the processors down than to take the time to gain further information. Thus, the system designer must plan for a graceful degradation of the system. A graceless degradation could happen in seconds and destroy a system without providing the necessary trails for corrective action.

Sorting Considerations

Chapter 2 deals extensively with the subject of sorts, so this discussion is limited to the design of processes which require data to be in a different sequence than that in which it currently resides.

Which sort is used is generally a function of the size of the file, the machine time involved, those processes which can overlap the sort, what applications await the data to be sorted, etc. By and large, the more data you can move to memory the quicker the sort can be. Design of applications which require sorts may well require the data to appear a specific way in a report—but consider sorting only the selected records. Modern systems designers will perform an extract phase, especially on files which are extensive. If, from a file of 1000,000 records, you were to report on only 10,000, then the wise thing to do is to extract the records, select those which apply to the process, and then sort what's left before producing the report. This is why the COBOL SORT and REPORT WRITER facilities are so popular.

Input Timing

It has always been difficult to keep the central processing unit of the computer busy. The speeds of processors have been such that no input mechanism was fast enough. Direct input has involved data communications, but even that is slow unless the transmitting unit has been used for slave input, that is, batch and forwarding. If this is done enough, the timing becomes a concern of communications contention.

A real-time system produces a myriad of problems. The availability of many inquiry units introduces priority problems. Some systems bog down under heavy terminal use. The systems designer must evaluate the queuing and servicing schemes of the software to ensure that they fit the environment. Many organizations have had to modify the communications software to meet specific requirements. The on-line system has unique timing considerations—not the least of which is that transactions must occur in a specified sequence. If transactions are produced in a batch environment, they can be sorted. No such facility exists for the on-line environment. Thus, the on-line environment must be used to ensure that transactions are received in a prescribed sequence.

Charting the System

The charting methods shown in the prior discussion of structuring techniques are those which are currently predominant. We should not forget their predecessors, however, and while we'll not go into detail here, we'll mention the traditional, the general systems flowchart and the Hierarchial Input Process Output (HIPO) chart. Examples of both are presented here, quoted from IBM publication GC20-1851, "HIPO—A Design Aid and Documentation Technique," with permission.

A general systems flowchart is a graphic representation of the system in which data provided by a source document are converted into final documents. These flowcharts are maps that show the processing procedures. The American National Standards Institute has developed a set of standard symbols and rules which have been nearly universally adopted. Each symbol has a specific use, and currently available templates carry the symbols (see Chapter 2).

There are several types of general systems flowcharts. They are often used as briefing or sales tools. For this, the chart is very general. In contrast, a systems flowchart can be very detailed. Too many systems are developed without this step. Where used, it should be dynamic, and should be modified as required, as it is the tool which integrates the entire work effort.

A more recent advancement in the area of systems design documentation works along the concept of structured systems. The HIPO chart is a documentation tool to support structured systems design and structured programming. It is a graphic representation of the movement from general to specific.

Controls

In view of the fact that the computer no longer merely keeps track of the money and is instead the money itself, the use of controls in an EDP system is not only desirable, but mandatory. Control can be exercised internally (by the computer) or externally (by the system auditor).

The best source of control information is from the Institute of Internal Auditors, and their book, *Systems Auditability & Control,* is highly recommended. According to them, controls are required at source document origination, authorization, DP input preparation, source document retention, and source document error handling. Included in the control types are written procedures, system designs, document storage, document handling, transaction identification, batching, logging, transmittal, error detection, error procedures, correction of errors, and resubmission.

Here is a brief checklist for controls:

1. Input controls:
   a. Simple/standard forms
   b. Batch controls
   c. Transaction counts
   d. Turnaround documents
   e. System anticipation of input
   f. Visual checking
   g. Data conversion
2. Editing controls:
   a. Limit checks
   b. Historical checks
   c. Logical relationship checks
   d. Field checks
   e. Sign checks
   f. Validity (to table value) checks
   g. Self-checking numbers

   h. Record counts
   i. Sequence checks
   j. Hash totals
   k. Crossfoot methods
   l. Code/date relationships
   m. Diagnostic checks
3. In-Process controls:
   a. Label checks
   b. Record counts
   c. File totals
   d. Address checks
   e. Suspense accounts
   f. Intervention records
   g. Protected records
   h. Checkpoint procedures
   i. Sequence checks
4. Output controls:
   a. Tests of reason
   b. Statistical and control data
   c. Exception control data

Controls should originate as close to the source of the action or information as possible. They should be planned for and established during the initial design of the system. Both program and human controls should be considered. Requirements for editing programs should be dictated by the total systems requirements. Standards should be developed for consistent and uniform application. Controls should be simple but adequate to accomplish their objectives. They should be thoroughly checked out during the testing stage to ensure accuracy, feasibility, and adequacy. Controls should be automated and computer-performed wherever possible. Wherever a control indicates an error, it should be clearly indicated and a procedure to effect correction should be documented and available.

The Cost of Systems Design

The identification of costs in systems design is a complex and debatable issue. Reliable cost data for a design project just isn't available. While each development project is different, the techniques of systems design remain relatively stable. Three types of cost must be considered: development cost, one-time conversion costs, and recurring costs.

Development cost is incurred in the systems design phase. The cost of systems design is considered to be two-thirds the cost of systems development, exclusive of hardware costs. It includes the cost of specialized training required by designers, the cost of machine time for simulation of design alternatives, the cost of consultants or outside assistance, the cost of travel to other locations doing similar work, etc. By far, the major development cost is the personnel costs, which varies from one project to another. Thus, it is necessary to estimate man-years to obtain a cost estimate. There has been very little historical statistical data to aid in this estimation. To keep the design costs within a reasonable span, most organizations amortize them over the life of the project.

The one-time conversion cost is that cost incurred when the current system is phased out and the new system is installed. The addition of new physical facilities for equipment and personnel makeup but one portion of this cost. The conversion cost could include duplicate facilities and a series of special programs necessary to prepare new files from current files. Conversion programs will have a one-time use, and will be discarded after current files have been purged and edited according to new rules. The most significant one-time cost is the cost of parallel operation. Few organizations dare to simply install a new system "cold turkey," though that approach is necessary under some circumstances. Personnel efforts will be duplicated, perhaps requiring more people, or some temporary people, or some extended operating hours. The systems team is charged with managing the parallel effort and costs.

The recurring costs are inherent in a system, whether a new system is developed or not. There will always be a certain amount of personnel costs. Equipment and maintenance costs now seem to be a way of life for most organizations. Supplies, utilities, and training are always necessary. Some recurring costs are treated as neutral costs in that they are unaffected by the system, while others are system-dependent but recurring, nevertheless.

The Analyst and the Programming Effort

It often happens that the analyst functions also as a programmer or as a project leader with the responsibility to oversee the programming effort. While programming considerations have been outlined in Chapter 2, it would be useful to document the kinds of questions the analyst must ask or the kinds of answers he must ensure are available:

1. Has a structured walkthrough been performed? Does the system conform to the practices, standards, and systems design?
2. What test cases were used in the walkthrough? Were they representative?
3. Is the test plan developed? Does lit include cases to test the mainline logic; to test each routine; exceptions; end-of-job; unusual mixtures and sequences of data?
4. Were standards observed?
5. Are there complex routines which require intensive auditing, testing, or the close supervision of an internal/external auditor?
6. Have the diagnostic errors been resolved, the logic errors been ironed out, the audit trails tested?

Documentation

Belatedly, documentation has been recognized as the keystone of the computer-based system. Documentation is extremely important because of its scope. The computer operator cannot function without it; the decision-maker cannot bless a development project without the analyst's documentation; the functional specialists need to know what the designer has proposed; the designer must show the programmer his design; etc.

Documentation is a seven-step process:

1. Analyzing the need for and uses of documentation.
2. Planning for production-the responsibility for writing and review must be fixed, procedures must be established, and distribution and controls must be set.
3. Writing and receiving of the documents—the contents and formats must be established, the technical and editorial review must be enforced, and provisions must be established for the draftsmen and illustrators.
4. Duplicating, preparing the illustrations, printing, collating, and binding.
5. Distributing the finished product.
6. Storing and retrieving copies to meet unforeseen demands.
7. Maintenance of the documentation—any new, modified, or corrected information must be incorporated, while all obsolete information must be purged; all of these changes must be properly disseminated to ensure compliance.

Analysts move from one job to another with great rapidity. When they depart, they take all unwritten information with them. Without documentation, it is most difficult to carry out any type of program maintenance. If a programmer is asked to adapt an existing program to a new machine, he must have the documentation for the existing program. Documentation can indicate what work has been performed on the development project. Others view documentation as the only tangible product furnished which can be used as a basis for agreement among personnel. Thus, documentation is not only an implementation and operations vehicle, but is also a managerial tool during the various phases of the development cycle.

Maintenance of Systems Documentation

The preparation of the documentation often seem a minor task when compared to the maintenance of it. Errors occur in the original writing. Systems are so dynamic that new or modified information reflecting systems changes appear at frequent intervals. In addition, the changes make a great deal of the information in the manuals obsolete. The computer specialists must control and regularize the processing of changes to the documentation.

The maintenance of systems documentation is a major problem in this era of centralized systems development. Many large organizations do not duplicate DP staff throughout their firms. Instead, they establish one agency whose sole responsibility is to design systems for use throughout the organization. Documentation is crucial to the success of each subunit. The subunit receives a system and must have the correct, formal documentation to operate it. If errors are found by the development agency or any subunit, there must be a way to communicate the documentation changes to all the subunits. Most central development agencies have control rooms staffed expressly for this function. Under this method, the documentation must be simple and direct. The development agency must at all time remember that the system's users know the system only through its documentation. There must be a firm communication and coordination network between the development agency and the subunit to ensure that the flow of documentation is unhindered.

Systems Documentation Considerations

The following are the types of documentation which should be prepared and maintained. The person who should be responsible is indicated in parenthesis:

1. Analytical Documentation:
   a. User request—a statement of the problem requirement (user/analyst)
   b. Analytical report—an evaluation of the cost and feasibility of the system (analyst)
   c. Design requirements statement—the objective, design parameters, and operating capabilities of the system (analyst)
2. Systems Specification:
   a. System summary—a general description of the entire system, including a narrative summary and system flowchart or HIPO chart (analyst)
   b. File specifications—definition of permanent data files including data element descriptions, edit criteria, and source references (analyst)
   c. Transaction specifications—definition of system output (analyst)
   d. Output specifications—definition of system inputs (analyst)
   e. Segmented processing specifications—a functional definition of each logical segment of the system identifying I/O requirements and specifying required operating capabilities (analyst/programmer)
   f. System test plan—definitive design for validating system performance, including plan, schedule, and test cases (analyst)

3. Program Documentation:
   a. Program specification—a logical description of the processing functions performed by the program, including I/O requirements, special techniques, formulas, and timing constraints (analyst)
   b. Input/output specifications—file, transaction, and output specifications associated with a program (programmer)
   c. Instructive output specifications—detailed and illustrated definition of diagnostic, instructional, and error messages emitted (programmer/analyst)
   d. Internal flow specification—general semidetailed flow diagrams, Chapin Charts, or decision tables showing program logic (programmer)
   e. Program test plan—definitive design for validating the logic of the program (programmer/analyst)
4. Job Operating Instructions:
   a. System operating instructions—sequence in which programs are run within the system, including frequencies and optional variations (analyst)
   b. Program operating instructions—program setup and execution (programmer)
5. Data Management Instructions:
   a. Data collection and preparation instructions—original preparation of data; eventually constitutes transaction files, including batching, transmission, submission, and scheduling requirements (analyst)
   b. Input control instructions—definition of the controls and audit trails required for input handling, validation, and security (analyst)
   c. Output review and control instructions—specifications of procedures for validation, quality assurance, land distribution of output (analyst)
6. User Aids:
   a. Management summary—a compilation of abstracts describing in nontechnical terms the files systems and reports available
   b. Reference manuals—expanded guides to the use and contents of files, systems, and reports

Implementing The System

Pre-Installation Review and Evaluation

Prior to installing the system, the designer must make a final check to ensure that the system is in agreement with the performance specifications. With the system in its final form, the designer can now simulate the system in a more precise fashion. He can now specify in detail the processing methodology as well as the input and output. The model can now be refined so it is ''near real.'' From the simulation, the designer can check assumptions and try modifications to improve the system efficiency.

Now the planning can be done for releasing the system to the user. Perhaps the hardest task here is convincing the user that the new system will not be perfect. Like most other new products, the system will have limitations. Levels of acceptance must be negotiated. The systems team schedules an acceptance test in which the performance of the system must meet the objective criteria. The user will inspect and officially acknowledge receipt of the new system.

Implementation of the system is the final step in the systems development cycle. This phase can become very complex land difficult if the installation of the system is concurrent with the physical installation of the equipment, because the systems team must separate systems problems form equipment problems. Consequently, computer specialists should recommend advanced installation and checkout of the hardware and its many components. Only after a thorough checkout should a team attempt the installation of a system.

Scheduling Installation

The desired outcome is to install the new system with a minimum of disruption. When and how it will actually occur will depend on the following:

1. The system should be installed after the hardware configuration has been accepted. The hardware should be tested for at least a month before acceptance.
2. Provisions must be made for the parallel processing which will take place during installation.
3. All necessary supplies for the new system must be on hand.
4. If other systems share the same computer, time must be scheduled for the installation.
5. The systems team should plan for the parallel operation, its features and duration.
6. Work schedules should be coordinated with available machine time to ensure responsiveness.
7. Documentation should be available two to four weeks before system installation.
8. The systems team is responsible to schedule the necessary training for users and operators.

Planning the Conversion

The pressure to attain maximum use increases after the equipment is accepted. This pressure is the critical test of the adequacy of all prior planning; hence, an established plan for an orderly conversion is imperative. Such a plan is also useful for evaluating the progress of conversion. The conversion is divided into two phases: (1) data clean-up and file build-up and (2) system test. Data clean-up can begin far in advance of the actual conversion. The user must realize that his existing data contain discrepancies in varying degrees of severity. In addition, some data may not pass edit checks in the new system even though the data are correct. The existing data must be subjected to the edit procedures of the new system. Any data which do not pass the edits are corrected and replaced in the system for subsequent ''final'' conversion.

The data clean-up must be accomplished before the building of new system files. File build-up is generally performed by a computer-based system designed for that specific task. The environment of the present system file determines the complexity of this system. The general approach is to extract data from the existing file in a format identical to that required for a new record. The generated transaction is then input to the formal scheme of programs, and the file is built. This method works equally well for any input file medium. Another approach is the direct conversion of one file to another without going through the step of generating input. In either of these methods, the validity of the input data must be beyond question to ensure a usable initial data file.

Subsequent to the file build-up, the system test phase begins. The test method used is generally one of parallel operation. It can vary from the complete duplicate processing of all input data to the more practical scheme of having the new system handle a sample of transactions. The system test randomly selects input data, processes it through the new system, and compares the results with those obtained from the current system. The current system continues to be the primary source of information during the test. When the reliability of the new system has been proven by using the sample of inputs, the systems team can shift all processing to the new system. The current system may operate for a brief additional period to verify the accuracy of results and to safeguard against system failure during conversion.

Special Controls and Audits

Conversion is the time when activities are able to clean house. Usually, a conversion subforce of the systems team is charged with the responsibility of doing the actual conversion. They have programmers, analysts, designers, and functional specialists available to speed this costly operation. With the pressures of short deadlines and the limited availability of the talent, many shortcuts can be and are taken. Audit trails become mazes during data clean-up and file build-up. For this reason, it is imperative that one member of the conversion subforce be an auditor.

Test Cases

If the system is a new system which replaces nothing; if the new system is radically different than the system which it replaces; then special consideration must be given to the system test. Test data must include valid system input as well as invalid and unknown inputs. The task then becomes one of comparing new system results with the known results that were produced manually.

Systems Maintenance and Follow-Up

Once the system is installed, the organization must keep the system current. Frequently, the task of systems maintenance becomes as time-consuming as the development effort. The actions taken are referred to as systems maintenance, modification, exploitation, optimization, and various other terms.

Post-Installation Changes

Changes in new systems become necessary because of system inadequacies and environmental changes. Most changes result in programming modifications of varying degrees. A small patch may be necessary to correct minor programming malfunctions. The problems in a system may necessitate many changes which are accumulated and implemented as a block. Environmental changes or a major system logic error may dictate a small development effort requiring systems analysis, design, etc. The predominant condition is the accumulation of changes.

Although management may assume that the majority of the development staff is now free to work on new projects, this is far from true. One example is in the use of programmers. There have been instances where 20% more programmers were needed to maintain a system than were required to write the programs, but this is extreme. Most agree that 30–60% of the original programming staff is needed to maintain the system. This number will decrease over time. Management must plan the orderly phaseout of the development staff and turn the system over to an operations staff. The world of current-generation hardware and software is so complex that systems are many times not fully understood until they are installed in the operating environment.

Periodic Reviews

A system need periodic review and evaluation. The performance specifications are the standards of excellence against which the system is compared. Documentation is the written specification against which the procedure is compared. The review of a DP installation is a task which should be performed by a team of disinterested, knowledgeable persons. Some organizations depend upon outside consultants to perform the task.

Most organizations consider a periodic review an essential part of the management function. They realize that data processing consumes a large portion of their budget and that a review program can not only reduce costs, but also improve management benefits. EDP systems are a remarkably powerful and versatile tool, and efficient use requires skill, imagination, and hard work. It results in a level of control and efficiency not otherwise obtainable in a large, complex organization.

Collecting and Analyzing Operating Costs

One operating cost is that of input preparation. Experience indicates that unless the system is radically changed, this cost under the new system will usually be higher than under the old method. Included are such items as salaries of data entry clerks land equipment operators, supplies, and rental machines. The persons collecting and analyzing the cost of input preparation must exercise caution to segregate the DP costs from the non-DP costs.

The second operating expense is that of amortization of the capital investment. Included in this category are investment in equipment, investment in the physical installation, and other change costs. If equipment is purchased, the IRS suggests a 10-year depreciation schedule. Rental costs include an allowance for obsolescence. The user, not the manufacturer, usually pays for obsolescence. Building costs and improvements are amortized in a manner similar to methods used in any industry. During the systems development cycle, the decision was made as to whether the equipment should be leased or purchased. The post-installation review determines whether that decision was wise. The amortization schedule produced during the cycle shows the breakeven point on the equipment at some future time, and management must be kept informed of the progress being made toward this goal.

The third type of operating cost is the labor cost of operating personnel as opposed to personnel performing input and output operations. This cost is one of the largest operating costs and is, potentially, the one which can get out of control. Personnel staffs have a natural tendency to grow. If a computer is not efficiently loaded at first and does not have enough work to keep it busy, it may be loaded with insignificant jobs to show full utilization until the major development work is completed. This requires unplanned-for people. Sound planning, realistically accounting for slack time, slow production, etc., prevents these situations which generate additional expense.

There are other operating expenses which require review and evaluation. The costs of taxes and insurance vary, based on the contractual agreements. Sometimes they are paid by the vendor and other times by the user. The cost of producing outputs is another expense. This includes the personnel salaries, miscellaneous service charges, and printed forms. Another expense could be a charge for floor space. These are examples of the types of operating costs that should be examined. The actual costs once the system is installed are compared to the costs which were proposed during the development cycle. Major discrepancies become a source of management concern.

Back-Cast

Let's take a backward glance to a couple of points which have been explained in narrative, but deserve final reinforcement in pictorial form before the chapter comes to an end. The first has to do with the mixture of design and user activities. Figure 7.33 demonstrates that the design process begins without the user's involvement. The window for user contributions lies in the design and development periods. From that point, the die is cast and the level of commitment has been reached. The organizational learning and adaptation process, on the other hand, starts very slowly and climbs equally slowly until after the implementation. And, as can be seen from the *Y* axis, the degrees of freedom in that design close as the effort increases geometrically along the *X* axis.

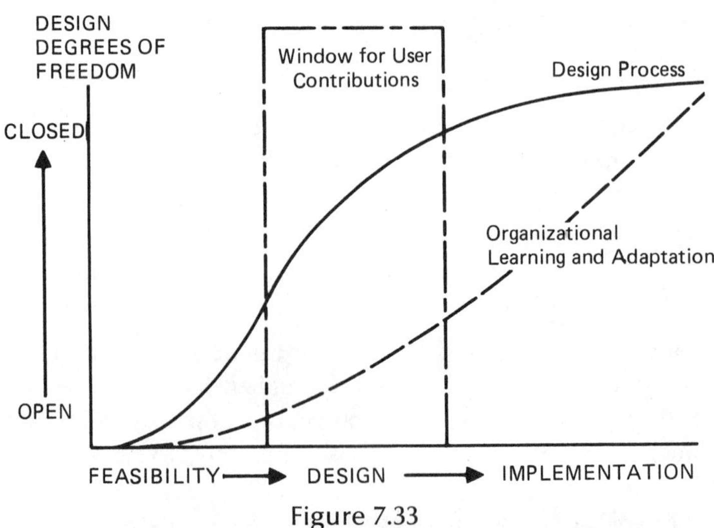

Figure 7.33

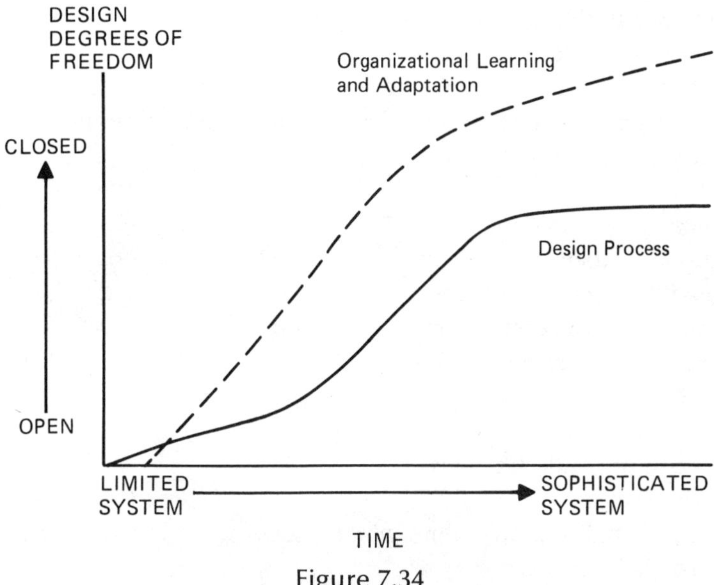

Figure 7.34

And lastly, Figure 7.34, using the same variables, draws the distinction between the limited (and therefore somewhat simple) and the sophisticated (with a high degree of complexity) system. In this instance, the organizational learning and adaptation accelerate quickly, but because of the complexity, the design effort climbs slowly.

That ends this chapter—and the traditional part of the book (though we have moved the database material). Because the field of work for the systems analyst has expanded both linearly and geometrically, two chapters have been added to the book—both within the systems section. Chapter 8 is a combined chapter on the subjects of communications, database, decision support systems, and office automation. Each section could well be a much larger chapter—but the CDP Examination is just beginning to explore topics in these areas. This beginning will no doubt receive a major expansion with the next edition.

QUESTIONS

1. Work Simplification:
   A. Consists of the normal daily improvements found by managers
   B. Is a new technique for systems analysis
   C. Is used exclusively by computer specialists
   D. Is designed for complex, business systems

2. A principal reason for difficulties experienced in using computers to solve business problems is:
   A. Failure to build efficient computers
   B. Failure to train managers to write computer programs
   C. Lack of standards for measuring computer efforts
   D. Lack of procedural languages

3. The primary reason for selecting a specific file organization is to:
   A. Maximize storage costs versus access requirements
   B. Gather logical data element groups
   C. Compress a file
   D. Maximize channel usage

4. The difference between traditional and nontraditional computer-oriented business systems is:
   A. Traditional systems are, largely, manual systems
   B. Traditional systems are broader in scope than nontraditional systems.
   C. Nontraditional systems include communications and word processing.
   D. Nontraditional systems do not follow the life-cycle methodology.
5. Process charts show:
   A. The general flow of the process
   B. The interrelation of processes
   C. Successive detailed steps in a process
   D. Where processing work is done in an organization
6. The information services organization has:
   A. Vertical linkages
   B. Horizontal linkages
   C. Both vertical and horizontal linkages
   D. No linkages whatsoever
7. A systems tool for analysis of a procedure which shows activities, quantities, time consumed, and distance moved is called a:
   A. Flow process chart
   B. Gantt chart
   C. Control chart
   D. SIMO chart
8. A business is
   A. A process that converts an output into an input
   B. A life-cycle management technique
   C. A system of systems
   D. A combination of production and services enterprises
9. A Feasibility Study is:
   A. The result of systems design
   B. A data processing proposal
   C. A special kind of management study
   D. A dollar value systems study
10. A code based on measurable physical characteristics is
    A. A mnemonic code
    B. An alphabetic derivation code
    C. A group classification code
    D. A significant digit code
11. Simscript and GPSS are examples of:
    A. Numerical control
    B. Source data automation
    C. Systems simulation
    D. Operating system subsets
12. XX XXX XXXX is an example of the format for
    A. A mnemonic code
    B. An alphabetic derivation code
    C. A group classification code
    D. A significant digit code
13. The selected area for a feasibility study is usually:
    A. That which produces the greatest benefits

B. Dependent on previous successes in the area
C. Determined by management
D. Not changed during the study

14. The __________ has the responsibility to decide what data is to be collected by a form.
A. Forms manufacturer
B. Systems Analyst
C. Programmer
D. User

15. Methods and Procedures staffs deal with:
A. Programming
B. Data base design
C. Paper flow mechanisms
D. Keypunch procedures

16. Why are tables useful to the systems analyst?
A. They are an effective method to express movement
B. They are an effective means to summarize relationships
C. They are the only method for presenting quantitative data
D. They should be used in place of charts wherever possible

17. The first tasks in systems analysis is:
A. Environmentally dependent
B. Programming
C. Orientation and fact-finding
D. The study of the processing operation

18. A network that describes the flow of data and the processes that change, or transform data through a system is called a:
A. Flowchart narrative
B. Hierarchy chart
C. Data flow diagram
D. Decision tree

19. Printing forms ''two-up'' means:
A. A transaction record is printed along with the documents
B. Documents are printed side-by-side
C. A carbon copy is printed along with the original
D. Off-line printing on the line printer

20. The chart which is used to record the details of manual procedures is called a:
A. Flow Process Chart
B. Hierarchy Chart
C. Data Flow Diagram
D. HIPO Chart

21. The product of systems analysis is:
A. System team charter
B. Application study
C. Feasibility study
D. Cost analysis study

22. The process of transferring information from one point to another is defined as:
A. Feedback
B. Dissemination

C. Presentation or technical writing
D. Communication

23. Management-by-Exception reporting means:
A. A report is generated upon management request only
B. A report is generated when an exceptional condition occurs
C. Only a sample of the data base is included in the report
D. Items failing an update editing are listed in a report

24. ________ are broad written guidelines and ________ are specific statements that tell how the guidelines are to be carried out.
A. Policies, procedures
B. Procedures, policies
C. Narratives, manuals
D. Manuals, narratives

25. The content of the systems analysis product is heavily oriented toward:
A. Cost
B. Data processing operation
C. Application processing
D. Management

26. Playscript is a format that frequently is used for laying out:
A. Reference manuals
B. Specifications
C. Policies and procedures
D. Narratives

27. In evaluation of a computer language in which to program an application, the analyst should:
A. Always pick COBOL because it's the standard language
B. Always pick FORTRAN, PL/1, APL, BASIC, or C for processing speed
C. Consider the nature of the application and select the input/output versus computing mix necessary
D. Do all programming in assembly language

28. The user and the systems analyst develop a contract of sorts between them. It is called
A. An information systems request
B. A project plan
C. A project request/directive
D. An Information memorandum

29. The application study is the:
A. Documentation of systems design
B. Cost study of systems design
C. Same as the feasibility study
D. Documentation of systems analysis

30. The identification of duplicate data is accomplished by a fact analysis technique that is called
A. Data element analysis
B. Recurring data analysis
C. Input/Output analysis
D. Report use analysis

31. Generally speaking, which of the following is not a prerequisite for using a benchmark problem to evaluate a hardware proposal?
A. At least 60% of the data processing requirements are known
B. No major application programs may dominate systems usage

C. The benchmark computer configuration must be known
D. The rate at which the data processing applications must operate

32. Success is measured in the ''value'' system of the
A. Analyst
B. Principal user
C. Manager of information systems
D. Programmer

33. The systems specification is the:
A. Same as the application study
B. Documentation of the design for the vendor
C. Expanded application study
D. Compressed application study

34. Which of the following is *not* a step in the definition of system performance?
A. Statement of general constraints
B. Identification and ranking of specific objectives
C. Description of inputs
D. Description of outputs

35. Which of the following is *not* an objective of an audit trail?
A. Tracing an original transaction to its final document
B. Tracing an entry on a final document back to an original entry
C. Providing program checks to determine the accuracy of the computer hardware
D. These are all objectives

36. A tentative selection of an output media is made by the
A. User
B. Analyst
C. Programmer
D. MIS manager

37. The document used to communicate systems development information to the vendor is the:
A. Feasibility study
B. Application study
C. System specification
D. Request for proposal

38. What item of information listed below is *not* contained on the data element list?
A. Description
B. Layout
C. Size
D. Format

39. The ''systems approach'' to problem solutions involves:
A. The development of a plan to subdivide the problem and control on each subdivision
B. The establishment of rigid and strictly enforced standards
C. The use of CPM or PERT to manage the project
D. The involvement of an auditor in establishing controls

40. The purpose of the preliminary evaluation of candidate systems is to:
A. Prepare detailed descriptions of each candidate
B. Formalize the functional differences between the candidates with a candidate system matrix
C. Reduce the candidates to a manageable number
D. Familiarize the team with available hardware devices

41. Benchmarks are:
    A. Representative routines for system timing
    B. Simulator programs
    C. Actual system programs
    D. Vendors' software applications
42. Which of the following is *not* part of the external performance section of the performance specifications?
    A. System output descriptions
    B. System input descriptions
    C. Information-oriented flowchart
    D. Process-oriented flowchart
43. When planning a fact-gathering interview with a user management individual, the analyst should begin with:
    A. Setting objectives for the interview
    B. Identifying the human relations problems he will experience in dealing with a user
    C. Defining the authority and responsibility of the user within the organization
    D. Whether or not to take notes
44. The decision to proceed with the design phase is the responsibility of the:
    A. Systems analyst
    B. Manager of Information Systems
    C. Representative of other affected organizations
    D. Principal user
45. Source data automation is:
    A. A selection criterion
    B. The use of software to capture data
    C. Capturing the data near a computer
    D. Capturing data at point of generation
46. Allocation of functions refers to:
    A. Dividing processing functions between computer program components
    B. Assigning functions to programmers, analysts, and users
    C. Distinguishing between study, design, and development phase activities
    D. Assigning functions to humans, to equipment, and to computer programs
47. When presenting a proposed system to user management, the detailed objectives of that system should:
    A. Satisfy all of the user's needs
    B. Be those with highest ROI
    C. Be those which satisfy legal requirements
    D. Be those which eliminate nuisance symptoms or "put out the fire"
48. Interface management is a term that refers to the:
    A. Planning of related database systems
    B. Interaction between users, analysts, and programmers
    C. Interface between hardware and software within one system database
    D. Interface between documentation and schedules
49. Which is *not* a technique for the validation of vendor bids?
    A. Time only
    B. Cost only
    C. Weighted scoring
    D. Cost value

50. The storage efficiency of a magnetic disk ________ as the blocking factor is increased
   A. Increases
   B. Decreases
   C. Varies
   D. Is not affected
51. Updating a file in-place often occurs in a real-time processing environment. When a system is designed to do this:
   A. Sequential data files cannot be used
   B. Audit trails are most critical
   C. Operator actions will make it happen
   D. Programming language selection is most critical
52. The ________ shows the size and data format characteristics for each field contained in an output record.
   A. Output data element source analysis sheet
   B. Magnetic disk schematic
   C. Record layout worksheet
   D. Direct access storage facility worksheet
53. SCERT is:
   A. An application program
   B. A computer evaluation by modeling technique
   C. A hardware monitor
   D. A manual evaluation of a computer system
54. Test requirements are established in the:
   A. Design phase
   B. Operation phase
   C. Development phase
   D. Study phase
55. The "relative" method of the file organization requires all records to:
   A. Be organized sequentially
   B. Have key fields which correspond to physical addresses
   C. Be indexed
   D. Be located by algorithm
56. Preliminary operational schedules are part of the
   A. System specification
   B. Changeover plan
   C. Operational plan
   D. Operator's reference manual
57. Human factors would be of primary interest to a:
   A. Programmer
   B. Computer operator
   C. Forms designer
   D. Data base designer
58. Turnaround time is the time
   A. For work to flow through the machine room
   B. Between the release of input data by the user and his receipt of output
   C. Required for the systems analyst to turn the system over to the principal user
   D. Between the arrival of data at the computer center and its availability for pickup

59. If a test file were created containing the following fields, the most stringent edit should be performed on which one?
   A. Employee number field
   B. Gross pay field
   C. Name field
   D. Rate of pay per hour field

60. The trend in the location of the data processing function is toward reporting to:
   A. An executive primarily responsible for information services
   B. The senior financial executive
   C. The senior general administrator
   D. The president of the company

61. The systems approach:
   A. Encompasses all source data required by a firm
   B. Includes fragmented systems
   C. Is different from the total system concept
   D. Applies to equipment selection

62. The individual responsible for maintaining the integrity of all of the system files is called the:
   A. Control clerk
   B. Librarian
   C. Supervisor of data preparation
   D. Database manager

63. The primary purpose for including a cost/benefit analysis when doing a preliminary study is to:
   A. Provide the user management with an idea as to what skills must be used to build the system
   B. Provide the basis for evaluating the system once it is in operation
   C. Justify its technical feasibility
   D. Argue for the need to do an analysis

64. The three basic types of decisions that management review of system life cycle activities can produce are:
   A. Obtain hardware, obtain software, obtain personnel
   B. Input, output, process for each day, week or month
   C. Proceed to next phase, cancel project, re-do certain parts of previous phase
   D. Budget approval, design approval, development approval

65. The simplification approach to design is:
   A. Called the efficiency approach
   B. The most limited approach
   C. Generally a hugh design workload
   D. Used when the user is displeased with his system

66. Which of the following is *not* a function of a systems analyst:
   A. Analyze a business system with problems and design a new or modified system to solve those problems
   B. Operate the computer console and log any malfunctions or failings
   C. Prepare and maintain manuals to communicate company policies and procedures
   D. Design various business forms used to collect data and to distribute information

67. To determine the volume and type of data rejected by an editing function, an analyst should consult:
   A. Keypunch personnel, since they must correct the errors
   B. User personnel, since they may have caused the error
   C. I/O control, since they must review the ''error log''
   D. Systems and programming personnel because errors must not occur

68. The new postal zip-plus-4 code is an example of a:
A. Simple sequence code
B. Block sequence code
C. Group classification code
D. Numeric zone code

69. The data system redesign approach to design generally:
A. Involves new equipment
B. Is a major system overhaul
C. Follows a ''flip-flop'' of a system
D. Is the same as the mechanization approach

70. In evaluating a form's effectiveness, the systems analyst should consider:
A. The artistic value of the form and that the cost is the lowest possible.
B. That the form can be used with all the different printers and that it incorporates a detachable stub set.
C. That it collects needed data, is cost effective, and is easy to complete and use.
D. That it be printed in blue, which is nonreproduceable

71. The cost of a control should be:
A. The ''rerun'' time cost
B. Borne is all instances by the user
C. Estimated in terms of the impact of loss due to the lack of control
D. Inclusive of all ''people coordination'' time to correct the error

72. Forms control
A. Is important to prevent a flood of new and modified forms from each department of the company
B. Is not needed in most businesses
C. Is the responsibility of the in-house reproduction center
D. Does not exist in any organization

73. Significant reductions in cost arise from design simulation through:
A. Changing simulator programs
B. Bad systems design
C. Modeling
D. Varying internal conditions

74. All decision tables have the following four parts
A. Title, line chart, summary, and conclusion
B. Condition stub, action stub, condition entries, and action entries
C. Title, instructions, body, and conclusion
D. heading, subtotal, total, and approval

75. The ''cutover'' form of systems implementation is most useful when:
A. Communications systems are to be used
B. People are to be displaced
C. The user is skeptical about systems performance
D. A parallel is too expensive

76. A __________ is used to depict a project schedule and to report progress:
A. Histogram
B. Decision table
C. Pie chart
D. Gantt chart

77. System requirements are:
A. Furnished by the user

B. Products of the environment
C. The results of the analysis phase
D. Initially determined by the systems team

78. To present a current picture of project performance, we need:
A. A bar chart, a pie chart, and a decision table or tree
B. A project plan, project cost report, and status report
C. Structured English outline of the project and a decision table or tree
D. A set of written specifications outline report contents

79. Data records best suited for storage in a tape-oriented master file would:
A. Have a high "hit" incidence but no response requirement
B. Have a low response requirement
C. Be valid only for use in on-line systems
D. Be so voluminous that they cannot be organized onto any direct access medium

80. The type of transformations of data streams that occur in processing in a system are:
A. Printing, display, or punching
B. Combining, splitting, or modifying
C. Sorting, storing, or retrieving
D. Table lookup, descending sort, coded classification

81. Intermediate and final output differ in:
A. Frequency
B. Media
C. Use
D. Format

82. Computer program flowcharts are used to depict program logic. The term "logic" here means:
A. The use of ones and zeroes by the computer
B. The binary numbering system
C. The types of instructions executed by the computer
D. A branch of mathematics called propositional calculus

83. A new system should be tested with data produced:
A. By vendor utility programs
B. By using existing files
C. Manually by analysts and users
D. By programs written expressly for that purpose

84. The two formal noncomputer communication-oriented activities that systems analyst perform most often are:
A. Technical writing and presentations
B. Printed reports and screen displays
C. Charts and structure diagrams
D. Coding sheets and printed listings

85. How many physical records does a tape with 10,000 logical records have?
A. 80,000
B. In excess of 10,000
C. Not fewer than 5,560
D. Between 1 and 10,000

86. To communicate problem statements, background discussions or summaries, the recommended type of writing is the:
A. Policy
B. Narrative

C. Specification
D. Playscript

87. The user should review the system design to ensure:
A. Information content, error handling, and file retention
B. Auditing methods, programming specifications, and error handling
C. Program specifications, information content, and output usability
D. Input/output processing, man-machine interfaces, and output usability

88. The systems analyst working in the business environment must realize that:
A. As a professional, any system he or she designs must be as technically perfect as possible within the present technology
B. Management is prepared to spend the time and resources needed to get the best system that can be designed
C. Often a system that meets basic needs and can be done quickly and inexpensively is all that is required for a project
D. Management must be forced to realize that the best, though expensive, is what is needed

89. Randomizing is:
A. A method of file organization
B. An addressing technique
C. Similar to the Monte Carlo method
D. A tool of operation research

90. Structured walkthroughs should be conducted:
A. With management present to enhance communication
B. As part of the standard employee evaluation for promotion
C. In a positive and nonthreatening manner using a peer group of the project developer
D. As an interview between the project designer and the MIS manager.

91. Simulation of a system's design permits:
A. Testing of probabilistic parameters
B. Two noncompatible pieces of hardware to work together
C. Market models to be built
D. Exception reporting to be done

92. In using screen displays, the systems analyst should:
A. Use the same format with related screens for an application or input sequence
B. Vary the screen formats for related screens to heighten interest in the user
C. Put as much data as possible on the screen to save time and space
D. Use separate and different screen and form designs for variety and a pleasing effect

93. Batch processing is:
A. Accumulating transactions for future processing
B. Processing transactions as they occur
C. Environmentally dependent
D. The same as real-time processing

94. The procedures for safeguarding the system fall within the systems analyst's influence. Such procedures should require:
A. Unlimited access to the computer room
B. Adjacent data storage libraries
C. Periodic preventative maintenance of the hardware
D. Periodic housecleaning

95. The internal design requirements of the design specification include:
A. Requirements for the computer program and for its subprograms

B. The computer equipment specifications
C. The personnel and training requirements
D. Systems test requirements

96. In computer system testing:
A. Formal test plans should be developed and a written test report prepared.
B. An ad hoc approach for checking the validity of the programs is the less expensive and quickest method
C. Murphy's Law should dictate the testing approach
D. The bottom-up method works best

97. An on-line system is:
A. Always real-time
B. One with an associated communication network
C. Environmentally independent
D. Generally smaller than a batch system

98. The general methods of changeover are:
A. hierarchical changeover, networked operation, relational replacement
B. Parallel operation, cutover (immediate replacement), and phased changeover
C. Sequential operation, direct changeover, indexed operation
D. Systems replacement, forms changeover, computer-based operation

99. A post-installation meeting serves which of the following purposes?
A. It allows the users to determine additional objectives
B. It allows both the user and the systems group to determine if objectives have been met
C. It allows the user and the systems team to prepare final documentation
D. It allows the user to be trained in the operation of the system

100. The use of punched cards as an input medium is declining rapidly because of:
A: The increase in cost-effective, on-line, transaction-oriented computer systems
B. The fact that there are a number of different types of punched cards and card readers fragment that market
C. The difficult of designing card input as opposed to screen terminal input
D. The cost of producing punched cards has risen dramatically in the last few years.

ANSWERS

1. A	**16.** B	**31.** D	**46.** D
2. C	**17.** C	**32.** B	**47.** B
3. A	**18.** C	**33.** B	**48.** A
4. C	**19.** B	**34.** C	**49.** A
5. C	**20.** A	**35.** C	**50.** C
6. C	**21.** C	**36.** B	**51.** B
7. A	**22.** D	**37.** D	**52.** C
8. C	**23.** B	**38.** B	**53.** B
9. C	**24.** A	**39.** A	**54.** A
10. D	**25.** A	**40.** C	**55.** B
11. C	**26.** C	**41.** A	**56.** B
12. C	**27.** C	**42.** D	**57.** C
13. A	**28.** C	**43.** A	**58.** D
14. D	**29.** A	**44.** D	**59.** A
15. C	**30.** B	**45.** D	**60.** A

61. A	**71.** C	**81.** C	**91.** A
62. D	**72.** A	**82.** C	**92.** A
63. B	**73.** D	**83.** C	**93.** A
64. C	**74.** B	**84.** A	**94.** D
65. B	**75.** B	**85.** D	**95.** A
66. B	**76.** D	**86.** B	**96.** A
67. C	**77.** D	**87.** A	**97.** B
68. C	**78.** B	**88.** C	**98.** B
69. C	**79.** A	**89.** B	**99.** B
70. C	**80.** B	**90.** C	**100.** A

TUTORIAL

1. Generally, work simplification is the improvements made in the day to day workings of the operation.
2. The whole idea behind standards is the efficient operation of the computer business. The idea is to find the most efficient, albeit not the most creative, set of solutions.
3. Storage costs are high and the available space can be misused. Access requirements are such that the record can be found with the minimum number of accesses. As a disk track gets used, and the blocking factor is changed, the ratio of space used to space not used (and fragmented) changes. At a given point, the efficiencies drop.
4. The question now is what is the definition of traditional. Traditional is that which has transaction-oriented input, detail or summary intermediate processes, and report of file output. The nontraditional system, then, goes beyond into integration of word processing and communication functions.
5. The process chart has symbols for filing, transportation, annotation, etc. It represents a manual process in much the same way a program flowchart represents a logical process.
6. It has vertical linkages because of the reporting process through the traditional hierarchy. It has horizontal linkages because it must serve organizational entities at the same horizontal level.
7. The flow process chart shows the activities, time consumed, distances, and operations performed, essentially in a manual system.
8. Each of the organizational entities has its own business system. The organization, then, is a system of systems.
9. The feasibility study is a management study which is used to detail the likely characteristics and costs of a proposed system.
10. Significant digit is a measurement analagous to a class point in a histogram. It is numeric, is descriptive of the group, but not a classification of the group.
11. These two software packages are illustrations of simulation systems, designed to simulate the operation of a system before the development process is undertaken.
12. This is an example of a group classification code, such as that which might be used in a clothing store, where XX is the store number, XXX is the department number, and XXXX is the garment style number.
13. Feasibility includes financial advisability. In an organization where resources are scarce, opportunity competes with opportunity, and the project with the greatest potential benefits is the one which is selected.
14. The user has the ultimate responsibility in all phases of systems development, as he or she is paying the bill. Unfortunately, users tend to abdicate responsibility more often than not.
15. Methods and Procedures staff deal with manual paper flow systems.
16. Not only effective, but concise. They provide an organization to the data and are the basis of several file organization schemes, specifically the relational database.

17. In the preliminary phase, the analyst becomes familiar with the user's area and some initial examination of the circumstances which occasion the study.
18. The data flow diagram is fundamental to the structured analysis process.
19. The size of the form, if it is too small, makes it difficult to use in a large line printer. When this is the case, a pair are printed side-by-side. And, of course, it cuts the amount of printing time.
20. The flow process chart, with several manual symbols, details the flow of a paperwork system.
21. Some will think that this is not entirely accurate, as they will separate the preliminary phase, with its feasibility study, from the analysis phase, with its statement of findings.
22. Communications will be a larger portion of future systems, as capabilities increase and functions become more highly integrated.
23. The idea of management-by-exception is that a parameter frame set is established and data which falls outside that set is highlighted on the report. The next level is to generate the report only when the exception has occurred.
24. Policies are established by top-level management. These policies evolve into procedures.
25. It's probably not the only choice, but the best amongst the answers. In the analysis phase, assuming that you consider the feasibility study, cost is a primary concern.
26. Playscript is a procedure writing language. It was not included in this chapter, but you will find reference to it in the Office Automation section.
27. Every computer language has strong and weak points. Ideally, one should select the language to fit the characteristics of the application. Unfortunately, because of the need for maintainability and the higher numbers of people capable of handling a common language, the common language is used, despite any inefficiencies.
28. Here we're splitting hairs. Some organizations begin with an information services request. Others begin with the project request/directive. The hair split comes from the recognition that we're really talking about a project.
29. When the analysis is completed, there is some documentation, and some will say that that is the application study. We'd prefer to feel that the application study is an examination of the area of concentration and a solution set to overcome any problems in that area.
30. The definition of "recurring" is that it happens again.
31. The benchmark exists to compare hardware using the same software and applications. The rate at which they MUST operate is of no consequence. We're interested in the rate at which they *do* operate.
32. The user is predominant—if he or she is not satisfied, according to his or her value system, the results of the systems effort are for naught.
33. The specification becomes a bidding document. The vendor can be in-house or out-of-house.
34. Inputs are random, imperfect, and not timed. They cannot be considered in performance specifications or statistics.
35. Audit trails are a feature of financial applications software, essentially. They are applied to other systems where recovery is required.
36. The analyst is theoretically the "expert," and should select the output media. Here again, we all recognize that large organizations or hardware availabilities dictate a certain degree of uniformity. Where the output media should be different, the analyst has the responsibility to try to sell the idea.
37. The request for proposal (RFP) will be sent to the vendor as an invitation to bid on a systems project.
38. The data layout goes beyond an individual data element level, and is usually applied to a record description.
39. The systems approach is, essentially, the scientific method, which breaks a problem down into its component parts.

40. "Candidate" merely means one of the available choices for selection. The preliminary evaluation is a screening process.

41. The benchmark compares the application run in a given language on more than one piece of hardware. It is a timing consideration process.

42. Here external means outside of the system. The process flow chart is to describe the program logic.

43. If you don't know what you wish to accomplish, you'll accomplish it. Set objectives for the fact-gathering interview.

44. The user has the final decision authority over the systems effort. It is the user which is paying the bill.

45. The idea of Source Data Automation (SDA) is to capture the data at its origin.

46. The responsibility of the analyst gets into some management functions, and that allocation of resource to problem resolution becomes a part of the new systems design.

47. While not all systems have a financial base, the majority of them do, and the highest return on investment (ROI) is more often than not the deciding factor.

48. It's simply a term which is meaningful to database-oriented systems people.

49. Not everything can be done yesterday, and not every vendor has the most outstanding (and frequently most expensive) staff. If your interest is to get the work done, the most consideration you should give to time is to a reasonable estimate.

50. The efficiency varies. It increases as the blocking factor increases, but at some point the cost in time of accessing very large blocks intersects with the cost of storage allocation. If the concept is large blocks, then the number of times divisible into a track size and the left-over space become primary considerations.

51. The update in-place changes the record and leaves no trace of what the record was. Audit trails, then, generally contain before and after pictures of the record.

52. The record layout worksheet is used to detail the size and characteristics of the data by field.

53. SCERT is a modeling technique used to detail the aspects of a prospective (candidate) system before it is built.

54. Since the design is the system as it will ultimately run, the test data must test that design. Therefore, the test requirements should be established at that time.

55. Relative usually means relative to logical zero. Logical zero can be at any disk address, but the key fields will correspond to physical addresses from that point.

56. Don't jump at the obvious, D. The analyst must establish a changeover plan which includes planning preliminary operational schedules.

57. Of the available list, these factors, called "ergonomics," are of most concern to the forms designer—eye movement, color, spacing, hand movement, etc.

58. Turnaround time is really an operational term, despite the fact that some may feel that it is the time between RJE (remote job entry) submission and the next mail distribution.

59. The most stringent editing should be done on the employee number field, as it is the key which unlocks a confidential record.

60. This movement has been around for a few years—essentially to put it at the VP level. However, with the advent of information centers under the office automation concept, the chief information officer (CIO) is fast becoming a fact of life. The CIO, then, has oversight responsibility for DP and OA.

61. We're looking at the information needs of an organization, and, therefore, all the source data of the firm.

62. Database managers or database analysts are probably a unique function in only large organizations and may be the additional responsibility of another person in the small organizations.

63. A preliminary study should include the feasibility analysis, an exploration of a systems likely characteristics and costs. Those explorations should include estimates of benefits.
64. Management has a choice—go, no go, or conditional go.
65. The idea of work simplification is to clean up the existing system in the places where efficiency can be added. It is not a broad brush approach.
66. The analyst should not be allowed to run the applications. The auditors would have some justified concern if this were the case.
67. In larger organizations, an input/output control section will normally monitor the error processes.
68. The classification is by postal zone and location within zone. It is said that the Canadian postal code localizes the mail to the specific block of the street.
69. It's but a cute way to say that the system laid over and died. It's at that point where a redesign is absolutely necessary.
70. It's got to be easy to use, reasonably priced, and gather the data which is necessary to run the system.
71. Theoretically, if the loss could be a thousand dollars, then $999 could be spent and you'd still be ahead of the game. Much less is required, of course, but the nature of the control should cover the importance of the data or process.
72. A new form is as near as the closest copy machine in an uncontrolled environment—and that can get mighty expensive.
73. In any model, if the conditions are varied—according to a plan—the output results can be measured.
74. Those listed are the four component parts of a decision table. If you were looking for "rule," recall that a rule is a combination of condition and action entries.
75. When people are displaced, a quick change is best, as it avoids unhappiness and, sadly, sabotage.
76. Gantt charts show the progress of the tasks (*Y* axis) over time (*X* axis).
77. The systems team has the skills necessary to identify the system requirements. The user, however, has the money, and therefore, the approval power.
78. The elements of reporting will the original plan, against which the progress is measured; a status report which shows the progress against that plan, and a cost report which also shows progress against that plan.
79. Tape records are best used where most of the records are to be "hit." They are entirely unsuitable where a response requirement is required.
80. Transformations (and transactions) involve the changes, during processing, of the data. B best fits the description of what must be done.
81. Intermediate data are used prior to summary. Output data are used for final reports.
82. Logic is a description of the program steps executed by the computer.
83. All data should be contrived data. Using production data gives misleading results.
84. The systems analyst must do the documentation and make the sales pitches. That requires good writing and presentation skills.
85. It can be one block of 10,000 records or 10,000 blocks of one record each, or anything in between.
86. Narrative presents the information as it is known, without any attempt to structure it.
87. The user is responsible for the presence of all the pieces. The analyst will not be so knowledgeable in the application area.
88. If there is anything which has spurred the use of microcomputers and driver software in the user areas, it is the fact that they are told that whatever they want to do is a full-fledged project which will take many months and cost many thousands of dollars.
89. Randomizing is generally the process whereby a direct access file. There is an algorithm (formula) drawn on the key. Those keys which duplicate produce what are called synonyms.

90. The idea is to find what has been missed. The lower the personal risk, the better will be the product. It should involve peers.

91. Probabilistic parameters are switches turned on in relation to their probability. Those switches redirect the program flow.

92. Whenever there is a large number of similar screens, work for uniformity, to avoid confusion.

93. When I run a batch, it's generally the accumulation of a period's worth of transactions. There is no response requirement to such a system.

94. Cleanliness is next to system safety, I always say.

95. The key word is ''internal''—we're looking to design the program requirements.

96. Testing must be a planned exercise—and the report of test should become part of the documentation of the system.

97. On-line implies communications.

98. Parallel operates the current and new system simultaneously. Cutover, or immediate replacement, drops the current system in favor of the older system. Phased, which would be best, works the pieces as they come on line. This may not always be possible, due to incompatibilities.

99. More often than not, we do not measure whether the objectives were met. It should be the case.

100. Communications cost are coming down, making as-required transaction processing possible. Also, we don't keep card files very much anymore.

8

MISCELLANEOUS SYSTEMS TOPICS

COMMUNICATIONS

Communications. The ability to communicate between your computer and the outside world. The ability to tap into services and into remote databases. Communications is something more than simply purchasing a modem and dialing up The Source, Dow Jones, or Compuserve—or any of the more than 5,000 other available services. It's communicating from computer to computer, from computer to terminal, and from terminal to terminal. It's micro to mainframe, host to network, global networks and local area networks. It's satellites and services, and a whole lot more, and, of course, there isn't the room here to cover it all—we'll leave that task to James Martin. But we will take time to learn enough about communications to understand what is happening when we do it using the computer.

The World of Data Communications and Teleprocessing

There must be something more to data communications than simply plugging the computer into the the telephone network and seeing what occurs, right? Right. Telecommunications (which we will hereinafter occasionally refer to as "TC") is a business consideration. There simply has to be a valid reason for doing it—the line charges would become simply too exorbitant otherwise.

Why Telecommunications?

One of the reasons for TC is document transmission. Historically, businesses have transmitted data using paper tape readers/punches, card readers/punches, magnetic card readers, badge readers, plate readers, optical document readers (facsimile), MICR readers, and mark-sensing devices. To do this, a variety of equipment and media have been required: microfilm, magnetic tapes, tape cassettes, and magnetic disks. The types of devices have included: keyboard devices, teleprinters, telephone (dial, touch-tone, direct connection), light pen, coupled stylus (graphics pad), facsimile machines, plate and badge readers, smart and dumb terminals, and now personal computers. Expect intelligent copiers to have such functions in the not too distant future.

Similarly, TC devices have included response and answerback devices such as typewriters, printers, teleprinters, passbook printers, display boards, screens and tubes, light panels, microfilm projectors, graphics plotters, strip recorders, readout guages, voice answerback, facsimile, and telemetry.

Categories of Data Transmission Systems

There are two predominant categories of TC systems, those which are on-line and those which are off-line. In simple terms, the difference is whether or not they are directly connected to a host computer.

On-line systems include terminals or personal computers which are in direct connection to a distant computer. There are no intermediate steps. A variety of entries are made directly to the host computer, and the host computer provides a variety of outputs to that terminal or other system. The host computer controls transmission process. Such on-line services can include:

- Devices using a slow scan rate (minutes). Applications of this concept would include temperature graphing and map transmission.
- Devices using a fast scan rate (milliseconds). Applications of this concept would include detection of critical temperatures and critical voltages.
- Transmission from computers—with response, including slow scan (data collection) and fast scan (interactive exchanges).
- Transmission from humans, including slow scan (not time sensitive) and fast scan (time sensitive).

Off-line applications, conversely, have no direct connection to the computer, may receive transmission from computers but be unable to respond. Included in this list are data collection devices, real-time or non-real-time. A real-time application is one which affects its environment on the basis of its input. The sensing of a critical temperature, for example, permits the computer-controlled nuclear reactor to change its environment by adding cooling. Included in this category are devices with both slow and fast scan rates, depending upon the nature of the application, or where no on-line response is required.

There are also the differences between an interactive environment and a non-interactive environment. The interactive environment is one which permits dialogue and change of the computer's environment. Generally, there is a user-initiated transaction. The host computer controls communication, processes a query and provides a response. This differs significantly from the non-interactive (or static) environment, which would include telemetry, data collection, or constant display. There is a world of difference in the quantity of transmissions among these, including the transmission of whole files, Yes/No interchanges, keyword entries, and transactions one-by-one or in batches. And, as you can imagine, the quantity transmitted may vary from a few bits (such as for an alarm system) to several million bits (for a downloaded or uploaded file).

Those services you are likely to encounter as a private individual would include information utility systems or time sharing systems. The utility systems, including bulletin board systems, will be limited function systems, designed for a specific purpose, such as legal research, chemical abstracts, financial insight systems (e.g., Dow Jones), or specific limited systems, wherein user files may be maintained or public domain files are available.

The time sharing systems you are likely to encounter will provide some considerable flexibility in the use of shared programming capability. And, of course, should you care to access specific networks or even to provide your own intercompany services, these are the types of services you'll likely encounter, not all of which you'll necessarily have direct access to commercial real-time systems and information utilities, such as:

Airline reservation	Savings Account
Banking	Stock brokerage
Sales Inquiry	Travel service
Sales-order entry	Professional billing
Point of sale data collection	Engineering
Credit information	Graphic design
EFTS	Document retrieval
Stockbroker	Data retrieval
Hospital	General Purpose
Text editing	Credit information
Document retrieval	Financial exchange
Information retrieval	Hospital and medical
Library catalog	Educational and teaching
Museum catalog	Hotel reservation
Hotel booking	Railroad information

Stores	Publishing
Inventory Control	Radio/TV brokerage
Production control	System bulletin boards
Production data collection	Retail and distribution
Management Inquiry	Insurance
Engineering Design	Merchandising and Advertising
Financial Analysis	Public survey and polling
Statistical	Sport and theater tickets
Specialized functions	Tax service
Labor negotiations	Career and employment networks
Real estate networks	Legal research
Legal citation	Post Office ECOM
MCI-Mail	Marketing Research
Criminal intelligence (NCIC)	Typing and Editing
Professional offerings	Personal Communications

These are not all, of course, but provide some insight into the power you have at your disposal.

A Twenty-Minute Communications Theory Course

Pumping Data

Think back to pictures you may have seen of firemen fighting a battle in the days when fire engines were drawn by horses. Recall that there was not one man holding the hose nozzle; there were several. In those days, mechanical pumps were of the surge variety, pushing water out of the hose only when the chamber compressed. Many an old-time fireman was knocked to a tender part of his anatomy, primarily due to Newton's second law of motion: "For every force or action there is an equal and opposite reaction." As time went on, an expansion bell was added to the line. The expansion bell took the surge and maintained the pressure necessary to keep a steady stream on the hose. This is the concept of standpipes and reservoirs to this day.

But as we think of the fireman's plight, we can learn something about communications. First, the hose is of a finite size. If we were to greatly increase the diameter of the hose and maintained the same volume of water, there would be a drop in the pressure. The same is true of data communications. Look around at the microwave towers. They exist to boost the pressure at intermediate points, like a pumper truck boosts the pressure at intermediate points in the transmission line between the source of the water and its final delivery. In a digital data communication system, the process in called a regenerative repeater, one which amplifies the signal without amplifying the line noise. These services, called digital channels, contain not only regenerative repeaters, but provides nearly noise-free services and not conversion equipment. Unfortunately, it is prohibitively expensive.

In an analog communication system, such as the telephone network, there are a few other problems with signal strength, thermal and line noise, sensitivity of heat and miscellaneous magnetic waves, and the ever-present hiss, all of which helps the computer-generated data signal to drown in the noise.

Either way, transmissions fall into one of three general categories of service: simplex, half-duplex, and full-duplex (called simply duplex). A simplex service is a one-way communication, and is most commonly used for data collection devices. A half-duplex service permits two-way communication, one way at a time, in turn. And a duplex service permits two-way communication, simultaneously. Full-duplex systems are generally in-house or devoted systems, although some of the systems you will encounter will be full-duplex systems.

The telephone network is a half-duplex network, but the manufacturers of the devices necessary encode the signals (MODEMs) have found a way to obtain full-duplex service from a half-duplex medium. The system is an analog, not a digital, system. It was built to carry the human voice. There are no digital repeaters, only amplifiers—of both signal and noise (distortion). It provides a fairly narrow range of frequencies (between 300 and 3,300 Hertz), and has bandwidth not dissimilar to the rate of oscillation of light. Like a violin string, there are fundamental notes and harmonics. A collection of frequencies is called a band, and the band in use for the telephone system is 3,000 cycles wide.

Into this 3,000 cycles is packed the speech spectrum [30 cycles per second (cps) to 20,000 cps]. These are the frequencies which can be heard. "Cycles per second" (cps) is synonymous with "Hertz." Using processes called "clipping" and "filtering," the audio range of 19,700 cps is compressed into the 3,000 cps bandwidth of the telephone system. Again, recall that the telephone system was designed to convey human intelligence, not human high-fidelity. And when it comes to using the service for data communications—particularly sensitive data communications—that's another matter entirely.

Computers are digital beasts. The communications medium is an analog critter. The only way, then, to get the former to communicate with the latter, is to change the nature of the signal. That's done using a device call the *modem.* It is the responsibility of the MODEM to prepare the signal for transmission on the analog network and to receive the signal from the analog network and prepare it for use by the computer again. The modem, then, is the data pump.

It's The Only Way . . .

As with any language, some standardization has been required in order to promote communication. There have been (and are) many standards, but you should research the topic in an extensive book on data communications if you want a thorough understanding. Those communications standards which directly affect us are a product of the International Standards Organization (ISO), of which the American National Standards Institute (ANSI) is a member. ISO has developed seven-layer model for telecommunications:

Layer 1—Physical Control. This element applies to the physical hardware. Interface cables and connectors, such as the RS-232 (serial interface), RS-449 (parallel interface), and the various DIN connections lie in this area. Devices for larger networks, such as multiplexors and concentrators, terminal control units and front-end communications processors also fall within the jurisdiction of this layer.

Layer 2—Link Control. This section of the standard covers the mechanisms for the transfer of data blocks. It governs the information which must precede and follow blocks of data and defines the transmission protocols which are used.

Layer 3—Network Control. This section governs the processes for communicating between computers which are not necessarily connected. It covers those services you are likely to use when you use MCI-Mail, for example.

Layer 4—Transport Control. This section governs message integrity. Includes standards for echo, parity, and standard user interface. We'll cover those shortly.

Layer 5—Session Control. This section is responsible for establishing or terminating a communication session. It checks to ensure proper communication. If communication was not proper, it controls the correction or termination of the process.

Layer 6—Presentation Control. This section governs the character set and data codes. It includes printer and screen displays, character set conversion, and compression of the bit stream.

Layer 7—Process Control. Here is the interface to applications database, file activities.

Well and good, you say, but how does this apply to my system? Parts of it obviously apply, though you may not realize you are directly affected by them. But if you have visions of developing an on-line system, then the communications handling programming which must be obtained must meet the criteria of these standards.

Examining the Signal

Let's examine the signal itself. That begins by examining the coding system. For example, the ASCII code for the letter "A" is 65. In binary, that looks like Figure 8.1.

Two data transfer models are shown next. First is the parallel model (Figure 8.2). Last is the serial model (Figure 8.3). The serial model is the one we'll use.

To begin with, as we have already discussed in this book, the byte is the unit of measurement in memory. And a byte, you will recall, is 8 bits. However, the standard language of communication is ASCII, which is 7 bits. The 8th bit is used by many hardware systems for graphics. However, there is the option to use the 8th bit when communicating, as the 8th bit is customarily used for parity, a concept which will be explained shortly.

Parallel (digital) transmission is a transmission on a bit-by-bit basis. It doesn't necessarily mean that there are eight distinct wires strung, though it could mean such in an in-plant communication network. It might mean eight distinct frequency allocations in a bandwidth. However, the digital network is not the same network which is used to carry telephone calls. It's frightfully expensive, requires equally expensive high-speed transmission equipment, and is somewhat out of the range of the average owner of an system. There must then be another way. That way is serial transmission, as shown by Figure 8.3.

Thus, as you can see, the bits are turned end-to-end and transmitted serially. That process of moving a character serially is called a *pulse train,* and there will be seven bits and a parity bit, or eight bits (with no parity bit) transmitted in this pulse train. Actually, there will be more, as we shall see, but the additional bits will be overhead bits.

Parity is the means to determine if a character has been transmitted and received correctly. Parity generally involves adding up the bits in the first seven bits and determining of the count is odd or even. If the system is even parity, the parity bit will be turned on if the count is odd. If the system is odd parity, the parity bit will be turned on if the count is even. There is no requirement to use parity bit. In fact, five types of parity consideration are available:

1. *None.* No parity bit is transmitted, and none is expected. The 8th bit can be used for data, and must be used if communication is to a system which uses the 8-bit character, commonly called the Extended Binary Decimal Interchange Code (EBCDIC).

Place Value	128	64	32	26	8	4	2	1
Character "A"	0	1	0	0	0	0	0	1
Bit Position	8	7	6	5	4	3	2	1

Figure 8.1

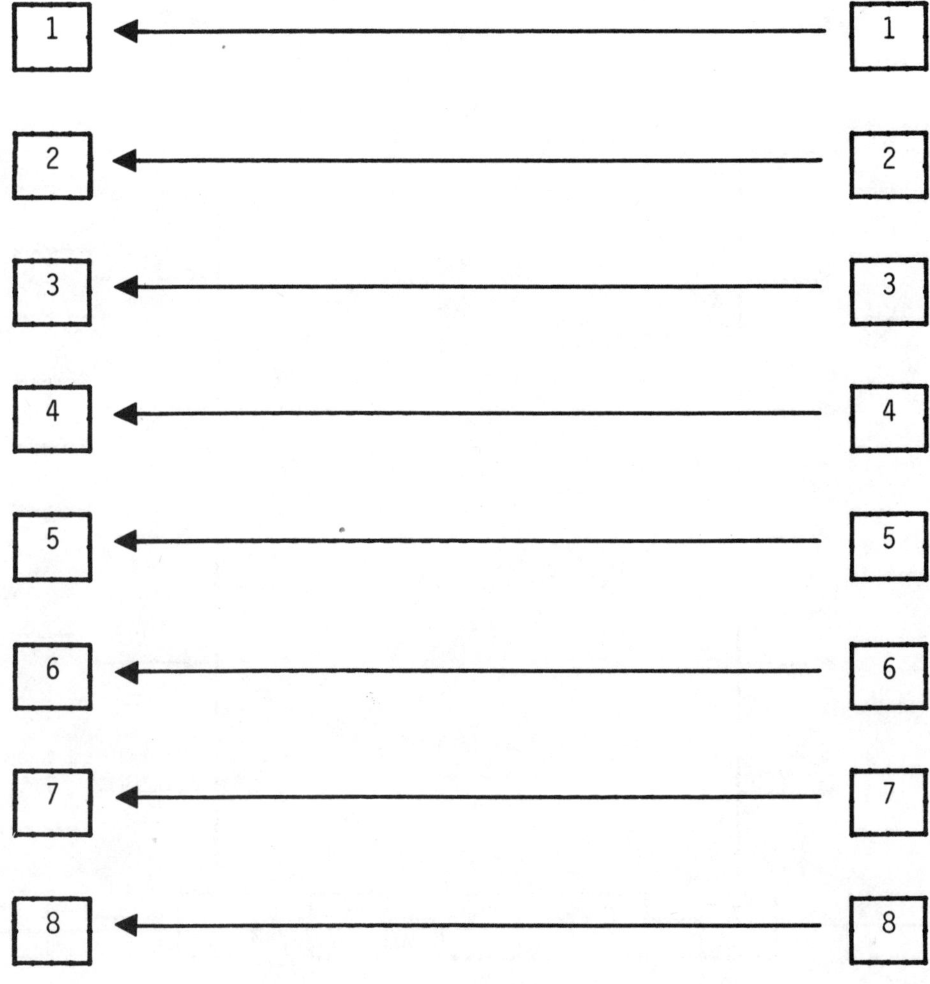

Figure 8.2

2. Mark parity. Always a binary 1-not used as quality check.
3. Space. Always a binary 0; also a position filler.
4. Even parity, as described.
5. Odd parity, as described.

Those services which have specific parity considerations will so specify. Again, you'll be on the terminal end of things, and you'll establish your communications protocol. How you handle parity detection and error correction will be a function of the sophistication of the communications handling program you will use.

Bit/Time

Enter a new concept: *bit/time.* The serial—otherwise known as "asynchronous"—method of communication uses a concept of standard time measurement. That standard time measurement is called "baud," and no doubt you'll be using equipment which is operating in either 300 baud or 1200 baud. Faster equipment is available for ranges above 14,000 baud. In any event, a *baud* is a unit of bit/time, a spacing of bits wherein it can be determined if a *one-bit* or a *zero-bit* has been transmitted. The pulse train is a *sine-wave train,* in which the bit/times are marked as shown in Figure 8.4, which is, of course, the character portion of the pulse train for the character "A."

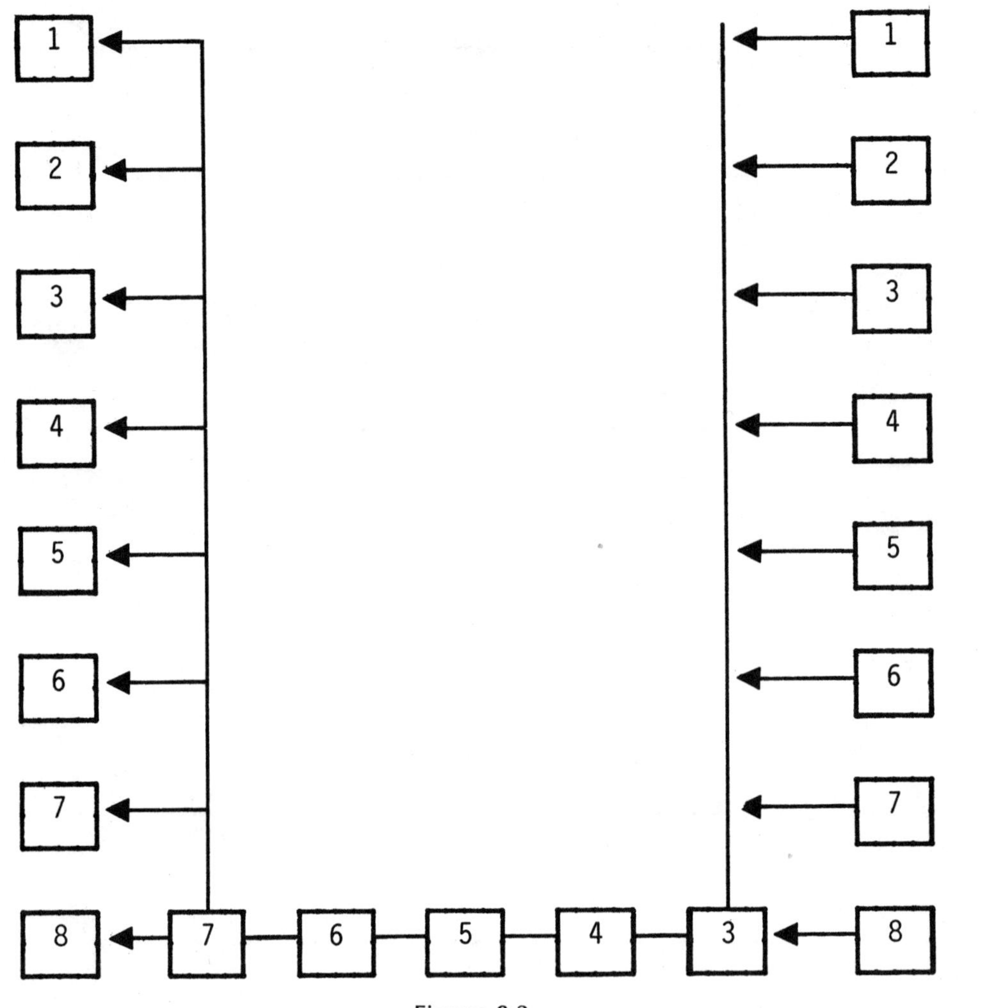

Figure 8.3

Asynchronous communication is customarily called *start/stop* communication. The reason for this is that once a connection is made, the host computer generates a tone, or *carrier.* This carrier is referred to as the *mark state.* The mark state is the steady transmission of binary 1s. The process begins by the transmission of a *start bit,* which is a binary zero. After that, the character follows, in *bit serial mode.* If the parity bit is used, then it follows next, else the 8th character will be a data bit. Because of the bit/time concept, the computer knows that once the start bit has been received, the *stop bit* will be eight bits down the line. The stop bit is a binary 1, and puts the line back into the marking state. Figure 8.5 shows how it looks.

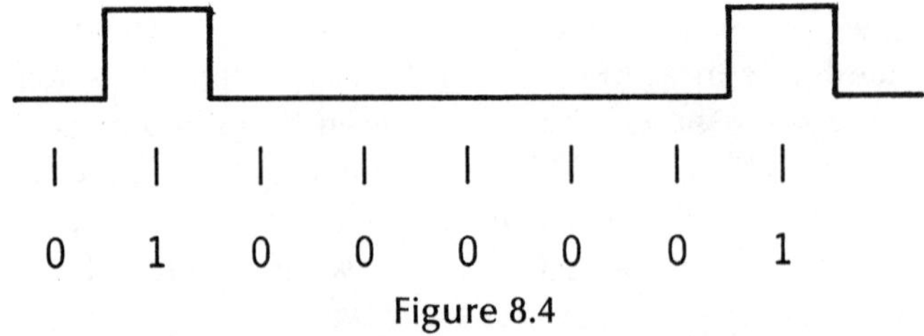

Figure 8.4

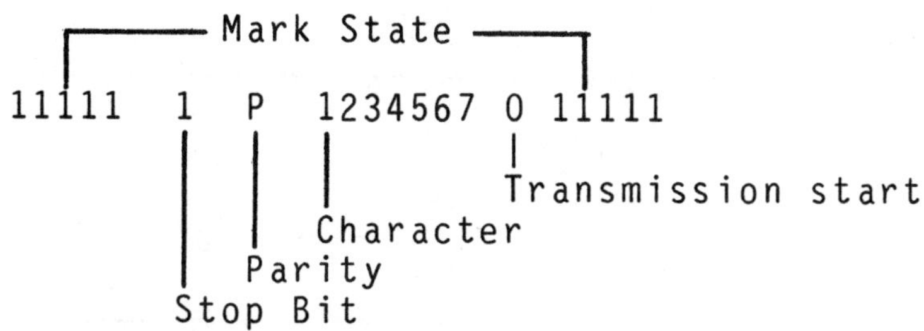

Figure 8.5

In asynchronous communications, this transmission is done *a character at a time,* each with a start bit and a stop bit. in the slower speeds a second stop is required, and occasionally you will see a choice of one or two stop bits offered. Again, listen to the requirements of the system you will be using. Generally at 300 baud and above, only a single stop bit is required. This start/stop nature permits manual keying of individual characters, but it is, of course, very slow, because it has a 30% overhead. Where this gets in the way is that this character-by-character transmission is also used when you are transmitting data files—and that slows things down measurably.

The Modems

The *modem,* frequently called a *data set* (a Bell System term) is actually comprised of three distinct parts:

- The UART (Universal Asynchronous Receiver/Transmitter). It is the function of the UART to acquire data from the computer's "Bus" and to pass it on to a signal amplifier. In the opposite direction, it receives data from the amplifier and transmits it to the computer's bus.
- The amplifier's function is to give the signal substance, in either direction.
- The Data Access Arrangement (DAA). The DAA is a line conditioner which ensures that the signal is not over-amplified (which means too high a voltage) to place too potent a signal on the analog network.

Because the telephone system is analog and not digital, the digital signal must be converted, or "modulated." The digital signal is made to provide sound within the same range of frequencies as are used for voice transmission and reception. On the sending end, the process is called *modulation*; on the receiving end, the process is called *demodulation. Modem* stands for *mo*dulate/*dem*odulate.

Modems can be categorized according to speed, communications protocols, features, and intelligence.

- Speed is measured in bits per second (baud):

  600 or less is considered low speed
  1200 to 9600 is considered to be medium speed
  More than 9600 is high speed.

- Protocol is the specific communications service. Most are asynchronous. The protocol for low speed is known as the Bell 103. For medium speed, there are two, the Bell 212A or Racal-Vadic protocols. The modems are designed to fit, so the specifics are not germane for our discussion.
- Modems have a variety of features, such as Auto-dial, which uses stored numbers from disk or in modem memory and Auto-answer, which is an unattended operation feature.

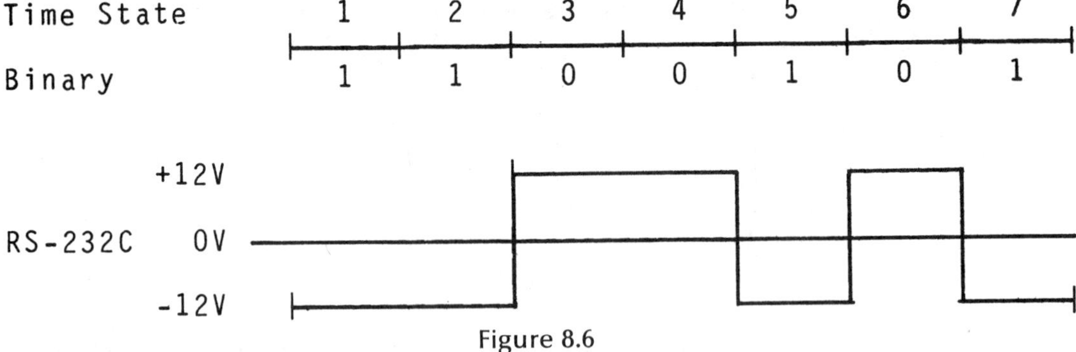

Figure 8.6

The asynchronous serial interface is also known as the RS-232 interface. This interface has the specification shown in Figure 8.6. The signal is a function of voltage.

While the telephone system spectrum is used for data communications, the entire width is not used. There are specific frequency assignments. Figure 8.7 shows the low speed modem originate-mode frequency diagram, and Figure 8.8 shows the low speed modem answer-mode frequency diagram:

The Bell 103 asynchronous protocol requires the frequencies to be shifted, and uses frequency modulation (FM).

The requirements, then, are for one modem to be in originate mode while the other is in answer mode. This must be as a function of understanding, prior agreement, or within the capabilities of the modem to shift.

The following are features which are available in one or more of the commercially available modems.

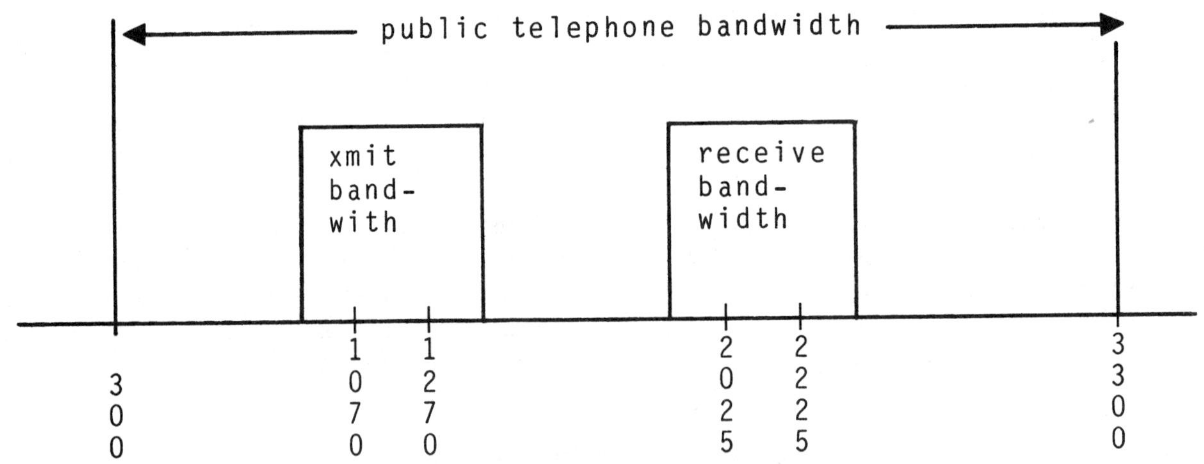

Direction	Signal Logic	Frequency (Hz)
Transmit	0	1070
Transmit	1	1270
Receive	0	2025
Receive	1	2225

Figure 8.7

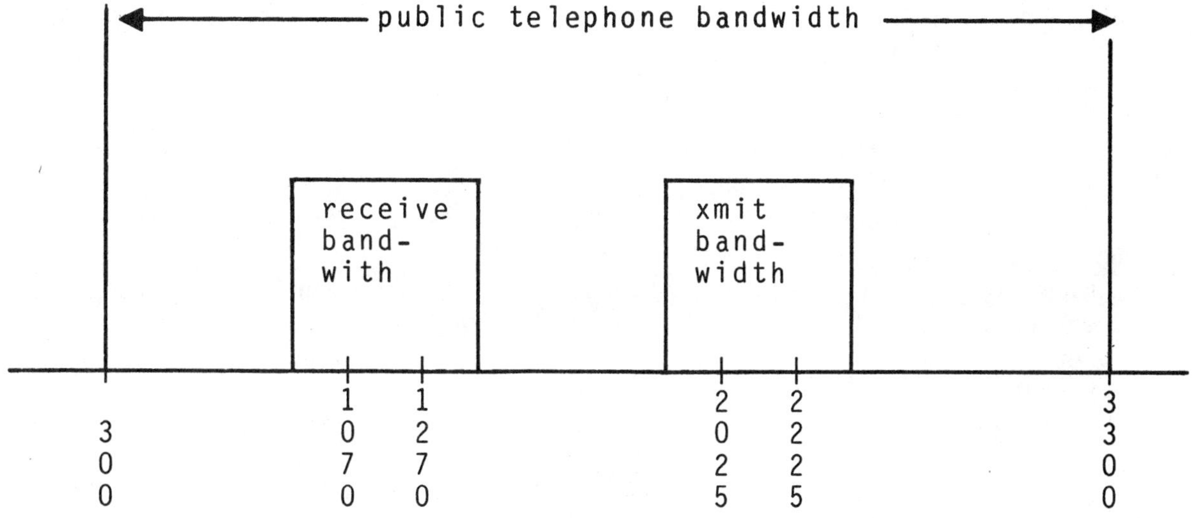

Figure 8.8

- Help command—provides brief explanations for common problems on the screen
- Command modes—a manufacturer's entry sequence
- Command recognition—speed and parity configuration—set and reset
- Command abort—interrupts the calling sequence
- Quit command—turns the modem off and on under software control; required to accomplish protocol changes
- Manual dial—permits manual dialing from the keyboard; mechanisms for batch mode calling using prefixes and suffices
- Dialing directory—stores frequently called numbers on a menu and responds to the menu
- Dial tones—pulse or touch-tone dialing; dial-tone wait commands
- Name selection dialing—enter a name and the number is selected and called
- Last number redial—self-explanatory, software actuated
- Repeat dialing—a predetermined number of times
- Number linking—a secondary number if the first is busy or does not answer; used for systems with multiple access; permits a circle of numbers to be established, thus permitting polling; may include successful-connection alarm
- Directory modification—establish directory items, wildcard or total clear, list
- Auto-answer— detail the number of rings, specify a force to answer or force to dial condition
- Busy mode—take the computer off the hook without shutting it off; bulletin board appears busy, not inoperative
- Protocol detect and switch—baud change, and back; requires data speed switch; can also be accomplished through software
- Set answerback string—transmit a specific string of characters after originating or answering a call; between 16 and 32 characters, internally buffered; bypasses repeated log-in sequences.
- Set backspace character— ASCII 008 (Ctl-H) is standard backspace, but ASCII 127 also works; other codes may be designated.
- Set attention character—on-line and off-line operating modes: *off line,* the modem is in an interactive command mode and responds to commands; *on line,* the modem is in a transparent mode while transmitting and receiving, and is not interruptable except via the attention character

- Set disconnect character—the character string which "hangs up," i.e., severs the connection; technically called "on hook"
- Modem register contents—Interfaces with communications software—needed for bulletin boards for protocol, speed, parity, and databit data
- Modem switches—existence of special signals; switch for Data Terminal Ready must be on to change parameters; software-controlled
- Built-in self-tests—pattern generator and error-checking; tests ability to send and receive data accurately; there are three types of tests:
  - Analog loop-back self test—checks the modem's transmitter to modem's receiver and compares the patterns
  - Digital loop-back self test—performs a test on a remote modem; data are sent to the remote and looped there; the patterns are compared
  - Remote digital loop-back—this is a transmission to the remote and back again

Standalone vs. Internal Modems

Modems may be obtained in one of two styles. You may obtain standalone units, units which are external to the computer. Or you may obtain modem cards which may be installed in the computer itself. There is something to be said for (and against) each.

Standalone modems can be used with any computer or terminal, and can be moved from one to another should you have more than one. Among the benefits of a standalone modem are these:

- It has indicator lights that show action and status.
- The heat load is external to the computer system unit.
- It can be removed from the serial port so the port can be used for another application.
- The communications port can be used between computers for faster transfer.
- It has a power on/off switch for last resort modem reset.
- It has internal switches which are easily reset.
- It has been well-proved.

There are a few disadvantages, as well:

- It requires space adjacent to the computer.
- It must be transported separately on a trip.
- It requires a power supply connection.
- It requires an RS-232 cable.
- It requires a serial communications adapter device.

The internal modem likewise has advantages and disadvantages:

- It requires no space outside the computer system.
- It requires no serial port connection.
- It requires no RS-232 cable.
- It requires no external power supply.
- It eliminates switches that can be vendor reset.
- Its switches can be software controlled.
- It does not have to be transported separately.
- It eliminates direct connection of a communications port to another computer through a null modem.

- It occupies an expansion slot which might be used for other facilities.
- It must be used with a compatible computer.
- It provides no indicator lights to show action and status.
- It provides no hardware default value reset switch.
- It adds significant heat load inside the system unit.
- It requires installation inside the system.

Micro-to-Mainframe Links

Communications is a hot topic at this point, as they are essentially the way that host (mainframe) computers will communicate with microcomputers. The concept is, of course, that the combination of the two devices will make the microcomputer an effective and inexpensive workstation. Insofar as direct communications is concerned, the communication capabilities exist—modems on both ends and communications driver software to handle the movement of data.

Consider Figure 8.9. The first box is the microcomputer. This is the most critical portion of the linkage setup. Questions of compatibility, software adaptability, communications adaptation, etc., must be addressed. Don't put yourself into having to write communications monitors for mongrel equipment. The second box is the emulator or modem. Insofar as modems are concerned, there are several for the micros and several for the mainframes and the compatibility and reliability of major brands are well established. Here you must establish common protocols, set common speeds, establish character control, etc.

The third box is the mainframe itself. Here there is little flexibility. Either the link is compatible or nothing will be operational. Terminal Control Units (TCU) and Front End Communications Processors (FECP) form a major component of these linkages. Finally, the software interfaces will be critical, especially if you are looking to transport data from a micro application to a mainframe application, and back again, recognizing that few applications operate in both environments. The Interactive Financial Planning System (discussed later in this chapter of the book) has both a microcomputer and mainframe component. Lotus 1-2-3 does not. In the later section on Office Automation there is also some discussion of Fourth Generation Languages which applies here.

There is much on the communications horizon which may affect you in the form of what is known as the Microcom Networking Protocol (MNP). Since the MNP uses a Link Protocol, and since Link Protocol is one of the synchronous protocols, we'd better spend a little time on other forms of communication. We'd like this book to have some value for the day after tomorrow. Next Saturday, we're not sure about.

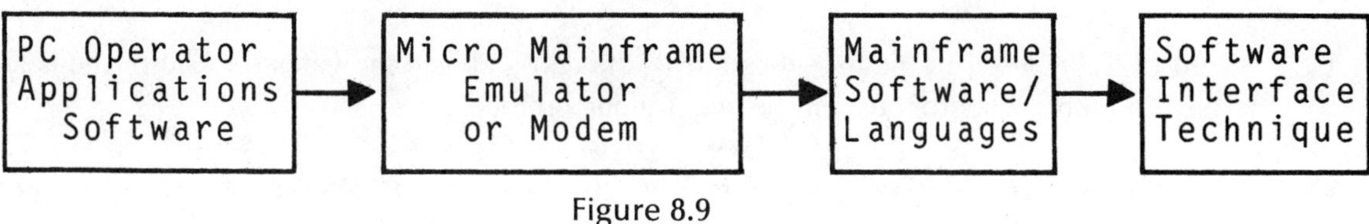

Figure 8.9

Another Communications Theory Course

Transmission Characters and Control Sets

Data communications is, of course, not new. Ever since the days of the teletype, we've been communicating electrically, and subsequently electronically. The teletype machine replaced the Morse code, but the concept wasn't terribly different. In the days when Baudot devised the five-channel teletype code, there was a limit of 32 characters which could be sent. Our concern is for the 7-bit ASCII code (which permits 128 characters) and the 8-bit extended ASCII code (and EBCDIC code) which permits 256 different characters. In any character set, some of the characters are reserved for control characters, such as end of record, carriage return, etc.

Recall that the 8th bit was available as a parity bit. The process of adding a 1 or 0 is customarily called a vertical redundancy check. When we get away from the limitation of sending characters in a start/stop configuration at the character level, it becomes possible to combine the transmitted characters into longer strings, permitting the addition of parity characters, counted lengthwise along the bits. This is called the horizontal redundancy check. Later, when we have investigated the topic more thoroughly, we'll discuss another similar concept, the cyclic redundancy check.

Communications Characters

The first 32 characters of the ASCII character set have special meanings, beginning with NUL. Many of the ASCII characters have special meanings, especially those above ASCII 127, but the first 32 and the very last character in the ASCII character set (255) have special meanings to communications. Those which are indicated as "CC" are specifically *communication control characters.* Those which are identified as "FE" are *format effector characters.* Those marked "IS" are *information separators* (and have special meaning to the system and system). And those which are marked as "SC" are special control characters. The codes are listed in Figure 8.10.

What might be more interesting yet is the realization that there are some commonalities amongst the codes. In the early days of telecommunications, many of the control sequences were achieved through the use of the shift key. Note the same characters, arranged by the bit equivalents, differing only by the high-order "shift" bit in Figure 8.11.

Let's now define the purpose of each of the characters:

NUL No character (" "). Used for filling in time or filling space on tape where there is no data. Prints nothing, but does take time. Frequently used to allow hard copy devices to move the print head to the left margin. (Requires at least 2 null characters). Some packages require a specified number of null characters to be transmitted.

SOH Start of Heading. Used to indicate the start of a heading which may contain address or routing information. Used in Bisync data streams exclusively. Used to signal the continuous transfer of files. Used also with XMODEM file transfer protocol to signal 128Byte block transfer (1 sector of a diskette).

STX Start of Text. Used to indicate the start of the text and also indicates the end of the heading. Used in both asynchronous and bisynchronous protocols.

ETX End of Text. Used to terminate the text which was started with STX. Used with bisynchronous to signal the beginning of block check characters.

EOT End of Transmission. Used to terminate the end of a transmission, which may have included one or more "texts" with their headings. The end frame of a transmission which began with SOH. Used to indicate the end of a block transfer in XMODEM.

ENQ Enquiry. A request for a response from a remote station. It may be used as a "WHO ARE YOU" request for a station to identify itself. Also used to facilitate repeated transmissions. See also ACK and NAK. These three are used to protocol data transmission that does not require interaction—and are transparent to the user.

```
000  CC  (NUL)  Null character -- used as filler
001  CC  (SOH)  Start of Heading
002  CC  (STX)  Start of Text
003  CC  (ETX)  End of Text
004  CC  (EOT)  End of Transmission
005  CC  (ENQ)  Enquiry
006  CC  (ACK)  Acknowledge affirmative
007  SC  (BEL)  Audible Alarm
008  FE  (BS)   Backspace
009  FE  (HT)   Horizontal Tab
010  FE  (LF)   Line Feed
011  FE  (VT)   Vertical Tab
012  FE  (FF)   Form Feed
013  FE  (CR)   Carriage Return
014  SC  (SO)   Shift Out
015  SC  (SI)   Shift In (also ITB -- see text)
016  CC  (DLE)  Data Link Escape
017  SC  (DC1)  Device Control 1 - XON or resume
018  SC  (DC2)  Device Control 2
019  SC  (DC3)  Device Control 3 - XOFF or pause
020  SC  (DC4)  Device Control 4
021  CC  (NAK)  Negative Acknowledgement
022  CC  (SYN)  Synchronous Idle
023  CC  (ETB)  End of Transmission Block
024  SC  (CAN)  Cancel
025  SC  (EM)   End of Medium
026  SC  (SUB)  Substitute
027  SC  (ESC)  Escape
028  IS  (FS)   File Separator
029  IS  (GS)   Group Separator
030  IS  (RS)   Record Separator
031  IS  (US)   Unit Separator
032  IS  (SP)   Space
255  SC  (DEL)  Delete
```

Figure 8.10

ACK Acknowledge. A character transmitted by a receiving device as an affirmation response to a sender. It is used as a positive response to polling messages. Used in data transmission error detection. ACK used to respond if there is no error. See also ENQ and NAK. These three are used to protocol data transmission that does not require interaction—and are transparent to the user.

BEL Bell. Used when there is need to call human attention. It may control alarm or attention devices. Can occur with CTRL-G (and often printed on keyboard), when using manual mode. Transmitted to the line printer in BASIC using LPRINT CHR$(7).

BS Backspace. Indicates movement of the printing mechanism or display cursor backwards in one position. Backspace delete. Clears print buffer.

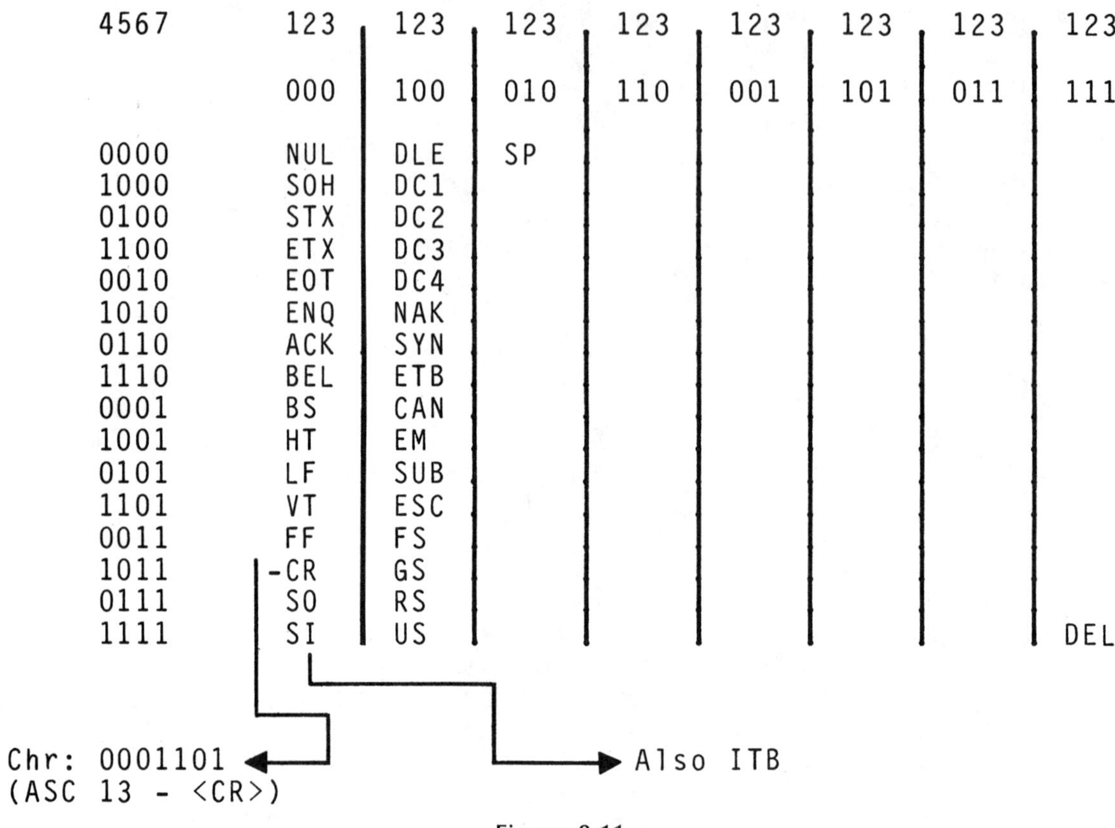

Bits

4567	123	123	123	123	123	123	123	123
	000	100	010	110	001	101	011	111
0000	NUL	DLE	SP					
1000	SOH	DC1						
0100	STX	DC2						
1100	ETX	DC3						
0010	EOT	DC4						
1010	ENQ	NAK						
0110	ACK	SYN						
1110	BEL	ETB						
0001	BS	CAN						
1001	HT	EM						
0101	LF	SUB						
1101	VT	ESC						
0011	FF	FS						
1011	-CR	GS						
0111	SO	RS						
1111	SI	US						DEL

Figure 8.11

HT Horizontal Tab. Indicates movement of the printing mechanism or display cursor backwards in one position. Tab key on console. LPRINT CHR$(9) on printer.

LF Line Feed. Indicates movement of the printing mechanism or display cursor to the next line, but not necessarily to the beginning of the next line. A carriage return is required for that.

VT Vertical Tab. Indicates movement of the printing mechanism or display cursor to the next of a series of preassigned printing lines. Works same as LF on IBM.

FF Form Feed. Indicates movement of the printing mechanism or display cursor to the starting position of the next page, form, or screen. Requires that the printer be on line. If off line and then on line, form feed will not be complete. Used to clear the screen and place the cursor at the home position.

CR Carriage Return. Indicates movement of the printing mechanism or display cursor to the starting position of the same line. CR without LF will cause overstrikes. It becomes very important to edit downloaded files to insert CR characters where linefeeds are.

SO Shift Out. Indicates that the code combinations which follow shall be interpreted as *outside* the standard character set until a SHIFT IN character is reached. Used in IBM for special printer characters—graphics, extended, etc. Terminated by a DC4 on the IBM.

SI Shift In. Indicates that the code combinations which follow shall be interpreted according to the standard character set. Resets receiving device. Uses for compressed print until DC2 is received. Also used for interrupt and resume command (ITB).

DLE Data Link Escape. A character which shall change the meaning of one or more contiguously following characters. It can provide supplementary controls, or permits the sending of data characters having any bit combination. Used in bisynchronous to signal start and end of transparent mode.

DC1 through DC4 are device control characters for the control of ancillary devices or special terminal features. These are specially used toggle switches.

DC1 Device Control 1. This is the XON character used to reinstate the transfer of data temporarily halted by the XOFF character.

DC2 Device Control 2. Turns off the compressed printing mode and empties the buffer.

DC3 Device Control 3. This is the XOFF, and halts the transmission of data. Used to suspend transmission until receiving device has caught up. A speed compensating or buffering device.

DC4 Device Control 4. Turns off the double-width printing mode.

NAK Negative Acknowledgement. A character transmitted by a receiving device as a negative response to the sender. It is used as a negative response to polling messages. See also ENQ and ACK.

SYN Synchronous/Idle. Used as a synchronous transmission system to achieve synchronization. When no data is being sent, a synchronous transmission system may sent SYN characters continuously.

ETB End of Transmission Block. Indicates the end of a block of data for communications purposes. It is used for blocking data where the block structure is not necessarily related to the processing format.

CAN Cancel. Indicates that the data which precedes it in a message or block should be disregarded (usually because an error has been detected). The command is vendor specific.

EM End of Medium. Indicates the physical end of a card, tape, or other medium, or end of the used portion of the medium.

SUB Substitute. Substituted for a character that is found to be erroneous or invalid.

ESC Escape. A character intended to provide code extension in that it gives a specified number of contiguously following characters an alternate meaning.

FS File Separator
GS Group Separator
RS Record Separator

US Unit Separator
Information separators to be used in an optional manner, except that their hierarchy shall be alphabetical (FS to US). The IBM system uses them for, in sequence, cursor right, cursor left, cursor up, and cursor down.

SP Space, a non-printing character used to separate words or to move the printing mechanism or display cursor forward by one position.

DEL Delete, used to obliterate unwanted characters. This is the standard delete mechanism (Hex FF).

Transparent Codes

If you've any experience at all in BASIC, you're aware of the fact that you cannot enclose quotes directly in a string variable. A$ = "KEN" gives KEN in A$. If, for some reason it is imperative to have that quote sign as a part of the literal, then you must find another means to include it. That is with the use of ASCII codes: A$ = CHR$(34) + "KEN" + CHR$(34) gives "KEN". The same concept is at work with the communications codes, The assigned codes cannot themselves be transmitted. The way around it is to have the system shift into transparent mode.

The communication code DLE puts transmission into transparent mode, allowing the control codes to be transmitted and to have meaning inside the DLE. Example:

DLE STX: Initiate transparent text mode
DLE ETB: Terminate transparent transmission
DLE ITB: Terminate transparent transmission, but resume regular transmission

What may not be immediately apparent is that the codes in use have a twofold meaning. First, they are meaningful to the communication handler program assigned to work in a specific communications protocol. And secondly, even though they may not be used specifically with the communications handler, they may have special meanings to the receiving applications software. The communications handler programs make use of several of these ASCII codes, even though they may have no specific meaning to the Asynchronous Transmission protocol.

Multitone Transmission

The Touch-Tone transmission media is based on signal generation on selected pairs from 8 audible frequencies, located at 697, 770, 852, 941, 1209, 1336, 1477, and 1633 hertz. Pressing of a key produces a discordant combination of two of these frequencies. The first group of four is called the low frequency group; the other is the high frequency group. In Figure 8.12, you can see how the numbers relate to the keys on the telephone handset. If your telephone doesn't happen to have 16 keys, don't be concerned. Lots of military phones do.

There are 16 potential frequencies—12 of which are used under normal circumstances. Other transmission modes use more.

Comparing The Modes

You'll recall that we said that in the asynchronous transmission mode, the transmission was done at the character level. In the synchronous transmission mode, you may transmit anything from one character to several hundred. There is continuity in transmission. You can transmit a record which is the length of a standard data processing card (80 characters), the length of a print line (80 or 132 characters), or the size

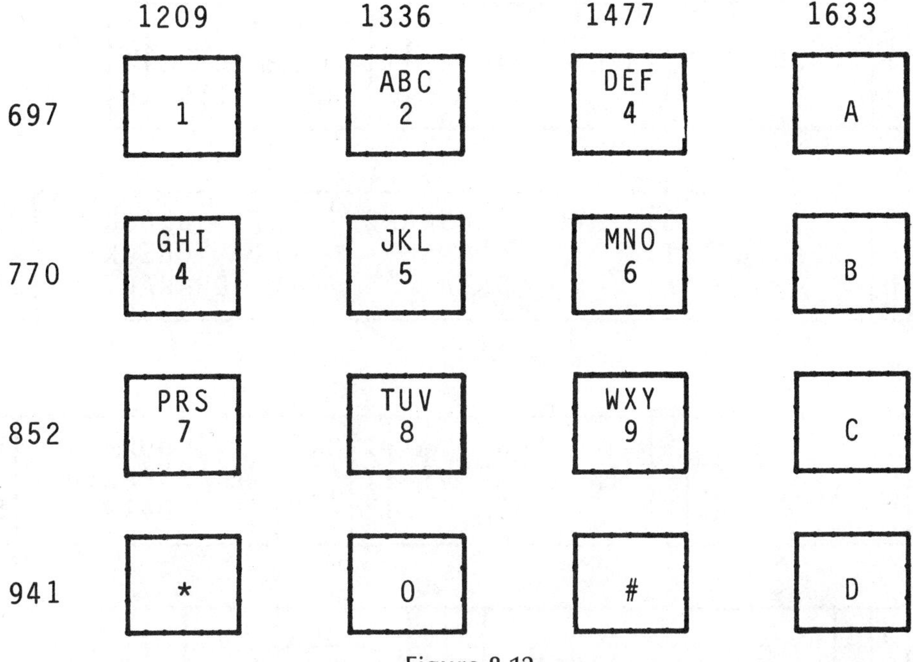

Figure 8.12

of a buffer (generally in multiples of 1,024 bytes). Because there are fewer gaps there is a higher speed of transmission.

One of the synchronous methods of transmission you may encounter is called the Binary Synchronous Protocol. Like the asynchronous mode, it is character oriented. However, synchronizing bits are not provided at the character level. Once connection is made, an alerting sequence is inserted at the beginning of the message in the form of PAD characters—alternating 0 and 1 bit. End of message padding exists in the form of continuous padding with 1 bits only. Once the padding has been detected, synchronous idle characters (SYN) are generated. The receiver "hunts" for SYN character. The process is called *handshaking.* Once detected, the receiver is alerted to incoming data. These are communication controls which have meaning to the binary synchronous transmission protocol:

SYN	SOH
PAD (START = 1010101010. . .)	STX
PAD (END = 1111111111. . .)	ITB
DLE	ETB
ENQ	ETX

Figure 8.13 shows examples of binary synchronous data transmission formats:

Recall the discussion of parity. VRC—vertical redundancy check—is the vertical parity at the character level. LRC—longitudinal redundancy check—is the horizontal parity across the length of the transmission block. In these illustrations, it is shown as a block check character (BCC). Where the system uses the CRC—cyclic redundancy check—a mathematical algorithm is used to divide a constant into the numeric binary value of all bits in the block, discarding the quotient and keeping the remainder as a BCC.

You will encounter a concept called SDLC (synchronous data link control). SDLC and its packet communication counterpart (HDLC) are the world standards for business communications. The only difference between the two is that a routing address is included in the HDLC block. Packet communications is much too deep a topic to get into here. In SDLC, the data transmitted is called an *information field.* It

PAD	PAD	SYN	SYN	STX	NON-TRANSPARENT DATA	ETX	BLOCK CHECK CHARACTER	PAD

PAD	PAD	SYN	SYN	SOH	HEADING	STX	NON-TRANSPARENT DATA	ETX	BLOCK CHECK CHARACTER	PAD

PAD	PAD	SYN	SYN	SOH	HEADING	STX	NON-TRANSPARENT DATA	ITB	BCC	STX	NON-TRANSPARENT DATA	ETB	BCC	PAD

PAD	PAD	SYN	SYN	DLE	STX	TRANSPARENT DATA	DLE	ETX	BLOCK CHECK CHARACTER	PAD

PAD	PAD	SYN	SYN	SOH	HEADING	DLE	STX	TRANSPARENT DATA	DLE	SYN	TRANSPARENT DATA	DLE	ETX	BLOCK CHECK CHARACTER	PAD

PAD	PAD	SYN	SYN	SOH	HEADING	DLE	STX	TRANSPARENT DATA	DLE	ITB	BCC	DLE	STX	TRANSPARENT DATA	DLE	ETB	BCC	PAD

Figure 8.13

may be any length. It is a bit-oriented data stream, and the receiver must break the characters down. Figure 8.14 shows the SDLC transmission block.

The next standard you'll encounter is the SNA—the systems network architecture. The Microcom Networking Protocol (MNP) is built upon the SNA. The SNA is the IBM Standard for network products and uses SDLC. Figure 8.15 will give you some idea of the interrelationship.

Under SNA, the transmitted block looks like Figure 8.16. You can well imagine that other vendors have adopted the standard.

SNA communications are done between logical units. A logical unit may be either hardware components or program code. On the system/system it is a combination of communications equipment and software. As you can see from Figure 8.16, there are Request/Response Units (RU), a Request/Response Header (RH), and Transmission Headers (TH). Put them all together (RU + RH + TH) and you end up with what is called a Path Information Unit (PIU). Add a Link Header and a Link Trailer, and you have an SDLC frame called a Basic Link Unit (BLU).

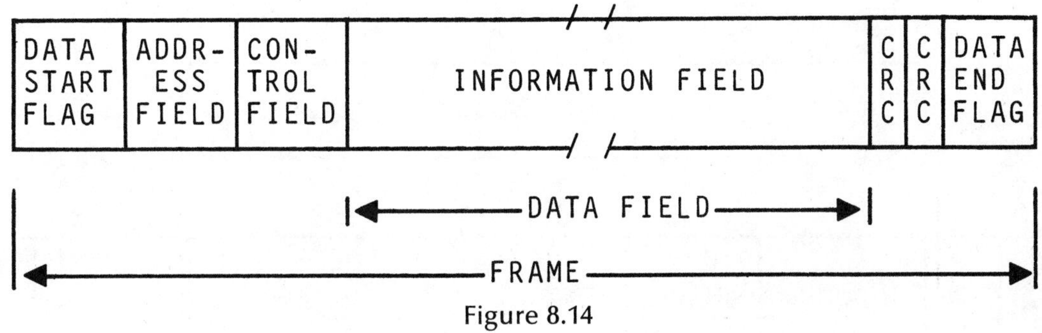

Figure 8.14

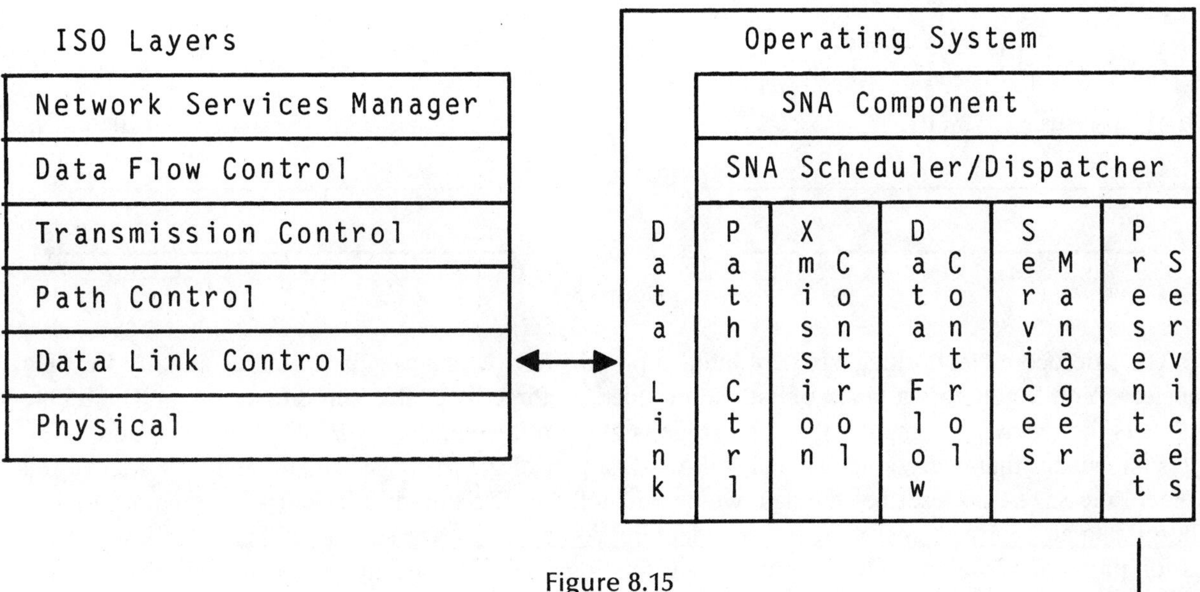

Figure 8.15

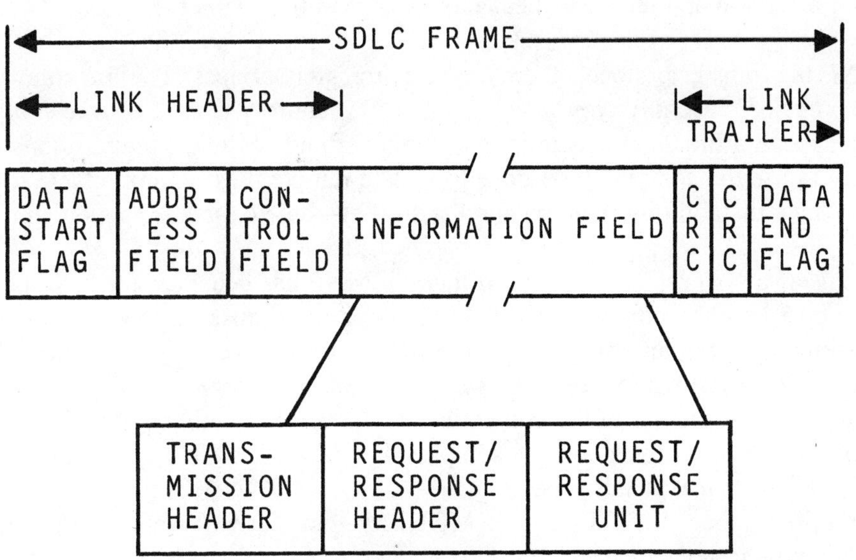

Figure 8.16

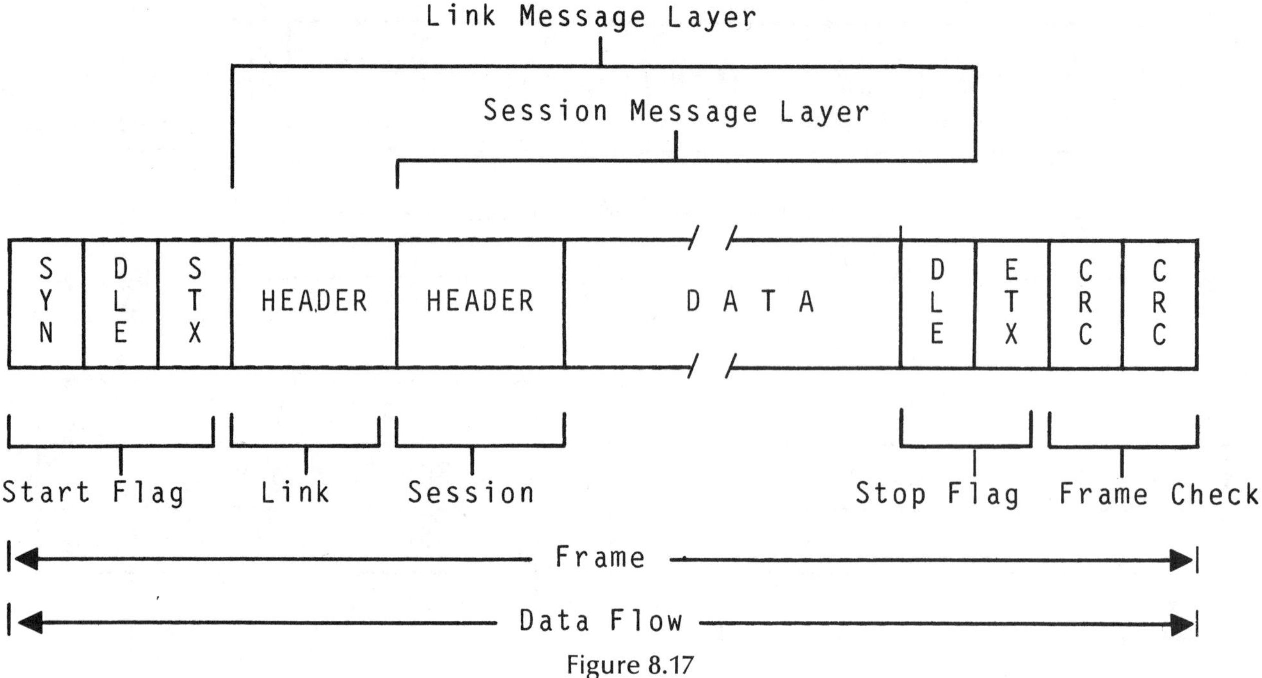

Figure 8.17

The Microcom Networking Protocol builds upon the SDLC concept. It is used essentially for file transfers. You'll note that a block of data is preceded by three bytes that act as a start flag. The SYN byte tells the receiving computer that a message is about to arrive; the combination of DLE and STX bytes announces that everything else that follows is a part of the message. Next comes a header, a link protocol message that describes the data which will follow. The link data header will contain protocol control data and perform such functions as identification and message stamping. This is followed by the session protocol header, which will provide information about this specific block of data. Then, after the data has been transmitted, the DLE and ETX bytes are the stop flag, signifying that the next two bytes will be the frame check sequence. The binary values that represent data are run through a polynomial and then divided by a constant on both ends of the transmission, to ensure data integrity. We'll talk briefly about error detection and recovery mechanisms later in the chapter. Figure 8.17 shows the MNP protocol.

With the MNP file transfer protocol, there are three transfer services. The first allows you to send a file to a distant computer. Secondly, you may receive a file sent to you by the same computer. And thirdly, you may append a file to an existing file at the other end of the communications link. This will provide the ability to use the computer you have to update remote files, an important facet if you're traveling. You'll also have the ability to manipulate distant files—delete them, rename them, display the directory.

If all this seems away over your head, know that the MNP has been accepted by both IBM and Apple (and probably others by the time you read this), essentially because of its virtual file capabilities. Virtual means essentially transparent to the nature of the hardware itself. The protocol will find its way into implementation under the UNIX operating systems, soon to emerge. Know that one of the reasons for doing so is to provide some file-to-file compatibility amongst dissimilar systems. At the time this is being written, IBM still has not released its token passing Local Area Network standard, so we cannot provide any information on that at this time.

There is one more protocol we'll discuss—XMODEM—but that will wait until a little later, for it is well used with the asynchronous mode.

Standard Cabling

Direct communications connections will, of course, be a function of the engineering of the mainframe computer. Connection to the microcomputer modem, however, makes use of an RS-232 cable to connect the two. The RS-232 cable is built according to an Electronic Industry Association standard, and has the connection shown in Figure 8.18.

About the only thing which will change will be the positioning of pins 2 and 3, when we discuss the use of a null modem, later in the chapter.

Speed Adjustment

Now you've had a concept of how to use the modem for one form of communications. Let's now entertain one of the common communications problems—the transmission which arrives faster than it can be handled. So long as we're using the 300 baud modem to transmit, we'll never have to worry about sending the data too fast—and by and large the majority of available services will be able to adapt to your rate of transmission. But in case you are in communication with someone whose modem is a faster modem, then the communication programming you have must be capable of asynchronous speed matching. There are a number of available data transfer flow control options. You can toggle the data flow on and off (XON and XOFF). You can utilize one or more of the temporary data storage mechanisms, such as a communications buffer-memory (RAM) which is used to compensate for differences in speed. And you can download to disk (store the received transmission on a disk file).

Conceptually, when a buffer is used, blocks of communications are transferred from the communications line to the buffer and then to disk. The buffer operates on a first-in, first-out (FIFO) basis. In a less sophisticated communication program, the size of the buffer allocation is crucial to the success of the communication, for it is possible to overrun the buffer. Generally what happens is that reading (sampling) of the data line is halted temporarily, while buffer blocks are written to disk. Then more data are read. Transmit buffers aren't generally very large; usually 255 bytes, the size of a variable. The receive buffer is most crucial, as receive buffer overflow can result in lost data.

The speed control exercised in many communications programs is called the XON/XOFF data flow control protocol, and can be used either on transmission, as it has been used here, or on reception. It

RS-232 Cable	
Pin	Connection
1	Protective Ground
2	Transmit Data
3	Receive Data
4	Request to Send
5	Clear to Send
6	Data Set Ready
7	Signal Ground
8	Carrier Detect
15	I/O Transmit
17	Receiver Clock
20	Data Terminal Ready
24	Transmit Clock

Figure 8.18

toggles (turns on and off) to prevent communications buffer overflow. As you could see, the transmission buffer was designated to be 128 characters, and the transmission program took on the responsibility to control the flow.

The concept isn't different on reception, except that a quality transmission receiving program will make decisions upon the amount of data received. When the buffer is nearing full, the software sends XOFF to the host. That can also be achieved by sending a CTRL-S, a concept with which you may be familiar in that pressing that combination temporarily suspends screen display. When the buffer is nearing empty, the software sends XON to the host. This may also be achieved by pressing CTRL-Q.

Protocol Transfer

The MNP protocol is a new, as we discussed, file transfer protocol. It is the successor to an older, and still widely used file transmission method, the XMODEM protocol. The XMODEM protocol uses few of the special characters, including ENQ, ACK, NAK, SOH, and EOT. It is designed for simplicity and for the most fundamental of error checking.

The SOH contains 2 characters. The first is a block number, assigned in sequence. This helps sort out any garbled messages received. The second characters is a 1's complement (to obtain a 1's complement, subtract the number from 255) of the block number to be transferred next. The transfer is limited to fixed length data—128 bytes. There is an error checking checksum provided. If the receiving checksum balances the transmitted checksum, acknowledgement (ACK) is given. If not, negative acknowledgement (NAK) is given, and the process is repeated. Figure 8.19 demonstrates these concepts.

And that, dear friends, brings up the nasty subject of errors in the transmission.

Line Error Detection and Remedies

A transmission may be garbled for a number of reasons, and the effects could be devastating. Errors which might occur include noise on the telephone lines. There can be "white noise," which is background noise. The noise might be thermal. Generally, on an unconditioned line, there are noise spikes, particularly where there is atmospheric disturbances along the way. The effect is that such noise destroys or switches bits, ruining the message of course, but destroying the checksum characters. These situations may also be caused by poor line isolation, cross talk, electrical pickup, atmospheric static, voltage fluctuation, or stray noises.

Errors will occur. A typical error rate is 1 bit in 100,000 (.0000001), and varies with modem design. Since the purpose of the modems is to maximize data rate (narrow the peaks and valleys), the receiver must be highly sensitive. The receiver, in this case, may well be the communications program you select.

Even more interesting to the business user is the effect of such errors. A "bit perfect" system may be technically impossible, and the problem may be less the line than the operator. Thus, it becomes important in any communications-based systems you design to ensure accuracy controls for human input. This will be necessary as protection against abuse or embezzlement, against lost or double entries when hardware failures occur, and against cumulative file errors. Design your system so you know what error rate is expected and acceptable: should some error be permitted? How should errors be reported?

Why is this important? If the error rate is 1 bit in 100,000 and your file has 10,000 records; if file items are updated 100 times a month and one of 20 five-bit characters is in error, allowing the data to be updated incorrectly, after 6 months, 4500 file records may be incorrect. It's important.

Let's examine the noise issue again. The major categories are applied noise and distortion. And the distortion problem is also quite large. Distortion is of two types; systematic and fortuitous. Systematic distortion is that distortion which is anticipated on a specific line—narrow pulses, phase delays, etc. It might include lost data, attenuation distortion, delay distortion, harmonic distortion, frequency offset,

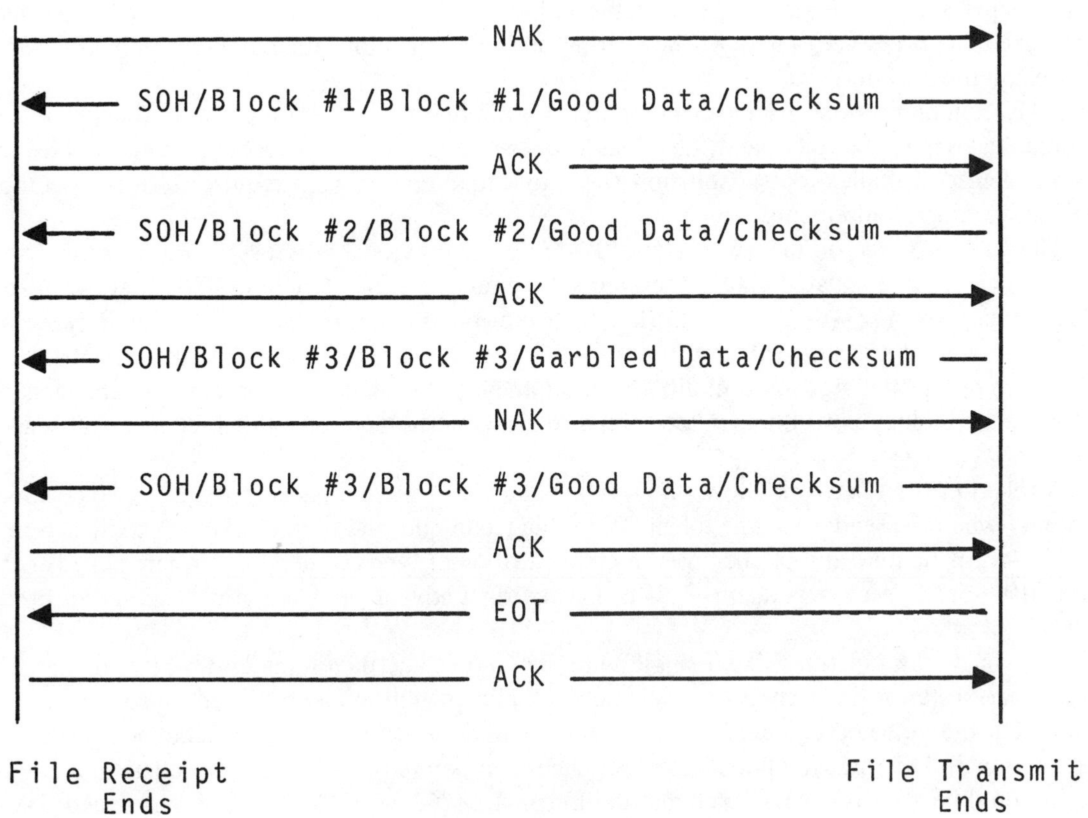

XMODEM Protocol Transfer

Figure 8.19

bias distortion, and characteristic distortion. Fortuitous distortion occurs at random and is not predictable, except by probabilities.

Noise categories include white noise, impulse noise, switchgear chatter, crosstalk, atmospheric noise, intermodulation noise, echoes, changes in signal phase, losses of signal amplitude, radio frequency interference (RFI), line outages, fading, jitter, and dropouts,

Lest this seem hopeless, simply remember that if you are losing a lot of your transmissions, these are some of the problems you might encounter, and you could contact those communication companies with whom you do business to discuss line conditioning. Or wait until a time of day (3 a.m.?) when nobody else is using the telephone lines.

Local Area Networks

Local area networks interconnect dissimilar information processing devices to allow high-speed communication and resource sharing among them. Devices that can be networked by a LAN system include computers, terminals, printers, and plotters, as well as the variety of automated equipment used in factories. Such factory automation equipment includes robots, programmable controllers, material handling systems, test equipment, machine tools, process control systems, machine vision systems, computer-aided design systems, and computers.

LANs are unique in their use of very high-speed shared communications media which permit a single device to use the entire available bandwidth of the system at transmission speeds ranging from one to 50 megabits per second. This high speed enables large blocks of data to be moved between workstations and centralized databases very rapidly. The sharing of communications media allows immediate access to all devices on the network.

LAN communications systems can incorporate a range of different topologies (bus, star, ring, tree), communications media (baseband, broadband, fiber-optic, thin coaxial cable), and access techniques (Carrier Sense Multiple Access/Collision Detection, token passing) as required to meet a company's specific networking requirements.

The LAN is based on the seven-layer ISO protocol, previously discussed. Each of these seven layers represents a group of related data processing and communications functions. The first two layers specify a broadband, token-passing, bus network. The use of broadband, or cable TV technology, to pass data has two important advantages. First, it allows more than one network to share the same cable, transmitting different types of signals from different equipment at the same time on different channels. Second, TV cable technology is well understood, readily available in large quantities, economical, and very reliable.

A token-passing network allows the sending station to move a packet of data to the destination station only when the sender has the token. With this technique, the time it takes for each station to access the network is definite and predictable, in contrast to other types of networks where signals can collide, forcing stations to start over again. This is an important advantage when critical timing of procedures is necessary.

A bus network functions like a single wire that allows any data transfer device to be plugged into it. In contrast to star or ring networks, a bus network allows additional equipment to be added or moved easily. Thus, automated equipment can be plugged into the network at any predefined point and at any time, in much the same way household appliances can be plugged into power outlets in the home.

It would be a mistake to assume that the Local Area Network, or LAN, as it is called, is a microcomputer phenomenon only. It encompasses mainframe computers, minicomputers, and now the micro. Although the advantages of using a local area communications system are more clearly defined today than just a few short years ago, the LAN market has become increasingly confusing, because the number of vendors competing in the marketplace has grown significantly. Included in the number now is an ever widening array of computer manufacturers, network suppliers, and telecommunications vendors. Adding to the confusion is the variety of available networks.

Public versus Private Systems

Data communications systems fall into two broad categories: private networks and public networks. Public data networks move digital information between subscribers through expensive wide-area telecommunications facilities such as satellites and microwave radios. Local area networks, though based on the packet-switching structures and protocols often used in public data networks, are privately owned communications systems that transport information through inexpensive media such as coaxial cable. They can transparently transport information between electronic devices installed within a single building, a cluster of buildings such as a campus, or—with the use of "bridges" operating over wide-area telecommunications facilities—in buildings in widely dispersed locations.

Typically, public communications systems are regulated by one or more governmental organizations. Because these systems are closely regulated and extremely capital intensive, the public communications systems market is dominated by a few large vendors. The private communications systems market, on the other hand, is a relatively unregulated market that is not capital intensive. It is characterized by rapid technological change and intense competition.

Within the private communications systems market, there are again two distinct categories. One category consists of small organizations with relatively simple information processing requirements. The other consists of large organizations—businesses, factories, laboratories, or educational institutions—that require extensive, complex information processing systems.

The PBX

Private branch exchanges (PBXs) were originally developed to network telephones. Later, computer terminal networking capabilities were added, because a PBX can provide the low-speed, point-to-point communications capability required to network terminals. However, neither PBXs nor the more recently introduced "integrated voice/data" PBXs have the speed, the interconnect capacity, or the intelligence necessary to effectively network large numbers of devices such as powerful workstations, host computers, and personal computers. This is the reason that every major computer company in the world has announced plans to interconnect their machines using LANs.

LANs were developed to provide the flexible, high-speed communications required for the powerful information processing devices that are so prevalent in today's offices, laboratories, and factories. To provide this enhanced communications capability, LAN vendors are using new techniques and transmission media rather than tying themselves to the low performance cabling systems used in PBXs. In short, PBXs and LANs are two separate solutions to two separate problems.

Proprietary LANs

Integrated into information processing systems by a computer systems vendor, proprietary LANs are optimized to sell that vendor's own equipment. These networks do not have the capability to interconnect the equipment of most other vendors.

The reasons are threefold. First, it is often not in the economic interest of computer companies to interconnect equipment manufactured by other vendors. Computer systems manufacturers are primarily in the business of selling more of their own information processing equipment, not networks.

Second, large computer companies have large installed bases that are incompatible with today's emerging standards. To obsolete and retrofit the billions of dollars of installed hardware and applications software that base represents will require many years and complex product transition strategies.

Finally, there are literally hundreds of permutations and combinations of worldwide de facto and de jure standards. Within each one of these standards exist places where the vendor must make specific implementation decisions. The result? The industry standards and open architectures necessary for all computers to readily converse with one another are many, many years away.

Therefore, to choose a proprietary network is to select one vendor's solution to networking. Moreover, once the choice is made, the end user is locked into this vendor for future product deliveries.

Special Purpose LANs

Local area networks that have been designed and optimized to network together clusters of similar types of devices are referred to as "special purpose" LANs. These networks support very limited types of devices. For example, Etherseries from 3COM or PC Network from IBM are designed to interconnect only personal computers. In the case of PC Network, the network is further restricted—to only IBM PCs and their compatibles. Another network, Network Systems' HYPERchannel, is designed for the computer-room environment and ties together mainframes over a high-speed coaxial cable.

To integrate multiple special purpose or proprietary LANs into an establishment-wide network requires high-performance gateways between the individual systems. Unfortunately for those organizations that would like this interconnection, such gateways are not available and are not likely to exist for many years. As a result, organizations that take the special purpose or proprietary LAN approach will have very limited interdepartmental communication capabilities, a severe limitation in large establishments.

General Purpose LANs

Unlike proprietary and special purpose LANs, general purpose networks are capable of linking together everything from mainframes, minicomputers, word processors, and personal computers to process control devices and robots manufactured by a very wide range of vendors. Today, most large organizations recognize that systems capable of providing high-level services across a large variety of information processing resources are far more valuable than systems that require them to use a single vendor's equipment. That, of course, has created a market of its own, and players such as IBM, Xerox, Orchid, Ungerman-Bass, Corvus, and Novell all participate.

CSMA/CD

The networks which have been in existence for many years have had "crash" problems. If two messages happened to be targeted identically and simultaneously, lockout and message mixing occurred. The vendors developed an algorithm for determining this and it has acquired the name CSMA/CD, which stands for "Carrier Sense Multiple Access/Collision Detection." The idea is to be able to determine the bit weight on the line and to hold back one source until the other has passed. This is not an easily implemented scheme, particularly in the packet switching environment. This is technically possible through an electronic circuit known as the Collision Condition Determination (CCD) circuit.

So Pick A Vendor

It is difficult to illustrate these points generically, so we're going to explore the Ungerman-Bass Net/One, a system designed to tie mainframe computers to microcomputers through a series of network interfaces. This should not be construed as anything other than the fact that Ungerman-Bass provided a considerable amount of material for this presentation. The system is built around a Network Interface Unit that looks like Figure 8.20.

The individual sections should be somewhat self-explanatory. The network interface section interfaces with the rest of the network by use of shared media. The control/communications processor is the software driver which keeps the concept working. And then, the I/O section performs the physical links to the individual computers.

This system is used to successfully integrate different types of information-processing devices into a coherent system of data exchangers, without regard to manufacturer. It is a high speed, high performance mixture of equipment, software, and communications capabilities that is independent of the media tech-

NETWORK INTERFACE UNIT		
NETWORK INTERFACE Media control Packet Handling Intelligence Access Techniques Media type Data type Topology	CONTROL/ COMMUNICATIONS PROCESSOR Network protocols Network management functions	I/O SECTION Physical links to user devices User device protocols

Figure 8.20

nology used—baseband, broadband, optical fiber, coaxial cable, or combinations thereof. There are products to fit the majority of different distribution systems, be it Ethernet, EIA or IEEE standards. The Network Interface Unit (NIU) contains the intelligence to reconcile differences in physical and software protocols, making high-speed communications possible. It performs many functions, including controlling traffic over circuits, Carrier Sense Multiple Access/Collision Detection (CSMA/CD).

Using special components, the network provides the ability to install the network from building to building, around campuses, and across continents. *Local bridges* can interconnect any physically adjacent systems, including those using different types of communications media. *Remote bridges* connect distant systems through public networks such as the telephone system, satellite links, or private facilities such as point-to-point microwave radio. *Gateways* are network interface units equipped with protocol converting software to connect the network to other network architectures. *Repeaters* allow the extension of cable length and topology, where a network strategy includes baseband or optical fiber, for much greater flexibility in making connection between floors, buildings, or wherever longer reaches of cable are necessary. By regenerating the signal from one segment to the other, repeaters extend the maximum end-to-end channel length, allowing a network with more complex topology.

Looking at Networks

Let's look a bit at how these networks could be deployed. Figure 8.21a shows the implementation configuration of a broadband or baseband network in a multi-building environment.

Under the Ungerman-Bass implementation, this can be accomplished by one of the following connection schemes:

BROADBAND/BASEBAND NETWORK MULTI-BUILDING ENVIRONMENT

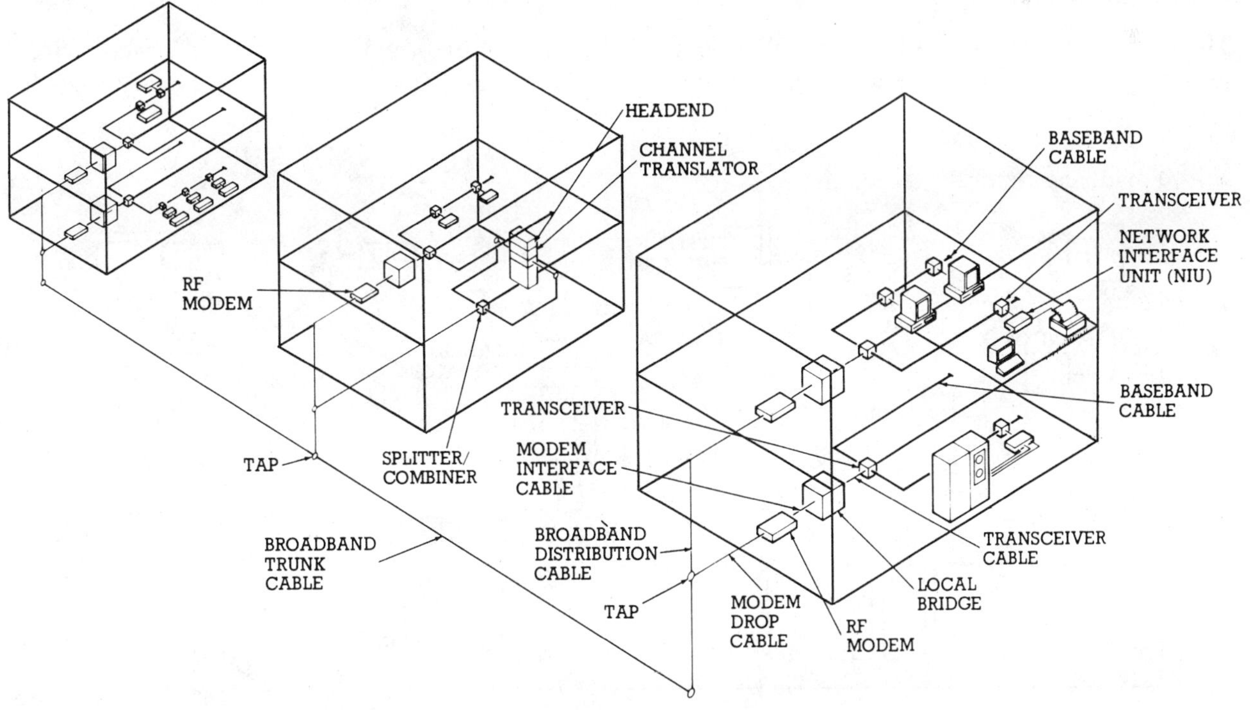

Figure 8.21a

- Broadband
- Thin Coaxial Baseband
- Ethernet Baseband

Broadband

This system is a general purpose local area network (LAN) communication system that can operate on broadband CATV coaxial cable systems. Up to five CATV channels can be used for networks, each operate at 5 megabits per second. The cable system can reach virtually any location within a building complex, providing easy network access as well as the flexibility to relocate equipment without reworking the design. It provides CSMA/CD capability and has the ability to function over a wide geographical area. Local bridges are available to connect the broadband network to other broadband networks or to other types of network on broadband, baseband, and optical fiber cable systems. Figure 8.21b is a network schematic for a broadband network.

Thin Coaxial Baseband

This system is a general purpose LAN that can operate on baseband RG 58 A/U coaxial cable systems. It is a high-speed network, providing reliable data exchange among computers and other digital devices within a small geographic area. As a system, it is generally less expensive than other media used for local area networks and is suitable for networking personal computers. The baseband system has an interface to the coaxial system, effecting the host to microcomputer interface. It provides CSMA/CD capability, works with dissimilar equipment, handles network switching, supports a variety of services. Its limitations include maximum cable lengths of 200 meters, repeaters, up to 600 meters between stations, maximum number of units at 30, etc. It is compatible with the Ethernet system. Figure 8.22 shows the schematic of the thin coaxial baseband network.

Ethernet Baseband

The Ethernet Baseband is a LAN capable of operating on the Xerox-originated Ethernet. Conceptually, its arrangement is a little different, but otherwise the concept is the same. Figure 8.23a shows the single

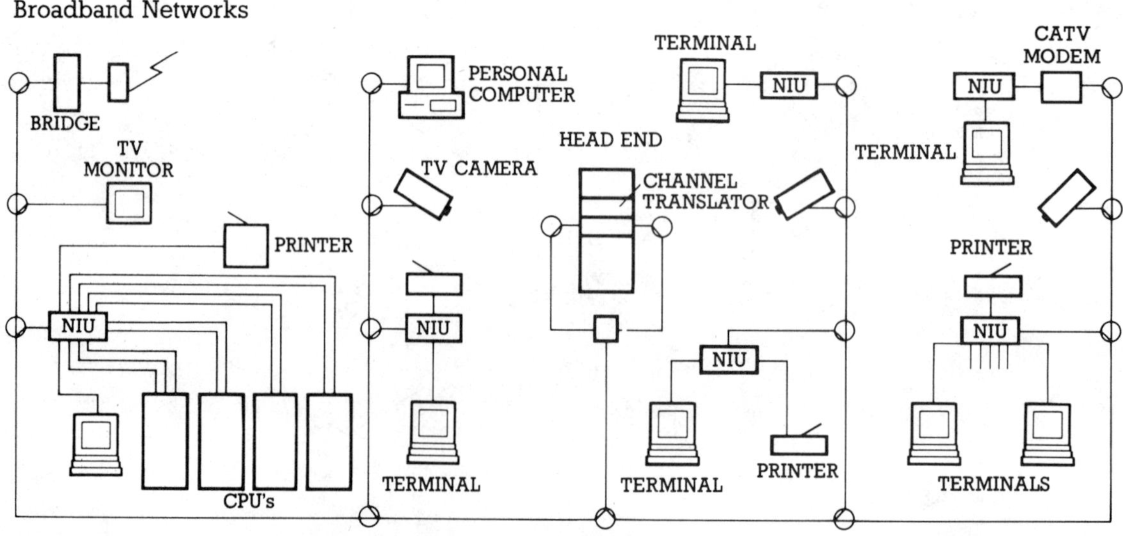

Figure 8.21b

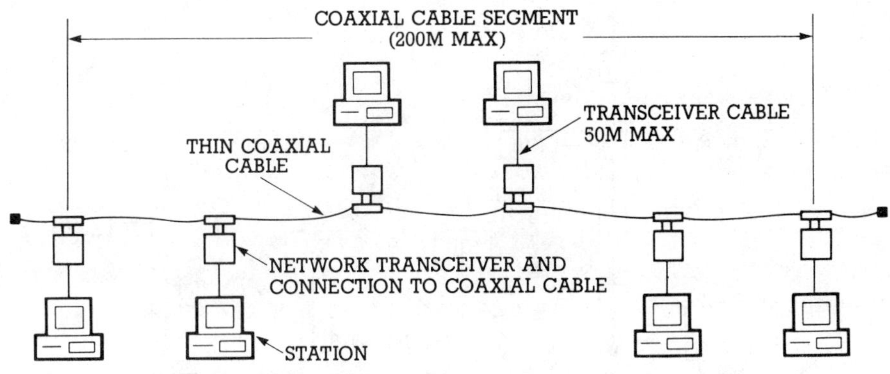

Figure 8.22

ethernet cable segment configuration, while Figure 8.23b shows a multiple Ethernet cable segment configuration.

Figure 8.24 shows the implementation configuration of an optical fiber network in a multi-building environment.

Optical Fiber

Optical fiber may be the transmission medium of the future for local area networks. There are no spurious magnetic forces or signals which could interfere with other equipment; therefore, optical fibers need not be shielded. The nature of fiber optics makes it secure, making it acceptable for outside installation between buildings. It is immune to industrial plant impulse noise, radar, lightning-induced surge, and other electromagnetic interferences which affect signals. It is not susceptible to crosstalk problems. It may be used in combustible areas because it is not prone to short circuits and fire hazards.

This system also includes optical star couplers and Ethernet-compatible optical transceivers. Baseband systems may be interfaced and provide the capability to mix network types. The star coupler provides multiple access and broadcast functions. The network repeater units can be used to extend the range of the transmission medium beyond single segments.

The outstanding feature of the system is its speed—10 megabits per second data rate. Like the other system, many vendors can be supported, and there are CSMA/CD capabilities. One of the things the

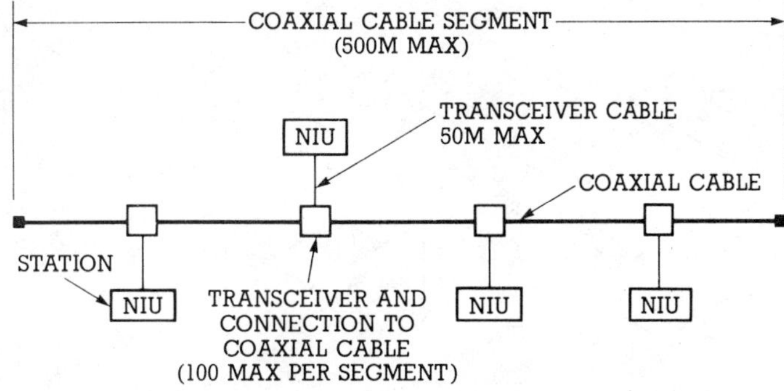

Figure 8.23a

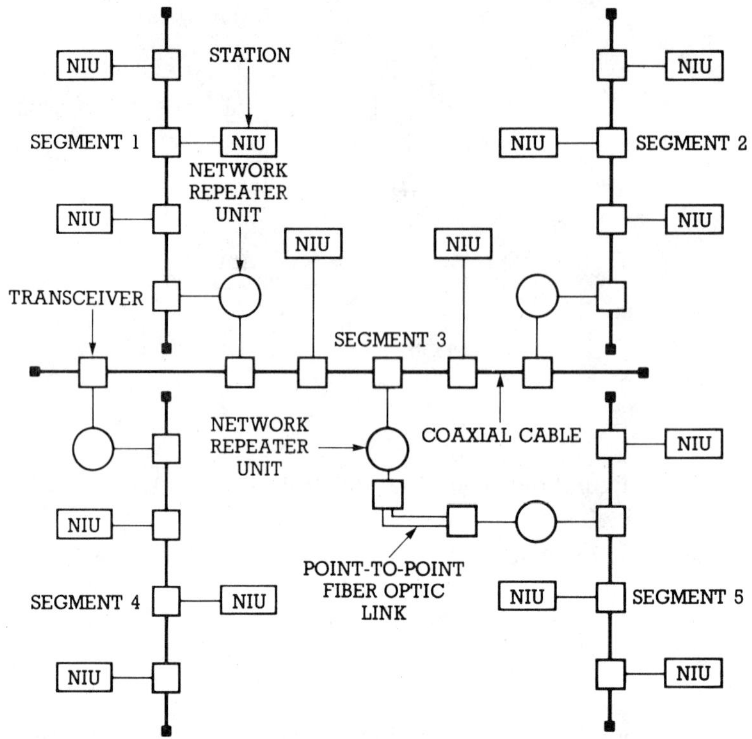

Figure 8.23b

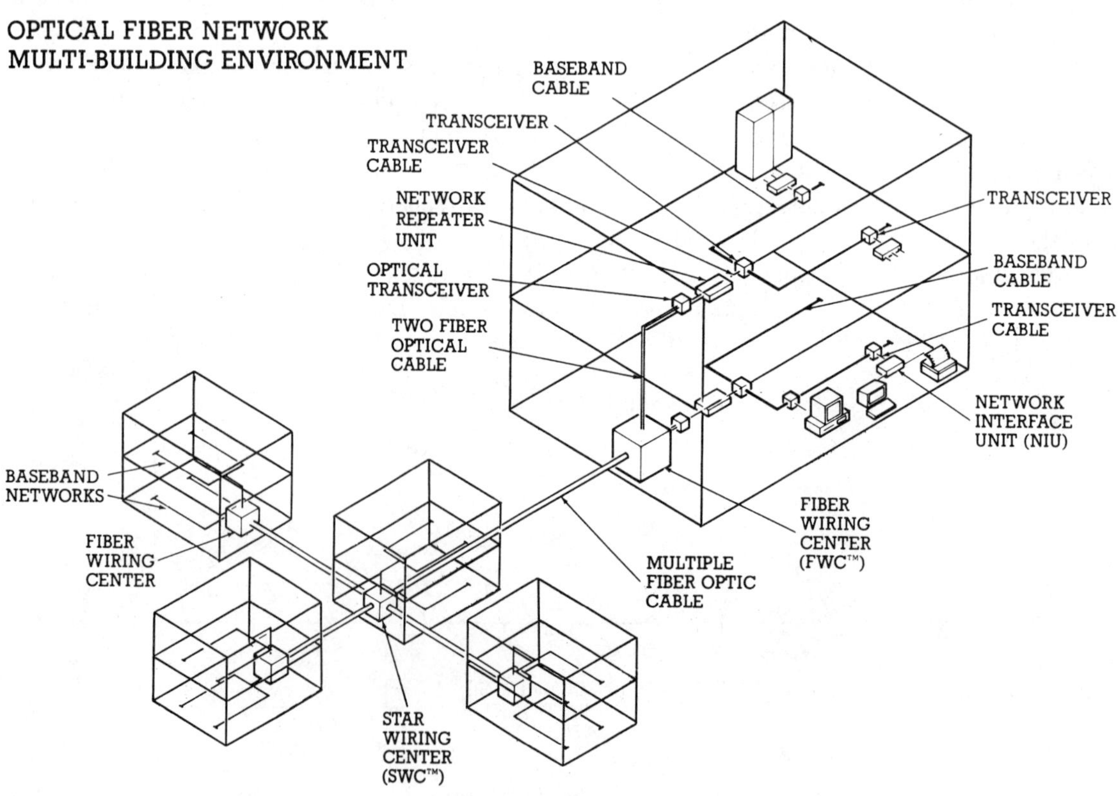

Figure 8.24

MULTIPLE SEGMENT CONFIGURATION

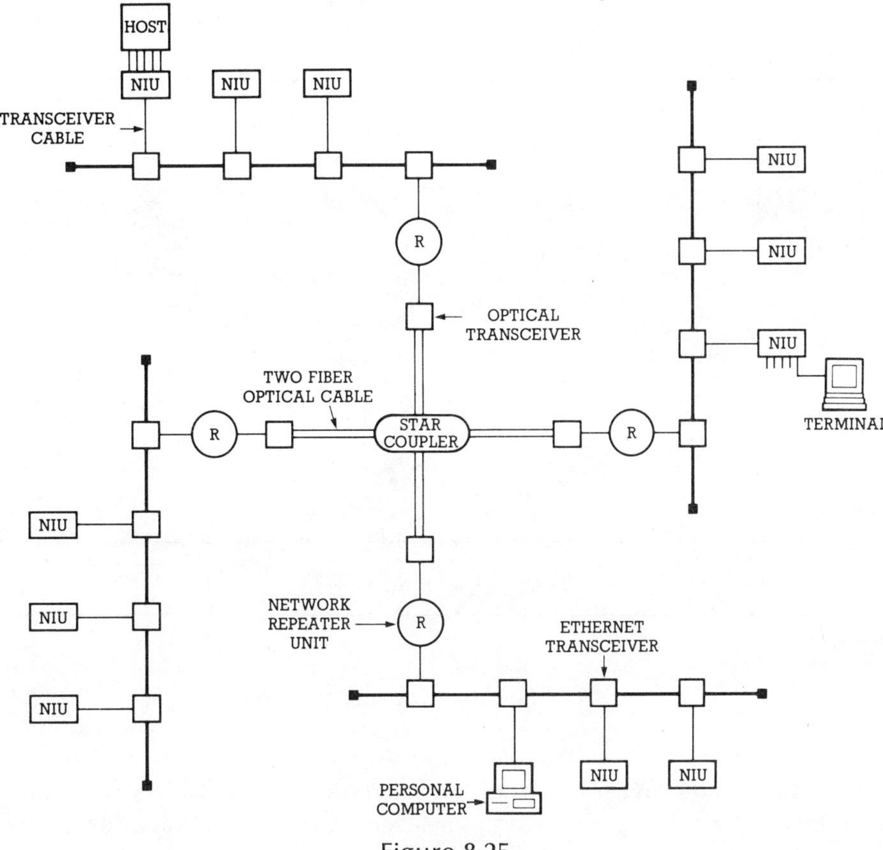

Figure 8.25

optical fiber system does provide, however, is the ability to work with and manage the network without having to take it down.

Figure 8.25 shows a multiple segment optical fiber configuration.

MORE ABOUT LOCAL AREA NETWORKS

Just as this manuscript was going to press, IBM formally introduced the first portion of its long-awaited ''token-ring'' local area network. Because it is a new departure, the subject of the LAN is further expanded. The information provided has been drawn from the newly published IBM Publication GC20-8203-1, *An Introduction to Local Area Networks.*

LAN TOPOLOGY

As mentioned before, the three basic topologies (the physical layout of the network connection medium) are the star, bus, and ring.

The Star Topology

The star topology has a number of nodes, each connected to a central controller as shown in Diagram A. All communications from node to node pass through the central controller, making this topology suitable for telephone networks and for simplistic computer networks. Generally the main computer will accept the responsibility for polling the other devices on the network.

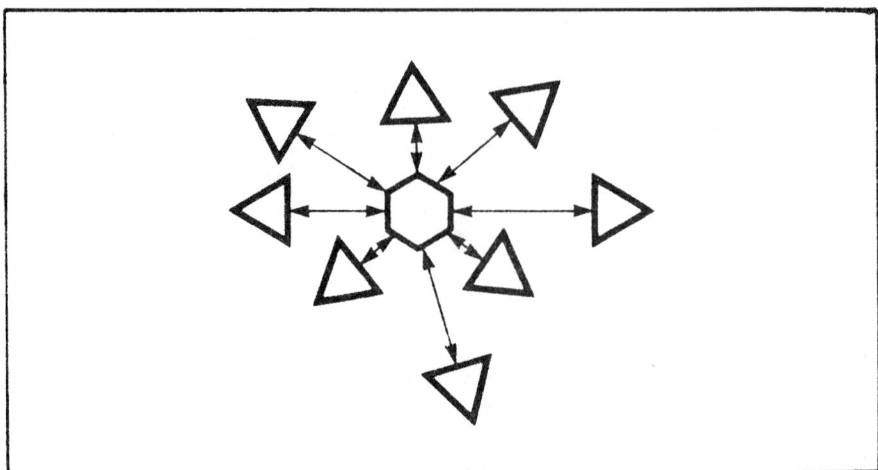

A. Ring Topology

The Bus Topology

The bus topology (see Diagram B) utilizes a wired bidirectional communication path with defined (addressed) terminus points. As the signal is sent by the computer along the bus (the common data path) or from the terminal itself, each node attached to the bus checks the transmission for its specific address. When there is a match, the computer or terminal accepts the transmitted data. Otherwise, that data are ignored. Control does not reside in a central controller. This is often referred to as a demand system.

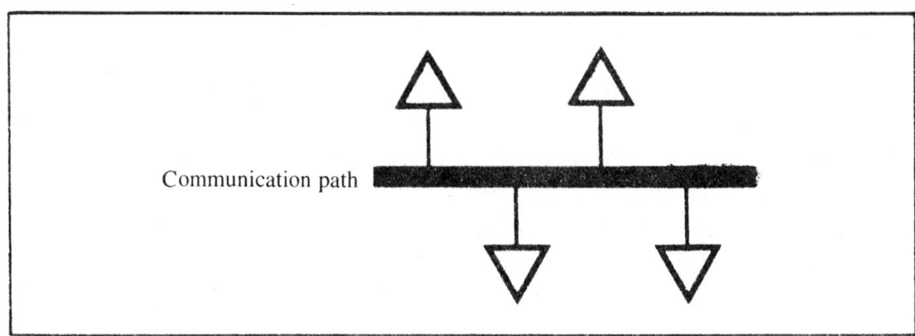

B. Bus Topology

The Tree Topology

The tree topology (Diagram C) is a bus-type topology whose branches are simply extended. This system is used for Community Antenna TeleVision (CATV) systems.

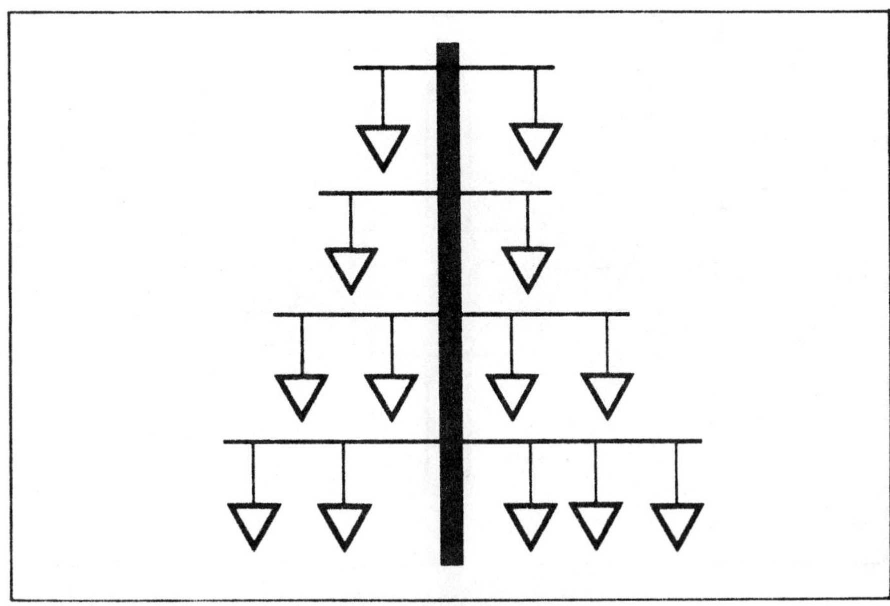

C. Tree Topology

The Ring Topology

The ring topology (Diagram D) is structured in a circular connection, with no defined ends. The ring topology provides good error detection and correction capabilities, and can even be configured as a ring/star (Diagram E).

In a token-ring network, computers, printers and other devices communicate electronically by passing the data from unit to unit is a prescribed order. Token passing is similar to polling, but the system does not need a central controller.

In the token-ring network, the "token" is simply the electronic carrier for the data being transferred. The token includes a number of bits for controlling transmission and is transferred from one node to the next, providing each node the opportunity to add its own message to the ring. The token-ring technique for a local area network can be compared to a tape recorder—the token—being passed around a round conference table—the ring. Those seated at the table who have nothing to say pass the recorder until someone who wants to send a message intercepts the recorder. The tape recorder is then passed from seat to seat until it reaches the person to whom the message is addressed. Should one person need to leave the table, the flow of information is not interrupted. Diagram D illustrates the point.

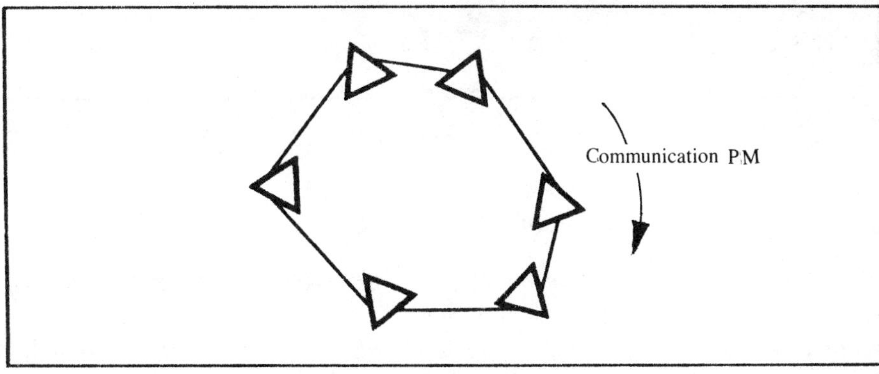

D. Token Ring Passing.

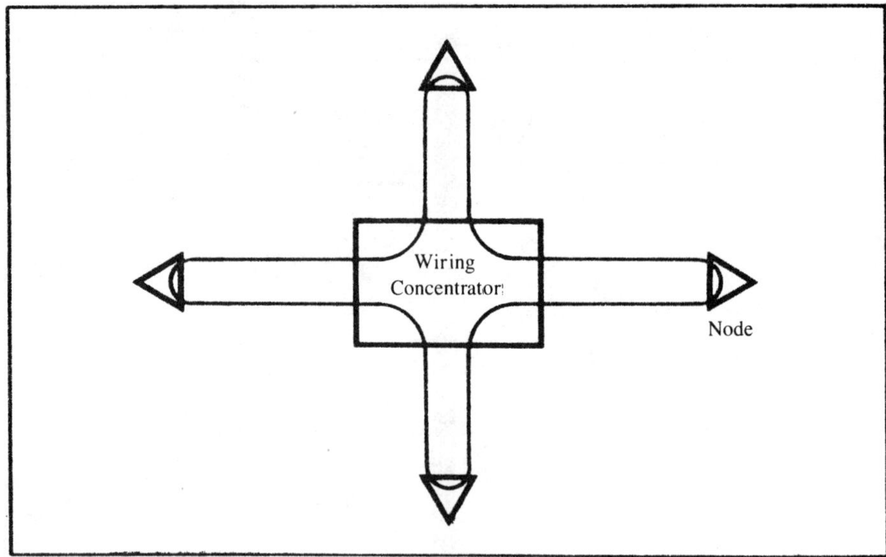

E. Star Ring

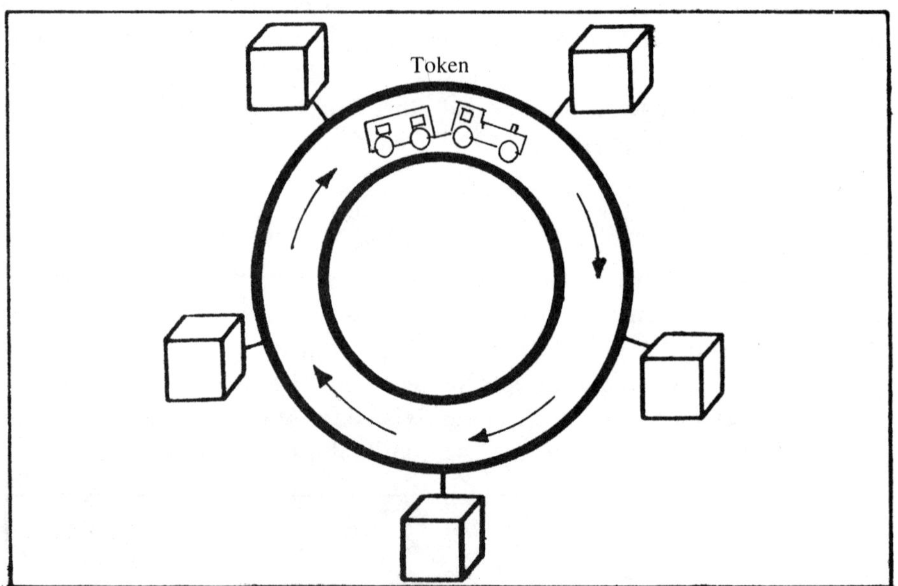

F. Token Ring

Token Ring Connectivity

The purpose of the token ring (shown above) can be something more than strictly "local." It shows the relationship between the token ring and other equipment.

There is, of course, much more to cover on the subject of communications. This will cover what I found in the 1985 exam.

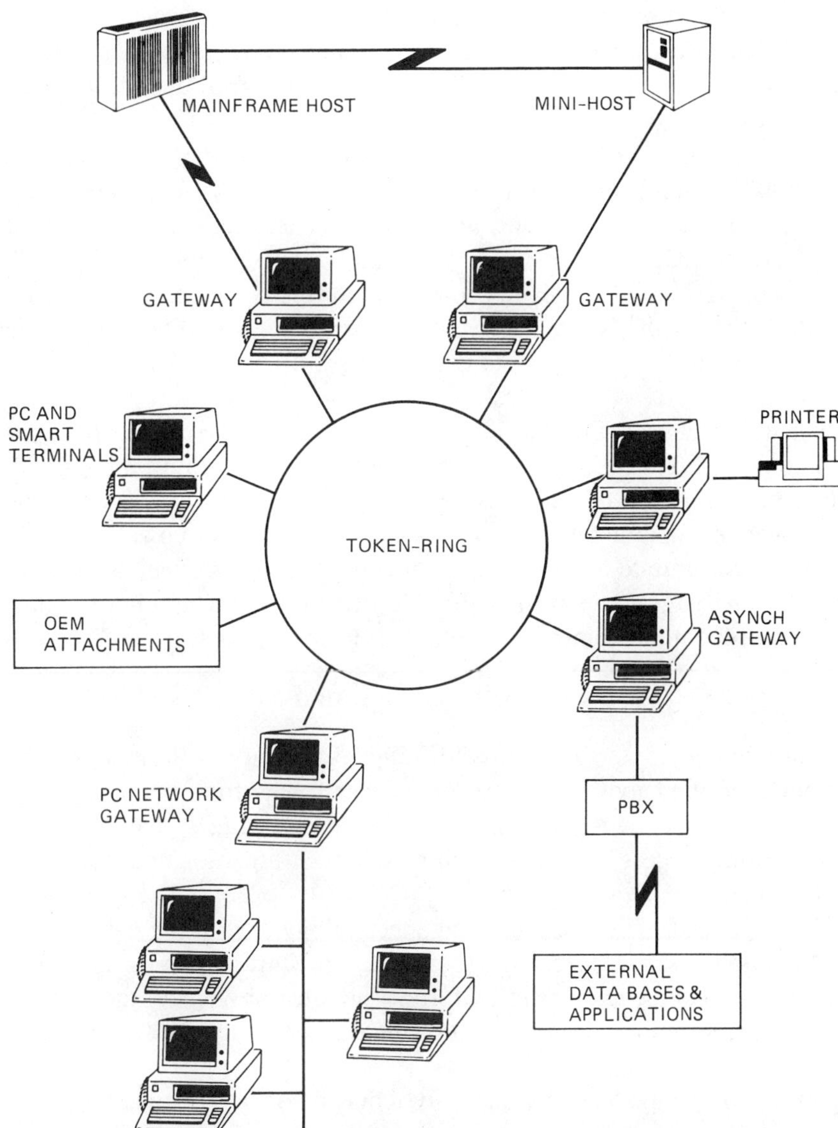

G. Token-Ring Network Connectivity

DATABASE CONCEPTS

The Pervasive Database

If spreadsheet applications were those which "made" the microcomputer, database applications have to be in a close second place. The reason for this is simple, if it isn't obvious. Traditionally, a programmer sat down at the computer and wrote a program in which he developed files. Those files were relatively simple—we call them "flat files"—and generally were able to supply all the immediate need for the program itself. Then, if another report was needed, another program was developed, and often another file. The user was totally dependent upon the programmer to develop both the files of data and the programs which manipulate that data. As the number and sizes of flat files proliferated, we began to call the aggregation of data a "database."

The face of data processing had been changing for some years when the microcomputer appeared. People had learned that the duplication of data had been both absurdedly redundant and outrageously expensive. The proliferation of programs necessary to capture and access this data had itself increased at an alarming rate. Projects were delayed, costs escalated, and user frustration mounted. But we learned that extensive collections of data could be developed (and therefore duplicate and redundant data could be eliminated) and alternative methods of accessing this information could be found. What remained was a useful and easy-to-use method to extract from that data useful reports. And then along came the microcomputer.

The microcomputer brought with it both data and operational independence. It put the power of the larger computer into the hands of the microcomputer user. And though it brought with it a higher degree of complexity than any prior item of office equipment, as we have seen, and will continue to see in this book, it brought a phenomenal amount of power. A major part of that power lies in the database application. Forgive us if we concentrate more on the microcomputer than on the mainframe, for as the database application found its genesis in the mainframe world, any observer would have to acknowledge that it has found its fruition in the microcomputer. The concepts are the same.

A Little Background . . .

The proliferation of microcomputers brought with it the ascention of information power, essentially because it put that power in the hands of the user of the data, away from the data processing fiefdom. As stated, files of data had been growing at a rapid pace, so rapid, in fact, that 20% of the US GNP is devoted to the collection, processing, and dissemination of information and knowledge. That is not all computerized, of course.

Something else happened—advances in storage technology caused the cost of a bit of storage to drop rapidly at the same time the same technology found ways to store drawings, on-line collections of data, and communications between people in digital form. The most obvious of these is the on-line conversions, as it brings a heightened access to computerized data. As capacities increased, cost per bit decreased.

These changes in storage media simultaneously reduced cost and increased speed. The solid-state memory devices provided microsecond access times. This differs from the older magnetic bubble memory (which provided millisecond access time), electromagnetic storage (whose access time was in fractions of a second) and electromechanical storage (much slower, and not used today). To drive home the point, the first trillion-bit on-line storage devices exist today in the mainframe world.

Technology hasn't stopped there. There have been quantum expansions in communications capabilities. We've gotten smarter about how to "talk" to the computer, and man–computer dialogues have steadily been improving. Database packages now give us the ability to easily develop the files, browse them, modify the data stored, add new data, and using very sophisticated extraction and manipulation languages, solve problems using the data. And today, it is the user, not the professional programmer, who is solving these problems. The information age now resides in the hands of Everyman.

Design Alternatives

When one develops a database package there are many needs to be met, some of which may be mutually exclusive. Not only is there a need to structure a mechanism to contain the data, there is a need to provide the facility to use the data with a wide variety of applications. The intent is to be able to do so with a minimal amount of restructuring of that data. The initial way this is done is by concentrating more upon defining the data and less upon designing the process. The whole idea is to develop a cache of data which is independent of any program(s) which will use that data, for if that can be achieved, the data can be modified without the accompanying requirement to modify the program, long a problem for data processing activities. This means that the data must be structured to remove redundancy, and that standards for definitions and dictionaries had to be set. It also means that some basic decisions had to be made: what's more important: storage or time? These are interlocking questions for which there are no easy solutions. However, new devices. new techniques, and new data base types have allowed us to pretty much have both.

Basic Terminology

Despite your advanced knowledge, permit us a bit of space to define some common database terms. These database terms apply both to micros and to their larger mainframe brothers. The list is designed to provide a flavor of what you will encounter.

- Peripheral (Secondary) Storage Devices. These are the tapes, disk units, drums, and demountable cells or cartridges, generally in use on the larger machines. For the microcomputer, these are the diskette drives and the hard disk drives.
- Volumes. These are the demountable tapes, disk packs, and cartridges. They are also drum and other nondemountable storage media. For the microcomputer, they are the diskettes themselves and the allocation of space on the hard disk. In essence, they are the physical unit of any peripheral storage medium accessible to one or more read/write mechanisms.
- Module. This is the hardware that holds one volume.
- Direct-Access Storage Device (DASD). A unit of modules. Data may be allocated to abbreviate the searching for the data.
- Track. Data which can be read or written by a single reading head without changing its position. May be on drum or disk.
- Cylinder. An access mechanism with many reading heads, each of which can read one track. A group of tracks which can be read without moving the access mechanism.
- Cell. Generic word to mean either track, cylinder, module, or zone delimited by a hardware boundary.
- Logical Data/Physical Data. Logical is the way the programmer sees it. Physical is the way the software arranges the data on the physical device. There are therefore these relationships: the logical relationship to the physical relationship; the logical structure to the physical structure; and the logical data description to the physical data description.
- Byte. 8 bits—the addressable character.
- Data Item. Smallest unit of named data (field, data element).
- Data Aggregate. Logical collection of data items (DATE is composed of data items MONTH, DAY, and YEAR).
- Record. A named collection of data items or data aggregates. The number of records in a logical structure is unlimited. The number of data items or data aggregates within the logical record will be limited.
- Segment. Another name for record. The basic quantum of data which passes to and from the application programs under control of the data base management software.
- File. A collection of the occurrences of a given type of (logical) record. Fixed file has the same

number of data items. In complex files, the records may have a varying number of data items (variable) because of the existence of repeating groups.

- Database. A collection of the occurrences of multiple record types with relationships established between records, data aggregates, and data items.
- Database System. A collection of multiple databases. Sometime referred to as a data bank.
- Block of Stored Records. Group of data which composes a physical record.
- Extent. Overflow records from anywhere; physically contiguous.
- Data Set. A named collection of physical records. Includes both data and indices. May be contained on multiple volumes.
- Bucket. A temporary storage of a stored record or collection of stored records. Often called a pocket or slot.

So What is a Database?

Now that we've defined these terms let's simply say that the developers of quality database packages have made much of that transparent. Why did we tell you? Because we're going to explain how things work, and it best to do so with some understanding of the terms.

A database is not all things to all people. In general, it is a collection of data which serves a limited number of applications, as follows:

- It is a collection of interrelated data stored together without harmful or unnecessary redundancy to serve multiple applications. Data are stored so they are independent of programs which use the data and require a common and controlled approach for adding or modifying data.
- It is a workable combination of on-line and batch processing. On-line means while you're sitting at the console, dealing with items on a one-by-one basis; batch processing means you have set up a program to process many data items.
- It must be designed to reduce redundancy and duplication of data. However, a database is not nonredundant. Some duplication is required to minimize access time. Therefore, it is best to have controlled redundancy, minimal redundancy, and the absence of harmful redundancy.
- It needs to change and grow constantly. Databases can easily grow linearly; geometric growth presents problems. However, database also provides data independence, causing the database to need frequent reorganization.
- The ability to support the multiple relationships necessary for multiple applications, while satisfying concerns for security and recovery and providing the ability to generate access to unanticipated data.

The Evolution of Database Concepts

And Then There Were Flat-Files . . .

Until the advent of database, files were organized in a serial manner. These are the so-called "flat-files." The file was composed of records that were known as "fixed-format" records, that is, each record was precisely the same size and they were strung one after the other on a storage medium—generally in sequence on some common field (called the "key field"). Therefore, the physical data structure was essentially the same as the logical file structure. These records were processed in a batch mode, and there was no real-time access. Several copies of the file were stored because previous generations of data were kept. Several variations of the file were kept because it was often necessary to access the data in something other than the key field sequence.

Key Field Employee Nr.	Last Name	First Name	Street Addr.	City	State	Zip	Other Data

Figure 8.26

The software which handled the flat files was designed to perform only the input/output operations. The application programmer designed the physical file layouts and embedded them into the application programs. And every time the data structure or storage device was changed, the application program had to be rewritten, recompiled, and retested. This means that the data was usually designed and optimized for one application, and rarely used across applications. It also means a high level of redundancy between data files.

Figure 8.26 shows an example of the "flat-file record." A collection of flat-file records produces a flat-file. Each record is fixed in nature; the identically named fields are stored in precisely the same relative location on the record and the records are stored contiguously on the media. Location of a specific record in the middle of the file was a virtual impossibility.

Flat-file database approaches have been to build a series of indices containing the keys of the flat files. This means that, on diskette, an index could be searched, the address of the specific record obtained, and the record itself obtained with the shortest possible process. Other fields of the flat-file record could likewise be indexed. This became known as the inverted form of database, shown in Figure 8.27.

That's fine, with but one exception. We know that there is one employee number per person, and no two people will have the same employee number. Zip code, on the other hand, may be common among several people. In this example we have shown one zip code entry per record. Duplicate zip codes would then be stored in the index, because they represented different records. The searching method would then require extensive searching of the index, now in zip code sequence, for all those individuals with common zip codes. There will be another method—the network method, which we'll discuss shortly.

Enter the Hierarchical File

As time progressed and we got smarter about how to organize data, we reasoned that it would be necessary to extend the indexing concept to permit either serial or random access to records. Not only did we need to maintain the batch processing capabilities, but also on-line, real-time applications were necessary. It was at this point that the logical and physical file organization were distinguished, and the form it took was the hierarchy, or tree. Figure 8.28 shows the first application of this concept, the so-called TREE.FRUIT.APPLE model, fashioned by IBM.

In this model, TREE became an index of an assortment of trees, FRUIT became an index of an assortment of fruits, and APPLE identified the specific fruit. At the APPLE level was where the record really was stored. These indices, when stored in memory, provided extremely fast access to records—but the records still maintained the flat-file structure. The currently-available hierarchical databases have been grossly improved over earlier models of hierarchical databases.

There are some advantages. Storage units can be changed without changing the application program. Data structures, usually serial, indexed sequential, or simple direct access, made location of data quite easy. Its disadvantages? Multiple-key retrieval is generally not used. Data security measures may be used by are rarely very secure. Data still tends to be designed and optimized primarily for one application. And much data redundancy still exists.

And the Network

The database network has much going for it. With it, multiple different logical files can be derived from the same physical data. The same data can be accessed in different ways by applications with different

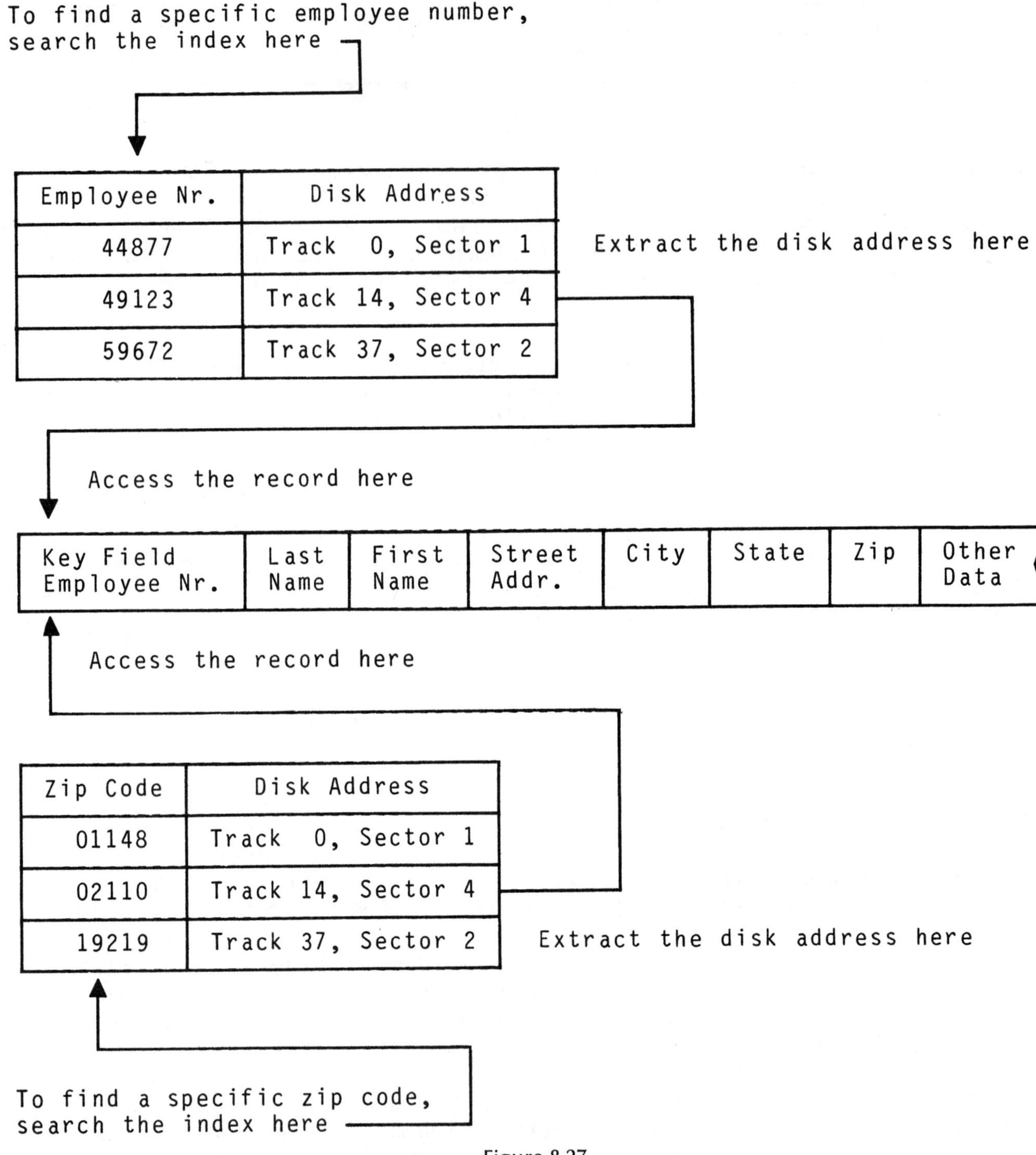

Figure 8.27

requirements. The software provides the means to lessen data redundancy. And data elements are shred between diverse applications. Absence of redundancy facilitates data integrity. The physical storage organization is independent of the application programs. It may be changed often in order to improve the data base performance without application program modification.

In the network database, the data is addressable at the field or group level, as opposed to the record

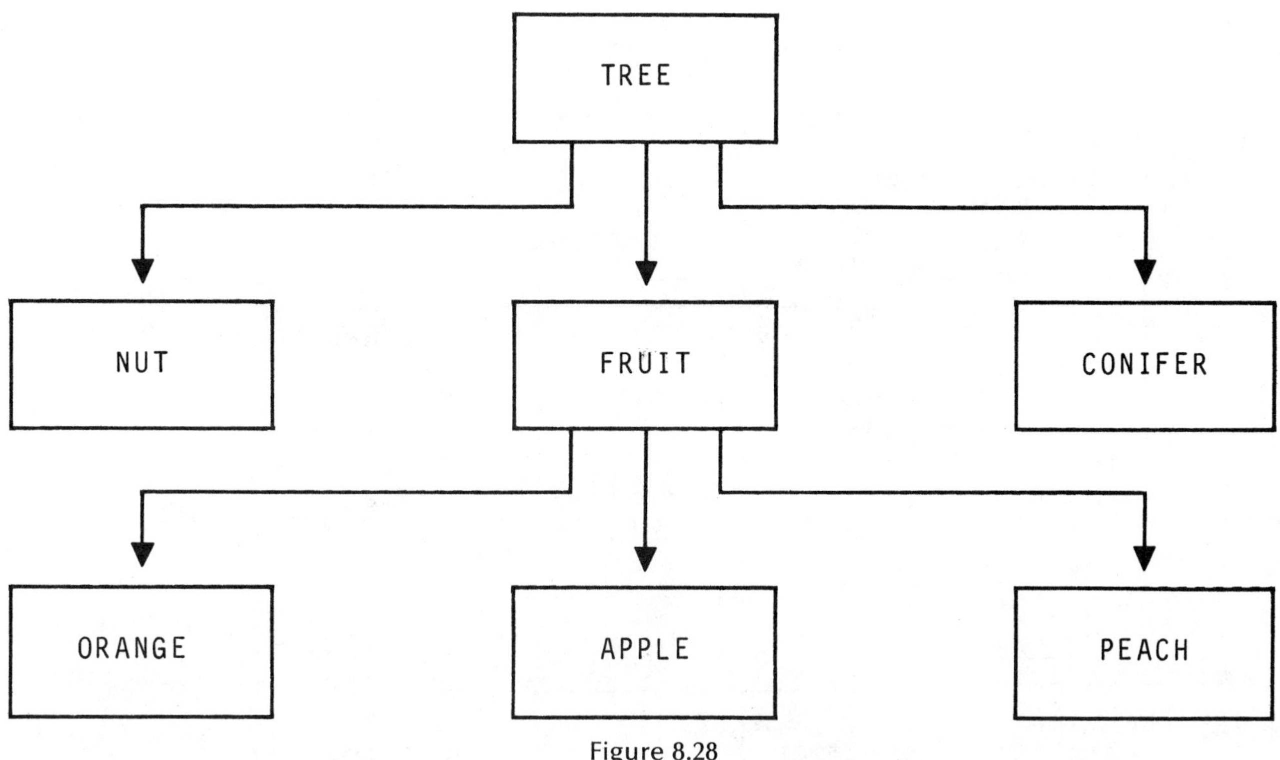

Figure 8.28

level requirements of the flat-file or hierarchical file structure. Multiple-key retrieval can be used. Complex forms of data organization are used without complicating the application programs. The software provides logical as well as physical data independence, allowing a global logical view of the data to exist independently of certain changes in the application programs' view of data or the physical data layouts. Network databases have data independence capabilities.

In the network system, the database may evolve without incurring high maintenance costs. Facilities are provided for a Data Base Administrator to act as controller and custodian of the data, and ensure that its organization is the best for the users as a whole. If your organization is a large one, then use of the database administrator might be a wise investment.

It cuts deeper than that. Effective procedures are provided for controlling the privacy, security, and integrity of the data. Data migration is facilitated. Inverted files are used on some systems to permit rapid data base searching. Good Database Management Systems (DBMS) have the power to provide answers to unanticipated forms of information request.

We've been using the terms "Logical and Physical Data Independence." By logical data independence it is meant that the overall logical structure of the data may be changed without changing the application programs. The changes may not remove any of the data used by the application programs. Physical data independence means the physical layout and organization of the data may be changed without changing either the overall logical structure of the data or the application programs.

The Conceptual Model of the Data—the Schema

In any database, there is a pattern to the data, established by the software. From the perspective of that pattern, both the programmer's view of the data and the allocation of the physical storage devices can change:

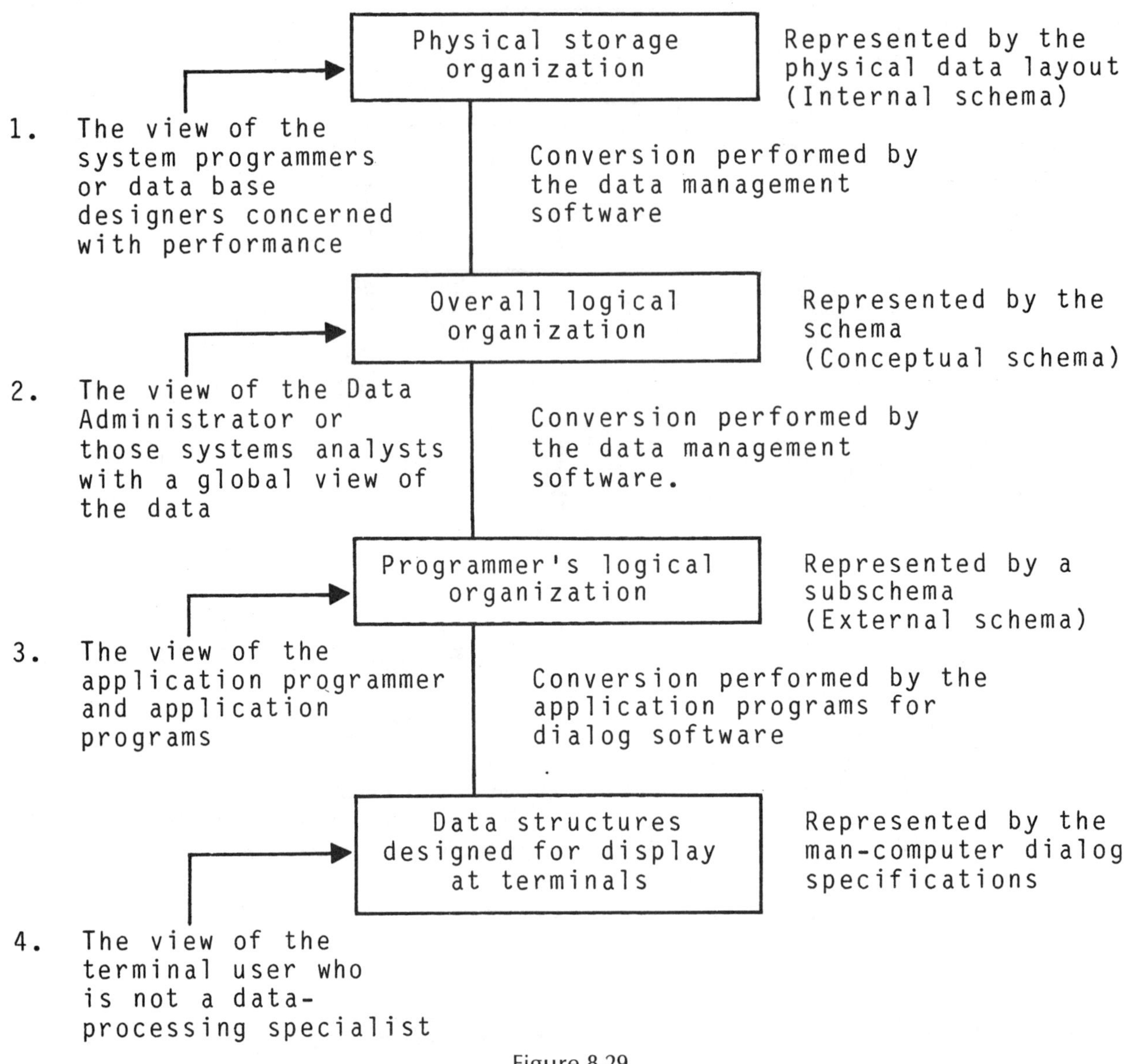

Figure 8.29

- External organization. This allows the programmer to describe the data as a file.
- Global logical data organization. The conceptual model for the database. It is the logical view of the data, different from the physical storage organization.
- Physical storage organization. Concerned with the physical representation and layout and the organization of data on the storage units—indices, pointers, chains, and other location means.

Figure 8.29 is a schematic of the network concepts thus far.

Objectives of Database Organization

It isn't enough, we feel, to assume that a database is simply a means to store data and gain access to it in a number of ways. We feel that the objectives of the database form of organization are useful knowledge, as well. These, then, are the primary and secondary objectives with which a good database package is built:

Primary Objectives

- The database is the foundation stone of future application development. It is easier, cheaper, faster, and more flexible than any other form of data storage and access.
- The data can have multiple uses. Data may be employed in different ways.
- Intellectual investment is protected. Existing programs and logical data structures need not be changed.
- Clarity and ease of use: users can easily know and understand what data are available. Access is in simple fashion. The database management system hides the complexity. Flexible usage allows the ability to search via multiple paths.
- Unanticipated requests for data can be handled quickly. Spontaneous requests for data can be handled without the creation of special programs. A good DBMS provides report generation capabilities.
- Change is easy. The database can grow and change without interfering with established ways of using the data.
- Low cost. The cost of storing and using data is low, reducing the high cost of making changes.
- Less data proliferation. New applications can be built using existing data.
- Performance. Data requests can be satisfied with speed suitable to the use of the data.
- Accuracy and Consistency. Accuracy controls are used on unproliferated data.
- Privacy. Unauthorized access may be prevented; and there are levels of restricted use.
- Protection from loss or damage. Data will be protected from failures and catastrophies, criminals, vandals, incompetents, and unauthorized access.
- Availability. The database is available in times of critical need for the data.

Secondary Objectives

- Physical data independence. storage hardware and physical storage techniques can be changed without causing application program rewriting.
- Logical data independence. New data items can be added, or the overall logic structures expanded, without existing programs having to be rewritten.
- Controlled redundancy. Data items will be stored only once except where there are technical or economic reasons for redundant storage.
- Suitably fast access. Access mechanisms and addressing methods will be fast enough for the usage in question.
- Suitably fast searching. The need for fast spontaneous searching of the data will grow as interactive systems usage spreads.
- Data standardization within an organization. Interdepartmental agreement is needed on data formats and definition. This will provide standards for compatible data.
- High-level programmer interface. The user can be the programmer. Using a DBMS there is no need of a specialized programmer. It provides an end-user language, with high-level query or report generation language for data extraction.
- Integrity controls. The DBMS provides a plethora of error-checking, such as range checks and logical checks.
- Fast recovery from failures. There is no loss of transactions.

Entities and Attributes

A database entity is a tangible object, such as employee, part number, bin location. It may also be a nontangible object, such as an event, job title, customer account, etc. It has properties: color, monetary value, name.

A collection of similar entities is called an entity set (file). Each field has a name and a data entity type, which will ultimately end up in a Data Dictionary. See Figure 8.30. There is also a set of attributes for these entities. There is the data class (N = Numeric; A = Alphabetic; B = Binary). And there is the length (V = Variable; the number for its own length). But this is true no matter what type of database organization is used. What, then, is the difference? The difference lies in how the media is used in the storage of flat-files, hierarchical files, and network files.

A flat-file, you will recall, was a collection of data in contiguous storage. Space is allocated on the disk for the file, which is presented in two-dimensional structure. The hierarchical file places the data in a fashion similar to the flat-files, but builds one or more indices which permit access to the data directly. The network database apportions the data to available spots on the disk on the basis of fields. But when it is all brought back together by the DBMS, the leftmost column identifies the entities (e.g., EMPLOYEE-NUMBER) and the data appears on the screen like it never was apart. In this environment, a record is called an entity record, and the same field in the record is called a set type. Therefore think, for a minute, how that might look. The database might show you the entire record or it might show you a column of fields named NAME. Actually, database people call these fields "tuples." A file is a set of *N*-tuples.

The key field (EMPLOYEE-NUMBER) is called an Entity Identifier. An entity identifier is just another word for the means whereby we will identify data using the primary key. The entity identifier may be either a single tuple (EMPLOYEE-NUMBER) or a combination of data items (tuples), such as FLIGHT-NUMBER and DATE. Such a combination is called a *concatenated key*, in that two tuples (FLIGHT-NUMBER + DATE) have been combined dynamically to locate a specific entity record. More can be required (e.g., MOVIE + THEATER + DATE), and if your business were as the owner of this string of movie theaters, it would become an unique identifier for a revenue record, as shown in Figure 8.31.

Value Redundancy

Insofar as media storage is concerned, the conventional flat-file, and to an extent, the hierarchical filing system, duplicate data unnecessarily. Figure 8.32 shows an employee number file with indication of where the employee is lodging.

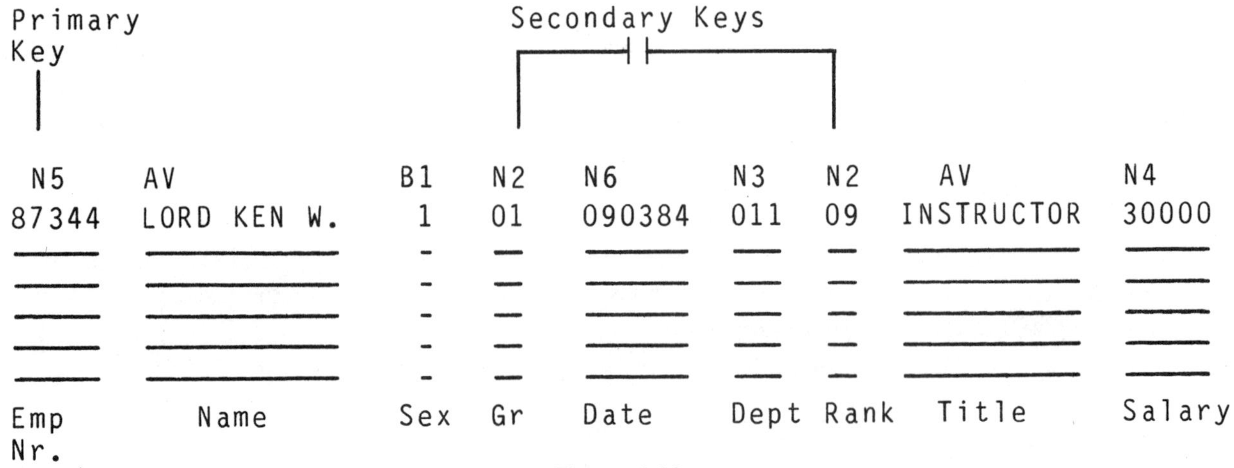

Primary Key   Secondary Keys

N5	AV	B1	N2	N6	N3	N2	AV	N4
87344	LORD KEN W.	1	01	090384	011	09	INSTRUCTOR	30000
___	___	_	__	___	___	__	___	___
___	___	_	__	___	___	__	___	___
___	___	_	__	___	___	__	___	___
___	___	_	__	___	___	__	___	___
___	___	_	__	___	___	__	___	___
Emp Nr.	Name	Sex	Gr	Date	Dept	Rank	Title	Salary

Figure 8.30

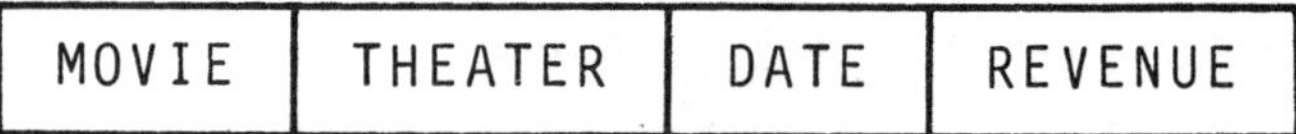

MOVIE	THEATER	DATE	REVENUE

Figure 8.31

Emp	Lodging
123	Statler Hilton
410	Best Western
411	Holiday Inn
420	Motel 6
700	Motel 6
714	Statler Hilton
760	Statler Hilton
800	Holiday Inn
802	Statler Hilton
804	Holiday Inn

Figure 8.32

Even in microcosm, one can see how much space is wasted. A more efficient way is to condense the data as much as possible by using pointers. This means that the individual key fields are separated from the data itself into an index. Recall that there will be one of those for every record. The next step, then, is to condense the data into its unique types. Figure 8.33 gives an indication of how this will occur.

Secondary Keys

Secondary keys are possible, on such data items as color, Zip Code, etc. The reason for having secondary keys is that there is no time to sort files in the interactive environment. This, then, gives rise to new index tables: Inverted List, Secondary Key + Primary Key, and Secondary Key + Record Address.

A completely inverted file would show every entity identifier with every value of every attribute. A partially inverted file is more common.

Data Models: Schemas and Subschemas

Though it isn't immediately obvious, a database consists of a series of schemas and subschemas. Bear with us, and we'll tell you what they are and what is the difference between them.

The data item by itself is useless. (Figure 8.34)

It has meaning only when it is associated with something else. (Figure 8.35)

The database, internally, has a data map that shows the logical relationships. Use of the data map shows the organization without concern for physical relationships.

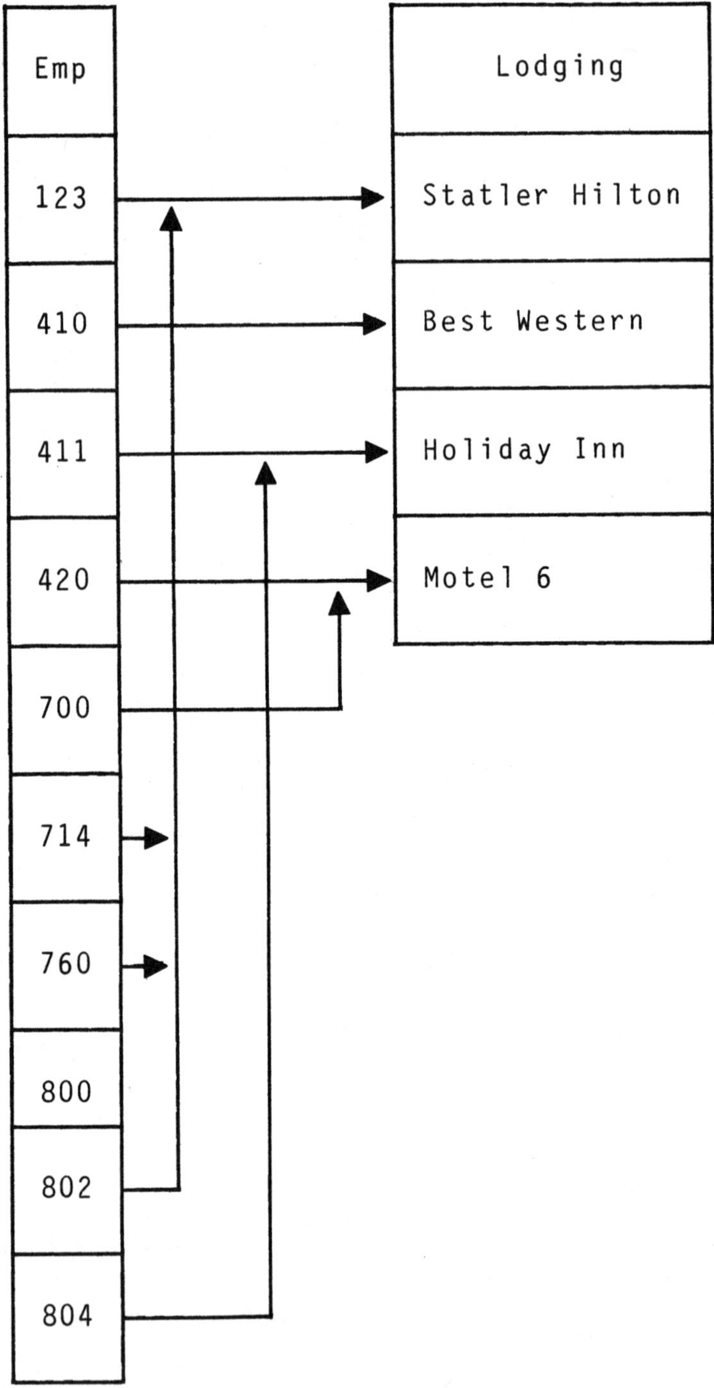

Figure 8.33

Salary

Figure 8.34

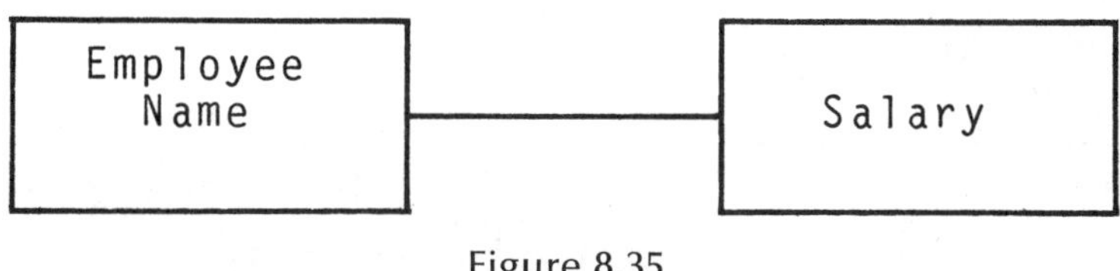

Figure 8.35

The schema is the overall database description, a chart of the types of data that are used, including the names of the entities, their attributes, and the specifics of the interrelationships. It is the framework into which the VALUES may be fitted. The schema has no values in and of itself. The *instance of a schema* is the definition applied to the database. Data will change in the format when the instance of the schema changes. There is some considerable difference between the instance of the personnel record and the personnel record of John Jones. Figure 8.36 demonstrates this point using several individual records from a Purchasing database.

Relationships and Cross References

In the illustration the lines between SUPPLIER # and PART # and between PART # and ORDER # represent relationships. The other lines are cross references. The PURCHASE-ORDER record is connected to the LINE-ITEM records for which the purchase order is composed. The SUPPLIER record is connected to the QUOTATION records showing the parts that that supplier can provide and the price quotations given. PART-NAME and PART-DESCRIPTION are in the PART record, cross-referenced. Likewise, SUPPLIER-NAME and SUPPLIER-ADDRESS.

Relationships convey information not inherent in the data items themselves. The PURCHASE ORDER record does not say what the parts are for. When coupled to the LINE-ITEM record, it is complete.

Cross references convey no information. They are merely file linkages to extend the information. The SUPPLIER # is meaningful in and of itself. If not coupled to SUPPLIER-NAME, no meaning is lost.

So the database system is tripartite. The Subschema is the programmer's data description (file organization). You will define that every time you use the database. The Schema is a chart of the entire logical database—the overall view (done by a data dictionary). It is also known as a global logical data-base description. And the physical database description is a chart of the physical layout of the data on the storage devices.

Hierarchical Structure

A hierarchical structure is often called a tree. It is composed of a hierarchy of elements known as *nodes*. The uppermost node is called the *root*. Unlike most trees, the hierarchical structure is upside down. See Figure 8.36a.

This tree has a *height* of 4 (the number of levels), a *moment* of 22 (the number of nodes), a *weight* of 16 (the number of leaves), and a *radix* of 1 (the number of roots). A node which has four new nodes at the next level has four *degrees*. A level which has five nodes, irrespective of their next level up, has a *count* of 5. All the nodes at a single level belonging to a single parent are called a *family*. The number of nodes belonging to that parent is called a *dimension*.

A *path* diagram details a consecutive number of nodes at a progressively lower level. A *maximal path* diagram begins at the root and continues to the furthest leaf.

Trees can be balanced or unbalanced. See Figures 8.37 and 8.38 for examples.
Note that no element has more than one *parent*. They are called *binodal*: they are related to one and only one node. The ultimate element in any path is a *leaf*.

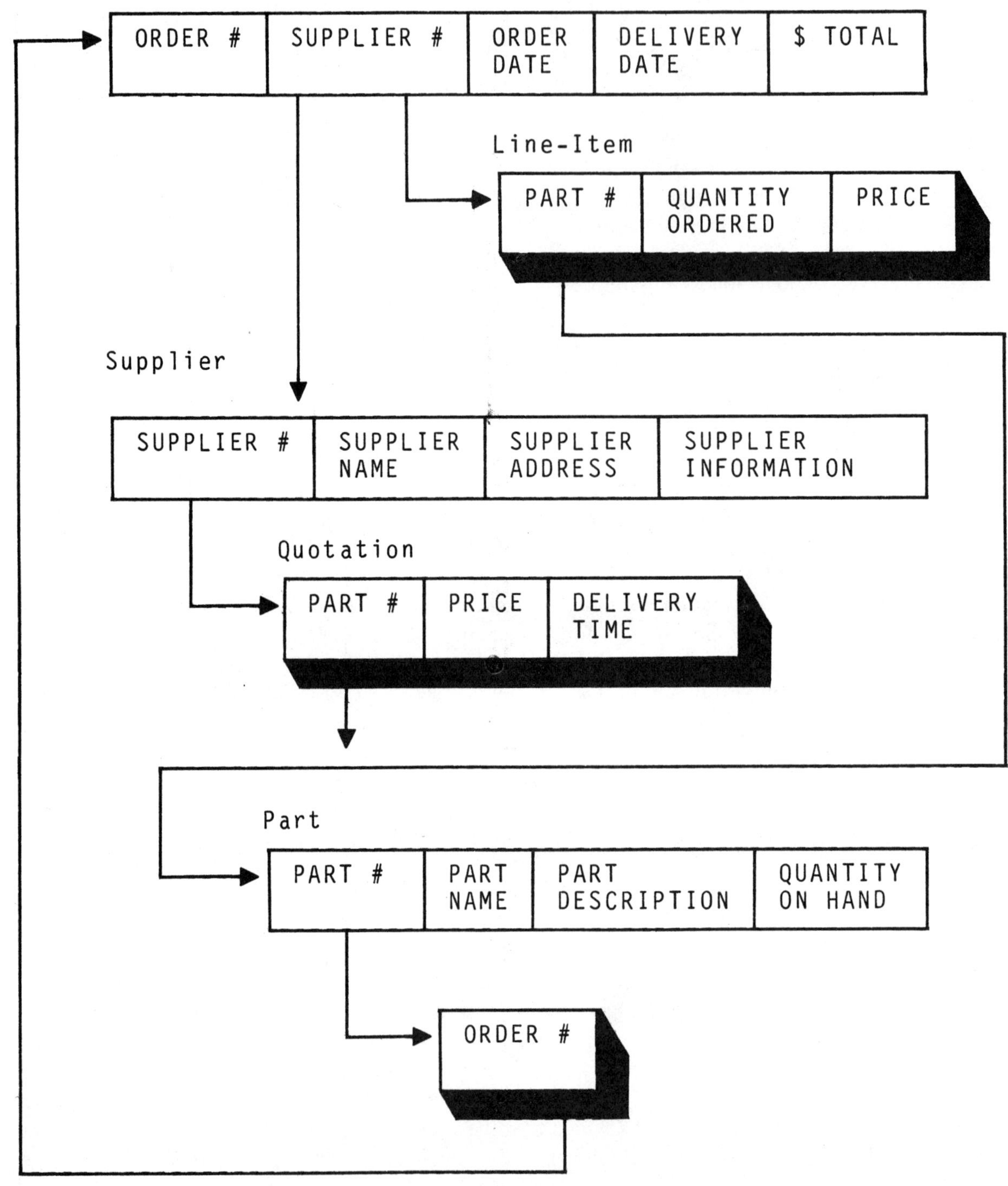
Purchase Order
ORDER #
SUPPLIER #
ORDER DATE
DELIVERY DATE
$ TOTAL
Line-Item
PART #
QUANTITY ORDERED
PRICE
Supplier
SUPPLIER #
SUPPLIER NAME
SUPPLIER ADDRESS
SUPPLIER INFORMATION
Quotation
PART #
PRICE
DELIVERY TIME
Part
PART #
PART NAME
PART DESCRIPTION
QUANTITY ON HAND
ORDER #

Figure 8.36

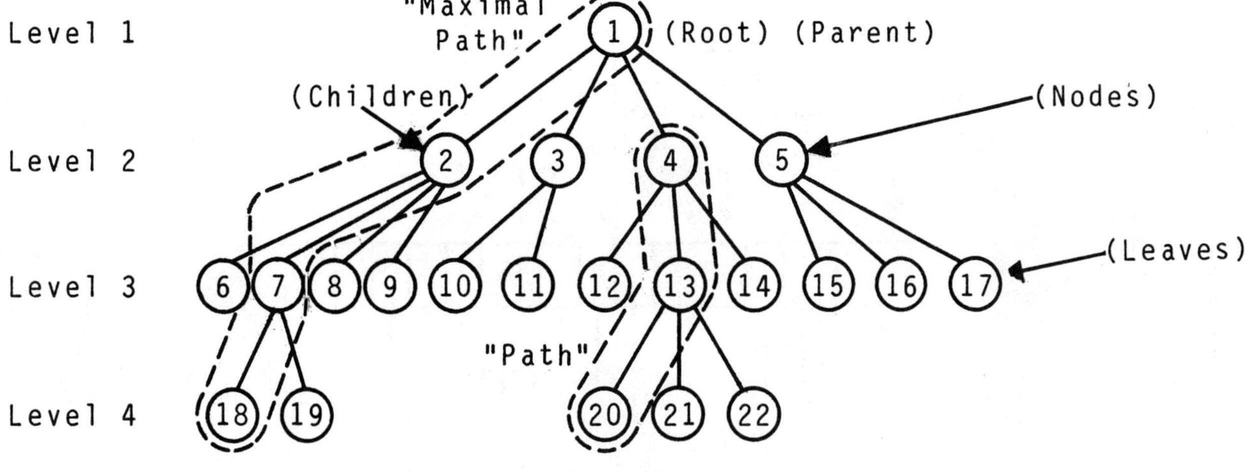

Figure 8.36a

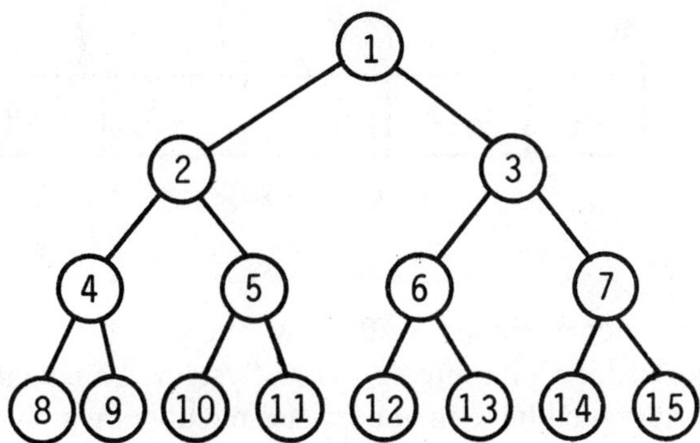

Figure 8.37. Example of a balanced tree.

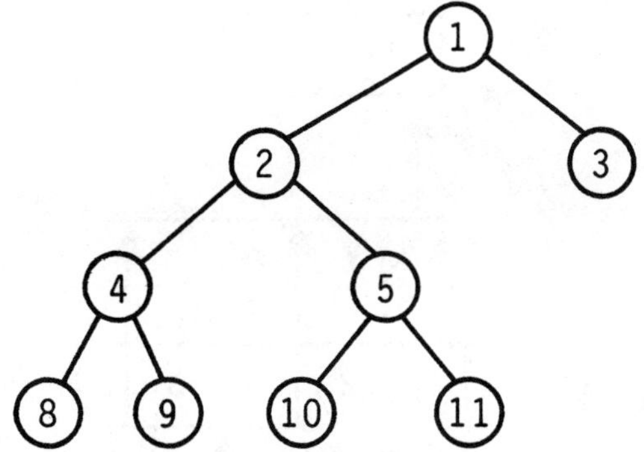

Figure 8.38. Example of a unbalanced tree.

Fractionalized Data

Because the records (in the case of the hierarchical database) and the data elements (in the case of the network database) exist in random parts of the diskette or hard disk, they must be tied together using pointers. A pointer is an address, contained in a record, referring to another record. In this case, the address is contained in the parent record and refers to one or more of its children. Figure 8.39 is an example of a parent with multiple child pointers.

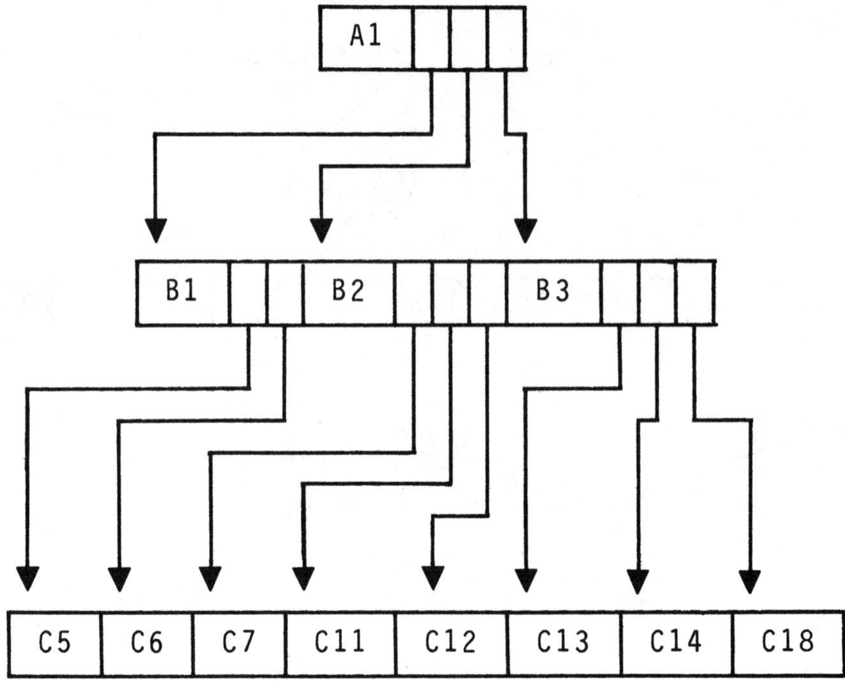

Figure 8.39

The same process works in reverse. Figure 8.40 shows the pointers from the children to the parents.

The Data Base Task Group of the Committee on Data Systems Languages (CODASYL) defines data sets as records which are owners,which have members and members which are owners and they themselves have members. This is illustrated in Figure 8.41.

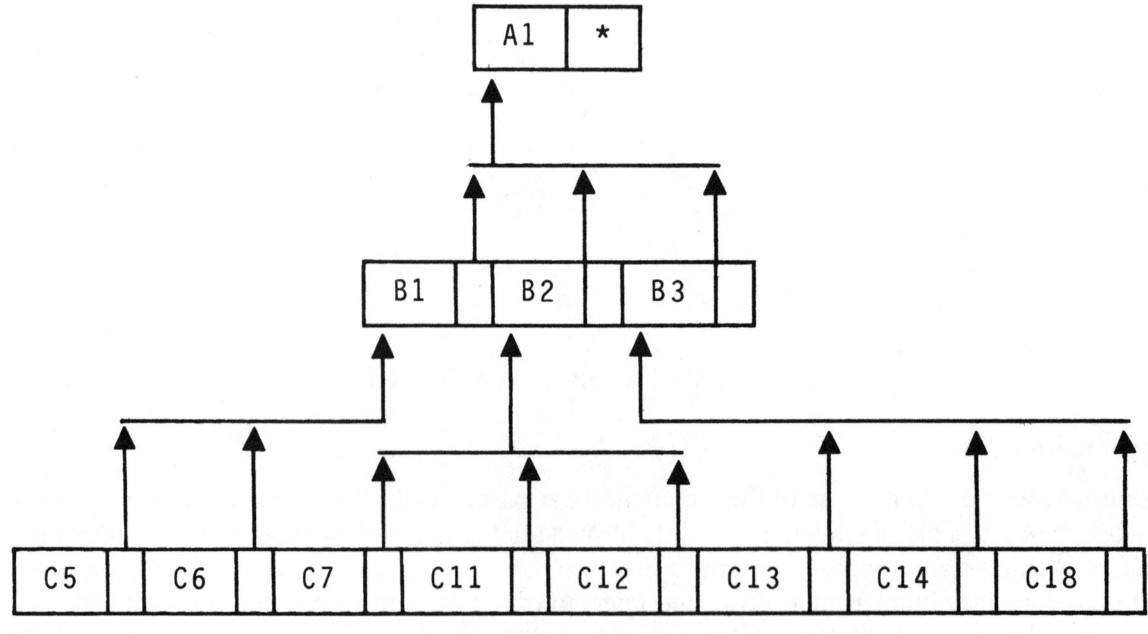

Figure 8.40

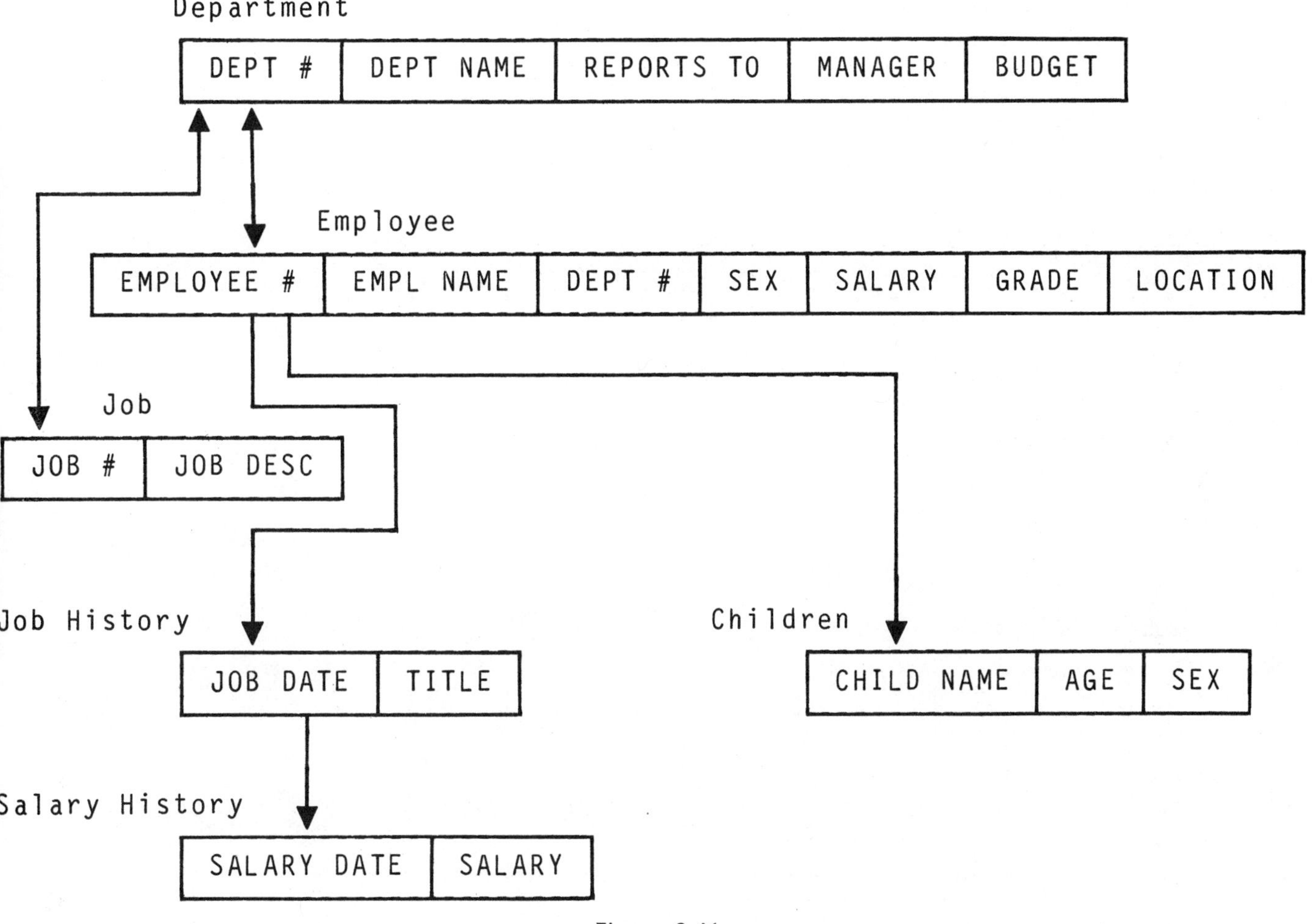

Figure 8.41

Introduction to Plex (Network) Structures

If a child in a data relationship has more than one parent, or a parent has more than one child, this is a network (or plex) structure. There are four types of plex structure. See Figure 8.42.

Any item in a plex structure can be linked to any other item. In Figure 8.43, each (2 and 3) child has two parents (1 and 4).

In Figure 8.44, the lowest node will have two parents.

Figure 8.45 shows an illustration where every data element is a parent:

Figure 8.46 is a more complex example, where the parents are not all on the same level.

And in Figure 8.47 the lowest node has four parents:

To more adequately illustrate the concept, Figure 8.48 is a simple plex structure. Here we have an example wherein suppliers, parts, quotations, purchase orders, and the item purchased all have an interrelationship. Figure 8.49 illustrates the concept involving multiple parts from multiple suppliers:

Mapping—Simple and Complex

With but a minor number of exceptions, we have been mapping in what is called the simplex manner (one arrow in one direction). It's time now to discuss complex mapping, called M:M (multiple to multiple) mapping. Figure 8.50 shows the four possibilities of complex mapping.

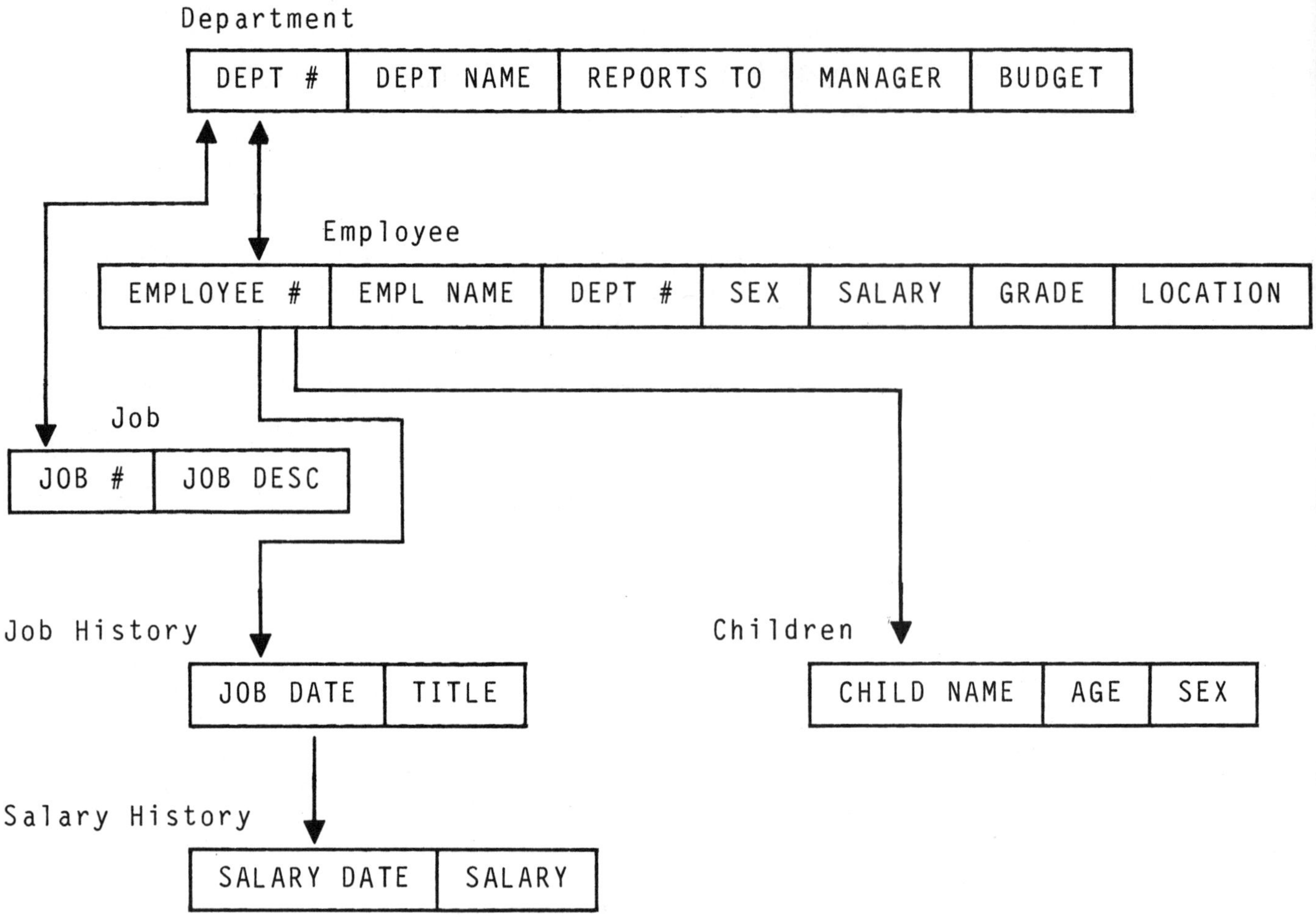

Department
DEPT #
DEPT NAME
REPORTS TO
MANAGER
BUDGET
Employee
EMPLOYEE #
EMPL NAME
DEPT #
SEX
SALARY
GRADE
LOCATION
Job
JOB #
JOB DESC
Job History
JOB DATE
TITLE
Children
CHILD NAME
AGE
SEX
Salary History
SALARY DATE
SALARY

Figure 8.42

1
2
3
4
1
2
3
1
2
3
4
5
6
7
8
9
10
11
1
2
3
4
5

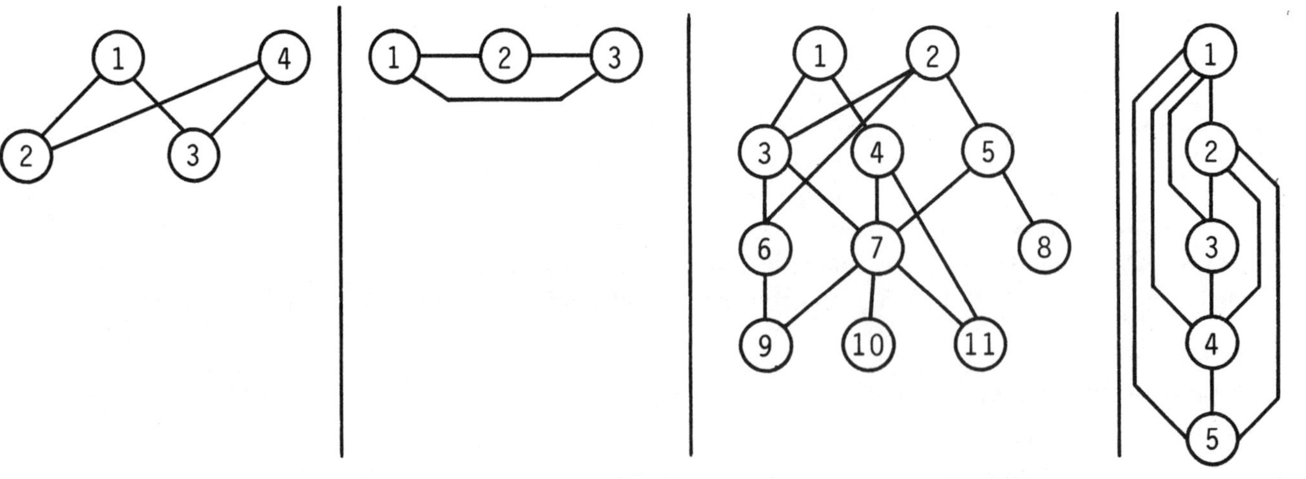

Figure 8.43

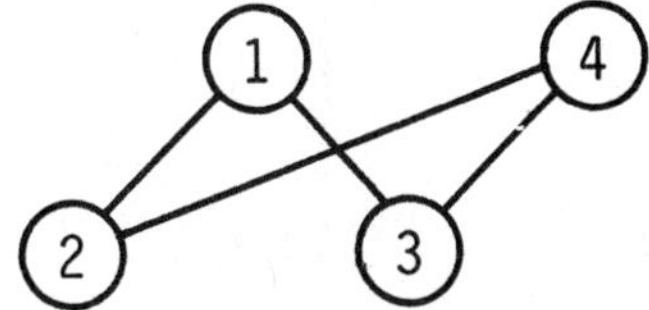

Figure 8.44

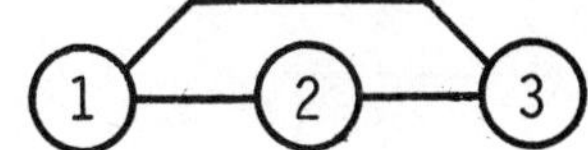

Figure 8.45

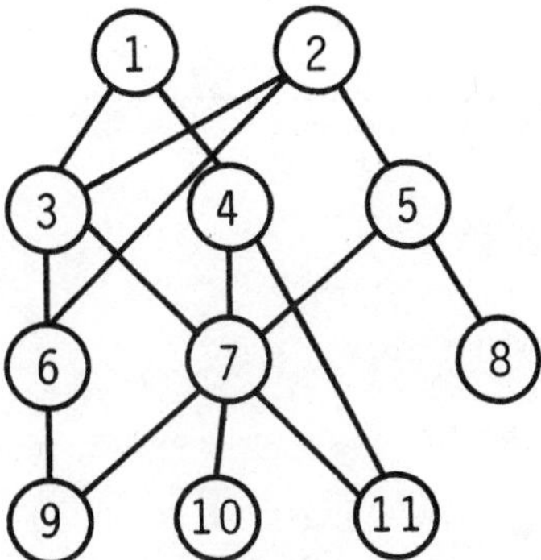

Figure 8.46

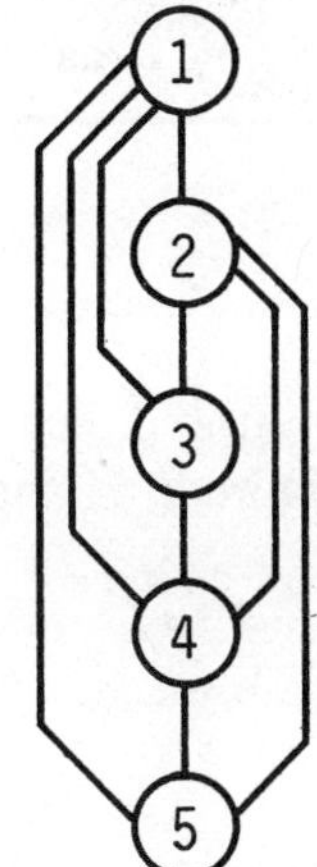

Figure 8.47

This delightful illustration (and several others in this section) is drawn from *Database Concepts*, James Martin, Prentice Hall.

Intersection Data

Intersection data is data that is related to the association between data. An example of this would be found in Figure 8.51, the schematic for a Bill of Materials database.

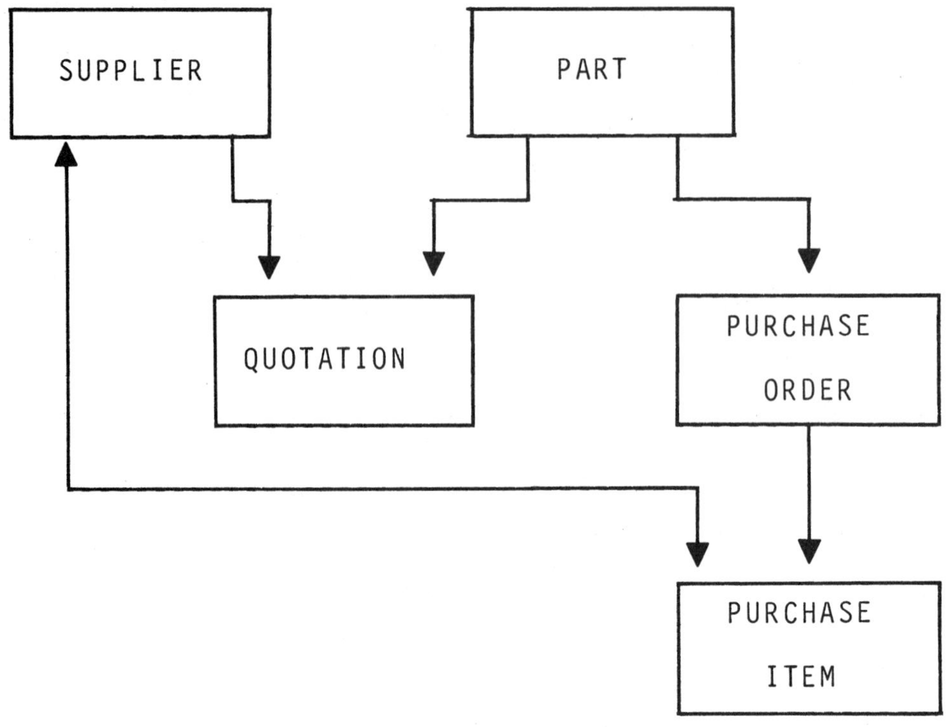

Figure 8.48

The same concept works where there is concatenation, as per Figure 8.52.

Likewise, the concept works not only with concatenation, but with complex mapping, per Figure 8.53.

Chains

A chain is a group of records scattered throughout the files and connected by pointers. It is a hardware consideration, not a software consideration. Figure 8.54 shows how it appears to the DBMS, and Figure 8.55 shows how it appears to you.

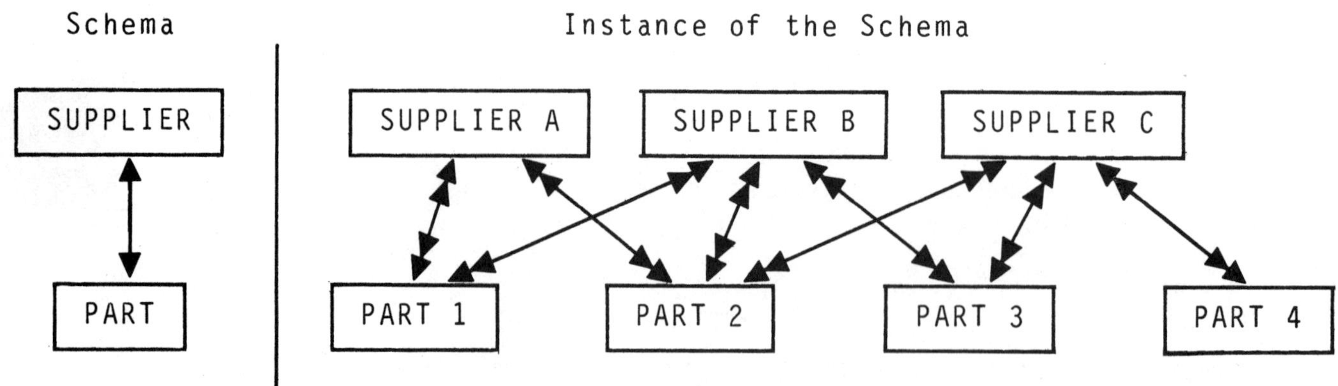

Figure 8.49

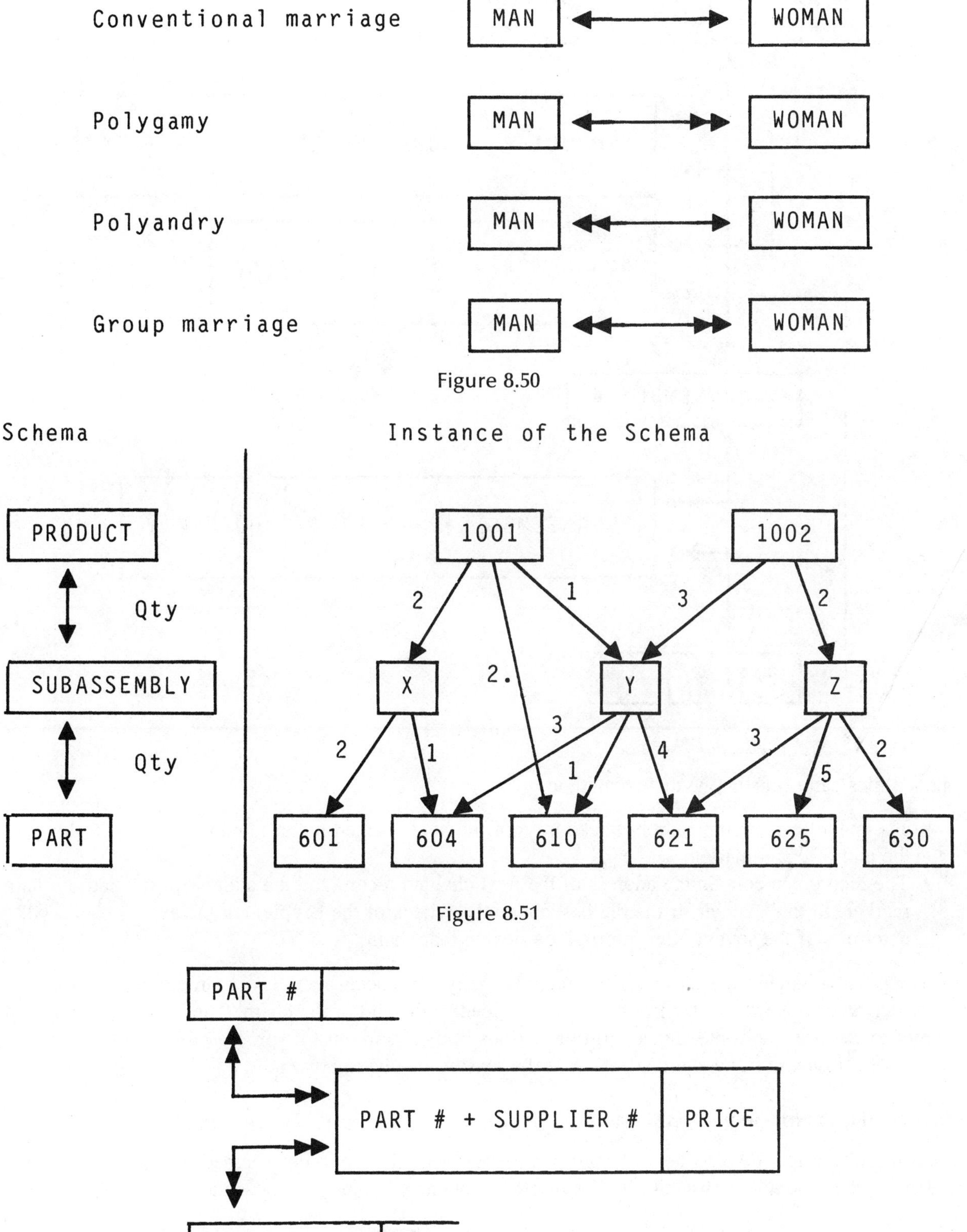

Figure 8.50

Figure 8.51

Figure 8.52

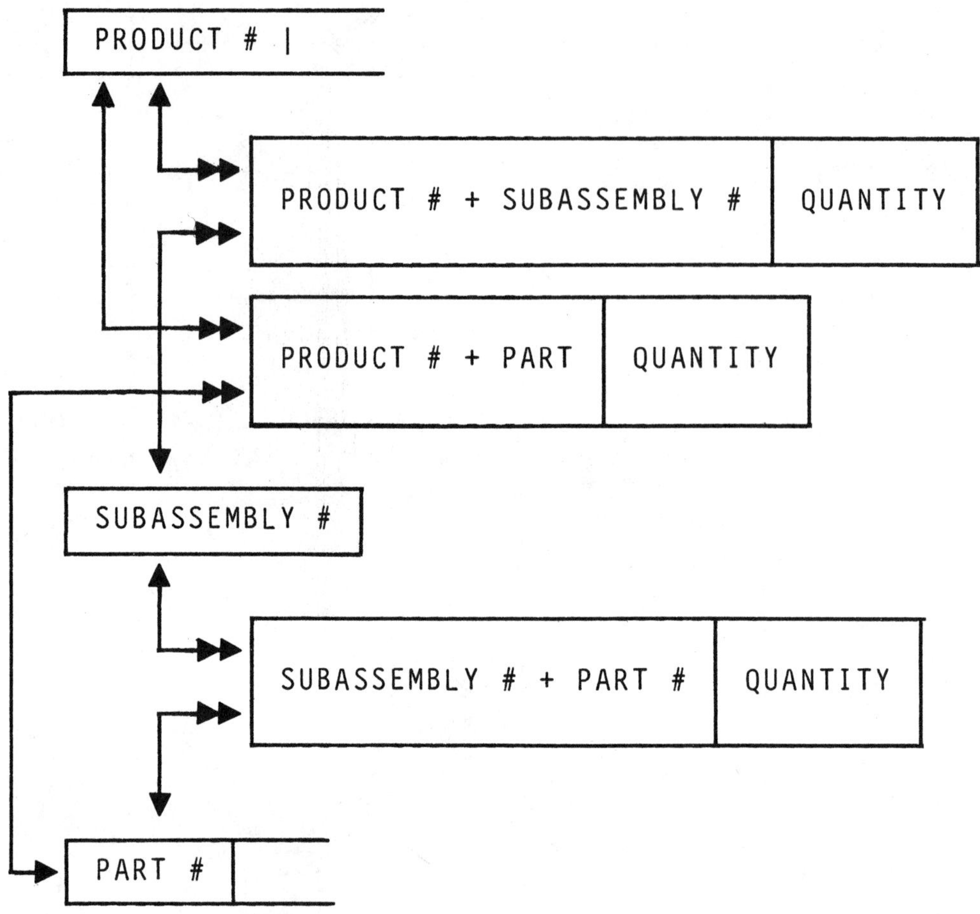

Figure 8.53

Chained files can occur in one of two methods:

- The record can contain simply the address of the next chained record, and the chain is followed to the end-of-chain marker.
- The record can contain the address of the next chained record and the address of the end-of-chain marker. In this manner, if the file is sequential, a check of the key field at the end-of-chain will determine if the sought-after information lies on that chain.

The process handles master and detail records easily. The detail records are simply chained on after the master record. Newly added transactions are added to the end of the chain. The disadvantage is that in order to acquire a current balance, all transactions in the chain must be processed. Therefore, frequent archival of transactions and summarization of the master may be important.

Sequenced and Non-Sequenced Chains

A text file would require a sequenced chain, as the text would have to be accessed in sequence. A non-sequenced chain permits transactions to be inserted anywhere, as processing sequence is not important.

Optimization

Optimization means cutting down the seek time via reorganization. It is possible for sequenced chains only to cut the number of seeks. It is periodically necessary for non-sequenced chains, as these might be spread all over the disk.

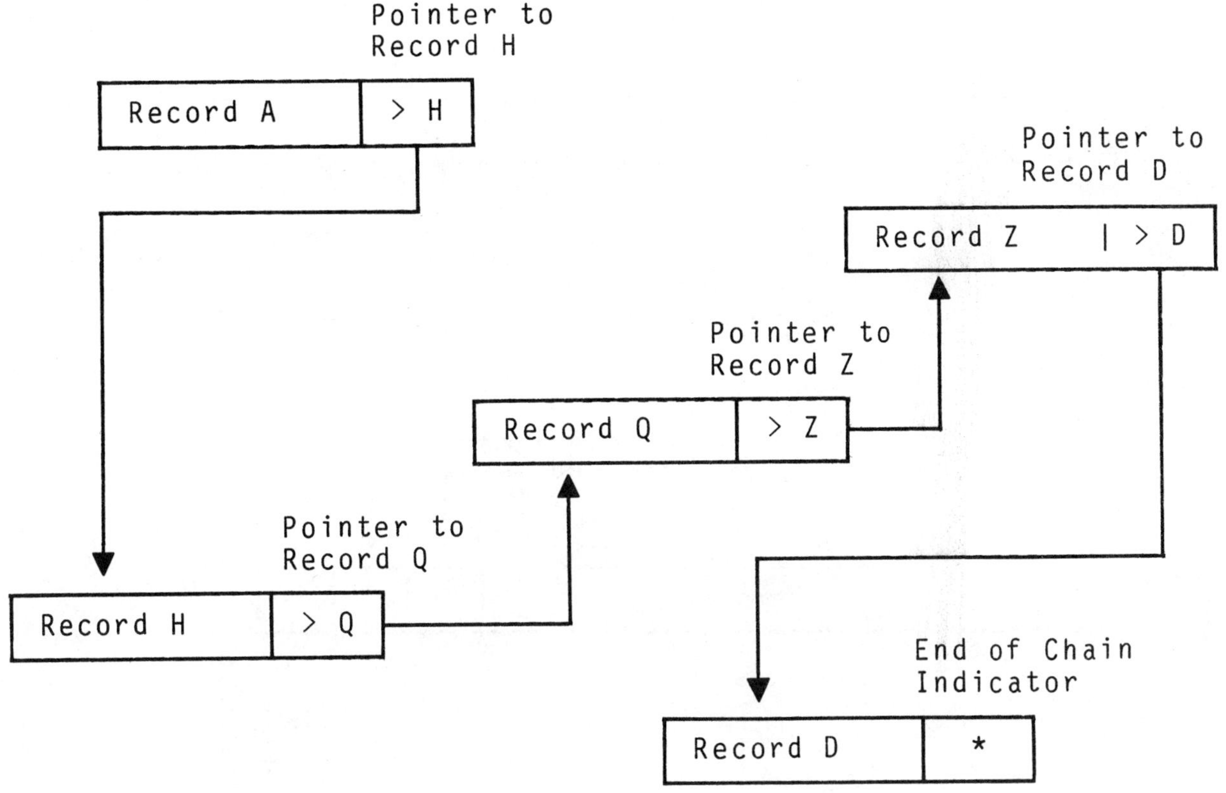

Figure 8.54

Record A	> H
Record H	> Q
Record Q	> Z
Record Z	> D
Record D	*

* This will be the end of chain marker—it is not an asterisk. More than likely it will be a special character known only to the DBMS.

Figure 8.55

Additions and Deletions

Additions and deletions require relinking the chain from the addition or deletion point to the end of the chain. Until the newly-constructed file is properly indexed, access will not be strictly by the chain.

Deletion is a problem where there are intersecting chains (two chains have a common element). Fig-

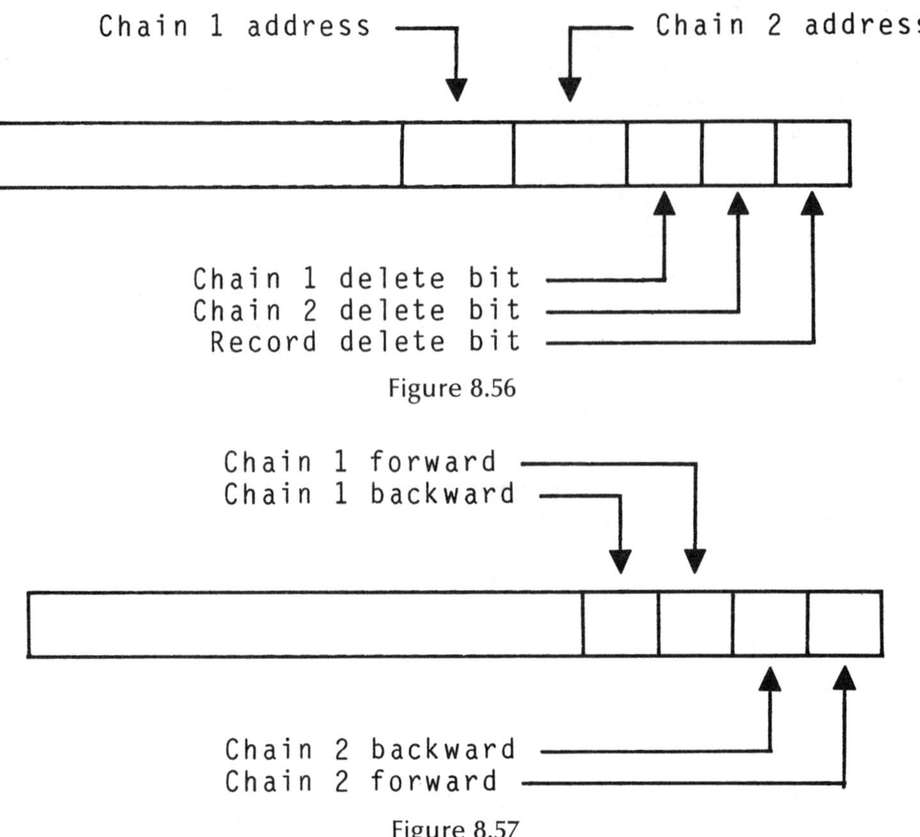

Figure 8.56

Figure 8.57

ure 8.56 shows how this problem is solved. The record contains two addresses, one for each chain in the intersection. If one chain is deleted, the deletion bit for that chain is posted. If both chains are deleted, the deletion bit for the record is posted.

Relinking is time consuming, and the deleted record doesn't drop off until reorganization anyway. This problem is solved somewhat by chain-forward and chain-backward pointers, as shown in Figure 8.57.

Ring Structures

There are several kinds and variations of ring structures. We'll concentrate upon just two, Figures 8.58 and 8.59. The first is called the one-way list, and the concept is that the data is strung together by a single address pointer. In this manner, the data records or the data elements can be sprinkled all over the diskette and can still be located by following the chain. If, for some reason, the chain is broken, then data will be lost.

The second is called the two-way chain. The records are strung together forward, as before. However, this time, the records include an additional address permitting a backwards chain. This time, should a reference be broken (and assuming that the entire record is not destroyed, the linkages can be reconstructed.

Search Strategies

What makes any of this work are the search strategies. Just how are things found. Well, there is sequential, of course. Searching can be done in sequence, either forward or backward. There is skip search-

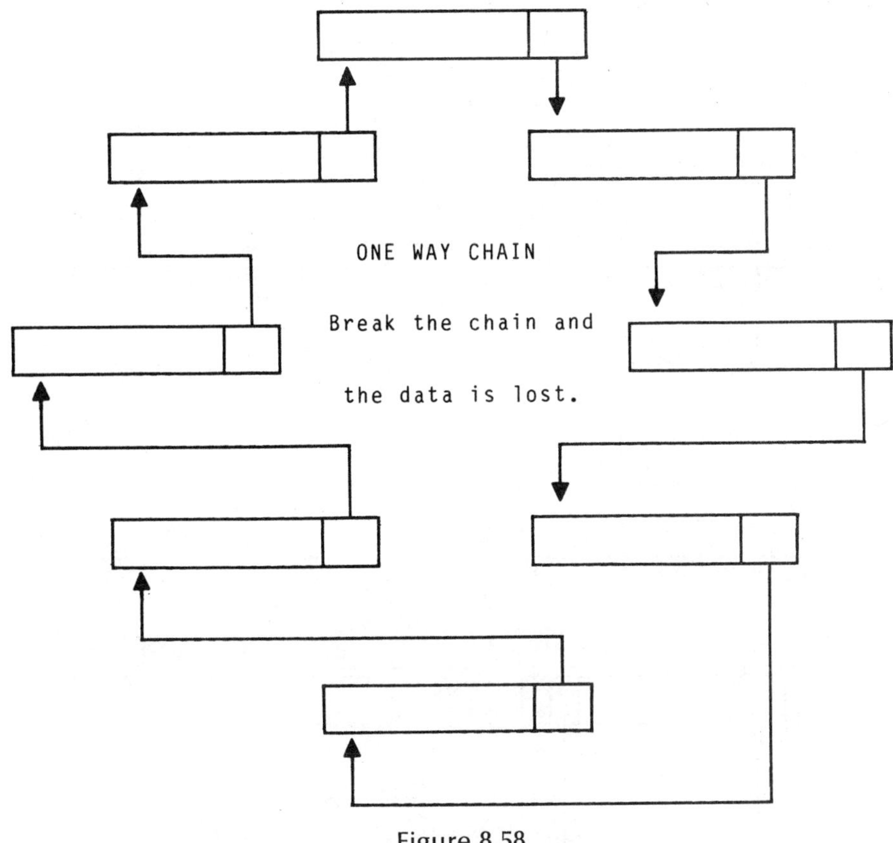
ONE WAY CHAIN
Break the chain and
the data is lost.

Figure 8.58

ing—a technique similar to a binary search but which works only with two-way lists. There are primary and secondary indices, and multilist chains. A discussion of each is coming up.

Before we do so, however, let's review. The primary key is that key on which the file has been sequenced—either on the disk or on the index. The physical position on the file is determined by this key. This key will uniquely identify the record. An example would be PART-NUMBER. The secondary key(s) are located elsewhere within the record and do not necessarily uniquely identify the record. And example would be PRODUCT-TYPE. There can be several secondary keys. Figure 8.60 shows a database organized according to PART-NUMBER, and containing a secondary key of PRODUCT-TYPE. Here we have a file which is sequenced on the PART-NUMBER. There may or may not be an index on PART-NUMBER. There is, however, a secondary key, and that secondary key has been indexed. The toys, in this case, are accessed through the head of the list from the secondary key. That is, the first of a product type category is pointed to by the secondary key. From that point on they are strung together by product type in a one-way list. A two-way ring could be just as easily defined.

So could another secondary key. Figure 8.61 depicts the same toys database, organized on PART-NUMBER, and containing the secondary index according to PRODUCT-TYPE. This time, however, we have added a second secondary key (not tertiary), which will access that portion of the record called COLOR.

Index Organization

There are several ways to organize the index. The index can be set up to include a count of the number of data elements in the chain (Figure 8.62). It might include multiple lists (Figure 8. 63). Or it could include imbedded keys (Figure 8.64)

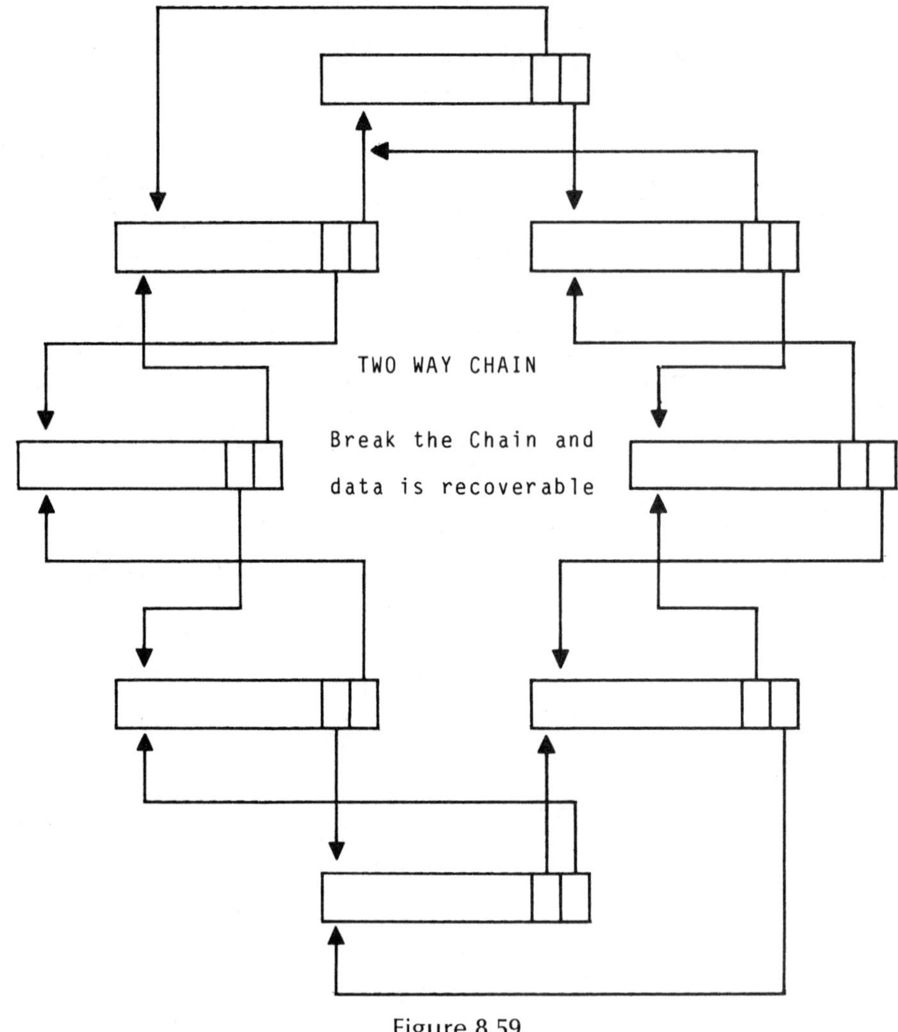

Figure 8.59

Count

The index can be constructed to store a chain count with the index. The advantage of this is that it provides an abbreviated search. If it is wished to examine blue cars, the shorter search would be by KEY 3, the second secondary key. If it is wished to examine white planes, then the shorter search would be by KEY 2, the first secondary key.

Multilist Organization

In the multilist organization we seek to break down the number of records into groups, something like labeling a file cabinet. The index is built to point to the head of a shorter chain. This example is established with sets of 2. Larger sets would be used. Extend that same concept to KEY 3, and you can see how quickly searching will be when the inquiry reads:

LIST THE ON-ORDER ITEMS FOR THE LUMBER INDUSTRY CUSTOMERS IN OREGON.

WHAT WERE THE SALES FOR THE LUMBER INDUSTRY IN JANUARY?

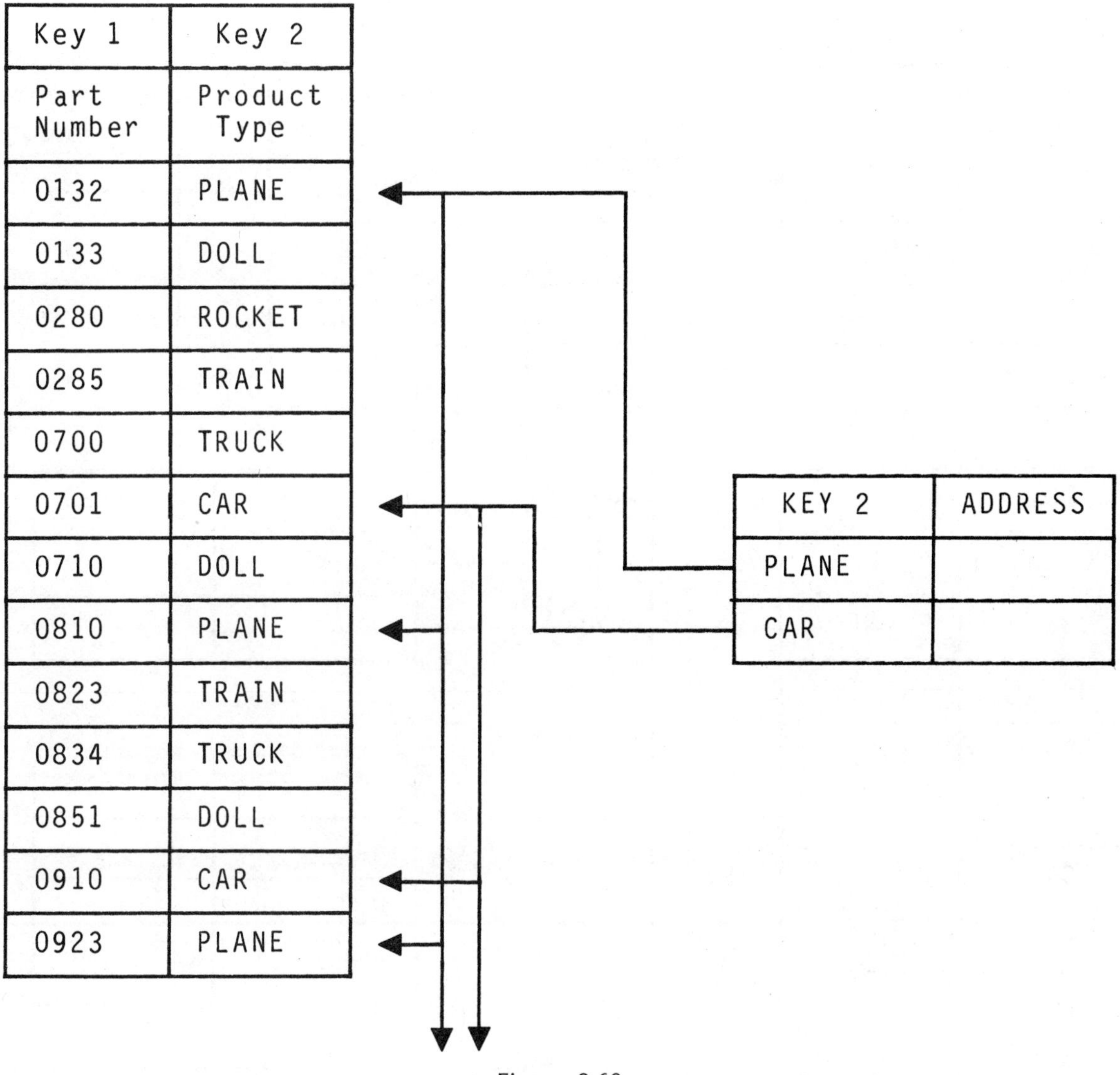

Figure 8.60

Inverted List Index

A variation is the inverted list index, where there are no chains. Each index entry simply points to a record. See Figure 8.65.

Chains Within the Indices

Yet another variation for searching is the location of the chains within the indices. In this manner, the keys are removed from the record and placed in the index. As you can well imagine, the search time is quite abbreviated.

The Relative File—The Relative Database

Most recent database efforts are drawn upon the concepts of the relative file (Figure 8.67). In the relative file, the key and the record location have something in common. The are generally used for records of contiguous items, are generally sequential files, and take on database proportions via chains.

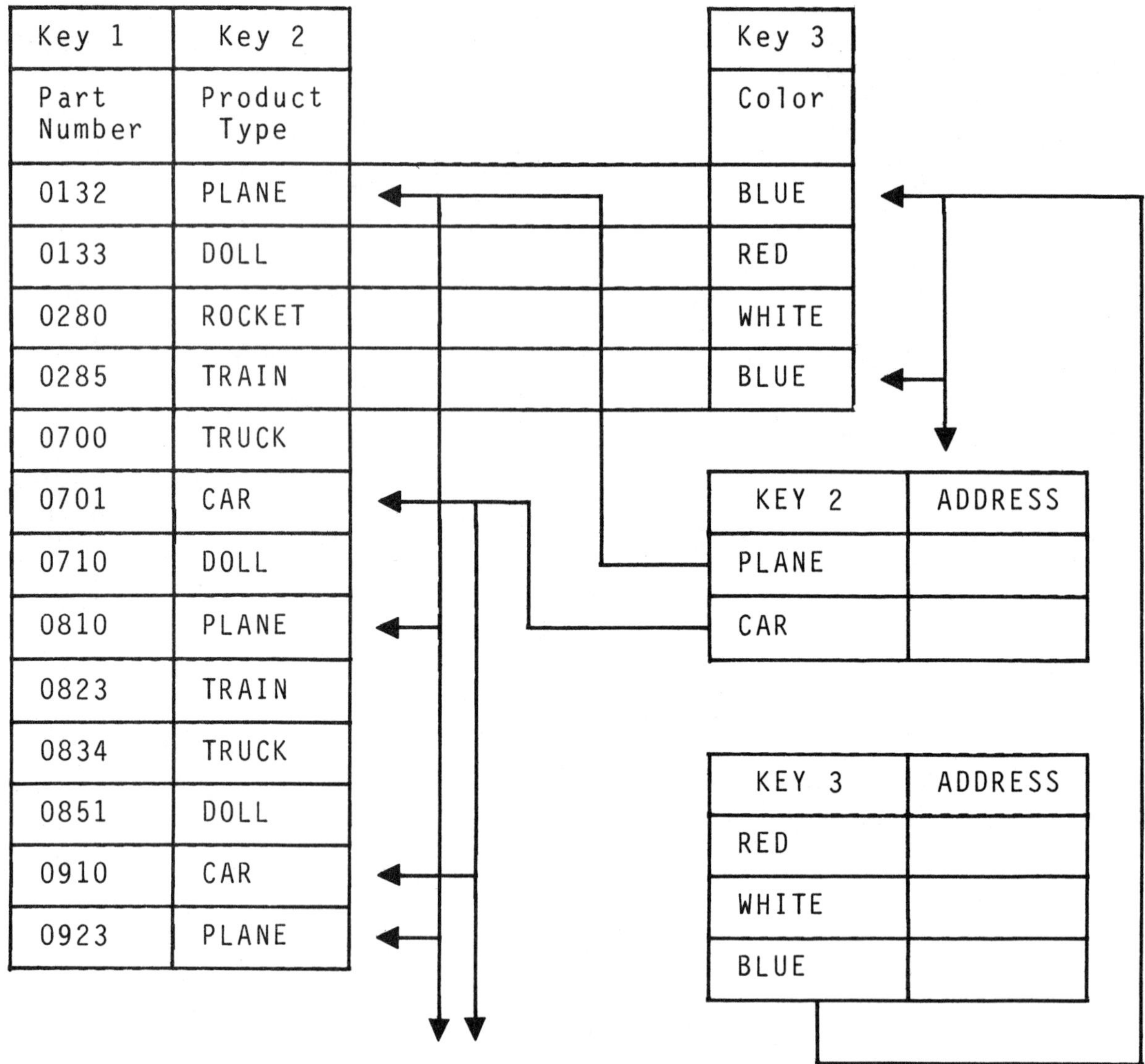

Figure 8.61

Relational Databases

The idea of a relational database is to provide an interface to the user which can be easily understood no professional programming training. This makes it possible to add new data items, records, and associations without changing existing subschemas, and permits maximum flexibility for spontaneous inquiries.

Relational databases define the data in tables. Each entry represents one data item; no repeating groups. They are column homogeneous—all items in a column are the same to the respective record. Each column is assigned a distinct name. All rows are distinct; no duplicates. Both rows and columns can be viewed in any sequence. Our hotel file (Figure 8.68) is a relational database:

Here we have 10 sets of 2 tuples each. There are, of course, some rules:

- A Table consists of only one type of record. A relational table can be viewed as a flat file.
- Each row or record has a fixed number of data elements, and each data element has a unique name.

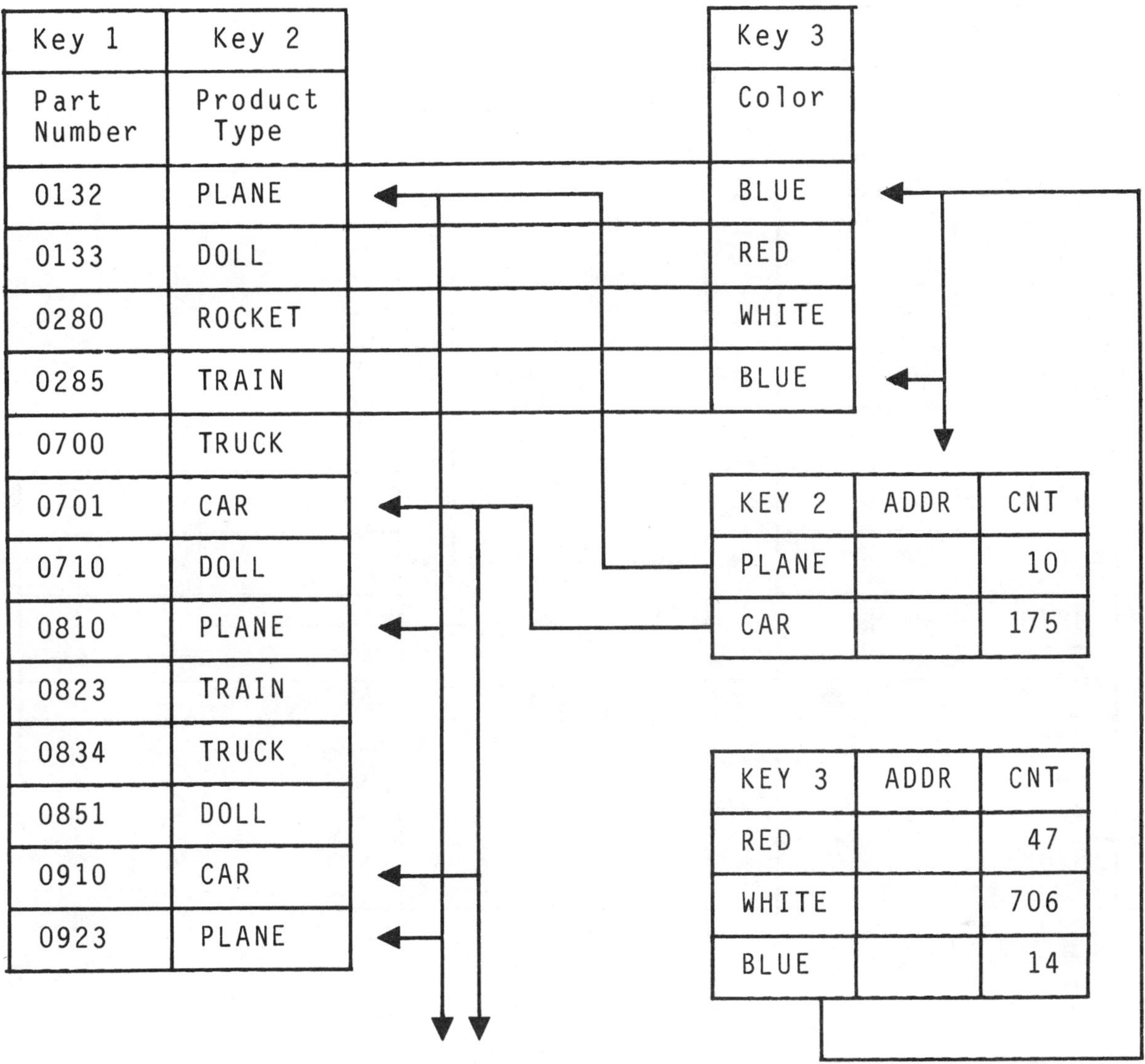

Figure 8.62

- Each data element exists once in a record. There are no repeating elements or groups.
- Records do not have a predetermined sequence in the file.
- New tables can be produced as subsets of tables.
- Old tables may be joined to form a new one. This is not a merge. It is an extract on similar values.
- It is possible to include selection, to build a new table from a subset of previous tables.
- You can form a projection, technically an extraction and consolidation.

DBMS Design Considerations

A modern database management system is self contained (integrated). It has its own command structure and language. It is both command and parameter driven. It may be commanded through the keyboard or via batch-processed parameter files. It has its own programming language.

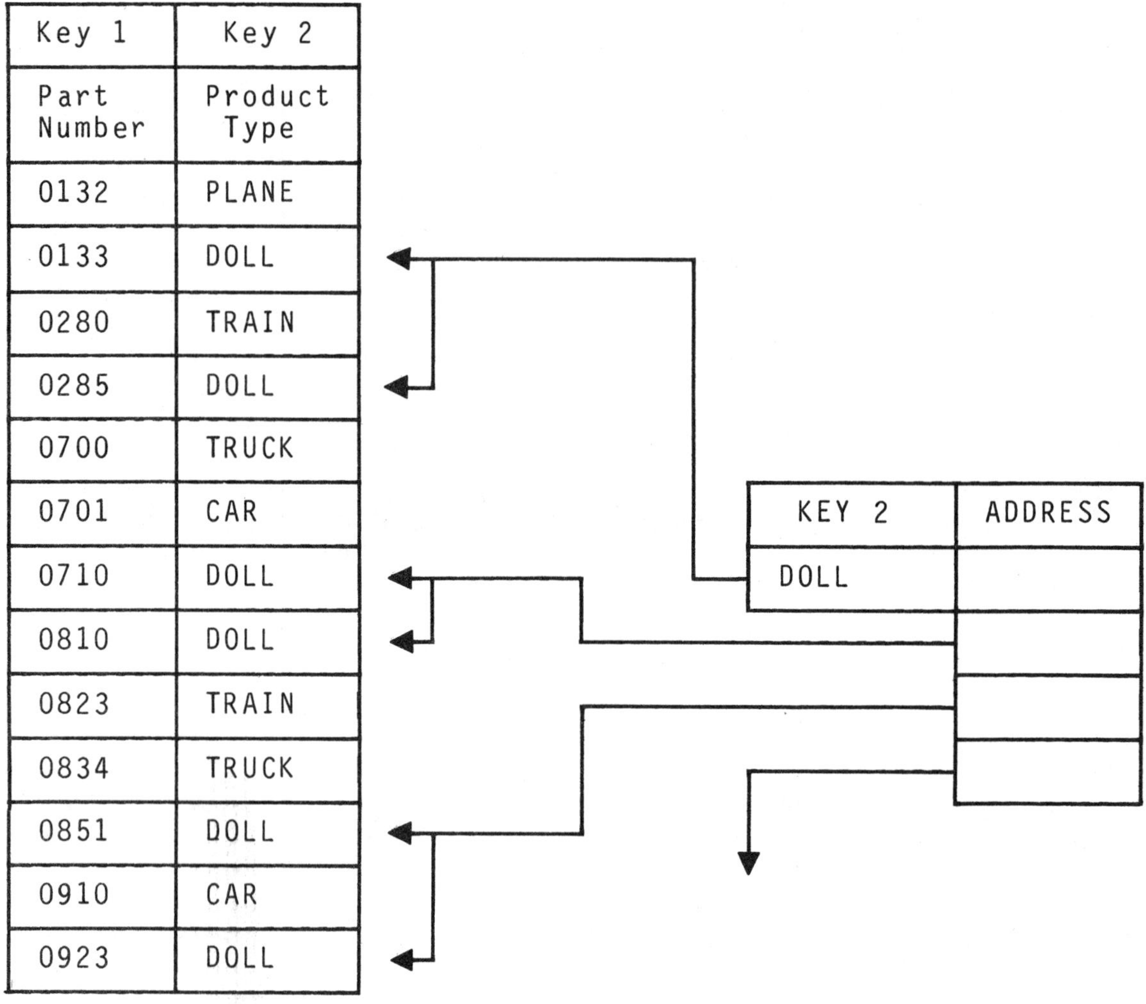

Figure 8.63

The main features include:

- The ability to define the database
- The ability to design the screen(s)
- The ability to design one or more reports
- The ability to specify processing steps
- The ability to edit and change data
- The ability to access records physically and logically.
- The ability to make data secure and private and to prevent unauthorized access
- Multilevel access (control vs input operations)
- Provides for backup and recovery
- Provides integration—functional and physical

And, increasingly, you will find the database management systems to be integrated with other functions, notably spreadsheet, word processing, graphics, and communications. And, you will find that the data-

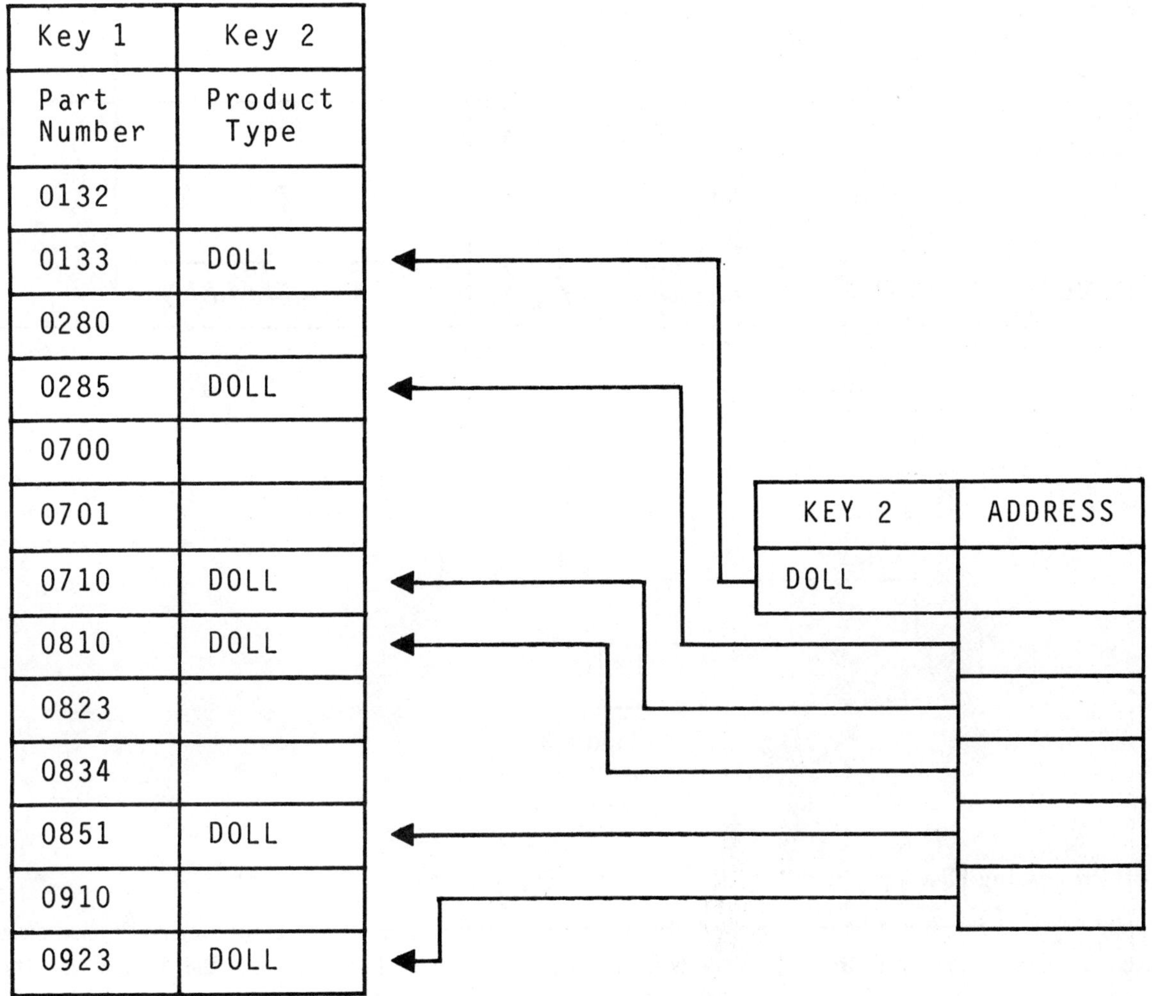

Figure 8.64

base is an integral part of these integrated packages, available for some time on microcomputers and appearing more and more on mainframe systems. Figure 8.68a is an example of the kind of work, integrated around the database, available in these systems.

Will there be more than one record within each of the categories? Certainly. That should be immediately obvious, as a word processing document will have many. More database references, more spreadsheet references, more of just about everything—tied together with macros.

DECISION SUPPORT SYSTEMS

In the 1985 CDP Exam, there was more than one question which alluded to the subject of decision support systems. In this portion of this final chapter, then, we'll deal briefly with the concepts of these systems. As a minimum, decision support systems include a word processing capability, a database capability, a spreadsheet capability, and a modeling capability. We have already dealt with the subject of database under that heading. We'll now fill in the blanks.

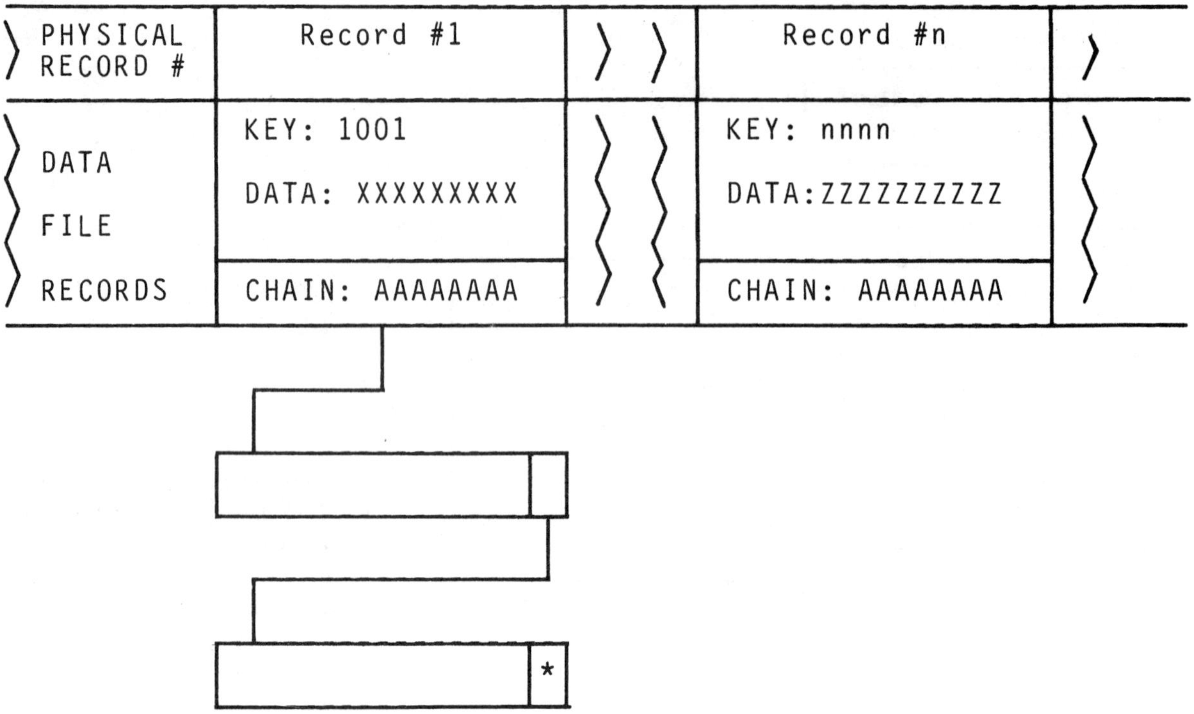

PHYSICAL RECORD #	Record #1	Record #n
DATA FILE RECORDS	KEY: 1001 DATA: XXXXXXXXX	KEY: nnnn DATA:ZZZZZZZZZZ
	CHAIN: AAAAAAAA	CHAIN: AAAAAAAA

*

Figure 8.65

Word Processing

Word Processing History

No doubt some computer historian will be able to pinpoint the origins of the computerized processing of words. My first exposure to the concept was in the service in the early 1960s, and the device was known as the Friden Flexowriter. In concept, this device was essentially an output device used for what we now call "power typing." To use the Flexowriter, it was necessary to punch a paper tape using one of the then prevalent paper tape coding structures. This tape was then fashioned into an endless loop and the device was used to produce repetitive letters, stopping only long enough to allow the human operator to enter a name and address. My recollection is that the device was also used in a large number of insurance companies.

As the computer age went under full steam, IBM devised a method to produce magnetic tape on either a selectric typewriter on by encoding the tape on a computer, and the power typing function was performed by the Magnetic Tape Selectric Typewriter (MTST), again, pausing only long enough for human intervention. That would be followed by a device called the MCST (for Magnetic Card Selectric Typewriter), and by this time the concept of magnetic storage of words, canned paragraphs, and a limited set of letters was born.

Next came the microcomputer chip and we were storing words and processes on cassette tapes and finally upon 8″ diskettes. Early names in vogue for such devices were Wang, CPT, Redactron, XEROX, Linolex, 3M, Entrex, and many others. The storage of processes is very important, for at this point we were able to develop procedures to combine portions of documents, or to do what we now call MAIL-MERGE, using files of customer names and addresses for combination with letters. Again, the concept was power typing, and letters were produced, saved, massaged, merged, extracted. In fact, "the processed word" became a concept which was the harbinger of office revolution yet to come. The seeds of what has become known as integrated office automation were sown. While memory typewriters and elec-

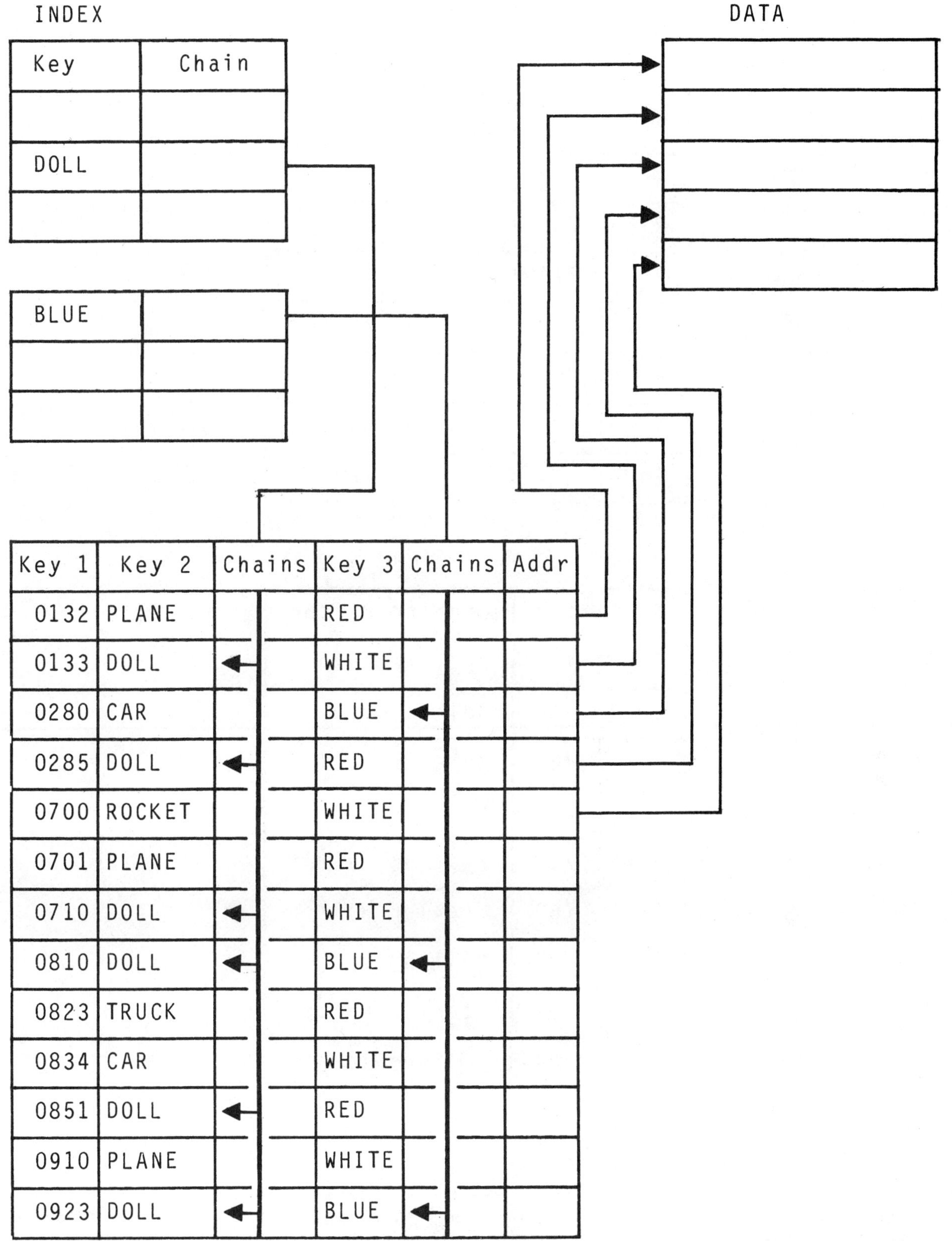
INDEX
Key
Chain
DOLL
BLUE
DATA
Key 1
Key 2
Chains
Key 3
Chains
Addr
0132 PLANE RED
0133 DOLL WHITE
0280 CAR BLUE
0285 DOLL RED
0700 ROCKET WHITE
0701 PLANE RED
0710 DOLL WHITE
0810 DOLL BLUE
0823 TRUCK RED
0834 CAR WHITE
0851 DOLL RED
0910 PLANE WHITE
0923 DOLL BLUE

Figure 8.66

R 1	123	Statler Hilton
R 2	410	Best Western
R 3	411	Holiday Inn
R 4	420	Motel 6
R 5	700	Motel 6
R 6	714	Statler Hilton
R 7	760	Statler Hilton
R 8	800	Holiday Inn
R 9	802	Statler Hilton
R10	804	Holiday Inn

Figure 8.67

S 1	123	Statler Hilton
S 2	410	Best Western
S 3	411	Holiday Inn
S 4	420	Motel 6
S 5	700	Motel 6
S 6	714	Statler Hilton
S 7	760	Statler Hilton
S 8	800	Holiday Inn
S 9	802	Statler Hilton
S10	804	Holiday Inn

Figure 8.68

tronic typewriters have come along with the revolution, the real advances have been made using the personal computer, the microcomputer dressed up in the guise of a "do everything" machine. The personal computer gave us the ability to use the device for many purposes other than the processing of words. Word processing became just one of the many functions of the personal computer—it was just another program to be run. Later versions of word processors would provide capability the folks at Friden could only have imagined in the early days.

ID # Parent Rcd	File Name of Inform.	Record Type	Comments or Look-Up Tables and References	NE XT
1001-00	ACCTING	SS	Check Register	01
1001-01	PERSONNEL	DB	Employee Records	02
1001-02	CORRESP	WP	Correspondence	03
1001-03	PERFORM	GR	Performance Graphics	04
1001-04	REPORT	COM	Weekly Reports (via MCI)	**

Figure 8.68a

The Word Processing Program

A word processing program is a computer program that turns the microcomputer into a most powerful typewriter. This powerful typewriter can not only absorb the machinations of the ten digit human interface, it can also be programmed to extract data from other sources, such as the database files we've just discussed, the spreadsheet files we are about to discuss, and to incorporate all that into a document which contains graphic representations.

As a typewriter/data entry device, it allows you to type all sorts of documents without once having to use paper. The actual preparation and shaping of the document occurs in the computer's memory and is committed to hardcopy (paper) only when the originator has ensured that it is accurate, sightly, and correct, both grammatically and syntactically. Because the text of the document is created in the computer's memory, the text of that document can easily be manipulated and refined.

Today's integrated word processing system consists of several parts. There is the editor program which allows you to develop and manipulate the document in the computer's memory. There are syntax and grammar checkers. There are spelling checkers which are an inordinate help to most of us whose spelling skills are not what they should be. There are features which will extract information from one document and include it in another. Some of the software permits footnoting, internal indices, etc. Finally, there is the program which will take that document and place it onto paper or onto the communication media. There are even features which can be used to initiate colored slides. The capabilities seem to be limited only to one's imagination. There are even programs which will allow concurrent working with two documents using a concept called ''windowing,'' wherein a part of each document is displayed in an area on the monitor screen.

The predominant advantage of being able to type directly into the computer's memory is that the text can easily be modified. Because the text is in the computer's memory instead of being printed on paper, you can overtype the text without erasing, insert new text into the middle of a document, restructure a sentence, eliminate a paragraph, etc., without making erasures or retyping pages of text.

A word processing program allows you to write your thoughts rapidly then go back and correct the spelling, sentence structure, grammar, etc. easily. Documents produced by a word processor typically look better than those produced by a typewriter. There are no typing corrections on the paper, and the formatting is typically better. A word processor can even justify the text so that the right margin is evenly aligned, instead of the ragged right margin that is typical of typed documents.

Features of the Word Processing Program

Word processing programs present an interesting design problem for programmers. Because a word processor is an attempt to create the ''ideal'' typewriter, the programmer must decide what an ''ideal'' typewriter is. The problem is that no one knows exactly what they want included in the "ideal" typewriter. The nontypist who is just starting out on a word processor has no idea of what needs to be included in the program. The typist who is just making the transition to a word processing program wants a program that is simple to learn and closely simulates the functions of a typewriter.

After using a word processor for a while, each user has different requirements. Technical writers want a word processor that can use mathematical symbols. Some users want a word processor that allows the use of graphic symbols within the body of the text. Still other users want to do multi-column text so that the resulting document looks like a newspaper or a magazine article. Still other users find spelling checking support programs, grammar-checking programs, and form letter programs essential.

Typically, word processing users go through a cycle. When first beginning to use a word processor, users are awed by the variety of features in the word processing program. Most beginning word processing users request a simple program. They want to minimize the number of commands to be used and memorized. Some users are content with a simple word processor because they seldom use the word processor and desire to get the job done with a minimum of effort. Such word processors as QWERTY and Bank Street Writer have provided such capability. Of course there are things that neither can do—but there are also people who don't need those features. However, most users quickly master the features incorporated in a simple word processing program and demand even more features and flexibility. That, in turn, raises the demand for word processing systems.

More Features of the Word Processing Program

A good word processing system incorporates at least these features:

- Insert, replace, and delete text anywhere you want.
- Search for a piece text and replace it with other text.
- Move and copy blocks of text from one place to another, in the document you're working on or in another document.
- Set margins and tabs, reformat and justify paragraphs.
- Underlined and boldface text using font characters.
- Print your text in pages with headers and footers.
- Search and replace with "wild card" match characters.
- Very fast operation lets you edit efficiently.

Of course, there are many advantages to using a word processor from an integrated package. Most important, however, is the fact that the incorporation of features leaves many of the operations common to the balance of the package. Do some word processors have fewer capabilities? Yes. Are there some word processors with more powerful features? Yes. Among the more important features (advantages) of an integrated program are:

- *In-memory operation.* The word processor should use the computer's Random Access Memory (RAM) to store text while you are creating, editing, or printing a document. Because of this, the document size cannot exceed the size of the computer's memory. If the document is larger than memory, the document must be broken down into several sections, like chapters in a book. This concept differs from other word processors which will parcel documents in and out of memory as needed.
  Some word processing programs use both RAM memory and a disk file in combination. This disk file and memory combination provides the advantage of allowing continuous typing of very large documents, but these file oriented word processing programs are much slower in operation as a consequence of dependence on disk operations that are much slower than memory operations.

Although both types of systems have their advantages, the memory based word processors are more than adequate for most documents and the speed of total memory based operation makes the programs much more pleasant to use.

- *Instant help.* One of the nicest features of today's word processor program is the quick and easily available help screens. Normally, a function key will always get you to the help screen while you are editing a document. The help screen appears instantly, and are fairly complete. After a brief period of familiarization, documentation is rarely necessary. The help screens provide most of the information needed. the quickness of the help screens is a particularly nice feature. You can hardly judge the time between pressing the help key and the appearance of the help screen. If you have experience with disk based word processors that typically take a couple of seconds to bring up a help screen you will appreciate the advantage of an instant help screen.
- *Tailorability.* Most word processing programs are judged by their completeness and their support of a wide variety of printers and printer features, using a variety of installation procedures.
- *Professional programming.* Look for a word processor that is a truly professional program. The program is as "Bug Free" as the highest quality commercial grade programs, and it is designed to be as "user friendly" as is possible for a complex program.

The available packages are not without disadvantages, however:

- *Document size.* The in-memory orientation of many word processor programs can only be fully utilized with the larger memory sizes. In-memory access provides speed, and the cost of that speed should be weighed against the cost and availability of diskette storage.
- *Extensive mailmerge capabilities.* One of the major uses for a word processor is the automatic creation of the same letter or document addressed and modified for each person in a group. The mailmerge function is particularly useful in the corporate environment where mass produced letters can be frequently used. The program provides for the creation of standard letters and for creation of operator entry to fill in the names, addresses, etc. However, most word processing packages do not provide a mechanism for creating a file with a list of addressees and the automatic creation of letters based on the names contained in the address file. The limitations of the mailmerge program may not seem important when you first start using a word processor, but the need for the mass mailing capability often becomes apparent and necessary after some word processing familiarity is acquired.

Common Features of a Word Processor

Most word processing programs include basically the same features. How the individual word processing program implements these features is specific to the program being used. Most of these features are inherent to a quality word processor.

Insertion

The insertion feature allows the operator to type into the middle of text. Because the text is not being typed directly onto paper, but is instead being typed into the computer's memory, the computer is able to move the text around. The insertion feature allows you to move the cursor to any point in the text and add new text. The preexisting text that follows is automatically moved downward in the document. The insertion feature is extremely useful. It allows you to add new new paragraph, line, or word without retyping the whole document.

Deletion

The deletion feature is much more than just an eraser. It allows the elimination of a character, word, sentence, or paragraph from text without leaving a hole in its place. When using a word processor, each time a character is deleted, the text that follows the character is automatically relocated so as to fill up the gap left by the elimination of the character. When using a typewriter, you could eliminate a character using an eraser or a "whiteout" cover-up. However, the text that followed the eliminated character would remain in exactly the same place.

The combination of insertion and deletion capabilities provides tremendous convenience for users who are creating original text (like this manuscript) on the computer. Writers find their productivity greatly increased because they can change the text instantly, without crossing out or retyping the text. Typists find these features convenient, because errors can be corrected without impacting the appearance of a document or retyping a page. Many typists increase their typing speed twofold because they are less concerned about making errors.

Search and Replace

Word processing programs normally contain features to search for the occurrences of words. For instance, you could tell a word processor to search for every occurrence of the word "Environment" in a long document. This feature is often used to locate points that need alternation in the text.

An extension of the same feature is the REPLACE function. For instance, the word "Enviornment" (as appears in this sentence) is misspelled. By using the REPLACE feature of a word processor, the misspelled word could be replaced by "Environment" throughout the text of the document.

Reformatting

Reformatting of text is one of the most important and powerful features of a word processing program. The user can change the margins and style of presentation at will. Because the text of the document is contained in the memory of the computer, it can be restructured at will. You can print a document, decide that the appearance is inappropriate, change the margins, and reprint the document, without retyping the text.

Blocking Text

The blocking of text is a major function in word processing. Blocking is the process of marking a segment of the text within a document for purposes of moving, copying, deleting, saving to a separate file, etc.

Blocking involves marking the initial character of the text that is to be marked and then marking the ending character of the marked segment of the text. The computer program will then highlight (mark) the text between these two points. Blocking is important because it is a way to tell the computer that just one segment of the text is to be worked upon. It is the equivalent of using a felt marker to highlight a segment of a document that had been printed on paper.

Once a segment of text has been highlighted, most word processors have features that allow the highlighted segment of the text to be worked on by the computer. Movement of the highlighted segment to another location in the text is achieved by moving the cursor to the point in the document that you would like the first character to begin. Once you have positioned the cursor, the word processor will have a command that causes the highlighted text to be moved to the new location.

When you use the move command, the highlighted text is transferred to the new location and deleted from the old location. In a way, text movement is like using a scissors and glue (cut and paste) to cut a section of the document out, then relocate that section of the document elsewhere in the document.

Copying is another function that uses the BLOCKING function. The text that has been highlighted using the BLOCKING function can be duplicated anywhere in the document. The COPYING function operates similarly to the MOVE function. The primary difference is that the COPY function duplicates the highlighted text, whereas the MOVE function relocates the highlighted text.

Block Deletion

Getting rid of a large segment of text can be a chore when you deleting only one character at a time. the BLOCK DELETE function, normally available in a word processor, makes elimination of a paragraph or a page much easier. BLOCK DELETION is performed by first highlighting the section of the text to be deleted using the BLOCK commands and then using the BLOCK DELETE function. The segment of the text that has been highlighted is eliminated and the text that exists below the deleted section is moved upward in the document to fill in the gap caused by the deletion.

Block File Transfers

The blocking function is also used to mark a section of text to be transferred to another document. For instance, assume that you have a paragraph in one document that you would like to use in another document. When you are using a word processor, you do not have to retype the paragraph in one document that you would like to use in another document. Instead, merely bring up the first document that contains the desired paragraph, mark it, use the word processor's function to write that marked portion to a disk file, bring up the second document, and use the word processor's function to read the disk file you have created into the document. Some word processors allow you to bring up both documents simultaneously on a split screen and then simply transfer from one document to another.

Other Features

Depending upon whose word processor you use, there are other features—character transposition, integration to a communications facility, the ability to insert graphics with text, the ability to pass data from a document to a file and vice-versa or from a spreadsheet to the document and back. Some of the packages use a "pop-up" window concept. The use of color distinguishes a few. Some have scientific capabilities. Some have multi-lingual capabilities.

Page-Oriented Word Processors

Page-oriented word processors are programs which operate on a single page of text at a time. These word processors create documents on the screen and those documents are exactly like the documents that will be printed. Each page is treated as a separate document. Each page is formatted exactly as it will be printed. Each page is stored to disk before a new page is started. In some ways, the page-oriented word processors are easier to use than the scrolling-type word processors. When you are trying to precisely format the appearance of the page, these page-oriented word processors allow you to easily determine the appearance of the page. You can precisely position the place on the page where text will begin and end. You can prepare signature blocks that fall on a precise position on the page, because the page will be printed exactly as it appears on the screen. In these page-oriented word processing packages, the pages are stored on the diskette (or other storage media) after each page. If the computer stops operating for any reason, (e.g., a power failure) the only part of the document that may be lost is the last page you are working on. It should also be stated that the software is programmed to provide the "saving services" automatically.

Page-oriented word processors have other advantages. The repositioning of text to other page locations is typically quite easy. Page 1 can easily be reassigned to become page 14. This is a particularly nice feature when you are creating a long document where you would like to resequence the document (e.g., making Chapter 1 into Chapter 2, etc.).

Just as page-orientation has advantages, it has complementary disadvantages. The page-oriented word processors typically have slower operating characteristics. They are forced to store the document to diskette after each page. This continual accessing of the disk drive can be distracting and annoying to the operator. Ask a professional writer (me).

Another disadvantage is the continual need for the operator to be concerned with page format. Typically, the page-oriented word processors require the operator to determine the end of page point and press a key in order to advance to the next page. Because some documents do not require precise page formatting, the page-orientation causes unnecessary complexity.

Perhaps the most outstanding disadvantage of the page-oriented word processor is need to continually worry about reformatting when inserting text into the middle of a long document. It would be like trying to insert a paragraph into the center of a typical typewritten page of text. If you inserted a paragraph, it would make the text too long to fit on to a single sheet of paper. The page-oriented word processing programs solve this problem by giving you document reformatting functions. This causes text to be moved from one page to the next page automatically. The function places text from one page on the next page and then checks the number of lines on the new page. If there are too many lines on that page, it takes lines off of the bottom of that page and move them to the next. . . . This process continues until the end of the document is reached. The text-moving process takes time, and destroys the precise layout of the pages that follow.

Scroll-Oriented Word Processors

Scroll-oriented word processors deal with the entire document as a single entity. Imagine that the computer is working with a scroll of paper instead of a group of individual pages of text. The text is written continuously on the scroll and no effort is made to change sheets of paper. This concept is easier to implement on a computer than the concept of individual sheets of paper. When insertions are made into the middle of the text, the information following insertion is merely moved down in the scroll. In the page-oriented word processor, each page must be treated individually. Insertions into the middle of a document require reformatting of all of the pages which follow the inserted text.

In the scroll-oriented word processors, the page printing segment of the program is more complex than the printing function in a page-oriented word processor. The scroll must be divided into individual pages by the printing program. This requires program to count the number of lines printed and insert top and bottom margins at the appropriate time.

One of the tricks for advanced use of a scroll-based word processor is to insert page breaks at appropriate points where precise formatting is required. These page break points cause the printer to eject the remainder of the page and start a new page immediately following the paper break. By inserting a page break, you can achieve precisely formatted pages. Because you know the position of the beginning of the page, you can count the number of lines which occur before entering text that must be precisely positioned. For instance, it might be important to have ten lines of continuous text area for insertion of an illustration. By insertion of a page break and leaving 10 lines at the beginning of the next page, you can be sure that the ten lines will not be interrupted by another page break. In spite of any reformatting required to accomodate inserted text, these ten lines will always be located at the beginning of a page.

Insert and Overstrike Modes

There are two insertion modes—the *insert mode* and the *overstrike mode.* The insert mode is frequently referred to as the ''Pushright'' mode. This mode allows the insertion of text into the middle of the document. All of the text to the right of the cursor is moved down and the new text is inserted before the text that follows. Without pressing the carriage return ([ENTER] key), the program will automatically cut the text into lines of the proper length to fit into the margins that are set. The margins can be set at a width of typically up to 240 characters. Why would anyone want text that wide? You'd have to use a program like one of those which will print the document lengthwise on continuous paper—or you may have as your object a typesetting operation.

In the overstrike mode, the word processing program replaces the existing text with the new text that you type. If you type into the middle of the text while in the overstrike mode, you will replace one character of the existing text for each character that you type. The overstrike mode has one other unusual feature. When in the overstrike mode, the word processor typically ignores the right margin and allows you to type up to 240 continuous characters on a line despite the margin settings.

Wordwrap

When in the insert mode, it is not necessary to press the [ENTER] key at the end of each line. The word processor will cut the long line of text that you type into appropriate segments to fit within the set margins. When you have typed too many characters to fit within the margin, the word processor will move the last word of the line down to the next line and continue inserting from that point. The operation works quickly and the words look as if they fairly jump. Text that is entered while in the overstrike mode can be reformated to comply with the current format by pressing a combination of keys or a function key. Ragged or justified edges will result.

Starting New Paragraphs

New paragraphs can be inserted by any of four techniques:

- By pressing the [ENTER] key
- By leaving one or more blank lines in the text (pressing the down arrow key then continuing text entry)
- By creating a format line in the middle of the text
- By inserting a page break into the document

Different word processing systems treat the end of a paragraph differently. Most insert a special character to indicate the end of a paragraph. When in the right-justify mode, most will not insert spaces in the last line of a paragraph in order to try to make the last character in the line align to the right margin.

Indented Text

There are many occasions when it is necessary to temporarily indent the left margin to highlight text of special significance. This is accomplished easily in most systems by pressing an indentation or tab key. Some indentation keys will cause a special symbol to appear on the screen (often a right arrow). This has the effect of moving the left margin to the right of its normal position until the next hard carriage return is encountered.

Hard Spaces

Hard spacing is an important consideration for advanced word processing system users. In the process of right-justifying text, the processor will typically place multiple spaces between words. This results in a a document in which the right margin always ends with the last character of the last word on each line, perfectly aligned with the right margin. However, there are occasions where it is not appropriate to have more than one space between words. Likewise, there are occasions where you do not want words split up at the end of a line. For instance, you might want the title "Gone With The Wind" to appear uninterrupted on one line. These goals can be accomplished by inserting hard spaces instead of normal spaces between words. These hard spaces are interpreted as though they were normal alphabet characters so the word is connected to the next word as though it was one continuous word. Hard spacing can be accomplished by different methods in various systems.

Blocking Text

Text blocking is an important concept in word processing. Blocking is the process of marking text which will be used for other actions. If you were working with regular paper, blocking would be equivalent to marking text. For instance, you might use a highlighter to mark a segment of your text for some activity when your secretary retyped the document. Blocking likewise highlights an area of text on most processors. For instance, you might block (highlight) a segment of the text to be moved to another area of the text. Another use is for erasure of text. You may wish to highlight an area of text that is to be erased.

Several of the commands incorporate this blocking function. These commands include:

- Copy. The blocking function allows you to mark the area that is to be copied.
- Move. The blocking function allows you to mark the area to be moved.
- Erase. The blocking function allows you to mark the area to be erased.

The blocking function has several features that increase its utility. These features apply to all of the commands that use the blocking function. When the function asks for "from what block," you will be able to use these features.

- Unanchor. The starting point of the block will automatically come up anchored to the current cursor position. However, you may not want to start the area to be highlighted at the current cursor position. To unanchor the starting point in the block, press a designated key.
- Anchor. Once you have unanchored the cursor, the function of reanchoring the cursor can be accomplished using the designated key.

One Key Commands

Many of the word processing systems have commands have been implemented as function keys. These commands will automatically be available. Otherwise these keys will have other functions when you are positioned at other types of windows. These one-key commands can be supplemented by other one-key commands based on macro programming. Normally these macro-based one-key commands will involve implementation of some of the menu functions so that they will be accessible using one keystroke.

Standard Wording

Still another function you may wish to provide in your master document creation worksheet is a series of standard phrases to be used, depending upon the situation. These are commonly called "boilerplate." This particular function can save you a tremendous amount of time. If you typically use the phase "Our customers are our primary concern," you could establish a special two key sequence to make the phrase easily available.

The function of auto-typing standard phrases can be extended to the use of paragraphs (more "boilerplate") which can be combined according to the unique requirements of the item of correspondence. If much of your correspondence uses similar content, you can create a paragraph book of these phrases. This helps the person who does the correspondence use dictation that assists the secretary doing the typing. The dictator then can use the title of the paragraph instead of dictating the whole paragraph. The typist has only to call the titled paragraph into the document with a few keystrokes. This procedure saves both time and mistakes.

Using Two Documents

One of the easiest ways to use standard paragraphs is to use two document windows. Some of the available systems permit this capability. The idea is to place the new document in the first window and the standard text can be stored in the second document window. By using the copy command or a macro that accomplishes the same function, you can make quick transfers of text from the second document into the first.

Integration

One of the major attributes of the more sophisticated word processors is the ability to use the spreadsheet's capabilities within the confines of a document. Generally, you must perform your spreadsheet functions in the spreadsheet environment. The integration extends to graphics, communications, and database, as well.

Creating Batch Letters

One of the most productive uses for a word processor is the function of batch letters. Properly used, the batch letter function can be a highly productive function that can change the way you run your business or personal life. The batch letter function involves the combination of the functions of data basing and the function of document creation. The word processing document becomes a part of the output format for the data base. For each name and address in a name and address data base, a separate letter or memo is created. The utility of this function will be realized only as you use it and incorporate it into your daily work methodology.

For instance, you may use the batch letter function to send memos to all salesmen in a division. You might likewise use it to send letters to all customers who are sixty days delinquent on accounts receivable. You could also use it for sending newsletters individualized to all of your friends. attorneys could use this function to send greetings to each of their clients who have a birthday or anniversary during the current month. The list of applications is limited only by your imagination.

Creating a batch letter involves the creation of a letter in which spreadsheet lines can be substituted for word processing text. Rather than switching back and forth between the document mode and spreadsheet mode, it is normally more convenient to create the entire batch document in the document mode then insert the necessary spreadsheet functions into the document. To do this you need to get into the habit of creating documents that are designed for easy substitution by spreadsheet cells.

The Electronic Spreadsheet

It could be said that the face which launched a thousand ships for microcomputers was the electronic worksheet, what we have come to call the spreadsheet. When we consider the history of computing, it is a marvel that such a tools was never developed in the mainframe world. We certainly had all the horsepower needed to do so. What we did not have, however, was the concept of a spreadsheet on every manager's desk, for the terminals of yesteryear were largely data-entry, and not management presentation, devices.

Though he may never every gain the accolades and the wealth, credit for the concept of the electronic spreadsheet must go to Delbert S. Jones, Jr., then operating an organization known as the Bottom Shelf, for his 1978 TRS-80 program, Analysis Pad. Somewhat ahead of his time, Del produced, for market, a rudimentary spreadsheet program which was distributed on a TRS-80 cassette tape. From that point, whether building upon his work or on original thought, two entrepreneurs—Bricklin and Frankston—went on to develop VisiCalc. Success brought others with better products into the marketplace, and Lotus 1-2-3 has, as of this writing, maintained its dominance of the spreadsheet market. Further, it has just been announced that VisiCalc has been withdrawn from the marketplace. Time marches on.

Years ago there was a popular toy which, which while it is still around, can hardly compete with Barbie and Ken (Mattel dolls), or the microcomputer. That toy was called a magic slate (my apologies to anyone who may hold the copyright for that device). The magic slate consisted of a cardboard-backed, paraffin-covered slate, covered by a sheet of acetate. One caused impressions to appear on the acetate by "writing" upon it with a wooden stylus. The stylus would cause an image to be inscribed directly through the acetate onto the paraffin. To "erase" the slate, one had only to lift the acetate away from the paraffin base, and begin again. In essence, the electronic spreadsheet works precisely the same way. It can be thought of as a tapestry of calculations. In much the same manner as you would perform calculations of a tabulation nature (add a list of figures), or develop a worksheet matrix, the spreadsheet can be established to perform any form of calculation desired, can be "cleaned" like the magic slate, and can perform again. And it does so at lightning speed, allowing for the hardcopy production of your work.

While in its execution, the spreadsheet still fits the concept of the accounting analysis pad, at the same time, it has given rise to a concept called the information expression. The coordinates which form the rows and columns of a spreadsheet are called "cells." A cell is comparable to an array element. Naturally, an array or matrix provides the location whereby cells are manipulated. And, by design, one array would contain the data while a second array would contain your directions (the information expression) for using the data. The program, then, would map the latter over the former when performing calculations.

In most spreadsheets, the entire cell is highlighted in reverse video in what is commonly called a "cell cursor" or "cell pointer." In these cells will be placed the titles that provide reference and the references to variable data and constant data that will be operational values assigned to a covering pattern of formulas and the directions (the information expression). The programmer calls the entire package an expression, an expression that consists of those variable and constant data and which must be resolved to provide a useful solution. The information expression is a formula, applied to a single cell, designed to manipulate data located there or in concert with other cells.

When speaking of spreadsheets it is hard not to use the phrase "What if . . . ?". The electronic spreadsheet allows you to look at data in several different ways. The businessperson might ask the question "What if we hired 10 more workers?" With the spreadsheet, wages can be extended, taxes can be calculated, and contributions to profit can be ascertained. After knowing the answer to that question you might ask "What would be the effect on the company if instead of hiring 10 new workers we were to hire 20?" With a spreadsheet you can make one change and nearly instantly obtain a new answer to the revised question. With paper and pencil it could well take 30 minutes. While it is often thought that spreadsheets are restricted to dealing with dollars, any relationship that involves numbers can make use of a spreadsheet.

Spreadsheet Basics

Let's look at the concepts of the computerized worksheet. To do so, we should concentrate upon:

- Appearance of the worksheet
- Movement around the worksheet
- Entry of data to a cell
- Commands and their usage
- Entry of formulae

- Development of Macros
- Use of Ranges

Worksheet Appearance

Were you to purchase a pad of analysis paper, you would no doubt obtain paper of either a notebook size or an extended format, generally with 25 rows and with up to 20 or so columns. If it were necessary to have more rows or columns that information would have to be extended to other forms. Often the forms were taped together, and the whole process became somewhat unwieldy.

With the electronic worksheet you do not have that limitation. If you need more columns than the screen allows, you simply move to the right of the screen and keep moving right. If you need more rows than the screen allows, you simply move to the bottom of the screen and keep moving downward. In fact, the size of the spreadsheet will depend upon the available memory installed in the computer, and the design point of the software program. Some spreadsheets programs are written for low memory computers, and therefore must be limited in their numbers of rows columns.

Movement

Most worksheet programs will provide the ability to move around within the worksheet itself. Most generally the movement attributes are a function of the package's design. In general, however, you'll find that movement amongst the cells is accomplished by the cursor (arrow) keys.

From that point, they may differ. But even while the mechanics of operation differ, the concept is precisely the same. The purpose of the GoTo function is to move directly to a specific line and column. On the surface that might not seem like much, and while you're on the same screen, it isn't. However, the screen as you see it is simply a window (the logical spreadsheet—that portion you can see) upon the entire spreadsheet (the physical spreadsheet). The logical spreadsheet is frequently called the ''active area.'' The concept is not dissimilar to reading the newspaper through a magnifying glass. So the GoTo function, however it's executed, can be used to move you from your present location to somewhere off the logical spreadsheet to elsewhere on the physical spreadsheet. Should you do this a row or column at a time, the process could become very lengthy, as with the emergence of each new row or column, the spreadsheet would be repositioned. And that can become time consuming.

Another movement feature of the spreadsheet package will be the ability to move right or left, up or down, in increments of one logical screen. This will be accomplished, generally, by the PgUp, PgDn, Ctrl, or Alt keys, either alone or in combination with the cursor keys. Those are IBM PC keys; other machines and terminals have similar functions.

Yet another pair of movements is accomplished by the Home and End keys. The Home key will move the cell cursor to the upper left corner of the logical spreadsheet. The End key will move the cell cursor to the lower right corner of the logical spreadsheet. Used with another key, each may move to the very beginning or the very end of the spreadsheet.

There is also the ability to simply pick up data and move it or copy it to another cell, a feature which is particularly useful when building macros to handle data which has been ''imported'' from other packages in other formats.

Cell Entry

Data is entered to a cell by one of four methods:

- Keyboard entry
- Copy or Move data from another cell

- Loading data from a disk file.
- Via communication from another option directly into the worksheet.

Two sorts of data may be entered from the keyboard—alphabetic data and numeric data. A cell may be declared as alphabetic or as numeric. Generally the alphabetic is used for titles, frames, and the like. There is often the opportunity to identify that data as left-justified, right-justified, or centered. That alphabetic data will customarily be loaded to the location of the cell cursor.

Loading the table from a file is another important feature. Many of the commercially used spreadsheets use the Data Interchange Format (DIF). This format is one which was designed by the designers of VisiCalc and has found somewhat universal acceptance amongst other software producers of not only spreadsheets, but word processors and graphics programs. Naturally no spreadsheet file can be loaded which has not first been saved by either the spreadsheet or by another software package.

Commands

Every spreadsheet has a series of commands, which can either be used dynamically or can be batched to form a sort of procedure for operating upon the data. In VisiCalc and Lotus 1-2-3, for example, it is not unusual for a command to begin with a special character, such as a slash (/) or a commercial at sign (@). Command-line functions are the functions available to the operator to modify, create, or work with the templates used in the spreadsheet environment.

Formulas

The raison d'etre for the spreadsheet is the calculation process. The formula methods for all spreadsheets are algebraic, with all the rules of algebra. Requirements for the formula will be operands, operations, and results. It will be necessary to specify the spreadsheet row and column as an operand. Often, because the result will be located in the same location as one of the operands on the spreadsheet (such as if you were adding a value to an accumulator), it will be necessary that the location where the answer is to be located be specified first. Naturally all the algebraic calculation symbols may be used. A good spreadsheet also includes function operations, such as @SUM, @AVG, etc., as well as the logical operators #AND#, #OR#, and #NOT#.

Formulas are used to create the spreadsheet template. The formulas use functions that are common to most users who are familiar with algebra. In addition, the formulas allow the creation of functions that work with "Strings." These formulas can incorporate the use of nonnumeric data in a programmed manner.

The extended formula functions involve the use of a special group of operators that either simplify formula creation or extend the number of operators available to the user. These extended formula functions are typically referred to as @ functions.

Macros and Ranges

The more sophisticated spreadsheet packages provide the ability to work within ranges of the spreadsheet and to develop keyboard macros which which may be used over and over, as you have already learned previously in this book. The range concept has to do with the spreadsheet's ability to identify subordinate portions by the assignment of names, to calculate within that specific range, and to perform a number of services upon that range along within the spreadsheet. This is frequently used where the spreadsheet is developed as an entity, but is subdivided. The macro concept is where a good spreadsheet's tremendous power lies. A macro will be a command, function, or formula that can either be generated by the touch of one or two keyboard keys or incorporated into macro programs. Macros are commonly used to save repetitive typing.

Entry Systems

One of the major problems with spreadsheet programming is the high level of operator understanding needed just to do simple data entry. The high level of knowledge needed for entry of data often results in managers and higher level employees doing data entry themselves instead of delegating the task to less highly qualified and less expensive personnel. In most cases, the person that programs the spreadsheet performs the task of data entry instead of letting a secretary or clerk do the job.

Input entry screen features will eliminate this problem. The person that designs the spreadsheet template will also create screens that prompt the operator on how to do data entry. These data entry screens will take entry from the operator and transfer the data to the proper locations in the spreadsheet. The operator need not be concerned with the spreadsheet only. Very limited computer knowledge will be needed for data entry to these entry screens.

Multiple Spreadsheet Programming

Many spreadsheet applications are three dimensional in nature. For instance, the nurse at a doctor's office might fill in a daily patient report using a spreadsheet. At the end of the month, a summary of each day's patient activity would be another spreadsheet application. The summary report would be three dimensional in nature because it draws from other daily reports. Other spreadsheets require manual transfer of selected information in order to assemble a summary report. However, the more sophisticated spreadsheets provide features that allow programming of multiple spreadsheet functions so the task could be done automatically.

Enhanced "IF" Processing

The ''IF'' function provided by most spreadsheets is rather rudimentary. The function provides the capability to do different calculations in different circumstances. For instance, you might want to perform a different function when negative numbers were entered to a cell in the spreadsheet, than if positive numbers were entered. Some of today's spreadsheets only allow for one or two ''IF'' functions per formula. A good spreadsheets allow many different functions to be performed based on a wide variety of circumstances. The mechanism most favored for expanded ''IF'' processing is tabled procedures.

Table Lookup of Procedures

Many spreadsheets allow the creation of data look up tables. Based on the information contained in one column, the table function will return the information contained in another column. This feature has been greatly enhanced in more recent spreadsheets. Tabled procedures will allow inexperienced users to construct very advanced spreadsheet applications.

Multilevel Tables

Most spreadsheets allow reference to two dimensional tables. An example of a two dimensional table is a mileage look up table. You look up one of the cities on the side of the table and look up the other city across the top of the table. The mileage between the two cities is positioned where the two lines intersect.

Spreadsheet Report Generators

One of the less advanced sections of spreadsheet programming until recently has been the reporting capability. The spreadsheet template has been designed in the eventual report format instead of the most functional model format. The layout of the spreadsheet template is the only report format available. With macros, recent spreadsheets give us the nearest thing to report generators which are capable of organizing the information contained in the spreadsheets for numerous types of reports.

Range Processing Reporting

A common function typically incorporated in computer programming languages is looping. The For/Next loop function allows repetition of a function or group of functions for a specified number of cycles or until a condition changes. the spreadsheet, again using macros, incorporates this function. Looping will allow automatic creation of a range of reports. For instance, a range of budget reports could be generated to show a range of salary increases from 5% to 10%. Looping will make spreadsheet programming more versatile. When looping is incorporated into spreadsheet programs, many applications that can only be accomplished today using a custom program, will be accomplished using spreadsheets.

Relative and Absolute Addressing—and the Copy Command

Of particular importance is the understanding of the differences between relative and absolute addressing. When the original formulas are copied to the destination address they will be modified to perform the same operation in different locations. For instance, the formula +C1+(C1*D1) might be copied to a series of cells below it. The copied formulas would change to reflect their new positions.

There are some instances where it will be desired for the references not to change. It could be that you would want at least a portion of the formula to maintain an absolute address. To accomplish this function, the location reference must be an absolute addressing reference. Absolute addressing involves the use of the "$" symbol to specify portions of a location that are not to be modified, as follows:

- The completely absolute address. Coded as $C$1, the dollar sign pins down both the column (C) and the row (1). This example will refer to only one cell—cell C1.
- The absolute column. Coded as $C1, the dollar sign now pins down the column only, but allows the copy command to modify the row number.
- The absolute row. Coded as C$1, the dollar sign pins down the row only, but allows the copy command to modify the column.

The Move Command

The move command works precisely as the copy command, except that after the copy has been accomplished, the original cells are erased.

The Erase Command

The erase command will be frequently used. It clears the contents of a range of cells. The screen highlighting feature may be used to designate the area to be erased, enter a range by typing it, or by entering a preassigned range name. If you want to erase the current cell quickly and conveniently. To make the programming function easier, you may wish to create a macro in your spreadsheet.

The Insert Command

The insert command is accessed from the spreadsheet menu by pressing a designated key. Accessing the insert command will cause the a secondary submenu. The insert submenu provides the choice of inserting columns, rows, or making global insertions, as follows:

- Columns will insert a column within the restrictions of the window in which you are currently operating.

- Rows will insert rows within the restrictions of the window in which you are operating.
- Global is different. It is not bound by the restrictions of the window. The global command will give you the option of inserting columns or rows throughout the worksheet. The addition of a column or row will affect all other segments of the worksheet.

A good spreadsheet will automatically adjust all formulas throughout the worksheet to reflect the changes caused by the insert command. Important point: both absolute and relative addresses will be modified to reflect the change caused by inserting a row or column.

The Delete Command

The delete command is similar to the insert command, except that it is used to eliminate columns or rows rather than add. The delete command also has a global command. Like the global function used with the insert command, the global function of the delete command should be used with caution, because it can have a major effect upon other portions of the worksheet outside of the window within which you are operating.

The Width Command

The width command is used to adjust the column width from the default (9 characters) to another count more suited to the needs of the worksheet.

The Format Command

The format command lets you choose numeric display formats. It offers a wide variety of choices for display of the numbers. You may choose currency, date, time, percent and other ways of displaying the numbers. The format command also provides a procedure for hiding the contents of a cell or a range of cells. This allows you to create portions of the spreadsheet that are invisible to the user.

Another feature of the format command that can prove useful is the ability to format cells so that the formula is displayed rather than the values that result from those formulas. This is particularly valuable when you are attempting to debug a template. To do this, it is first necessary to modify the width of a column within a range so that the complete formulas may be displayed, and then you may perform a printout on that section. The spreadsheet format for display of formulas can be easier to review than the normal formula printout technique.

Range Commands

The range commands provide *some* of the range functions. Other range functions are provided through other commands such as Move, Copy, Goto, etc. The range command provides a series of functions that affect ranges, such as these:

- *Range Name.* The range name function is used to create a named range, modify the name, or delete the range. The range name function is also used to create a series of range names using the range name label function. The range name label function can create a series of range names by assigning the label adjacent to a value in a spreadsheet as a range name.
  The range name table function is used to move a listing of range names to the worksheet. You are requested to provide a range (worksheet area) to be used as a place to provide a listing of the range names and locations.
- *Range Transpose.* The range transpose function is used to change the storage structure of the information contained within a range. Columns of data are converted to rows of data. Rows of data

are converted into columns of data. This function is used only to transpose data. Unlike the move or copy commands, the range transpose command does not readjust relative formulas. It is used only for data cells.

- *Range Values.* The range values function is used to copy the cell values to another section of the spreadsheet. Key point: only the *values* of the range are copied. The formulas that generated those values are not copied. This allows the spreadsheet programmer to use the values as they appeared at the time of extraction, removing them from consideration for recalculation. This would be particularly useful for extracting moving average data.
- *Range Label-Alignment.* This function adjusts the placement of label cells within the designated range. You will be requested to make a selection of Left, Center, or Right. Your selection will change the placement of all label cells within the designated range. This command has a one-time impact. If you enter labels within the range after having used this command, the labels will follow the format of the label prefix that you use or the default label prefix.
- *Range Protect.* The range protect function is used to protect an area from changes by the operator. The range protect function is integrated with the functions of Global-Protection and the Settings security function. The range protect function is used to designate which cells are to be blocked from user modification. The designation of ''allow changes'' or ''prevent changes'' will be assigned to each cell in the range. However, changes will still be allowed until Global-Protection is turned on. Even then, changes will be allowed if the Global-Protection feature is turned back off. Users will be allowed access to the Global-Protection feature to turn the protection on or off until the Settings Security function is used to assign a password to the worksheet. Once a password has been assigned using this Settings Security function, the only way that the Global-Protection function can be changed is by entry of the sheet's password. Hope you remember it!
- *Range Fill.* The range fill function is used to fill an area with a sequence of numbers. All of the cells designated will be filled with the sequence until the sequence is completed or the number of cells in the range is filled. The spreadsheet puts the start value in the upper left hand corner of the fill range and then moves cell by cell down each column of the range, adding the Step value to the previous value until either the range fills, or the Stop value is reached, whichever comes first. This same feature can be used to create tables based upon formulas. The formula can be substituted for any or all of the Start, Step, or Stop values. The values that result from these formulas will be placed in the cells, not the formula itself.
- *Range Distribution.* The range distribution function is a function that is used to analyze the contents of a range. It requires a column which indicates the values you would like to compare for, and another column to store the results of the range distribution analysis.
- *Range What-If.* The range what-if function is a complex function but extremely useful. It is used to provide a list of results based upon feeding a formula one or two series of values. The function has two options. The first option is used to provide for one list of variables being used in sequence with the formula. The second option is used when two lists of values are provided to a formula. This function is particularly useful for creating tables.

Graph

The graph function of the more sophisticated spreadsheets provides access to the Graph functions, and will not be covered in this book.

Query Commands

The query commands are used in conjunction with database areas of the integrated spreadsheet. The database has been covered extensively in this chapter. However, the query function provides some functions that are not otherwise available.

- *Query Settings.* The query settings command is used to fill in one or more database settings sheets These database settings sheets record specifications that define many of the operations you can per form with a database.
- *Query Find.* The query find command is used to highlight selected records in a database. The highlighting is based upon the selection criteria contained in the criteria range. The database records that meet the criteria are displayed as a horizontal row of cells, each cell corresponding to a field from the database record. Using up and down arrows, you may move between records that meet the criteria you have selected. The query find command does not allow you to modify, delete, or otherwise edit the records that are found. It only allows you to view the records that meet the selection criteria. To perform editing functions upon records that meet selection criteria, it is necessary to use an editing method.
- *Query Extract.* The query extract command is extremely useful to the advanced programmer. It allows you to copy selected records from a database in whole or in part to another area in the worksheet. To use this command, you must use the database settings sheet to designate an output range. The output range should contain a row of labels that contain the field names to be extracted from the database. When this command is selected, the record portions which have been identified will be copied to the output range if the record in the database meets the selection criteria you have provided.
- *Query Unique.* The query unique function operates similarly to the query extract function. However, the query unique command filters the extracts so that no duplicate records are allowed to pass through the filter. If you used this command with a one column output range, the spreadsheet can extract a complete list of all different values that occur in a field. For example, you may wish to have a list of all of the different salaries paid to employees. By performing a query unique on the database, and extracting only the salary field, you will get a resulting list of only those salaries that are different from all other salaries. The command is not foolproof; there is no guarantee that there will be no duplicate copies in the output range. The reason for the possibility of duplicates is that you may not be using the entirety of the database record in the output range. If duplicates could cause a problem, be sure to use the query unique function in place of the query extract function.
- *Query Delete.* The query delete command is used to delete groups of records that meet a selection criteria. The query delete function allows large scale deletion of records that meet specific selection criteria. This function should of course be used with caution, and having a backup copy of the data would seem to be a wise decision. The command can, however, be extremely useful. It becomes particularly useful if a date field is used in the database record. The query delete function can then be used to delete old records based upon date criteria. Some element of positive control should be used to ensure that only what you wished to have deleted was actually deleted.
- *Query Record Sort.* The query record sort is similar to the record sort function found in the FORMS window section. It uses the sort key criteria in the database settings sheet to accomplish a sort upon the entire database.
- *Query Parse.* The query parse command is used to create new database records by dividing lines of text into field entries. The query parse function will be covered in more detail in the communications section of this book.

Illustrations in this section have been drawn from *Symphony,* from Lotus Development Corporation. There is not room to identify all of Symphony's features. We've hit the spreadsheet highlights.

Decision-Making Skills

Supporting a decision with computer software and hardware is insufficient if we have no specific idea of the kinds of decisions to be made. The quality of management depends heavily upon the decisions made by those persons. A manager must evaluate alternatives and select from the available options as many of the "right" alternatives as possible. He or she is under examination. The ratio of "hits" to "misses" must weigh favorably in the direction of the hits. A constant pattern of failure disqualifies a person for management status. This is why there has been such a push over the last two decades in the fields of computers and management information systems. With information there may be power—but more specifically, there needs to be accuracy.

Decision-making is the process of evaluating alternatives and choosing from among them. There are personal decisions available, but involvement in others' personal decisions must be merely to assist evaluation of alternatives. Any involvement is at risk, and therefore the manager should concentrate upon professional decisions. These decisions are of high visibility, often offer immediate results, tend to be goal focused and directive. Prespecified and routine decisions, those policies and procedures which appear on paper are designed to provide time to the manager, to remove him or her from the more mundane aspects of day-to-day operation. Nonroutine decisions are situation oriented. Routine decisions are nonroutine decisions made as one rises in the management ranks.

Decision Processes

There are at least two types of decision processes:

- Intuitive. We often call this women's intuition. Intuitive decisions are shaped by experience. They are the result of informal processes, and general experience a low rate of success, as experience is often limited.
- Scientific. This is an observation of events which begins with the formulation of a hypothesis, the participation in experimentation, the verification of results.

Which should the manager use? Both.

Environmental Constraints

There are several constraints upon the effectiveness of a decision. Among these are where in the organization the decision is to be made. There are a number of forces that apply upon the decision, including regulatory pressures, stockholder values, market forces, and the work force.

The Decision-Making Process

Any decision process begins with an awareness of the problem. This then requires a specification of that problem, a means to distinguish the illness from the symptom. Next, the decision maker must assess the decision shaping forces, develop available alternatives, evaluate those alternatives, select and implement what is perceived to be the best alternative, and finally he or she must evaluate the process and learn from it, hopefully allowing room for mistakes.

The decision shaping forces include risk, time, quality, and quantity. The risks are financial and personal. Time is needed for evaluation vs. "spot" decisions, particularly when there are time pressures for payoff potential. The quality vs. quantity of decisions will always be the hallmark of an effective decision maker.

The Decision Problem

The first problem of any decision is the decision maker himself. There will always be the mixture of responsibility vs. accountability. Complicate that by the fact that the decision maker is always under inspection for his decision-making skill, and you can see the problem is a bit larger than anticipated.

Next comes the problem content. There is a desired to move toward the "optimum" solution. But solutions are not universal, and the world is imperfect. There are courses of action, of course, and they demand alternatives to avoid ''knee-jerk'' reactions. Often a good decision is limited by time or other resources. Payoff relationships require specificity. The better ones can be scientifically measured, can be assessed by probability tools, decision trees, and payoff matrices. And then after all that, there is the state of nature—the world/art/situation. Decision making involves the element of choice. The decider needs to know the objective environment and to be able to assess the precise vs. the imprecise relationships.

Enter The Decision Model

There would be little point to have good hardware and software for evaluating alternatives if they didn't effect the assessment desired. To properly assess, it is necessary to build a model, and there are several, such as physical models, schematic models, and mathematical models. Physical models are generally something inanimate—and this is our general concept of models. An animate model is our vision of how things are or should be, as in a photograph. Physical models are easily tested—by operation or by inference and reasoning. Schematic models depict flows and relationships. Generally, they are flexible models which may be developed to scale. Mathematical models are used to present a scientific picture. They provide simulation—''What if'' games—and that is one of the great strengths of the spreadsheet. The rules for decisions made under uncertainty have not changed, just the ease with which they are tested.

Naturally, the computer has an impact here. It can quickly test all probabilistic outcomes, provide instant feedback, and lays bare all responsibility. If desired, it can be used for continuous sampling, instantaneous feedback and analysis, projection, simulation, and sensitivity analysis.

Planning vs. Decision-Making

Some experts feel that planning is, in fact, decision-making. Others believe that decision-making is but one of the sequential steps of the planning process. Administrative processes are decision processes. Decision theory, therefore, is the modeling of the decision process and the integration of techniques, primarily quantitative in nature, into the decision model. It is preferred to be a choice from among alternatives.

The decision requires the selection of a course of action and a commitment to it. It is also one of the steps in the systematic planning process. In the final analysis, the staff must be the ones to carry out the steps which result in the decision. Factors which influence decision-making include: (1) the background bias of the individual with the decision responsibility; (2) the wresting of decisions which should rightfully be delegated to subordinates; (3) the timing of the decision; and (4) the results of previous decisions obtained via feedback.

Decision Models

The classic decision model is the three-step process suggested by Herbert Simon in *The Science of Management Decisions*:

1. Intelligence activity—searching the environment for conditions calling for a decision
2. Design activity—inventing, developing, and analyzing available courses of action
3. Choice activity—selecting a specific course of actions from those available

Of particular interest is the concept of intelligence activity. The manager must seek out the events which call for a decision. In this regard, the decision should be considered as an opportunity to influence the behavior of the organization; it is creative and innovative.

Simon also divides decisions into those which are programmed and those which are unprogrammed.

The programmed decision, associated primarily with middle management, lends itself to fixed decision rules and can be adapted to the computer. Unprogrammed decisions will continue to require human judgment.

A slightly modified decision model has been suggested by Joseph Massie in *Essentials of Management*:

1. Identify the problem.
2. Isolate the limiting factor.
3. Develop alternatives and assumptions.
4. Decide.
5. Implement (communicate, direct, control).

This listing is not unlike Peter Drucker's sequential planning steps. A comparison of Massie's and Simon's models demonstrates divergent perspectives. Massie takes a limited viewpoint of starting with a problem; Simon starts with the search for an opportunity for a decision. Unrecognized problems may have the greatest need for a decision, however, and the identification of the real problem may be the most difficult step in the entire process. Massie does introduce the concept of the limiting factor, or strategic factor. This means that the decision-maker should focus on those few factors which are critical to the success of, or significantly differentiate between, the alternatives. Massie also shows that implementation is an essential step in the decision process.

Decision Techniques

From time immemorial, man has searched for ways to make faultless decisions for future time on the basis of incomplete data. All decisions made about future time are made under uncertainty. It therefore behooves the manager to acquire the skills and tools to narrow the degree of uncertainty.

There are different kinds of decisions. Routine administrative decisions are treated within the framework of policy and procedure and can be adopted to clerical or computer processes. Operational decisions which lend themselves to one-time or nonrepetitive solution by quantitative analysis form a second decision type. Included in this category would be machine time, inventory levels, distribution activities, etc. The third type of decision is the ill-structured, complex, one-of-a-kind decision—the exception. While there are techniques to be applied, the final disposition is judgmental. Decision techniques, then, become largely synonomous with quantitative approaches or mathematical analysis. Some of these are statistical analysis, financial, mathematical, and others, including game theory, linear programming, simulation, and operations research.

Game theory was developed by John von Neumann and Oskar Morgenstern to provide a means for selecting the highest payoff strategy in a competitive situation.

Linear programming is a means to determine the optimum combination of limited resources to meet a particular objective.

Simulation is a systematic, step-by-step, trial-and-error approach to the solution of complex problems through the exercise of a mathematical model. Results of various courses of action under alternative assumptions or forecasted conditions can be compared.

Certain disadvantages of any decision technique should be recognized. The business environment is a complex one, and many of these techniques require simplifying assumptions which render their validity doubtful. Because of the doubt, and because of the math involved, quantitative solutions frequently are set aside in favor of the intuitive judgment.

Often related to decision techniques is the separate field of Operations Research (OR). The crux of OR is an application of the scientific method to the definition and solution of problem areas with emphasis on the logical analysis of the situation through the use of mathematical or symbolic models. It cannot be denied that OR and the use of quantitative techniques have improved the rationality of managerial decisions.

Modeling

Introduction to Modeling

A model is comprised of variables and objectives. The structuring of those objectives and attributes of the problem is the purpose of building the model. The trick is to know when the set of objectives and attributes is right.

The variables of a quantitative model include a mathematical description of the relationship amongst variables. These variables are categorized in this manner:

- Decision variable. This variable is controlled by the decision maker, and varies in accordance with the alternative selected.
- Intermediate variable. This links decisions to outcomes, and functions as a consolidation variable.
- Output variable. This is used to measure decision performance and is referred to an ''attribute.''

Let's illustrate that. A rancher runs his cattle using a whistle and a German shepherd. The third variable of this problem is the location in the south forty of the cattle. In this problem, the whistle is decision variable—it is controlled by the rancher (the decision maker) according to the alternative selected. The location of dog is the intermediate variable. It links the decisions to the outcomes and is a consolidation variable. The location of the cattle in the south forty is an outcome variable.

There are several types of variables. Binary variables take the value of 0 or 1 and are used for go or no-go decisions. Discrete variables are used for any of a finite number of values. Questions of ''Which'' and ''When,'' are represented as specific discreet values. This data need not be continuous (example: automobiles may be purchased with 4, 5, 6, or 9 seats. Continuous variables, however, present an infinite number of possible values, and all values lie within a specific range. Variables have other characteristics. They can be random variables which model uncertainty and are expressed as probabilities. They can be exogenous variables—variables which are external to the model and which cannot be influenced by decision variables.

A Sample Model

The problem is the capital investment and design of a product line. These are the variables:

Decision Variables	
Size of plant?	Continuous
Makes products A and B or just A?	Binary
Which manufacturing machines?	Discrete
Intermediate Variables	
Investment capital	Continuous
Working capital	Continuous
Production expenses (R)	Continuous
Unit sales (R)	Continuous
Demand for product (R, E)	Continuous
State of the economy (E)	Continuous
Competitive action (E)	Continuous

Output Variables	
Operating profit	Continuous
Cash flow	Continuous
Net present value	Continuous
Internal rate of return	Continuous
Market share	Continuous
Retention of scarce skilled workers	Continuous

The modeler must decide:

- Which variables are discrete, random, or continuous
- What variables are "significant" to the purpose of the model
- What variables fall within/without the boundaries of the model

Models are abstractions of systems, substitutes for the real system. They involve a large number of assumptions about the nature of the environment in which the system works, about the operating characteristics of its components, and about the way people will behave. A model is a set of relations, a continuum of complexity (from one variable to many), of uncertainty (from deterministic to probabilistic), and of time (from static to dynamic). That can be best illustrated with figure 8.69.

Corner 1 is the simplest situation, a deterministic model that involves only one variable and does not involve time. Deterministic means cause and effect. Accounting models are deterministic. Forecasting models are probabilistic. An example of the statement of a deterministic model would be:

TOTAL COST = UNIT COST * NUMBER OF UNITS

Corner 2 is deterministic and dynamic. There is an element of time. Such a model would be the present value of a savings account.

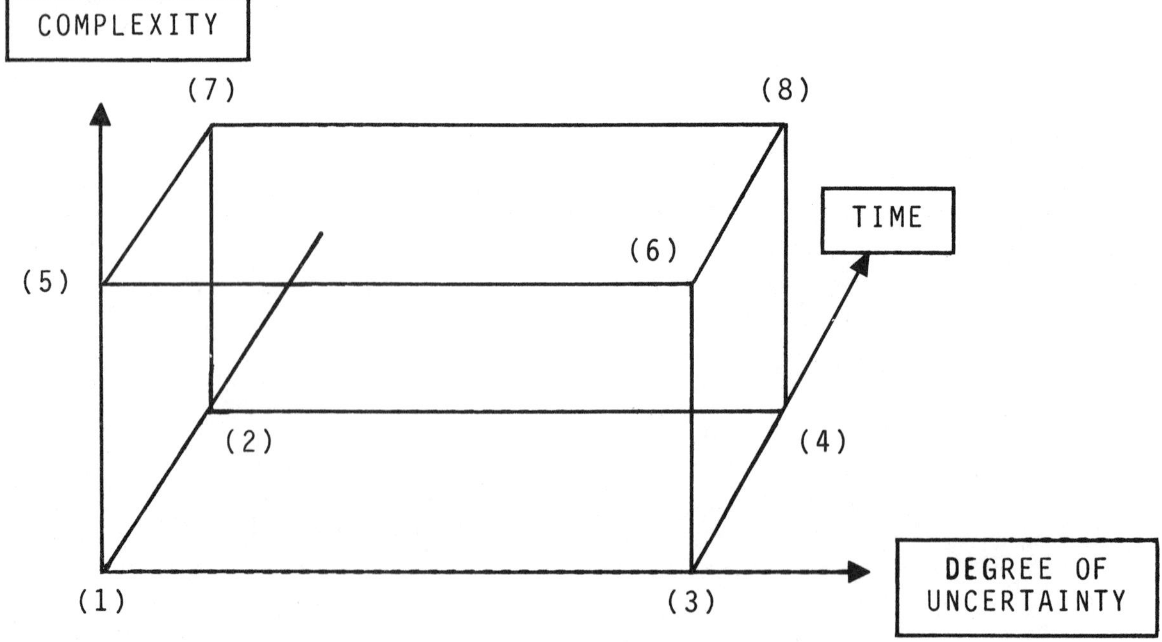

Figure 8.69. Decision Model.

$$\text{PRESENT VALUE} = \text{FUTURE VALUE}_n\ (1 + \text{INT RATE})^{-n}$$

Corner 3 is probabilistic and static. There is no time dimension and there is a degree of uncertainty. Such a model would apply to sales this month:

$$\text{SALES} = \text{SALES}_{(1)} + \text{SALES}_{(2)} \ldots \text{SALES}_{(31)}$$

Corner 4 is probabilistic and dynamic. There is a degree of uncertainty about it. An example would be the price of a share of stock:

$$\text{PAYBACK} = \text{SHARES} * \text{MARKET PRICE}$$

Corner 5 represents the addition of complexity in the form of more than one variable. Here simultaneous equations are calculated, such as the time to cross a mountain:

Standard distance formula: $D = R * T$

$$T = \frac{D}{R}$$

Add the element of altitude:

$$T = \left(\frac{D}{R}\right) * A_{(1 \ldots n)}$$

The complexity of the model increases with either the addition of time or uncertainty.

Corner 6 is probabilistic, static, and complex. Here we can add to the model consideration for differences in weather.

Corner 7 is dynamic, complex, and deterministic. Add to the model consideration for a handicap, such as the climber wearing crutches.

Corner 8 is dynamic, probabilistic, and complex. Here we take everything about the model discussed thus far, plus additional considerations for terrain.

Many problems can be solved at Corner 1 and at the corners adjacent to 1 with relatively simple models. Problems at Corner 8 require deep understanding of the problem.

Let's take this example: the value of a savings account. The minimum balance is $1,000. First Pelican Bank pays 5.25% simple annual interest on the minimum balance. The model is:

$$\text{BALANCE} = \text{PRINCIPAL} + \text{INTEREST}$$

where:

$$\begin{aligned} \text{PRINCIPAL} &= 1000 \\ \text{INTEREST RATE} &= 0.0525 \\ \text{INTEREST} &= \text{PRINCIPAL} * \text{INTEREST RATE} \end{aligned}$$

That shows up in the Interactive Financial Planning System (IFPS) in the manner shown in Figure 8.69a.

```
MODEL FIRSTPELICAN VERSION OF 5/17/85  15:32
10    COLUMNS 1-6
20    BALANCE = PRINCIPAL + INTEREST
30    PRINCIPAL = 1000,PREVIOUS BALANCE
40    INTEREST RATE = 0.0525
50    INTEREST = PRINCIPAL*INTEREST RATE
END OF MODEL
? solve
MODEL SECONDPELICAN VERSION OF 5/17/85  15:32 -- 6 COLUMNS 4 VARIABLES
ENTER SOLVE OPTIONS
? all
```

	1	2	3	4	5	6
BALANCE	1053	1108	1166	1227	1292	1359
PRINCIPAL	1000	1053	1108	1166	1227	1292
INTEREST RATE	.0525	.0525	.0525	.0525	.0525	.0525
INTEREST	52.50	55.26	58.16	61.21	64.42	67.81

Figure 8.69a

There are available on the market a number of interactive modeling systems. MicroProphit, Point Five, and IFPS are but three. We've selected IFPS because it is available on both the mainframe and microcomputers.

As you can see from the above illustration, IFPS produces a spreadsheet. Nothing is seemingly remarkable about that. The really remarkable aspect of IFPS is the modeling language. IFPS is used to model an actual business situation, generally in a financial context. Thus, the unit that you create to reflect the business environment is the model of that business. A model contains statements, which take the form of a series of equations or other operations. Statements are an abstraction of the business reality; they express the situation by presenting assumptions about values and the relationships between various components (variables) of the business.

It is convenient to think of a model's solution as a matrix of rows and columns. The rows of the matrix correspond to the user-defined variables, and the columns usually correspond to time periods. Columns may also represent other things, such as the different divisions or departments within a corporate organization. The model then describes the interactions of these variables over a period of time (or the interactions within each individual division of the company).

Market Models

Market models test the variables under uncertainty of the product in the marketplace. To the economist, this is experimentation with supply and demand curves. Because it's mathematically based, a spreadsheet or a financial modeling system can be used to depict the potential impact of changes in market forces. Consider Figure 8.70.

There are some assumptions which must be made:

- As the price decreases, the demand for the commodity will increase.

$$\text{DEMAND} = \text{A} - (\text{B} * \text{PRICE}) \tag{1}$$

- As the price increases, the supply of the commodity available will increase.

$$\text{SUPPLY} = \text{C} + (\text{D} * \text{PRICE}) \tag{2}$$

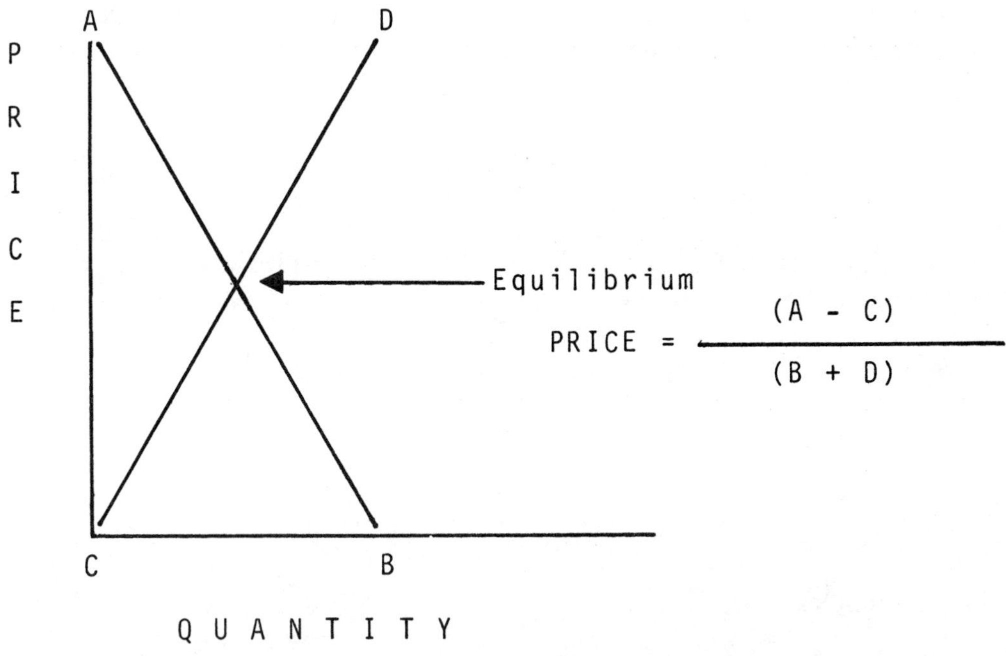

Figure 8.70

- The supply will equal the demand

$$\text{SUPPLY} = \text{DEMAND} \tag{3}$$

These three relations form the market model.

For this model to match the assumptions, B and D must be positive so that supply goes up and demand goes down as price increases. A must be positive so that if price becomes high enough, the demand goes to 0.

Given that A = 500, B = 1000, C = −40, and D = 800, we would see that:

Equilibrium price is 30 cents

$$\text{PRICE} = \frac{(A - C)}{(B + D)} = \frac{500 - (-40)}{1000 + 800} = \frac{540}{1{,}800} = .30$$

Recalculating through formulas [1] and [2], supply and demand are 200:

$$\begin{aligned} \text{DEMAND} &= A - (B * \text{PRICE}) \\ &= 500 - (1000 * .30) = 200 \\ \text{SUPPLY} &= C + (D * \text{PRICE}) \\ &= -40 + (800 * .30) = 200 \end{aligned}$$

This model is at Corner 5. The model has these characteristics:

- It represents a situation in quantitative terms.
- It contains major assumptions which have to be verified.
- There is no element of time.

We can make the model more realistic. In real markets, information lags the current situation. This would move the model from Corner 5 to Corner 7. Assume that the current supply is based on price in the previous period—modify the assumptions about supply:

DEMAND = A − (B * PRICE)

SUPPLY = C + (D * PREVIOUS PRICE)

PRICE = (A − C − (D * PREVIOUS PRICE))/B

This is derived as follows:

$$\text{PRICE} = \frac{(A - C) - D}{(B + D) - D}$$

So now, it would seem that the model-building process follows the schematic of Figure 8.71.

Model Building Principles

Models must pass these tests:

- Relevance. The condition must fit the problem
- Accuracy. Will be variable, depending upon the decision to be made
- Aggregation. Grouping number of individual quantities into a larger quantity.

From that point, you find a way to express it mathematically and fit it into the matrix.

OFFICE AUTOMATION

It would appear that a goodly portion of the future for systems analysts lies in the field of office automation, often called office information systems. The advent of the microcomputer has brought with it the concept of an integrated workstation, what AT&T calls the IVDT (the integrated voice/data terminal). The existence of a departmental computer which supports and controls these workstations and has a mainframe linkage is certain to change the way organizations work. At the same time, the handwriting should be on the wall—there will be fewer mainframes and minicomputers (assuming the latter survive at all) and more and more of the micro and supermicro. In fact, we will see the lines blurred between the distinctions.

Touche Ross, one of the nation's largest accounting firms, refers to the integrated office as the "glue" concept. In this environment, the integrated work station will have these capabilities: graphics, spreadsheets, electronic mail, word processing systems, mapper systems (for the time being let's call them the fourth generation languages), mainframe applications, sociological systems (such as SPSS, the Statistical Package for the Social Sciences), electronic filing, conference calling, and computer-aided design (CAD). That's a lot of power to place on a workstation capability, but recall that this workstation will interface not only with clerical personnel, but also with middle-level professionals and high-level managers. Thus, the glue becomes the hub of the wheel. The spokes then become functional software, network control, remote connection, local connection, and the physical configuration. Attached to the wheel will be the mainframes and peripherals of many vendors.

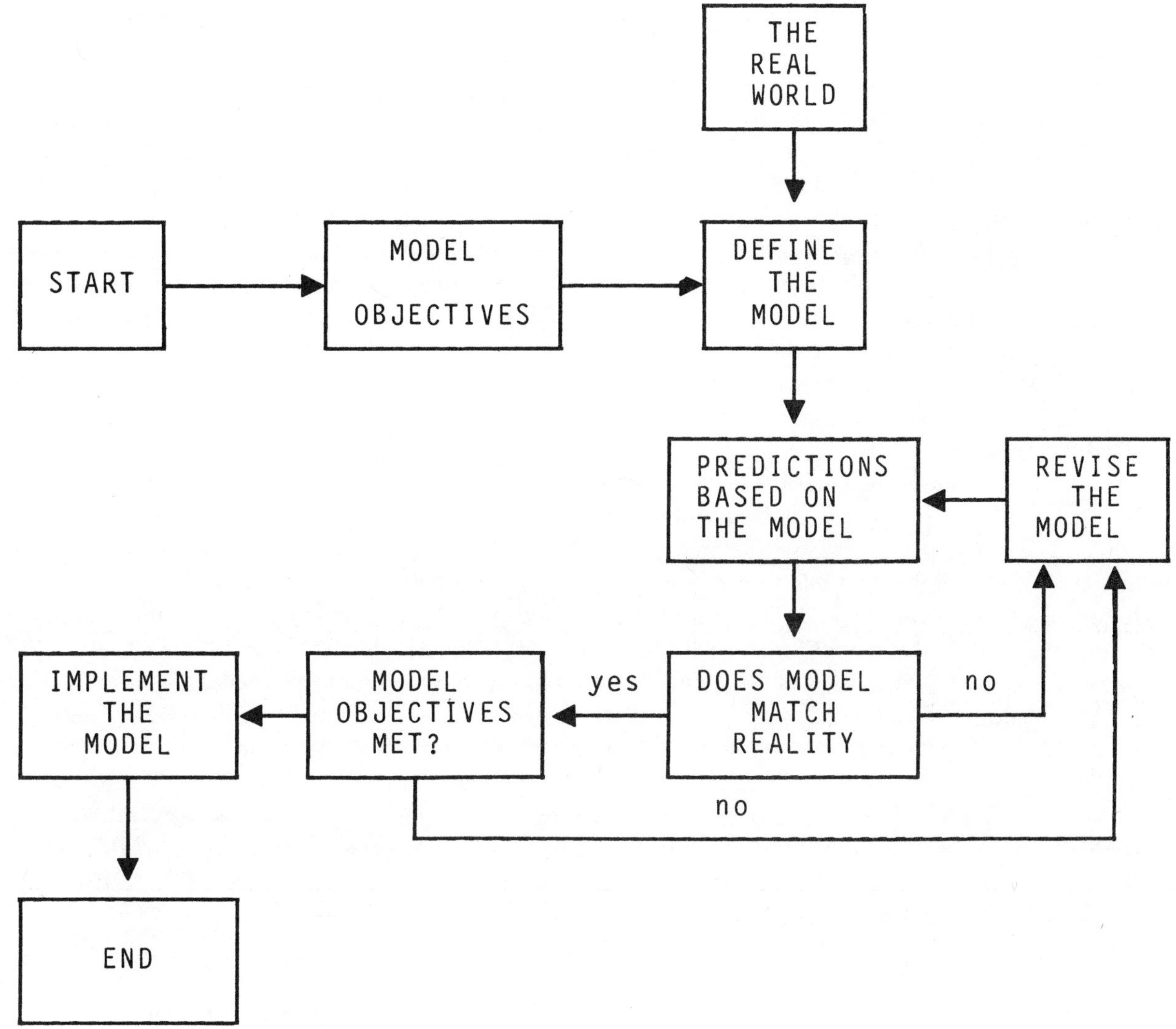

Figure 8.71

Integrating Word Processing into Office Automation

Word processing is, without question, the first move made by any office into the automated office. By and large, these incursions have been standalone and involved a typist or secretary. Vendors of word processing hardware have improved the technology with shared logic systems, where typing pools or a distribution of clerical personnel can access and share the resources of a central processors. But microcomputers have made the capability available to anyone in the office, making the data processing technology available to word processing functionality.

The Office—the Hub of Information Technologies

Analysts have a great future who become involved with the growing move to office automation, for the office will begin to share the limelight with data processing for use of the information resource. Under the leadership of a Chief Information Officer (CIO), there will come into existence mini-computer centers known as ''information centers.'' In essence, this will be a functional duplication of the larger mainframe DP activities, and EDP is but one of the information technologies to be tapped in the office information system. Personal computing will continue to be a part of the process, with spreadsheet, modeling, and graphics capabilities being available to knowledgeable management personnel. Word processing and list management will become a part of the system, supported by clerical personnel. Image processing—intelligent copiers, sophisticated printers, facsimile, and a host of other image products and services—will become a part of the office information system. But communications offers the most startling of future enhancements. Voice annotation of documents, data transmission, teleconferencing, and document transmission are all part of the future of the office automation package. Think, for a minute of integration as applied to the electronic document. It will receive image processing when the company's logo and name are printed in fancy script at the top of the letter, and an electronic signature is placed at the end. It will receive text, when the letter is printed. It will receive data when information is inserted in that letter. It will receive graphics when the histogram is placed in the letter. It will receive voice when the letter has a voice annotation. And the whole thing will be communications-based. We've only scratched the surface.

The jury is still out on whether the technology forced the automated office or the change in people did so. For years, we have been talking about the paperless office, or the office without walls. We not only haven't removed paper, we've generated more of it. So, yes, it could be that office automation is equipment in search of applications. But that is not unusual. Technology has led this entire information revolution. But at the same time, white collar jobs have received unprecedented growth in this century. In 1900 it was 17.6% of the workforce; in 1920, 24.9%; in 1940, 31.1%; in 1960, 40%; in 1980, 51.2%; and it is predicted to be 60% by 1990. Again, white collar employment has been spurred by the existence and application of technology. That's certainly true. But at the same time, there has been a more than 100% increase in available information for each 10% growth of the white collar workforce.

In much the same way as we all could not become telephone operators in the traditional sense, we cannot be information workers in the traditional sense. The current term, and it is most applicable, is *knowledge workers*. According to IBM, the salary and benefits of a professional employee in 1975 was $35,000. A terminal to support that professional then cost $14,000. Today, again according to IBM, the cost of the person has risen to $70,000 and the cost of the terminal (aka personal computer) has dropped to $3,500. I'm not sure where my $70,000 is, but the price of the currently available terminal is in that ball park.

So we have a mandate for the office systems analyst between now and the end of the century. We must find ways to increase the speed and quality of communication, improve productivity, reduce paper, reduce manual filing, improve information access, improve document quality, and to prove the consistency of information. Figures 8.72 and 8.73 are examples of information presentation available today. They are examples of the types of integrated reports which can be obtained from a laser printer. These were run on an Apple McIntosh computer and printed on the Apple LaserWriter. This will show what is possible.

The Nature of the Near Future

Figure 8.74 shows the dimensions of the office automation activity as it is beginning to happen. The three dimensions of people (width), functions (height), and information (depth) are as they can be predicted now, in 1986. It is certain to be different.

The OA Need

According to AT&T Information Systems, who should have some insight on the situation, there will be nearly a 300% increase in the OA market by the end of the decade, while the traditional DP market will

Financial Report

The Watermill Restaurants, Inc.

1984 Year in Review

	March 31	June 30	Sept. 30	Dec. 31
TOTAL RESTAURANT SALES	$115,600	$125,790	$139,723	$153,660
COSTS AND EXPENSES				
Cost of Sales	61,460	65,035	71,994	76,140
Operating, G &A (see Note 1)	32,722	36,400	40,542	42,890
Interest (long-term)	251	226	185	96
	94,433	101,661	112,721	119,126
Income before Federal Taxes	21,167	24,129	27,002	34,534
Provision for Federal Income Taxes	10,374	12,003	13,902	16,976
NET INCOME	$10,793	$12,126	$13,100	$17,558
NET INCOME PER SHARE	$1.08	$1.20	$1.31	$1.76
CASH DIVIDENDS	$0.20	$0.20	$0.20	$0.20

(Dollars in thousands, except per share amounts.)

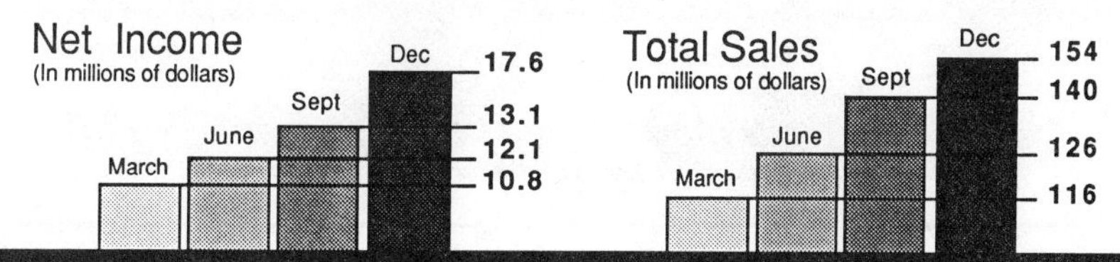

Note 1. Six restaurants owned by others, including certain directors and officers of the Company, are managed by the Company under contracts entered into in fiscal year 1972. As consideration for managing the restaurants, the Company receives 35% of the restaurants' net operating income as defined in the agreements. The Company compensates the restaurant managers out of its management fees.

This document was created using the Apple LaserWriter and MacDraw.

Figure 8.72

experience a decline. In the OA market, there will be a large front office expansion—information centers, desktop computers, and an even larger integration of communications. The vendors, say AT&T, will deal in these categories of products:

The office is a functional unit which processes and communicates information. The information in at the clerical level comes out as decisions at the management level:

- Clerical. Interrupt driven, routine, structured, message preparation, storage, and administration
- Middle level. Professional, technical, sales; client driven, analysis, seeking information, unstructured.
- Management level. Information driven, review, negotiation, decision.

Among the things you'll find as you work into the office is that the executive secretary spends 5% typing, and of course that's where the best typewriter or word processor goes. Middle management secretarial spends 50% typing of an enormous amount of paperwork, and gets lesser machinery—perhaps

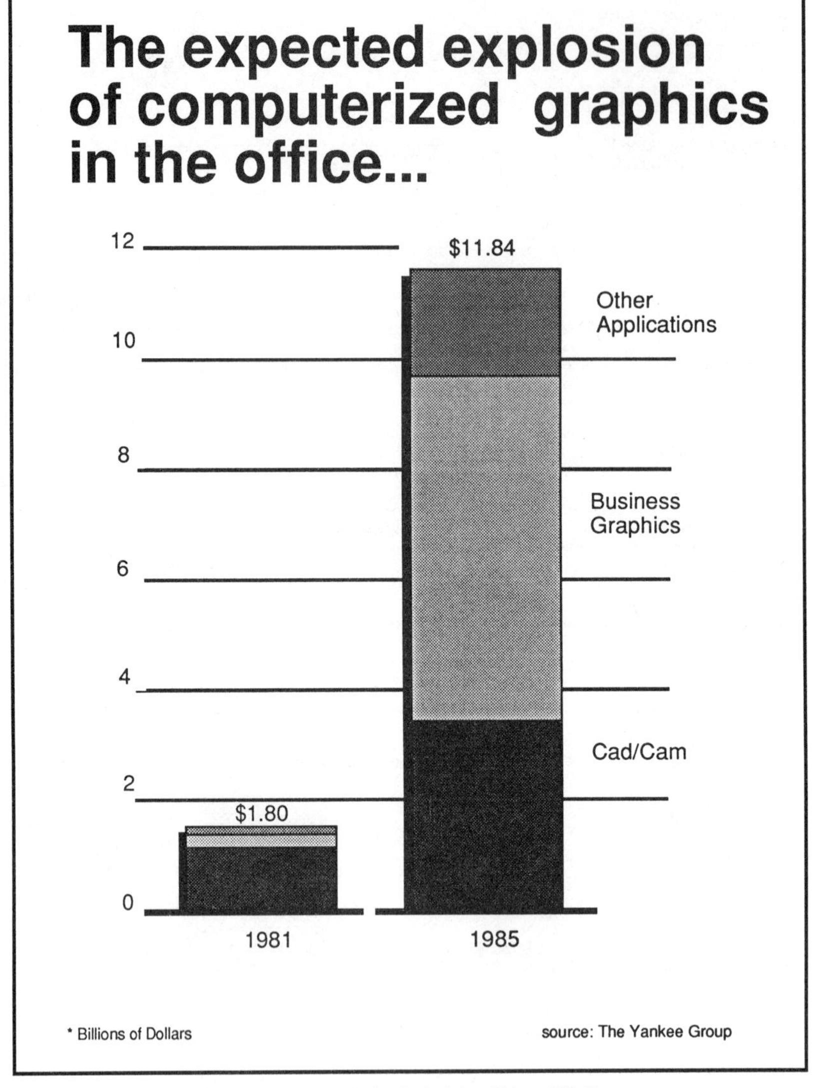

This document was created using the Apple LaserWriter and MacDraw.

Figure 8.73

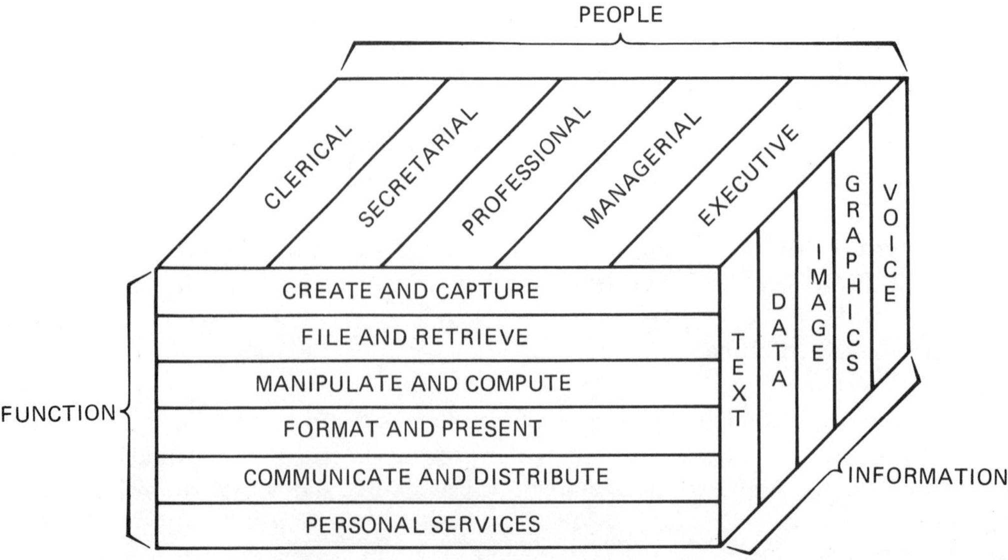

Figure 8.74

Category	User	Vendor
Core Processors Workstations Operating systems Messaging Switching	Basic functions System foundations Vendor competition Standardization High level of need	Strength Differentiation R&D focus Base for future markets
Secondary Printers Displays Facsimile Applications software	Critical to complete configurations Media conversions Manual backup	Many niches Multiple sources for systems Rapid changes
Tertiary Vertical applications Specialized displays Turnkey software	Wide variety of needs Customized	Specialized vendors Value-added retailers Distributors

Figure 8.75

has to share. Clerical spend 90% typing, and have a full need—and have virtually none of the better equipment.

The mixture of communication tasks show something interesting, as well. Secretarial personnel spend 41% of their time communicating on the phone. Managers spend 28%. Sales spends 8%. Professional and technical spends 25%. 98% of the offices have communications or voice station. Office stations account for 9%, and data stations account for 18%. That will change radically. The IVDT—Integrated voice/data/terminal—will be used to support office automation processes. It will provide these messaging services: telephone, electronic and voice mail, facsimile, database inquiry, teleconferencing, and copy/print services. it will provide these processing services: word processing, spreadsheet, business graphics, personal programming, file management, decision support. Executive penetration at this point is but 4%. It must increase.

Also coming—intelligent programmable copiers, which will do FAX (facsimile), communication (E-mail), laser printing, optical scanning to optical disk, and provide cheap storage.

Today, the human does the integration—the present systems do not integrate well. There is no profit to spend $2K to $8K for a system and then put the paper into the USPS mail. Time will tell just how much benefit will be derived from production graphics in support of decision support systems (DSS). The needs of the future are shown in Figure 8.76.

The secretary is the hub of the office. At the moment, the messaging/processing mix for clerical is 60%/40%; for professional/technical, it's 70%/30%; for managerial, it's 90%/10%. Users require messaging communications and processing functionality. At the moment 65% of the office access is for word processing.

AT&T will be in "folder portables," workstations, and LAN. They will provide products for the casual user ($1,800 upgradable), for the heavy user ($5K–$6K multifunction), for technical and engineering ($10K range)—8.5 × 11 screen with bit graphics, and secretarial, via workstations. Expect AT&T to work in LAN layers: workstation to workstation communications; departmental communications, and corporate/campus-wide communications. Expect the intelligent copier to be tied to a multimedia communication packet and digital controllers to work among people, databases, and systems.

	Clerical	Professional/Technical	Managerial
High Need	Telephone Document preparation Mail Copying Filing Forms Administration	Telephone Calculation Mail Document preparation Database inquiry Graphics File management	Telephone Administration Mail
Moderate Need	Graphics Urgent mail Archives	Copying Archives Personal programming Conference Forms Statistics Urgent mail	Conference Graphics Urgent mail Archives Calculations
Low Need	Conference Calculations Statistics		Copying Document prep. Personal prog. Forms Statistics

Figure 8.76

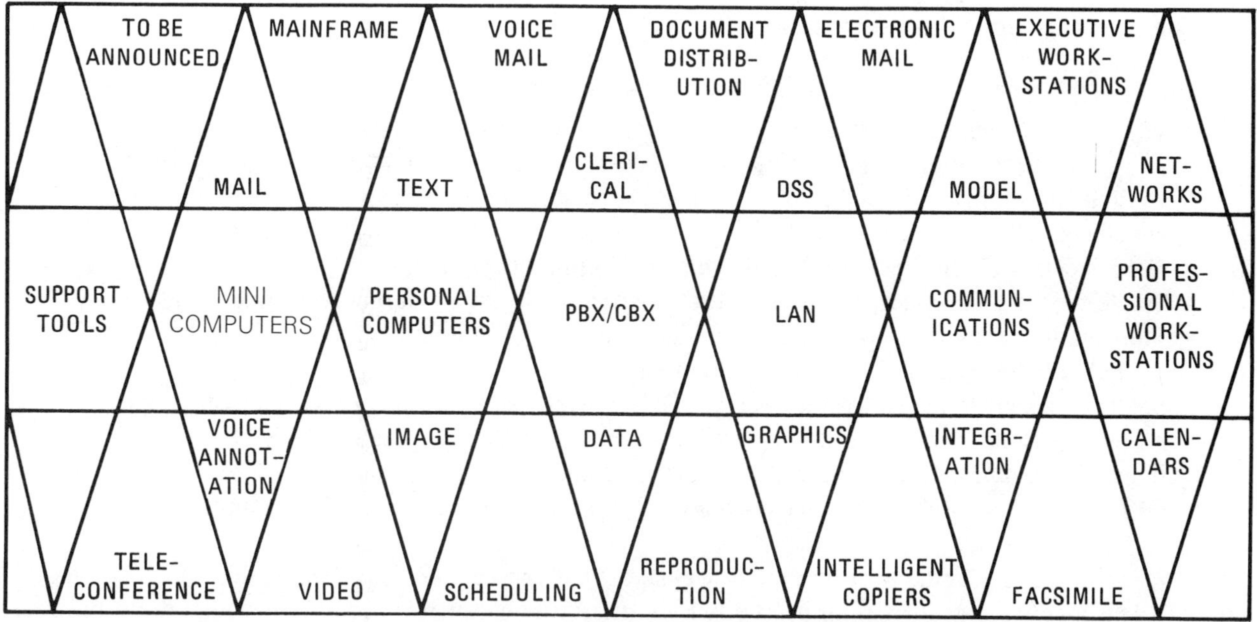

Figure 8.77

How To Get There

So, you say, an office information is just another system? In many ways that is true—the traditional systems analysis skills are more than sufficient to get going, but they are just the beginning. The beginning is, like any other system, a master plan for the office information system. Figure 8.77 is an example of the puzzle of technology you'll be facing as you move into the office information systems area. And this is far from complete.

Strategies for Integration of OIS

We've now seen that the OIS integration is of data, text, voice, image/video, and graphics. What sets OA apart from DP? OA has been word processing, electronic mail, decision support systems, calculations. DP has been electronic data processing and telecommunications. The functions are now blurred—any function which provides support is called OIS—most noticeable in the voice annotation of data.

These are the OIS market shares as of 1986: IBM 28%, DEC 6%, WANG 4%, Other 62% taken up by vendors with 1% or less. New competitors include AT&T, HP, Japan, Inc. Those others are big names: Burroughs, Honeywell, NCR, Philips, Prime, Sperry, Xerox—and small names: A.B. Dick, Compucorp, Datapoint, Harris/Lanier, Exxon, Pitney Bowes, Raytheon.

The existing technology is imbedded: hardware, software, data/text, technical staff, and training. The incoming technology must fight for its place. But as it does, come to grips with one very troublesome fact: *the mainframe is now a peripheral to the workstation in an integrated environment. It's but a server.* As stated, there is a move to create the Chief of Information position to which both EDP and OA will report.

At this point, benefits are hard to measure. They are significant, but soft. It's a critical mass issue. E-Mail, for example, requires a critical mass. The workstation is not a standard executive tool. The organization will spend $10K to $20K for office furniture for the executive with no questions asked, but a $3K terminal or personal computer must be justified extensively. OIS system methodologies are lacking. Tradition is the square peg; OIS is the round hole. Tradition is not up to integration, and integration is where it is going.

These are the current OIS strategies:

- Integration with business planning has to consider OIS.
- There must be an OIS master plan for the organization. The organizational impact is great, right or wrong. It sucks top management into the process. The cost of not planning is incredible.
- Organization is critical. Get a CIO, as high as possible. Don't underestimate training. The CIO envelopes DP.
- Get a steering committee with key players and technologies involved.
- Single workstation concept—build everything you need into a single workstation.
- The data gathering concepts are different and much more difficult. There is a large interview list, for E-Mail, for example. It's a multiple function survey
- Solution design concepts—get all key people involved, and a sample of the clerical people. Survey *all* others. Build in flexibility, upgradeability, and estimate that you will have double or triple the indicated volumes. Recognize that access to the mainframe is inevitable.
- OIS will be "the glue" which keeps the integrated workstation OA environment together.

And, as you do so, remember that today we have what can best be described as the "disintegrated office." It is a concept of marketing people, whose interest is hardware. It did not emanate from the user areas. There is an unawareness of benefits and increases in productivity. Edison DeCastro (President of Data General) says that 90% of corporate America doesn't know what OA is. But the process is fraught with difficulty. Presently, there is a mixture of media and system solutions which new technology will obsolete. *Present unintegrated systems were designed and built by choosers, not users.* And they will be obsoleted by the IVDT.

And as you deal with the user's information workers, remember that they are aided and abetted by manufacturers and carriers, but don't really care about technology, per se, in the same manner as they didn't care about the plumbing, the electricity, or whether communications were broadband or baseband. The user is application oriented. Thus, OA must consist of people: executives, managers, and professionals; the process of decision making; a place to house the working group, and the available products and technologies. The benefits will be easier jobs, easier tasks, increases in workflow. But it will not come easy. Secretaries will want to change roles. Managers will want to maintain roles. The office runs as a social order—OA must take that into account.

Current OA expectations may be unreasonable—it is a powerful tool, but not an end-all. There is a misunderstanding of documents. We were promised the paperless office; instead, we got more paper. And those who claim to be in the know, claim that the reason was that the task was placed in the hands of computer people. Whether this is true is open to question; but the fact remains that it will be you, the systems analyst, that will become the first office automation analysts. The new directions include shared tenant services, and that puts you squarely into the act.

There are factors which will tend to keep the office disintegrated. Today, everybody has his own phone, but everybody does not have his own data terminal, and in fact may resist the placement of a terminal on his desk. It is known that people do resist sharing a desktop with terminal. And it is known that people resist sharing a terminal located elsewhere. It's an enigma, and one of the greatest you must deal with.

OA must be an extension. It will not necessarily be computer driven. It will be DSS based—not a streamlining tool. OA is a workplace technology. We've moved from a pencil sharpener to an integrated office system—rapidly. New buildings must take automation into consideration. Old buildings must be reconstructed. We will be building the OA building. Simply computerizing disorganization will not correct problems. You're dealing with people who have made a rapid transition from coffee pot to computer. The Information Center will become the centralized service. The end user is now a paraprogrammer—no intensive training, low skill level—but who is productive for useful technical tasks.

Artificial Intelligence will accelerate the shift. Driver programs will assist. The user has the intensive knowledge of the subject and a cursory knowledge of the computer, and that may be enough. This will be truly user programming.

It is useful to liken OA to music. The individual plays his tune (standalone PC user), but for there to be music, the group must play the same tune (centralization), otherwise noise will result (disintegration). The conductor (CIO) can get the desired results only if managers are sufficiently aware of the desired results. When one recognizes that one laser printer in one week can produce enough information for 666 people to read in 8 hours, it seems obvious that some consideration must be given to how we do it.

The OIS Master Plan

These are the elements of an effective OIS master plan. It is necessary to determine:

- Functional information processing requirements
- Hardware requirements
- Software requirements
- Communication requirements
- Organizational issues
- Training
- Timeframes
- Workplan

Don't simply accept the traditional DP master plan as sufficient. To begin with OA uses many more technologies. it spans the entire organization. There are multiple vendors. The users have a diversity of sophistication. And the productivity and quality benefits are entirely different.

There are some key considerations about direction. The OA analyst must understand the business plan and the role of information in achieving the strategic objectives of the organization. The flow of information must be traced. There must be management commitment to the process. The interference with the user will be much different than with DP—there will be much more. The coordination of multiple vendors is not an easy task. And when you get to prototyping, everybody must help.

How then to go about it? Get a multidisciplinary project team. Carefully promote the understanding of the project objectives. Perform extensive interviewing and surveying. Catalog the information processing requirements as to their technical and functional requirements. Review the technical alternatives. Prototype the system. Deal with the organizational issues early on. And then conduct a phased installation. That's not different from DP, you say? Please tell me that after you've automated your first office.

Training and Support for OA

Training is extremely important in the OA environment. There is a considerable amount of fear—but that is just the tip of the iceberg. Indeed, these are the training requirements, according to Mary Ruprecht, co-author of *Office Automation: A Management Approach* (Wiley):

- Technical skills. If it is expected that the office people are to keep things together. At the very least, these skills are required of the OA analyst.
- Personnel skills. The nature of the workplace changes, and the interrelationships therein.
- Management skills. The knowledge worker now becomes involved in the managerial tasks, as a means to facilitate decision support.
- Financial skills. And, it could be added "modeling" skills. The knowledge worker must have something more than a high school education.

Training must be accomplished at three levels: orientation, acquaintance, and competency. Training for the organization's office automation analyst need not be dissimilar to other systems training done by the organization: That person will need to know how to:

- Perform a user needs analysis
- Select a system to fit the need
- Install and support the various components to fulfill the need.
- Measure use and acceptance
- Evaluate and improve the system.

Of course, the office automation analyst will have to have a working knowledge of the kinds of things we cover in this book, plus a few more upon which we will touch only casually, for once office automation catches on, tradition has been that both the complexity of the systems and the desire to use them will increase.

At the 1985 convention of the Office Automation Society International, Mr. Ray Fortune of Bell Northern Research placed the issue clearly into focus: ''What we learned: implementation was not as planned—more definition was needed. Level of use was higher than anticipated, and the type of use was different from what was anticipated. There was a tremendous productivity impact as people began to rely exclusively on the systems. We learned that there was a turndown phase—something had to be thrown away. And we learned that the implementation was only the beginning for us, as the impact was assessed, traffic was measured, and tuning had to be done.'' Training? ''Don't give out 15 inches of user manual. Try it out before installing it, to ensure a stable environment. Do not train until the system is ready to use, and use a professional trainer, not an available analyst.''

Mr. Fortune also stated that BNR had found these support statistics important—one support person per *n* operators:

User support	1 : 5 to 1 : 3
OA	1 : 20
WP	1 : 50
DP	1 : 100
Telephone	1 : 500

Fourth Generation Languages

OA brings with it sophisticated database maintenance and extraction/query capability known as fourth generation software. Fourth generation languages are application development tools which allow end users to build applications without resorting to a computer language. There has been a beginning of standards in these areas, with the UNIX operating system and SQL, the structured query language.

The UNIX operating system, developed by AT&T and adopted by several vendors, provides the capability to integrate applications much like *Symphony* (previously mentioned product of Lotus Development Corporation. In fact, it is often referred to as a ''Symphony of UNIX.'' Under UNIX, applications written in C will become commonplace, and work best under UNIX. It is widely felt that UNIX will emerge as a standard OS for OA.

The computer user's appetite is voracious. As computer power increases and software capability increases, the user's appetite grows and successful applications are required. New approach with fourth generation languages is to prototype it quickly, try it, change it, and use it. This will have an impact on current practices in structured programming, to be certain. It is doubtful that office personnel will have to learn C, but there is no doubt that they must be trained in the application of UNIX and the integration of applications in the UNIX shell.

```
Query Next Previous Add Update Remove Table Screen Current Master Detail ■
  Output Exit

COMPANY PERSONNEL and PROJECTS                    ** 1 Personnel Table **

Number   [[1011   ]]          Name  [Dorothy    ]  [Oester          ]

Title    [energy specialist    ]   Social Security  [415-84-2212]
Project  [[220    ]]
                                   Date Hired       [02/28/79 ]
                                   Salary           [$44500.00]
Post        [[141    ]]  Anchorage Last Review      [04/15/83 ]
Date Posted [09/07/81]             Last Raise       [1.08 ]

POST ADDRESS                       HOME ADDRESS
---------------                    ---------------
34 Roundlake Rd.                   Address [980 Elm St.     ]
Anchorage                          City [Brookside          ]
AK  98520                          State [VA] Zip[02040]
```

Figure 8.78

This is not the place to teach about fourth generation languages in detail, but it would be useful to examine some samples made available by Relational Database Systems of Palo Alto, California. Their system, Informix-SQL, is a combination database and user-developed form system for entry, query, extraction, and reporting that can be done by the user himself. It's not a simple system—but it is extremely capable. Figure 8.78 is an example of the ease with which the user can prepare his own data entry screens.

The structured query which accompanies the package provides any sort of logical, sequential, or combinatorial extraction. A typical SQL query is shown in Figure 8.79. An example of a more complicated extraction is shown in Figure 8.80:

The names used look a little strange, but are those names which have been defined by the SQL data definition, shown in Figure 8.81. And in case you thought that getting a report was difficult, Figures 8.82 a and b show a sample report:

Errors and Omissions

Of course there is more to the subject of office automation. We've barely scratched the surface. Some of the applicable elements have been covered in other parts of the book, and we're about to deal with one of the more important of the topics, ergonomics. But as we close this part of the chapter, let's remember that the future holds great promise if we think rather than daydream about it, if we plan rather than wait for it, if we accept rather than reject the inevitability of change.

ERGONOMICS

There is an area of scientific study aimed at adapting the work done and the tools used by people to suit their anatomical, physiological, and psychological needs. This field is called ''ergonomics'' (human factors). It would be nice to be able to say that ergonomics came about as a result of consideration of these factors, and certainly it did to an extent. However, like many workplace improvement concerns, it came about as a result of products in the market and labor union pressures.

TYPICAL SQL QUERY

```
RDSQL        New Run Modify Use-editor Output Save Choose Info Exit
Run the current RDSQL statements
--------------------------------- company -------- Press CTRL-W for Help --

select proj_num, start_date, end_date, manager
   from projects
   order by proj_num
```

Figure 8.79

NESTED SQL QUERY

```
select lname last_name, salary, personnel.proj_num, end_date
  from personnel, projects
     where personnel.proj_num = projects.proj_num and
     personnel.proj_num IN

        (select proj_num from projects
           where end_date>

              (select start_date from projects
                 where proj_num =245))

  order by end_date
```

Figure 8.80

SQL DATA DEFINITION

```
create table personnel
  (pers_num   serial,
   fname       char(15),
   lname       char(20),
   hire_date   date,
   title       char(25),
   salary      money(8),
   last_review date,
   last_raise  smallfloat,
   proj_num    smallint);
```

Figure 8.81

SAMPLE REPORT

```
database
  company
end

select lname, title, proj_num, salary
   from personnel
   where proj_num > 220
   order by proj_num
end
```

Figure 8.82a

SAMPLE REPORT
(Continued)

```
format
  page header
    print 20 spaces, "STAFF ON PROJECTS ABOVE 220"
    skip 2 lines
    print "NAME",
      column 21, "POSITION",
      column 46, "NUM.",
      column 58, "SALARY"
      skip 1 line
  on every row
    print lname, title, proj_num, salary using "$$$,$$$.&&"
  on last row
    skip 1 line
    print "TOTAL SALARIES",
      column 52, total of salary using "$$$,$$$.&&"
end
```

Figure 8.82b

Keystroking a terminal certainly isn't as dangerous as working with radioactive materials, but long-term exposure to uncomfortable furniture, inadequate lighting, and insufficient ventilation can produce a myriad of illnesses, ranging from tendonitis to a reduced ability to distinguish colors. Concern over these health hazards has led to government-funded research in this country and abroad, to determine methods of coping with computer-related physical as well as emotional ailments—ranging from blood clots due to uncomfortable seating to feelings of worker isolation. As a result of growing public concern over these health hazards, some states have considered legislation to govern the office use of video-display units. The legislation calls for safeguards such as mandatory eye exams, work rotation, and adjustable desks and chairs. Studies of computer users point out that a well-designed workplace is critical to worker comfort and safety. And they have shown that with proper display design, lighting and work stations, terminal-oriented work need not cause any unique visual problems.

The arrival of computer technology in the office means that people and organizations now have a powerful tool which can make their work both more efficient and more fun. The computer's ability to carry out, at great speed, uninteresting routine tasks involving huge quantities of information is an excellent complement to the human ability to interpret results, to make decisions and to perform creative tasks.

In the past, the ergonomics of working methods and equipment have improved as a result of natural development, but in recent years, and largely under union pressures, a more scientific approach has been applied. In spite of this, the development of computer technology has been so rapid that the task of adapting it to meet the needs of its human users has often been relegated to second place. However, demands for improved ergonomics have grown at the same rate as computers and data terminals have become more common tools in our offices.

The design of a good workplace must take into account the user's well-being, both physical and mental. Psysiological factors such as lighting, noise levels, and work posture are often easy to measure and to improve. Rather more difficult, through no less important, are the measurement and quantification of psychological and social factors, such as how people react to tasks and the way they are organized. Today we know that the properly planned and executed introduction of terminal workplaces into a company can create an enhanced work environment and office ergonomics. And this, in turn, creates new openings for the improvement of both job satisfaction and productivity.

Where Ergonomics Began

Furniture manufacturers have begun to pay more attention to ergonomics—from the Greek *ergos* (work) and *nomos* (natural laws)—the study of designing the work environment to meet human needs. This behavioral science, also known as ''human factors engineering,'' had its start during World War II in the design of aircraft controls and pilot seating. During the past two decades, ergonomics has increasingly focused on product design, drawing upon the fields of anatomy, physiology, and psychology.

With the growth of automated work and the white-collar sector, office furniture has become more ergonomic and now includes a variety of products—introduced since the 1970s—that exclusively support the desktop computer. Many of the most advanced designs come from Europe. European manufacturers adhere to strict government regulations, as a result of pressure from strong white-collar unions in countries such as West Germany and Sweden.

American furniture manufacturers have rushed to keep pace with these foreign imports, but this country has no mandatory standards governing design, manufacture, or use of computer-support furniture. nevertheless, the number of products on the market has never been greater. They range from work surfaces that you can lower or raise up to six inches—with separate surfaces for monitors and keyboards—to chairs that you can angle, tilt, and swivel in almost any directions.

If you want to set up a computerized or terminal work area, what should you look for? Begin by determining how frequently folks use the computer or terminal. Ergonomics becomes really important when you spend more than a third of your time at the computer. For a constant user, insist on adjustable chairs, work surfaces, and lighting, so that the environment may be adjusted to suit the user's comfort.

Offices As They Are

Backplanning

Few existing office environments were planned with computerization in mind. Computer equipment requires power supply and cable-laying. Video display units and keyboards create new lighting requirements. Printers may increase noise levels and all electrical equipment generates heat energy which increases the room temperature.

Few companies have the opportunity to reconstruct their offices from the ground up so that they are perfectly adapted to modern computer equipment. it therefore becomes necessary to adapt equipment to suit the office. The colors should be so neutral that the equipment will easily blend into the office environment without creating unpleasant contrasts.

Terminals and printers should be easy to place in the office environment. They should generate a minimum of heat, and be capable of adaptation to suit individual work posture and lighting conditions. Casings should be scratchproof and reflection-free. Terminals and printers should operate quietly. It should, where necessary, be easy to fit printers with sound-proof hoods.

Furniture Design

The most rapid advances in ergonomic furniture design center on the chair, no doubt because back disorders are the number one cause of worker absenteeism, affecting 50–80% of the population. A 1980 Louis

Harris poll conducted for Steelcase, the largest U.S. manufacturer of furniture, found that 54% of surveyed workers felt that the comfort of their chairs affected their performance. Indeed, the current preoccupation with increased productivity on the part of American management has boosted the development of ergonomic chairs that incorporate a high degree of built-in design flexibility to accomodate a variety of postures and body sizes. The research these designs reflect shows that computer work involves a variety of sitting positions—from leaning over the desk to reclining—that change every eight to ten minutes. Sitting is an athletic activity. Tasks such as typing put a 30% additional load on the spine.

Although experts agree that a "good" chair design must pay attention to the lumbar region of the spine just above the pelvic bone, to the buttocks, and to the backs of the thighs, translating these anatomical concerns into physical reality has produced various results. Ergonomics is not a hard science in the sense that some sciences are. If it were, chairs would tend to look more alike than they do now.

What the ergonomic specialists agree on is that seating should conform to several criteria: a rounded front edge, support for the lumbar vertebrae, a lightly padded seat, a backrest high enough to reach the lower shoulder, adjustable seat height, and tiltable seat and back. The aim of current ergonomic chair design is to allow users to customize seating to their specific body proportions and sitting postures. A chair should be in proportion to the person using it. It has to fit.

Similarly, the design of the desk should be flexible enough to adapt to the user's particular style of working. In supporting the computer, it must accomodate two separate tasks: viewing data on a monitor at eye level and entering data via keyboard at typing level. Swivel, tilt, and height adjustments on chairs are not enough. All furniture should be able to be adjusted to meet the needs of the computer user. As a result, furniture manufacturers have responded by offering adjustable desktops; retractable keyboard trays, and separate shelves for monitors, keyboards, and peripherals. Some experts predict that this furniture will give way to workstations that integrate electronics.

To fit a chair, check to ensure that the sitter's hips and knees are at right angles and your feet flat on the floor. Remember, though, that few people maintain this posture for long. A sitter changes positions every eight to ten minutes. Be sure that the seat of the chair can be raised or lowered; experts recommend six to nine inches of movement, from a height of 16 to 22 inches. Many so-called ergonomic chairs now incorporate gas-lift mechanisms, which make seating adjustments as easy as pressing a button under the seat.

The front edge of a seat should be rounded or "scrolled" so that it doesn't cut into the back of your legs and restrict blood flow to the thighs and feet. The seat cushion should be lightly padded so that any pressure exerted on the buttocks can be shifted. If too soft, a cushion can cause pressure under the thighs and thrust the hip bones forward. It should be constructed in a material that "breathes," to avoid trapping body heat and perspiration, which can lead to rashes and other infections.

To support the lumbar region of the spine properly, a chair's backrest should fit snugly into the small of your back and tilt backward and forward to accommodate seated movement—at an angle of 80 to 120 degrees, measured from the seat. To adjust to the lower back, the backrest should be able to move up and down two inches or more.

If the chair reclines, it should have a headrest, but it should not push the head forward. Armrests are important in reducing shoulder and arm fatigue. They should be short enough to allow the chair to be drawn up to the work surface and, ideally, be adjustable in height.

To provide stability, the base of the chair should be five-pronged. If a leg should break off from this type of base, the remaining prongs will remain firmly and safely on the floor. For mobility, choose a swivel base on casters.

Factors that contribute to an ergonomic chair design:

- Thoracic support. The contoured backrest adjusts up and down, forward and backward, and remains in constant contact with the user's back, regardless of the tilt angle.

- Lumbar (lower back) support: Contoured seat sides support pelvic rotation and backward and forward motion, regardless of the tilt angle. Seat angle adjustment: the pivot allows the feet to remain on the floor.
- The foam construction is not too soft. It is firm enough to cushion and support the body
- Pneumatic height adjustment.
- Five-pronged base provides extra stability and balance, and casters allow smooth, friction-free movement.
- Waterfall front edge aids thigh circulation, reduces leg fatigue, and lets the feet rest comfortably flat on the floor.

Working Surfaces

Ideally the desk should be a flexibly designed as the chair. For a relaxed hand position, keyboards and displays should be positioned at different heights, the keyboard lower than the standard 29-inch desk height. Many of the computer-support desks and terminal stands current available feature separately adjustable surfaces for monitors and keyboards, which can be moved up, down, or sideways with a lever, crank, or other mechanism. Some monitor-support surfaces can tilt up to 15 degrees, so viewing angles can be adjusted and rotated for shared use.

Lighting Design

Of the complaints associated with computers, the most common are related to the eyes. Research conducted by the National Institute of Occupational Safety and Health (NIOSH) shows that 91% of the computer operators surveyed reported eyestrain, and 80% experienced burning eyes. Many of these visual problems stem directly from harsh lighting that produces glare. If you find yourself shielding your eyes or your monitor from irritating reflections, you, too, may be suffering from glare.

Glare can be either direct or indirect. Direct glare occurs when light shines from a fixture directly into the eyes. Indirect glare occurs when light emitted from one source onto a surface reflects back from that surface and into the eyes. This type of glare is referred to as a "veiling reflection," since it causes the surface onto which it is reflected to appear washed out, as if the viewer were looking through a veil.

The easiest way to prevent glare is to make sure that the computer is positioned away from a window and away from direct sunlight. Irritating reflection from shiny and brightly colored ceilings, walls, desktops, and clothing can be avoided by placing neutral, matte-finished objects and surfaces in front of the the computer, with darker finishes behind you to absorb the light.

Crucial to reducing both glare and eyestrain is proper lighting design to illuminate the monitor, adjacent paper documents, and the room itself. The challenge in lighting the computer, which is a source of light itself, is to find a way to balance two different sets of activities: reading printed copy, which assumes a sight line 20 to 40 degrees lower than the horizontal at a distance of 16 inches, while viewing the screen, which assumes a horizontal sight line at a distance of 24 inches from the monitor to the eyes.

Glare and poor lighting design may not be the only factors behind computer-related eyestrain. Often the major reason people have display tube-related eye problems is that they have not been tested for this type of work. It is highly recommended that people using terminal displays receive annual eye checkups for testing of near-point acuity, binocularity, and convergence—visual skills which come into play when working at a video display. Another visual problem that may plague computer users more than others is presbyopia (*presby*—old; and *opio*—eyes), a type of reading difficulty that begins to affect people who are 35 and older, involving loss of lens accomodation and decrease in pupil size.

The vogue for many is the contact lense. However, the eyeglasses or contact lenses worn may not be corrected for computer-screen viewing distances. Normal reading eyeglasses are designed for use with a 12-to 16-inch distance between the eyes and the paper; the computer screen requires a distance of 24 inches. Bifocal wearers encounter fatigue by looking from lower (reading) lenses to upper lenses. As a bifocal wearer, the author found it necessary to obtain special multiple lenses for computer viewing, and it is necessary to wear them, depending on the conditions in their workspace. Filtered prescription glasses that screen out rays provide protection from a video display's ultraviolet light—a leading cause of cataracts and retinal damage.

One of the simplest ways to avoid eyestrain is to take a 15 minute break away from your computer every two hours. Another way is to position the monitor so that the viewing angle is 10 to 20 degrees below the horizontal plane at eye level.

Be sure that the computer or terminal is properly maintained to ensure a sharp screen image, display contrast, and proper refresh rate. You can cure a computer that flickers during use in a brightly lit room by dimming the room lighting and adjusting the brightness level of the screen.

Since ordinary office work requires good ambient lighting, most offices often have large windows, light-colored walls and perhaps powerful ceiling lighting. Desks are normally located so that the light from windows falls from the side to provide effective working light. Since most people are right-handed, the light should come from the left so that shadows are not cast on documents by the hands and arms. Additional lighting, independent of overhead fixtures, should be available for left-handed persons.

The same applies to terminals. They should be located so that light from windows and light fittings comes from the side. Curtains or blinds can be used to reduce strong daylight and any reflections caused by windows. Reflections from the walls can be reduced by using darker colors. Light from powerful ceiling lights should be dispersed by fitting them with baffles.

The ambient lighting must be adjusted to suit the tasks, the type of equipment and the individual lighting needs of the people working there. If using display screens with negative presentation (light characters on a dark background) the general level should not, however, be higher than 30 footcandles. For positive presentation (dark characters on light background) on the other hand, the general lighting level can be 50–60 footcandles. If the ambient lighting is supplemented with adjustable work lamps, lighting can be adapted to suit individual needs, both in intensity and direction. The eye requires balanced contrast ratios if it is to avoid fatigue. Luminance ratios between the work surface, the terminal, the walls, the ceiling, and the floor are therefore important.

Selecting the proper lighting for your computer workstation is a much more difficult task than choosing furniture or accessories, since it is dependent on specific room conditions and the placement of the computer monitor. Not only must the lighting fixture illuminate the screen—a source of light and reflection in itself—but it must also light the keyboard and adjacent paper documents on the desk. In addition, the general level of room lighting should be bright enough to avoid the eyestrain that comes from sharp contrasts between the brightness of the screen and surrounding work areas, yet subdued enough to prevent glare. The American Optometric Association (AOA) recommends screen brightness to three to four times the lighting level of the room.

A way to achieve this balance is to combine the ambient lighting in the room to illuminate the work space indirectly—by shining lights against the walls or ceiling with a directly focused, adjustable task lamp on the side of your desk that you use for paperwork. The brightness of the ambient lighting should range from 30 to 50 footcandles (about half the level of brightness in an ordinary, paper-pushing office), and task lighting should be at a level of 70 footcandles. (A light meter that gives a reading in footcandles is available from the General Electric Company). If you use overhead fixtures to illuminate the computer screen, the incidence of light should be as close to a 45 degree angle as possible on the monitor to avoid veiling reflections and glare.

Filters that fit over the computer screen are another way of reducing glare, but they may diminish contrast, character visibility, and brightness. Another way is to use a computer or terminal with black characters on a white background. Known as "negative contrast" or "positive presentation," this type of display reduces the effects of veiling reflections on the screen and may help to reduce problems of adapting to the different luminance levels of the VDT and surrounding objects."

If the user works near a window, be sure that the monitor is placed at right angles to it, so that incoming sunlight doesn't shine directly into your eyes or from behind you onto the screen. Stick to neutral tones when choosing colors for your work surface, in order to prevent extreme, competing contrasts in brightness between desktop and display. Matte, rather than shiny, finishes, are recommended to prevent light bouncing off the work surface onto the screen.

When choosing light fixtures, try to stay away from fluorescent tubes. Not only do some of these tubes produce an unnatural, greenish-white light, but they also have a tendency to flicker when tubes are wearing out or circuits are faulty. Some researches believe fluorescent lamps cause long-term health risks, from fatigue to cell mutations.

More soothing to the eyes—and to the psyche—are halogen lamps; common incandescent bulbs; and the newly developed Norelco PL13 fluorescent bulb and Vita Lite, manufactured by the Duro-Test Corporation of North Bergen, NJ. All of these luminaries emit bright, warm light. Vita Lite produces a mix of broad-spectrum colors that simulate natural daylight, which, according to recent studies, have been found to cure everything from depression to jet lag.

Noise

Noise can also be a source of problems in modern offices. What is noise? People who revel in powerful disco music when awake may be disturbed by the ticking of an alarm clock when they try to sleep. In simple terms, noise is "undesirable sounds." People's reaction to noise, in other words, is highly individual. What disturbs your neighbors may not bother you. And vice versa.

An effort must be made to prevent all noise in order to permit optimum levels of comfort and concentration. Street noise, for instance, can be reduced by installing triple-glazed windows. Curtains, textile wall-coverings and upholstered furniture all contribute to lower noise levels. Acute sources of noise, such as telex units and printers, can be located off to one side, perhaps even separated by internal screens or walls and with sound absorption materials in the ceiling.

Environmental

Other factors to consider in setting the scene for your computer are the environmental conditions surrounding your work area. Room humidity should be within the 40–60% range. Air that is too dry generates static electricity, which can interfere with a computer's electromagnetic field, and air that is too moist can be detrimental to disk and paper storage.

Be sure the work area is adequately ventilated to cope with the heat output from the computer. Fresh-air circulation is important to prevent the buildup of airborne toxins from common materials such as plywood, particle board, and foam insulation, all of which give off formaldehyde, a cause of skin, eye, and respiratory irritation.

Finally, don't forget aesthetics when you buy furniture, lighting, or any other computer-support item. No matter how ergonomic they are, you probably won't use them if their designs are completely at odds with your decor and sense of well-being. Don't hesitate to consult a local architect or interior designer for information on how to order the latest products. Remember, beauty may lie in the eye of the beholder, but comfort keeps the eyes open and bright.

Finishing Touches

For a truly ergonomic work space, consider purchasing computer-support accessories that are designed to keep the most dedicated full time computer user comfortable and productive. You can customize the desk with tilting stands for adjusting monitor viewing angles and augment your chair with a footrest to promote leg circulation, for example. Figure 8.83 shows important factors in user comfort.

Some companies offer whole lines of peripheral support products, including hanging cartridges to

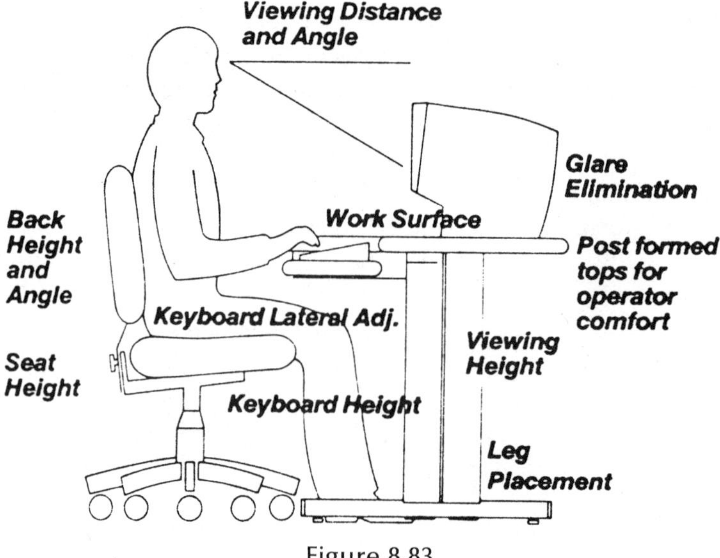

Figure 8.83

store printout paper, diskette holders; and mobile carts for transferring papers, disks, and manuals from place to place. Should you find yourself continually straining your eyes and shifting your head sideways to read paper documents on your desk and input data, you may want to invest in a document holder that places the paper on the same vertical plane as that of the display screen.

If the clatter of the printer drives you crazy, consider purchasing a specially engineered acoustic housing. In addition to reducing noise, this type of cabinet offers shelving for a variety of printer sizes and baskets in which to store printouts.

Another environmental enhancement worth pursuing is a desktop fan to provide increased air circulation and relief from terminal-heat buildup.

The Terminal Workstation

Just as in the case of the general design of the system it is important that the user is involved at an early state of the process and is permitted to influence the selection of terminal equipment and furniture.

There is no "correct" solution to what an efficient terminal workstation should look like. The answer has to do with what the individual user requires from his or her workplace and how the workplace is intended to function.

What type of work is to be done at the workplace? Is it long-term terminal work or just occasional query activities? And does the operator also need to have eye-contact with visitors on the other side of the desk? Do several different operators use the same workplace? And how much time does each of them spend there? What other tasks have to be carried out at the same workplace? Handling paper? Manuscripts? In data registration, the work itself is often regulated by the document. In the case of inquiries or registration of orders, the location of the telephone is important.

Some terminals are intended to function is a customer-oriented environment. Here, the handling of money or tickets may be the principal function and the visual display unit and keyboard play no more than a subordinate role.

Much has been said about the design of terminal workstations. But one thing is certain: it is always individual, and there should be definite insistence on the use of flexible equipment. There are, however, certain fundamental factors which should always be taken into account.

- The terminal equipment must be able to be sited individually. A separate keyboard and, where necessary, a separate numeric keypad should be standard. The VDU must be able to be tilted vertically and rotated horizontally.

- The chair plays a central role. It must provide a correct sitting position so that the load on the lower spine in minimized.
- Some terminals are to be used by people in a standing position. Terminals for customers, for instance. Or an input terminal on a production line. In such cases it is naturally important that the terminal be located at the right height so there is no need for the operator to bend each time he/she uses the terminal.

What kind of tasks are to be carried out at the workplace? Continuous, intensive use of the terminal, or just the occasional query? Does the user need to maintain eye contact with customers or visitors at the opposite side of the desk? It is also of benefit to be able to regulate the height of the table surface. The guideline here is that the height of the table should be capable of adjustment so that the lower arm is parallel with the table-top when the hands are placed on the keyboard. This minimizes the load on the arm muscles. Special terminal tables are usually better than ordinary desks. And it is particularly important to take account here of the luminance ratio between table, paper, keyboard, and VDU.

As to printers, the requirements vary widely from one installation to another. In some offices, many users work at high-speed printers, while other workstations each have their own near-letter-quality printer. There are many printing techniques in use, just as there are many different speeds and typefaces to choose from. If the printer is located close to workplaces, the noise which it emits should not exceed 55 dB when printing. If it is higher, a hood should be used. This should be effective, but at the same time, lightweight and easy to put on and take off. Today, there is no need to accept anything less than good print quality, and if you use carbon copies, these should also be of a good standard. You should be able to read what is being printed, even when the printer is covered by a hood. And there must be easy access to the printer, in order to refill the paper or change the type ribbon, for instance.

The Visual Display Unit

Many new users are somewhat suspicious about working at VDUs. They may have heard people talking about radiation, eye fatigue, and headaches. There is no basis in fact for the belief that working at modern terminals can be hazardous to health. The criticism arises from the fact that many of the VDUs in use some years ago were not good. They often presented fuzzy displays with a great deal of flicker, which caused eye-strain, leading to things like headaches.

Things have changed since then. Many manufacturers today produce bright and easily read characters which are clearly presented without any noticeable flicker. This means you should ensure that your supplier satisfies high requirements with regard to presentation on the screen. Most of today's screens are based on the cathode ray tube, the technology used in an ordinary TV set. An electronic ray sweeps in a series of lines over a phosphor layer which lights up. What decides the clarity of the characters is the closeness of the sweeps across the screen, how often the sweeps are repeated, and the type of phosphor used. Different types of phosphor radiate for varying lengths of time. Other types of screen technology are today the subject of experimental research, for example plasma and floating crystal technology.

Each character on the screen is made of dots within the framework for a dot matrix. In principle, one can say that the more dots there are, the clearer the character. Today, 7×9 dots is recommended as an absolute minimum. Of course, the size and the design of the characters is also important for readability. Here there is a good deal of variation from one manufacturer to another, but lower case character height should be 0.15 inch for normal reading distances. The distance between the rows should be at least 70% of the character height. The typeface used should be simple in design, permit varying stroke widths, and should not be slanting. Figure 8.84 shows the relationship of the characters.

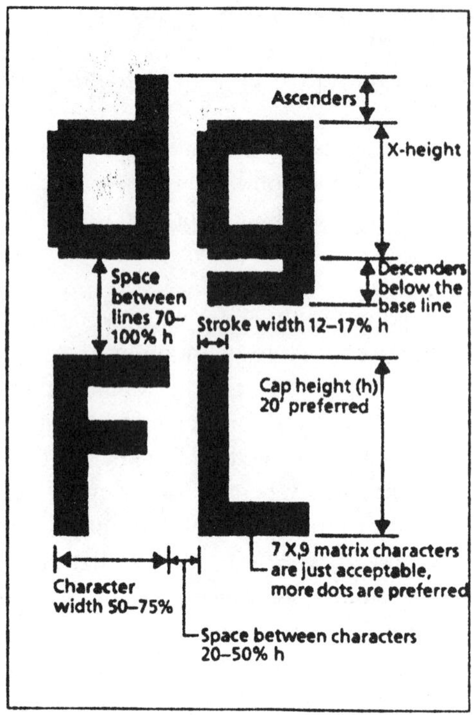

Figure 8.84

Guidelines for Screen Presentation

The number of scan lines per character, the refresh rate, the number of dots in the dot matrix, and the type of phosphor used all vary greatly between different terminal types and manufacturers. While it is difficult to lay down general guidelines, some are listed here.

General:

- There should be at least 10–12 scan lines per character.
- The dots in the matrix should be round or square, not elliptical or rectangular.
- Character spacing should be as even as possible.
- Height of the characters should be 0.15 inch at normal reading distance.
- A 7 × 9 dot matrix is an absolute minimum. The more dots in the matrix, the greater the readability of the character.

For light characters:

- Refresh rate 50–60 Hz, depending on the type of phosphor used.
- The contrast between character and background between 8 : 1 and 10 : 1.
- The brightness of the characters should be adjustable. The character must not lose its sharpness at maximum brightness.

For dark characters:

- Refresh rate must be at least 70 Hz.
- Contrast between character and background between 1 : 8 and 1 : 12.
- The brightness of the background should be adjustable.

There are several common error risk characters for typefaces based on 7 × 9 dot matrices. It is important to check that the terminal manufacturer has selected a font involving as few risks of error as possible. As you design systems for use in the office, consider the types of errors which arise from mutual confusion and from one-way confusion:

Mutual Confusion	*One-Way Confusion*
O and Q	C read as G
T and Y	D read as B
S and 5	H read as M or N
I and L	J, T read as I
X and K	K read as R
I and 1	2 read as Z
	B read as R, S, or 8

The Keyboard

The keyboard itself is probably the most extensively studied and developed part of a terminal workstation. This is easy to understand, since the work of developing keyboards has been going on ever since the typewriter was first introduced over 100 years ago. Equally significant, the design of the keyboard is of vital importance in terminal work. This is particularly true for operators who perform long-term and intensive terminal work.

The most important factor is the freedom to place the keyboard anywhere on the work surface, independent of the location of the display. The numeric keypad should be capable of being placed separately, which is important for left-handed people. It is also important that the keyboard have a low profile so that the hand can rest against the surface of the table when not working. If the keyboard is too high to permit this, it should be fitted with a special hand-wrist support.

The keys must provide finger-tip space, at the same time as it is often desirable that the keyboard be as small as possible. It has been found that the best size for terminal keys is between 0.5 inch square, and the distance between the centers of the keys should be about 0.75 inch.

A degree of concavity in the key feels comfortable to the user. Certain keys can have a deeper form, the so-called "home keys" (F and J on the QWERTY keyboard). The 5 key on the numeric keypad should have a "wart" to help the operator locate the fingers without having to look at the keyboard.

The color of the keyboard is important, too. There must be sufficient contrast between the keyboard, the keys, and the work surface. In addition, the keyboard and the keys should have a matte finish, in order to avoid irritating reflections.

Today, an angle or slope of 5 to 11 degrees is recommended for keyboards, but the ideal solution is naturally for the keyboard to be adjustable so that users can easily select the angle that suits them best.

Just as important as slope is the height of the keyboard above the table surface, since this sets the angle of the hand and wrist, and thereby the work position. Keyboards which are too high should therefore be inset into the surface of the table to avoid unnecessary loading on arms and neck.

European standards recommend that the middle row of the keyboard, the one beginning with A, S, D, shall not be higher than 1.2 inch from the work surface, but in principle one can say the slimmer the keyboard, the better the work position.

Another important detail is the marking of the keys. The characters used must not be too small (at least 0.1 inch) and abbreviations on the keys must follow a clear and logical pattern which is easy for users to identify.

There are three alternative keyboard layouts: QWERTY, Dvorak, and alphabetic. When working with English text, the traditional QWERTY allots 57% of the work to the left hand. The DVORAK layout gives 56% of the work to the right hand, which is better since more than 80% of all people are right-handed. The investment in QWERTY is, however, so enormous that it is not probable that any other layout will take over its dominant position.

Naturally, the markings must not wear away after some time in use, but should preferably be engraved or stamped into the surface of the key itself.

New users in particular often prefer to have some kind of feedback when a key is depressed. This may be an audible click, or some form of counter-pressure. Even modern keyboards should be equipped to provide such tactile feedback, but in the case of audible feedback, the sound should be adjustable in both loudness and pitch. Consequently, different users in the same environment can have different levels of audible feedback on their keyboards or they can remove the sound completely should they so wish.

Software Ergonomics

In the future, more and more people with no computer training will use different kinds of computers and terminals in their day-to-day work. This calls for the development of a new area of application of ergonomics known as "software ergonomics."

Software ergonomics has to do with the design of the system itself, not the hardware used to operate it. With the communication between users and the computer. With the language and the procedures which are used in this communication. With response times for different situations. With the discovery and correction of errors. With help functions which make the terminal work easier.

This is one area where relatively little has been done up until now. The people who designed today's information handling systems often assumed that the user was motivated to understand the language of the computer. For this reason the languages used in dialogues between the computer and its human operator are often difficult to understand, cryptic. Such messages may even prevent the user from working creatively. The time may instead often have to be spent in seeking help from manuals and other documentation.

We must think differently in the future. We must start out with the basis that the user does not understand how the computer works, and, additionally, is not interested in learning to communicate with the machine on the machine's own terms. We must create effective means of communicating so that the user can work efficiently at the terminal and not need long periods of training.

When the first stages of the system design process are beginning, a dialogue must be established between the user and the system designer. Their attitudes to the dialogue must be coordinated at an early stage and, as far as possible, be based on the user's requirement of a natural language in communication. This is a major and highly interesting field of work, and many users are going to be involved in the analysis and design of the user-friendly information systems of the future.

Some thoughts about the near future in the world of software ergonomics:

- Command language. The command language will be changed from a formal to a natural language to which the user is accustomed. In the future, we shall probably have commands which are not simply one word, but rather a series of 5-6 synonyms which all reflect the meaning of the command and which are accepted by both the human user and the computer, even when spelled incorrectly.
- Layout of the display. If the display layout is poor, this leads to the user making mistakes, the rate of working is reduced and the time needed to learn to operate the system increases. It is important to define at an early stage, together with the user, how the display is to be used, which information content is to be presented and where the different elements of information should be placed. If paper forms are used in conjunction with the work at the terminal, the display layout should be similar to these. Information on the screen should be grouped on the basis of user logic.
- Error messages. Most error messages in the systems in use today appear cryptic to the user. A question mark is merely frustrating, and an error code all too often leads to long periods spent

hunting through manuals. The error message must be simple, and in the user's own language. It should always be presented at the same place on the screen, and should inform the user of the nature of the error, and the remedy. In the systems of tomorrow, this must take the form of a "conversation" between the computer and the user.

- Help functions. In a modern information system there must be sophisticated help functions by which the computer assists the user when the user presses a special HELP key or simply types the word "HELP" on the screen. Further help commands and queries should enable the system to guide the user through the documentation so that it quickly becomes clear what the user must do.
- Response times. There are few things more irritating than long response times, but at the same time, too-short response times can, in certain situations, subject the user to stress too, since he or she may then feel compelled to respond at the same rate. In such situations, the system can be designed with delay functions. Guidelines for the response times which are acceptable to users in different situations:

Time from key depression to display of character	0.2 sec
Time from issuing a command to response	2.0 sec
Response time for a simple query	2.0 sec
Response time for a complex query	5.0 sec
Display new page	1.0 sec
Scrolling	0.5 sec
Time between entry of error and error message	2.0 sec

Influencing the Work Environment

In just a few years there will be a terminal of some kind at almost all office workplaces. We shall nearly all be computer users, and we shall all influence the design of systems.

If we do not do something to influence the work environment in good time this is going to mean that even more people are going to experience the problems which can arise in connection with poorly designed workstations and badly planned work environments.

Between the ages of 20 and 60 the focal length of the eye changes. Older people need more light. So it is important to ensure that workstation lighting is arranged to suit the individual. Many people do not discover that they need glasses until they begin working at terminals. If you work at terminals for a good deal of your working day, it is important to have regular eye checks to ensure that you have the correct glasses and avoid straining your eyes unnecessarily.

Poor lighting and incorrect contrast relationships result in fatigue. Incorrect work posture caused by wrongly located keyboards, displays, manuscript holders or perhaps just the wrong kind of chair often cause neck and back problems. Symptoms like those of physical ailments can appear which are in fact disguised psychological problems, and in fact connected with poor motivation and uncertainty in the face of new challenges. This can be treated with a dose of information and through involvement in the planning and design of systems and routines.

In the criticism which is sometimes directed against working at computer terminals, eye problems are often discussed. It has often happened that someone commencing terminal work discovers through working at the terminal that his or her sight is not what it was. Around the age of 40, the eye's ability to focus at short distances deteriorates. Most people have to get reading glasses, which are normally designed for a reading distance of about 14 inches. Many of these people in turn use bifocal lenses so that they can also see clearly at longer distances.

These types of glasses are actually not of any use for terminal work and result in poor work postures since the display on the screen is at a distance in between the two focal lengths of the lenses. The best way to avoid this type of problem is to have regular eye tests. In this way, accomodation and other vision problems are discovered early, and special glasses better suited to terminal work can be arranged.

Consequently it is important for everyone, at an early stage, to be allowed to influence his work environment and the tools and aids to be used. Set up demands for equipment and aids: thorough training, for instance, and proper documentation which is easy to understand and use.

Ensure that the working surroundings are right, and that the prerequisites for correct work environment exist. Make sure that you sit correctly, that you are working at the correct height, and the equipment and documents are located so that your movements are minimized. Adapt your workplace so that it suits you and your pattern of movement. Find out by trial and error what the best working position is at the terminal.

But even if you have the perfect working position, certain muscles are always continuously load-bearing, which results in reduced circulation and fatigue in the muscles. For this reason it is important that you also learn how to stimulate the body and to avoid fatigue. Rest pauses, exercise, and the possibility of variation in the tasks, such as switching between sitting and standing work, help to loosen up stressed joints and muscles.

Here are some summary checklists which can be used.

Chairs

In choosing a chair, consider the following:

- Is the chair height easily adjustable from the seated position?
- Does the backrest adequately support the lower-lumbar region of the spine?
- Does the backrest tilt backward and forward?
- Can it be adjusted up and down?
- Do armrests interfere with movement?
- Does the seat have a rounded front edge?
- Is the chair adequately padded?
- Does the chair feature a five-legged base with casters.

Lighting

When selecting your lighting, be sure to consider the following points:

- Is the level of illumination from the fixture adequate for computer use?
- Is the light flicker-free?
- Is the fixture covered with glare shields or an adjustable shade?
- Can you easily position the lamp to avoid glare and reflections?
- Are the windows near your work space covered with blinds, curtains, or other means of controlling daylight?

Work Surfaces

Consider the following questions when you are planning your work surface:

- Are there separate work surfaces for keyboards and displays?
- Can you tilt the work surfaces and adjust their height?
- Does adequate space exist for storing copies, manuals, documents, and personal belongings?
- Is the work surface deep enough so that you can place your monitor at a preferred distance?
- Is the legroom adequate to accomodate different postures?
- Can you rest your arms when you are not typing?

- Can you route the computer wiring out the way through the desktop?
- Are work surfaces nonreflective?

Accessories

Review this checklist as you shop for related accessories for your work space:

- Are you buying to accessory to complement your work space or to compensate for an initial wrong choice in furniture and lighting design?
- Do the accessories support computers or other manufactured hardware and software; are they flexible enough for both?
- Do the binders, files, holders, and other storage devices fit the sizes of your printouts, disks, and diskettes?
- Can the size of your current work space accomodate the storage of additional peripherals and accessories?

Keyboard Requirements

- The keyboard should be separate from the display unit. The numeric keypad should also, if possible, be separate from the main keyboard.
- Remember that color, contrast, and matte-finished keys are important factors in the choice of keyboards.
- The keyboard should have built-in hand-wrist support or be low enough for the hand and wrist to be rested on the table surface.
- The slope is important and should naturally be adjustable, if possible. An angle of 5 to 11 degrees is recommended.
- The marking of the keys should not be too small, and should, of course, resist wear. Abbreviations printed on the keys must be logical and easy to understand.
- Broad keys should also be designed so that they move straight up and down, even when pressed off-center. Off-center pressure must not lead to wear or to the key depression not being registered.

Guidelines for Ergonomics

The following is a list of ergonomic considerations extracted from the book *The Human Factor (Designing Computer Systems FOR PEOPLE)*, by Richard Rubinstein/Harry Hersh, Digital Press, 1984—highly recommended reading. To each I have added a comment.

1. *Designers make myths; users make conceptual models.* Get the user involved.
2. *Separate design from implementation.* Do the design work.
3. *Describe before you leap.* Know where you're going; it'll be easier to get there.
4. *Develop an explicit use model.* The world is full of theoreticians; make the model concrete.
5. *Maintain a consistent myth.* Don't constantly change direction.
6. *Don't supply kits.* Do it yourself projects don't work.
7. *Limit the scope of systems.* Concentrate, concentrate.
8. *Limit states.* Diminish the number of differences.
9. *Make states visible and visibly distinguished.* Make the differences different.
10. *Minimize conceptual load.* Explicit, that's the word.
11. *Respect the rules of human conversation.* Computer gobbledygook just won't do.
12. *Interrupt with care.* Make soft changes and redirections.

13. *Respond with an appropriate amount of information.* Not codes—information; don't leave them wondering.
14. *Don't misrepresent capabilities.* The oversell is as dangerous as the undercapacity.
15. *Do not violate the rules of human language.* Syntax! Construction! Accuracy! Clarity! Completeness!
16. *Be consistent in the use of language.* It's useful to build a glossary.
17. *Teach by example, not by formalism.* Guide gently; don't force structure.
18. *Avoid arbitrary syntax.* Don't write your own language.
19. *Use application terminology.* When in Rome. . .
20. *Use standard language.* Avoid translation, transliteration and nuance.
21. *Coordinate all system responses.* Make certain they are germane and relative.
22. *Make metaphors make sense.* What's a meta for? It would be better to avoid them.
23. *Correct spelling.* Spelling counts; the eye is a bad interpreter.
24. *Eliminate obviously (and less obviously) bad terms.* Tailor to your audience and keep it clean.
25. *Icons are concrete.* Any graphics terminal can use them.
26. *Avoid complex queries.* Nothing worse than not knowing what to do, in what sequence, when.
27. *Consider voice I/O for use in "hands busy" or "eyes busy" environments.* It's new technology, but it's coming.
28. *Avoid lengthy segments of speech output.* We have synthetic speech capability; the messages should be brief and pointed.
29. *Structure the voice input so that only one- or two-word commands are required.* No interpretation necessary.
30. *Treat learning aids as part of the system.* The price of not helping is greater than the cost of helping.
31. *Write the user's guide first.* If it makes sense on paper, it'll make sense at the terminal. Better yet, get the user to write the guide.
32. *Support clear conceptual models for documentation.* Avoid the fifteen inches of binder.
33. *Examples, examples, examples.* Assume nothing.
34. *An index is an information retrieval system.* Use it.
35. *Verify that help helps.* Train a novice and listen carefully.
36. *Don't let help interfere with the task.* Allow the user to escape the help and return to work.
37. *Integrate help and error processing.* Recovery, rejection, help—provide the answers.
38. *Avoid multiple style modes.* Don't mix text with command structure.
39. *Don't rely on punctuation to carry meaning.* Use the words to emphasize, not the punctuation.
40. *Keep menus short.* And keep them simple.
41. *Label menus.* This will simplify your prototyping.
42. *Use a pointing device.* Move a block cursor, use a mouse or a light pen.
43. *Respond to direct manipulations in real time.* Don't allow the user to doze awaiting a response.
44. *Match objects in the interface to the external myth.* Make it do what you said it would do.
45. *Let the user choose the order of tasks.* Menu options and selectable command structures avoid putting the user in a tight structure.
46. *Acknowledge user actions—quickly.* Again—respond.
47. *Provide an easy way out.* No rope to hang; no limb to cut.
48. *No surprises.* If the user must wonder what to do next, it will be a mistake.
49. *Confirm information content, not literal input.* As we get into artificial intelligence systems, this will be easier.
50. *Don't distract.* Avoid the cute, the complex, the garish.

51. *Report errors simply and in context.* The user needs to know what the error is and how to correct it without researching volumes of reference manual.
52. *Be polite.* Empathize. Gently.guide as you would touch a delicate flower.
53. *Don't blame the user.* Help.
54. *Avoid error codes.* Avoid any codes. Use plain language.
55. *Don't mislead.* Guide accurately.
56. *Fix problems.* Revise, learn, modify—dynamically, if possible.
57. *Don't personify the computer.* Don't call it "Harry," Dirty or otherwise.
58. *Distinguish between success and failure.* And don't preach. Help.
59. *State errors in terms of the external myth. Design against the objective.*
60. *Make it easy to correct mistakes.* Don't leave them guessing; they won't be laughing.
61. *Combine error and help processing.* Progress is the key; help them to progress.
62. *Design the error behavior of the system.* Make it conversational and helpful.
63. *Allow people to work in real time.* Long waits not only waste time—they kill momentum.
64. *Announce long delays.* If you must wait, notify the operator, permitting the working at other tasks.
65. *Make delays make sense.* Logic, clarity, expectancy.
66. *Respect the rules of good presentation on paper.* Logic, clarity, format.
67. *Present lists vertically.* The best way to design the screen.
68. *Identify output data.* This is, after all, a system.
69. *Number from 1; measure from 0.* Zero is a number to computer people only.
70. *Use formatting and ordering to clarify structure.* Structure is explainable.
71. *Use graphs and charts.* Particularly in documentation.
72. *Avoid clutter.* Clutter confuses.
73. *Visual attributes must compose correctly.* Clear space, color, typestyle: they must look right.
74. *Don't overwhelm the user with visual attributes.* Some colors clash; overbusy screens and reports require more time to clarify than the cost of extra paper.
75. *Make semantics of attributes clear and consistent.* Explain everything; leave nothing open to interpretation.
76. *Allow flexibility in formatting input data.* New languages allow the user to develop format styles.
77. *Provide prompting or cuing for input.* Don't leave anyone with just a question mark.
78. *Allow shorthand and abbreviations in input.* Provided there is a glossary.
79. *Make frequent inputs easy to express. And easy to repeat. Key-condensed input is helpful here.*
80. *Design keyboards as a part of systems.* Single key entry if possible. Two and three key entries are confusing and error prone.
81. *Simplify keyboard layouts.* Really only applicable to use of special and function keys.
82. *Group keys according to function.* Focus the eye movement.
83. *Separate text and control on keyboards.* Don't multifunction the keys—the result will be errors and confusion.
84. *Avoid multiplexing keys.* Again, don't multifunction the keys—the result will be errors and confusion.
85. *Articulate the evaluation goals.* You must measure to see if you did accomplish that which you set out to do.
86. *Select subjects who are unfamiliar with the system.* It's the novices, trying to use the system for the first time, who will spot a majority of errors.
87. *Select subjects who are representative of the target user population.* It helps to have some consistency of people.

88. *Use representative tasks.* It helps to have some relevance of tasks.
89. *Standardize the tasks.* Nothing bizarre.
90. *Use the design guidelines to structure an evaluation.* If the design was by the objective, the measurement will fall into place.

As you go through this list you no doubt wondered about "the myth." Simply stated, the myth is the system you sold; not necessarily the one you installed. This list will not match the book numerically, because some of the numbered points were left out of the book. I've renumbered them. Also, as a final point, the authors have suggested repeating Frank and Lillian Gilbreth's time and motion study concepts. The Gilbreths did the first work in the area of functional ergonomics by taking movies. The authors suggest it is useful to videotape the subjects.

As you've looked at this list, it should be plain that ergonomics—human factors—go far beyond the design of the furniture. For an in-depth study of the relationship of systems to people, it is recommended that you read James Martin's book on the design of man-computer dialogs.

Chewing Our Cabbage (a Second Time) in Summary

More than a hundred years ago, after the invention of the telephone, someone predicted that everybody would have to become a telephone operator. Though not exactly as was envisioned, the prognostication has come true—we have all become "telephone operators." In 1955, on the television program *See It Now,* Edward R. Murrow predicted that unless something changed, every woman in the country would be called upon to work a telephone switchboard. Murrow did not live to see the population decline nor the geometric expansion of the demand for telephone and related community services. The direct distance dialing Bell System Network took away the switchboard and made us all communications workers. Today, the DDD remains as the premiere hallmark of a burgeoning communications service, where selection is king and unheard of capacity and capability has become the queen.

The automation of the office—and let's be very careful to isolate the concept from the sheer electrification of mechanical and office-related tasks—now encompasses so large a selection of options and capabilities as to at-once enhance the office's traditional functions while simultaneously creating vistas of unparalleled capacity. For some, this is progress. For others, this is fear. For yet others, this is economic survival and ultimate profitability.

"The Office" has traditionally been the glue which holds the organization together. Orders moved from *the office* to the factory. Time cards moved from the factory to *the office.* Customers dealt with *the office.* Personnel and payroll were all located at *the office.* In short, take awaya the office's predominant administrative position, and the office ceases to exist as the cohesive force which binds together all other equal or subordinate forces of the organization.

Automation of the administrative function can be traced largely along the scribing pathway. The quill pen gave way to the steel point pen, to the fountain pen. The invention of printing mechanisms with finger-selectable type is a 20th Century phenomenon. Electrification of this process added to speed, quality, uniformity, and ease of use. The electronification of the process, while making quantum leaps in these areas, still came up against an upper and largely physical limitation—the speed of the typist. Two copies required carbon paper. Accuracy demanded care, extra skills, or chemical coverings. As late as 1960 it was still necessary to type something a second time to get two "good" copies. Xerography changed that, and the xerographic and electrostatic copiers would change the way the office ran—its speed and directions. While not everyone in the office had learned to be a type operator, just about everybody could easily become a copy operator—and did, to the chagrin of many a manager's budget.

During this time, the office workforce, largely female, derived status by the type of typewriter one was given. The executive secretary received the Selectric typewriter, irrespective of the volume (low) and quality (moderate) needs of the output from the machine. Other clerical persons whose volumes were considerably higher were allocated the older, slower, sometimes manual equipment. Technical people took pot luck. Typewriting was "woman's work"; good typewriting machines went where they would be used as status symbols; and communications by the fingertips were made difficult, at the least. The manager would be criticized if he (and later, she) did so—so he never learned. The "glue" to the office automation was the office automaton, Sarah Secretary. Only now is the folly of that mindset apparent.

It was the technical folks who came and changed it all. They knew where the glue was. It wasn't in typewriters and secretaries. It was in terminals and microchips. Computers were the glue to hold the organization together. Computers would do the personnel and payroll functions. Computers would schedule the factory, report the progress, ship the goods. It was structuring, to be sure, but pervasive, and the technocrats invaded, one by one, the various significant organizational functions, reducing each to a number and a construct of logic. The technicians would have their say. But at the same time, the field of office automation may well surpass anything we have ever known in the field of data processing. It would behoove the DP analyst with an eye to the future to ensure his or her knowledge base in what promises to be an exciting new direction of the field.

And there it is.

QUESTIONS

1. The categories of data transmission systems include:
   A. Twisted pair, corrugated cable
   B. On-line, off-line
   C. Integrated, segregated
   D. Hardwire, soft-sector
2. A disk cylinder is characterized by its
   A. Modules
   B. Access heads
   C. Cells
   D. DASD
3. A word processor which allows concurrent editing of two documents uses a concept called:
   A. MailMerge
   B. Windowing
   C. Block transfer
   D. Move and replace
4. Five functions which have been implemented in the integrated workstation are:
   A. CAD, CAM, DTF, word processing, database
   B. CAI, spreadsheet, mapping, processing, editing
   C. Graphics processor, process control, manufacturing monitoring, word processing
   D. Word processing, database, spreadsheet, graphics, and communications
5. Devices using a slow scan rate would include:
   A. Temperature graphing and map transmission
   B. Detection of critical temperatures and voltages
   C. Transmission from computers
   D. Transmission from humans
6. The difference between logical data and physical data is:
   A. Physical data is relative to the computer; logical data is relative to the software
   B. Physical data is relative to the software; logical data is relative to the hardware
   C. Physical data can be picked up by hand
   D. Logical data can pass tests of reason

7. The predominant value of a word processing system is:
 A. The ability to tie to a database or spreadsheet
 B. The ability to scroll from window to window
 C. The ability to concurrently enter while printing
 D. The ability to modify text in memory

8. Criteria for an ergonomically-sound keyboard include:
 A. Standard design, highlighted keys
 B. Separate, sloped, matte color, key marking, key size
 C. Clicking sound, adjustable key spacing
 D. Separable, infrared, multifunction keys

9. The best definition of a real-time application:
 A. Changes its environment on the basis of its output
 B. Senses it environment on the basis of temperature
 C. Always posts records quickly
 D. Affects its environment on the basis of its input

10. A disk file extent is:
 A. the distance one will go to use database
 B. the DBMS executive
 C. the extension of the file from track to overflow
 D. the cylinder overflow indicator

11. A serious limitation to an in-memory word processing system is:
 A. Limited mailmerge capability
 B. Limited document size
 C. No memory for overlay processing
 D. No window processing

12. The information center concept will consolidate OA and DP under a person called the:
 A. CEO
 B. CIO
 C. CIA
 D. CDP

13. An interactive environment may best be described as:
 A. A user-initiated dialogue and response
 B. A machine-initiated dialogue and response
 C. A user-received correspondence
 D. A machine-received correspondence

14. The nature of a flat file is generally:
 A. Sequential, fixed format
 B. Random, variable format
 C. Sequential, variable format
 D. Random, fixed format

15. A model must pass three tests:
 A. Relevance, accuracy, aggregation
 B. Junction, disjunction, conjunction
 C. And, or, and nor
 D. Stub, entry, and rule

16. Eyestrain is a constant problem when using the terminal and screen. It is particularly acute for folks who are:
 A. Myopic
 B. Older than 40

C. Nearsighted
D. Farsighted

17. The nature of a static communications environment could include:
A. Telemetry, data collection, or constant display.
B. Card readers, punches, and printers
C. Microwave, closed loop, and LAN
D. Telephone, telegraph, television

18. The inverted form of database is essentially:
A. A DASD file which is built in ISAM
B. A random file which has hashed keys
C. A ring structured file with reverse keys
D. A flat-file on which one or more indices have been built

19. The ability to change margins and style of presentation is a feature of what word processing function?
A. Insertion
B. Reformating
C. Blocking
D. Deletion

20. Among the capabilities of the integrated workstation is graphics. Graphics will be used for:
A. Creating visuals for classrooms
B. Picturephone communications
C. Image processing and electronic composition
D. Calculating budgets

21. Computer communications is *least* efficiently conducted in
A. A digital communications system
B. An analog communications system
C. A modem communications system
D. A microwave communications system

22. The TREE.FRUIT.APPLE model by IBM is an example of:
A. A multiple-tuple
B. A leaf/node database
C. A flat file
D. A hierarchical file

23. To test the variables of a supply and demand model, the economist would use what decision support tool?
A. A financial modeling system
B. A statistical modeling system
C. A database modeling system
D. A spreadsheet modeling system

24. Software ergonomics includes consideration of: Command language, layout of the display, error messages and help functions, response times. Which did the author consider to be most important?
A. Command language
B. Display layout
C. Error messages and help functions
D. Response times

25. The three types of computer transmission service are:
A. Simplex, complex, duplex
B. Duplex, complex, perplex

C. Half-Simplex, half-duplex, full-simplex
D. Simplex, half-duplex, full-duplex

26. If multiple different logical files can be derived from the same physical data, we're talking about what kind of database?
A. Inverted
B. Indexed
C. Network
D. Token

27. When a paragraph has been highlighted, is is marked for what kind of operation?
A. Blocking
B. Editing
C. Printing
D. Sorting

28. There are three alternative keyboard layouts: QWERTY, Dvorak, and alphabetic. Which is fastest?
A. QWERTY
B. Dvorak
C. alphabetic
D. numeric

29. A full-duplex system is normally used for:
A. Process control of chemical plants
B. Satellite business systems
C. In-house or devoted systems
D. Telephone communications

30. The difference between physical and logical data independence is:
A. Logical means the application programs don't have to be changed; physical means the organization may be changed
B. Logical means the application programs may not be changed; physical means the organization may be changed only if the programs are changed
C. Physical means the application programs must be changed; logical means the organization may be changed.
D. Physical means the application programs may not be changed; logical means the organization must be changed.

31. The decision model has three dimensions. They are:
A. Left, right, and up
B. Amplitude, certitude, and etude
C. Simplicy, dimension, dependency
D. Complexity, time, degree of undertainty

32. Poorly designed workstations and badly planned work environments require consideration of:
A. Economics
B. Aquanautics
C. Ergonomics
D. Statistics

33. Because the telephone system is used for computer communications,
A. The computer interface must be parallel
B. The computer interface need not be serial
C. The modem must interface to a half-duplex service
D. The modem must interface to a full-duplex service

34. The conceptual model for the database is called the:
A. Global physical data organization

B. Local physical data organization
C. Global logical data organization
D. Local logical data organization

35. Page-oriented word processors are better than scrolling word processors. Why?
A. A complete page, as it will be printed, is shown
B. A screen which adjusts to the size of the document is shown
C. The page is legal size, so anything can fit
D. The statement is inaccurate; it's not any better

36. Integration, as applied to the electronic document, includes:
A. Image, text, data, graphics, voice
B. Heading, body, salutation, signature
C. Assembly, mailmerge, addressing, franking
D. Typing, posting, filing, mailing

37. The bandwidth of the telephone system, in cycles is:
A. 3,000
B. 4,800
C. 9,600
D. 14,200

38. Data structures designed for display at terminals:
A. Are the view of the terminal user who is not a data processing specialist.
B. Are the view of the systems analyst who is a qualified data processing specialist
C. Are the view of the database administrator who is qualified in the database software.
D. Are the view of the terminal administrator who is qualified in the terminal interface software

39. In addition to deciding which variables are pertinent to a problem, and where the boundaries are, the modeler must also select variables which are:
A. Jointed, disjointed, conjointed
B. Discrete, random, continuous
C. Random, collected, sampled
D. Inverse, obverse, and coverse

40. Which describes screen presentation guidelines?
A. Pixels, raster, formatted, sectors
B. Scan, matrix, ribbon, pins
C. Formatted, linear, scrolling, page
D. Scan, dots, matrix, refresh, contrast, brightness

41. In order to communicate using the DDD, there must be an interface to accomplish:
A. Conversion of analog to digital using a TCU
B. Conversion of digital to analog using a MODEM
C. Conversion of parallel to serial using a FECP
D. Conversion of serial to parallel using a synthesizer

42. The primary objectives of a database should include consideration of:
A. Retrofitting old files
B. Tailoring to the available computer languages
C. Availability of applications development
D. Transferrability to alternate hardware

43. The insert and overwrite modes of word processors differ by a single facet. It is:
A. Insert pushes the line right; overwrite does not
B. Insert does not shift the line; overwrite does
C. Neither insert nor overwrite affect the line length
D. Both insert and overwrite affect the line length

44. A definition of the term "knowledge worker" could be:
A. The traditional secretary/clerical person
B. Middle management-level technical employee
C. The warehouse and distribution personnel
D. The labor union in the manufacturing operation

45. The International Standards Organization (ISO) has developed a seven-layer model for telecommunications. Included are:
A. Physical, motor, transmission
B. Link, presentation, process
C. Session, bus, and network
D. Stop, start, pulse

46. The secondary objectives of a database should include consideration of:
A. Low cost
B. Availablility for applications development
C. Retrofitting old files
D. Controlled redundancy

47. Wordwrap is a feature of the word processor which:
A. Automatically places a carriage return at the end of each line
B. Adjusts a ragged right edge to align to the rightmost side of the text
C. Moves a word which is too wide for the line to the next line
D. Truncates the line to fit the margins

48. For a truly ergonomic work space, consider purchasing:
A. Halogen lamps
B. Halon fire extinguishers
C. Adjustable work surfaces
D. Anti-static floor mats

49. Parallel vs. serial transmission of computer signals means:
A. Parallel means all 7 ASCII bits are sent simultaneously
B. Serial means all 7 ASCII bits are sent simultaneously
C. Parallel means all 7 ASCII bits are masked
D. Serial means all 7 ASCII bits are masked

50. A collection of similar database entities is called:
A. A quadruple-tuple
B. Hashed file
C. An entity set
D. Indexed network

51. The variables of a quantitative model include a mathematical description of the relationship amongst variables. These variables are categorized in this manner:
A. Quantitative, qualitative, instrumental
B. Decision, process, tabulate
C. Input, process, output
D. Decision, intermediate, output

52. The laser printer with suitable software provides the facility to provide such special output as:
A. Integrated documents
B. Standard report formats
C. Pie charts and histograms
D. Dispersed documents

53. That process of moving a character serially is called a:
A. Character move

B. Bit stream
C. Character set
D. Pulse train

54. The minimum entries in a data dictionary are:
A. Size and class
B. Name and entity type
C. Name and size
D. Entity type and class

55. A hard space is:
A. A space which is coded from the keyboard
B. A space which will not be removed when the text is reformated
C. A space which will be removed when the text is reformated
D. A space which is used for indentation

56. The text states these differences between "front office" and "back office" functions:
A. Front office functions will not change; back office functions will increase
B. Increases will be found in both the front and back office locations
C. Decreases will be found in both the front and back office locations
D. Front office functions will increase; back office functions will decrease

57. A mark parity is:
A. A means to hold the communication line
B. A means to flag or annotate the pulse stream
C. A means to acknowledge a transmission
D. A means to disconnect the line

58. The entry identifier is also known as the:
A. Field description
B. Index identifier
C. Tuple count
D. Key field

59. Decision techniques include:
A. Ordinary, timely, random
B. Statistical, financial, quantitative
C. Sampling, inferential, stochastic
D. Administrative, clerical, managerial

60. The most important considerations for lighting design among the answers given is:
A. Direct and indirect glare
B. Near-point acuity, binocularity, and convergence
C. Sharp screen image, display contrast, and proper refresh rate
D. Balancing the activities of reading copy and reading the screen

61. The standard time measurement of a communication service is:
A. The bit
B. The byte
C. The baud
D. The boot

62. The dynamic combination of two tuples could be called a:
A. Truncated field
B. Concatenated key
C. Contiguous element
D. Concurrent network

63. The coordinates which form the rows and columns of a spreadsheet are called ''cells.'' Relate the cell to the operation of a computer.
A. A cell is a canned procedure
B. A cell is a variable
C. A cell is an array element
D. A cell is a constant

64. Which of the following statements is true when considering the use of noise to achieve optimum comfort
A. No extraneous noise at all should be permitted
B. Some extraneous noise of a soothing nature is acceptable
C. Some extraneous noise of a raucous nature is acceptable
D. There need be no restrictions on noise

65. The purpose of the UART is to:
A. Interface the DDD to the computer
B. Interface the DAA to the DDD
C. Interface the computer's bus to the modem
D. Interface the network to the computer's bus

66. The concept of value redundancy deals with
A. Excessive media usage
B. Diminished processing time
C. Changes in network organization
D. Duplicate records

67. Data is entered to a cell by one of four methods. They are:
A. Keyed entry, calculated, derived, and developed
B. Keyboard, Copy or Move, Loading, and communication
C. 10 key pad, Dvorak keyboard, diskette, and Bernoulli
D. Mouse, light pen, graphics pad, and keyboard

68. Which of the following organizational levels is client-driven?
A. Clerical
B. Administrative
C. Middle management
D. Top management

69. Micro-to-mainframe linkages may be effected by the use of:
A. Digital coding systems
B. FECPs and TCUs
C. Modems and CPUs
D. TCUs and arithmetic registers

70. The rationale for having secondary keys is:
A. Alternate field access without resorting
B. Simplified filing
C. Diminished access time
D. Decreased processing time

71. The formula methods for spreadsheets are:
A. Literal
B. Numeric
C. Alphabetic
D. Algebraic

72. The IVDT (integrated voice/data/terminal) does *not* include:
A. Messaging services

B. Intelligent copiers
C. Unique outputs
D. Processing services

73. The Microcom Network Protocol is a:
A. Asynchronous protocol
B. Synchronous protocol
C. Bisynchronous protocol
D. Trisynchronous protocol

74. The purpose of the database schema is:
A. To detail the database to an application
B. To diminish access time by input/output procedures
C. To reorganize the database upon finding synonyms
D. To provide a description and chart of data

75. The Range feature of a spreadsheet performs what function?
A. Labels a portion of the spreadsheet to locate the object of operations
B. Defines an area for the SUM operation
C. Is the way to do an array operation
D. Is the way to do a matrix transformation

76. The voice annotation of data is
A. Not currently possible
B. A cassette recording which accompanies the printout
C. A digitally produced voice recording "attached" to the data or graphics record
D. A synthetic speech output of a word processing program

77. The number of characters which can be transmitted in the ASCII system is:
A. 32
B. 128
C. 256
D. 512

78. Distinguish between relationships and cross references.
A. Neither convey information
B. One is dependent; the other is independent
C. Both are dependent
D. Both are independent

79. A spreadsheet macro can function
A. As a data transfer program
B. As a driver program
C. As a specification program
D. As a calculation program only

80. The statement "The mainframe is now a peripheral to the workstation in an integrated environment. It's but a server" means:
A. The DP Manager's job is in jeopardy
B. It is possible to append the host computer to the microcomputer, reversing roles
C. It is impossible to append the host computer to the microcomputer; they are always separate
D. The host and the mainframe cannot communicate

81. The Carrier Sense Multiple Access/Collision Detection (CSMA/CD) uses:
A. DDD
B. SOS
C. BCD
D. CCD

82. Distinguish between the schema and the subschema.
A. Schema describes the application; subschema describes the database
B. Schema is a global description; subschema is a local description
C. Schema is ordinate; subschema is inordinate
D. Schema is defined in a COBOL program; subschema defined in a data definition language

83. Many spreadsheets allow the creation of data look up tables. How?
A. The table is contained in the first column and that column must be searched
B. One column is used as a reference to a second column, which contains the table
C. A table is nothing more than the rows and columns of a spreadsheet summed horizontally
D. A table lookup is a special function of the most sophisticated word processor.

84. The design element of an ergonomic chair design which include the ''waterfall'' feature is important because of
A. Viewing angle
B. Arm and wrist fatigue
C. Thigh circulation
D. Thoracic and lumbar support

85. The world standard for business communications is currently:
A. SNA/DMSA
B. SDLC/HDLC
C. HDLC/SDA
D. SDLC/MNP

86. The elements of a hierarchical structure are known as:
A. Tuples
B. Modules
C. Nodes
D. Leaves

87. The difference between relative and absolute addressing of a spreadsheet is:
A. A relative address is adjusted on copy operations; an absolute address is not
B. A relative address is not adjusted on copy operations; an absolute address is
C. A relative address gets an annual card
D. An absolute address is a certainty

88. The statement ''E-Mail is a critical mass issue'' means:
A. It isn't beneficial unless the number of potential users is significant
B. The preponderance of users must be from an overwhelming number of subscribers
C. There is a point at which the service will blow up.
D. There is a point at which E-Mail becomes an infeasible solution.

89. A commonly used data transmission speed control is:
A. ACK/NAK
B. ETC/DLE
C. XON/XOFF
D. TRON/TROFF

90. The purpose of a pointer is to:
A. Conjoin the fractured data elements
B. Refer to the adjacent data element
C. Point to the application in which the database is used
D. Define hierarchical relationships

91. The purpose of the Format command is:
A. To structure the margins on the worksheet

B. To align decimal points on all cells
C. To select display presentations of structured data
D. To display formulas in cells

92. Factors which will *not* tend to keep the office disintegrated:
A. The reticence of managerial personnel to use a keyboard
B. The easy availability of telephones; the nonavailability of IVDTs.
C. The availability of intelligent copy machines
D. The movement toward electronic publishing

93. The predominant purpose of the local area network (LAN) is:
A. Collection of similar devices
B. Collection of dissimilar devices
C. Word processor to word processor interface
D. Word processor to telephone network interface

94. A plex database structure may be defined as:
A. One with neither parent nor child
B. One with parent but no child
C. One with more than one parent or child
D. One with child but no parent

95. The format for passing spreadsheet data to and from other software packages is:
A. DTF
B. DIF
C. ACF
D. SSF

96. The four required skills of an OA analyst, according to industry expert Mary Ruprecht are:
A. Clerical, organizational, managerial, and technical
B. Analytical, systematic, clerical, and administrative
C. Systematic, analystical, managerial, and administrative
D. Technical, personnel, management, and financial

97. Optical Fiber is a new means to send:
A. Local area network signals
B. Computer to DDD interface signals
C. Microwave data transmission
D. Analog to analog transmission

98. The purpose of optimization is:
A. Resequence the chains
B. Diminish the seek time
C. Increase the latency
D. Shake up the records

99. Distinguish between a routine and a nonroutine decision.
A. A routine decision is procedural; a nonroutine decision is judgmental
B. A routine decision is determinant; a nonroutine decision is holistic
C. A routine decision is democratic; a nonroutine decision is autocratic
D. A routine decision is random; a nonroutine decision is specific

100. OA training must be accomplished at three levels. They are:
A. Judgment, dexterity, and proficiency
B. Orientation, acquaintence, and competency
C. Integration, familiarization, and utilization
D. Familiarization, dexterity, and competency

ANSWERS

1. B	**26.** C	**51.** D	**76.** C
2. B	**27.** A	**52.** A	**77.** B
3. B	**28.** B	**53.** D	**78.** B
4. D	**29.** C	**54.** B	**79.** C
5. A	**30.** A	**55.** B	**80.** B
6. A	**31.** D	**56.** D	**81.** D
7. D	**32.** C	**57.** A	**82.** B
8. B	**33.** C	**58.** D	**83.** B
9. D	**34.** C	**59.** B	**84.** C
10. C	**35.** A	**60.** D	**85.** B
11. B	**36.** A	**61.** C	**86.** C
12. B	**37.** A	**62.** B	**87.** A
13. A	**38.** A	**63.** C	**88.** A
14. A	**39.** B	**64.** A	**89.** C
15. A	**40.** D	**65.** C	**90.** A
16. B	**41.** B	**66.** A	**91.** C
17. A	**42.** C	**67.** B	**92.** C
18. D	**43.** A	**68.** C	**93.** C
19. B	**44.** B	**69.** B	**94.** C
20. C	**45.** B	**70.** A	**95.** A
21. B	**46.** D	**71.** D	**96.** D
22. D	**47.** C	**72.** B	**97.** A
23. D	**48.** C	**73.** B	**98.** B
24. C	**49.** A	**74.** D	**99.** A
25. D	**50.** C	**75.** A	**100.** B

TUTORIAL

1. There are two predominant categories of TC systems, those which are on-line and those which are off-line. In simple terms, the difference is whether or not they are directly connected to a host computer.
2. A cylinder is an access mechanism with many reading heads, each of which can read one track. A group of tracks which can be read without moving the access mechanism.
3. A program which will allow concurrent working with two documents is a using a concept called "windowing," wherein a part of each document is displayed in an area on the monitor screen.
4. The integrated work station will have these capabilities: graphics, spreadsheets, electronic mail, word processing systems, mapper systems (for the time being let's call them the fourth generation languages), mainframe applications, sociological systems electronic filing, conference calling, and computer-aided design (CAD).
5. Devices using a slow scan rate (minutes). Applications of this concept would include temperature graphing and map transmission.
6. Logical is the way the programmer sees it. Physical is the way the software arranges the data on the physical device. There are therefore these relationships: the logical relationship to the physical relationship; the logical structure to the physical structure; and the logical data description to the physical data description.
7. The predominant advantage of being able to type directly into the computer's memory is that the text can easily be modified. Because the text is in the computer's memory instead of being printed

on paper, you can overtype the text without erasing, insert new text into the middle of a document, restructure a sentence, eliminate a paragraph, etc., without making erasures or retyping pages of text.

8. The keyboard should be separate from the display unit. The numeric keypad should also, if possible, be separate from the main keyboard. Color, contrast, and matte-finished keys are important factors in the choice of keyboards. Slope is important and should naturally be adjustable, if possible. An angle of 5 to 11 degrees is recommended. The marking of the keys should not be too small, and should, of course, resist wear. Abbreviations printed on the keys must be logical and easy to understand. Broad keys should also be designed so that they move straight up and down, even when pressed off-center. Off-center pressure must not lead to wear or to the key depression not being registered.

9. The real-time system affects its environment on the basis of its input. The sensing of a critical temperature, for example, permits the computer-controlled nuclear reactor to change its environment by adding cooling.

10. Extent—overflow records from anywhere; physically contiguous.

11. Document size: The in-memory orientation of many word processor programs can only be fully utilized with the larger memory sizes. In-memory access provides speed, and the cost of that speed should be weighed against the cost and availability of diskette storage.

12. Under the leadership of a Chief Information Officer (CIO), there will come into existence mini-computer centers known as ''information centers.'' In essence, this will be a functional duplication of the larger mainframe DP activities, and EDP is but one of the information technologies to be tapped in the office information system.

13. The interactive environment is one which permits dialogue and change of the computer's environment. Generally, there is a user-initiated transaction. The host computer controls communication, processes a query and provides a response.

14. It's generally a fixed format, sequential record. The physical data structure is essentially the same as the logical file structure.

15. Models must pass these tests: Relevance—the condition must fit the problem; accuracy— will be variable, depending upon the decision to be made; aggregation—grouping number of individual quantities into a larger quantity.

16. Around the age of 40, the eye's ability to focus at short distances deteriorates. Most people have to get reading glasses or bifocal lenses so that they can also see clearly at longer distances. Special glasses with appropriate focal lengths are required. The best way to avoid this type of problem is to have regular eye tests.

17. A static communications environment would include telemetry, data collection, or constant display.

18. The inverted form of database consists of a flat-file with a series of indices containing the keys of the flat files. This means that, on diskette, an index could be searched, the address of the specific record obtained, and the record itself obtained with the shortest possible process. Other fields of the flat-file record could likewise be indexed.

19. Reformatting of text is one of the most important and powerful features of a word processing program. The user can change the margins and style of presentation at will. Because the text of the document is contained in the memory of the computer, it can be restructured at will. You can print a document, decide that the appearance is inappropriate, change the margins, and reprint the document, without retyping the text.

20. Image processing—intelligent copiers, sophisticated printers, facsimile. No doubt a few visuals will be made.

21. In an analog communication system, such as the telephone network, there are a few other problems with signal strength, thermal and line noise, sensitivity of heat and miscellaneous magnetic waves, and the ever-present hiss, all of which helps the computer-generated data signal to drown in the noise.

22. A multiple-hierarchical indexing scheme to a flat file.

23. Market models test the variables under uncertainty of the product in the marketplace. To the economist, this is experimentation with supply and demand curves. Because it's mathematically based, a spreadsheet or a financial modeling system can be used to depict the potential impact of changes in market forces.

24. Much consideration was given to error messages and help functions by the author. They're all important, for different reasons.

25. Transmissions fall into one of three general categories of service: simplex, half-duplex, and full-duplex (called simply duplex).

26. The database network permits multiple different logical files to be derived from the same physical data. The same data can be accessed in different ways by applications with different requirements.

27. A blocking operation will highlight the text between the parameters, preparatory to a move, copy, or delete operation.

28. When working with English text, the traditional QWERTY allots 57% of the work to the left hand. The Dvorak layout gives 56% of the work to the right hand, which is better since more than 80% of all people are right-handed. The investment in QWERTY is, however, so enormous that it is not probable that any other layout will take over its dominant position.

29. Full-duplex systems are generally in-house or devoted systems, although some of the systems you will encounter will be full-duplex systems.

30. By logical data independence it is meant that the overall logical structure of the data may be changed without changing the application programs. The changes may not remove any of the data used by the application programs. Physical data independence means the physical layout and organization of the data may be changed without changing either the overall logical structure of the data or the application programs.

31. Models are abstractions of systems, substitutes for the real system. They involve a large number of assumptions about the nature of the environment in which the system works, about the operating characteristics of its components, and about the way people will behave. A model is a set of relations, a continuum of complexity (from one variable to many), of uncertainty (from deterministic to probabilistic), and of time (from static to dynamic).

32. Ergonomics is the study of human factors, and has become a large consideration of system designers.

33. The telephone network is a half-duplex network, but the manufacturers of the devices necessary encode the signals (modems) have found a way to obtain full-duplex service from a half-duplex medium.

34. The global logical data organization is the conceptual model for the database. It is the logical view of the data, different from the physical storage organization.

35. Page-oriented word processors are programs which operate on a single page of text at a time. These word processors create documents on the screen and those documents are exactly like the documents that will be printed. Each page is treated as a separate document. Each page is formatted exactly as it will be printed. Each page is stored to disk before a new page is started. In some ways, the page-oriented word processors are easier to use than the scrolling-type word processors.

36. It will receive image processing (logo, name, and electronic signature), text, data, graphics, voice, and communications-based.

37. The telephone system provides a fairly narrow range of frequencies (between 300 and 3,300 Hertz), and has bandwidth not dissimilar to the rate of oscillation of light.

38. Data structures designed for display at terminals is the view of the terminal user who is not a data processing specialist.

39. The modeler must also decide which variables are discrete, random, or continuous. *Conjointed* and *coverse* are not bona fide words.

40. Consideration for hardware acquisition should consider these elements: scan rate, dots or pixel resolution, matrix resolution, refresh rate, contrast, and brightness.

41. It is the responsibility of the modem to prepare the signal for transmission on the analog network and to receive the signal from the analog network and prepare it for use by the computer again.

42. The database is the foundation stone of future application development. It is easier, cheaper, faster, and more flexible than any other form of data storage and access.

43. The insert mode is frequently referred to as the ''Pushright'' mode. This mode allows the insertion of text into the middle of the document. All of the text to the right of the cursor is moved down and the new text is inserted before the text that follows.

44. It is easy to jump at the secretary/clerical person because we have a mindset which says that office automation is merely a way to speed those functions. There is no doubt that some of those folks will become knowledge workers. But the middle management stratum is the level where the knowledge worker is currently employed.

45. The ISO model includes: Layer 1, Physical Control; Layer 2, Link Control; Layer 3, Network Control; Layer 4, Transport Control; Layer 5, Session Control; Layer 6, Presentation Control; and Layer 7, Process Control.

46. One of the secondary objectives of a database is controlled redundancy. Data items will be stored only once except where there are technical or economic reasons for redundant storage.

47. The word processor will cut the long line of text that you type into appropriate segments to fit within the set margins. When you have typed too many characters to fit within the margin, the word processor will move the last word of the line down to the next line and continue inserting from that point.

48. Any of these is of benefit for use under specific circumstances, but only one of them applies to the subject of ergonomics—the adjustable work surfaces.

49. A parallel transmission, such as used with a digital network or coaxial cable, allows simultaneous transmission of all bits of the signal, be they the 7-bit ASCII or the 8-bit EBCDIC characters.

50. A collection of similar entities is called an entity set (file).

51. Decision variable—this variable is controlled by the decision maker, and varies in accordance with the alternative selected. Intermediate variable—this links decisions to outcomes, and functions as a consolidation variable. Output variable—this is used to measure decision performance and is referred to an ''attribute.'

52. The text provides a couple examples of the integrated document, which is really the wave of the paper-oriented communication future, and is largely a feature of the laser printer.

53. That process of moving a character serially is called a *pulse train,* and there will be seven bits and a parity bit, or eight bits (with no parity bit) transmitted in this pulse train.

54. Each field has a name and a data entity type, which will ultimately end up in a Data Dictionary.

55. There are occasions where you do not want words split up at the end of a line. For instance, you might want the title ''Gone With The Wind'' to appear uninterrupted on one line. These goals can be accomplished by inserting hard spaces instead of normal spaces between words. These hard spaces are interpreted as though they were normal alphabet characters so the word is connected to the next word as though it was one continuous word.

56. In the OA market, there will be a large front office expansion—information centers, desktop computers, and an even larger integration of communications. Back office functions, such as the traditional computer room, will experience a decline.

57. A mark parity–always a binary 1–and not used as quality check, keeps the line ''busy.''

58. The key field is called an Entity Identifier. An entity identifier is just another word for the means whereby we will identify data using the primary key.

59. Decision techniques are largely synonomous with quantitative approaches or mathematical analysis. Some of these are statistical analysis, financial, mathematical, and others, including game theory, linear programming, simulation, and operations research.
60. The challenge in lighting the computer, which is a source of light itself, is to find a way to balance two different sets of activities: reading printed copy, which assumes a sight line 20 to 40 degrees lower than the horizontal at a distance of 16 inches, while viewing the screen, which assumes a horizontal sight line at a distance of 24 inches from the monitor to the eyes.
61. That standard time measurement is called "baud," and no doubt you'll be using equipment which is operating in either 300 baud or 1200 baud. Faster equipment is available for ranges above 14,000 baud. In any event, a *baud* is a unit of bit/time, a spacing of bits wherein it can be determined if a *one-bit* or a *zero-bit* has been transmitted.
62. Such a combination is called a *concatenated key,* in that two tuples can be have been combined dynamically to locate a specific entity record.
63. A cell is comparable to an array element. Naturally, an array or matrix provides the location whereby cells are manipulated. And, by design, one array would contain the data while a second array would contain your directions (the information expression) for using the data. The program, then, would map the latter over the former when performing calculations.
64. An effort must be made to prevent all noise in order to permit optimum levels of comfort and concentration.
65. The UART (Universal Asynchronous Receiver/Transmitter). It is the function of the UART to acquire data from the computer's "Bus" and to pass it on to a signal amplifier. In the opposite direction, it receives data from the amplifier and transmits it to the computer's bus.
66. Value redundancy is when media storage is concerned, the conventional flat-file, and to an extent, the hierarchical filing system, duplicate data unnecessarily.
67. Keyboard entry, Copy or Move data from another cell, Loading data from a disk file, and by communication from another option directly into the worksheet.
68. The clerical level is interrupt driven. The middle management level is client driven. The top management level is information driven.
69. Micro-to-mainframe links may be direct, through terminal control units (TCU) and front end communications processors (FECPs).
70. The rationale is to have access to the record through an alternate index, which will allow the file to be used without resorting.
71. The formula methods for all spreadsheets are algebraic, with all the rules of algebra. Requirements for the formula will be operands, operations, and results.
72. There will no doubt be communication with intelligent copiers, but they are not, at this time, planned to be a part of the IVDT.
73. The Microcom Networking Protocol (MNP) uses a Link Protocol, and Link Protocol is one of the synchronous protocols.
74. The schema is the overall database description, a chart of the types of data that are used, including the names of the entities, their attributes, and the specifics of the interrelationships. It is the framework into which the *values* may be fitted. The schema has no values in and of itself.
75. The range concept has to do with the spreadsheet's ability to identify subordinate portions by the assignment of names, to calculate within that specific range, and to perform a number of services upon that range along within the spreadsheet. This is frequently used where the spreadsheet is developed as an entity, but is subdivided.
76. It's new technology and it's exciting. It works by taking voice input, digitizing it, and recording the digitized voice as a special record with the data. That record is then produced in a synthetic speed output when the data is accessed.

77. In the days when Baudot devised the five-channel teletype code, there was a limit of 32 characters which could be sent. Our concern is for the 7-bit ASCII code (which permits 128 characters) and the 8-bit extended ASCII code (and EBCDIC code) which permits 256 different characters.
78. Relationships convey information not inherent in the data items themselves. The PURCHASE-ORDER record does not say what the parts are for. When coupled to the LINE-ITEM record, it is complete. Cross references convey no information. They are merely file linkages to extend the information. The SUPPLIER # is meaningful in and of itself. If not coupled to SUPPLIER-NAME, no meaning is lost.
79. The macro concept is where a good spreadsheet's tremendous power lies. A macro will be a command, function, or formula that can either be generated by the touch of one or two keyboard keys or incorporated into macro programs. Macros are commonly used to save repetitive typing.
80. If the host can use the microcomputer as an appendage, there is no logical, or electronic, reason not to do so. In the scenario, the host computer, or mainframe, becomes a database machine to the microcomputer or workstation.
81. The idea is to be able to determine the bit weight on the line and to hold back one source until the other has passed. This is not an easily implemented scheme, particularly in the packet switching environment. This is technically possible through an electronic circuit known as the Collision Condition Determination (CCD) circuit.
82. Whereas the Schema is a chart of the entire logical data base—the overall view (done by a data dictionary, and also known as a global logical database description), the Subschema is the programmer's data description (file organization).
83. Based on the information contained in one column, the table function will return the information contained in another column. This feature has been greatly enhanced in more recent spreadsheets. Tabled procedures will allow inexperienced users to construct very advanced spreadsheet applications.
84. The waterfall front edge of a chair aids thigh circulation, reduces leg fatigue, and lets the feet rest comfortably flat on the floor.
85. SDLC and its packet communication counterpart (HDLC) are the world standards for business communications.
86. A hierarchical structure is often called a tree. It is composed of a hierarchy of elements known as *nodes*. The uppermost node is called the *root*. Unlike most trees, the hierarchical structure is upside down.
87. When the original formulas are copied to the destination address they will be modified to perform the same operation in different locations. For instance, the formula +C1+(C1*D1) might be copied to a series of cells below it. The copied formulas would change to reflect their new positions.
88. An E-Mail activity on even a local area network takes a significant number of users to justify the cost. A national service, such as MCI Mail could never have happened without the justifying numbers.
89. The speed control exercised in many communications programs is called the XON/XOFF data flow control protocol, and can be used either on transmission or on reception. It toggles (turns on and off) to prevent communications buffer overflow.
90. Because the records (in the case of the hierarchical database) and the data elements (in the case of the network database) exist in random parts of the diskette or hard disk, they must be tied together using pointers. A pointer is an address, contained in a record, referring to another record.
91. The format command lets you choose numeric display formats. It offers a wide variety of choices for display of the numbers. You may choose currency, date, time, percent and other ways of displaying the numbers. The format command also provides a procedure for hiding the contents of a cell or a range of cells.

92. Intelligent copy machines will assist the integrated office, but won't keep it from becoming integrated. However, managerial fear of key-driven devices and the mindset that thought entry into a computer media is low level work might well delay the integration functions. Electronic publishing will be very much a part of the integrated office.

93. Local area networks interconnect dissimilar information processing devices to allow high-speed communication and resource sharing among them.

94. If a child in a data relationship has more than one parent, or a parent has more than one child, this is a network (or plex) structure.

95. The Data Interchange Format (DIF) was devised by the inventors of VisiCalc for passing data to and from a spreadsheet. DIF never became a standard; there are several versions.

96. The person will need these skills because the position will become something other than clerical or administrative. The schools have a lot of training to do.

97. Optical fiber may be the transmission medium of the future for local area networks. It is self-contained, not spurious, secure, immune to exterior forces.

98. Optimization means cutting down the seek time via reorganization. It is possible for sequenced chains only to cut the number of seeks. It is periodically necessary for non-sequenced chains, as these might be spread all over the disk.

99. Nonroutine decisions are situation oriented and judgmental. Routine decisions are nonroutine decisions made as one rises in the management ranks, and tend to be proceduralized.

100. Training must be accomplished at three levels: orientation, acquaintance, and competency.

EPILOG

And thus ends one of the most ambitious projects I've ever undertaken. When the third edition was published, an acquaintance told me that it was like taking a year of college. This edition has been expanded to give him the impression that he can now go after the whole degree.

The expansion of this book was no mean feat, and involved much research. I am indebted to the vendor literature, brochures, and squibs from which much was extracted for this edition. Special mention should be made of three of James Martin's books from which information was extracted and illustrative material was adapted: *Computer Data-Base Organization, Telecommunications and the Computer,* and *Structured Techniques for Computing.* I'd used these for my class notes and drew from those notes in several places in the book. All three are worthwhile purchases from Prentice-Hall. Many other references were used over the years to develop this book. Most are credited specifically, where necessary. My thanks also to the speakers at the 1985 convention of the Office Automation Society International meeting in Minneapolis. You gave me food for thought and were the sources of many ideas for the section dealing with that topic.

Like the last few editions, this edition found much more information being added than was being dropped. This would seem to be evidence of the broadening of our field, and certainly the expansion of the systems topics in this edition would give testimony to what I think is happening to the field. In the 1985 exam, only a few questions dealt with the items in these expansions. But they were there, and, of course, I'd like for this manual to find broader use than just for the CDP examination.

This edition is the first to have tutorial answers to the questions—and the question pool in this book went from 400 to 800, a major undertaking.

We went to great lengths to overcome the deficiencies of the last edition. Particular attention was paid to the questions and answers, as that's where the problem seemed to be last time. As always, any help you can offer to correct deficiencies—and there will be some: we haven't published a perfect book yet—would be more than welcomed.

Finally, I wish to again mention that the rights for this book are for sale. I've rewritten it three times now. My career has taken some shifts and a younger person with his or her career before should consider taking over the responsibility. The book has been offered to the ICCP and they have demurred. I'll not give it away, but we can find acceptable terms, I'm sure. The alternative will be to have this book die at the end of its useful life, and too many people owe their CDP Certificate to the book to allow that to happen. It would be kind of nice to have ICCP recognize that.

Good luck on the exam!

Kenniston W. Lord, Jr., CDP, CSP

INDEX